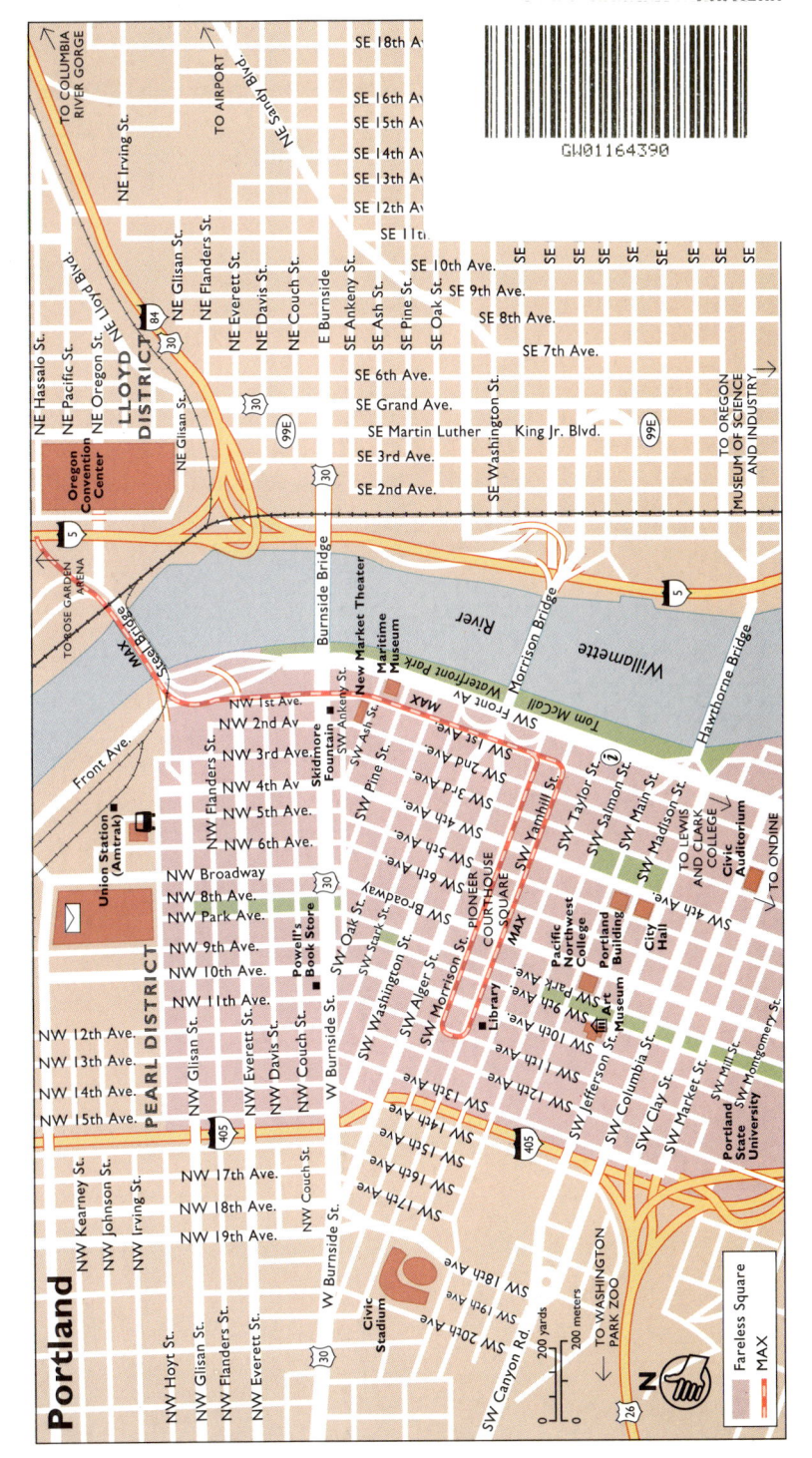

Portland

Seattle

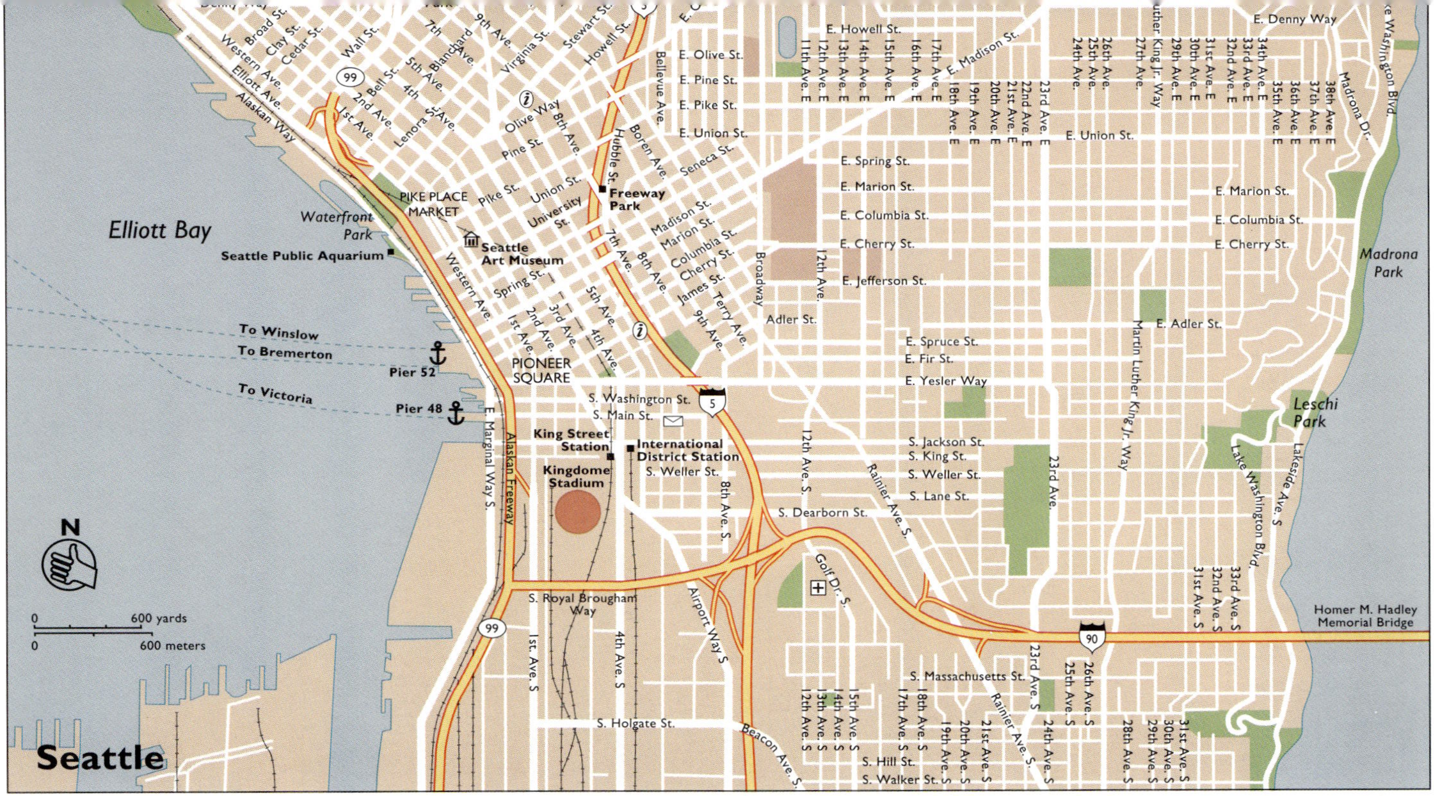
Seattle
Elliott Bay
Seattle Public Aquarium
Waterfront Park
PIKE PLACE MARKET
Seattle Art Museum
Freeway Park
PIONEER SQUARE
King Street Station
International District Station
Kingdome Stadium
To Winslow
To Bremerton
To Victoria
Pier 52
Pier 48
Madrona Park
Leschi Park
Homer M. Hadley Memorial Bridge
Alaskan Way
Alaskan Freeway
E. Marginal Way S.
Western Ave.
Elliott Ave.
1st Ave.
2nd Ave.
3rd Ave.
4th Ave.
5th Ave.
7th Ave.
8th Ave.
9th Ave.
Terry Ave.
Broadway
12th Ave.
Boren Ave.
Bellevue Ave.
Hubble St.
Olive Way
Pine St.
Pike St.
Union St.
University St.
Seneca St.
Spring St.
Madison St.
Marion St.
Columbia St.
Cherry St.
James St.
Wall St.
Bell St.
Lenora St.
Blanchard
Virginia St.
Stewart St.
Howell St.
Broad St.
Clay St.
Cedar St.
E. Howell St.
E. Olive St.
E. Pine St.
E. Pike St.
E. Union St.
E. Madison St.
E. Spring St.
E. Marion St.
E. Columbia St.
E. Cherry St.
E. Jefferson St.
Adler St.
E. Adler St.
E. Spruce St.
E. Fir St.
E. Yesler Way
E. Denny Way
Madrona Dr.
Lake Washington Blvd.
Lakeside Ave. S
Martin Luther King Jr. Way
11th Ave. E
12th Ave. E
13th Ave. E
14th Ave. E
15th Ave. E
16th Ave. E
17th Ave. E
18th Ave. E
19th Ave. E
20th Ave. E
21st Ave. E
22nd Ave. E
23rd Ave. E
24th Ave.
25th Ave.
26th Ave.
27th Ave.
29th Ave. E
30th Ave. E
31st Ave. E
32nd Ave. E
33rd Ave. E
34th Ave. E
35th Ave. E
36th Ave. E
37th Ave. E
38th Ave. E
S. Washington St.
S. Main St.
S. Jackson St.
S. King St.
S. Weller St.
S. Lane St.
S. Dearborn St.
Rainier Ave. S.
12th Ave. S.
8th Ave. S.
23rd Ave.
Golf Dr. S.
Airport Way S
S. Royal Brougham Way
1st. Ave. S
4th Ave. S
S. Holgate St.
Beacon Ave. S.
S. Massachusetts St.
S. Hill St.
S. Walker St.
12th Ave. S
13th Ave. S
14th Ave. S
15th Ave. S
17th Ave. S
18th Ave. S
19th Ave. S
20th Ave. S
21st Ave. S
23rd Ave. S
24th Ave. S
25th Ave. S
26th Ave. S
28th Ave. S
29th Ave. S
30th Ave. S
31st Ave. S
32nd Ave. S
33rd Ave. S
99
5
90
N
0
600 yards
600 meters

Vancouver

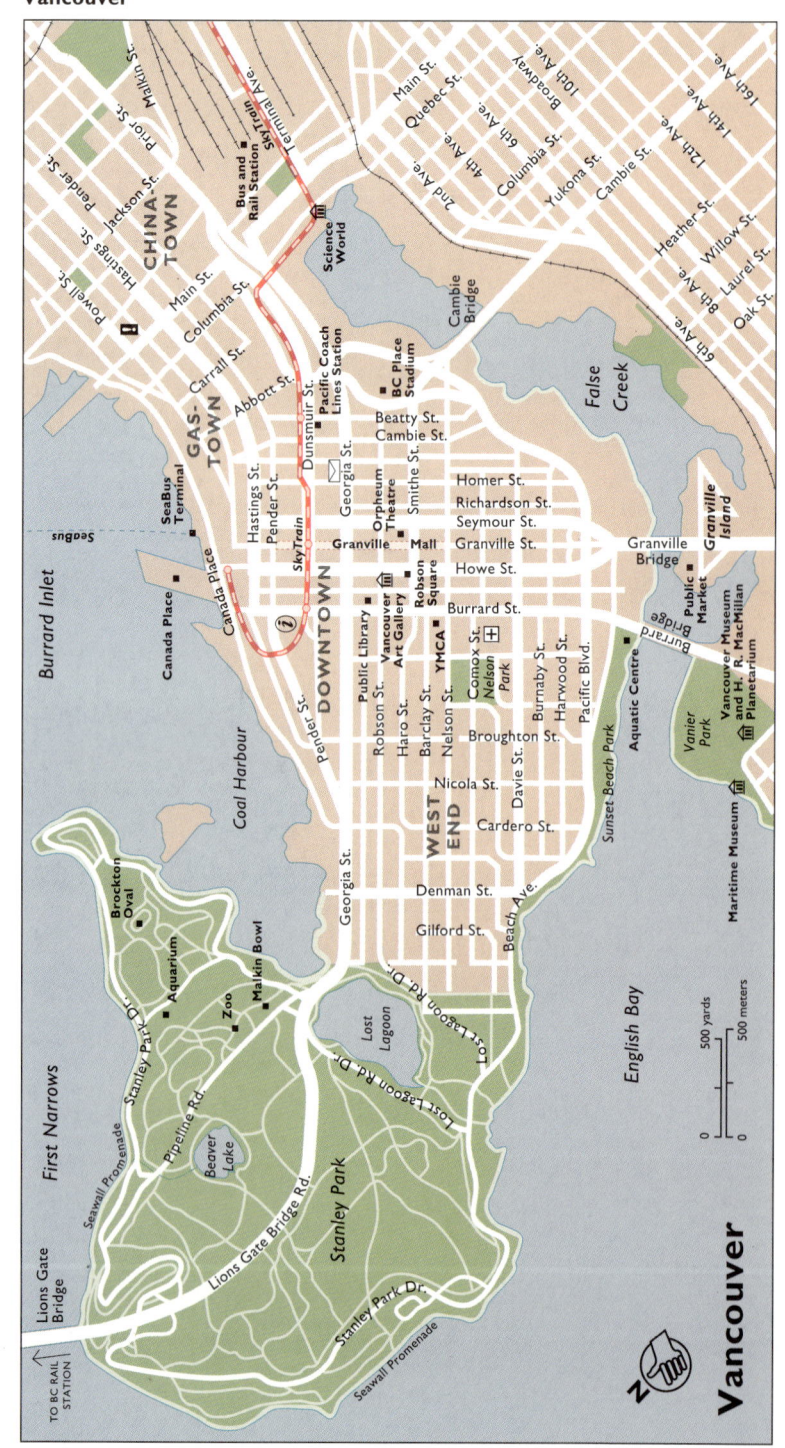

Let's Go writers travel on your budget.

"Guides that penetrate the veneer of the holiday brochures and mine the grit of real life."
—The Economist

"The writers seem to have experienced every rooster-packed bus and lunar-surfaced mattress about which they write."
—The New York Times

"All the dirt, dirt cheap."
—People

Great for independent travelers.

"The guides are aimed not only at young budget travelers but at the independent traveler; a sort of streetwise cookbook for traveling alone."
—The New York Times

"A guide should tell you what to expect from a destination. Here *Let's Go* shines."
—The Chicago Tribune

"An indispensable resource, *Let's Go*'s practical information can be used by every traveler."
—The Chattanooga Free Press

Let's Go is completely revised each year.

"A publishing phenomenon...the only major guidebook series updated annually. *Let's Go* is the big kahuna."
—The Boston Globe

"Unbeatable: good sight-seeing advice; up-to-date info on restaurants, hotels, and inns; a commitment to money-saving travel; and a wry style that brightens nearly every page."
—The Washington Post

All the important information you need.

"*Let's Go* authors provide a comedic element while still providing concise information and thorough coverage of the country. Anything you need to know about budget traveling is detailed in this book."
—The Chicago Sun-Times

"*Let's Go* guidebooks take night life seriously."
—The Chicago Tribune

Let's Go Publications

Let's Go: Alaska & the Pacific Northwest 2002
Let's Go: Amsterdam 2002 **New Title!**
Let's Go: Australia 2002
Let's Go: Austria & Switzerland 2002
Let's Go: Barcelona 2002 **New Title!**
Let's Go: Boston 2002
Let's Go: Britain & Ireland 2002
Let's Go: California 2002
Let's Go: Central America 2002
Let's Go: China 2002
Let's Go: Eastern Europe 2002
Let's Go: Egypt 2002 **New Title!**
Let's Go: Europe 2002
Let's Go: France 2002
Let's Go: Germany 2002
Let's Go: Greece 2002
Let's Go: India & Nepal 2002
Let's Go: Ireland 2002
Let's Go: Israel 2002
Let's Go: Italy 2002
Let's Go: London 2002
Let's Go: Mexico 2002
Let's Go: Middle East 2002
Let's Go: New York City 2002
Let's Go: New Zealand 2002
Let's Go: Paris 2002
Let's Go: Peru, Ecuador & Bolivia 2002
Let's Go: Rome 2002
Let's Go: San Francisco 2002
Let's Go: South Africa with Southern Africa 2002
Let's Go: Southeast Asia 2002
Let's Go: Southwest USA 2002 **New Title!**
Let's Go: Spain & Portugal 2002
Let's Go: Turkey 2002
Let's Go: USA 2002
Let's Go: Washington, D.C. 2002
Let's Go: Western Europe 2002

Let's Go *Map Guides*

Amsterdam
Berlin
Boston
Chicago
Dublin
Florence
Hong Kong
London
Los Angeles
Madrid
New Orleans
New York City
Paris
Prague
Rome
San Francisco
Seattle
Sydney
Venice
Washington, D.C.

Let's Go

ALASKA
& THE PACIFIC NORTHWEST
2002

Stephen M. Davis editor
Natalie M. Carnes associate editor

researcher-writers
Brice Conklin
Ashley Dayer
Emily Russin
Nathaniel Towery
Michael Weller
Jessica Yin

Jenna Robins map editor
Brian R. Walsh managing editor

Macmillan

HELPING LET'S GO If you want to share your discoveries, suggestions, or corrections, please drop us a line. We read every piece of correspondence, whether a postcard, a 10-page email, or a coconut. Please note that mail received after May 2002 may be too late for the 2003 book, but will be kept for future editions. **Address mail to:**

> Let's Go: Alaska & The Pacific Northwest
> 67 Mount Auburn Street
> Cambridge, MA 02138
> USA

Visit Let's Go at **http://www.letsgo.com**, or send email to:

> **feedback@letsgo.com**
> Subject: "Let's Go: Alaska & The Pacific Northwest"

In addition to the invaluable travel advice our readers share with us, many are kind enough to offer their services as researchers or editors. Unfortunately, our charter enables us to employ only currently enrolled Harvard students.

Published in Great Britain 2002 by Macmillan, an imprint of Pan Macmillan Ltd.
20 New Wharf Road, London N1 9RR
Basingstoke and Oxford
Associated companies throughout the world
www.panmacmillan.com

Maps by David Lindroth copyright © 2002, 2001, 2000, 1999, 1998, 1997, 1996, 1995, 1994, 1993, 1992, 1991, 1990, 1989, 1988 by St. Martin's Press.

Published in the United States of America by St. Martin's Press.

Let's Go: Alaska & The Pacific Northwest. Copyright © 2002 by Let's Go, Inc. All rights reserved. Printed in the United States of America. No part of this book may be used or reproduced in any manner whatsoever without written permission except in the case of brief quotations embodied in critical articles or reviews. For information, address St. Martin's Press, 175 Fifth Avenue, New York, NY 10010, USA.

ISBN: 0-333-90578-4
First edition
10 9 8 7 6 5 4 3 2 1

Let's Go: Alaska & The Pacific Northwest is written by Let's Go Publications, 67 Mount Auburn Street, Cambridge, MA 02138, USA.

Let's Go® and the thumb logo are trademarks of Let's Go, Inc.
Printed in the USA on recycled paper with biodegradable soy ink.

ADVERTISING DISCLAIMER All advertisements appearing in Let's Go publications are sold by an independent agency not affiliated with the editorial production of the guides. Advertisers are never given preferential treatment, and the guides are researched, written, and published independent of advertising. Advertisements do not imply endorsement of products or services by Let's Go, and Let's Go does not vouch for the accuracy of information provided in advertisements.
If you are interested in purchasing advertising space in a Let's Go publication, contact: Let's Go Advertising Sales, 67 Mount Auburn St., Cambridge, MA 02138, USA.

HOW TO USE THIS BOOK

You hold in your hands the key to successful travel in Alaska and the Pacific Northwest. Consider this book a treasure map that will guide you to the diamonds in the rough that is the northwest. A witty treasure map that actually gives you a description of the treasure. And very explicit directions on how to get it.

ORGANIZATION OF THIS BOOK

GETTING TO KNOW A&P. The first chapter, **Discover Alaska and the Pacific Northwest,** provides you with an overview of travel in the region, including **Suggested Itineraries** that give you an idea of what you shouldn't miss and how long it will take to see it. **Pacific Northwest: Unauthorized and Uncensored** provides you with a general introduction to the history, cultue and arts. The **Essentials** section outlines the practical information you will need to prepare for and execute your trip.

FINDING YOUR REGION. The guide is organized geographically by political region. The chapters begin with Oregon and move up the coast through Washington and British Columbia, and then cut inland briefly to the Rockies in Alberta, before moving ever north to the Yukon territory, the Alaska Panhandle, and Central Alaska, finishing the last section with a glimpse at Arctic Alaska. The **black tabs** in the margins will help you to navigate between chapters quickly and easily.

APPENDIX. The appendix contains a useful table for the road tripper, providing the distances between all the major destinations in the Pacific Northwest.

A FEW NOTES ABOUT LET'S GO FORMAT

RANKING ESTABLISHMENTS. In each section (accommodations, food, etc.), we list establishments in order from best to worst. Our absolute favorites are so denoted by the highest honor given out by Let's Go, the Let's Go thumbs-up (👍).

> **THIS IS A GRAYBOX** Every once in a while, we stick in a graybox. These boxes provide interesting facts and tales about the places we list along with a bit of history (and maybe even a recipe).

PHONE CODES AND TELEPHONE NUMBERS. The **area code** for each region, city, or town appears opposite the name of that region, city, or town, and is denoted by the ☎ icon. **Phone numbers** in text are also preceded by the ☎ icon.

AHEM. WE'D LIKE TO DRAW YOUR ATTENTION TO. . .
Let's Go: Alaska and the Pacific Northwest 2002 is proud to debut a new outdoors format that provides expanded coverage of hiking, kayaking, fishing, and skiing for outdoors enthusiasts. Our coverage of art, music, and nightlife, has also been twisted, tweaked, and generally pained to emerge sleeker and *chic*-er than ever. Amidst these pages of cities, towns, parks, and drives, seek and ye shall find Woodstock-esque music festivals, free winery tours (with equally free tastings), native dance competitions, Shakespeare theater, and good old-fashioned rodeos.

> **A NOTE TO OUR READERS** The information for this book was gathered by *Let's Go* researchers from May through August of 2001. Each listing is based on one researcher's opinion, formed during his or her visit at a particular time. Those traveling at other times may have different experiences since prices, dates, hours, and conditions are always subject to change. You are urged to check the facts presented in this book beforehand to avoid inconvenience and surprises.

Cruise Prince William Sound or Kenai Fjords National Park

Kenai Fjords National Park & Prince William Sound are natural wonders you will want to make part of your Alaska adventure. Let our experienced captains & crew make the difference as you explore abundant marine wildlife, glaciers and unmatched scenic beauty. Our custom boats are designed to give you the most from this unique, once-in-a-lifetime experience. Come find out why locals have named us *"Alaska's #1 Wildlife & Glacier Cruise!"*

Call Today Toll-Free 800-468-8068

Located in Anchorage at 513 W. 4th Avenue (907) 276-6249

www.kenaifjords.com
www.princewilliamsound.com

KENAI FJORDS TOURS
An Alaska Heritage Tours Company

Prince William Sound Cruises & Tours
Operated by Stan Stephens
An Alaska Heritage Tours Company

CONTENTS

DISCOVER 1
When to Go 2
Things to Do 3
Suggested Itineraries 6

PACIFIC NORTHWEST 11
R-e-s-p-e-c-t: The Indigenous People 11
The Europeans Arrive 12
Betrayal: Policy toward The Native People 15
Rising Again: The Indigenous People today 16
Contemporary Culture 18

ESSENTIALS 22
Documents and Formalities 22
Money 25
Safety and Security 28
Health 30
Packing 33
Accommodations 33
Camping and The Outdoors 37
Keeping in Touch 42
Transportation 44
Additional Information 55
Alternatives to Tourism 58

OREGON 63
PORTLAND 65
Mount Hood 80
Columbia River Gorge 82
THE COAST: US 101 86
Astoria 87
Seaside 90
Cannon Beach 92
Tillamook 94
The Three Capes Loop 95
Lincoln City 96
Depoe Bay and Otter Crest Loop 97
Newport 97
Oregon Dunes and Reedsport 100
Coos Bay, North Bend, and Charleston 102
Bandon 104
Brookings 105
INLAND VALLEYS 106
Salem 106
Corvallis 108
Eugene 110
Grants Pass 115
Ashland 116
CENTRAL AND EASTERN OREGON 122
Bend 122
Sisters 126
Crater Lake and Klamath Falls 128
Pendleton 131
Hells Canyon & Wallowa Mtns. 133
Burns 137
Lakeview 140
Baker City 143

WASHINGTON 146
SEATTLE 146
PUGET SOUND 171
Olympia 171
Vashon Island 176
Whidbey Island 177
Bellingham 179
Mount Baker 181
SAN JUAN ISLANDS 182
San Juan Island 183
Orcas Island 187
Lopez Island 189
OLYMPIC PENINSULA 190
Olympic National Park 190
Port Townsend 194
Port Angeles 198
PACIFIC COAST 204
THE CASCADE REGION 206
Mount St. Helens 206
Mount Adams 212
Mount Rainier National Park 214
Chelan 217
Stehekin 219
EASTERN WASHINGTON 224
Yakima 225
Spokane 226
Pullman 230

BRITISH COLUMBIA 233
VANCOUVER 235
Sechelt Peninsula 249
Whistler 252
VANCOUVER ISLAND 254
Victoria 257
Near Victoria: Gulf Islands 262
Salt Spring Island 262
Pender Island 264
Pacific Rim Natl. Park 265
West Coast Trail 265
The Broken Group 266
Long Beach 267
Up Island 269
Nanaimo 269
Comox Valley 273
Strathcona Provincial Park 276
Port Hardy 278
Cape Scott Provincial Park 279
INTERIOR BRITISH COLUMBIA 280
Fraser River Canyon 280
Kamloops 283
Shuswap Lake Region 284
The Okanagan Valley 286
Kelowna 286
Penticton 289
Nelson 290
Valhalla Provincial Park 293
Fernie 295
Revelstoke 296
Glacier National Park 299
Yoho National Park 300
Kootenay National Park 301
NORTHERN BRITISH COLUMBIA 303
Quesnel 306

Prince George 307
Terrace 312
Prince Rupert 314
QUEEN CHARLOTTE ISLANDS/ HAIDA GWAII 317
Queen Charlotte City 318
Massett 322
Gwaii Haanas National Park Reserve/Haida Heritage Site 326
APPROACHING THE YUKON 328
Stewart, BC and Hyder, AK 329
Dease Lake 332
Dawson Creek 335
Fort Nelson to the BC/Yukon Border 337

ALBERTA 339
EDMONTON 339
CALGARY 346
THE ROCKIES 353
Banff National Park 354
Jasper National Park 363

THE YUKON 369
WHITEHORSE 369
Kluane National Park 379
Dawson City 384
Inuvik, Nt 392

THE PANHANDLE 394
Ketchikan 394
Prince Of Wales Island 403
Wrangell 406
Petersburg 409
Sitka 412
Tenakee Springs 417
Juneau 418
Gustavus 424

Glacier Bay National Park 425
Haines 426
Skagway 430
Yakutat 435

CENTRAL ALASKA 438
ANCHORAGE 439
Girdwood 449
Portage 450
Wrangell-St. Elias National Park 451
Glennallen 452
Mccarthy and Kennicott 455
PRINCE WILLIAM SOUND 458
Valdez 458
Cordova 462
KENAI PENINSULA 466
Seward 467
Homer 472
Kodiak 480
Kodiak National Wildlife Refuge 485
Unalaska and Dutch Harbor 487
Soldotna 492
Kenai 493
Ninilchik 495
INTERIOR ALASKA 497
Denali Nat'l Park and Preserve 497
Talkeetna 506
Fairbanks 510
Tok 520
Eagle 522
ARCTIC ALASKA 524
Nome 526
Barrow 530

APPENDIX 533
INDEX 535

MAPS

Chapter Divisions ix
The Pacific Northwest, Western Canada, and Alaska x-xi
Transportation 10

OREGON
Oregon 64
Portland Overview 65
Downtown Portland 68
Eugene 111
Ashland 117
Near Bend 125
Hells Canyon Region 134

WASHINGTON
Washington 147
Seattle Overview 148
Seattle 152-153
Puget Sound and the Olympic Peninsula 172
Olympia 173
Bellingham 180
San Juan Islands 183
Olympic National Park 191

Mt. St. Helens, Mt. Ranier, and Vicinity 207
Spokane 227

BRITISH COLUMBIA
Vancouver Overview 234
Downtown Vancouver 236
Vancouver Island 255
Victoria 256
Southern British Columbia 281
Nelson 291

ALBERTA
Alberta 340
Edmonton Overview 341
Downtown Edmonton 342
Calgary Overview 346
Downtown Calgary 347
The Rockies 353
Banff Townsite 359
Jasper Townsite 363

THE YUKON
British Columbia and the Yukon

Territory 370
Whitehorse 371
The Alaska Highway 376
Dawson City 384

THE PANHANDLE 394
Southeast Alaska (The Panhandle) 395
Alaska! 396-397
Ketchikan 398
Petersburg 410
Sitka 413
Juneau 419
Skagway 431

CENTRAL ALASKA 438
Southcentral Alaska 438
Anchorage 440
Kenai Peninsula 466
Homer 473
Kodiak 480
Denali National Park 498
Fairbanks 511
Downtown Fairbanks 513

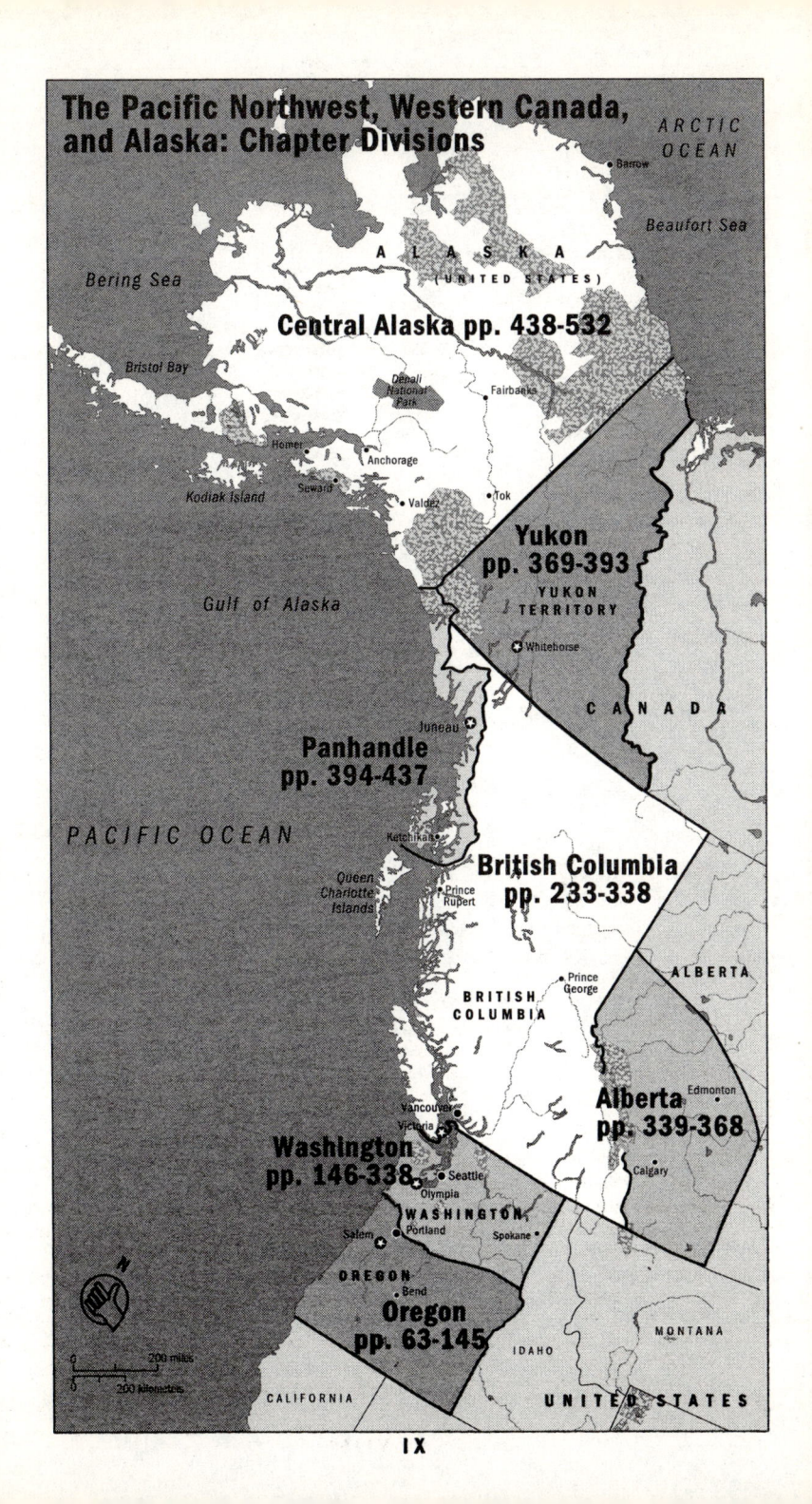

The Pacific Northwest, Western Canada, and Alaska: Chapter Divisions

x

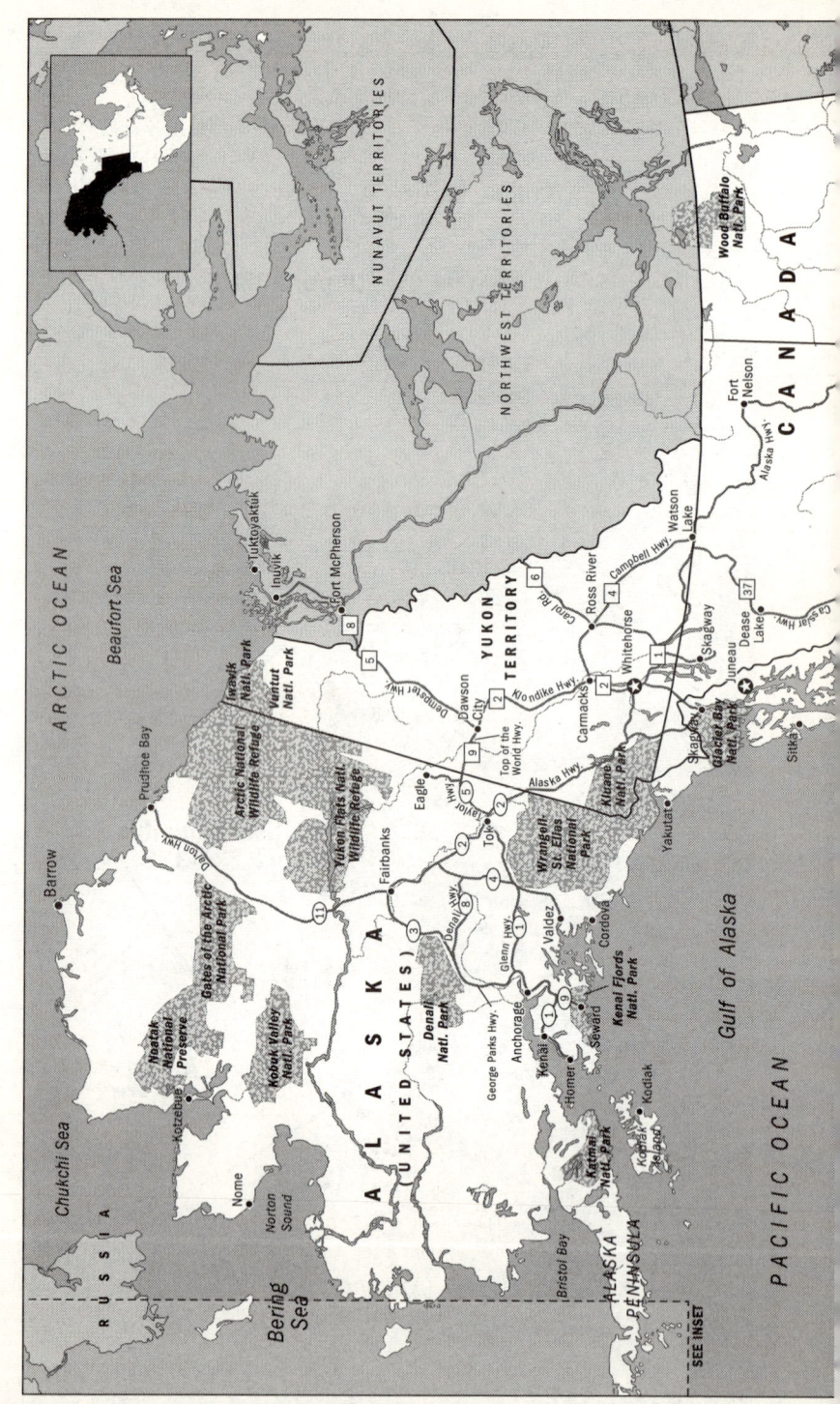

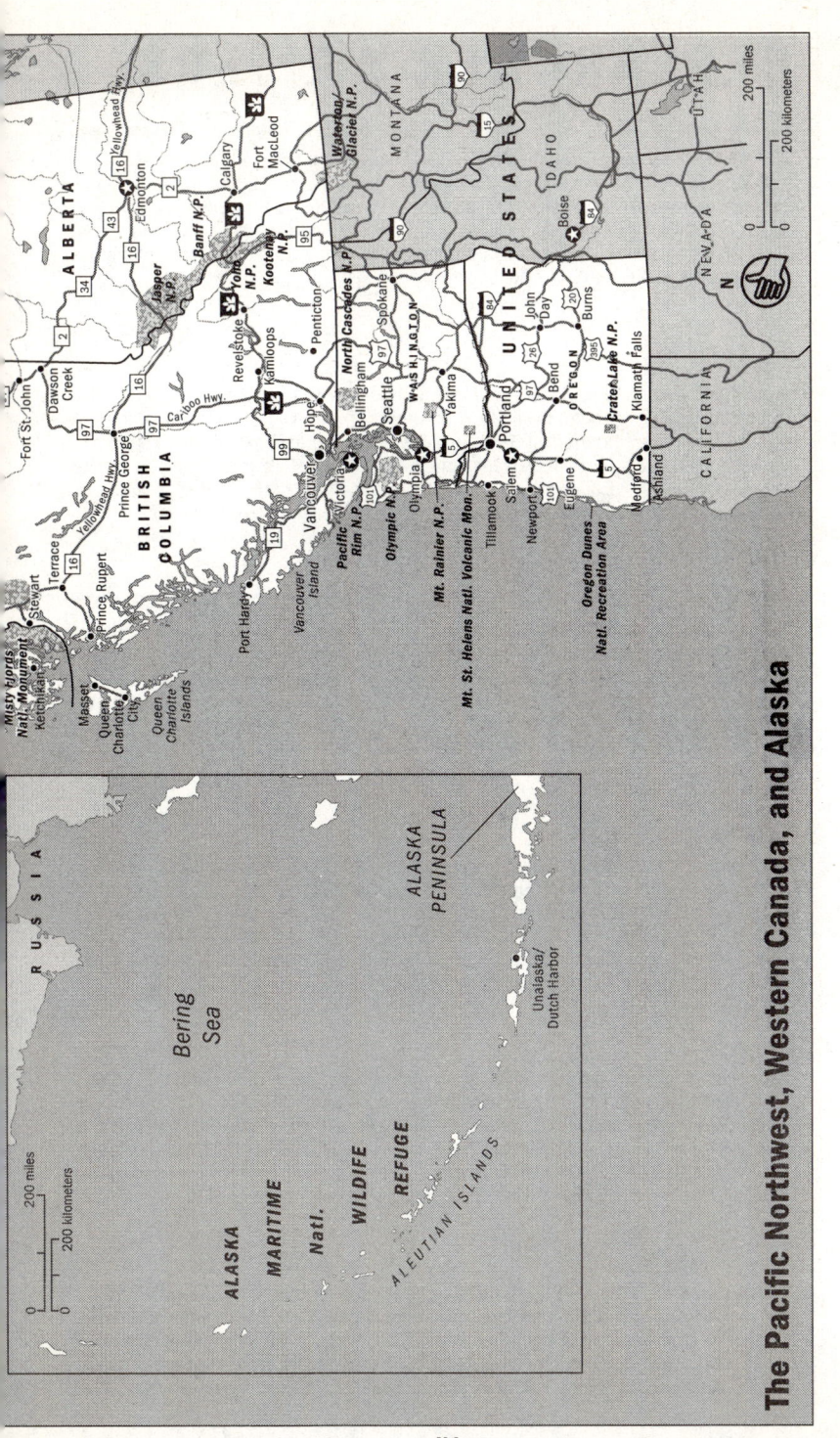

The Pacific Northwest, Western Canada, and Alaska

RESEARCHER-WRITERS

Ashley Dayer *Yukon, Northern BC, and Central Alaska*

The gorillas had Jane Goodall; the sea had Jacques Cousteau; but the Yukon and Northern BC had Ashley Dayer, animal-lover, marine expert, and the most hard-core traveler who ever drove 10,000 miles in 50 days. Her researching prowess and find-it-all skills earned her the titles of Animal-Sitings-Record-Holder and Canadian-Boys-Heartbreaker, accolades second only to her achievement in seeking out the cheapest, zaniest, and best of every site she visited.

Brice Conklin *Central and Arctic Alaska*

Brice dazzled hostel owners across Central Alaska with his rugged charm and dry humor. As he rode through the state, this Anchorage native put his regional knowledge to good use, expanding outdoors coverage, recovering hidden establishments, and spotting the tourist-traps with a singularity of purpose. He took on the roughest trails, wrestled the toughest bears, and traveled to the farthest reaches of the arctic that we might have a more intimate knowledge of his home state.

Emily Russin *Panhandle, Central, and Arctic Alaska*

With sleuth-like skills, Emily dug up precious insider information as she skipped up the southeast coast of Alaska. She blended in with the local populations—debating logging, chilling with anglers, dodging polar bears—and transcribed her adventures with wit and style which sparkles even from the well-worn pages of a trusty travel guide. Leaving the relative warmth of the panhandle, she charged northward to Barrow, where she did it all again, arctic-style.

Jessica Yin *BC and Alberta*

Overcoming a chaotic beginning, Jess recovered admirably to to capture the spirit of western Canada. This mountaineering expert sized up the national parks of Banff and Jasper with remarkable precision before she headed out to Vancouver to club her way through Canada's favorite city. Along the way, she churned out award-deserving research for her readers and dropped pearls of wisdom for her editors: wildlife ain't tame and scenery, it just *is*, man.

Mike Weller *Washington and Oregon*

After a brief, albeit glorious, brush with fame in the pages of the *Boston Globe*, Mike blazed through Oregon and Washington with an enthusiasm which even the laziest car transmission failed to dampen. Navigating the big cities of Portland and Seattle with the grace of a ballerina, Mike was equally facile as he danced through the national parks in between. Lightning Bill will never forget his tell-it-to-me 'tude, and we're all the richer for Mike's ability to locate the soul of the northwest.

Nathaniel Towery *Oregon, Washington, and Southern BC*

Nate stunned us all with his endurance as he drove nearly 10,000 miles in six weeks. With the speed of a man possessed, he checked establishments and parks across the great state of Oregon before heading north to the corners of Washington and BC. With an abundance of phone calls and emails, Nate kept the office in good cheer as he researched his way around the Pacific Northwest.

ACKNOWLEDGMENTS

The Let's Go 2002 series is dedicated to the memory of Haley Surti

The A&P team would like to thank: Our sweet and sassy RW team who weathered all kinds of disasters to turn in fabulous copy. Our ME Harris, one of the top ten Aladdin's of the office, hands down, and Jen, our mapper. To all the nameless proofers for your corrections. The gods-across-the-partition for random corrections. And, of course, Diamond Tooth Cody and the Basement Dancehall Gang: Klondike Nat(e!), Sarah Snake-hips Lulu, Ethel "Tom" the Moose, and Nellie the Ben. You girls made the the plagues of Basement 2002 bearable, nay, fun.

Steve thanks: Nat, champion of defenseless trees and keeper of the one who lived; I couldn't have asked for anyone better. Mike the headless chicken, the Webster's pronunciation guide, and the domestic pod that gave them life—you kept me sane in our lightless office. The plumber, maintenance men, and assorted others who tried to keep the rainwater, garlic smell, and sewage from our files. And of course, mom and pop, the Purple Flower Consortium, my three-*cum*-four roommates, and Sarah.

Natalie thanks: The unsinkable Molly Fewclothesteve, a great editor, awesome guy, and budding Joan of Arc. My fantastic fam—Mom, Dad, Tori, and Ros—for all the luvin'. Ben and Mare, my Jude and Shazzer of a very BJ summer. Gab and Gladys, you are absolutely the br—I mean!—best. Jana my love, Princecily, Madame Prez Cindy, and the Club Wilson crew. All my peeps in Boston for a great three months. The basement of comedians: the most fun, chill, and, quirky group of people I could ever have hoped to work with. Most of all, to God, from whom all good things come. And to online dictionaries with pronunciation guides. Who knew life could be so grand?

Editor
Stephen M. Davis
Associate Editors
Natalie M. Carnes
Managing Editor
Brain R. Walsh
Map Editor
Jenna Robins

Publishing Director
Sarah P. Rotman
Editor-in-Chief
Ankur N. Ghosh
Production Manager
Jen Taylor
Cartography Manager
Dan Barnes
Design & Photo Manager
Vanessa Bertozzi
Editorial Managers
Amélie Cherlin, Naz F. Firoz, Matthew Gibson, Sharmi Surianarain, Brian R. Walsh
Financial Manager
Rebecca L. Schoff
Marketing & Publicity Managers
Katharine Douglas, Marly Ohlsson
New Media Manager
Kevin J. Yip
Online Manager
Alex Lloyd
Personnel Manager
Nathaniel Popper
Production Associates
Steven Aponte, Chris Clayton, Caleb S. Epps, Eduardo Montoya, Melissa Rudolph
Some Design
Melissa Rudolph
Office Coordinators
Efrat Kussell, Peter Richards

Director of Advertising Sales
Adam M. Grant
Senior Advertising Associates
Ariel Shwayder, Kennedy Thorwarth
Advertising Associate
Jennie Timoney
Advertising Artwork Editor
Peter Henderson

President
Cindy L. Rodriguez
General Manager
Robert B. Rombauer
Assistant General Manager
Anne E. Chisholm

HOSTELLING INTERNATIONAL
SEATTLE

Quality downtown accommodations-just $18-21 per night!

Downtown Location.
HI-Seattle is just blocks from the Seattle Art Museum and the famous Pike Place Market, full of eateries, shops and other fun attractions. Walk down to the waterfront, take a scenic ride on a Washington State Ferry, or stroll into Myrtle Edwards Park for a panoramic view of the Olympic Mountains across Puget Sound. The Space Needle, Pioneer Square, and the new Experience Music Project are also just a short walk away!

Quality Budget Accommodations.
HI-Seattle is consistently listed as one of the highest-rated hostels in the world! Reviewers and guests have said ...

"It's the best American hostel I've seen yet."
"... a gold star for service and courtesy."
"... the Club Med of budget lodging."

Great Perks!
* Discounts from local merchants
* 24-hour access
* Free lockers and day storage
* Full kitchen and laundry facilities
* Major credit cards accepted
* Internet Access

Open 24 hours.
HI-Seattle
84 Union Street
Seattle, Washington 98101
Telephone: (206) 622-5443
For reservations, call:
(888) 622-5443
(free from Canada or USA)
Just $18-21 per night!

The best hostels in the best places. Experience Hostelling International.

Visit us on the web:
www.hiseattle.org

HOSTELLING INTERNATIONAL®

DISCOVER ALASKA & THE PACIFIC NORTHWEST

MEET YOUR TERRITORY: AN INTRODUCTION IN FACTS AND FIGURES

OREGON: FOR THE YOUNG AND THE "SPIRITED."
Best place to feel the spirit: Portland, the city with more microbreweries than any other.
Deepest lake in the US: Crater Lake.
Deepest river gorge in North America: Hells Canyon.

WASHINGTON: BETTER THAN CALIFORNIA, DARNIT.
Number of wineries in 1981: 19. Number of wineries in 2001: 160.
Though (grrr) second in premium wine production in the US, Washington boasts more awards and competitions proportional to its production than any other wine region in the world. And they have sunlight 2hr. longer per day than California. And they receive more rain than California.

BRITISH COLUMBIA: CALI-WHO?
British Columbia's rank among the film and TV production centers in the world: 3.
Number of films shot in British Columbia in year 2000: 192.
Total area in square kilometers of California: 400,000.
Total area in square kilometers of British Columbia: 950,000. Booyah!

ALBERTA: "STRONG AND FREE." AND HITTING ITS GROOVE.
Number 1 export: oil. Number 2 export: marijuana. Number 3 export: high oilmen.
Km of road: 180,000. Km of paved roads: 31,000. Km of pipelines for oil: 184,000.

YUKON: YES, YUKON.
Lowest temperature ever recorded in Canada: -62.8°C (northwest of Kluane Lake).
Most famous resident: Jack London.
Close runners-up: Klondike Kate and the Yukon Dancehall Girls (Diamond Tooth Gertie, Mollie Fewclothes, Nellie the Pig, Ethel the Moose, and Snake-hips Lulu).

ALASKA: LAND OF THE BIG AND HARD CORE.
17 of the 20 highest peaks in the US are in Alaska, and the longest river in North America is the 2000-mile Yukon River. Alaska has more active glaciers and icefields than any other place in the inhabited world, including the Malespina glacier, which spans 850 sq. mi. Come, all ye adventurers, and she will give you risks.

From the dense, misty rainforests of Oregon to the last desolate, treeless island in the Aleutian chain, North America's northwest coast is a land of staggering natural beauty. Along the coast, sharp young peaks soar skyward from the water's edge, spilling pieces of glacier into the ocean at their bases. Human settlements of varying sizes and degrees of polish mark the spots where rivers meet the coast, pointing the way to the country's interior. There, peaks give way to sometimes arable land, desert, tundra, and more mountains, peppered with more cities and towns.

For thousands of years, human settlement in the region has relied on natural resources. In the last two hundred years, human activities have significantly impacted the land—enthusiastic logging, mining, and fishing proved the land isn't inexhaustible—but the birth of the environmental spirit in the late 20th century is revitalizing the region. That spirit, the explosive growth of tourism, and the adoption of sustainable practices by resource-based industries have helped modern governments see old-growth forests as something more than raw lumber.

While you are assured of seeing many visitors wherever you go, with a minimum of effort you are just as able to lose the crowds. For example, while Banff National Park, in the Rockies, welcomes five million visitors a year, the right dayhike—or a visit to one of the park's lesser-known neighbors—is all it takes to find solitude. For those overwhelmed by the boundless backcountry, a community of welcoming hostels, quirky communities, and laid-back cities anchor the wilderness.

Winter visits promise hundreds of miles of skiing, snowboarding, snowshoeing, and snowmachining out of snow-bound cities where locals cheerily entertain themselves and love the diversion of guests. Farther south along the coast, winter isn't so much white as wet, and the litany of snow sports is restricted to higher elevations. The look of the Northwest under that much gray is sober but saturated, with stretches of ash-colored beach offset by craggy, ice-laced peaks.

However audacious it is to gloss this many miles of coast and this deep an interior in a single book, the present attempt is culled from what our researchers insisted they would do again if they could turn around and do their trips over. The sample itineraries that follow are intended to help you picture what your own trip might look like. For practical trip-planning resources, including campground reservation numbers, road reports, climate charts, Internet resources, and preferred outdoor publishing companies, see the **Essentials** (p. 22) chapter, and begin thumbing through the rest of *Let's Go: Alaska and the Pacific Northwest 2002*.

WHEN TO GO

In general, tourist season in the US and Canada runs from late May to early September. In Canada, the beginning is marked by the Victoria Day long weekend; in the US, the Memorial Day long weekend. Summer ends with the Labour/Labor Day long weekend at the beginning of September. In the off season, accommodations may be cheaper and less crowded, but sights you traveled so far to see may also be closed, and camping is not nearly as pleasant. On national holidays, many sights and all banks and government offices will be closed, and transportation may run on restricted schedules. The coastal cities are justly famous for rain, which pours down 10 months of the year. The rain-producing ocean also keeps coastal temperatures moderate year-round. In Portland and Vancouver, a few snow days a year are the norm, but it doesn't stick around at lower elevations. To the east of the coastal mountains, expect less precipitation, warmer summers, and colder winters. The same variation is experienced up north, only on a shifted scale—winters in the interior of the Yukon and Alaska are bitterly cold, while summers are merely cool. As in the south, things are more even on the coast. Festivals add spice to local culture, and a full listing of them can be found on p. 21.

NATIONAL HOLIDAYS

USA Date in 2002	Holiday
January 1	New Year's Day
January 21	Martin Luther King, Jr. Day
February 18	Presidents' Day
May 27	Memorial Day
July 4	Independence Day
September 2	Labor Day
October 7	Columbus Day
November 11	Veterans Day
November 28	Thanksgiving
December 25	Christmas Day

CANADA Date in 2002	Holiday
January 1	New Year's Day
April 15	Easter Sunday
April 16	Easter Monday
May 20	Victoria Day
July 1	Canada Day
September 2	Labour Day
October 14	Thanksgiving
November 11	Remembrance Day
December 25	Christmas Day
December 26	Boxing Day

THINGS TO DO

ON FOOT

The vast scenic lands in Alaska and the Pacific Northwest provide the hiker with limitless opportunities. Known for its natural beauty, impressive landscape, and clean waters, this region is arguably the most desirable place in North America to hit the trails. The national, provincial, and state parks provide some of the best and most varied hiking anywhere and are well-staffed, well-maintained, and well worth it. Reading the **Outdoor Activities** sections of a few parks should give a sense of the possibilities. Though popular destinations often limit the number of visitors, campsites may be hard to secure, and crowds will surely be on hand, one need not be in a designated park to enjoy the outdoors in the Northwest. Trails through virgin lands more beautiful than you can imagine abound. Contact the visitors center in your specific area for more info on how to break fresh ground. Experienced hikers may wish to consider the following multi-day (month) hikes:

CHILKOOT TRAIL. This three- to five-day (33 mi./53km) hike starts in Skagway, AK, and passes through a dramatic variety of climates, terrain, and vegetation, both above and below treeline, on its way through the Interior. Originally a trade route protected by the Tagish and Tlingit people, the trail was the route to the Interior during the Yukon gold rush of the 1890s. For more info, see p. 379.

PACIFIC CREST TRAIL. This 2650 mi./4260km trail stretches from California's border with Mexico to Washington's border with Canada. First explored in the 1930s, the system of trails is now a federally protected Scenic Trail that takes five to six months to hike. Pick up the trail in any of the national parks along the range or in the Columbia River Gorge (see p. 82). The Pacific Crest Trail Association (PCTA) maintains the trail and sells comprehensive trail guides, videos, and PCTA mouse pads on its website. (☎ 916-349-2109; www.pcta.org. Call 888-728-7245 for free info pack or trail condition report.)

WEST COAST TRAIL. This spectacular trail winds through 48 mi./77km (five to seven days) of coastal forest and beach along the Pacific Ocean in the Pacific Rim National Park on the west coast of Vancouver Island. Reservations are necessary to hike the trail. See p. 265 for info.

ON WATER

Most of Oregon's commercial trips float on the beautiful **Rogue** (see Grants Pass, p. 115) and **Deschutes** (see Bend, p. 122) rivers. Interior BC offers adrenaline rush runs on **Adam's River** p. 284, in the Shuswap. In Jasper, two rivers present prime rafting: the **Athabasca** and the faster **Sunwapta**, p. 363. Expect professionalism from a rafting outfit. If the rafts have patches, the life jacket supply is sparse, or the paddles are different shapes and sizes, you may want to take your business elsewhere.

Kayaking in Alaska's rivers couldn't be finer (unless the water were a little warmer). The small boat allows almost unlimited access to the coastline, and is perfect for investigating small coves and inlets and losing the cruise ship crowd. The West Coast of Vancouver Island, particularly **The Broken Islands,** p. 266, is another popular place to explore by kayak.

Alaska doesn't jump to mind for water sports that entail being *in* the water, but **Cordova,** p. 465, and **Yakutat,** p. 435, are places that both should. Both offer **surfers** incredible breaks, with Yakutat giving a bit bigger ride on a stunning black beach. **Long Beach** and **Cox Beach,** in Pacific Rim National Park, p. 265, offer sweet rides in BC. Seward, AK offers the ultimate in cold-water fun. In the third weekend in January, the **Polar Bear Jump,** p. 467, brings bravado to the fore when residents plunge into the ice waters to raise funds for cancer research; don't lose face by using a wet-suit. The best medicine for the icy Pacific is to bear inland to the many **hot springs.** An ideal place to warm up or to soothe aching muscles, this natural phenomenon is a favorite pastime. For a start, try **Circle Hot Springs, AK,** p. 519, **Cougar Hot Springs** in Eugene, OR, p. 110, **Canyon Hot Springs,** in Revelstoke, BC, p. 310, or **Hot Springs Cove** in the Pacific Rim National Park in BC, p. 265.

Nothing makes a better combination in the Northwest than water and wind. The gods smiled fondly on **Columbia River Gorge,** p. 82, blessing it with a river, gracing it with steep canyons, and consecrating it with a howling wind. Out of this, the **windsurfing** cult arose. Although the Gorge is eminent in the minds of windsurfers, other sites abound, by virtue of good breeze off the Pacific and moderate weather.

ON SNOW

The skiing and riding in the northern Rockies, the Cascades, and Coast range are some of North America's best. The best mega-resort is **Whistler-Blackcomb,** p. 252, a 1½hr. drive north of Vancouver, BC, which draws nearly two million international visitors a year. Most remarkable about the skiing, though, is the fact that many areas are only minutes from urban centers. Hostels in Washington, Oregon, Alberta, and BC all offer ski-and-stay packages. **Fernie Alpine Resort,** p. 295, is working to gain the title of megalith; with its new expansion, the resort now covers more than 2500 acres. The sleeper resort to watch is **Powder Springs Resort,** p. 310, in Revelstoke. With the largest vertical drop in North America and the interest of an Austrian family who already owns 36 resorts in Europe, it may only be a matter of time...Much to the joy of snowboarders across North America, ski hills have finally accepted that shredders are here to stay. Terrain parks are sprouting up left, right, and center. Valdez, AK hosts the **King and Queen of the Hill Snowboard Competition,** p. 458, to pay homage to the sport. The **World Extreme Skiing Championship** also takes place in Valdez. **Cross-country skiing** tends to get overshadowed by its vertical counterparts in the Northwest, but dump tons of snow on beautiful hiking trails, and what do you get but miles and miles of skiing trails.

ON CRACK

In the past decade, outdoor sports have battled to top the thrill that plain old Mother Nature provides. Pain, unfortunately seems to be a requisite for the rating of extreme. The **Chad Ogden Ultramarathon,** p. 480, is a 43 mi. race from Chiniak to Kodiak, AK that truly tests the mettle of racers. The **Ski to Sea Race,** p. 180, in Bellingham, WA, on Memorial Day weekend, is the mother of all relays with skiing, running, canoeing, and kayaking stages covering the terrain from Mt. Baker to Bellingham Bay. Golf is taken to extremes at the **Mt. Fairweather,** p. 425, course in Gustavus, AK. A measly nine holes gains its reputation as hard-core because it is open year-round. Defy gravity in Nanaimo, BC at the **Bungy Zone,** p. 269, and defy it again at the **Skaha Bluffs, BC,** p. 289, with phenomenal rock climbing. Firefighters train to sky-dive into forest fires at the **Smoke Jumpers Base,** p. 223, between Winthrop and Twisp, WA. Tiny Lakeview, OR, p. 140, the **hang gliding** capital of the US, lets you get away from things in a whole new way. You can off-road on the **Sand Dunes,** p. 100 along the coast of Oregon or **ski *sans* snow,** p. 307, in August on the sandy bluffs of the Nechako Cutbanks, in Prince George, BC.

NATIVE CULTURE

The Northwest is home to some of the finest exhibits of Native American and First Nation (the preferred terms for the indigenous people of the US and Canada, respectively) culture on the continent, and is the birthplace of some of their most popular traditions, such as potlatch, cedar carving, and long houses. Major museums in the region are the **Royal British Columbia Museum** in Victoria, BC, p. 257; the **Museum of Anthropology** in Vancouver, BC, p. 246; and the **Museum at Warm Springs,** OR, p. 3. Unfortunately, museums often give a sterile feeling to native cultures. For a more enlivened experience, watch a performance by the **Alutiiq Dancers,** (see Kodiak, p. 480), wander mist-shrouded **totem poles** in Ketchikan, AK, p. 394, or visit the **petroglyphs** on the beach in Wrangell, AK, p. 406. For more options, the Alaska Native Brotherhood halls are good resources for events and demonstrations.

BREWERIES AND VINEYARDS

Up and down the coast of Washington and Oregon, small companies turn out unique beverages that have won more awards per liter of output than any state in the Union. The wine counterculture is on the upswing—wine bars are cropping up and wine tastings are becoming an institution. In Washington, **Yakima Valley**, p. 225, is in the heart of the Wine Country. With the same rich volcanic soils and latitude of Bordeaux, France, Yakima is able to turn out award-winning wines en masse. **Spokane**, p. 226, **Salem**, p. 106, and **Lopez Island**, p. 189, have their fair share of vintners. In the fertile crescent of Interior BC, **Kelowna**, p. 286, and **Penticton**, p. 289, harbor prize-winning vintages. Stop by Kelowna for the **Okanagan Wine Festival** in October. A must-see for true connoisseurs is the **Shallon winery** in Astoria, p. 89, to sample rarities such as lemon meringue pie wine.

Beer rules the roost in Alaska. Fairbanks, p. 510, hosts the **Alaskan Microbrew Festival**, celebrating the finer craft of small-scale production. Haines hosts its own homage to hops at the **Craft Beer and Home Brew Festival**, p. 426. Small breweries are open for tours: try the **Skagway Brewing Co.**, in Skagway, p. 430. In the lower 48 visit the **Oregon Brewers Guild**, p. 65, in Portland and the **Rogue Ale Brewery**, p. 97, in Newport. And of course, dropping into Canada will prove the old adage: American macro-brews taste like piss once you try the smooth, flavorful Canuck brews.

LET'S GO PICKS

BEST SPORTING EVENTS: Catch a **baseball game** under the midnight sun on the solstice itself in Fairbanks, AK. The **Mountain Marathon**, in Seward, AK, p. 467, cuts to the chase, ascending 3000 ft. in 45min., while the **Equinox Marathon** in Fairbanks, p. 510, is considered one of the five hardest marathons in the country for gaining 3500 ft. over 26.2 mi.

BEST (NON-FOOT) RACES: The Chuckwagon Derby and the bathtub race highlight the tests of brawn and skill during Klondike Days in Edmonton, AB, p. 344.

BEST BICYCLE RIDE: Through breathtaking glaciers from Jasper to Banff along the **Icefields Parkway**, p. 362.

BEST WAY TO GET IN TOUCH WITH SANTA CLAUS: You always knew the 'rents were holding back when they said Santa was crap. Get **proof**—Santa promises to write you back for $5, p. 509.

BEST BOOKSTORE: Cavernous **Powell's City of Books** swallows patrons whole in hallowed book-lined walls, p. 74.

BEST PLACE TO FIND ALLIGATOR SKIN BOOTS: Undoubtedly, **The Stampede** in Calgary, where locals celebrate their rough-and-tumble heritage, p. 350.

BEST WAY TO GET HIGH: Scale the infamous **Denali**, p. 497.

SECOND BEST WAY TO GET HIGH: Matanuska Valley Thunderfuck is incredibly potent, although Let's Go does not endorse using illegal substances for relaxation at the end of a long day. p. 447.

BEST ANIMAL ENCOUNTERS: Get intimate with buffalo skeletons at **Head-Smashed-In Buffalo Jump**, AB, p. 351, to learn how a native tribe could destroy a herd of buffalo in an afternoon. In the land of winter, what would replace the earthworm, but the **iceworm?** Rangers in Portage dispel myths about the wee beasties who call glaciers home, p. 450. Cordova honors them with an annual Ice Worm Festival in February, p. 465.

BEST WAY TO RUB ELBOWS WITH STAR ATHLETES: As deadweight in his sled, you can be part of the training process for Mitch Seavey's dogs as they get in shape for the famous **Iditarod**, p. 471.

BEST ILLEGAL FISHING: When the **Childs Glacier** calves, waves are sent up into the surrounding forest, stranding fish in the trees. Look but don't touch—it's illegal to harvest these beauties, p. 465.

SUGGESTED ITINERARIES

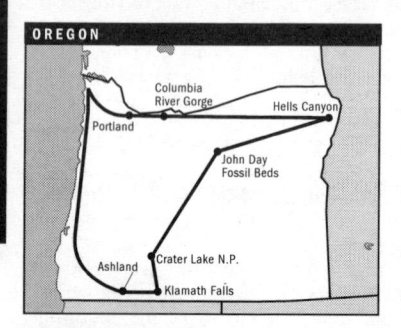

OREGON (2 WEEKS). Any journey through Oregon should begin and end in **Portland** (4 days, p. 65). Visitors could wile away weeks in this phenomenal city that combines cosmopolitan flare, crunchy outdoors, and youthful money. After satisfying the city dweller in you, embark on the open road to venture into **Columbia River Gorge** (2 days, p. 82), where you can trade the car in for a surfboard and let loose on windsurfing heaven. Remove yourself from the coast by driving out to **Hells Canyon** (2 days, p. 133), whose barren landscape resembles a cratered moonscape. Continuing down through the hot interior, visit the **John Day Fossil Beds** (1 day, p. 143), where fossilized remains of tropical rainforests defy the naked eye. The unusual landscape continues at **Klamath Falls,** where **Crater Lake** plunges to a depth of 1932 feet (1 day, p. 128). Unfortunately the water is unattainable; it's forbidden to swim in the lake. Withdrawing from the rugged outdoors, stop into **Ashland** (2 days, p. 116) to sample some of the country's best Shakespeare. Gradually meander back up the coast to Portland on US 101, with stops to play in the sand and surf (2 days).

WASHINGTON (3 WEEKS). Seattle (1 week, p. 146) creates its own small cosmos revolving and pulsing to the beat of the city. With a plethora of trips within driving distance from the city, it provides an ideal base. Jump on a ferry with a small bag to spend several days hopping between the **San Juan Islands** (5 days, p. 182) and their beautiful beaches. This archipelago is perfect for kayaking. Touch base in Seattle to provision for a journey to **Mt. Baker** (3 days, p. 181). A mecca for skiing in the winter, it provides gorgeous vistas, challenging hikes, and breathtaking drives for summer visitors. To taste the international, visit **Leavenworth** (1 day, p. 217), a small town that pretends to be nestled in the Alps. A final must-see stop is the **Olympic National Park** (5 days, p. 190), an outdoors lover's playground; true solace can be found within its rugged boundaries.

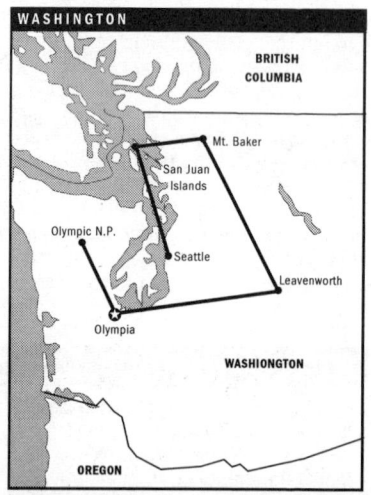

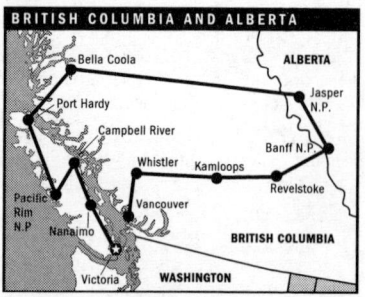

BRITISH COLUMBIA AND ALBERTA (4 WEEKS). When discovering western Canada, there is no better starting point than British Columbia's biggest metropolis, **Vancouver** (5 days, p. 235), which features a variety of sights, museums, and exciting nightlife. After you've had enough of the big city trek out to **Whistler** (4 days, p. 252); don't forget to pack the skis. Together with Blackcomb, these sister mountains provide some of North America's best downhill skiing. Allow yourself a day's rest in **Kamloops** (p. 283) before starting the National Parks escapade. Start in smaller **Revelstoke** (2 days, p. 310), a favorite with hikers and bikers, before heading to monster **Banff** (3 days, p. 354) and **Jasper National Parks** (3 days, p. 363). The **Icefields Pkwy.** accesses major portions of both parks.

SUGGESTED ITINERARIES

While hiking is the premier activity, climbing, kayaking, and rafting also keep the outdoor lover satisfied. Strike west on the Yellowhead Hwy. to **Bella Coola.** Overnight here before hopping on a ferry to **Port Hardy** (2 days), on the northern tip of Vancouver Island. Meander to the southern tip, and visit the **Pacific Rim National Park** (3 days, p. 265). Perched on the sea, this park has an entirely different landscape than the inland parks. Meander down Hwy. 19, stopping in towns such as **Campbell River** and **Nanaimo** (2 days). Finally, allow at least four days for **Victoria,** at the southern tip of the island. In the most British-feeling city in British Columbia, you'll definitely want to experience high tea.

gest town you'll see after leaving Edmonton. Make a final stop in **Dawson City** (p. 384) to provision for the drive up the **Dempster** (p. 390). The twelve-hour drive on brutal gravel is bound to torment tires. At the end of the road is **Inuvik** (p. 392), where you can stop and dip your toes into the Beaufort Sea. Flightseeing to **Tuktoyaktuk** brings you within sight of the polar caps.

DESOLATION (2-3 WEEKS, DEPENDING ON YOUR PACE). The Northwest is inundated with tourists for the summer. All it takes to get away is a car and the backroads. Fly into **Edmonton** (p. 339) to overstep Calgary's mobs, and go north. Cut across the AB/BC border and sojourn in **Dawson Creek** (p. 335), which has the unfortunate luck of sharing a name with the kitschy teenybopper TV show. Get onboard the **Alaska Hwy.** (p. 334) to get the scenic overhaul of northern BC. Stop in towns like **Fort Nelson** (p. 337) for eats and shut-eye only: the drive *is* the attraction. **Whitehorse** (p. 375) is the big-

CENTRAL ALASKA AND THE NORTHERN YUKON (3 WEEKS). Anchorage (3 days, p. 439) is the hub of the largest state in the US. While not a metropolis by "continental" US standards, Anchorage has a couple of great museums, entertainment options, and jaw-dropping views. Outside Anchorage is **Denali National Park** (3 days, p. 497), home to the largest peak in North America, Mt. McKinley. Arguably the world's most amazing sight, Denali (as locals call it) alone will make your trip worthwhile. After glimpsing the giant, drive north to **Fairbanks** (4 days, p. 510), North America's northernmost hub, where there is a remarkable amount going on in and around town. It can be a base for rugged adventures to Arctic to places such as **Barrow** and **Prudoe Bay.** From Fairbanks, gear up to take in small-town Alaska and experience the "Alaska effect"—things on the map are farther than they appear. Travel southeast on Rte. 2, and across the Canadian border to Kluane

8 ■ SUGGESTED ITINERARIES

National Park, which is part of one of the world's largest protected wilderness areas. Be prepared for Dall sheep, bald eagles, large glaciers, and untouched landscape (1 week). Finish your trip in nearby **Whitehorse** (4 days, p. 375), the Yukon's largest city.

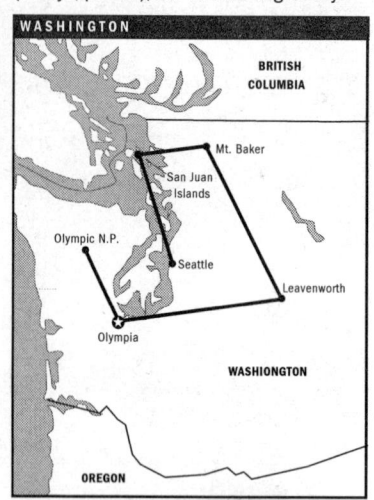

THE PANHANDLE (2 WEEKS). The Panhandle is best enjoyed afloat. Fly into **Seattle,** and bus up to **Bellingham** (p. 179). Get on board the **Alaska Marine Hwy.** for the trip to **Juneau** (3 days). In Juneau, set up base camp (3 days, p. 418). The plethora of ferries and prop planes connect the inlets, islands, and coves of the Panhandle. Visit **Glacier Bay National Park** for beautiful kayaking (3 days, p. 425). **Ketchikan** (2 days, p. 394) has priceless totem poles and a long house waiting to be explored. The **Misty Fiords** (1 day, p. 403) are another national park begging for your attention. Fly to **Prince Rupert** and from there embark on the ferry to the **Queen Charlotte Islands** (4 days, p. 317), affectionately dubbed the 'Canadian Galapagos.' There you can visit one of the most vibrant native communities in Canada. The **Gwaii Haanas National Park Reserve** and portions of Moresby have been declared a World Heritage Site by UNESCO, and will give you a flavor of the Northwest before Europeans arrived.

IF I HAD A MILLION DOLLARS (6+ WEEKS). The farthest reaches of Alaska hold a tenuous position in a budget travel guide. Very few places on earth, however, can give the sense of solitude, loneliness, and insignificance that the Arctic does. The rural nature of the communities makes traveling this area prohibitive for most people. To see the wildest that Alaska has to offer, base yourself in **Anchorage** (p. 439). Trips require much preparation to ensure that you are ready to tangle with Mother Nature at her wildest. The highlights of this trip are the great outdoors—cultural events are isolated up north. Hop on a plane to **Barrow** (p. 530) to visit the northernmost point of the US and to dip your toes into the **Arctic Ocean.** A trip out to **Nome** (p. 526) will put you down in a town with a rich gold mining history. The most exciting event of the year is the Iditarod dogsledding race, which starts or finishes here on alternating years. The **Gates of the Arctic National Park** is accessible by flight service from **Bettles** (p. 525). Incorporate some down-time in Anchorage to enjoy the city and recharge the batteries before heading out to **Kotzebue** (p. 528). For the northern native communities this serves as a trading post, but for the traveler it is also a gateway to parks well above the Arctic Circle. Flying to **Kodiak** (p. 480) brings you to a rugged town that was the first Russian capital in Alaska. Mother Nature doesn't smile on Kodiak, unleashing earthquakes and tsunamis with frightening regularity, but mountains abound on the island, harkening to altitude junkies. **The Katmai Wilderness** (p. 477) and its Valley of 10,000 Smokes will have you reconsidering what beautiful is about in the landscape left by one of the 20th century's most cataclysmic events: the eruption of Novarupta. With a week and a kayaking or canoe partner, the **Savanoski Loop** is one of the finest routes in the state. **The Aleutian Islands** (p. 486) stretch into nothing but dark water and storms. The islands support fewer than twenty trees, and the velvety green ridgelines of the volcanoes billowing out of the North Pacific are truly one of the most remarkable features of the Alaskan landscape.

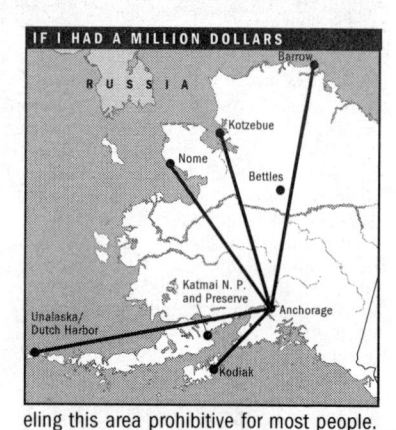

Sheep Tickets.

Visit **StudentUniverse.com** for real deals on student travel anywhere.

StudentUniverse.com   Real Travel Deals

800.272.9676

10 ■ SUGGESTED ITINERARIES

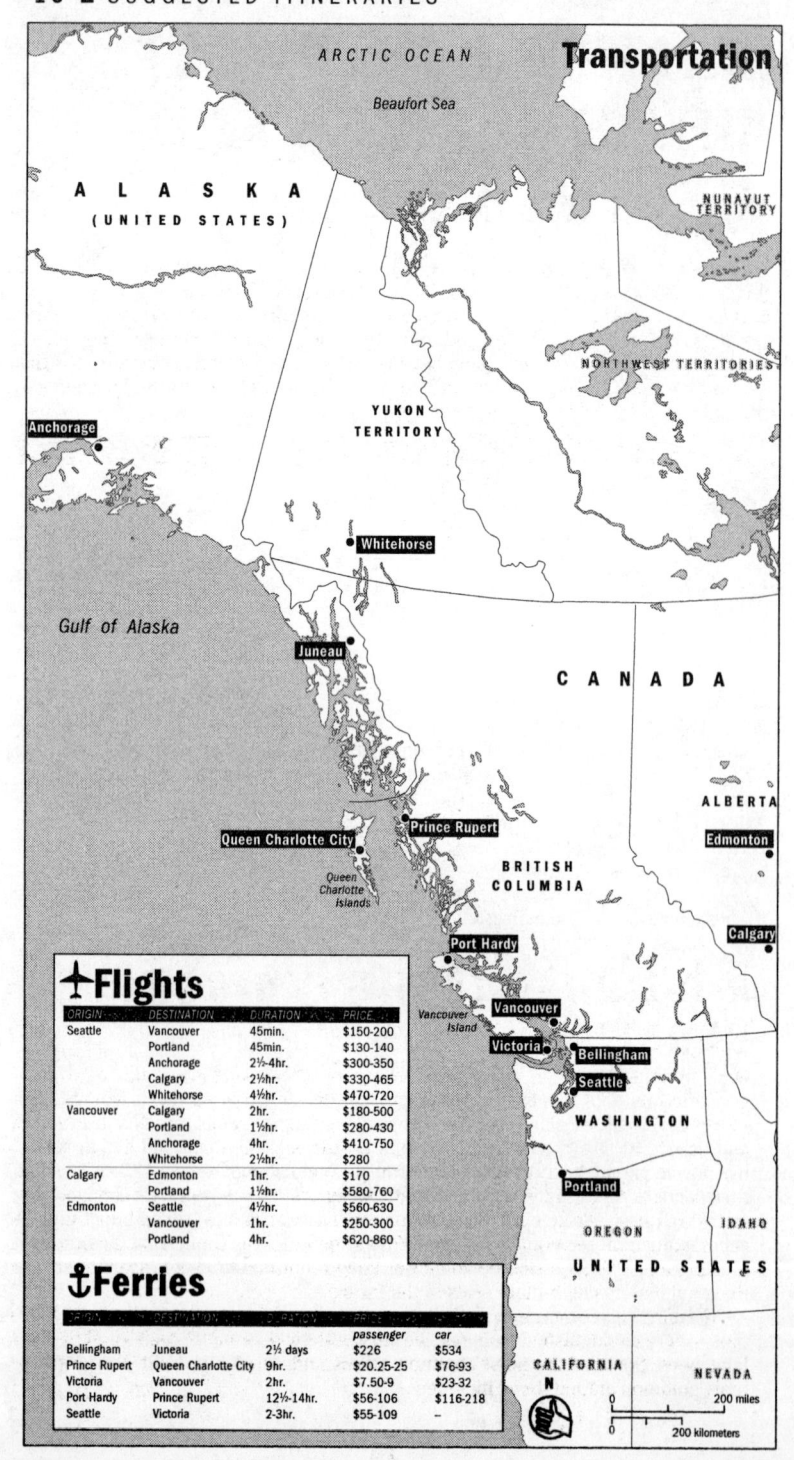

Transportation

✈ Flights

ORIGIN	DESTINATION	DURATION	PRICE
Seattle	Vancouver	45min.	$150-200
	Portland	45min.	$130-140
	Anchorage	2½-4hr.	$300-350
	Calgary	2½hr.	$330-465
	Whitehorse	4½hr.	$470-720
Vancouver	Calgary	2hr.	$180-500
	Portland	1½hr.	$280-430
	Anchorage	4hr.	$410-750
	Whitehorse	2½hr.	$280
Calgary	Edmonton	1hr.	$170
	Portland	1½hr.	$580-760
Edmonton	Seattle	4½hr.	$560-630
	Vancouver	1hr.	$250-300
	Portland	4hr.	$620-860

⚓ Ferries

ORIGIN	DESTINATION	DURATION	PRICE passenger	car
Bellingham	Juneau	2½ days	$226	$534
Prince Rupert	Queen Charlotte City	9hr.	$20.25-25	$76-93
Victoria	Vancouver	2hr.	$7.50-9	$23-32
Port Hardy	Prince Rupert	12½-14hr.	$56-106	$116-218
Seattle	Victoria	2-3hr.	$55-109	–

PACIFIC NORTHWEST: UNAUTHORIZED AND UNCENSORED

This is a story about passion. A passion whose unrelenting wildness is matched only by its object: the land of the Pacific Northwest. For years different groups fought one another for control over her resources, lured by the vision of sparkling waters, lush forests, unconquered mountains, and virgin wilderness. Mesmerized by her wild beauty, these groups have resorted to any means necessary for this land. The history of the Pacific Northwest is a history of these groups struggling to claim her. Meet the players in the story:

PLAYER	MOTIVATION	WEAPONS/ASSETS
Indigenous Nations	Sense of kinship with and deep respect for the land which supports them	First dibs
Settlers/Industrialists	Money (exploitation)	Big guns, little mercy
Conservationists	True love	1) Lobbyists and legislation 2) Willingness to chain selves to trees and engage in life-endangering demonstrations for cause Tough combo.
Tourists (You)	A few (unbelievably awesome) thrills	*Let's Go: Alaska and the Pacific Northwest*, for the wise among them

This is not to say that the players experienced a single motivation—many who rushed to the Pacific Northwest for gold, fur, or farmland, subsequently discovered and were overwhelmed by the beauty of the land—but these are their motivations distilled for the purposes of comparison, an incomplete portrait of their identities and desires. Who, then, *are* the groups and what did they really want? And who has won the battle for the Pacific Northwest? Read on, fair reader, for the exciting, tragic, and twisted story of these groups and their relationships with Alaska and the Pacific Northwest.

R-E-S-P-E-C-T: THE INDIGENOUS PEOPLE

Once upon a time, approximately twelve to sixty thousand years ago, a group of nomadic hunters bravely traipsed across the (frozen) Bering Strait from Siberia into present-day Alaska and eventually moved farther south into North America and the Pacific Northwest. True to popular imagination, many did live in igloos, use dogsleds for transport (commemorated in the **Iditarod**, see p. 443), and sustain themselves by hunting whales and other sealife. They depended on the land, but some sign of reverence for the land or other reciprocal gesture almost always accompanied these people's use of it. For example, in the Yupik tribe the first time a young man caught a seal he could not keep it but had to give it away to secure the good luck to catch more seals in the future.

The different communities—including the Aleutians, Yuits, Inuits, and Eskimos—were distinguished from one another both by their mythologies and by their languages. Some of the most common words and phrases in Inuit, the language most common among them, include:

12 ■ THE EUROPEANS ARRIVE

ENGLISH	INUIT	ENGLISH	INUIT
How are you?	Qanuipit?	I am hungry	Kaaktunga
I am fine	Qanuingittunga	What is it?	Una suna?
What is your name?	Kinauvit?	I am sick	Aaniajunga
I want to take your picture	Ajjiliurumajagit	I have to use the washroom	Quisuktunga
Thank you	Qujannamiik	Where am I?	Namiippunga?
You are welcome	Llaali	I want to go fishing	Iqalliarumajunga
How much is it?	Qatsituqqa?	I want to go by dogteam	Qimuksikkuurumavunga
Expensive	Akitujuq	Good-bye (to one)	Tavvauvutit
Yes, No	Li, Aakka	Good-bye (to all)	Tavvauvusi

CULTURE

The languages may have defined the differences among the groups, but the land created their commonalities. The rich supply of salmon and halibut sustained these communities, and daily life centered around fishing. The economy of coastal groups focused around three main subsystems, all related to fish: fishing, construction of plank houses for smoking and drying fish, and later transportation, which provided access to the fish. Almost all native groups adjusted their lifestyles according to the season, moving between different settlements that favored the harvesting of available game, fish, and living materials. The coastal culture, prevalent throughout much of the Northwest, was one of waterside villages of cedar plank houses, wooden sculptures, massive dugout canoes, and **potlatch festivals.**

Although large-scale potlatch festivals no longer occur, another remnant of the native culture remains a defining aspect of the Pacific Northwest: the totem pole. Particularly noticeable in British Columbia, the totem pole peppers parks, sites, and tourist shops (see "Top Five Things You Never Should Have Learned About Totem Poles", p. 16). In their images, these poles tell the stories of families, clans, and individuals, a trait which reflects the family-oriented organization of the tribes. Several tribes, including the Athabascans and Tlingit, were organized **matrilinearly,** with the mother shouldering the headship of the household. These were the indigenous cultures which the Europeans encountered when they arrived.

THE EUROPEANS ARRIVE

The indigenous tribes and the land of the Pacific Northwest enjoyed an amiable relationship that was upset by the arrival of the Europeans. Instead of arriving all at once, though, the Europeans first came in the form of a few celebrated figures:

EXPLORER	YEAR	NATIONALITY	CLAIM TO FAME
Francis Drake	16th century	English	Circumnavigated the globe; claimed Oregon for the English and affectionately described the coast as wrapped in "vile, thicke, and stinking fogges."
Vitus Bering	1741	Danish, working for Russia	Led the Russians to the Aleutian Islands.
Aleksei Chirko	mid-18th century	Russian	Explored Alaska; brought reports of seals and skilled hunters to Russia, which catalyzed an interest in the fur trade.
Juan Perez and Bruno Heceta	1774-75	Spanish	Claimed Nootka Sound for Spain and re-initiated European interest in the Pacific Northwest.
James Cook	1778	English	Searched for a polar trade route; voyaged from Oregon to Alaska's westernmost tip
George Vancouver	1792	English	Cartographer who accompanied Cook and mapped out the Pacific Northwest; got an island and The Major City in BC named after him (see p. 235 and p. 254).
Alexander Mackenzie	1793	English	Completed an overland exploration of the Pacific Northwest.

WHAT IS THIS POTLATCH FESTIVAL?
Potlatch festivals were an opportunity for villagers to exchange and display wealth, celebrate important transitions such as adoptions or aging, and to enact stories and history. Derived from a Chinook word meaning "gift" or "giving," the Potlatch was a feast marking an important event in a person's life and required that the host lavishly give of himself, even if he had no resources for daily living. The amount one gave increased the respect he garnered from the community. At intertribal potlatches, rival chiefs might destroy hundreds of blankets and canoes just to demonstrate the excesses of their wealth. Banned for some time by both US and Canadian governments as part of a policy of integration, potlatch festivals are now starting to come back

Early Russian explorers eagerly recognized the value of trading with the skilled Aleut hunters they encountered. The Aleuts, likewise, eagerly parted with their otter pelts for beads that, while common to the Russians, the Aleuts saw as portals for spirits. A short while after Britain increased its trading activity in the south, a permanent Russian settlement was established on Kodiak Island. By the time of Vancouver's voyage, Russian control of the Arctic seal hunt was beginning to replace trade; already a small population of Aleuts had been relocated from the Pribilof Islands, a rich seal breeding ground. In 1799 the Russian-American Company was established in Sitka (see p. 412), and its brokerage clout was felt as far south as California. The Russians' aggressive imposition upon the Native Alaskans incited the Tlingit, a powerful coastal nation, to raze the Russians' settlement and massacre nearly every inhabitant in 1802. Two years later, the Russians returned to bombard the Tlingit fort. The Tlingit withdrew from the area after 10 days' fighting exhausted their ammunition. Prior to this intense conflict, the Europeans considered the indigenous nations autonomous and profitable trading partners. But the coast had become a lucrative asset for a number of well armed and well organized outsiders. During the coming decades, it would be bargained for among England, Russia, and the US while indigenous nations would be forced out of their role as partners in the coastal economy.

THE EUROPEANS START TO TURN
Trade, according to most Europeans, was mutually beneficial: Europeans took valuable furs and pelts and natives received weapons with which they could defend themselves and their property. The Europeans also brought less welcome gifts with them: smallpox, venereal infections, and other contagious diseases. Ultimately, this trade crippled the indigenous people's power.

THE RISE AND FALL OF THE 1763 ROYAL PROCLAMATION
The British recognized the continent's unexplored territory—much of what lay west and north of the thirteen colonies—as the "Hunting Grounds" of independent indigenous nations under the Crown's protection. Several developments contributed to the erosion of these amicable relations. First, political conflict with the American government no longer required that the British maintain a network of allies on the continent. Second, as Europeans pushed west, they developed the means to harvest the land's resources themselves. Lastly, newcomers were frustrated by the indigenous peoples of the West; natives were suspicious of outsiders and didn't help the new settlements. They had no interest in adopting their manners of dress and custom.

THE HIDDEN HERO
At 17, Sacagawea was both the youngest member of the Lewis and Clark expedition and the only woman. Though she received none of the monetary or land rewards her master-husband did, she played what was arguably a more vital role. Sacagawea served as interpreter, navigator, and ambassador to the Native Americans. Her importance to the mission is less disputed than the pronunciation of her name. Experts advise: Sah-cah'-gah-wa-ah, not Sa'-ca-jah-wee-ah.

14 ■ THE EUROPEANS ARRIVE

CULTURE

HOW MANY WORDS DO THE ESKIMOS HAVE FOR SNOW?
An idle question? Perhaps for some, but others have leaked pages of ink in vitriolic responses to the debate it has spawned. While the common answer has been that the Eskimos have nine or ten words for snow, estimates for the West Greenlandic tribes shoot up to 49. Not everyone is so quick to embrace these numbers or their significance, though. In his book *The Great Eskimo Vocabulary Hoax*, Geoff Pullman contests the idea that the Eskimos have an unusually large vocabulary for snow. He points out that English speakers also have many words for snow, including ice, sleet, powder, and flakes. Those committed to the many-snow-words theory contend that English cannot touch the precision of some Eskimo languages. In West Greenlandic, for example, there is a word for "lumps of ice stranded on the beach" (issinnirit), not to be confused with "lump of old ice frozen into new ice" (tuaq) which is distinct from "new ice formed in crack in old ice" (nutarniq). Lexicons are available online for many Native American and First Nation languages for those who wish to settle this debate themselves.

THE COMPETITION MOUNTS AND PEOPLE GET... *COMPETITIVE*
As more people streamed into western Washington and Oregon in the middle of the 19th century, Europeans and natives had to compete not only against one another, but also against the United States. As Thomas Jefferson sensed the British beginning to take hold of the region, he organized the first US overland exploration of the West, headed by **Meriwether Lewis and William Clark.** Jefferson sent the Lewis and Clark expedition west in 1804 with political, scientific, and commercial goals. He believed the nation that controlled the fabled Northwest Passage would control the continent's destiny. Jefferson outlined many tasks, including announcing American sovereignty in the uncharted region. The team traveled from St. Louis to the Pacific Ocean and back, returning in 1806 with information about plants, animals, rivers, mountains, and native cultures. While the team did not find a Northwest passage, its safe return and promising discoveries encouraged many families to migrate west.

Hundreds departed for the West along the famed **Oregon Trail.** The trail extended from Independence, Missouri, to the mouth of the Columbia River and took four to six months to travel. While the Trail offered settlers the opportunity to stake claim in unexplored lands, it also came with great risk. The journey was often filled with the hardships of poor equipment, illness, and attacks from Natives. To provide for families on the frontier and the establishment of communities, the **1862 Homestead Act** made 160 acres of land available for free to any married man who would live on and cultivate the land for five years. The same act barred the ownership of land by non-whites. The argument by Natives that this was their land, and therefore not the US government's to give away, failed to sway those in power. Settlers created a provisional government in 1843, lobbied for territorial status in 1848, and joined the Union as Oregon 11 years later.

HOW THE WEST WAS DOMESTICATED
Gold and oil discoveries along the West Coast in the late 19th century also supported settlement in the Northwest. These finds not only encouraged cities surrounding the gold and oil but also helped supplying towns grow. For example, gold in the Klondike in 1895 drew thousands to the interior of what would be staked out as the Yukon Territory (see p. 369) three years later. Seattle (see p. 146) and Skagway (see p. 430) proudly lay claim to their roles as the Klondike's outfitters. The San Francisco gold rush precipitated the building of Portland (see p. 65), which was well positioned to supply the California town with timber and wheat. Only one territorial acquisition of the period was considered unsound. When Russia offered the sale of Alaska to the US in 1867, the icy expanse was considered a depleted resource, as evidenced by the Russian's lackluster seal trade. It was not until years later that US Secretary of State William Seward was celebrated for purchasing the vast oil field for a piddling 2¢ per acre.

> **EIGHT THINGS THAT YOU DIDN'T KNOW ABOUT THE OREGON TRAIL:**
> 1. One in ten people died traveling it.
> 2. Oxen or mules rather than horses were the animals of choice for the wagons.
> 3. Because their wagons were already too full, the emigrants could not sit in the wagons and be pulled along by the horses–er, oxen. Most of them walked. Barefoot.
> 4. The biggest killer on the trail was cholera.
> 5. As trees and fuel for the fire became scarce around 1849 when the trail got crowded, travelers resorted to using buffalo dung to get their fires going.
> 6. Some travelers had to wait for up to two hours for a buffalo stampede to pass.
> 7. Most people began their journeys by loading their wagons with over a ton of cargo, but within one day of their journey, most would already have begun unloading their wagon by throwing things out into the world.
> 8. Two hundred would-be travelers signed up to ride in the wind-wagon, a forerunner of the airplane, but the contraption never got off the ground.

By the end of the 19th century, the indigenous culture was dying rapidly. The number of newcomers flooding the land and governmental intervention forced the native peoples onto small reservations. The indigenous nations were devastated by disease, enslavement, murder, and the strain of relocation. They had begun to develop new economic patterns more dependent upon white American and British manufactured goods. Traditional means for fishing using canoes and spears were replaced by gasoline engines, power gears, and navigation with tables, compasses, and charts. Even the aggressive warrior tribes of Northwest Coast Indians never mounted a major war against the Europeans. Not cowardice, but the vulnerability of their coastal villages to naval gunfire, motivated the decision to share the land. Unfortunately, there peaceful response was not reciprocated, and the situation turned uglier for the indigenous people.

BETRAYAL: POLICY TOWARD THE NATIVE PEOPLE

While tribes farther east were exiled from their traditional land, the indigenous people of the Pacific Northwest seem to have retained their home court advantage. While not victims of the **Kill and Banish the Indians** policy of the 16th, 17th, 18th, and early 19th centuries, they couldn't escape the **Destroy the Indians' Culture** policy of Canada and the **Take the Indians' Land** policy of the US.

From the birth of the United States until 1924 when Congress granted Native Americans citizenship, US policy consisted of a series of broken promises for land. Laws such as the **Indian Removal Act** left little doubt of government intentions and led to the Cherokee's forced relocation known as the **Trail of Tears**. Conditions improved slightly with President Roosevelt's 1934 **Indian Reorganization Act,** in which indigenous communities were recognized as tribes and directed to create their own constitutions. The effect of this policy was mitigated by a subsequent reversal of policy in **Operation Relocation** (1952), in which large groups of Native Americans were relocated from reservations into cities. The gesture had an unexpected effect as, for the first time in generations, Native Americans who lived off reservations began to recognize themselves as an ethnic group against the backdrop of mainstream society. This was the beginning of the modern native revival.

The Canadian policy toward the First Nations was not any more just or kind. The **1876 Indian Act** gave the government complete control over every person that it declared to be Indian. Children were separated from their families, forbidden to speak with their siblings, and even prohibited from speaking their native language. Those who refused to submit to this policy were severely punished, and many children were physically and sexually abused. Adults were taught methods of farming, untenable in many of the regions where it was attempted, and traditions of community life were disallowed. A few rights were granted after World War II, and in 1969, presaging the trend toward euphemism, the government ended the policy of **assimilation** in favor of a new policy of **integration**. By the time residential schools were closed, some as late as the 1970s, an entire generation had been raised in isolation from their land and weakened by alcoholism, poverty, and the neglect of their traditions.

Since the 1970s, tribes in both countries have been making slow gains as the descendents of their conquerors grant them more autonomy. Much of their culture is gone forever, as are most native tongues, but for many tribes in the Pacific Northwest now is a time of renewal.

METHOD	HOW IT WORKED	LONG-TERM EFFECT
Germs	Lacking evolutionary defenses, some ninety-five percent of Native Americans and First Nations were killed by diseases that Europeans brought with them from the old world.	Plagues so depopulated the continent that Europeans believed the land to be deserted. Because no one was using the land, the Europeans felt justified in moving in on it.
Guns	Settlers occupied land that belonged to Native Americans and First Nations. When the indigenous owners tried to defend their land, the settlers shot them.	Tribes in the East were driven off their land very quickly. Resistance grew as settlers moved West, but the native peoples had neither the weapons nor the numbers to defend themselves.
Government (early policy)	The US and Canadian governments signed treaties with native peoples promising them some land in exchange for vacating their homelands. These treaties were universally broken, leading to later treaties. Each step took more and more land from the native people	Indigenous people were steadily exiled to the West, then given reservations, then given smaller reservations, and ultimately were left with tiny tracts of worthless land.
Government (later policy)	A policy of integration prohibited native languages, religious ceremonies, and native dress.	Many tribes lost parts of their heritage forever. While this policy caused the fewest deaths, it has probably done the most damage to native communities.

RISING AGAIN: THE INDIGENOUS PEOPLE TODAY

In the last ten years, the census showed that roughly 16% of the Alaskan population is Native American, and recently they have been asserting their rights more forcefully.

TOP FIVE THINGS YOU NEVER SHOULD HAVE LEARNED ABOUT TOTEM POLES...
because they are wrong:
1. The totems in the Pacific Northwest are thousands of years old.
The oldest date from 1835, and most are under 100 years old.
2. Totem pole carving is a disappearing art form.
After a bout in the earlier half of the twentieth century in which authentic totem building virtually vanished, totem carving experienced a renaissance in the latter half.
3. Totems were built to be worshiped.
Totems tell stories and stand for particular values, people, and ideas, but they are not objects of worship.
4. The totem poles in Stanley Park (see p. 246) are fake.
They are actually authentic and among the most valuable totems in the world.
5. Totem poles were used to ward off evil spirits.
A popular myth, but a myth nonetheless.

> **THE MOTHER OF EVE** Though lacking a creation story for woman, the Inupiat boast one of the most original mythologies for the birth of man. Before people aged, before time governed the universe, there lived a woman who remained forever young. As the only person alive, she became rather bored and lonely and one day decided she needed a companion. Taking the pooya she was chewing out of her mouth, the woman artfully fashioned it into a pretty image which she completed with a raven's beak atop head of the sculpture. Flushed in the triumph of her creation, the woman delighted herself by playing with the image until she was so exhausted that she fell fast asleep, her image resting lifelessly beside her. The next morning she gleefully discovered that her creation had become animated. Thus was the first man born.

NEGOTIATING WITH THE GOVERNMENT. First Nations (the indigenous people of Canada) and Native American (the indigenous people of the United States) tribes have once again begun to flourish as independent communities. Some indigenous people live on reservations within cities that serve as little more than suburbs; others have settled land claim negotiations and are living on their traditional territory and resurrecting their customs. There is a whole range of intermediate stages, depending on the health of the communities involved, what lands they claim, and with which governments they are negotiating. Most indigenous communities that are federally recognized reservation tribes in the US, or administered under the Indian Act in Canada, are allowed hunting and fishing rights, as well as the right to use specified lands for ceremonial purposes. Some communities seek first and foremost to preserve the cultural heritage of their traditional lands. In British Columbia, for example, Haida tribesmen oversaw the use of ancient village sites in the disputed territory of the Queen Charlotte Islands and lobbied heavily for its preservation from logging. After the federal government purchased the land, the Haida's role in the stewardship of the spectacular **Gwaii Haanas National Park Reserve** became officially recognized. The indigenous people have been working with the government to re-assert their presence and reclaim their love: the land.

THE 1960S. Throughout the 1960s, Native Alaskans watched with increasing frustration as the federal and state governments divvied up vast tracts of land that the Inuit, Aleut, Tlingit, Haida, and Athabasca had claims upon. After the discovery in 1968 of immense oil deposits in the Beaufort Sea on Alaska's northern coast, Native Alaskans increased the pressure to settle the claims that had been so long ignored and sought a share in the anticipated economic boom

DECEMBER 1971. The US government finally made some degree of peace with Native Alaskans, state and federal courts, and environmental groups by passing the **Alaska Native Claims Settlement Act.** Sixty thousand Native Alaskans received a total of one billion dollars and 40 million acres of land.

1993. Yukon First Nations negotiated a settlement for self-government and land claims under a general framework known as the **Umbrella Final Agreement.**

1997. In the **Delgamuukw** decision of 1997, the Supreme Court of Canada allowed the Wet'suwet'en and Gitksan to cite ceremony and oral tradition to prove that their use of disputed lands preceded the arrival of Europeans.

AUGUST 1998. Negotiations continue over items of self-government and the right to self-determination. In August of 1998, after years of talks between government officials and the **Nisga'a** band of northern British Columbia, representatives signed a controversial landmark treaty granting the Nisga'a a form of self-government and control over natural resources in 1940 square kilometers of their traditional lands.

1999. The Supreme Court of Canada instructed the government to revise the Indian Act so that communities, and not the government, have the power to allow non-residents to vote in band elections. It also passed Bill C-49, or the **First Nations Land Management Act,** which created a framework for First Nations to develop their own land-use laws. Most dramatically, on April 1, 1999, the Canadian government split the Northwest Territories in half and granted the densely Inuit-populated eastern portion, **Nunavut** ("Our Land"), self-government.

APRIL 11, 2001. An association of tribes signed an agreement with state of Alaska which would lay the ground rules for future dialogue between the groups. The agreement said little that was earth-shattering, but it did affirm the right of the tribes to form their own governments and conduct their own affairs.

CONTEMPORARY CULTURE

CONSERVATION AND HARVEST

Political entities in the Northwest strive to compete and to protect their independent interests within the framework of federal legislation. Inevitably, relations don't go smoothly. The central political tensions are between conservation and harvest, where **harvest** is synonymous with jobs, and **conservation** is synonymous with tradition. These are particularly difficult to balance in Oregon, Washington, and Alaska, home to the most federally and state-protected land in the United States. The outright challenge of co-managing renewable resources is exacerbated in British Columbia and the Yukon by the involvement of vast quantities of land in territorial disputes with First Nations. The work of co-managing the resources that these states and provinces share—like the Pacific salmon fishery—has been the most dramatic and drawn-out subject of reconciliation.

Policies of environmental stewardship emerged in response to a variety of pressures, from civic consciousness to political activism. Oregon has led the pack in reform beginning in 1967, when the **Oregon coast,** was preserved for free and uninterrupted use by the public. Moreover, Oregon's 1971 **Bottle Bill** was the first recycling refund program in the US.

On the animal front, Washington and Oregon's **spotted owl** remains a symbol of conflict between conservationists and industrialists after vast tracts of the bird's old-growth forest habitat were protected. A vociferous battle has also been fought of the gray whale, an interesting case in which the government waited until 1937 to ban commercial harvesting of these creatures. In many cases indigenous communities lead conservation efforts, suspending their hunting and trapping before sluggish government wheels begin to roll toward curbing industries. On Vancouver Island residents rallied to save the **endangered marmot**; efforts culminated with a "Marmot-aid" benefit concert.

In general, things go best for all when projects are undertaken together. For example, the collaboration between Washington State University Wood Materials and Engineering Laboratory and the logging industry produced significant results. Materials that fifty years ago would have been considered waste were used to create six billion board feet of alternative wood product, equivalent to the total amount of board feet expected to be cut in Washington and Oregon in 2001.

THE WILD THINGS

The wildlife in Alaska and the Pacific Northwest is one of its biggest draws. Some of the critters running around the area include:

THE MAKAH WHALE CONTROVERSY was not a traditional conflict between industrialists and conservationists but one between conservationists and Native Americans. In the 1990s, when the endangered gray whales had rebounded to a viable population, the Makah applied to the International Whaling Commission, with US support, for a cultural exemption to the continuing ban. The five-whale allowance granted to the Makah enraged conservationists. Regardless, Makah returned to the ceremonial and subsistence hunt in 1999 among protest and publicity.

BROWN BEARS. Alaska has about 30,000 brown bears, or one per square mile, which is more than 98% of the United States' brown bear population. Bears usually prefer solitude, so they shouldn't hassle tourists. Still, hikers are advised to purchase bear spray before venturing out into the back country.

CARIBOU. Better known in the popular imagination as reindeer, the caribou was made to travel over land. These animals travel across more land each year (3000 miles) than any other animal, and they can get up to speeds of over 50 mph, making them faster than any car on the Dempster highway (see p. 390).

MOUNTAIN GOATS. Unlike the fast-moving caribou, mountain goats move at a more deliberate pace. Patience seems to be a virtue of these creatures. Male goats ("billies") crawl on their bellies when they are pursuing a female goat ("nannies").

WOLVES. Contrary to popular myth, gray wolves do not always mate for life. Divorce rates have been rising among the wolf population in recent years. Experts are unsure as to why, but *Let's Go* suggests that perhaps male wolves could learn from the billies.

BLACK BEAR. The black bear fares even worse in the romance department. Male and female bears are never together except to breed. As soon as breeding is over, the male bear ditches, leaving the female to raise the cubs.

RED FOX. Though red is the usual color of these foxes, these animals often have different colors at different times of their life. The foxes can be found with black coats, silver coats, or with a black and brown cross on their back.

BALD EAGLE. Chosen because it is unique to North America, the bald eagle fortunately beat out Ben Franklin's choice of the wild turkey as the emblem of the United States. After the population dwindled due to hunters and pesticides, the bald eagle is staging a promising comeback.

CULTURE AND THE ARTS

Years ago, cities like Vancouver were middle-class port towns with a burgeoning counter-culture. In the years since, they've exploded and the entire Pacific Rim seems to have breached its humdrum roots: tourists have poured in, technological industries have expanded, and resource-driven industries are grinding to a halt under environmental pressures. Yet none of the communities of the Northwest stray far from their origins—port towns remain port towns, and the festivals that first brought communities together continue to do so—lending an authenticity to the cities. The laid back lifestyle of the Northwest results from this seamless blending, and their love for the land is expressed in its aggressive defense.

The influx of money and people has infiltrated even the most backwater communities to create a worldly atmosphere. As a result the Northwest has come to support everything the tasteful traveler could hope for: from famed stagings of **Shakespeare** in Ashland, OR (p. 116), to the celebration of the **Oosic Stout,** the microbrew named for a male walrus' maleness, in Skagway, AK (p. 430).

MUSIC AND THEATER

Music lovers wouldn't hesitate to say that **Seattle** stole the show from California at the close of the millennium. As the birthplace of **Jimi Hendrix** and the cradle of grunge, it's undeniable that rock's greatest influences emanate from the Northwest. Artists who hit it big in the 90s included **Pearl Jam, Nirvana, Alice in Chains,** and **Soundgarden,** who pioneered the **grunge** sound and look. Today, rock still reigns supreme in Seattle at the **Experience Music Project,** which opened in June, 2000 (see p. 164). Designed by Frank Gehry, architect of the famed Guggenheim Museum in Bilbao, Spain, the $250 million project was the brain child of Paul Allen, Microsoft's co-founder. Although prowling record executives signing contracts with everything in plaid have departed Seattle, the Northwest has been identified as a breeding ground for **riot-grrrl** rock and **guitar-timbre** bands. Seattle also has a **repertory theater** community third in size only to those of Chicago and New York, and its **opera** is internationally renowned for its Wagner productions. Bryan Adams, of Vancouver and Pop, has charged that **"CanCon"** laws, which require TV and radio to air a minimum amount of Canadian content, breed mediocrity in Canadian arts. Beyond Adams' own syrupy ballads, there is scant evidence to support his complaint.

MOVIE	ACTORS	YEAR	LOCATION
Dr. DooLittle 2	Eddie Murphy	2001	Wrangell, AK (p. 406)
Mystery Alaska	Russell Crowe, Hank Azaria	1999	Banff National Park, BC (p. 354)
Independence Day	Will Smith, Bill Pullman, Jeff Goldblum	1996	Grants Pass, OR (p. 115)
Maverick	Mel Gibson, Jodie Foster, James Garner	1994	Columbia River Gorge (p. 82)
Free Willy	Jason James Richter	1993	Astoria and Portland, OR (Cannon Beach, p. 92)
The Goonies	Sean Astin, Josh Brolin	1985	Astoria, OR (p. 87)
Indiana Jones and the Temple of Doom	Harrison Ford, Kate Capshaw	1984	Grand Coulee Dam, WA (p. 218)
The Shining	Jack Nicholson	1980	Timberline Lodge, OR (p. 80)
One Flew Over the Cuckoo's Nest	Jack Nicholson	1975	Salem, OR (p. 106)
Call of the Wild	Clark Gable, Loretta Young	1935	Mt. Baker Lodge, WA (p. 181)

VISUAL ART

Not to be outdone, the visual arts hold their own place of prominence for having cultivated the continent's oldest art forms and for being at the center of their revitalization: the cedar **masks, totems,** and **longhouses** of indigenous coastal nations have long been recognized as some of the world's most notable artistic achievements. Native carving is a versatile art that entwines religious lineage and cultural heritage, with current attention being focused on turning out a marketable product. **Bill Reid** (1920-1998), a Haida carver and Vancouver native, is one of many artists celebrated for revitalizing communities through carving, dance, song, and potlatch, all art forms suppressed by law during the last hundred years.

Government support reflects the public's commitment to the arts. Portland and Seattle, for example, funnel a 1% tax on capital improvements into the acquisition and creation of public art. While government cutbacks have compromised the health of famed centers for arts in Western Canada, artist communities and colonies are alive and thriving among the San Juan and Gulf Islands of Washington and British Columbia and in small towns like Atlin, BC, and Homer, AK (p. 472). Where government comes up short, philanthropists step in: in 1998-9, the Patrons of Northwest Civic, Cultural, and Charitable Organizations, **PONCHO,** had its best year yet, dispensing $2 million in Puget Sound; since 1962, the group has poured $21 million into the region's arts organizations.

FESTIVALS

Communities throughout the Northwest, both rural and urban, thrive on **festivals**. Every community has its own tradition of celebration and new venues and organizers are always cropping up to peddle everything from folk and bluegrass to rock, to pot-smoking (see p. 240), golfing, and outhouse racing (see **Delta Junction**, p. 519). Orchestral music aficionados flock to the **Bach Festival** in Eugene, WA. The Seattle's **Bumbershoot** festival and a whole range of vibrant **nightlife** in the environs support new music in Portland (p. 65), Seattle (p. 146), Olympia (p. 171), Spokane (p. 226), and Bend (p. 122). Shakespeare enthusiasts will appreciate Ashland's **Oregon Shakespeare Festival** (p. 120).

FESTIVALS (2002)

DATE	NAME & LOCATION	DESCRIPTION
Beginning March 3	Iditarod AK: Anchorage to Nome	The bravest of the brave hitch up a team of hardy huskies and mush over tundra and mountains across 1150 mi. of Alaska.
July 1	Canada Day Anywhere in Canada	Typically quiet Canada struggles with an irresistible urge to whoop it up for the anniversary of Confederation.
July 4	Independence Day Anywhere in the US	Fireworks, fireworks, beer, fireworks, beer, beer, fireworks, hot dogs and hamburgers on the grill, and some fireworks.
July 12-14	Oregon Country Fair Eugene, OR	Craft booth concessionaires and earnest crystal-worshippers converge on Eugene to eat, play, discuss sustainable energy, and hug.
July 5-14	Stampede Calgary, AB	One of the biggest rodeos in the world; international contestants, hundreds of thousands of visitors, and many cows.
July 19-21	Folk Music Festival Vancouver, BC	A modern-day Woodstock of the West, Vancouver attracts folk musicians from around the world to don their Birkenstocks and jam.
Third weekend in July	Rhythm & Blues Festival Winthrop, WA	Just what its name says. Ample rhythm and plentiful blues invade a self-proclaimed wild Western town.
Labor Day weekend	Bumbershoot Seattle, WA	Seattle's block party for the arts draws hundreds of thousands of groovsters to watch every sort of big-name act, from Sir Mix-A-Lot to the Indigo Girls to Sky Cries Mary.
September 12-15	Round-Up Pendleton, OR	A whole week of tribal dances, bucking broncos, and country line dancing. Yeee-haw!
Mid-February to October	Shakespeare Festival Ashland, OR	Dude, that's a lot of drama.

ESSENTIALS

DOCUMENTS AND FORMALITIES

> **ENTRANCE REQUIREMENTS**
> **Passport** (p. 23). Required for all visitors to the US and Canada.
> **Visa** (p. 24). In general, required for visiting US and Canada, but requirement can be waived. (See p. 24 for more specific information.)
> **Work Permit** (p. 59). Required for all foreigners planning to work in the US or Canada.

EMBASSIES AND CONSULATES ABROAD

Contact your nearest embassy or consulate to obtain info regarding visas and passports to the US and Canada. Listings of foreign embassies within the US as well as US embassies abroad can be found at www.embassyworld.com. A US **State Department** web site provides contact info for key officers at US overseas stations: www.state.gov/www/about_state/contacts/keyofficer_index.html. The Canadian Ministry of Foreign Affairs is at www.dfait-maeci.gc.ca/dfait/missions/menu-e.asp.

US CONSULATES AND EMBASSIES

Australia, Moonah Pl., Yarralumla ACT 2600 (☎02 6214 5600; www.usis-australia.gov/embassy); MLC Centre, 19-29 Martin Pl., 59th fl., Sydney NSW 2000 (☎02 9373 9200); 553 St. Kilda Rd., P.O. Box 6722, Melbourne VIC 3004 (☎03 9526 5900); 16 St. George's Terr., 13th fl., Perth WA 6000 (☎08 9202 1224).

Canada, 490 Sussex Drive, Ottawa, ON K1N 1G8 Canada (☎613-238-5335; www.usembassycanada.gov); 1095 West Pender St., Vancouver, BC V6E 2M6 (☎604-685-4311); 615 Macleod Trail SE, Room 1000, Calgary, Alberta T26 4T8 (☎403-266-8962).

Ireland, 42 Elgin Rd., Ballsbridge, Dublin 4 (☎01 668 8777; www.usembassy.ie).

New Zealand, Yorkshire General Bldg., 4th fl., 29 Shortland St., Auckland (☎09 303 2724); 29 Fitzherbert Terr., Thorndon, Wellington (☎04 472 2068; www.usembassy.state.gov/wellington).

South Africa, Broadway Industries Centre, P.O. Box 6773, Heerengracht, Foreshore, Cape Town (☎021 214 280); 1 River St., c/o Riviera, Killarney, Johannesburg (☎011 646 6900); 877 Pretorius St., Arcadia 0083, P.O. Box 9536, Pretoria 0001 (☎012 342 1048; www.usembassy.state.gov/pretoria).

UK, 24 Grosvenor Sq., London W1A 1AE (☎ 0207 499 9000; www.usembassy.org.uk).

CANADIAN CONSULATES AND EMBASSIES

Australia, Commonwealth Ave., Canberra ACT 2600 (☎02 6270 4000; www.dfait-maeci.gc.ca/australia); 111 Harrington St., Level 5, Sydney NSW 2000 (☎02 9364 3000); 123 Camberwell Rd., Hawthorn East, Melbourne VIC 3123 (☎03 9811 9999); 267 St. George's Terr., Perth WA 6000 (☎08 9322 7930).

Ireland, 65 St. Stephen's Green, Dublin 2 (☎01 478 1988).

New Zealand, 61 Molesworth St., 3rd fl., Thorndon, Wellington (☎04 473 9577).

South Africa, Reserve Bank Bldg., St. George's Mall St., 19th fl., Cape Town 8001 (☎021 423 5240); 1103 Arcadia St., Hatfield, Pretoria 0083 (☎012 42 3000).

UK, 30 Lothian Rd., Edinburgh, Scotland EH2 2XZ (☎0131 220 4333; fax 0131 245 6010); Canada House, Trafalgar Square, London, SW1Y 5BJ (☎0207 258 6600).

US, 1251 Ave. of the Americas, New York, NY 10020 (☎212-596-1658); 550 S. Hope St. 9th fl., Los Angeles, CA 90071 (☎213-346-2700); 2 Prudential Plaza, 180 N. Stetson, Ave., Ste. 2400, Chicago, IL 60601 (☎312-616-1860); 501 Pennsylvania Ave. NW, Washington, D.C. 20001 (☎202-682-1740).

EMBASSIES IN THE US AND CANADA

IN WASHINGTON, D.C. (US)

Australia, 1601 Mass. Ave. NW, 20036 (☎202-797-3000; www.austemb.org).
Canada, 501 Penn. Ave., 20001 (☎202-682-1740; www.canadianembassy.org).
Ireland, 2234 Mass. Ave. NW, 20008 (☎202-462-3939; www.irelandemb.org).
New Zealand, 37 Observatory Circle, 20008 (☎202-328-4800; www.nzemb.org).
UK, 3100 Mass. Ave., 20008 (☎202-588-6500; www.britainusa.com/consular/embassy).
South Africa, 3051 Mass. Ave., 20008 (☎202-232-4400; http://usaembassy.southafrica.net).

IN OTTAWA, ONTARIO (CANADA)

Australia, 50 O'Connor St. #710, K1P 6L2 (☎613-236-0841; www.ahc-ottawa.org).
Ireland, 130 Albert St. #700, K1P 5G4 (☎613-233-6281).
New Zealand, 99 Bank St. #727, K1P 6G3 (☎613-238-6097; www.nzhcottawa.org).
UK, 310 Summerset St., K2P 0J9 (☎613-230-2961; www.britain-in-canada.org).
US, 100 Wellington St., K1P 5T1 (☎613-238-5335; www.usembassycanada.gov).
South Africa, 15 Sussex Dr., K1M 1M8 (☎613-744-0330).

PASSPORTS

REQUIREMENTS. All non-Canadian and non-US citizens need valid passports to enter the US and Canada, and to re-enter their own country. Returning home with an expired passport is illegal and may result in a fine. US citizens can enter Canada (and vice versa) with proof of citizenship and a photo ID. A driver's license and birth certificate should suffice.

PHOTOCOPIES. Be sure to photocopy the page of your passport with your photo, passport number, and other identifying information, as well as any visas, travel insurance policies, plane tickets, or traveler's check serial numbers. Carry one set of copies in a safe place, apart from the originals, and leave another set at home. Consulates also recommend that you carry an expired passport or an official copy of your birth certificate in a part of your baggage separate from other documents.

LOST PASSPORTS. If you lose your passport, immediately notify the local police and the nearest embassy or consulate of your home government. To expedite its replacement, you will need to know all information previously recorded and show ID and proof of citizenship. In some cases, a replacement may take weeks to process, and it may be valid only for a limited time. Any visas stamped in your old passport will be irretrievably lost. In an emergency, ask for immediate temporary traveling papers that will permit you to re-enter your home country.

NEW PASSPORT. File any new passport or renewal applications well in advance of your departure date. Most passport offices offer rush services for a steep fee. Citizens of Australia, Canada, Ireland, New Zealand, and the United Kingdom can apply for a passport at the nearest post office, passport office, or court of law.

VISAS

Citizens of most European countries, Australia, New Zealand, and Ireland can waive US visas through the **Visa Waiver Pilot Program**. Visitors qualify if they are traveling only for business or pleasure (*not* work or study), are staying for fewer than 90 days, have proof of intent to leave (e.g. a return plane ticket), an I-94W form (arrival/departure certificate attached to your visa upon arrival), and are traveling on particular air or sea carriers. Citizens of South Africa and some other countries need a visa in addition to a valid passport for entrance to the US. To obtain a visa, contact a US embassy or consulate.

All travelers planning a stay of more than 90 days (180 days for Canadians) also need to obtain a visa; contact the closest US embassy or consulate. The **Center for International Business and Travel (CIBT)**, 23201 New Mexico Ave. NW #210, Washington, D.C. 20016 (☎ 202-244-9500 or ☎ 800-925-2428), secures travel "pleasure tourist," or **B-2**, visas to and from all possible countries for a variable service charge (six month visa around US$45). If you lose your I-94 form, you can replace it at the nearest **Immigration and Naturalization Service (INS)** office (☎ 800-375-5283; www.ins.usdoj.gov), although it's unlikely that the form will be replaced within the time of your stay. **Visa extensions** are sometimes attainable with a completed I-539 form; call the forms request line (☎ 800-870-3676). Be sure to double-check on entrance requirements at the nearest US embassy or consulate, or consult the Bureau of Consular Affair's web site (www.travel.state.gov/visa;visitors.html).

Citizens of Australia, Ireland, New Zealand, the UK, and the US may enter Canada without visas for stays of 90 days or less if they carry proof of intent to leave; South Africans need a visa to enter Canada (CDN$75 for a single person, CDN$400 for a family). Citizens of other countries should contact their Canadian consulate for more info. Write to Citizenship and Immigration Canada for the booklet *Applying for a Visitor Visa* at Information Centre, Public Affairs Branch, Jean Edmonds Tower South, 365 Laurier Ave. W, Ottawa, ON K1A 1L1 (☎ 613-954-9019 or 800-242-2100), or consult it online at http://cicnet.ci.gc.ca. Extensions are sometimes granted; phone the nearest Canada Immigration Centre.

IDENTIFICATION

When you travel, always carry two or more forms of identification on your person, including at least one photo ID; a passport combined with a driver's license or birth certificate is usually adequate. Many establishments, especially banks, may require several IDs in order to cash traveler's checks. Never carry all your forms of ID together; split them up in case of theft or loss.

STUDENT AND TEACHER IDENTIFICATION. The **International Student Identity Card (ISIC)**, the most widely accepted form of student ID, provides discounts on sights, accommodations, food, and transport. The ISIC is preferable to an institution-specific card (such as a university ID) because it is more likely to be recognized (and honored) abroad. All cardholders have access to a 24-hour emergency helpline for medical, legal, and financial emergencies (in North America call 877-370-ISIC) and US cardholders are also eligible for insurance benefits (see **Insurance**, p. 32). Many student travel agencies issue ISICs, including STA Travel in Australia and New Zealand; Travel CUTS in Canada; *usit* in the Republic of Ireland and Northern Ireland; SASTS in South Africa; Campus Travel and STA Travel in the UK; Council Travel and STA Travel in the US (see p. 46). The card is valid from September of one year to December of the following year and costs AUS$13, UK£5, or US$22. Applicants must be degree-seeking students of a secondary or post-secondary school and be of at least 12 years of age. Because of the proliferation of fake ISICs, some services (particularly airlines) require additional proof of student identity, such as a school ID. The **International Teacher Identity Card (ITIC)** offers the same insurance coverage but with limited discounts. The fee is AUS$13, UK£5, or US$22. Find more info at www.istc.org.

CUSTOMS ■ 25

YOUTH IDENTIFICATION. The International Student Travel Confederation also issues a discount card to travelers who are 26 years old or under, but are not students. This one-year **International Youth Travel Card** (**IYTC**; formerly the **GO 25** Card) offers many of the same benefits as the ISIC. Most organizations that sell the ISIC also sell the IYTC (US$22).

CUSTOMS

Upon entering the United States or Canada, you must declare certain items from abroad and pay a duty on the value of those articles that exceed the allowance established by the US or Canada's customs service. Keeping receipts for larger purchases made abroad will help establish values when you return. Upon returning home, you must declare all articles acquired abroad and pay a **duty** on the value of articles that exceed the allowance established by your country's customs service. Goods and gifts purchased at **duty-free** shops abroad are not exempt from duty or sales tax at your point of return; you must declare these items as well. "Duty-free" merely means that you need not pay a tax in the country of purchase. For more specific information on customs requirements, contact the following information centers.

> **AMERICAN AND CANADIAN CUSTOMS DECLARATIONS**
> Entering the **US** as a *non-resident,* you are allowed to claim US$100 of gifts and merchandise if you will be in the country for 72hr. *Residents* may claim $400 worth of goods. If 21, you may bring in 1L of wine, beer, or liquor. 200 cigarettes, 50 cigars (steer clear of Cubans), or 2kg of smoking tobacco are also permitted. Entering **Canada,** *visitors* may bring in gifts, each of which may not exceed CDN$60 in value. *Residents* who have been out of the country for 24hr. may claim CDN$50 exemption. After 48hr. they may claim CDN$200, and after 7 days CDN$750. If you are of the legal drinking age in the province, and have been out of the country for 48hr. or more, you may bring in 1.5L of wine, 1.14L of liquor, or 24x355mL cans or bottles of beer or ale. You may also bring in 200 cigarettes, 50 cigars, 200 tobacco sticks, or 200g of manufactured tobacco.

Australia: Australian Customs National Information Line (in Australia call 01 30 03 63, from elsewhere call 61 2 6275 5366; www.customs.gov.au).

Canada: Canadian Customs, 333 Dunsmuir St., Vancouver, BC V6B 5R4 (☎800-461-9999 in Canada or 506-636-5064; www.revcan.ca).

Ireland: Customs Information Office, Irish Life Centre, Lower Abbey St., Dublin 1 (☎01 878 8811; fax 878 0836; taxes@revenue.iol.ie; www.revenue.ie/customs.htm).

New Zealand: New Zealand Customhouse, 17-21 Whitmore St., Box 2218, Wellington (☎04 473 6099; fax 473 7370; www.customs.govt.nz).

South Africa: Commissioner for Customs and Excise, Privat Bag X47, Pretoria 0001 (☎012 314 9911; fax 328 6478; www.gov.za).

UK: Her Majesty's Customs and Excise, Passenger Enquiry Team, Wayfarer House, Great South West Rd., Feltham, Middlesex TW14 8NP (☎020 8910 3744; fax 8910 3933; www.hmce.gov.uk).

US: US Customs Service, 1330 Pennsylvania Ave. NW, Washington, D.C. 20229 (☎202-354-1000; fax 354-1010; www.customs.gov).

MONEY

Money is easily accesible throughout the Northwest. The American dollar is accepted in many Canadian establishments, although manners dictate that you should ask whether a store will take it before handing it to someone. It is better not to pay with American dollars because private establishments often give a poor exchange rate. It is also better to exchange money in advance or pay with plastic.

NOTE. Throughout this guide, prices in Canada (British Columbia, Alberta, and the Yukon) are in Canadian dollars, and prices in the US (Oregon, Washington, and Alaska) are in US dollars.

CURRENCY AND EXCHANGE

The main unit of currency in the US and Canada is the **dollar ($),** which is divided into 100 **cents (¢).** Paper money is green in the US; bills come in denominations of $1, $5, $10, $20, $50, and $100. Coins are 1¢ (penny), 5¢ (nickel), 10¢ (dime), 25¢ (quarter), and $1. Paper money in Canada comes in denominations of $5, $10, $20, $50, and $100, which are color-coded by denomination. Coins are 1¢, 5¢, 10¢, 25¢, $1, and $2. The $1 coin is known as the **Loonie** and the $2 coin is affectionately dubbed the **Toonie.** The chart below is based on rates in late August, 2001.

THE GREENBACK (US DOLLAR)	
CDN$1 = US$0.65	US$1 = CDN$1.54
UK£1 = US$1.43	US$1 = UK£0.70
IR£1 = US$1.15	US$1= IR£0.87
AUS$1 = US$0.52	US$1= AUS$1.91
NZ$1 = US$0.43	US$1 = NZ$2.32
ZAR1 = US$0.12	US$1 = ZAR8.29

THE LOONIE (CANADIAN DOLLAR)	
US$1 = CDN$1.54	CDN$1 = US$0.65
UK£1 = CDN$2.20	CDN$1 = UK£0.46
IR£1 = CDN$1.76	CDN$1= IR£0.57
AUS$1 = CDN$0.80	CDN$1= AUS$1.25
NZ$1 = CDN$0.66	CDN$1 = NZ$1.51
ZAR1 = CDN$0.19	CDN$1 = ZAR5.39

Banks generally have the best rates. Elsewhere, you can expect steep commission rates. A good rule of thumb is to use banks or money-exchanging centers that have at most a 5% margin between buy and sell prices. Convert in large sums to avoid numerous penalties, but no more than you'll need. ATM and credit cards (see p. 27) often get very good rates.

TRAVELER'S CHECKS

Traveler's checks (**American Express** and **Visa** are the most recognized) are one of the safest and least troublesome means of carrying funds, although they are gradually becoming obsolete in the US because of the increased availability of ATMs. Several agencies and banks sell them for a small commission. Each agency provides refunds if your checks are lost or stolen, and many provide additional services, such as toll-free refund hotlines abroad, emergency message services, and stolen credit card assistance.

While traveling, keep check receipts and a record of which checks you've cashed separate from the checks themselves. Also leave a list of check numbers with someone at home. If your checks are lost or stolen, immediately contact a refund center (of the company that issued your checks) to be reimbursed; they may require a police report verifying the loss or theft. Ask about toll-free refund hotlines and the location of refund centers when purchasing checks, and always carry emergency cash.

American Express: Call 800-25-19-02 in Australia; in New Zealand 0800 441 068; in the UK 0800 521 313; in the US and Canada 800-221-7282. Elsewhere call the US collect +1 801-964-6665; www.aexp.com. Traveler's checks are available at a 1-4% commission at AmEx offices and banks, or commission-free at AAA offices (see p. 52). *Cheques for Two* can be signed by either of 2 people traveling together.

Citicorp: In the US and Canada call 800-645-6556; elsewhere call US collect +1 813-623-1709. Traveler's checks (available only in US dollars, British pounds, and German marks) at 1-2% commission. Call 24hr

Thomas Cook MasterCard: In the US and Canada call 800-223-7373; in the UK call 0800 62 21 01. Checks available in 13 currencies at 2% commission. Thomas Cook offices cash checks commission-free.

Visa: In the US call 800-227-6811; in the UK call 0800 89 50 78; elsewhere call UK collect +44 20 7937 8091. Call for the location of their nearest office.

CREDIT CARDS

Credit cards are generally accepted in all but the smallest businesses in both the US and Canada. Major credit cards—**MasterCard** (along with its European counterparts **Euro Card** or **Access**) and **Visa** (with its European counterparts **Carte Bleue** or **Barclaycard**) are welcomed most often—can be used to extract cash advances in dollars (both US and Canadian) from associated banks and teller machines throughout both countries. Credit card companies get the wholesale exchange rate, which is generally 5% better than the retail rate used by banks and other currency exchange establishments. **American Express** cards also work in some ATMs, as well as at AmEx offices and major airports. All such machines require a **Personal Identification Number (PIN).** You must ask your credit card company for a PIN before you leave; without it, you will be unable to withdraw cash with your credit card outside your home country. If you already have a PIN, check with the company to make sure it will work in Canada and the US.

CREDIT CARD COMPANIES. Visa (US ☎ 800-336-8472) and MasterCard (US ☎ 800-307-7309) are issued in cooperation with banks and other organizations. American Express (US ☎ 800-843-2273) has an annual fee of up to US$55. AmEx cardholders may cash personal checks at AmEx offices abroad, access an emergency medical and legal assistance hotline (24hr.; in North America call 800-554-2639, elsewhere call US collect +1 715-343-7977), and enjoy American Express Travel Service benefits (including plane, hotel, and car rental reservation changes; baggage loss and flight insurance; mailgram and international cable services; and held mail). The Discover Card (in US call 800-347-2683, elsewhere call US +1 801-902-3100) offers cashback bonuses on most purchases.

CASH (ATM) CARDS

Cash cards—popularly called ATM cards—are widespread in the US and Canada. Depending on the system that your home bank uses, you can most likely access your personal bank account from abroad. ATMs get the same wholesale exchange rate as credit cards, but there is often a limit on the amount of money you can withdraw per day (around US$300). There is typically also a surcharge of US$1-2 per withdrawal. Also, if your PIN is longer than four digits, ask your bank whether you need a new number.

The two major international money networks are **Cirrus** (US ☎ 800-424-7787) and **PLUS** (US ☎ 800-843-7587). To locate ATMs around the world, call the above numbers, or consult www.visa.com/pd/atm or www.mastercard.com/atm. Most ATMs charge a transaction fee that is paid to the bank that owns the ATM.

DEBIT CARDS

Debit cards are a hybrid between credit and cash cards. They bear the logo of a major credit card, but purchases and withdrawals made with them are paid directly out of your bank account. Using a debit card like a credit card often incurs no fee (contact the issuing bank for details), gives you a favorable exchange rate, and frees you from having to carry large sums of money. When given the option to use your card as either an ATM card or a credit card (as you will be at self-serve gas stations), it's usually cheaper to choose to use it as a credit card. Be careful, though: debit cards lack the theft protection that credit cards usually have.

GETTING MONEY FROM HOME

AMERICAN EXPRESS. Cardholders can withdraw cash from their checking accounts at any of AmEx's major offices and many representative offices (up to US$1000 every 21 days; no service charge, no interest). AmEx "Express Cash" withdrawals from any AmEx ATM in the US and Canada are automatically debited from the cardholder's checking account or line of credit. Green card holders may withdraw up to US$1000 in any seven-day period (2% transaction fee; minimum US$2.50, maximum US$20). To enroll in Express Cash, cardmembers may call 800-227-4669 in the US; elsewhere call the US collect +1 336-668-5041.

WESTERN UNION. Travelers from the US, Canada, and the UK can wire money abroad through Western Union's international money transfer services. In the US, call 800-325-6000; in Canada, 800-235-0000; in the UK, 0800 83 38 33. To wire money within the US using a credit card (Visa, MasterCard, Discover), call 800-CALL-CASH (225-5227). The rates for sending cash are generally US$10-11 cheaper than with a credit card, and the money is usually available at the place you're sending it to within an hour. To locate the nearest Western Union location, consult www.westernunion.com.

FEDERAL EXPRESS. Some people choose to send money abroad in cash via FedEx to avoid transmission fees and taxes. While FedEx is reasonably reliable, note that this method is **illegal**. In the US and Canada, FedEx can be reached by calling 800-463-3339; in the UK, 0800 12 38 00; in Ireland, 800 535 800; in Australia, 13 26 10; in New Zealand, 0800 733 339; and in South Africa, 011 923 8000.

COSTS

The cost of your trip will vary considerably, depending on where you go, how you travel, and where you stay. The single biggest cost of your trip will probably be your round-trip **airfare** to Alaska and the Pacific Northwest (see **Transportation: By Plane,** p. 44). If you choose to rent a car (necessary for travel through many places), that will be another major expense (see **Transportation: By Car** see p. 51). Before you go, spend some time calculating a reasonable per-day **budget** that will meet your needs.

STAYING ON A BUDGET. On land, **accommodations** start at about $12 per night in a hostel bed, while a basic sit-down meal costs about $10 depending on the region. If you stay in hostels and prepare your own food, you'll probably spend from $30-40 per person per day. A slightly more comfortable day (sleeping in hostels/guesthouses and the occasional budget hotel, eating one meal a day at a restaurant, going out at night) would run US$50-65; for a luxurious day, the sky's the limit. Transportation costs will increase these figures. **Gas** prices have risen significantly in the US over the past year. A gallon of gas now costs about $1.60 per gallon (40¢ per L), but prices vary widely according to state gasoline taxes. In Canada, gas costs CDN60-70¢ per L (CDN$2-2.65 per gallon). Before you go, spend some time calculating a reasonable per-day **budget** to meet your needs. Don't forget to factor in emergency reserve funds (at least $200) when planning how much money you'll need.

SAFETY AND SECURITY

> **EMERGENCY = 911.** For emergencies in the US and Canada, dial **911**. This number is toll-free from all phones, including coin phones. In a very few remote communities, 911 may not work. If it does not, dial 0 for the operator and request to be connected with the appropriate emergency service. In national parks, it is usually best to call the **park warden** in case of emergency. Let's Go always lists emergency contact numbers.

PERSONAL SAFETY

EXPLORING. To avoid unwanted attention, try to blend in as much as possible and familiarize yourself with the area before you set out. The gawking camera-toter is a more obvious target for thieves and con artists than the low-profile traveler. Carry yourself with confidence; if you must check a map on the street, duck into a shop. If you are traveling alone, be sure someone at home knows your itinerary, and **never admit that you're traveling alone.** Whenever possible, *Let's Go* warns of unsafe neighborhoods and areas, but there are some good general tips to follow. When walking at night, stick to busy, well-lit streets and avoid dark alleyways. Do not attempt to cross through parks, parking lots, or other large, deserted areas. Buildings in disrepair, vacant lots, and unpopulated areas are all bad signs. Keep in mind that a district can change character drastically between blocks and from day to night. Look for children playing, women walking in the open, and other signs of an active community. If you feel uncomfortable, leave as quickly and directly as you can, but don't allow fear of the unknown to turn you into a hermit. Careful, persistent exploration will build confidence and make your stay even more rewarding.

SELF DEFENSE. There is no sure-fire way to avoid all the threatening situations you might encounter when you travel, but a good self-defense course will give you concrete ways to react to unwanted advances. A rule of thumb though: if you are in physical danger, it is best to give the attacker what he asks for; your life is more important than your wallet. **Impact, Prepare,** and **Model Mugging** can refer you to local self-defense courses in the US which both men and women are invited to attend (☎ 800-345-5425) and Vancouver (☎ 604-878-3838). Workshops (2-3hr.) start at US$50; full courses run US$350-500.

GETTING AROUND. For long drives in desolate areas, invest in a cellular phone and a roadside assistance program (see p. 52). Drive with doors locked at night and in unsafe neighborhoods. Don't stop to assist a stranger whose car has broken down; instead call for help. Park in well-lit areas and don't leave valuables in plain view when parked and use a steering wheel locking device in larger cities.

Bicycling can also be a viable option in many of the isolated communities in the Pacific Northwest and Alaska. Wearing a bike helmet and locking your bike should eliminate most risks associated with this form of self-propelled travel. Most towns have bike rental shops where bikes and appropriate safety gear can be obtained. For info on **hitchhiking**, see p. 54.

TRESPASSING. Much wilderness is owned or controlled by private citizens, Native Americans, First Nations, or companies. Each has their own reasons for being sensitive to **trespassing** and none take it lightly. Poking around lumber yards, quarries, or fishing docks will not be appreciated by workers (and is often dangerous). Look out for and respect signs; when in doubt ask park rangers, public lands offices, or locals before making camp or setting out into the backcountry.

FINANCIAL SECURITY

PROTECTING YOUR VALUABLES. There are a few steps you can take to minimize the financial risk associated with traveling. First, **bring as little with you as possible.** Leave expensive watches, jewelry, cameras, and electronic equipment at home; chances are you'll break them, lose them, or get sick of lugging them around anyway. Second, buy a few combination **padlocks** to secure your belongings either in your pack—which you should **never leave unattended**—or in a hostel locker. Third, **carry as little cash as possible;** instead carry traveler's checks and ATM/credit cards, keeping them in a **money belt**—not a "fanny pack"—along with your passport and ID cards. Fourth, **keep a small cash reserve separate from your primary stash.** This should entail about US$50 (about CAN$75) sewn into or stored in the depths of your pack, along with your traveler's check numbers and important photocopies.

ACCOMMODATIONS AND TRANSPORTATION. Never leave your belongings unattended; crime occurs in even the most demure-looking hostel or hotel. Bring your own **padlock** for hostel lockers, and don't ever store valuables in any locker.

Be particularly careful on **buses, subways,** and **trains;** horror stories abound about determined thieves who wait for travelers to fall asleep. Carry your backpack in front of you where you can see it. When traveling with others, sleep in alternate shifts. When alone, use good judgement in selecting somewhere to nap: use a lock to secure your pack to something and stay in sight of people. Try to sleep on top bunks with your luggage stored above you (if not in bed with you), and keep important documents and other valuables on your person.

If traveling by **car,** don't leave valuables (such as radios or luggage) in it while you are away. If your tape deck or radio is removable, hide it in the trunk or take it with you. Similarly, leave baggage in the trunk.

DRUGS AND ALCOHOL

If you carry **prescription drugs** while traveling, it is vital to have a copy of the prescriptions to present at US and Canadian borders. The importation of **illegal substances** into the Canada or the US is (needless to say) illegal, highly risky, and a punishable offense. Border guards of both countries have unlimited rights to search your baggage, your person, and your vehicle. They will seize vehicles on the spot that are found to be involved in smuggling even small quantities of illegal substances. US border guards can also ban you on the spot from re-entering the country for years. If you are not a US citizen, you may have no right to appeal such decisions. Away from borders, police attitudes vary widely, but the old standards—marijuana, LSD, heroin, cocaine—are illegal in every province and state.

In the US, the drinking age is 21; in Canada it is 19, except in Alberta, Manitoba, and Québec, where it is 18. Drinking restrictions are strict; the youthful should expect to be asked to show government-issued identification when purchasing any alcoholic beverage. Drinking and driving is prohibited everywhere, not to mention dangerous and idiotic. Open beverage containers in your car will incur heavy fines; a failed breathalyzer test will mean fines, a suspended license, and possibly imprisonment. Most localities restrict where and when alcohol can be sold under restrictions known as "blue laws." Sales usually stop at a certain time at night and are often prohibited entirely on Sundays.

HEALTH

Travelers complain most often about their feet and their gut, so take precautionary measures: drink lots of fluids to prevent dehydration and constipation, wear sturdy, broken-in shoes and clean socks, and use talcum powder to keep your feet dry.

BEFORE YOU GO

Preparation can minimize the likelihood of contracting a disease and maximize the chances of receiving effective health care in the event of an emergency. For tips on packing a basic **first-aid kit** and other health essentials, see p. 33.

In your **passport,** write the names of any people to be contacted in case of a medical emergency, and list any allergies or medical conditions. Matching a prescription to a foreign equivalent is not always possible or safe. Carry prescriptions or a statement from your doctor stating the medication's trade name, manufacturer, chemical name, and dosage. Keep your medication with you while traveling.

MEDICAL ASSISTANCE ON THE ROAD

When traveling in the Pacific Northwest, keep in mind that major cities are few and far between. Depending on where you are, the best medical facilities could be several hundred miles away. As you travel into more rural areas, facilities become more limited. With that in mind, think twice before exploring remote areas if you have a serious medical condition that might require immediate attention.

If you are concerned about being able to access medical support while traveling, there are special support services you may employ. The *MedPass* from **Global Emergency Medical Services (GEMS)**, 2001 Westside Dr., #120, Alpharetta, GA 30004, USA (☎ 800-860-1111; fax 770-475-0058; www.globalems.com), provides 24-hour international medical assistance, support, and medical evacuation resources. The **International Association for Medical Assistance to Travelers (IAMAT;** US ☎ 716-754-4883, Canada ☎ 416-652-0137, New Zealand ☎ 03 352 2053; www.sentex.net/~iamat) has free membership, lists doctors worldwide, and offers detailed info on immunization requirements and sanitation. If your regular **insurance** policy does not cover travel abroad, you may wish to purchase extra coverage (see p. 32).

Those with medical conditions (diabetes, allergies to antibiotics, epilepsy, heart conditions) may want to obtain a stainless-steel **Medic Alert** ID tag (first-year US$35, $15 annually thereafter), which identifies the condition and gives a 24-hour collect-call number. Contact the Medic Alert Foundation, 2323 Colorado Ave., Turlock, CA 95382, USA (☎ 800-825-3785; www.medicalert.org).

ENVIRONMENTAL HAZARDS

While the Pacific Northwest enjoys a temperate climate, summer temperatures can reach triple digits. Heat exhaustion, caused by dehydration and salt deficiency, can lead to fatigue, headaches, and dizziness. Avoid it by drinking plenty of fluids, eating salty foods (e.g. crackers), and avoiding dehydrating beverages (e.g. alcohol, coffee, tea, and caffeinated soda). Heat stress can lead to heatstroke, characterized by a rising temperature, severe headache, and cessation of sweating. Victims should be cooled off with wet towels and taken to a doctor.

On the opposite end of the spectrum, the extreme cold and dampness makes hypothermia and frostbite very real dangers. Victims may shiver, feel exhausted, have poor coordination or slurred speech, hallucinate, or suffer amnesia. Do not let hypothermia victims fall asleep, or their body temperature will continue to drop and they may die. To avoid hypothermia, keep dry, wear layers, and stay out of the wind. Watch out for frostbite when the temperature is below freezing. If skin turns white, waxy, and cold, do not rub the area. Drink warm beverages, get dry, and slowly warm the area with dry fabric or steady contact until a doctor can be found. For climbers, several of the mountains in the region reach dangerously high altitudes. Allow your body a couple days to adjust to less oxygen.

Environmental pests in the Northwest include Rydberg's Poison Ivy and Western Poison Oak. The plants secrete oils that can cause unbearable itchiness, hives, and inflammation of the affected areas. Calamine lotion or topical cortisones (like Cortaid) may stop itching.

WATER-BORNE DISEASES

When you are camping all water needs to be treated either by boiling it, filtering it, or using purification tablets. Remember that boiling will not get rid of all pathogens. Common reactions to untreated water include nausea, bloating, diarrhea, and malaise. Try quick-energy, non-sugary foods with protein and carbohydrates to keep your strength up. Over-the-counter anti-diarrheals (e.g. Immodium) may counteract the problems, but can complicate serious infections. The most dangerous side effect is dehydration; drink 8 oz. of water with ½ tsp. of sugar or honey and a pinch of salt, try uncaffeinated soft drinks, or munch on salted crackers. If you develop a fever or your symptoms don't go away after 4-5 days, consult a doctor. Consult a doctor for treatment of diarrhea in children.

OTHER INFECTIOUS DISEASES

Giardia (a.k.a. Beaver Fever): Found in streams and lakes, *Giardia lamblia* is a bacterium that causes gas, cramps, and violent diarrhea. Symptoms can last 1-2 weeks. To protect yourself, bring water to a boil for at least one minute or purify it with iodine tablets before drinking or cooking with it.

Lyme's Disease: Tick-borne diseases, like Lyme's disease, can be very serious. Only 3 cases of Lyme's disease in Alaska have ever been reported, but infection is more common in Western Canada and the Pacific Northwest. A Lyme's infection can cause a circular rash of two inches or more that looks like a bull's eye. Other symptoms are flu-like: fever, headache, fatigue, or aches and pains. Left untreated, Lyme's can cause dangerous problems in joints, the heart, and the nervous system. A vaccine has recently been brought to market; see your doctor for details. Lyme's can be treated with antibiotics if caught early. The ticks that spread this disease are too small to see with the naked eye, so watch for symptoms and wear bug repellent when hiking. Tucking pants into socks and wearing insect repellent with DEET can also help.

Red Tide: Refers to any number of harmful algal blooms in sea water, which sometimes, but not always, give the water surface a reddish tinge. Shellfish feed on these toxic algae, and toxin accumulates in their muscle tissue. The two most serious classes of toxins, which can cause fatal paralytic shellfish poisoning (PSP) and amnesic shellfish poisoning in humans, are both found regularly in shellfish on the Pacific Coast from Alaska to Oregon. The highest incidence of PSP in the world is in Southeast Alaska. The virtually unreported diarrhetic shellfish poisoning (DSP), which causes intestinal problems, is even more common. *Do not eat shellfish without assurance from a local health authority that they are free from toxins.*

INSURANCE

Travel insurance generally covers four basic areas: medical/health problems, property loss, trip cancellation/interruption, and emergency evacuation. Although your regular insurance policies may extend to travel-related accidents, you should consider purchasing travel insurance if the cost of potential trip cancellation, interruption or emergency medical evacuation is greater than you can absorb. Prices for travel insurance purchased separately generally run about US$50 per week for full coverage, while trip cancellation/interruption may be purchased separately at a rate of about US$5.50 per US$100 of coverage.

Medical insurance (especially university policies) often covers costs incurred abroad; check with your provider. **US Medicare** covers foreign travel only in Mexico and Canada. **Canadians** are protected by their home province's health insurance plan for up to 90 days after leaving the country; check with the provincial Ministry of Health or Health Plan Headquarters for details. **Homeowners' insurance** (or your family's coverage) often covers theft during travel and loss of travel documents (passport, plane ticket, railpass, etc.) up to US$500.

ISIC and **ITIC** (see p. 24) provide basic insurance, including US$100 per day of in-hospital sickness for up to 60 days, US$3000 of accident-related medical reimbursement, and US$25,000 for emergency medical transport. Cardholders have access to a toll-free 24-hour helpline for medical, legal, and financial emergencies overseas (US and Canada ☎ 877-370-4742, elsewhere call the US collect +1 715-345-0505). **American Express** (US ☎ (800) 528-4800) grants most cardholders automatic car rental insurance (collision and theft, but not liability) and ground travel accident coverage of US$100,000 on flight purchases made with the card.

INSURANCE PROVIDERS. Council and **STA** (see p. 46) offer a range of plans that can supplement your basic coverage. Other private insurance providers in the US and Canada include: **Access America** (☎ 800-284-8300); **Berkely Group/Carefree Travel Insurance** (☎ 800-323-3149; www.berkely.com); **Globalcare Travel Insurance** (☎ 800-821-2488; www.globalcare-cocco.com); and **Travel Assistance International** (☎ 800-821-2828; www.worldwide-assistance.com). Providers in the **UK** include **Campus Travel** (☎ 01865 25 80 00) and **Columbus Travel Insurance** (☎ 020 7375 0011). In **Australia**, try **CIC Insurance** (☎ 9202 8000).

PACKING

PACK LIGHT. Lay out only what you absolutely need; the less you have, the less can lose (or store, or carry on your back). Any extra space left will be useful for any souvenirs or items you might pick up along the way. If you plan to do a lot of hiking, also see **Outdoors,** p. 37.

LUGGAGE. If you plan to cover most of your itinerary on foot—or even if you plan on moving around a lot—a sturdy **frame backpack** is unbeatable. Toting a **suitcase** or **trunk** is fine if you plan to live in one or two cities and explore from there, but a very bad idea if you're going to be moving around a lot. In addition to your main piece of luggage, a **daypack** (a small backpack or courier bag) is a must.

CLOTHING. Dressing in layers is best when traveling and hiking. Even in summer, the Pacific Coast and Alaska can get cold, so don't go overboard on shorts and sandals. Don't skimp on raingear, however, as every season is the rainy season in the Pacific Northwest. Remember that wool, fleece, and polypropylene insulate when wet, whereas wet cotton is colder than wearing nothing at all. No matter when you're traveling, always bring a **warm jacket** or wool sweater, a **rain jacket** (Gore-Tex® is both waterproof and breathable), sturdy shoes or **hiking boots,** and **thick socks. Flip-flops** or waterproof sandals are crucial for grubby hostel showers.

SLEEPSACK. Some hostels require that you either provide your own linen or rent sheets from them. Save cash by making your own sleepsack: fold a full-size sheet in half the long way, then sew it closed along the long side and one of the short sides.

FIRST-AID KIT. For a basic first-aid kit, pack bandages, aspirin, antibiotic cream, a thermometer, a Swiss Army knife, tweezers, moleskin, decongestant, motion-sickness remedy, diarrhea or upset-stomach medication (Pepto Bismol or Immodium), an antihistamine, sunscreen, insect repellent, and burn ointment.

FILM. Developing film in the US and Canada costs $7-10 for 24 exposures. Less serious photographers may prefer **disposable cameras** over expensive permanent ones. Despite disclaimers, airport security X-rays *can* fog film, so buy a lead-lined pouch at a camera store or ask security to hand inspect it. Always pack it in your carry-on luggage, since higher-intensity X-rays are used on checked luggage.

OTHER USEFUL ITEMS. For safety purposes, you should bring a **money belt** and small **padlock.** Basic **outdoors equipment** (plastic water bottle, compass, waterproof matches, pocketknife, sunglasses, sunscreen, hat) are also essential. Quick repairs of torn garments can be done on the road with a **needle and thread;** also consider bringing electrical tape for patching tears. Doing your **laundry** by hand (where it is allowed) is both cheaper and more convenient than doing it at a laundromat—bring detergent, a small rubber ball to stop up the sink, and string for a makeshift clothes line. **Other things** you're likely to forget: a rain jacket; sealable **plastic bags** (for damp clothes, soap, food, shampoo, and other spillables); a travel **alarm clock;** safety pins; rubber bands; a flashlight; earplugs; and garbage bags.

ACCOMMODATIONS

HOSTELS

Hostels are generally dorm-style accommodations, often with large single-sex rooms with bunk beds, although some hostels do offer private rooms for families and couples. Some have kitchens and utensils for your use, bike or moped rentals, storage areas, and laundry facilities. There can be drawbacks: some hostels close during certain daytime "lockout" hours, have a curfew, don't accept reservations, impose a maximum stay, or, rarely, require that you do chores. In the Northwest, a bed in a hostel will average $15 and slightly more in the major cities.

34 ■ ACCOMMODATIONS

HOSTELLING INTERNATIONAL

Joining the youth hostel association in your own country (listed below) automatically grants you membership privileges in **Hostelling International (HI)**, a federation of national hosteling associations. HI hostels are scattered throughout the US and Canada, and many accept reservations via the **International Booking Network** (Australia ☎02 9261 1111; Canada ☎800-663-5777; England and Wales ☎1629 58 14 18; Northern Ireland ☎1232 32 47 33; Republic of Ireland ☎01 830 1766; NZ ☎03 379 9808; Scotland ☎8701 55 32 55; US ☎800-909-4776; www.hostelbooking.com). HI's umbrella organization's web page (www.iyhf.org), lists the web sites and phone numbers of all national associations and can be a great place to begin researching.

Most HI hostels also honor **guest memberships**—you'll get a blank card with space for six validation stamps. Each night you'll pay a nonmember supplement (one-sixth the membership fee) and earn one guest stamp; get six stamps, and you're a member. Most student travel agencies (see p. 46) sell HI cards, as do all of the national hosteling organizations listed below. All prices listed below are valid for **one-year memberships** unless otherwise noted.

- **An Óige (Irish Youth Hostel Association),** 61 Mountjoy St., Dublin 7 (☎01 830 4555; www.irelandyha.org). IR£10, under 18 IR£4.
- **Australian Youth Hostels Association (AYHA),** Level 3, 10 Mallett St., Camperdown NSW 2050 (☎02 9565 1699; www.yha.org.au). AUS$52, under 18 AUS$16.
- **Hostels Association of South Africa,** 3rd fl. 73 St. George's St. Mall, P.O. Box 4402, Cape Town 8000 (☎021 424 2511; www.hisa.org.za). ZAR45.
- **Hostelling International-American Youth Hostels (HI-AYH),** 733 15th St. NW, #840, Washington, D.C. 20005 (☎202-783-6161; www.hiayh.org). US$25, under 18 free.
- **Hostelling International-Canada (HI-C),** 400-205 Catherine St., Ottawa, ON K2P 1C3 (☎800-663-5777 or 613-237-7884; www.hostellingintl.ca). CDN$35, under 18 free.
- **Hostelling International Northern Ireland (HINI),** 22-32 Donegall Rd., Belfast BT12 5JN, Northern Ireland (☎02890 31 54 35; www.hini.org.uk). UK£10, under 18 UK£6.
- **Scottish Youth Hostels Association (SYHA),** 7 Glebe Crescent, Stirling FK8 2JA (☎01786 89 14 00; www.syha.org.uk). UK£6.
- **Youth Hostels Association (England and Wales) Ltd.,** Trevelyan House, 8 St. Stephen's Hill, St. Albans, Hertfordshire AL1 2DY, UK (☎0870 870 8808; www.yha.org.uk). UK£12.50, under 18 UK£6.25, families UK£25.
- **Youth Hostels Association of New Zealand (YHANZ),** P.O. Box 436, 193 Cashel St., 3rd Floor Union House, Christchurch 1 (☎03 379 9970; www.yha.org.nz). NZ$40.

REGIONAL HOSTEL INFORMATION IN WESTERN CANADA

- **HI British Columbia Region:** #402-134 Abbott St., Vancouver, BC V6B 2K4 (☎800-661-0020 or in BC 800-663-5777 or 604-684-7111; fax 604-684-7181; www.hihostels.bc.ca) web site offers online reservations.
- **HI Southern Alberta Region:** 1414 Kensington Rd. NW #203, Calgary, AB T2N 3P9 (☎403-283-5551; www.hostellingintl.ca/Alberta). Online reservations and info on ski and stay packages at ski areas in the Rockies.
- **HI Northern Alberta Region:** 10926-88 Avenue Edmonton, AB T6G 021 (☎780-432-7798; www.hostellingintl.ca/Alberta). Online reservations and info on northern Alberta.

HOTELS AND MOTELS

Many visitors centers, especially those off major thoroughfares, have hotel coupons. Even if you don't see any, ask. Budget motels are often clustered off highways several miles from town. It is fortunate that the Canadian hostel system is somewhat more extensive than that of the US because the country has a dearth of cheap motels. US budget motel chains cost significantly less than the chains catering to the next-pricier market, such as Holiday Inn. Chains also

HOTELS AND MOTELS ■ 35

DENALI MOUNTAIN MORNING HOSTEL & LODGE

private cabin

Wake to mountain peaks and the sound of Carlo Creek!

BUNKS: $25
PRIV. ROOMS: $65 for 2
PRIV. CABINS: $75-100+

Rooms and cabins sleep 4 - 7
Beautiful log cabins, great atmosphere

Contact us for expedition river trips and daily Park adventures!! Outdoor gear rentals, FREE shuttles, kitchen, hot showers, store...

Ben and Becky
www.hostelalaska.com
(907) 683-7503
Near National Park entrance

ESSENTIALS

Seaside International Hostel

HOSTELLING INTERNATIONAL

A European Tradition
on the Oregon Coast

Private Rooms & Dorms
On the River (canoes & sea kayaks)
4 Blocks to the Beach
On Site Espresso Bar
Common Kitchen & Lounges
Outdoor Decks & Lawn
Movies shown every evening

Also visit our Portland Hostel
Portland Int'l. Hostel - NW
1818 NW Glisan, Portland
503-241-2783
800-909-4776

www.2oregonhostels.com

Rated in top 10 hostels in U.S.A.

Seaside International Hostel
930 N. Holladay Drive
Seaside, Oregon 97138
Seaside@Teleport.com
503-738-7911
800-909-4776

36 ■ ACCOMMODATIONS

have more predictable standards of cleanliness and comfort than locally-operated budget competitors. Contact chains for free directories, and always inquire about discounts for seniors, families, frequent travelers, groups, or government personnel: **Motel 6** (☎ 800-466-8356; www.motel6.com); **Super 8 Motels** (☎ 800-800-8000; www.super8.com); **Choice Hotels International** (☎ 800-424-6423; www.choice hotels.com); **Best Western International** (☎ 800-528-1234; www.bestwestern.com).

YMCAS AND YWCAS

Young Men's Christian Association (YMCA) and **Young Women's Christian Association (YWCA)** lodgings are usually cheaper than a hotel but more expensive than a hostel. Not all locations offer lodging; those that do are often located in urban downtowns. Many YMCAs accept women and families; some will not lodge those under 18 without parental permission.

YMCA of the USA, 101 North Wacker Drive, Chicago, IL 60606 (☎ 888-333-9622; fax 312 977-0031; www.ymca.net). Provides a listing of the nearly 1000 Ys across the US and Canada. Offers info on prices, services available, telephone numbers and addresses, but no reservation service.

YMCA Canada, 42 Charles St. East, 6th fl., Toronto, ON M4Y 1T4 (☎ 416-967-9622; fax 967-9618; www.ymca.ca), offers info on Ys in Canada.

YWCA of the USA, Empire State Building, #301, 350 Fifth Ave., New York, NY 10118 (☎ 212-273-7800; fax 465-2381; www.ywca.org). Publishes a directory (US$8) on YWCAs across the USA.

World Alliance of YMCAs, 12 Clos Belmont, 1208 Geneva, Switzerland (☎ +41 22 849 5100, fax +41 22 849 5110; office@ymca.int; www.ymca.int).

HOTELS AND GUESTHOUSES

Budget hotel singles in the US cost about $40 per night, doubles $60; in Canada they are less common and also have steeper prices. Keep in mind, however, that prices rise with the size of the city. You'll typically share a hall bathroom; a private bathroom will cost extra, as will hot showers. Some hotels offer "full pension" (all meals) and "half pension" (no lunch). Smaller **guesthouses** are often cheaper than hotels. If you make **reservations** in writing, indicate your night of arrival and the number of nights you plan to stay. The hotel will send you a confirmation and may request payment for the first night. Not all hotels take reservations, and few accept checks in foreign currency. Enclosing two International Reply Coupons will ensure a prompt reply (each US$1.05; available at any post office).

BED AND BREAKFASTS (B&BS)

For a cozy alternative to impersonal hotel rooms, B&Bs (private homes with rooms available to travelers) range from the acceptable to the sublime. Hosts will sometimes go out of their way to be accommodating by accepting travelers with pets, giving personalized tours, or offering home-cooked meals. On the other hand, many B&Bs do not provide phones, TVs, or private bathrooms. In many northern communities, B&Bs are the only indoor accommodation option. The cheapest rooms in cheap B&Bs in the region generally cost $40-60 for a single and $60-80 for a double. For more info on B&Bs, see **Bed & Breakfast Inns Online,** P.O. Box 829, Madison, TN 37116 (☎ 615-868-1946; info@bbonline.com; www.bbonline.com), **Inn Finder,** 6200 Gisholt Dr. #105, Madison, WI 53713 (☎ 608-285-6600, fax 285-6601; www.inncrawler.com), or **InnSite** (www.innsite.com). Also try **Bed & Breakfast Central Information (BBCI),** P.O. Box 38279, Colorado Springs, CO 80937 (615-868-2318; email bbci@bbonline.com; www.bbonline.com/bbci).

UNIVERSITY DORMS

Many **colleges and universities** open their residence halls to travelers when school is not in session; some do so even during term-time. These dorms are often close to student areas—good sources for information on things to do—and are usually very clean. Getting a room may take a couple of phone calls and require advanced planning, but rates tend to be low and many offer free local calls.

CAMPING AND THE OUTDOORS

Camping is about the most rewarding way to slash traveling costs, particularly in Alaska and the Pacific Northwest. Traveling in a group of two or three means that the burdens of carrying gear and paying for sites (up to $20 in built-up areas, but often free to $5 for rustic sites) can be shared. *Let's Go* lists camping options town-by-town, including free camping on public lands. Campgrounds run by the provincial governments in Canada are usually spread out among forested areas and are generally more pleasant and less expensive than commercial sites. State campgrounds in the US blur the line between RV haven and treed tenter refuge. In British Columbia permits for Forest Service sites (CDN$8 per night, annual CDN$27) must be bought in town or from Forest Service employees, but enforcement in the more remote campgrounds of Northern BC and the Yukon is reportedly sporadic. Many sites have maximum stays of 14 days.

USEFUL RESOURCES

A variety of publishing companies offer hiking guidebooks to meet the educational needs of novice or expert. For information about camping, hiking, and biking, write or call the publishers listed below to receive a free catalog.

The Milepost, 619 E Ship Creek Ave., Anchorage, AK 99501 (☎(800) 726-4707 or 706- 722-6060; www.themilepost.com). An annual trip planning publication—essential for a trip to Alaska, but also useful for British Columbia, Alberta, and the Yukon.

The Mountaineers Books, 1001 SW Klickitat Way, #201, Seattle, WA 98134, USA (☎800-553-4453 or 206-223-6303; www.mountaineersbooks.org). Over 400 titles on hiking, biking, mountaineering, natural history, and conservation.

Sierra Club Books, 85 Second St., 2nd fl. San Francisco, CA 94105, USA (☎415-977-550; www.sierraclub.org/books). Publishes general resource books, as well as books on hiking in British Columbia and Alaska.

Wilderness Press, 1200 Fifth St., Berkeley, CA 94710, USA (☎800-443-7227 or 510-558-1666; www.wildernesspress.com). Over 100 hiking guides/maps for the western US, including *Camp Free in BC*, which lists hundreds of free campsites.

NATIONAL PARKS

National parks protect some of the US and Canada's most precious wildlife and spectacular scenery. The parks also offer activities such as hiking, skiing, and snowshoe expeditions. Most have backcountry camping and developed campgrounds; others welcome RVs, and a few offer opulent living in grand lodges.

Entry fees vary from park to park. In US parks pedestrian and cyclist entry fees tend to range from US$2-10, while vehicles cost US$5-20. National parks in the US offer a number of passes. The **National Parks Pass** (US$50 a year) admits the bearer and accompanying passengers in a vehicle (or family members where access is not by vehicle) entry into most US parks. For an additional $15, the Parks Service will affix a **Golden Eagle Pass** hologram to your card which will allow you access to sites managed by the US Fish and Wildlife Service, the US Forest Service, and the Bureau of Land Management. The

Golden Age Passport ($10 one time fee), available to those aged 62 or more, and the **Golden Access Passport,** free to travelers who are blind or permanently disabled, allows access to US national parks and 50% off camping and other park fees. Passes are available at park entrances.

The **Western Canada Annual Pass,** available for both individuals and groups, offers a similar deal at Canadian national parks in the four western provinces (CDN$35, seniors over 64 CDN$27, ages 6-16 CDN$18, groups of up to 7 adults CDN$70, groups of up to 7 which include at least one senior $53).

Let's Go lists fees for individual parks and contact information for park visitors centers (check the index for a complete listing). Every national park in the US and Canada has a web page, accessible from www.nps.gov or http://parkscanada.pch.gc.ca, which lists contact info, fees, and reservation policies.

US Forest Service, Outdoor Recreation Information Center, 222 Yale Ave. N, Seattle, WA 98109 (☎206-470-4060; www.fs.fed.us).

Parks Canada, 220 4th Ave. SE Room #550, Calgary, AB T2G 4X3 (☎800-748-7275; fax 292-4408; www.parkscanada.pch.gc.ca).

Alaska Public Lands Information Center, 605 W. 4th Ave. #105, Anchorage, AK 99501 (☎907-271-2737, in Fairbanks 456-0527; fax 907-456-0532; www.dnr.state.ak.us).

STATE AND PROVINCIAL PARKS

> **CAMPING RESERVATION NUMBERS. Reservations Northwest** (☎888-755-6900 or 206-935-1055; www.reservationsnorthwest.com) books campsites at many Oregon and Washington state parks (no reservation fee). The Oregon state parks info line (☎800-452-5687; www.prd.state.or.us) and its Washington equivalent (☎800-233-0321; www.parks.wa.gov) provide info on all state parks, including those not listed with the reservations center, and can refer callers to the agencies responsible for all other campsites in the state. The National Recreation Reservation service partners with the **US Forest Service (USFS)** to offer a reservations line (☎877-444-6777; www.reserveUSA.com) reserves selected campgrounds in national forests in Washington, Oregon, Alaska, and USFS cabins in southeast Alaska. For info on USFS campgrounds, cabins, and fire lookouts in Washington and Oregon not listed with the nationwide network, contact **Nature of the Northwest,** 800 NE Oregon St. #177, Portland, OR (☎503-872-2750; www.naturenw.org). **BC Discover Camping** (☎800-689-9025 or 604-689-9025; www.discovercamping.ca) reserves sites at many of the BC provincial parks. (CDN$12-20 per night; reservation fee CDN$6.42 per night for first 3 nights). For info on other, non-reservable provincial park campsites, call 250-387-4550. **Supernatural British Columbia** (☎800-663-6000; www.hellobc.com) can refer you to private campgrounds throughout BC. State campgrounds in Alaska are all first come, first serve, and cost about US$10.

In contrast to national parks, the primary function of **state and provincial parks** is usually recreation. Prices for camping at public sites are usually better than those at private campgrounds. Don't let swarming visitors dissuade you from seeing the larger parks—these places can be huge, and even at their most crowded they offer opportunities for quiet and solitude. Most campgrounds are first come, first serve, so arrive early. Some limit your stay and/or the number of people in a group. See above for camping reservation lines. For general information, contact:

Alaska Department of Natural Resources Public Information, 550 W. 7th Ave. #1260, Anchorage, AK 99501 (☎907-269-8400; fax 269-8901; www.dnr.state.ak.us/parks). Information on cabins ($25-65 per night) in Alaska state parks.

Alberta Park and Protected Areas, 9820 106 St., 2nd fl., Edmonton, AB T5K 2J6 (☎780-427-7009; fax 427-5980; www.gov.ab.ca/env/parks.html).

British Columbia Ministry of Environment, Lands, and Parks, P.O. Box 9338, Stn. Prov. Govt., Victoria, BC V8W 9M1 (☎ 250-387-1161; www.elp.gov.bc.ca/bcparks).

Oregon State Parks and Recreation Department, 1115 Commercial St. NE, Suite 1, Portland, OR 97301 (☎ 800-551-6949 or 503-378-6305; fax 503-378-5002; www.prd.state.or.us).

Washington State Parks and Recreation Commission, 7150 Cleanwater Lane, P.O. Box 42650, Olympia, WA 98504, info 800-233-0321; www.parks.wa.gov).

Yukon Parks and Outdoor Recreation, Box 2703, Whitehorse, YT Y1A 2C6 (☎ 867-667-5648; fax 393-6223).

US NATIONAL FORESTS

If national park campgrounds are too developed for your tastes, **national forests** provide a purist's alternative. While some have recreation facilities, most are equipped only for primitive camping; pit toilets and no running water are the norm. (See **Camping Reservation Numbers** p. 38, for reservations.) For general information, including maps, contact the **US Forest Service, Outdoor Recreation Information Center,** 222 Yale Ave. N, Seattle, WA 98109 (☎ 206-470-4060; www.fs.fed.us).

Backpackers can enjoy specially designated **wilderness areas,** which are even less accessible due to regulations barring vehicles (including mountain bikes). **Wilderness permits** (generally free) are required for backcountry hiking.

In Alaska, the Forest Service oversees more than 200 scenic and well-maintained **wilderness cabins** for public use, scattered throughout the southern and central regions of the state. Reservations and user permits are required along with a fee of $25-65 per party per night. Steep fines are levied for neglecting to obtain these. Three major agencies, along with several smaller agencies, are in charge of the cabins. The best way to find out information about all the cabins is by calling the **Alaska Public Lands Information Center** (☎ 907-269-8400; www.nps.gov/aplic.) They can answer further questions, redirect your inquiries, or mail out maps and brochures.

Many trailhead parking lots in Oregon and Washington National Forests require a Trail Park Pass ($3 per day per vehicle; annual pass for two vehicles $25). Passes are available at area outfitters and convenience stores, but not at trailheads.

The US Department of the Interior's **Bureau of Land Management (BLM)** offers a variety of outdoor recreation opportunities on the 270 million acres it oversees in ten western states and Alaska, including camping, hiking, mountain biking, rock climbing, river rafting, and wildlife viewing. Unless otherwise posted, all public lands are open for recreational use. Write the Alaska State office (☎ 907-269-8400) in Anchorage at 222 W 7th Ave. #13, Anchorage, AK 99513, or the Washington/Oregon office (☎ 503-952-6002) at 1515 SW 5th Ave., P.O. Box 2965, Portland, OR 92208 for a guide to BLM campgrounds, many of which are free.

CAMPING AND HIKING EQUIPMENT

WHAT TO BUY...

Good camping equipment is both sturdy and light. Camping equipment is generally more expensive in Australia, New Zealand, and the UK than in North America.

Sleeping Bag: Most sleeping bags are rated by season ("summer" means 30-40°F at night; "three season" means 20°F; and "four-season" or "winter" often means below 0°F). These temperatures represent the minimum temperature that the user would still be comfortable. Sleeping bags are made either of **down** (warmer, lighter, more expensive, and miserable when wet) or of **synthetic** material (heavier, more durable, and not as bad when wet). Prices range from US$80-210 for a summer synthetic to US$250-300 for a good down winter bag. **Sleeping bag pads** include foam pads (US$10-20), air mattresses (US$15-50), and Therm-A-Rest self-inflating pads (US$45-80). Bring a **stuff sack** to store your bag and keep it dry.

Tent: The best tents are free-standing (with their own frames and suspension systems), set up quickly, and only require staking in high winds. Low-profile dome tents are the best all-around. Good 2-person tents start at US$90, 4-person at US$300. Seal the seams of your tent with waterproofer, and make sure it has a rain fly. Other tent accessories include a **battery-operated lantern,** and a **plastic groundcloth.**

Backpack: Internal-frame packs mold better to your back, keep a lower center of gravity, and flex adequately to allow you to hike difficult trails. **External-frame packs** are more comfortable for long hikes over even terrain, as they keep weight higher and distribute it more evenly. Make sure your pack has a strong, padded hip-belt to transfer weight to your legs. Any serious backpacking requires a pack of at least 4000 in^3 (16,000cc), plus 500 in^3 for sleeping bags in internal-frame packs. Sturdy backpacks cost anywhere from US$125-420—this is one area in which it doesn't pay to economize. Fill up any pack with something heavy and walk around the store with it to get a sense of how it distributes weight before buying it. Either buy a **waterproof backpack cover,** or store all of your belongings in plastic bags inside your pack.

Boots: Be sure to wear hiking boots with good **ankle support.** Boots are the most important piece of gear you will buy. They should fit snugly and comfortably over a pair of thick wool socks and thin liner socks. Break in boots before you leave in order to spare yourself from painful and debilitating blisters.

Other Necessities: Synthetic layers, like those made of polypropylene, and a **pile jacket** will keep you warm even when wet. An amazingly compact **"space blanket"** will help you to retain your body heat and doubles as a groundcloth (US$5-15). Plastic **water bottles** are virtually shatter- and leak-proof. Bring **water-purification tablets** for when you can't boil water. For those places that forbid fires or the gathering of firewood, you'll need a **camp stove** (the classic Coleman starts at US$40) and a propane-filled **fuel bottle** to operate it. Also don't forget a **first-aid kit, pocketknife, insect repellent,** and **waterproof matches** or a **lighter.**

...AND WHERE TO BUY IT

The mail-order/online companies listed below offer lower prices than many retail stores, but a visit to a local camping or outdoors store is invaluable to getting a good sense of the look and weight of certain items.

Cabela's, www.cabelas.com.

Discount Camping, 880 Main North Rd., Pooraka, South Australia 5095, Australia (☎ 08 8262 3399; www.discountcamping.com.au).

L.L. Bean, Freeport, ME 04033 (US and Canada ☎ 800-441-5713; UK ☎ 0800 891 297; elsewhere, call US +1 207-552-3028; www.llbean.com).

Mountain Designs, P.O. Box 1472, Fortitude Valley, Queensland 4006, Australia (☎ 07 3252 8894; www.mountaindesign.com.au).

Mountain Equipment Co-op, 130 Broadway St., Vancouver, BC V5Y 1P3 (☎ 888-847-0770 or 604-709-6241; www.mec.ca).

Recreational Equipment, Inc. (REI), Sumner, WA 98352, USA (☎ 800-426-4840 or 253-891-2500; www.rei.com). Also has several other locations in the US.

YHA Adventure Shop, 14 Southampton St., London, WC2E 7HA, UK (☎ 020 7836 8541). The main branch of one of Britain's largest outdoor equipment suppliers.

WILDERNESS SAFETY

Stay warm, stay dry, and stay hydrated. The vast majority of life-threatening wilderness situations can be avoided by following this simple advice. Prepare yourself for an emergency, however, by always packing raingear, a hat and mittens, a first-aid kit, a reflector, a whistle, high energy food, and extra water.

Check **weather forecasts** and pay attention to the skies, since weather patterns can change suddenly. Always let someone know when and where you are going hiking—either a friend, your hostel, a park ranger, or a local hiking organization. Do not attempt a hike beyond your ability—you may be endangering your life. See **Health,** p. 30, for information about outdoor ailments and basic medical concerns.

If you are hiking in a park or wilderness area that might be frequented by bears, ask local rangers for information on bear behavior before entering, and obey posted warnings. No matter how cute a bear appears, don't be fooled—they're powerful and unpredictable animals that are not intimidated by humans. If you're close enough for a bear to be observing you, you're too close. If you see a bear at a distance, calmly walk (don't run) in the other direction. If it seems interested, back away slowly while speaking to the bear in firm, low tones and head toward a settled area. If you are attacked by a bear, get in a fetal position to protect yourself, put your arms over the back of your neck, and play dead. In all situations, remain calm, as loud noises and sudden movements can trigger an attack.

Don't leave food or other scented items (trash, toiletries, the clothes that you cooked in) near your tent. **Bear-bagging,** hanging edibles and other good-smelling objects from a tree out of reach of hungry paws, is the best way to keep your toothpaste from becoming a condiment. Bears are also attracted to any **perfume,** as are bugs, so cologne, scented soap, deodorant, and hairspray should stay at home. Like dogs, their power of smell is stronger than yours, so you'll need to bearbag even dishes and film. For more information, consult *How to Stay Alive in the Woods,* by Bradford Angier (Macmillan Press, US$8).

> **ENVIRONMENTALLY RESPONSIBLE TOURISM.** The idea behind responsible tourism is to leave no trace of human presence behind. A campstove is the safer (and most efficient) way to cook. If you must make a fire, keep it small and use only dead branches or brush rather than cutting vegetation. Make sure your campsite is at least 150 ft. (50m) from water supplies or bodies of water. If there are no toilet facilities, bury human waste (but not paper) at least four inches (10cm) deep, but not more than eight inches (20cm), and 150 ft. or more from any water supplies and campsites. Always pack your trash in a plastic bag and carry it with you until you reach the next trash receptacle. For more information on these issues, contact one of the organizations listed below.
>
> **Earthwatch,** 3 Clock Tower Place #100, Box 75, Maynard, MA 01754, USA (☎800-776-0188 or 978-461-0081; info@earthwatch.org; www.earthwatch.org).
>
> **Ecotourism Society,** P.O. Box 668, Burlington, VT 05402, USA (☎802-651-9818; ecomail@ecotourism.org; www.ecotourism.org).
>
> **National Audobon Society,** Nature Odysseys, 700 Broadway, New York, NY 10003 (☎212-979-3066; travel@audobon.org; www.audobon.org).
>
> **Tourism Concern,** Stapleton House, 277-281 Holloway Rd., London N7 8HN, UK (☎020 7753 3330; www.tourismconcern.org.uk).

CAMPERS AND RVS

Renting an RV will always be more expensive than tenting or hostelling, but it's cheaper than staying in hotels and renting a car (see **Rental Cars,** p. 51). The convenience of bringing along your own bedroom, bathroom, and kitchen makes it an attractive option, especially for older travelers and families with children. Rates vary widely by region, season (July and August are the most expensive months), and type of RV. A week long rental can run US$1000-1400.

Cruise America, (US ☎800-327-7799, Canada 888-278-1736; www.cruiseamerica.com). Offices in Anchorage, Calgary, Vancouver, Seattle, and Portland.

ABC Motorhome and Car Rentals, 3875 W. International Airport Rd., Anchorage, AK 99502 (☎ 800-421-7456 or 907-279-2000; fax 243-6363; www.alaskan.com/abcmotorhomes).

El Monte RV, 316 SW. 16th St., Renton, WA 98055 (☎ 800-367-3687 or 425-687-8441; www.elmonterv.com).

Candan RV Rentals, 20257 Langley Bypass, Langley, BC V3A 6K9 (☎ 604-530-3645; fax 530-1696; www.candan.com). Also has an office in Alberta at 540 Meridian Rd., Calgary, AB T2A 2N7 (☎ 403-272-7870; fax 402-272-5860).

KEEPING IN TOUCH

MAIL

SENDING MAIL TO THE US AND CANADA

Mail should be marked "air mail" or "par avion" to avoid being sent by sea.

Australia: Allow 4-6 work days for regular **airmail** to US; 5-7 work days to Canada. **EMS** can get a letter to the US or Canada in 2-5 work days for AUS$30. www.auspost.com.au/pac.

Ireland: Allow 4-6 work days for regular airmail to the US and Canada. www.anpost.ie.

New Zealand: Allow 4-10 work days for regular airmail to the US and Canada. www.nzpost.co.nz/nzpost/inrates.

UK: Allow 4-6 days for airmail to the US and Canada. www.royalmail.co.uk/calculator.

Federal Express (Australia ☎ 13 26 10; US and Canada ☎ 800-247-4747; New Zealand ☎ 0800 73 33 29; UK ☎ 0800 12 38 00; www.fedex.com) handles express mail services from most of the above countries to the US and Canada; for example, they can get a letter from Sydney to New York in one day for US$32.

RECEIVING MAIL

General Delivery: Mail can be sent to North America through **General Delivery** to almost any city or town with a post office. Address letters as in the following example:

Benjamin SILBERMANN
General Delivery
Post Office Street Address
Seattle, WA 98101 or VANCOUVER, BC V8W 1L0
USA or Canada.

The mail will go to a special desk in the central post office unless you specify a post office by street address or postal code. As a rule, it is best to use the largest post office in the area, and mail may be sent there regardless of what is written on the envelope. It is usually safer and quicker to send mail express or registered. When picking up your mail, bring a form of photo ID, preferably a passport. There is generally no surcharge, and if there is, it generally does not exceed the cost of domestic postage. If the clerks insist that there is nothing for you, have them check under your first name as well. *Let's Go* lists post offices in the Practical Information section for each city and most towns.

American Express's travel offices throughout the world will act as a mail service for cardholders if you contact them in advance. Under this free **Client Letter Service,** they will hold mail for up to 30 days and forward upon request. Address the letter in the same way shown above, but with the address of the local AmEx office. Some offices will offer these services to non-cardholders (especially those who have purchased AmEx Traveler's Cheques), but you must call ahead to make sure. A complete list of offices is available free from AmEx (☎ 800-528-4800).

SENDING MAIL HOME FROM THE US AND CANADA

Aerogrammes, printed sheets that fold into envelopes and travel via air mail, are available at post offices. It helps to mark "air mail," although "par avion" is universally understood. Most post offices will charge exorbitant fees or simply refuse to send aerogrammes with enclosures. Airmail from the US averages four to seven work days, although times are more unpredictable from smaller towns. A **standard letter** costs $1; a postcard 55¢. For packages up to 4 lbs., use **Global Priority Mail,** which delivers to major locations in three to five work days for a $5 flat-rate.

If regular airmail is too slow, **Federal Express** (for international operator, US ☎ 800-247-4747) can get a letter from New York to Sydney in two work days for a whopping US$30. By **US Express Mail,** a letter from New York to Sydney would arrive within four work days and would cost $15.

Surface mail is by far the cheapest and slowest way to send mail. It takes one to three months to cross the Atlantic and two to four months to cross the Pacific—appropriate for sending large quantities of items you won't need to see for a while. When ordering books and materials from abroad, always include one or two **International Reply Coupons (IRCs)**—a way of providing the postage to cover delivery. IRCs should be available from your local post office and those abroad ($1.05).

TELEPHONES

> **PLACING INTERNATIONAL CALLS.** To call the US or Canada from home or to place an international call from the US or Canada, dial:
> 1. The **international dialing prefix.** To dial out of **Australia,** dial 0011; the **Republic of Ireland, New Zealand,** or the **UK,** 00; **South Africa,** 09; **Canada** or the **US,** 011.
> 2. The **country code** of the country you want to call. To call **Australia,** dial 61; the **Republic of Ireland,** 353; **New Zealand,** 64; **South Africa,** 27; the **UK,** 44; **Canada** or the **US,** 1.
> 3. The **city** or **area code.** *Let's Go* lists the area codes next to the town name.
> 4. The **local number.**

CALLING HOME FROM CANADA AND THE US

A **calling card** is probably your best and cheapest bet. Calls are billed either collect or to your account. **MCI WorldPhone** also provides access to MCI's Traveler's Assist, which gives legal and medical advice, exchange rate information, and translation services. Other phone companies provide similar services to travelers. **To obtain a calling card** from your national telecommunications service before you leave home, contact the appropriate company below.

- **US: AT&T** (☎ 888-222-0300); **Sprint** (☎ 800-877-4646); or **MCI** (☎ 800-444-4141; from abroad dial the country's MCI access number).
- **Canada:** Bell Canada **Canada Direct** (☎ 800-565-4708).
- **UK:** British Telecom **BT Direct** (☎ 0800 34 51 44).
- **Ireland:** Telecom Éireann **Ireland Direct** (☎ 800 250 250).
- **Australia:** Telstra **Australia Direct** (☎ 13 22 00).
- **New Zealand:** Telecom New Zealand (☎ 0800 000 000).
- **South Africa:** Telkom South Africa (☎ 09 03).

Wherever possible, use a calling card for international phone calls; long-distance rates for national phone services are often exorbitant. You can usually make direct international calls from pay phones, but if you aren't using a calling card you may need to drop your coins as quickly as your words. Prepaid phone cards and occasionally credit cards can be used for direct international calls, but they are still less cost-efficient. In-room hotel calls invariably include a surcharge.

The expensive alternative to dialing direct or using a calling card is using an international operator to place a **collect call.** An operator from your home nation can be reached by dialing the appropriate service provider listed above. They will typically place a collect call even if you don't possess their phone cards.

CALLING WITHIN THE US AND CANADA
The simplest way to call within the country is to use a coin-operated phone. You can also buy **prepaid phone cards,** which carry a certain amount of phone time depending on the card's denomination. The time is measured in minutes or talk units (e.g. one unit/one minute), and the card usually has a toll-free access telephone number and a personal identification number (PIN). To make a phone call: dial the access number, enter your PIN at the voice prompt, and enter the phone number of the party you're trying to reach. Phone rates tend to be highest in the morning, lower in the evening, and lowest on Sunday and late at night.

TIME DIFFERENCES
The six time zones in the US are (east to west, each zone one hour earlier than the preceding): **Eastern, Central, Mountain, Pacific, Alaskan and Hawaii.** Eastern time is five hours behind Greenwich Mean Time (GMT). Thus, when it is noon in New England, it is 11am in the Great Lakes, Texas, and the rest of the South, 10am in the Southwest and Rockies, 9am on the West Coast and Nevada, and 8am in Alaska. From April 7, 2002, to October 27, 2002, daylight savings time will be in effect. In April, clocks are moved forward one hour; in October, they are moved back one hour. Indiana, Arizona, and Hawaii do not observe daylight savings time, so from April to October they are out of sync with their time zone. Canada has two additional time zones: **Newfoundland** and **Atlantic,** which are three and a half hours and four hours behind GMT, respectively.

EMAIL AND INTERNET

As the birthplace of the Internet, the US has widespread coverage and easy accessibility as does Canada. The Internet can be accessed at Internet cafes, copy centers, libraries, and many college campuses. *Let's Go* lists where to access the Internet in the Practical Information of city listings. **Cybercafe Guide** (www.cyberiacafe.net/cyberia/guide/ccafe.htm) can help you find cybercafes in the US and Canada. Libraries usually offer free access. Though in some places it's possible to forge a remote link with your home server, in most cases this is a much slower (and thus more expensive) option than taking advantage of free **web-based email accounts** (e.g., www.hotmail.com and www.yahoo.com).

TRANSPORTATION

BY PLANE

When it comes to airfare, a little effort can save you a bundle. If your plans are flexible enough to deal with the restrictions, courier fares are the cheapest. Tickets bought from consolidators and standby seating are also good deals, but last-minute specials, airfare wars, and charter flights often beat these fares. The key is to hunt around, be flexible, and to persistently ask about discounts. Students, seniors, and those under 26 should never pay full price for a ticket.

> **Timing:** Airfares to the US and Canada peak in the summer, and holidays are also expensive periods in which to travel. Midweek (M-Th morning) round-trip flights run $40-50 cheaper than weekend flights, but the latter are generally less crowded and more likely to permit frequent-flier upgrades. Return-date flexibility is usually not an option for the budget traveler; traveling with an "open return" ticket can be pricier than fixing a return date when buying the ticket and paying later to change it.

BY PLANE ■ 45

Mooooore Room.

Real American Airlines deals for students and faculty, online at StudentUniverse. Earn AAdvantage miles and enjoy *more room throughout Coach only on American*.

StudentUniverse.com

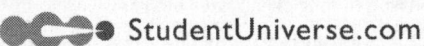

featuring
AmericanAirlines

800.272.9676

RESTRICTIONS: A portion of or all travel may be on American Eagle, American's regional airline affiliate. American Airlines, American Eagle and AAdvantage are marks of American Airlines, Inc. American Airlines reserves the right to change AAdvantage program rules, regulations, travel awards and special offers at any time without notice, and to end the AAdvantage program with six months notice. AmericanAirlines is not responsible for products or services by other participating companies. *Only American has removed rows of seats throughout Coach to provide more room for more Coach passengers than any other airline. Now available on all two-class aircraft; three-class aircraft reconfiguration in progress; not available on American Eagle.

ESSENTIALS

46 ■ TRANSPORTATION

Route: Round-trip flights are by far the cheapest; "open-jaw" (arriving in and departing from different cities) and round-the-world, or RTW, flights are pricier but reasonable alternatives. If the Pacific Northwest is only 1 stop on a more extensive globe-hop, consider a round-the-world (RTW) ticket. Tickets usually include at least 5 stops and are valid for about a year; prices range US$1200-5000. Try **Northwest Airlines/KLM** (US ☎800-447-4747; www.nwa.com) or **Star Alliance**, a consortium of 22 airlines including United Airlines (US ☎800-241-6522; www.star-alliance.com). Patching one-way flights together is the least economical way to travel. Flights between capital cities or regional hubs will offer the most competitive fares.

Boarding: Whenever flying internationally, pick up tickets well in advance of the departure date, and confirm by phone within 72 hours of departure. Most airlines require that passengers arrive at the airport at least 2 hours before departure.

BUDGET AND STUDENT TRAVEL AGENCIES

While knowledgeable agents can make your life easy and help you save, they may not spend the time to find you the lowest possible fare—they get paid on commission. Travelers holding **ISIC and IYTC cards** (see p. 24) qualify for big discounts from student travel agencies. Most flights from budget agencies are on major airlines, but in peak season some may sell seats on less reliable chartered aircraft.

Council Travel (www.counciltravel.com). Countless US offices, including branches in Atlanta, Boston, Chicago, L.A., New York, San Francisco, Seattle, and Washington, D.C. Check the website or call 800-2-COUNCIL (226-8624) for the office nearest you.

CTS Travel, 44 Goodge St., **London** W1T 2AD (☎0207 636 0031).

STA Travel, 7890 S. Hardy Dr., Ste. 110, Tempe AZ 85284 (24hr. reservations and info ☎800-777-0112; fax 480-592-0876; www.statravel.com). A student and youth travel organization with countless offices worldwide (check their website for a listing of all offices), including US offices in Boston, Chicago, L.A., New York, San Francisco, Seattle, and Washington, D.C. Ticket booking, travel insurance, railpasses, and more. In the UK, walk-in office 11 Goodge St., **London** W1T 2PF or call 0870-160-6070. In New Zealand, 10 High St., **Auckland** (☎09 309 0458). In Australia, 366 Lygon St., **Melbourne** Vic 3053 (☎03 9349 4344).

StudentUniverse, 545 Fifth Ave., Suite 640, New York, NY 10017 (toll-free customer service ☎800-272-9676, outside the US 212-986-8420; www.studentuniverse.com), is an online student travel service offering discount ticket booking, travel insurance, railpasses, destination guides, and much more. Customer service line open M-F 9am-8pm and Sa noon-5pm EST.

Travel CUTS (Canadian Universities Travel Services Limited), 187 College St., **Toronto,** ON M5T 1P7 (☎416-979-2406; fax 979-8167; www.travelcuts.com). 60 offices across Canada. Also in the UK, 295-A Regent St., **London** W1R 7YA (☎0207-255-1944).

usit world (www.usitworld.com). Over 50 **usit campus** branches in the UK (www.usitcampus.co.uk), including 52 Grosvenor Gardens, **London** SW1W 0AG (☎0870 240 10 10); **Manchester** (☎0161 273 1880); and **Edinburgh** (☎0131 668 3303). Nearly 20 **usit NOW** offices in Ireland, including 19-21 Aston Quay, O'Connell Bridge, **Dublin** 2 (☎01 602 1600; www.usitnow.ie), and **Belfast** (☎02 890 327 111; www.usitnow.com). Offices also in Athens, Auckland, Brussels, Frankfurt, Johannesburg, Lisbon, Luxembourg, Madrid, Paris, Sofia, and Warsaw.

Other organizations that specialize in finding cheap fares include:

Cheap Tickets (☎888-878-8849; www.cheaptickets.com). Cheap flights in the US.

Travel Avenue (☎800-333-3335). Rebates commercial fares to or from the US and offers low fares for flights anywhere in the world. They also offer package deals, including car rental and hotel reservations, to many destinations.

COMMERCIAL AIRLINES ■ 47

> **FLIGHT PLANNING ON THE INTERNET.** The Web is a great place to look for travel bargains—it's fast, convenient, and you can spend as long as you like exploring options without driving your travel agent insane. Many airline sites offer special last-minute deals on the Web. Other sites do the legwork and compile the deals for you—try www.bestfares.com, www.onetravel.com, www.lowestfare.com, and www.travelzoo.com. **STA** (www.sta-travel.com), **Council** (www.counciltravel.com), and **StudentUniverse** (www.studentuniverse.com) provide quotes on student tickets, while **Expedia** (msn.expedia.com) and **Travelocity** (www.travelocity.com) offer full travel services. **Priceline** (www.priceline.com) allows you to specify a price, and obligates you to buy any ticket that meets or beats it; be prepared for antisocial hours and odd routes. **Skyauction** (www.skyauction.com) allows you to bid on both last-minute and advance-purchase tickets. Finally, the cheapest tickets on the web come from **Hotwire** (www.hotwire.com). They quote you a price based on the dates you submit. You don't learn the exact times or the airline until after you purchase the ticket. An indispensable resource on the Internet is the *Air Traveler's Handbook* (www.cs.cmu.edu/afs/cs/user/mkant/Public/Travel/airfare.html), a comprehensive listing of links to everything you need to know before you board a plane. Just one last note—to protect yourself, make sure that the site uses a secure server before handing over any credit card details. Happy hunting!

COMMERCIAL AIRLINES

The commercial airlines' lowest regular offer is the **APEX** (Advance Purchase Excursion) fare, which provides confirmed reservations and allows "open-jaw" tickets. Generally, reservations must be made seven to 21 days ahead of departure, with seven- to 14-day minimum-stay and up to 90-day maximum-stay restrictions. These fares carry hefty cancellation and change penalties (fees rise in summer). Book peak-season APEX fares early; by May you will have a hard time getting your desired departure date. Use **Microsoft Expedia** (expedia.msn.com) or **Travelocity** (www.travelocity.com) to get an idea of the lowest published fares, then use the resources outlined here to try and beat those fares. Low-season fares should be appreciably cheaper than the high-season (mid-June to Aug.).

STANDBY FLIGHTS

Traveling standby requires considerable flexibility in arrival and departure dates and cities. Companies dealing in standby flights sell vouchers rather than tickets, along with the promise to get to your destination (or near your destination) within a certain window of time (typically one to five days). You call in before your specific window of time to hear your flight options and the probability that you will be able to board each flight. You can then decide what flights you want to try to make, show up at the appropriate airport at the appropriate time, present your voucher, and board if space is available. Vouchers can usually be bought for both one-way and round-trip travel. You may receive a monetary refund only if every available flight within your date range is full; if you opt not to take an available (but perhaps less convenient) flight, you can only get credit toward future travel. Carefully read agreements with any company offering standby flights as tricky fine print can leave you in a lurch. To check on a company's service record in the US, call the Better Business Bureau (☎212-533-6200). It is difficult to receive refunds, and clients' vouchers will not be honored when an airline fails to receive payment in time. One established standby company in the US is **Whole Earth Travel,** 325 W. 38th St., New York, NY 10018 (☎800-326-2009; fax 212-864-5489; www.4standby.com) and Los Angeles, CA (☎888-247-4482).

TICKET CONSOLIDATORS

Ticket consolidators, or **"bucket shops,"** buy unsold tickets in bulk from commercial airlines and sell them at discounted rates. The best place to look is in the Sunday travel section of any major newspaper (such as the *New York Times*), where many bucket shops place tiny ads. Call quickly, as availability is typically extremely limited. Not all bucket shops are reliable, so insist on a receipt that gives full details of restrictions, refunds, and tickets. Pay by credit card (in spite of the 2-5% fee) so you can stop payment if you never receive your tickets. For more info, see www.travel-library.com/air-travel/consolidators.html or pick up Kelly Monaghan's *Air Travel's Bargain Basement* (Intrepid Traveler, US$10).

TRAVELING FROM THE US AND CANADA

Travel Avenue (☎800-333-3335; www.travelavenue.com) searches for best available published fares and then uses several consolidators to attempt to beat that fare. Other consolidators worth trying are **Interworld** (☎305-443-4929; fax 443-0351); **Pennsylvania Travel** (☎800-331-0947); **Rebel** (☎800-227-3235; travel@rebeltours.com; www.rebeltours.com); **Cheap Tickets** (☎800-377-1000; www.cheaptickets.com); and **Travac** (☎800-872-8800; fax 212-714-9063; www.travac.com). Yet more consolidators on the web include the **Internet Travel Network** (www.itn.com); **Travel Information Services** (www.tiss.com); **TravelHUB** (www.travelhub.com); and **The Travel Site** (www.thetravelsite.com). Keep in mind that these are just suggestions to get you started in your research; *Let's Go* does not endorse any of these agencies.

TRAVELING FROM THE UK, AUSTRALIA, AND NEW ZEALAND

In London, the **Air Travel Advisory Bureau** (☎0207 636 5000; www.atab.co.uk) can provide names of reliable consolidators and discount flight specialists. From Australia and New Zealand, look for consolidator ads in the travel section of the *Sydney Morning Herald* and other papers.

DISCOUNT TICKETS

Many airlines offer special passes to international travelers. You must purchase these passes outside North America. A voucher is good for one flight on an airline's domestic system; typically, travel must be completed within 30 to 60 days. The point of departure and destination for each coupon must be specified at the time of purchase, but travel dates may be changed during your trip (often at no extra charge). **America West Air, US Airways, United, Continental, Delta,** and **TWA** all sell vouchers. Call the airlines for specifics. TWA's **Youth Travel Pack** offers a similar deal (four one-way flight coupons for $550) to students ages 14-24, including North Americans. **Canada 3000** (see below) flies cheaply between Whitehorse, YT; Anchorage, AK; Victoria and Vancouver, BC; and Calgary, AB.

- **Air Canada,** (☎888-247-2262; www.aircanada.ca). Discounts for ages 12-24 on standby tickets for flights within Canada.
- **Alaska Airlines,** (☎800-252-7522; www.alaskaairlines.com).
- **America West Air,** (☎800-235-9292; www.americawest.com).
- **American Airlines,** (☎800-433-7300; www.americanair.com).
- **Canada 3000,** (☎888-226-3000 or 416-259-1118; www.canada3000.ca)
- **Continental Airlines,** (☎800-525-0280; www.flycontinental.com).
- **Delta Airlines,** (☎800-241-4141; www.delta-air.com).
- **Northwest Airlines,** (☎800-225-2525; www.nwa.com).
- **United Airlines,** (☎800-241-6522; www.ual.com).
- **US Airways,** (☎800-428-4322; www.usair.com).

> **FURTHER READING** Check out *The Worldwide Guide to Cheap Airfare*, Michael McColl. Insider Publicaions (US$15), *Discount Airfares: The Insider's Guide*, George Hobart, Priceless Publications (US$14).

BY TRAIN

Locomotives are one of the most scenic ways to tour the US and Canada, but keep in mind that air travel is much faster, and often much cheaper, than train travel. As with airlines, you can save money by purchasing your tickets as far in advance as possible, so plan ahead and make reservations early. It is essential to travel light on trains; not all stations will check your baggage.

AMTRAK. (☎800-USA-RAIL/872-7245; www.amtrak.com) The only provider of intercity passenger train service in most of the US. Their informative web page lists schedules, fares, arrival and departure info, and takes reservations. Discounts on full rail fares are given to: senior citizens (15% off), students with a Student Advantage card (15% off; call 877-2JOINSA to purchase the $20 card; www.studentadvantage.com), travelers with disabilities (15% off), children ages 2-15 accompanied by an adult (50% off up to two children), children under two (free for one child), and US veterans (10% off with a VeteransAdvantage membership card). "Rail SALE" offers online discounts of up to 90%; visit the Amtrak web site for details and reservations.

VIA RAIL. (888-VIARAIL; www.viarail.ca) Amtrak's Canadian equivalent offers **discounts** on full fares: students 18-24 with ISIC card (35% off full fare); youth 12-17 (35% off full fare); seniors 60 and over (10% off); ages 11 and under, accompanied by an adult (free). Reservations are required for first-class seats and sleep car accommodations. "Supersaver" fares offer discounts between 25-35%. The **Canrail Pass** allows unlimited travel on 12 days within a 30-day period on VIA trains. Between early June and mid-October, a 12-day pass costs CDN$658 (seniors and youths CDN $592). Off-season passes cost CDN$411 (seniors and youths CDN$370). Add CDN$33-$56 for additional days of travel. Call for information on seasonal promotions such as discounts on Grayline Sightseeing Tours.

ALASKA RAILROAD CORPORATION (ARRC). (☎800-544-0552; 907-265-2300; fax 907-265-2323; www.akrr.com). AARC covers 470 mi. of track once per day in each direction from mid-May to mid-September. It connects Seward and Whittier in the south with Anchorage, Denali National Park, and Fairbanks. Children aged 2-11 travel for 50% off. See specific locations for fares, details, and rail options.

BY BUS

Buses generally offer the most frequent and complete service between the cities and towns of the US and Canada. Often a bus is the only way to reach smaller locales without a car. Laidlaw, the company that owns Greyhound Canada, acquired Greyhound USA in 1999. That summer, North America-wide specials began to appear. *Russell's Official National Motor Coach Guide* ($17.30 including postage) is an invaluable tool for constructing an itinerary. Updated each month, *Russell's Guide* has schedules of every bus route (including Greyhound) between any two towns in the US and Canada. Russell's also publishes two semiannual *Supplements* that are free when ordered with the May and December issues; a Directory of Bus Lines and Bus Stations, and a series of Route Maps (both $8.40 if ordered separately). To order any of the above, write Russell's Guides, Inc., P.O. Box 278, Cedar Rapids, IA 52406 (☎319-364-6138; fax 365-8728).

GREYHOUND

Greyhound (☎800-231-2222; www.greyhound.com) operates the most routes in the US, but does not serve Alaska. Schedule information is available at any Greyhound terminal or agency, on their web page, or by calling them toll-free.

> **Advance purchase fares:** Reserving space far ahead of time ensures a lower fare, although expect a smaller discount during the busy summer months. For tickets purchased more than 14 days in advance, fares anywhere in the US will be no more than $109 one-way. Fares are often reduced even more for 21-day advance purchases on many popular routes; call up to the date pricing or consult their web page.

50 ■ TRANSPORTATION

Discounts on full fares: Senior citizens (10% off); children ages 2-11 (50% off); students with a Student Advantage card (up to 15% off); travelers with disabilities and special needs and their companions ride together for the price of one. Active and retired US military personnel and National Guard Reserves (10% off with valid ID) and their spouses and dependents may take a round-trip between any 2 points in the US for $179. With a ticket purchased 3 or more days in advance during the spring and summer months, a friend can travel along for free (some exceptions).

Ameripass: Call 888-GLI-PASS (454-7277). Allows adults unlimited travel through the US for 7-day ($209 for adults, $188.10 senior citizens and students with valid ID), 10-day $259, $233; 15-day $319, $287; 21-day $369, $232; 30-day $429, $368; 45-day $469, $422; or 60-day $599, $539. Passes that allow travel through the US and Canada are 15-days $399, $359 student and senior; 21-day $439, $395; 30-day $499, $449; 45-day $569, $512; 60-day $639, 575. For travel exclusively through western US and Canada, there is a 15-day option $299, $269; and a 30-day option $399, $359. Children's passes are half the price of adults. The pass takes effect the first day used. Before purchasing an Ameripass, total up the separate bus fares between towns to make sure that the pass is more economical, or at least worth the unlimited flexibility it provides.

International Ameripass: For travelers from outside the US. A 4-day pass to travel through the US is $135; a 7-day pass $185, $166 students with a valid ID and senior citizens; a 10-day pass $239, $215; 15-day pass $285, $257; 30-day pass $385, $347; 45-day pass $419, $377; 60-day pass $509, $458. Travel through the US and Canada for 15-day runs $339, $305; 21-day $389, $350; 30-day $449, $404; 45-day $499, $449; 60-day $559, $503. The western US and Canada pass is available for 15-day $299, $269; or 30-day $399, $359. Call 888-GLI-PASS (454-7277) for info. International Ameripasses are not available at the terminal; they can be purchased in foreign countries at Greyhound-affiliated agencies; telephone numbers vary by country and are listed on the web page. Passes can also be ordered at the web page, or purchased in Greyhound's International Office, in Port Authority Bus Station, 625 Eighth Ave., New York, NY 10018 (☎800-246-8572 or 212-971-0492; intlameripass@greyhound.com).

GREYHOUND CANADA TRANSPORTATION

Greyhound Canada Transportation, 877 Greyhound Way, Calgary, AB T3C 3V8 (☎800-661-TRIP); www.greyhound.ca) is Canada's main intercity bus company. The web page has full schedule info.

Discounts: Seniors (10% off); students (25% off with an ISIC; 10% off with other student cards); a companion of a disabled person free; ages 5-11, 50%; under 4 free. If reservations are made at least 7 days in advance, a friend travels half off. A child under 15 rides free with an adult if reserved 7 days in advance.

Canada Pass: Offers 7-, 10-, 15-, 21-, 30-, 45-, and 60-day unlimited travel from the western border of Canada to Montreal on all routes for North American residents, including limited links to northern US cities. 7-day advance purchase required. 7-day pass CDN$249, $224; 10-day pass CDN$319, CDN$287; 15-day pass CDN$379, CDN$341; 21-day CDN$419, CDN$377; 30-day pass CDN$449, CDN$404.10; 45-day pass CDN$535, $482; 60-day pass CDN$599, CDN$539. The Canada Plus Pass includes coast to coast travel and is slightly more expensive.

GREEN TORTOISE

Green Tortoise, 494 Broadway, San Francisco, CA 94133 (☎800-867-8647 or 415-956-7500; www.greentortoise.com; email tortoise@greentortoise.com), offers a more slow-paced, whimsical alternative to straightforward transportation. Green Tortoise's communal "hostels on wheels"—remodeled diesel buses done up for living and eating on the road—traverse the US on aptly named Adventure Tours. Prices include transportation, sleeping space on the bus, and tours of the regions through which you pass, often including such treats as hot springs and farm stays. Meals are prepared communally and incur an additional food charge. Cross-country trips run Feb.-Oct. between Boston or New York City and San Francisco, Los Angeles, or Seattle (14 days: $429, plus $131). The Grand Alaska Extravaganza takes 30 days to work up from San Francisco to Alaska, and several shorter tours will begin in Alaska itself (call for prices). Prepare for an earthy trip; buses have no toilets and little privacy. Reserve one to two months in advance; deposits ($100 or $500 for Alaska) are generally required. Many trips have space available at departure. Reservations can be made over the phone or through the web.

BY CAR

Before you leave, tune up the car, pack an easy-to-read repair manual, and learn a bit about minor automobile maintenance and repair—it may help you limp into the nearest garage. Always carry: a **spare tire** and **jack, jumper cables, extra oil, road flares**, a **flashlight**, and, in case you break down at night or in winter, **safety candles, matches**, and **blankets**. In summer, carry extra **water** for you and your radiator. In extremely hot weather, use the air conditioner with restraint; turning the heater on full blast will help cool the engine. If radiator fluid is steaming, turn off the car for 30 minutes—never pour water over the engine to cool it. If you plan to drive in snow, you should also carry a **shovel, traction mats** (burlap sacks or car floor mats make a good substitute in a bind), and **sand** or **kitty litter**.

Carry emergency **food and water** if there's a chance you may be stranded in a remote area. A cell phone is the perfect companion on a road trip, although beware of spotty coverage in rural areas. Always have plenty of **gas** and check road conditions ahead of time (see **Road Conditions**, below), particularly during winter. The huge travel distances of North America will require more gas than you might at first expect. To burn less fuel, make sure your tires have enough air.

> Sleeping in a vehicle parked on the highway or in the city is extremely dangerous—even the most dedicated budget traveler should not consider it an option.

Be sure to **buckle up**—seat belts are required by law in almost every region of the US and Canada. The **speed limit in the US** varies considerably from region to region and road to road. Most urban highways have a limit of 55 mph (88km per hr.), while the limit on rural routes ranges from 60-80 mph (97-128km per hr.). The **speed limit in Canada** is generally 50km per hr. in cities and towns, and 80-110km per hr. (50-68 m.p.h.) on highways.

In the 1950s, US President Dwight "Ike" Eisenhower began the **interstate system**, a federally funded hwy. network. Even-numbered interstates run east-west, and odd ones run north-south, increasing in number toward the north and east. If the interstate has a three-digit number, it is a branch of another interstate (i.e., I-235 is a branch of I-35) and is often a bypass skirting around a large city. An even digit in the hundreds place means the branch will eventually return to the main interstate; an odd digit means it won't.

> **ROAD CONDITIONS.** Both **Oregon** (☎800-977-6368 or 503-588-2941; www.tripcheck.com) and **Washington** (☎800-695-7623 or 206-368-4499; www.smarttrek.org) have comprehensive web sites with live traffic cameras and up-to-date reports on construction and snow conditions in mountain passes. In **British Columbia**, check the web site www.th.gov.bc.ca/th. The site has links to road conditions in **Alberta** and the **Yukon** as well.

DRIVING PERMITS

If you do not have a license issued by a US state or Canadian province or territory, you might want an **International Driving Permit (IDP).** While the US allows you to drive with a foreign license for up to a year and Canada allows it for six months, the IDP may facilitate things with police if your license is not in English. You must carry your home license with your IDP at all times. It is valid for a year and must be issued in the country of your license, and you must be 18 to obtain one.

52 ■ TRANSPORTATION

Australia: Contact your local Royal Automobile Club (RAC) or the National Royal Motorist Association (NRMA) if in NSW or the ACT (☎ 08 9421 4444; www.rac.com.au/travel). Permits AUS$15.

Ireland: Contact the nearest Automobile Association (AA) office or write to the UK address below. Permits IR£4. The Irish Automobile Association, 23 Suffolk St., Rockhill, Blackrock, Co. Dublin (☎ 01 677 9481), honors most foreign automobile memberships (24hr. breakdown and road service ☎ 800 667 788; toll-free in Ireland).

New Zealand: Contact your local Automobile Association (AA) or their main office at Auckland Central, 99 Albert St. (☎ 9 377 4660; www.nzaa.co.nz). Permits NZ$10.

South Africa: Contact the Travel Services Department of the Automobile Association of South Africa at P.O. Box 596, 2000 Johannesburg (☎ 11 799 1400; fax 799 1410; http://aasa.co.za). Permits ZAR28.50.

UK: To visit your local AA Shop, contact the **AA Headquarters** (☎ 0870 600 0371), or write to: The Automobile Association, International Documents, Fanum House, Erskine, Renfrewshire PA8 6BW. For more info, see www.theaa.co.uk. Permits UK£4.

AUTO CLUBS

Membership in an auto club, which provides free emergency road-side assistance 24 hours per day, is an important investment for anyone planning to drive on their vacation. AAA and CAA have reciprocal agreements, so a membership in either is good for road service in Canada, or America.

American Automobile Association (AAA), (Emergency road service ☎ 800-AAA-HELP (222-4357); www.aaa.com). Offers free trip-planning services, road maps, guidebooks, 24hr. emergency road service anywhere in the US, limited free towing, commission-free traveler's checks from American Express with over 1,000 offices scattered across the country. Discounts on Hertz car rental (5-20%), Amtrak tickets (10%), and various motel chains and theme parks. AAA has reciprocal agreements with auto associations of many other countries, which often provide you with full benefits while in the US. Membership hovers between $50-60 for the first year and less for renewals and additional family members; call 800-564-6222 to sign up.

Canadian Automobile Association (CAA), 1145 Hunt Club Rd. #200, Ottawa, ON K1V 0Y3 (☎ 800-CAA-HELP/800-222-4357); www.caa.ca). Affiliated with AAA (see above), the CAA provides nearly identical membership benefits. Basic membership is CDN$63 and CDN$32 for associates; call 800-564-6222 to sign up.

Mobil Auto Club, 200 N. Martingale Rd., Schaumburg, IL 60174 (information ☎ 800-621-5581; emergency service ☎ 800-323-5880). Benefits include locksmith reimbursement, towing, roadside service, and car-rental discounts. $7 per month covers you and another driver.

RENTING

Car rental agencies fall into two categories: national companies with hundreds of branches, and local agencies that serve only one city or region. National chains usually allow you to pick up a car in one city and drop it off in another (for a hefty charge, sometimes in excess of $1000), and by calling their toll-free numbers, you can reserve a reliable car anywhere in the country. Generally, airport branches have more expensive rates. Most branches rent to ages 21-24 with an additional fee, but policies and prices vary from agency to agency. If you're 21 or older and have a major credit card in your name, you may be able to rent where the minimum age would otherwise rule you out. **Alamo** (☎ 800-462-52663; www.alamo.com) rents to ages 21-24 with a major credit card for an additional $25 per day, **Enterprise** (☎ 800-736-8222; www.enterprise.com) rents to customers age 21-24 with a variable surcharge, and many **Dollar** (☎ 800-800-4000; www.dollar.com) and **Thrifty** (☎ 800-367-2277; www.thrifty.com) locations do likewise for varying surcharges. Some branches of **Budget** (☎ 800-527-0700; www.budget.com) rent to drivers under 25 with a surcharge that varies by location. **Hertz** (☎ 800-654-3131; www.hertz.com) policy varies with city.

Most rental packages offer unlimited mileage, although some allow you a certain number of miles free before the charge of 25-40¢ per mile takes effect. Quoted rates do not include gas or tax, so ask for the total cost before handing over the credit card; many large firms have added airport surcharges not covered by the designated fare. Return the car with a full tank unless you sign up for a fuel option plan that stipulates otherwise. And when dealing with any car rental company, be sure to ask whether the price includes insurance against theft and collision. There may be an additional charge for a collision and damage waiver (CDW), which usually comes to about $12-15 per day. Major credit cards (including MasterCard and American Express) will sometimes cover the CDW if you use their card to rent a car; call your credit card company for specifics.

CAR INSURANCE
Some credit cards cover standard insurance. If you rent, lease, or borrow a car, and you are not from the US or Canada, you will need a **green card,** or **International Insurance Certificate,** to certify that you have liability insurance and that it applies abroad. Green cards can be obtained at car rental agencies, car dealerships (for those leasing cars), some travel agents, and some border crossings.

BY BICYCLE

Before you rush onto the byways of the Pacific Northwest, remember to make a few preparations. Bike **helmets** are required by law in most of the region and are essential safety gear. A good helmet will cost about $40 to buy; get help to ensure a correct fit. A white **headlight** and red **taillight** (and not just reflectors) are likewise both required and indispensable. **Anybody's Bike Book** ($12) provides vital info on repair and maintenance during long-term rides.

Bikeways Local Network (www.bikeways.com/maps2/mapsframe.htm). A compilation of road and cycling maps in British Columbia. Key in route planning.

The Bicycling Visitor's Guide to Seattle (www.cascade.org/visitors_guide.html). Bike routes and information on cycling in and around Seattle.

Oregon Department of Transportation (☎ 503-986-3556; www.odot.state.or.us/techserv/bikewalk). *Oregon Bicycling Guide* and *Oregon Coast Bike Route Map* outline bike routes and campgrounds. Free; order by email (daryl.m.bonitz@state.or.us) or phone.

Adventure Cycling Association, P.O. Box 8308-P, Missoula, MT 59807 (☎ 800-755-2453 or 406-721-1776; fax 721-8754; www.adv-cycling.org). A national, nonprofit organization that maps long-distance routes and organizes bike tours for members. Membership $30 in the US, $35 in Canada, $45 overseas.

The Canadian Cycling Association, 702-2197 Riverside Drive, Ottawa, ON K1H 7X3 ☎ 613-248-1353; www.canadian-cycling.com). Sells maps, books, and guides to regions of Canada, Alaska, and the Pacific Coast. Pick up *The Canadian Cycling Association's Complete Guide to Bicycle Touring in Canada* (CDN$24).

BY FERRY

Along the Pacific Coast, ferries are an exhilarating and often unavoidable way to travel. Only a small portion of the Panhandle is accessible by road; most of this area can be reached only by the **Alaska Marine Hwy.** Beyond providing basic transportation, the ferries give travelers the chance to enjoy the beauty of the coast. Ferry travel can become quite expensive, however, if you bring a car along. The web site www.ferrytravel.com provides schedules for **Washington State Ferries, Alaska Ferries, BC Ferries,** and seven independent companies.

ALASKA MARINE HWY.
The **Alaska Marine Hwy.,** Homer Ferry Terminal, 4667 Homer Spit Rd., Suite #1, Juneau, AK 99603 (☎ 800-382-9229; TDD 800-764-3779; www.akmhs.com) connects the Northwest Coast from Washington to Alaska. The **southeast,** or **Inside Passage,** system runs from Bellingham, WA and Prince Rupert, BC up the coast to Skagway,

AK, stopping in Juneau, Ketchikan, Haines, and other towns in southeast Alaska. All southeast ferries have free showers, cafes, and a heated top-deck "solarium" where cabinless passengers can sleep comfortably in sleeping bags; some boats offer lectures on history and ecology. The **southcentral** network serves such destinations as Kodiak Island, Seward, Homer, and Prince William Sound. These two systems are connected by a once-a-month boat going from Juneau to Valdez and Seward. The **southwest** network runs from Kodiak to the Aleutian Islands. There is a slight additional charge for stopovers, which should be reserved at the same time as the rest of your trip. A free printed schedule may be ordered from their web site or by calling or writing.

Those who intend to hit the water running, and keep running, might check out the **AlaskaPass,** P.O. Box 351, Vashon, WA 98070 (North America ☎ 800-248-7598 or international 206-463-6550; www.alaskapass.com). It offers unlimited access to most of Alaska's railroads, ferries, and buses. A 15-day pass goes for $649 (ages 2-11 $325), and a 22-day pass for $749 (ages 2-11 $375). A flex-pass allows travel on eight non-consecutive days over a 12-day period costs $549 (ages 2-11 $275); one good for 12 out of 21 days goes for $699 (ages 2-11 $350). It services most buses, trains, and ferrries. Plan carefully for your trip: short ferry hops in the panhandle cost as little as $18, and a bus from Anchorage to Fairbanks costs $55. A lot of mileage is required to make the pass worthwhile.

OTHER FERRIES

Information about fares, reservations, vehicles, and schedules often vary with the season. Consult each ferry company when constructing your itinerary in order to clear up any additional questions before finalizing your plans.

- **BC Ferries** (☎ 888-223-3779 in BC, 250-386-3431 outside BC; fax 381-5452; www.bcferries.bc.ca/ferries). Passenger and vehicle ferry service throughout coastal BC. Service is frequent and reservations are recommended on the longer routes through the **Inside Passage** and **Discovery Coast Passage,** and to the **Queen Charlotte Islands.** Heavy traffic on weekends, particularly in the summer.
- **Black Ball Transport, Inc.** (in Victoria ☎ 250-386-2202, fax 386-2207; in Port Angeles ☎ 360-457-4491, fax 457-4493; www.northolympic.com/coho). 2-4 ferries daily between **Port Angeles** and **Victoria.** 90min. $7.50 each way, car and driver $29.50, motorcycle and driver $17.50. Bicycles $3.50 extra. Reservations not accepted.
- **Victoria Clipper,** 2701 Alaskan Way, Pier 69, Seattle, WA 98121 (☎ 800-888-2535, in Seattle 206-448-5000, in Victoria 250-382-8100; www.victoriaclipper.com). Daily passenger service between **Seattle, WA** and **Victoria, BC.** 2-3hr. $66 one-way, return $79-109 (order 14 days in advance for best prices); bike $10 each way.
- **Washington State Ferries,** 801 Alaskan Way, Seattle, WA 98104 (in Seattle ☎ 206-464-6400 or in Victoria 250-381-1554; www.wsdot.wa.gov/ferries). Ferries to **Sidney, BC,** and throughout **Puget Sound.** No reservations, except for travel to the **San Juan Islands** or **British Columbia.** Service is frequent, but traffic is heavy—especially in summer, when waits of over an hour to board a ferry are not uncommon. Fares fluctuate, but stay reasonable. Bikes $10.

BY THUMB

> Let's Go urges you to consider the risks and disadvantages of hitchhiking before thumbing it. Hitching means entrusting your life to a stranger who happens to stop beside you on the road. While this may be comparatively safe in some areas of Europe and Australia, it is **NOT** in most of North America. We do **NOT** recommend it. Don't put yourself in a situation where hitching is the only option.

SPECIFIC CONCERNS ■ 55

That said, if you decide to hitchhike, there are precautions you should take. **Women traveling alone should never hitch in the United States.** Refuse a ride if you feel in any way uncomfortable with the driver. If at all threatened or intimidated, ask to be let out no matter how uncompromising the road looks. Have a *back-up plan* in case you get stranded or face an emergency. Carrying a cellular phone for emergency use is a good idea, although coverage is spotty in some isolated areas. In rural areas, hitching is reportedly less risky than in urban areas. Many people hitchhike in the North, but it is not unusual to get stranded on a sparsely traveled route. A wait of a day or two between rides is not uncommon on certain stretches of the Alaska Hwy. Alaska state law prohibits moving vehicles from not picking up stranded motorists, as the extreme weather conditions can be life-threatening. However, hitchhikers may only legally thumb for rides on the on-and-off ramps of highways—not on the highways themselves. In fact, all states prohibit hitchhiking while standing on the roadway itself or behind a freeway entrance sign; hitchers more commonly find rides near intersections where many cars converge and well-lit areas where they can see their prospective rider and stop safely. Hitchers riding across the **USA-Canada border** should be prepared for a series of queries about citizenship, insurance, contraband, and finances, and for an auto inspection. Walking across the border avoids the hassle.

ADDITIONAL INFORMATION

SPECIFIC CONCERNS

WOMEN TRAVELERS

Women exploring on their own inevitably face some additional safety concerns, but it's easy to be adventurous without taking undue risks. Women are targeted for muggings and swindlings, as well as general harassment because criminals see them as easier prey. If you are concerned, consider staying in hostels that offer single rooms that lock from the inside or in religious organizations with rooms for women only. Communal showers in some hostels are safer than others; check them before settling in. If you are camping in isolated areas or traveling in big cities with which you are unfamiliar, try to travel with partners. In more rural areas, rowdy bars can also be sketchy. Wherever you go, walk purposefully and self-confidently; women who look like they know what they are doing and where they are going are less likely to be harassed. Always carry extra money for a phone call, bus, or taxi. Consider approaching older women or couples if you're lost or feel uncomfortable. Memorize the emergency numbers in places you visit, and consider carrying a whistle or airhorn on your keychain.

BISEXUAL, GAY, AND LESBIAN TRAVELERS

American cities are generally accepting of all sexualities, and thriving gay and lesbian communities can be found in most cosmopolitan areas. Most college towns are gay-friendly as well. However, homophobia still rears its ugly head. The more rural you get, the more rampant it is likely to be. Listed below are contact organizations that offer materials addressing some specific concerns. **Out and About** (www.planetout.com) offers a bi-weekly newsletter addressing travel concerns.

International Gay and Lesbian Travel Association, 52 W. Oakland Park Blvd., Fort Lauderdale, FL 33311, USA (☎800-448-8550 or 954-776-2626; www.iglta.com). An organization of 1200 companies serving gay and lesbian travelers worldwide.

Gay's the Word, 66 Marchmont St., London WC1N 1AB (☎+44 20 7278 7654; www.gaystheword.co.uk). The largest gay and lesbian bookshop in the UK, with both fiction and non-fiction titles. Mail-order service available.

Giovanni's Room, 1145 Pine St., Philadelphia, PA 19107 (215-923-2960; www.queerbooks.com). An international lesbian/feminist and gay bookstore with mail-order service (carries many of the publications listed below).

International Lesbian and Gay Association (ILGA), 81 rue Marché-au-Charbon, B-1000 Brussels, Belgium (+32 2 502 2471; www.ilga.org). Provides political information, such as homosexuality laws of individual countries.

FURTHER READING

Damron Men's Guide, Damron Road Atlas, Damron's Accommodations, and *The Women's Traveller.* Damron Travel Guides (US$14-19). For more info, call 800-462-6654 or visit www.damron.com.

Ferrari Guides' Gay Travel A to Z, Ferrari Guides' Men's Travel in Your Pocket, and *Ferrari Guides' Inn Places.* Ferrari Publications (US$16-20). Purchase the guides online at www.ferrariguides.com.

The Gay Vacation Guide: The Best Trips and How to Plan Them, Mark Chesnut. Citadel Press (US$15).

Gayellow Pages USA/Canada, Frances Green. Gayellow pages (US$16). They also publish smaller regional editions. Visit Gayellow pages online at www.gayellowpages.com.

TRAVELERS WITH DISABILITIES

US federal law dictates that all public buildings should be handicap accessible, and recent laws governing building codes have made disabled access more the norm than the exception. Businesses, transportation companies, national parks, and public services are complied to assist the disabled in using their facilities. However, traveling with a disability still requires planning and flexibility.

Those with disabilities should inform airlines, buses, trains, and hotels of their disabilities when making arrangements for travel; some time may be needed to prepare special accommodations. Call ahead to restaurants, hotels, parks, and other facilities to find out about the existence of ramps, the widths of doors, the dimensions of elevators, etc. Major airlines and Amtrak accommodate disabled travelers if notified at least 72 hours in advance. Amtrak offers 15% discounts to disabled passengers, and hearing impaired travelers may contact Amtrak using teletype printers (800-872-7245; www.amtrak.com). **Greyhound** (see p. 49) provides free travel for a companion; if you are traveling alone, call Greyhound (800-752-4841) at least 48 hours, but no more than a week, before you leave and they'll arrange assistance where needed. Hertz, National, and Avis **car rental** agencies have hand-controlled vehicles at some locations (see **Renting,** p. 52). If planning to visit a national park or any other sight managed by the US National Park Service, you can obtain a free **Golden Access Passport** (see **National Parks,** p. 37).

Access-Able Travel Source, LLC, P.O. Box 1796, Wheat Ridge, CO 80034 (303-232-2979; fax 239-8486; www.access-able.com). A database on traveling the US for disabled travelers, started by two avid disabled travellers. Provides info on access, transportation, accommodations, and various other resources.

Moss Rehab Hospital Travel Information Service (215-456-9600; www.mossresourcenet.org). A telephone and Internet information resource center on travel accessibility and other travel-related concerns for those with disabilities.

Society for the Advancement of Travel for the Handicapped (SATH), 347 Fifth Ave., #610, New York, NY 10016 (212-447-7284; www.sath.org). An advocacy group that publishes free online travel information and the travel magazine *OPEN WORLD* (US$18, free for members) and a wide range of info on disability travel facilitation and accessible destinations. Annual membership US$45, students and seniors US$30.

Directions Unlimited, 123 Green Ln., Bedford Hills, NY 10507 (☎800-533-5343). Books individual and group vacations for the physically disabled; not an info service. Specializes in arranging individual and group vacations, tours, and cruises for the physically disabled or blind travelers.

MINORITY TRAVELERS

Racial and ethnic minorities sometimes face blatant and, more often, subtle discrimination and/or harassment, although regions in the US and Canada differ drastically in their general attitudes toward race relations. Verbal harassment is now less common than unfair pricing, false information on accommodations, or inexcusably slow or unfriendly service at restaurants. The best way to deal with such encounters is to remain calm and report individuals to a supervisor, and establishments to the Better Business Bureau for the region (the operator will provide local listings). Contact the police in extreme situations. *Let's Go* always welcomes reader input regarding discriminating establishments.

In larger cities, African-Americans can usually consult chapters of the Urban League and the **National Association for the Advancement of Colored People (NAACP)** (www.naacp.org) for info on events of interest to African-Americans.

TRAVELERS WITH CHILDREN

Family vacations often require that you slow your pace, and always require that you plan ahead. When deciding where to stay, remember the special needs of young children. If you pick a B&B or a small hotel, call ahead and make sure it's child-friendly. If you rent a car, make sure the rental company provides a car seat for younger children. Be sure that your child carries some sort of ID in case of an emergency or in case he or she gets lost.

Museums, tourist attractions, accommodations, and restaurants often offer discounts for children. Children under two generally fly for 10% off the adult airfare on international flights (this does not necessarily include a seat). International fares are usually discounted 25% for children from two to 11. Finding a private place for **breast feeding** is often a problem while traveling, so pack accordingly.

DIETARY CONCERNS

> **FURTHER READING**
> *Backpacking with Babies and Small Children,* Goldie Silverman. Wilderness Press (US$10).
> *How to Take Great Trips with Your Kids,* Sanford and Jane Portnoy. Harvard Common Press (US $10).
> *Have Kid, Will Travel: 101 Survival Strategies for Vacationing With Babies and Young Children,* Claire and Lucille Tristram. Andrews and McMeel (US$9).

Vegetarians should have no problems getting by in Alaska and the Pacific Northwest, especially with our help. We consistently try to list vegetarian-friendly establishments, grocery stores, and public markets. The **North American Vegetarian Society,** P.O. Box 72, Dolgeville, NY 13329 (☎518-568-7979; www.navs-online.org), sells several travel-related titles in the US and Canada including Transformative Adventures, a Guide to Vacations and Retreats (US$15), and the Vegetarian Journal's Guide to Natural Food Restaurants in the US and Canada (US$12).

Travelers who keep **kosher** should contact synagogues in larger cities for information on kosher restaurants. If you are strict in your observance, you may have to prepare your own food on the road. A good resource is the *Jewish Travel Guide,* by Michael Zaidner (Vallentine Mitchell; US$17).

For more information, visit your local bookstore, health food store, or library, and consult *The Vegetarian Traveler: Where to Stay if You're Vegetarian,* by Jed and Susan Civic (Larson Publications; US$16).

ALTERNATIVES TO TOURISM

For an extensive listing of "off-the-beaten-track" and specialty travel opportunities, try the **Specialty Travel Index,** 305 San Anselmo Ave., #313, San Anselmo, CA 94960, USA (☎888-624-4030 or 415-455-1643; www.specialtytravel.com; US$6). **Transitions Abroad** (www.transabroad.com) publishes a bimonthly online newsletter for work, study, and specialized travel abroad.

STUDYING ABROAD: UNIVERSITIES

If you are currently studying as an undergraduate and would like to get credit for schoolwork completed abroad check with universities in your home country to see if they offer exchanges with particular North American schools. The web site at www.studyabroad.com lists term-time and summer study opportunities around the world. Citizens of Australia, New Zealand, the UK, and Ireland can contact their local member organization of the **Experiment in International Living,** P.O. Box 676 Brattleboro, VT 05302, USA (☎802-257-7751; fax 258-3428; www.experiment.org), also known as the **School for International Training (SIT)** and **World Learning.** They can help arrange homestays, academic study abroad, study at language schools, and volunteer work. The **Council on International Educational Exchange (CIEE;** ☎800-2-COUNCIL; www.ciee.org) does all this and also has a new program aimed at helping foreigners find short-term work in the US.

Thanks go government subsidies, the tuition at Canadian schools is almost sane compared to their counterparts in the US. Although foreign students pay more than Canadian citizens, the total cost can be less than half of American schools.

If you want more general information on schools in the US, check out your local bookstore for college guides. The *Fiske Guide to Colleges*, by Edward Fiske (NY Times Books; $23), and *Barron's Profiles of American Colleges* ($25) are very useful. MacLean's (www.macleans.ca), a Canadian news magazine, puts out a yearly issue ranking Canadian universities.

Foreign students who wish to study in the US or Canada must apply to schools first, be admitted, and then begin the application for the appropriate visa. Studying in the US requires either an M-1 visa (vocational studies) or an F-1 visa (for full-time students enrolled in an academic or language program). Studying in Canada requires a student authorization (IMM 1208) in addition to the appropriate tourist visa. Students must prove sufficient financial support, and be in good health (see **Entrance Requirements,** p. 22). If English is not your native language, you will probably be required to take the **Test of English as a Foreign Language (TOEFL),** which is administered in many countries. The international students' office at the institution you will be attending can give you more specifics.

Most American undergraduates enroll in programs sponsored by US universities. Those relatively fluent in English may find it cheaper to enroll directly in a local university (although getting credit may be more difficult). Some schools in the Northwest that offer study abroad programs to foreigners are listed below.

University of Alaska, Anchorage. Summer Sessions, 3211 Providence Dr., Anchorage, AK 99508, USA (☎907-786-6740).

University of Alaska, Fairbanks. P.O. Box 756340, Fairbanks, AK 99755, USA (☎907-474-5266; ffjsk@aurora.alaska.edu).

LANGUAGE SCHOOLS

Several American and foreign companies offer courses in English at various centers and in the US and Canada. A few companies that have locations in the Pacific Northwest include:

American Cultural Exchange, 200 W. Mercer St. Suite 504, Seattle WA 98119 (☎206-217-9644; fax 217-9643; www.cultural.org) offers courses at **Pacific Lutheran University, Seattle Pacific University,** and at the **North Seattle Center** among others.

American Language Academy, 1401 Rockville Pike, Suite 550, Rockville MD 20852 (☎ 301-309-1400; fax 309-0202; www.ala-usa.com) offers courses in Portland at the **University of Portland** and in Ashland at **Southern Oregon State University.**

Eurocentres, 101 N. Union St. #300, Alexandria, VA 22314, USA (☎ 703-684-1494; www.eurocentres.com) or in Europe, Head Office, Seestr. 247, CH-8038 Zurich, Switzerland (☎ +41 411 485 50 40). Eurocenters has a branch in Vancouver, BC called the **Pacific Language Institute** 300-755 Burrard St., Vancouver, BC V6Z 1X6.

WORKING AND VOLUNTEERING ABROAD

US. Foreign students living in the US are prohibited from taking an off-campus job during the first year of their study and can only accept such a job after the first year upon permission from the INS. Technical students are allowed to work only as a function of their training. Visitors to the US under the regular visitation visa (the B-2 visa) are prohibited from taking any type of employment.

To work in the US without immigrating, one must obtain a work visa or participate in a cultural exchange program. Work visas are difficult to procure and require the presence of extraordinary circumstances, such as extensive education or prominence in a particular academic or professional field. Cultural exchanges are easier to arrange and are intended to facilitate multi-culturalism in education, arts, and sciences. The US Information Agency organizes a variety of cultural exchanges (www.usinfo.state.gov).

CANADA. Foreign students living in Canada are allowed to work only under exceptional circumstances, such as unforeseen loss of expected funding. In order to work in Canada without immigrating, one must be sponsored by a Canadian employer who can prove that foreign assistance is needed to fill a Canadian employee market shortage. An Employment Authorization (EA) can be issued to a foreign worker only if he or she is sponsored by a Canadian employer and if a Human Resources Development Canada officer agrees that the foreign worker will produce a net benefit for Canada and Canadians.

WORKING FOR A LIVING

ALASKAN CANNERIES. Seafood harvesting and processing jobs are no pleasure cruise. While it's possible to earn a lot in a brief time, you must be willing to put in long, hard hours (upward of 80 per week) at menial and unrewarding tasks. As the **Alaska Employment Service** eloquently states, "Most seafood processing jobs are smelly, bloody, slimy, cold, wet, and tiring because of manual work and standing for many hours. The aroma of fish lingers with workers throughout the season. Most get used to it. Those who can't generally leave." If you're interested, the Alaska Department of Labor lists available jobs online (www.labor.state.ak.us) and through an info line (☎ 907-465-8900). Be sure you understand whether your potential employer will provide housing, food, and transportation costs.

TREEPLANTING. Planting trees is the Canadian equivalent of work in the canneries—the smell is better, but hours are long and hard, and the bugs can be horrific. Planters are usually paid between 10 and 30¢ per tree; an experienced planter can plunk enough trees in the ground to earn more than CDN$200 a day. Most treeplanters are university students who work from late spring to mid-summer at remote camps. The companies that hire them range from well-run, professional organizations to exploitative rip-off operations. The web site at http://web.radiant.net/harihari contains lists and reviews of companies, straight-up and detailed discussion of the work, and advice from veterans on everything from spotting good and bad companies to customizing your shovel.

60 ■ ALTERNATIVES TO TOURISM

OTHER OPPORTUNITIES. Childcare International, Ltd., Trafalgar House, Grenville Place, London NW7 3SA (☎+44 020 8906 3116; fax 8906 3461; www.childint.co.uk) offers *au pair* positions in Canada and the US, and provides info on required qualifications. The organization prefers a long placement but does arrange summer work. UK£100 application fee. Members of **Willing Workers on Organic Farms (WWOOF**; www.phdcc.com/sites/wwoof) receive a list of organic farms looking for short-term employees to work in exchange for room and board. US membership ($10) is available only to US citizens. (☎413-323-4531; P.O. Box 608, Belchertown, MA 01007, USA.) Canadian membership costs CDN$30. (☎250-354-4417; wwoofcan@uniserve.com; Rural Rte. 2, S. 18, C. 9, Nelson, BC Canada VIL 5P5.)

VOLUNTEERING

Volunteer jobs are readily available and many provide room and board in exchange for labor. You can sometimes avoid high application fees by contacting the individual workcamps directly. Volunteer work is much easier to arrange for foreign visitors than paid work.

COMMUNITY SERVICE

Action Without Borders, 350 Fifth Ave. #6614, New York, NY 10118 USA (☎212-843-3973; www.idealist.org), maintains a web site which lists volunteer opportunities at 18,000 nonprofits in 130 countries including the US and Canada, and has links to organizations that help arrange international volunteering stints.

Americorps, (www.cns.gov/americorps), the domestic equivalent to America's Peace Corps, places US citizens in community development programs throughout the US, usually for a one-year term. You can also contact Americorps' umbrella organization, the Corporation for Public Service, 1201 New York Ave., NW, Washington, D.C. 20525 (☎202-606-5000).

Earthwatch, 3 Clocktower Pl., P.O. Box 75, Maynard, MA 01754 (☎800-776-0188 or 978-461-0081; www.earthwatch.org). Arranges 1- to 3-week programs to promote conservation of natural resources. Programs average US$1600.

Habitat for Humanity International, 121 Habitat St., Americus, GA 31709, USA (☎800-422-4828; www.habitat.org). Offers international opportunities to live with and build houses in a host community. Costs range US$1200-3500.

OUTDOORS

Student Conservation Association (SCA), Box 550 Charlestown, NH 03603 (☎603-543-1700; www.sca-inc.org). A clearinghouse for volunteer positions and internships in US National Parks and on other public lands lasting from 4 weeks to 12 months. Some positions are part of the Americorps program (see above). A free 4-5 week program for high school students provides food and lodging on month-long trail maintenance gigs. **SCA Northwest Office,** 1265 S. Main St. Suite 210, Seattle, WA 98144 (☎206-324-4649; fax 324-4998).

Parks Canada National Volunteer Program (☎888-773-8888; www.parkscanada.pch.gc.ca) suggests potential volunteer opportunities to Canadians and foreign nationals who email (via the web site) or write (Coordinator, Parks Canada National Volunteer Program, 25 Eddy St., 4th fl., Hull, QC K1A 0M5) with their qualifications and dates for which they seek placement. The deadline for summer placements is Dec. 1; for winter and spring placements June 30. Candidates may also contact individual parks; addresses are listed on the web site.

OTHER RESOURCES

Let's Go tries to cover all aspects of budget travel, but we can't put *everything* in our guides. Listed below are books and web sites that can serve as jumping off points for your own research.

MAPS AND ROAD GUIDES

Rand McNally's Road Atlas, (☎800-234-0679 or 206-264-6277; www.randmcnally.com; $11) covers highways throughout the US and Canada. Available at bookstores, gas stations, and from the publisher. Provides driving directions online.

The Milepost, 619 E. Ship Creek Ave. #329, Anchorage, AK 99501, USA (☎800-726-4707 or 907-272-6070; www.themilepost.com; US$24.95) is a mile-by-mile guide to the highways in northern BC, the Yukon, and Alaska. It's available up north or direct from the publishers.

Delorme Atlas and Gazetteer, 2 Delorme Dr., P.O. Box 298, Yarmouth, ME 04096, USA (☎800-511-2459 or 207-846-7000; www.delorme.com). Topographical maps (1:150,000-1,400,000) available for all 50 states including dirt roads, campsites, boat launches, and established trails on public land ($17-20, plus $5 shipping in US). Their Topo software (US$100, Pacific coast states including Alaska $50) for Windows computers shows 20ft. intervals and includes 300,000 mi. of trails. Users can generate elevation profiles for custom routes, 3-D views of landscapes, and custom maps.

United States Geological Survey Topographical Maps, USGS Information Services, 345 Middlefeild Rd., Menlo Park, CA 94025 (☎888-275-8747 or 650-853-8300; www.usgs.gov). "7½-minute" series of topographic maps at 1:24,000 (available for the lower 48 states and near urban centers in Alaska), "15-minute" maps at 1:63,360 (covering nearly the rest of Alaska), geological maps, and maps of national parks may be purchased online ($4 per sheet) as well as at hundreds of stores. Free catalogue.

ITMB, 530 W Broadway, Vancouver, BC V5Y 1E9 (☎604-879-3621, fax 879-4521; www.itmb.com) distributes government topographical maps of BC and the Yukon, as well as their own, up-to-date topo maps of popular recreational areas near Vancouver, BC locations.

THE WORLD WIDE WEB

Almost every aspect of budget travel (with the most notable exception, of course, being experience) is accessible via the web. Even if you don't have Internet access at home, seeking it out at a public library or at work would be well worth it. Within 10 minutes at the keyboard, you can make a reservation at a hostel, get advice on travel hotspots or find out exactly how much a ferry costs. Each state and province in the Northwest has a tourism web page: *Washington* www.tourism.wa.gov; *Oregon* www.traveloregon.com; *British Columbia* www.hellobc.com; *Alberta* www.discoveralberta.com; *Yukon* www.touryukon.com; *Yukon First Nations* www.yfnta.org; *Alaska* www.dced.state.ak.us/tourism.

LEARNING THE ART OF BUDGET TRAVEL

How to See the World: www.artoftravel.com. A compendium of great travel tips, from cheap flights to self-defense to interacting with local culture.

Recreational Travel Library: www.travel-library.com. A fantastic set of links for general information and personal travelogues.

INFORMATION ON THE USA AND CANADA

CIA World Factbook: www.odci.gov/cia/publications/factbook/index.html. Tons of vital statistics on American and Canadian geography, government, economy, and people.

62 ■ ALTERNATIVES TO TOURISM

MyTravelGuide: www.mytravelguide.com. Country overviews, with everything from history to transportation to live web cam coverage of the US and Canada.

Atevo Travel: www.atevo.com/guides/destinations. Detailed introductions, travel tips, and suggested itineraries.

Columbus Travel Guides: www.travel-guides.com. Practical info.

TravelPage: www.travelpage.com. Links to official tourist office sites throughout the Northwest.

PlanetRider: www.planetrider.com. A subjective list of links to the "best" web sites covering the culture and tourist attractions.

OTHER INTERNET RESOURCES

Microsoft Expedia: www.expedia.com. Allows you to compare flight quotes, generate driving maps, with turn-by-turn instructions.

About (a.k.a. MiningCo.): www.about.com. City-specific sites assembled by local "guides" with info on area activities, history, transportation, and extensive link collections for Calgary, Seattle, Eugene, Portland, Spokane, Fairbanks, and Vancouver.

USWest Yellow Pages: www.uswestdex.com. Comprehensive phonebook-style listings of businesses in western states, including Oregon, Washington, and Alaska.

AND OUR PERSONAL FAVORITE...

Let's Go: www.letsgo.com. Our constantly expanding website features photos and streaming video, online ordering of all our titles, info about our books, a travel forum buzzing with stories and tips, and links that will help you find everything you ever wanted to know about the US and Canada.

OREGON

> **OREGON'S... Capital:** Salem. **Population:** 3,082,000. **Area:** 97,060 mi.² **Motto:** "She flies with her own wings." **Animal:** Beaver. **Nickname:** Beaver State. **Fish:** Chinook salmon. **Rock:** Thunderegg. **Dance:** Square Dance.

"Discovered" by Lewis and Clark on their overland expedition to the Pacific Ocean, Oregon soon became a hotbed of exploration and exploitation. Lured by plentiful forests and promises of gold and riches, entire families liquidated their possessions and sank their life savings into covered wagons, corn meal, and oxen, high-tailing it to Oregon in search of prosperity and a new way of life. This population of outdoors-enthusiasts and fledgling townspeople joined the Union in 1859, and has ever since become an eclectic mix of treehuggers and suave big-city types. Today, Oregon remains as popular a destination as ever for backpackers, cyclists, anglers, beachcrawlers, and families alike.

The wealth of space and natural resources that supported the prospectors and farmers of old continues to provide the backbone of Oregon today: four out of ten Oregonians are involved in some way in the most diversified agricultural center in the US. More than half of Oregon's forests lie on federally owned land, hopefully preserving them for future generations of outdoor explorers, but 80,000 workers depend on an timber industry that is threatened by over-logging, by the Endangered Species Act, and by disputes over ownership of the remaining land and rights. Nevertheless, Oregon deserves its environmentalist reputation, having created the country's first recycling refund program and spearheaded wide-scale preservation of coastline for public use.

The caves and cliffs of the coastline remain a siren call to Oregon's most precious non-natural resource: tourists. For those in search of big city life, Portland's laid-back and idiosyncratic personality—its name was determined by a coin toss (the flip side would have christened it "Boston, Oregon")—draws the microchip, mocha, and music crowds, while the college town of Eugene embraces hippies and Deadheads from around the West. From excellent microbrews to snow-capped peaks, a visit to Oregon is still worth crossing the Continental Divide.

OREGON'S HIGHLIGHTS

CRATER LAKE NATIONAL PARK (see p. 128) protects a placid, azure pool in the maw of an ancient and enormous volcano.

THE HIGH DESERT MUSEUM in Bend (see p. 122) bolsters appreciation for nature.

THE COLUMBIA RIVER GORGE (see p. 82) cuts a stunning chasm.

ASHLAND'S SHAKESPEARE would make Will proud (see p. 120).

CANNON BEACH'S (see p. 92) silky soft stretch of sand is the ultimate getaway.

DUNE BUGGIES gear it up in **Oregon Dunes National Recreation Area** (see p. 100).

PERUSE Portland's **Rose Garden** to see why it's dubbed the City of Roses (see p. 76).

64 ■ OREGON

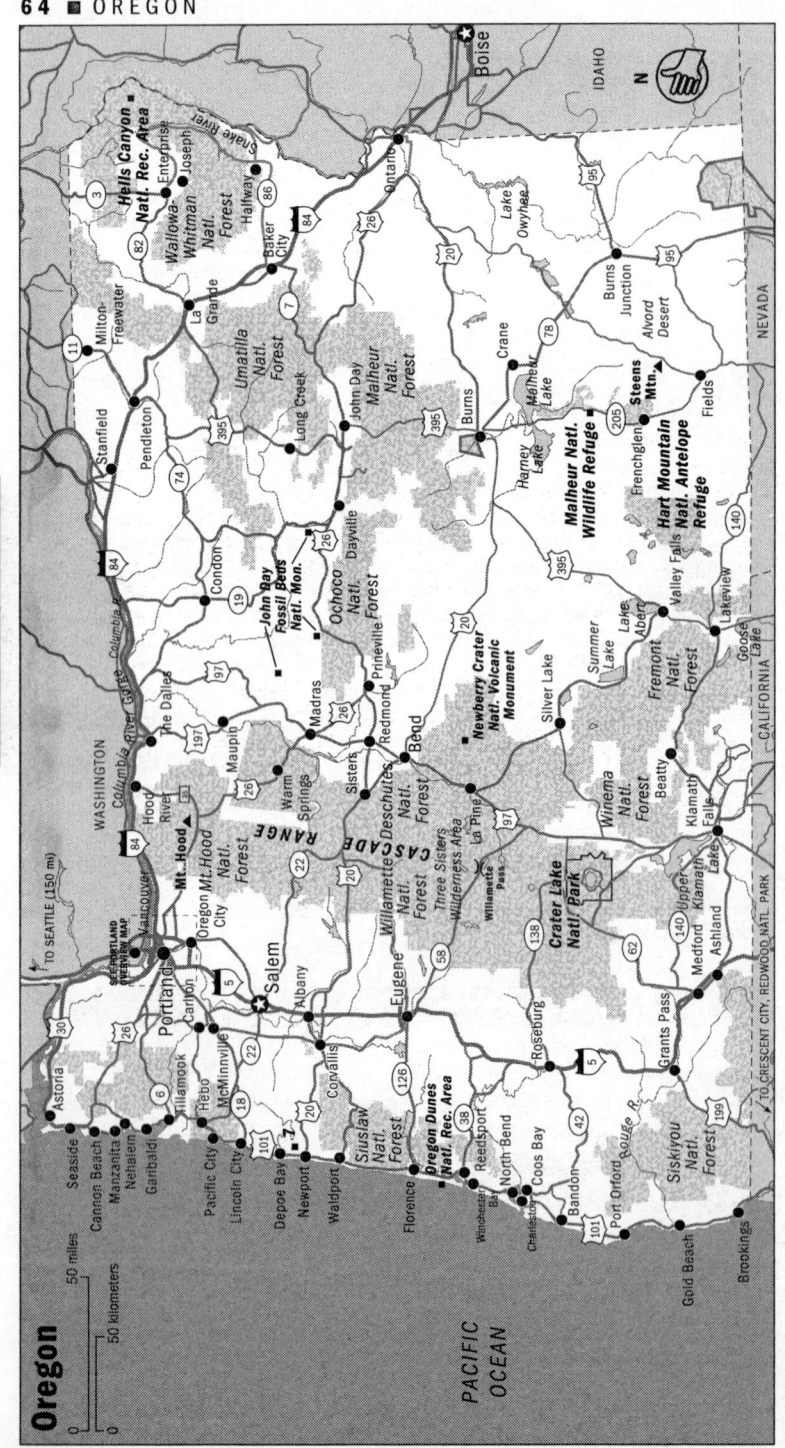

PORTLAND ☎ 503

As a slate of "best places to live" awards attest, Portland is no longer the secret it once was. Increasingly popular and populous, the City of Roses is still the quietest and mellowest of the West Coast's big cities. With over 200 parks, the pristine Willamette River, and snow-capped Mt. Hood in the background, Portland is an oasis of natural beauty. An award-winning transit system and pedestrian-friendly streets make it feel more like a pleasantly overgrown town than a metropolis. Yet with over one million people in the metropolitan area, as well as industry giants like Nike and Intel, Portland is a thriving component of the West Coast economy.

Culture is constantly cultivated in the endless theaters, galleries, and bookshops around town. Powell's City of Books engulfs an entire city block, making it the largest independent bookstore in the country. A 1% public art tax on new construction funds an ever-growing body of outdoor sculpture. Local artists fill galleries and cafes with paint and plaster and the street with murals. Improvisational theaters are in constant production, and open-mic night is in vogue all over town. The city's venerable orchestra, the oldest in the western United States, maintains the traditional side of Portland's cultural scene.

Other Portland institutions marry art and entertainment in the microbrewery capital of America. During the rainy season, Portlanders flood neighborhood pubs and coffeehouses for shelter and conversation, but not even America's best beer can keep hikers, bikers, and runners from their sylvan surroundings. The Willamette River and its wide park reach all the way downtown, and dense forests in the West Hills cloak miles of well-manicured hiking trails. Not too far out of town, Portlanders head to Mt. Hood in the east and the Pacific Coast in the west.

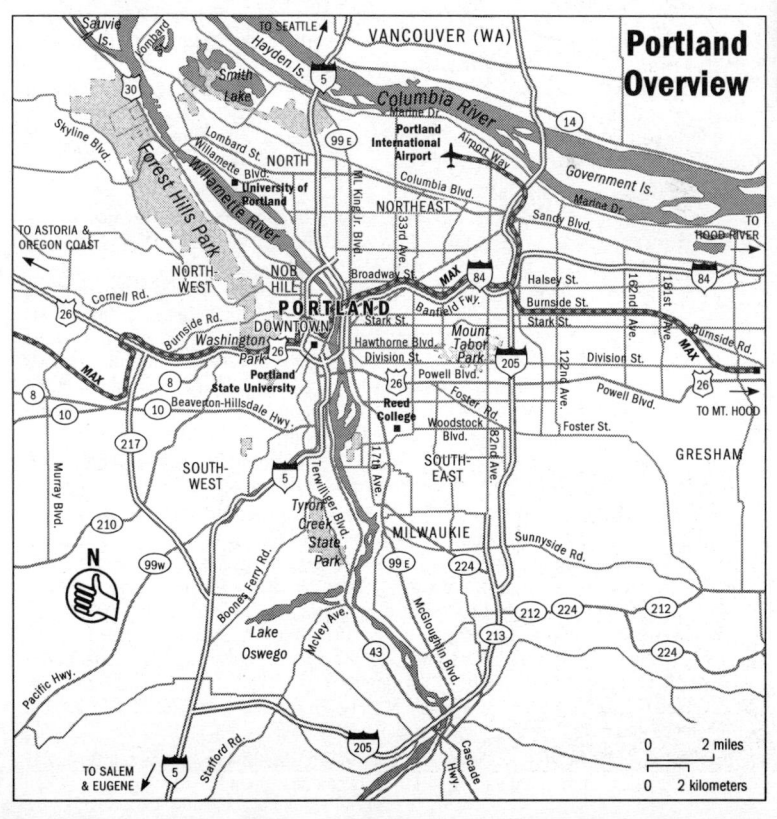

INTERCITY TRANSPORTATION

Flights: Portland International Airport (☎460-4234), is served by almost every major airline. The airport is connected to the city center by the **MAX** Red Line, an efficient light rail system. (38min.; every 15min. daily 5am and 11:30pm; $1.55.) Another option is Tri-Met bus #12 (Sandy Blvd.) outside baggage claim, which passes south through downtown on SW 5th Ave. (45min.; 6 per morning hr., 2 per eveninghr.; $1.20). **Gray Line** (☎285-9845) provides **airport shuttles,** which stop at most major hotels in Portland, as well as 5th Ave. (every 45min. from 5:15am-midnight, $15).

Trains: Amtrak, 800 NW 6th Ave. (☎273-4866; reservations 800-872-7245), at Hoyt St. in weathered yet regal Union Station. Ticket counter open daily 7:45am-9pm. To **Seattle** (4hr., 4 per day, $23-36), **Eugene** (2½hr., 2 per day, $15-28), and **San Francisco** (19hr.; 1 per day; $78-130, sleeper $152-244).

Buses: Greyhound, 550 NW 6th Ave. (☎243-2310 or 800-231-2222), at NW Glisan by Union Station. Ticket counter open 5am-1am. To **Seattle** (3-4½hr., 9 per day, $22); **Eugene** (2½-4hr., 9 per day, $14); **Spokane, WA** (about 8hr., 6 per day, $40). Student Advantage (15%), senior (10%), and military (10%) discounts. Lockers $5 per day.

LOCAL TRANSPORTATION

The award-winning **Tri-Met bus system** is one of the most logically organized and rider-friendly public transit systems in America. The downtown **transit mall,** closed to all but pedestrians and buses, lies between SW 5th and 6th Ave., where over 30 covered passenger shelters serve as stops and info centers. Southbound buses stop along SW 5th Ave., northbound along SW 6th Ave. Bus routes and stops are colored according to their **service areas,** each with its own lucky charm: red salmon, orange deer, yellow rose, green leaf, blue snow, purple rain, and brown beaver. Most of downtown is in the **Fareless Square.** For directions and fares outside this zone, see **Public Transportation,** below.

Most downtown streets are **one-way.** The city's **Smart Parks** are common and well marked. (Near Pioneer Sq. 95¢ per hr., $3 per hr. after 4hr., $2 after 6pm, max. $10; weekends $5 per day.) Parking is cheaper farther from city center. **Tri-Met** is the best bet for day-long excursions downtown.

Public Transportation: Tri-Met, 701 SW 6th Ave. (☎238-7433; www.tri-met.org), in Pioneer Courthouse Sq. Open M-F 9am-6pm. Several **information lines** available: **Call-A-Bus** info system ☎231-3199; fare info ☎231-3198; TDD info ☎238-5811; special needs ☎962-2455; lost and found ☎962-7655. Buses generally run 5am-midnight with reduced hours on weekends. Fare $1.20-1.50, ages 7-18 90¢, over 65 or disabled 55¢, free in the downtown. All-day pass $4; 10 fares for $10. All buses and bus stops are marked with one of seven symbols and have bike racks ($5 permit available at area bike stores). **MAX** (☎228-7246), based at the Customer Service Center, is Tri-Met's light-rail train running between downtown, Hillsboro in the west, and Gresham in the east. A new line, opened late in 2001, serves the airport from the main line's "Gateway" stop. Transfers from buses can be used to ride MAX. Runs M-F 4:30am-1:30am.

Taxis: Radio Cab (☎227-1212), $2.50 base, $1.50 per mi. **Broadway Cab** (☎227-1234), $2.50 base, $1.50 per mi. Airport to downtown $25-30.

Car Rental: **Crown Rent-A-Car,** 1315 NE Sandy Blvd. (☎230-1103). A tiny building with limited selection, Crown is by far the cheapest option for anyone under 25. 18-21 must have credit card and proof of insurance. 22 must have credit card. Transport from airport available upon request. From $25-40 per day, $140-160 per week. Open M-F 8:30am-5pm. **Rent-a-Wreck,** 1800 SE M.L. King Blvd. (☎233-2492 or 888-499-9111). From $20-30 per day, $110-150 per week, with 100 free mi. per day. Older cars. Will occasionally rent to under-25. Open M-F 7:30am-5pm, weekends by appointment only. **Dollar Rent-a-Car** (☎800-800-4000), at airport. From $30 per day, $170 per week, with unlimited mileage. Extra 15% airport fee. Must be 25 with credit card, or 21 with proof of insurance and a $19 per day surcharge. Open 24hr.

AAA: 600 SW Market St. (☎222-6777 or 800-AAA-HELP/222-4357), between Broadway and 6th Ave., near the Portland State University campus. Open M-F 8am-5pm.

DON'T NEED A TICKET TO RIDE? Portland is home to one of the best inventions the budget traveler has seen for a long time: the **No-Fare Zone.** Anywhere north and east of 405, west of the river and south of Hoyt St. all of the city's public transportation is free—that's right, no ticket needed to ride. Just get on and off the MAX or the bus within this area and you can walk away without paying a cent. It takes a little getting used to, but once it becomes second nature the possibilities are endless. It speeds up club hopping, makes running across town to eat at that special place a breeze, even going a few blocks to put money in the meter is no problem. So go ahead—take a ride. No one is going to stop you.

ORIENTATION

Portland lies in the northwest corner of Oregon, where the Willamette (wih-LAM-it) River flows into the Columbia River. **I-5** connects Portland with San Francisco (659 mi., 11-14hr.) and Seattle (179 mi.; 3-3½hr.), while **I-84** follows the route of the Oregon Trail through the Columbia River Gorge, heading along the Oregon-Washington border toward Boise, Idaho. West of Portland, **US 30** follows the Columbia downstream to Astoria, but **US 26** is the fastest path to the coast. **I-405** runs just west of downtown to link I-5 with US 30 and 26.

Every street name in Portland caries one of five prefixes: **N, NE, NW, SE,** or **SW,** indicating what part of the city the address is to be found. East and west are separated by the Willamette River, and **Burnside St.** provides separation between north and south. Plain ol' north is separated from northeast by **Williams Ave.** While the directions help keep travelers oriented, the real unit in Portland geography is the neighborhood. It seems like the name of the area changes every few blocks, so we will only list the major ones here.

Close to the city center, Northwest Portland is home to Chinatown and most of Old Town. Nob Hill and Pearl District, the recently revitalized home to most of Portland's beautiful people, are found further north, while Washington Park is found further west. Forest Park is a huge wooded area that stretches along the river, providing a boundary to the north of this whole area. Southwest Portland includes downtown, the southern end of Old Town, and a slice of the wealthier West Hills. Portland State University fills a large space south of the city center. Southeast Portland contains parks, factories, local businesses, residential areas of all brackets, and a rich array of cafes, stores, theaters, and restaurants, particularly around Hawthorne Blvd. east of SE 33rd St. Reed College, with its wide green quadrangles and brick halls, lies deep within the southeast district at the end of Woodstock Ave., which has a life and culture of its own. Northeast Portland is highly residential, but like the southeast, has pockets of activity. Unlike the southeast, though, the northeast does not have any accommodations, so venturing out is a little more difficult. Some of the northeast's biggest draws are near the river, and include the Lloyd Center Shopping Mall and the Oregon Convention Center. The north of Portland is almost all residential, and receives next to no tourist traffic.

PRACTICAL INFORMATION

TOURIST SERVICES

Visitor Information: Portland Oregon Visitors Association (POVA), 701 SW Morrison St. (☎275-9750; www.travelportland.com). Located in Pioneer Courthouse Sq. Walk through the crowds of screaming kids and between the fountains to enter. All the pamphlets you could want, plus a 12min. interpretive movie. Free *Portland Book* has maps and comprehensive info on local attractions. Open M-Sa 9am-6pm, Su 10am-4pm. Also houses a **Tri-Met Service Counter** and **Ticket Central Portland,** a counter that sells tickets to sporting events and almost any show in town, plus day-of-show half-price tickets. They only serve walk-in customers, but do have a number to call for ticket availability (☎275-8358). Open M-F 9am-6pm, Sa 10am-4pm, Su noon-4pm.

68 ■ PORTLAND

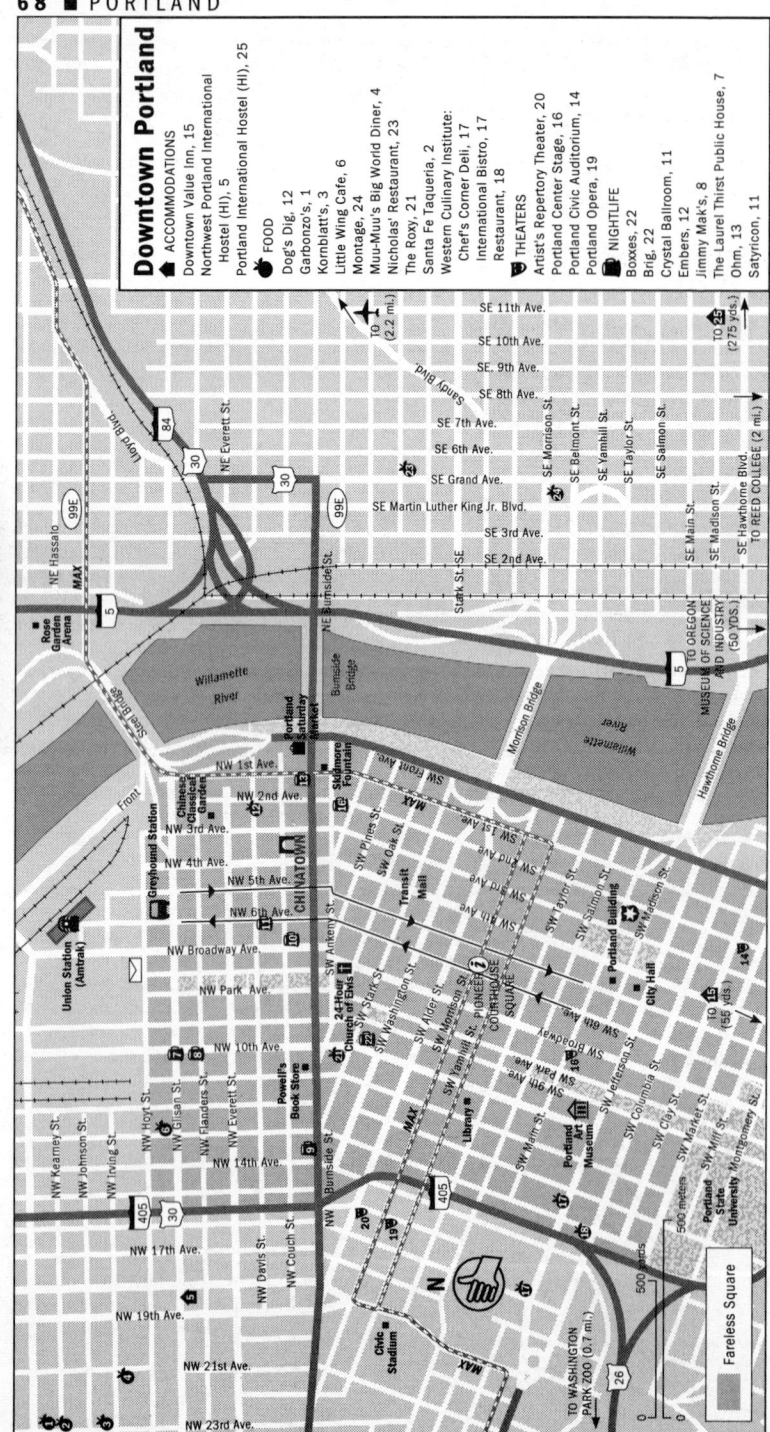

Downtown Portland

ACCOMMODATIONS
- Downtown Value Inn, 15
- Northwest Portland International Hostel (HI), 5
- Portland International Hostel (HI), 25

FOOD
- Dog's Dig, 12
- Garbonzo's, 1
- Kornblatt's, 3
- Little Wing Cafe, 6
- Montage, 24
- Muu-Muu's Big World Diner, 4
- Nicholas' Restaurant, 23
- The Roxy, 21
- Santa Fe Taqueria, 2
- Western Culinary Institute: Chefs Corner Deli, 17
- International Bistro, 17
- Restaurant, 18

THEATERS
- Artist's Repertory Theater, 20
- Portland Center Stage, 16
- Portland Civic Auditorium, 14
- Portland Opera, 19

NIGHTLIFE
- Boxxes, 22
- Brig, 22
- Crystal Ballroom, 11
- Embers, 12
- Jimmy Mak's, 8
- The Laurel Thirst Public House, 7
- Ohm, 13
- Satyricon, 11

Outdoor Information: Portland Parks and Recreation, 1120 SW 5th Ave. #1302 (☎823-2223), in the Portland Building between Main and Madison St. Offers a wealth of information including maps and pamphlets on Portland's parks. Open M-F 8am-5pm. **Nature of Northwest,** 800 NE Oregon St. #117 (☎872-2750; www.naturenw.org), 2 blocks east of the Convention Center on NE 7th Ave. A multitude of hiking maps, guidebooks and raw information are on tap at this U.S. Forest Service-run shop. Pick up a Northwest Forest Pass here, required for parking in most National Forests in Washington and Oregon ($5 per day, $30 annually). Open M-F 9am-5pm. Closed holidays.

LOCAL SERVICES

Bookstore: See **Powell City of Books,** p. 74. **Powell's Travel Store** (☎228-1108). Adjacent to the **Tourist information** in Pioneer Courthouse Sq. Has a huge selection of road maps, hiking maps, guidebooks and travel literature. Open M-F 9am-7pm, Sa 10am-6pm, Su 10am-5pm. A **Thomas Cook's** is also found inside of Powell's Travel for any money-changing needs. Open M-F 9am-5:30pm, Sa 10:30am-2pm, closed Su.

Outdoors Equipment: U.S. Outdoor Store, 219 SW Broadway (☎223-5937). Located just around the corner from the **Church of Elvis** (see **Sights**), this store has a huge selection of gear for almost any outdoor activity, summer or winter. Open M-F 9am-8pm, Sa 10am-6pm, Su noon-5pm.

Gay and Lesbian Info: Portland's best resource for queer info is the biweekly newspaper **Just-Out** (☎236-1252), available free around the city.

Tickets: Ticketmaster (☎224-4400). Surcharge $1.50-7.75. **Fastixx** (☎224-8499) Surcharge $2-3 per order, plus an additional $1 per ticket ordered. Also try **Ticket Central Portland** (see **Tourist Services,** above).

Laundromat: Springtime Thrifty Cleaners and Laundry, 2942 SE Hawthorne Blvd. (☎232-4353). 150 ft. from the Hawthorne hostel. Wash $1.25, dry 25¢ per 10min. Open daily 7:30am-9pm.

Public Pool: Call 823-5130 for a list of 16 public pools. $2.50; under 17 $1.50.

EMERGENCY AND COMMUNICATION

Emergency: ☎911. **Police:** 1111 SW 2nd Ave. (non-emergency response ☎823-3333; info ☎823-4636; lost and found ☎823-2179), between Madison St. and Main St.

Crisis and Suicide Hotline: ☎655-8401. **Women's Crisis Line:** ☎235-5333. 24hr.

Late Night Pharmacies: Walgreen's (☎238-6056), intersection of 39th St. and Belmont St. Open 24hr.

Hospital: Legacy Good Samaritan, 1015 NW 22nd St. (☎413-8090; emergency 413-7260), between Lovejoy and Marshall. **Adventist Medical Center,** 10123 SE Market (☎257-2500).

Internet Access: Library, 801 SW 10th Ave. (☎248-5123), between Yamhill and Taylor. Open M-W 9am-9pm, Th-Sa 9am-6pm, Su 1-5pm. Free 1hr. Internet access. **Internet Arena,** 1016 SW Taylor St. (☎224-2718), across the street from the main library. $6 per hr., minimum $2. Open M-F 11am-8pm.

Post Office: 715 NW Hoyt St. (☎800-275-8777). Open M-F 7am-6:30pm, Sa 8:30am-5pm. **ZIP Code:** 97208.

ACCOMMODATIONS

Although downtown is studded with Marriott-esque hotels and the smaller motels are steadily raising prices, Portland still welcomes the budget traveler. Two Hostelling International locations provide quality housing in happening areas. Prices tend to drop away from the city center and inexpensive motels can be found on SE Powell Blvd. and the southern end of SW 4th Ave. Portland accommodations fill up, especially during the Rose Festival, so early reservations are wise.

HOSTELS AND MOTELS

Portland International Hostel (HI), 3031 SE Hawthorne Blvd. (☎236-3380), at 31st Ave. across from Artichoke Music. From downtown mall take bus #14 to SE 30th Ave. About a 20min. ride. Lively and inexpensive with much common space and a huge porch. Kitchen, laundry, and Internet access ($1 per 20min.). All-you-can-eat pancakes ($1). Staff will also help arrange daytrips. Fills early in summer. Reception daily 8am-10pm. No curfew. 34 beds. Dorms $15, nonmembers $18. Private rooms $41-46.

Northwest Portland International Hostel (HI), 1818 NW Glisan St. (☎241-2783) at 18th Ave. From downtown mall take bus #17 down Glisan to corner of 19th Ave. The snug Victorian building has a kitchen, laundry, and Sunday sundaes ($1). Tours to Mt. Hood, the Columbia River Gorge and Mt. St. Helens ($39). Permits available for roadside parking ($5 deposit). 34 dorm beds (co-ed available). Reception 8am-11pm. No curfew. $14-16 plus tax, with a $3 fee for nonmembers. Two private doubles, $40-50.

McMenamins Edgefield, 2126 SW Halsey St. (☎669-8610 or 800-669-8610), in Troutdale. By car, take I-84 east to Exit 16, turn right at the exit, and then left at the first stoplight onto SW Halsey St. Continue down Halsey, turn right just before Edgefield's vineyards. Take MAX east to the Gateway Station, then Tri-Met bus #24 (Halsey) east to the main entrance. This beautiful 38-acre former farm is a posh escape that keeps two hostel rooms. Wine tasting, 3 pubs (hamburgers $5), massage service, and more. Lockers and linens included. Two single-sex dorm-style rooms with 12 beds each ($20 plus tax) are the budget option. Call ahead in the summer. No curfew. Reception 24hr.

Downtown Value Inn, 415 SW Montgomery St. (☎226-4751), at 4th Ave. Take bus #12 through downtown to the corner of 5th Ave., or by car follow signs to the city center and Montgomery. An inexpensive option cleaner than the price would suggest. Pizza hangout downstairs. Phones, cable TV, laundry. Reception 24hr. Check-out 11am. Reservations recommended. Singles from $45; doubles from $55; rooms with jacuzzi $65.

CAMPGROUNDS

Both camping options are a little too distant from Portland to make commuting for more than a day or two an attractive option, but they do provide good spots to stop on the way in or out.

Ainsworth State Park (Oregon Park Info Center ☎800-551-6949 or 695-2301, M-F 8am-5pm). 37 mi. east of Portland, Exit 35 off I-84 on US 30, in Columbia Gorge. Wooded and lovely, but hwy. noise prevails. Showers, toilets, hiking. Non-camper showers $2. Open Apr.-Oct. Tent sites $13, full hookups $18.

Champoeg State Park, 8239 NE Champoeg Rd. (☎678-1251 or reservations 800-452-5687). Take I-5 south 27 mi. to Exit 278; follow signs west for 6 mi. Play along miles of paved bikeway or hike by the Willamette River. Water, electricity. Little privacy. Cabins that sleep 5, $35; yurts $27; RV and tent sites $19; 6 walk-in sites $15. If you walk or bike in, $4 sites are available. A $3 per vehicle day use fee is charged to non-campers.

◘ FOOD

Portland has more restaurants per capita than any other American city, and dining is seldom dull. Downtown tends to be expensive, but restaurants and quirky cafes in the NW and SE quadrants offer great food at reasonable prices.

PEARL DISTRICT AND NOB HILL

Trendy eateries line NW 21st and 23rd St. **Food Front,** 2375 NW Thurman St., a small cooperative grocery, has a superb deli and a wonderland of natural foods, fruit, and baked goods. (☎222-5658. Open daily 9am-10pm; winter 9am-9pm.) The Pearl District is popping out new restaurants at unprecedented rates making it an ideal locale if you are dining on a whim.

FOOD ■ 71

Little Wing Cafe, 529 NW 13th Ave. (☎228-3101) off Glisan. Take bus #17. Art-hunters gather at this all-homemade cafe. Sandwiches like the Eggplant Supreme ($6). Open M-Th 11:30am-4pm and 5:30-9pm; F-Sa 11:30am-4pm and 5:30-10pm.

Muu-Muu's Big World Diner, 612 NW 21st Ave. (☎223-8169), at Hoyt St. Bus #17. Where and high and low culture smash together. Muu-Muu's specializes in meals like the Shroom-wich (mushrooms and cheese in wine sauce $7). Open M-F 11:30am-1am.

Kornblatt's, 628 NW 23rd Ave. (☎242-0055), at Irving. Take bus #15. This New-York-style, kosher deli uses fluent deli-speak, from rugelach to kishka, while dishing up matzoh ball soup ($4) and big sandwiches ($5-10). Open Su-Th 7am-8pm, F-Sa 7am-9pm.

Garbonzo's, 922 NW 21st Ave. (☎227-4196), at Lovejoy. Sit amid the wire reliefs and watch the friendly staff bring your falafel to life. Falafel pita $3.75. Open Su-Th 11:30am-midnight, F-Sa 11:30am-2am. Also at 3433 SE Hawthorne Blvd.

Santa Fe Taqueria, 839NW 23rd St. (☎220-0406). Bus #15. Busy Nob Hill Mexican joint. Tacos $3. Restaurant open daily 11am-midnight; bar open to 1am.

DOWNTOWN AND OLD TOWN

The center of town and tourist traffic, Southwest Portland gets expensive. Streetcarts offer an array of portable food and bento boxes (lunches of meat or vegetables on a bed of rice), making a quick, healthy meal in one of downtown's many parks easy. **Snow White House** on 9th and Yamhill serves great crepes. Speedy ethnic restaurants also peddle cheap eats on Morrison St. between 10th and 11th Ave. For groceries, a 24hr. **Safeway** supermarket is found just behind the PAM (see **Sights**), 1025 SW Jefferson St.

▩ Western Culinary Institute (☎294-9770), would leave the Frugal Gourmet speechless. WCI has 4 eateries, each catering to a different budget niche, all of them reasonable. **Chef's Diner,** 1231 SW Jefferson, opens mornings to let cheerful students serve, taste, and discuss sandwiches, the breakfast special, or the occasional all-you-can-eat buffet ($5). Open Tu-F 7am-noon. **Chef's Corner Deli,** 1239 SW Jefferson, is good for a quick meal on-the-go (around $1 per dish, 3 make a nice meal). Open Tu-Th 8am-5:30pm, F 8am-6pm. Moving up the price scale, the elegant **Restaurant,** 1316 SW 13th Ave., serves a classy 5-course lunch ($10) rivaled by its superb 6-course dinner (Tu, W and F, $20). Reservations recommended. Open Tu-F 11:30am-1pm; dinner 6-8pm. An **International Bistro** opened in late 2001, serving food at a price range just below the restaurant. It is 3 blocks west of the Deli on Jefferson St. Call for details.

The Roxy, 1121 SW Stark St. (☎223-9160). Giant crucified Jesus with neon halo, pierced waitstaff, and quirky menu. Quentin Tarantuna Melt $6. Open Tu-Su 24hr.

Dogs Dig Vegetarian Deli, 212 NW Davis St. (☎223-3362). Vegetarian and vegan sandwiches, soups, and burgers served in a tiny storefront adorned with bad jokes and snapshots of nearly every dog in Portland. Soup and sandwich $5. Open M-F 9am-5pm.

SOUTHEAST PORTLAND

Anchored at happening Hawthorne Blvd., Southeast Portland is a great place to people-watch and tummy-fill. Eclectic eateries with exotic decor and economical menus hide in residential and industrial neighborhoods. Granola-seekers glory in **Nature's,** 3016 Division St. (☎233-7374. Open daily 9am-10pm.) **Safeway,** 2800 SE Hawthorne, at 28th Ave. is one among plenty. (☎232-5539. 24hr.) Most of Chinatown's good restaurants have moved east to E 82nd and Division.

▩ Nicholas' Restaurant, 318 SE Grand Ave. (☎235-5123), between Oak and Pine opposite Miller Paint. Bus #6 to the Andy and Bax stop. Lebanese and Mediterranean food at incredible prices. Sandwiches $4-8. Open M-Sa 10am-9pm, Su 11am-7pm.

Montage, 301 SE Morrison St. (☎234-1324). Bus #15, to the end of the Morrison Bridge and walk under it. Louisiana-style cooking. Munch gator ($10) or oyster shooters ($1.50), while pondering a mural of *The Last Supper*. Open M-Th 11:30am-2pm and 6pm-2am, F 11:30am-2pm and 6pm-4am, Sa 6pm-4am, Su 6pm-2am.

OREGON

Cafe Lena, 2239 SE Hawthorne Blvd. (☎ 238-7087). Bus #14. Would-be Whitmans come for open-mic poetry (Tu 9:30pm), while others just enjoy the chill atmosphere. Open Tu 8am-midnight, W-Th 8am-9:30pm, F-Sa 8am-10pm, Su 8am-3pm.

Thanh Thao Restaurant, 4005 SE Hawthorne Blvd. (☎ 238-6232). Bus #14. Offers Vietnamese and Thai that draw crowds of locals. Main entrees are large enough to feed two, and cost $6.50-8. Open M and W-F 11am-2:30pm and 5-10pm, Sa-Su 11am-10pm.

Barley Mill Pub, 1629 SE Hawthorne Blvd. (☎ 231-1492). Bus #14. This pub is a smoky temple to Jerry Garcia, honored by the hearty burgers they serve; upbeat, yet mellow, like the man himself. McMenamins beer and 20 other kinds on tap ($3-4). Happy hour M-F 4-6pm. Open M-Sa 11am-1am, Su noon-midnight.

Cup and Saucer, 3566 SE Hawthorne Blvd. (☎ 236-6001). Ask Chef Karen to cook you a world-famous garden scramble any time of day. Ani DiFranco has been spotted here, and the staff promises that you'll at least hear her on their stereo. Open daily 7am-9pm.

Hawthorne Street Cafe, 3354 SE Hawthorne Blvd. (☎ 232-4982). Bus #14. Two ginormous marionberry pancakes ($5.50) will more than do, and that is only the tip of the menu iceberg. Breakfast all day. Open M-F 7:30am-2:30pm, Sa and Su 8am-3pm, and dinner W-Su 5-10pm.

NORTHEAST PORTLAND

The northeast is distant from any hostel, but the food is worth a short trip. Places to eat line Broadway east of the river, and other pockets of commerce turn out good eats for Portland's most residential area.

Counter Culture, 3000 NE Killingsworth St. (☎ 249-3799). Take bus #10 to Killingsworth, or bus #6, and transfer to #72. One of the hottest restaurants in town, these rebels churn out upscale vegan cuisine that has everyone ooh-ing and ahh-ing. Seasonal menu, entrees $9-11. A dessert list finishes off the animal-free extravaganza. Open Tu-Sa 5:30-10pm, Su 5:30-9pm; brunch Sa-Su 9am-2pm.

Saigon Kitchen, 835 NE Broadway (☎ 281-3669). Perhaps the most honored Vietnamese and Thai restaurant in town. The chả giò rolls, deep-fried and served with fresh herbs and sauce ($7), are a favorite. Most entrees $7-9. Lunch specials $5-6. Also at 3829 SE Division St. (☎ 236-2312). Open M-Sa 11am-10pm, Su noon-10pm.

Dragonfly, 1411 NE Broadway (☎ 288-3960). A vibe so cool they should only serve ice cream. Affordable "nouvelle pan-Asian cuisine." Lunch $6-9, dinner $8-12. $30 table minimum with lunch. Open M-F 11:30am-2:30pm and 5-9:30pm, Sa-Su 5-9:30pm.

◨ CAFES

Coffee Time, 712 NW 21st Ave. (☎ 497-1090). Sip a cup of chai ($2-3) while locals play or watch chess at almost every table. The intelligentsia mingle on the couches; bohemians chill to music in the tapestried parlor. Lattes $2-3. Open daily, 6am-3am.

Palio Dessert & Espresso House, 1996 SE Ladd (☎ 232-9214), on Ladd Circle. Bus #10 stops right in front of the cafe, or walk south three blocks on SE 16th Ave. from Hawthorne. Tucked in the park-like Ladd neighborhood, this tranquil cafe sports mosaic floors, Mexican mochas ($2.50), and espresso mousse ($4). Bring a book and enjoy the outside seating. Open M-F 8am-midnight, Sa-Su 10am-midnight.

Pied Cow Coffeehouse, 3244 SE Belmont St. (☎ 230-4866). Bus #15. Sink into the velvety cushions in this quirky Victorian parlor. Espresso drinks $1-3, pot of tea $1.50. Open Tu-Th 4pm-midnight, F 4pm-1am, Sa noon-1am, Su noon-midnight. Closed Jan.

Rimsky Korsakoffeehouse, 707 SE 12th Ave. (☎ 232-2640), at Alder St. Bus #15 to 12th St., then walk 2 blocks north. Unmarked and low-key, this red Victorian house is a hidden gem with a frenzy of desserts. Ask for a "mystery table." Live classical music nightly. Open Su-Th 7pm-midnight, F-Sa 7pm-1am.

SIGHTS

Parks, gardens, open-air markets, and innumerable museums and galleries bedeck Portland. For $1.20, Bus #63 delivers passengers to at least 13 attractions. Catch the best of Portland's dizzying art scene on the first Thursday of each month, when the Portland Art Museum and small galleries in the Southwest and Northwest stay open until 8pm. For more info, contact the **Regional Arts and Culture Council,** 620 SW Main St. #420 (☎823-5111), across from the Portland Centre for the Performing Arts, or grab the *Art Gallery Guide* at the Visitors Center.

DOWNTOWN

Portland's downtown centers on the pedestrian and bus mall, which run north-south on 5th and 6th Ave. between W Burnside Blvd. on the north end and SW Clay St. on the south. On the **South Park Blocks,** a cool and shaded park snakes down the middle of Park Ave., enclosed on the west by **Portland State University (PSU).** The area is accesible by any bus from the Transit Mall; then set out on foot.

PORTLAND ART MUSEUM (PAM). PAM sets itself apart from the rest of Portland's burgeoning arts scene by the strength of its collections, especially in Asian and Native American art. The **Northwest Film Center** (see **Cinema**) shares space with the museum, and shows classics, documentaries, and off-beat flicks, almost every day. *(1219 SW Park, at Jefferson St. on the west side of the South Block Park. Bus #6, 58, 63. ☎226-2811. Open Tu-Sa 10am-5pm, Su noon-5pm, and until 8pm on the first Th of the month. $7.50, seniors and students $6, under 19 $4, under 5 free; special exhibits may be more.)*

PIONEER COURTHOUSE SQUARE. The fully-functioning **Pioneer Courthouse,** at 5th Ave. and Morrison St., is the centerpiece of the **Square.** Since opening in 1983 it has become "Portland's Living Room." Urbanites of every ilk hang out in the brick quadrangle, plus a good dose of tourists, too. During July and Aug., **High Noon Tunes** draw music lovers in droves. *(701 SW 6th Ave. Along the Vintage Trolley line and the MAX light-rail. Events hotline ☎223-1613. Music W noon-1pm.)*

FOUNTAINS. Nineteen large fountains provide plenty of cool spots to sit on sunny days; the free *Portland's Municipal Fountains* is available at the visitors center. **Salmon St. Springs,** in Waterfront Park at SW Salmon St., is controlled by an underground computer that synchronizes its 185 jets according to the city's mood. About 60 **Benson Bubblers,** miniature fountains in their own right, dot downtown.

ARCHITECTURE. The most controversial structure downtown is Michael Graves's **Portland Building,** 1120 SW 5th Ave., on the mall. This conglomeration of pastel tile and concrete, the first major work of postmodern architecture to be built in the US, has been both praised as PoMo genius and condemned as an overgrown jukebox. Nearby, the **Standard Insurance Center,** 900 SW 5th Ave., between Salmon and Taylor, has sparked controversy over **The Quest,** a sensual white marble sculpture more commonly known as "Five Groins in the Fountain."

NO ROOM FOR MUGGERS In 1948, a hole was cut through the sidewalk at the corner of SW Taylor St. and SW Naito Pkwy. (Front St.). It was expected to accommodate a mere lamp post, but greatness was thrust upon it. The streetlamp was never installed, and the 24-inch circle of earth was left empty until noticed by Dick Fagan, a columnist for the *Oregon Journal*. Fagan used his column, "Mill Ends," to publicize the patch of dirt, pointing out that it would make an excellent park. After years of such logic-heavy lobbying, the park was added to the city's roster in 1976. At 452.16 square inches, Mill Ends Park is officially the world's smallest. Locals have enthusiastically embraced it, planting flowers and hosting a hotly contested snail race on St. Patrick's Day.

OLD TOWN AND CHINATOWN

The section of downtown above SW Stark running along the Willamette River comprises **Old Town**. Although not the safest part of Portland, Old Town has been revitalized in recent years by storefront restoration, new shops, restaurants, and nightclubs. On weekends, **Saturday Market** draws all of Portland for food, crafts, hackey-sacks, and live entertainment. Just west of Old Town the arched **China Gates** at NW 4th Ave. and Burnside provides an entrance to a chinatown that, apart from a few restaurants and shops, seems more about business than Asian culture.

SHANGHAI TUNNELS. Downtown's waterfront district is laced with a complex web of underground passages known as the **Shanghai tunnels**. Urban lore has it that seamen would get folks drunk, drag them down to the tunnels, and store them there until their ship sailed. Forced aboard and taken out to sea, these hapless Portlanders would provide a free crew ("Behave or I'll make you a galley slave" is a common parental threat in Portland).

SKIDMORE FOUNTAIN. Intended as a place where "horses, men, and dogs" might drink, **Skidmore Fountain,** at SW 1st Ave. and SW Ankeny St., is now a popular people-watching spot and marks the end of **Waterfront Park,** a 20-block swath of grass and flowers along the Willamette River. Resident Henry Weinhard's offer to run beer through the fountain upon its opening in 1888 was rejected by city officials.

CLASSICAL CHINESE GARDENS. The newest addition to Portland's long list of gardens, this city block is done in the Suzhou style, the largest one found outside of China. While the plantings are still growing in and the buildings lack a weathered feeling, the large pond, winding paths, and ornate decorations do provide a quiet retreat in the middle or Portland. A tea house also offers a chance to experience authentic Chinese tea for $4-6. *(NW 3rd and Everett; ☎ 228-8131. Open Apr.-Oct. 9am-6pm., Nov.-Mar. 10am-5pm. $6, seniors, students, and children 6-18 $5, under 6 free.)*

THE PEARL DISTRICT

Opposite the North Park Blocks, between NW 8th and Park Ave., the up-and-coming **Pearl District** buzzes. Stretching north from Burnside to I-405 along the river, this former industrial zone is packed with galleries, loft apartments, and warehouses-turned-office buildings. Storefronts and cafes make the area welcoming, but boxy architecture hulks on.

■ **POWELL'S CITY OF BOOKS.** The largest independent bookstore in the world, Powell's is a must-see for anyone who gets excited about the written word. If you like to dawdle in bookshops, bring a sleeping bag and rations. Nine color-coded rooms house books on everything from criminology to cooking. The **Anne Hughes Coffee Room** inside serves bagels, cookies, and coffee for those who can't find their way out. Poetry and fiction readings and an extensive travel section on the Pacific Northwest make Powell's a worthy stop. *(1005 W Burnside St. on the edge of Northwest district. Bus #20. ☎ 228-4651 or 800-878-7323; www.powells.com. Open daily 9am-11pm.)*

24-HOUR CHURCH OF ELVIS. The flagship (and only) church for "Realisticism," this space borders somewhere between installation art and childhood nightmare. As the proprietor says, "What we can't get rid of, we might as well worship." Where does the King fit in? That is one we are still trying to figure out. Visits to the gift store grant exit from the land of eternal grace. Tours and non-binding weddings, $5. *(720 SW Ankeny St. ☎ 226-3671; www.churchofelvis.com. Usually open M-Th 2-4pm, F-Sa noon-5pm and 8pm-midnight, Su noon-5pm, but call ahead.)*

GALLERIES. *First Thursday* (free at PAM) is a guide to local galleries. For a nice selection, walk north on NW 9th Ave., turn left on NW Glisan and right on NW 12th. Ave. On the way you'll pass some of the area's most engaging spaces, including the **Mark Woolley Gallery,** 120 NW Ninth Ave., and the visiting artist's exhibition space at the **Pacific Northwest College of Art,** at 1241 NW Johnson. **Quintana Galleries,** 501 SW Broadway, displays work by contemporary Native American artists working in traditional styles.

NORTH AND NORTHEAST PORTLAND

Nicknamed "Munich on the Willamette," Portland is the uncontested **microbrewery** capital of the US; residents are proud of their beer. The visitors center hands out a list of 26 metro area breweries, most of which happily give tours if you call ahead.

BREWERIES. Widmer Bros. Brewing Co., half a mile north of the Rose Garden, offers free tours that include a video, viewing the facilities, and free samples. *(929 N Russell. ☎ 281-2437. Tours F 3pm, Sa 1pm and 2pm.)* Many beer factories are brew pubs, sometimes offering live music with their beers. Try the **Lucky Labrador Brew Pub,** where dogs rule the loading dock for Miser Monday pints. *(915 SE Hawthorne Blvd. ☎ 236-3555. Pints $3.25. Open M-Sa 11am-midnight, Su noon-10pm.)* Also try the **Bridgeport Brewing Co.** (see **Nightlife**). Visit the **Oregon Brewers Guild** to learn how these alchemists work magic on water and hops grain. *(510 NW 3rd Ave. ☎ 295-1862 or 800-440-2537; www.oregonbeer.org. Open M-F 10am-4pm.)*

THE GROTTO. Minutes from downtown on Sandy Blvd., a 62-acre Catholic sanctuary houses magnificent religious sculptures and shrines, as well as running streams and gardens. At the heart of the grounds is "Our Lady's Grotto," a breathtaking cave carved into a 110-foot cliff, and a replica of Michelangelo's *Pietà*. An elevator ($2) ascends from the Meditation Chapel for a serene view that takes in a life-size bronze of St. Francis of Assisi. *(US 30, at NE 85th. ☎ 254-7371. Open daily May-Oct. 9am-8pm; Nov.-Jan. 9am-4pm; Feb.-Apr. 9am-6:30pm. Exact closing time can vary.)*

SOUTHEAST PORTLAND

Southeast Portland is largely residential but is scattered with pockets of activity.

OREGON MUSEUM OF SCIENCE AND INDUSTRY (OMSI). The flocks of kids are mesmerized by the Paleontology Lab where staff work on real dinosaur bones. The motion simulator ($3.50) spruces up the immobile exhibits and the Omnimax Theater provides an experience like no other. The Murdock Planetarium presents astronomy matinees and moonlights with rockin' laser shows. The Pink Floyd show comes highly recommended. While at OMSI, visit the Navy's last diesel submarine, the U.S.S. Blueback. She never failed a mission, starred in the 1990 film *The Hunt for Red October*, and gets fantastic mileage. *(Right next to the river at 1945 SE Water Ave., two blocks south of Hawthorne Blvd. Bus #63. ☎ 797-4000; www.omsi.edu. Open daily Labor Day to Memorial Day 9:30am-7pm; winter daily 9:30am-5:30pm. Museum and Omnimax admission each cost $7, ages 4-13 and seniors $5. Omnimax ☎ 797-4640. Shows start on the hr. Su-Tu 11am-4pm, and W-Sa 11am-7pm. Th 2-for-1 tickets after 7pm. Planetarium ☎ 797-4646. Matinees daily $4; laser shows evenings W-Su $6.50. U.S.S. Blueback ☎ 797-4624. Open Tu-Su 10am-5pm. 40min. tour $4. OMSI offers a package, as well: admission to the museum, an Omnimax film and either the planetarium or the sub, $16, kids and seniors $12.)*

CRYSTAL SPRINGS RHODODENDRON GARDEN. Over 2500 rhododendrons of countless varieties surround a lake and border an 18-hole public golf course. Unwind among ducks, waterfalls, and 90-year-old rhodies. The flowers are in full bloom from March to May. *(SE 28th Ave., at Woodstock. Just west of Reed College. Bus #63. Open daily Mar. 1 to Labor Day dawn-dusk; Oct.-Feb. 8am-7pm. $3, under 12 free.)*

WASHINGTON PARK

Ever wonder where Nike's craze for trail running shoes came from? Once you visit Washington Park, with its miles of beautiful trails, serene gardens, and myriad versions of natural beauty, you won't ask again. Holding some of Portland's premier (and least expensive) attractions, the park is shaped in a large "V." Take the MAX to "Washington Park" and you will be rocketed via elevator to the bottom of this V, where the **Zoo** and **World Forestry Center** are found. The Washington Park Shuttle, free with valid MAX ticket, stops in the Zoo parking lot, at the **Rose Garden** and **Japanese Garden**, through a posh neighborhood, and then to the **Hoyt Arboretum's** visitors center. From there the bus completes its circuit with another 5min. ride back to the MAX and zoo.

INTERNATIONAL ROSE TEST GARDEN. An eminent source of Portland pride, during the summer the Rose Garden is a sea of blooms, arresting the eye and confirming Portland's title of the City of Roses. Blooms reach their peak in June. *(400 SW Kingston. ☎ 823-3636. Open daily 5am-10pm. Free, but donations appreciated.)*

JAPANESE GARDENS. Just across from the Rose Garden, these grounds complete the 1-2 punch of what is perhaps Portland's best destination. Planned and planted in the early 60s, the gardens shift gracefully between various styles of landscape design. The Dry Landscape Garden (*Karsansui*) is an amazing example of Zen simplicity and beauty. *(611 SW Kingston Ave. ☎ 223-1321. Open Apr.-Sept. Tu-Su 10am-7pm, M noon-7pm, last admission 6:30pm; Oct.-Mar. Tu-Su 10am-4pm, M noon-4pm. Tours daily at 10:45am and 2:30pm. $6, seniors $4, students $3.50, under 6 free.)*

OREGON ZOO. Apparently happy, captive animals live in scrupulous re-creations of natural habitats. The zoo has gained fame for its successful elephant breeding. Recent additions include a Cascade Mountains-like goat habitat, and a marine pool as part of the zoo's "Great Northwest: A Crest to Coast Adventure" exhibit. A steam engine pulls passengers on a mini railway out to Washington Park gardens and back, giving a better view of the flowers and animals. *(30min.; $2.75, seniors and ages 3-11 $2.)* The zoo features weekend educational talks and has a **children's petting zoo.** For over 22 years, from late June to August, nationally touring artists have performed at the **Rhythm and Zoo Concerts** at the sculpture garden. *(☎ 234-9694. W-Th 7pm; free with zoo admission.)* **Zoobeat Concerts** feature artists in blues, bluegrass, pop, and world beat on selected summer weekend evenings. *(4001 SW Canyon Rd. ☎ 226-1561. Open 9am-6pm. $6.50, seniors $5, ages 3-11 $4; 2nd Tu of each month free after 1pm.).*

HOYT ARBORETUM. Forming the wooded backdrop against which the rest of Washington Park's sights stand out, Hoyt features 180 acres of trees and 12 mi. of trails, including the charming, wheelchair-accessible **Overlook** and **Bristlecone Pine Trails.** The 26 mi. **Wildwood Trail** winds through Washington and Forest Parks, connecting the Arboretum to the Zoo and Japanese Garden. *Let's Go* recommends purchasing a map ($1) at the visitors center as trails are sometimes poorly marked, and have fooled at least one *Let's Go* researcher. *(4000 SW Fairview Blvd. ☎ 228-8733. visitors center open daily 9am-4pm.)*

FOREST PARK. Just north of Washington Park stretches a 5000-acre tract of wilderness. Washington Park provides access by car or foot to this sprawling sea of green, the largest park completely enclosed within a US city. A web of trails leads into lush forest, past scenic overviews, and through idyllic picnic areas. The **Pittock Mansion,** within Forest Park, was built by Henry L. Pittock, founder of the daily *Oregonian.* Enjoy a striking panorama of the city from the lawn of this 85-year-old, 16,000 sq. ft. monument to the French Renaissance.

🎵 ENTERTAINMENT

Prepare for culture. Upon request, the Visitors Association (see **Practical Information** p. 67) will fork over a thick packet outlining the month's events. Outdoor festivals are a way of life in Portland; the city's major daily newspaper, the **Oregonian,** lists upcoming events in its Friday edition. The city's favorite free cultural reader, the Wednesday **Willamette Week,** is a reliable guide to local music, plays, and art. Drop boxes are all over town, and their office is just across from the library. **The Rocket** (bimonthly, free) provides comprehensive coverage of alternative and punk music for the whole Northwest. Yuppies find their interests represented weekly in **Ourtown,** which lists downtown goings-on. Also call the *Oregonian's* Inside Line (☎ 225-5555) for up-to-date information on happenings in the area.

MUSIC

Although first-rate traveling shows never miss Portland, and many have bargain tickets available, some of the greatest shows are free and outdoors. Live music venues are listed under **Nightlife,** below.

ENTERTAINMENT ■ 77

Oregon Symphony Orchestra, 923 SW Washington St. (☎228-1353 or 800-228-7343). Box office open M-F 9am-5pm; during Symphony Season Sa 9am-5pm, as well. Classical and pop Sept.-June $15-60. Students and seniors can purchase tickets half-price 1hr. before showtime. "Symphony Sunday" afternoon concerts ($10-15). "Monday Madness" offers $5 student tickets one week before showtime. Call for park performance info. Wheelchair accessible. Infrared listening devices available.

High Noon Tunes (☎223-1613), at Pioneer Courthouse Sq. Jammed concerts early July-Aug. W noon-1pm. A potpourri of rock, jazz, folk, and world music.

Sack Lunch Concerts, 1422 SW 11th Ave. (☎222-2031; www.oldchurch.org), at Clay St. and the Old Church. Classical and jazz music W at noon (usually 1hr.).

Chamber Music Northwest, 522 SW 5th Ave. #725 (☎294-6400). Performs late June-July M, Th, and Sa at Reed College Kaul Auditorium; Tu and F at Catlin Gabel School. Call for directions. Shows at 8pm. Additional shows occur periodically throughout the year. $17-33, ages 7-14 and students with ID $5.

THEATER

Theater in Portland meets all tastes, ages, and budgets. The **Portland Center for the Performing Arts (PCPA)** is the fourth-largest arts center in the US. Free **backstage tours** begin in the lobby of the Newmark Theater, at SW Main and Broadway. (☎248-4335; www.pcpa.com. Tours every 30min. W and Sa 11am-1pm. Any bus to the Transit Mall; walk from there.) **Friends of the Performing Arts Center** (☎274-6555) stages the monthly **Brown Bag Lunch Series,** a glimpse of free professional productions on weekdays around noon. The *Oregonian* has details.

Portland Center Stage (☎274-6588), in Newmark Theater of PCPA at SW Broadway and SW Main. Classics, modern adaptations, and world premiers run late Sept. to Apr. Tu-Th and Su $21-38, F-Sa $21-44. $10 youth matinee seats sometimes available (25 and under). Half-price student rush tickets sometimes available 1hr. before curtain.

Oregon Ballet Theater, 1120 SW 10th Ave. (☎222-5538 or 888-922-5538). One of the best companies on the West Coast. Six productions Oct.-June. $5-80; half-price student rush often available 1hr. before curtain; check tourist office for discount tickets.

Artists' Repertory Theater, 1516 SW Alder St. (☎241-1278). Puts on top-notch, low-budget, and experimental productions that are loaded with fresh talent. W, Th, Su matinees $24, seniors $18; F-Sa $28. Students always $15.

CINEMA

Portland is a haven for cinema lovers. With the help of the *Oregonian*, a full-price ticket to just about any screen can be scrupulously avoided, and McMenamins' theater-pubs are one of a kind.

Mission Theater and Pub, 1624 NW Glisan (☎225-5555 ext. 8830), serves home-brewed ales and sandwiches ($6-7). Watch popular second-run flicks while lounging on couches or in the old-time balcony. Shows begin 5:30pm, 8pm, and 10pm. $2-3. 21+.

Bagdad Theater and Pub, 3702 SE Hawthorne Blvd. (☎225-5555 ext. 8831 or 236-9234). Bus #14. This cine-pub is housed in a former vaudeville theater, with a separate pub in front. First show s at 5:30pm, and two others follow at approximately 2hr. intervals. Pub open M-Sa 11am-1am, Su noon-midnight. $2-3. 21+.

Cinema 21, 616 NW 21st St. (☎223-4515), part of Nob Hill's bustling strip. Mean, clean, and pistachio green. Mostly documentary, independent, and foreign films. $6, students $5, under 12 and seniors $3; first matinee Sa-Su $3.

Northwest Film Center, 1219 SW Park Ave. (☎221-1156; www.NWfilm.org), screens documentary, foreign, classic, experimental, and independent films at the historic **Guild Theatre,** 829 SW 9th Ave., 2 blocks north of PAM, as well as in the museum's auditorium. Every Feb. the center also hosts the **Portland International Film Festival,** with 100 films from 30 nations. Screenings begin sometime between 7pm and 9pm. Box office opens 30min. before each show. $6.50, students and seniors $5.50.

Cinemagic, 202 SE Hawthorne (☎ 231-7919), at Hawthorne and 20th. Art-house and independent films. First show 5:30pm, two more follow. Two titles run every night. Some matinees Sa and Su. $6, students, seniors and children $4.

SPORTS

When Bill Walton led the **Trailblazers** (☎ 321-3211) to the 1979 NBA Championship, Portland went berserk—landing an NBA team in the first place had been a substantial accomplishment for a city of Portland's size. In 2000, the Blazers came close to a title repeat by losing to the Los Angeles Lakers in the Western Conference Championships. The Blazers play November to May in the sparkling new **Rose Garden Arena** by the Steel Bridge in Northeast Portland, with its own stop on MAX. Portland is also home to the Portland **Fire** of the WNBA professional women's basketball league. The **Winter Hawks** of the Western Hockey League play September to March in the Rose Garden Arena and at the **Coliseum.** Take bus #9 or MAX. (☎ 238-6366. Tickets $12-20.) The **Civic Stadium,** 1844 SW Morrison St., on the other side of town, is home to the **Portland Rockies,** the Colorado Rockies' baseball team, who played their inaugural season in 1995. (☎ 223-2837. June-Sept. $6-7.)

FESTIVALS

Cinco de Mayo Festival (☎ 222-9807; www.cincodemayo.org), on the weekend closest to May 5th spanning a total of four days. Portlanders celebrate Mexican Independence with sister city Guadalajara at Waterfront Park.

Rose Festival, 5603 SW Hood Ave. (☎ 227-2681), during the first 3 weeks of June (for 2002, May 31-June 24). Like Alpacas? Then check out the Alpaca show. Portland's premier summer event offers concerts, celebrities, auto racing, an air show, and the largest children's parade in the world. Larger events require tickets, but smaller stuff is free.

Waterfront Blues Festival (☎ 282-0555 or 973-3378), Early July. Outrageously good entertainment featuring blues, folk, and other artists on three stages with open air seats. Suggested donation is $3-5 and 2 cans of food to benefit the Oregon Food Bank.

Oregon Brewers Festival (☎ 778-5917; www.oregonbrewfest.com), on the last full weekend in July. The continent's largest gathering of independent brewers parties at Waterfront Park (72 breweries). $1 per taste, $3 per mug. Under 21 must be with parent.

Mt. Hood Festival of Jazz (☎ 219-9833, www.mthoodjazz.com), on the first weekend in Aug. at Mt. Hood Community College in Gresham. Take I-84 to Wood Village-Gresham exit and follow the signs, or ride MAX to the end of the line. The PNW's premier jazz festival. Wynton Marsalis and the late Stan Getz have been regulars. Tickets from $29 per night, more through Ticketmaster. Three-day passes $70-130. Reserve well in advance.

The Bite: A Taste of Portland (☎ 248-0600), Mid-Aug., in Waterfront Park. Samples of food, wine, and beer from over 20 Portland restaurants ($2-5), free music, and stand-up comics. Proceeds benefit Special Olympics Oregon. $3 suggested donation.

NIGHTLIFE

Once an uncouth and rowdy frontier town, always an uncouth and rowdy frontier town. Portland's nightclubs cater to everyone from the iron pumping college athlete to the nipple-pierced neo-goth aesthete. Bigger, flashier clubs rule **Old Town** and central **Downtown,** where mixed crowds dance shoulder-to-shoulder down the street from grooving reggae beatsters. In the **Pearl District** and **Nob Hill,** yuppies and college kids kick back together in spacious bars. In the **Southeast,** cramped quarters make for instant friends over great music and drinks. Hidden in the Northeastern suburb of **Laurelhurst,** locals gather in intimate clubs to listen to the best of the city's folk and rock. The plentiful neighborhood pubs often have the most character and the best music. Mischievous minors be warned: the drinking age is strictly enforced, but spectacular all-ages venues provide thrills without swills.

DOWNTOWN AND OLD TOWN

Ohm, 31 NW 1st Ave. (☎223-9919), at Couch under the Burnside Bridge. A venue dedicated to electronic music and unclassifiable beats. Tu brings Dhalia, W Breakbeat and Trance, Th Spoken word, and weekends often bring big-name live DJs. Cover $5-15. Open M-W 8pm-2:30am, Th-F 8pm-3:30am, Sa 8pm-4am, Su 8pm-3am. After-hours for some shows and special events stretch past 6am. Kitchen service until 2am.

Brig, The Nightclub Fez, Red Cap Garage and **Boxxes,** 341 SW 10th St. (☎221-7262; www.boxxes.com), form a network of clubs along Stark St. between 10th and 11th. On weekdays the clubs are connected, but on weekends they are often sealed off. Check at the door to see what is happening where. The 23-screen video and karaoke bar is where matchmaking magic happens. Cover $2-5. Open F-Sa 9pm-4am, Su-Th noon-2:30am.

Satyricon, 125 NW 6th Ave. (☎243-2380), on the bus mall. A venue perfectly suited for punk and alternative. They don't open unless a show's booked. This intimate space hosted the Northwest's bests acts long before grunge rock was even the new kid on the block. Nightly cover $4-10, bigger draws $10-15. 21+. Open daily 10pm-2:30am.

Kells Irish Pub, 112 SW 2nd Ave. (☎227-4057). With a cigar bar and wood and brass interior, Kells caters to a more upscale crowd, but a great space and live music every night of the week makes sure that crowd is always buzzing. 21+. Happy hour M-F 4-7pm and 11pm-1am. Open Su-W 11:30am-1am, Th-Sa 11:30am-2am.

Embers, 110 NW Broadway (☎222-3082), at Couch St. Follow rainbows to the dance floor, or watch fish swim in the bar counter. Retro and house music. A mixed gay, bisexual, and straight crowd enjoys the nightly drag show at 10pm. Happy hour until 7pm. Special events on Thurs. Open daily 11:30am-2:30am.

Crystal Ballroom, 1332 W Burnside Blvd. (☎225-0047), near I-405. Look past the grand ballroom's immense paintings, gaudy chandeliers, and arching balcony, and jump onto the newest in stage technology: the infamous "floating dance floor." Tina Turner and the Grateful Dead have jammed here. Open daily 11:30am-2:30am.

SOUTHEAST AND HAWTHORNE

Produce Row Cafe, 204 SE Oak St. (☎232-8355). Bus #6 to SE Oak and SE Grand; walk west along Oak toward the river. A huge deck, bleeding-edge staff and enough beers to give a German a headache. 30 beers on tap and over 150 in bottles. Rotating line-up of bands (jazz, rock, bluegrass) and open-mic. Domestic bottles $2, pints $3. Open M-Th 11am-midnight, F-Sa noon-1am, Su noon-11pm.

La Cruda, 2500 SE Clinton (☎233-0745), serves huge veggie burritos ($5). Their name means "hangover" in Spanish. After a night of downing their killer mango margaritas ($4.50), you'll understand why. Open daily 11am-2:30am; full kitchen until midnight.

Mulligan's, 3518 SE Hawthorne Blvd. (☎235-6390). An intimate local watering hole, with $2 pints on Th and Sa and a nice selection of local beers on tap. A small kitchen out back turns out the bar fare (fries $2.50). Open daily 2pm-3:30am.

LAURELHURST

The Laurel Thirst Public House, 2958 NE Glisan St. (☎232-1504), at 30th Ave. Bus #19. Local talent makes a name for itself in two intimate rooms of groovin', boozin', and schmoozin'. Burgers and sandwiches $5-8. Free pool Su-Th before 7pm. Cover $3-8 after 8pm. Open Su-Th 9am-1:30am, F-Sa 9am-2am. M mornings opens at noon.

Beulahland, 118 NE 28th Ave. (☎235-2794), at Couch opposite the Coca-Cola bottling plant. Bus #19. A small venue with local art on the walls, and huge inflatable toys hanging from the ceiling. DJs on F, often spinning Ska; live music Sa. No cover. Happy hour 4-7pm. Open Su-Th 7am-midnight, F-Sa 7am-2:30am.

PEARL AND NOB HILL DISTRICTS

Jimmy Mak's, 300 NW 10th Ave. (☎295-6542), 3 blocks from Powell's Books at Flanders. Jam to Portland's renowned jazz artists. Shows 9:30pm-1am. Cover $3-6. Vegetarian-friendly Greek and Middle Eastern dinners ($8-17). Open Tu-Sa 11am-2am.

Bridgeport Brewing Co., 1313 NW Marshall (☎241-3612), at 13th St. The zenith of beer and pizza joints in a wood-beamed rope factory. Tables cut from old bowling alleys. Sheltered outdoor eating. On-site microbrewery produces a range of British-style ales. Open M-Th 11:30am-11pm, F-Sa 11:30am-midnight, Su 1-9pm. Also at 3632 SE Hawthorne (☎233-6540).

DAYTRIP FROM PORTLAND: SAUVIE ISLAND

From I-405, Vaughn or Yeon Ave., take US 30 W (direction: "Mount St. Helens"). After about 20 min. watch for Sauvie Island signs to the right; or take bus #17 (St. Helens Rd.) from SW 6th and Salmon (40-50min.).

Peaceful Sauvie Island is part nature preserve, part farming community, found at the confluence of the Columbia and Willamette Rivers, just northwest of downtown Portland. A bridge connects Sauvie to the mainland at its southern tip, where produce-growing farms dominate, broken up only by pick-your-own berry stands and farmers markets. Most Portlanders head to Sauvie for its **beaches,** located on the northeast side of the island, which, along the rest of the northern half of the island, form the bird-laden **Sauvie Island State Wildlife Preserve.** Parking in the preserve requires a permit, and is efficiently enforced (daily permit $3.50, yearly $11). To get one stop at **Sam's Cracker Barrel Grocery,** and grab a 10¢ map of the island while you're there. Sam's is located just over the bridge, about 50 yd. north on Sauvie Island Rd. (☎621-3960. Open daily 7am-8pm.) Plan ahead; Sam's is several miles from the beaches and is the most convenient place on the island to buy a permit. To get to the beaches head east and north from Sam's along Gillihan Loop Rd., and after 5 mi. bear right onto Reeder Road. Go another 4 mi. on Reeder and the beaches will be to your right. The local park office should know if there are any current advisories against dipping. The **Fish and Wildlife Office** (☎621-3488) is on the western side of the island, just north of where Reeder Rd. and Sauvie Island Rd. meet; they'll also be able to recommend nice routes for a short hike around the preserve (the preserve is closed to hikers late Sept. to mid-April). Sauvie is short on roofed accommodations, but camping is available at **Sauvie Cove RV Park,** 31421 NW Reeder Rd., just south of the beaches. (☎621-9881. Sites with water and firepits $17. RV sites also available for short and long-term stays.)

NEAR PORTLAND

MOUNT HOOD ☎503/541

The snow-capped peak of Mt. Hood, at 11,235 ft., juts above its cohorts, Adams and Bachelor—evidence of its much more recent volcanic activity. This recent seismic activity doesn't seem to bother thousands of outdoor enthusiasts, though. From rabid downhill skiers and snowboarders to the trail-loving cross-country skiers in the winter, and the climbers, hikers, bikers, and fishers in the summer, Mt. Hood offers an unbeatable outdoor experience.

ORIENTATION AND PRACTICAL INFORMATION

Mt. Hood stands near the junction of US 26 and Hwy. 35, 1½hr. east of Portland via US 26. For a more scenic drive, take I-84 along Columbia River Gorge to Exit 64, and approach from Hood River (see p. 82) on Hwy. 35. The town **Government Camp,** 50 mi. east of Portland, has food, accommodations, and gear rental.

MOUNT HOOD ■ 81

Greyhound (☎800-231-2222) buses leave from the Huckleberry Inn (☎503-272-3325) in Government Camp to **Portland** (2hr., two per day, $9) and **Bend** (3hr., one per day, $19). **Emergency:** ☎911. **Hospital:** None in Government Camp, nearest is in either Portland or Hood River. **Post office:** 88331 E Govt. Camp Loop Rd., in Government Camp. (☎800-275-8777. Open M-F 8:30am-5pm.) **ZIP Code:** 97028. **Area code:** 503 to the west and south of Mt. Hood; 541 for Hood River and the northeast.

Hood River Ranger District Station, 6780 Hwy. 35 (☎541-352-6002), 11 mi. south of Hood River and 25 mi. north of the US 26 and Hwy. 35 junction, has more specialized info on the three ranger districts in the vicinity, as well as a variety of trail maps ranging from free to $5. (Open Memorial Day to Labor Day daily 8am-4:30pm; closed Sa-Su in winter.) **The Mt. Hood Info Center,** 65000 E US 26, 16 mi. west of the junction of US 26 and Hwy. 35 and 30 mi. east of Gresham, at the entrance to the Mt. Hood village, has topo maps and info on ranger districts. The friendly staff will also direct you to the best trails. (☎503-622-7674 or 888-622-4822; www.mthood.org. Open June-Oct. daily 8am-6pm; daily Nov.-May 8am-4:30pm.)

ACCOMMODATIONS AND CAMPING

Most campgrounds in Mt. Hood National Forest cluster near the junction of US 26 and Hwy. 35, although they can be found along the length of both highways as well, on the way to Portland or Hood River. For a much more expensive, less outdoorsy, and probably more relaxing experience, stay in a hotel in Government Camp or on the mountain itself. For **reservations** for the campgrounds below, except Alpine and Lost Lake, call 877-444-6777.

Lost Lake Resort (☎541-386-6366). From Hwy. 35, turn east onto Woodworth Dr., right onto Dee Hwy., then left on Lost Lake Rd. (Forest Service Rd. 13). Offers sites with water, showers, and toilets. A 3 mi. hike around the lake provides stunning views of Mt. Hood. Rent a canoe ($8), boat ($10-20), or fish in the trout-stocked lake for free. 121 sites; $15, on lake $20. RV sites without electricity $18; cabins $45-100.

Trillium Lake, 2 mi. east of the Timberline turn-off on US 26, has trails around the crystal-clear lake, paved sites, water, and toilets. Paved areas and large sites mean more RVs. Sites $12, lakeside $14.

Still Creek, just 1 mi. west of Trillium Lake down a dirt road off US 26, offers sites that are unpaved and have a quieter, woodsy feel ($13). Potable water, toilets, few RVs.

Sherwood, 14 mi. north of US 26 and just off Hwy. 35, beside a rambling creek. Potable water, pit toilets, no showers. Sites are $10.

SIGHTS

Six miles up the road, just east of Government Camp, stands the historic **Timberline Lodge** (☎622-7979), built by hand in 1937 by unemployed craftspeople under the New Deal's Works Progress Administration. On the Timberline grounds is the **Wy'East Day Lodge,** offering complimentary ski storage in the wintertime, so skiers can trek into the **Wy'East Kitchen,** a cafeteria alternative to Timberline's expensive main dining. (Entrees $4-7. Open in summer M-F 6:30am-2pm, Sa-Su 6:30am-3pm; in winter M-F 7:30am-4pm, Sa-Su 8am-4pm. Open 7:30am-9pm.) At the **Ram's Head,** on the third floor of the lodge, you can pay a pretty penny to eat with a view (lunch $10-15; dinner $16-36). For a view that beats them all, Timberline's **Magic Mile express lift** carries passengers above the clouds for spectacular views of the Cascades ($6, ages 7-12 $4, under 7 free).

In summer, Mount Hood Ski Bowl opens its **Action Park,** with fun for the entire family, featuring Indy Kart racing ($5 per 5min.), horseback riding ($25 per hr.), mini-golf ($3), batting cages ($1 for 10 pitches), helicopter rides ($20), bungee jumping ($25), and an alpine slide for $5. (☎222-2695. Open M-F 11am-6pm, Sa-Su 10am-6pm.) The Ski Bowl maintains 40 mi. of bike trails ($4 trail permit), and **Hurricane Racing** rents mountain bikes mid-June to October ($10 per hr.; half-day $25, full-day $35; trail permit included). The Mt. Hood Visitors Center also lists **free** hiking trails on which mountain biking is allowed.

HIKING

Hiking trails circle Mt. Hood; simple maps are posted around **Government Camp.** The free *Day Hikes* booklet describes 34 trails in the area and is available from the Mt. Hood Information Center (see **Orientation and Practical Information,** p. 80). A Northwest Forest parking pass is required at several trailheads. ($5 per day or $30 per year; available at the Mt. Hood Info Center). **Mountain Tracks Nordic Ski Shop** in the Huckleberry Inn, Government Camp, and visitors information have details on more ski trails. (☎503-272-3380. Closed summers.)

Mirror Lake Trail (6 mi. loop, several hours). Trailhead at a parking lot off US 26, 1 mi. west of Government Camp. A very popular dayhike, this trail winds its way to the beautiful Mirror Lake through the forest. Easy to moderate hiking.

Timberline Trail (41 mi., overnight). Trailhead at **Timberline Lodge** (see **Downhill Skiing,** below) was constructed by the New Deal Civilian Conservation Corp in the 1930s and circles the mountain, offering incomparable views of the Cascades. Strenuous.

Old Salmon River Trail (5 mi. round-trip, 2-3hr.). Take Hwy. 26 to Welches, OR. 1 mi. east of the signal, turn onto Salmon River Rd. (2618) and go for 2½ mi. Winds up gentle grades through the forests and meadows, and creek-crossings in spring. Moderate.

Trillium Lake Loop (4½ mi. loop, 1-2hr.). Trailhead in the day-use area of the Trillium Lake campground. A lakeside trail offering wildlife viewing and alpine wetlands that becomes a challenging cross-country ski course in winter. Easy to moderate.

SKIING

Three respectable Mt. Hood area resorts are more convenient to Portland. All offer **night skiing** and **snowboard parks.**

Timberline (☎622-0717; snow report ☎503-222-2211). Off US 26 at Government Camp. A largely beginner and intermediate area with a 2600 ft. vertical drop and the longest season in North America, Timberline features a high-speed lift on the Palmer Snowfield that is open year-round. Lift tickets $34. Ski rental package $21, ages 7-12 $13; snowboard package $33, ages 7-12 $23. Open winter daily 9am-4pm; spring and fall 8:30am-2:30pm; summer 7am-1:30pm. Night skiing Jan.-Feb. W-F 4-9pm, Sa-Su 4-10pm.

Mount Hood Ski Bowl, 87000 E US 26 (☎503-222-2695 or 800-754-2695). In Government Camp 2 mi. west of Hwy. 35. Just a little guy, with a vertical drop of 1500 ft. The season is shorter (mid-Nov. to May) because of its lower elevation. However, with 34 lit trails they offer the most night skiing in America and have a badass terrain park. Lift tickets $16, under 12 $11; $16 per night. Ski rental package $18, ages 7-12 $13; snowboard package $26, $20 per night. Open M-Tu 3:30-10pm, W-Th 9am-10pm, F 9am-11pm, Sa 8:30am-11pm, Su 8:30am-10pm.

Mount Hood Meadows (☎337-2222; snow report 503-227-7669 or 541-386-7547). 9 mi. east of Government Camp on Hwy. 35. This is the largest and nicest resort in the area, offering a wide range of terrain, and the most high-speed lifts. At a medium elevation, it often stays open through May. Mt. Hood Meadows offers $20 lift tickets through participating hotels, including the Bingen School Hostel (see p. 83). Lift tickets $41, ages 7-12 $21. Night skiing Dec.-Mar. W-Su 4-10pm, $17. Ski rental package $20, ages 7-12 $15; snowboard package $28, ages 7-12 $21. Beginner package with lift ticket, lesson, and rental $45. Open mid-Nov. to May daily 9am-4pm.

COLUMBIA RIVER GORGE ☎541/509

Stretching 75 stunning miles east from Portland, the Columbia River Gorge carries the river to the Pacific Ocean through woodlands, waterfalls, and canyons. Heading inland along the gorge, heavily forested peaks give way to broad, bronze cliffs and golden hills covered with tall pines. Mt. Hood and Mt. Adams loom nearby, and breathtaking waterfalls plunge over steep cliffs into the river. The river wid-

COLUMBIA RIVER GORGE ■ 83

ens out and the wind picks up at the town of Hood River, providing some of the world's best windsurfing. Once fast and full of rapids, the Columbia is more placid now, as the upstream dams have taken the rough side out to preserve the salmon.

TRANSPORTATION

To follow the gorge, which divides Oregon and Washington, take **I-84** east from Portland to Exit 22. Continue east uphill on the **Historic Columbia River Hwy. (US 30)**, which follows the crest of the Gorge and affords unforgettable views. Or stay on I-84, which follows the Columbia River; **Hwy. 14** runs the length of the Washington side of the river. **Hood River, OR**, at the junction of I-84 and **Hwy. 35**, is the hub of activity in the Gorge. It gives access to the larger city of **Dalles, OR**, to the east and **Mt. Hood** (see p. 80) to the south. **Bingen, WA** (BIN-jin), across the Hood River Bridge (75¢ toll), gives access to the forests of **Mt. Adams** (see p. 212). **Maryhill, WA**, is 33 mi. west of Bingen on Hwy. 14.

- **Trains: Amtrak** (☎800-872-7245) disgorges passengers at foot of Walnut St. in **Bingen, WA**, across from Monterey Bay Fiberglass in the Burlington-Northern Santa Fe terminal. One train leaves per day for **Portland** (2hr., $10-18) and **Spokane** (6hr., $30-63).
- **Buses: Greyhound,** 600 E Marina Way (☎386-1212 or 800-231-2222), in the Hood River DMV building. Off I-84 at Exit 64, take a left at the intersection before the toll bridge and follow the signs to the DMV, the second building on the right. Open M-F 8:30-11:30am and 1:30-4:30pm. To **Portland** (1¼hr., 4 per day, $12).
- **Public Transportation: Columbia Area Transit (CAT;** ☎386-4202) provides door-to-door service within the Hood River area for $1.25; call for pickup. Also provides weekend shuttle to Meadows during ski season ($3). Open daily 8am-4:30pm.

PRACTICAL INFORMATION

- **Visitors Information: Hood River County Chamber of Commerce,** 405 Portway Ave. (☎541-386-2000 or 800-366-3530; www.hoodriver.org), in the Expo Center north off Exit 63. Helpful information on events in the region complements a plentiful collection of maps. Open Apr.-Oct. M-F 9am-5pm, Sa-Su 10am-5pm; Nov.-Mar. M-F 9am-5pm. Many other visitors centers also line the gorge.
- **Outdoor Information: Columbia Gorge National Scenic Area Headquarters,** 902 Wasco St. #200 (☎541-386-2333; www.fs.fed.us/r6/columbia), in Sprint's Waucoma Center Building, Hood River. Forest Service camping map ($4). Open M-F 7:30am-5pm.
- **Internet Access: Hood River Library,** 502 State St. (☎541-386-2535), Hood River, up the hill near Wy'East Whole Foods. 2 computers with 30min. Internet access for free, but sign up well in advance. Open M-Th 8:30am-8:30pm, F-Sa 8:30am-5pm. **Hood River Wine and Internet Bar,** 106 3rd St., Hood River (☎541-386-3239) has 2 computers with Internet access; $5 per hr. Wine bar features a variety of local and regional wines by the glass ($3-8). Open M-Th 4-11:30pm, F-Sa noon-11:30pm, Su noon-8pm.
- **Weather:** ☎541-386-3300.
- **Emergency:** ☎911.
- **Hood River Police:** 211 2nd St. (non-emergency ☎541-386-3942).
- **Hospital: Hood River Memorial,** 13th and May St. (☎541-386-3911). 24hr. emergency.
- **Post Office:** 408 Cascade Ave. (☎800-275-8777), Hood River. Open M-F 8:30am-5pm. **ZIP Code:** 97031.

ACCOMMODATIONS

Hotel rooms in Hood River typically start around $50 and spiral upward from there. Cheaper motels line the west end of Westcliffe Dr., north off I-84 Exit 62, although they're usually full on the weekends. As for camping, the state parks along the river offer an affordable experience. **Ainsworth State Park** is also readily accessible (see **Portland: Accommodations and Campgrounds,** p. 69). For a full list of camping facilities, contact the visitors center.

84 ■ NEAR PORTLAND

Bingen School Inn Hostel/Columbia Gorge Outdoor Center (☎509-493-3363; www.bsi-cgoc.com). Take the third left after the yellow blinking light onto Cedar St.; from there it's 1 block up the hill on Humbolt St. An outdoorsy converted schoolhouse, with airy rooms, 2 dorm style and 7 private. In the summer, **windsurfing lessons** ($65 per 3hr., beginner to advanced) and **rentals** ($30 per day, $185 per week) are available. Kitchen, laundry, climbing wall, volleyball net, outdoor grill, TV/VCR, school lockers, and linen are available. Winter guests score $20 Hood Meadows lift tickets. Beds $15; 5 large private rooms $35 for 2 people, $10 per additional person.

Beacon Rock State Park (☎503-427-8265). 7 mi. west of the Bridge of the Gods on Washington's Hwy. 14, has 28 secluded, woodsy sites and easy access to hiking, mountain biking, fishing, and rock climbing. Primitive sites $8; sites with water, flush toilets, and showers $14.

Viento State Park (☎541-374-8811 or 800-452-5678). 8 mi. west of Hood River off I-84. Sandwiched between I-84 and the river, with a railroad alongside, this campsite offers a noisy but pleasant experience, as well as easy access to hiking and the river. Showers and toilets. 13 tent sites $14, 61 hookups $16. Handicap facilities available.

Lone Pine Motel 2429 Cascade St., Hood River (☎541-387-8882 or 541-490-9000), just west of Safeway, rents comfortable hostel-style rooms with fridges, microwaves, and TV for almost nothing, but rarely has openings. Rooms $25-35, or $125 for week.

🍴 FOOD AND NIGHTLIFE

For groceries, find **Safeway,** 2249 W Cascade St., on the west side of Hood River. (☎541-386-1841. Open daily 24hr.) For the organically inclined, **Wy'East Whole Food Market,** 110 5th St., off Oak St. in Hood River, complements its natural food selection with handmade sandwiches ($4-5) and a java, smoothie, and juice bars. (☎541-386-6181. Open M-F 7:30am-6:30pm, Sa 9am-6pm, Su 10am-5pm.)

River City Saloon, 207 Cascade Ave. (☎541-0387-2583) sports a remodeled shine in its long wood bar and spacious stage, which it fills with bluegrass, rock, and everything in between. Parmesan chicken sandwich is $9. Happy Hour 4:30-6:30pm, with $2.50 microbrews. Also offers **Internet access,** at $1 per 15min. Open daily 4:30pm-2am.

Full Sail Brewing Company and Pub, 506 Columbia Ave. (☎541-386-2247, www.fullsailbrewing.com). Take 5th St. 2 blocks toward the river from Oak St. Relax on the deck with a view of the river. Grill food ($6-12). Open daily noon-9pm.

Sage's Cafe, 202 Cascade Ave. (☎541-386-9404). Cheap, hearty breakfasts ($3-6) and lunchtime options including quiche or a sandwich ($2.50 and $4.50). Open M-F 7am-6pm, Sa 8am-6pm, Su 8am-5pm.

👁 SIGHTS

VISTA HOUSE. Completed in 1918 as a memorial to Oregon's pioneers, the House is now a visitors center in **Crown Point State Park**. Located at the edge of the canyon, it has exhibits about the Gorge's history and terrain. For a lofty view, drive up the **Larch Mountain Rd.,** which splits from US 30 just above the Vista House and winds up 4000 ft. over 14 mi. From the Larch Mountain Lookout, a steep 20min. hike through woods leads to a picnic area with views of Mount St. Helens, Mt. Rainier, Mt. Adams, Mt. Hood, and Mt. Jefferson. *(From I-84 Exit 22 take Corbett Hill Rd. to top of hill, turn left for 3 mi. ☎503-695-2230. Open daily mid-Apr. to mid-Oct. 8:30am-6pm.)*

MARYHILL MUSEUM OF ART. This elegant museum sits high above the river on the Washington side. Built in the 1920s by Sam Hill, a great benefactor of the area and instigator of the historic preservation of the Columbia Gorge, was a friend of Queen Marie of Romania, whose coronation garb is displayed along with Rodin plasters. Two more floors contain watercolors, chess sets, and native artifacts, as well as a collection of 27 in. tall mannequins dressed in haute couture from Parisian fashion houses, who pose on sets built to scale. *(35 Maryhill Museum Dr. Hwy. 14 from Bingen or I-84 to Biggs, Exit 104, cross Sam Hill Bridge, then turn left onto Hwy. 14 for 3 mi. ☎509-773-3733. Open daily mid-Mar. to mid-Nov. 9am-5pm. $7, seniors $6, ages 6-12 $2.)*

COLUMBIA RIVER GORGE ■ 85

STONEHENGE. Sam Hill built this full-scale replica of the English monument out of reinforced concrete as a memorial to the men of Klickitat County killed in WWI. Hill, a Quaker, thinking that the original monument was used in sacrificial rituals before its astronomical properties became known, designed this pagan symbol to express that "humanity still is being sacrificed to the god of war on fields of battle." People gather here on patriotic holidays, as well as for pagan celebrations. Hill's crypt is just south of the bluff. (*3 mi. farther east along Hwy. 14.*)

OUTDOOR ACTIVITIES

OUTDOOR GAMES

Hood River hosts the **Subaru Gorge Games** (☎866-467-4301; www.gorge-games.com) on the third weekend of July in 2002. World class athletes gather to compete in one of the most highly regarded outdoor adventure competitions, with events including kayaking, windsurfing, kiteboarding, climbing, paragliding, and a 24hr. mountain bike race to rival Le Mans waterfalls.

A string of waterfalls adorns the Historic Columbia River Hwy. (US 30) east of Crown Point; pick up a waterfall map at the Vista House (see **Sights**, p. 84), or at the visitors center in Hood River. A short paved path leads to the base **Latourell Falls**, 2½ mi. east of Crown Point. East another 5½ mi., **Wahkeena Falls**, beautiful and visible from the road, splashes 242 ft. down a narrow gorge. The base of the falls, is less than ½ mi. farther east on Historic Columbia River Hwy. From I-84 Exit 31, take the underpass to the lodge. On a platform, you can watch the falls crash into a tiny pool, and then drain under the gracefully arching Benson Bridge. For a more strenuous hike, follow the **Larch Mountain Trail** to the top of the falls. Multnomah Falls visitors center in the lodge has free trail maps. (☎504-695-2372. Open daily July-Aug. 9am-8pm; June and Sept. 9am-7pm; Oct.-May 9am-5pm.)

> **A SAIL...A KITE???** Yes, ladies and gentlemen, there is a new player in the aquatic playground of the Columbia River. While the section of the Columbia known as Hood River has always been justly famous for its fabulous windsurfing and sailboarding, it is also gaining ground as a perfect place to practice your kiteboarding techniques. Kiteboarding, or standing on a piece of fiberglass the size of a snowboard while harnessed to a rather large kite as you whip across the river at nearly 30 m.p.h., is the new rage for the younger crowd of windsurfers. Offering opportunities to jump 10 ft. in the air, propelled by the kite 100 ft. above, kiteboarding provides an often irresistible allure. If you care to try, be sure to take a few lessons so you spend your time over the water rather than in it.

WINDSURFING

Frequent 30mph winds make Hood River a windsurfing paradise. Considered one of the best sites in the world for freestyle sailboarding (the professional term for windsurfing), Hood River attracts some of the best windsurfers around, making watching as interesting as participating. The venerated **Rhonda Smith Windsurfing Center**, in the Port Marina Sailpark, Exit 64 off I-84, under the bridge and left after the blinking red light, offers classes. (☎541-386-9463. $125 for two 3hr. classes. Includes free evening practice.) Lessons are also available from the **Bingen School Inn** (see **Accommodations**). **Big Winds**, 207 Front St., at the east end of Oak St., has cheap beginner rentals, as well as plenty of helpful advice and a wealth of equipment. (☎541-386-6086. $8 per hr.; $15 per half-day; $25 per day.) There are a variety of other shops in town offering 0rentals, repairs, and lessons.

- **The Hook,** a shallow, sandy cove, off I-84 Exit 63, where beginners learn the basic techniques of starting, handling, and jibing before moving out to the deep water of the river.
- **Spring Creek Fish Hatchery, a.k.a. "The Hatch,"** Hwy. 14 west from Bingen at the fish hatchery sign. The place to watch the best in the business. There is plenty of parking, and the shore offers a view of the most popular stretch of water.

Event Site, off Exit 63 behind the visitors center, is another excellent spot to watch the action. All-day parking costs $3, but free to sit and watch.

MOUNTAIN BIKING

The Gorge also has excellent mountain biking, with a wide variety of trails for bikers of all skill levels. **Discover Bicycles,** 205 Oak St. (☎541-386-4820; www.discover-bicycles.com) rents mountain bikes ($5 per hr., $25 per day), suggests routes, and sells maps ($2-5). Open M-Sa 9am-7pm, Su 9am-5pm.

Seven Streams Canyon Loop (8 mi. loop, 1-2hr.). To get to the trailhead, take Oak St. from Hood River past where it merges with W Cascade, and then turn left on Country Club Rd. After 1½ mi., take a right on Post Canyon Rd. and park on the right where the road becomes gravel. The trail offers great views as it winds through canyons. Moderate.

Mosier Twin Tunnels (4½ mi., 1hr.). A segment of the Historic Columbia River Hwy. that is too narrow for cars, located between Hood River and Mosier. Parking is available at both the east and west end of the tunnels for $3. Offers mainly an on-road ride, with views of the river and the tunnels. Easy to moderate.

Surveyor's Ridge Trail (22 mi. round-trip, several hours). To get to the trailhead, take Rte. 35 south from Hood River for 11 mi. to Pinemont Dr. (Rd. 17), and go east for 6 mi. Turn right onto the dirt road at the "Surveyors Ridge" sign and park in the area by the power lines. Trail mainly follows the ridgeline and offers spectacular views of the Hood River Valley, Mt. Hood, and Mt. Adams. Open June-Oct. Moderate to strenuous.

HIKING

Mazama Trail (7½ mi., several hours). Take Hwy. 35 for 13 mi. to Woodworth Rd., then Woodworth 3 mi. to Dee Hwy. (281). Turn right and go 5 mi. before turning and following the signs to Lost Lake for 7 mi. on Rd. 18, then turn left onto rd. 1810. Take 1810 to 1811, and drive 3 mi. to trailhead. This trail begins in the forest with Mt. Hood acting as a magnificent backdrop, then climbs up a steep ridge and through a dense forest to flowered glades and amazing vistas. Open June-Oct. $3 permit required. Strenuous.

Catherine Creek Trail (1¼ mi. round-trip, less than 1hr.). From Bingen, go east on Hwy. 14 and turn left on County Rd. 1230 at Rowland Lake. After about 1½ mi., park at the Catherine Creek lot. An easy walk along a paved path on the Washington side through wildflowers with dramatic views of the Columbia River and Mt. Hood.

Mt. Hamilton Trail (4½ mi. round-trip, several hours). Follow the directions in **Accommodations,** above, to **Beacon Rock State Park,** and park in the lot east of Beacon Rock, 848 ft. neck of an old volcano. Climbing 2250 ft. up Mt. Hamilton on the Washington side of the river, the trail leads hikers up switchbacks to find the summit bursting with wildflowers in June and July. Moderate to difficult.

THE COAST: US 101 ☎503

If not for the renowned US 101, Oregon's sandy beaches and dramatic seaside vistas might be only a beautiful rumor to those on the interior. From the Long Beach peninsula and Astoria in the north to Brookings in the south, the highway hugs the shoreline along the Oregon Coast, linking a string of touristy resorts and small, unspoiled fishing villages. Wherever the windy, bustling two lanes of US 101 part from the coast, a narrower road sticks to the stretches of unspoiled coast. Oregon's beaches are some of the largest and most beautiful you will ever see. Miles of untouched sand will keep the most picky beach comber content, and those brave enough to face the cold will enjoy the ocean waves. Touristy but gorgeous resort towns like Canon Beach and small communities like Bandon that line the Pacific Ocean make the Oregon Coast a worthy destination.

ASTORIA ■ 87

> **PORTRAIT OF A MONSTER** A standard primate chest-expansion program may have created the Bigfoot (English) or Sasquatch (Chinook Indian tribe) which grow to approximately 2000 lb. and 7 ft. 3½ in. Sasquatch lurk in the Cascades and cross up into BC. While every culture has its own big scary monster, from the Scots' Nessie to the Tibetan's Yeti, there is evidence of a Sasquatch. Plaster-cast footprints and a video of a man in a hairy suit are enough to convince many, not only that there is a Sasquatch, but also that the government is involved in an elaborate cover-up. While this may be stretching it, *Let's Go* still recommends caution around giant hairy mythical beasts.

INTERCITY TRANSPORTATION

Gasoline and grocery **prices** on the coast are about 20% higher than in inland cities; the smaller coastal villages tend to be cheapest and most interesting. There are 17 major state parks along the coast, many of which offer **campgrounds** with electricity and showers. While most of the traffic seems to be tourists in RVs, some savvy travelers choose to experience the coast by **bicycle**, a rewarding yet exhausting ride. Cyclists can contact virtually any visitors center or chamber of commerce on the coast for a free copy of the Oregon Coast Bike Route Map, which provides invaluable info on campsites, hostels, bike repair facilities, temperatures, and wind conditions. In summer, prevailing winds also blow southward, keeping at the backs of cyclists and easing their journey. As the shoulders of US 101 and other coastal highways often narrow to nonexistent, and enormous log trucks lumber around tight turns, cyclists must be very vigilant about safety concerns as well. **Buses** run up and down the coast, stopping in most sizeable towns. Many local lines are affiliates of Greyhound and make connections to major urban centers like Seattle, Portland, and Eugene. The fastest way to experience the coast, however, is by car.

ASTORIA ☎ 503

Established in 1811 by John Jacob Astor's trading party, Astoria is the oldest US city west of the Rocky Mountains. Originally built as a fort to guard the mouth of the Columbia, it quickly became a port city for ships heading to Portland and Longview, WA. A much more pleasant and less expensive destination than the overrun resort cities to the south, Astoria offers the same beautiful views of the Pacific Ocean from nearby Fort Stevens State Park. Its Victorian homes, bustling waterfront, rolling hills, and persistent fog suggest San Francisco on a smaller scale.

ORIENTATION AND PRACTICAL INFORMATION

Astoria is a peninsula extending into the Columbia River and is located approximately 7 mi. from the ocean beaches in both Ft. Stevens and nearby Washington. From Astoria, **US 30** runs 96 mi. to Portland. Astoria can also be reached from Portland on **US 26** and **US 101** via Seaside (see p. 90). Astoria is a convenient link between Washington and the Oregon coast. Two bridges run from the city: the **Youngs Bay Bridge** leading southwest where **Marine Dr.** becomes US 101, and the **Astoria Bridge,** which spans the **Columbia River** into Washington. All streets parallel to the water are named in alphabetical order except for the first one.

Buses: Pierce Pacific Stages (☎ 692-4437). A Greyhound affiliate. Pickup at Video City, 95 W Marine Dr., opposite the chamber of commerce. To **Portland** (3hr., $22). **Sunset Empire Transit,** 465 NE Skipanon Dr., Warrenton (☎ 861-7433 or 800-766-6406). Pickup at Duane and 9th St. To **Seaside** (7 per day; $2.25; seniors, students, and disabled $1.75). **Astoria Transit System** (contact **Sunset Empire** for info, above). Local bus service M-Sa 7am-7pm. 75¢; students, seniors, disabled 50¢.

88 ■ THE COAST: US 101

Taxis: Yellow Cab (☎ 325-3131 or 861-2626). Base $2, $1.80 per mi. Runs 6am-10pm.

Visitor Information: 111 W Marine Dr. (☎ 325-6311), just east of Astoria Bridge. Loads of info on Astoria and the surrounding attractions. Open June-Sept. M-F 8am-6pm, Sa 9am-6pm, Su 9am-5pm; Oct.-May M-F 8am-5pm, Sa-Su 11am-4pm.

Internet Access: Astoria Library, 450 10th St. (☎ 325-7323). Free 1hr. of Internet access, sign up a day in advance, or 15min. walk-up (ID required). Open Tu-Th 10am-7pm, F-Sa 10am-5pm, Closed Su-M. **Community Information Center,** 1335 Marine Dr. (☎ 325-8502; www.ctrf.net). 5¢ per min. or $3 per hour on broadband connections. Open M-F 9am-8pm, Sa 9am-5pm, Su 1-5pm.

Laundromat: Maytag Self-Service Laundry, 127 W Bond St. (☎ 325-7815), one block away from Marine Dr. Wash $1, dry 25¢ per 10min., or 50¢ per 40 min., detergent 75¢. Open daily 8am-9pm, last wash load at 7:45pm.

Emergency: ☎ 911. **Crisis line:** ☎ 800-562-6025

Police: 555 30th St. (☎ 325-4411).

Hospital: Columbia Memorial, 2111 Exchange St. (☎ 325-4321) 24hr.

Post Office: 748 Commercial St. (☎ 800-275-8777). Open M-F 8:30am-5pm. **ZIP Code:** 97103.

ACCOMMODATIONS AND CAMPING

Motel rooms can be expensive and elusive during summer. US 101 both north and south of Astoria is littered with clean, scenic campgrounds.

Fort Stevens State Park (☎ 861-1671; reservations 800-452-5687), over Youngs Bay Bridge on US 101 S, 10 mi. west of Astoria. Rugged, empty beaches and hiking and bike trails surround the campground. Toilets, showers, and water. Reservations ($6) recommended. Wheelchair accessible. 600 sites, $18; full hookups $21; hiker/biker sites $4.25 per person; yurts $29.

Grandview B&B, 1574 Grand Ave. (☎ 325-0000 or 325-5555; www.pacifier.com/~grndview). Intimate, cheery, luxurious rooms. Includes delicious breakfast. Rooms with shared bath from $45, with private bath from $71. Off-season, 2nd night is $36.

Lamplighter Motel, 131 W Marine Dr. (☎ 325-4051 or 800-845-8847), between the Pig'n'Pancake diner and visitors center. Spotlessly clean, well lit rooms with cable TV and phones. Large bathrooms, refrigerators. Coffee is available in the lobby all day. Rooms $49-55, less in winter. Senior discount in winter.

Hideaway Hotel and Hostel, 443 14th St. (☎ 325-6989), in a converted apartment building in the heart of town. Separate dorms with shared bath. $15.

FOOD

Safeway, 1153 Duane St., provides groceries (☎ 325-4662). Open daily 6am-midnight.) A small but growing **farmer's market** is in the parking lot behind the Maritime Museum (see **Sights,** below) each summer Saturday.

Columbian Cafe, 1114 Marine Dr. (☎ 325-2233). Local banter, wines by the glass, and fantastic pasta and seafood dishes ($10-15, lunches $5-8) make it worthwhile. Try "Chef's Mercy"—name the heat your mouth can stand and the chef will create you a meal ($7-8). Open Tu-F 8am-2pm, Sa-Su 9am-2pm; dinner W-Th 5-9pm, F-Sa 5-10pm.

Home Spirit Bakery and Cafe, 1585 Exchange St. (☎ 325-6846; www.home-spirit.com). Eat a fabulous meal in a restored Victorian Home just a block away from the Shallon Winery. Open M-Sa 11am-2pm for lunch, W-Sa 5:30-8pm for dinner. Call ahead.

Someplace Else, 965 Commercial St. (☎ 325-3500). Complementing the delicious Italian fare is the nightly special ($5-14), a popular dish from a different country every night. Open W-Su 11:30am-2pm and 4-9pm.

WINE AND CHEESE, TOGETHER AT LAST

One block up from the Maritime Museum is the **Shallon Winery**, 1598 Duane St., where owner Paul van der Velt presides over a kingdom of fantastic wines. A self-proclaimed connoisseur of fine food, he insists that visitors call him at any time of day or night before considering a meal at any restaurant within 50 mi. Samplers taste wines made from local berries and the world's only commercially produced whey wines (from the cheese factories in Tillamook). Approach the cranberry-and-whey wine with caution; the fruity taste belies its high alcohol content. Sampling lemon meringue pie wine is likely to be the highlight, and Paul's chocolate orange wine is more candy than beverage. Others have spent millions trying to reproduce this chocolate delicacy to no avail. (☎ 325-5978; www.shallon.com. Must be 21 to drink. Open almost every afternoon. Gratuities and purchases appreciated.)

Wet Dog Cafe and Pacific Rim Brewing Co., 144 11th St. (☎ 325-6975). Astoria's only venue for live music. Crowds pack in every weekend for burgers ($5.50-8) and anything from alternative to blues ($3-6), nursing their pints of Peacock Spit Golden Ale ($3.25) from the brewery out front. Game room. DJ Th-F. Live music Sa. Opens daily at 11am, closes Su-T 10pm, W 11pm, Th 1am, and F-Sa 2am. Dinner until 9pm.

SIGHTS

The clouds around **Astoria Column** lift every so often to reveal a stupendous view of Astoria cradled between Saddle Mountain to the south and the Columbia River estuary to the north. Completed in 1926, the column on Coxcomb Hill Rd. encloses 164 steps past newly repainted friezes depicting local history. (Open dawn-10pm. Free.) The cavernous, wave-shaped **Columbia River Maritime Museum,** 1792 Marine Dr., on the waterfront, is packed with marine lore, including displays on the salmon fisheries that once dominated Astoria. Among the model boats is the 1792 vessel that Robert Grey first steered into the mouth of the Columbia River. (☎ 325-2323. Open daily 9:30am-5pm. $5, seniors $4, ages 6-17 $2, under 6 free.) The **Scandinavian Festival,** on the third weekend in June, attracts throngs of celebrants. ($6, children $3, under 6 free.) The **Astoria Regatta** (☎ 861-2288), held the second week of August, dates to 1894 and is still going strong. It features food and craft booths, a watershow, boat rides, fireworks, dances, and sailboat races.

DAYTRIPS FROM ASTORIA

FORT CLATSOP NATIONAL MEMORIAL. 5 mi. SW of town on US 101 south from Astoria to Alt. Rte. US 101; follow signs 3 mi. to park. (☎ 861-2471.) This National Memorial reconstructs Lewis and Clark's winter headquarters from journal descriptions. The fort has been completely restored and contains exhibits about their quest for the Pacific Ocean. In summer, rangers robed in feathers and buckskin demonstrate quill writing, moccasin sewing, and musket firing. *(Open mid-June to Labor Day daily 8am-6pm; winter 8am-5pm. $2; under 17 free; families $4 per car.)*

FORT STEVENS STATE PARK. Located off US 101 on a narrow peninsula 10 mi. west of Astoria, Fort Stevens was constructed in 1863 to prevent attack by Confederate naval raiders and was significantly upgraded in 1897 with the addition of 8 concrete artillery batteries. Several of these remaining batteries are the focus of a self-guided walking tour (about 2hr.) that begins up the road from the campground area. *(☎ 861-2000. Day-use pass costs $3. Get a map and pass from the camp registration.)* Battery Russell (☎ 861-2471), in the park 1 mi. south of the historical area, is the only mainland American fort to have endured enemy fire since the War of 1812. A restored 1954 Army cargo truck takes visitors on narrated tours, daily in the summer at 11am, 12:30, 2:30, and 4pm, and leaves from the Fort Stevens Military Museum and Interpretive Center. *(☎ 861-2000. Open daily 10am-6pm; winter 10am-4pm. $2.50; under 13 $1.25.)* **Equipment Rental: Bikes and Beyond,** 1089 Marine Dr. (☎ 325-2961) rents bikes ($15 per half-day, $25 per day) and boats.

SEASIDE ☎ 503

In the winter of 1805-1806, explorers Lewis and Clark made their westernmost camp near Seaside. While the amenities were few and far between at that time, after the development of a resort in 1870 the situation improved rapidly and visitors began pouring in. Years of visitors, indoor mini-golf, and barrels of salt taffy have transformed Seaside from a remote outpost to a bustling, beachfront tourist mill. For those uninterested in video arcades, Seaside still has merit as a base for exploring the beautiful Oregon coast. Also to its credit, Seaside is less expensive than nearby Cannon Beach, and its hostel is one of the best in the Northwest.

ORIENTATION AND PRACTICAL INFORMATION

Seaside lies 17 mi. south of Astoria and 8 mi. north of Cannon Beach along **US 101.** The most direct route between Seaside and Portland is **US 26,** which intersects US 101 just south of Seaside near Saddle Mountain State Park. The **Necanicum River** runs north-south through Seaside, two blocks from the coastline. In town, US 101 splits into **Roosevelt Dr.** and **Holladay Dr.** All three are bisected by **Broadway,** the town's main street and a tourist-dollar black hole. Streets north of Broadway are numbered, and those south of Broadway are lettered. The **Promenade** (or "Prom") is a paved foot-path that hugs the beach for the length of town.

Buses: Pierce Pacific Stages (☎ 692-4437; call Greyhound at 800-231-2222 for schedules and fares), a Greyhound affiliate, departs the hostel at 3pm for **Portland** (3¼hr., $24) and **Seattle, WA** (5½hr., $37, via **Kelso, WA**). **Sunset Empire Transit** (☎ 861-7433 or 800-776-6406), runs between **Astoria** and **Cannon Beach** 7 times per day M-Sa, stopping at the hostel in addition to the bus stops. Round-trip fare $5; seniors, disabled, students, and ages 6-12 $3.25; under 6 free. Tickets available from drivers.

Visitor Information: Chamber of Commerce, 7 N Roosevelt Dr. (☎ 738-6391 or 800-444-6740), on US 101 and Broadway. The **Seaside Visitor Bureau** (☎ 738-3097 or 888-306-2326; www.seasideor.com) is in the same building. Open June-Aug. daily 8am-5pm; Oct.-May M-F 9am-5pm, Sa-Su 10am-4pm.

Equipment Rental: Prom Bike Shop, 622 12th Ave. (☎ 738-8251), at 12th and Holladay, rents bikes, in-line skates, beach tricycles, and surreys. Most $5-6 per hr., $25-30 per day. Excellent repair work. Must be 18. Open daily 10am-6pm. Also at 151 Ave. A.

Taxis: Yellow Cab ☎ 738-5252. $1.50 base, $1.40 per mi.

Internet Access: Seaside Library: 60 N Roosevelt Dr. (☎ 738-6742). Free 30min. of Internet access. Open Tu-Th 9am-8pm, F-Sa 9am-5pm, Su 1-5pm.

Laundry: Clean Services, 1223 S Roosevelt Dr. (☎ 738-9513). Wash $1.25, dry 25¢ per 6-8min. Detergent 75¢. Open daily 7:30am-10pm.

Emergency: ☎ 911. **Police:** 1091 S Holladay Dr. (☎ 738-6311). **Coast Guard:** 2185 SE Airport Rd. (☎ 861-6214) in Warrenton.

Hospital: Providence Seaside Hospital, 725 S Wahanna Rd. (☎ 717-7000).

Post Office: 300 Ave. A, off of Columbia Ave. (☎ 800-275-8777). Open M-F 8:30am-5pm, Sa 8:30-10:30am. **ZIP Code:** 97138.

ACCOMMODATIONS AND CAMPING

Seaside's expensive motels are hardly an issue for the budget traveler thanks to the large hostel on the south side of town. Motel prices are directly proportional to their proximity to the beach and start at $50 (less during the off-season). The closest state parks are **Fort Stevens** (☎ 861-1671; see p. 89), 21 mi. north, and **Saddle Mountain** (☎ 800-551-6949), 10 mi. east, off US 26 after it splits with US 101.

SEASIDE ■ 91

Drive 8 mi. northeast of Necanicum Junction, then another 7 mi. up a winding road to the base camp. (Drinking water. 10 sites $7 Oct.-Apr., $10 May-Sept.) Sleeping on the beach in Seaside is illegal.

Seaside International Hostel (HI), 930 N Holladay Dr. (☎ 738-7911). Free nightly movies, a well-equipped kitchen, an espresso bar, and a grassy yard along the river make this hostel a pastoral wonderland. Kayak and canoe rental ($7-8 per 2hr.). Call well ahead. 34 large bunks. $15, nonmembers $18; private rooms with bath and cable TV sleep 4 $38, nonmembers $58. $2 off for touring cyclists. Office open 8am-11pm.

Colonial Motor Inn, 1120 N Holladay Dr. (☎ 738-6295 or 800-221-3804). With lovely colonial furniture, free snacks, and clean, quiet rooms, this little motel is a standout for the price. Creeekside gazebo. Singles $54, doubles $59; less in winter.

Riverside Inn, 430 S Holladay Dr. (☎ 738-8254 or 800-826-6151; www.riversideinn.com). Cozy bedrooms, fresh flowers, and ceilings with skylights make this B&B a secret garden amid the Seaside motel madness. Rooms have private bath and TV. Homemade breakfast. Riverfront deck. Doubles from $65; Oct.-Apr. from $60.

FOOD

Prices on Broadway, especially toward the beach, are outrageous. **Safeway,** 401 S Roosevelt Dr., stocks bread and water. (☎ 738-7122. Open daily 6am-midnight.)

The Stand, 220 Ave. U (☎ 738-6592), at the south end of town, serves the cheapest meals around to a local crowd. Burritos $1.75-3.75. Open M-Sa 11am-8pm.

Morning Star Cafe, 846 Ave. C (☎ 717-8188), across from Safeway. Comfy beat-up couches and aging boardgames transport diners to old basement rec rooms. Enjoy a sandwich ($3-4) or quiche ($3.50) with a mocha ($3). Open daily 7am-3pm.

Harrison's Bakery, 608 Broadway (☎ 738-5331). Seaside's famous beach bread and a font of frosted treats made every day at low tide. Hosteling discounts and plate-sized doughnuts. Open W-M 7:30am-4:30pm, F-Sa 7:30am-5:30pm.

Sherry's on Broadway, 604 Broadway (☎ 738-5992), stages a mouth-watering parade of Italian dishes (dinners $6.50-10) amid old Broadway memorabilia. Hot sandwiches star at lunchtime ($4.50-7). Open M-F 11am-7 or 8pm, Sa-Su 11am-9pm.

SIGHTS AND ENTERTAINMENT

Perhaps the US's premier recreation road race, the **Hood to Coast Relay** is the ultimate team running event. Held annually at the end of August, runners tear up the trails between Mt. Hood and Seaside (195 mi.) to the cheers of 50,000 spectators. About 750 12-person teams run three 5 mi. shifts in this 1-2 day relay race. Contact Bob Foote (☎ 227-1371) for more info.

Seaside's tourist population, often larger than the real population, swarms around **Broadway,** a garish strip of arcades and shops running the half mile from Roosevelt (US 101) to the beach. "The Arcade" as it is called, is the focal point of downtown and attracts a youthful crowd. Bumper cars, basketball games, and other methods of fleecing visitors abound. **The Turnaround** at the end of Broadway signals the official (read: arbitrary) end of the Lewis and Clark Trail.

Seaside's **beachfront** is sometimes crowded despite bone-chilling water and strong undertows that make swimming a risky business. For a slightly quieter beach, head to **Gearhart,** 2 mi. north of downtown off US 101, where long stretches of dunes await exploration. **Cleanline Surf,** 719 1st Ave., rents surfing gear. (☎ 738-7888, or 888-546-6176. Open M-Sa 9am-7pm, Su 10am-6pm.)

The **Seaside Aquarium,** 200 N Prom, is smaller than its companion in Newport, but it makes up for its small size by giving visitors the chance to feed playful harbor seals. (☎ 738-6211. Open Su-Th 9am-6pm, F-Sa 9am-8pm; winter open W-Su 9am-6pm. $6, seniors $4.75, ages 6-13, families of 6 $19. Seal feeding 50¢.)

CANNON BEACH ☎ 503

Many moons ago, a rusty cannon from the shipwrecked schooner *Shark* washed ashore at Arch Cape, giving this town its name. Today, home to a veritable army of boutiques, bakeries, and galleries, Cannon Beach presents a somewhat more refined version of Seaside and Astoria's crass commercialism. Arguably the most desirable location on the entire Oregon Coast because of its amazing ocean views and interesting shops, Cannon Beach fills with Portlanders and other tourists, who vacation at the beach community and breathtaking sand strip of Cannon Beach.

ORIENTATION AND PRACTICAL INFORMATION

Cannon Beach lies 8 mi. south of Seaside, 42 mi. north of Tillamook on US 101, and 79 mi. from Portland via US 26. The four exits into town from US 101 all lead to **Hemlock**, the town's main drag.

Buses: Sunset Transit System (☎ 800-776-6406). To Seaside (75¢) and Astoria ($2.25). Cannon Beach Shuttle traverses downtown; to board, just signal to the driver. Runs daily 9am-6pm. 75¢ donation requested.

Visitor Information: Cannon Beach Chamber of Commerce and Visitor Info, 207 N Spruce St. (☎ 436-2623), at 2nd St. Chamber open M-F 9:30am-5pm. Visitor Info open M-Sa 10am-5pm, Su 11am-4pm.

Equipment Rental: Mike's Bike Shop, 248 N Spruce St. (☎ 436-1266 or 800-492-1266), around the corner the from Chamber of Commerce. Mountain bikes $6-8 per hr., $20-30 per day. Beach tricycles $8 per 90min., electric bikes for $12 per hr. Open daily 10am-5pm. **Cleanline Surf,** 171 Sunset Blvd. (☎ 436-9726; www.cleanline-surf.com). Surfboards and boogieboards $15 per day; wetsuits $20 per day, or a complete package for $35. Open M-Sa 10am-6pm, Su 10am-5pm; winter daily 10am-5pm.

Emergency: ☎ 911.

Police: 163 Gower St. (☎ 436-2811).

Medical Care: Providence North Coast Clinic, 171 Larch St. (☎ 717-7000), in Sandpiper Sq. Non-emergency care only, nearest emergency care in Seaside (see p. 90). Open M-F 8:30am-noon and 1:15-4:30pm.

Internet Access: Cannon Beach Library, 131 N Hemlock (☎ 436-1391). $6 per hr. Open M-W, F 1-5pm, Th 1-7pm. **Copies and Fax,** 1235 S Hemlock (☎ 436-2000). $5 for first 30 min., then $5 for each additional hour. Open M-F 10am-6pm.

Post Office: 163 N Hemlock St., 97110 (☎ 436-2822). Open M-F 9am-5pm. **ZIP Code:** 97110.

ACCOMMODATIONS AND CAMPING

At the pleasant motels along Hemlock St., family units can make a good deal for groups. In winter, inquire about specials; most motels offer two-for-one deals. Real budget deals are a short drive away: the **Seaside International Hostel** is 7 mi. north (see p. 91), and **Oswald West State Park** (see p. 94), 10 mi. south of town, has a stunning campground, and **Nehalem Bay State Park,** only a few miles farther south than Oswald West outside of **Nehalem,** has plentiful camping options.

McBee Cottages, 888 S Hemlock (☎ 436-2569), but the office is in the Sandtrap Inn at 539 S Hemlock. Bright and cheerful rooms a few blocks from the beach. Some kitchen units and cottages available. $59; winter $39.

Wright's for Camping, 334 Reservoir Rd. (☎ 436-2347), off Hwy. 101. Sites among the trees make this family-owned campground a relaxing retreat from RV mini-cities. Showers, toilets. Wheelchair accessible. Reservations advised in summer. 19 sites, $17.

FOOD

The deals are down Hemlock, in mid-town. **Mariner Market,** 139 N Hemlock St. holds 7000 grocery items on its expansive shelves. (☎ 436-2442. Open July-Sept. Su-Th 8am-10pm, F-Sa 8am-11pm; Oct.-June Su-Th 8am-9pm, F-Sa 8am-10pm.)

CANNON BEACH TO TILLAMOOK ■ 93

Lazy Susan's Cafe, 126 N Hemlock St. (☎436-2816), in Coaster Sq. A Cannon Beach favorite. Excellent homemade scones. Homemade soup $3.50, tuna apple hazelnut salad $8. Open M-Th and Su 8am-5pm, F-Sa 8am-8pm; winter M, W, Th 8am-2:30pm, F 8am-8pm, Su 8am-5pm.

Midtown Cafe, 1235 S Hemlock St. (☎436-1016), in Haystack Sq. Everything is homemade, from the hand-carved door to the jams on the tables. Start your day with an apple oat scone ($2). Lentil burgers $8. Open M and W-F 7am-2pm, Sa-Su 8am-2pm.

Bill's Tavern, 188 N Hemlock St. (☎436-2202). A local favorite for down-to-earth eatin'. Beer on tap is brewed upstairs. Basic pub grub $3-8.25. Pints $3. Open Th-Tu 11:30am-midnight, W 4:30pm-midnight. Kitchen closes around 9:30pm.

SIGHTS AND OUTDOOR ACTIVITIES

Cannon Beach is a gauntlet of expensive, sporadically elegant galleries and gift shops. A stroll along the 7 mi. stretch of flat, bluff-framed beach suits many better. **Coaster Theater,** 108 N Hemlock St., is a small playhouse that stages theater productions, concerts, dance performances, comedy, and musical revues year-round. Schedule varies, so call or check the website. (☎436-1242; www.coastertheater.com. Tickets $12-15. Box office open W-Sa 1-8pm.) A huge **Sand Castle Competition** transforms Cannon Beach into a fantastic menagerie on June 8, 2002. Contestants begin digging in the early morning to construct ornate sculptures from wet sand. Call the Chamber of Commerce (See **Visitor Information,** p. 92) for more info. To **surf** a set, rent boards from **Cleanline Surf,** 171 Sunset Blvd. (☎436-9726. Surfboards and boogieboards $15 per day; wetsuits $20 per day. Open M-Sa 9am-7pm, Su 10am-6pm; winter daily 10am-5pm.)

HIKING

The park attracts picnickers and hikers. Ecola Point offers a view of hulking Haystack Rock, which is spotted with (and by) gulls, puffins, barnacles, anemones, and the occasional sea lion. (☎436-2844. $3 entrance fee.) Ecola Point also affords views of the Bay's centerpiece, the Tillamook Lighthouse. Decommissioned in 1957, the now privately-owned lighthouse can be reached only by helicopter to deposit the ashes of the dead.

Indian Beach Trail (2 mi, about 1hr.), leads to Indian Beach and its tide pools, which teem with colorful and fragile sea life. Easy to moderate.

Tillamook Head (12 mi. round-trip, several hours). Leaves from Indian Beach, and hugs the coast to the mini-cape that separates Seaside Beach from Cannon Beach. The trail passes the top of Tillamook Head (2 mi. up the trail), where 5 hiker sites await those willing to make the trek for free camping. Moderate.

Saddle Mountain Trail (5 mi. round-trip, several hours), 14 mi. east of Cannon Beach on US 26, is named after the highest peak in the Coast Range. The trail leads to the mountain's 3283 ft. summit and ends with astounding views of the Pacific Ocean, Nehalem Bay, and the Cascades. Moderate to difficult.

CANNON BEACH TO TILLAMOOK ☎503

In the summer of 1933, the Tillamook Burn reduced 5 sq. mi. of coastal forest near Tillamook to charcoal. While nature has restored Tillamook State Forest to health, coastal towns to the west are still nastily scarred. The gift shops that line the hwy. hide behind fading paint and crooked telephone poles. The coastline alongside these tiny towns, however, is much less crowded than Seaside and Cannon Beaches. Tourist info for the area is available at the visitors center in Tillamook (see p. 94) or the **Rockaway Beach Chamber of Commerce,** 103 S 1st St., off US 101. (☎355-8108. Open M-F 10am-3pm.) For **Internet access** in Rockaway Beach, head to **Kristi's Cyber Cafe,** 344 S US 101, in Rockaway Beach, (☎355-3335). An hour on the net will set you back $7, or $5 for students and seniors.

OSWALD WEST STATE PARK. Ten miles south of Cannon Beach, Oswald West State Park is a tiny headland rainforest of hefty spruce and cedars. Locals call the park **Short Sands Beach.** Although the beach and woodsy **campsites** are only accessible by a ¼ mi. trail off US 101, the park provides wheelbarrows for transporting gear from the parking lot to the 29 sites, which teem with surfers. (Open Mar.-Nov. Sites $15.) From the park, the 4 mi. round-trip **Cape Falcon Trail** leads over the headland to the 1661 ft. **Neahkahnie Mountain.**

NEHALEM. Eight miles south of Oswald State Park, a cluster of made-in-Oregon-type shops along US 101 make up **Nehalem.** The **Nehalem Bay Winery,** 34965 Hwy. 53, 3 mi. south of town, provides free tastings of local cranberry and blackberry vintages. The winery sponsors performances in a small **theater,** an annual **bluegrass festival,** a **fun express train** on weekends, and is a general forum for bacchanalian revelry. (☎368-9263. Open daily 9am-6pm; winter 10am-5pm, or later if Ray's.)

WHEELER. A few miles south of Nehalem and 22 mi. north of Tillamook, the small town of Wheeler is a surprise find. **Wheeler on the Bay Lodge,** 580 Marine Dr., in addition to their expensive rooms, rents **kayaks.** (☎368-5858. Singles $15 per hr., $38 per day; doubles $20 per hr., $44 per day. Includes 10min. training session for beginners. Open daily 8am-7pm.) The **Wheeler Marina** (☎368-5780) rents crabbing nets on the bay south of Wheeler and will often cook the crabs for you ($4).

TILLAMOOK ☎503

Although the word Tillamook (TILL-uh-muk) translates to "land of many waters," to the Northwest it is synonymous with cheese. The cows that dot the surrounding hills produce a nationally famous cheddar. Still a small farming town at heart, Tillamook gets its share of tourist traffic and funnels most of it to the Tillamook Cheese Factory. Visitors say cheese, take a picture, and shuffle off to the coast.

☛⚐ ORIENTATION AND PRACTICAL INFORMATION. Tillamook lies 49 mi. south of Seaside and 44 mi. north of Lincoln City on **US 101.** It's also 74 mi. west of Portland on **Rte. 6** and **US 26.** Tillamook's main drag, US 101, splits into two one-way streets downtown. **Pacific Ave.** runs north and **Main Ave.** runs south. The cross streets are labeled numerically. The **Tillamook Cheese Factory** sits north of town (1½ mi.). **Ride the Wave Bus Lines** (☎800-815-8283) runs locally (M-Sa; $1) as well as **Portland** (2½hr., 5 per week, $10). Find a list of campsites and hiking trails in Tillamook County at the **Tillamook Chamber of Commerce,** 3705 US 101 N, in the big red barn near the Tillamook Cheese Factory. (☎842-7525. Open M-Sa 9am-5pm, Su 10am-4pm; winter M-F 9am-5pm, Sa 10am-4:30pm, Su 10am-2pm.) **Emergency:** ☎911. Internet Access: **Tillamook County Library,** 210 Ivy Ave. (☎842-4792) offers 3 computers with free 30min. of Internet access. Open M-Th 9am-9pm, F-Sa 9am-5:30pm. **Police:** 210 Laurel St. (☎842-2522), in City Hall. **Coast Guard:** ☎322-3531. **Post office:** 2200 1st St. (☎800-275-8777. Open M-F 9am-5pm.) **ZIP Code:** 97141.

⚐ ACCOMMODATIONS AND CAMPING. Motels are steep, but the camping is some of the area's finest. The only reasonably priced motel in town is the **MarClair Inn,** 11 Main Ave., at the center of town, which rents huge, beautiful rooms. Enjoy the outdoor pool, hot tub, and sauna. (☎842-7571 or 800-331-6857. Singles $64; doubles $73. 10% AAA discount. Credit card required.) **Cape Lookout State Park,** 13000 Whiskey Creek Rd., lies 12 mi. southwest of Tillamook on the Three Capes Loop (see p. 95). Some sites are only 20 yards from the beach, while others offer more privacy and shade. (☎842-4981; reservations 800-452-5687. $3, day-use fee. Non-camper showers $2. 176 tent sites, $13-16; 38 full hookups, $16-20; 4 yurts, $27; walk-ins $4 per person.) **Kilchis River Park,** 6 mi. northeast of town at the end of Kilchis River Rd., which leaves US 101 1 mi. north of the factory, has 35 sites between a mossy forest and the Kilchis River, with a baseball field, volleyball court, horseshoes, swimming, and hiking. (☎842-6694. Water, toilets, no showers. Open May-Oct. Tent sites $10; walk-ins $5.)

◘ **FOOD.** Tillamook may be a cheese-lover's paradise, but other food choices in town are lacking. Pick up Velveeta at **Safeway,** 955 US 101. (☎842-4831. Open daily 6am-11pm.) The **Blue Heron French Cheese Company,** 2001 Blue Heron Dr., north of town and 1 mi. south of the factory, is a country-style store, which focuses on brie. Gourmet sandwiches cost $6.25; salad trio goes for $5.75. Tastings of local and often unusual dips, jams, wines, and, yes, brie, are free. (☎842-8281. Open daily 8am-8pm; winter 9am-5pm. Deli open 11:30am-4pm.) The **Tillamook Association of Performing Arts** (☎815-8272) puts on plays upstairs; tickets are sold at the Blue Heron. **La Casa Modelo,** 1160 US 101 N, makes mild Mexican food and serves it in a beautiful wood-paneled dining room. Small lunch specials run $5-7; foot-long tacos are $8. (☎842-5768. Open daily 11:30am-9pm, winter 11:30am-8pm.) **Blue Moon Cafe,** 2104 2nd, offers breakfast and lunch in a simple, busy environment. Huge sandwiches run $3.25-4.50, or have a salad ($3.50-5) and stay for a slice of the $2.50 homemade pie. (☎842-3155. Open M-F 7:30am-4:30pm.)

◙ **SIGHTS.** The **Tillamook Cheese Factory,** 4175 US 101 N, is a shrine to dairy delights, a cradle of curdled creations, and a thinly disguised tourist trap. Wander through the amusing exhibits, taste award-winning tidbits, and then get lured into buying pounds of cheddar. (☎842-4481. Open mid-June to Labor Day daily 8am-8pm; Sept. to mid-June 8am-6pm.) The impressive **Tillamook Naval Air Station Museum,** 6030 Hangar Rd., lies 2 mi. south of town. This hulking 1940s seven-acre hangar is the largest wooden clear-span structure in the world. The airy cavern is home to over 34 fully functional warplanes, including a P-38 Lightning, a PBY-5A Catalina, and an F-14 Tomcat. (☎842-1130. Open daily 10am-5pm. $8; over 65 $7; ages 13-17 $4.50; 12 and under free.) West of the highway, downtown, the **Tillamook County Pioneer Museum,** 2106 2nd St., at Pacific Ave., features dioramas of pioneer days. The real head-turners here, however, are the stuffed animals preserved by taxidermist and big game hunter Alex Walker. He donated his remarkable collection to the museum, a move which has inspired lesser-known local taxidermists to do the same. (☎842-4553. Open M-Sa 8am-5pm, Su 11am-5pm. $2; seniors $1.50; ages 12-17 50¢; under 12 free.)

THE THREE CAPES LOOP ☎503/541

Between Tillamook and Lincoln City, US 101 wanders east into wooded land, losing contact with the coast. The Three Capes Loop is a 35 mi. circle to the west that connects a trio of spectacular promontories—Cape Meares, Cape Lookout, and Cape Kiwanda State Parks—that make for a sweet Sunday drive. Narrow twists and a rocky road make the trip tricky for those on two wheels. The loop leaves US 101 at Tillamook and rejoins US 101 about 10 mi. north of Lincoln City.

CAPE MEARES STATE PARK. Cape Meares State Park, at the tip of the promontory jutting out from Tillamook, protects one of the few remaining old growth forests on the Oregon Coast. The **Octopus Tree,** a gnarled Sitka spruce with six candelabra trunks, is an eight-year-old's ultimate fantasy. The **Cape Meares Lighthouse** operates as an illuminating on-site interpretive center. (☎503-842-5270. Open May-Sept. daily 11am-4pm; Oct. and Mar.-Apr. F-Sa 11am-4pm. Free.)

CAPE LOOKOUT STATE PARK. Another 12 mi. southwest of Cape Meares, **Cape Lookout State Park** (☎503-842-4981), offers a small, rocky beach with incredible views of Cape Meares Lighthouse. It also has some fine camping near the dunes and the forests behind them. From here, the 2½ mi. **Cape Trail** heads past the 1943 crash site of a military plane to the end of the lookout where a spectacular 360° view featuring **Haystack Rock** awaits.

CAPE KIWANDA STATE PARK. Cape Kiwanda State Park (☎800-551-6949), 1 mi. north of Pacific City, is the southernmost promontory on the loop and home to one of the most sublime beaches on the Oregon shore. The sheltered cape draws beachcombers, kite-flyers, volleyball players, jetskiers, windsurfers. The park is open from 8am until the sun slips down behind magnificent Haystack Rock. The flat-bottomed dory fleet is one of the few fishing fleets in the world that launches beachside. If the surf is up, head to **South County Surf,** 33310 Cape Kiwanda Dr., in Pacific City. (☎503-965-7505. Surfboard rental $20 until 5pm; boogie board $10; wetsuit $15. Open daily 9am-6pm.)

PACIFIC CITY. Pacific City is a hidden gem that most travelers on US 101 never even see. If you plan to stay overnight, the **Anchorage Motel,** 6585 Pacific Ave., offers homey rooms. (☎541-965-6773 or 800-941-6250. Singles from $37; doubles from $42.) The town hides away some surprisingly good restaurants. The **Grateful Bread Bakery,** 34805 Brooten Rd., creates monuments to the art of dining: get anything from a vegetarian stuffed foccaccia ($6) to a dilled shrimp salad sandwich. (☎965-7337. Open M-Sa 8am-6pm, Su 8am-5pm; winter closed W-Th.)

LINCOLN CITY ☎541

The City is actually five towns wrapped around a seven mile strip of ocean-front motels, gas stations, and souvenir shops along US 101. Nothing draws as much money for the city as the new Chinook Winds Siletz Tribal Gaming Convention Center. Otherwise known as "the Casino," swingers and glassy-eyed tourist come here to gamble away days, nights, and life savings. For the shop-til-you-drop types, Lincoln City is also known for its gigantic array of factory outlet stores. Bicyclists will find Lincoln City hellish, and hikers would do well to cut three blocks west to the seashore to avoid the hilly landscape.

ORIENTATION AND PRACTICAL INFORMATION. Lincoln City lies between Devils Lake and the deep blue sea 42 mi. south of Tillamook, 22 mi. north of Newport, 58 mi. west of Salem, and 88 mi. southwest of Portland. Despite its oblong shape, Lincoln City is divided into quadrants: **D River** (marked "the smallest river in the world") is the north-south divide; US 101 divides east from west. **Greyhound buses,** 3350 NW US 101 (☎800-454-2487) depart from Wendy's at the north end of town to **Portland** (2½hr., 2 per day, $13) and **Newport** (50min., 2 per day, $7). Tickets are available at the visitors center (see below). **Robben-Rent-A-Car,** 3244 US 101 NE, rents for $28 per day and 15¢ per mi. after 50 mi. Must be 21 with credit card. (☎994-2454 or 800-305-5530. Open daily 8am-5pm.) At the **Lincoln City Visitor and Convention Bureau,** 801 US 101 SW #1, opposite Burger King and next to the Price and Pride, a 24hr. telephone board connects with local motels at the push of a button, and volunteers are happy to share their wealth of brochures. (☎994-8378 or 800-452-2151. Open M-F 8am-8pm, Sa 9am-5pm, Su 10am-4pm; winter M-F 8am-5pm, Sa 9am-5pm, Su 10am-4pm.) The **Oregon Surf Shop,** 4933 US 101 SW, rents a wetsuit and surfboard for $30 per day, or wetsuit and boogie board for $25. (☎996-3957 or 877-339-5672. Open Su-Th 10am-6pm, F-Sa 9am-6pm.) **Internet Access:** The **Driftwood Library,** 801 US 101 SW, near the visitors center, provides free 1hr. of Internet access. (☎996-2277. Open M-W 9am-9pm, Th-Sa 9am-5pm.) **Public showers** ($1.25) are yours at the Lincoln City Pool, 2150 NE Oar Place. (☎994-5208. Open in summer M-F 5:30am-9pm, Sa 11am-9pm, Su noon-4:30pm; call for winter hours.) **Emergency:** ☎911. **Police:** 1503 East Devils Lake Rd. SE (☎994-3636). **Hospital: Samaritan North Lincoln,** 3043 NE 28th St. (☎994-3661). **Post office:** 1501 East Devils Lake Rd. SE, 97367, one block east of US 101. (☎800-275-8777. Open M-F 9am-5pm.) **ZIP Code:** 97367.

ACCOMMODATIONS AND FOOD. Beautiful, small rooms await at the **Captain Cook Inn,** 2626 US 101 NE. (☎994-2522 or 800-994-2522. Singles $48; doubles $52.) The **Sea Echo Motel,** 3510 US 101 NE, sits high above the highway overlooking the coast. Rooms are standard but quiet. (☎994-2575. Singles $45; 2 beds $58-64.) **Devils Lake State Park,** off 6th St. NE from US 101 NW, grants access to fishing and boating on the lake. (☎994-2002 or 800-452-5687. Wheelchair accessible. Non-camper showers $2. Reservations recommended. 55 tent sites, $17; 32 full hookups, $22; 10 yurts, $29; walk-ins $4.25.) Lincoln City has decent dining if you can navigate the fast-food shoals. **Dory Cove,** 5819 Logan Rd., at the far north of town, is the locals' unanimous choice for affordable seafood. Dinners start at $10 a plate. (☎ 994-5180. Open M-Sa 11:30am-8pm, Su noon-8pm; winter M-Th 11:30am-8pm, F-Sa 11:30am-9pm, Su noon-8pm.) Skor bars and 7-up are at **Safeway,** 4101 NW Logan Rd., at the north end of town. (☎ 994-8667. Open daily 6am-midnight.)

SIGHTS AND ENTERTAINMENT. Shop till you drop at the 100 plus **Factory Stores,** at E Devils Lake Rd. and US 101. (☎ 996-5000. Open M-Sa 10am-8pm, Su 10am-6pm.) To finish off a day of spending, join the slot-junkies at the 24hr., climate-controlled **Casino,** 1777 44th St. NW (☎ 888-244-6665). Turn left at Lighthouse Sq. on Logan Rd. NW and look to your left: it's the hulking yellow stucco structure. The casino sponsors **Concerts-by-the-Sea** (☎ 888-624-6228; $10-70) generally every few weeks from May to December. The windy beaches of Lincoln City host the **Fall** and **Spring International Kite Festivals** late September to early October and in early May at River Park.

DEPOE BAY AND OTTER CREST LOOP ☎ 541

Rest stops and beach-access parking lots litter the 30 mi. of US 101 between Lincoln City and Newport. Diminutive **Depoe Bay** boasts **gray whale viewing** along the town's low seawall, at the Depoe Bay State Park Wayside and at the Observatory Lookout, 4½ mi. to the south. Go early in the morning on a cloudy day during annual migration (Dec.-May) for the best chance of spotting the giants. **Tradewinds Charters** (☎ 765-2345 or 800-445-8730), on the north end of the bridge on US 101 downtown, has 5hr. ($55) and 6hr. ($65) fishing and crabbing trips, and 1hr. ($13) and 2hr. ($19) whale-watching trips. **Dockside Charters** offers similar trips; turn east at the only traffic light in Depoe Bay. They're next to the Coast Guard. (☎ 765-2545 or 800-733-8915. 5hr. fishing $50; 1hr. whale-watching $15, ages 13-17 $11, ages 4-12 $8.) Just south of Depoe Bay, detour from US 101 on the renowned **Otter Crest Loop,** a twisting 4 mi. excursion high above the shore that affords spectacular vistas at every bend and includes views of Otter Rock and the Marine Gardens. The loop is now open only to bikers/hikers, making for a much more peaceful trip. A lookout over **Cape Foulweather** has telescopes (25¢) for spotting sea lions lazing on the rocks. The **Devil's Punch Bowl,** formed when the roof of a seaside cave collapsed, is also accessible off the loop. It becomes a frothing cauldron during high tide when ocean water crashes through an opening in the side of the bowl.

NEWPORT ☎ 541

After the miles of malls along US 101, Newport's renovated waterfront area of pleasantly kitschy restaurants and shops is a delight. Newport's claim to fame, however, is the world-class Oregon Coast Aquarium. Best known as home to Willy the orca of *Free Willy* (whose "real" name is Keiko), the aquarium offers several interesting exhibits. This, in addition to the Mark Hatfield Marine Science Center and loads of great seafood, make Newport a marine lover's starred attraction.

ORIENTATION AND PRACTICAL INFORMATION

Corvallis lies 55 mi. east on **US 20,** Lincoln City is 22 mi. north on **US 101,** and Florence sits 50 mi. south. Newport is bordered on the west by the foggy Pacific Ocean and on the south by Yaquina Bay. A suspension bridge carries US 101 traffic across the bay. US 101, known in town as the **Coast Hwy.,** divides east and west Newport. US 20, known as **Olive St.** in town, bisects the north and south sides of town. Just north of the bridge, **Bay Boulevard** circles the bay and runs through the heart of the port. Historic **Nye Beach,** bustling with tiny shops, is on the northwest side of town in between 3rd and 6th St.

Buses: Greyhound, 956 10th St. SW (☎265-2253 or 800-454-2487), at Bailey St. Open M-F 8-10am and 1-4:15pm, Sa 8am-1pm. To **Portland** (4hr., 2 per day, $18), **Seattle** (9hr., 2 per day, $45), and **San Francisco** (16½-21hr., 3 per day, $76).

Taxis: Yaquina Cab Company (☎265-9552). $2.25 base, $2.25 per mi.

Visitor Information: Chamber of Commerce, 555 Coast Hwy. SW (☎265-8801 or 800-262-7844; www.discovernewport.com). 24hr. info board outside. Open M-F 8:30am-5pm; summer also Sa-Su 10am-4pm.

Internet Access: Newport Public Library: 35 Nye St. NW (☎265-2153), at Olive St., offers free 30min. of Internet access every day on 6 computers. Open M-Th 10am-9pm, F-Sa 10am-6pm, Su 1-4pm.

Laundry: Eileen's Coin Laundry, 1078 Coast Hwy. N (☎265-5474). Wash $1.25, dry 25¢ per 8min. Open daily 6am-11pm.

Emergency: ☎911. **Weather and Sea Conditions:** ☎265-5511.

Police: 810 Alder St. SW (☎265-5331). **Coast Guard:** ☎265-5381.

Hospital: Pacific Communities Hospital, 930 Abbey St. SW (☎265-2244).

Post Office: 310 2nd St. SW (☎800-275-8777). Open M-F 8:30am-5pm, Sa 10:30am-1:30pm. **ZIP Code:** 97365.

ACCOMMODATIONS AND CAMPING

Motel-studded US 101 provides affordable, yet sometimes noisy rooms. Nearby monster camping facilities often fill on summer weekends.

Beverly Beach State Park, 198 123rd St. NE (☎265-9278; reservations 800-452-5687), 7 mi. north of Newport and just south of Devil's Punch Bowl. Year-round campground of gargantuan proportions. Non-camper showers $2. 129 tent sites, $17; 76 electrical, $20; 53 full hookups, $22; 21 yurts, $29; hiker/biker $4.25.

City Center Motel, 538 Coast Hwy. SW (☎265-7381 or 800-627-9099), opposite the visitors center. Spacious, oddly empty rooms. Singles $30, doubles $45.

Money Saver Motel, 861 SW Coast Hwy. (☎265-2277 or 888-461-4033). Friendly management distinguish this motel. Singles $39; 2 beds $52; suite with kitchen $75.

South Beach State Park, 5580 Coast Hwy. S (☎867-4715), 2 mi. south of town. Sparse conifers offer little shelter and no privacy. Showers $2 for non-campers. 238 electric hookups, $21; 16 yurts, $29; 6 primitive sites, $14; hiker/biker sites $4.25.

FOOD

Food in Newport is surprisingly varied, yet seafood is the choice dining option. **Oceana Natural Foods Coop,** 159 2nd St. SE, has a small selection of reasonably priced health foods and produce. (☎265-8285. Open daily 8am-8pm.) **J.C. Sentry,** 107 Coast Hwy. N, sells standard supermarket stock. (☎265-6641. Open 24hr.)

Mo's Restaurant, 622 Bay Blvd. SW (☎265-2979). This local favorite has such a following that Mo's granddaughters have opened up a whole host of Mini Mo's. Go for the clam chowder ($4-6). Open daily 11am-10pm.

April's, 749 3rd St. NW (☎265-6855), down by Nye Beach, is the undisputed pinnacle of local dining. The serene ocean view and good food are worth every penny. Tables fill early, especially on weekends. Dinners $12-19; daily specials are pricier. Towering chocolate eclairs $4. Reservations suggested. Open Tu-Su for dinner from 5pm.

Canyon Way Restaurant & Bookstore, 1216 SW Canyon Way (☎265-8319). Browse through the charming bookstore before or after meal. Try the vegetable sandwich ($7) for lunch. Dinner entrees are pricier ($16-21). Restaurant open Tu-Sa: lunch 11am-3pm, dinner 5:30-9pm. Bookstore open M-Sa 10am-9pm. Deli open Tu-Sa 10am-4pm.

Rogue Ale & Public House, 748 Bay Blvd. SW (☎265-3188). They "brew for the rogue in all of us," and bless 'em for it. Plenty of brew on tap, and garlic ale bread to boot ($2.25). Locals pack it in for F and Sa night trivia. Fish'n'chips with Rogue Ale batter $8. Open daily 11am-2:30am; food until 11:30pm.

ENTERTAINMENT AND EVENTS

The **Newport Performing Arts Center,** 777 W Olive St., hosts theater and dance performances, film festivals, and excellent orchestral and band concerts. (☎265-2787. Box office M-F 9am-5pm and 1hr. before shows. Tickets $6-18.) The **Newport Seafood and Wine Festival,** during the last weekend in February, showcases Oregon wines, food, music, and crafts ($8 per day; 21+). The three-day **Lincoln County Fair and Rodeo** comes to the Newport Fairgrounds on the third weekend in July. (☎265-6237. Th-Su $6 per day; ages 6-12 $3; under 6 free. For all four days $18; children $9.) Contact the Chamber of Commerce for info on all seasonal events.

SIGHTS

MARK O. HATFIELD MARINE SCIENCE CENTER. The Center is the hub of Oregon State University's coastal research. While the live octopus can't be played with, a garden of sea anenomes, slugs, and bottom-dwelling fish all await your curious fingers in the touch tanks. *(At the south end of the bridge on Marine Science Dr. ☎867-0100. Open daily 10am-5pm; winter Th-M 10am-4pm. Admission by donation.)*

OREGON COAST AQUARIUM. More famous, less serious, and much more expensive than the Science Center is the **Oregon Coast Aquarium.** This world-class aquarium housed Keiko, the much-loved *Free Willy* Orca, during his rehabilitation, before he returned to his childhood waters near Iceland two years ago. The Passages of the Deep exhibit features a new 200-foot undersea tunnel; experience being surrounded by sharks, rays, and fish. *(2820 Ferry Slip Rd. SE, at the south end of the bridge. ☎867-3474; www.aquarium.org. Open May-June 9am-6pm, July-Sept. 9am-8pm, winter 10am-5pm. $10.25, seniors $9.25, ages 4-13 $6.25.)*

ROGUE ALE BREWERY. The Brewery has won more awards than you can shake a pint at. Cross the bay bridge, follow the signs to the Hatfield Center. Their line of 20 brews, including Oregon Golden, Shakespeare Stout, and Dead Guy Ale are available at the pub in town (see **Food,** above) or upstairs at **Brewers by the Bay,** where taster trays of four beers cost $4. *(2320 Oregon State University Dr. SE. Brewers by the Bay ☎867-3664. Brewery ☎867-3660. Open M-F noon-8pm, Sa-Su 11:30am-8pm. Free tours of the brewery leave daily at 4pm, depending on demand.)*

NEWPORT TO REEDSPORT ☎541

From Newport to Reedsport, US 101 slides through a string of small towns, beautiful campgrounds, and spectacular stretches of beach. The **Waldport Ranger District Office,** 1049 Pacific Hwy. SW/US 101, is located 16 mi. south of Newport in Waldport. The office describes hiking in **Siuslaw National Forest,** a patchwork of three wilderness areas along the Oregon Coast, and furnishes detailed maps ($4-6) and advice on the area's campgrounds. (☎563-3211. Open M-F 8am-4pm.)

CAPE PERPETUA. Cape Perpetua, 11 mi. south of Waldport, and 40 mi. north of Reedsport, is the highest point on the coast (803 ft.) and has a number of exciting sea-level trails. The **Cape Perpetua Interpretive Center,** 2400 US 101, just south of the viewpoint turn-off, has informative exhibits about the surrounding area. (☎547-3289. Open M-Sa June-Aug. 9am-5pm, Su noon-5pm; Sept. W-Su 10am-4pm; Oct.-May M-F 10am-4pm, Sa-Su 10am-4pm.) Well-worn offshore attractions like **Devil's Churn** (¼ mi. north of the visitors center down Restless Water Trail) and **Spouting Horn** (¼ mi. south down Captain Cook Trail) demonstrate the power of the waves. **Cape Perpetua Campground,** at the viewpoint turn-off, has 37 sites alongside a tiny, fern-banked creek. (Water, toilets. Firewood $5. Sites $14.) The **Rock Creek Campground,** 8 mi. farther south, has 16 sites under mossy spruces a half-mile from the sea. (Drinking water, toilets. $14.)

ALPHA FARM. Escape the coast's bourgeois tourism at an unusual communal alternative, **Alpha Farm.** Drive 14 mi. east of **Florence,** a far-too-long strip of fast-food joints and expensive motels 50 mi. south of Newport, to the tiny community of **Mapleton;** press on 30min. along Rte. 36 and then 7 mi. up Deadwood Creek Rd. Anyone willing to lend a hand with the chores is welcome to camp out or stay in the beautiful, simple bedrooms. Visitors are welcome from Monday to Friday for up to three days, but call ahead. The **Alpha Bit Cafe,** in Mapleton on Rte. 126, is owned and staffed by members of Alpha Farm. (Farm ☎ 964-5102; cafe 268-4311. Open Sa-Th 10am-6pm and F 10am-9pm.)

OREGON DUNES AND REEDSPORT ☎ 541

Millennia of wind and water action have formed the Oregon Dunes National Recreation Area, a 50 mi. expanse between Florence and Coos Bay. Endless mounds of sand rise 500 ft. above the water, shifting so quickly that the entire face of a dune can disappear and reform in the course of a day. In many places, no grass or shrubs grow, and the vista presents nothing but sand, sky, and tire tracks. In other spots, hidden lakes and islands of trees offer a green oasis amid what is technically a desert. Although more than half the dunes area is closed to traffic, campgrounds fill up early with dirtbike and dune buggy junkies. With them come blaring radios, thrumming engines, and a hard-partying ethic.

ORIENTATION AND PRACTICAL INFORMATION

The dunes' shifting grip on the coastline is broken only once, where the Umpqua and Smith Rivers empty into **Winchester Bay.** On the south side of the bay is a small town of the same name, on the north is **Reedsport.** At the junction of **Rte. 38** and **US 101,** Reedsport is 185 mi. southwest of Portland, 89 mi. southwest of Eugene, and 71 mi. south of Newport.

Visitor Information: Oregon Dunes National Recreation Area Visitor Center, 855 US 101 (☎ 271-3611; www.fs.fed.us/r6/siuslaw/odnra.htm), at Rte. 38 in Reedsport, just south of the Umpqua River Bridge. Has displays, a 10min. video on dune ecology, and essential info on fees, regulations, hiking, and camping. Maps $4-6. Open June-Oct. daily 8am-4:30pm; Nov.-May M-F 8am-4:30pm, Sa 10am-4pm. The **Chamber of Commerce** (☎ 271-3495 or 800-247-2155), at the same location and open the same hours, has dune buggy rental info and motel listings.

Laundromat: Coin Laundry, 420 N 14th St. (☎ 271-3587), next to McDonald's. Wash costs $1.25, a dry 25¢ per 7½min. Open daily 8am-9:30pm.

Internet Access: Public Library, 395 Winchester Ave. (☎ 271-3500). Free 1hr. of Internet access. Open M 2-8:30pm, Tu-W and F 10am-6pm, Th 2-6pm, Sa-11am-2pm.

Emergency: ☎ 911.

Police: 146 N 4th St. (☎ 271-2100). **Coast Guard:** ☎ 271-2138.

Post office: 301 Fir Ave. (☎ 800-275-8777), off Rte. 38. Open M-F 8:30am-5pm. **ZIP Code:** 97467.

ACCOMMODATIONS AND CAMPING

Although they often fill in summer, motels with singles from $40 abound on US 101. Fourteen campgrounds, many of which are very near the dunes, also dot the coast. During the summer, RVs dominate local campsites. Permits for dispersed camping (allowed on public lands 200 ft. from any road or trail) are required year-round and available at the Dunes Information Center. The national recreation area is administered by Siuslaw National Forest. The campgrounds that allow dune buggy access—**Spinreel** (36 sites), parking-lot style **Driftwood II** (69 sites), **Horsfall** (showers; 69 sites), and **Horsfall Beach** (34 sites)—are rowdy in the summer. (Toilets, water. $13.) Limited reservations ☎ 800-280-2267; call five days in advance.

Harbor View Motel, 540 Beach Blvd. (☎271-3352), off US 101 in Winchester Bay, is so close to the marina that there are boats in the parking lot. Aging rooms are comfortable and clean. Friendly management. Singles $34; doubles $40. Kitchens $2 more.

William M. Tugman State Park (☎759-3604; reservations 800-452-5687), 8 mi. south of Reedsport on US 101. Close to gorgeous Eel Lake. Slightly less privacy, but still well-sheltered. Hiker/biker camping is the most private ($4). Water and electricity. Non-camper showers $2. Wheelchair accessible. 115 sites, $15; yurts $29.

Carter Lake Campground, 12 mi. north of Reedsport on US 101. Boat access to the lake; some sites lakeside. Well-screened sites, as quiet as it gets out here. No ATVs. Nice bathrooms, but no showers. Open May-Sept. 23 sites, $13.

Eel Creek Campground, 10 mi. south of Reedsport. Sandy, spacious sites hidden from the road and each other by tall brush. Trailhead for the 2½ mi. Umpqua Dunes Trail, one of the best dune walks. Toilets, water. No hookups or ATVs. 53 sites, $13.

FOOD

Cheap, tasty food prevails in Winchester Bay and Reedsport. Grab a shrink-wrapped T-bone and a box of fudgesicles at **Safeway,** right off US 101 in Reedsport (open daily 7am-11pm). The **Bayfront Bar and Bistro,** 208 Bayfront Loop, in Winchester Bay, is a classy but casual choice on the waterfront. For lunch, a salmon burger is $6, and grilled oysters are $8. Dinner is pricey ($9-16), but good. (☎271-9463. Open Tu-Su 11am-9pm.) The exterior of **Back to the Best,** on US 101 at 10th St., may be dated, but the food is fresh. Sandwiches with such fineries as smoked gouda cost $4.25. (☎271-2619. Open M-F 6am-6pm, Sa-Su 8am-6pm.)

OUTDOOR ACTIVITIES

DUNES. At times, the dunes may seem like a maze of madcap buggy riders, but the sand actually houses a complex ecosystem and a network of quiet trails. A stop at the National Recreation Area visitors center (see **Visitor Information,** p. 100) can unlock some of the hidden attractions of Oregon's giant sandbox. At the very least, travelers should stop at the **Oregon Dunes Overlook,** off US 101, located about halfway between Reedsport and Florence. Here, wooden ramps lead to views of the dunes and a glimpse of the ocean. The **Tahkenitch Creek Loop,** actually three separate trails, plows 3½ mi. through forest, dunes, wetlands, and beach. ($1 parking fee. Overlook staffed daily Memorial Day to Labor Day 10am-3pm. Guided hikes available.) The revamped **Umpqua Scenic Dunes Trail** makes another excellent hike. Be wary of quicksand in the low, wet areas. For an unmuffled and undeniably thrilling dune experience, venture out on wheels. Plenty of shops between Florence and Coos Bay rent and offer tours.

For an unmuffled and undeniably thrilling dune experience, venture out on wheels. While there are no accurately defined buggy trails through the dunes because the buggy traffic constantly shifts the boundaries, just follow other riders for the best action in the sand. Plenty of shops between Florence and Coos Bay rent and offer tours. **Dune Country ATV,** 1 mi. off Hwy. 101 in Winchester Bay at the Discovery Point Resort, is just one of the many. Rent a Suzuki ($30 per hr., $93 per 4hr.) or a Polaris Quad ($40 per hr., $132 per 4 hr.; both require a $100 deposit) and explore over 10,000 acres of dunes. (☎271-9357. Open M-Sa 8am-7pm, Su 9am-6pm; call for winter hours.)

OTHER ACTIVITIES. Umpqua Lighthouse State Park has an excellent **gray whale viewing** station. The best times to see these massive creatures are during their migrations. They head north in two waves from March through May and south in late December and early January. **Bird watching** is also popular around Reedsport. Lists of species and their seasons are available at the NRA visitors center. Throughout August, the **Crab Bounty Hunt** offers a $3000 reward for catching a particular tagged crab. Traps can be rented in Winchester Bay anytime.

102 ■ THE COAST: US 101

> **EATING RIGHT FOR LONGER LIVING** Each year, over 22,000 gray whales *(Eschrichtius robustus)* migrate northward from their warm winter calving grounds in Mexico to an Arctic summer smorgasbord born of increased energy from the midnight sun. During the 19th century, these whales were hunted almost to extinction. Whalers would kill a calf, wait for its mother to investigate, and then harpoon her, too. Today, gray whales have regained their high population levels so successfully that native groups like the Makah Nation have renewed ceremonial and subsistence whale hunts with international support. The secret of the whales' success might be in their diet. Unlike the slowly rebounding humpbacks, which eat major commercial fish species, the gray whales feed on creatures that would make a human's stomach turn: fish roe, mud shrimp, and crab larvae.

COOS BAY, NORTH BEND, AND CHARLESTON ☎ 541

The largest city on the Oregon Coast, Coos Bay still has the feel of a down-to-earth working town. Nearby North Bend blends into Coos Bay, while tiny Charleston sits peacefully a few miles west on the coast. This is one of the few places on the coast where life slows down as you near the shore, with a string of state parks along the coastline. Coos Bay was also home to Steve Prefontaine, the US Olympian and distance running legend who died in a tragic car accident in his early 20s.

ORIENTATION AND PRACTICAL INFORMATION

US 101 jogs inland south of Coos Bay, rejoining the coast at Bandon. From Coos Bay, **Rte. 42** heads east 85 mi. to **I-5**, and US 101 continues north over the bridge into dune territory. **Coos Bay** and **North Bend** are so close together that one town blends seamlessly into the next, but street numbers start over again at the boundary. US 101 runs along the east side of town, and **Cape Arago Hwy.** runs along the west side, connecting Coos Bay to **Charleston**.

Buses: Greyhound, 275 N Broadway (☎267-4436), Coos Bay. Open M-Th 6:30am-5pm, F-Sa 6:30am-4pm. To **Portland** (6½hr., 4 per day, $30) and **San Francisco, CA** (14hr., 2 per day, $65).

Taxis: Yellow Cab (☎267-3111). $5 anywhere within town, and $1 per mi. outside.

Car Rental: Verger, 1400 Ocean Blvd. (☎888-5594), Coos Bay. Cars from $26, 100 mi. per day free then 20¢ per mi. thereafter. Must be 21 with credit card. Open M-F 8am-5:30pm, Sa 9am-5pm.

Equipment Rental: High Tide Rental, 8073 Cape Arago Hwy. (☎888-3664). Charleston, diagonally across from the Charleston Visitor Center rents every piece of gear necessary to fully enjoy the land and water of Coos Bay. Kayaks $20 for 2hr., bikes $15 per day, and crab pots $8. Open daily 7am-6pm.

Visitor Information: All the following cover the whole area. **Bay Area Chamber of Commerce,** 50 E Central Ave. (☎269-0215 or 800-824-8486), off Commercial Ave., Coos Bay. Open M-F 9am-5pm, Sa 10am-4pm; in summer Su noon-4pm. **North Bend Visitor Center,** 1380 Sherman Ave. (☎756-4613), on US 101, just south of North Bend bridge. Open M-F 8am-5pm, Sa 10am-5pm, Su 12:30-5pm; winter M-F 8am-5pm. **Charleston Visitor Center** (☎888-2311), at Boat Basin Dr. and Cape Arago Hwy. Visitor info with vim and vigor. Open daily May-Sept. 9am-5pm.

Outdoor Information: Oregon State Parks Information, 89814 Cape Arago Hwy. (☎888-8867), Charleston. Open M-F 8am-noon and 1-5pm.

Internet Access: Coos Bay Library, 525 W Anderson St. (☎269-1101), Coos Bay. Free 30min. of Internet access. Open M-W 10am-8pm, Th-F 11am-5:30pm, Sa 11am-5pm.

COOS BAY, NORTH BEND, AND CHARLESTON ■ 103

Laundromat: Wash-A-Lot, 1921 Virginia Ave. (☎756-5439), North Bend. Wash $1.50; dry 25¢ per 6min. Open 24hr.

Emergency: ☎911. **Police:** 500 Central Ave. (☎269-8911), Coos Bay.

Coast Guard: 63450 King Fisher Rd. (☎888-3266), Charleston.

Women's Crisis Line: ☎756-7000. 24hr.

Hospital: Bay Area Hospital, 1775 Thompson Rd. (☎269-8111), Coos Bay.

Post Office: 470 Golden Ave. (☎800-275-8777), at 4th St., Coos Bay. Open M-F 8:30am-5pm. **ZIP Code:** 97420.

ACCOMMODATIONS AND CAMPING

Budget-bound non-campers should bunk at the affordable **Sea Star Hostel**, 23 mi. south on US 101 in **Bandon** (☎347-9632. See p. 104). Campers, rejoice: the nearby state-run and private sites allow full access to the breathtaking coast.

2310 Lombard (☎756-3857), at the corner of Cedar St., North Bend. A tiny home with a beautiful garden. Breakfast from a wonderful hostess. Reservations always recommended. Two twin beds $35; double bed $40.

Bluebill Campground (☎271-3611), off US 101, 3 mi. north of North Bend. Follow the signs to the Horsfall Beach area, then continue down the road to this US Forest Service campground. ½ mi. to the ocean and dunes. Closed in winter. 18 sites, $13.

Sunset Bay State Park, 89814 Cape Arago Hwy. (☎888-4902; reservations 800-452-5687), 12 mi. south of Coos Bay and 3½ mi. west of Charleston. Akin to camping in a well-landscaped parking lot. Fabulous Sunset Beach is worth it. 138 sites, $17; full hookups $20; yurts $27; hiker/biker sites $4.

FOOD

For grocery needs, **Safeway** holds court at 230 E Johnson Ave. off US 101 north, at the southern end of town. (Open daily 6am-1am.)

Blue Heron Bistro, 100 Commercial Ave. (☎267-3933), at the corner of Broadway. Delicious sandwiches, both hot and cold ($8), and handmade dinners with international flavors ranging from Italy to Germany ($9-13). Knock back a glass of Liefmaus Framboise ($5), and call it a meal. Open M-Sa 11am-10pm, Su 5-10pm.

Cheryn's Chowder House (☎888-3251), at the east end of Charleston Bridge. Boats moored beyond the parking lot testify to the freshness of the fish. From grilled shrimp and cheese ($6) and a fish and chips basket ($7) to a bowl of clam chowder ($3.60), it's all fresh and cooked just right. Open daily 7am-9pm; winter 8am-8pm.

Cranberry Sweets, 1005 Newmark St. (☎888-9824), Coos Bay. This far-from-average candy factory serves up enough samples of ambitious ventures like beer squares and cheddar cheese fudge to make lunch moot. Open M-Sa 9am-6pm, Su 11am-4pm.

SIGHTS AND EVENTS

Four miles south of Charleston up Seven Devils Rd., the ■**South Slough National Estuarine Research Reserve** is one of the most fascinating and under-appreciated venues on the central coast. Spreading out from a small interpretive visitors center, almost 7 sq. mi. of salt- and freshwater estuaries nurture all kinds of wildlife, from sand shrimp to blue herons to deer. Hiking trails weave through the sanctuary, and free guided walks leave from the center. (☎888-5558; www.southsloughestuary.com. Open June-Aug. daily 8:30am-4:30pm; Sept.-May M-F 8:30am-4:30pm. Trails open year round dawn-dusk.) Inland 24½ mi. from Coos Bay, at **Golden and Silver Falls State Park,** three trails lead to the awesome Golden Falls, a 210 ft. drop into the abyss, and the beautiful Silver Falls, thin sheets of water cascading down a rock face. From Coos Bay, take the Eastside-Allegany Exit off US 101, and follow it along a narrow, gravel road.

For two weeks in mid-July, Coos Bay plays host to the **Oregon Coast Music Festival** (☎ 267-0938), the most popular summer music event on the coast. A week of jazz, blues, and folk (tickets $6-10) is followed by a week of performances by the renowned festival orchestra ($12-17). Art exhibits, vessel tours, and a free classical concert in Mingus Park spice up the festival even for the ticketless. In September, Oregon remembers one of its favorite native sons in the **Steve Prefontaine 10K Memorial Run** named after the great Olympic athlete who died in an automobile accident. The race draws world-class runners. (☎ 269-1103. Entrance fee $14-17.)

OUTDOOR ACTIVITIES

Sunset Bay, 11½ mi. from Coos Bay on Cape Arago State Hwy., has been rated one of the top 10 American beaches. Sheltered from the waves by two pincer-like cliffs, the warm, shallow bay is perfect for **swimming.** The magnificent **Shore Acres State Park** rests a mile beyond Sunset Bay on the Cape Arago Hwy. (☎ 503-888-3732. Open daily 8am-9pm; winter 8am-dusk. $4 per car. Wheelchair accessible.) Once the estate of local lumber lord Louis J. Simpson, the park contains elaborate botanical gardens that outlasted the mansion and a short trail to peaceful Simpson Beach. Come December, the rose garden is festooned with 200,000 lights, and the park serves free hot drinks. At the south end of the hwy. is breezy **Cape Arago,** notable for the rich life of its tide pools. Paved paths lead out toward the tip of the cape and provide an excellent view of Shell Island, a quarter-mile offshore, which is a protected elephant and harbor seal rookery. Fishing enthusiasts can hop on board with **Bob's Sportfishing,** operating out of a small building at the west end of the Charleston Boat Basin, where they can by one day fishing licenses for $8. (☎ 888-4241 or 800-628-9633. 6hr. rock fishing trip $60 March to mid-May; 5hr. salmon fishing trip $55 mid-May to Sept.)

BANDON ☎ 541

Despite a steady flow of tourists in the summer, the small fishing town of Bandon-by-the-Sea has refrained from breaking out the pastels and making itself up like an amusement park. A fine hostel and a number of outdoor activities make Bandon a worthwhile stop on a tour of the coast.

PRACTICAL INFORMATION. Bandon is 24 mi. south of Coos Bay and 27 mi. north of Port Orford on US 101. **Greyhound** (☎ 800-231-2222) departs the hostel (see below) for **Portland** (7¼hr., 11am, $34) and for **San Francisco, CA** (13hr., 4:40am and 4:20pm, $63.50). The **visitors center** is at 300 SE 2nd St., in the Old Town next to US 101. (☎ 347-9616. Open daily 10am-5pm; winter 10am-4pm.) **Post office:** 105 12th St. SE (☎ 800-275-8777). Open M-F 8:30am-4:30pm. **ZIP Code:** 97411.

ACCOMMODATIONS AND FOOD. Bandon's rambling ■**Sea Star Hostel (HI),** 375 2nd St., on the right as you enter Old Town from the north, is a laid-back installment in the HI series. A noon check-out and open-24-hours policy make for a relaxed place to pass the night. (☎ 347-9632. Kitchen, laundry. $13, nonmembers $16. Family rooms for 2, members $28, nonmembers $34. Guest house $40-95.) The beautiful Mediterranean exterior of the **Bandon Wayside Motel,** on Rte. 42 south, just off US 101, gives way to small rooms with cable. (☎ 347-3421. Singles $32; doubles $36.) Two miles north of town and across the bridge, **Bullard's Beach State Park** houses the **Coquille River Lighthouse,** built in 1896. (☎ 347-2209. 185 sites, $19; yurts $27; hiker/biker sites $4 per person.)

For a tasty and healthy morsel, step into **Mother's Natural Grocery and Deli,** 975 US 101, near the junction with Rte. 42 south, where you can have a piece of homemade quiche ($3.50) or a plate of vegan tamales ($4.25) after the shopping is done. (☎ 347-4086. Open M-Sa 10am-6pm.) The best seafood is at **Bandon Boatworks,** 275 Lincoln St. SW, through Old Town and South Jetty Rd. Lunches ($6-9) are more affordable than dinners ($12-22), when the Boatworks breaks out the wine glasses. (☎ 347-2111. Open M-Sa 11:30am-9pm, Su 11am-8:30pm; winter closed M.)

◎ SIGHTS AND EVENTS. The **West Coast Game Park,** 7 mi. south of Bandon on US 101, is home to a variety of wildlife. (☎347-3106. Open daily 9am-7pm; winter 9am-5pm. $9, over 60 $8, ages 7-12 $7, ages 2-6 $5.) A stroll around **Old Town** is pleasant, as is exploring the beach on a horse from **Bandon Beach Riding Stables.** (☎347-3423. $25 for 1hr.) The well-marked beach loop road that leaves from Old Town and joins US 101 5 mi. south passes **Table Rock, Elephant Rock,** and **Face Rock,** three of the coast's most striking offshore outcroppings. Known as the "Cranberry Capital of Oregon," Bandon celebrates the fall harvest with the **Cranberry Festival** (☎347-9616) parade and food fair in the second weekend of September

Between Bandon and Brookings, the best deals for the weary traveler are two campgrounds near Port Orford that offer access to the shore. **Cape Blanco State Park,** 4 mi. north of Port Orford and 5 mi. west of US 101, nestles in a grove of pines just south of the cape and its lighthouse. (☎332-6774. 54 sites with water and electricity, $18: hiker/biker $4.) Six miles south of Port Orford, **Humbug Mountain State Park,** has 101 tightly packed sites. (☎332-6774. Showers and toilets. Tents $16; water and electricity $18; hiker/biker sites $4; 4 cabins $35 per night.)

BROOKINGS ☎541

Brookings is the southernmost stop on US 101 before California and one of the few coastal towns that remain relatively tourist-free. Here, hardware stores are easier to find than trinket shops, and the beaches are among Oregon's most unspoiled. The city also sits in Oregon's "banana belt" (a.k.a. California's "arctic circle"): warm weather is not rare in January, and some Brookings backyards even boast scraggly palm trees. For exhaustive coverage of all that is hot and cool down south, consult *Let's Go: California 2002.*

🛈 PRACTICAL INFORMATION. US 101 is called Chetco Ave. in town. Strictly speaking, there are two towns here, separated by the **Chetco River**—Brookings to the north and **Harbor** to the south—which share everything and are referred to as Brookings Harbor. The **Greyhound** station is at 601 Railroad Ave., at Tanbark. (☎469-3326. Open M-F 8:45am-noon and 4-6:30pm, Sa 8:45am-noon.) Two buses per day run to **Portland** (9hr., $46) and **San Francisco, CA** (12hr., $53). The **Brookings Welcome Center,** 1650 US 101, welcomes from just north of town. (☎469-4117. Open May-Sept. M-Sa 8am-6pm, Su 9am-5pm; Apr. and Oct. M-Sa 8am-5pm, Su 9am-5pm.) The **Chamber of Commerce,** 16330 Lower Harbor Rd., is across the bridge to the south. (☎469-3181 or 800-535-9469. Open M-F 9am-5pm, Sa 9:30am-1pm; winter closed Sa.) The **Chetco Ranger Station,** 555 5th St., distributes info on the **Siskiyou National Forest.** (☎469-2196. Open M-F 8am-4:30pm.) Clean up at **Econ-o-Wash,** next door to the Westward Motel on Chetco Ave. (Wash $1.25, dry 25¢ per 7½min. Open daily 7:30am-10pm, last wash 9pm.) Rent a wetsuit and boogie board for $14 at **Escape Hatch,** 642 Railroad Ave. (☎469-2914. Open M-F 10am-5:30pm, Sa 10am-5pm.) Free 1hr. of **Internet access** at the **library,** 405 Alder. (☎469-7738. Open M and F 10am-6pm; Tu and Th 10am-7pm; W 10am-8pm, Sa 10am-5pm.) Also at **Java Java,** 612 Chetco Ave., for $5 per hr. (☎412-7444. Open M-F 7am-4pm, Sa 9am-4pm.) **Post office:** 711 Spruce St. (☎800-275-8777). Open M-F 9am-4:30pm. **ZIP Code:** 97415.

🏨🍴 ACCOMMODATIONS AND FOOD. The Bonn Motel, 1216 US 101, has recently refurbished buildings and a heated indoor pool. (☎469-2161. Singles $48, doubles $56; less in winter.) **Harris Beach State Park Campground,** at the north edge of Brookings, has 63 tent sites set back in the trees. (☎469-2021 or 800-452-5687. Showers, laundry. Sites $17; full hookups $20; hiker/biker sites $4; yurts $28.) For campsites off the beaten path, travel 15 mi. east of Brookings on North Bank Rd. to the charming **Little Redwood Campground,** alongside a salamander-filled creek. (Drinking water and pit toilet. 12 sites. $10.) **Redwood Bar** (drinking water), across the way, charges $5. Contact the Chetco Ranger Station for info (☎469-2196.)

A half-sandwich and a cup of excellent soup or chili goes for $4.50 at the **Homeport Bagel Shop,** 1011 Chetco Ave. (☎469-6611. Open M-F 7am-5pm.) A number of seafood spots can be found near the harbor. The locals' favorite is **Oceanside Diner,** 16403 Lower Harbor Rd. (☎469-7971. Open daily 4am-3pm.)

◉ ⚠ SIGHTS AND OUTDOOR ACTIVITIES. Brookings is known statewide for its flowers. In downtown's **Azalea Park,** large some more than 300 years old, azaleas encircle pristine lawns and bloom from April to June. The pride of Brookings is its **Azalea Festival** (☎469-3181), held in Azalea Park over Memorial Day weekend. The **Chetco Valley Historical Society Museum,** 15461 Museum Rd., 2½ mi. south of the Chetco River, has exhibits on the patchwork quilts of settlers and Native American basketwork. (☎469-6651. Open May-Sept. W-Su noon-5pm; Oct.-Apr. F-Su noon-5pm. Donations welcome.) The museum is hard to miss; look for the largest Monterey cypress tree in Oregon out front. **Boardman State Park** enfolds US 101 north of Brookings, overlooking the beach for 8 mi. and housing a series of picnic sites. Thirty miles north of Brookings in **Gold Beach,** you can ride a boat up the **Rogue River. Mail Boat Hydro-Jets,** 94294 Rogue River Rd., offers 64, 80, and 104 mi., 6-7hr. whitewater daytrips. (☎247-7033 or 800-458-3511. May-Oct. $30-75.)

INLAND VALLEYS

While jagged cliffs and gleaming surf draw tourists to the coast, many Oregonians opt for the inland Willamette and Rogue River Valleys for their vacations. Vast tracts of fertile land support agriculture and a burgeoning wine industry, and for decades the immense forests maintained a healthy timber industry. Since the fortunes of logging are now uncertain, tourism has become the industry of choice in small-town Oregon. With festivals galore, Ashland, Eugene, Corvallis, and Salem all attract their fair share of visitors.

SALEM ☎ 503

The home of Willamette University and the third-largest urban center in Oregon, Salem gives off the vibes of a much smaller city. Boasting fine museums, several renowned wineries, and attractions like the Oregon State Fair, Salem draws its throngs of visitors, though it's hardly a hopping inland tourist destination.

▣ TRANSPORTATION

Salem is 51 mi. south of **Portland** and 64 mi. north of **Eugene** on **I-5. Willamette University** and the **capitol building** dominate the center of the city, and the nearby shops anchor the heart of downtown. To reach downtown, take Exit 253 off I-5. Street addresses are divided into quadrants: the **Willamette River** divides east from west. East of the river, **State St.** divides SE from NE.

- **Trains: Amtrak,** 500 13th St. SE (☎588-1551 or 800-872-7245), across from the visitors center. Open daily 6:15am-7pm. To **Portland** (1½hr., 2 per day, $8-15); **Seattle** (5-7hr., 2 per day, $27-46); and **San Francisco, CA** (17hr., 1 per day, $76-120).
- **Buses: Greyhound,** 450 Church St. NE (☎362-2428), at Center St. Station. Open daily 6am-8:30pm. Lockers $1 per day. To **Portland** (1½hr., 9 per day, $7-8); **Eugene** (1½-2hr., 10 per day, $10-11); and **Seattle, WA** (6hr., 8 per day, $26-28).
- **Local Transportation: Cherriots Customer Service Office,** 183 High St. NE (☎588-2877), provides bus maps and monthly passes. Routes leave from High St., between State and Court St., in front of courthouse. All buses have bike racks on them. Adults 75¢; over 60 and disabled 35¢; under 19 50¢. Every hr. M-F 6am-9pm, Sa 7am-9pm.
- **Taxis: Salem Yellow Cab Co.** (☎362-2411). $2.20 base, $1.80 per mi.
- **AAA:** 2909 Ryan Dr. NE (☎861-3118 or 800-962-5855). Open M-F 8am-5pm.

PRACTICAL INFORMATION

Visitor Information: 1313 Mill St. SE (☎ 581-4325 or 800-874-7012; www.scva.org), in the Mission Mill Museum complex. Open M-F 8:30am-5pm, Sa 10am-4pm.

Internet Access: Salem Public Library, 585 Liberty St. SE (☎ 588-6315). Free Internet access on 15 computers. A wealth of metered parking available in the garage next door. Open June-Aug. Tu-Th 10am-9pm, F-Sa 10am-6pm; Sept.-May also open Su 1-5pm.

Laundromat: 11:05 Suds City Depoe, 1785 Lancaster Dr. NE (☎ 362-9845), at Market St. Snack bar, and big-screen TV. Wash $1, dry 25¢ per 15min. Open daily 7:30am-9pm.

Lancaster Self-Service Laundry, 2195 Lancaster Dr. NE, next to Bi-Mart. Wash 18 lb. for $1.75, or 50 lb. for $4.25. Dry 25¢ per 10min. Open daily 8am-10pm, last load at 9pm.

Emergency: ☎ 911.

Police: 555 Liberty St. SE (☎ 588-6123), in City Hall room 130.

24hr. Crisis Line: ☎ 581-5535. **24hr. Women's Crisis Line:** ☎ 399-7722.

Hospital: Salem Hospital, 665 Winter St. SE (☎ 561-5200).

Post Office: 1050 25th St. SE (☎ 800-275-8777). Open M-F 8am-5:30pm. **ZIP Code:** 97301.

ACCOMMODATIONS AND CAMPING

The visitors center has a list of B&Bs, which provide a comfortable and often classy setting (from $45). A number of cheaper hotels line Lancaster Dr. along the length of I-5, and camping options within a reasonable distance are also available; inquire at the visitors center for a list of the best.

Silver Falls State Park, 20024 Silver Falls Hwy. Rte. 214 (☎ 873-8681; reservations ☎ 800-452-5687). Take Rte. 22 (Mission St.) east for 5 mi., then take the exit for Rte. 214 N (Silver Falls Rd.), and follow it for about 18 mi. Warm showers, toilets, water. Day hikes to 10 waterfalls and volcanic caves, and vistas of the Willamette River Valley. Wheelchair accessible. 60 tent sites, $16. 44 RV hookups, $20. 14 cabins $35.

Alden House Bed and Breakfast, 760 Church St. (☎ 363-9574 or 877-363-9573). Choose from 6 theme rooms (romantic, cowboy), all of which have a TV/VCR and private baths. Breakfast in the elegant dining room at 9am. Reservations advised. $45-65.

Cozzzy Inn, 1875 Fisher Rd. NE (☎ 588-5423). Take I-5 Exit 256 to Lancaster Dr., then to Sunnyview to Fisher Rd. Comfortable rooms, bargain prices. Singles $35, double $38.

FOOD

Busy Lancaster Dr. (just east and parallel to I-5) woos burger lovers into the wee hours (most are restaurants at 900 SE block). Aisle upon aisle of grocery goodness awaits at **Roth's,** 702 Lancaster Dr. NE. (☎ 585-5770. Open daily 6am-11pm.) Hit the **Farmer's Market** at the corner of Marion and Summer St., for local produce and crafts. (☎ 585-8264. Open Sa 9am-3pm.)

La Hacienda Real, 3690 SE Commercial (☎ 540-5537), serves up Mexican specialties in large quantities ($5-15). Fresh-made tortillas ($3 per dozen) and generous lunch specials ($5-7). Open Su-Th 11am-10pm, F-Sa 11am-11pm.

Off-Center Cafe, 1741 Center St. NE (☎ 363-9245). Colorfully named breakfasts such as Green Chile Tortoise ($6.25), are enormously satisfying. Standard dinner fare. Open Tu-F 7am-2:30pm, Th-Sa 6-9pm for dinner, Sa-Su 8am-2pm for brunch.

Fuji Rice Time, 159 High St. SE (☎ 364-5512), serves traditional Japanese food to the local lunch crowd, who enjoy watching the chef at work in the sushi bar ($4-6). Tempting yaki-soba ($5.25). Open M-F 11am-2:30pm and 5-9pm, Sa 4-9pm.

Arbor Cafe, 380 High St. NE (☎ 588-2353), offers up a wide range of espresso and teas ($1-3), as well as delicious pastries ($1-2) for breakfast; paninis and sandwiches for lunch and dinner ($4-6). Open M-Th 7:30am-9pm, F-Sa 7:30am-10pm.

SIGHTS AND ENTERTAINMENT

STATE CAPITOL. The gigantic marble exterior topped by a 23 ft. gilt-gold statue of the "Oregon Pioneer," is located in the heart of Salem. In summer, a free tour to the top of the rotunda leaves every 30min., and tours of the various chambers leave every hour; call for off-season tours. *(900 Court St. NE. Bounded by Court St. to the north, Waverly St. to the east, State St. to the south, and Cottage St. to the west.* ☎ *986-1388. Open M-F 7:30am-5:30pm, Sa 9am-4pm, Su noon-4pm.)*

OREGON STATE FAIR. Salem celebrates the end of summer in the 12 days leading up to Labor Day with the annual Oregon State Fair. With a whirl of livestock shows and baking contests, country-folk invade the city and transform it from a picture of complacent suburbia to a barnyard celebration. *(2330 17th St. NE. At the Expo Center.* ☎ *947-3247 or 800-833-0011; www.fair.state.or.us. Open Su-Th 10am-10pm, F-Sa 10am-11pm. $6-7, seniors $3-5, ages 6-12 $2-4.)*

SALEM ART FAIR AND FESTIVAL. During the third weekend of July, the Salem Art Association hosts the free **Salem Art Fair and Festival** in Bush's Pasture Park. While the food booths do brisk business and the local wineries pour from their most recent vintage, the artsy and crafty display their wares as bands strum away the afternoon. The visitors center has info on the fair and on local **wineries.**

SALEM CINEMA. This single screen theater offers relief from the sports-cum-tropical-themed bar scene with its indie film selection. *(Pringle Plaza, 445 High St. SE* ☎ *378-7676; www.salemcinema.com. $7, students $5.50, seniors and 12 and under $4, bargain matinees $4.)*

CORVALLIS ☎ 541

Unlike so many Oregon towns, this peaceful residential community in the central Willamette Valley has no historic pretensions. Covered in black and orange for nine months, the colors of the local university Oregon State (OSU), Corvallis is at heart a college town. Also boasting a gigantic Hewlett-Packard facility, Corvallis keeps pace with the technological world. Life bustles downtown all year, but like any college town, Corvallis mellows in the summer, hosting a few choice festivals and some outdoor exploration in the nearby Willamette and Deschuetes National Forests. Corvallis makes a nice stop on the way to bigger, better places.

ORIENTATION AND PRACTICAL INFORMATION. Corvallis is laid out in a checkerboard fashion that quickly degenerates outside the downtown area; numbered streets run north-south and streets named for lesser-known American presidents (Van Buren, Polk, Buchanan) run east-west. **Rte. 99 W** splits in town and becomes two one-way streets: northbound **3rd St.** and southbound **4th St. 2nd St.** becomes US 20 north of town and leads to Albany and I-5.

Greyhound, 153 4th St. NW runs to: **Portland** (2½hr., 6 per day, $15); **Seattle, WA** (7hr., 6 per day, $28); **Newport** (7½hr., 2 per day, $12); **Eugene** (1hr., 4 per day, $8). Lockers $1 per day. (☎757-1797 or 800-231-2222. Open M-F 6am-1pm and 2-6pm, Sa-Su 7am-1pm.) **Corvallis Transit System** runs public transit. Fare 50¢. Service M-F 6:30am-7pm, Sa 9:30am-4:30pm. **A-1 Taxi** (☎754-1111). $2 per mi., $7 minimum. 24hr. **Chamber of Commerce** (☎757-1505) and **Convention and Visitor Bureau** (☎757-1544 or 800-334-8118; www.visitcorvallis.com), are both at 420 2nd St. NW, the first right past the bridge coming from the east. The visitor bureau sells a detailed $2 map of Corvallis and Albany, and provides an excellent map of the bike trails in the area for free. Both open M-F 8am-5pm. **Oregon State University** (☎737-0123; events info 737-6445) has its main entrance and info booth at Jefferson and 14th St. Booth open M-F 8am-5pm. **Peak Sports,** 129 2nd St. NW (☎754-6444), sells trail maps ($2-10) and rents mountain bikes ($25 for first day, $15 each day after). Open M-Th and Sa 9am-6pm, F 9am-8pm, Su noon-5pm. **Corvallis Public Library,** 645 Monroe St. NW, offers free Internet access, 1hr. max. (☎757-6926. Open M-F 9am-9pm, Sa 9am-6pm, Su noon-6pm.) **Campbell's Laundry,** 1120 9th St. NW, offers wash $1.25, dry 25¢ per 10min. (☎752-3794. Open daily 6am-1am. Adjoining coffee shop with TV.) **Emergency:** ☎911. **Police:** 180 5th St. NW (☎757-6924). **Medical Services: Corvallis Clinic,** 3680 Samaritan Dr. NW. (☎754-1150; walk-in service ☎754-1282). Take 9th St. north from downtown. Open M-F 8am-8pm, Sa-Su 10am-5pm. **Post Office:** 311 2nd St. SW. Open M-F 8am-5:30pm, Sa 9am-4pm. **ZIP Code:** 97333.

ACCOMMODATIONS. The few campgrounds in and around Corvallis are not the RV mini-cities of their counterparts up and down Western Oregon. The few motels are reasonably priced, but occasionally fill during important college weekends or for conventions. The **Budget Inn Motel,** 1480 SW 3rd St., has decently sized rooms for undersized prices. (☎752-8756. Fridges, A/C, TV with cable. Kitchenettes $4 extra. Singles $34; doubles $38.) Small, pleasant sites in sight of tractors and cow barns are available at **Benton County Fairgrounds,** 110 53rd St. SW. Follow Rte. 34 W, then left onto 53rd St., or take the Rte. 3 CTS bus. (☎757-1521. Closed mid-July to early Aug. for the fair. Sites $12; hookups $15.) Then there's **EconoLodge,** 345 2nd St. NW, right off US 20. A clean, non-descript manifestation of the mega-chain. (☎752-9601. Laundry; $1 wash, dry 25¢ for 15 min. Singles $42; doubles $48.)

FOOD AND NIGHTLIFE. Corvallis has a smattering of collegiate pizza parlors, noodle shops, and Mexican-like food. OSU students prowl Monroe Ave. for cheap filling grub. **First Alternative Inc.,** 1007 3rd St. SE, is a co-op stocked with a range of well-priced, natural products. (☎753-3115. Open daily 9am-9pm.) **Safeway,** 450 3rd St. SW, offers everyone a place to grocery shop. (☎753-5502. Open daily 6am-2am). Though sporting the requisite adobe and neon facade, **Bombs Away Cafe,** 2527 Monroe St. NW, is not your typical Mexican eatery. A self-proclaimed "funky taqueria," it serves up Mexican entrees from sopitos ($6) to the $7 "Wet Burrito." (☎757-7221. Open M-F 11am-midnight, Sa 5pm-midnight, Su 5-10pm. 21+ after 10pm.) At **Nearly Normal's,** 109 15th St. NW, purple cottage turned veggie-haven with masses of flowers and hanging plants which whet the appetite for the low-price ($4-8) vegetarian options with large portions. (☎753-0791. Open M-F 8am-9pm, Sa 9am-9pm.) **McMenamins,** 420 3rd St. NW, has by far the best pub fare in town. Have a sandwich ($5-7), or a specialty like Rockin' Randy's Red Wine Beef Stew ($7.50). Try a taster of 6 hand-brewed ales. (☎758-6044. Open M-Sa 11am-1am, Su noon-midnight.) After hours try **La Conga,** 360 NW 5th St., the only place in Corvallis open when the bars close. Chicken, beef, or fish tacos $1.50, burritos $3-5. (☎757-2441. Open 24hr.) If college beer bashes are your thing, find your way to the University frat houses. For the more musically oriented, the **KBBR concert line** (☎737-3737) lists concerts.

ENTERTAINMENT. Corvallis gets kickin' the third weekend of July, when Oregonians gather to celebrate Leonardo da Vinci's contributions to art, science, and technology in the **Da Vinci Days Festival.** Renaissance men and women compete in the 10th **Kinetic Sculpture Race,** in which people-powered, all-terrain works of art vie for a crown, and everyone joins in the fun of the Sidewalk Chalk Art Competition. (☎800-334-8118; www.davinci-days.org. $7 per day, under 13 $4; all 3 days $11, under 13 is $6.)

While not as large as Da Vinci Days, the **Fall Festival,** held the third weekend in September in Central Park, combines food, music, and an excellent crafts fair together into a raucous, family-friendly event. Contact the Visitor Bureau for more information (see **Practical Information** above.) Ten miles east in **Albany** (off US 20 before I-5), the **River Rhythms** concert series attracts thousands each Thursday night from mid-July through August for free music in the picturesque Monteith River Park. Musical acts vary from bluegrass to candy-coated pop. Each week in July, a special Monday night show features local performers. Call the **Albany Visitor Center** for more info. (☎928-0911. Open M-F 9am-5pm, Sa 9am-3pm, Su 10am-2pm.)

110 ■ INLAND VALLEYS

MOUNTAIN BIKING. Mountain biking is a way of life in Corvallis, and all roads seem to lead to one bike trail or another. In fact, almost any point within the city can be reached by bike within 15min. A map of the trails around Corvallis can be found at the visitor bureau (see **Practical Information,** above). Those searching for a hard-core mountain biking experience, however, would be better served in the Willamette or Deschutes National Forests near **Sisters.**

Oregon State University's McDonald Forest. Go west out of town on Harrison for 4½ mi., then turn right on Oak Creek Rd. until the pavement dead-ends at OSU's lab. Over 10 mi. worth of trails cover the forest from the lab, and although mostly flat, they provide a nice afternoon of fairly unchallenging riding.

Chip Ross Park. North on 3rd St., then left on Circle Blvd., and right on Highland. After 1 mi., look left on Lester Ave. for a tiny blue sign. On a clear day, the trails here offer splendid views of the Cascade Valley. Maps for this park and other biking destinations are available at **Peak Sports** ($5; see **Practical Information,** above).

EUGENE ☎ 541

The home of the University of Oregon, and known as the track capital of the USA due to legends such as Coach Bowerman (inventor of the artificial track) and his runner Steve Prefontaine, Eugene takes due credit for its role in the running revolution of the 80s. Fitness enthusiasts flock to this running mecca, which is also the original hometown of Nike, Inc. (now based in Beaverton). Home to both a biking revolution and an active hippie movement, which celebrates itself each year during the Oregon Country Fair, Eugene has also earned itself a liberal reputation.

TRANSPORTATION

Eugene is 111 mi. south of **Portland** on **I-5,** just west of **Springfield. Franklin Blvd.,** also known as Rte. 129 and Rte. 99, runs from I-5 to the city center. East-west streets are numbered beginning at Willamette St. **Hwy. 99** splits in town—**6th Ave.** runs west and **7th Ave.** goes east. The **pedestrian mall** is downtown, on Broadway between Charnelton and Oak St. Eugene's main student drag, **13th Ave.,** leads to the **University of Oregon (U of O),** in the southeast of town. The city is a motorist's nightmare of one-way streets, and virtually none of the little parking available downtown is free. The most convenient way to get around is by bike—every street has at least one bike lane, and the city is quite flat. Most city **parks** are officially open from 6am to 11pm. The **Whittaker,** around Blair Blvd. near 6th Ave., has higher crime levels and may be unsafe at night.

Trains: Amtrak, 433 Willamette St. (☎687-1383 or 800-872-7245), at 4th Ave. Baggage storage $1.50 per item per day. Open daily 5:15am-7pm. To **Seattle, WA** (6-8hr., 2 per day, $31-58); **Portland** (2½-3hr., 2 per day, $15-27).

Buses: Greyhound, 987 Pearl St. (☎344-6265 or 800-231-2222), at 10th Ave. Open daily 6:15am-9:35pm. Lockers $1 per day for passengers. To **Seattle, WA** (6-9hr., 9 per day, $31); **Portland** (2-4hr., 9 per day, $13).

Public Transportation: Lane Transit District (LTD; ☎687-5555). **Maps** and timetables at the LTD Service Center at 11th Ave. and Willamette St. Runs M-F 6am-11:40pm, Sa 7:30am-11:40pm, Su 8:30am-8:30pm. Wheelchair accessible, and bike rack equipped. $1; seniors and 18 and under 50¢.

Taxis: Yellow Cab, ☎746-1234. $2 base, $2 per mi. 24hr.

Car Rental: Enterprise Rent-a-Car, 810 W 6th Ave. (☎344-2020). $33 per day; unlimited mileage within OR. Out-of-state 25¢ per mi. over 200 mi daily. Will beat any competitor's price. 10% county tax. Must be 21. Credit card required for out-of-town customers. Open M-F 7:30am-6pm, Sa 9am-noon.

AAA: 983 Willagillespie Rd. (☎484-0661), near Valley River Center Mall, 2 mi. north of the U of O campus. Open M-F 8am-5pm.

EUGENE ■ 111

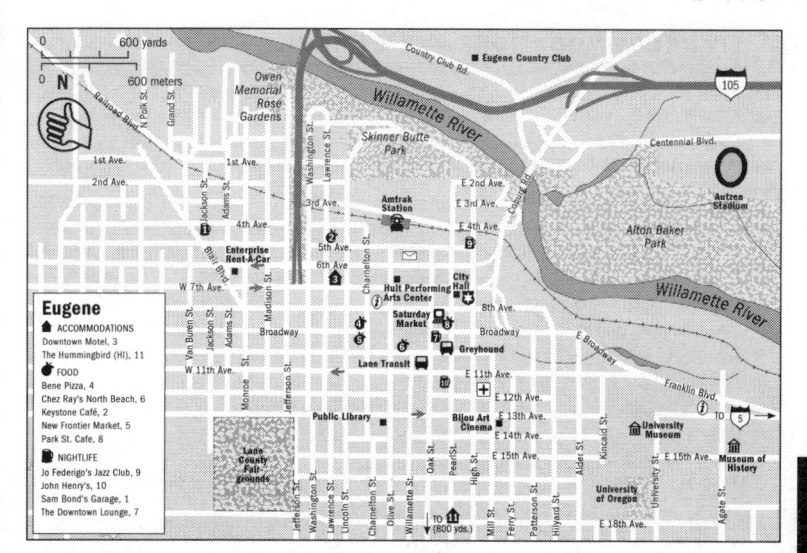

Eugene

ACCOMMODATIONS
Downtown Motel, 3
The Hummingbird (HI), 11

FOOD
Bene Pizza, 4
Chez Ray's North Beach, 6
Keystone Café, 2
New Frontier Market, 5
Park St. Cafe, 8

NIGHTLIFE
Jo Federigo's Jazz Club, 9
John Henry's, 10
Sam Bond's Garage, 1
The Downtown Lounge, 7

PRACTICAL INFORMATION

Visitor Information: 115 W 8th Ave. #190 (☎484-5307 or 800-547-5445; www.visitlanecounty.org.), but the door is on Olive St. Courtesy phone. Sells an indexed **map** for $4, or ask for an equally good free one. The friendly staff will be happy to assist you with anything you ever wanted to know about Eugene. Open May-Aug. M-F 8:30am-5pm, Sa-Su 10am-4pm; Sept.-Apr. M-Sa 8:30am-5pm.

University of Oregon Switchboard, in the Rainier Building at 1244 Walnut St. (☎346-3111). Great info on anything, from rides to housing to directions. Open M-F 7am-6pm.

Outdoor Information: Willamette National Forest, 211 E 7th Ave. (☎465-6521), in the Federal Building. Map $6. Open M-F 8am-4:30pm.

Equipment Rental: Paul's Bicycle Way of Life, 152 W 5th Ave. (☎344-4105). Friendly staff. City bikes $12 per day, $60 for a week. Open M-F 9am-7pm, Sa-Su 10am-5pm. Also at 2480 Alder St. (☎342-6155) and 2580 Willakenzie (☎344-4150). **High Street Bicycles,** 535 High St. (☎687-1775), downtown. Mountain bikes $20 per day. Open M-Sa 9am-5:30pm, Su 10am-5pm. Credit card required.

Internet Access: Eugene Public Library, 100 W 13th Ave. (☎682-5450) at Olive St. 1hr. free, 3 times per week. Be prepared to wait. Internet room with 8 more computers is open M-Tu 2pm-7pm, W-Sa 2pm-5pm. **CS Internet Cafe,** 747 Willamette Ave. (☎345-0408). First 15 min. of Internet access is $2, $7.20 per hour. Open M-F 8am-5pm

Laundromat: Express-o-Wash, 595 E 13th Ave. (☎343-3240), at Patterson. Big-screen TV, video games, espresso bar, and tanning facilities. Wash $1, dry 25¢ per 10min. Detergent 50¢. Open daily 6am-11pm; last load 9:30pm.

Emergency: ☎911. **Police:** 777 Pearl St. #107 (☎682-5111), at City Hall.

Medical Services: White Bird Clinic, 341 E 12th Ave. (☎800-422-7558). Free 24hr. crisis counseling. Low-cost medical care at the clinic's **medical center,** 1400 Mill St. Open M and W-F 9am-12:30pm, by appt. only 12:30-5pm.

Post Office: 520 Willamette St. (☎800-275-8777), at 5th Ave. Open M-F 8:30am-5:30pm, Sa 10am-2pm. **ZIP Code:** 97401.

ACCOMMODATIONS AND CAMPING

A choice hostel, inexpensive hotels, and accessible campgrounds make Eugene particularly budget friendly. Ask at the visitors center for directions to the cheap hotel chains scattered about the town. Farther east on Rte. 58 and 126, the immense **Willamette National Forest** is also packed with campsites (drinking water, $6-16; without water, usually free).

The Hummingbird Eugene International Hostel (HI), 2352 Willamette St. (☎349-0589). Take Bus #24 or 25 from downtown; get off at 24th Ave. and Willamette. A wooden fence guards this home-turned-hostel, which is set back from the street. A bookshelf-lined living room with TV and stereo complements the lovely backyard garden. Check-in 5-10pm. Check-out at 10am. Lockout 11am-5pm. Kitchen open 7:30-9:30am and 5-10pm. Cash or traveler's check only. Members and students $16, non-members $18; private rooms from $39.

Pine Meadows (☎942-8657 or 877-444-6777). Take I-5 South to Exit 172, then head 3½ mi. south, turn left on Cottage Grove Reservoir Rd., and go another 2½ mi. Alongside a reservoir with plenty of RV and jet ski traffic. Showers, toilets. Open just before Memorial Day to Labor Day. 92 sites $12. 15 primitive sites ¼ mi. down the road, $6.

Schwarz Park (☎942-1418 or 877-444-6777), off Exit 174 (I-5 S), about 15min. south of Eugene. Go straight down the off-ramp and left at the first traffic light, then go past the village green for about 5½ mi. The camp lies below beautiful and swimmable Dorena Lake. Flat and quiet. Showers, toilets, and water. 82 sites, $10.

Downtown Motel, 361 W 7th Ave. (☎345-8739 or 800-648-4366), located near downtown and the highway, but still quiet and peaceful. Cable TV, fridges, and free sweets. Strong coffee in the morning. Reserve early by credit card. Singles $35; doubles $42.

FOOD

Eugene offers those on a budget ample opportunity to enjoy the local cuisine. The student hang-out zone at 13th Ave. and Kincaid has cheap grab-and-go options. The **New Frontier Market, with the Broadway Bistro and Wine Bar,** at 200 W Broadway at Charnelton (☎685-0790) is an organic store that also features an amazing wine bar and take-out lunch counter. For groceries, head to **Safeway,** 145 E 18th Ave. at Oak. (☎485-3664. Open daily 6am-2am.)

Keystone Cafe, 395 W 5th St. (☎342-2075). For 22 years, the creative menu and entirely organic ingredients have given diners a true taste of Eugene. A small kitchen and crowds of devotees make for slow service, but all will be forgiven after a mouthful of their famous pancakes ($3.25). A host of vegan and vegetarian options is available. Breakfast served all day ($3-7). Open daily 7am-5pm.

Bene Gourmet Pizza, 225 W Broadway Ave. (☎284-2700) This simple yet elegant cafe serves a wide range of truly gourmet pizzas, from the basic to a pie with turkey sausages, roasted peppers, and roasted hazelnuts ($12-17). A pizza slice, salad, and drink is the $6.50 lunch special. Open M-Th 11am-9pm, F 11am-10pm, Sa-Su 4-10pm.

Park St. Cafe, 776 W Park (☎485-2089). Look for the sign as the restaurant is off the street in a knot of shops. Delicious breakfasts, from "eggs and things" to oatmeal ($2.50-6), and sandwiches for lunch ($7). 3-4 daily lunch specials, such as kebabs or chicken pot pies ($7). Open M-F 9am-3pm.

Chez Ray's North Beach, 44 W 10th Ave. (☎344-1530). Dine among tie-dyed bar stools. Breakfast all day runs $6-8, and Chez Ray's world famous-salmon burger is $6.50. Dinner specials soar to $18.50, but reasonable options persist (burgers $6-9). A wide range of live entertainment every night. Open Su-F 9am-11pm, Sa 9am-1am.

NIGHTLIFE

According to some, Eugene's nightlife is the best in Oregon outside Portland. Not surprisingly, the string of establishments by the university along 13th St. are dominated by the college crowd. Refugees from this scene will find a diverse selection throughout town. Check out *Eugene Weekly* for club listings.

Sam Bond's Garage, 407 Blair Blvd. (☎431-6603). Bus #50 or 52. A supremely laid-back gem in Whittaker neighborhood. Groove to country power pop every night, with the popular Bluegrass Tuesdays, and eight microbrews ($3 per pint). Open daily 3pm-1am.

The Downtown Lounge/Diablo's, 959 Pearl (☎343-2346). The **Downtown Lounge,** upstairs in the large building, offers the casually dressed, younger set four pool tables bathed in red light and a long bar and stage in back. Live music. Open daily 11am-2:30am. Downstairs, in **Diablo's,** over 500 clubbers in the hippest clothes possible party in the flame-covered nightclub (cover $2-3). Open W-Sa 9pm-2:30am.

Jo Federigo's Jazz Club and Restaurant, 259 E 5th Ave. (☎343-8488), across the street from 5th St. Public Market. A restaurant with New Orleans flair and jazz club that swings every night (usually at 9:30pm). W is Blues night. Restaurant open for lunch Tu-F 12:30pm-2pm, dinner daily 5-10pm. Jazz club open daily 8:30pm-1am.

John Henry's, 136 E 11th Ave. (☎342-3358). In the heart of downtown, this cavernous warehouse-style venue hosts a different genre every night from Grrl Variety (Fierce Pussy Posse) to Beergrass (Jackass Willie). Microbrew pints $3. Cover usually $3-7. Call for a schedule. Free pool until 10pm. Open M-Sa 4pm-1am.

ENTERTAINMENT AND SIGHTS

The *Eugene Weekly* (www.eugeneweekly.com) has a list of concerts and local events, as well as features on the greater Eugene community. The Community Center for the Performing Arts operates the **WOW Hall,** 291 W 8th Ave., a historic dance hall on the National Register of Historic Places. All kinds of musical acts, public speaking, dance, theater, workshops, and classes are held here. Tickets are available at the Hall and at local ticket outlets. (☎687-2746. Open M-F 3-6pm. Tickets free-$15.) High-brow culture finds a home at the extravagant **Hult Performing Arts Center,** One Eugene Center at 7th Ave. and Willamette St. The two theater halls host a variety of music from blues to Bartók, as well as theater and opera. (Info ☎682-5087, ticket office 682-5000, 24hr. event info 682-5746. Free tours Th and Sa at 1pm. Tickets $8-45; some student and senior discounts. Box office open Tu-F 11am-5pm, Sa 11am-3pm, and 1hr. before curtain.) The **Bijou Art Cinema,** 492 E 13th Ave., at Ferry St. is a local favorite, where indie and art films are screened in the sanctuary of an old Spanish church. (☎686-2458. Box office open 20min. before the first screening. Th-Sa $6.50, Su-W $5, seniors $4. Late night shows run for $3.)

OREGON COUNTRY FAIR. The fair takes place in **Veneta,** 13 mi. west of town on Rte. 126, and is by far the most exciting event of the summer. Started in 1969 as a fundraiser for a local Waldorf school, the fair has become a magical annual gathering of hippies, artists, musicians, misfits, and activists. From July 12-14, 2002, 50,000 people, many still living in Haight Ashbury happiness, flock from across the nation to experience this festival unlike any other. Hundreds of performers crowd onto seven different stages, and 300 booths fill with art, clothing, crafts, herbal remedies, exhibits on alternative energy sources, and food. Lofty tree houses, parades of painted bodies, dancing 12-foot dolls and thousands of revellers transport travelers into an enchanted forest of frenzy. Parking is extremely limited ($5) and the fair requires advance tickets. Most people park for free at Civic Stadium, at 19th and Willamette in Eugene. From there, free buses run every 10min. from 10am until the fairgrounds close at 7pm. (☎343-4298; www.oregoncountryfair.org. Tickets F and Su $10, Sa $15; not sold on site.) Nearby camping $30-36 per person for the weekend available through Fastixx (☎800-992-8499).

114 ■ INLAND VALLEYS

OREGON BACH FESTIVAL. The Oregon Bach Festival is entering its 32nd year. From June 28-July 14, 2002, conductor Helmuth Rilling leads some of the country's finest orchestral musicians in a 33-year-old celebration of Bach and his contemporaries. (☎346-5666 or 800-457-1486; www.bachfest.uoregon.edu. Concert and lecture series $13; main events $20-45; ages 6-18 $10.)

SIGHTS

UNIVERSITY OF OREGON. Take time to pay homage to the ivy-covered halls that set the scene for *National Lampoon's Animal House* at Eugene's centerpiece, the University of Oregon. Tours issue from the reception desk at **Oregon Hall.** *(At E 13th Ave. and Agate St. ☎346-3014. Tours M-F 10am and 2pm, Sa 10am. Reception desk open M-F 8am-5pm.)*

MUSEUM OF NATURAL HISTORY. A few blocks away, the Museum of Natural History, at Agate, shows a collection of relics from indigenous cultures worldwide, including the world's oldest pair of shoes. *(1680 E 15th Ave. ☎346-3024. Open T-Su noon-5pm. Suggested donation $2.)*

NIKE STORE. More shoe history is at the Nike Store, which houses an exhibit that pays homage to the athletic shoe giant's beginnings. View the waffle iron used to make the first waffle outsole, and the back of the first distribution vehicle used by Nike—a white VW. *(296 E 5th Ave. ☎342-5155. Open daily 10am-6pm.)* The store is part of the **5th St. Public Market,** a cluster of restaurants and galleries located downtown. *(At the corner of 5th Ave. and High St. ☎484-0383.)*

OUTDOOR ACTIVITIES

KAYAKING AND RAFTING. There are plenty of kayaking opportunities in the area. To fill a free hour, canoe or kayak the **Millrace Canal,** which parallels the Willamette for 3 mi. The visitors center has a full list of outfitters and other details. If whitewater is what you crave, check out **Oregon Whitewater Adventures** (☎746-5422 or 800-820-RAFT; www.oregonwhitewater.com). The guides can arrange trips to any of the nearby rivers, from floating to class IV rapids. Call for details.

DRIVING. To see the country as 19th-century settlers saw it, take Rte. 126 east from Eugene. The highway follows the beautiful McKenzie River, and on a clear day, the mighty snow-capped **Three Sisters** are visible. Just east of the town of **McKenzie Bridge,** the road splits into a scenic byway loop. Rte. 242 climbs east to the vast lava fields of **McKenzie Pass,** while Rte. 126 turns north over Santiam Pass and meets back with Rte. 242 in Sisters (see p. 126). Rte. 242 is often blocked by snow until the end of June. The exquisite drive winds its narrow way between **Mt. Washington** and the **Three Sisters Wilderness** before rising to the high plateau of McKenzie Pass. Here, lava outcroppings once served as a training site for astronauts preparing for lunar landings. The Civilian Conservation Corps-built **Dee Wright Observatory** affords incredible views on clear days. The **McKenzie Ranger Station,** 3 mi. east of McKenzie Bridge on Rte. 126., has more info. (☎822-3381. Open daily 8am-4:30pm; winter M-F 8am-4:30pm.) Check with the ranger about hiking permits (usually free) before going to the trailheads. The **Willamette National Forest** (see **Practical Info,** p. 111) has an information packet on the McKenzie Pass.

HOT SPRINGS. Cougar Hot Springs, also known as the Terwilliger Hot Springs on Cougar Lake, is a popular soaking spot. To get there, go 4 mi. east of Blue River on Rte. 126, turn right onto Aufderheide Dr. (Forest Service Rd. #19), and follow the road 7 mi. along the side of Cougar Reservoir. The hot springs used to be a bathing-suit-optional destination for the most free-spirited of the Eugene scene. Suits now required. The Forest Service can suggest other hot springs in the area.

HIKING. The 26 mi. **McKenzie River Trail,** starts 1½ mi. west of the ranger station (see **Driving** above, trail map $1) and ends north at Old Santiam Rd. near the Fish Lake Old Growth Grove. Parallel to Rte. 126, the trail winds through mossy forests, and leads to some of Oregon's most spectacular waterfalls, Koosah Falls and Sahalie Falls. These falls flank Clear Lake, a volcanic crater now filled with crystal-clear waters. The entire trail is also open to mountain bikers. A number of Forest Service campgrounds cluster along this stretch of Rte. 126. More ambitious hikers can sign up for overnight permits at the ranger station and head for the high country, where the hiking opportunities are endless.

GRANTS PASS ☎ 541

Workers building a road through the Oregon mountains in 1863 were so overjoyed by the news of General Ulysses S. Grant's Civil War victory at Vicksburg that they named the town Grants Pass after the burly President-to-be. Today, the city colonizes the hot, flat valley with espresso stands and fast-food joints. A fine place to sleep, but real adventure lies in the Rogue River Valley and Illinois Valley regions.

◪ PRACTICAL INFORMATION. The town lies within the triangle formed by **I-5** in the northeast, **Rte. 99** in the west, and the **Rogue River** to the south. In town, Rte. 99 splits into one-way **6th** and **7th** streets, which run through the heart of downtown and separate east from west. The railroad tracks (between G and F St.) divide north and south addresses. Within the confines of historic downtown, north-south streets are numbered and east-west streets are lettered. **Greyhound,** 460 NE Agness Ave. (☎476-4513), at the east end of town, runs to **Portland** (5½hr., 5 per day, $30) and **San Francisco, CA** (12hr., 4 per day, $49; open M-Sa 6am-6:45pm). **Grants Pass Cab,** charges $2.25 per mi. on top of a $2.50 base. (☎476-6444. 24hr.) **Enterprise,** 1325 NE 7th St., rents cars from $30 plus 25¢ per mi. after 150 mi. (☎471-7800. Must be 21 with a credit card. Open M-F 7:30am-6pm, Sa 9am-noon.) The **Chamber of Commerce,** 1995 NW Vine St., off 6th St., provides info beneath an immense plaster caveman. (☎476-7717 or 800-547-5927. Open M-F 8am-5pm, Sa 9am-5pm, Su 10am-4pm; winter closed Sa and Su.) **MayBelle's Washtub,** 306 SE I St., at 8th St. (☎471-1317), is a laundromat. Wash $1.25, dry 25¢ per 8min. Open daily 7am-10pm; last wash 8:30pm. **Emergency:** ☎911. **Police:** 500 NW 6th St. (☎474-6370). **Hospital:** 500 SW Ramsey Ave. (☎472-7000), just south of town. **Internet Access:** The **Josephine County Library,** at 200 NW C St. (☎474-5480), has 1hr. free, fast Internet access on three computers. Open M-Th 10am-7pm, F-Sa 10am-5pm. **Post office:** 132 NW 6th Ave. at F St. (☎800-275-8777). Open M-F 9am-5pm. **ZIP code:** 97526.

⛺⛺ ACCOMMODATIONS AND CAMPING. Grants Pass supports one of every franchise motel on earth, from Motel 6 to the Holiday Inn Express. The one-of-a-kind cheapo motels are farther back from the interstate on 6th St. and cost $25-35. The owner of the huge hold house **Fordson Home Hostel (HI),** 250 Robinson Rd., gives tours of the antique tractors and vortex on his 20 secluded acres. Perks include free bike loans and $2 off the nearby Oregon Caves entrance fee. 38 mi. southwest of Grants Pass. Follow US 199 to Rte. 46 east. After 6 mi., turn onto Upper Holland Loop Rd., and after 1 mi., you'll hit Robinson Rd. (☎592-3203. Reservations mandatory. $12, nonmembers $15. Bicyclists, backpackers, and students with ID $2 off.) For clean and welcoming, if aging, rooms, the **Parkway Lodge,** 1001 NE 6th St., off Exit 58, fits the room and provides cable to boot and fridges on request. (☎476-4260. Singles $28, doubles $32; winter $5 less.) Of the camping options, **Valley of the Rogue State Park,** is your best choice. The valley is just wide enough for the river, a row of tents, RVs interspersed with a few trees, and the noise of the interstate. 12 mi. east of town off I-5 Exit 45B. (Tents $15; electric $17; full hookups $18; yurts $27.)

FOOD. For spatulas and spaghetti noodles, try **Safeway,** 115 SE 7th St., at G St. (☎479-4276. Open daily 24hr.) The **Growers' Market** (☎476-5375), held in the parking lot between 4th and F St. on Saturday mornings 9am and 1pm, is the state's largest open-air market with arts and crafts, produce, food, and music everywhere. ◪**Thai Barbecue,** 428 SW 6th St., at J St., is decorated like an English teahouse but serves authentic Thai. Excellent *pad thai* and most lunch dishes $5.25, with many dinner entrees only a few dollars more. (☎476-4304. Open M-Sa 11am-9pm.) **Matsukaze,** 1675 NE 7th St., at Hillcrest, is the only Japanese for miles, and some of the best anywhere. Traditional entrees run $4-15. (☎479-2961. Open M-Th 11am-2pm and 5-9pm, F 11am-2pm and 5-9:30pm, Sa 5-9:30pm only; winter closes 30min. earlier.) **Old Town Cafe,** at 6th Ave. and F St. in the Old Town Building. Breakfast is cheap and plentiful. Lunch fare runs from $2.25 for a stuffed potato to $5 for a double bacon cheeseburger. (☎955-1886. Open M-F 9am-5pm, Sa 9am-3pm.)

RAFTING AND KAYAKING. The **Rogue River** is the greatest draw for the town of Grants Pass. One of the few federally protected "Wild and Scenic Rivers," the Rogue can be enjoyed by raft, jetboat, mail boat, or simply by foot. Anglers are in good company—Zane Grey and Clark Gable used to roam the Rogue River with tackle and bait. For more information on fishing licenses and the best places to go, head to the ranger station off of I-5 at Exit 58. For those wishing to be more involved with their water, rafting is prime on a 35 mi. stretch of Class III and IV rapids—the whitest in the Rogue—starting just north of Galice. Rafting this restricted area requires a guide. Much of the rest of the river, though, provides great floating opportunities and plenty of sights. The river can be found just outside of **Merlin,** where the necessary equipment can be procured as well. To get there, head west off I-5 Exit 61. **White Water Cowboys,** 209 Merlin Rd., rents rafts, and offers shuttle and pickup services. (☎479-0132. Discounts possible in May, early June, and late Sept., as well as for multi-day rentals. $65-95 per day). **Orange Torpedo Trips,** in the same building, runs tours down every section of the Rogue river in inflatable orange kayaks. The first to use these interesting contraptions all the way back in 1969, Orange Torpedo Trips is one of the oldest and best in the business. (☎479-5061 or 800-635-2925; www.orangetorpedo.com. 2hr. for $30; half-day for $49; full-day for $69, all on the Rogue; under 12 10% off.)

SPELUNKING. The **Oregon Caves National Monument,** 30 mi. south of Grants Pass via US 199 through plush, green wilderness to Cave Junction, and then 20 mi. east along Rte. 46. Here, in the belly of the ancient Siskiyous, enormous pressure and acidic waters created some of the only caves with walls of glistening marble in North America. A typical guided cave tour ($7.50; seniors $6.50) runs 1½hr. and begins every 15min. in the summer and every hour from Sept. to Dec. The temperature inside is 42°F, and the walk can be rather strenuous. Tours last 1¼hr. An "off-trail" tour for those who like their exploration a bit more extreme leaves every summer morning at 10am and lasts 4hr. (☎592-2100 or 593-3400; www.nps.gov/orca/cavetour.htm. $25; reservations recommended. Open mid-Mar. to Nov. daily 9am-6:30pm; closed Dec. to mid-Mar.)

ASHLAND ☎541

Set near the California border, Ashland mixes hip youth and British literary history to create an unlikely but intriguing stage for the world-famous Oregon Shakespeare Festival. From mid-February to October, drama devotees can choose from 11 plays—several of them written by dramatists other than Shakespeare—which are performed in Ashland's three elegant theaters. The town happily embraces the festival, giving rise to such Bard-bandwagon businesses as "All's Well Herbs and Vitamins," and fosters a vibrant community of artists, actors, and Shakespeare buffs. And for those who can look past the stage, Ashland also offers great eats and a wide range of unspoiled outdoor adventures.

ASHLAND ■ 117

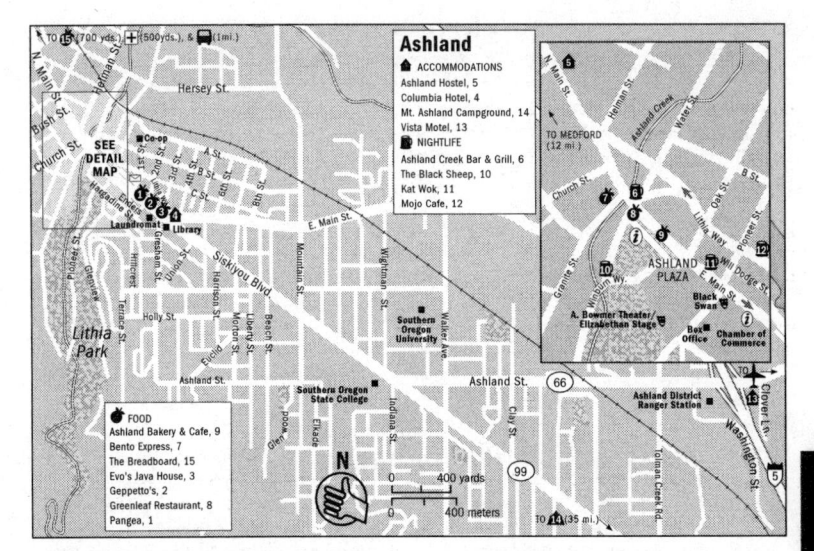

Ashland

♠ ACCOMMODATIONS
Ashland Hostel, 5
Columbia Hotel, 4
Mt. Ashland Campground, 14
Vista Motel, 13
■ NIGHTLIFE
Ashland Creek Bar & Grill, 6
The Black Sheep, 10
Kat Wok, 11
Mojo Cafe, 12

♦ FOOD
Ashland Bakery & Cafe, 9
Bento Express, 7
The Breadboard, 15
Evo's Java House, 3
Geppetto's, 2
Greenleaf Restaurant, 8
Pangea, 1

JOURNEY'S END

Ashland is located in the foothills of the Siskiyou and Cascade Ranges, 285 mi. south of Portland and 15 mi. north of the California border, near the junction of **I-5** and **Rte. 66**. **Rte. 99** cuts through the middle of town on a northwest-southwest axis. It becomes **N Main St.** as it enters town, then splits briefly into **E Main St.** and **Lithia Way** as it runs through downtown. Farther south, Main St. changes name again to **Siskiyou Blvd.,** where Southern Oregon University (SOU) is flanked by affordable motels and bland restaurants.

Buses: Greyhound (☎ 482-8803). Pickup and drop-off at Mr. C's Market, at the intersection of Rte. 99 N and Valley View Rd., which extends from I-90 Exit 280. To: **Portland** (8hr., 3 per day, $43), **Sacramento, CA** (7hr., 3 per day, $45), and **San Francisco, CA** (11hr., 3 per day, $49).

Public Transportation: Rogue Valley Transportation (RVTD; ☎ 779-2877), in Medford. Bus schedules available at the Ashland Chamber of Commerce. The #10 bus runs between the transfer station at 200 S Front St. in **Medford** and the plaza in Ashland (35min.), then makes several stops on a loop through downtown Ashland. An in-town fare is 25¢. #10 runs through Ashland every 30min. daily 5am-7pm.

Taxis: Yellow Cab (☎ 482-3065), $2.50 base, $2 per mi. 24hr.

Car Rental: Budget, 3038 Biddle Rd. (☎ 779-0488), at the airport in Medford. $30 per day, 20¢ per mi. after 200 mi. Must have credit card. Ages 21-24 $10 extra per day.

HERE CEASE MORE QUESTIONS

Visitor Info: Chamber of Commerce, 110 E Main St. (☎ 482-3486), next to the Black Swan. Also, there is an **info booth** in the center of the plaza. Open summer M-Sa 10am-6pm, Su 11am-5pm.

Outdoor Information: Ashland District Ranger Station, 645 Washington St. (☎ 482-3333), off Rte. 66 by I-5 Exit 14. Offers Pacific Crest Trail tips, as well as up-to-date sno-park info. Ranger station open M-F 8am-4:30pm; welcome desk inside open M-Sa 10am-6pm, Su 9am-5pm.

Equipment Rental: Ashland Mountain Supply, 31 N Main St. (☎ 488-2749). Rents internal frame backpacks $5 per day. Mountain bikes $13 for 2hr., $30 per day; $20 per day for 2-5 day rentals. Cash deposit or credit card required. Open daily 10am-6pm.

118 ■ INLAND VALLEYS

Tours: The Adventure Center, 40 N Main St. (☎488-2819 or 800-444-2819; www.raftingtours.com), guides rafting trips on the Rogue, Klamath, and Umpqua rivers. Half-day $69; full-day $119-139; bike tours around Mt. Ashland $69 for 3hr., $119 per day.

Laundromat: Main Street Laundromat, 370 E Main St. (☎482-8042). Wash $1.25, dry 25¢ per 8min. Open daily 7am-11pm, last wash at 10pm.

Emergency: ☎911. **Police:** 1155 E Main St. (☎482-5211).

Crisis Line: ☎779-4357 or 888-609-4357. 24hr.

Hospital: Ashland Community Hospital 280 Maple St. (☎482-2441). 24hr. emergency service.

Internet Access: Ashland Library, 410 Siskiyou Blvd. (☎482-1151), at Gresham St. Free 30min. of Internet access. Open M-Tu 10am-8pm, W-Th 10am-6pm, F-Sa 10am-5pm. **Ashland Community Food Store Co-op,** 237 N 1st St. (☎482-2237), and **Evo's Java House,** 376 E Main St. (☎482-2261) both offer free access.

Post Office: 120 N 1st St. (☎800-275-8777), at Lithia Way. Open M-F 9am-5pm. **ZIP Code:** 97520.

TO SLEEP, PERCHANCE TO DREAM

In winter, Ashland is a budget traveler's paradise of motel vacancy and low rates; in summer, every room in town, including the amazing hostel, fills in the blink of an eye and rates rise sky high. Only foolish players arrive without a reservation. RVTD buses (see **Public Transportation,** p. 117) travel to Medford, 12 mi. away, where midsummer nights see motel vacancies. There, the depressingly similar motels along Central and Riverside Ave. are $8-10 cheaper than the chains along the highway, and every room is at least $10 cheaper than its Ashland counterpart. The **Cedar Lodge,** 518 N Riverside Ave., is among the nicest of the non-chains, and offers a relaxing pool in which to pass the time between plays. (☎773-7361 or 800-282-3419.) Singles $45; doubles $49; 10% AAA discount.) The nearest state park offering a decent-sized campground is the **Valley of the Rogue State Park** (see p. 2), about 30 mi. north on I-5.

Ashland Hostel, 150 N Main St. (☎482-9217). The Victorian parlor, sturdy bunks, and front-porch swing play host to travelers and money-wise, theater-bound families. Laundry. Kitchen. Check-in 5-10pm. Lockout 10am-5pm. Curfew midnight. Reservations recommended. Dorms $18; two private rooms for $45. Cash or traveler's checks only.

Mt. Ashland Campground, about 25min. south of Ashland off I-5 Exit 6. Follow signs to Mt. Ashland Ski Area and take the high road from the far west end of the lot, at the sign for Grouse Gap Snowpeak. 7 sites in the forest overlook the valley and Mt. Shasta. Can be snowy in June. Fire pits and pit toilets, no drinking water. Suggested donation $3.

Columbia Hotel, 262½ E Main St. (☎482-3726 or 800-718-2530). A reading alcove, morning tea time, and spacious rooms make this historic home turned European-style hotel a pleasant experience. Only 1½ blocks from the theaters. May-Oct. rooms start at $65; private baths begin at $95; Feb.-May $55-75. 10% HI discount in off-season.

Vista Motel, 535 Clover Lane (☎482-4423 or 888-672-5290), just off I-5 at Exit 14, behind a 76 gas station. The small building conceals plush, newly renovated rooms with cable TV and A/C. A small pool and good rates make the deal even sweeter. Singles $39; doubles $45. Spring and winter discounts $8.

FOOD OF LOVE

The incredible selection of foods available on North and East Main St. has earned Ashland a great culinary reputation. Even the ticketless come from miles around to dine in Ashland's excellent (although expensive) restaurants. Beware of the pre-show rush—a downtown dinner planned for 6:30pm can easily become a late-night affair, as pushy theater-goers fight to finish by 8:15pm. In lieu of prepared food, **Ashland Community Food Store Co-op**, 237 N 1st St., at A St., has a lively spirit and great organic produce and natural foods, as well as Internet access. (☎482-2237. 5% senior discount. Open M-Sa 8am-9pm, Su 9am-9pm.) Cheaper groceries available at **Safeway**, 585 Siskiyou Blvd. (☎482-4495. Open daily 6am-midnight.)

- **Pangea**, 272 E Main St. (☎552-1630), offers a menu of creative, filling wraps and grilled panini sandwiches. The Wrap of Khan is a meal in itself ($7). Almost anything on the menu can be made without meat. Open daily 11:30am-9pm.

- **The Breadboard**, 744 N Main (☎488-0295). In the morning, this joint is hoppin' with locals hungry for pumpkin pancakes ($4.50). Lunch features comfort food like the philly cheesesteak ($7.50). Gorgeous views of the mountains. Open W-Su 7am-2:30pm.

- **Bento Express**, at the corner of Granite St. and N Main St., is a tiny restaurant offering large portions of rice and cheap *bento* lunches to go. *Bao* and potstickers are $1.75, *bento* meals are $4.25. Open M-Sa 11am-6pm, Su noon-5pm.

- **Geppetto's**, 345 E Main St. (☎482-1138). An intimate dining room. Have a pesto or smoked salmon omelette ($8.50), "World Famous Eggplant Burger" ($4.75), and dinner from $10.50. Open daily 8am-midnight.

- **Greenleaf Restaurant**, 49 N Main St. (☎482-2808). Healthy food near a picturesque creek. For breakfast, *kasha* ($5) is delicious. Salads ($3-10), pastas ($5-9.50), and spuds ($3-7) are meals in themselves. Open daily 8am-9pm. Closed Jan.

🍸 DRINK DEEP ERE YOU DEPART

Ashland remains a cultural center even after the festival ends. Local and touring artists alike play throughout the year to the town's enthused audiences. The **Oregon Cabaret Theater**, at 1st and Hagardine St., stages light musicals in a cozy former church with drinks, dinners, and Sunday brunch. Tickets $15-22, food not included; dinner and brunch reservations required 48hr. in advance. (☎488-2902; www.oregoncabaret.com. Box office open Th-Sa, M 11am-6:30pm, and Su 4-6:30 when there is a performance.) Small groups, such as the **Actor's Theater of Ashland** (☎535-5250), **Ashland Community Theatre** (☎482-7532), and **Southern Oregon University's (SOU)** theater department (☎552-6346) also raise the curtains sporadically year-round. Ashland also finds space for great music. When in town, the traveling **Rogue Valley Symphony** (☎770-6012) performs in the Music Recital Hall at SOU and at Lithia Park. Tickets run from $20-34, students $10. In July and August, the **State Ballet of Oregon** graces the stage in a variety of venues Monday nights. Monday nights in late June find the **Palo Alto Chamber Orchestra** giving hit performances at the Elizabethan Theatre, weather permitting. (☎482-4331. Tickets $10.)

- **Kat Wok**, 62 E Main St. (☎482-0787), rocks with a tiny dance floor wedged between the restaurant tables and a glow-in-the-dark pool. For sustenance before the party, try the pan-Asian cuisine ($7-17) or the new sushi bar. 21+. Open Th-Sa lunch 11:30am-2:30pm; dinner Su-M 5-8pm, T-Sa 5-9pm; club W-Su 9pm-2am.

- **The Black Sheep**, 51 N Main St. (☎482-6414). Probably the only English pub in Oregon. "Eclectic fayre" features scones ($3.50), and dinner ($11-17) includes homegrown herbs. Imperial pints (20 oz.) from $4. 21+ after 11pm. Open daily 11am-1am.

- **Ashland Creek Bar & Grill**, 92 N Main St. (☎482-4131). A huge outdoor deck and dedication to live music (every Th-Sa) have created a strong local following. The traditional grill menu features burgers and the like ($4.50-9). 21+ after 9pm. Open Th-Sa 11am-2am, Su-W 11am-1am. Cover ranges from $1-5, depending on fame of the entertainers.

- **Mojo Cafe**, 140 Lithia Way (☎552-1302), features both a healthy dose of soul food and a busy music scene. Have fried catfish lunch ($6.25) before the jazz or blues show starts (around 9pm). Cover ranges from free to $8. Open M-Sa from 11am, Su 9am-4pm brunch, then 5pm-close. The night usually ends between midnight and 2am.

MIDSUMMER MADNESS

The Oregon Shakespeare Festival (☎482-4331; www.osfashland.org.), began in 1935 by local college teacher Angus Bowmer as a nighttime complement to the daytime boxing matches in the old **Chautauqua Dome**. Today, on the site of the dome stands the festival's feature theater, and instead of local college students, professional actors perform 11 plays in repertory, five or six of which are contemporary and classical plays. Performances run on the three Ashland stages from mid-February through October, and any boxing now is over scarce tickets. The 1200-seat **Elizabethan Stage,** an outdoor theater modeled after an 18th-century London design, is open from mid-June to mid-October, and hosts three Shakespeare plays per season. The **Angus Bowmer Theater** is a 600-seat indoor stage that shows one Shakespearean play and a variety of dramas. The **newest theater,** yet unnamed, will open its doors for the first time for the 2002 season and seat 260-350, serving as a modern replacement for the intimate 138-seat **Black Swan,** which will be used for rehearsal rather than production in 2002. The 2002 season will feature *As You Like It* and *Titus Andronicus* in the Elizabethan, *Julius Caesar* and Edward Albee's *Who's Afraid of Virginia Woolf* in the Bowmer, and *Macbeth* in the new theater.

TICKETS. Ticket purchases are recommended six months in advance. The **Oregon Shakespearean Festival Box Office,** 15 S Pioneer St., is next to the Elizabethan and Bowmer Theaters, and across the street from the New Theater. (☎482-4331; www.osfashland.org. Open Tu-Su 9:30am-8:30pm, M 9:30am-5pm.) General mail-order and phone ticket sales begin in January, and many weekend shows sell out within the first week. Tickets cost $22-39 for spring previews and fall shows, summer shows $29-52, plus a $5 handling fee per order for phone, fax, or mail orders. Children under 6 are not admitted to any shows. Those under 18 receive 25% discounts in the summer and 50% in the spring and fall. For complete ticket info write **Oregon Shakespeare Festival,** P.O. Box 158, Ashland, OR 97520, or visit the website.

Last-minute theater-goers should not abandon hope. At 9:30am, the box office releases any unsold tickets for the day's performances. Prudence demands arriving early; local patrons have been known to leave their shoes in line to hold their places. When no tickets are available, limited priority numbers are given out. These entitle their holders to a designated place in line when the precious few returned tickets are released (1:30pm for matinees, 6pm for evening shows). For those truly desperate for their Shakespeare fix, the box office also sells twenty clear-view **standing room tickets** for sold-out shows on the Elizabethan Stage ($11, available on the day of the show). Half-price **rush tickets** are occasionally available 1hr. before performances not already sold out. Some half-price matinees are offered in the spring and in October, and all three theaters hold full-performance **previews** in the spring and summer at considerable discounts. Although scalping is illegal, unofficial ticket transactions take place all the time just outside the box office. Ticket officials advise those "buying on the bricks" to check the date and time on the ticket carefully and pay no more than the face value.

BACKSTAGE TOURS. Backstage tours provide a wonderful glimpse of the festival from behind the curtain. Tour guides (usually actors or technicians) divulge all kinds of anecdotes—from the story of the bird songs during an outdoor staging of *Hamlet* to the time when a door on the set used for most every stage entrance and exit locked itself midway through the show, provoking over 30min. of hilarious improvising before it was fixed during intermission. (Tours leave from Black Swan Tu-Sa. Start at 10am and last 2hr. Call box office in case of changes. $10, ages 6-17 $7.50; no children under 6.) In mid-June, the **Feast of Will** celebrates the annual opening of the Elizabethan Theater with din-

ASHLAND ■ 121

ner and merry madness in Lithia Park. ($19. Call the box office for details.) Finally, Festival Noons, a mix of lectures, concerts, and talks held in the courtyard just outside the Elizabethan Theatre where the old Chautauqua dome stood, occur almost every day at noon beginning in mid-June. Mostly free, but some require tickets ($2-10) available at the box office.

THE GILDED MONUMENTS

LITHIA PARK
Before it imported Shakespeare, Ashland was naturally blessed with **lithia water** containing dissolved lithium salts reputed to have miraculous healing powers. It is said that only one other spring in the world has a higher lithium concentration. To try the water, hold your nose (thus avoiding sulfur salts) and head for the circle of fountains in the plaza's center. Besides aquatic phenomena, Lithia Park features free concerts, readings, and nature walks around hiking trails, a Japanese garden, and swan ponds. On summer weekends, the park fills with an artisans market.

EMIGRANT LAKE PARK
Scads of kids and kids-at-heart flock to the 280-foot **waterslide** at **Emigrant Lake Park**, 6 mi. east of town on Rte. 66. (Slide info ☎774-1200, ext. 2145). Popular for boating, hiking, swimming, and fishing, the park offers fantastic views of the valley. $3 entry fee. Ten slides for $5 or unlimited slides and for 3hr. $10-12. Park open daily 8am-sunset, waterslide May-Sept. noon-6:30pm.

MT. ASHLAND
If your muscles demand a little abuse after all this theater-seat lolly-gagging, head out to Mt. Ashland for some serious **hiking** and **biking.** Both hiking and biking on and around Mt. Ashland require a trailhead parking pass, available at the ranger station for $5. The ranger station can also provide an excellent and comprehensive guide to hiking and biking in the area for free. The folks at the **Adventure Center** (see **Equipment Rental,** p. 117) can give tips on biking trails.

Pacific Crest Trail (3½ mi. one-way, 2hr.). Forest boundary to Grouse Gap. Take Exit 6 off I-5 and follow the signs along the Mt. Ashland Access Rd. for 7¼ mi. to the sign denoting the Rogue River National Forest Boundary. This section of the Pacific Crest Trail begins to climb Mt. Ashland, passing through forests and meadows covered with wildflowers, and ends at the Grouse Gap shelter. Moderate.

Wagner Butte Trail (5¼ mi. one-way, several hours). From Ashland, take Rte. 99 north of town to Rapp Rd. in Talent. Turn left and drive 1 mi. to the junction with Wagner Creek Rd. and then 8 mi. to Forest Rd. #22. Turn left and drive 2 mi. to the trailhead across from a parking area. This trail climbs 3000 ft. through a landslide area and stands of old-growth fir to the top of Warner Butte. Breathtaking views on sunny days. Strenuous.

Horn Gap Mountain Bike Trail (3 mi. one-way or 9 mi. loop, 1-3hr.). To reach the trailhead from Lithia Park, take Granite St. along Ashland creek 1 mi. to Glenview, and park alongside the road. This is the upper trailhead; the lower trailhead is 4 mi. down the road. This ride offers both incredible views of Mt. Ashland with technical fun in steep slopes and several slalom courses. It can be linked with Rd. 2060 to create the 9 mi. loop. Moderate.

SKIING
At the top of the 9 mi. road leading from I-5 Exit 6 is **Mount Ashland,** a small ski area with 23 runs, a vertical drop of 1150 ft., a new half pipe and over 100 mi. of free **cross-country** trails. (☎482-2897; snow report ☎482-2754; www.mtashland.com. Lift tickets $27, ages 9-17 and seniors $22, 8 and under free. Starting the beginning of Jan., lift tickets on Tu are only $15. Ski rentals $17 per day, snowboards $25. Open from late Nov. to mid-Apr. daily 9am-4pm. Night skiing Th-Sa 4-10pm.)

CENTRAL AND EASTERN OREGON

Central Oregon stretches between the peaks of the Cascades to the west, and Eastern Oregon spans gorges, desert mountain ranges, and alkali flats to the east. Except for Portlanders, most Oregonians live in Central Oregon, west of the Willamette Valley. Tourists come to eastern Oregon for the rodeos and festivals, or to toe the Oregon Trail. Backcountry hikers hunger to hit majestic Mt. Hood, Hells Canyon—the deepest gorge in the US—and the isolated volcanic features and wildlife preserves of the southeast. The severe landscape has changed little but never ceased to test the resolve of its inhabitants. The fertility of the land and the harshness of winter have, nurtured and taken their toll upon game, hunters, wheat, and farmers, and make this part of Oregon the outdoor destination it is today.

THE CASCADES

The Cascade range connects California's Mt. Shasta with Washington's Mt. Rainier. Once highly volcanic, the Cascades have settled down enough for wind and water to have their way. Slicing Oregon almost completely from north to south, the Cascades create a natural barrier for moisture and lush vegetation. Central Oregon's towns are dotted throughout the mountains and receive most of the precipitation from the Pacific Ocean; more arid, less populated regions lie to the east.

BEND   ☎ 541

Defined by a dramatic landscape—volcanic features to the south, the Cascades to the west, and the Deschutes River running through its heart—Bend attracts its share of Oregon's visitors. Settled in the early 19th century as "Farewell Bend," a waystation on a pioneer trail along the Deschutes, Bend lost its small-town feel in the 1970s. A flood of young urbanites from California, Portland, and Seattle arrived in search of the perfect blend of urban excitement and pristine wilderness. Today, while malls and outlets flood the banks of US 97, downtown has grown into a charming crowd-pleaser, and the outdoor opportunities have only gotten better.

ORIENTATION AND PRACTICAL INFORMATION

Bend is 144 mi. north of Klamath Falls on **US 97** and 100 mi. southeast of Mt. Hood via **US 26E** and **Rte. 97S.** The city is bisected by US 97, which becomes **3rd St.** in town. **Wall** and **Bond St.** are the main arteries. Downtown lies to the southwest along the **Deschutes River.** From east to west, Franklin Ave. becomes Riverside Blvd; at the edge of Drake Park, Tumalo St. becomes Galveston Ave.; Greenwood Ave. becomes Newport Ave.; 14th St. becomes Century Dr. and is the first leg of the **Cascade Lakes Hwy.** Before you explore, get a map at the **visitors center.**

Buses: Greyhound, 63076 US 97N, across the street from the Visitor Information (☎382-2151). Open M-F 8am-1:30pm and 2:30-5pm, Sa 8:30am-3pm, Su 8:30am-2pm. Call for info on other bus and van lines. To **Portland** (1 per day, 4½hr., $24) and **Eugene** (1 per day, 2½hr., $21).

Taxis: Owl Taxi, 1919 NE 2nd St. (☎382-3311). $2 base, $2 per mi.

Visitor Information: 63085 US 97N (☎382-3221; www.visitbend.org). Full-time ranger on duty. Offers a motherlode of brochures in addition to an *Attractions and Activities Guide* and a clear map of the area. Open M-Sa 9am-5pm, Su 11am-3pm.

Outdoor Information: The forest headquarters maintains an info desk in the visitors center. A *Recreation Opportunity Guide,* which can be found there as well as the ranger stations, covers each of the 4 ranger districts. **Deschutes National Forest Headquarters,**

1645 20E (☎383-5300) and **Bend/Fort Rock District Ranger Station,** 1230 NE 3rd St. #A262 (☎383-4000; www.fs.fed.us/r6/deschutes), have additional info on Deschutes National Forest. Both open M-F 7:45am-4:30pm. **Oregon Dept. of Fish and Wildlife,** 61374 Parrell Rd. (☎388-6363) has fishing licenses for $8 per day; inquire about hunting permits. Open M-F 8am-5pm.

Equipment Rental: Hutch's Bicycles, 725 NW Columbia Ave. (☎382-9253). Mountain bikes $15 for 4hr., $20 per day. Open M-F 9am-7pm, Sa-Su 9am-6pm. **Sunnyside Sports,** 930 NW Newport Ave. (☎382-8018; www.sunnysidesports.com). Front suspension bikes for $20 per day, each additional day $10. Cross-country skis $10 per day, each additional day $5. Open M-Th 9am-7pm, F 9am-8pm, Sa-Su 8am-6pm. **Pine Mountain Sports,** 133 SW Century Dr. (☎385-8080). Mountain bikes $20 per day. Also rents skis and snowshoes ($25 and $10). Open M-Sa 9am-6pm, Su 10am-5pm. Full suspension models at all shops are $45 per day.

Laundromat: Westside Laundry and Dry Cleaners, 738 NW Columbia Ave. (☎382-7087). Wash $1.25, dry 25¢ per 10min. Open daily 6:30am-9:30pm, last wash at 8:15pm.

Emergency: ☎911.

Police: 711 NW Bond St. (☎388-0170).

Hospital: St. Charles Medical Center, 2500 NE Neff Rd. (☎382-4321).

Internet Access: Try the **Deschutes County Library,** 601 NW Wall (☎388-6679). Free fast Internet access on the second floor next to the reference desk. Open M-Th 10am-8pm, F 10am-6pm, Sa 10am-5pm, Su 1-5pm. **Cafe Internet,** 141 SW Century Dr. (☎318-8802) offers broadband Internet access and a wide variety of games. $2 for 15 minutes, $10 for an entire Saturday of network gaming. Open M-Sa 10am-6pm.

Post Office: 2300 NE 4th St. (☎800-275-8777), at Webster. Open M-F 8:30am-5:30pm, Sa 11am-1pm. **ZIP Code:** 97701.

ACCOMMODATIONS AND CAMPING

Bend treats budget travelers right: the hostel and B&Bs provide phenomenal deals for tuckered-out travelers. Cheap motels line 3rd St. just outside of town. **Deschutes National Forest** maintains a huge number of lakeside campgrounds with toilets along the **Cascade Lakes Hwy.** west of town. Those with potable water cost $8-12 per night on average; the rest are free. Backcountry camping in the national forest area is free. Parking permits may be required. Contact the **Bend/Ft. Rock Ranger District Office** (see above) for more info.

Bend Cascade Hostel, 19 SW Century Dr. (☎389-3813 or 800-299-3813). From 3rd St., take Greenwood west until it becomes Newport, then take a left on 14th St. Beds, pillows, sleepsacks, and blankets are provided. Laundry $1 wash, dry 50¢. Kitchen. 3 private rooms. Lockout 9:30am-4:30pm. Curfew 11pm. $15; seniors, students, cyclists, and HI $14; under 18 with parents half-price.

Tumalo State Park, 62976 OB Riley Rd. (☎382-3586 or 800-551-6949). 4 mi. north of Bend off US 20W. Pastoral riverside campsites go early despite road noise. Solar showers available. 65 sites, $16-18; 22 full hookups $20; 4 yurts $29.

FOOD

There should be no problem finding somewhere to eat; Bend has a huge number of restaurants. Four mega-markets line south 3rd St. **Devore's Good Food Store and Wine Shop,** 1124 Newport NW, peddles all things organic plus wine and cheese. (☎389-6588. Open M-Sa 8am-7pm, Su 10am-6pm.)

Taqueria Los Jalapeños, 601 NE Greenwood Ave. (☎382-1402). A simple space filled by a steady stream of locals devoted to good, cheap food. Filling bean and cheese burritos for $1.75; combo plates $7. Open M-Sa 11am-8pm; winter 11am-7pm.

Mother's Juice Cafe, 1255 NW Galveston St. (☎318-0989). Friendly staff blend exquisite smoothies ($4). Enjoy the Mt. Everest sandwich, a veritable mountain of veggies on wheat ($5.75, $3.75 for half). Open M-Sa 7am-8pm; winter 7am-7pm; Su 11am-5pm.

Westside Bakery and Cafe, 1005 NW Galveston (☎382-3426). Watch out; you won't be able to peel your eyes away from the tempting case of sugary desserts (under $3) on the way to your table. Burgers and sandwiches ($5.50-7). Open daily 6:30am-2:30pm.

Kuishinbo Kitchen, 114 NW Minnesota St. (☎385-9191), between Wall and Bond St. Grab a Japanese lunch to go. Bento ($5.25-6.75) is good, but most people order yaki soba noodles with tofu or meat ($4-6). Open M-F 11am-6:30pm, Sa 11am-4pm.

SIGHTS AND EVENTS

HIGH DESERT MUSEUM. The museum is one of the premier natural and cultural history museums in the Pacific Northwest. Stunning life-size dioramas recreate rickety cabins and cramped immigrant workshops. An indoor desertarium offers a peek at shy desert creatures. Hourly interpretive talks wind through river otter and porcupine habitats, and a new 7000 sq. ft. wing featuring birds of prey in their natural habitats includes the endangered spotted owl. A Native American wing with exhibits on post-reservation Indian life is insightful. *(59800 Hwy. 97 S, 3½ mi. south of Bend on US 97. ☎382-4754; www.highdesert.org. Arrive early to beat crowds. Open daily 9am-5pm. $7.75, ages 13-18 and over 65 $6.75, ages 5-12 $3.75, under 5 free.)*

DRAKE PARK AND THE CASCADE FESTIVAL OF MUSIC. Picnic by the river with Canadian geese at beautiful Drake Park. The park hosts many events and festivals, most notably the Cascade Festival of Music, a week-long series of classical and pop concerts during the week before Labor Day. *(Between Mirror Pond and Franklin St., one block from downtown. ☎382-8381; www.cascademusic.org. Tickets $16-25, rush tickets and students under 12 half-price. Call the office or write to 842 NW Wall St. #6.)*

BEND SUMMER FESTIVAL. The annual festival, held during the second weekend in July, showcases the work of artisans and performers from across central Oregon. Downtown is closed as the streets are flooded with all sorts of people selling arts, crafts, and food. *(☎385-6570. All events free. Parking limited.)*

OUTDOOR ACTIVITIES

The outdoor activities in Bend are limitless, and without peer in Oregon. From skiing, snowboarding, and snowshoeing in the winter to hiking, biking, and rafting in the summer, Bend can be an inexpensive outdoor adventure waiting to happen.

SKIING. Those who ski the 9065 ft. **Mount Bachelor** with its 3365 ft. vertical drop, are in good company—Mt. Bachelor has been home to the US Ski Team and the US Cross-Country Ski Team, and hosts many of the largest snowboarding competitions in the country. The ski season runs September to June. (☎800-829-2442; snow report 382-7888. Alpine day tickets $43, ages 7-12 $22.) A shuttle bus service runs the 22 mi. between the parking lot at the corner of Simpson and Columbia in Bend and the mountain (Nov.-May; $2). Many nearby lodges offer **ski packages** (contact Central Oregon Visitor's Association at ☎800-800-8334 for info). **Chairlifts** are open for sightseers during the summer. (Open daily 10am-4pm. $10, seniors $9, ages 7-12 $6.) A parking permit is necessary for all cars on the mountain ($5 per day from the ranger). See **Orientation and Practical Info** for equipment rental info.

MOUNTAIN BIKING. Though biking is not allowed in the wilderness area itself, mountain bikers have many options for intense riding in the Bend area. The **Three Sisters Wilderness Area,** north and west of the Cascade Lakes Hwy., is one of Oregon's largest and most popular wilderness areas. A parking permit is required at most trailheads; pick one up at any of the ranger stations or at the visitors center ($5 per day). Try **Deschutes River Trail** (6 mi.) for a flat, forested trail ending at **Deschutes River.** To reach the trailhead, go 7½ mi. west of Bend on Century Dr. (Cascade Lakes Hwy.) until Forest Service Rd. 41; turn left and follow the signs to Lava Island Falls (21 mi. round-trip). For a technical ride, hit **Waldo Lake Loop,** a grueling 22 mi. around the lake. To get there, take Cascade Lakes Hwy. to Forest Service Rd. 4290. A slick guide to mountain bike trails around Bend ($9) and *Mountain Biking Route Guide* (free) are available at the **Bend/Ft. Rock District Ranger Station** but the hottest trails aren't on maps; talk to locals or folks in the bike shops.

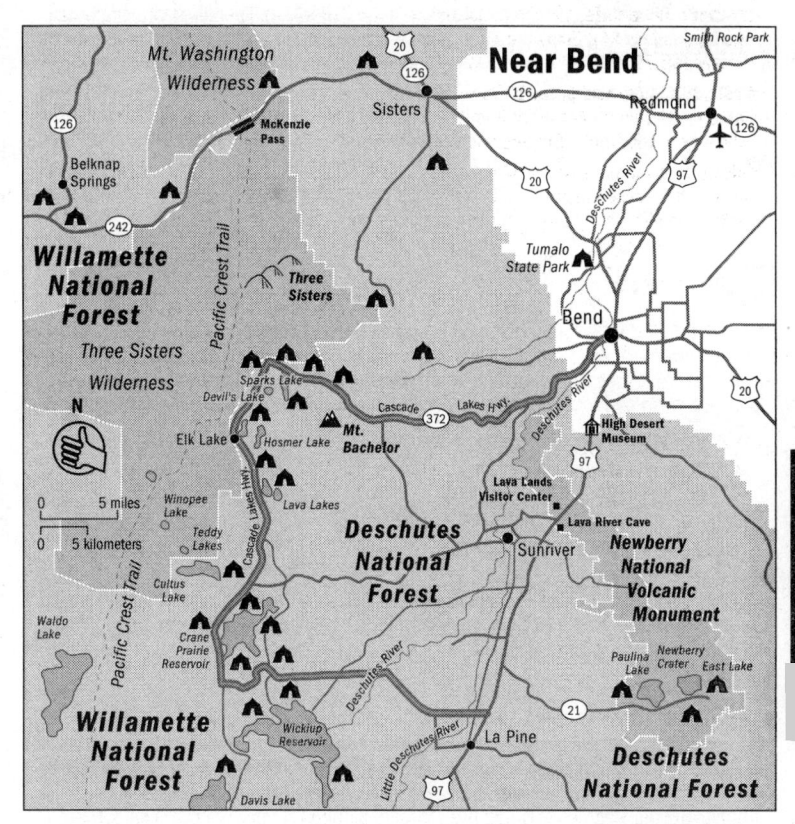

RAFTING. As if skiing, hiking, and biking, weren't enough, Bend also offers miles of Class IV rapids for intrepid rafters. Whitewater rafting, although costly, is one of the most popular local recreational activities. Half-day trips usually last three hours and cover the fairly tame waters of the upper Deschutes. Full-day trips require a 1hr. drive to Maupin to run the Class III+ rapids of the lower Deschutes. In addition to trips on the Deschutes, rafters find fun on nearby rivers like the Clackamas, Owyhee, Klickitat, and the class V rapids of the Wind. Sun Country Tours runs half-day and full-day trips out of the Sun River Resort, 17 mi. south of Bend off US 97, and at 531 SW 13th St. in Bend. (☎800-770-2161. Half-day $40; full day $95-105, ages 6-12 $80-105.) River Drifters (☎800-972-0430; www.riverdrifters.net) offers trips on the Deschutes as well, but also trips to other rivers close by. Trips on the Deschutes are $65-75 per day for adults, $55-65 for kids. Trips to other rivers such as the Klickitat and the Sandy Gorge run for $75.

126 ■ THE CASCADES

DAYTRIP FROM BEND: NEWBERRY NATL. MONUMENT

The Newberry National Volcanic Monument was established in 1990 to link and preserve the volcanic features in south Bend. Featuring such volcanic wonders as **Lava Butte, Lava River Cave,** and **Newberry Crater,** and **the Paulina Lakes,** the Newberry National Monument offers visitors plenty of sights and a wealth of hiking. Immediately behind the **Lava Lands Visitor Center** is **Lava Butte,** a 500-foot cinder cone from which lava once flowed. Between Memorial Day and Labor Day, you can drive 2 mi. up the narrow road (no RVs) that leads to the butte. *(13 mi. south of Bend on US 97.* ☎ *593-2421. Required parking fee $5, free with a Golden Eagle Passport. Open mid-May to Labor Day daily 9am-5pm; Apr. to mid-May and Labor Day to Oct. W-Su 9:30am-5pm.)* The monument's centerpiece is **Newberry Crater,** the remains of what was the Newberry Volcano, one of three volcanoes in Oregon likely to erupt again "soon." The 500 sq. mi. caldera contains Paulina Lake and East Lake. *(13 mi. south of Lava Lands Visitor Center on US 97, then 13 mi. east on Rte. 21. Parking within the national monument requires a $5 permit, available from the ranger or the visitors center; parking free with a Golden Eagle Pass.)*

- **Obsidian Flow Trail** (½ mi.). Hike along one of the most recent geological events in the Cascades, the Big Obsidian Flow. Formed only 1300 years ago by an eruption of the Newberry volcano, the 170 million cubic yards of obsidian is crossed by this trail. Easy.

- **Paulina Lake Trail** (7 mi.). Beginning at the visitors center and circumnavigating the gorgeous Paulina Lake, this trail provides views of the wildlife surrounding the lake. Paulina Lake also offers excellent fishing. Easy to moderate difficulty.

- **Crater Rim Trail** (21 mi.). Encircling the entire Newberry Caldera, the trail offers vistas of the entire Bend area as well as the surrounding mountains. While hikers share this trail with bikers and horseback riders, there are plenty of sights to go around. Difficult.

SISTERS ☎ 541

A gateway to the nearby **Deschutes National Forest** and the **Cascade Lakes,** Sisters offers those in town and those just passing through the same warm welcome. Located 20 mi. northwest of Bend on US 20, Sisters features an old West look, which is authenticated by the annual Sisters Rodeo and the popular Outdoor Quilt Show. Sisters also provides access to climbing facilities in nearby Smith Rock State Park and the sights of the Warm Springs Indian Reservation.

■⁊ ORIENTATION AND PRACTICAL INFORMATION. From Sisters, **Rte. 126** heads east to **Redmond** (20 mi.) and **Prineville** (39 mi.), and to the west joins **US 20** to cross the Cascades. **Rte. 242** heads southwest over McKenzie Pass (see p. 127) to rejoin Rte. 126 and blend into **Cascade St.** The **visitors center,** 164 N Elm St., is one block from Cascade St. (☎549-0251; www.sisters-chamber.com. Open M-F 9am-5pm; Sa-Su hours vary, call ahead.) Sisters' **Deschutes National Forest Ranger District Station,** on the corner of Cascade and Pine St., has info on nearby campgrounds, local day hikes and biking trails, and sells the required $5 parking permit for the park. (☎549-7700. Open M-F 7:45am-4:30pm, Sa 8am-4pm; winter M-F 7:45am-4:30pm.) **Equipment Rental: Eurosports,** 182 E Hood St., rents mountain bikes, snowshoes, snowboards, and cross-country and alpine skis. (☎549-2471. Bikes: front suspension $20 per day, $100 per week; full suspension $25 per day, $125 per week. Snowshoes, shaped skis, and snowboards $12-25 per day. Open daily 9am-5:30pm; winter M-F 9am-5:30pm, Sa-Su 8am-5:30pm.) **Epicure Exchange,** 391 W Cascade St., has **Internet** for $5 per hr. (☎549-0536. Open daily 8am-5pm.)

⚡🛏 CAMPING AND FOOD. Budget travelers generally pass up expensive Sisters for Bend's cheap lodging (see **Bend Accommodations,** p. 123). Camping, however, is as good as it gets in the Deschutes National Forest. The Ranger District maintains many spectacular **campgrounds** near Sisters; most of them cluster around **Camp Sherman,** a small community on the Metolius River 16 mi. northwest of Sisters. Two noteworthy sites are **Riverside,** 10 mi. west on Rte. 20 and 4 mi. northeast on Rd. 14 (pumped water, 16 sites, $10), and **Allingham,** 1 mi. north of the Camp Sherman store on Rd. 14 (piped water, 10 sites, $12). Both are maintained by Hoodoo Recreation Services through the ranger. Contact Hoodoo at 822-3799 or www.hoodoo.com for more info. Riverside's walk-in sites provide refuge from motor vehicles, and Allingham's drive-in sites perch right on the river, with ample fishing opportunities (with an $8 license).

Plan on exploring Sisters during the daylight hours; things are slow at 6pm and dead by dark. Overpriced food is available anytime at the faux-western tourist joints, but delis that close by 5, or even 3pm, are better for palette and purse. **Sisters Bakery,** 251 E Cascade St., has all kinds of baked goods, including marionberry cobbler ($2.25) top-notch bread ($3), and heavenly homemade pastries under $2. (☎ 549-0361. Open daily 5am-6pm.) **The Harvest Basket,** 110 S Spruce St., features organic groceries, and fresh fruit smoothies. (☎ 549-0598. Open daily 9am-6pm.)

◙ SIGHTS AND EVENTS. The annual **Sisters Rodeo,** over the second weekend in June, draws big-time wranglers to this tiny town for 3 days and nights of bronco-riding, calf-roping, and steer-wrestling, all in pursuit of the purse of $100,000. Have a rip-roaring time at the Rodeo Parade and the Buckaroo Breakfast in the company of the Pepsi Girls and the Dodge Pickup Guys. (☎ 549-0121 or 800-827-7522. $8-12. Shows often sell out.) **The Outdoor Quilt Show,** held annually for over a quarter of a century, features over 900 colorful quilts hung on storefronts throughout the town. Some of the quilts are offered for sale. (☎ 549-6061. Second Sa of July; 9:30am-5pm.) **The Museum at Warm Springs** is located off Hwy. 26 north of Sisters and Bend (look for the signs), on the Warm Springs Indian Reservation. A stunning piece of architecture, it documents the tribal history of the Wasco, Paiute, and Warm Springs Indians by interactive and informative exhibits. (☎ 553-3331. Open daily 10am-5pm. $6; seniors $5; ages 5-12 $3.) The reservation is also home to the **Indian Head Casino** in the **Kah-Nee-Ta Resort.** For more info call 553-1112.

◪ HIKING. A $5 per day use permit, available at the trailheads or from the ranger in Sisters is required for most activities. The ranger station in Sisters also offers guides to popular hiking and biking trails in the region for free.

Metolius River Trail (10 mi.). West on Rte. 20 from Sisters, then make a right at the sign for Camp Sherman (Rd. 14). Proceed 7 mi. on Rd. 14 past the "Head of the Metolius" and park at the Wizard Falls Fish Hatchery, right on the Metolius River. (☎ 595-6611. Open daily 8am-5pm.)

Black Crater (8 mi.). About 11 mi. west of sisters off the left side of Rte. 242. Deeper in the mountains, the strenuous round-trip hike up Black Crater offers unsurpassed views of snow-capped peaks and lava flows on McKenzie Pass, and intimate encounters with volcanic debris. Access is often limited due to snow.

McKenzie Pass (15 mi.). West of Sisters on Rte. 242. The site of a relatively recent lava flow which created barren fields of rough, black **A'A** (AH-ah) lava. The ½ mi. trails from the Dee Wright Observatory winds among basalt boulders, cracks, and crevices.

◪ OTHER OUTDOOR ACTIVITIES. Opportunities for both novice and hard core **mountain biking** abound near Sisters. No bikes or motor vehicles are allowed in official wilderness areas, but most other trails and little-used dirt roads are open to bikes. The ranger station distributes a packet detailing local trails, or talk to the friendly owner of Eurosports for the info on the best trails (see **Practical Info** above). Half an hour from Sisters, the majestic rock spires of **Smith Rock State Park** are a popular **rock climbing** destination. Pick up a trail guide from the ranger or at the park. Bivouac camping is also available for $6 a night. For learning climbers, **First Ascent** offers lessons. (☎ 800-325-5462. Take Rte. 126 to Redmond, then north for 9 mi. on US 97 and follow the signs from the town of Terrebonne. $175 per day, $95 per person per day for 2 people, $80 per person per day for 3 or more people.)

128 ■ THE CASCADES

CRATER LAKE AND KLAMATH FALLS ☎ 541

The deepest lake in the US, the 7th deepest in the world, and one of the most beautiful anywhere, Crater Lake is one of Oregon's signature attractions. Formed about 7700 years ago in an eruption of the huge Mt. Mazama, it began as a deep caldera and gradually filled itself with centuries worth of melted snow. The circular lake plunges from its shores to a depth of 1936 ft., which means that it remains iceless in the winter, although its banks, which reach 6176 ft. up to the sky, are snow-covered until July. Visitors from all over the world circle the 33 mi. Rim Drive, carefully gripping the wheel as the clear blue water enchants them. Sure to bring even more visitors than usual, Crater Lake will celebrate 100 years as a national park during the 2002 summer. Klamath Falls, one of the nearest towns, makes a convenient stop on the way to the park and houses most of the services, motels, and restaurants listed below.

TRANSPORTATION

Rte. 62 skirts the park's southwestern edge as it arcs 130 mi. between Medford in the southwest and Klamath Falls, 56 mi. southeast of the park. To reach Crater Lake from Portland, take **I-5** to Eugene, then **Rte. 58** east to **US 97** south. From US 97, **Rte. 138** leads west to the park's north entrance, but Crater Lake averages over 44 ft. of snow per year, and snowbound roads can keep the northern entrance closed as late as July. Before July, enter the park from the south. **Rte. 62** runs west from US 97, through the small town of **Fort Klamath** (the closest town to the national park) and on to the south access road that leads to the caldera's rim. From there, Rte. 62 intersects US 97 about 40 mi. south of the park, and another 20 mi. of southward travel on US 97 brings you to Klamath Falls.

- **Trains: Amtrak** (☎ 884-2822 or 800-872-7245; www.amtrak.com). At the east end of Main St., turn right onto Spring St., then left onto Oak St. Open daily 6:45-10:15am and 9-10:30pm. Once a day to **Portland** ($36-60) and continues north.

- **Buses: Greyhound**, 3817 US 97 N, in Mollie's Truck Stop (☎ 882-4616). Once a day to **Bend** (3hr., $20), **Eugene** (10hr., $40), and **Redding, CA** (4hr., $30). Open M-F 6am-2:30pm and midnight-12:45am, Sa 6-9am and midnight-12:45am.

- **Public Transportation: Basin Transit Service** (☎ 883-2877), runs 6 routes. Runs M-F 6am-7:30pm, Sa 10am-5pm. 90¢, seniors and disabled 45¢.

- **Taxis: Classic Taxi** (☎ 850-8303). $2 base, $2 per mi. 24hr.

- **Car Rental: Budget** (☎ 885-5421), at the airport. From S 6th St., go south on Washburn Dr. and follow the signs. $25 per day M-F, 25¢ per mi. after 100 mi. $28 per day Sa-Su, 200 free mi. per day. Open M-F 7am-10pm, Sa 8am-10pm, Su 9am-10pm.

PRACTICAL INFORMATION

- **Visitor Information: Chamber of Commerce**, 507 Main St. (☎ 884-0666 or 800-445-6728; www.klamathcountytourism.com). Open M-F 9am-5pm.

- **Outdoor Information: William G. Steel Center** (☎ 594-2211, ext. 402), 1 mi. from the south entrance. Open daily 9am-5pm. **Crater Lake National Park Visitors Center** (☎ 594-2211, ext. 415), on the lake shore at Rim Village. Open daily June-Sept. 8:30am-6pm.

- **Park Entrance Fee:** Cars $10, hikers and bikers $5. Free with Golden Eagle Passport.

- **Internet Access: Klamath County Library**, 126 S 3rd St. (☎ 882-8894). Has 6 computers with 1hr. free Internet access. Open M and F-Sa 10am-5pm, Tu-Th 10am-8pm.

- **Laundromat: Main Street Laundromat**, 1711 Main St. (☎ 883-1784). Wash $1.25, dry 25¢ per 10min. Open daily 8am-8pm; last wash 7pm.

CRATER LAKE AND KLAMATH FALLS ■ 129

Emergency: ☎911. **Police:** 425 Walnut St. (☎883-5336).

Crisis Line: ☎800-452-3669. 24hr. **Rape Crisis:** ☎884-0390. 24hr.

Hospital: Merle West Medical Center, 2865 Daggett Ave. (☎882-6311). From US 97 N, turn right on Campus Dr., then right onto Daggett. 24hr. emergency room.

Post Office: Klamath Falls, 317 S 7th St. (☎800-275-8777), at Walnut St. Open M-F 7:30am-5:30pm, Sa 9am-noon. **Crater Lake,** in the Steel Center. Open M-Sa 10am-noon and 1-3pm. **ZIP Code:** 97604.

ACCOMMODATIONS AND CAMPING

Klamath Falls has plenty affordable hotels that make easy bases for Crater Lake. If you'd rather live in the trees, **Forest Service campgrounds** line **Rte. 62** through Rogue River National Forest to the west of the park. The park itself contains two campgrounds, both of which are closed until roads are passable. **Backcountry camping** is allowed in the park; a backcountry permit, free from the Steel Center, is required.

Mazama Campground (☎594-2255), near park's south entrance off Hwy. 62. Tenters and RVs swarm this monster facility when it opens in mid-June, and some don't leave until it closes in Oct. Mostly tent sites. Few electrical hookups. **Loop G** is more secluded and spacious. Toilets, laundry, telephone, and gas. Showers 75¢ for 4min. Wheelchair accessible. No reservations. 200 sites, tents $15; RVs $17; electric hookups $19.

Townhouse Motel, 5323 S 6th St. (☎882-0924). 3 mi. south of Main, on edge of strip-mall land, offers clean, comfy rooms at unbeatable prices. Cable, A/C, no phones. Fridges and microwaves are $4 extra if available. Double bed $30; two-bed rooms $35.

Lost Creek Campground (☎594-2255), in the southeast corner of the park, 3 mi. on a paved road off Rim Dr. Mid-sized sites are set amid pines. Water and toilets. No reservations. Usually open mid-July to mid-Sept., but check with Steel Center. Tent sites $10.

Collier Memorial State Park and Campground (☎783-2471), 30 mi. north of Klamath Falls on US 97, offers small tent and RV sites with little privacy just off the Williamson River. With toilets, showers, and laundry, though, this is a good place to crash for the night. Sites $15, Full hookups $18. Down the same road, the **Williamson River Campground** offers tent sites with pit toilets and no water for $6 per night.

FOOD

Eating cheap ain't easy in Crater Lake, with dining limited to a cafeteria, restaurant, and cafe in Rim Village. **Klamath Falls** has some affordable dining and a **Safeway** at Pine and 8th St., one block north of Main. (☎882-2660. Open daily 6am-11pm.) The **Fort Klamath General Store,** 52608 Hwy. 62, offers canned goods, sells gas, and houses a cafe. (☎381-2263. Open daily 7am-10pm; winter 7am-8pm.)

Waldo's Mongolian Grill and Tavern, 610 Main St. (☎884-6863). Pile your choice of veggies and meats into a bowl and watch as it sizzles on the grill. Medium bowl is $8.50, all-you-can-eat $10. The tavern has 81 beers, including 15 microbrews. Grill open M-Sa 11am-9pm; tavern open M-Th 11am-11:30pm, F-Sa 11am-1am.

Klamath Grill, 712 Main St. (☎882-1427). Offers daily specials and delicious homemade grub. Cold deli sandwiches and burgers are $4-6, specials are $6. Open M-F 6am-2:30pm, Sa-Su 7am-2pm.

Bountiful Bakery, 513 Main St. (☎273-1462). Basic homemade goodness hits the spot in this small cafe on the main drag. Be like the locals and have soup and a sandwich for $5.50 or stick with salad ($3-6). Open M-F 6am-9pm.

Cattle Crossing Cafe (☎381-9801), on Hwy. 62 in Fort Klamath. Waffle breakfasts ($3-7), burgers ($5-6), and delicious dinners ($7-12) are capped off by mouth-watering homemade pie ($2.75 a slice). Open Apr.-Oct. daily 6am-9pm.

OUTDOOR ACTIVITIES

The area around Crater Lake is filled with all sorts of outdoor adventures. With ample options for hiking and biking, as well as easy access to the backcountry regions outside the park, you may feel overwhelmed with options. A good jumping off point is the Steel Center (see **Outdoor Information**), or up at the Rim Village where the information center and the Crater Lake Lodge are located. **Crater Lake Lodge** (☎ 594-2255) is a few hundred yards east of Sinnott Memorial Overlook in the rim village. Rooms aren't budget, but fun in the lodge can be had for free: make a quick visit to the rustic "great hall," rebuilt from its original materials, and warm yourself by the fire or relax in a rocking chair on the observation deck. The friendly staff will be happy to help you find any info on the Lake that you need.

DRIVING. Rim Drive, often not open until mid-July, loops 33 mi. around the rim of the caldera, high above the lake. Pull-outs are strategically placed along the road wherever a view of the lake might cause an awe-struck tourist to drive off the cliff.

HIKING. Most visitors never stray far from their vehicles as they tour the lake, so hiking provides a great way to get away from the crowds. Trailheads are scattered along the rim, so just park and hike away from the road. The Steel Center has a trail map and info about which trails are closed due to weather.

   Watchman Peak (¾ mi. one-way, 1hr.). Begins on the west side of the lake. This short climb provides a great outlook over Wizard Island, 1 of the 2 active cindercones in the lake. Moderate.

   Mt. Scott (5 mi. round-trip, 2-3hr.). The trailhead is 17 mi. clockwise from Rim Village. Although steep, the ascent to the top of 9000 ft. Mt. Scott and the historic fire tower on top affords a beautiful panoramic view of the lake. Moderate to strenuous.

   Cleetwood Cove Trail (2¼ mi. round-trip, 2hr.), leaves from the north edge of the lake and is the only route down to the water and the park's most traveled trail. It drops 700 ft. in 1 mi. to get to the shore. Moderate to strenuous.

ON THE LAKE. In the summer, park rangers lead hour long boat tours from the end of the Cleetwood Cove Trail. Aside from giving a comprehensive history of the lake and its formation, the tours provide breathtaking views of both **Wizard Island,** a cinder cone rising 760 ft. above the lake, and **Phantom Ship Rock,** a spooky rock formation. ($19.25, under 11 $11.50. Tours run daily 10am-4:30pm between late June and mid-Sept.) Land-lubbers may prefer picnics and fishing at the bottom of the trail. Unfortunately, the water is too nutrient-poor to support much life; rainbow trout and kokanee alone inhabit the lake. Swimming is prohibited as the melted snow of the lake reaches a maximum temperature of only 50°F (10°C).

BACKCOUNTRY EXPLORATION. A hiking trip into the park's vast **backcountry** leaves all the exhaust and tourists behind. Hiking or climbing inside the caldera is prohibited. Other than near water sources, dispersed camping is allowed anywhere in the area but is complicated by the absence of water and the presence of bears. Get info and required backcountry permits for free at either visitors center. **Pacific Crest Trail** (various distances and times), begins from the trailhead ¾ mi. west of the south entrance. The ultimate backcountry trail passes through the park and three backcountry campsites, giving great views of mountain meadows, old-growth timber, and, of course, the lake. Another excellent loop begins at the **Red Cone trailhead** on the north access road, passing the less-traveled **Crater Springs, Oasis Butte,** and **Boundary Springs trails.** However, it is impaired by the snow until July and opens only at the discretion of the ranger. Contact the Steel Center for more information.

PENDLETON ☎ 541

This agricultural town is best known for its once locally processed wool and for the bustling Pendleton Round-Up. In mid-September, the population of this small northeastern Oregon town triples to 50,000 as cowfolks and horsedudes gather for the rodeo of a lifetime, Pendleton's annual celebration of machismo. Other than Round-Up weekend, Pendleton proves to be a worthwhile stop-over in a trip to the beautiful national forests that surround it, or on the way to better things.

ORIENTATION AND PRACTICAL INFORMATION

Pendleton is at the junction of I-84, Rte. 11, and US 395, just south of the Washington border, roughly equidistant (200-230 mi.) from **Portland, Spokane, WA**, and **Boise, ID**. Pendleton is divided into quadrants: east-west by Main St. and north-south by the Umatilla River. Streets parallel to the river are named alphabetically, with the main thoroughfares being Court Ave., Emigrant Ave., and Dorian Ave.; streets parallel to Main St. are numbered.

Buses: Greyhound, 320 SW Court Ave. (☎276-1551 or 800-231-2222). Open daily 9am-1pm, 3-9pm, and midnight-3am, mainly based on when the buses arrive. To: **Portland** (4-8hr., 3 per day, $32), **Seattle** (6hr., 2 per day, $56) and **Walla Walla, WA** (1hr., 2 per day, $11). 15% discount with a Student Advantage Card.

Taxis: Elite Taxi, ☎276-8294. Open M-Sa 4am-3am, Su 6am-3am.

Car Rental: Round-Up Rent-A-Car, 309 SW Emigrant Ave. (☎276-1498). $20 per day, 15¢ per mi. over 50 mi. Unlimited free mileage on weekly rentals ($140). Must be 25 with credit card. Open M-Sa 8am-5pm.

Visitor Information: Pendleton Chamber of Commerce, 501 S Main St. (☎276-7411 or 800-547-8911; www.pendleton-oregon.org). Cheerful help with housing, directions, and Round-Up tickets. Open M-F 8am-5pm, Sa 9am-5pm; winter M-F 8:30am-5pm.

Outdoor Information: Umatilla Forest Headquarters, 2517 SW Hailey Ave. (☎278-3716; www.fs.fed.us/r6/uma), up the hill from I-84 Exit 209. Answers all questions about the Umatilla National Forest. Open M-F 7:45am-4:30pm.

Emergency: ☎911. **Police:** 109 SW Court Ave. (☎276-4411). 24hr.

Hospital: St. Anthony's, 1601 SE Court Ave. (☎276-5121).

Internet Access is available at the **Library,** 502 SW Dorian Ave., in the City Hall Complex. Free Internet access for 1hr. for locals. Open M-Th 11am-8pm, F-Sa 11am-5pm.

Post Office: 104 SW Dorian Ave. (☎800-275-8777), in the Federal Building at SW 1st St. Open M-F 9am-5pm, Sa 10am-1pm. **ZIP Code:** 97801.

ACCOMMODATIONS

For most of the year, lodging in Pendleton is inexpensive. During the Round-Up, rates double, and rooms are booked up to two years in advance. The nearest decent camping is 25 mi. away at Emigrant Springs State Park, or in the **Mountain View RV park:** 1375 SE 3rd St, (☎276-1041), where tents pay RV rate of $15. Fortunately, the Round-Up provides an additional 1500 spots at schools around town (tents $10, RVs $15). Call the Chamber of Commerce after April 1 to lasso a spot.

Tapadera Budget Inn, 105 SW Court (☎276-3231 or 800-722-8277), near the town center. Relax in the big rooms, all featuring cable TV and HBO, or after dinner at the in-house restaurant and bar. Singles $34; doubles $44.

Relax Inn, 205 SE Dorian Ave. (☎276-3293), 2 blocks east of Main St. Offers dimly lit but clean rooms, some with fridges, at unbeatable prices. Singles $25; doubles $30.

Emigrant Springs State Park (☎983-2277; reservations 800-452-5687), 26 mi. southeast of Pendleton off I-84 Exit 234. Get away from the Up in this shady grove of evergreens at a historic Oregon Trail camp. Some highway noise, hot showers, and flush toilets. Wheelchair accessible. 33 tent sites $13, 18 full hookups $17.

FOOD

Vegetarians will have more luck grazing in the surrounding wheat fields than in most of the restaurants—Pendleton offers steak and little else. For groceries, head to **Albertson's,** opposite the Round-Up. (☎276-1362. Open daily 6am-midnight.)

▨ **Great Pacific Cafe,** 403 S Main St. (☎276-1350). This cool establishment hosts wine tastings every other F at 4:30pm ($1.50 per half-glass) and bluegrass every Sa afternoon. Many come for coffee and sandwiches ($4-7). Open M-Sa 8:30am-8pm.

Cimmiyottis, 137 S Main (☎276-4314). The local place to see and be seen in the evenings offers great steaks ($13-19) and Italian food. Open M-Sa from 4pm.

Circle S Barbecue, 210 SE 5th St. (☎276-9637). A neighborhood restaurant built on the premise that it is not possible to eat too much meat. BBQ is $10.50 for 1 meat, $11.50 for 2. Open Tu-Th 7am-8:30pm, F-Sa 7am-9pm, Su 7am-2pm.

The Cookie Tree, 30 SW Emigrant Ave. (☎278-0343). A buzzing little shop known mainly for its large, delicious sandwiches ($3.25-6.50). Vegetarians can delve into the Avocado Deluxe or the Veggie Delight ($5.50 each). Open M-F 6am-3pm.

SIGHTS AND EVENTS

PENDLETON ROUND-UP. At heart, Pendleton is a fervent, frothing rodeo town. This has been one of the premier events in the national circuit since 1910 and is known as the "fastest moving rodeo in America." Ranchers from all over the US flock to Pendleton for steer-roping, bulldogging, bareback competitions, buffalo chip tosses, wild-cow milking, and greased-pig chases. Tickets go on sale 22 months in advance (mid-Nov.) and often sell out. Get yours today (for next year, of course) through the Chamber of Commerce. Lucky callers may even snag a resell to this year's event. Those who fail sometimes try the ever-present scalpers. *(☎276-2553 or 800-457-6336. Sept. 12-15, 2002. Tickets $10-16 per day.)*

▨ **THE TAMASTSLIKT CULTURAL INSTITUTE.** A huge and carefully designed tribute to the Confederated Tribes of the Umatilla Reservation. It tells the story of the Oregon Trail from the Indian perspective. The museum features hours of taped and filmed interviews with tribal elders and activists, as well as a real tule mat winter lodge and a 12,000 year-old mammoth tooth. See the beautiful beadwork in the gift shop afterward. *(At the Wildhorse Resort, 4 mi. east of Pendleton off I-84 Exit 216. ☎966-9748. Open daily 9am-5pm. $6; over 55, children, and students $4; under 5 free.).*

PENDLETON UNDERGROUND TOURS. This is the town's great year-round attraction, retelling Pendleton's wild history from its pinnacle (when the town claimed 32 bars and 18 brothels within 4 blocks) to unscrewing of the last red lightbulb (well into the 1950s). The 1½hr. tour meanders through former speakeasies, inhuman living quarters for Chinese laborers, a brothel, and an opium den. *(37 SW Emigrant Ave. ☎276-0730 or 800-226-6398. Reservations highly recommended in summer. Call for tour times and reservations. $10, children 12 and under $5. AAA discount $1.)*

PENDLETON WOOLEN MILLS. Manufacturing the wool blankets and clothing bearing their name since 1909, the mills now draw devotees eager to own a Native American patterned blankets or a thick wool shirt. *(1307 SE Court Place. ☎276-6911. Open May-Dec. M-Sa 8am-5pm, Su 11am-3pm. Free 20min. tour M-F 9, 11am, 1:30, and 3pm. Blanket seconds go for $50-89, perfect patches $140-200, shirts $45.)*

OUTDOOR ACTIVITIES

EN ROUTE TO BLUE MOUNTAINS AND UMATILLA. Pendleton makes a good stop-off on the way to the **Blue Mountains** in the **Umatilla National Forest** (yoo-ma-TILL-uh). The abundance of hiking, fishing, boating, and other recreational activities makes the Umatillas a popular yet still pristine place to explore. To get there,

HELLS CANYON & WALLOWA MTNS. ■ 133

take Rte. 11 north for 20 mi. to Rte. 204 E. After 41 mi., Rte. 204 meets Rte. 82 on the east side of the mountains at **Elgin**. There are five main **campgrounds** along this route, all with picnic tables, drinking water (save Woodland), and none with showers or electricity. All 5 offer great hiking trails; check with the ranger station for maps and suggestions. The most convenient are **Woodward** (18 sites; $10) and **Woodland** (7 sites; free), just before and just after the town of **Tollgate** off Rte. 204. **Target Meadows** (20 sites; $10) is an isolated spot only 2 mi. off the hwy. (take Forest Rd. 640 north from Toilgate off Rte. 204). **Jubilee Lake**, 12 mi. northeast of Tollgate, is popular for swimming, boating, and fishing. It also offers rowboats for $6 per hr. (turn north onto Forest Rd. 64 at Tollgate, 22 mi. east of the junction of Rte. 204 and Rte. 11, and follow the signs. Wheelchair accessible. 51 sites $14.) This portion of Rte. 204, between Rte. 11 and Elgin, winds through dense timber and creeks, near two wilderness areas: the small **North Fork Umatilla** (20,144 acres) to the south, and the large **Wenaha-Tucannon Wilderness** (177,465 acres) to the north. Both are little-used and offer 200 mi. of more challenging hiking trails, as well as real solitude to hunters, fishers, horseback riders.

RAFTING. In April and May it is possible to raft Class III rapids on the north fork of the **John Day River**. The 40 mi. journey begins at Dale, south of Pendleton on I-395, and ends at the town of Monument; call the ranger for details.

WINTER. In the winter, **snowmobiling** is a popular pastime; the north half of the Umatilla National Forest is crisscrossed with over 200 mi. of groomed trails. Ask for the *Winter Sports on the Umatilla National Forest* brochure at the Chamber of Commerce for information on specific trails. **Cross-country skiers** will find marked trails at Horseshoe Prairie, 7 mi. south of Tollgate on the west side of Rte. 204, and are welcome (along with snowmobiles), on forest roads in winter. Contact the ranger for trailhead **parking permits.** Further info on the Umatilla National Forest is available at the Umatilla Forest Headquarters in Pendleton.

HELLS CANYON & WALLOWA MTNS. ☎541

The northeast corner of Oregon is the state's most rugged, remote, and arresting country, with jagged granite peaks, glacier-gouged valleys, and azure lakes. East of La Grande, the Wallowa Mountains (wa-LAH-wah) rise abruptly, looming over the plains from elevations of more than 9000 ft. Thirty miles east, North America's deepest gorge plunges to the Snake River. It may take a four-wheel-drive vehicle to get off the beaten path, but those with the initiative and the horsepower will find stunning vistas and heavenly solitude in the backcountry.

▐ TRANSPORTATION

There are three ways to get to the **Wallowa Valley,** which lies between the **Hells Canyon National Recreation Area** and the **Eagle Cap Wilderness.** From **Baker City,** Rte. 86 heads east through **Halfway** (also known as **Half.com,** the world's first dot-com city) to connect with Forest Rd. 39, which winds north over the southern end of the Wallowas, meeting Rte. 350 (also known as Little Sheep Creek Hwy.) 8 mi. east of **Joseph.** From **La Grande,** Rte. 82 arcs around the north end of the Wallowas, through the small towns of Elgin, Minam, Wallowa, and Lostine, continuing through **Enterprise** and **Joseph,** and terminating at **Wallowa Lake.** From **Lewiston, ID,** Rte. 129 heads south into Washington, then over Rattlesnake Pass, becoming Rte. 3 in Oregon and joining Rte. 82 in Enterprise.

▐ ORIENTATION AND PRACTICAL INFORMATION

Three main towns offer services within the area: Enterprise, Joseph, and Halfway. Joseph lies 6 mi. east of Enterprise on Rte. 82. In **Enterprise,** Rte. 82 is called North St., and in Joseph it goes by Main St. **Halfway** is about 65 mi. south of Joseph. To get

134 ■ THE CASCADES

there, take E Wallowa Rd., off Main St. in Joseph, and follow the signs to Halfway (the drive takes 2hr., the majority of which is on **Forest Rd. 39,** a paved but brutally curvy route). Other major roads in the area are **Rte. 350,** a paved route from Joseph 30 mi. northeast to the tiny town of **Imnaha,** and the **Imnaha River Rd.** (a.k.a. Country Rd. 727 and Forest Rd. 3955), a good gravel road that runs south from Imnaha to reconnect with Forest Rd. 39 about 50 mi. southeast of Joseph. The invaluable and free Wallowa County Visitor Map is available in visitors centers and ranger stations, as are current road conditions information.

Buses: Moffit Brothers Transportation (☎569-2284) runs the **Wallowa Valley Stage Line,** which makes one round-trip M-Sa between **Joseph** and **La Grande.** Pickup at the **Chevron** on Rte. 82 in Joseph, the **Amoco** on Rte. 82 in Enterprise, and the **Greyhound terminal** in La Grande. Will stop and pickup at Wallowa Lake with advance notice. One-way from **La Grande** to: **Enterprise** ($11); **Joseph** ($12); and **Wallowa Lake** ($17).

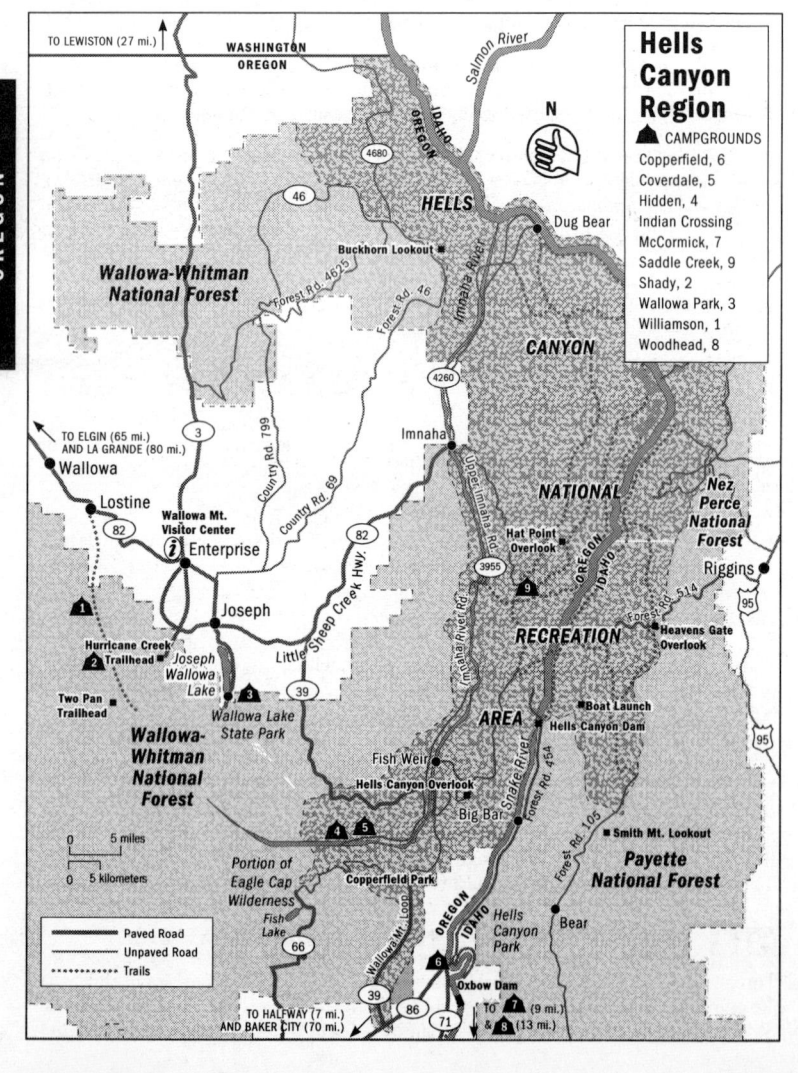

HELLS CANYON & WALLOWA MTNS. ■ 135

Visitor Information: Wallowa County Chamber of Commerce, 936 W North St. (☎426-4622 or 800-585-4121), in Enterprise. General tourist info as well as the comprehensive and free *Wallowa County Visitor Guide.* Open M-F 8am-5pm, Sa 9am-4pm. **Hells Canyon Chamber of Commerce** (☎742-4222), in the office of Halfway Motels (see **Accommodations,** below), provides info on accommodations, outfitters, and guides.

Outdoor Information: Wallowa Mountains Visitor Center, 88401 Rte. 82 (☎426-5546; www.fs.fed.us/r6/w-w), on the west side of Enterprise. $6 map a necessity for navigating area roads. Open Memorial Day-Labor Day M-Sa 8am-5pm, Su noon-5pm; Labor Day to Memorial Day M-F 8am-5pm. **Hells Canyon National Recreation Area Office,** 2 mi. south of Clarkston, WA on Rte. 129 (☎509-758-0616) carries all sorts of information on Hells Canyon. Open M-F 7:30-11:30am and 12:30-4:30pm.

Laundromat: Joseph Laundromat and Car Wash, on Rte. 82 in Joseph, across from the Indian Lodge Motel. Wash $1, dry 25¢ per 8min. Open daily 6am-10pm.

Emergency: ☎911. **Police:** State police ☎426-3036. Enterprise, 108 NE 1st St. (☎426-3136), at the corner of North St.

Fire: ☎426-4196.

Hospital: Wallowa Memorial, 401 NE 1st St. (☎426-3111), in Enterprise.

Internet Access: The **Enterprise Public Library,** 101 NE 1st St. (☎426-3906), at Main St., charges $4 for 30min. and $6 per hr. Open M, F noon-6pm, T-Th 10am-6pm.

Post Office: 201 W North St. (☎800-275-8777), on Rte. 82 in Enterprise. Open M-F 9am-4:30pm. **ZIP Code:** 97828.

▟▟ ACCOMMODATIONS AND CAMPING

Most of the towns along Rte. 82 have motels with plenty of vacancy during the week. On weekends rooms are more scarce. Campgrounds here are plentiful, inexpensive, and sublime. Pick up the free *Campground Information* pamphlet at the Wallowa Mountains Visitor Center (see p. 135) for a complete listing of sites in the area. Many campgrounds are not fully serviced, and are therefore **free,** but recent improvements to some campgrounds (water and pit toilets) have resulted in fees ($5-8) for formerly free campsites. On the whole, showers and toilets are non-existent, and insect repellent is a must in summer. There are many potential campsites, but because of adverse road conditions, most campgrounds are only open from June to September.

Indian Lodge Motel, 201 S Main St. (☎432-2651 or 888-286-5484), on Rte. 82 in Joseph. Elegant rooms with dark wood furniture and plush blue carpet. A/C, cable, coffeemakers, fridges. Singles $37; doubles $49. Winter singles $32; doubles $40.

Country Inn Motel, 402 W North St. (☎426-4986 or 877-426-4986 toll free), in Enterprise. Reminiscent of a country farmhouse. Rooms stay remarkably cool without A/C. Cable, coffeemakers, fridges. Singles $42, doubles $50. Rates lower in winter.

Wallowa Lake State Park Campground (☎432-4185; reservations 800-452-5687) at the eastern end of Rte. 82. Books solid 11 months in advance. Full-service camping. Flushing toilets, potable water, showers. Tent sites $17, full hookups $21.

Copperfield, at the northern end of Hwy. 86; **McCormick** 12 mi. south of Copperfield off of Hwy. 71; and **Woodhead,** 4 mi. south of McCormick on Hwy. 71, are 3 campgrounds along the **Snake River** near Oxbow and Brownlee Dams that are the only sites open year-round (☎785-3323). Tent and RV sites, restrooms. Hot showers at Woodhead. No reservations. $6, hookups $10.

Saddle Creek Campground. From Rte. 82, turn on E Wallowa Rd. (a.k.a. Rte. 350) in Joseph. When you reach Imnaha, drive 19 mi. to the campground on the unpaved and steep Hat Point Rd. (Forest Rd. 4240). 7 sites perched on the lip of Hells Canyon. Unbelievable views. 1½hr. from Joseph. Toilets, no water. Wheelchair accessible. Free.

Imnaha Lake Campgrounds include 3 campgrounds by the Imnaha River. Take Forest Rd. 39 from Joseph or Halfway for 1hr. to Forest Rd. 3960 at the Imnaha Lake Campgrounds sign. The first campground, **Coverdale** (11 sites), is 5 mi. up Forest Rd. 3960. **Hidden** campground (13 sites) lies 3 mi. farther, and 2 mi. beyond that is **Indian Crossing** (14 sites, trailhead access). All 3 have water, pit toilets, and are $5 per night.

FOOD

If heading out onto the hairy roads of Hells Canyon, bring some provisions—a flat or breakdown could require a roadside meal or two. Find groceries at **Safeway,** 601 W North St., on Rte. 82 in Enterprise. (☎ 426-3722. Open daily 6am-10pm.) In Halfway, the **Old Pine Market,** 130 S Main St. (☎ 742-4366. Open daily 7:30am-8:30pm.)

Wildflour Bakery, 600 N Main St. (☎ 432-7225), in Joseph, offers an amazing selection of scrumptious baked goods, as well as giant sourdough and cornmeal pancakes ($2 per cake). Sit on the patio and enjoy the day with a chicken sausage sandwich or giant burrito ($5). Open M and W-Sa 7am-3pm, Su 7am-1pm. Breakfast til 11am.

Embers Brew House, 206 N Main St. (☎ 432-2739), in Joseph. In the summer, the patio is packed outside this popular dinner spot. Sample 5 of 17 microbrews ($5). Fries $4. Open June-Sept. daily 11am-11pm; winter Su-Th 11am-8pm, F-Sa 11am-11pm.

Old Town Cafe, 8 S Main St. (☎ 432-9898), in Joseph. Sit in the outdoor grotto and dig into a bottomless bowl of homemade soup ($3) or a giant fresh baked cinnamon roll ($1.75). Breakfast all day. Open F-W 7am-2pm.

Vali's Alpine Delicatessen Restaurant, 59811 Wallowa Lake Hwy. (☎ 432-5691), in Wallowa Lake. For 25 years in this small, alpine-esque cottage, Mr. Vali has cooked one authentic European dish each night and Mrs. Vali has served it. Hungarian Kettle Goulash $8.50; schnitzel $12. Reservations required for dinner. Breakfast W-Su 9am-11am, dinner seatings W-Su at 5 and 8pm. In winter, Sa and Su only.

OUTDOOR ACTIVITIES: HELLS CANYON

The canyon's endearing name comes from its legendary inaccessibility and hostility to human habitation. The walls of Hells Canyon drop over 8000 ft. to the **Snake River,** which makes it the deepest canyon in North America.

LOOKOUTS. Hells Canyon Overlook, the most accessible of the lookout points, is up Forest Rd. 3965. The road departs Rd. 39 about 5 mi. south of the Imnaha River crossing. The broadest and most eye-popping views are from the **Hat Point Lookout Overlook,** where visitors can climb a 90 ft. wooden fire lookout. To get there, go 24 mi. up a steep but well-maintained gravel road (not recommended for trailers) from Imnaha (Forest Rd. 4240, a.k.a. Hat Point Rd.), and follow the signs. There are pit toilets at the overlook and several picnic sites for day use. The **Buckhorn Lookout** lies far off the beaten path, 42 mi. northeast of Joseph, and offers lofty views of the Imnaha River Valley. Take Rte. 82 north 3 mi. out of Joseph or 3 mi. south out of Enterprise, and look for the green sign for Buckhorn. Turn off and follow Zumwalt Rd. (a.k.a. Country Rd. 697, which turns into Forest Rd. 46) for approximately 40 bumpy miles to Buckhorn—about a half-day round-trip. Also at that end of the canyon, the immense **Hells Canyon Dam** lies 23 mi. north of Oxbow on Rte. 86, (turns into Forest Rd. 454). This drive is one of only three ways to get near the bottom of the canyon by car, and the dam is the only place to cross.

HIKING. There are over 1000 mi. of trails in the canyon, only a fraction of which are maintained. Most are only open in April. The dramatic 56 mi. **Snake River Trail** runs by the river for the length of the canyon. At times, the trail is cut into the side of the rock with just enough clearance for a horse's head. This trail can be followed from **Dug Bar** in the north down to the Hells Canyon Dam or accessed by steep trails along the way. From north to south, **Hat Point, Freezeout,** and **P.O. Saddle** are access points. To reach Dug Bar, get a high-clearance 4WD vehicle and hit the steep, slippery Forest Rd. 4260 for 27 mi. northeast from **Imnaha.** Bring snakebite kits, boots, and water. Rangers patrol the river by boat at least once a day.

WATER. The easiest way to see a large portion of the canyon is on the Snake River by jet boat or raft; both pursuits are guaranteed to drench. Numerous outfitters operate out of Oxbow and the dam area; the Wallowa Mountains Visitors Center (see p. 135) and all local chambers of commerce have a list of the permittees. **Hells Canyon Adventures,** 4200 Hells Canyon Dam Rd., 1½ mi. from the Hells Canyon Dam in Oxbow, runs a wide range of jet boat and raft trips. (☎ 785-3352 or 800-422-3568. Jet boats 2hr. $30, 3hr. $40, full day $95. Whitewater rafting $140 for a day trip.)

OUTDOOR ACTIVITIES: WALLOWA MOUNTAINS

Without a catchy, federally approved name like "Hells Canyon National Recreation Area," the Wallowas often take second place to the canyon. They are equally magnificent, however, as their canyons echo with the rush of rapids and their jagged peaks cover with wildflowers in spring.

HIKING. Over 600 mi. of **hiking trails** cross the **Eagle Cap Wilderness** and are usually free of snow from mid-July to October. Deep glacial valleys and high granite passes make hiking this wilderness difficult. It often takes more than a day to get into the most beautiful areas, so carry adequate supplies and prepare for sudden weather changes. The 5 mi. hike to **Chimney Lake** from the **Bowman** trailhead on the Lostine River Rd. (Forest Rd. 8210) traverses fields of granite boulders sprinkled with a few small meadows. A little farther on lie the serene **Laverty, Hobo,** and **Wood Lakes,** where the road is less traveled. The **Two Pan** trailhead at the end of the Lostine River Rd. is the start of a forested 6 mi. hike to popular **Minam Lake,** which makes a good starting point for those heading to other back country spots.

By far the most popular area in the Eagle Cap Wilderness is the **Lakes Basin** (a 7-9 mi. hike from the Two Pan trailhead), where explorers can find unsurpassed scenery, good fishing, and hikes to Eagle Cap Peak. While it is possible to escape the crowds in the basin during the week, the lake is packed on weekends. **Steamboat, Long,** and **Swamp Lakes** (also accessible from the Two Pan trailhead) are as magnificent as the Lakes Basin but receive only half as many visitors. Rangers at the visitors center can also recommend more secluded routes. Many excellent day hikes to **Lookingglass, Culver, Bear, Eagle, Cached, Arrow,** and **Heart Lakes** start from the Boulder Park trailhead, on Forest Rd. 7755, on the southern side of the Eagle Cap Wilderness (accessible from Baker City and Halfway).

FISHING. Fishing in the alpine lakes of Eagle Cap is incredible, but it's illegal even to catch and release without a permit. Some fish, such as bull trout, are entirely protected. Get permits ($8 per day, $49 per year) and the *Oregon Sport Fishing Regulations* booklet at any local sporting store.

BURNS ☎ 541

Tiny Burns and its even tinier neighbor Hines serve as way-stations and supply centers for travelers. Packed with cheap motels and fast food joints, Burns offers sustenance, shelter, and a wealth of information on the surrounding country. And what great outdoor country it is. Ideally situated between the Ochoco and Malheur National Forests, the Malheur National Wildlife Refuge, Steens Mountain, and the Alvord Desert, Burns is the center for outdoor activities in the otherwise uninhabited wilderness of southeastern Oregon.

ORIENTATION AND PRACTICAL INFORMATION. US 20 from Ontario and US 395 from John Day converge 2 mi. north of Burns, continue through Burns and Hines as one, and diverge about 30 mi. west of town. US 20 continues west to Bend and the Cascade Range; US 395 runs south to Lakeview, OR, and California; Rte. 205 runs south to Frenchglen and Fields (see below). Although buses and vans run to and from some of the nearby towns, there is no public transportation to the surrounding outdoors. **Harney County Chamber of Commerce,** 76 E Washington

St., has excellent maps and info on both towns. (☎573-2636. Open M-F 9am-5pm.) Even more useful are the **Burns Ranger District (Malheur National Forest)** and **Snow Mountain Ranger District (Ochoco National Forest)**, in Hines. These outdoor resources share an office on the main drag about 4½ mi. south of Burns, and provide information on camping, hiking, and every other wilderness activity imaginable in the surrounding countryside. (☎573-4300. Open M-F 7:30am-4:30pm.) **Burns Bureau of Land Management (BLM)**, US 20 West, is a few miles west of Hines. The BLM office, and the BLM website, provide essential information on the federally controlled areas of Southeastern Oregon, including Steens Mountain and the Malheur Wildlife Refuge. (☎573-4400; www.or.blm.gov/burns. Open M-F 7:45am-4:30pm.) **Emergency:** ☎911. **Police:** 242 S. Broadway (☎573-6028). **Hospital:** 557 W Washington St. (☎573-7281). 24hr. emergency care. **Post Office:** 100 S Broadway. (☎800-275-8777. Open M-F 8:30am-5pm.) **ZIP Code:** 97720

ACCOMMODATIONS AND FOOD. The **Bontemps Motel**, 74 W Monroe St., provides comfortable rooms with firm beds and some damn cool lampshades. Cable TV and A/C come standard; fridges and microwaves are $5 more. (☎573-2037 or 800-229-1394. Singles $32; doubles $38; pets $5.) **Idlewild,** just off of US 395 17 mi. north of town, is the only convenient official campground. Ponderosa pines surround. (☎573-4300. Pit toilets and drinking water. No hookups. 23 sites, $7.) **Safeway**, 246 W Monroe St. (☎573-6767. Open daily 5am-11pm.) **Broadway Deli**, 528 N Broadway Ave., sells cheap but filling sandwiches ($4.75) and homemade soup ($2 per bowl). A great alternative to the fast food fare. (Open M-F 8:30am-5pm.)

NEAR BURNS ☎541

MALHEUR NAT'L WILDLIFE REFUGE & DIAMOND CRATERS

About 40 mi. south of Burns, miles of sagebrush give way to the grasslands and marshes of **Harney** and **Malheur Lakes,** where thousands of birds end their migratory flight paths each year at **Malheur National Wildlife Refuge.** Stretching 35 mi. south along Rte. 205, the refuge covers 185,000 acres and is home to 58 mammal species and over 320 species of birds, including grebes, ibis, plovers, shrikes, owls, wigeons, and waxwings. Malheur is the sole National Refuge that contains remnants of earlier civilizations; any discovered arrowheads cannot be removed.

The refuge headquarters, 6 mi. east of Rte. 205 on a well-marked turn-off between Burns and Frenchglen, houses a useful **visitors center** that provides trail directions and area info. (☎493-2612. Open M-F 7am-3:30pm, Sa-Su 8am-4pm.) No camping is allowed within the refuge, but **accommodations** are available at the **Malheur Field Station** an old government training camp a few miles from headquarters. Make reservations in advance, especially for spring, fall, and holiday weekends. Toilets and potable water. (☎493-2629. Three-meal package $20. Kitchen access $2. 36 dorm-style bunks $18; singles $30; doubles $45; RV hookups $16.)

The refuge is open to exploration by foot or vehicle year-round during daylight hours. It takes 2hr. to traverse, and some areas require a 4WD vehicle. The drive leaves from the visitors center and provides some of the best wildlife viewing in Oregon. Hundreds of bird species nest here in spring and bald eagles are often seen in the coldest months, and hiking is generally allowed only along roads.

HIKING. Two short hiking trails depart from the visitors center, and a couple others are available. The **Loop Trail** (11 mi. loop, several hr.) largely unmarked and primitive, departs from P-Ranch, just before Frenchglen off the Steens Mt. Loop. This moderately difficult trail offers great opportunities to see migratory birds.

DIAMOND CRATERS. A well-marked turn-off 30 mi. south of Burns on Hwy. 205 leads to the **Diamond Craters,** located just east of the Malheur Refuge. The nearest facilities are in Burns, 55 mi. to the northwest. The 100-year-old **Hotel Diamond,** 12 mi. east of Rte. 205 on Diamond Lane, seems young in relation to the craters, but proves a sophisticated rest stop for the dedicated explorer. Children—not old enough to be considered historical—are not allowed. (☎ 493-1898; www.central-oregon.com/hoteldiamond. Breakfast $1.50-4.75; dinner $10-15, for guests only. A small, but historic, double with shared bath starts at $55.)

This outstanding national area contains some of the most diverse basaltic volcanic features in the country. The BLM has created a self-guided tour for those wishing to educate themselves about the area. Pick up a brochure detailing the 13 stops and sights of the tour in any visitors center, ranger station, or at the Hotel or Mercantile in Frenchglen. Stay on established trails lest your car/bike/ankles become fixed in soft volcanic cinder. Bring water and watch out for rattlesnakes.

FRENCHGLEN ☎ 541

An hour south of Burns along Rte. 205, Frenchglen provides access to wildlife refuges and the western side of the Steens Mountain via the Steens Mtn. Loop. **Fields,** 55min. farther south of Frenchglen on Rte. 205 at the southern tip of the mountain, provides access to the eastern face and the Alvord Desert. Both towns are little more than a few buildings along the highway, but they can provide food, shelter, and sound advice. **Frenchglen Mercantile** (☎ 493-2738), on Rte. 205, has gas, canned goods, and from June through August they also offer pre-made deli sandwiches for $4.50. They recommend and sell *Oregon's Outback*, a helpful book that outlines an auto tour of southeastern Oregon. The owners also run a bar and a guesthouse connected to the main store, with two very comfortable rooms in which to end a long day. (☎ 493-2738. Double bed $65. Open daily 7am-8pm.) The **Steens Mountain Resort,** North Steens Mt. Loop Rd. just 3 mi. outside of town, also has a small general store with canned goods and laundry facilities. (☎ 493-2415 or 800-542-3765. Wash 75¢, dry 50¢ for 20min. Open daily 8am-6pm.)

FIELDS ☎ 541

Consisting of only a few houses, the rambling **Fields Station** is home to four businesses owned by the same family. The general store and gas station are the last of each for miles. The cafe serves remarkably large burgers ($4.25), scrumptious onion rings ($2), and 6000 milkshakes a year ($3). The small motel and campground next door to the cafe rents rooms. (☎ 495-2275. Singles $30; doubles $40; RV hookups $7.50; tenting areas free.)

STEENS MOUNTAIN ☎ 541

Oregon's most unearthly landscape lies in the southeast, where the **Steens Mountain** rises nearly 10,000 ft. above inhospitable sagebrush to the west; to the east lies an uninhabited, bone-dry alkali flat. Steens is the highest mountain in southeastern Oregon and the view from the top pans across four states. Contact the Burns District BLM for road info and get **maps** of the area at the **Frenchglen Hotel** and the **Steens Mountain Resort.** There are four **campgrounds,** all with pit toilets and drinking water; all charge $6 per night. Each is just off the Steens Mt. Rd., which leaves from Frenchglen. **Page Springs** only 5 mi. from Frenchglen, is accessible year-round (36 sites); **Fish Lake,** 19 mi. in and nearly 1½ mi. up toward the mountain, has 23 sites and a boat ramp; **Jackman Park,** 3 mi. farther in (6 mountainside sites); and **South Steens,** a few miles farther (21 sites and 15 equestrian sites).

DRIVING. Nearly all visitors to Steens Mountain are vehicle-shackled; walking even a short distance from the road leaves behind all but occasional bighorn sheep and pronghorn antelope. To further discourage foot exploration, the nearest water source is five mi. in any direction from most anywhere along the road and the temperature hovers around a toasty 100 degrees. The 66 mi. dirt track **Steens Mountain Loop Rd.** (open July-Oct.), climbs the west slope of the mountain from Rte. 205 near Frenchglen, and rejoins the hwy. only 8 mi. farther south.

OTHER EXPLORATION. Some of the best **fishing and hiking** is on the mountain's steep east face. Usually beginning just off the road, trails lead to lakes and cliffs, and enjoy great views of the surrounding country. One popular and moderately difficult hike is along **Blitzen River** (4 mi. one-way, several hours), which follows along the river, crossing in places to avoid steep cliffs, to some great places to fish. Watch out for rattlesnakes and stinging nettles.

ALVORD DESERT ☎ 541

From Fields, a 25 mi. trek up the Alvord Desert Rd. towards Andrews avails the **Alvord Hot Springs,** an easy-to-miss tin shack on the right side of the road. The mineral-rich bath emerges from the ground into an open pool at a scalding 174ºF, but the enclosed pool next door is much cooler and skinny-dipping is common. About 20 mi. farther north, **Mann Lake** is home to excellent fishing and a free campsite with pit toilets and water. Winding its way from Nevada through the Alvord Desert and up Steens Mountain, the **Desert Trail** links with the Fremont National Trail to provide an challenge equal to the Pacific Crest Trail. The first section of trail begins at the Page Springs campground on Steens Mountain (see above) and runs 25 mi. to the summit. The next section runs 15 mi. down to the Alvord Desert. Hiking the strenuous 40 mi. trail takes about eight days. **Trail guides** and info are available from the Desert Trail Association (☎475-2960) in Burns.

HART MOUNTAIN NATIONAL ANTELOPE REFUGE ☎ 541

Sixty-five miles northeast of Lakeview, a 275,000-acre refuge where the deer and antelope play, is accessible from a well-marked turn-off from Rte. 140 about 15 mi. east of Lakeview. The nearest services are in the town of **Plush,** 25 mi. away. Headquarters, on the main road near the center of the refuge, houses a 24hr. **visitors and viewing room** where you can pick up a free backcountry permit and some information on the refuge inhabitants. The lookout point 7 mi. south along the Blue Sky Rd. provides excellent wildlife viewing, but much of the refuge is accessible only to 4WD vehicles. A free **campground** with pit toilets but no water is next to the **Hart Mountain Hot Springs,** a few mi. south of headquarters on a clearly marked road. Fires are prohibited mid-summer through fall. **Rock Creek,** which passes by the refuge headquarters, has excellent **fishing.** From August to October, the refuge bustles with it's main influx of visitors: **hunters** eager to bag antelope, bighorn sheep, and deer. In winter, some of the surviving antelope gallop south to the **Sheldon National Refuge,** just across the border into Nevada.

LAKEVIEW ☎ 541

The incentives to visit friendly, dusty Lakeview (what with the lake having dried up) may seem few. They are, in fact, two. Lakeview makes an agreeable stop on the way to the great outdoors of southern Oregon because, first, the high buttes with unusually strong updrafts surrounding Lakeview have transformed this otherwise unremarkable town into the hang-gliding capital of the west. While no formal instruction is available within 500 mi. of town, extremely lucky and daring visitors may be able to hitch a tandem ride with a visiting pilot. Second, those happily on the ground are even closer to the vast Fremont National Forest.

⚡🛈 ORIENTATION AND PRACTICAL INFORMATION. Lakeview lies 15 mi. north of California, at the junction of Rte. 140 and Rte. 395. **Red Ball Stage Lines,** 619 Center St. (☎884-6460), runs two buses per day to **Klamath Falls** (one-way $17). The **Ford** dealership, 351 North O St. (☎947-4965), rents **cars** for $59 per day with unlimited mileage. **Visitor info** can be found at the **Chamber of Commerce,** 126 North E St. A good collection of info on trails in the area is also available. (☎947-6040. Open year-round M-F 8am-6pm; additionally, in summer Sa-Su 9am-5pm.) Visit the **Lakeview Ranger District,** located on Hwy. 395 just north of town. (☎947-3334; www.fs.fed.us/r6/fremont for outdoor info. Open M-F 7:45am-4:30pm.) **Equipment rental,** for at least skis if not parasails, is available at **D&M Ski,** 118 N L St., behind the blue house). This family-run shop rents ski and snowboard packages, provides information about the Warner Canyon Ski area, and is open when the ski area is open. (☎947-4862. Skis $12.50 per day, snowboards $13.50 per day. Call D&M or the ranger to check if they're open.) **Internet Access** can be found at **Gooselake Internet Services,** 102 North E.

St., for $10 per hr. (☎947-4513; www.gooselake.com. Open M-F 9am-5:30pm, Sa 10am-3pm), and at **Lake Cyber Outpost,** 510 N 1st St., next to the town hall, for $4 per hr. (☎947-5236. Open M-Th 2-6pm.) Wash up after a hard day at **Diane's Corner Laundromat,** on the corner of N K St. and N 4th St. (☎947-3886. Open daily 8am-9pm. Wash $1.25, dry 25¢ for 10min.) **Police:** 245 North F St., (☎947-2504). **Crisis line:** ☎947-2449. 24hr. **Post office:** 18 South G St. (☎800-275-8777. Open M-F 9:30am-5pm.) **ZIP Code:** 97630.

ACCOMMODATIONS AND CAMPING. The **Lakeview Lodge Motel,** 301 North G St., has friendly management and quietly elegant rooms. This "best value inn" also sports an exercise room, sauna, hot tub, and cable. (☎947-2181. Singles $60; doubles $50; kitchenettes $4 extra. 10% AAA discount.) Farther from town lies **Rim Rock Motel,** 727 South F St. Not every motel needs to be elegant. Instead, Rim Rock has cheap, adequate rooms featuring fridges, microwaves (when available), and cable. (☎947-2185. Singles $30; doubles $35.)

Popular **Goose Lake Campground,** 14 mi. south of Lakeview on Rte. 395 has quiet, somewhat private sites around a popular lake. Toilets and showers make it even better. (☎947-3111. Hookups and tent sites $15. Showers $2 for non-campers.) The Lakeview Ranger District rents two cabins in the summer: **Aspen Cabin** and **Drake Peak Lookout Cabin.** Both are located off Forest Rd. 3615 north of Rte. 140 east of Lakeview. Each rents for $25 per night and sleeps four. Aspen has a wood burning stove; Drake Peak has propane and wood stoves; neither has drinking water. The ranger can also direct you to free **campgrounds** in the forest. **Dog Lake,** one of the closest, is 25min. from Lakeview on Lake Rd. To get there, take Rte. 140 west of town to Forest Rd. 4017, which is denoted by a small sign on the side of the road, and follow it to Dog Lake. In addition to the rustic camping in eight sites, Dog Lake has excellent year-round bass and trout fishing. Pit toilets. Open May-Oct.

FOOD. Food choices in Lakeview are somewhat limited. Stock up on enriched rice and Evian at **Safeway,** 244 North F St. which glistens under a giant cowboy. (☎947-2324. Open daily 7am-11pm.) The popular **Indian Village,** 508 North 1st St., is decorated with artifacts that museums would kill for. The portions are large and breakfast is served all day. Buffalo burger $5.75. (☎947-2833. Open M-Sa 5am-9pm, Su 5am-3pm.) **Green Mountain Deli and Bakery,** 510 Center St., serves sandwiches ($3.75-6) in a cafe whose freshly-made donuts (40-85¢) hypnotize customers. (☎947-4996. Open M-F 4am-4pm, Sa 4am-2pm.)

NEAR LAKEVIEW

FREMONT NATIONAL FOREST ☎541

The **Fremont National Forest** provides a multitude of opportunities for hiking, fishing, canoeing, and cross-country skiing, all within a couple hours from Lakeview. For the angler, **fishing licenses** are available for $8 per day or $20 per year at **Lakeview Boot and Shoe Repair and Sporting Goods,** 221 North F St., opposite Safeway. (☎947-4486. Open M-Sa 9am-5:30pm.) Also at the **True Value Hardware Store** at the corner of E St. and Center St. (☎947-2210. Open M-Sa 8:30am-6pm, Su 9am-4pm.) If snow is more your idea of a good time, grab a **parking permit** ($10 per year) for the sno-parks in the area at the **Department of Motor Vehicles,** on S F St. just before S 9th St. (open M-F 9am-12:30pm and 1:30-5pm). Some of the hiking trails in the region require a trailhead permit, available at the ranger station for $5.

FISHING. Camping and fishing are great at Mud Creek, 18 mi. northeast of Lakeview on Forest Rd. 3615 off Hwy. 140. Watch out for the mosquitoes in the spring. While the area can be busy in the summer, during the runs in the spring and fall it can become a solitary fishing dream. Dog Lake (see Accommodations above) also combines its rustic camping with a great place to fish.

SKIING. Two state **Sno-parks** in the forest provide access to snowmobile trails, skiing, and winter back-country opportunities. One of them is **Warner Canyon**, located off Hwy. 140 east of town (follow the signs). In addition to cross-country skiing and snowmobiling trails, Warner Canyon offers downhill skiing at the Warner Canyon Ski area (lift tickets $16 per day, rentals from D&M see above).

HIKING. In the forest, hiking is generally moderate, although the weather can quickly complicate things. Water is often hard to find the farther the trails wander from Lakeview. Access to the **Fremont National Recreation Trail**, which when completed will run 175 mi. through the Fremont National Forest and connect to the Pacific Crest Trail at the Desert Scenic Trail, is at Silver Creek Marsh. The best directions are from the ranger. The difficult **Blue Lake/Palisades Rocks Trail** (6-8 mi. one-way from Corral Creek) runs through the Gearhart Mountain Wilderness, past the Palisade rock formation to pristine Blue Lake. Directions are complicated and can be found at either the Chamber of Commerce or the ranger.

HOT SPRINGS. Warm up after skiing at **Geyser Hot Springs,** about a mile north of town on Hwy. 395. Although at heart simply a big bathtub, it still does feel good after a long day exploring. Another option is at the **Summer Lake Hot Springs,** about 50 mi. north of Lakeview on Rte. 30 at the southern end of Summer Lake.

JOHN DAY FOSSIL BEDS ☎ 541

The John Day Fossil Beds National Monument is one of Eastern Oregon's most precious gems. The rich geologic history of fossils spanning 40 million years is divided into three isolated units, each representing a different stretch of time: the **Sheep Rock Unit,** the **Painted Hills Unit,** and the **Clarno Unit.** While the monument shares its namesake with the town of John Day, the latter is at best a stopover.

ACCOMMODATIONS. The campground of **Strawberry,** located only 25min. from John Day, offers its 12 sites ($6) along with **McNaughton Spring** (3 sites) and **Slide Creek** (3 sites), both free to the intrepid camper (only Strawberry has potable water). These 3 campgrounds are located off Forest Rd. 6001 near the beginning of the **Strawberry Basin Trail,** the area's main access point (take County Rd. 60 South from Prairie City). The trail runs 1 mi. toward Strawberry Lake and Strawberry Mountain, the forest's highest peak; a 12 mi. loop passes other lakes. **Magone Lake** (mah-GOON) is another popular campground with 23 sites, fishing, hiking, and swimming. (Potable water. $10.) To get there from John Day, take US 26 east 9 mi. to Keeney Forks Rd. North (watch for the tiny sign) and follow the signs for 15 mi. to the campground. An excellent map of both the Strawberry and Monument Rock Wildernesses is available for $4 at the ranger station.

Clyde Holiday State Park, 7 mi. west of town on US 26, provides grassy sites with a less-than-primitive aura. It offers electricity, showers, and teepees that have electricity, carpeting, and foam mattresses. Showers for non-campers are $2. (☎932-4453, reservations 800-452-5687. Hiker-bicyclist sites $4, 30 sites with electricity $16, 2 tepees $28.) For those preferring a real bed, **Dreamer's Lodge,** 144 N Canyon Blvd., has large rooms with A/C, fridges, microwaves, and cable TV. (☎575-0526 or 800-654-2849. Singles $48; doubles $52; ask about AAA discount.)

FOOD. Pick up groceries at **Chester's Thriftway,** 631 W Main St., in John Day Plaza. (☎575-1899. Open daily 7am-9pm.) Sit down and have a burger or a steak at the **Grubsteak Mining Co.,** 149 E Main St. Pool and beer are available in the saloon in the back. Or just go for breakfast at 5am ($3-7) before heading out to the fossil beds. (☎575-1970. Open M-Th 5am-2pm and 4-10pm, F-Sa 4-11pm, and Su 11am-9pm.) Enjoy a sit-down meal at **Dayville Cafe,** 212 W Franklin St. (Rte. 26), in Dayville. Big breakfasts, grilled sandwiches ($5-6) and country dinners ($10-15) are served in a calico country atmosphere. Everything is fresh and homemade in house by mom and pop. (☎987-2132. Open daily 7am-8pm. No credit cards.)

BAKER CITY ■ 143

🔺 **OUTDOOR ACTIVITIES.** The **Sheep Rock Unit** presents some of the best hiking of the three units, with trails that show off fossils of the prehistoric animals that once roamed this area. It also contains the **visitors center;** on Rte. 19, 2 mi. north of US 26. The center has displays, exhibits, and an award-winning video produced by high school students that explains the history of the fossil beds. (☎987-2333. Open daily 9am-5pm.)

In the **Sheep Rock Unit,** the **Blue Basin** area (3 mi. up the road from the visitors center) provides two distinct hiking opportunities: the **Island in Time Trail,** an easy 1 mi. round-trip into the canyon which passes by a blue-green rock formation, and the **Blue Basin Overlook Trail,** a more challenging 3 mi. loop up to the basin's rim, where the entire Unit as well as the John Day river valley can be seen. The Island Trail's fossilized sea turtles and saber-toothed carnivores are intriguing, but are surpassed by the Overlook Trail's views of brightly colored badland spires.

Five miles north of US 26 from the turn-off, 3 mi. west of Mitchell, the **Painted Hills Unit** offers several short hikes that present a better way to examine the beautifully colored mounds, once tropical rainforests. It focuses on an epoch 30 million years ago when the land was in geologic transition. Smooth mounds of brilliant red, yellow, and black sediment are most vivid at sunset and dawn, or after rain when the whole gorge glistens with brilliantly colored layers of claystone.

The **Clarno Unit,** the monument's oldest section, on Rte. 218, is accessible by US 97 to the west or Rte. 19 to the east. Its trails wind through ancient ash-laden mudflows from volcanic eruptions. While all of the hikes are short, and many more scenic than strenuous, all offer up ample opportunities to witness the stark beauty of this National monument.

In addition to the three units, John Day is surrounded on three sides by the massive grasslands of sagebrush and juniper, and forests of pine and fir, of **Malheur National Forest** (mal-HERE; see p. 138). This vast region of timbered hills and jagged ridges is seeing rising use as its two designated wilderness areas, **Strawberry Mountain** and **Monument Rock,** are being discovered by city folk searching for an escape. The forest offers over 250 mi. of hiking and riding trails during the summer and fall, as well as extensive snowmobiling, cross-country skiing, and ice fishing in the winter. The **Bear Valley/Long Creek District Ranger Station,** 431 Patterson Bridge Rd., off Rte. 26., offers free info and a detailed map of the region for $4 (☎575-3000. Open M-F 7:15am-5pm.). Camping is permitted anywhere in the forest out of sight of the road, but using existing sites is preferred.

BAKER CITY ☎541

The elegant storefronts that line Main St. are a reminder of Baker City's past prosperity, but little remains of this time. Baker boasts Oregon's tallest building east of the Cascades (10 stories), but it's the nearby natural wonders—Elkhorn Ridge, Wallowa-Whitman National Forest, and Hells Canyon—that draw most visitors.

■■⚑ ORIENTATION AND PRACTICAL INFORMATION. Baker City is on **I-84** in NE Oregon, 43 mi. southeast of **La Grande.** From Baker City, Rte. 86 leads east to Hells Canyon and Rte. 7 leads west to connect with US 26. Streets running parallel to I-84 are numbered in increasing order the farther they are from the hwy. Two principal streets intersect **Main St.: Washington** in the east and **Broadway** in the middle. **Campbell St.** intersects I-84 east of town.

Greyhound, 515 Campbell St. (☎523-5011 or 800-231-2222), by I-84 in Baker Truck Corral. Open daily 7-9am and 5-8pm. To **Portland** (7hr., 3 per day, $44-47). Catch a cab with **Baker Cab Co.** (☎523-6070). Up to $4.50 within Baker City, $1.25 per mi. outside city limits. 24hr. **Visitor Information: Baker County Visitor and Convention Bureau,** 490 Campbell St. (☎523-3356 or 800-523-1235; www.visitbaker.com), off I-84 Exit 304. Open June-Aug. M-F 8am-5pm, Sa 8am-4pm, Su 9am-2pm; Sept.-May M-F 8am-5pm. **Wallowa National Forest Ranger Station** and the **Bureau of Land Management,** 3165 10th St. (☎523-4476), have info on the Elkhorns and the Anthony Lakes Recreation Area. Sells area maps ($3-6). Open M-F 7:45am-4:30pm. 1hr. of **Internet**

144 ■ THE CASCADES

access is free at the **Library,** 2400 Resort St. (☎523-6419). First left after the river on Campbell St. as you drive west away from I-84. Open M-Th 10am-8pm, F 10am-5pm, Sa 10am-4pm, Su noon-4pm. **Laundromat and Public Showers** are available at **Baker City Laundry,** 815 Campbell St. (☎523-9817). Showers $5. Wash $1.25, dry 25¢ per 8min. Open daily 7am-10pm. **Emergency:** ☎911. **Police:** 1655 1st St. (☎523-3644). **Hospital: St. Elizabeth,** 3325 Pocahontas Rd. (☎523-6461). **Post Office:** 1550 Dewey Ave., in the Federal Building. Open M-F 8:30am-5pm. **ZIP Code:** 97814.

ACCOMMODATIONS AND CAMPING. Baker City has reasonably priced motels on 10th St. Generally, deals get better the farther the motel is from the Interstate. After a long day traveling, leave your covered wagon in the parking lot and relax in the pool at the **Oregon Trail Motel,** 211 Bridge St. (☎523-5844; reservations 800-628-3982). Fridges, microwaves are available upon request. (Reception daily 7am-11pm; ring bell if you arrive later. Singles $35; doubles $48. $3 pet charge.) Enjoy bright turquoise doors and beds equipped with "magic fingers" relaxation service (25¢ per 15min.) at the **Western Motel,** 3055 10th St. (☎523-3700; reservations 800-481-3701. Reception 24hr. Singles $25, doubles $30; slightly higher on holidays.) For camping try **Union Creek Campground** (☎894-2505), at Phillips Lake. Follow Rte. 7 for 20 mi. south toward Sumpter. Sparse pines mean high RV visibility. Tent sites are woodsier. Swimming area, boat ramp, toilets, no showers. (12 tent sites, $10. 58 hookups, $14-16. 50% senior discount with Golden Age Passport.) Cheaper sites are available at **Anthony Lake Recreation Area,** 34 mi. from Baker City on Anthony Lake Hwy. Take Rte. 30 north past Haines and turn west onto Anthony Lake Hwy. Three campgrounds located in the area: **Anthony Lake** (21 sites, $8), **Grande Ronde Lake** (8 sites, $5), and **Mud Lake** (8 sites, $5). On tranquil lakes set in jagged peaks. Draws large weekend crowds. Pit toilets, water. Open early June-Aug.

FOOD. Baker City will surprise and delight the diner expecting more of the Eastern Oregon staple steak and potatoes. While gigantic truck stop breakfasts, burgers, and steak dominate I-84 and 10th St., cafes along Main St. offer welcome alternatives, such as salads that are more green than white. **Albertsons,** 2300 Resort St., fulfills all your grocery needs. (☎523-6306. Open daily 6am-11pm.) The elegant and friendly **Baker City Cafe/Pizza à Fetta,** 1915 Washington Ave., makes everything from scratch, including a fabulous gourmet pizza. (☎523-6099. Slices $2.25-2.75; 14 in. pies $13-14. Open M-F 11am-5pm.) Eat your continental breakfast ($5) in the beautiful 3-story dining area of Historic Landmark, **Geiser Grand Hotel,** 1996 Main St., or go for dinner and have pasta or fresh salmon ($8-15). Lunch ($5-8). (☎523-1889. Open daily 7am-10pm.) **El Erradero,** 2100 Broadway (☎523-2327), is where locals go for pioneer-sized Mexican meals. Burrito with everything or chicken enchiladas both $7. Tequila margaritas make a Mexican meal complete ($4). Open Su-Th 11am-9:30pm, F-Sa 11am-10pm.

SIGHTS AND EVENTS. The National Historic Oregon Trail Interpretive Center, 5 mi. east of Baker City off I-84 Exit 302, does its best to upstage Baker City's other museums. The multi-million dollar facility offers dramatic panoramic views of the snow-capped mountains near North Powder in addition to relating the history of the Oregon Trail. Over 4 mi. of outdoor trails (some wheelchair accessible), lead to scenic overlooks and interpretive sites while bringing visitors within arm's reach of the wagon ruts of the original trail that run alongside the path. Excellent **lectures and performances** are held periodically; call for the schedule. (☎523-1843. Open Apr.-Oct. daily 9am-6pm; Nov.-Mar. 9am-4pm. $5, ages 62+ and 6-17 $3.50.)

The **Miners' Jubilee** (July 18-21, 2002), in City Park, is a show and sale of arts with live music, and also includes a parade, bronco- and bull-riding, and mining demonstrations. The intense **gold-panning championship** determines the state's foremost gold panner. A schedule is available at the visitors bureau.

OUTDOOR ACTIVITIES. Elkhorn Ridge, towering steeply over Baker City to the west (follow the signs along Rte. 7 south), provides local access to the Blue Mountains. Oregon Trail pioneers avoided this jagged peak, but a paved loop called **Elkhorn Drive** (a National Scenic Byway for good reason) now leads over the range, providing drivers along its 106 mi. with lofty views and lots of hiking and fishing. The drive begins in Baker City and heads north out of town on Rte. 30; from there follow the signs. A map of the route is available at the visitor bureau. The **Hells Canyon National Scenic Loop Drive** (see p. 136) begins and ends in Baker City.

GOLD...IN OREGON??

Don't believe it? Neither could the settlers who found the first nuggets in Griffin Gulch, which is named after the lucky prospector who found gold in 1861. The town of Sumpter quickly sprang up near the strike, and from 1870-1915 over $16 million worth of gold, at $25 an ounce, was excavated from mines and streams with the help of smelters that could crush over 100 tons of rock per day. Then, in 1917, tragedy struck. A spark in one of the smelters led to a fire that engulfed the town, burning everything to the ground. Devastated, many gold seekers went elsewhere, leaving Sumpter and nearby Baker City as virtual ghost towns. Those who remained found work on gold dredges, 500 ton behemoths that dug rock and soil and filtered it through an intricate processing system to recover the gold particles, then dumped the remaining rock out the back. The final dredge, started up in 1935, dug up $4.5 million worth of gold in its 19-year history. It also left over 8 mi. of mercury-poisoned tailings, a mixed legacy for these massive mining machines. Tour the last dredge in Sumpter, 30 mi. west of Baker City.

WASHINGTON

> **Washington State Capital:** Olympia. **Population:** 5,685,300. **Area:** 66,582 mi.^{2}
> **Motto:** *"Alki,"* "by and by" in Salish. **Nickname:** Evergreen State. **Flower:** Coast rhododendron. **Gem:** Petrified wood. **Tree:** Western hemlock. **Folk Song:** "Roll On, Columbia, Roll On." **Fishing Hotline:** 360-902-2500. **Shellfish Hotline:** 360-796-4601.

What is now Washington was home to only some 400 settlers when Oregonians rallied for territorial recognition in the 1840s. The indigenous nations of the coast and plains still outnumbered the newcomers when Washington was made a territory in 1853 (encompassing much of present-day Idaho and Montana). By 1863 4000 settlers had journeyed along the Oregon Trail and the state had attained roughly its present shape. Over the 20th century, the development of the state's towns depended on the course of railroads linking the west with the east. During World War II, Seattle's resource-driven economy was transformed by the nation's need for ships and aircrafts.

On Washington's western shore, concert halls and art galleries offer cosmopolitan entertainment within easy reach of Puget Sound, its gorgeous islands, and the temperate rainforests of the Olympic Peninsula. Seattle is the home of coffee, grunge, Microsoft, scattered hilly neighborhoods, fantastic parks, and miles of waterfront. The lush San Juan Islands boast puffins, sea otters, and sea lions. Pods of orcas circle the islands, followed by pods of tourists in yachts and kayaks. Vashon Island, closer to Seattle, is a beautiful, less touristed artsy retreat. Due west of the Emerald City, the stunning Olympic National Park is the backdrop for settlements where fishing and logging support a small local population. At Neah Bay, an hour from the rainforests of the park's western rim, an ancient Makah settlement buried in a landslide has earned the nickname "Pompeii of the Pacific."

Buses cover most of Washington, although navigating the Olympic Peninsula requires some dexterity with a patchwork of county schedules. The train from Los Angeles to Vancouver makes many stops in western Washington; another line extends from Seattle to Spokane and on to Chicago.

WASHINGTON'S HIGHLIGHTS

EMP in Seattle lets you tap into the American rock n' roll experience (see p. 164).

ONP the massive national park on the Olympic Peninsula lets you have it all in the micro-environments it encloses (see p. 190).

BURN with envy at the excitment of the North Cascades Smokejumpers Base (p. 224).

HIKE spectacular Mt. Rainier (see p. 214).

CONSUME java straight from the source in Seattle (see p. 146).

BRATWURST is dished up in Bavarian Leavenworth (see p. 217).

SEATTLE ☎ 206

Seattle's serendipitous mix of mountain views, clean streets, espresso stands, and rainy weather proved to be the magic formula of the 1990s. Although a slowdown in the tech sector has turned some computer magnates' smiles into frowns, the setting and culture continue on in Seattle without missing a beat. The city is one of the youngest and most vibrant in the nation. A nearly epidemic fixation on coffee has also made it one of the most caffeinated. The droves of newcomers provide an interesting contrast to the older residents who remember Seattle as a city-town,

WASHINGTON ■ 147

not a thriving metropolis bubbling over with young millionaires. Computer and coffee money have helped drive rents sky high in some areas, but the grungy, punk-loving street culture seems to prevail in others. In the end, there is a nook or cranny for almost anyone in Seattle.

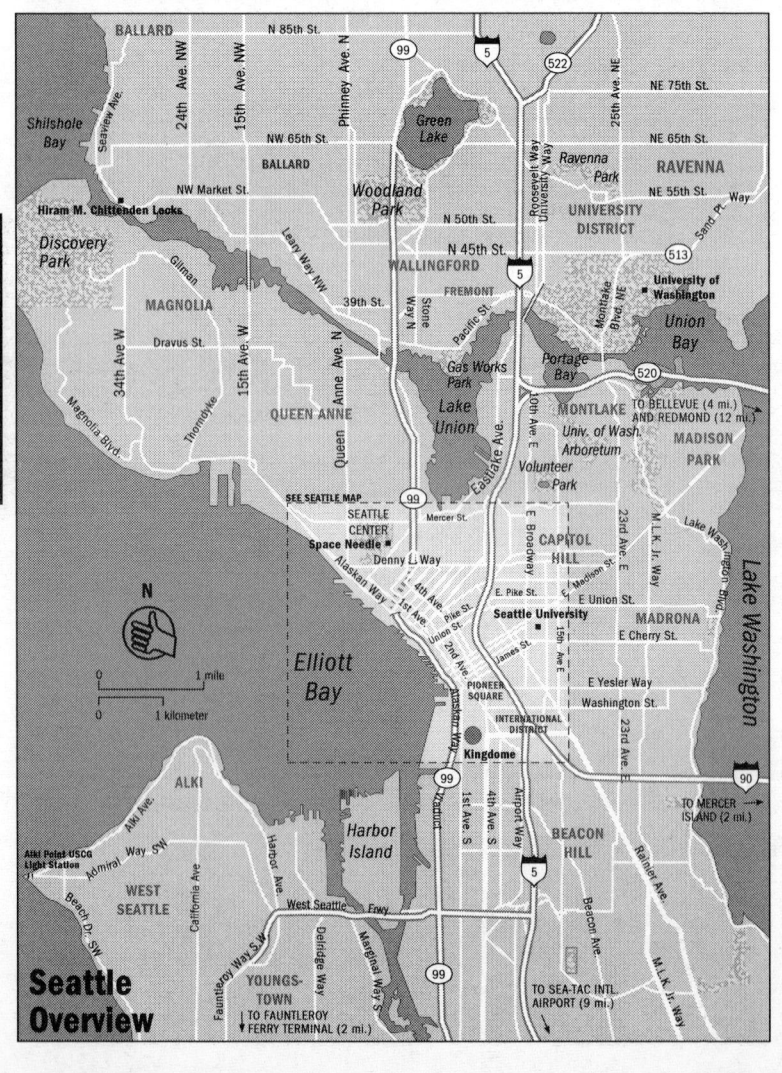

The Emerald City sits on an isthmus, with mountain ranges to the east and west. Every hilltop in Seattle offers an impressive view of Mt. Olympus, Mt. Baker, and Mt. Rainier. To the west, the waters of Puget Sound glint against downtown skyscrapers and nearly spotless streets. Although daytrips beckon in any direction, the city's nine neighborhood hills beg for exploration. Plan to get wet and bag the umbrella, a tool that only outsiders use. The city's artistic landscape is as varied and exciting as its physical terrain. Opera always sells out, and the *New York Times* has complained that there is more good theater in Seattle than on Broadway. When Nirvana introduced the world to their discordant sensibility, the term "grunge" and Seattle became temporarily inseparable, and the city that produced Jimi Hendrix again revitalized rock and roll. Good bands thrive in grunge's wake, keeping the Seattle scene a mecca for edgy entertainment. Bill Gates of Microsoft and Howard Shultz of Starbucks have built vast and perhaps only marginally evil empires on the backs of software and coffee beans.

■ INTERCITY TRANSPORTATION

Flights: Seattle-Tacoma International (Sea-Tac; ☎ 431-4444), on Federal Way, 15 mi. south of Seattle, right off **I-5** (signs are clear). Bus #194 departs the underground tunnel at University St. and 3rd Ave. (30min.; every 20-35min., 5:25am-8:45pm; $1.25-1.75, children 50¢) and #174 departs Union & 2nd Ave. (45min.; every 15-30min., 5:25am-3:30am; $1.25-1.75) for the airport. These routes leave from the airport for Seattle from outside the baggage claim (every 15min., 4:45am-2:45am; $1-1.75).

Trains: Amtrak (☎ 800-USA-RAIL, arrival/departure times 382-4125), King St. Station, at 3rd and Jackson St., 1 block east of Pioneer Square next to the stadiums. Ticket office and station open daily 6:15am-8pm. To: **Portland** (4 per day, $26-36); **Tacoma** (4 per day, $9-14); **Spokane** (1 per day, $45-81); **San Francisco, CA** (1 per day, $97-162); and **Vancouver, BC** (1 per day, $23-34).

Buses: Greyhound (☎ 628-5526 or 800-231-2222), at 8th Ave. and Stewart St. Try to avoid night buses, since the station can get seedy after dark. Ticket office open daily 6:30am-2:30am. To: **Spokane** (6 per day, $30); **Vancouver, BC** (16 per day, $23); **Portland, OR** (14 per day, $24); and **Tacoma** (9 per day, $5). **Quick Shuttle** (☎ 604-940-4428 or 800-665-2122; www.quickcoach.com) makes 8 cross-border trips daily from Seattle (Travelodge hotel at 8th and Bell St.) and the Sea-Tac airport to the **Vancouver, BC** airport and the Holiday Inn on Howe St. in downtown Vancouver (4-4½hr.; $31 from downtown, $39 from Sea-Tac). **Green Tortoise Bus Service** (☎ 800-867-8647; www.greentortoise.com) has run trips south to San Francisco in the past—service is expected to resume 2002. Ask at the hostel for details.

Ferries: Washington State Ferries (☎ 464-6400 or 888-808-7977; www.wsdot.wa.gov/ferries) has two terminals in Seattle. The main terminal is downtown, at Colman Dock, Pier 52. From here service departs to **Bainbridge Island** (35min.; $4.50, $8-10 with car), **Bremerton** on the Kitsap Peninsula (1hr.; passenger-only boat 30min.; $4.50-$5.50, $8-10 with car), and **Vashon Island** (25min., passengers only, $5.50). From the waterfront passenger-only ferries leave from Pier 50. The other Seattle terminal is in **Fauntleroy;** to reach the terminal drive south on I-5 and take Exit 163A (West Seattle) down Fauntleroy Way. Sailings from Fauntleroy to **Southworth** on the Kitsap Peninsula (35min.); **Vashon Island** (15min.); both $2.90, $10.25-13 with car. If ferry travel is in your plans we strongly suggest picking up a copy of both the *Sailing Schedule* and the *Fares* pamphlet. Services are tricky, so it is worth spending a few minutes perusing the schedule or calling the toll-free info line. Most ferries leave daily and frequently 6am-2am. **Victoria Clipper** (☎ 800-888-2535; reservations 448-5000) takes passengers from Seattle to **Victoria** only. Departs from Pier 69 (3hr.; 2-4 per day; one way $66-75, round-trip $109-125; under 12 half-price. Bicycles $10).

Car Transport: Auto Driveaway (☎ 253-850-0800, 800-235-5052), on Pacific Highway S, near the airport. Recruits people to drive cars to locations across the US. The management loves to hear from *Let's Go* readers. $300 cash deposit. Open M-F 8am-5pm.

Ride Board: Ground floor of **Husky Union Building** (HUB), behind Suzallo Library on University of Washington main campus. Matches cars and riders, within geographical reason. Also check board at **Seattle HI** (p. 155) and the **Green Tortoise Hostel** (p. 154).

▊ LOCAL TRANSPORTATION

Although navigating Seattle seems daunting at first glance, even the most road-weary drivers can learn their way around the Emerald City like so many singing munchkins. Street parking creates many blind pull-outs in Seattle, so be extra careful when turning onto cross roads. Downtown, **avenues** run northwest to southeast, and **streets** run southwest to northeast. Outside downtown, everything is simplified: with few exceptions, avenues run north-south and streets east-west. The city is in **quadrants:** 1000 1st Ave. NW is a far walk from 1000 1st Ave. SE.

When driving in Seattle, **yield to pedestrians.** They will not look, so make sure you do. Locals drive slowly, calmly, and politely; police ticket frequently. Downtown driving can be nightmarish; parking is expensive, hills are steep, and one-way streets are ubiquitous. Read the street signs carefully, as many areas have time and hour restrictions; ticketers know them by heart. **Parking** is reasonable, plentiful, and well-lit at **Pacific Place Parking** between 6th and 7th Ave. and Olive and Pine St., with hourly rates comparable to the meters and at **Seattle Center,** near the Space Needle. (☎ 652-0416. 24hr. $2 per hr.; $19 per day.) Park at the Needle and take the monorail to the convenient **Westlake Center** downtown. Public transportation on the whole in Seattle is not stellar. The size and population of the city warrant a subway, but instead, inhabitants and visitors alike must settle for the above-ground replacements. Although buses are large and schedules are flexible, the transit is slower and less frequent that the average person needs.

The **Metro ride free zone** includes most of downtown Seattle (see **Public Transportation,** below). The **Metro** buses covers King County east to North Bend and Carnation, south to Enumclaw, through to Snohomish County, where bus #6 hooks up with **Community Transit.** This line runs to Everett, Stanwood, and into the Cascades. Bus #174 connects to Tacoma's Pierce County System at Federal Way.

Seattle is a **bicycle-friendly** city. All buses have free, easy-to-use bike racks (bike shops have sample racks on which to practice). Between 6am and 7pm, bikes may only be loaded or unloaded at stops outside the ride free zone. Check out Metro's *Bike & Ride,* available at the visitors center. For a bike map of Seattle, call **City of Seattle Bicycle Program** (☎ 684-7583).

Public Transportation: Metro Transit, Pass Sales and Information Office, 201 S Jackson St. (☎ 553-3000 or 24hr. 800-542-7876; www.transit.metrokc.gov). The bus tunnel under Pine St. and 3rd Ave. is the heart of the downtown bus system. Open M-F 9am-5pm. Fares are based on a 2-zone system. **Zone 1** includes everything within the city limits (peak hours $1.50, off-peak $1.25). **Zone 2** includes everything else (peak $2, off-peak $1.25). Ages 5-18 always 50¢. **Peak hours** in both zones M-F 6-9am and 3-6pm. Exact fare required. Weekend day passes $2.50. Ride free daily 6am-7pm in the downtown **ride free area,** bordered by S Jackson on the south, 6th and I-5 on the east, Blanchard on the north, and the waterfront on the west. Free **transfers** can be used on any bus, including a return trip on the same bus within 2hr. Transfers are often helpful, as nearly all routes pass through the center of town. All buses have free **bike racks** and most are **wheelchair accessible** (info ☎ 684-2046). The **Monorail,** runs from Space Needle to Westlake Center, on the 3rd floor. Every 15min. 9am-11pm; $1.25, seniors 50¢, ages 5-12 75¢.

Taxi: Metro Cab (☎ 901-0707). $1.50 base, $1.60 per mi. **Farwest Taxi** (☎ 622-1717), $1.80 base, $1.80 per mi.; **Orange Cab Co.** (☎ 522-8800), $1.80 base, $1.80 per mi.

Car Rental: U Save Auto Rental, 16223 Pacific Hwy. S (☎ 242-9778). $33 per day for compacts, plus 22¢ per mi. over 100 mi. unlimited mileage in BC and WA. Must be 21, with a major credit card. **Enterprise,** 11342 Lake City Way NE (☎ 364-3127). $50 per day for compacts, plus 20¢ per mi. over 150 mi. Airport location 15667 Pacific Hwy. S (☎ 242-4533) charges an additional 10% tax.

ORIENTATION

Seattle is a long, skinny city, stretching from north to south on an isthmus between **Puget Sound** to the west and **Lake Washington** to the east, linked by locks and canals. The city is easily accessible by car via **I-5,** which runs north-south through the city, and by **I-90** from the east, which ends at I-5 southeast of downtown. Get to **downtown** (including **Pioneer Square, Pike Place Market,** and the **waterfront**) from I-5 by taking any of the exits from James St. to Stewart St. Take the Mercer St./Fairview Ave. Exit to the **Seattle Center;** follow signs from there. The Denny Way Exit leads to **Capitol Hill,** and, farther north, the 45th St. Exit heads toward the **University District.** The less crowded **Rte. 99,** also called **Aurora Ave.** or the Aurora Hwy., runs parallel to I-5 and skirts the western side of downtown, with great views from the

Alaskan Way Viaduct. Rte. 99 is often the better choice when driving downtown or to **Queen Anne, Fremont, Green Lake,** and the northwestern part of the city. For more detailed directions to these and other districts, see the individualized neighborhood listings under **Food** (p. 155), **Nightlife** (p. 161), and **Sights** (p. 162).

PRACTICAL INFORMATION

TOURIST AND FINANCIAL SERVICES

Visitor Information: Seattle-King County Visitors Bureau (☎461-5840), at 8th and Pike St., on the 1st floor of the convention center. Helpful staff doles out maps, brochures, newspapers, and Metro and ferry schedules. Open June-Oct. M-F 8:30am-5pm, Sa-Su 10am-4pm; Nov.-May M-F 8:30am-5pm.

Outdoor Information: Seattle Parks and Recreation Department, 100 Dexter Ave. N (☎684-4075). Open M-F 8am-5pm for info and pamphlets on city parks. **Outdoor Recreation Information Center,** 222 Yale Ave. (☎470-4060), in REI (see **Equipment Rental,** below). A joint operation between the Park and Forest services, this station is able to answer any questions that might arise as you browse REI's huge collection of maps and guides. Unfortunately, the desk is not set up to sell permits. Free brochures on hiking trails. Open Tu-F 10:30am-7pm, Sa 9am-7pm, Su 11am-6pm; winter hours may be shortened.

Equipment Rental: REI, 222 Yale Ave. (☎223-1944), near Capitol Hill. The mothership of camping supply stores rents everything from camping gear to technical mountaineering equipment (see **Outdoor Activities,** p. 168). Open M-F 10am-9pm, Sa 10am-7pm, Su 11am-6pm. **The Bicycle Center,** 4529 Sand Point Way (☎523-8300), near the Children's Hospital. Rents mountain and hybrid bikes ($3 per hr., $15 per day; 2hr. minimum). Credit card deposit required. Open M-Th 10am-8pm, F 10am-7pm, Sa 10am-6pm, Su 10am-5pm. **Gregg's Greenlake Cycle,** 7007 Woodlawn Ave. NE (☎523-1822). Wide range of bikes conveniently close to Green Lake and Burke-Gilman bike trails ($7 per hr., $20-30 per day, $25-35 per 24hr; each additional day $10). Photo ID and cash or credit card deposit required. Also rents in-line skates ($7 per hr., $20 per day, $25 per 24hr.). Open M-F 10am-9pm, Sa-Su 10am-6pm.

Currency Exchange: Thomas Cook Foreign Exchange, 400 Pine St. (☎682-4525), on the 3rd floor of the Westlake Shopping Center. Open M-Sa 9:30am-6pm, Su 11am-5pm. Also behind the Delta Airlines ticket counter and at other airport locations.

Travel Agencies: Council Travel, 4311 University Way (☎632-2448). Open M and W-F 9am-5:30pm, Tu 10am-5:30pm, Sa 10am-3pm. Also at 424 Broadway Ave. E (☎329-4567), in Capitol Hill. Open M-F 10am-6pm, Sa 11am-3pm. **STA Travel,** 4341 University Way (☎633-5000; www.statravel.com), at NE 45th. Open M-F 9:30am-6:30pm, Sa 10am-5pm.

LOCAL SERVICES

Bookstores: Elliott Bay Books, 101 S Main St. (☎624-6600), in Pioneer Sq. Vast collection with 150,000 titles. Sponsors a reading and lecture series almost every day, all year long. Most readings are at 7:30pm. Coffeehouse in the basement. Open M-Th 9:30am-10pm, F-Sa 9:30am-11pm, Su 11am-7pm.

Ticket Agencies: Ticketmaster (☎628-0888) in Westlake Center and every Tower Records store. **Ticket/Ticket,** 401 Broadway E (☎324-2744), on the 2nd floor of the Broadway Market, sells half-price day-of-show tickets for theatres, music, clubs, cruises, tours, and more. Cash only purchases in person. Open Tu-Sa noon-7pm, Su noon-6pm. Also in **Pike Place Market information booth** at 1st Ave. and Pike St. 30min. free parking in garage under Harrison St. with ticket purchase. Open Tu-Su noon-6pm.

Laundromat: Sit and Spin, 2219 4th St. (☎441-9484). A laundromat local hot spot (see **Nightlife,** p. 161). Wash $1.25, dry 25¢ per 15min. Open Su-Th 9am-midnight, F-Sa 9am-2am. **University Maytag,** 4733 University Way (☎985-3887), is another alternative. Wash and dry $1.50 each. Open daily 9am-9pm.

152 ■ SEATTLE

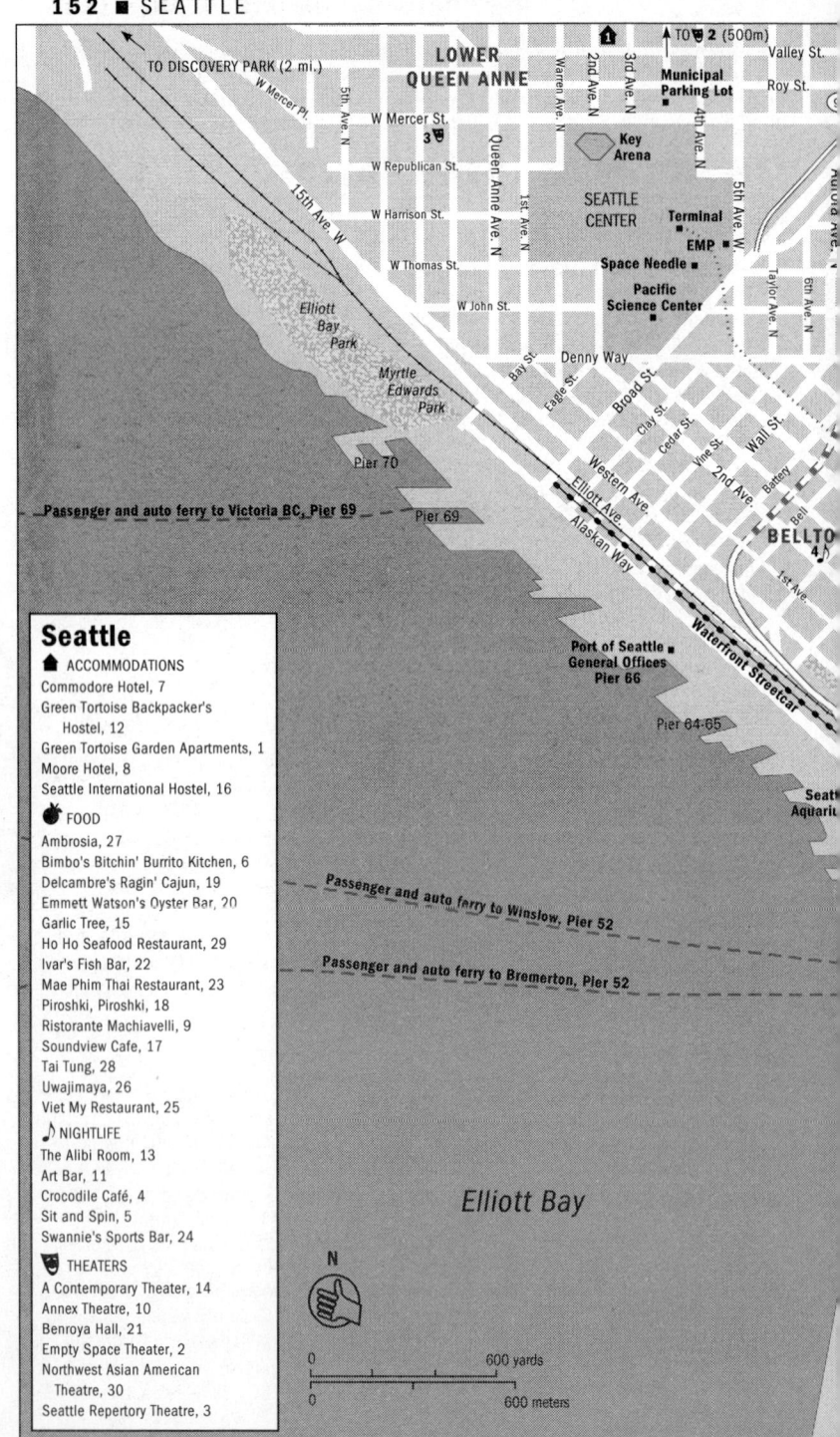

Seattle

🏠 ACCOMMODATIONS
Commodore Hotel, 7
Green Tortoise Backpacker's Hostel, 12
Green Tortoise Garden Apartments, 1
Moore Hotel, 8
Seattle International Hostel, 16

🍎 FOOD
Ambrosia, 27
Bimbo's Bitchin' Burrito Kitchen, 6
Delcambre's Ragin' Cajun, 19
Emmett Watson's Oyster Bar, 20
Garlic Tree, 15
Ho Ho Seafood Restaurant, 29
Ivar's Fish Bar, 22
Mae Phim Thai Restaurant, 23
Piroshki, Piroshki, 18
Ristorante Machiavelli, 9
Soundview Cafe, 17
Tai Tung, 28
Uwajimaya, 26
Viet My Restaurant, 25

♪ NIGHTLIFE
The Alibi Room, 13
Art Bar, 11
Crocodile Café, 4
Sit and Spin, 5
Swannie's Sports Bar, 24

🎭 THEATERS
A Contemporary Theater, 14
Annex Theatre, 10
Benroya Hall, 21
Empty Space Theater, 2
Northwest Asian American Theatre, 30
Seattle Repertory Theatre, 3

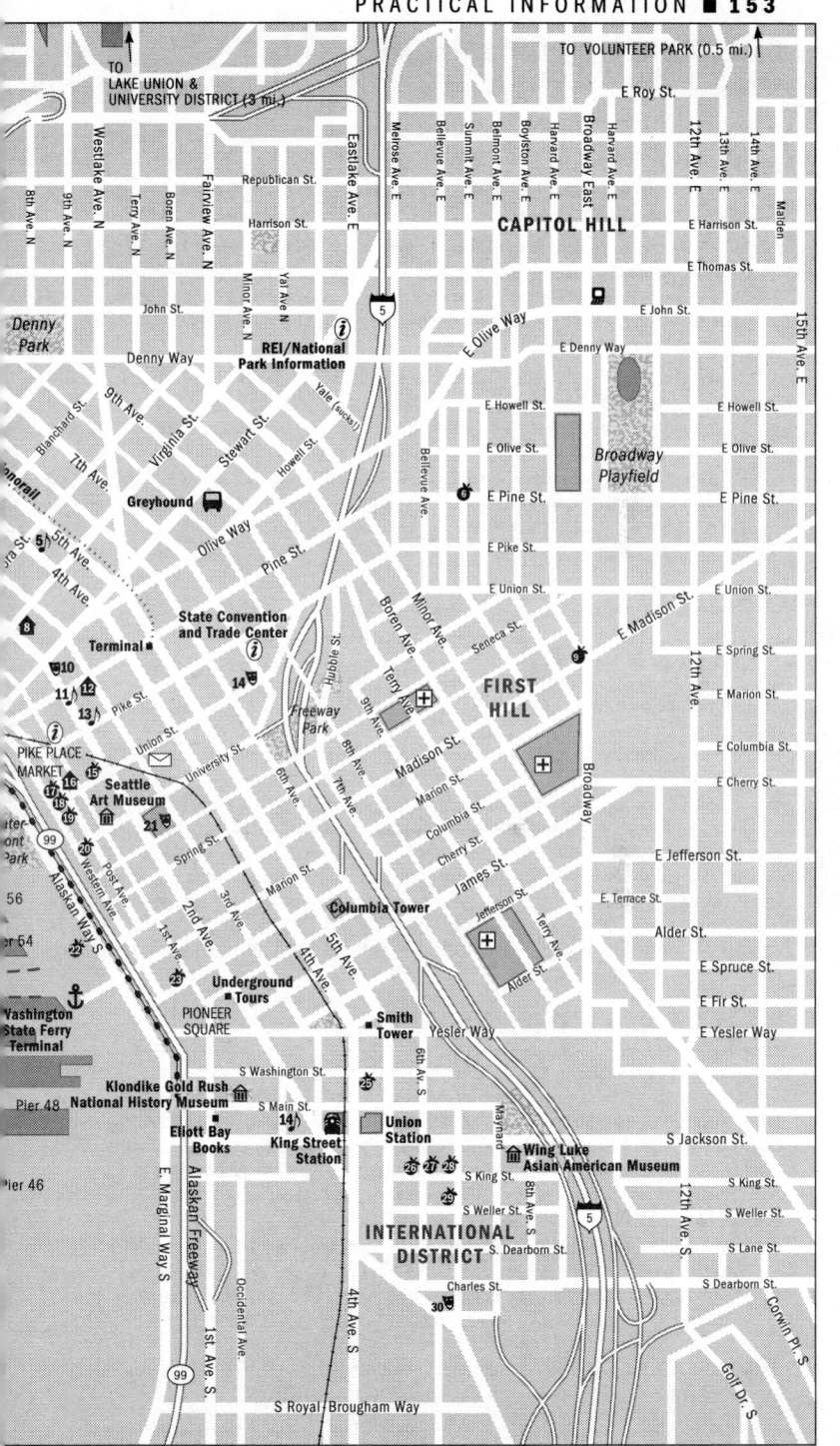

PRACTICAL INFORMATION ■ 153

EMERGENCY AND COMMUNICATIONS

Emergency: ☎911.

Police: 810 Virginia St. (☎625-5011).

Crisis Line: ☎461-3222.

Rape Crisis: King County Sexual Assault Center (☎800-825-7273). Crisis counseling and advocacy. **Harborview Medical,** ☎521-1800. Both 24hr.

Medical Services: International District Emergency Center, 720 8th Ave. S, Suite 100 (☎461-3235). Medics with multilingual assistance available. Clinic 9am-6pm, phone 24hr. **Health South Medical Center,** 1151 Denny Way (☎682-7418). Walk-in. 7am-6pm. **Swedish Medical Center, Providence Campus,** 500 17th Ave. (☎320-2111), for urgent care and cardiac. 24hr.

Internet Access: The **Seattle Public Library,** 800 Pike St. (☎386-4636; TDD 386-4697), is stashed away in a temporary building near the convention center until fall 2003, when a brand-new Rem Koolhaas building will open. A visitor's library card lasts 3 months ($15). Free 45min. Internet access with photo ID. Open M-Th 9am-9pm, F 10:30am-6pm, Sa 9am-6pm, Su 1-5pm. **Capitol Hill Net,** 219 Broadway Ave. E #23 (☎860-6858), upstairs in Alley Mall charges $6 per hr. Here, *Let's Go* readers and all hostelers get 15min. free. Open M-F 9am-midnight.

Post Office: (☎800-275-8777), at Union St. and 3rd Ave. downtown. Open M-F 8am-5:30pm, Sa 8am-noon. General delivery window open M-F 10am-noon and 1pm-3pm. **ZIP Code:** 98101.

PUBLICATIONS

The city's major daily, the *Seattle Times* (☎464-2111; www.seattletimes.com), lists upcoming events in its Thursday "Datebook" section. Its major "competitor," (well, actually its partner) the *Seattle Post-Intelligencer,* has an award-winning sports section and great news coverage, but does not publish on Sunday. The Thursday listings of the *Seattle Weekly* (www.seattleweekly.com) are free and left-of-center. Even farther over is *The Stranger* (free), which covers music and culture, materializing Thursdays at music, coffee, and thrift shops. *The Rocket,* a bimonthly publication, relays music and entertainment info from all over the Northwest. *Arts Focus,* free at most bookstores, covers performing arts. *Seattle Arts,* published by the Seattle Arts Commission, is especially good on visual arts. Both are monthlies. The weekly *Seattle Gay News* sells on Fridays at newsstands.

ACCOMMODATIONS

Seattle's hostel scene is not amazing, but there are plenty of choices and establishments to fit all types of personalities. **Pacific Bed and Breakfast Association** arranges B&B singles in the $50-65 range. (☎800-648-2932; www.seattlebedandbreakfast.com. Open M-F 9am-5pm.) The **Vashon Island Hostel** is probably the best bedding in the area, most certainly the most relaxing (see **Accommodations** p. 176).

DOWNTOWN

Green Tortoise Backpacker's Hostel, 1525 2nd Ave. (☎340-1222; fax 623-3207; www.greentortoise.net), between Pike and Pine St. on the #174 or 194 bus route. A young party hostel downtown; lots of people, lots of activities. The place in Seattle for extroverts. Often free beer Tu and F; pub-crawls F. Laundry, kitchen. Internet access $1 per 5min. $20 cash key deposit required. Bring your own linens and blankets; blanket $1 with $9 deposit. Free continental breakfast 7-9:30am. Free dinner on M night. Reception 24hr. No curfew. 185 beds in 37 rooms. $18-20, $1 less with cash, $1 off with HI or ISIC card. 10 private rooms $50; winter $40.

Seattle International Hostel (HI), 84 Union St. (☎622-5443 or 888-622-5443; www.hiseattle.org), at Western Ave., right by the waterfront. Take Union St. from downtown; follow signs down the stairs under the "Pike Pub & Brewery." Great location that overlooks the water; the space itself can feel like a cramped dorm on full nights. Coin laundry. Internet access 15¢ per min. 7-night max. stay in summer. Reception 24hr. Check-out 11am. No curfew. Reservations recommended. 199 beds, 6-10 per room; $19, nonmembers $22. Private rooms sleep 2-3. $54, nonmembers $60.

Moore Hotel, 1926 2nd Ave. (☎448-4851 or 800-421-5508; www.moorehotel.com), at Virginia, 1 block east from Pike Place Market, next to historic Moore Theater. Open lobby, cavernous halls, and attentive service makes the Moore more reminiscent of the 20s. Singles $39, with bath $59; doubles (one bed) $49, with bath $67. Big room with 2 beds and bath $74. Large suites, some with kitchen, $85-120. HI discount 10%.

Commodore Hotel, 2013 2nd Ave. (☎448-8868), at Virginia. Pleasant decor, only a few blocks from the waterfront. Front desk open 24hr, no visitors past 8pm. Internet access 15¢ per min. Singles $59, with bath $79; 2 beds and bath $89.

OUTSIDE DOWNTOWN

For inexpensive motels farther from downtown, drive north on Hwy. 99 (Aurora Ave.) or take bus #26 to the neighborhood of Fremont. Budget chain motels like the **Nites Inn,** 11746 Huron Ave. N, line the highway north of the Aurora bridge. (☎365-3216. Singles from $50, doubles $55.) Look for AAA approval ratings.

Green Tortoise Garden Apartments, 715 2nd Ave. N (☎340-1222; fax 623-3207), on the south slope of Queen Anne Hill, 3 blocks east from the Space Needle and the Seattle Center. Long-term accommodations for travelers staying over a month. Backyard, kitchen, garden, laundry, free tea and coffee. Applications available at the Green Tortoise Hostel (allow a few days for processing). Beds $300 per month and $95 per additional week (one month minimum stay), 4 people per room. $300 deposit.

The College Inn, 4000 University Way NE (☎633-4441; www.speakeasy.org/collegeinn), at NE 40th St. Quiet place near UW campus and its youthful environs. Rooms are small, but turn-of-the-century bureaus and brass fixtures are s'durned charming. Free continental breakfast. Singles from $49; doubles $60-70. Double with 2 beds $75-85. Credit card required.

🛈 FOOD

Although Seattleites appear to subsist solely on espresso and steamed milk, they do occasionally eat. When they do, they seek out healthy cuisine, especially seafood. The finest fish, produce, and baked goods are at **Pike Place Market** (see below). The **University District** supports inexpensive and international cuisine. The **Chinatown/International District** offers tons of rice, pounds of fresh fish, and enough veggies to keep your mother happy, all at ridiculously low prices. **Puget Sound Consumer Coops (PCCs)** are local health food markets at 7504 Aurora Ave. N, (☎525-3586) in Green Lake, and at 6514 40th NE, (☎526-7661) in the Ravenna District north of the university. Capitol Hill, the U District, and Fremont close main thoroughfares on summer Saturdays for **farmers markets.**

PIKE PLACE MARKET AND DOWNTOWN

In 1907, angry citizens demanded the elimination of the middle-man and local farmers began selling produce by the waterfront. Not even the Great Depression slowed business, which thrived until an enormous fire burned the building in 1941. The early 1980s heralded a Pike Place renaissance, and today thousands of tourists mob the market daily. (Open M-Sa 9am-6pm, Su 11am-5pm. Produce and fish open earlier; restaurants and lounges close later.) In the **Main Arcade,** on the west side of Pike St., fishmongers compete for audiences as they hurl fish from shelves to scales. Cutthroat competition will have you paying only pennies for mouthwatering cherries. The market's restaurants boast stellar views of the sound.

Even if you aren't hungry, merchants sell assorted gifts, and several stands offer stunning flower arrangements at a quarter of the cost of most florists. Be prepared to fight the masses during lunch. An **information booth** faces the bike rack by the Main Arcade, at 1st Ave. and Pike St. (☎461-5800. Open Tu-Su 10am-noon.) Restaurants south of Pike Place cater mostly to suits on lunch breaks and tourists, but there are many sandwich and pastry shops covering downtown.

Piroshki, Piroshki, 1908 Pike Pl. (☎441-6068). The *Russian Piroshki* is a croissant-like dough baked around sausages, mushrooms, cheeses, salmon, or apples doused in cinnamon. *Let's Go* does not recommend having all ingredients at once...($3-4). Watch the *piroshki* process in progress while awaiting your order. Open daily 8:30am-6pm.

Delcambre's Ragin' Cajun, 1523 1st Ave. (☎624-2598), near Pike Place. A tremendous portion of spicy red beans with *andouille* (a flavorful sausage) was enjoyed by former President Clinton in 1995. Lunch $6-8. Dinner almost twice that. Open in summer daily 11am-3pm and 5-9pm. Closed for dinner early in the week during winter.

Soundview Cafe (☎623-5700), on the mezzanine in the Pike Place Main Arcade, follow the neon blue sign. Self-serve breakfast. The sandwich-and-salad bar is a good place to brown-bag a moment of solace. Open M-F 7am-5pm, Sa 7am-5:30pm, Su 9am-3pm.

Garlic Tree, 94 Stewart St. (☎441-5681), one block up from Pike Place Market. The smell will drag you in. Loads of fabulous veggie, chicken, and seafood stir-fries ($7-9). Open M-Th 11am-8pm, F-Sa 11am-9pm.

Emmett Watson's Oyster Bar, 1916 Pike Place (☎448-7721), enhance your manliess while treating the lady to a splendid dinner in the courtyard. Oyster Bar Special—2 oysters, 3 shrimp, bread, chowder—is $6.25. Shelves of bottles show off the large selection of brews. Open M-Th 11:30am-8pm. F-Sa 11:30am-9pm. Su 11:30am-6pm.

THE WATERFRONT

Budget eaters, steer clear of Pioneer Square: instead, take a picnic to **Waterfall Garden,** on the corner of S Main St. and 2nd Ave. S. The garden sports tables and chairs and a man-made waterfall that masks traffic outside. (Open daily 8am-6pm.)

Mae Phim Thai Restaurant, 94 Columbia St. (☎624-2979), a few blocks north of Pioneer Sq. between 1st Ave. and Alaskan Way. Slews of pad thai junkies crowed in for cheap, delicious Thai cuisine. All dishes $5. Open M-F 11am-7pm, Sa noon-7pm.

Ivar's Fish Bar, Pier 54 (☎624-6852), north of the square, is named for late Seattle shipping magnate Ivar Haglund. A fast-food window that serves the definitive Seattle clam chowder ($2). Their specialty is fish and chips ($6). Open daily 11am-2am.

INTERNATIONAL DISTRICT

Along King and Jackson St., between 5th and 8th Ave. east of the Kingdome, Seattle's International District is packed with great eateries. Competition keeps prices low and quality high, and unassuming facades front fabulous food. Lunch specials are particularly appealing, and long lines move quickly.

Uwajimaya, 600 5th Ave. S (☎624-6248). A district veteran that just moved to bigger, better quarters. The new Uwajimaya Center is a full city block of groceries, gifts, videos, CDs, and everything else you can stick a price tag to. There is even a food court, plying goodies such as Korean BBQ and Taiwanese-style baked goods. A great place for groceries for the hostel, or just to grab a quick bite. Open M-Sa 8am-11pm, Su 9am-10pm.

Tai Tung, 655 S King St. (☎622-7372). Select authentic Chinese and Mandarin cuisine from one of the largest menus around. Grab a bite at the bar, where menus are plastered on the wall. Entrees $5-12. Open Su-Th 10am-11:30pm, F-Sa 10am-1:30am.

Ho Ho Seafood Restaurant, 653 S Weller St. (☎382-9671). Generous portions of tank-fresh seafood. Great place for large parties to share food on round, spinning tables. Stuffed fish hanging from ceilings and large mirrors make for an interesting atmosphere. Lunch $5-7 (until 4pm), dinner $7-12. Open Su-Th 11am-1am, F-Sa 11am-3am.

Viet My Restaurant, 129 Prefontaine Pl. S (☎382-9923), near 4th and Washington St. Consistently delicious Vietnamese food at great prices. Stare into the kitchen from your table and watch your meal come to life. Most meals under $5. Open M-F 11am-9pm.

Ambrosia, 619 King St. (☎623-9028), serves up mouth-watering "foaming milk tea"—a mixture of Taiwan tea, milk, black tapioca pearls, and fresh fruit flavors. Fight by the regulars to choose from 100 different flavors. Our suggestion: the HoneyDew Milk Tea ($2.50). Open Su-Th 11am-9pm, F-Sa 11am-midnight.

CAPITOL HILL

With bronze dance-steps on the sidewalks and neon storefronts, **Broadway** is a land of espresso houses, imaginative shops, elegant clubs, and plenty of eats. Although not the cheapest place to eat, it has a great variety of cuisine options catering to most budgets and taste buds. Bus #7 runs along Broadway; bus #10 runs through Capitol Hill along more sedate **15th St.** Free parking is behind the reservoir at Broadway Field, on 11th Ave.

■ Bimbo's Bitchin' Burrito Kitchen, 506 E Pine (☎ 329-9978). The name explains it, and the decorations prove it (fake palm trees and lots of plastic). An experience, and if that's not enough, walk right on through the door to the **Cha Cha,** a similarly-decorated bar. Spicy Bimbo's burrito $4. Open M-Th noon-11pm, F-Sa noon-2am, Su 2-10pm.

Caffe Minnie's, 611 Broadway E (☎860-1360). The original Caffe Minnie (☎448-6263) is at 1st and Denny Way. Famous tomato basil soup ($4). Breakfast all day and a huge menu to chose from. Both open 24hr.

Ristorante Machiavelli, 1215 Pine St. (☎621-7941), right across the street from Bauhaus (see **Cafes,** below). A small Italian place that locals fiercely love. Not too far of a walk from downtown, either. Pasta $7-9. Open M-Th 5-10pm, F-Sa 5-11pm.

HaNa, 219 Broadway Ave. E (☎328-1187). Packed quarters testify to the popularity of the sushi here. Sushi combo platter with rice and soup (lunch $6.25, dinner $8.75). Open M-Sa 11am-10pm, Su 4-10pm.

Honey Hole Sandwiches, 703 E Pike (☎ 709-1399). The primary colors and veggie filled sandwiches make you feel healthy and happy. The hummus-loaded "Daytripper" is a treat ($5). Open daily 10am-7pm.

UNIVERSITY DISTRICT

The neighborhood around the immense University of Washington ("U-Dub"), north of downtown between Union Bay and Portage Bay, supports funky shops, international restaurants, and yes, coffeehouses. The best of each lies within a few blocks of University Way, known as "Th' Ave." Restaurants run rampant here. The Ave. supports everything from Denny's to bubble tea. Think student budget: this place is probably the cheapest place to eat in the city. To get there, take Exit 169 off I-5 N, or take one of buses #70-74 from downtown, or #7 or 9 from Capitol Hill.

Flowers, 4247 University Way NE (☎633-1903). This 20s landmark was a flower shop. The mirrored ceiling tastefully reflects an all-you-can-eat vegetarian buffet ($7). Great daily drink specials: $2 tequila shots W, $3 well sours Th, $3 margaritas Sa. Open W-Sa 11am-2am, Su-Tu 11am-midnight; kitchen closes for all but snacks at 10pm.

Mamma Melina, 4759 Roosevelt Way NW (☎632-2271). Right underneath the Seven Gables cinema, this restaurant is a little slice of southern Italy transplanted onto Seattle's sodden soil. The food is fantastic, and the atmosphere great. Tu 5-9pm is when the real action happens; wine is half price, and Pappa sings his favorite Neapolitan songs. Pasta $9-12. 10% off with ticket stub from a show upstairs. Service begins 4:30pm.

Pizzeria Pagliacci, 4529 University Way NE (☎632-0421; 726-1717 for delivery), also on Capitol Hill at 426 Broadway Ave. E (☎323-7987). Seattle's best pizza since 1986. M-F 2pm-5pm buy 2 slices, get a free drink. Open Su-Th 11am-11pm, F-Sa 11am-1am.

Tandoor Restaurant, 5024 University Way NE (☎523-7477). The lunch buffet ($6) is a great deal (11am-2:30pm), as is Sunday brunch ($7). Classiness is evidenced by the higher dinner prices. Open M-Sa 11am-2:30pm and 4:30-10pm, Su 11am-3pm.

Wing Dome, 4545 University Way NE (☎632-1033). Wing lovers have met their match. Hotness ranges from 1 to 5 alarms. Several other types for the weak. 10 for $6. M, 29¢ wings all day; W, 25 wings and pitcher of beer $20; Th, 50 wings $20. Open M-Sa 11:30am-11pm, Su noon-10pm.

Shultzy's, 4114 University Way NE (☎548-9461). As they proudly say, "Seattle's Wurst Restaurant." Sausage made from damn near anything: Bratwurst, chicken, hot Italian...sausage. All $4. Open daily 11am-11pm.

CAFES

The coffee bean is Seattle's first love. One cannot walk a single block without passing an institution of caffeination. The city's obsession with Italian-style espresso drinks has even gas stations pumping out thick, dark, soupy java.

CAPITOL HILL

Bauhaus, 305 E Pine St. (☎625-1600). The Reading Goddess looks from above the towering bookshelves, protects patrons, and oversees service of drip coffee ($1) or Kool-Aid ($1). Open M-F 6am-1am, Sa-Su 8am-1am.

The Globe Cafe, 1531 14th Ave. (☎324-8815). Seattle's next literary renaissance is brewing here. Quotes overheard at the Globe are plastered on the tables. Fabulous all-vegan menu. Stir-fry tofu $5.50. Internet access $6 per hr. Open Tu-Su 7am-7:30pm.

B&O Cafe, 204 Belmont (☎322-5208), takes its name from the Monopoly RR. Weekend brunches till 3pm. Delicious desserts $5.50. Open M-Th 7am-midnight, F 7am-1am, Sa 8am-1am, Su 8am-midnight.

UNIVERSITY DISTRICT

Espresso Roma, 4201 University Way NE (☎632-6001). Pleasant patio, and quasi-former-warehouse interior result in spacious tables with an open air feel. Probably the Ave's cheapest coffee; mocha $1.65. Internet access $6 per hr. Open daily 7am-11pm.

Ugly Mug, 1309 43rd St. (☎547-3219), off University Way. Offbeat in a 10,000-Maniacs-Thrift-store sort of way. Eclectic chair collection is quite comfortable. Wide sandwich selection (turkey focaccia $4). Open M-F 7:30am-6pm, Sa and Su 9am-6pm.

Gingko Tea, 4343 University Way NE (☎632-7298). Gentle classical music supplies the background; tasteful wood furniture and floral cushions provide the foreground. Five types of chai ($2.55); bubble tea ($2.45). Open M-Th 10am-10pm, F-Su 11am-8pm.

ENTERTAINMENT

Seattle has one of the world's most notorious underground music scenes and the third-largest theater community in the US (second to New York and Chicago), and supports performance in all sorts of venues, from bars to bakeries. Risers seem to grow from the asphalt in spring, when street fairs and outdoor theater come to life. The big performance houses regularly sell half-price tickets and alternative theaters offer high-quality drama at downright low prices. The free **Out to Lunch** series (☎623-0340) brings everything from reggae to folk dancing to parks, squares, and office buildings during summer. The **Seattle Public Library** screens free films as part of the program and hosts daily poetry readings.

MUSIC AND DANCE

The **Seattle Opera** performs favorites from August to May. Come January 2002 they will move out of the Seattle Center Opera House and into the Mercer Arts Arena, next door, to make room for renovations. Buffs should reserve well in advance, although rush tickets are sometimes available. (☎389-7676; www.seattleopera.org. Students and seniors can get half-price tickets 1½hr. before the performance. From $31.) The **Pacific Northwest Ballet** performs at the Opera House from (Sept.-June). In 2002, look for *Song and Dance* (May), *Tango Tonight* (Apr.), and

SEATTLE CityPass

1 Low Price, 6 Famous Attractions, No Ticket Lines!
It's a Great New Way to Enjoy Seattle!

CityPass Includes Admission to:
The Space Needle • Pacific Science Center & IMAX
Seattle Aquarium • Museum of Flight
The Woodland Park Zoo • Argosy Cruises Harbor Tour

Only $35.50 a $71.00 Value!

CityPass is **on sale at all** of the above attractions. Ask for it at the first one you visit! Good for 9 days. For more information visit **www.citypass.com** or call (707) 256-0490.

New York City · San Francisco · Philadelphia · Boston · Chicago · Hollywood

---

Cinderella (Feb.; ☎ 441-9411. Tickets from $15. Half-price rush tickets available to students and seniors 30min. before showtime.) The **Seattle Symphony,** performs in the new Benaroya Hall, 200 University St. at 3rd Ave., from September to June. (☎ 212-4700; tickets 215-4747. From $10, most from $25-39; seniors half-price; students $10. Rush tickets from $6.50. Ticket office open M-F 10am-6pm, Sa 1-6pm.) Even if you won't be hearing the symphony, drop by the new concert hall to take in Chihuly glass chandeliers and a Rauchenberg mural. (☎ 215-4895. Tours M-F noon and 1pm.) Free organ concerts bring out large crowds on the 1st Monday of the month at 12:30pm as well. The **University of Washington** offers its own program of student recitals and concerts by visiting artists. The **World Series** showcases dance, theater and chamber music (tickets $25-40). Some lectures and dances are much cheaper ($5-10). Contact the Meany Hall box office, 4001 University Way. (☎ 543-4880). Half-price student rush tickets available half an hour before show at the box office. (Open Sept.-June M-F 10am-6pm; summer M-F 10:30am-4:30pm.)

THEATER

The city hosts an exciting array of first-run plays and alternative works, particularly by many talented amateur groups. Rush tickets are often available at nearly half price on the day of the show (cash only) from **Ticket/Ticket** (☎ 324-2744).

The Empty Space Theatre, 3509 Fremont Ave. N (☎ 547-7500; www.emptyspace.org), 1½ blocks north of the Fremont Bridge. Comedies in the small space attract droves. Season runs Oct. to early July. Tickets $22-30. Under 25 and previews (first 4 shows of a run) $10. Half-price tickets 30min. before curtain. Box office open Tu-Su from noon.

Seattle Repertory Theater, 155 Mercer St. (☎ 443-2222; www.seattlerep.org), at the wonderful Bagley Wright Theater in the Seattle Center. Contemporary and classic winter productions (and Shakespeare). Tickets $15-45 (cheaper on weekdays), seniors $31, under 25 $10. Rush tickets 30min. before curtain. Box office open M-F 10am-6pm, weekends noon-6pm during season.

A Contemporary Theater (ACT), 700 Union St. (☎ 292-7676). Summer season of modern and off-beat premieres. $20-45. Under 25 $10. Office open daily noon-7pm.

Annex Theatre (☎ 728-0933). A rogue theater group without a regular space—call their number to find out where they are performing. Refreshing emphasis on company-generated material and unconventional theater. Shows usually Th-Sa at 8pm and Su at 7pm. Pay-what-you-can previews. Tickets $10-12.

Northwest Asian American Theater, 409 7th Ave. S (☎ 340-1445), in the International District, next to the Wing Luke Asian Museum. Excellent new theater with pieces by Asian Americans. Season runs year-long. Prices $6-12. Students and seniors sometimes get discounts. Box office M-F 10am-6pm.

CINEMA

Seattle is a cinematic paradise. Most of the theaters that screen non-Hollywood films are on Capitol Hill and in the University District. Large, first-run theaters are everywhere, including the mammoth 16-screen **Loews Cineplex Meridian** (☎ 223-9600) at 7th Ave. and Pike. **Seven Gables,** a local company, has recently bought up the Egyptian, the Metro, the Neptune, and about 25 other theaters. $28 buys admission to any five films at any of their theaters. Call ☎ 443-4567 (movie phone) for local movie times and locations. On summer Saturdays, **outdoor cinema** in Fremont begins at dusk at 670 N 34th St., in the U-Park lot by the bridge, behind the Red Door Alehouse. Enter as early as 7pm to catch live music that starts at 8pm. Management offers prizes for best costumes. (☎ 767-2593. $5.) **TCI Outdoor Cinema** shows everything from classics to cartoons for free at the Gasworks Park. (☎ 720-1058. Live music 7pm-dusk.) Aspiring independent filmmakers or actors/actresses should check out the Alibi Room for readings (see **Nightlife,** below). Unless specified, the theaters below charge $5 for matinees and $8 for features.

The Egyptian, 801 E Pine St. (☎ 32-EGYPT), at Harvard Ave. on Capitol Hill. This Art Deco art-house is best known for hosting the **Seattle International Film Festival** in the last week of May and first week of June. The festival's director retrospective features a personal appearance by said director. Festival series tickets available at a discount.

The Harvard Exit, 807 E Roy St. (☎ 323-8986), on Capitol Hill, near the north end of the Broadway business district. Quality classic and foreign films. Converted women's club that has its own ghost, and an enormous antique projector.

Seven Gables Theater, 911 NE 50th St. (☎ 632-8820), in the U District just off Roosevelt, a short walk west from University Way. Another art-house cinema in an old house showing art, independent, and international films. Entrance is shaded by trees.

Grand Illusion Cinema, 1403 NE 50th St. (☎ 523-3935), in the U District at University Way. Plays world cinema flicks and exciting international films. Frequently revives old classics and hard to find films. One of the last independent theaters in Seattle. $7, seniors and children $3.50; matinees $4.50.

Little Theatre, 608 19th Ave., at Mercer St. on Capitol Hill (☎ 675-2055) Documentaries and independent films. $7, seniors and children $3.50, matinees $4.50.

SPORTS

Seattleites cheered last summer when the home team, the **Mariners,** moved out of the Kingdome, where in 1995 sections of the roof fell into the stands. The "M's" are now playing baseball in the half-billion dollar, hangar-like **Safeco Field,** at First Ave. S and Royal Brougham Way S, under an enormous retractable roof. Saving the game from frequent rain-outs is simply a matter of pushing a single button labelled "Go" and costs a mere $1.50 in electricity. (Tickets ☎ 622-4487. From $10.) Seattle's football team, the **Seahawks,** are stuck playing in UW's Husky Stadium until construction on their stadium is finished. (Tickets ☎ 628-0888. From $10.)

On the other side of town and at the other end of the aesthetic spectrum, the sleek **Key Arena** in the Seattle Center hosts Seattle's NBA basketball team, the **Supersonics** (☎ 628-0888). The men now share their turf with their female counterparts: the WNBA expansion team, the **Seattle Storm** (☎ 628-0888; www.storm.wnba.com). For college sports fans, the **University of Washington Huskies** football team has dominated the PAC-10 for years and don't plan to let up. Call the Athletic Ticket Office (☎ 543-2200) for Huskies schedules and prices.

NIGHTLIFE

Seattle has moved beyond beer to a new nightlife frontier: the cafe-bar. The popularity of espresso bars in Seattle might lead one to conclude that caffeine is more intoxicating than alcohol, but often an establishment that poses as a diner by day brings on a band, breaks out the disco ball, and pumps out the microbrews by night. Many locals tell tourists that the best spot to go for guaranteed good beer, live music, and big crowds is Pioneer Square, where UW students from frat row dominate the bar stools. You may prefer to go to Capitol Hill, or up Rte. 99 to Fremont, where the atmosphere is usually more laid-back than in the Square. Wherever you go, but especially downtown, do stay alert—Seattle is big city, with the homelessness, crime, and dark alleys that come with size.

DOWNTOWN

The Alibi Room, 85 Pike St. (☎ 623-3180), across from the Market Cinema in the Post Alley in Pike Place. A local indie filmmaker hangout that is remarkably friendly in its air of culture. Bar with music open 7 nights, a downstairs dance floor opens F and Sa. Brunch Sa and Su. No cover. Open daily 11:30am-2am.

Sit and Spin, 2219 4th Ave. (cafe and laundromat ☎ 441-9484), between Bell St. and Blanchard St. Board games keep patrons busy while they wait for their clothes to dry or for alternative bands to stop playing in the back room. F-Sa nights cover $6-8. The cafe sells everything from local microbrews on tap to bistro food. Artists cut albums in the **Bad Animal** studio down the street where R.E.M. once recorded. Open Su-Th 9am-midnight, F-Sa 9am-2am. Kitchen opens daily at 11am.

Art Bar, 1516 2nd Ave. (☎ 622-4344), opposite the Green Tortoise Hostel. Gallery and bar. DJs and dancing all week. Tu funk, Th Dancehall Reggae, F jungle, Sa hip-hop. Pints $2.50 from 4-9pm. Cover $5-6. Open M-F 11am-2am, Sa-Su 6pm-2am. Sa after-hours house music 4-10am.

Crocodile Cafe, 2200 2nd Ave. (☎ 448-2114; www.thecrocodile.com), at Blanchard in Belltown. Cooks from scratch by day, and plays host to local and national bands by night. House W. Shows usually start 9:30; some need tix in advance. 21+ after 9pm. Cover $5-20. Open Tu-Sa 8am-2am, Su 9am-3pm for brunch.

PIONEER SQUARE

Pioneer Square provides a happening scene, dominated by twenty-somethings, frat kids, and cover bands. Although the local scene took a beating when several bars closed due to earthquake damage, the vibe is still largely intact. Most of the area bars participate in a joint cover (F-Sa $10, Su-Th $5) that will let you wander from bar to bar to sample the bands. The larger venues are listed below. Two smaller venues, **Larry's Greenfront,** 209 1st Ave. S (☎ 624-7665) and **New Orleans,** 114 1st Ave. S (☎ 622-2563) feature great blues and jazz nightly. Not part of the Pioneer Square joint cover because it's often free, **J and M Cafe and Cardroom,** 201 1st Ave. (☎ 292-0663) is in the center of Pioneer Square, often blasting rock and blues (Th, no cover) or disco and top 40 (W $5). Most of the Pioneer Square clubs shut down at 2am Friday and Saturday nights, and around midnight during the week.

Bohemian Cafe, 111 Yesler Way, (☎ 447-1514) pumps reggae every night. 3 sections, a cafe, a bar and a stage, all of them adorned with art of Jamaica. Live shows six nights per week, often national acts on weekends. Happy hour 4-7pm. Part of the joint cover. Open M-Sa 4pm-2am. After-hours electronica F and Sa 2-8am.

Central Tavern, 207 1st Ave. S. (☎ 622-0209), was one of the early venues for grunge, and in a weird twist has now become a favorite for bikers. Live rock six nights a week, at 9:30pm. Part of the joint cover. Open daily 11:30am-2am, kitchen closes 8ish.

Last Supper Club, 124 S. Washington St. (☎ 748-9975) at Occidental. Two dance floors, DJed with everything from 70s disco (F); funky house, drum & bass, and trance (Sa). Su nights salsa at 8:30pm. Cover F-Sa $10; W, Th, Su $5. Open W-Su 4pm-2am.

162 ■ SEATTLE

Swannie's Sports Bar, 222 S Main St. (☎622-9353). Share drink specials with pro ballplayers who stop by post-game. Any Seattle sports junkie will swear this is the place to be. Drink specials change daily. Open M-F 11:30am-2am; Sa-Su 4pm-2am.

CAPITOL HILL

East off of Broadway, Pine St. is cool lounge after cool lounge. Find your atmosphere and acclimatize. West off of Broadway, Pike St. has the clubs that push the limits (gay, punk, industrial, fetish, dance) and break the sound barrier.

Linda's, 707 Pine St. E (☎325-1220). A very chill bar that is a major post-gig scene for Seattle rockers. Live DJ playing jazz and old rock (Su, Tu, and Th; no cover). Expanded menu, liquor, and breakfast on weekend. Open M-F 2pm-2am, Sa-Su 10am-2am.

Vogue, 1516 11th Ave. (☎324-5778) off Pike St. If this club were a country, black leather would be the national outfit. Be prepared to dress for the night; e.g., no one is allowed in not wearing black for fetish night. Live music (Tu), Goth (W), live music (Th), fetish (F and Su), 80s/90s New Wave (Sa), Cover $2-5. Open Tu-Su 9pm-2am.

Neighbors, 1509 Broadway (☎324-5358; www.neighboursonline.com). Enter from the alley on Pike. A very gay dance club priding itself on techno slickness. Midnight drag shows (Su, and Tu-Th). House (M, W, F-Sa), 80's (Tu, Th), Latin (Su). Cover Su-Th $1; F-Sa $5. Open Su-W 9pm-2am, Th 9pm-3am, F-Sa 9pm-4am.

Garage, 1130 Broadway (☎322-2296), between Union and Madison. An automotive warehouse turned upscale pool hall, this place gets suave at night. Happy hour 3-7pm. 18 pool tables $6-14 per hr.; $4 per hr. during happy hour; $5 per hr. (M); free for female sharps on Ladies' Night (Su). Open daily 3pm-2am.

◉ SIGHTS AND FESTIVALS

ANNUAL EVENTS

Pick up a copy of the visitors center's *Calendar of Events*, published every season, for event coupons and an exact listing of innumerable area happenings. The first Thursday evening of each month, the art community sponsors **First Thursday,** a free and well-attended gallery walk. Watch for **street fairs** in the University District during mid- to late May, at Pike Place Market over Memorial Day weekend, and in Fremont in mid-June. The International District holds its annual two-day bash in mid-July, featuring arts and crafts booths, East Asian and Pacific food booths, and presentations by a range of groups from the Radical Women/Freedom Socialist Party to the Girl Scouts. For more info, call **Chinatown Discovery** (☎382-1197), or write P.O. Box 3406, Seattle 98114.

Puget Sound's yachting season begins in May. **Maritime Week,** during the third week of May, and the **Shilshole Boats Afloat Show** (☎634-0911) August 14-18, 2002, gives area boaters a chance to show off their crafts. Over the 4th of July weekend, the Center for Wooden Boats sponsors the free **Wooden Boat Show** (☎382-2628) on Lake Union. Blue blazers and deck shoes are *de rigeur*. Size up the entrants (over 100 wooden boats), then watch a demonstration of boat-building skills. The yearend blow-out is the **Quick and Daring Boatbuilding Contest,** when hopefuls go overboard trying to build and sail wooden boats of their own design, using a limited kit of tools and materials. Plenty of music, food, and alcohol make the sailing smooth.

Northwest Folklife Festival (☎684-7300), on Memorial Day weekend. One of Seattle's most notable events, held at the Seattle Center. Dozens of booths, artists, musicians, and dancers congregate to celebrate the area's heritage. $5 suggested donation.

Bite of Seattle (☎232-2982), in mid-July. Bite size to full meals from free to $8. Decide for yourself what is the best of Seattle. Free.

Seattle Seafair (☎728-0123), spread over 4 weeks beginning in early July. The biggest, baddest festival of them all. Each neighborhood contributes with street fairs, parades large and small, balloon races, musical entertainment, and a seafood orgy. Major city wide torch run culminates the event.

Bumbershoot (☎ 281-7788), over Labor Day weekend. A massive, 4-day arts festival that caps off the summer, held in the Seattle Center. Attracts big-name rock bands, street musicians, and a young, exuberant crowd. 4 days $44; 2 days $28; 1 day $16. Tickets are cheaper if you buy them in advance. Additional tickets may be needed for certain big-name, major concerts or events. Prices subject to change.

Opening Day (☎ 325-1000), First Sa in May. A celebration of spring, water, and boats. Highlight is the Montlake Cut parade of yachts and the Windermere Cup crew races.

It takes only three frenetic days to get a decent look at most of the city's major sights, since most are within walking distance of one another or the Metro's ride free zone (see p. 149). Seattle taxpayers spend more per capita on the arts than any other Americans, and the investment pays off in unparalleled public art installations throughout the city (self-guided tours begin at the visitors center), and plentiful galleries. The investments of Seattle-based millionaires have brought startlingly new and bold architecture in the Experience Music Project and International Fountain. Outside cosmopolitan downtown, Seattle boasts over 300 areas of well-watered greenery (see **Waterways and Parks,** p. 167).

DOWNTOWN

SEATTLE ART MUSEUM. Housed in a grandiose building designed by Philadelphia architect and father of Postmodernism Robert Venturi, the SAM does a good job of balancing special exhibits, a strong collection of African, Native American, and Asian art and an eclectic bunch of contemporary western painting and sculpture. Is the giant hammering man out front hammering his way into Seattle's consciousness? Call for info on special musical shows, films, and lectures. Admission is also good for the **Seattle Asian Art Museum** (a branch housed in the museum's former building; see p. 165) for a week. *(100 University Way, near 1st Ave. Recording ☎ 654-3100, person 654-3255, or TDD 654-3137. Open Tu-W and F-Su 10am-5pm, Th 10am-9pm. Free tours 1 and 2pm, as well as several later in the day. $7, students and seniors $5, under 12 free; first Th of the month free.)*

SEATTLE ART MUSEUM GALLERY. Inside the Museum Plaza Building at 1st Ave., the free **Seattle Art Museum Gallery** displays work by local artists. *(Open M-F 11am-5pm, Sa-Su 11am-4pm.)*

PUBLIC ART. Beside the Westlake monorail stop, **Westlake Park's** Art Deco brick patterns are surprisingly dry. **Wall of Water** is a good place to kick back and listen to steel drums on Pike St., between 4th and 5th Ave. **Pike Place Market** is nearby (see **Food,** p. 155). The **concrete waterfalls** of **Freeway Park,** which straddles I-5 between Pike St. and Spring St., are designed to mimic a natural gorge and block freeway noise.

THE WATERFRONT

The **Pike Place Hillclimb** descends from the south end of Pike Place Market past chic shops and ethnic restaurants to the Alaskan Way and waterfront. (An elevator is available.) The waterfront is lined with fish and chip shops, harbor cruise companies, and t-shirt shops armed to share "authentic" Seattle with you. Needless to say, you will not be lonely in the harbor.

THE SEATTLE AQUARIUM. The aquarium's star attraction is a huge underwater dome, but harbor seals, fur seals, otters, and plenty of fish don't disappoint, either. Touch tanks and costumes delight kids. A one-million-dollar salmon exhibit and ladder teaches about the state's favorite fish. Feedings occur throughout the day and shouldn't be missed. Next door, the **Omnidome** cranks out Imax films, many of them focusing on natural events or habitats. *(Pier 59, near Union St. ☎ 386-4320, TDD 386-4322. Open daily 10am-8pm; winter 10am-6pm; last admission 1hr. before closing. $9, seniors $8, ages 6-18 $6.25, ages 3-5 $4.25. Omnidome ☎ 622-1868. Films daily 10am-10pm. $7, seniors $6.50, ages 6-18 $6. Aquarium and Omnidome combo ticket $14.50, seniors and ages 13-18 $13.50, ages 6-13 $10.75, ages 3-5 $4.25.)*

164 ■ SEATTLE

STREETCAR. Dispel the myth—streetcars exist outside San Francisco and they present the perfect means to explore the waterfront. The 20s-era cars were brought in from Melbourne after Seattle sold its originals to San Francisco as "cable cars" (posers!). Streetcars are wheelchair-accessible, and run from the Metro opposite the King St. Station in Pioneer Square north to Pier 70 and Myrtle Edwards Park. *(Every 20-30min. M-F 7am-11pm, Sa 8am-11pm, Su 9am-11pm; winter until 6pm. $1.25, $1.50 during peak hours; children 50¢. Weekend or holiday day pass $2.50. Under 12 with a paying passenger free on Su. Metro passes accepted.)*

THE SEATTLE CENTER

The 1962 World's Fair demanded a Seattle Center to herald the city of the future. Now it houses everything from carnival rides to ballet, although Seattleites generally leave the center to tourists and suburbanites. The center is bordered by Denny Way, W Mercer St., 1st Ave., and 5th Ave., and has eight gates, each with a model of the Center and a map of its facilities. It is accessible via a short **monorail** which departs the third floor of the Westlake Center. The center's anchorpoint is the Center House, which holds a food court, stage and **Information Desk.** A brand-new International Fountain squirts water 20 ft. in the air from all angles off its silver, semispherical base. The grass around it is a wonderful place to sit and relax. *(Monorail: every 15min. M-F 7:30am-11pm, Sa-Su 9am-11pm. $1.25, seniors 50¢, ages 5-12 50¢. Info Desk: open daily 11am-6pm. For info about special events and permanent attractions, call 684-8582 (recorded info) or 684-7200 for a real live person.)*

EXPERIENCE MUSIC PROJECT (EMP). Undoubtedly the biggest and best attraction at the Seattle Center is the new, futuristic, abstract, and technologically brilliant Experience Music Project. The museum is the brainchild of Seattle billionaire Paul Allen, who originally wanted to create a shrine to worship his music idol Jimi Hendrix. But nothing this man does is small. Splash together the technological sophistication and foresight of Microsoft, dozens of ethnomusicologists and multimedia specialists, a collection of musical artifacts topping 80,000, the world-renowned architect Frank Gehry, and enough money to make the national debt appear small (OK, OK...it was only $350 million), and you guessed it, you have the rock and roll museum of the future. The building alone—consisting of sheet metal molded into abstract curves and then acid-dyed gold, sliver, purple, light-blue, and red—is enough to make the average person gasp for breath. Walk in and strap on your personal computer guide (MEG) that allows you to interact with the exhibits. Hear clips from Hendrix' famous "Star Spangled Banner" as you look at the remnants of the guitar he smashed on a London stage. Move into the Sound Lab and test your own skills on guitars, drums, and keyboards linked to computer teaching devices and cushioned in state-of-the art sound rooms. When you are ready, step over to On Stage, a first class karaoke-gone-haywire, and blast your tunes in front of a virtual audience. Expect to spend several hours testing your creativity, jamming to punk/hip-hop/blues/folk and much, much more—in fact, locals tend to make a day out of it, using readmission to go in and out several times. Unfortunately this much to do does come with a hefty price tag. *(325 Fifth St. at Seattle Center. From I-5 take Exit 167 and follow signs to Seattle Center. Bus #15, 4, 3. ☎ 367-5483 or 877-367-5483; TDD 770-2771; www.emplive.com. Open in summer daily 9am-11pm; winter Su-Th 10am-6pm, F-Sa 10am-11pm. $20, seniors and ages 13-17 $16, children $15. Free live music Tu-Sa in the lounge; national acts perform for a price almost every F and Sa in the Sky Church.)*

SPACE NEEDLE. Until the EMP came to town, the **Space Needle** appeared to be something from another time—now it matches quite well with its futuristic neighbor. The Needle provides a great view (insert "on a clear day" here) and an irreplacable landmark for the disoriented. The elevator ride itself is a show—operators are hired for their unique talents. The needle houses an observation tower and a high-end 360° rotating restaurant. *(☎ 905-2100. $11, seniors $9, ages 5-12 $5.)*

SIGHTS AND FESTIVALS ■ 165

PACIFIC SCIENCE CENTER. The get-down-and-dirty approach of this museum ropes kids into loving to learn. Ride a high rail bike, tread water in a giant hamster wheel, or play virtual basketball. The tropical butterfly garden is fantastic and the Center also houses a **laserium** that quakes to rock as well as two **IMAX theaters.** *(200 2nd Ave. N. Monorail or Bus #1, 2, 3, 4, 6, 8, 19, 24.* ☎ *443-2001; www.pacsci.org. Exhibits open in summer daily 10am-9pm; winter 10am-5pm. $8, seniors and ages 3-13 $5.50, under 3 free. Laserium* ☎ *443-2850. Laser shows nights Th $5, F-Su $7.50. IMAX* ☎ *443-4629. Shows daily from 10am-7pm. $7.50, seniors or ages 3-13 $6.50. Various combo tickets are sold, ranging from $12.50-24.50 for adults.)*

PIONEER SQUARE AND ENVIRONS

From the waterfront or downtown, it's just a few blocks south to historic **Pioneer Square,** centered around Yesler Way and 2nd Ave., home of the first Seattleites. The 19th-century buildings, restored in the 1970s and now home to chic shops and trendy pubs, retain their historical intrigue and great crowds of tourists. Pioneer Square is extra busy on game day as baseball moms and dads walk their children to Safeco Field Baseball Park to see the Mariners in action.

UNDERGROUND TOUR. Originally, downtown stood 12 ft. lower than it does today. The tour guides visitors through the subterranean city of old. Be prepared for lots of company, comedy, and toilet jokes. Tours depart from Doc Maynard's Pub, 610 1st Ave. "Doc" Maynard, a charismatic and colorful early resident, gave a plot of land here to one Henry Yesler to build a steam-powered lumber mill. The logs dragged to the mill's front door earned the street its epithet, **Skid Row,** and the smell of the oil used to lubricate the slide was so overwhelming that the self-respecting Seattleites of the day left the neighborhood to gamblers and prostitutes. *(*☎ *682-4646 or 888-608-6337; www.undergroundtour.com. 90min. tours daily, roughly hourly 10am-6pm. $9, seniors and students ages 13-17 $7, children $5; Cash only.)*

KLONDIKE GOLD RUSH NATIONAL HISTORIC PARK. The park houses a spiffy interpretive center that details the history of gold rush stampeders and the ghost towns they left in their wake. Gold digging artifacts and timelines tell the story. Rangers lead tours, but for park info head over to the REI park desk. *(117 S Main St.* ☎ *553-7220; www.nps.gov/klse/home.htm. Open daily 9am-5pm. Tours of Pioneer Square daily at 10am; gold panning demonstration 1 and 3pm, summers only. Free.)*

THE INTERNATIONAL DISTRICT/CHINATOWN

Seattle's **International District/Chinatown** is three blocks east of Pioneer Square, up Jackson on King St.

■ **Wing Luke Memorial Museum.** This hole-in-the-wall gives a thorough description of life in an Asian-American community, investigates different Asian nationalities in Seattle, and work by local Asian artists. Special exhibits add even more to the tight space. The museum also hands out the very helpful *Walking Tour of the International District*. *(407 7th Ave. S* ☎ *623-5124. Open Tu-F 11am-4:30pm, Sa-Su noon-4pm. $4, seniors and students $3, ages 5-12 $2. Free first Th of the month.)*

■ **SEATTLE ASIAN ART MUSEUM.** What do you do when you have too much good art to exhibit all at once? Open a second museum; which is just what SAM did, creating a wonderful stand-on-it-own attraction. The collection is particularly strong in Chinese art, but most of East Asia is admirably represented. *(In Volunteer Park, just beyond the watertower.* ☎ *654-3100. Open Tu-Su 10am-5pm, Th 10am-9pm. $3, under 12 free; free with SAM ticket from the prev. 7 days; SAAM ticket good for $3 discount at SAM.)*

■ **UNIVERSITY OF WASHINGTON ARBORETUM.** The Arboretum nurtures over 4000 species, trees, shrubs, and flowers, and maintains superb trails. Tours depart the **Graham Visitor Center,** at the southern end of the arboretum on Lake Washington Blvd. *(10 blocks east of Volunteer Park. Bus #11 from downtown.* ☎ *543-8800. Open daily sunrise to sunset, visitors center 10am-4pm. Free tours Sa and Su at 1pm.)*

PUBLIC ART. Landmarks of the International District include the abstract Tsutakawa sculpture (corner of Maynard and Jackson), and the gigantic dragon mural and red-and-green pagoda in Hing Hay Park (S King and Maynard St.). Although you will not find many trees in the park, the pagoda provides a nice respite from the sun (or rain).

VOLUNTEER PARK. Although it is unsafe (and closed) at night, the park is a popular afternoon destination. The **outdoor stage** often hosts free performances on summer Sundays. Scale the **water tower** at the 14th Ave. entrance for a stunning 360° panorama of the city and the Olympic Range. The **glass conservatory** houses dazzling orchids. *(Between 11th and 15th Ave. at E Ward St., north of Broadway. Open daily 10am-4pm; summer 10am-7pm. Free.)*

JAPANESE TEA GARDEN. The tranquil 3½ acre park is a retreat of sculpted gardens, fruit trees, a reflecting pool, and a traditional tea house. *(☎684-4725. At the south end of the U-W Arboretum, entrance on Lake Washington Blvd. Open Mar.-Nov. daily 10am-dusk. $2.50; seniors, disabled, students, and ages 6-18 $1.50; under 6 free.)*

UNIVERSITY DISTRICT, FREMONT, AND BALLARD

The northern districts of Seattle include neighborhoods that seem to be entirely at odds with each other, and yet somehow eek out a peaceful co-existence. The University district is a young and multi-cultural scene revolving around the main drag "The Ave." Fremont is a small community, busy with plans of secession from the nation. Scandinavians have concentrated in Ballard.

■ **HENRY ART GALLERY.** Specializing in modern and contemporary, the Henry reflects its curators' enthusiasm with unconventional installations and rarely-seen artists. A beautiful space right in the middle of campus. *(Located at the intersection of 41st NE and 15th NE Ave. ☎616-9894. Open Tu-Su 11am-5pm, Th 11am-8pm. $6, seniors $4.50, all students free. Free Th after 5pm.)*

UNIVERSITY OF WASHINGTON. With over 36,000 students, the university (U-Dub) comprises the state's educational center of gravity. The U District swarms with students year-round, and Seattleites of all ages take advantage of the area's many bohemian bookstores, shops, taverns, and restaurants. Looming gothic gargoyles, lecture halls, red brick, and rose gardens make the campus a bower fit for hours of strolling. The area surrounding the campus has a more built-up feel than the other residential areas of Seattle, but then again, there are so many better things to think about it this area than the architecture such as beer, food; food, beer. The red concrete basin in the center of campus is a hub of student radicalism and skateboarding known as **Red Square.** Stop by the friendly **visitors center,** which is usually manned by helpful college students. *(Visitors center 4014 University Way NE at NE Campus Way. Buses #71-73 from downtown, or #7, 9, 43, or 48 from Capitol Hill. ☎543-9198. Open M-F 8am-5pm. Guided tours leave from center at 10:30am.)*

THOMAS BURKE MUSEUM OF NATURAL HISTORY AND CULTURE. Savor the chance to see the only dinosaur bones on display in Washington and a superb collection on Pacific Rim cultures. You will enjoy kid-friendly explanations of the natural history of Washington's formation. Across the street, the astronomy department's old stone **observatory** is open to the public. *(45th St. NE and 17th Ave. NE. In the northwest corner of the campus. ☎543-5590; www.washington.edu/burkemuseum. Open daily 10am-5pm and til 8pm on Th. $5.50, seniors $4, students $2.50, under 5 free. Special exhibits occasionally more. Observatory ☎543-0126.)*

FREMONT. This area is home to residents who pride themselves on their love of art and antiques, and the liberal atmosphere of their self-declared "center of the world" under Rte. 99. Twice in the past ten years Fremont has applied to secede from the United States. A statue entitled **"Waiting for the Inner-City Urban"** laments the loss of the neighborhood's public transportation to downtown. The **immense troll** beneath the Aurora Bridge on 35th st. grasps a Volkswagen Bug with a confounded expression. Some say kicking the bug's tire brings good luck; others say it hurts the foot. A flamin' **Vladimir Lenin** resides at the corner of N 36th and N Fremont Pl.; this work from the former Soviet Union will be around until it's bought by a permanent collection, presumably of Soviet artwork.

Fremont is a perfect place for lazing around a coffee shop all day as it rains, or checking out the thrift shops and other counter-culture essentials that line the small business district. If a drink is what you are after, check out **Triangle Lounge,** 3507 Freemont Pl. N, a small bar with a lot of character. (☎ *632-0880 Bar snacks $4-8. Lots of brew. Open daily 11:30am-2am.)*

NORDIC HERITAGE MUSEUM. Just east of the U District, the primarily Scandinavian neighborhood of **Ballard** offers a wide variety of Scandinavian eateries and shops along Market St. The museum presents realistic exhibits on the history of Nordic immigration and influence in the US. Stumble over cobblestones in old Copenhagen, or visit the slums of New York City that turned photographer and Danish immigrant Jacob Riis into an important social reformer. The museum hosts a **Viking festival** (☎ 789-5708) the weekend after the 4th of July and a series of **Nordic concerts** by national and international musicians throughout the year. *(3014 NW 67th St. Bus #17 from downtown, and bus #44 from the U District, transferring to #17 at 24th and Market. ☎ 789-5707. Open Tu-Sa 10am-4pm, Su noon-4pm. $4, seniors and students $3, ages 6-18 $2.)*

WATERWAYS AND PARKS

Thanks to the foresight of Seattle's early community and the architectural genius of the Olmsted family, Seattle enjoys a string of parks and waterways.

LAKE UNION. Sailboats fill Lake Union, situated between Capitol Hill and the University District, and the **Center for Wooden Boats** can supply it, with a moored flotilla of new and restored craft for rent. **Gasworks Park,** at the north end of Lake Union fills the grounds of a retired oil-refining facility, necessitating frequent EPA checks. Fittingly, the park hosts a ■**4th of July Fireworks show,** and is a celebrated kite-flying spot. **Gasworks Kite Shop** provides the high-flying vehicles. **Urban Surf** rents surfboards, in-line skates, snowboards and kiteboards. *(Center for Wooden Boats: 1010 Valley St. ☎ 382-2628; www.cwb.org. Open daily noon-6pm. Rowboats weekends $20-30, weekdays $13-19; sailboats weekends $25-38, weekdays $16-24. Fireworks: Take bus #26 from downtown to N 35th St. and Wallingford Ave. N. Gasworks. Kite Shop: 3333 Wallingford N, one block north of the park. ☎ 633-4780. Open M-F 10am-6pm, Sa 10am-5pm, Su 11am-5pm. Urban Surf: 2100 N Northlake Way, opposite park entrance. ☎ 545-9463. Boards $15 per day. Skates $5 per hr., $16 per day. Open M-F 10am-7pm, Sa 10am-5pm, Su 11am-5pm.)*

WOODLAND PARK AND WOODLAND ZOO. Next to Green Lake are Woodland Park and the Woodland Park Zoo. The park is mediocre, but the zoo has won a bevy of AZA awards (the zoo Oscars, if you will) for best new exhibits. The African Savanna and the Northern Trail exhibits are both full of zoo favorites: grizzlies, wolves, lions, sasquatch, giraffes, and zebras. *(5500 Phinney Ave. N I-5 50th St. Exit or N 50th St. Bus #5 from downtown. ☎ 684-4800. Park open daily 4:30am-11:30pm. Zoo open May to mid-Sept. daily 9:30am-6pm; mid-March to April and mid-Sept. to mid-Oct. until 5pm; winter until 4pm. $9, seniors $8.25, ages 6-17 $6.50. Prices will rise slightly in 2002.)*

DISCOVERY PARK. Across the canals and west of the locks lie the 534 bucolic acres of **Discovery Park,** at 36th Ave. W and W Government Way, on a lonely point west of the Magnolia District and south of Golden Gardens Park. Grassy fields and steep, eroding bluffs, while dangerous for hikers, provide a haven for birds forced over Puget Sound by bad weather around the Olympic Mountains. . A **visitors center** is right by the entrance. A popular beach and lighthouse are also open for exploration, but only via free **Shuttle.** The **Daybreak Star Indian Cultural Center** at the park's north end is operated by the United Indians of All Tribes Foundation as a social, cultural, and educational center. *(Discovery Park: ☎ 386-4236. Open daily 6am-11pm. Visitor Center: 3801 W Government Way. Open daily 8:30am-5pm. Bus #24 or 33. Beach: open June-Sept. Sa-Su 11:45-4:30pm. By donation. Cultural Center: ☎ 285-4425. Open M-F 9am-5pm, Sa 10am-noon, Su noon-5pm. Free.)*

SEWARD PARK. At the south end of a string of beaches and forest preserves on the west shore of Lake Washington, this area offers sweeping views of the lake and Mercer Island, and a popular bike loop half-way around the lake. *(Bus #39.)*

OUTDOOR ACTIVITIES

BIKING. Over 1000 **cyclists** compete in the 19 mi. **Seattle to Portland Race** in mid-July. Call the **bike hotline** (☎ 522-2453) for info. On five **Bicycle Sundays** from May to September, Lake Washington Blvd. is open exclusively to cyclists from 10am to 6pm. Call the **Citywide Sports Office** (☎ 684-7092) for info. The **Burke-Gilman Trail** makes for a longer ride from the University District along Montlake Blvd., then along Lake Union and all the way west to Chittenden Locks and Discovery Park.

WHITEWATER RAFTING. Although the rapids are hours away by car, over 50 **whitewater rafting** outfitters are based in Seattle and are often willing to undercut one another with merciless and self-mutilating abandon. **Washington State Outfitters and Guides Association** (☎ 877-275-4964) provides advice; although their office is closed in summer, they do return phone calls and send out info. The **Northwest Outdoor Center,** 2100 Westlake Ave., on Lake Union, gives instructional programs in whitewater and sea kayaking, and leads three-day kayaking excursions through the San Juan Islands. (☎ 281-9367). Kayak rentals $10-15 per hr. Weekdays 3rd and 4th hours are free. Make reservations. Open M-F 10am-8pm, Sa-Su 9am-6pm.)

DAYTRIPS TO THE EAST

EAST SOUND. Seattleites leave the city en masse to play in what is a biker's, picnicker's, and suburbanite's paradise rolled into one. Entirely unnecessary Range Rovers and outdoor shopping plazas litter the landscape. Companies buy up expanses of East Sound land, smother them in sod and office complexes, and call them "campuses"—witness **Microsoft,** which has nearly subsumed the suburb of Redmond. Rapid growth has had its benefits, though. The wealthy and beautiful suburb of **Bellevue** is home to Bill Gates, among others. The small but interesting **Bellevue Art Museum** stands strong in a new building surrounded by malls and parking lots. The museum focuses mainly on contemporary art, and makes a good destination for a rainy day. The July **Bellevue Jazz Festival** attracts both local cats and national acts. *(Museum, 510 Bellevue Way NE. ☎ 425-519-0770. In central Bellevue just south of NE 8th St., west of I-405. Open W-F noon-8pm, Tu and Sa 10am-5pm, Su noon-5pm. $6, students $4. Festival, cross Lake Washington on one of two floating bridges to arrive in East Sound.)*

JIMI HENDRIX'S GRAVE. Rock pilgrims trek out to the grave of Seattle's first rock legend, **Jimi Hendrix,** to pay homage. Jimi's grave is in Greenwood Cemetery, in the town of Renton. Plan on spending some time driving labyrinthine streets, but once you make it the grave is located toward the back of the cemetery, just in front of the sun dial. *(Bus #101 from downtown to the Renton Park'n'Ride, then switch to #105 to Greenwood Cemetery. Drivers take the Sunset Blvd. Exit from Rte. 405—follow Sunset Blvd., not Park—turn right onto Branson, and right again on NE 4th. The Cemetery is on a hill, just next to a McDonalds.)*

LAKE SAMMAMISH STATE PARK AND FURTHER EAST. The exits along I-90 east of the city contain several hidden treats. Swim, water-ski, and play volleyball to your heart's content within **Lake Sammish State Park,** a weekend hotspot on the eastern shores of the lake. *(Take I-90 east to Exit 15, and follow the very large brown signs.)*

Further away, in the town of **Snoqualmie,** 29 mi. east of Seattle, is the **Northwest Railroad Museum.** The museum is made up of the state's oldest operating depot, as well as several working locomotives and vintage railroad cars. The real highlight is a 7 mi., hour-long roundtrip train ride that real fans can take to the neighboring town of North Bend. *(109 King St. On Rte. 202. Take the Snoqualmie Parkway exit from I-90, and turn right at 202. ☎ 452-888-9311; www.trainmuseum.org. Museum open Th-M year-round, but the train only runs April-Sept. Sa-Su 11am-4pm. Rides depart on the hour. Round-trip $7.)*

FLYING DAYTRIPS ■ 169

While in Snoqualmie be sure to view the astounding **Snoqualmie Falls,** just outside of town. Formerly a sacred place for the Salish, the 270 ft. wall of water has generated electricity for Puget Power since 1898. Five generators buried under the falls work hard to provide energy for 1600 homes. It is particularly spectacular in spring, when the falls are swollen with melt-off.

As I-90 leaves the sound it rises into mountains that offer some fantastic **dayhikes.** You can really take your pick—for information the **Issaquah Chamber of Commerce** (☎425-392-7024), at 155 NW Gilman in downtown Issaquah, just past the State Park, sells maps ($5-6), and can help set you up with a route.

▣ FLYING DAYTRIPS

BOEING. The Seattle area is surrounded by the vast factories of **Boeing,** the city's most prominent employer and site of the largest covered structure in North America. Boeing courts industrial espionage by offering **public tours** of the facilities in Everett, about 15min. north of the city, where 747s, 767s, and 777s are made. Just seeing how such large pieces are moved and assembled makes the tour worth it. Arrive early because the limited tickets often run out in the summer. The tour includes a theater show and a short walk of the facilities. *(Take I-5 north to exit 189, and then go west on 526. Signs are clear.* ☎*800-464-1476. $5, seniors and under 16 $3. Tours M-F 9am-3pm. Tickets reservations $10.)*

MUSEUM OF FLIGHT. South of Seattle at Boeing Field is the wheelchair-accessible **Museum of Flight.** The cavernous structure enshrines flying machines, from canvas biplanes to chic fighter jets, hanging from a three-story roof. An exhibit on the Apollo space shuttle missions, which landed the first man on the moon, includes a life-sized replica of the command module. Tour Eisenhower's old Air Force One, or fly in a nauseatingly realistic flight simulator ($3.50) and explore the red barn where William E. Boeing founded the company in 1916. Photographs and artifacts trace the history of flight from its beginnings through the 30s. *(9404 E Marginal Way S. Take I-5 south to Exit 158 and turn north onto E Marginal Way S and follow for ½ mi. Bus #174.* ☎ *206-764-5700. Open F-W 10am-5pm, Th 10am-9pm. Free tours of the museum every 30min., 10am-3:30pm. $9.50, seniors $8.50, ages 5-17 $5, under 5 free. Free after 5pm on 1st Th of the month.)*

▣ DAYTRIPS TO THE WEST

BREMERTON. Nosing into Puget Sound between the Olympic Peninsula and Seattle, the Kitsap Peninsula's deep inlets seemed a natural spot in which to park a fleet of nuclear-powered submarines. The instant you set foot in **Bremerton,** the hub of the peninsula, you see that is exactly what happened. *(Washington State Ferries* ☎ *206-464-6400 or 800-84-33779; www.wsdot.wa.gov/ferries. 2 boats run between downtown Seattle and Bremerton. A daily regular ferry runs daily; 1hr.; $4.50, car and driver $8-10. Passenger only ferry runs M-F; 30min.; $5.50; departs Pier 50. Bremerton Area Chamber of Commerce, 301 Pacific Ave.* ☎ *360-479-3579; www.bremertonchamber.org. Open M-F 9am-5pm; booth at ferry dock open on weekends.)*

BREMERTON NAVAL MUSEUM AND USS TURNER JOY. The museum, replete with WWII photos, 10 ft. models of ships, and a 14th-century wicker basket from Korea believed to be the world's oldest existing cannon, is sure to please any Navy buff. *(*☎*360-479-7447. Open M-Sa 10am-5pm, Su 1-5pm. Donations appreciated.)*

Behind the museum, explore the destroyer **USS Turner Joy,** the ship that fired the first American shots of the Vietnam War. It is managed by the Bremerton Historic Ships Association. For a closer view of the retired ships that fill Bremerton harbor, join the **Navy Ship Tour** at the *Turner Joy* and scoot along mothballed submarines and aircraft carriers. Tours leave from the Ship's Store in Port Orchard, across the harbor, but stop in Bremerton before heading to the boats. *(USS Turner Joy:* ☎*360-792-2457. Self-guided tours $7, seniors $6, children $5. Navy Ship Tour:* ☎*360-792-2457. Daily June-Aug.; May and Sept. Sa and Su only. Tours last 45min. $9, seniors $8, children $6.)*

DROP THE PACK. After a few months backpacking it's no surprise that your shoulders start bruising like unrefrigerated steaks. Fortunately, there is a cure: sea kayaks. Kayaking is the perfect way to explore the nooks of Washington's labyrinthine Puget Sound, and rental boats are readily available. A truly unique resource is the Cascadia Marine Trail, a network of seaside campsites and launching spots maintained specifically for paddlers and sailors. The trail stretches from the San Juans south to Olympia, has over 40 places to pitch a tent along the way, and has been recognized as one of 16 Millennium Trails in the country. Routes in the south of the Sound tend to be shorter and more protected, perfect for beginner to intermediate boaters. Paddling in the north sound can be dangerous due to ship traffic and fast tides, so be sure you know your stuff before biting this off. Companies that rent often offer moderately-priced guided trips for anywhere from half-day to multi-day excursions. Fees for camping vary site to site, from free to $10. For information and help planning a trip contact the Washington Water Trails Association, 4649 Sunnyside Ave. N, Room 305 (☎545-9161; www.wwta.org).

KITSAP HISTORICAL MUSEUM. This museum adds real-life history to the floating war machines. A highlight is the coat made from long-haired monkeys in the late 20s. Outside, stroll the Bremerton Boardwalk. *(280 4th St. ☎360-479-6226. Open Tu-Sa 9am-5pm; until 8pm first F of every month. $2, seniors and students $1, under 18 free.)*

DAYTRIP TO TACOMA

Although spending time in Tacoma rather than Seattle may seem like hanging out in Newark, New Jersey instead of New York, New York, Tacoma's lively art scene and beautiful park make it worth a daytrip. As Washington's third largest city, Tacoma offers the standard food and accommodations. However, if you are looking for anything besides the standard $50 per night motel, the hostels of Seattle remain your best bet.

Tacoma lies on I-5, 32 mi. (30min.) south of Seattle and 28 mi. (30min.) northeast of Olympia. Take Exit 132 from I-5 and follow the signs to the city center. Several options exist for getting to Tacoma: **SoundTransit** runs two of these. The **Sounder** is a commuter train the runs from Tacoma in the morning, and from Seattle in the evening (1hr.; $4). Express **Buses** run more frequently, and offer more options (1hr.; $2). Pick up a schedule booklet from Union Station in Seattle. Both SoundTransit options arrive at the Puyallup Ave. Station in Tacoma, which is shared with **Greyhound.** (510 Puyallup Ave. ☎383-4621. Open daily 8am-9pm.) They also run buses to **Seattle** (8 buses per day, $5), and **Portland.** Point Defiance is Tacoma's ferry terminal. Get the skinny on Tacoma at the **Pierce County Visitor Information Center,** 1001 Pacific Ave. #400 (☎627-2836 or 800-272-2662; open M-F 9am-5pm), or from the desk in the back of the Washington State Museum gift shop (see **Sights,** below; open M-Sa 10am-4pm, Su noon-5pm). The superb *Pierce County Bicycle Guide Map* shows bike routes and lists trails near Mt. Rainier. Tacomans are bicycle enthusiasts.

WASHINGTON STATE HISTORY MUSEUM. The shiny new 40 million dollar museum houses interactive, stereophonic exhibits on Washington's history through the 1800s. A sprawling model train on the fifth floor is a highlight for children, railroad buffs, and child railroad buffs. A museum of glass, showcasing Dale Chihuly among others, is scheduled to open nearby in late 2002. *(1911 Pacific Ave. ☎888-238-4373. Open M-W and F 10am-4pm, Th 10am-8pm, Sa 10am-5pm, Su noon-5pm. $7, seniors $6.25, students $5; family $20. Free Th 5-8pm.)*

TACOMA ART MUSEUM. The museum takes a refreshingly offbeat approach to its limited space. Exhibits anticipated for 2002 include American Design (winter), Jack Dollhausen: Electric Sculpture (spring) and The Art of Gordon Parks (fall). A permanent retrospective of the works of popular native glass artist Dale Chihuly is no less intriguing. Look out in 2003; the museum will move to a new location near Union Station. *(1123 Pacific Ave., at 12th St. ☎ 272-4258. Open Tu-W and F-Su 10am-5pm, Th 10am-8pm. $5, seniors and students $4, 6 and under free. Free third Th of every month.)*

COMMENCEMENT ART GALLERY. In recent years, Tacoma's cheap rent has lured a dynamic art scene from Seattle, reflected in the parade of strong local work that comes to Commencement Art Gallery. *(901 Broadway, in the Pantages building, facing Commencement St. ☎ 591-5341. Open Tu-Sa noon-5pm. Free.)*

ANTIQUE ROW. Rummage through found objects for your new aesthetic treat in any one of a number of funky shops. Together they form **Antique Row(s)**. **Tacoma's Farmers Market** takes over Antique Row on Thursdays. *(East of 9th on Broadway and St. Helens St.; Market June to mid-Sept.)*

POINT DEFIANCE PARK. The park is a wonderful spot to pass time on a warm day, but it's a secret everyone knows about. Besides a spot to relax, the park is excellent for other more active and visual pursuits. A 5 mi. driving and walking loop passes all the park's attractions, offering postcard views of Puget Sound and access to miles of woodland trails. In spring, the park is bejewelled with flowers; a rhododendron garden lies nestled in the woods along the loop. **Owen Beach** looks across at Vashon Island and is a good starting place for a ramble down the shore. The loop then brushes by the spot where in 1841 defiant US Navy Capt. Wilkes proclaimed that he could take on the world if he had the appropriate arsenal. The park's prize possession is the **Point Defiance Zoo and Aquarium.** Penguins, puffins, polar bears, beluga whales, and sharks intrigue visitors. The meticulously restored **Fort Nisqually** was built by the British Hudson Bay Company in 1832 as they expanded their trade in beaver pelts. The series of 19th century cabins contain museum-like exhibits of the lives of children, laborers, and natives. *(Park: Rte. 16 to the 6th Ave., go east on 6th Ave., then head north on Pearl St. ☎ 305-1000. Open daily from dawn until 30min. after dusk. Zoo: 5400 N Pearl St. ☎ 404-3678; www.pdza.org. Open daily 10am-7pm; Labor Day-Memorial Day 10am-4pm. $8, seniors $7, ages 4-13 $6, under 4 free. Fort: ☎ 591-5339. Open daily June-Aug. 11am-6pm; Sept.-Apr. W-Su 11am-4pm. $3, seniors $2, ages 5-12 $1.)*

PUGET SOUND

Stretching from Admiralty Inlet to Whidbey Island this unusually deep body of water runs a full 100 mi. up to the Straits of Juan de Fuca and Georgia. Sharing the seas with the shipping trade frequenting the harbors of Seattle, Tacoma, Everett, and Port Townsend, naval submarines and battleships are based in Bremerton. The Alaska Marine Highway also ends its voyage here in the Sound. Originally discovered by George Vancouver, he generously decided that an island and major city were enough for him and gave naming rights to his second lieutenant Peter Puget.

OLYMPIA ☎ 360

Due to crazy zoning laws drastically limiting the height of buildings, Olympia grows out rather than up (poor thing). Inside of what seems like an interminable network of suburbs there yet lurks a grungy, dyed core flavoring the otherwise bland suburbia. The liberal Evergreen State College campus lies a few miles from the city center, and its highly-pierced tree-hugging student body spills into the mix in a kind of chemistry experiment that gets progressively weirder when the Olympia-as-state-capital politicians join in. The product of this grouping resists definition, but it is worth experiencing for yourself. Named Olympia because of its suburb view of the Olympic mountains, the city is also a logical launching pad into Olympic National Park.

172 ■ PUGET SOUND

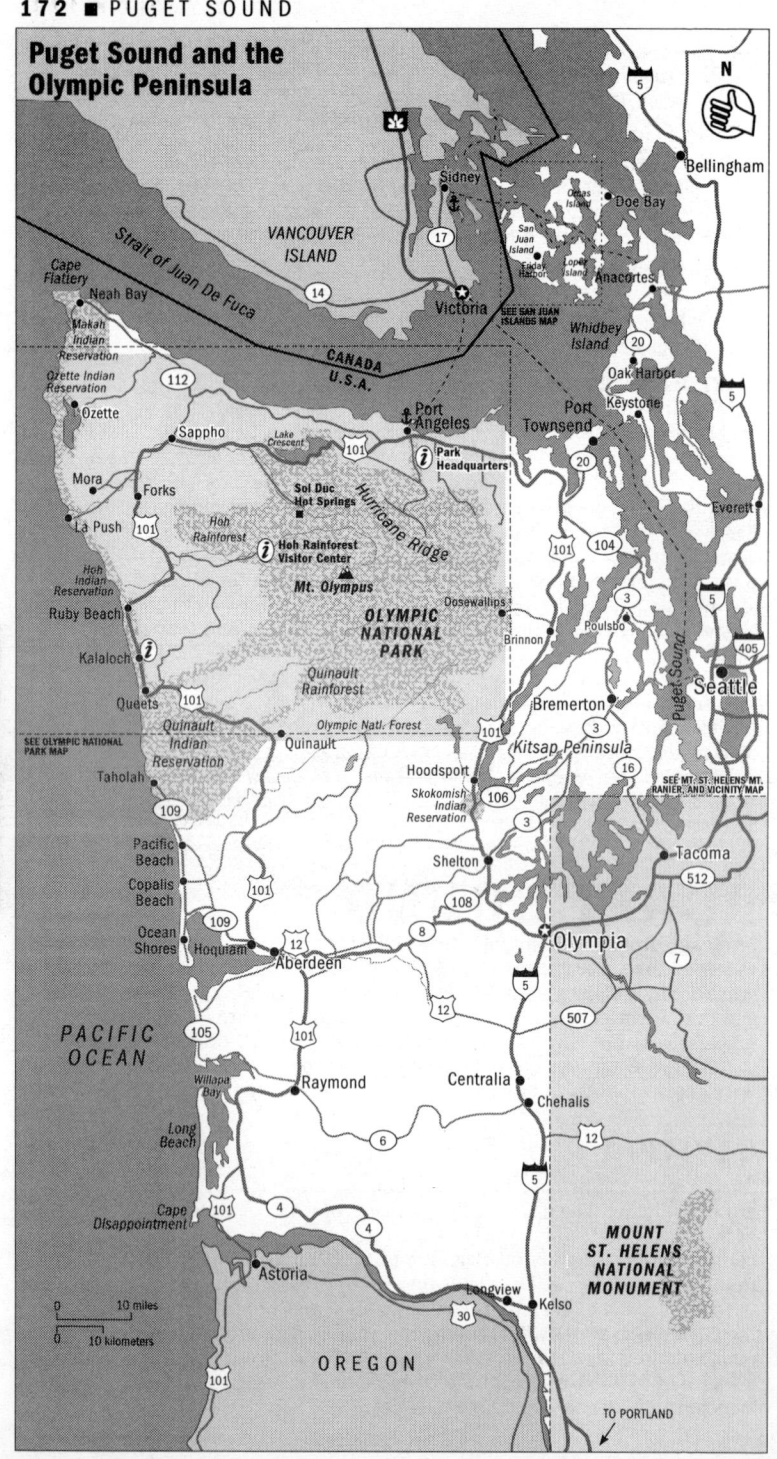

Puget Sound and the Olympic Peninsula

Olympia

ACCOMMODATIONS
Capital Forest Area, 13
Golden Gavel Motor Hotel, 11
Grays Harbor Hostel, 3
Millersylvania Park, 12

FOOD
Crazee Espresso, 5
Farmers Market, 3
Saigon Rendez-Vous, 9
Santosh, 2
The Spar Cafe & Bar, 4

NIGHTLIFE
4th Ave. Alehouse, 6
Eastside Club & Tavern, 7
Fishbowl Brewpub, 10
Thekla, 8

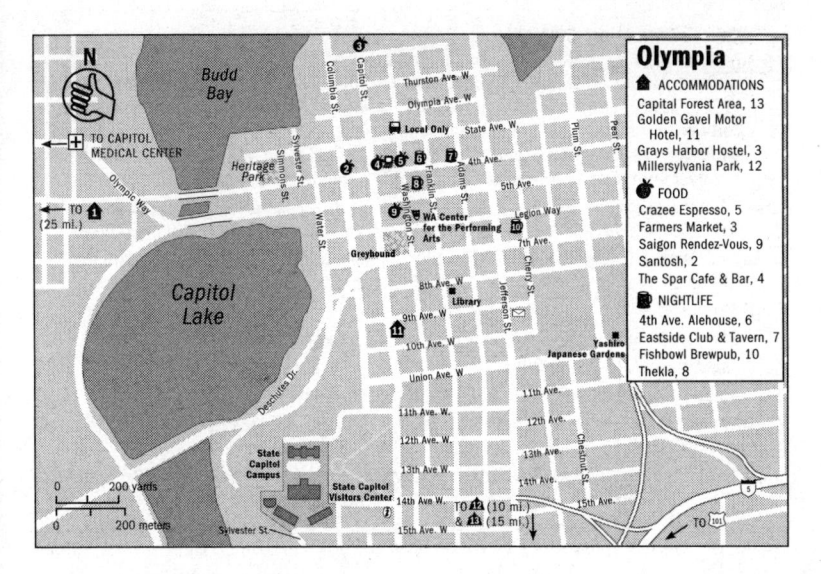

TRANSPORTATION

Settled at the junction of **I-5** and **US 101,** Olympia makes a convenient stop on any north-south journey, wedged between **Tumwater** (to the south, I-5 Exit 102) and **Lacey** (to the east, I-5 Exit 108). I-5 Exit 105 leads to the **Capitol Campus** and **downtown** Olympia. The west side of downtown borders freshwater **Capitol Lake** and salty **West Bay,** also known as **Budd Bay.** The **4th Ave.** bridge divides the two bodies of water and leads to the city's fast-food-chain-infested section. Navigating Olympia's one-way streets on **bike** or **foot** is easy, and all public buses have bike racks.

- **Trains: Amtrak,** 6600 Yelm Hwy. (☎923-4602 or 800-872-7245). In neighboring Lacey (I-5 exit 108), but bus #64 runs between downtown and station. Open daily 8-11:30am, 12:45-3:30pm, and 5:30-8:15pm. To **Seattle** (1¾hr., 4 per day, $10-18), and **Portland** (2½hr., 4 per day, $13-24).

- **Buses: Greyhound,** 107 E 7th Ave. (☎357-5541 or 800-231-2222), at Capitol Way. Office is open daily 8:30am-10pm. To **Seattle** (1¾hr., 6-7 per day, $8-9; but check out the **Olympia Express,** below), **Portland** (2¾hr., 6-7 per day, $22-24), and **Spokane** (9hr., 2 per day, $30).

- **Public Transportation: Intercity Transit (IT;** ☎786-1881 or 800-287-6348). Reliable and flexible service to almost anywhere in Thurston County, even with a bicycle. Schedules at the visitors center or at Transit Center, 222 State Ave. Open M-F 7:30am-5:30pm. 75¢ per ride. Day passes $1.50. The most useful route is #42, which runs from the Capitol Campus to downtown, eastside, and westside (every 15min., 6:45am-5:45pm). **Olympia Express** runs between Olympia and **Tacoma** (55min., M-F 5:50am-6pm, $2. Tacoma to Seattle costs $1.50. Olympia and Lacey to Sea-Tac $2).

- **Taxis: Red Top Taxi,** ☎357-3700. **Capitol City Taxi,** ☎357-4949.

- **AAA:** 2415 Capitol Mall Dr. (☎357-5561 or 800-562-2582). Open M-F 8:30am-5:30pm.

PRACTICAL INFORMATION

- **Visitor Information: Washington State Capitol Visitor Center** (☎586-3460), on Capitol Way at 14th Ave., south of the State Capitol; follow the signs on I-5, or from Capitol Way turn west at the pedestrian bridge. Open M-F 8am-5pm.

174 ■ PUGET SOUND

Outdoor Information: State Natural Resources Building, 1111 Washington St. (☎902-1000 or 800-527-3305), houses the **Department of Natural Resources (DNR)** in a maze of offices. The **Maps Department** (☎902-1234), the **Fish and Game Office** (☎902-2200), and the **Washington State Parks and Recreation Commission Information Center** (☎800-233-0321) are a couple places you'll stumble across. The **Olympic National Forest Headquarters,** 1835 Black Lake Blvd. SW (☎956-2400), provides info on forest land. Open M-F 8am-4:30pm. For Olympic National Park info, call 565-3000.

Outdoors Equipment: Pick up essentials or go on a buying spree at **Olympic Outfitters,** 407 E 4th Ave. (☎943-1114). Open M-F 10am-8pm, Sa 10am-6pm, Su noon-5pm.

Laundromat: Westside Laundry, 2103 Harrison Ave. NW (☎943-3857), in a strip mall on the west side of town. Wash $1.75, dry 25¢ per 7min. Open 8am-10pm daily.

Emergency: ☎911.

Police: 900 Plum St. SE (8am-5pm ☎753-8300; 5pm-8am ☎704-2740), at 8th Ave.

Crisis Line: ☎586-2800. 24hr.

Women's Services: Safeplace ☎754-6300 or 800-364-1776.

Hospital: Providence St. Peter Hospital, 413 Lilly Rd. NE (☎491-9480). Follow signs northbound on I-5, Exit 107; southbound Exit 109. Emergency 24hr.

Internet Access: Olympia Timberland Library, 313 8th Ave. SE (☎352-0595), at Franklin St. A nice place to find some quiet, and provides up to an hour of free Internet access. Open M-Th 10am-9pm, F-Sa 10am-5pm, Su 1-5pm. **Olympia World News,** 116 E 4th Ave. (☎570-9536), off Washington St. 50¢ per 10min. Open M-W 8:30am-9:30pm, Th 8:30am-11pm, F-Sa 8:30am-midnight, and Su 9am-9:30pm.

Post Office: 900 Jefferson SE (☎357-2289). Open M-F 7:30am-6pm, Sa 9am-4pm. **ZIP Code:** 98501

🏠 ACCOMMODATIONS AND CAMPING

Olympia motels cater to policy-makers ($60-80), but options in Tumwater are more affordable. Try **Motel 6,** 400 W Lee St. (☎754-7320. Singles $44; doubles $50.)

■ **Grays Harbor Hostel,** 6 Ginny Ln. (☎482-3119), just off Rte. 8 in Elma, 25 mi. west of Olympia. Bus #40 (Grays Harbor) from Olympia, or take the Grays County Fairground Rd. Exit off Rte. 8 (reached via 101), then make the first right. Instantly feels like a home away from home. Kitchen, two common rooms, a disc golf course, and shed for bike repairs. Check-in 5-9pm. Lockout 9:30am-5pm. The Klemps are working on moving the hostel to Olympia, so call ahead. 14 beds. $14; private room $28 as a single, $42 as a double. (Motor)cyclists camp on the lawn for $10.

The Golden Gavel Motor Hotel, 909 Capitol Way (☎352-8533). A few blocks north of the Capitol building. Clean, spacious, 70s-style rooms are a siren call for travelers not on the corporate account. Singles $45-49; doubles $51-61. AAA/senior discount $2.

Millersylvania State Park, 12245 Tilly Rd. S (☎753-1519; reservations ☎800-452-5687), 10 mi. south of Olympia. Take Exit 95 off I-5 N or S, turn onto Rte. 121 N, then take a left at the stop sign to 6 mi. of trails and Deep Lake. A few secluded sites, usually in the back of the park. Some kitchens available. 10-day max. stay. Showers 25¢ per 3min. Wheelchair accessible. 180 sites. $14; hookups $20; sites for bicyclists $6.

Capital Forest Multiple Use Area, 15 mi. southwest of Olympia. Take Exit 95 off I-5. Pick up a forest map at the state DNR office (see **Practical Information** above) or the Central Region DNR office (☎748-2383) in nearby Chehalis. 60 campsites spread among 7 campgrounds, administered by the DNR. No showers. Some sites have water.

🍴 FOOD

Diners, veggie eateries, and Asian quickstops line bohemian 4th Ave. east of Columbia. Get slightly upscale groceries at the 24hr. **Safeway,** 520 Cleveland Ave. (☎943-1830), off Capital Blvd. in Tumwater, a quarter-mile south of the Capitol building. The **Olympia Farmer's Market,** 700 N Capitol Way, is a great place to stroll, people-watch, and grab cheap eats from small vendors. (☎352-9096. Open Apr.-Oct. Th-Su 10am-3pm; Nov.-Dec. Sa-Su 10am-3pm.)

The Spar Cafe & Bar, 114 E 4th Ave. (☎ 357-6444), has been a hot spot for beer, burgers ($7), and cigars for decades. Recognized as a national historic monument and still operating to the tunes of live jazz every Sa night (8pm-midnight). Cafe open M-Th 6am-10pm, F-Sa 6am-11pm, Su 6am-9pm. Bar open M-Th 11am-midnight, F-Sa 11am-2am.

Saigon Rendez-Vous, 117 W 5th Ave. (☎ 352-1989). The queen of Olympia's many Vietnamese restaurants, this cheery space may offer the largest vegetarian menu anywhere in WA outside of Seattle. Entrees $5-8. Open M-Sa 10:30am-10:30pm, Su noon-9pm.

Santosh, 116 4th Ave. (☎ 943-3442), west of Capitol Way. All-you-can-eat Indian lunch buffet $6. Regular dishes $8-12. Open daily 11am-3pm and 5-9pm, F-Sa until 10pm.

Crazee Expresso, 124 4th Ave. (☎ 754-8187), at N Washington St. The artsy flock here for a cuppa joe and conversation. Open M-Th 7am-7pm, F 7am-11pm, Sa 8am-11pm.

Happy Teriyaki, 106 E Legion Way (☎ 705-8000), at Capitol Way. Cheerfully prepares quality Japanese meals ($6-8) in a fast-food style setting. Open M-Sa 11am-10pm.

NIGHTLIFE

Olympia's ferocious nightlife seems to have outgrown its daylife. Labels like K Records and Kill Rock Stars, with their flagship band Bikini Kill, have made Olympia a crucial pitstop on the indie rock circuit. *The Rocket* and the city's daily *Olympian* list shows. Except occasional nights at Thekla, all venues open only to the 21+ crowd.

Eastside Club and Tavern, 410 E 4th Ave. (☎ 357-9985). Old and young come to play pool and sip pints of microbrews in what can only be described as a perfect atmosphere for Olympia. Drink specials often. M pints $1.75, Th $2. Happy hour daily 4-7pm, pints $1.75. Open M-F noon-2am, Sa-Su 3pm-2am.

Thekla, 524 Franklin St. (☎ 352-1855), under the neon arrow off N Washington St. between 4th Ave. and Capitol, in a retro-meets-space-age refitted bank building. This gay-friendly dance joint offers swing (W, Sa), karaoke (Tu, Su), disco (Th), funk (F), house and hip-hop (Sa) and 80s tunes (Su). Cover $2-5. Open Tu-Su 5pm-2am.

Fishbowl Brewpub & Cafe, 515 Jefferson St. SE (☎ 943-3650), 2 blocks south off 4th. Fish on outside walls, paintings, and aquarium. British ales ($3.25) named after fish in this, the only microbrewery in town. Full kitchen daily until 11pm offers sandwiches and pasta ($3.50-7). Occasional live music. Open M-Sa 11am-midnight, Su noon-10pm.

4th Ave. Alehouse & Eatery, 210 E 4th Ave. (☎ 956-3215). Townfolk gather for "slabs" of pizza ($2.25), seafood baskets ($5-6), and one (or several) of the 26 draft micropints ($3) in Oly's old Town Hall. Live tunes, from blues to rock to reggae (Th-Sa 9pm). Cover $3-10. Restaurant open M-F 11:30am-8pm, F-Sa noon-8pm.

SIGHTS AND EVENTS

The main draw to Olympia is definitely its political scene, so don't miss the chance to see WA state tax dollars in action. The state capitol, as well as a variety of parks and gardens, highlights the list of must see sights in Olympia.

STATE CAPITOL. Olympia's crowning glory is the State Capitol, a complex of state government buildings, carefully sculpted gardens, veterans' monuments, and fabulous fountains, including a remarkable replica of Copenhagen's Tivoli fountain. Get a free tour of the **Legislative Building** which was styled after Rome's St. Peter's Basilica. The newly renovated interior enshrines a six-ton Tiffany chandelier and six bronze doors depicting the state's history. Unfortunately, the building's spectacular stone dome is closed to the public. *(I-5 to Exit 103. Visitors Center ☎ 586-3460. Call 586-8687 for more info and options for the disabled. Free tours depart from front entrance daily on the hour 10am-3pm. Open for tourists to explore M-F 8am-5:30pm, Sa-Su 10am-4pm.)*

WOLF HAVEN INTERNATIONAL. See wolves in their natural habitat on guided tours of the haven, which houses wolves reclaimed from zoos or illegal owners. During the summer weekly **Howl-ins** are a sort of vaudeville-inspired wolf-and-human romp. *(3111 Offut Lake Rd. 10 mi. south of the capitol, near Millersvania Park. Take Exit 99 off I-5, turn east, and follow the brown signs. ☎ 264-4695 or 800-448-9653;*

176 ■ PUGET SOUND

www.wolfhaven.org. Open May-Sept. W-M 10am-5pm; Oct. and Apr. 10am-4pm. Nov.-Jan. and Mar. Sa and Su 10am-4pm. Closed Feb. 45min. tours on the hr.; last tour leaves 1hr. before closing. $6, ages 5-12 $4. Howl-ins June to early Sept. F-Sa 6:30-9:30pm. $10, children $8.)

PARKS AND GARDENS. The Yashiro Japanese Garden is a small and often deserted garden guarded by high walls. Come to read or just to sit. *(At Plum and Union, next to City Hall. Northeast of the State Campus.* ☎ *753-8380. Open daily 10am-dusk to picnickers and ponderers.)* The $620,000 interactive fountain at **Heritage Park** provides a place for politicians and children in underoos to partake in the good life. On hot days, the fountain is bustling with activity. *(4th Ave. and Sylvester St.)* Built by the Olympia Brewery, **Tumwater Falls Park** is perfect for salmon-watching, picnicking, or a run. *(Less than a mile south of town on I-5 at Exit 103.)*

NISQUALLY NATIONAL WILDLIFE REFUGE. Nisqually National Wildlife Refuge shelters 500 species of plants and animals and miles of open trails. People come to walk, and above all birdwatch. Bald eagles, shorebirds, and northern spotted owls nest here. The trails are open daily from dawn to dusk and are closed to cyclists, joggers, and pets. Visitors center offers free binocular loans and info packets—just leave behind an ID. *(Off I-5 between Olympia and Tacoma at Exit 114.* ☎ *753-9467. Visitors centers office open W-Su 9am-4:30pm. Park open dawn to dusk. $3 per person or family.)*

VASHON ISLAND ☎ 206

Although it's only a 25min. ferry ride from Seattle and an even shorter hop from Tacoma, Vashon (VASH-in) Island has remained inexplicably invisible to most Seattleites. With forested hills and expansive sea views, this artists' colony feels like the San Juan Islands without the tourists or an economy to cater to them. Add to this the best hostel in the Seattle area, and Vashon becomes the perfect place for a one-day trip, a multi-day exploration, or a base from which to explore Seattle.

TRANSPORTATION. Vashon Island stretches between **Seattle** and **Tacoma** on its east side and between **Southworth** and **Gig Harbor** on its west side. The town of **Vashon** lies at the island's northern tip; ferries stop at both the south and north ends of the island. The steep hills on Vashon don't keep bikes from being the recreational vehicle of choice. **Washington State Ferries** (☎ 464-6400 or 888-8008-7977; www.wsdot.wa.gov/ferries), runs ferries to Vashon Island from four different locations. A passenger ferry departs downtown **Seattle** (25min., 8 per day M-F, $5.50), while ferries from **Fauntleroy** in West Seattle and **Southworth** in the Kitsap Peninsula take cars and walk-on passengers. (Fauntleroy ferries 15min., Southworth ferries 10min.; both $3, car and driver $10-13.) A fourth ferry departs from **Point Defiance** in Tacoma (see p. 170) and arrives in Tahlequah (15min.; $3, car and driver $10-13). To get to the Fauntleroy terminal on the mainland from Seattle, drive south on I-5 and take Exit 163A (West Seattle/Spokane St.) down Fauntleroy Way. To get to Point Defiance in Tacoma, take Exit 132 off I-5 (Bremerton/Gig Harbor) to Rte. 16. Get on 6th Ave. and turn right onto Pearl; follow signs to Point Defiance Park and the ferry. Seattle's **King County Metro** services the downtown ferry terminal, Fauntleroy ferry terminal, and Vashon Island. Buses #54, 116, 118, and 119 run between Seattle and Fauntleroy. Bus #54 picks up at 2nd and Pike St. Save your transfer for the connection on Vashon. Buses #118 and 119 service the island's east side from the north ferry landing through Vashon to the south landing. Bus #117 service the west side of the island. The island is in a different fare zone than Seattle. (☎ 553-3000 or 800-542-7876. 30min., buses every 30min. 5:15am-1:40am. One zone $1.25. Between zones $1.75.)

PRACTICAL INFORMATION. The local **Thriftway** (see **Food,** below) provides maps, as does the Vashon-Maury **Chamber of Commerce,** 17637 SW Vashon Hwy. (☎463-6217). The **library,** 17210 Vashon Hwy., provides free **Internet access.** (☎463-2069. Open M-Th 11am-8:30pm, F 11am-6pm, Sa 10am-5pm, Su 1-5pm.) **Laundry: Joy's,** 17318 Vashon Hwy. (☎463-9933. Wash $1.25, dry 25¢ per 10min. Open daily 7am-8:30pm.) **Vashon Pharmacy:** 17617 Vashon Hwy. (☎463-9118. Open M-F 9am-7pm, Sa 9am-6pm, Su 1am-1pm.) **Emergency:** ☎911. **Police:** ☎463-3783. **Post office:** 1005 SW 178th St., on Bank Rd. (☎800-275-8777. Open M-F 8:30am-5pm, Sa 10am-1pm.) **ZIP Code:** 98070.

WHIDBEY ISLAND ■ 177

ACCOMMODATIONS AND FOOD. The **Vashon Island AYH Ranch Hostel (HI)**, 12119 SW Cove Rd., 1½ mi. west of Vashon Hwy., is an oasis just 30min. away from Seattle. Though this frontierland packed with teepees and logcabin bunkhouses, is a destination in its own right, the hostel is also a perfect pace to dump a car so you can ferry downtown Seattle. Free pancake breakfast and 100 acres of hiking and biking. (☎463-2592. Free 1-gear bikes, mountain bikes $6 per day. Open May-Oct. Bicyclists $10; members $11, nonmembers $14; sleeping bag $2. Private double $45; nonmembers $55; $10 per extra person. 24hr. check-in.) A shuttle to the morning ferry is $1.25. The hostel's new B&B, **The Lavender Duck,** just north on Vashon Hwy., has pleasant, themed rooms and a beautiful living room and kitchen. Check in at hostel. The meadows are the island's only legal place to **camp,** and campers can use the hostel's kitchens, showers, and common space. Dirk makes pickups during reasonable hours. Get creative in the hostel's kitchens with supplies from the large and offbeat **Thriftway,** downtown at 9740 SW Bank Rd. All buses from the ferry terminal stop there, and a free phone connects to the hostel. (☎463-2100. Open daily 8am-9pm.) The **Stray Dog Cafe,** 17530 Vashon Hwy., has tasty vegetarian (mushroom burger $6.25) and vegan options. (☎463-7833. Open M-Tu 7am-3pm, W-F 7am-3pm and 6-9pm, Sa 8am-3pm, Su 8am-4pm.) **Bishop's Cafe and Lounge,** 17618 Vashon Hwy., has plenty of meals for meat-lovers and many options for the nightowl in all of us as well: video games, pool, big screen TVs, and pints o' beer. (☎463-5959. Restaurant open daily 10am-10pm. Bar 11am-2am.)

SIGHTS AND OUTDOOR ACTIVITIES. Vashon Island provides wonderful but strenuous biking, a sometimes-unbalanced relationship celebrated at the **Bicycle Tree,** where a misbehaving little two-wheeler is lodged in the woods past Sound Food, off the Vashon Hwy. **Point Robinson Park** is a gorgeous spot for a picnic, and **free tours** (☎217-6123) of the 1885 **Coast Guard lighthouse** are available. From Vashon Hwy., take Ellisburg Rd. to Dockton Rd. to Pt. Robinson Rd. **Vashon Island Kayak Co.,** at Burton Acres Park, Jensen Point Boat Launch, runs guided tours (from $48) and rents sea kayaks. (☎463-9527. Open F-Su 10am-5pm. Call and leave a message for weekday rentals. Singles $14 per hr., $35 per half-day, $50 per day; doubles $20, $50, $65.) More than 500 acres of woods in the middle of the island are interlaced with mildly difficult **hiking trails.** The Vashon Park District can tell you more. (☎463-9602. Open daily 9am-5pm.) Lastly, count on some culture no matter when you visit—one in 10 residents of Vashon is an artist. **Blue Heron Arts Center,** 19704 Vashon Hwy., has a small gallery showcasing local artists, coordinates activities such as free gallery openings on the first Friday of each month (7-9:30pm) and publishes *Island View,* a guide to current goings on. (☎463-5131. Open Tu-F 11am-5pm, Sa noon-5pm.)

WHIDBEY ISLAND ☎ 360

Clouds wrung dry by the mountains west of Seattle release a scant 20 in. of rain each year over Whidbey Island, a beach-ringed strip of land that offers peaceful relaxation to travelers passing through on the way to the San Juan islands. This is prime road-biking country, with easy slopes and rustic scenery. The town of **Coupeville,** in Whidbey's middle, has delightful shops and a peaceful waterfront. It is a great place to start exploring the four state parks and historic reserve, where rocky beaches meet bluffs crowded with wild roses and blackberries. MacGregor's free *Whidbey Island* is full of maps and info on coastal towns.

TRANSPORTATION. Washington State Ferries (☎206-464-6400 or 800-843-3779; www.wsdot.wa.gov/ferries) provides frequent service from the mainland to the island. One ferry connects mainland **Mukilteo,** 10 mi. south of Everett and 19 mi. north of Seattle, with **Clinton,** on the south end of the island (20min.; every 30min.; $2.70, car and driver $5-6.25, bike 90¢). The other connects **Port Townsend** on the Olympic Peninsula with the **Keystone terminal** near Ft. Casey State Park (see **Accommodations,** below), at the "waist" of the island (30min., every 45min.; $2, car and driver $7-8.75, bike 35¢). You can drive onto the island along Rte. 20, which heads

ZOUNDS! MOUNDS!

Baffling scientists since the mid-1800s, Mima (my-mah) Mounds have spawned wild speculation about their origins. An evenly spaced network of small, perfectly rounded hills covers the prairies just outside the Capital Forest, 12 mi. southwest of Olympia. Anthropology fanciers attribute the mounds' existence to the arcane labors of a nation of yesteryear, biology buffs cite giant gophers, and delusional paranoids cry government conspiracy. The scientific community is torn among hypotheses ranging from glacial action to seismic shock waves; by 1999, no fewer than 159 Mima-related papers had been published. Today, the Mounds inhabit some of the last remaining prairie in the Pacific Northwest, providing visitors with an opportunity to learn about the region's natural history and mystery. To reach the Mounds, take Exit 95 off I-5 and follow the signs to Littlerock. From Littlerock, follow more signs to the Capital Forest and watch for the marked dirt road to the parking lot and trailhead. (Open daily 8am-dusk. For info, call the DNR ☎ 748-2383.)

west from I-5, 12 mi. south of Bellingham, at Exit 230. **Rte. 20** and **Rte. 525** meet near Keystone and form the transportation backbone of the island, linking significant towns and points of interest. **Island Transit** (☎ 678-7771 or 321-6688) provides free, hourly public transportation all over the island and has info on connections to and from **Seattle**, but no service Sundays. All buses have bike racks that hold up to two bikes. Flag a bus down anywhere safe for it to stop. The **Visitor Info Center**, 207 Main St., is a self-serve station filled with maps and brochures. Just look for the tiny building with a giant American flag. For **Traveler Info,** tune to 1610AM. The **Whidbey Cybercafe & Bookstore,** in Clinton, deals books, lattes, and **Internet access.** (8898 Hwy. 525. ☎ 341-5922. $6 per hr., 15min. minimum. Open M-Sa 11am-7pm.)

ACCOMMODATIONS. Ebey's Landing, a Department of the Interior protected beach, covers much of the peninsula and has great views of the islands, the surrounding Olympic Mountains, and Port Townsend. In total, this historical reserve covers 44 mi., including the Sunnyside Cemetery, Ft. Casey State Park, Monroe Landing, and the Crockett Blockhouse. Two State Parks lie near Ebey's Landing: **Fort Ebey State Park** just north and east off Rte. 20 (☎ 678-4636; open daily 6:30-dusk; 50 sites; $13, RV $20) and **Fort Casey State Park** just south, home to old bunkers and military paraphernalia on a peninsula with unsheltered, slightly crowded sites with views of the straits. (☎ 800-452-5687. Pay showers 25¢ per 3min. $14; no RV hookups.). An interpretive center lies at the **Admiralty Point lighthouse** (open Apr.-Oct. Th-Su 11am-5pm.) To avoid the busier state parks, try the free **Rhododendron campground,** 1½ mi. before Coupeville; look for the small tent sign on eastbound Rte. 20/525; if you see the recycling plant you've just passed it. (Ballfields, picnic sites, restrooms. 6 primitive sites.) The beautiful **South Whidbey State Park,** amidst old growth forest by the beach, was once a favorite camp of the Skagit and Snohomish tribes. Numerous trails cut through the woods and beach. (☎ 206-321-4559; reservations 800-452-5687. 54 sites, $14; hookups $20, hiker/biker $6.)

FOOD. La Paz, 8898 Hwy. 525 right off of the ferry dock, is a baja-style Mexican restaurant in Clinton, replete with loud colors and beans. Seafood taco and rice $7. (☎ 341-4787. Open daily noon-3pm for lunch and 5-8pm for dinner; open F-Sa until 9pm for dinner.) Seaside **Coupeville,** Washington's second oldest town, makes for a nice stroll, and at the bakery, **Knead and Feed,** 4 Front St., you can eat fabulous soup and enjoy a waterfront view. (☎ 678-5431. Lunch $3-8. Open M-F 10am-3pm, Sa-Su 9am-4pm.) For coffee, a book, and a pizza ($4) walk down the stairs to **Great Times Espresso,** 12 Front St. (☎ 678-5358. Open M-F 7am-7pm, Sa-Su 8am-7pm.)

SIGHTS AND OUTDOOR ACTIVITIES. At the north tip of the island, on Rte. 20, the crowded **Deception Pass Bridge,** the nation's first suspension bridge, connects Whidbey Island to the Anacortes Islands. A secret cave at one end held 17th-century prisoners who were forced to make wicker furniture. Deception Pass itself is a thin sliver of water that can be brought to the boil by tides; occasionally white-water kayakers come out to test their mettle against the salt-water rapids. **Deception Pass State Park,** 41229 SR (☎675-2417), surrounds the pass itself, and is the most heavily used of Whidbey's four state parks (especially on weekends), largely because its views are magnificent. There are camping facilities, a saltwater boat launch, and a freshwater lake good for swimming, fishing, and boating. The campground is subjected to jet noise from EA6B Navy attack aircraft from nearby Whidbey Island Naval Air Station, in Oak Harbor. (☎800-452-5687. Reservations suggested. 168 sites, $14; 83 hookups.)

BELLINGHAM ☎360

Strategically situated between Seattle and Vancouver, Bellingham is the southern terminus of the Alaska Marine Hwy., an amazingly inexpensive way to go north. Most travelers who stay the night are contemplating or completing an overseas journey to or from Alaska. Somehow Bellingham manages to blend its role as small town, college town, harbor town, and transportation hub into a seamless identity. Bellingham also serves as the gateway to the ruggedly beautiful Mt. Baker area, one of Washington's favorite winter-time playgrounds.

TRANSPORTATION. Bellingham lies along **I-5,** 90 mi. north of **Seattle** and 57 mi. south of **Vancouver, BC.** Downtown centers on **Holly St.** and **Cornwall Ave.,** next to the Georgia Pacific pulp mill (Exits 252 and 253 off I-5). **Western Washington University (WWU)** sits atop a hill to the south. The hip town of **Fairhaven,** where the ferries, buses, and trains stop, is directly south of town and serviced by public transit. Catch a train at **Amtrak,** 401 Harris Ave. (☎734-8851 or 800-872-7245), in the bus/train station next to the ferry terminal. (Counter open daily 8:45am-12:30pm and 1-4:30pm.) Two per day to **Seattle** (2½hr., $16-24) and **Vancouver, BC** (1½hr. $11-16). **Greyhound,** in the same station, next to the ferry terminal. (☎733-5251 or 800-231-2222. Open M-F 6-6:30am and 8am-6pm, Sa-Su 8am-6pm.) To **Seattle** (2hr., 8 per day, $14-15); **Mt. Vernon** (30min., 5-6 per day, $6.50-7.50); and **Vancouver, BC** (2hr., 4-6 per day, $10.50-11.50). Private shuttles run ferries to the nearby San Juan Islands (see p. 182). **Public Transportation** routes all start at the Railroad Avenue Mall terminal, between Holly and Magnolia St. (☎676-7433. M-F 5:50am-6:30pm. 50¢, under 6 and over 84 free. No transfers. Buses run every 15-60min. One night route runs M-F 7:30-11pm.) **City Cab** (☎773-8294 or 800-281-5430) and **Yellow Cab** (☎734-8294) service the town.

PRACTICAL INFORMATION. Services include a friendly, well-organized **Visitors Info Center,** 904 Potter St. Take Exit 253 (Lakeway) from I-5. (☎671-3990. Open daily 8:30am-5:30pm. **Equipment Rental: Fairhaven Boatworks,** 501 Harris Ave. (☎647-2469) rents kayaks (single $6-8 per hr, $25-40 per day; double $8-10 and $40-50), as well as sailboats ($8-200 per day) and rowboats. **Fairhaven Bikes,** 1103 11th St. (☎733-4433), rents bikes ($20-30 per day) and in-line skates. **Bellingham Cleaning Center,** 1010 Lakeway Dr., offers a wash for $1.25, and a dry 25¢ per 10min. (☎734-3755. Open M-F 7am-8pm, Sa 8am-8pm, Su 10am-7pm. Check your email at the **library,** 210 Central Ave., at Commercial St. opposite City Hall. Free **Internet access;** just ask for a guest pass at the desk. (☎676-6860. Open M-Th 10am-9pm, F-Sa 10am-6pm; also Sept.-May Su 1-5pm). **Emergency:** ☎911. **Police:** 505 Grand Ave. (☎676-6913. Open M-F 8am-5:30pm.) **Crisis Line:** ☎800-584-3578. **Hospital: St. Joseph's General,** 2901 Squalicum Pkwy. (☎734-5400). Open 24hr. **Post Office:** 315 Prospect. Open M-F 8am-5:30pm, Sa 9:30am-3pm. **ZIP Code:** 98225.

ACCOMMODATIONS. Bellingham's hostel recently closed, but plans are in the works to reopen in a new location—ask at the tourist office, as this would be the best budget option by far. Currently, **Bellingham Inn,** 202 E Holly St. is one of the best alternatives, with queen beds, clean rooms, and cable TV. Take I-5 Exit 253. Just a walk from everything you need. (☎734-1900. Singles $42, doubles $50). **Cascade Inn,** 208 N Samish Way offers a big TV, desk, and chairs in bedrooms. Exit 252 off I-5. (☎733-2520. Single $40, doubles $50.) If you prefer camping, try

Bellingham

ACCOMMODATIONS
Bellingham Inn, 3
Cascade Inn, 4
Larrabee St. Park, 6

FOOD
Casa Que Pasa, 2
Old Town Cafe, 1
Tony's, 5

Larrabee State Park, on Chuckanut Dr., 7 mi. south of town, among trees on Samish Bay. Tide pools and alpine lakes nearby. Toilets, tables, and firepits, but camp is short on space. (☎ 676-2093; reservations 800-452-5687. 87 sites, $14; hookups $20. Open year-round; reservations suggested. Park open daily 6:30am-dusk.)

FOOD. The **Community Food Co-op**, 1220 N Forest St., at Maple St., has all the essentials for the healthy eater, plus a tasty cafe in the back. (☎ 734-8158. Open daily 8am-9pm, cafe closes at 8pm.) The Saturday **Bellingham Farmer's Market**, at Chestnut St. and Railroad Ave., has 115 vendors with fruit, vegetables, seafood, and homemade doughnuts. (☎ 647-2060. Apr.-Oct. Sa 10am-3pm, Su 11am-3pm.) For humongous burritos starting at $3 and 80 different tequilas, try **Casa Que Pasa**, 1415 Railroad Ave. Gallery space for local artists. (☎ 738-8226. Open daily 11am-11pm.) Bang out a few songs on the piano at **The Old Town Cafe**, 316 West Holly St., which makes delectable breakfasts with ingredients from the market. Buttermilk pancakes $3.75. (☎ 671-4431. Open M-Sa 6:30am-3pm, Su 8am-2pm.) **Tony's**, 1101 Harris Ave. Garden and cafe with stained-glass windows serves ice cream, bagels, and the infamous Toxic Milkshake, made with coffee and espresso grounds ($4.25). Adjoining **Harris Ave. Cafe** in Fairhaven Village, blocks from the ferry, has tasty $5-10 breakfasts. (☎ 738-4710. Open M-F 7am-9pm, Sa-Su 7:30am-9pm.)

SIGHTS AND ENTERTAINMENT. The **Whatcom Museum of History and Art**, 121 Prospect St., occupies four buildings along Prospect St., most notably the bright red, old city hall. Photographs of turn-of-the-century Pacific Northwest logging scenes by Darius Kinsey are a highlight. Climb to the third floor of the old city hall to watch clock tower innards at work. (☎676-6981. Open Tu-Su noon-5pm. Wheelchair accessible. Free.) **Big Rock Garden Park,** 2900 Sylvan St., is a 3-acre sculpture Japanese-style garden, featuring mostly contemporary work. Take Alabama St. east, then go left on Sylvan for several blocks. Call ahead for a schedule. (☎676-6985. Park open in summer 7am-9pm, winter 8am-6pm.)

In the second week of June, lumberjacks from across the land gather for axe-throwing, log-rolling, and speed-climbing contests at the **Deming Logging Show.** To reach the showgrounds, take Rte. 542 (Mt. Baker Hwy.) 12 mi. east to Cedarville Rd., turn left and follow signs. (☎592-3051. $5, ages 3-12 $3.) The **Bellingham Festival of Music** brings symphony, chamber, folk, and jazz musicians from around the world during the first two weeks of August. All concerts are in Western Washington University Auditorium at 8pm. (☎676-5997. Tickets $18-23; students half-price.) Memorial Day weekend sees the mother of all relays, the **Ski to Sea Race** (☎734-1330). Participants sand-ski, run, canoe, bike, and sea kayak their way from Mt. Baker to the finish line at Bellingham Bay. Families, friends, and spectators join the participants in a grand parade and festival at the race's conclusion.

◪ **OUTDOOR ACTIVITIES.** The 2½ mi. hike up **Chuckanut Mountain** leads through a quiet forest to a view of the islands that fill the bay. On clear days, Mt. Rainier is visible from the top. The trail leaves from Old Samish Hwy., about 3 mi. south of city limits. The beach at **Lake Padden Park,** 4882 Samish Way, has the warmest water in the Puget Sound; take bus #44 1 mi. south of downtown. The park also has tennis courts, playing fields, hiking trails, a boat launch (no motors allowed), and fishing off the pier. (☎676-6985. Open daily 6am-10pm.) The popular **Interurban Trail** (great for biking) runs 5½ mi. from **Fairhaven Park** to **Larrabee State Park** along the relatively flat route of the old Interurban Electric Railway. Occasional breaks in the trees permit a glimpse of the San Juan Islands. Several trails branch off the main line and lead up into the Chuckanut Mountains or down to the coast; pick up a map from the visitors center.

NEAR BELLINGHAM: BLAINE AND BIRCH BAY

A small border town 20 mi. north of Bellingham, Blaine is a busy port of entry between Canada and the US. The lines to cross the border can be tedious in either direction, especially on weekends. Directly on the Canada/US border, Blaine's main attraction is the **Peace Arch State Park,** a good place to get out and stretch before waiting in line to cross the border. The Peace Arch contains relics of early US and Canadian ships of discovery and commemorates the Treaty of Ghent, which ended the War of 1812 and inaugurated the long era of peace between Canada and the US (see p. 185 for an exception). To reach the park, take I-5 Exit 276, then turn north onto 2nd St. (☎332-8221. Open daily 8am-dusk.) The **Harbor Cafe,** 295 Marine Dr., halfway down Blaine's main pier, serves the best seafood in town. (☎332-5176. Open daily 6am-10pm; winter closes at 9pm.)

MOUNT BAKER ☎360

Crowning the **Mt. Baker-Snoqualmie National Forest,** Mt. Baker received the greatest snowfall recorded in one season in the US—1140 in. (95 ft.)—in 1999. The yearly average of 615 in. (51¼ ft.) makes for excellent snowboarding and skiing. No high speed lifts here; just great bowls, chutes, glades, and cheap lift tickets. During the summer, hikers and mountaineers challenge themselves on its trails. To get to this hotbed of outdoor activity, take I-5 Exit 255, just north of Bellingham, to Rte. 542, known as the **Mt. Baker Hwy.;** 58 mi. of roads through the foothills afford views of Baker and other peaks in the range. The highway ends at **Artist Point** (5140 ft.), with spectacular wilderness vistas. The road closes at Mt. Baker Ski Area in winter. For trail maps, **backcountry permits,** or further info about both the National Forest and National Park, stop by the **Glacier Ranger Station,** located on 542 just before the National Forest (☎586-5700. Open daily May-Sept. 8am-4:30pm.)

CAMPING. Silver Lake Park, 9006 Silver Lake Rd., is 3 mi. north of the highway at Maple Falls. The park has 73 sites, swimming, hiking, and fishing. (☎ 599-2776. Sites $14; hookups $16.) More primitive and closer to the mountain is **Douglas Fir Campground,** at Mile 36 off Rte. 542 (30 sites, $12), and **Silver Fir Campground,** at Mile 46 off Rte. 542 (21 sites, $12; water).

WINTER SPORTS. Baker is arguably the birthplace of the snowboard, and it is wildly popular here. The volcano packs soft powder for longer than any other nearby ski area, staying open from early November through May. The ski area has eight lifts and the lowest lift ticket rates in the Northwest. There is no snow-making or shaping on the mountain's 1500 vertical feet of runs. Contact the **Mt. Baker Ski Area Office** in Bellingham for more info. (☎ 734-6771; www.mtbakerskiarea.com. Lift tickets Sa-Su and holidays $34, Th-F $26, M-W $24; under 16 and seniors $26, $21, $20.) In the winter many trails become impromptu cross-country ski trails and snowshoe tracks. Additionally, the forest service maintains a few plowed **SnoParks,** lots that are plowed for easy access. Call the Sedro-Wooley station for info and permits.

HIKING. Trails remain closed late into the spring, so call ahead. The Baker area is very popular in summer with weekend hikers. The **Lake Ann Trail** (5 mi., multi-day), is one of the favorites in the area. This steep trail leads 5 mi. to the lake of the same name, then continues to the Lower Curtis Glacier. Hikers can make the inevitable Robert Frost references along the **Fire and Ice Trail,** a picturesque a half-mile loop beginning on Rte. 542. The first part of the trail is wheelchair accessible. For a hike up to a beautiful, remote lake, head up to **Tomyhoi Lake Trial** (4 mi. one-way, full day). Take forest service road 3065 north from the highway as far as it will go.

SAN JUAN ISLANDS

With hundreds of tiny islands and endless parks and coastline, the San Juan Islands are an explorer's dream. Many locals consider their cars a sad alternative to their kayaks, and the San Juan Islands offer ample opportunity to commune with cedars and tidepools in relative seclusion. To avoid the summer tourist rush but still enjoy good weather, visit in late spring or early fall; many businesses open only upon request during the winter. The *San Juanderer* has tide charts and ferry schedules, and is free on ferries or at visitors centers. A trip San Juan Island requires thinking ahead as the info you need may be available only in Seattle. Book early in the summer weeknds the accommodations and ferries fill up as fast as the kelp grows (up to 14 in. per day in waters around San Juan).

INTER-ISLAND TRANSPORTATION

Washington State Ferries (☎ 206-464-6400 or 888-808-7977; www.wsdot.wa.gov/ferries), has frequent daily service to **Lopez** (45min.), **Shaw** (1¼hr.), **Orcas** (1½hr.), and **San Juan Island** (2hr.), from **Anacortes;** check the schedule available at visitors centers in Puget Sound. To save on fares, travel directly to the westernmost island on your itinerary, then return: eastbound traffic travels for free. The ferries are packed in summer, so arrive at least 1hr. (2hr. on weekends) prior to departure. ($6.80, vehicle $17-28.25 depending on destination, inter-island (westbound) free for passengers, $9-11.25 for cars. Cash only.) To reach the terminal from Seattle, take **I-5** north to Mt. Vernon, then **Rte. 20** west to Anacortes and follow signs. The **Bellingham Airporter** (☎ 800-235-5247) runs shuttles between **Sea-Tac** (see p. 149) and **Anacortes** (10 per day M-F, 7 per day Sa-Su; $31, round-trip $56).

Victoria Clipper (☎ 800-668-7758) departs **Seattle's** Pier 69 daily for San Juan Island, arriving at Spring St. Landing, one block north of the state ferry dock in **Friday Harbor** (2½hr.; $32, round-trip $49) or at **Rosario Resort** on Orcas Island (3¼hr.; mid-May to mid-Sept.; $38, round-trip $59; 1 week advance discount; children half-price). **Island Commuter** (☎ 734-8180 or 888-734-8180) departs **Bellingham** for **Rosario**

Resort (1¼hr.), **Friday Harbor** (2¼hr.), and islands on the way ($25, round-trip $35, ages 6-12 half-price, under 6 free; bicycles $5). **Kenmore Air** (☎800-543-9595) flies to San Juan from Seattle (5 times per day; one-way $99-$110, round-trip $159-183).

SAN JUAN ISLAND ☎360

The furthest trek from Anacortes, yet the most popular of the islands, San Juan Island was discovered by the tourist world in the early 1980s. San Juan is the last stop on the ferry route and home to Friday Harbor, the largest town in the archipelago. It is also the easiest island to explore, since the ferry docks right in town, the roads are good for cyclists, and a shuttle bus services the island. Limekiln State Park is the only designated whale-watching park in the world. Even if you don't make it to the park, there are more than a dozen whale-watching boats leaving from Friday Harbor. But popularity has its price: Seattle-weekenders flood the island throughout the summer, bringing all sorts of traffic.

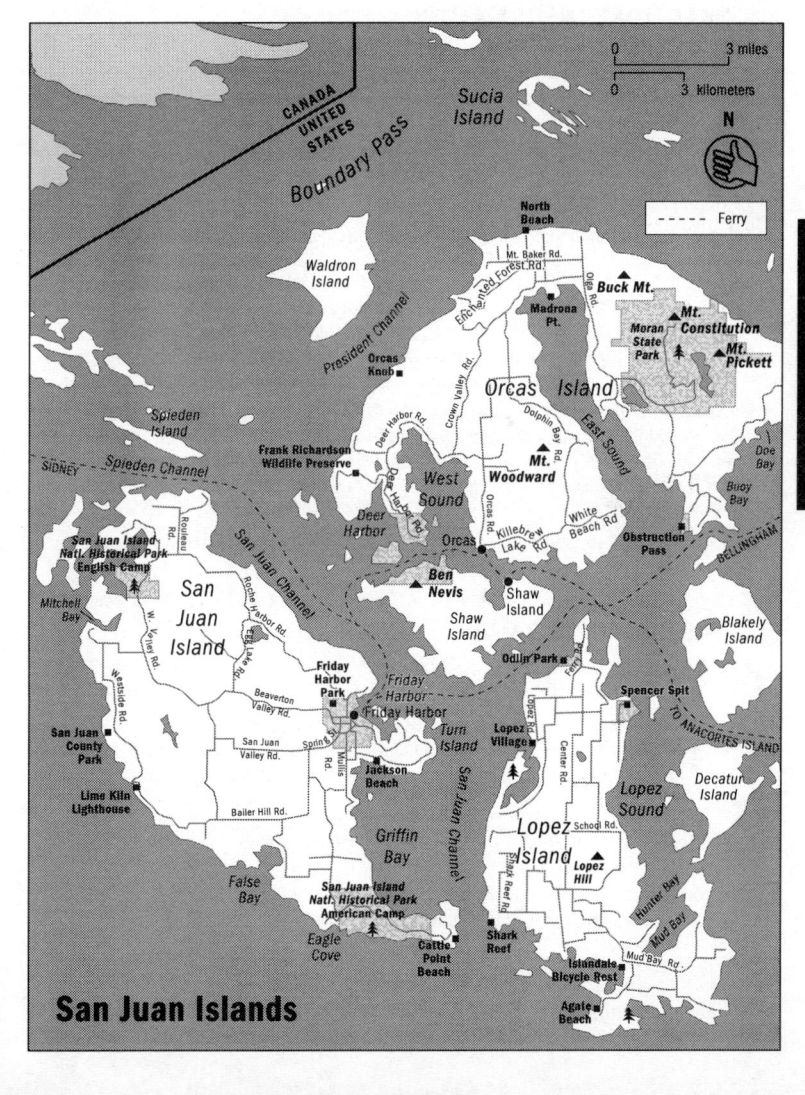

LOCAL TRANSPORTATION

With bicycle, car, and boat rentals within blocks of the ferry terminal, **Friday Harbor** is a convenient base for exploring San Juan. Miles of poorly marked roads access all corners of the island. It's wise to carefully plot a course on a free **map** available at the visitors centers, real estate offices, and gas stations.

Buses: San Juan Transit (☎378-8887 or 800-887-8387; www.san-juan.net/transit.com) circles the island every 35-55min. and will stop upon request. Point-to-point $4; return trip $7; day pass $10; 2 day pass $17, seniors $16, children under 12 $8 (good on Orcas Island). Tours $18, seniors $16 (twice a day; reserve ahead.)

Ferries: Washington State Ferries, see **Transportation,** above.

Taxis: San Juan Taxi (☎378-3550). $4 base, $1 per person, $1 per mi. after the first mi.

PRACTICAL INFORMATION

Visitor Information: Chamber of Commerce, 1 Front St. #2a (☎378-5240; www.sanjuanisland.org), is accessible from a small passageway on Spring St., just next to Amigo's Restaurant.

Outdoor Information: San Juan National Historic Park Information Center (☎378-2240; www.nps.gov/sajh), on the corner of 1st and Spring St. Open M-F 8:30am-4:30pm; winter until 4pm.

Tours: A host of companies offer tours; shopping around (especially fliers at the tourist office) pays! **San Juan Boat Tours** (☎800-232-6722), at Spring St. docks, a block right from ferry, has a 66-passenger boat that has speakers to pick up the Orcas' chat. (3hr.; $39, children $29.) **Sea Quest Expeditions** (☎378-5767), a non-profit education, research, and conservation group, runs kayaking tours. Call to arrange trips. May-Oct. half-day $39; full day $59; longer trips available. **Crystal Seas Kayaking** (☎378-7899) offers 3hr., multi-day, and custom tours from $49; leaves from Friday Harbor.

Equipment Rental: Island Scooter and Bike Rental, 85 Front St. (☎378-8811), next to Friday's Crabhouse, rents scooters for $16 per hr.; $48 per day. Bikes $6 per hour, $25 per day. Open daily 9am-6pm. **Island Bicycles,** 380 Argyle St. (☎378-4941), up Spring St., rents bikes for $6 per hr.; $30 per day. Rentals require a credit card. Open daily 9am-6pm.

Laundromat: Sail-In Laundromat, on East St. behind the waterfront strip. Wash $2.50, dry 25¢ per 10min. Open daily 8am-9:30pm.

Emergency: ☎911. **Police:** 135 Rhone St. (non-emergency ☎378-4151), at Reed St.

Domestic Violence/Sexual Assault Services: ☎378-8680.

Pharmacy: Friday Harbor Drug, 210 Spring St. (☎378-4421). Open M-Sa 9am-7pm, Su 10am-4pm. **Red Tide Hotline:** ☎800-562-5632.

Medical Services: Inter-Island Medical Center, 550 Spring St. (☎378-2141), at Mullis Rd. Open M-F 8:30am-4:30pm, Sa 10am-1pm **Crisis:** ☎378-2345. 24hr.

Internet Access: Menu Bar, 435-B Argyle Rd. (☎378-1987). $6 per hr. Open M-F 9am-6pm, Sa 10am-4pm.

Post Office: 220 Blair St. (☎378-4511), at Reed St. Open M-F 8:30am-4:30pm. **ZIP Code:** 98250.

ACCOMMODATIONS AND CAMPING

The popularity of San Juan and its few budget accommodations make finding a bed challenging. The campgrounds are wildly popular; reservations are imperative. Often beautiful, the B&Bs are also prohibitively expensive; contact **San**

SAN JUAN ISLAND ■ 185

DIE, IMPERIALIST PIG! Back in 1859, when Washington was officially part of "Oregon Country" and the San Juan Islands lay in a territorial liminality between British Vancouver Island and the United States, one hungry hog unwittingly gave his life for what turned out to be truth, justice, and the American Way. Seventeen Americans farmed on San Juan Island when the British Hudson's Bay Company claimed it for England. When Lyman Cutlar caught a British pig making a royal mess of his potato patch, he understandably shot it dead. The Brits threatened to arrest him, and the Americans looked to Uncle Sam for protection. Three months, five British warships, and several American cannons later, war between the two nations looked inevitable. Although the standoff soon cooled down, the "Pig War" stalemate lasted 12 years. Both countries occupied the island until 1872, when Kaiser Wilhelm of Germany, invited to settle the dispute, granted it all to the US. In the end, the pig was the conflict's only casualty. But, hey, martyrdom and everlasting fame beat a life of wallowing in the mud any day!

Juan Central Reservation (☎888-999-8773; www.fridayharbor.com) for help. If you miss out on hosteling and camping options, your best bet is taking the evening ferry back to Anacortes where a plethora of cheap motels line Commercial Ave., the main street leading up to the ferry. Their prices are less than half of what they charge on the island. The **Gateway Motel**, 2019 Commercial Ave., is a decent deal. (☎293-2655. Open 8am-11pm. Singles $40; doubles $58; with kitchen $10 more.)

- **Wayfarer's Rest**, 35 Malcolm St. (☎378-6428), a 10min. walk from the ferry up Spring onto Argyle St., and left at the church. This house turned-hostel has beautiful homemade driftwood bunks, a huge living area, a garden, a full kitchen, and the best linens around. Occasional fresh eggs from resident chickens add a country touch. Coin showers, washers, and dryers. Check-in 2-9pm. $20, private room $45, private cabin $50.

- **San Juan County Park**, 380 Westside Rd. (☎371-1842), 10 mi. west of Friday Harbor, along the bay. The 20 sites are on a bluff, with have views of whales (maybe) and great sunsets (almost definitely). Water, toilets, no showers. Open daily 7am-10pm. Office open daily 9am-7pm. Vehicle sites $18; walk-ins $5.

- **Lakedale Campgrounds**, 4313 Roche Harbor Rd. (☎378-2350 or 800-617-2267), 4 mi. from Friday Harbor, just west of Egg Lake Rd. Some sites set near lakes. Reservations suggested, but management boasts that they've never turned a camper away. Open Mar. 15 to Oct. 15; cabins year-round. Fishing permits $4 per day, non-campers $8 per day. Boat rental. Vehicle sites $24, plus $5.75 per person after 2; hiker/biker sites $8 per person; 4-person tent-cabins from $45. Cheaper rates in off-season.

FOOD

The king needs his wine! **King's Market**, 160 Spring St., stocks it. (☎378-4505. In summer open M-Sa 7:30am-10pm, Su 7:30am-9pm.) Vegetarian food flourishes, but a cheap dinner can be hard to find. Most small places close at 6 or 7pm.

- **Thai Kitchen**, 42 1st St. (☎378-1917), next to the Whale Museum. A popular dinner spot with a beautiful patio for flower-sniffing or star-gazing. Lunch dishes around $7, dinners $8-12. Open M 5-9pm, Tu-Sa 11:30am-3pm and 5-9pm.

- **San Juan Donut Shop**, 225 Spring St. (☎378-2271). Bottomless coffee ($1.25) at the town rumor mill. Stop in for a donut or call for a sack lunch. Open daily 7am-5pm.

- **Hungry Clam Fish and Chips**, 130 First St. (☎378-3474), serves up excellent, fresh, beer-battered Alaskan Cod (fish and chips $5.50-8.50). Open daily 11am-7pm.

- **Hard Clay Cafe**, 10 N First St. (☎378-5544). Mingle with the local ladies in the back room. One of the few cafes open past 5pm. Open daily 7:30am-8pm; maybe later F-Sa.

WASHINGTON

186 ■ SAN JUAN ISLANDS

SIGHTS

Driving around the 35 mi. perimeter of the island takes about 2hr.; on bike it makes for the perfect day-long tour. The **West Side Rd.** traverses gorgeous scenery and provides the best chance for sighting **orcas** from three resident pods. To begin a tour of the island, head south and west out of Friday Harbor on Mullis Rd. (Bikers may want to do this route in the opposite direction, as climbs heading counter-clockwise around the island are much more gradual.)

WHALE MUSEUM. The museum has a rich collection of artifacts and whale skeletons. Call their whale hotline at 800-562-8832 to report sightings and strandings. *(62 1st St. ☎ 378-4710 or 800-946-7227. Open daily June-Sept. 9am-5pm; Oct.-May 10am-5pm. $5, seniors $4, students and ages 5-18 $2, under 5 free.)*

SAN JUAN ISLAND NATIONAL HISTORICAL PARK. The San Juan park preserves the two sites where the tensions of the Pig War (see graybox, p. 185) are most manifest. **American camp**, where the American army built its barracks, is the more elaborate of the park's two halves. The **visitors center** explains the history of the curious conflict, while a self-guided trail leads from the shelter, through the buildings, and past the site of a British sheep farm. **English Camp,** on the island's north end, forms the second half of the Park and boasts an audiovisual program in the barracks to detail the British side. During the summer Saturday afternoons at one of the two camps are made lively by volunteers in period costume re-enacting daily Pig War-era life. *(To get to American Camp follow Cattle Point Rd. south from Friday Harbor. British Camp can be reached by Roche Harbor Rd. ☎ 378-2902. Camp open daily June-Aug. dawn-11pm, Sept.-May Th-Su. Visitors Center open daily 8:30am-5pm. Guided walks. June-Sept. Sa 11:30am. Re-enactments June-July 12:30-3:30pm. Free.)*

HOTEL DE HARO AND MASONIC MAUSOLEUM. The Hotel de Haro was the first hotel in Washington. The free brochure *A Walking Tour of Historic Roche Harbor*, available at the info kiosk in front of the hotel, leads through this old mining camp. *(At the Roche Harbor Resort, on Roche Harbor Rd. at the northern end of the island. ☎ 378-2155.)* Don't miss the vaguely unsettling **Masonic mausoleum.** *(Follow signs to Roche Harbor and stop at lot behind the airfield. Signs guide visitors to mausoleum foot path.)*

OUTDOOR ACTIVITIES

San Juan Island has whales on the brain, and it is no surprise; in the ocean to the west of the island several pods of Orcas are to be seen all summer long. **Limekiln Point State Park,** along West Side Rd., is renowned as the best **whale-watching** spot on the island. Take the short hike to the whale-watching balconies, where cliffside crowds watch as killer whales prowl for salmon between occasional acrobatics. The most determined whale-watchers shell out for a **cruise**; most operations charge $45 (children $35) for a 3-4hr. boat ride. Get a brochure at the chamber of commerce or the park visitors center. But keep in mind, San Juan has almost as many whale-watching boats as it does whales. When you are choosing your company, ask about boat size and how much the captain narrates the tour. Keep in mind that smaller boats can usually get closer to the whales.

The island provides several places for the land-bound to stroll. If the sky is clear, make the half-mile jaunt down the road to **Cattle Point** for views of the distant Olympic Mountains, or stop by **South Beach,** a stretch of shoreline that dazzles beach walkers and whale stalkers. Also in the south, **Eagle Beach** and **Grandma's Cove,** are considered some of the finest beaches on the island. Heading east from West Side Rd., Mitchell Bay Rd. leads to a steep half-mile trail to **"Mount" Young,** a good tall hill within looking range of Victoria and the Olympic Range. The gravel False Bay Rd., heading west from Cattle Point Rd., runs to **False Bay,** where **bald eagles** nest. During spring and summer, nesting eagles are visible at low tide along the northwestern shore.

ORCAS ISLAND ☎ 360

Mount Constitution overlooks much of Puget Sound from its 2407 ft. summit atop Orcas Island. A small population of retirees, artists, and farmers dwell here in understated homes surrounded by green shrubs and the red bark of madrona trees. With a commune-like campground and resort and the largest state park in Washington, Orcas has the best budget tourist facilities of all the islands. Unfortunately, much of the beach is occupied by private resorts and closed to the public. Beauty and solitude can be found at Doe Bay, while Eastsound provides the civilization—it offers a movie theatre, several restaurants, a museum, and shopping.

ORIENTATION AND PRACTICAL INFORMATION

Orcas is shaped like a horseshoe, lending a commonsensical name to the main thoroughfare, **Horseshoe Hwy.** The ferry lands on the southwest tip at **Orcas Village**. **Eastsound,** the main town, is at the top of the horseshoe, 9 mi. northeast. **Olga** and **Doe Bay** are another 8 and 11 mi. down the eastern side of the horseshoe, respectively. Stop in one of the four shops at the ferry landing to get a free **map.**

- **Ferries: Washington State Ferries,** see p. 182.
- **Public Transportation: San Juan Transit** (☎376-8887). Service every 1½hr. to most parts of the island. From the ferry to Eastsound $4, as is all other point to point travel.
- **Taxis: Orcas Island Taxi,** ☎376-8294.
- **Visitor Information:** San Juan Island houses the more official tourist facilities. **Pyewacket Books** (☎376-2043), in Templin Center, in Eastsound at N Beach Rd., has good island books.
- **Equipment Rental: Wildlife Cycles** (☎376-4708), 350 North Beach Rd., at A St. in Eastsound. Bikes $7.50 per hr., $30 per day. Open M-Sa 10am-5:30pm, Su 11am-2pm. **Dolphin Bay Bicycles** (☎376-4157), near the ferry, $25 per day, $55 for 3 days (the perfect length to explore the island).
- **Emergency:** ☎911. **Domestic Violence/Sexual Assault Services:** ☎376-1234.
- **Pharmacy:** Ray's (☎376-2230, after-hours emergencies 376-3693), in Templin Center in Eastsound at N Beach Rd. Open M-Sa 9am-6pm.
- **Internet Access: Library,** (☎376-4985), at Rose and Pine in Eastsound; walk up the path from Prune Alley. Open M-Th 11am-6pm, F-Sa 11am-5pm. **Orcas Online,** 254 N Beach Rd. (☎376-4124), in Eastsound. $5 per 30min. Open M-F 9:30am-4:30pm, Sa noon-3pm.
- **Post Office:** (☎376-4121), 221 A St. in Eastsound. Open M-F 9am-4:30pm. **ZIP Code:** 98245.

ACCOMMODATIONS AND CAMPING

B&Bs on Orcas charge upwards of $85 per night; call 376-8888 for advice. Camping is the cheapest option on Orcas. Reservations are important during summer.

- **Doe Bay Resort** (☎376-2291), off Horseshoe Hwy. on Pt. Lawrence Rd., 5 mi. east of Moran State Park. A former commune and then Human Potential Center, this retreat keeps the old feel in its guise as vacation spot. Cafe, treehouse, and a coed clothing-optional hot tub and steam sauna. Sauna $4 per day, non-guests $7; one free pass for guests. Office open 10am-1pm and 3-7pm. Kayak rentals through Shearwater Adventures (see **Outdoors Information,** below). Private rooms start at $65; yurts $75; camping $25.
- **Moran State Park,** State Rte. 22 (☎376-2326 or 800-452-5687). Follow Horseshoe Hwy. straight into the park, 14 mi. from the ferry on the east side of the island. The most popular camping in the islands, but sites are often very cosy. Two major lakes. Swimming, fishing, hiking trails. Rowboats and paddleboats $12-13 per hr., $35-45 full day. 4 campgrounds, 151 sites. About 12 sites are open year-round. Sites from $14.

188 ■ SAN JUAN ISLANDS

Obstruction Pass. Accessible by boat or foot. Turn off the Hwy. just past Olga, and head south (right) on Obstruction Pass Rd. Follow the gravel road marked Obstruction Pass Trailhead to the trailhead and parking lot. Pit toilets, no water. Access to nice pebble beaches on Puget Sound. 11 free sites.

FOOD

Essentials can be found in Eastsound at **Island Market,** 469 Market St. (☎376-6000. Open M-Sa 8am-9pm, Su 10am-8pm.) For a large selection of groceries, medicines, and vegan cheeses, make a bee-line for **Orcas Homegrown Market,** on N Beach Rd. Try their deli and seafood specials for lunch; most specials are $5-6 and there are always vegetarian options. (☎376-2009. Open daily 8am-9pm.) For loads of fresh local produce, visit the **Farmer's Market** in front of the museum (Sa 10am-3pm).

- **Comet Cafe** (☎376-4220), in Eastsound Sq. on N Beach Rd. Two sisters run a bright, happy-go-lucky cafe. One bakes sweets, the other makes the savory stuff. Homemade soups and ice cream, as well as cooked-to-order breakfasts. Open Tu-Sa 9am-3pm.
- **Chimayo** (☎376-6394), on N Beach Rd. A Southwest theme and comfy booths. Fresh burrito ($5-9). A taco bar dishes out low-priced eats for lunch. Open M-Sa 11am-7pm.
- **Lower Tavern** (☎378-4848), at the corner of Horseshoe Hwy. and Prune Alley. One of the few cheap spots open after 5pm. Dig into burgers and fries for $6-7. Open Su-Th 11am-midnight, F-Sa 11am-2am; kitchen closes M-Sa 9pm, Su 5pm.

OUTDOOR ACTIVITIES

Travelers on Orcas Island don't need to roam with a destination in mind; half the fun lies in rambling around, although much of the land is private property. The trail to **Obstruction Pass Beach** is the best way to clamber down to the rocky shores. Taking up the majority of Orcas' eastern half, **Moran State Park** is the last large undeveloped area on the San Juans, making it a star outdoor attraction. This is a hands down must-see during even a brief sojourn on the island. Ample trails, steep mountains, and several lakes keep the landscape varied and the sweat running. For those who want to glimpse the outdoors without hiking it, try the **Orcas Tortas,** a green bus that slowly drives from Eastsound campground to the peak of Mt. Constitution. (☎376-4156; $8.)

HIKING

Over 30 mi. of hiking trails cover the park, providing hikes for all levels of desire. Find a good map and detailed trail descriptions in the free *Guide to Moran State Park*, available at the **registration station.** (☎376-2326. Rangers on duty daily Apr.-Aug. 6:30am-dusk, Sept.-Mar. 8am-dusk.)

- **Cold Springs Trail** (4¼ mi. one-way, 1 day) is the park's most challenging trail, going from the North End Campground up to the summit of Mt. Constitution. Since a road also runs to the summit, those with a little less spunk can catch a ride back down to the camping areas. 2000 ft. gain.
- **Mountain Lake Trail** (4 mi. loop, 2-3hr.) starts from the cabin near Mountain Lake campground and loops around Mountain Lake, the larger and more secluded of the parks two big lakes. A more mellow trail.

WATER SPORTS

Within the park, two freshwater lakes are accessible from the road, and rowboats and paddleboats are rented at **Cascade Lake** for both ($12-14 per hr.). Anglers also hit Moran's water with glee. Outside of the park and on salt water, Orcas is probably the best place to kayak in the San Juans, with a wide variety of conditions and far fewer crowds than San Juan Island. **Shearwater Adventures** runs fascinating **sea kayak tours** and classes, and their store in Eastsound is a great information source for more experienced paddlers. (☎376-4699. 3hr. tour with 30min. of dry land training $45. Full-day and multi-day trips available.) **Crescent Beach Kayak,** on the highway 1 mi. east of Eastsound, rents kayaks for paddling the mellow waters of the East Sound. (☎ 376-2464. $10 per hr., $25 per half-day. Open daily 9am-5pm. Owner will not rent when there are white caps in the water.)

LOPEZ ISLAND ☎ 360

Smaller than either Orcas or San Juan, "Slow-pez" lacks some of the tourist facilities of the larger islands. Lopez Island is ideal for those seeking solitary beach-walking, bicycling, or a true small-town experience. Free of imposing inclines and heavy traffic, the island is the most cycle-friendly in the chain.

■■ **ORIENTATION AND PRACTICAL INFORMATION.** **Lopez Village,** the largest town, is 4½ mi. from the ferry dock off Fisherman Bay Rd. To get there, follow Ferry Rd. then take a right onto the first street after Lopez Center (before the Chevron station). It's best to bring a bicycle, unless you're up for the hike. In a singular Lopez tradition, motorists wave to one another as they drive, so get your hands ready. To rent a bike or kayak, head to **Lopez Bicycle Works** and **Lopez Kayak,** both south of the village next to the island's Marine Center. Get an excellent map here or at the visitors center. (☎ 468-2847. Bikes open July-Aug. daily 9am-9pm Apr.-June and Sept.-Oct. 10am-5pm; kayaks open daily 10am-5pm. Bikes $5 per hr., $25 per day. Single kayaks $12-15 per hr., $40-60 per day; doubles $20 per hr., $60-80 per day. 2hr., 3hr., and day-long trips available.) For a taxi, call **Angie's Cab** (☎ 468-2227). Keep it so at **Keep It Clean,** south of the winery. (Wash $2, dry 25¢ per 5min. Open M-F 8:30am-7pm, Sa-Su until 5pm.) **Domestic violence/sexual assault services:** ☎ 468-4567. **Emergency:** 911. **Clinic:** ☎ 468-2245. **Post Office:** on Weeks Rd. (☎ 468-2282). Open M-F 8:30am-4:30pm. **ZIP Code:** 98261.

■■ **ACCOMMODATIONS AND FOOD.** When spending the night on Lopez, camping is the only bargain. **Spencer Spit State Park,** on the northeast corner of the island about 3½ mi. from the ferry terminal, has six sites on the beach and 25 nicely secluded wooded sites up the hill. Spencer Spit offers good **clamming** in the late spring, unless there is red tide (☎ 800-562-5632; permit required). The park is closed November 1 to February 2. (☎ 468-2251; reservations ☎ 800-452-5687. Toilets, no showers or hook-ups. Reservations necessary for summer weekends. Open until 10pm. Sites $14.) Voted one of the 10 best places to woo by MSNBC, **Lopez Farm Cottages and Tent Camping,** just north of town on Fisherman Bay Rd. is a beautiful spot to enjoy. Each campsite comes equipped with a hammock and chairs. Minimum age is 14. Free morning coffee. Showers that open to the sky. Few campgrounds are designed as well, and the cottages are even better (☎ 800-440-3556. Sites $28 for double occupancy, cottages $99-150 depending on time of year). **Odlin Park** is close to the ferry terminal, 1 mi. south along Ferry Rd., and offers running water, a boat launch, volleyball net, and baseball diamond as well as nice beaches and pleasant walks. (☎ 468-2496; reservations 378-1842. 30 sites. $15-17.) Although it doesn't boast the selection of restaurants that the other two islands do, a good meal is readily had. Play *boules* while brown-bagging in the grassy park adjacent to the **Village Market,** which has a complete meat and produce department. (☎ 468-2266. Open daily 8am-8pm.) Across the street, sample fresh pastries, bread, and pizza at **Holly B's.** (☎ 468-2133. Open M and W-Sa 7am-5pm, Su 7am-4pm.) The **Farmer's Market** demonstrates island bounty (Sa 10am-2pm).

■■ **OUTDOOR ACTIVITIES AND SIGHTS.** Lopez is attractive more for the lack of things to do. People are so friendly that you will probably just find yourself trading stories. If explore you must, the small **Shark Reef** and **Agate Beach County Parks,** on the southwest end of the island, have tranquil and well-maintained hiking trails. Watch in wonder at the waves crashing against the rocky beaches at Shark Reef Park or stroll down Agate's calm and deserted shores. **Lopez Island Vineyards,** 724 Fisherman Bay Rd., San Juan's oldest vineyards, permits visitors to sample all of their wines for $2 per person. (☎ 468-3644. Open summer W-Sa noon-5pm, and year-round by appointment.)

OLYMPIC PENINSULA

Due west of Seattle and its busy Puget Sound neighbors, the Olympic Peninsula is a remote backpacking paradise. Olympic National Park dominates much of the peninsula, and it prevents the area's ferocious timber industry from threatening the glacier-capped mountains and temperate rainforests. With the pick of three ecosystems—rainforest, beach, or mountain—outdoors enthusiasts have a full plate. Outside of the park, a smattering of Indian reservations and logging and fishing communities lace the peninsula's coastline along US 101. To the west, the Pacific Ocean stretches to a distant horizon; to the north, the Strait of Juan de Fuca separates the Olympic Peninsula from Vancouver Island; and to the east, Hood Canal and the Kitsap Peninsula isolate this sparsely inhabited wilderness from the sprawl of Seattle.

OLYMPIC NATIONAL PARK

Olympic National Park (ONP) is certainly the centerpiece of the Olympic Peninsula, sheltering one of the most diverse landscapes of any region in the world. The park's accolades speak much for the place. With glacier-encrusted peaks, river valley rainforests, and jagged shores along the Pacific Coast, the park has something to offer to everyone. Roads lead to many corners of Olympic National Park, but they offer only hint at the depths of its wilderness. A dive into the backcountry leaves summer tourists behind and reveals the richness and diversity of the park's many faces. Many try to make this trip in a day or two, but beware: the breadth and distances in the park make it difficult to enjoy in under three or four days.

ORIENTATION

The entire **Olympic Mountain Range** is packed into the peninsula's center, where conical peaks ring huge quantities of moisture from heavy Pacific air. Average precipitation in the park varies, but an annual 12 ft. of rain and snow are common. At altitudes above 3500 ft. it is not rare to encounter snow in late June. The mountains steal so much water that some areas are among the driest in Washington.

Temperate rainforests lie on the west side of ONP, along the coast, and in the **Hoh, Queets,** and **Quinault River valleys.** Moderate temperatures, loads of rain, and summer fog support an emerald tangle dominated by Sitka spruce and Western Red cedar. The rest of the park is populated by lowland forests of Douglas fir and hemlock, with silver fir at higher elevations. Ancient Native American **petroglyphs** and boxy offshore bluffs called **sea stacks** lend a sacred quality to the beaches along the coastline. Swaths of **Olympic National Forest** and private land separate these seaside expanses from the rest of the park. The park's perimeters are well-defined but are surrounded by **Forest Service** land, **Washington Department of Natural Resources (DNR)** land, and other public areas. It's important to remember that the ONP and ONF are maintained by separate organizations. Their usage, purposes, facilities, rules, and regulations differ accordingly.

Each side of the park has one major settlement—**Port Townsend** in the east, **Port Angeles** to the north, and **Forks** is the west. Their size and services decline as you go go west, as does the traffic. The park's vista-filled eastern rim runs up to Port Townsend, from where the much-visited northern rim extends westward. Along a winding detour on Rte. 112, off US 101 westward, the tiny town of **Neah Bay** and stunning **Cape Flattery** perch at the northwest tip of the peninsula; farther south on US 101, the slightly larger town of Forks is a gateway to the park's rainforested western rim. Separate from the rest of the park, much of the peninsula's Pacific coastline comprises a gorgeous coastal zone.

OLYMPIC NATIONAL PARK ■ 191

Olympic National Park

▲ ACCOMMODATIONS
Rainforest Hostel, 7
Ruffles Motel, 32

▲ CAMPGROUNDS
Altaire, 30
Bear Creek, 23
Copper Mine Bottom, 13
Cottonwood, 6
Deer Park, 33
Dosewallips, 21
Eagle, 26
Fairholm, 25
Falls Creek, 16
Graves Creek, 18
Heart O' Hills, 31
Hoh Rain Forest, 27
Kalaloch, 8
Klahowya, 24
Lake Cushman State Park, 20
Minnie Peterson, 9
North Fork, 17
Pillar Point, 22
Salt Creek, 29
South Fork, 10
Staircase, 19
Queets, 14
Upper Clearwater, 12
Willaby, 15
Willoughby Creek, 4
Yahoo Lake, 11

WASHINGTON

192 ■ OLYMPIC PENINSULA

July, August, and September are the best months for visiting Olympic National Park. Much of the backcountry remains snowed-in until late June, and only summers are relatively rain-free. The Park Service runs free interpretive programs such as guided forest hikes, tidepool walks, and campfire programs out of its ranger stations. For a schedule of events, pick up a copy of the *Bugler* from ranger stations or the visitors center (see below). Erik Molvar's *Hiking Olympic National Park* ($15) is a great resource for hikers, with maps and step-by-step trail logs for over 585 mi. of trails. Although it lacks coverage of coastal areas and can be slightly outdated, Robert Wood's comprehensive *Olympic Mountains Trail Guide* ($15) is the classic book for those planning to tackle the backcountry. *Custom Correct* maps provide detailed topographic information on various popular hiking areas. However, with the density of helpful ranger stations and adequate signs, most visitors who are sticking to park campgrounds will have little need to purchase additional literature.

TRANSPORTATION

The peninsula provides quite a few transportation options for a place so remote. Driving, highway 101 forms an upside-down "U", passing through almost every place listed. A combination of roads also heads straight west from Olympia, allowing one to bypass the park and then head north on 101, skipping the crowds and going straight to the rainforest. Local buses link Port Townsend, Port Angeles, Forks, and Neah Bay, cost 50¢-$1, and accommodate bicycles. From there rides can be cobbled together to get further into the park. Vans lines, ride-sharing, and taxis are all options. When combined with bus, bicycling can move a traveler quickly and is much more versatile. The only place to be aware of is the stretch of 101 that runs along Lake Crescent—it is poor for bikers. Roads into the park are accessible from US 101 and serve as trailheads for over 600 mi. of hiking. No roads cross the entire park, necessitating some degree of backtracking.

Actually getting to the peninsula to begin the trip requires a bit more foresight, but can be rewarding: the trip from Seattle to the farthest end of Olympic National Park can cost as little as $7 (7hr. via Pierce, Grays Harbor, and West Jefferson Transits). A ferry is probably the fastest bet and can work well for those driving, too. For more info, contact Washington State Ferries (☎888-808-7977 or 206-464-6400); Greyhound (☎800-231-2222); King in Seattle (☎800-542-7876); Pierce in Tacoma (☎206-581-8000); Intercity in Olympia (☎800-287-6348); Kitsap in Kitsap and Bainbridge (☎360-373-2877). For service on the peninsula, Jefferson in Port Townsend (☎360-385-4777); Clallam in Port Angeles (☎800-858-3747); Grays Harbor in Aberdeen (☎800-562-9730); West Jefferson in the southwest (☎800-436-3950); and Mason in the southeast (☎800-374-3747). The hostels around the peninsula know the terrain and will help anyone navigate transit routes around the park.

PRACTICAL INFORMATION

Entrance Fee: $10 per car; $5 per hiker or biker. Charged at Hoh, Heart o' the Hills, Sol Duc, Staircase, and Elwha entrances. Covers 7 days access to the park; keep that receipt! Backcountry users must pay $2 extra per night to ranger offices. The National Forest requires a Northwest Forest Pass at most parking areas ($5 daily, $30 annually).

Visitor Information: Olympic National Park Visitor Center, 3002 Mt. Angeles Rd. (☎565-3130; www.nps.gov/olym/home.htm), off Race St. in Port Angeles (see p. 198). ONP's main info center. Contains a children's natural history room, extensive exhibits, and plays a 12min. movie that gives an overview of the park. The info center also distributes an invaluable **park map.** Open daily 9am-5:30pm; winter 9am-4pm.

OLYMPIC NATIONAL PARK ■ 193

Park Headquarters, 600 E Park Ave. (☎565-3000), in Port Angeles, is an administrative office but can answer questions by phone. Open M-F 8am-4:30pm. For the many local **ranger stations,** see specific regions below.

Fishing: Fishing in park boundaries requires a license except when along the Pacific Ocean. A booklet with all of the park's regulations is published mid-spring and is available at stations on request.

Backcountry Information: Olympic National Park Wilderness Information Center (☎565-3100; www.nps.gov/olym/wic), behind the visitors center, provides trip-planning help and info on food storage and leave-no-trace techniques. Call here for backcountry reservations. Pay the ONP wilderness user fee here or at any ranger station.

Emergency: ☎911. **Park Headquarters** (☎565-3000). Staffed daily 7am-midnight; winter 7am-5:30pm. Or call the nearest ranger station and report your exact location.

Park Weather: ☎565-3131. 24hr.

Park Radio: 530 AM for road closures and general weather conditions. 610 AM for general park rules and information, 1610 AM in Lake Crescent and Quinault areas.

CAMPING

Competition for sites on the peninsula can get fierce, but there is sufficient space for the entire population of Washington to camp there at once if it so chose. It just takes a little driving to uncover all the treasures of hidden sites. On top of numerous national park sites there is a network of state and county sites and several hostels well spaced across peninsula.

STANDARD CAMPING. Ask at the Olympic National Forest Headquarters in Olympia (see p. 173) about **ONP** campgrounds throughout its boundaries (sites $8-12). **ONF** maintains six free campgrounds in the Hood Canal Ranger District and other campgrounds within its boundaries; **Seal Rock, Falls View,** and **Klahowya** can be reserved. (☎800-280-2267; www.reserveusa.com. Open daily 8am-midnight. Sites $8-12.) In addition to **Ft. Worden** and **Ft. Flagler,** there are four **state parks** on the peninsula. (Reservations ☎800-452-5687. Sites $14, hookups $20, hiker or biker $6.) **Dosewallips** (☎796-4415) and **Lake Cushman** (see Eastern Rim, below) are to the east. **Sequim Bay,** is northeast of Sequim. (☎683-4235. Table and stove at each site. Restrooms.) Most **drive-up camping** is first come, first served.

BACKCOUNTRY CAMPING. Whether in rainforest, high country, or along the coast, backcountry camping in the park requires a **backcountry permit.** Park offices maintain **quota limits** on backcountry permits for popular spots, including **Lake Constance** and **Flapjack Lakes** in the eastern rim (see below); **Grand Valley, Badger Valley,** and **Sol Duc** in the northern rim (see p. 198); **Hoh** in the western rim (see p. 202); and the coastal **Ozette Loop.** Make **reservations** in advance, especially for the Ozette area, where reservations are required. Contact the Wilderness Info Center to secure a spot. Backpackers should prepare for varied weather conditions. Even in summer, parts of the park get very wet. Pack appropriately for the weather. **Giardia,** a nasty diarrhea-inducing bacterium, lives in the water here. Water purification tablets are available at the visitors center and most outfitters. **Black bears** and **raccoons** pose another backcountry hazard; when issuing backcountry permits, ranger stations instruct hikers on hanging food out of animals' reach. Cougars have also become a concern, and ranger officials will give you extensive advice on how to maximize your safety. For more on wilderness safety, see p. 40. Above 3500 ft., **open fires** are prohibited; below 3500 ft. maps and signposts indicate whether they are allowed. Before any trip, inquire about **trail closures;** winter weather often destroys popular trails.

WASHINGTON

EASTERN OLYMPIC PENINSULA

The area of the peninsula most accessible from Puget Sound City, the Olympic's eastern edge suffers from a heavy traffic of weekend cabin-renters and short day trippers. Still, the eastern edge of the Park, generously padded with a thick strip of National Forest, houses some fun (and generally dry) trails. The big draw, though, is the town that serves as the peninsula's social capitol, Port Townsend. PT is the one settlement west of Olympia that doesn't qualify as "sleepy," making it a welcome change of pace for travelers who have been taking advantage of the park's solitude for a little too long.

PORT TOWNSEND ☎ 360

Set apart from the rest of the Olympic Peninsula on a small peninsula of its own, Port Townsend nonetheless rules the local roost for culture. During the late 1800s, the city's predominance in the entire state of Washington seemed secure. Every ship en route to Puget Sound stopped here for customs inspection, and speculation held that the bustling port would become the capital of the new state. When rumors circulated that rail would connect the town to the east, wealthy families flocked to the bluffs overlooking the port, constructing elaborate Victorian homes and stately public buildings. When rail passed the town by, "the inevitable New York" was left a ghost town, perched on the isolated northeast tip of the Olympic Peninsula to subsist by paper milling and logging. In the 1970s, Port Townsend's neglected Victorian homes were discovered by artists and idealists who turned the town into a vibrant, creative community. Now the business district stands restored, recently declared a national landmark, and the town takes advantage of its 19th-century feel to entice those heading to the park onto Rte. 20 and into town. It is a turn that few who make it regret.

ORIENTATION AND PRACTICAL INFORMATION

Port Townsend sits at the terminus of **Rte. 20** on the northeastern corner of the Olympic Peninsula. Over land, it can be reached by **US 101** on the peninsula, or from the Kitsap Peninsula across the Hood Canal Bridge. **Kitsap County Transit** meets every ferry and runs to Poulsbo. From Poulsbo, **Jefferson County Transit** runs to PT. The ferry also crosses frequently to and from Keystone on Whidbey Island (see p. 177). Ferries dock at **Water St.**, west of touristy downtown, which is along **Water** and **Washington St.** where restaurants, hotels, and motels. Laid-back uptown, with a small business district of its own, is four steep blocks up, on **Lawrence St.**

Local Transportation: Jefferson County Transit (JCT; ☎ 385-4777; www.jeffersontransit.com). Peninsula towns are serviced by JCT and neighboring transit systems. Buses run between Ft. Worden and Downtown, and also connect to Seattle and Port Angeles. 50¢; seniors, disabled travelers, and ages 6-18 25¢; extra-zone fare 25¢. Day passes $1.50. A **shuttle** runs between downtown and the Park 'n' Ride lot, right next to the Safeway. There is usually ample parking in town, although usually limited to 2hr.

Taxis: Peninsula Taxi, ☎ 385-1872. $2 base plus $1.75 per mi.

Visitor Information: Chamber of Commerce, 2437 E Sims Way (☎ 385-2722 or 888-365-6978; www.ptguide.com), lies 10 blocks southwest of town on Rte. 20. Open M-F 9am-5pm, Sa 10am-4pm, Su 11am-4pm.

Equipment Rental: P.T. Cyclery, 100 Tyler St. (☎ 385-6470), rents mountain bikes for $7 per hr., $25 per day. Maps $1.75. Ages 100+ free. Open M-Sa 9am-6pm. **Kayak Port Townsend,** 435 Water St. (☎ 385-6240 or 800-853-2252; www.kayakpt.com), is part of PT's burgeoning sea kayaking scene. Rents singles $25 per 4hr.; doubles $40 per 4hr. Windrider sailing craft $25 per hr., $60 per day; ages 84+ free.

PORT TOWNSEND ■ 195

Emergency: ☎911. **Police:** 607 Water St. (☎385-2322) at Madison. 24hr.

Crisis Line: ☎385-0321 or 800-659-0321. 24hr. **Sexual Assault Line:** ☎385-5291.

Pharmacy: Safeway Pharmacy, 442 Sims Way (☎385-2860). Open M-F 8:30am-7:30pm, Sa 8:30am-6pm, Su 10am-6pm.

Hospital: 834 Sheridan (☎385-2200 or 800-244-8917), off Rte. 20 at 7th St.

Internet Access: Library, 1220 Lawrence (☎385-3181). Free Internet access, 15min. drop in, up to 75min. by appointment. Open M-W 11am-8pm, Th-Sa 11am-6pm. **Cafe Internet,** 2021 E Sims Way (☎385-9773). $10 per hr. Open M-F 8:30am-6pm.

Post Office: 1322 Washington St. (☎385-1600). Open M-F 9am-5pm, Sa 10am-2pm. **ZIP Code:** 98368.

ACCOMMODATIONS AND CAMPING

Many of the town's Victorian homes are B&Bs; inquire at the Chamber of Commerce. **Water St. Hotel,** 635 Water St., is a newly renovated Victorian building right downtown with fabulous views of the water and Port Townsend streets. (☎385-5467 or 800-735-9810. $50 for double with shared bath, $85 private.)

■ **Olympic Hostel (HI;** ☎385-0655), in Fort Worden State Park 1½ mi. from town. Follow the signs to the park at "W" and Cherry St. A converted WWII barracks, the Olympic offers nice clean beds, but the biggest attraction is the surrounding park and conference center—laundry, tennis courts, frequent concerts, trails, and beaches. Private rooms available. Check-in 5-10pm, check-out 9:30am. Book ahead, especially in summer. Beds $14; nonmembers $17; hikers/bikers $2 off.

Fort Flagler Hostel (HI; ☎385-1288), in Fort Flagler State Park, on gorgeous **Marrowstone Island,** 20 mi. from Port Townsend. Take State Rte. 20 to State Rte. 19 South, go 3 mi., and turn left on State Rte. 116 for 9 mi. into Fort Flagler State Park. Old military building that is a short hop to the beach but further from town. Check-in 5-10pm, lockout 10am-5pm. Open Mar.-Sept. Call if arriving late. Book ahead for weekends. Beds $14, nonmembers $17, hikers/bikers $2 off.

Fort Flagler State Park (☎385-1259). Camping in same place as the hostel. Some sites on the beach. 115 sites. Tents $14, RVs $20, hikers/bikers $6. Book ahead.

Oak Bay Jefferson County Parks (☎385-9129), off Oak Bay Rd. Open 9am-4pm. Head to Marrowstone island but turn off Rte. 116 and onto Oak Bay Rd. before you reach any island. No reservations. Lower Oak Bay: 22 sites on the shore $8. Upper Oak Bay: 22 sites $8, hookups $10.

FOOD

The **Food Coop,** 414 Kearney St., is in a converted bowling alley. Every Wednesday 3:30-6pm there is a market in their parking lot. (☎385-2883. Open M-Sa 8am-9pm, Su 9am-7pm.) **Safeway,** 442 Sims Way (☎385-2860), is open 24hr.

■ **The Elevated Ice Cream Co.,** 627 Water St. (☎385-1156), ironically on the ground floor. Serves homemade ice cream that receives rave reviews. Single scoop $1.75. If you don't want frozen treats, try the sweet shop next door. Open daily 10am-10pm.

Waterfront Pizza, 953 Water St. (☎385-6629), offers little historic ambiance but churns out a damn good pizza on a sourdough crust. 12 in. Foccaccia $4. Open daily 11am-10pm. Summer weekends 11am-11pm.

Bread and Roses, 230 Quincy St. (☎385-1044). Serves baked goods, sandwiches ($3-7), and muffins in cozy environs; the garden is gorgeous. Open daily 6:30am-4pm.

Burrito Depot, 609 Washington St. (☎385-5856). Quick, tasty Mexican food, and Thai thrown in, too. Big burritos $4-6. Open M-Sa 10:30am-8:30pm, Su 11:30am-8:30pm.

THE GIFT THAT JUST WON'T STOP GIVING.

In the early part of this century, elk were shipped from Washington to Alaska in an effort to provide more game for hunting, and mountain goats were sent from Alaska to Washington in return. The goats proliferated in Olympic National Park long after hunting was prohibited, damaging endangered native plants by grazing, trampling, wallowing, and loitering. Park Service authorities tried many ways of removing the goats, including live capture and sterilization darts, but nothing really worked. In 1995, they resolved to liquidate the goats once and for all by shooting them from helicopters. Washington Congressman Norm Dicks got this measure postponed, and has since has proposed reintroducing the native gray wolf to the park. Wolves were eliminated in the early part of this century, in an effort to provide more game for hunting. To add to the mess, a 2000 study concluded that the goats neither belong in, but nor do they substantially damage, the environment. For now, the goats are left hiding peacefully deep in the interior of the park.

SIGHTS

Port Townsend is full of huge Queen Anne and Victorian mansions. Of over 200 restored homes in the area, some have been converted into B&Bs, and two are open for tours. Free *Visit Port Townsend* has a map with short descriptions of historic buildings (available at the visitors center or museum). For more details, buy the humorous *Historic Homes* booklet ($4.50) at the **Jefferson County Museum**, at Madison and Water St., in the old brick city hall, built 1891. Here, vestiges of the town's raucous past are displayed, including a kayak parka made of seal intestines and a jail rumored to have held Jack London for a night. (☎385-1003; www.jchsmuseum.org. Open M-Sa 11am-4pm, Su 1-4pm; Jan. and Feb. weekends only. $2, under 13 $1.) The **Ann Starret Mansion**, 744 Clay St., is renowned for its frescoed ceilings and three-tiered spiral staircase. (☎385-3205 or 800-321-0644. Tours daily from noon-3pm. $2.)

Point Hudson, where Admiralty Inlet and Port Townsend Bay meet, is the hub of a small shipbuilding area and forms the corner of Port Townsend. North of Point Hudson are several miles of **beach** and the beautiful **Chetzemoka Park**, a (guess what) Victorian park at Garfield and Jackson St. **Fort Worden State Park** is a sprawling complex most easily accessed through the gates at "W" and Cherry St. (Open daily 6:30am-dusk.) In the 1900s, Fort Worden was part of the "Triangle of Fire," a defence for Puget Sound formed by **Worden** (☎344-4400), **Fort Flagler** across the bay, and **Fort Casey** on Whidbey Island. Fort Worden re-entered service in 1981 as the set for *An Officer and a Gentleman*. Three museums are on the grounds. The **Commanding Officer's Quarters** is stuffed with Victorian furniture. (Open daily June-Aug. 10am-5pm; Mar.-May and Sept.-Oct. Sa-Su 1-4pm. $1.) The **Coast Artillery Museum** is clean-cut. (☎385-0373. Open Tu-Su 11am-4pm, closed Oct.-Mar. $1.) Sea life lives above the Fort Worden pier at the **Marine Science Center**. (☎385-5582. Open Tu-Su noon-6pm; fall and spring Sa-Su noon-6pm. $3, children $2.)

ENTERTAINMENT

Port Townsend's music scene is surprisingly lively. *This Week* has the scoop on the nightlife. Steep-side **Sirens**, 823 Water St., hosts live folk and blues (F-Sa) on the deck, which has a great view. (☎379-1100. Open M-Th 4pm-2am, F-Sa noon-2am. Happy hour 4-6pm. Occasional cover.) **Upstage**, 923 Washington St., supports music from classical to country from Thursday to Saturday. (☎385-2216. Cover $3-14. Open daily 4pm-midnight.) The **Rose Theatre**, 235 Taylor St., is one fine arthouse theater which claims to make the best popcorn in the Northwest. (☎385-1089. $6, seniors $5, children $4; matinees $5.)

Every summer, **Centrum Foundation** (☎ 385-5320 or 800-733-3608; www.centrum.org) sponsors festivals in Fort Worden Park, including the **Port Townsend Blues Festival** (tickets $20) at the beginning of August, the **Festival of American Fiddle Tunes** (tickets $14) in early July, and **Jazz Port Townsend** (tickets $19-24) the third week of July. The **Port Townsend Writer's Conference** in mid-July is one of the finest in the Northwest. Well-attended guest-readings and lectures cost $5-6. Port Townsend's biggest gathering is the **Wooden Boat Festival** (☎ 385-3629), held the first weekend after Labor Day. It is organized by **The Wooden Boat Foundation**, 380 Jefferson St. (☎ 385-3628), an institute that supports lessons and races.

THE REST OF THE EASTERN PENINSULA

NEAR HOODSPORT

The first info area one passes on 101 from coming in from Olympia is the Hood Canal Ranger Station, just off of the highway in Hoodsport. (☎ 877-5254. Open daily 8am-4:30pm; winter M-F 8am-4:30pm.) This station is jointly run between the Forest and Park services, so it can answer questions about almost any destination on the peninsula. The station's turnoff also leads to two of the whole peninsula's most popular destinations. The first is a camping and hiking area on Lake Cushman known as Staircase. Staircase Campground is a major hub 16 mi. northwest of Hoodsport; take a left after 9 mi. on 119 and follow the signs. (☎ 877-5569. RV accessible. 65 sites. $10.) Lake Cushman State Park, on the way to Staircase, provides another base camp for extended backpacking trips. The park offers fine swimming beaches, showers (25¢ per 3min.), and toilets. (☎ 877-5491. Reservations 800-452-5687. 80 sites, $14. 30 full hookups, $20.) The other much sought-out place is the summit of Mt. Ellinor, also past the station. Follow Rte. 119 for 9 mi. to Forest Rd. 24, turn right and continue to Forest Rd. 2419, following signs to Jefferson Pass and Upper/Lower Trailhead. Look for signs to the Upper Trailhead along Forest Rd. #2419-04. Once on the mountain, hikers can choose either the three mile path or an equally steep but shorter journey to the summit. Those hiking on the mountain before late July should bring snow clothes.

DOSEWALLIPS (DOH-SEE-WALL-UPS)

This trailhead is reached via a long a steep drive, making it a very attractive option for people who want to reach the interior of the park without too many days of walking. At the trailhead there is a small seasonal Ranger Station to take care of any last minute needs (such as bear canisters). A pretty and popular multi-day trail leads from the trailhead across the park to a number of other well-traversed backpacking trails, including Hurricane Ridge (see p. 200). Another option is the **West Forks Dosewallip Trail,** a slightly strenuous 10½ mi. trek to the Anderson Glacier. This trail should reopen in late 2001 after being closed because of a downed bridge. Call ahead to see if this, the shortest route to any glacier in the park, is open. While there, check out **Dosewallips Campground,** at the end of Dosewallips Rd. off US 101, 27 mi. north of Hoodsport, has 30 campsites with pit toilets. Sites are spacious and very calm. (Forest Rd. 2610. No RVs. $10.)

QUILCENE

Thirty miles north of Hoodsport, the Quilcene Ranger Station (☎ 765-2200) is available to answer any questions that come up regarding the Nation Forest (Open daily 8am-4:30pm. Closed on weekends in winter.) Nearby, the Mt. Walker Viewpoint, 5 mi. south of Quilcene on US 101, is a very popular destination. A one-lane gravel road leads 4 mi. to the lookout, the highest viewpoint in the forest accessible by car. The road is steep, has sheer drop-offs, and should not be attempted in foul weather or with a temperamental car. Picnic tables perch on the east side; feast there while gazing at the north face of 7743 ft. Mt. Constance.

NORTHERN OLYMPIC PENINSULA

On the north side of the peninsula the mountains creep towards the shore, leaving only a thin strip of land that people have settled. Along this stretch of 101 spur roads regularly reach south into the park, delivering travelers to hot springs, trailheads, and mountain passes. The north strikes a good balance between the isolation of the west and the traffic of the east—solitude can be found, yet transportation is still easy to figure out, especially when using Port Angeles as a base. It is the right balance for someone with only a day or two to see the park, or who is looking to recover from a stint in the isolation of the western park.

PORT ANGELES ☎ 360

As 101 turns west on the peninsula, the traffic thins as only those headed to ONP remain. Port Angeles (PA) is the final stop: the point where the weekend traffic drops off and those here to explore remain. With the park headquarters, transportation connections, and a small, walkable downtown, it has always been a logical stop, but with the addition of a new hostel and several good places to eat, PA is now at least as much a place to recharge batteries and rest aching muscles as it is a place to pass through.

TRANSPORTATION

Buses: Olympic Bus Lines, 221 N Lincoln (☎417-0700), in the Doubletree Hotel parking lot. To **Seattle** (2½hr., 4 per day, $49 round-trip) and **Sea-Tac Airport** (3hr., 3-5 per day, $58 round-trip). **Olympic Van Tours, OVT** (☎452-3858), runs from the Olympics to **Hurricane Ridge** ($20) and **Hoh Rainforest** ($32). OVT also shuttles to trailheads.

Ferries: Two different vessels, one passengers-only, shuttle across the straits to **Victoria**. **M.V. Coho,** 101 E Railroad Ave. (☎457-4491; www.northolympic.com/coho), runs Mar.-Jan. (1¾hr.; 2-4 per day; $7.75, with bicycle $11.25, with car $30; children $4). **Victoria Express,** 115 E Railroad Ave. (☎800-633-1589; www.victoriaexpress.com), has passenger only service (1hr., $12.50, ages 5-11 $7.50, under 5 free). US and Canadian citizens crossing into Canada, children included, need valid proof of citizenship. Other internationals should check their own visa requirements. Day parking lots line Railroad Ave. near the docks ($5-8).

Public Transportation: Clallam Transit System, 830 W Lauridsen Blvd. (☎800-858-3747 or 452-4511; www.clallamtransit.com), serves **Port Angeles** and **Clallam County,** as far as **Neah Bay** and **Forks,** from the transport center on Railroad Ave. at Oak St., a block west of the ferry. Operates M-F 4:20am-5:30pm, Sa 7am-5pm. Downtown 75¢, ages 6-19 50¢, seniors 25¢; day pass $2.

Taxis: Peninsula Taxi, ☎385-1872. $2 base plus $1.75 per mi.

Car Rental: Evergreen Auto Rental, 808 E Front St. (☎452-8001). From $29 per day plus 20¢ per mi. after 100 mi. Must be 21 with proof of insurance.

PRACTICAL INFORMATION

Visitor Information: Chamber of Commerce, 121 E Railroad Ave. (☎452-2363 or 877-465-8372; www.portangeles.org), near the ferry. Ask for a guide to the town's art for a fun walking route. Open daily 10am-4pm, longer depending on staff size; winter M-F.

Outdoor Information: The **Olympic National Park (ONP) Visitor Center,** 3002 Mt. Angeles Rd. (☎565-3130), is just outside of town. See p. 190 for details. **Port Brook and News,** 104 E 1st St. (☎452-6367), has maps and advice on the region. Open M-Sa 9am-9pm, Su 10am-5pm.

Equipment Rental: Olympic Mountaineering, 140 W Front St. (☎452-0240; www.olymtn.com), rents sturdy gear (external frame pack $15 per day) with lower weekly rates. Offers climbing and hiking trips in ONP (from $75 per person for 2), as well as a small indoor climbing wall. Open M-Sa 9am-6pm, Su 10am-5pm. **Brown's Outdoor Store,** 112 W Front St. (☎457-4150), rents at low daily rates. Packs $10 per day, tents $10 per day. Call ahead. Open M-Sa 9:30am-6pm, Su noon-4pm. **Sound Bikes and Kayaks,** 120 E Front St. (☎457-1240) rents bikes for $9 per hr.; $30 per day. Leads half-day kayak trips for $40, kayak rentals alone $12 per hr. Open M-Sa 9am-5:30pm.

Laundromat: Peabody St. Coin Laundry, 212 Peabody St. at 2nd St. Wash $1.75, dry 25¢ per 10min. **24hr.**

Emergency: ☎911. **Police:** ☎452-4545. 24 hr.

Sexual Assault: Safehome, 1914 W 18th St. (☎452-4357).

Medical: **Olympic Memorial Hospital,** 939 Caroline St. (☎417-7000) at Washington St. on the waterfront. Open 24hr. **Pharmacy: Safeway** (☎457-0599), see **Food,** below.

Post Office: 424 E 1st St. (☎452-9275). Open M-F 8:30am-5pm, Sa 9am-noon. **ZIP Code:** 98362.

ACCOMMODATIONS

Countless motels are found in PA, and, keeping in mind that cleanliness is proportional to price, you can pay what you will. The least expensive motels line US 101 west of town, so cruise First St. to price shop. Winter rates drop $5-15. **Heart o' the Hills Campground,** just after the park entrance, overflows with vacationers poised to take Hurricane Ridge by storm. The campground has no hookups or showers but offers plenty of giant trees, fairly private sites, and wheelchair access. (105 sites. $10.) West on US 101 halfway between Port Angeles and Lake Crescent a 6 mi. spur road leads south to two **campgrounds** along the waterfall-rich Elwha River: **Elwha Valley** and the nearby **Altaire.** Both have drinking water, toilets, and fishing. (☎452-9191. Sites $10.) This road also has a trailhead that begins the trail to **Olympic Hot Springs,** an undeveloped spring 2½ mi. in.

Thor Town Hostel, 316 N Race St. (☎452-0931), 7 blocks east of the city center and 1 mi. north of ranger station. When the hammer stops and the dust settles (expected late '01) an 18 bed hostel in a renovated 100-year old house will be left standing. Bike rentals $8 per day, trailhead shuttles, and bus info. Reception 5-9pm. $12, doubles $28.

Ruffles Motel, 812 E 1st St. (☎457-7788), is slightly ahead in terms of the price-grime curve. Nice rooms, rose-trimmings, and cable, but no A/C. Singles $46, doubles $54.

FOOD

If Port Angeles had a nickname, it would be "City of Buffets." Every place has them, and they are often a good deal. For a breakfast buffet, try the **Best Western Olympic Lodge**, 140 Del Guzzia (☎452-4995), a $6 public all-you-can-eat. There is plenty of seafood in town—finding a cheap place to eat is the trick. Picnickers can shop at **Safeway,** 110 E 3rd St., at Lincoln St. (☎457-0788. Open 24hr.)

Thai Peppers, 222 N Lincoln. A new restaurant in town, this place keeps PA natives happy. Lunch specials $6, dinners $8-10, and the seafood is excellent. Open M-Sa 11am-2:30pm and 4:30-9pm. Sundays open for dinner only.

India Oven, 222 N Lincoln (☎452-5170). The centerpiece here is their daily all-you-can-eat, $7, and the food is good. Regular dishes $8-11. Open daily 11am-10pm.

La Casita, 203 E Front St. (☎452-2289). Seafood burritos ($8) stuffed with gobs of crab, shrimp, and fish. Free, all-you-can-eat tortilla chips to snarf between margaritas ($2). Open M-Th 11am-9pm, F-Sa 11am-10pm, Su noon-9pm.

Bella Italia, 118 E 1st St. (☎457-5442), gets rave reviews. Hungry vegetarians can sit down to a hunk of lasagna ($10) or a plate of spaghetti ($7) in a romantic, candle-lit booth. Open M-F 11am-10pm, Sa-Su 11am-11pm.

Sirens, 134 W Front St. (☎417-9152). Grab a final beer before hitting the trail. Open mic (Th). Local talent jams F-Sa ($3). Entrees $7-10. Open M-Th 11:30am-1:30am.

SIGHTS AND OUTDOOR ACTIVITIES

The main draw to Port Angeles is the National Park, which looms behind the town in the form of Mt. Angeles. Nevertheless, there are several places to enjoy outside of the park if a change of pace is what you are looking for.

The **Fine Arts Center,** 1203 E Lauridsen Blvd., near the national park visitors center, has art exhibits by Northwest artists in a small gallery space. The surrounding five acres show sculpture in a very entertaining art park. (☎457-3532; www.olympus.net/community/pafac. Open Tu-Su 11am-5pm. Free.) Several sights are found just to the east of PA in the Dungeness area. Take 101 east about 4 mi. and turn left. A 5 mi. (2hr.) trail out on the 7 mi. **Dungeness Spit,** the largest natural sandhook in the nation, leads to a lighthouse with free tours. (Open 9am until 2hr. before sunset.) The Dungeness Spit also houses a small **campground.** Nearby, the **Olympic Game Farm,** 1423 Ward Rd. (☎683-4295 or 800-778-4295; www.northolympic.com/gamefarm), off Woodcock St., is a zoo and retirement home for movie stars. Drive by zebras, llamas, rhinos, and bears or take a guided walking tour. (Open daily 9am-6pm for driving; 10am-3pm for walking. Driving tour 4 mi. $9, children $7. Walking tour 1hr. $10. Children $8.)

While most come to the ridge just to gawk, getting out on your feet is the best way to take in the views without the chatter of families and rangers. Before July, walking on the ridge usually involves snow-stepping. On weekends from late December to late March the Park Service organizes free guided **snowshoe walks** atop the ridge. **High Ridge** (½ mi. loop, 30min.) is a paved trail just off of the Hurricane Ridge parking lot, with access to a view north from **Sunset Point. Klahhane Ridge** (3¾ mi., 5hr.) is a more strenuous hike, leading 2¾ mi. on flat ground, and then turning for 1 mi. of tough switchbacking to actually get to Klahhane.

Accessible by road directly from Port Angeles, **Hurricane Ridge** boasts the best drive-up views of the park's mountainous interior. Clear days promise splendid views of Mt. Olympus and Vancouver Island, both set against a foreground of snow and indigo lupine. RVs and tourists crowd the ridge by day, but seclusion can be found at dawn and on many short trails that originate here. To get into the park, take Race Rd. south from 101 and turn right shortly after the **ONP Visitors Center.** The station posts info on visibility up above, or call ahead (☎565-3132).

LAKE CRESCENT

A massive body of water right in the center of the peninsula and just off 101 is a tempting destination and one that is not often bypassed. Just a short ride away from Port Angeles, it makes a good quick trip for sun and a swim. Storm King Ranger Station is on a small peninsula in the center of the lake and offers all of the regular services. (☎928-3380. Open daily in summer 10am-5pm.)

At the west end of the lake just past the Fairholm General Store there is a small road that heads to **Fairholm Campground,** which has wheelchair access, beautiful moss covered trees, picnic areas, and some sites right on the lakeshore. (☎928-3380. 87 sites, $10.) Several strenuous hikes head out from the lake up the steep slopes. Talk to the station to pick your poison. The **Lake Crescent Lodge,** next to the Storm King Station, rents rowboats to help in summertime seduction. (☎928-3211. Rentals 7am to an hour before dusk, $8.50 per hr.) There is also swimming along the shore. **Fishing** is popular on the water—but only catch-and-release is allowed.

SOL DUC HOTSPRINGS

One popular trail runs along **Sol Duc Hotsprings.** Just west of the tip of Lake Crescent a road turns south and follows the Sol Duc river south for 12½ mi. into a large green valley. At the end lies a beacon for every tired traveler—hot baths, in the **Sol Duc Hotsprings Resort.** Hiking is also good in the area; for information and permits the **Eagle Ranger Station,** just before the springs, is the place to stop (☎327-3534. Open daily in summer, 8am-4:30pm). With its location, it is no surprise that the **Sol Duc Hot Springs Campground,** often fills by 3pm. It is found just past the resort. (☎327-3534. Wheelchair-accessible restrooms. Picnic sites. 82 sites. $12.)

PORT ANGELES ■ 201

With trails leaving the resort, ranger station, and **Sol Duc Trailhead** (at the end of the road, 1 mi. from the campground), Sol Duc is a good leaping off point, or better yet given the hot baths, return point. **Lover's Lane Trail** (6 mi. loop, 2½hr.) departs the resort and leads to Sol Duc falls before looping back. The lazy or busy just go from the Sol Duc trailhead and make it there in 1½ mi. (1hr.). **Mink Lake** (2½ mi., 5hr.) climbs through a dense forest to a small mountain lake. After this there will be no guilt about pampering oneself in a hot spring. Strenuous. 1500 ft. gain.

The **Resort** is not inexpensive, but still affordable, with special end of day rates and all-day admission. Natural spring water is filtered into three man-made mineral pools. To avoid the hot water and sulfur smell, you can also jump in the large chlorinated swimming pool. (☎ 327-3583; www.northolympic.com/solduc. Open late May to Sept. daily 9am-9pm; spring and fall Th noon-6pm, F-Su 9am-6pm. $10; ages 4-12 $7.50; last 2 hrs twilight rate $6.50. Suit, locker, towel rental $3 each. Showers $3 without admission to the pool.)

NEAH BAY AND CAPE FLATTERY

At the westernmost point on the Juan de Fuca Strait and well away from the National Park is **Neah Bay,** the only town in the **Makah Reservation.** The community has recently become famous for its revival of its gray-whale hunt and is renowned for the "Pompeii of the Pacific," a remarkably-preserved 500-year-old Makah village buried in a landslide. Gorgeous **Cape Flattery** is the most northwesterly point in the contiguous US. James Cook gave the Cape its name in 1778, because it "flattered us with the hopes of finding a harbor." Flattery got them nowhere; the nearest port is Port Angeles, 50 mi. away.

You can reach Neah Bay and Cape Flattery by an hour-long detour from **US 101.** From Port Angeles, **Rte. 112** leads west 72 mi. to Neah Bay. Or, from the south, **Rte. 113** runs north from Sappho to **Rte. 112. Clallam Transit System** runs from Port Angeles; take bus #14 from Oak St. to Sappho (1¼hr.), then #16 to Neah Bay. (☎ 452-4511 or 800-858-3747. 4-5 times per day. $1; seniors 50¢; ages 6-19 50¢.)

ACCOMMODATIONS AND CAMPING. Neah Bay caters to those who fish, and it is not the best place to spend the night. Try to plan your day so you can do the round-trip and crash somewhere else. If stuck, try the oceanside **Cape Motel** on Rte. 112 for small but clean rooms, or sack out in a rustic shanty or tentsite. (☎ 645-2250. Office open 7:30am-10pm. Rooms $48-68; shanty singles $18; $25 as doubles; Sites $12.) **Shipwreck Pt. Campground,** 8 mi. east of Neah Bay, has tent sites close to thee beach along the Juan de Fuca Strait, and nice bathrooms. (☎ 963-2744. $15 for 2 adult, each extra guest $3; RVs $20.)

SIGHTS. The **Makah Cultural and Research Center,** in Neah Bay on Rte. 112, is just inside the reservation, opposite the Coast Guard station. The center presents beautiful artifacts preserved by a mudslide from the archaeological site at Cape Alava. The center also serves as the town's social and cultural center. The Makah Nation, whose recorded history is 2000 years old, lives, fishes, and produces artwork on this land. (☎ 645-2711. Open June-Aug. daily 10am-5pm; Sept.-May M-F 10am-5pm. $4; seniors and students $3; under 5 free. Free tours at 11am W-Su.) During Makah Days, in the last weekend in August, Native Americans from around the region come for canoe races, dances, and bone games (a form of gambling). Visitors are welcome and the salmon is delightful. Call the center for details.

Cape Flattery can be reached through Neah Bay, 8 mi. further northwest. Pick up directions at the Makah Center, or just take the road through town until it turns to dirt. Follow the "Marine Viewing Area" sign once you hit gravel, and continue for another 4 mi. to a small circular parking area, where a trailhead leads half a mile to Cape Flattery. At 3pm, a free, short guided hike leaves from the trailhead. You'll know you're close to the amazing views of **Tatoosh** and **Vancouver Island** when you hear the sound of Tatoosh's bullhorn. The road is excruciatingly bumpy, but the hike reveals some of the more beautiful stretches of ocean around. To the south, the Makah Reservation's **beaches** are solitary and peaceful; respectful visitors are welcome to wander.

Dayhikers and backpackers adore the 9 mi. loop that begins at Ozette Lake, an ONP area accessible from 112. The trail forms a triangle with two 3 mi. legs leading along boardwalks from Ozette through the rainforest. One heads toward sea stacks at **Cape Alava,** the other to a sublime beach at **Sand Point.** A 3 mi. hike down the coast links the two legs, passing ancient native petroglyphs. The entire area is mostly prairie and coastal forest but presents plenty of sand to slog through. Overnighters must make permit reservations in advance; spaces fill quickly in summer. The **Ozette Ranger Station** has further info. (☎963-2725. Open intermittently.) Call the visitors center outside of PA at 565-3100 for permit reservations.

WESTERN OLYMPIC PENINSULA

Swinging wildly between rainforest and empty beaches, highway 101 traces a manic path through what is a truly stunning landscape. The western park is wild in so many ways. Many fewer travelers drive the extra distance to this side of the peninsula. The landscape has been much less sculpted by humans, and the opportunities to enjoy the beauty are so many that people are quickly dispersed. The west side of the Olympic Peninsula is a truly magical place, one that will enchant a visitor for any period of time.

FORKS ☎907

Between ONP's northern and western rims lies the logging town of Forks, the perfect place to stop along US 101 and grab a bite to eat—in fact, the only place to stop. Forks lies two hours west of Port Angeles and offers the widest selection of services in the Western region.

■♫ **ORIENTATION AND PRACTICAL INFORMATION. Clallam Transit** (☎452-4511 or 800-858-374) Rte. #14 serves Forks from **Port Angeles** (M-F; 7 per day; $1.25, disabled and seniors and ages 6-19 $1). The **Forks Chamber of Commerce,** south of town, offers advice and maps, as well as tours through a real saw mill. (☎374-2531 or 800-443-6757. Open daily 10am-4pm.) The **Department of Natural Recources Main Office,** just off US 101 on the north side of Forks, right next to Tillicum Park, hands out maps of state land on the peninsula. Since tourists who actually stop here are a rarity, DNR is happy to help. (☎374-6131. Open M-F 8am-4:30pm.) **Police:** (☎374-2223), in the City Hall on E. Division. Open daily 6am-6pm. **Hospital:** (☎374-6271), just west of 101 on Bogachiel Way. **Post office:** At Spartan Ave. and A St., east of US 101. Open M-F 9am-5pm, Sa 10am-noon. **ZIP Code:** 98331.

┏┓ **ACCOMMODATIONS AND FOOD.** The best roof to sleep under on the Western peninsula, the **Rainforest Hostel,** 169312 US 101, is not in Forks, but 20 mi. south between Hoh Rain Forest and Kalaloch. Family rooms and dorms are available, as are outside trailers for couples or people allergic to the resident dog and cat. The Rain Forest is a true resource for travelers, with laundry ($2), snacks, ride-sharing, info on buses, and parking. To get there, follow the hostel signs off US 101, 6 mi. south of the Hoh turnoff or 4 mi. north of Ruby Beach. Buses travel to the hostel from North Shore Brannon's Grocery in Quinault daily 9am, 1pm, and 4:35pm. (☎374-2270; www.thortown.com, a URL shared with PA's hostel. Check-in 5-9pm. Morning **chore** required. Beds $12; family rooms $1 plus $12 per person, $6 per child. Camping available for bikers, hikers, and bussers for $6 per person.)

For eats, the **Raindrop Cafe,** 111 E A St., at S Forks Ave., serves up breakfast until 11am, names its burgers after clouds ($3.50-6.50), and serves seriously delicious $7 salads. (☎374-6612. Open M-Sa 6am-9pm, Su 6am-8pm; winter daily 6am-8pm.) Off the highway, grab groceries and coffee at **Forks Thriftway,** 950 S Forks Ave. (☎374-6161. Open M-Su 8am-10pm.)

MORA

A quiet beach and campsite that doubles as a trailhead for long beach-following hikes is found just 10 mi. west of Forks. In the morning, a haze hangs over the beach and next to no one is to be seen, making this area a perfect place to camp. This area is reached by taking Hwy. 110 west from just north of Forks.

Mora Campground is a sprawling 97-site campground that sees quite a bit of traffic from beach-goers. It offers evening programs on weekend nights, as well as toilets and water. (☎374-5460. Sites $10.) **Beach camping** is permitted both north and south of the **Mora Ranger Station.** For info north, see hiking below. To camp south a permit is required, as well as a short drive to just before **La Push.** From there a trail leads down the beach—camping is permitted south of Third Beach and north of Oil City. Before hiking or camping on the coast, pick up a required overnight permit, a park map, a tide table, and the useful *Olympic Coastal Strip Info* brochure at a ranger station. Set up camp well above the highest line of tidal debris. North from Mora's **Rialto Beach,** 17 mi. of secluded beach snakes up to **Shi-Shi Beach.** Camping is allowed anywhere north of Ellen Creek with overnight backcountry permit. The options for overnight are many, and dayhikers often choose to take an abbreviated version of the same route, stopping at **Hole-in-the-Wall** (1½ mi. round-trip, 2hr.). Rialto beach is a sight in itself. To get there, head 1½ mi. west from Mora Campground.

HOH RAIN FOREST

The place to go to see the western rain forests, Hoh bears the weight of many guests. The sights are spectacular, the growth is amazing, and the 18 mi. drive into the park from 101 is an enjoyable patchwork of old growth, wildflowers, and riverbeds. Turn off from 101 onto the Hoh Valley Rd., and drive about 12 mi. to the park entrance booth. Check out **Hoh Rainforest Visitors Center,** for backcountry permits and assistance in designing a backcountry route. (☎374-6925. Open daily mid-June to Labor Day 9am-6pm; Labor Day to mid-June 9am-4:30pm.) The park maintains 88 **campsites** near the visitors center ($10) with drinking water and toilets, but limited facilities for the handicapped. Two free DNR campsites closer to 101, **Minnie Peterson** and **Willoughby Creek** are primitive and without treated water. No reservations are taken, so they are worth checking out to see what is open.

Hikers regularly file into the Hoh parking lot, returning from several popular routes that thread into the park's interior from the rainforest. The Hoh River Trail parallels the Hoh River for 18 mi., a two-day trip that traces through old growth forests and lowlands to **Blue Glacier** on the shoulder of **Mount Olympus.** Shy Roosevelt elk, the ever-contested northern spotted owl, and the gods of ancient Greece inhabit this area. Several campsites lie along this hike; inquire at the visitors center for exact location. Closer by, the three-quarter-mile wheelchair-accessible **Hall of Mosses Trail** offers a whirlwind tour of rainforest vegetation. The slightly longer **Spruce Nature Trail** leads 1¼ mi. through old growth forest, passing more varied vegetation along the banks of the Hoh River.

LAKE QUINAULT

This large lake at the southwestern corner of ONP sustains a small enclave of weekend getawayers, anglers, and hikers, many of them bypassing the rest of the peninsula and coming straight north to the lake via Aberdeen. On the southern, more populated side of the lake, the Forest Service operates an info center at the **Quinault Ranger Station,** 353 S Shore Rd. (☎288-2525. Open M-F 8am-4:30pm, Sa-Su 9am-4pm; winter M-F 9am-4:30pm.) On the northern side of the lake the **Quinault River Ranger Station** performs similar services, but from within the national park, 6 mi. from the highway. (☎288-2444. Open daily 8:30am-5pm in summer; closed winters.) Campers can drop their gear lakeside in **Willaby Campgrounds,** a quarter-mile before the Forest Service Ranger Station along the south shore of the lake. (☎288-2213. Sites $14.) Be aware—like the rest of the area, this campsite fills quickly. The **Lake Quinault Lodge** (☎288-2900 or 800-562-6672), next to the southern ranger station, rents canoes ($12 per hr.), seacycles ($17), rowboats ($10), and kayaks ($15) from their posh establishment.

Lake Quinault is surrounded by a great network of trails. Stop at either ranger station and they will provide a detailed photocopy of trails in the area. **The North Fork trailhead** is 20 mi. up North Shore Rd. and starts one of the parks's most popular multi-day hikes. It stretches 44 mi. north across the park, finishing at **Whiskey Bend** on the north rim near Elwha campgrounds. The week-long trip is one of the easier ones into the heart of the Olympics and has 17 campsites along the way (backcountry permit required). **Three Lakes Point** is an exquisite summit that often remains covered with snow into July. The 7 mi. hike (one-way) from North Fork runs through yellow cedar and prime amphibian habitat. Give the trip several days. **Dayhikes** depart the Quinault Ranger Station, including the 4 mi. **Quinault Lake Loop** and the half-mile **Maple Glade Trail.** Many more are found on the north of the lake, including the new 1 mi. **Kestner Homestead Trail.**

PACIFIC COAST ☎ 360

Approaching its northern terminus, US 101 travels along the final of three states' coastal shores. Small towns, phenomenal shellfish, and sparkling beaches beckon. Unfortunately, red tide plagues the shellfish population with a bacteria that can be fatal to humans. Check with visitors centers or www.doh.wa.gov/ehp/sf/biotoxin.htm to see which beaches are open.

WILLAPA BAY ☎ 360

Willapa Bay stretches between the Long Beach Peninsula and the Washington mainland just north of the Washington-Oregon border and the mouth of the Columbia River. Home to the last unpolluted estuary in the nation, this is an excellent place to watch birdlife, especially in late spring and early fall. US 101 passes the bay as it winds along the Pacific Coast toward Oregon. From Olympic National Park to the north, the highway passes Grays Harbor and the industrial cities of **Aberdeen** and **Hoquiam** at the mouth of the **Chehalis River.** As US 101 passes through Willapa Bay's sparkling sloughs, fantastic views compensate for the protected bay's ban on swimming and sunning. From the north, stop at the headquarters of the **Willapa National Wildlife Refuge,** just off US 101 on the left, 12 mi. north of the junction between US101 and Rte. 103 by Chinook. The headquarters offer info on the Canada geese, loons, grebes, cormorants, and trumpeter swans. (☎ 484-3482. Open M-F 7:30am-4pm.) Rangers can give directions to several accessible hiking trails in the region, including **Leadbetter Point** at the tip of the Long Beach Peninsula. **Long Island** is home to five limited-use **campgrounds,** all inaccessible by car. Reaching the island requires finding a boat or bumming a ride on one (boats launch from the headquarters). After reaching the island, hike 2½ mi. along the island's main road to reach the **Trail of Ancient Cedars.**

LONG BEACH PENINSULA ☎ 360

The 28 mi. of unbroken sand that is Long Beach Peninsula is an overwhelming frenzy of kitsch and souvenir shops broken only sporadically by calm forests and beautiful ocean views. Accessible by US 101 and Rte. 103, every town has a clearly marked beach access road (unmarked roads end in private property). Fishing, swimming, boating, and kite-flying are how residents recuperate from pounding winter storms. **Clamming season** lasts from October to mid-March (but beware red tide). **Short Stop,** in the Shell Station across the street from the visitors center sells non-resident licenses (annual license $22, two-day license $7) along with tips and tide tables. The peninsula, with 500 acres of **cranberry bogs,** is one of only four regions in the US where cranberries are grown. Most of the bogs are in **Grayland** along Cranberry Rd., parallel to Hwy. 105; berries are harvested in October.

Like most other towns along the bay, **Ilwaco** was nearly devastated when depleted salmon stocks required a shutdown of the fishery for several years. Salmon steaks are plentiful along the waterfront where the industry is beginning to recover. **Pacific Salmon Charters** leads 8hr. fishing tours. (☎ 642-3466 or 800-831-2695. From $70. Open daily at 5:30am.) The **Long Beach Peninsula Visitors Bureau** is

5min. south of Long Beach on US 101. (☎ 642-2400 or 800-451-2542; www.funbeach.com. Open M-Sa 9am-5pm, Su 10am-4pm. Call for winter hours.) **Pacific Transit** sends buses from Long Beach as far north as Aberdeen. (☎ 642-9418. 85¢; exact change required.) **Local buses** run up and down the peninsula all day. Schedules are available in post offices and visitors centers on the peninsula (local service Sa-Su only). During the last week in August, flyers from Thailand, China, Japan, and Australia compete in the **International Kite Festival**.

Among the cheap places to hit the hay on the Peninsula is **Sand-Lo-Motel,** 1910 Pacific Hwy. (☎ 642-2600. Rooms $50 and up; rates drop in winter.) A haven from the craziness is **My Mom's Pie Kitchen,** 1113 S Pacific Hwy., a delicious respite from steak houses and greasy spoons. (☎ 642-2342. Open W-Sa 11am-6pm.) **Marsh's Free Museum,** 409 S Pacific Way (☎ 642-2188), is home to a mechanical fortune teller, Jake the petrified alligator-man, and honky-tonk souvenirs (open, ironically, whenever tourists bring money). For the best meal around, head down Hwy. 103 in Ocean Park to historic **Oysterville**. The star draw of this tiny, whitewashed town, is **Oysterville Sea Farms,** at 1st and Clark, which raises and dishes out a certain mollusk. (☎ 665-6585. Open daily 10am-5pm.)

THE COLUMBIA RIVER ESTUARY ☎ 360

Several miles south of Long Beach on Washington's southern border, **Cape Disappointment** guards the Columbia River Estuary. In 1788, British fur trader Captain John Meares, frustrated by repeated failures to cross the treacherous Columbia River sandbar, gave the large promontory guarding the river mouth its name. Over 300 years, almost 2000 vessels have been wrecked, stranded, or sunk where the Columbia meets the ocean, and even today the Coast Guard keeps busy during the frequent squalls. **Fort Columbia State Park** lies on US 101 northwest of the Astoria Megler Bridge, 1 mi. east of **Chinook** on the west side of the highway. The park **interpretive center** recreates life at the fort and describes the indigenous Chinook people who once occupied this land. (☎ 777-8221. Open Memorial Day to Oct. 1 daily 10am-5pm; call for winter hours.)

Three miles southwest of Ilwaco, at the southern tip of the Peninsula, **Fort Canby State Park** offers camping and a megadose of Lewis and Clark (open daily dawn-dusk). The park was the dynamic duo's final destination, and now boasts two lighthouses and a well-pruned campground packed with RVs. The sites fill up quickly in summer. (☎ 642-3078 or 800-452-5687. 240 sites $12; hookups $17; hiker/biker sites $6; cabins and yurts sleep 4 for $35. Reservation fee $6.) At the end of the main road, the spaceship-shaped **Lewis and Clark Interpretive Center** hovers above the ruins of the fort. Inside, a winding display documents their expedition from its Missouri origins to the party's arrival at the mouth of the Columbia. (Open daily 10am-5pm.) The **North Head Lighthouse,** built in 1898, is accessible by a gravel path in the northwest corner of the park. The **Cape Disappointment Lighthouse,** built in 1856, is the oldest lighthouse in the Pacific Northwest. In the southeast corner of the park, its distinctive red light can be reached by walking up a steep hill from the Coast Guard station parking lot, or by following a narrow, fairly steep trail from the interpretive center. For a magnificent beach-level view of both lighthouses, drive through the campground area past **Waikiki Beach** on the **North Jetty.** Waikiki is the only beach safe enough for swimming and is a solitary spot for winter beachcombing and ship watching.

> **THE CITY OF (NO) LIGHT.** You may notice dim lights in state buildings and supermarkets across the Northwest. An altruistic move by an environmentally-conscious state? Alas, young idealist, we fear the world is not so selfless; the motivation is less about altruism and more about blackmail. Because the western United States is connected by an electrical network, the northwest quickly felt the spring 2001 power shortage in California. Utilities demanded 10% reductions in usage or threatened to raise prices up to 300%. Folks responded with a lot of grumbling, especially about their (least) favorite state down south, but they have made changes, stalling drastic price raises.

THE CASCADE REGION

Sprawling in the rain shadow of the Cascades, the hills and valleys of the Columbia River Basin foster little more than sagebrush, tumbleweed, and tiny wildflowers among unirrigated dunes. Where the watershed has been tapped, however, a patchwork of farmland yields bumper crops of fruit and wine. Seeking the best of the region, travelers take high alpine routes through the Cascades, where dry hills give way to uncommonly green beauty in the mountains. The Cascades are most accessible in July, August, and September. Many high mountain passes are snowed in during the rest of the year, making access difficult and anything beside skiing and snowshoeing just about impossible. Mounts Baker, Vernon, Glacier, Rainier, Adams, and St. Helens are accessible by four major roads. The North Cascades Hwy. (Rte. 20) is the most breathtaking and provides access to North Cascades National Park. Scenic US 2 leaves Everett for Stevens Pass and descends along the Wenatchee River. Rte. 20 and US 2 are often traveled in sequence as the Cascade Loop. US 12 approaches Mt. Rainier National Park through White Pass and provides access to Mt. St. Helens from the north. I-90 sends four lanes from Seattle to the ski resorts of Snoqualmie Pass and eastward. From the west the state is accessible by bus on I-90 and US 2, and the train parallels I-90. Rainstorms and evening traffic can slow hitching; locals warn against thumbing Rte. 20.

MOUNT ST. HELENS ☎ 360

After two months of mounting volcanic activity, Mount St. Helens erupted with a cataclysmic blast on May 18, 1980, transforming what had been a perfect mountain cone into a crater one mile wide and two miles long. The force of the ash-filled blast crumbled 1300 ft. of rock and razed forests, strewing trees like charred matchsticks. Ash from the crater rocketed 17 mi. upward, circling the globe and blackening the region's sky for days. Debris from the volcano flooded Spirit Lake and choked the region's watersheds. Mt. St. Helens is made up of the middle third of the Gifford Pinchot National Forest, as well as the Mount St. Helens National Volcanic Monument. The monument is part National Park, part laboratory, and encompasses most of the area around the volcano affected by the explosion. This ashen landscape, striking for its initially bleak expanses, is steadily recovering from the explosion. Parts of the monument are off-limits to the public due to experiments, and hikers are obliged to keep to the handful of trails through such areas. Due to federal budget cuts many of the services currently offered on the mountain are slated to be cut back or cancelled. Call ahead to be sure, especially regarding early morning and winter hours.

✷ ORIENTATION

To make the **western approach** (the most popular and worthwhile of the approaches, see p. 208), take Exit 49 off **I-5** and use **Rte. 504,** otherwise known as the **Spirit Lake Memorial Hwy.** The brand-new 52 mi. road has wide shoulders and astounding views of the crater. For most, this is the quickest and easiest daytrip to the mountain, and includes the Mount St. Helens Visitor Center, the Coldwater Ridge Visitor Center, and the Johnston Ridge Observatory. A **southern approach** (see p. 209)on **Rte. 503** skirts the side of the volcano until it connects with **Forest Service Rd. 90.** From there, **Forest Service Rd. 83** leads to lava caves and the Climber's Bivouac, a launch pad for forays up the mountain. Views from the south side don't show the recent destruction, but the green glens and remnants of age-old lava and mud flows make up for it with great hiking and camping. To make a **northern approach** (see p. 210), take **US 12** east from I-5 (Exit 68). The towns of Mossyrock, Morton, and Randle along US 12 offer the **closest major services** to the monument. From US 12, **Forest Service Rd. 25** heads south to Forest Service Rd. 99,

ORIENTATION ■ 207

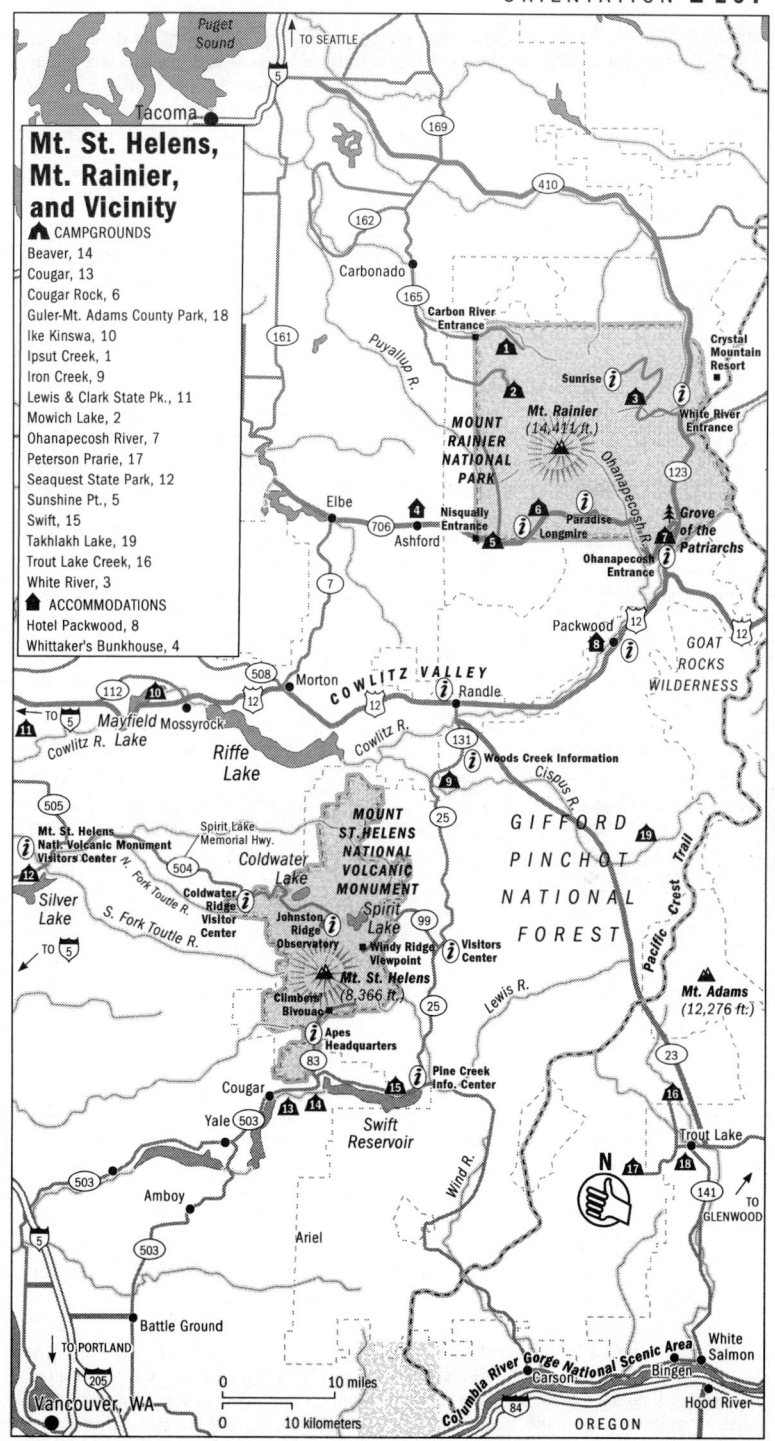

Mt. St. Helens, Mt. Rainier, and Vicinity

▲ CAMPGROUNDS
Beaver, 14
Cougar, 13
Cougar Rock, 6
Guler-Mt. Adams County Park, 18
Ike Kinswa, 10
Ipsut Creek, 1
Iron Creek, 9
Lewis & Clark State Pk., 11
Mowich Lake, 2
Ohanapecosh River, 7
Peterson Prarie, 17
Seaquest State Park, 12
Sunshine Pt., 5
Swift, 15
Takhlakh Lake, 19
Trout Lake Creek, 16
White River, 3

⌂ ACCOMMODATIONS
Hotel Packwood, 8
Whittaker's Bunkhouse, 4

which leads 16 mi. into the most devastated parts of the monument. Travelers can stop by the famous and majestic Spirit Lake, and marvel at the huge expanses of blown down forest. Although the monument itself contains no established **campgrounds,** a number are scattered throughout the surrounding national forest. See individual approaches for listings of campgrounds. Talking to a ranger is always your best option.

◨ PRACTICAL INFORMATION

Entrance Fee: There are 2 main types of fees associated with Mt. St. Helens. The first is the **Monument Pass**—this one-day, multi-site pass allows access to almost every center on the western approach, as well as Ape Cave. It can be purchased as a multi-site pass everywhere it is needed ($6, ages 4-15 $2, 3 and under free), or it can be purchased as a single site pass, which allows access to only one area ($3, ages 4-15 $1). Areas of the monument that do not require a Monument Pass most likely require the second fee, a **Northwest Forest Pass,** which will take care of the entire northern approach, as well as most of the southern area ($5 per day, $30 annually). Now for a twist: the purchase price of an **Annual Northwest Forest Pass** includes a card that entitles one person access to all areas requiring a Monument Pass. If that wasn't enough, climbing the mountain requires a whole separate set of permits (see **Climbing** p. 210).

Visitors Information: There are 9 visitors centers and info stations, listed below by approach. Those on the western approach are the most popular.

Publications: *The Volcano Review,* free at all visitors centers and ranger stations, contains a map, copious information, and schedules of activities. The *Road Guide to Mount St. Helens* ($6), available at visitors centers, is more thorough.

Forest Service Information: Gifford Pinchot National Forest Headquarters, 10600 NE 51st Circle, Vancouver, WA 98682 (☎891-5000, recording 891-5009; www.fs.fed.us/gpnf). Info on camping and hiking within the forest. Additional **ranger stations** and **visitor information** at **Randle,** 10024 US 12 (☎497-1100) and **Packwood,** 13068 US 12 (☎497-1172), both north of the mountain on US 12.

Monument Headquarters, 42218 NE Yale Bridge Rd., Amboy, 98601 (☎247-3900, recording 247-3903), 4 mi. north of Amboy on Rte. 503. This is *the* place to call or write for any questions prior to the trip: road conditions, permit availability, access, etc. Open daily 7:30am-5pm.

Radio: 530 AM. Road closures and ranger hours. Only in winter.

Emergency: ☎911.

WESTERN APPROACH: RTE. 504

◨ VISITORS CENTERS

Mount St. Helens Visitor Center (☎274-2100; 24hr. recorded info 274-2103), opposite Seaquest State Park. A great introduction to the explosive events of 1980. See the film, a manmade lava cave, and other interactive geological displays. Learn how a volcano works before you see its aftermath. A mile-long hike through 2500-year-old wetlands is also offered. Open daily 9am-5pm. 16min. film shown twice per hour.

Forest Learning Center (☎414-3439). The Weyerhaeuser Lumber Company sponsors this center, which houses interesting exhibits on logging and the reforestation of the surrounding timber downed by the explosion. Take the time and watch the video that explains how logging is done. Open May-Oct. 10am-6pm. Free.

Coldwater Ridge Visitor Center (☎274-2131; fax 274-2129). Superb view of the crater, along with trails leading to **Coldwater Lake.** Emphasis on the area's recolonization by living things through exhibits, a short film, and a ¼ mi. trail. Picnic areas, interpretive talks, and a gift shop and snack bar. Open daily 10am-6pm. Call for winter hours.

Johnston Ridge Observatory (☎274-2140), at the end of Rte. 504. Geological exhibits and the best view from the road of the steaming lava dome and crater. The center is named for David Johnston, a geologist who predicted the May 18, 1980 eruption, stayed to study it, and was killed. Fantastic wide screen 22min. film and exhibits emphasizing survivors of the blast. Open daily May-Oct. 10am-6pm.

ACCOMMODATIONS AND FOOD

The only non-camping options close to the park are a few expensive motels that cluster around I-5, Exit 49, near the intersection of Rte. 504. Despite high prices, they book solid in the summer. Try the **Mt. St. Helens Motel**, 1340 Mt. St. Helens Way NE in **Castle Rock**, 5 mi. from the Mt. St. Helens Visitor Center on Rte. 504. (☎274-7721. Free local calls, fridge, TVs, morning coffee, and laundry facilities. Singles $57; doubles $75.) **Seaquest State Park** opposite the Mt. St. Helens Visitor Center, is easy to reach off I-5, and the closest to the park with facilities. (☎274-8633, reservations 800-452-5687. Reservations essential. Wheelchair accessible. Pay showers. 92 sites, $14; 16 full hookups $20; 4 primitive walk-in sites $5.) If your coolers and stomachs are empty, Castle Rock is the best place to refuel. Supermarkets and convenience stores lie on the west side of Hwy. 5, while fast food joints and a few restaurants sit on the east. Papa Pete throws a mean and inexpensive pizza at **Papa Pete's Pizza,** 1163 Mt. St. Helens Way NE. (☎274-4271. Open daily 10am-11pm.)

HIKING

The 1hr. drive from the Mt. St. Helens Visitor Center to Johnston Ridge offers spectacular views of the crater and rebounding ecosystem, with plenty of opportunities to park the car and walk along short, well-marked trails. The **Boundary Trail** leads from the Johnston Ridge Observatory to Spirit Lake (3 mi. to the lake), and continues 52 mi. to Mt. Adams through sensitive terrain.

SOUTHERN APPROACH: RTE. 503

VISITORS CENTERS

Pine Creek Information Station, 17 mi. east of Cougar on Rd. 90, shows a short interpretive film of the eruption. Also the only place in the south of the park with free water to fill up bottles. Open June-Sept. daily 9:30am-5:30pm.

Apes' Headquarters, at Ape Cave on Rd. 8303, 3 mi. north of the Rd. 83-Rd. 90 junction (15min. from Cougar). Rangers dish out rental lanterns and guide 45min. lantern walks into the 1900-year-old lava tube daily from 10:30am-4:30pm, every hour on the half hour. On the weekends arrive early to snag a spot. Dress warmly—cave is 42°F. Open late-May to Sept. daily 10am-5:30pm.

CAMPING

Swift Campground, 30min. east of Cougar on Rd. 90 and just west of the Pine Creek Information Station, has 93 spacious sites on Swift Reservoir. It is one of the most popular campgrounds in the area. (☎503-813-6666. $12.) **Cougar Campground** and **Beaver Bay,** 2 and 4 mi. east of Cougar respectively, along Yale Lake; Cougar Lake has 60 sites ($15) that are more spread out and private than Beaver Bay's 78 sites ($15).

OUTDOOR ACTIVITIES

SPELUNKING

The **Ape Cave** lies 5 mi. east of Cougar, just off of Road 83. The cave is a broken 2½ mi. lava tube formed by a less explosive eruption over 1900 years ago. When exploring the cave, wear a jacket and sturdy shoes, and take at least two flashlights or lanterns. The Lower Cave's easy travel attracts the feet of most visitors, but the Upper Cave offers a more challenging scramble over rock rubble and lava breakdown. Budget 1¼hr. for the Lower Cave, 3hr. for the Upper Cave. A Monument Pass is required. Rangers lead guided cave explorations every day (see **Apes' Headquarters,** above), as well as rent lanterns. (Rentals $2 each, and stop at 4pm.) No free water is available at Apes.

HIKING
A quarter-mile before Ape Cave on Rd. 83 is the **Trail of Two Forests,** a lava-strewn and wheelchair-accessible boardwalk path above the forest floor. A beautiful forest has emerged, engulfed in lava from thousands of years ago. Rd. 83 continues 9 mi. farther north, ending at **Lahar Viewpoint,** the site of terrible mudflows that followed the eruption. On Rd. 83, 11 mi. northeast of its junction with Rd. 90, the **Lava Canyon Trail #184** hosts a range of challenges: an easy, wheelchair-accessible 40min. stroll yields spectacular views of the **Muddy River Gorge** and **Waterfall;** a more difficult route leads 3 mi. to the site of a now-defunct footbridge over Lava Canyon. Only the brave should venture farther; the trail then continues along a cliff and down a 25 ft. ladder to reach the canyon floor.

CLIMBING
The recently reshaped Mt. St. Helens draws hordes of people eager to gaze into the crater to see the source of so much power. It is now the most climbed mountain in the Northwest. Its popularity, combined with a fragile ecosystem, is an instant recipe for bureaucracy. The biggest challenge to climbing an otherwise very easy route is getting a permit. Between May 15 and Oct. 31, the Forest Service allows 100 people per day to hike to the crater rim. $15 permits are required to climb anywhere above 4800 ft. ($30 for an annual pass; reservations still required). Reserve in person or write to the Monument Headquarters (see **Practical Information**). Fifty permits per day may be reserved in advance after Feb. 1. Write early; weekends are usually booked by March, and weekdays often fill up as well. The reservationless can enter a 6pm lottery for the next day's remaining permits at **Jack's Restaurant and Country Store,** 13411 Louis River Rd., on Rte. 503, 5 mi. west of Cougar. (☎231-4276. I-5 Exit 21. Open daily 5:30am-9pm.)

Once that whole mess has been taken care of, the climber has a great route to look forward to. Although not a technical climb, the route up the mountain is a steep pathway of ash strewn with boulders. Often, the scree on the steep grade is so thick that each step forward involves a half-step back (5hr. up; 3hr. down). The view from the lip of the crater, encompassing Mt. Rainier, Mt. Adams, Mt. Hood, Spirit Lake, and the lava dome directly below, is magnificent. Bring sunglasses, sunscreen, sturdy climbing boots, foul-weather clothing, plenty of water, and gaiters to keep boots from filling with ash. Snow covers parts of the trail as late as early summer, making an ice axe a welcome companion. Free camping (no water) is available at the **Climber's Bivouac,** the trailhead area for the **Ptarmigan Trail #216A,** which starts the route up the mountain. The trail is located about 4 mi. up Rd. 83. Note: entry into the crater is strictly prohibited.

WINTER ACTIVITIES
The southern area of Mt. St. Helens has several **SnoParks** along Rte. 90 and Rte. 83, connected by semi-groomed trails. They are popular with cross-country skiers, snowshoers, and snowmobilers. Pick up a pass before going out; they are available in Cougar and Randle during the winter. Another SnoPark is found along Rd. 25, accessible only from Randle.

NORTHERN APPROACH: US 12

VISITORS CENTERS

Woods Creek Information Station, 6 mi. south of Randle on Rd. 25, from US 12. A small station that is designed mainly for drive-through-style quick questions. It is, however, the north's best option past the Randle station (see p. 211). Open June-Aug. daily 9am-4pm.

COWLITZ VALLEY/US 12 ■ 211

Windy Ridge Interpretive Site, at the end of Rd. 99 off Rd. 25, 1¼hr. from Randle. Rangers give 30min. talks about the eruption in the outdoor amphitheater before the stunning backdrop of the volcano. Talks every hour on the half-hour between 11:30am-4:30pm. The route to Windy Ridge is lined with several viewpoints, all of them looking onto the area most damaged by the eruption. Stopping is well worth the extra time.

CAMPING

Iron Creek Campground, just south of the Woods Creek Information Station, is the closest campsite to Mt. St. Helens, and has good hiking and beautiful forest along with a good location. The only downside of this campground is the crowds—all 98 sites can fill up on busy weekends. (Reservations ☎877-444-6777, strongly recommended in summer. Water. $12.50 per site, $14.50 for premium sites, $6 per extra vehicle.) The first stop for visitors traveling south on Rd. 25 from Randle and US 12 should be the **Woods Creek Information Station.**

HIKING

Independence Pass Trail #227, a moderate 3½ mi. hike, has overlooks of Spirit Lake and superb views of the crater and dome that only get better as you go along. A serious hike continues past the intersection with **Norway Pass Trail,** running through the blast zone to the newly reopened **Mt. Margaret peak.** Considered the best hike in the park, the trail is 8 mi. (7hr.) to the peak and back. Farther west, **Harmony Trail #224** provides a steep 2 mi. round-trip hike to Spirit Lake. Spectacular **Windy Ridge** is the exclamation point of Rd. 99. From here, a steep ash hill grants a magnificent view of the crater 3½ mi. away. The Truman Trail meanders 7 mi. through the Pumice Plain, where hot flows sterilized the land. The area is under constant scrutiny by biologists, so stay on the trail at all times.

COWLITZ VALLEY/US 12   ☎360

The **Cowlitz Valley** is a broad flat valley that stretches from the south of Rainier west to Interstate 5. While not remarkable in itself, because of its location between Rainier, St. Helens, and Adams it is almost inevitable that anyone touring the southern Cascades will end up here at some point. Don't despair; several lakes, plenty of inexpensive accommodations, services and roads leading to all of the major peaks makes it a good stop on almost any itinerary.

The main road running through the valley is **US 12.** To get beta on the next stop in your tour of the area, stop at the **Cowlitz Valley Ranger Station,** 10024 US 12, located in Randle, near the center of the valley, with lots of information on trails and other outdoor activities. (☎497-1100. Open June-Aug. daily 8am-4:30pm. In winter no weekend hours.) Info is also available 16 mi. to the east, at the **Packwood Visitor Information Center,** 13068 US 12. (☎497-1172. Open daily 7:45-11:30am, 12:30-4:30pm; winters closed on weekends.) **Packwood** has groceries and other essentials. **Mossyrock** and **Morton** are settlements with services nearer I-5.

There are several options for camping, including Northwest Forest Pass sites—ask at a station for info. **Ike Kinswa State Park** on Mayfield Lake's Rte. 122, a 30min. drive west of Randle and 14 mi. off US 12, offers camping, swimming (to non-campers, too) and **trout fishing** year-round. It boasts 101 private sites with abundant foliage, showers (50¢ per 3min.), and full access to the lake. (☎983-3402, reservations 800-452-5687 are strongly recommended in summer. Sites $14; full hookups $20; extra vehicle $6.) Thirteen miles to the west of Ike Kinswa along Rte. 12 on Jackson Hwy., the **Lewis and Clark State Campground** has sites amid old-growth forests. (☎864-2643 or reservations 800-452-5687. BBQs, horseshoes, kitchens. Group sites available. 25 sites, $13.) US 12 is also well stocked with **motels** between Morton and Packwood—shop around for good deals. The **Cowlitz River Lodge,** right across from the Packwood Information Center, offers very nice rooms for a decent price. (13069 US 12. ☎494-REST. Singles $50; doubles $67.)

MOUNT ADAMS ☎ 509

Weighing in at 12,276 ft., Mt. Adams is the second highest peak in Washington and also one of the most remote. Connected by pavement only to the south, and with the other gravel roads closed much of the year from snow, Adams and the area surrounding it are much quieter than the other big peaks in the South Cascades. Add rugged volcanic terrain and very few towns, and you have a good idea of what to expect on a trip out to see this massive glaciated peak.

ORIENTATION AND PRACTICAL INFORMATION. The **Mt. Adams District** is formed by the southern third of the **Gifford Pinchot National Forest**, as well as the **Mt. Adams Wilderness**. The entire area is most accessible from the south, by following Hwy. 141 north from Hood River, via Bingen and White Salmon. Other approaches include from the north, along Forest Rd. 23 (part of it unpaved), and from the west, following local roads from Goldendale. No public transportation gets very close—**Greyhound** (☎773-5525 or 800-231-2222; www.greyhound.com) stops 51 mi. to the west in Goldendale, at the Golden Lanes, 1005 S Columbus. It runs to **Portland** (3hr., $25) and **Yakima** (1½hr., $10.50). Southbound bus leaves 5:05pm, Northbound 1:40pm. **Amtrak** (☎800-872-7245) comes a little closer, stopping 20 mi. away in Bingen at the foot of Walnut St.; from **Portland** (2hr., $10-17) and **Spokane** (5½hr., $34-60).

Whichever way you come, the first stop should be **Trout Lake**, found on Highway 141. The main draw there is the **Mt. Adams District Ranger Station**, 2455 Hwy. 141 (☎395-3400), with uncommonly friendly staff who are generous both with advice and free photocopies of maps. While at the station be sure to pick up the appropriate permits as well (open M-F 8am-4:30pm, during summer additional weekend hours). Trout Lake also has a gas station and **General Store**, 2383 Hwy. 141, which boasts a small supply of food and essentials at a price that will make you regret not getting them elsewhere. (☎395-2777. Open daily 8am-8pm.) Sundries can also be found a long drive away at **Shade Tree Convenience Store** (see **Accommodations**).

Info about the area, as well as all of Washington and Oregon, is available in White Salmon, at the **Mt. Adams Chamber of Commerce Information Center**, just west of the toll bridge from Hood River. (☎493-3630; Open M-F 9am-5pm.) **Equipment rental** is best taken care of in Hood River (see **Columbia River Gorge**, p. 82). For **road conditions**, call 360-905-2958. **Emergency:** ☎911. **Police:** 180 W Lincoln, White Salmon (non-emergency ☎493-2660). **Post office:** 2393 Hwy. 141 (☎395-2108), in Trout Lake. **ZIP Code:** 98650 (Trout Lake).

CAMPING. The Mt. Adams area is crawling with places to pitch a tent, many of them requiring only a **Northwest Forest Pass**. The best plan is to stop at the ranger station, tell them what you want to do, and they will tell you the best site to use as a base. Most pay sites are so because they boast better facilities or desirable views. The closest to Trout Lake is the **Guler-Mt. Adams County Park**, one of the few areas with showers. To get there, take a left at the Post Office and follow signs. (Sites with water $10, water and electricity $14.) The biggest pay area near Trout Lake is **Peterson Prairie;** head 3 mi. on 141 after it enters the national forest and look to your right (30 sites; $11 per site). On the way, check to see if there is room at **Trout Lake Creek**, a forest-pass-only site just off 141; take a right on Forest Road 88 and follow signs. Perhaps the best camping is an hour north of Trout Lake, in the Takhlakh Lake area. There are several different campsites, but the best is **Takhlakh Lake Campsite**, which offers amazing views of Mt. Adams presiding over the lake ($11 per site, $13 for prime sites). To get there take the Mt. Adams Rec. Hwy. out of Trout Lake, then Forest Road 23 for an hour until you see signs.

The one budget option that will put a hard roof overhead is found in Glenwood, a 16 mi. drive from Trout Lake. This is the small but friendly **Shade Tree Inn**, a motel with attached **restaurant** and **convenience store**, 105 E Main. (☎364-3471. TV, A/C. Showers. Single $45; double $55. Reception and store daily 8am-9pm, restaurant 8am-7pm.) To get to Glenwood, take the Mt. Adams Rec. Hwy. out of Trout Lake, and then take the first right—a small sign will say Glenwood.

MOUNT ADAMS ■ 213

OUTDOOR ACTIVITIES. The Adams area has something for everyone, almost year-round. Quality can vary, though; a long thaw leaves many trails closed through spring, and bugs can make early summer very uncomfortable.

HIKING. The best resources in the Mt. Adams area for hiking are available at the ranger station: rangers' advice and the Forest Services *Trail Guide*. Hiking is generally very rewarding—most trails meander in and out of broken-up lava flows and occasionally open up onto good views. In order to park, many trailheads require a Northwest Forest Pass ($5 per day, $30 annually; available at the ranger station). The area can get very dry in the summer, so be sure to bring adequate water.

The options for dayhiking are huge; these are just two drops in a very large bucket: The half-mile trail to **Sleeping Beauty Peak** starts off at a small trailhead on the left side of Rd. 8810-040, about a quarter-mile from the Rd. 8810 junction (see directions to **Trout Lake campground,** above). The **Indian Heaven Wilderness Trail** is a mild 10 mi. loop through forest and meadow from Cultus Creek campground along four different trails. For multi-day hikes, the most popular is the **Round-the-Mountain Trail.** It does not go around the mountain at all, but instead stretches 8 mi. on the south of Mt. Adams, eventually ending at the border of the **Yakima Indian Reservation.** This is closed to hikers lacking tribal permission, so most parties turn around at this point, yielding a 2-3 day 16 mi. journey.

CLIMBING AND MOUNTAIN BIKING. Mt. Adams is traced with at least a dozen mountaineering routes, including the very popular (and relatively easy) **South Spur** and **Mt. Adams Summit Route.** All routes require crampons and an ice axe year round, and usually do not even open up until June. In addition, climbers should stop at the Ranger Station to register and purchase a **Cascade Volcano Pass** ($10 for trips on M-Th, $15 for a trip that touches either F, Sa or Su), required for all parties going higher than 7000 ft. on the mountain. Mountain biking is permitted on many of the trails in the National Forest. Trailhead signs are clearly marked; check ahead at the station to save time.

RAFTING AND KAYAKING. Both the **White Salmon** and **Klikitat Rivers** offer good whitewater, the White Salmon almost all year long. Two companies operate out of White Salmon—**Zoller's Outdoor Odysseys** (☎ 800-366-2004) and **All Adventures** (☎ 877-641-7238). **River Riders,** in Hood River, has competitive prices, too (☎ 800-448-7238). A day on the river can cost anywhere between $45 and $70.

HUCKLEBERRIES AND BIRDWATCHING. Mt. Adams boasts several huge fields of **huckleberries**. When ripe (mid-late summer) they can be picked with the help of a free permit (get one at the station). To reach the popular **Sawtooth Huckleberry Fields,** follow Hwy. 141/Rd. 24 for 11 mi. past the Rd. 60 intersection. Mushroom picking is also popular, but *Let's Go* does not recommend doing so without a little expertise. Birdwatching is also a favorite—guided trips leave the ranger station every Friday morning, and the **Conboy National Wildlife Refuge,** just outside of Glenwood (see **Accommodations**) is one of the few places in the Northwest where Sandhill cranes nest (open for day use only).

> **RUMBLE IN THE MOUNTAINS** A long time ago, when wishing still mattered and mountains fought for love, three rumples in the earth's crust were caught in a love triangle. Legend holds that Pah-toe (Mt. Adams) fought and defeated his brother Wy'East (Mt. Hood) for the love of Squaw Mountain. Dismayed, the broken-hearted Squaw Mountain laid at the feet of Pah-toe and fell asleep, becoming Sleeping Beauty Mountain. Pah-toe, once proud and tall, bowed his head in shame thus taking his current shape.

MOUNT RAINIER NATIONAL PARK ☎ 360

At 14,411 ft., Mt. Rainier (ray-NEER) presides regally over the Cascade Range. The Klickitat native people called it Tahoma, "Mountain of God," but Rainier is simply "the Mountain" to most Washington residents. Perpetually snow-capped, this dormant volcano draws thousands of visitors from all around the globe. Clouds mask the mountain for at least 200 days per year, frustrating those who come solely to see its distinctive summit. Rainier is so big it creates its own weather by jutting into the warm, wet air and pulling down vast amounts of rain and snow. Its sharp ridges, steep gullies, and 76 glaciers combine to make Rainier an inhospitable host for the thousands of determined climbers who attempt its summit each year. The non-alpinists among us can explore the old growth forests and alpine meadows of Mt. Rainier National Park. With over 305 mi. of trails through wildflowers, rivers, and hot springs, Mt. Rainier has a niche for all lovers of nature.

TRANSPORTATION

To reach Mt. Rainier from the **west**, take **I-5** to **Tacoma**, then go east on **Rte. 512**, south on **Rte. 7**, and east on **Rte. 706**. This road meanders through the town of **Ashford** and into the park by the Nisqually entrance, which leads to the visitors centers of **Paradise** and **Longmire**. Rte. 706 is the only access road open year-round; snow usually closes all other park roads from November to May. Mt. Rainier is 65 mi. from **Tacoma** and 90 mi. from **Seattle**.

All major roads offer scenic views of the mountain, with numerous roadside lookouts. The roads to **Paradise** and **Sunrise** are especially picturesque. **Stevens Canyon Rd.** connects the southeast corner of the national park with Paradise, Longmire, and the Nisqually entrance, unfolding superb vistas of Rainier and the Tatoosh Range. The summer draws hordes of visitors, making parking very difficult at many of the visitors centers and trailheads throughout the afternoon hours.

Rainier weather changes quickly, so pack warm clothes and cold-rated equipment. Before setting out, ask rangers for info on mountain-climbing and hiking and for equipment recommendations. Group size is limited in many areas, and campers must carry all waste out of the backcountry. Potable water is not available at most backcountry campsites. All stream and lake water should be treated for giardia with tablets, filters, or by boiling it before drinking. For more information on preparing for the outdoors, see **Camping and Hiking Equipment**, p. 39.

PRACTICAL INFORMATION

The section of the Mt. Baker-Snoqualmie National Forest that surrounds Mt. Rainier on all but its southern side is administered by Wenatchee National Forest, 301 Yakima St. (☎ 509-662-4314), Wenatchee 98807. The Gifford Pinchot National Forest (☎ 425-750-5000), to the south, has headquarters at 6926 E Fourth Plain Blvd., P.O. Box 8944, Vancouver, WA, 98668. The Packwood ranger station is nearest, south at 13068 US 12. (☎ 494-0600. Open 10am-5pm.)

> **Entrance Fee:** $10 per car, $5 per hiker. Permits good for 7 days. Gates open 24hr.
>
> **Buses: Gray Line Bus Service,** 4500 S Marginal Way, Seattle (☎ 206-624-5208 or 800-426-7532; www.graylineofseattle.com). From **Seattle** to Mt. Rainier daily May to mid-Sept. (1-day round-trip $54, under 12 $27). Buses leave from the Convention Center at 8th and Pike in Seattle at 8am and return at 6pm. The trip up takes 3½-4hr. (with a few stops at picturesque viewpoints) and allows 2½hr. at Paradise. **Rainier Shuttle** (☎ 569-2331) runs daily between **Sea-Tac Airport** and **Ashford** (2hr., 2 per day, $40), or **Paradise** (3hr., 1 per day, $45).
>
> **Visitor Information:** The best place to plan a backcountry trip is at the **Longmire Wilderness Center** (☎ 569-4453, for backcountry reservations only), 6 mi. east of the Nisqually entrance in the southwest corner of the park. Open Su-Th 7:30am-6:30pm, F-

Sa 7am-7pm. The **White River Ranger Station** (☎663-2273), off Rte. 410 on the park's east side, on the way to Sunrise, is also very good. Open Su-Th 8am-4:30pm, F-Sa 7am-7pm. On the north side, the **Wilkeson "Red Caboose" Ranger Station** (☎829-5127) is at Carbon River. Open M-Th 8am-4:30pm, F 8am-7pm, Sa 7am-7pm, Su 8am-6pm. These stations all distribute **backcountry permits.** The **Park Headquarters,** Tahoma Woods, Star Rte., Ashford 98304 (☎569-2211; www.nps.gov/mora) is the best place to call with phone inquiries. Open M-F 8am-4:30pm. The free **map** and *Tahoma News,* distributed at park entrances and ranger stations, are invaluable for maps, hiking recommendations, and safety precautions.

Equipment Rental: Rainier Mountaineering, Inc. (RMI; ☎569-2227; www.rmiguides.com), in Paradise across from the Paradise Inn. Rents ice axes ($12.50), crampons ($12.50), boots ($23), packs ($23), and helmets ($9) by the day. Expert RMI guides lead summit climbs, seminars, and special schools and programs. Open May-Oct. daily 9am-5pm. **White Pass Sports Hut,** 13020 US 12 (☎494-7321), in Packwood, rents skis. Alpine package $14 per day, Nordic package $12 per day. Also rents snowshoes ($9 per day) and boards ($20 per day). Open daily 9am-5pm; winter M-F 7am-6pm, Sa-Su 8am-6pm.

Climbing: Glacier climbers and mountain climbers intending to scale above 10,000 ft. must register in person at **Paradise, White River,** or **Wilkeson Ranger Stations** to be granted permits. Cost-recovery fee $15 per person. Annual pass $25.

Internet access: See **Whittacker's Bunkhouse,** below. $3 per 30min; $5 per hr.

Emergency: ☎911.

Hospital: The nearest medical facilities are in **Morton** (40 mi. from Longmire) and **Enumclaw** (5 mi. from Sunrise). **Tacoma General Hospital,** 315 Martin Luther King Way (☎253-552-1000), has 24hr. emergency facilities.

Post Office: In the **National Park Inn,** Longmire. Open M-F 8:30am-noon and 1-5pm. In the **Paradise Inn** (see below). Open M-F 9am-noon and 12:30-5pm, Sa 8:30am-noon. **ZIP Code:** Longmire 98397; Paradise 98398.

ACCOMMODATIONS

Longmire, Paradise, and Sunrise offer expensive accommodations. For a roof, stay in Ashford or Packwood. Otherwise, camp under the rooftop of the world.

Hotel Packwood, 102 Main St. (☎494-5431), in Packwood, 20min. south of Ohanapecosh or 1hr. south of Nisqually. A charmer since 1912. A sprawled-out grizzly graces the parlor. Grr. Singles and doubles with and without private bath $32-54.

Whittaker's Bunkhouse (☎569-2439), 6 mi. west of the Nisqually entrance. Owned by Lou Whittaker, a long-time RMI guide. View his accomplishment in the photos hanging from nearly every wall. Homey espresso bar, but no kitchen or bedding. Book ahead. Spacious co-ed dorms with 2 baths. Bunks $25; private rooms from $65-90.

Paradise Inn (☎569-2413; reservations 569-2275), in Paradise. Built in 1917 from Alaskan cedar at 5400 ft. Large, dining facility with exquisite food. Open late May-Oct. Book ahead. Very popular during the summer. Singles and doubles from $75, each extra person $12.

CAMPING

Backcountry camping requires a permit, free from ranger stations and visitors centers in person 24hr. beforehand, or by reservation up to two months in advance. (☎569-4453. $20 per group. Quotas limit group size.) Inquire about trail closures before setting off. Hikers with a valid permit can camp at well-established trailside, alpine, and snowfield sites (most with toilets and water source). Fires are prohibited except in front-country campgrounds.

Camping in **national forests** outside the park is free. Avoid eroded lakesides and riverbanks; flash floods and debris flows are frequent. **Campfires** are prohibited except during the rainy season. Check with ranger stations for details. There are six campgrounds within the park. For reservations, apply in person at the visitors centers, or after February call 800-365-2267 (international 301-722-1257) or visit http://reservations.nps.gov. National Park campgrounds are handicapped-accessible, but have no hookups or showers. Coin-op showers are available at **Jackson Memorial Visitors Center,** in Paradise. Alternatively, the Packwood RV park has pay showers for $3 at the corner of Main St. and US 12 in Packwood. **Sunshine Point,** a quarter-mile beyond Nisqually entrance, is in the south. (Open year round. Quiet hours 10pm-6am. 18 sites $10.) **Cougar Rock,** 2¼ mi. north of Longmire, in the southwest. Near a sometimes flowing river. (Quiet hours 10pm-6am. Open May-Sept. Reservation required June 28 to Labor Day. 200 individual sites. $15. Winter season $12. 5 group sites $3 per person.) **Ohanapecosh,** 11 mi. north of Packwood on Rte. 123, in the southeast, provides secluded sites with great scenery. (Open May-Sept. Reservations required June 28 to Labor Day. Often booked solid. 205 sites, $15; winter $12.) **White River,** 5 mi. west of White River on the way to Sunrise in the northeast. (Open late June-Sept. 112 sites, $10.)

FOOD

The general stores in the park sell only last-minute trifles like bug repellent (well worth it). Items are charged an extra state park tax, so stock up before you arrive. **Blanton's Market,** 13040 US 12 in Packwood, is the closest decent supermarket to the park and has an **ATM** in front. (☎494-6101. Open daily 6am-10pm.) **Highlander** (☎569-2953), in Ashford, serves standard pub-fare in a single dimly-lit room with a pool table and wooden Indian. Their specialty is the $3 homemade pie. Burgers $6-7. (Open daily 7am to anytime between 10pm and 2am. Restaurant closes at 9pm.) **Club Cafe,** 13016 Hwy. 12, in Packwood. A small down-home diner, eggs for breakfast and standbys for lunch and dinner. Their omelettes always elicit oohs and ahhs. (☎494-5977. Open daily 7am-7pm.)

OUTDOOR ACTIVITIES

Rainier's moody weather makes it a tricky destination. Clouds and freezing rain can sweep in on any day, making the fire in Paradise Inn the most attractive destination on the mountain. In winter huge volumes of snow close most of the park, and trails often remain snow-covered well into summer. But hit Rainier on a good day, and the rewards are huge. Hiking is probably the best bet, as ample views and fascinating terrain are easily reached.

HIKING. The hiking trails are way too numerous to list—it is easily Washington's most varied area. One option is ranger-led interpretive hikes, which delve into everything from area history to local wildflowers. Each visitors center conducts hikes and most of the campgrounds have evening talks and campfire programs. **Camp Muir** (9 mi. round-trip), the most popular staging ground for a summit attempt, is also a challenging dayhike. It begins on Skyline trail, and then heads north on Pebble Creek Trail. The latter half of the hike is covered in snow for most of the year.

CLIMBING. A trip to the **summit** of Rainier requires substantial preparation and expense. The ascent involves a vertical rise of more than 9000 ft. over 9 mi., and usually takes two days with an overnight stay at **Camp Muir** on the south side (10,000 ft.) or **Camp Schurman** on the east side (9500 ft.). Each camp has a ranger station, rescue cache, and toilet. Permits cost $15 per person. Only experienced climbers should attempt the summit; novices can be guided to the summit with **Rainier Mountaineering, Inc. (RMI;** see **Equipment Rental,** p. 215), after a day-long basic climbing course. For details, contact Park Headquarters or RMI (See **Practical Information,** p. 214).

WILLKOMMEN IN LEAVENWORTH! A true experiment in tourism. After the town's logging industry collapsed and the railroad switching station moved to nearby Wenatchee, Leavenworth needed a new *Weltanschauung*. Desperate officials launched "Project Alpine," a gimmick to transform the town into a German village: zoning and building codes necessitated Bavarian-style buildings, waiters learned about bratwurst, polka blasted over the loudspeakers, and German beer flowed. It worked: more than 1.5 million Americans came in 2000, with influxes peaking during the city's three annual festivals. Tasty pretzels and *Schnitzel*, oddly enough, compliment the nearby world-class rock climbing and camping. On the eastern slope of the Cascades, Leavenworth is near Washington's geographic center. To get there from Seattle, follow I-5 North to Everett (Exit 194), then US 2 East (126 mi., 2½hr.). From Spokane, follow US 2 West (184 mi., 4hr.). The Chamber of Commerce/Visitor Information Center, 220 9th St. at Commercial St., provides a plethora of pamphlets and brochures. (☎548-5807. Open M-Th 8am-5pm, F-Sa 8am-6pm, Su 10am-4pm; winter M-Sa 8am-5pm.) Indulge in the fabulous location of Bindlestiff's Riverside Cabins, 1600 Hwy. 2. Eight private cabins rest feet from the beautiful Wenatchee River where you can watch the rafters drift by, borrow the BBQ, and grill on your own private porch. (☎548-5015. Fridge. TV. No phones. One and two room cabins $63-83.) Camping is also available 8 mi. out of town on Icicle Creek Rd. at a National Forest Campground ($10). Predictably, Leavenworth's food mimics German cuisine; surprisingly, it often succeeds. German *Wurst* booths are tucked between buildings everywhere. When you've had your fill of tourist-watching and sausage-scarfing, embark on an adventure into Leavenworth's extensive hiking, biking, and climbing opportunities in the Wenatchee National Forest.

CHELAN ☎509

The serpentine body of Lake Chelan (sha-LAN) undulates some 55 mi. southeast through the Wenatchee National Forest and the Lake Chelan National Recreation Area toward the Columbia River and US 97. Here, the green mountains of North Cascades National Park transform into the bone-dry brown hills and apple orchards that surround the town of Chelan. Unfortunately, the town itself is disappointingly touristy—the economy is structured around family tourism that usually involves renting a house for an extended stay. There is little in town to draw the budget traveler. The real beckon of Chelan is at the docks, where several ferries leave for the beautiful wilderness further up the lake.

ORIENTATION AND PRACTICAL INFORMATION. The town of Chelan rests on the southeast end of Lake Chelan, along Hwy. 97, 190 mi. (4hr.) east of Seattle and west of Spokane. Alt. Rte. US 97 cuts through town along the lake and becomes its main street, **Woodin Ave.** Look out for speed traps near the lake.

Link, the local bus service, runs Rte. 21 and 31 hourly between the Chamber of Commerce and Wenatchee. (☎662-1155 or 800-851-5465; www.linktransit.com. 1¼hr., M-F 6am-6pm, 50¢-$1.) **Northwest Trailways** (☎800-366-3830, or through Greyhound 800-231-2222) departs Wenatchee for **Seattle** (3½hr., 2 per day, $23) and **Spokane** (3½hr., 1 per day, $23). For **ferry** service, see **Stehekin**, p. 219. The **Chamber of Commerce**, 102 E Johnson, off Manson Hwy., has info on the town. (☎682-3503 or 800-424-3526; www.lakechelan.com. Open M-F 9am-5pm, Sa 9am-4pm, Su 10am-3pm; winter M-F 9am-5pm.) The **Chelan Ranger Station**, 428 W Woodin Ave., on the lake, is the place to buy maps ($4) or Northwest Forest Passes ($5) for parking. (☎682-2549 or 682-2576. Open daily June-Sept. 7:45am-4:30pm; Oct.-May M-F 7:45am-4:30pm.) **Chelan Boat Rentals**, 1210 W Woodin, is one of the shops on the lake that rents small fishing boats ($55 per hr.), jet skis (from $30 per hr., $125 per day), and bikes ($10 per hr., $50 per day. ☎682-4444. Open daily 9am-8pm.) **Town Tub Laundry** is by the Pennzoil station on the east end of Woodin Ave. (Open daily

218 ■ MOUNT ST. HELENS

8am-9pm. Wash $1.75, dry 25¢ per 10min.) **Electrik Dreams,** 246 W Manson Rd., Suite 1 (☎ 682-8889) provides **Internet access** for $9 per hour. **Emergency:** ☎ 911. **Police:** 207 N Emerson St. (☎ 682-2588). **Crisis line:** ☎ 662-7105. 24hr. **Pharmacy:** In **Safeway** (see **Food,** below). Open M-F 9am-7pm, Sa 8am-6pm, Su 10am-6pm. **Hospital:** 503 E Highland St. (☎ 682-2531. Open 24hr.) **Post office:** 144 E Johnson (☎ 682-2625. Open M-F 8:30am-5pm.) **ZIP Code:** 98816.

ACCOMMODATIONS AND CAMPING.
With a few exceptions, most Chelan motels and resorts are rather pricey. The **Apple Inn,** 1002 E Woodin, boasts a hot tub, pool, and shuttle service. (☎ 682-4044. Single $49, double $59; winter $35, $39.) **Mom's Montlake Motel,** 823 Wapato, south off Woodin Ave. on Clifford, is a summertime mom-and-pop operation with clean, microwave- or kitchen-equipped rooms. (☎ 682-5715. Singles $49; doubles $59.) Most campers head for **Lake Chelan State Park,** a pleasantly grassy—albeit crowded—campground 9 mi. up the south shore of the lake with a beach, swimming area, small store, picnic sites, boat launch, playing fields, and jet ski rentals. (☎ 687-3710 or reservations 800-452-5687. Bus #21. Sites $14; full hookups $20.) **Twenty-Five Mile Creek State Park** is a smaller, but no less crowded, site; also boasts a beach, boat launch, and small store. (☎ 687-3610. ☎ 800-452-5687. Reservations recommended Apr.-Sept. 63 sites, $14; 23 hookups $20.) Campers are also free to pitch tents anywhere in the national forest, but may only light fires in established fire rings.

FOOD.
The cheapest food in Chelan is at local fruit stands, although a few good places are to be found slightly outside of town on E Woodin. **Safeway,** 106 W Manson Rd., has groceries. (☎ 682-2615. Open daily 6am-11pm.) **Bear Foods** (a.k.a. Golden Florin's General Store), 125 E Woodin Ave., provides food leaning more in the health-freak direction. (☎ 682-5535. Open M-Sa 9am-7pm, Su noon-5pm.) Behind the ivy-covered facade at **Local Myth,** 514 E Woodin Ave., Art and the gang create mind-blowing pizzas from wholewheat dough and fresh, hearty ingredients. The pizzas ($7 and up) and calzones ($6-9) are unbeatable. (☎ 682-2914. Open daily 4pm-9ish.) Pick up baked goods and throw down shots of wheatgrass ($2.50) or espresso ($1) next door at **The Rising Sun Bakery.** (☎ 682-8938. Open M-F 9am-5pm.) The unassuming **Dagwood's International Kitchen,** 246 W Manson Way, serves *pad thai* ($6.50) and burgers. (☎ 682-8630. Open daily 11am-10pm; winter M-F 11am-8pm.) For the coffee addict, **Flying Saucers,** 116 S Emerson, offers mochas, chai tea, cinnamon rolls (all $2), and aura galore in a converted 50s diner with flying saucers hanging from the ceiling. (☎ 682-5129. Open summer M-Sa 7am-8pm; winter M-F 7am-4pm.)

DAYTRIP FROM CHELAN: GRAND COULEE DAM

As the climate warmed 18,000 years ago, a small glacier blocking a lake in Montana gave way, releasing floodwaters that swept across eastern Washington, gouging out layers of soil and exposing the layers of granite and basalt below. The washout carved massive canyons called coulees into a region now known as the Channeled Scab Lands, which compose most of the striking, mesa-filled country south of the dam across its largest canyon, the Grand Coulee.

From 1934 to 1942, 7000 workers toiled on the construction of the Grand Coulee Dam, a local remedy for the agricultural woes of the drought and the Great Depression, but a travesty for conservationists and Native Americans. Nearly a mile long, this behemoth is the world's largest solid concrete structure and irrigates the previously parched Columbia River Basin as it generates more power than any other hydroelectric plant in the United States. The Columbia River, raised 350 ft. by the dam, forms both **Franklin D. Roosevelt Lake** and **Banks Lake,** where "wet-siders" from western Washington flock for swimming, boating, and fishing.

The dam hulks at the junction of Rte. 174 and Rte. 155, about 75 mi. east of Chelan and 90 mi. west of Spokane. The rotund **Visitor Arrival Center,** on Rte. 155 just north of Grand Coulee, is filled with disconnected exhibits on the construction, operation, and legacy of the dam. A guided tour of the third and newest powerplant begins every 30min. between 10am and 5pm (contact the visitors center for more info). On summer nights, a spectacularly cheesy, yet technically amazing 36min. laser show chronicles the structure's history on the spillway of the dam. Watch from the visitors center for guaranteed sound (and arrive at least an hour early to beat the crowds), or park at Crown Point Vista off Rte. 174 and tune in to 89.9 FM. (☎509-633-9265. Open daily June-July 8:30am-11pm; Aug. 8:30am-10:30pm; Sept. 8:30am-9:30pm; Oct.-May 9am-5pm. Show daily late May-July 10pm; Aug. 9:30pm; Sept. 8:30pm. Free.)

STEHEKIN ☎509

Stehekin (steh-HEE-kin) counts among the most magical places in Washington. An isolated village at the north end of Lake Chelan, its main connection to the rest of the world is via a 60 mi. ferry; the only other option is hiking or horse-riding in. This isolation has preserved a wild, beautiful place. With McGregor Mountain looming and silence a 5min. walk out of the small settlement, Stehekin is a destination that invites the outdoorsy for days on end.

INTERCITY TRANSPORTATION. Three **ferries** ply the lake in summer. The ferries proceed along a shoreline where mountain goats and brown bears roam: this alone makes the ride worthwhile. All are operated by the **Lake Chelan Boat Company,** 1418 W Woodin, about 1 mi. west of downtown Chelan. (☎682-2224 or reservations 682-4584; www.ladyofthelake.com. Open May-Oct.) The *Lady of the Lake II*, a 350-person ferry, makes one round-trip to Stehekin per day. (4hr. with a 1½hr. layover, 8:30am. Ferry $25. Daytime parking free, overnight $5.) This ferry also picks up from Fields Point, 16 mi. up South Shore Rd. near **Twenty-Five Mile Creek State Park** (9:45am; parking $3 per day, $17 per week). You can request that the ferry stop at **Prince Creek** or **Moore Point campgrounds** (free, no permit required) along the Lakeshore Trail (see **Outdoors,** below). Arrange in advance to be picked up, then flag them down with a bright article of clothing. The smaller *Lady Express* makes an express trip to Stehekin (2¼hr. with a 1hr. layover, $44). A combination ticket for the *Lady Express* or *Lady of the Lake II* to Stehekin and back also runs $41, and allows just over three hours in Stehekin. A new, high-speed catamaran, the *Lady Cat,* makes two round-trips per day (1¼hr. with a 1½hr. layover, 7:45am and 1:30pm, $89). Book ferry tickets in advance on summer weekends; they will not accept credit cards on the day of travel.

LOCAL TRANSPORTATION. Stehekin itself is small enough that you can see it all from one point—transport isn't a question. Getting further up the road to trailheads and campsites can be an issue, though. **Discovery Bikes** (☎686-3014) rents two-wheelers ($3.50 per hr., $10 per half-day, $25 per day). From mid-June to mid-Oct., a shuttle leaves from the ferry and runs up Stehekin Valley Rd. to **High Bridge** campgrounds (45min., 4 per day). The NPS shuttles continue on to **Bridge Creek** campground (30min.) and **Glory Mountain** (1hr.; July to mid-Oct. $5, children and bicycles $3). From mid-May to mid-June, the NPS shuttle runs to High Bridge upon request. Reservations, recommended for NPS shuttles, can be made at 856-5700, ext. 340 and 14, or at the Golden West Visitor Center.

CAMPING AND FOOD. The Park Service maintains 12 **campgrounds** along the Stehekin River off Stehekin Valley Rd. All except the area closest to Stehekin are geared to the hiker. **Purple Point,** right next to the ferry landing, is unique in its amenities: water, free showers, and bathrooms. All need reservations, so stop at the ranger station, and have them help you figure out how to get there. **Permits** are free, and required for backcountry camping and hiking. Stehekin's **Golden West Visitor Center** is the place to head for these, as well as info, bear canisters, and plenty of interpretive programs. (☎856-5700, ext. 340 and 14. Open daily 8:30am-5pm; call for spring and fall hours.) There are exactly three dining options in the valley. A delicious dinner at **Stehekin Valley Ranch,** 9 mi. from the dock, costs about $74.

(☎ 682-4677. Open M-F 9am-5pm. Reserve ahead. Bus to and from costs $2.) The **Lodge Restaurant,** at the landing, serves dinner. (☎ 682-4494. Entrees $6-17.) Two miles up the road, the **Stehekin Pastry Company** lures hikers out of the hills for sticky buns. (Open June-Sept. daily 8am-5pm; May 26-June 15 and Sept. 24-Oct. 8 Sa-Su 8am-5pm.) A "bakery special" fare applies for the shuttle ($1 one-way).

🛈 OUTDOOR ACTIVITIES. Some short, scenic dayhikes surround the landing. The simple three-quarter-mile **Imus Creek Trail** is an interpretive trail, offering great views of the lake, starting behind the Golden West Visitor Center. The moderately steep **Rainbow Loop Trail** offers stellar valley views. The 4½ mi. trail begins 2½ mi. from Stehekin; SAC runs to the trailhead five times a day, but it's close enough to walk, and residents rarely hesitate to provide a ride. From Purple Creek near the visitors center, take a right turn up the switchbacks of the steep 15 mi. (round-trip) **Purple Creek Trail.** The 5700 ft. climb is tough, but rewards effort with lake views and glimpses of nearby glaciers. The moderate 17½ mi., 2-3 day **Lakeshore Trail** begins by the visitors center and follows the shore of Lake Chelan to Prince Creek.

An unpaved road and many trails probe north from Stehekin into **North Cascades National Park.** Two hikes begin at High Bridge. The mellow **Agnes Gorge Trail** is the second trailhead on the left, 200 yards beyond the bridge, and travels a level 2½ mi. through forests and meadows with views of 8115 ft. Agnes Mountain. Behind the ranger cabin, the **McGregor Mountain Trail** is a strenuous straight shot up the side of the mountain, climbing 6525 vertical feet over 8 mi. and ending with unsurpassed views of the high North Cascades peaks. The last half-mile is a scramble up ledges. This extremely difficult trail is often blocked by snow well into July; check at the visitors center before starting out. The shuttle to Bridge Creek provides access to the **Pacific Crest Trail,** which runs from Mexico to Canada. The North Cascades portion of this trail has been called its most scenic by many who have completed the colossal journey.

The Rainbow Falls Tour, in Stehekin, is a guided bus tour that coincides with ferry arrival times. It zooms through the valley and its major sights: the Stehekin School, the last one-room schoolhouse in Washington; the Stehekin Pastry Company; and Rainbow Falls, a misty 312 ft. cataract ($7, ages 6-11 $4, under 6 free).

ALONG RTE. 20: NORTH CASCADES

A favorite stomping ground for grizzlies, deer, mountain goats, black bears, and outdoorsmen of all levels, the North Cascades are one of the most rugged expanses of land in the continental US. The dramatic peaks stretch north from Stevens Pass on US 2 to the Canadian border. The centerpiece of the area is **North Cascades National Park,** which straddles the crest of the Cascades. The green wilderness and steep peaks attract backpackers and mountain climbers from around the world. **Rte. 20** (open Apr.-Nov., weather permitting), a road designed for unadulterated driving pleasure, is the primary means of access to the area and awards jaw-dropping views. The backcountry extravaganza of untrammeled land, jagged peaks, and an Eden of wildlife and flora is mostly inaccessible without at least a day's uphill hike. Ira Springs's *100 Hikes in Washington: The North Cascades National Park Region* is a good guide for recreational hikers, while Fred Beckley's *Cascade Alpine Guide* targets the more serious high-country traveler.

Rte. 20 (I-5 Exit 230) follows the Skagit River east to the small towns of **Sedro Woolley, Concrete,** and **Marblemount** in the **Mount Baker-Snoqualmie National Forest.** The highway then enters North Cascades National Park via the **Ross Lake National Recreation Area,** one of the two designated recreation areas within the National Park. After passing through **Newhalem, Diablo Lake,** and **Ross Lake,** Rte. 20 leaves the National Park and enters the **Okanagan National Forest District,** crossing Washington Pass (5477 ft.) and descending to the Methow River and the dry Okanagan rangeland of Eastern Washington. The **Lake Chelan National Recreation Area** occupies the southern tip of the national park, bordered on the south by the Wenatchee National Forest. Mile Markers line the entirety of Rte. 20 and are the best points of reference if you are asking for directions from the ranger station. Police happily ticket speeders in town.

SEDRO WOOLLEY TO MARBLEMOUNT ☎ 360

SEDRO WOOLLEY. Although situated in the rich farmland of the lower Skagit Valley, Sedro Woolley is primarily a logging town. Volunteers at the **visitors center** work in the train caboose at Rte. 20 and Ferry St. (☎ 855-1841. Open daily 9am-4pm.) The town's main attraction is the annual **Sedro Woolley Loggerodeo** (☎ 855-1129 or 800-214-0800), held in the last week of June through the 4th of July weekend. Axe-throwing, pole-climbing, and sawing competitions share center stage with bronco-busting and calf-roping. Other events for the family include a parade, variety show, and street dance. Sedro Woolley houses the **North Cascades National Park and Mt. Baker-Snoqualmie National Forest Headquarters**, which will be moving down the street to 810 State Route 20, near the intersection with Route 9. If it isn't open yet, check back at 2105 Rt. 20, their old location. (☎ 856-5700. Open daily 8am-4:30pm. Closed on weekends in winter.) Helpful rangers and info on activities in the Park can help you move out of Sedro. Check out their 3-D topographical map. For **snow avalanche info** call 206-526-6677. Backcountry campers must contact the Wilderness Information Center in Marblemount (see below) for a permit.

AROUND CONCRETE. On Rte. 20, 32 mi. east of Sedro Woolley, lies the tiny town of Concrete, where rows of businesses made of concrete pay homage to an ethereal local industry. Six miles west of Concrete, south on Lusk Rd. and then east on Cape Horn Rd., **Rasar State Park** (RAY-sir) has 128 acres of lush trails to the Skagit River where you can watch eagles feed on salmon. (☎ 826-3942. 18 sites, $14; 20 utility sites, $20; hiker/biker $6.) East of Concrete, right before **Rockport State Park**, Sauk Mountain Rd. (Forest Rd. 1030) makes a stomach-scrambling climb up Sauk Mountain. The road is bumpy and a thorough dust bath; trailers, RVs, and the faint of heart should not attempt the ascent. Seven miles up and a right turn at Rd. 1036 to the parking lot leads to the **Sauk Mountain Trailhead**. This winds 3½ mi. past backcountry campsites near Sauk Lake to a 360° panoramic view of Mt. Rainier, Puget Sound, the San Juan Islands, and the Cascade Peaks. The park below has wheelchair-accessible trails and the nicest campsites in the area. (☎ 853-8461, reservation 800-452-5687. 8 sites, $14; 50 full hookups, $20; $6 per extra vehicle. 3-sided Adirondack cabins with 8-person bunk beds $19.)

Continue one mile east to Skagit County's **Howard Miller Steelhead Park**, on the Skagit River, where anglers come to catch the park's tasty namesake. (☎ 853-8808. Tent sites $12, hookups $16, 3-sided Adirondack lean-tos $16.) The surrounding **Mt. Baker-Snoqualmie National Forest** permits free camping closer to the high peaks, but requires trail park passes, available from the Forest Service and local businesses ($3 per day). These are not required when parking in **Ross Lake National Recreation Area** or in **North Cascades National Park** on Cascade River Rd. (see below).

AROUND MARBLEMOUNT. The major destination in Marblemount is the **Marblemount Wilderness Information Center**, 1 mi. north of West Marblemount on a well-marked road. This is the best resource for backcountry trip-planning in the North Cascades. Exploring the park can only be done well on a multi-day hiking trip; those serious about seeing the North Cascades should plan on passing through here. They are the only place to pick up backcountry permits, and have updates on trails and weather. (☎ 873-4500 ext. 39. Open July-Aug. Su-Th 7am-6pm, F-Sa 7am-8pm; winter call ahead.)

East on Rte. 20, the roadside shack for **Cascadian Farms**, at Mile 100.5, blends up frosty shakes ($3.50) with berries grown in the adjacent fields that are part of the largest organic operation in the US. (☎ 853-8173. Open in summer daily 8am-8pm.) Three miles west of Marblemount (Mile 103), **Clark's Skagit River Resort** offers camping. (☎ 873-2250 or 800-273-2606, www.northcascades.com. Tents $15; hookups $20; cabins from $59. Office open 9am-9pm.) Hundreds (no joke) of bunnies roam the groomed landscape. Eat dinner there at the **Eatery**, 58439 Rte. 20, famous valley-wide for the pie. (Open daily 6:30am-8pm.) Stock up on drinking water and firewood ($3 per bundle) at **Marblemount Mercantile Market**. (☎ 873-4274. Open 9am-9pm; winter 9am-7pm.)

A ROOM WITH A VIEW While on Rte. 20 anywhere east of Mazama, look north to the highest mountain, and on top you'll see a small hut: the Goat Peak Lookout, home to local celebrity Lightnin' Bill and his trusty dog Lookout Turk. Lightnin' Bill, so nicknamed not because he's speedy, but because he "loves to be up here during those lightnin' storms," inhabits one of the last manned (and dogged) fire lookouts in the state. What does he do for weeks at a time in a one-room hut, 7000 ft. in the sky? Bill writes poetry (he'll read you some when you reach the tower), enjoys the view, and chats with those who make the hike to his isolated home. To visit Bill and Turk, head east from Mazama 2 mi. on County Rd. 1163 to the gravel Forest Rd. 52. Continue almost 3 mi. along the dusty road and turn left on Forest Rd. 5225. Drive 6¼ mi. and turn right on Rd. 5225-200. Continue 2½ mi. to the end of the road and the beginning of the trailhead. (The directions are far more complicated than the actual driving.) Signs to Goat's Peak L.O. lead the way. The trail to the fire lookout is a steep 2½ mi. jaunt, and passes through colorful alpine meadows. Bill will show you everything in his little home, from the lightning rod above to the glass ashtrays under the bedposts that insulate him from electrical storms. Then he'll take your picture and you'll be recorded in his photo album forever.

Stay where the loggers and vagabonds of yore stayed, in the last surviving roadhouse built along this route, the **Log House Inn**, 60117 Hwy. 20. It offers primitive rooms with bathrooms in the hall. The restaurant downstairs sells hamburgers for $4.25. (☎873-4311. Singles $29-31; doubles $30-33.) When you leave Marblemount, **be prepared:** there are no major service stations for more than 69 mi.

MARBLEMOUNT TO ROSS LAKE ☎ 206

NORTH CASCADES NATIONAL PARK. East from Marblemount and across the Skagit River, Highway 20 enters into the wildest, most rugged park in Washington. The North Cascades National Park is unlike any other, for hardly any attempt is made to give the vehicle-bound a taste of the area's flavor. Those determined to penetrate the park should allot a stout pair of boots and several days toward that goal. Provide these, and the North Cascades will happily share the jagged rock and pine-scented air that keeps so many locals coming back. The National Park is divided into four sections. The North Unit reaches up to the Canadian border, and is the most remote area of the park. The few trails that do cross it begin mainly near Mt. Baker or Hozemon, a small camp accessible from British Columbia. The Ross Lake National Recreation Area runs along Hwy. 20 and north along Ross Lake. This is the most highly used area of the park, and the one to which most confine their stay. South Unit is pocked by glaciers and is accessible from trails leaving Hwy. 20 along its north and east sides, making in an inviting wilderness to explore. Finally, at the park's southernmost tip, the Lake Chelan National Recreation Area protects the beautiful wilderness around Stehekin and the northern tip of Lake Chelan. Most begin their trips via the Chelan ferry here. As with every National Park in Washington, the North Cascade is surrounded by ample National Forest. Know which you are headed into, as different agencies, permits, and rules apply. The Marblemount Wilderness Information Center, 4 mi. to the west of the park, provides backcountry permits, required for any overnight travel in the park, and info on hikes. Another source for hiking info is the North Cascades Visitors Center and Ranger Station. (☎386-4495. Open daily 8:30am-6pm; winter Sa-Su 9am-4:30pm.) Thunder Creek Trail is among the most popular hikes in the area. The 1½ mi. meander through old growth cedar and fir, begins at Colonial Creek Campground at Rte. 20, Mile 130. A more challenging variation is the Fourth of July Pass Trail. It begins 2 mi. into the Thunder Creek trail, is 3¼ mi., and climbs 3500 ft. toward boggling views of glacier-draped Colonial and Snowfield peaks.

The national park's Goodell Creek Campground at Mile 119, just west of Newhalem, is a beautiful, small area, with leafy sites suitable for tents and small trailers, and a launch site for whitewater rafting on the Skagit River. (21 sites, $10. Pit toilets, water shut off after Oct., when sites are free.) Newhalem Creek Campground, at Mile 120, shares a turn-off with the visitors center. It is a larger facility geared toward the RV folk (111 sites, $12).

The amazing, 3½ mi. Cascade Pass Trail begins 22 mi. from the bridge, and continues to Stehekin Valley Rd. where shuttles service the Bridge Creek campgrounds. Stehekin, at the northern tip of Lake Chelan, can be reached by boat (see Stehekin, p. 219). Apply to the electric company if you wish to settle in the controlled community of Newhalem, or pass through after the Ross Lake Recreation Area, a buffer between the highway and North Cascades National Park.

ROSS LAKE. Seattle City Light, in **Diablo,** operates a small museum and provides tours of the **Skagit Hydroelectric Project,** which generates 35% of Seattle's electricity. Tour highlights include a walk across **Diablo Dam,** a ride up the 560 ft. **Incline Railway,** and a boatride around the lake. A shorter tour, lacking the boatride, was cancelled in 2001 due to electricity shortages. Call to see if it is back up and running. (☎206-684-3030. Visitors center open Th-M 9am-4pm; 3hr. tours 11am, $20, children $10.) The artificial and astoundingly green-blue expanse of **Ross Lake,** behind **Ross Dam,** snakes into the mountains as far as the Canadian border. The lake is accessible by trails and is ringed by 15 primitive campgrounds, some accessible by trail, others by boat. Back in the planned powerstation town of **Newhalem,** grab necessities at the **Skagit General Store.** It has fishing licenses and basic groceries. (☎386-4489. Open M-Th 7:30am-5:30pm, F 7:30am-7:30pm, Sa-Su 10am-6:30pm; winter M-F 7:45am-5:30pm.)

ROSS LAKE TO WINTHROP ☎509

This is the most beautiful segment of Rte. 20. The frozen creases of a mountain face rise before you: snow and granite rise on one side of the road, sheer cliffs plummet on the other. Leaving the basin of Ross Lake, the road begins to climb, exposing the jagged peaks of the North Cascades. The **Pacific Crest Trail** (Mile 157) crosses Rte. 20 at **Rainy Pass** on one of the most scenic and difficult legs of its 2500 mi. course from Mexico to Canada (which provides another route to Stehekin, see p. 219). Near Rainy Pass, groomed scenic trails of 1-3 mi. can be hiked in sneakers, provided the snow has melted (about mid-July). Just off Rte. 20, an overlook at **Washington Pass** (Mile 162) rewards with one of the state's most dramatic panoramas, an astonishing view of the red rocks exposed by **Early Winters Creek** in **Copper Basin.** The area has many well-marked trailheads off Rte. 20 that lead into the desolate wilderness. The popular 2½ mi. walk to **Blue Lake** begins half a mile east of Washington Pass—it's usually snow-free by July and provides a gentle ascent through meadows. An easier 2 mi. hike to **Cutthroat Lake** departs from an access road 4½ mi. east of Washington Pass. From the lake, the trail continues 4 mi. farther and almost 2000 ft. higher to **Cutthroat Pass** (6820 ft.), treating determined hikers to a breathtaking view of towering, rugged peaks.

WINTHROP TO TWISP ☎509

WINTHROP

Farther east is **Winthrop,** a town desperately and somewhat successfully trying to market its frontier history. At the **Winthrop Information Station,** 202 Riverside, at the junction with Rte. 20, the staff laud the beauty of this nouveau Old West town, complete with boardwalks, blocky-letter signs and horse-drawn wagons. (☎996-2125. Open daily early May to mid-Oct. 10am-5pm.) Winthrop's summer begins and ends with rodeos on Memorial and Labor Day weekends. Late July brings the top-notch, three-day **Winthrop Rhythm and Blues Festival,** where big-name blues bands flock to don their boots, belt their tunes, endorse radio stations, and play cowboy. (☎996-2541. Tickets $40 in advance, $50 at the gate. On-site camping $15.) The town also rocks with the two-day **Country Musical Festival** in late July. Top-name bands fill the horse barns and saloons and thousands back in to listen. (☎996-2125. Tickets $40 in advance, $48 at the door.)

224 ■ EASTERN WASHINGTON

If you need more than a tent or a barn, the **Mt. Gardner Inn**, 611 Hwy. 20, will do the trick with A/C, fridges, and TVs. (☎996-2000. Queen-size bed singles $39, doubles $45-65.) The best local camping is 4 mi. outside of town at **Pearrygin Lake State Park**, a lakefront park with beach, showers and just enough shade. (☎996-2370 or 800-233-0321. Follow signs from Winthrop. 83 sites, $14; RVs $20.) Pan for gold at **Grubstake and Co**. If you don't strike it rich, settle for a sunflower burger ($7) or lemonade. (☎996-2375. Open daily 7am-8pm.) **Rocking Horse Ranch**, 18381 Hwy. 20, 10 mi. west of Winthrop on Rte. 20, gives guided trail rides and has campsites. (☎996-2768. $25 for 1½hr., $90 full day, or $105 overnight trip. Sites $12.) Rent a bike at **Winthrop Mountain Sports**, 257 Riverside Ave. (☎996-2886. Open M-F 9am-6:30pm, Sa 9am-7:30pm, Su 9am-6pm. $15-25 per 4hr., $20 per day.)

The **Methow Valley Visitor Center** (MET-how) is a National Forest information office, where info about the surrounding Okanagan N.F. is readily dispensed. (☎996-4000. Open daily 9am-5pm; call for winter hours.) In winter the biggest attraction is the cross-country skiing. Nearly 125 mi. of groomed cross-country skiing trails are linked by the **Methow Valley Community trail**, which parallels Rte. 20: the **Sun Mountain Trails** around Winthrop, the **Rendezvous Trails** near Rendezvous Mountain to the west, and the **Mazama Trails** around the town of Mazama. Call the **Methow Valley Sports Trail Association** for more info (☎996-3287; trail conditions 800-682-5787; www.mvsta.org).

Between Winthrop and Twisp on East Country Rd. 9129, the **North Cascades Smokejumper Base** is staffed by courageously insane smokejumpers who give a thorough tour of the base and explain the procedures and equipment used to help them parachute into forest fires and put them out. (☎997-2031. Open in summer and early fall daily 8am-6pm. Tours 10am-4:30pm.)

TWISP

Flee the Wild West of Winthrop and sleep in **Twisp**, named for the yellowjacket, or "T-wasp" in the local dialect. Nine miles south of Winthrop on Rte. 20, this village is more laid-back, less busy, and offers lower prices than its dressed-up neighbor to the north. The **Methow Valley Ranger Station**, 502 Glover St., can assist with camping and hiking. (☎997-2131. Open M-F 7:45am-4:30pm.) **Methow Valley Central Reservations** (☎996-2148) can help you with hotels. At the **Sportsman Motel**, 1010 E Rte. 20, a barracks-like facade masks tastefully decorated rooms with kitchens. (☎997-2911. Singles $39; doubles $44.) **Sisters Cafe**, 104 N Glover St., seems a little out of place in this old Western town, serving excellent California-style wraps. (☎997-1323. Open M-F 8am-5pm, Sa 9am-2pm.) Grab cinnamon "twisps" ($1.85), or a take-out lunch special ($2-5) at the **Cinnamon Twisp Bakery**, 116 N Glover St. (☎997-5030. Open M-F 7am-5pm, Sa-Su 7am-3pm.) The brewery/restaurant on 2nd St. also comes highly recommended from Lightnin' Bill.

There are many **campgrounds** and **trails** 15-25 mi. up Twisp River Rd., just off Rte. 20 in Twisp. Most of the campsites are primitive and cost $5. For camping closer to the highway, head to the **Riverbend RV Park**, 19961 Rte. 20, 2 mi. west of Twisp. Beyond an abundance of slow-moving beasts (RVs), Riverbend has plenty of tent sites along the Methow River. (☎997-3500 or 800-686-4498. Office open daily 9am-9pm. Sites $15; hookups $20; $2 per person after 2 people.) From Twisp, Rte. 20 leads east to **Okanagan** and Rte. 153 runs south to **Lake Chelan** (see p. 217).

EASTERN WASHINGTON

Lying in the Cascade's rain shadow, the hills and valleys of the Columbia River Basin foster little more than browning grass, sagebrush, and tumbleweed. The construction of the dam in centuries past has made irrigation possible, thereby transforming the region into a land of bountiful fruit crops and their dazzling by-product: tasty, high-quality wines. Sunshine fills the days and attracts the moody and depressed from rainy Western Washington ("wetsiders"). The region boasts some of world's best apples and proudly bronzes flocks of visitors from all of the world every year. The calm beauty of the region permeates gentle farmland, rolling sand dunes, numerous waterways, and precious parks.

YAKIMA ☎ 509

Lying in the middle of some of the planet's most fertile land for fruit, Yakima (Yak-ih-muh) is a large rural town *par excellence*. The saving grace of the town is an active conference center—because of it, affordable accommodations abound. With rooms beginning at $35, Yakima is an attractive overnight stop to wash up, grab a good Mexican meal and then push on in the morning.

ORIENTATION AND PRACTICAL INFORMATION

Yakima is on **I-82,** 145 mi. (2½hr.) southeast of **Seattle** and 145 mi. (2½hr.) northwest of **Pendleton, OR.** The **Yakima Valley** lies southeast of the city, along I-82. Southeastern downtown, especially near the fairgrounds, can be dangerous at night. Numbered streets line up to the east of the railroad tracks, numbered avenues to the west. **Greyhound,** 602 E Yakima (☎457-5131 or 800-231-2222), stops in Yakima on the way to **Portland, OR** (4½hr.; 1-2 per day; M-Th $30, F-Su $32) and **Seattle** (3½hr.; 3 per day; M-Th $22, F-Su $24). Open M-F 7:45am-5pm; Sa 7:45am-4:30pm; Su and holidays 7:45-8:15am, 10:30-11am, and 2:30-4:30pm. **Yakima Transit** (☎575-6175), based at 4th St. and Chestnut Ave., near the clock, runs local buses. (50¢, seniors 25¢, ages 6-17 35¢. Day Pass $1.50. Runs M-F 5am-7pm, Sa 8am-7pm.) **Yakima Valley Visitor and Convention Bureau,** 10 N 8th St. (☎575-3010 or 800-221-0751; www.visityakima.com), in the convention center. Open summer M-F 8am-5pm, Sa 9am-5pm, Su 10am-4pm; Nov.-Mar. M-F 8am-5pm. **Laundromat: K's,** 602 Fruitvale St. (☎452-5335. Open daily 7am-9pm. Wash $1.25-3.75, dry 25¢ per 10min.) **Police:** 200 S 3rd St. (☎575-6200), at Walnut Ave. **Crisis Line:** ☎575-4200. 24hr. **Hospital: Providence Medical Center,** 110 S 9th Ave. (☎575-5000), at W Chestnut. **Post Office:** 205 W Washington Ave. (☎800-275-8777), at 3rd Ave. Open M-F 8:30am-5:30pm, Sa 9am-3pm. **ZIP Code:** 98903.

ACCOMMODATIONS AND CAMPING

The fruit bowl is overflowing with reasonably priced, run-of-the-mill motels, and the best way to find a cheap room is to comparison shop on 1st St. (I-82 Exit 31). Cheap and pleasant **Forest Service campgrounds** (Ranger info ☎653-2205) lie along the Naches River on Hwy. 410, about 30 mi. west of town on the way to Mt. Rainier. Most sites with drinking water cost $6-18. A list of other sites is available from the **Naches Ranger Station,** 10061 Hwy. 12, in Naches, 16 mi. from town on Hwy. 12. (☎653-2205. Open M-F 7:45am-4:30pm, Sa 7am-noon; winter weekdays only. Front foyer with materials open 24hr.) **Red Apple Motel,** 416 N 1st St. is friendly and affordable with cable, A/C, laundry, and pool. (☎248-7150; www.redapplemotel.com. Reception 7am-1am. Singles Sa-Su $47, M-F $37; doubles $53, $42.) **Yakima Inn,** 1022 N 1st St., near I St. has large cheap rooms and a pool. (☎453-5615. Singles $32; doubles $37.)

FOOD

The *Yakima Valley Farm Products Guide*, distributed at the visitors center and at regional hotels and stores, lists local **fruit sellers** and **u-pick farms,** although the latter are fast disappearing because of liability concerns. **Fruit stands** are common on the outskirts of town, particularly on 1st St. and near interstate interchanges (look for several off I-82 Exit 37). A great place to buy fruit is on **Lateral A,** between Yakima and nearby Wapato (6 mi. south of town on Hwy. 12, on the right). In summer, the **Yakima Farmer's Market** (☎457-5765) closes off 3rd and Yakima Ave. in front of the Capitol Theater on Sundays from 9:30am-2:30pm. **Grant's Brewery Pub,** 32 N Front St., at A St., in the old train depot, is a comfortable, family-style pub with microbrews. It has live jazz, blues, and folk bands some weekends. (☎575-2922. Open M-Th 11:30am-11pm, F-Sa 11:30am-midnight, Su 2-8pm; kitchen closes 1-2hr. earlier.) Every day is Cinco De Mayo at **Espinoza's,** 1026 N 1st St. (☎452-3969. Open M-Th 11am-10pm, F-Sa 11am-11pm, Su 11am-9pm.)

SIGHTS AND EVENTS

Washington is the second-largest wine producer in the nation. The **vineyards** just east of the Cascades benefit not only from mineral-rich soil deposited by ancient volcanoes but also a rain shield that keeps the land dry and easily controlled by irrigation. For a complete list of wineries, pick up the *Wine Tour* guide at visitors centers or call the **Yakima Valley Wine Growers Association** (☎800-258-7270; www.yakimavalleywine.com). **Staton Hills Winery,** 71 Gangle Rd., in Wapato, 10min. south of Yakima, is the closest vineyard, as well as the classiest. From I-82 Exit 40, head east, looking up for the sign and vineyards on the hills above. Specializing in Cabernet and Merlot, **Sageland/Staton** (STAY-ten) **Hills** boasts an upscale tasting room trumped only by the panoramic view. (☎877-2112. Open daily 9am-5pm. 4 free 1 oz. servings.) The nearby town of **Zillah** lays claim to seven wineries, including the smaller **Bonair Winery,** 500 S Bonair, which boasts blue-ribbon Chardonnays ($11) and affordable Sunset Pinks ($6.50). Head east from I-82 Exit 52, turn left at the BP gas station onto Cheyne, left again onto Highland Dr., then left once more onto Bonair Rd. (☎829-6027; www.bonairwine.com. Open Apr.-Oct. daily 10am-5pm; call for winter hours.) The 10-day **Central Washington State Fair** (☎248-7160), held in late September, includes agricultural displays, cattle and horse shows, local arts and crafts, rodeos, and big-name entertainers.

DAYTRIP FROM YAKIMA: TOPPENISH

Toppenish, 19 mi. southeast of Yakima, is the gateway town of the **Yakama Reservation** (in 1991, as a gesture of independence from the state, the tribe re-adopted the original spelling of its name from its 1855 treaty with the US government). Toppenish brags about being the city where "The West still lives," as it holds tight to its railroads, rodeos, farming, and history. The **Yakama Nation Cultural Center,** in Toppenish, presents exhibits on the culture of the 14 tribes and bands that inhabit the Yakima Valley. The fabulous museum concentrates on the oral tradition of the native Yakama. (☎865-2800. Open daily 8am-5pm. $4, students and seniors $2, ages 7-10 $1, under 6 75¢.) Yakima yields 75% of the nation's hops production; to pay tribute, you can tour the **American Hop Museum,** 22 South B St. Learn how beer is preserved and flavored in a series of exhibits. (☎865-4777. Open daily 11am-4pm. Donations appreciated.) The Old Depot Museum, across the street from the tourist office, celebrates all things steam-driven and even organizes weekend antique train rides. Call or stop in for details. (☎865-1911. Open Th-Sa 10am-5pm, Su noon-4pm. Train rides $8, children $5.) **Treaty Days** (June 7-9), which celebrate the Treaty of 1855, feature parades, salmon dinners, and **Mural-in-a-Day** (first Saturday in June), during which the town creates a large, historically accurate mural (running total is 61). The **Toppenish Powwow Rodeo** happens during the weekend closest to July 4th on Division Ave. in Toppenish; it features a parade, games, dancing, and live music, in addition to the rodeo. (☎829-9407. Fair $2. Rodeo $10 plus $2 parking fee.) For more information on either event, contact the **Toppenish Chamber of Commerce,** 5A S Toppenish Ave. (☎865-3262 or 800-569-3982), at S Division.

SPOKANE ☎509

Ah, 1974: Gerald Ford in the White House, Elvis in the white suit, and Spokane (spoe-KAN) in the world's spotlight. Built on silver mining and grown prosperous as an agricultural rail link, Spokane found fame when the World's Fair came to town in 1974. Parks, department stores, and skyways sprang up in preparation for the city's promising future. Today, cafes catering to a college crowd and 50s-style burger joints make for a comfortable suburban atmosphere, and the melancholy remains of Spokane '74 slumber in Riverfront Park. A small-town America feel and the culture of a larger city make Spokane '02 worthy of a stopover.

Spokane

ACCOMMODATIONS
Boulevard Motel, 8
Downtowner Motel, 9
Riverside State Park, 2

PUBS
Dempsey's Brass Rail, 6
Satellite Diner & Bar, 4

FOOD
Dick's, 10
Fitzbillie's Bagels, 5
Frank's Diner, 7
Onion, 3
Spokane Marketplace, 1

MUSIC AND CLUBS
Avista Stadium, 11

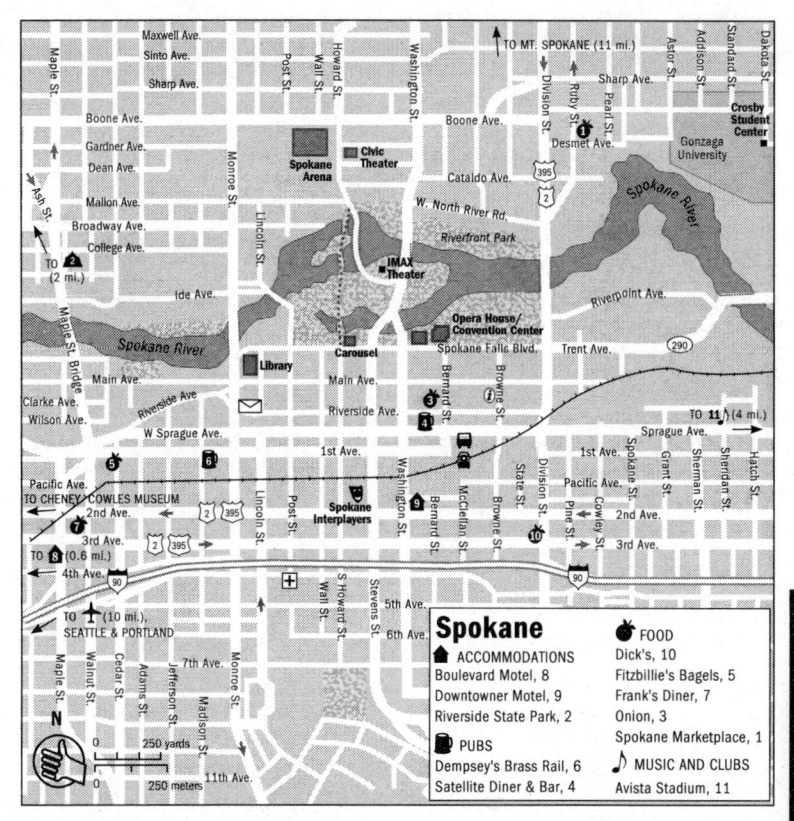

TRANSPORTATION

Spokane is 280 mi. east of Seattle on I-90, between Exits 279 and 282. Avenues run east-west parallel to the **Spokane River**, streets run north-south, and both alternate directions one-way. The city is divided north-south by **Sprague Ave.** and east-west by **Division St.** Downtown is the quadrant north of Sprague Ave. and west of Division St., wedged between I-90 and the river.

Airplanes: Spokane International Airport (☎ 624-3218), off I-90 8 mi. southwest of town. Most major carriers service **Seattle, Portland,** and beyond.

Trains: Amtrak, 221 W 1st Ave. (☎ 624-5144; 800-USA-RAIL), at Bernard St. Counter open M-F 10am-6pm, daily 10pm-6am. All trains depart 1-3am. 1 train per day to **Seattle** and **Portland, OR** ($35-75, depending on season and availability.)

Buses: Greyhound, 221 W 1st Ave. (☎ 624-5251), at Bernard St., in the same building as Amtrak. Ticket office open daily 7:30am-6:20pm and 12:15-2:20pm. One way to: **Seattle** (6hr., 4 per day, $26) and **Portland, OR** (8-10hr., 4 per day, $36). **Northwestern Trailways** (☎ 838-5262 or 800-366-3830) shares the same terminal, serving other parts of WA and large cities. Ticket office open daily 8am-6:45pm. Senior discounts.

Public Transportation: Spokane Transit Authority (☎ 328-7433) buses serve all of Spokane, including Eastern Washington University in Cheney. 75¢, under 5 free. The major downtown routes (along Sprague Ave. and Division St.) operate until 12:20am M-F.

Taxis: Checker Cab, ☎ 624-4171. **Yellow Cab,** ☎ 624-4321. Both run 24hr.

Car Rental: U-Save Auto Rental, 918 W 3rd St. (☎ 455-8018), at Monroe St. Cars from $27 per day, $150 per week. Unlimited mileage within WA for more than 3 days; otherwise 20¢ per mi. after 200 mi. Must be 21 with major credit card; $5 per day if under 25. Open M-F 7am-7pm, Sa 8am-5pm, Su 10am-5pm.

PRACTICAL INFORMATION

Tourist Office: Spokane Area Convention and Visitors Bureau, 201 W Main St. (☎ 800-248-3230). Exit 281 off I-90. Offers free Internet access and local phone calls. Open May-Sept. M-F 8:30am-5pm, Sa 9am-5pm, Su 10am-3pm; Oct.-Apr. M-F 8:30am-5pm.

Equipment Rental: Mountain Gear, 2002 N Division St. (☎ 325-9000 or 800-829-2009; www.mgear.com) rents canoes and kayaks ($45 per day), snowboards ($24), and skis ($10). Open M-F 9:30am-8pm, Sa 9:30am-6pm, Su 11am-5pm.

Internet Access: Spokane **Library**, 906 W Main St. (☎ 444-5333). Free 15min. Open M and Tu noon-8pm, W-F 10am-6pm. **Cybergate Coffee Cafe**, 506 W Indiana Ave. (☎ 327-4378). Access $5 per hr. A variety of drinks ($1.50-3). Open M 6am-8pm, Tu-Sa 6am-10pm, Su 8am-8pm. Also, see the **Visitors Bureau** above.

Laundromat: Otis Hotel Coin-Op, 110 S Madison St. (☎ 624-3111), at 1st Ave. $1 wash, dry 25¢ per 20min. Open daily 6am-6pm.

Emergency: ☎ 911. **Police:** ☎ 456-2233. 24hr. crime report line.

Crisis Line: ☎ 838-4428. 24hr.

Washington Road Conditions: ☎ 800-695-7623.

Medical Services: Rockwood Clinic, 400 E 5th Ave. (☎ 838-2531 or 459-1577), at Sherman St. Open daily for walk-ins 8am-8pm. **Deaconess Medical Center**, 800 W 5th Ave. at Lincoln St. (emergency ☎ 458-7100, info 458-5800). 24hr. emergency room.

Post Office: 904 W Riverside. Ave. (☎ 800-275-8777). Open M-F 6am-5pm. **ZIP Code:** 99210

ACCOMMODATIONS AND CAMPING

Cheaper motels are sprinkled among the chains along Rte. 2 toward the airport, and others can be found on the north end of town along Division Ave.

Boulevard Motel, 2905 W Sunset Blvd. (☎ 747-1060). Take 4th Ave. southwest from downtown to the I-90 Business Loop, which becomes Sunset Blvd. The recently-renovated rooms are so clean you could eat off the floor. Singles $34; doubles $40.

Downtowner Motel, 165 S Washington St. (☎ 838-4511), at 2nd Ave. Aging exterior and the mint green ivy motif. This motel's prices and convenient downtown location can't be beat. Continental breakfast and cable included. Singles $30; doubles $38.

Riverside State Park (☎ 800-233-0321; reservations ☎ 800-452-5687), 6 mi. northwest of downtown. Take the Maple St. Bridge north and turn left at the brown park sign; follow signs to Rte. 291 (Nine Mile Rd.), turn left onto Rifle Club Rd. and follow to the park. 101 newly rebuilt sites in a sparse ponderosa forest near the river. Showers 25¢ per 3min. $14, hookups $20, hiker/biker sites $6.

Falk's Lodge at Mount Spokane State Park, 24817 N Mt. Spokane Park Dr. (☎ 238-9114). 30 mi. northeast of Spokane at entrance to Mt. Spokane State Park. Take Rte. 2 north out of town and then follow Rte. 206 (Mt. Spokane Park Dr.) east to lodge. Showers and toilets. 6 tent sites, $10. 21 RVs, $13.

SPOKANE ■ 229

FOOD

Spokane offers great produce from local farmers. The **Spokane Marketplace,** 1100 N Ruby St., northwest of town at DeSmet St., sells fresh fruit, baked goods, and crafts. (☎456-0100. Open Apr. Sa 9am-4pm; May-Dec. W and Sa 9am-4pm.) Groceries are at **Safeway,** 1617 W 3rd St. (☎624-8852. Open 24hr.)

The Onion, 302 W Riverside Ave. (☎624-9965), at Bernard St. Head to the Onion for an amazing burger ($6-8), or stick with the huckleberry shake ($3) with throngs of locals and visitors who've been going to the Onion since 1978. Open daily 11am-about 11pm.

Frank's Diner, 1516 W 2nd Ave. (☎747-8798), at Walnut St. Voted the #1 breakfast in Spokane for the past 4 years. Breakfast (as well as lunch and dinner) all day long—a whopping 12,000 eggs and 2 tons of hash browns a month! More elegant than most pricey restaurants. 2 eggs with potatoes $5.50. Open M-Sa 6am-9pm, Su 6am-3pm.

Dick's, 10 E 3rd Ave. (☎747-2481), at Division St. Look for the huge panda sign near I-90 and find burgers by the bagful. This place is a time warp—customers eat in their parked cars and pay 1950s prices: burgers 59¢; fries 59¢; shakes 89¢. Always crowded. Open M-Th 8am-midnight, F-Sa 8am-1am, Su 9am-midnight; mid-June to Aug. open 1hr. later.

Fitzbillie's Bagel Bakery, W 1325 1st Ave. (☎747-1834), at Cedar St. Actually lives up to its promise of "New York Style," with the exception of the sunny patio. Truly satisfying bagels with flavored cream cheese $1.90; soup, salad, and sandwich combos $5-6. Open M-F 6am-5pm, Sa-Su 7am-3pm.

NIGHTLIFE AND SPORTS

Spokane has the best of both worlds—minor league teams for travelers in search of small-town USA and great nightlife for those desperate for a big-city fix. For local happenings, pick up the *Spokesman-Review* Friday "Weekend" section, or look for the *Inlander* or the *Wrap*, both available at the library.

Dempsey's Brass Rail, 909 W 1st Ave. (☎747-5362), has a hot dance floor, flashy decor, and free Internet access by the bar. Drag Diva shows (F-Sa) and rainbow-striped beer taps make Dempsey's "the place to be gay." Happy Hour 3-7pm daily. Kitchen serves dinner daily 3-8pm. Open Su-Th 3pm-2am, F-Sa 3pm-4am.

Satellite Diner and Bar, 425 W Sprague Ave. (☎624-3952), is always full and provides that crucial post-party breakfast. Voted the best after-midnight hangout in Spokane, it's a great place to people-watch until 4am over biscuits and gravy ($3.25). Microbrews $3. Open M-F 7am-4am, Sa-Su 6pm-4am; bar closes at 2am.

Baseball: The **Spokane Indians** play single-A baseball in the Northwest League of Professional Baseball from June to August in **Avista Stadium,** at the Spokane Fairgrounds, 602 N Havana St. (☎535-2922; www.ticketswest.com. Great seats only $4, seniors $3.)

Hockey: Sept.-Mar. the minor league **Spokane Chiefs** play hockey in the Canadian Hockey League in the **Spokane Memorial Arena.** (720 W Mallon Ave. Follow signs from the Maple St. Exit off I-5. ☎535-7825. Box office open M-F 10am-6pm. Seats $7-15.) The Arena also hosts musical talents from Godsmack to Ani DiFranco, as well as seasonal attractions like WWF wrestling. All Arena-sponsored events are ticketed by **Select-A-Seat.** (Select-A-Seat ☎325-7469; tickets 325-7328 or 800-325-7328; www.ticketswest.com). The ticket line is open 24hr. and requires credit card.

SIGHTS

MANITO PARK. Undoubtedly one of the most beautiful spots in Spokane, this park boasts five sections of lovingly maintained flowerbeds. Commune with the carp in the **Nishinomiya Japanese Garden,** overdose on the blooming

230 ■ EASTERN WASHINGTON

roses on **Rosehill** in late June, relax in the elegant **Duncan Garden,** or sniff around in the **David Graiser Conservatory** and the **Joel Farris Perennial Garden.** *(4 W 21st Ave. From downtown, go south on Bernard St. and turn left on 21st Ave.* ☎ *625-6622. Open 24hr.; buildings locked from dusk-8am. Free.)*

RIVERFRONT PARK. The centerpiece of downtown, the park is Spokane's civic center and the place for a pleasant stroll. Developed for the 1974 World's Fair, the park's 100 acres are divided down the middle by the rapids that culminate in Spokane Falls. In the park, the **IMAX Theater** houses your basic five-story movie screen and a projector the size of a Volkswagen Bug. **Serendipity Cycles,** in the park, rents surrey cycles and hot shots. The park hosts **ice-skating** in the winter. *(Park: 507 N Howard St., just north of downtown.* ☎ *456-4386. www.SpokaneRiverfrontPark.com. Theater:* ☎ *625-6686. Shows June-Sept. on the hour; call for winter schedule. Open daily 11am-9pm. $7, under 12 $5, over 62 $6. Carousel: Open Su-Th 11am-8pm, F-Sa 11am-10pm. $1.75 per whirl, under 12 or over 62 $1. A one-day pass, $15, covers both, plus a ferris wheel, park train, sky ride, and more. Cycling: Open daily June-Aug. 10am-9pm. $12 per hr., $20 per hr. with trailer. Ice skating: $4.50, under 12 and over 62 $3.50; skate rental $2.)*

CHENEY COWLES MEMORIAL MUSEUM. Still closed for a major expansion, the new museum is expected to open in late fall of 2001 and promises amazing views of the Spokane valley in addition to great new exhibits. It will cover the area's history from the Lewis and Clark expedition to Expo '74. *(2316 W 1st Ave. Follow 2nd Ave. west out of town, turn right onto and go two blocks along Poplar St.* ☎ *456-3931. Events will continue off site until the museum's completion. Call 363-5330.)*

CROSBY STUDENT CENTER. Located at Gonzaga University, this is a must-see for Bing Crosby devotees. The tiny Crosbyana Room is a shrine of records and relics from Gonzaga's most illustrious alum. The center also features a big screen TV, plush couches, and a cafe. *(502 E Boone St.* ☎ *323-4097. Open June-Aug. M-F 8:30am-4:30pm; Sept.-May M-F 8am-midnight, Sa-Su 11am-midnight. Free.)*

MUSIC. Spokane Symphony Orchestra calls the **Opera House** home. The opera house also hosts traveling **Broadway shows** and special performances. *(Opera House: 334 W Spokane Falls Blvd. Ticket Office: 601 Riverside in the Mezzanine of the Bank of America building.* ☎ *326-3136. Open M-F 9:30am-5:30pm. Box office at the Opera House: open M-F 10am-5pm. Orchestra: www.spokanesymphony.com.)* Known for locally produced shows, the **Civic Theater** has a downstairs space for experimental productions. *(1020 N Howard St., opposite the Spokane Veteran's Memorial Arena.* ☎ *325-2507 or 800-446-9576. $17, seniors $14, students $10.)* The **Spokane Interplayers Ensemble** is a resident professional theater. *(174 S Howard St.* ☎ *455-7529. Season runs Sept.-June Tu-Sa. $14-18, under 25 $8-10.)*

PULLMAN ☎ 509

Tiny Pullman has two main attractions: the undulating, green-and-yellow hills that supply the nation's lentils and make up Washington's Palouse (puh-LOOZ) region; and enormous Washington State University (WSU, a.k.a. "Wazoo"), alma mater of sociologist William Julius Wilson and Far Side cartoonist Gary Larson. The strong presence of the 20,000-student school is evident from the Cougar banners that line the streets and grace store windows: the college is the town.

◘ TRANSPORTATION. Pullman lies at the junction of Rte. 27 (which becomes Grand Ave. in town) and Rte. 270. US 195 passes the city just to the west on its way from Spokane (70 mi. north). In town, Rte. 270 becomes Davis Way in the west and Main St. in the east. The campus lies just east of town; Stadium Way, which intersects N Grand Ave. on one end and Main St. on the other, loops through its center. **Northwestern Trailways,** 1002 NW Nye St. (☎ 334-1412 or 800-366-3830; open M-F

6:45-7:30am, 10:30am-noon, and 1-5pm; Sa 6:45-7:30am, 10:30-11:15am, and 2-4:30pm), sends buses to **Seattle** (2 per day, $40) and **Spokane** (2 per day, $15). Public bus schedules are available around campus and at the visitors center. **Pullman Transit** runs from WSU to downtown. (☎332-6535. 50¢, under 18 and seniors 30¢. Runs M-F 7am-6pm.) **Wheatland Express** runs to the University of Idaho in Moscow, ID, just 15min. away and makes several stops in both Pullman and Moscow. (☎334-2200. In-town fare 75¢, children and seniors 50¢, between cities $2. Runs daily 6am-6pm; mid-May to mid-Aug. no Sa or Su service.) **Moscow-Pullman Cab** (☎208-883-4744). $2 base, $1.50 per mi. 24hr. **Car Rental: U-Save,** 1115 S Grand Ave. (☎334-5195). $31 per day, 25¢ per mi. after 200 mi. Must be 21 with major credit card. Open M-F 8am-5:30pm, Sa 9am-5pm.

■ PRACTICAL INFORMATION. Visitor Information: Chamber of Commerce, 415 N Grand Ave. (☎334-3565 or 800-365-6948; www.pullman-wa.com). Waxes eloquent on the lentil. Open M-F 9am-5pm. **Betty's Coin-Op Laundry,** at the intersection of North Grand and Stadium Way. Wash 75¢, dry 25¢ per 12min. Open 7am-11pm daily. **Police:** 260 SE Kamiaken St. (☎332-2521). For emergencies, **Pullman Memorial Hospital,** 1125 NE Washington Ave. (☎332-2541). Unlimited free Internet access is available in the cafeteria of the **WSU Compton student union,** on Wilson St., off Stadium Way. Also free 30min. at the public **library,** 210 N Grand Ave. (☎334-4555. Open M-W 10am-8pm, Th-F 10am-6pm, Sa-Su 1-5pm.) **Post Office:** 1135 S Grand Ave. (☎800-275-8777. Open M-F 8:30am-5pm, Sa 9am-1pm.) **ZIP Code:** 99163

■■ ACCOMMODATIONS AND FOOD. The steady stream of students through Pullman fosters a decent selection of no-frills motels. Rooms are easy to find, except on home football weekends, when rooms are booked one year in advance, and during commencement (the first week of May). Most rates drop in the summer, when the college students go home. **Manor Lodge Motel,** 455 SE Paradise St., at Main St., offers comfortable rooms with cable, fridges, microwaves, and nostalgia-inspiring shag carpet in varying hues of color. (☎334-2511. Singles $50; doubles $70; full kitchens $5 extra. $10 cheaper in summer.) **Nendels Inn,** 915 SE Main St., near Stadium Way, one block from WSU. (☎332-2646. Clean rooms. Fridges and microwaves available on request. Singles $45; doubles $49.) **American Travel Inn Motel,** 515 S Grand Ave., on US 195 has 35 spacious, spic 'n' span rooms. (☎334-3500. Cable, and a passable pool. Singles $42; doubles $46.) **Kamiak Butte County Park,** 10 mi. north of town on US 27, offers 10 forested campsites with water, toilets, and a view of the Palouse. (☎397-6238. Sites $10.)

Swilly's, 200 Kamiaken St., caters to the nicer crowd without busting the budget. Lunch is cheap, with sandwiches and calzones for $5-7, and dinners like pasta primavera or lasagna ($11 and $12) are delicious. (☎334-3795. Open M-Sa 11am-9:30pm.) **Sella's,** 1115 E Main St., has built its business on calzones. Build your own ($5.50) and top it off with a $5.50 gallon of beer. (☎334-1895. Open daily 11am-9pm in the summer; til 10pm during the school year.) **Ferdinand's** is on the WSU campus. From Wilson Ave., turn toward the tennis courts onto South Fairway and follow signs up to Ferdinand's. Ferdinand's Cougar Gold cheese ($14 for a 30 oz. tin) may be Pullman's biggest attraction. Excellent ice cream cone and a glass of milk will do your body good. (☎335-2141. Open M-F 9:30am-4:30pm.)

■■ OUTDOOR ACTIVITIES AND EVENTS. Pullman's gentle terrain and the broad, sweeping vistas of the pastoral Palouse region make the area ideal for exploration by bicycle or car. Professional photographers mass here to capture the purple-tinted prairies and wheat fields. **Kamiak,** 10 mi. north of town off Hwy. 27, and **Steptoe Buttes,** 28 mi. north off State Hwy. 195, both make enjoyable daytrips. Short hikes of medium difficulty to the top of each butte provide impressive views of the Palouse. Pack a lunch and head for the hills, or hit the paved **Chipman Trail** that runs the 8 mi. between Pullman and Moscow, ID. More hiking and a fabulous view of the **Palouse falls** cascading 198 ft. into a salt-rock canyon await at the Palouse Falls State Park, 80 mi. west of town on Hwy. 261. (☎549-3551. 10 free camping sites. Open Apr.-Oct.)

Sweltering summer temperatures and endless fields may spark a yearning for the high, cool forests of the **Blue Mountains.** One good approach is along Rte. 128 from the town of **Pomeroy,** a 62 mi. (about 1½hr.) drive southwest of Pullman. Follow US 195 south to **Clarkston,** and then proceed west on US 12. This area, including the vast, remote **Wenaha-Tucannon Wilderness,** is administered by the **Pomeroy Ranger District** of **Umatilla National Forest,** 31 W Main St., in Pomeroy. (☎843-1891. Open M-F 7:45am-4:30pm.) Info is also available at the **Walla Walla Ranger District office,** 1415 W Rose St., Walla Walla. (☎522-6290. Open M-F 7:45am-4:30pm.)

During the third weekend of August, the annual **National Lentil Festival** gets Pullman jumping with a parade, live music, a 5km fun run, and free samples of every type of food that you could possibly make out of lentils, including ice cream. Nearly all the lentils grown in the US come from the Palouse. In 2000, Pullman created a world-record-breaking 250-gallon bowl of lentil chili, simply because they could. For more info, write the National Lentil Festival, 415 N Grand Ave., Pullman 99163, or call 334-3565 or 800-365-6948.

BRITISH COLUMBIA

> **BRITISH COLUMBIA'S... Capital:** Victoria. **Population:** 4,067,200. **Area:** 947,796km^2. **Motto:** *Splendor sine Occasu* (splendor without diminishment). **Bird:** Steller's jay. **Flower:** Pacific dogwood. **Tree:** Western red cedar. **Holiday:** British Columbia Day, Aug. 1. **Sales Tax:** 7% PST plus 7% GST. **Drinking Age:** 19.

Traditional territory of Kwakwaka'wakw (historically known as the Kwagiulth or Kwakiutl), Nuu-cha-nulth (historically the Nootka), and Coast Salish nations among others, this region of the Northwest was the site of the earliest established trade between Europeans and coastal nations, and the resulting dispute between European nations over rights to the coast. Alexander MacKenzie reached Nootka Sound with his indigenous guides in 1793, the first instance of overland contact with the coastal nations. Eventually, gold was discovered north and east of Vancouver in 1858, bringing in a flood of prospectors. A minor saloon town with a small sawmill, the city of Vancouver blossomed on account of the Canadian Pacific Railroad, which made the town its western terminus in 1886.

Today, residents swear backwards and forwards that BC is the most beautiful place on earth, and most visitors share the opinion upon their departure. It's easy to see why. Small developed communities surround the city metropolis, and breathtaking wilderness is never more than a short drive away. Vancouver's relaxed populace enjoys the most diverse nightlife in western Canada, and gets two full months of summer to enjoy Burrard Inlet's sweeping beaches and snow-capped horizons. Vancouver's location on the mainland side of the Strait of Georgia affords immediate access to the Gulf Islands and Vancouver Island. Sechelt Peninsula, north along the mainland, is less developed than its surroundings and boasts amazing diving, kayaking, and hiking among the largest trees in Canada. Buses and ferries make for easy connections between Vancouver, Victoria, and Nanaimo, as well as the Gulf Islands and the Sechelt Peninsula.

BRITISH COLUMBIA'S HIGHLIGHTS

EDUCATE yourself on the Northwest's indigenous history and culture in Vancouver's famous **Museum of Anthropology** (see p. 246).

SKI to your heart content's at **Whistler/Blackcomb** (see p. 252), one of North America's premier resorts.

PICNIC by the beach at **Lighthouse Park** (see p. 248)

SOAK away your sorrows in **Radium Hot Springs** (see p. 303).

LEAP off a bridge in **Nanaimo** (see p. 269).

CHILL with the Haida on Moresby Island (see p. 326).

SCUBA DIVE off the **Sechelt Peninsula** (p. 249).

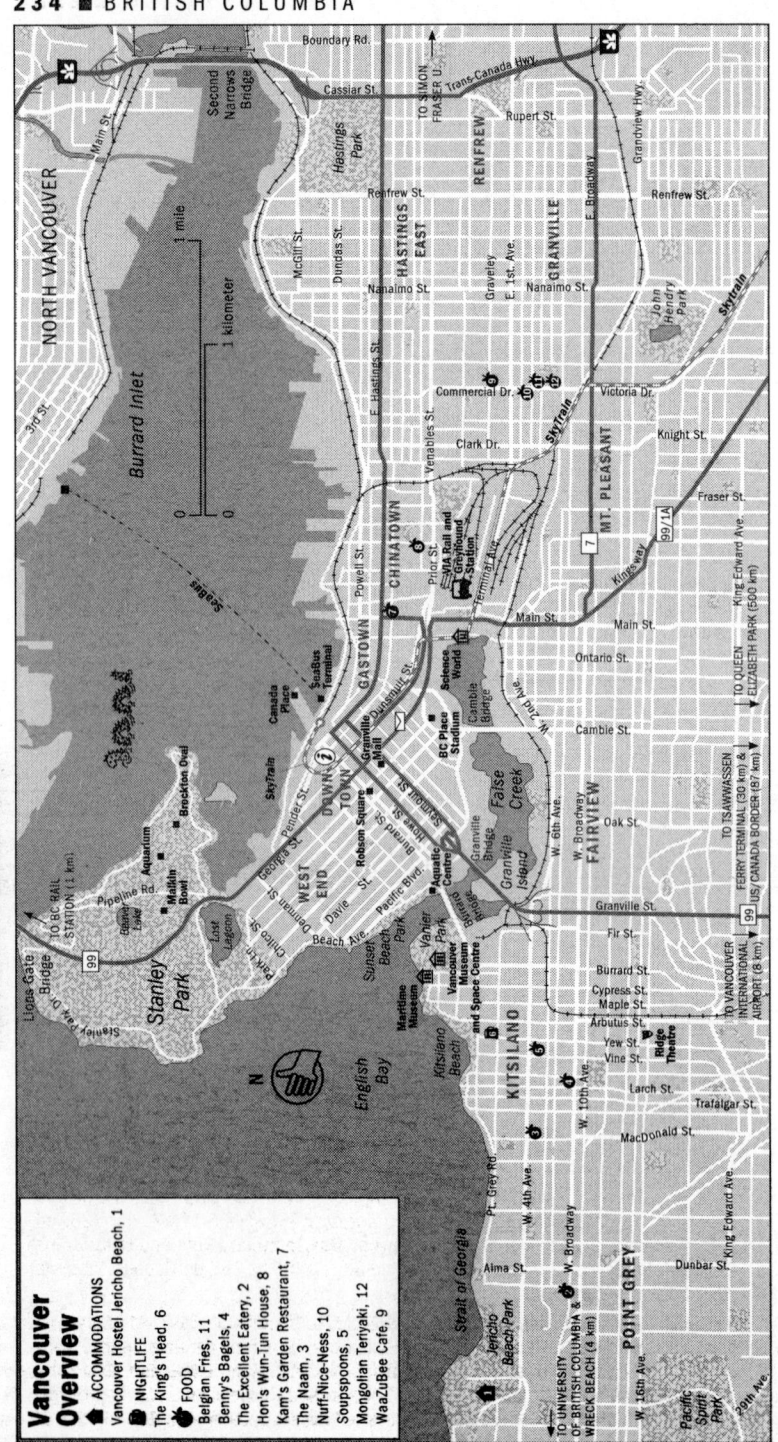

234 ■ BRITISH COLUMBIA

Vancouver Overview

ACCOMMODATIONS
Vancouver Hostel Jericho Beach, 1

NIGHTLIFE
The King's Head, 6

FOOD
Belgian Fries, 11
Benny's Bagels, 4
The Excellent Eatery, 2
Hon's Wun-Tun House, 8
Kam's Garden Restaurant, 7
The Naam, 3
Nurf-Nice-Ness, 10
Soupspoons, 5
Mongolian Teriyaki, 12
WaaZuBee Cafe, 9

INTERCITY TRANSPORTATION ■ 235

VANCOUVER ☎ 604/778

Like any self-respecting city on the west coast of North America, Vancouver boasts a thriving multicultural populace; the Cantonese influence is so strong that it is often referred to by its nickname, "Hongcouver." With the third largest Chinatown in North America and a strong influence of just about every other major culture from around the world, visitors are never hard-pressed to find exotic food or entertainment. And while this may be the norm for big cities, Vancouver mixes its diversity and urban excitement with stunning surroundings and ready access to outdoor adventure.

Wedged between the Pacific Ocean and the heavily forested Coast Mountain range, city founders recognized Vancouver's potential for getting freshly cut timber out to the ocean for sea transport. When the city incorporated in 1886, logging was its economic mainstay. In the years since, Vancouver has been routinely reshaped by waves of immigration. The thousands of Chinese immigrants whose work, at the turn of the century, made possible the completion of the trans-Canada railroad, settled at the line's western terminus, founding the city's Chinatown.

More recent developments on the cultural landscape include a tendency for young Canadians from all points east to migrate, seemingly instinctively, to this western city. This ongoing influx of immigrants has ensured that the city's pungent multicultural flavor will continue to invade the senses of anyone who wanders its streets. And while there is some degree of self-segregation among the city's neighborhoods, its inhabitants largely cherish the diversity. Perhaps the best evidence of (maybe even the reason for) this harmony is the abundance of fine restaurants of every imaginable cuisine and budget level.

> **PHONE CODES.** On August 11, 2001, Vancouver will switch to 10-digit dialing. All the old numbers will remain 604, but new numbers will have the area code 778. Should you encounter problems, confirm the area code of the number you are trying to reach at www.addthecode.com.

■ INTERCITY TRANSPORTATION

Flights: Vancouver International Airport (☎276-6101), on Sea Island, 23km south of the city center. A visitors center (☎303-3601) is on level 2. Open daily 8am-midnight. To reach downtown, take bus #100 "New Westminster Station" to the intersection of Granville and 70th Ave. Transfer there to bus #20 "Fraser." An **Airporter** (☎946-8866 or 800-668-3141) bus leaves from airport level 2 for downtown hotels and the bus station. 4 per hr.; 6:30am-midnight; $10, seniors $8, ages 5-12 $5.

Ferries: BC Ferries (☎656-5571 or 888-BC-FERRY; www.bcferries.com) connects Vancouver to **Vancouver Island**, the **Sechelt Peninsula**, and the **Gulf Islands**. Ferries to **Victoria** (1½hr.; 8-16 per day; $9, bikes $2.50, car and driver $30-32), **Nanaimo** (2hr.; 4-8 per day; $9, car $30-32), and the Gulf Islands leave from the **Tsawwassen Terminal,** 25km south of the city center (take Hwy. 99 to Hwy. 17). To reach downtown from Tsawwassen by bus (1hr.), take #640 "Scott Rd. Station" or #404 "Airport" to the Ladner Exchange, then transfer to bus #601. More ferries to **Nanaimo** (1½hr.; 8 times per day; $9, car $30-32) and the **Sechelt Peninsula** (fare charged only from Horseshoe Bay to Langdale; 40min., 8-10 per day; $8, ages 5-11 $4, car $28; off-season slightly cheaper) depart the **Horseshoe Bay Terminal** at the end of the Trans-Canada Hwy. in West Vancouver. Take "Blue Bus" #250 or 257 on Georgia St. to get there from downtown (40min.).

Trains: VIA Rail, 1150 Station St. (☎800-561-8630; US ☎800-561-9181) runs eastbound trains. Open M, W, Th, and Sa 9:30am-6pm; Tu, F, and Su 9am-7pm. 3 trains per week to eastern Canada via **Jasper, AB** (17hr., $193) and **Edmonton, AB** (23hr., $258). **BC Rail,** 1311 W 1st St. (☎984-5246), in North Vancouver just over the Lions Gate Bridge at the foot of Pemberton St., runs to Whistler and northern BC. Take the BC

BRITISH COLUMBIA

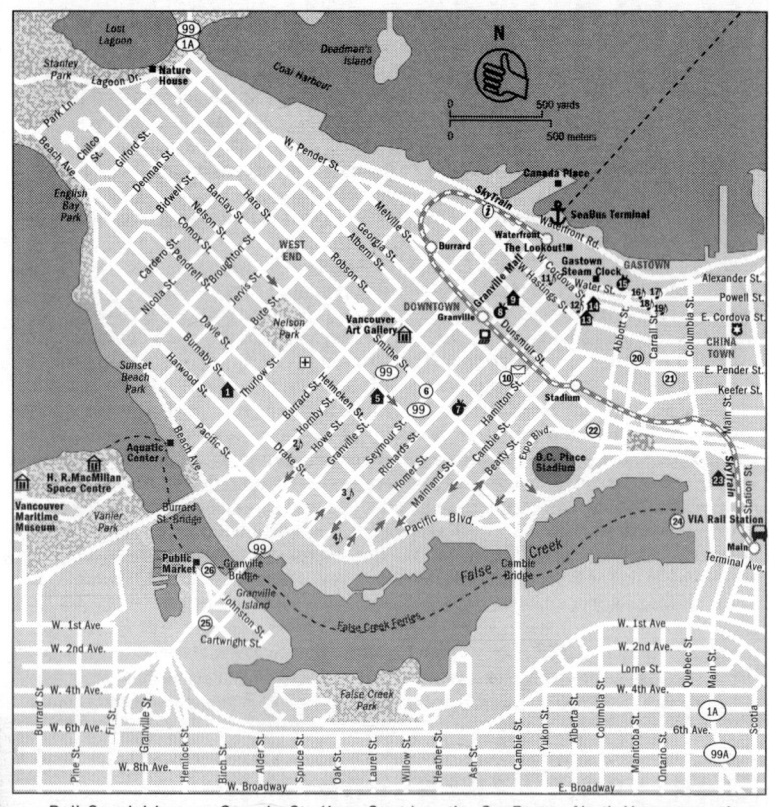

Rail Special bus on Georgia St. (June-Sept.) or the SeaBus to North Vancouver, then bus #239 west. Open daily 8am-8pm. Trains to **Whistler** (2¾hr., daily, $39); **Williams Lake** (10hr.; W, F, Sa at 7am; $143); **Prince George** (14½hr.; Su, W, F at 7am; $212).

Buses: Greyhound Canada, 1150 Station St. (☎482-8747 or 800-661-8747; www.greyhound.ca). Open daily 5am-12:30am. In the VIA Rail station. To **Calgary, AB** (15hr., 4 per day, $115); **Banff, AB** (14hr., 4 per day, $98); and **Jasper, AB** (2 per day, $98). **Pacific Coach Lines,** 1150 Station St. (☎662-8074), to **Victoria** every time a ferry sails (3½hr., $28.50 includes ferry). **Quick Shuttle** (☎940-4428 or 800-665-2122; www.quickcoach.com) makes 8 trips per day from the Holiday Inn on Howe St. downtown via the airport to **Bellingham, WA** (1½hr., $22), **Seattle, WA** (3½hr., $34), and the **Sea-Tac airport** (4hr., $44). **Greyhound USA** (☎800-229-9425 or 402-330-8552; www.greyhound.com) goes to **Seattle** (3-4½hr.; one-way US$20, round-trip US$36).

LOCAL TRANSPORTATION

If you're on the outskirts of Vancouver with a car, consider using the **Park 'n' Rides:** cheap or free parking lots at major transit hubs, where you can leave your car for the day and take public transit into town. From the southeast, exit Hwy. 1 at New Westminster and follow signs for the Pattullo Bridge. Just on the right over the bridge, a lot is on the corner of Scott Rd. and King George Hwy. Park for $1 per day and take the SkyTrain downtown. The Phibbs Exchange lot is on the North Vancouver side of the Second Narrows Bridge, and the Park Royal station is in West Vancouver near often-jam-packed Lions Gate Bridge at Taylor Way and Marine Dr. Parking, allowed only during the day, is free (except for Scott Rd.).

Downtown Vancouver

ACCOMMODATIONS
- Cambie Intl Hostel, 14
- C&N Backpackers Hostel, 23
- Seymour Cambie Hostel, 9
- Gastown Hostel, 13
- Global Village Backpackers, 5
- Vancouver Hostel Downtown, 1

FOOD
- La Luna Café, 15
- Lingo Cyberbistro, 8
- Subeez Café, 7

NIGHTLIFE
- The Blarney Stone, 19
- The Cambie, 12
- The Drink, 11
- The Irish Heather, 18
- Odyssey, 2
- The Purple Onion, 17
- Sonar, 16
- Sugar Refinery, 3
- Wett Bar, 4

OTHER
- Arts Club Theatre, 26
- Dr. Sun Yat-Sen Classical Chinese Garden, 21
- GM Place, 22
- Granville Island Brewing Co., 25
- Library, 10
- Orpheum Theatre, 6
- Science World, 24
- World's Skinniest Building, 20

Public Transit: Transit timetables are available at public libraries, city hall, community centers, and Vancouver Travel Infocentre (see **Practical Information**, below). The pamphlet *Discover Vancouver on Transit* lists bus numbers for every major site in the city. **Coast Mountain Buslink** (☎953-3333; www.translink.bc.ca) is the bus system that covers most of the city and suburbs, with direct transport or easy connections to airport and the ferry terminals (see **Intercity Transportation**, above). The city is divided into three concentric zones for fare purposes. Riding in the **central zone**, which encompasses most of Vancouver, costs $1.75. During peak hours (M-F before 6:30pm), it costs $2.50 to travel between 2 zones and $3.25 for 3 zones. During off-peak hours, all zones are $1.75. Ask for a **free transfer** (good for 90min.) when you board buses. **Day passes** $7; sold at all 7-11 and Safeway stores, SkyTrain stations, and HI hostels. Seniors and ages 5-13 for 1 zone or off-peak $1.25; 2 zones $1.75; 3 zones $2.25; day pass $5. Bikes can travel on the rack-equipped #404/#601 combination to the Tsawassen ferry terminal. **SeaBus** and **SkyTrain:** Same contact information as the buses, above. Included in the normal bus fare. The SeaBus shuttles passengers across the busy waters of Burrard Inlet from the foot of Granville St. downtown (Waterfront SkyTrain station) to **Lonsdale Quay** at the foot of Lonsdale Ave. in North Vancouver. **Bikes** may be brought on board the SeaBus, but not on the SkyTrain. The SkyTrain is a light rapid transit system, with a 28km track from Vancouver to **Burnaby, New Westminster,** and **Surrey** in 40min. 20 stations with service every 5min.

Car Rental: Resort Rent-a-Car, 3231 No. 3 Rd. (☎232-3060; www.resortcars.com) in Richmond (free pickup in Vancouver). From $34 per day, $164 per week; unlimited mileage. Must be 21. Open M-F 7am-9pm, Sa-Su 7am-7pm. Cheap Internet specials. Most major car rental companies are located at the airport.

Taxis: Yellow Cab, ☎681-1111 or 800-898-8294. **Vancouver Taxi,** ☎871-1111. **Black Top and Checker Cab,** ☎731-1111.

ORIENTATION

Vancouver lies in the southwestern corner of mainland British Columbia. It is divided into distinct regions, mostly by waterways. South of the city flows the **Fraser River,** and to the west lies the **Georgia Strait,** which separates the mainland from Vancouver Island. **Downtown** juts north into the Burrard Inlet from the main mass of the city and **Stanley Park** goes even further north. The **Lions Gate** suspension bridge over Burrard Inlet links Stanley Park with North and West Vancouver **(West Van),** known collectively as the **North Shore;** the bridges over False Creek south of downtown link downtown with **Kitsilano ("Kits")** and the rest of the city. West of Burrard St. is the **West End.** Gastown and Chinatown are just east of downtown. The **University of British Columbia (UBC)** lies to the west of Kitsilano on Point Grey, while the **airport** is on Sea Island in the Fraser River delta tucked between S. Vancouver and Richmond to the south. **Hwy. 99** runs north-south from the US-Canada border through the city along **Oak St.,** through downtown, then over the Lions Gate bridge. It joins temporarily with the **Trans-Canada Hwy. (Hwy. 1)** before splitting off again and continuing north to Whistler (see p. 251). The Trans-Canada enters from the east, cuts north across the **Second Narrows Bridge** to the North Shore, and ends at the Horseshoe Bay ferry terminal. Most of the city's attractions are grouped on the peninsula and farther west.

238 ■ VANCOUVER

> **VANCOUVER'S DISTRICTS** Getting around downtown is relatively easy when you know the signs to look for. Each of the main neighborhoods is decorated with colorful banners proclaiming its identity; Chinatown has "The Silk Road" dragon banners, while Davie Street has rainbow flags flying from the lightposts. All the lightposts in Chinatown bear bilingual street signs held up by little dragons; Gastown has red brick sidewalks, a vestige of the early days–stray from these cues and you could be wandering into the downtown east side (not good). Finally, if you see mountains through the maze of skyscrapers, know that you're looking north.

Vancouver is a major point of entry for heroin, has an active street trade in this drug and marijuana, and has a high addict population. While incidences of armed assaults, armed robbery, and murder are low by US standards, the rates for crimes are higher than in most other Canadian cities. Walking around by day is safe most anywhere and downtown is relatively safe at night on main streets. The area east of Gastown, especially around **Hastings** and **Main St.**, is home to many of Vancouver's down, out, and addicted, and should be avoided late at night if possible.

⚡ PRACTICAL INFORMATION

VISITOR AND LOCAL SERVICES

Visitor Information: 200 Burrard St., plaza level (☎683-2000), near Canada Place. BC-wide info on accommodations, tours, activities. Courtesy reservation phones. Open daily 8am-7pm.

Travel Outfitter: The Travel Bug, 2667 W Broadway (☎737-1122). Everything you need for getting around from maps to bags to guides. 10% HI discount on accessories. Open M-Tu 10am-6pm, W-F 10am-7:30pm, Sa noon-5pm, Su 10am-6pm.

Tours: The Gray Line, 255 E 1st Ave. (☎879-3363 or 800-667-0882). Narrated bus tours. The Double Decker Bus stops at over 20 sights. Unlimited use for 2 days $26; seniors $25; ages 5-12 $14. Buses run 8:30am-4:30pm. Hostels run sporadic tours.

Consulates: Canadian Consulate General, 412 Plaza 600 (☎443-1777). **British Consulate General,** 900 4th Ave., Suite 3001 (☎622-9255).

Equipment Rental: Stanley Park Cycle, 766 Denman (☎688-0087), near Stanley Park. Mountain bikes or 21-speed from $3.50 per hr., $10.50 per 5hr. Open daily 8am-9pm. **Vancouver Downtown Hostel** and **Jericho Beach Hostel** rent bikes for $20 per day. **Bikes and Blades,** 718 Denman St. (☎602-9899), a block up from Georgia St. Bikes $4.50 per hr., $12 per 5hr. In-line skates from $4.50 per hr., $10 per 5hr. Open daily 9am-9pm. The immensely popular and knowledgably staffed **Mountain Equipment Co-op (MEC),** 130 W Broadway (☎872-7858; www.mec.ca), rents tents, sleeping bags, and kayaks. Open M-W 10am-7pm, Th-F 10am-9pm, Sa 9am-6pm, Su 11am-5pm.

Laundry: Davie Laundromat, 1061 Davie St. (☎682-2717), $2.50 per load. Open daily 8am-9pm. **Swan's Coin Laundry** 1352 Burrard St. (☎684-0323). Numerous other locations along W Broadway in Kits.

Gay and Lesbian Information: The Centre, 1170 Bute St., offers counseling and info. *Xtra West* is the city's gay and lesbian biweekly, available here and around Davie St. in the West End. Open M-F 9:30am-7pm. Try www.gayvancouver.bc.ca for events.

Weather: ☎664-9010; www.weatheroffice.com.

Road Conditions: Talking Yellow Pages ☎299-9000. Select #7623.

EMERGENCY AND COMMUNICATION

Emergency: ☎911. **Police:** 312 Main St. (☎665-3321), at Powell.

Crisis Center: ☎872-3311. 24hr. **Rape Crisis Center:** ☎872-8212. 24hr.

ACCOMMODATIONS ■ 239

Pharmacy: Shoppers Drug Mart, 2979 W Broadway (☎ 733-9128), and 1125 Davie St. (☎ 669-2424). Open 24hr.

Hospital: Vancouver General Hospital, 899 W 12th Ave. (☎ 875-4111). **UBC Hospital,** 221 Westbrook Mall (☎ 822-7121), on the UBC campus.

Internet Access: Library: 350 W Georgia St. (☎ 331-3600). **Free email** terminals or pay $5 per hr. Open M-Th 10am-8pm, F-Sa 10am-5pm. Free email at 20 other branches; check white pages. **The Student Centre,** 616 Seymour St. (☎ 488-1441). $3.75 per hr. After 7pm, $2 per hr. Avoid 1:30 and 4:30pm, when students at the nearby Language School rush in. Open daily 10am-midnight. Also see **Lingo** (**Food,** p. 241).

Post Office: 349 W Georgia St. (☎ 662-5725). Open M-F 8am-5:30pm. **Postal Code:** V6B 3P7.

ACCOMMODATIONS

Greater Vancouver B&Bs are a viable option for couples or small groups (singles from $45, doubles from $55). The visitors center and agencies like **Town and Country Bed and Breakfast** (☎ 731-5942) and **Best Canadian** (☎ 738-7207) list options. HI hostels are a good bet for clean rooms and quiet nights; others can be rowdy or seedy.

DOWNTOWN AND WEST END

Vancouver Hostel Downtown (HI), 1114 Burnaby St. (☎ 684-4565 or 888-203-4302), in the West End. Sleek and clean 225-bed facility between downtown, the beach, and Stanley Park. Four-bunk rooms, game room, library, kitchen, rooftop patio, free linen, and tours of the city. Free shuttle to Jericho Beach Hostel. Internet $6 per hr. Pub crawls twice a week; activities every day. Travel agency in the lobby. Reservations crucial in summer. Open 24hr. $20, nonmembers $24; private doubles $55, nonmembers $64.

Global Village Backpackers, 1018 Granville St. (☎ 682-8226 or 888-844-7875; www.globalbackpackers.com), on corner of Nelson, next to Ramada Inn. Shuttle from bus/train station; call for details. Airporter Bus stops at Granville St. Funky technicolor hangout in an area with great nightlife. Internet, pool, laundry. Linen included. HI, ISIC, other hosteling members $21; doubles $57, with bath $62. Nonmembers $3 more.

Seymour Cambie Hostel, 515 Seymour St. (☎ 684-7757). The quieter of 2 downtown Cambie hostels. All rooms twins. Pub crawls (W), movie nights (Su-M), soccer games (Sa), free tours of Granville Island Brewery (Tu at noon, 2pm, and 4pm). Laundry and Internet access. No lockers, storage available for $2 per day. Open 24hr. Jul. 1-Sept. 30 $23, Oct. 1-Jun. 30 $20; private room $40.

C&N Backpackers Hostel, 927 Main St. (☎ 682-2441 or 888-434-6060), 300m north on Main St. from the train station. Dorms with 3-4 beds, and cheap meal deals with the Ivanhoe Pub across the street ($2.50 breakfast all day) make this hostel a real bargain. Kitchen, TV with video collection, Internet, laundry ($1 per wash or dry), bikes ($10 per day), smoking room. May-Sept. dorm $14; single, double, or family room $35. Off-peak $12; single $25; double $30. Weekly and monthly rates available.

GASTOWN

Cambie International Hostel, 300 Cambie St. (☎ 684-6466 or 877-395-5335). Atop the pub and grill of the same name, the Cambie offers easy access to—or a retreat from—the busy sights and sounds of Gastown. Common room, laundry. No kitchen, but free hot breakfast. Pool tables in the pub. Free airport pickup 9am-8pm. 24hr. reception. Dorms June-Sept. $20; Oct.-May $15. Private rooms $23.

Gastown Hostel, 340 Cambie St. (☎ 684-4664). No-frills accommodations close to Water St. and the heart of downtown. Laundry available. Single or double with shared bathroom $40. Reception at the bar of the attached pub. Open 11am-2am.

BRITISH COLUMBIA

CANNABUSINESS

British Columbia's buds fare well at Amsterdam's Cannabis Cup (the World Cup of pot smoking), and at an estimated $1 billion, generate half as much annual revenue as the province's logging industry. Most ganja dollars come from exports, and most exports go straight to the US. In 1998, Canada legalized hemp plants containing very low levels of its psychoactive compound THC, giving visitors and locals full legal freedom to enjoy fibrous rope. At some Vancouver cafes, however, public marijuana smoking is commonplace. What's the source of such seeming herbal impunity? Vancouver police don't seem to treat small-time pot smoking behind closed doors as a criminal offense, despite federal law. The fuzz does tend to have moments of forgetfulness, though, at which point they raid the shops. For a connoisseur's perspective and news on further legalization efforts, tune in to the mind-altering www.cannabisculture.com or www.pot-tv.net. Educate yourself on the issues by visiting the BC Marijuana Party Bookshop and HQ at 307 W. Hastings St., which has literature, clothing, and other party paraphernalia. (☎ 682-1172. Open M-Th 10:30am-6pm, F-Sa 10:30am-7pm, Su 11am-6pm.)

KITSILANO AND OTHER NEIGHBORHOODS

Vancouver Hostel Jericho Beach (HI), 1515 Discovery St. (☎ 224-3208 or 888-203-4303), in Jericho Beach Park. Follow 4th Ave. west past Alma, bear right at the fork, or take bus #4 from Granville St. downtown. Peaceful location with a great view across English Bay. 285 beds in 14-person dorm rooms. 10 family rooms. Kitchens, TV room, laundry, cafe (breakfasts around $5.50, dinner $6-7), free linen, parking $3 per day. Bike $20 per day. Stay-and-ski package with Grouse Mountain (see below) for $37. Reservations imperative in summer. $18, nonmembers $22; family rooms $50-60.

Pacific Spirit Hostel, 1935 Lower Mall (☎ 822-1000, fax 822-1001) at Place Vanier on the University of British Columbia campus. Bus #4 or #10 from city center, continue down University Blvd. from bus loop until you turn right on Lower Mall. Standard dorm singles for a hostel price. Laundry, free linen, TV lounges, shared microwave and fridge; pubs and food on campus. Free Internet. 10% HI or ISIC discount. Open May-Aug. $24.

Simon Fraser University (☎ 291-4503), McTaggart-Cowan Hall (pink building), in Burnaby, 20km east of the city center. From W. Hastings and Granville St. downtown, take bus #135 in daytime M-Sa (25min.), or #35 at night or on Su (40-45min.). Location atop Burnby Mountain offers great views. Fridges, kitchen (no pots and pans), patio, TV lounge. Parking $3 per night. Check-in after 3pm. Open May-Aug. 8am-midnight. Singles $19, with linens $25; twin with linens $48.

CAMPING

Capilano RV Park, 295 Tomahawk Ave. (☎ 987-4722; fax 987-2015), at foot of Lions Gate Bridge in North Van; closest RV park to downtown. Turn onto Capilano Rd., take first right on Welch, then right on Tomahawk. Showers, pool, laundry. Reception open daily 8am-11pm. 2-person sites $25-30, extra person $4; hookups $30-45.

Richmond RV Park, 6200 River Rd. (☎ 270-7878 or 800-755-4905), near Holly Bridge in Richmond, a 30min. drive from Vancouver. Follow the Westminster Hwy. west into Richmond from Hwy. 99, turn right on No. 2 Rd. then right on River Rd. Scant privacy. Showers. Open Apr.-Oct. 2-person sites $18; hookups $23-28. 10% AAA/CAA discount.

Hazelmere RV Park and Campground, 18843 8th Ave. (☎ 538-1167), in Surrey, a 45min. drive from downtown. Close to the US/Canada border. Off Hwy. 99A, head east on 8th Ave. Quiet sites on the Campbell River, 10min. from the beach. Showers 25¢ per 4min. 2-person sites $20; full hookups $26; additional person $2; under 7 free.

ParkCanada, 4799 Hwy. 17 (☎ 943-5811), in Delta about 30km south of downtown, near Tsawwassen ferry terminal. Take Hwy. 99 south to Hwy. 17, then go east for 2.5km. The campground, located next to a waterslide park, has a pool and free showers. 2-person sites $17; hookups $20-27; additional person $1-2.

FOOD ■ 241

🍴 FOOD

The diversity and excellence of Vancouver's international cuisine makes the rest of BC seem provincial. Vancouver's **Chinatown** and the **Punjabi Village** along Main and Fraser, around 49th St., serve cheap, authentic food. The entire world, from Vietnamese noodle shops to Italian cafes to succulent yet cheap sushi, seems represented along **Commercial Drive,** east of Chinatown. Produce peddled along "The Drive" puts supermarkets to shame.

Restaurants in downtown compete for the highest prices in the city. The **West End** caters to diners seeking a variety of ethnic cuisines, while **Gastown** lures tourists fresh off the cruise ships. Many cheap and grubby establishments along Davie and Denman St. stay open around the clock. Dollar-a-slice, all-night **pizza places** pepper downtown. In Kits, **Buy-Low Foods,** at 4th and Alma St., keeps it real. (☎ 222-8353. Open daily 9am-9pm.) Downtown, **SuperValu,** 1255 Davie St., is where it's at. (☎ 688-0911. Open 24hr.)

WEST END, DOWNTOWN, AND GASTOWN

- **Subeez Cafe,** 891 Homer (☎ 687-6107), at Smithe, downtown. Serves the cool kids in a cavernous and casual setting. Eclectic menu, from vegetarian gyoza ($6.50) to organic beef burgers ($9), complements a lengthy wine list and home-spun beats (DJs W and F at 10pm). Weekly "fresh sheet" specials. Entrees $7-15. Open M-F 11:30am-1am, Sa 11am-1am, Su 11am-midnight.

- **Cafe Oasis,** 1183 Davie St. (☎ 684-4760). Falafel sandwiches ($5), large tofu stew with rice ($7), breakfast wrap ($5.50), and hearty soups ($3.50) will fill a hungry stomach. Open daily 10am-1am. 10% HI discount.

- **La Luna Cafe,** 117 Water St. (☎ 687-5862), in Gastown. Loyal patrons swear by the coffee, roasted on premises. Cheap, satisfying sandwiches ($3.75-4.50), homemade soups ($3). Internet $1 per 12min. Open M-F 7:30am-5pm, Sa 10am-5pm.

- **Lingo Cyberbistro,** 547 Seymour St. (☎ 331-9345), downtown. Tasty, cheap sandwiches in fresh, decorative slices of bread for around $5.25. Internet $6.85 per hr. 10% student discount on beverages and Internet. Open M-F 7:30am-7:30pm, Sa 8am-4pm.

COMMERCIAL DRIVE AND EAST VANCOUVER

- **Mongolian Teryaki,** 1918 Commercial Dr. (☎ 253-5607). Diners fill a bowl full of meats, veggies, sauces, and noodles, and the chefs will fry it up and serve it with miso soup, rice, and salad for only $5 (large bowl $6). Open daily 11am-10:30pm.

- **WaaZuBee Cafe,** 1622 Commercial Dr. (☎ 253-5299), at E 1st St. Sleek, metallic decoration, ambient music, and artwork accompany the brilliantly prepared food. Veggie spinach and ricotta agnoilotti pasta $13, Thai prawns $8, veggie burger $7. Open M-F 11:30am-1am, Sa 11am-1am, Su 11am-midnight. Sister restaurant of **Subeez,** above.

- **Nuff-Nice-Ness,** 1861 Commercial Dr. (☎ 255-4211), at 3rd. Nice price and no fuss in this small Jamaican deli. Jerk chicken with salad and rice $7.50; beef, chicken, or veggie patties $2. Open M-Sa noon-9pm, Su noon-8pm.

- **Belgian Fries,** 1885 Commercial Dr. (☎ 253-4220). Small joint fries up what CBC Montreal hails as the "Best Poutine in BC." If you've never had it, try this concoction of fries, curds, and gravy. Huge portions serve two ($5). Open daily noon-10pm.

KITSILANO

- **The Naam,** 2724 W 4th Ave. (☎ 738-7151), at MacDonald St. Bus #4 or 7 from Granville Mall. The most diverse vegetarian menu around with great prices. Crying Tiger Thai stir fry $8.50; 5 kinds of veggie burgers under $7, tofulati ice cream $3.50. Live music nightly 7-10pm. Birthday discounts equal to the nearest decade of your new age (e.g. 22 years old=20% off!). Open 24hr.

- **Benny's Bagels,** 2505 W Broadway (☎ 731-9730). Every college student's dream. Serves the requisite beer ($3 per glass), bagels (70¢, $2.15 with cream cheese), and sandwiches and melts ($5-7.25). Open Su-Th 7am-1am, F-Sa 24hr.
- **The Excellent Eatery,** 3431 W Broadway (☎ 738-5298). Candlelight, sushi, and pop art. Reserve one of two canopied booths. Sushi $3-5. Mango-tuna-avocado sushi $4. Specials Sa-Th. Open M-Th 5pm-12:30am, F-Sa 5pm-1am, Su 5-11:30pm.
- **Soupspoons,** 2278 W. 4th Ave. (☎ 328-7687). This Parisian bistro offers panini and sandwiches ($5.50), salads ($3), and 10 ever-changing soups every day. For a great picnic, the Beachpack gets you a chilled soup, baguette sandwich, and drink for $6. Open daily 10am-10pm, in winter 10am-9pm.

CHINATOWN

The prettiest are usually the priciest in Chinatown and adjacent **Japantown**. For guaranteed good food, stop in restaurants that are crowded with locals. Lively afternoons make this a better place for lunch than dinner.

- **Hon's Wun-Tun House,** 268 Keefer St. (☎ 688-0871). Award-winning Cantonese noodle-house is the place to go (bowls $3.50-6). 334 options make reading the menu take almost as long as eating from it. Phenomenal service. Check the free *Georgia Straight* for 15% off coupon. Cash only. Open daily 8:30am-10pm; in summer F-Su until 11pm.
- **Kam's Garden Restaurant,** 509 Main St. (☎ 669-5488). Authentic, no-frills Chinese food. Huge noodle platters $5-9. Open daily 10:30am-8pm.

ENTERTAINMENT

MUSIC, THEATER, AND FILM

The renowned **Vancouver Symphony Orchestra** (**VSO;** ☎ 684-9100) plays September to May in the refurbished **Orpheum Theatre** (☎ 665-3050), at the corner of Smithe and Seymour. In summer, tours of the historic theater are given ($5). The VSO often joins forces with other groups such as the **Vancouver Bach Choir** (☎ 921-8012).

Vancouver has a lively theater scene. The **Vancouver Playhouse Theatre Co.** (☎ 873-3311), on Dunsmuir and Georgia St., and the **Arts Club Theatre** (☎ 687-1644), on Granville Island, stage low key shows, often including local work. **Theatre Under the Stars** (☎ 687-0174), in Stanley Park's Malkin Bowl, puts on outdoor musicals in the summer. Have some laughs at the **Theatresports League** at the Arts Club New Revue Stage on Granville Island. The world-famous improvisational theatre company performs competitive improv, comedies, and improv jam sessions W-Sa at 8pm and F-Sa at 10pm. (Box office ☎ 687-1644. Open M-Sa 9am-showtime. Tickets $15, students $12.)

The **Ridge Theatre,** 3131 Arbutus, shows nightly arthouse, European, and vintage film double features. See the last soundproofed "crying room" in the lower mainland in this 1950 theatre, where babies can bawl without disturbing the rest of the audience. (☎ 738-6311. $7, seniors and children $4; Tu $5, seniors and children $3; seniors free on M.) The **Hollywood Theatre,** 3123 W Broadway, shows a mix of arthouse and second-run mainstream double features for cheaper than the other prevalent theatres around downtown. (☎ 515-5864. $5, on M $3.50, seniors and children $3.50.) The **Blinding Light!! Cinema,** 36 Powell St., shows indie films and hosts special events such as the monthly Multiplex experimental music and film series. (☎ 878-3366; www.blindinglight.com. $5.) The **Paradise,** 919 Granville (☎ 681-1732), at Smithe, shows triple features of second-run movies for $4.

SPORTS

One block south of Chinatown on Main St. is **BC Place Stadium,** at 777 S Pacific Blvd., home to the Canadian Football League's BC Lions and the world's largest air supported dome (tickets from $15). At the stadium entrance, the Terry Fox Memorial honors the Canadian hero who, after losing a leg to cancer, ran over

Got ISIC?

ISIC is your passport to the world.

Accepted at over 17,000 locations worldwide.
Great benefits at home and abroad!

To apply for your International Student, Teacher or Youth Identity Card
CALL 1-800-2COUNCIL
CLICK www.counciltravel.com
VISIT your local Council Travel office

Bring this ad into your local Council Travel office and receive a free Council Travel/ISIC t-shirt! *(while supplies last)*

FALL/WINTER 2001 • FREE

student Travels

WORK, STUDY, TRAVEL ABROAD

CZECH IT OUT!
Exploring Prague and Other Pleasures in the Czech Republic

BOSTON
Weekend Wandering in Beantown

INSIDE
Your International Student Identity Card (ISIC) Application

PLUS
- Cuba
- Australia

Bedazzled By BRAZIL
Boundless Attractions From Beautiful Beaches to Spectacular Festivals to Lush Jungles

STOP IN FOR YOUR FREE COPY TODAY!

STUDENT TRAVELS MAGAZINE
is now available at all Council Travel offices.

This FREE magazine is the student guide to getting around the world - on a student's budget!

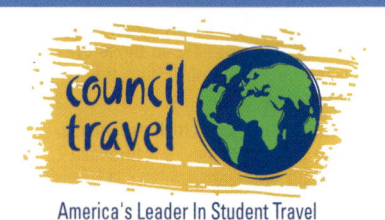

council travel
America's Leader In Student Travel

Find your local office at
www.counciltravel.com

1-800-2COUNCIL

NIGHTLIFE ■ 243

5300km across Canada to raise money for medical research. The NHL's **Vancouver Canucks** call the nearby **GM Place** home. Tickets for both are often available as late as game day (tickets start around $40). The **Vancouver Canadians** play AAA baseball in Nat Bailey Stadium, at 33rd. Ave. and Ontario, opposite Queen Elizabeth Park, offering some of the cheapest sports tickets going ($7.50-9.50). For tickets and info call **Ticketmaster** at 280-4400.

ANNUAL EVENTS

As with almost everything else, buying tickets in advance for these festivals often results in drastically reduced prices.

- **Chinese New Year** will fall between Feb. 7-11, 2002. Fireworks, music, and dragons in the streets of Chinatown and beyond.
- **Alcan Dragon Boat Festival,** End of June each year. (☎696-1888; www.canadadragonboat.com). Traditional food and dance from around the world, and dragon boat racing on False Creek. $9; seniors and youth $5; family $20.
- **Du Maurier International Jazz Festival Vancouver,** June 21-30, 2002. (☎872-5200 or 888-438-5200; www.jazzvancouver.com). Draws over 500 performers and bands for 10 days of hot jazz, from acid to swing. Some free concerts in Gastown, at the Roundhouse on Davie St., and around Granville Island. Other events range from $10-60.
- **Vancouver Folk Music Festival,** July 19-21, 2002 (☎602-9798 or 800-883-3655; www.thefestival.bc.ca). Performers from around the world give concerts and workshops in July. Very kid-friendly. $35-50 per day; $110 for the weekend. Ages 13-18 $22-25, $55; ages 3-12 $6. Under 2 and over 65 free.
- **HSBC-Power Smart Celebration of Light,** late July to early Aug. (☎738-4304; www.celebration-of-light.com). Pyrotechnicians light up the sky over English Bay on Sa and W nights. Hundreds of thousands gather to watch, closing off downtown streets. Displays coordinate with music aired on 101 FM.
- **Holy Pride!** Late July to early Aug. (www.vanpride.bc.ca). This is Vancouver's gay and lesbian festival. Events include dances, parties, games, music, and a parade. Tickets and info from Ticketmaster or Little Sisters (see above).
- **Vancouver International Film Festival,** late Sept. to early Oct. (☎685-0260; www.viff.orgtickets). This event showcases 275 movies from over 50 countries, with particular emphasis on Canadian films, East Asian films, and documentaries. $6-8.

◪ NIGHTLIFE

Vancouver's nightlife centers around dance clubs playing beats and DJs spinning every night. Local pubs inundate communities with relaxed options for a post-work or play drink. The free weekly **Georgia Straight** publishes comprehensive club and event listings, restaurant reviews, and coupons. **Discorder** is the unpredictable, monthly publication of the UBC radio station CITR. Both are available in record shops and cafes.

GASTOWN

- **Sonar,** 66 Water St. (☎683-6695). A popular 2-level beat factory. House Sa, hip-hop W, and turntablist F. Pints $3.50-4.75. Open M-Sa 9pm-2am, Su 9pm-midnight.
- **The Irish Heather,** 217 Carrall St. The second-highest seller of Guinness in BC, this true Irish pub and bistro serves up memories of the Emerald Isle. Draughts ($5.20), mixed beer drinks ($5.60), and a helping of bangers and mash ($14) will keep those eyes smiling. Lots of veggie dishes, too. Conservatory in the back, live music four times a week 8-11pm. Open M-F 3-11:30pm, Sa-Su 11:30am-12:30pm.
- **The Blarney Stone,** 216 Carrall St. (☎687-4332). For a more raucous Irish experience, join the mostly university crowd for live music by a band called Killarney, a fixture for 17 years. Cover $5-7, Th $5 cover goes to charity. Open W-Sa 7pm-2am.

Purple Onion, 15 Water St. (☎ 602-9442). Sucks in the crowd with an eclectic music selection and inviting lounge chairs. The lounge features live blues, R&B, jazz, and funk acts W-Sa. DJs spin acid jazz, disco, soul, and funk in the back room. M and W-Sa $3-8 cover; Tu no cover, Su $1. Open M-Th 8pm-2am, F-Sa 7pm-2am, Su 7pm-midnight.

The Cambie, 300 Cambie St. (☎ 684-6466). Young crowds from all over the cultural spectrum, picnic tables made from bowling lanes, loud music, sports TVs, and beer as cheap as it gets. Su beer pitchers $7.25, Tu nights $2.50 highballs, Su free pool. Burger and a beer $5 every night. Open daily 9am-1:30am.

DOWNTOWN

■ **Sugar Refinery,** 1115 Granville St. (☎ 683-2004). Artsy, retro lounge where the youth involved in film, art, and music go to relax. An ever-changing program of events, music, and spoken word entertains while the tasty vegetarian meals (entrees $7.50-9, big sandwiches $5-7.50) and decadent desserts such as the popular Molestic (vanilla gelato and chocolate brownies, $5.50) please the stomach. Tap beers served in mason jars $4.25-5.75. Open daily 5pm-3am, kitchen open throughout.

Wett Bar, 1320 Richards St. (☎ 662-7707). Candlelit dining booths and a weekend dress code. Wields one of the most advanced stereo and light systems in Vancouver. Hip-hop F, top 40 Sa, house W. Open M and W-Sa 9pm-2am, Tu 9pm-1am.

Odyssey, 1251 Howe St. (☎ 689-5256). Embark on a high-energy journey. F-Sa cranks out beats to a mainly gay crowd. Male go-go dancers spice it up F. Drag Night Su and W. $2-4. Open daily 9pm-2am.

The Drink, 398 Richards St. (☎ 687-1307). Nightclub with a diverse repertoire including alternative Tu, "Noche Havana" latin W, House Party Th with $2 drinks, and hip-hop and reggae Sa to get you dancing. Open W 8pm-2am, Th-Sa 9pm-2am, Su noon-2am.

KITSILANO

The King's Head, 1618 Yew St. (☎ 738-6966), at 1st St., in Kitsilano. Cheap drinks, cheap food, relaxing atmosphere, and a great location near the beach. Bands play acoustic sets on a tiny stage. Daily drink specials. $3 pints. Gullet-filling Beggar's Breakfast ($4). Open M-F 7am-1:30am, Sa 7:30am-2am, Su 7:30am-midnight.

Koerner's Pub, 6371 Crescent Rd. (☎ 822-0983), on UBC campus. Owned and operated by the Graduate Student Society, this is the place to meet a smart special someone. BBQ daily $2 burgers or dogs, meat or veggie. Mellow M's with live music and open jam, W techno night. Open late Aug. to mid-Apr. M-F noon-1am, Sa 4pm-1am; summer M-Sa 4pm-midnight.

◉ SIGHTS AND ANNUAL EVENTS

WORLD'S FAIR GROUNDS AND DOWNTOWN

■ **VANCOUVER ART GALLERY.** Host to fantastic temporary exhibitions and home to a good collection of contemporary art. An entire floor of the gallery is devoted to the landscape paintings of British Columbian Emily Carr. An immigrations officer who was murdered in 1914 is said to haunt the catacombs underneath the gallery, which is where the holding cells were located in this former courthouse. *(750 Hornby St. in Robson Square. ☎ 662-4700; www.vanartgallery.bc.ca. Open F-W 10am-5:30pm, Th 10am-9pm; call for winter hours. $12.50, seniors $9, students $7, under 12 free; Th 5-9pm pay-what you-can; 2-for-1 HI discount.)*

EXPO '86. On the city's centennial, the World Exposition brought attention, prestige, and roller-coasters to Vancouver. The fairgrounds are still there, on the north shore of False Creek, and are slowly evolving into office space, apartment towers, and a cultural center, near False Creek and Yaletown. The big-screen star of Expo '86 was the **Omnimax Theatre,** part of **Science World,** 1455 Quebec St., at the Main St. stop of the SkyTrain. In addition to the 27m spherical screen, Science World also

SIGHTS AND ANNUAL EVENTS ■ 245

features tons of hands-on exhibits and fact-crammed shows for kids. (☎ 268-6363. *Open daily July-Aug. 10am-6pm; call for winter hours. $12; students, seniors, and children $8. Omnimax shows Su-F 10am-5pm, Sa 10am-9pm. $10. Combined ticket $14.75; $10.50.)*

CANADA PLACE. The Canada Pavilion, or Canada Place, was built to resemble five giant sails; the masts provide a cavernous interior space free of support structures while the distinctive roof dominates the harbor. The shops and restaurants inside are outrageously expensive, but the promenades around the complex make for terrific gawking at luxury liners and their camera-toting cargo. *(SkyTrain from the main Expo site or walk across the street from the visitors center on Burrard St.)*

LOOKOUT! 555 W Hastings St., offers fantastic 360° views of the city! Tickets are expensive! But they're good for the whole day! Come back for a more sedate nighttime skyline! *(Skytrain to Waterfront Station. ☎ 689-0421. Open daily 8:30am-10:30pm; winter 10am-9pm. $9, students $6, seniors $8. 50% HI discount!)*

GASTOWN

One of the oldest neighborhoods in Vancouver, Gastown has collapsed into the tourist trap mold. Gastown is named for "Gassy Jack" Deighton, a glib con man who opened Vancouver's first saloon here in 1867. Today the area overflows with shops, nightclubs, restaurants, and boutiques. Many establishments stay open and well-populated at night. Stroll along Water St. and hear the rare **steam-powered clock** on the corner of Cambie St. whistle the notes of the Westminster Chimes every 15min. To find it, just look for the big crowd of people on the hour. *(Adjacent to downtown, bordered by Richards to the west, Columbia to the east, Hastings to the south, and the waterfront to the north.)*

CHINATOWN

The neighborhood bustles with restaurants, shops, bakeries, and **the world's narrowest building** at 8 W Pender St. In 1912, the city expropriated all but a 1.8m (6 ft.) strip of Chang Toy's property in order to expand the street; he built on the land anyhow. The serene **Dr. Sun Yat-Sen Classical Chinese Garden**, 578 Carrall St., maintains imported Chinese plantings, carvings, and rock formations in the first full-size authentic garden of its kind outside China. *(☎ 689-7133. Open daily May to mid-June 9:30am-5:30pm; mid-June to Aug. 9:30am-6:30pm; Sept. 9:30am-5:30pm; Oct.-Apr. 9:30am-4pm. Admission to part of the garden is free, while another section is $7.50, students $5, seniors $6, children free, families $18. Tours every hr. 10am-6pm.)* Don't miss the sights, sounds, smells, and tastes of the weekend **night market** along Pender and Keefer St. (F-Su 6:30-11pm), the first in North America. Chinatown itself is relatively safe, but its surroundings make up some of Vancouver's more unsavory sections. *(Chinatown is southeast of Gastown. Bus #22 north on Burrard St. leads to Pender and Carrall St., in the heart of Chinatown.)*

GARDENS

The city's temperate climate, which also includes ample rain most months of the year, allows floral growth to flourish. Locals take great pride in their private gardens, and public parks and green spaces also showcase displays of plant life.

■VANDUSEN BOTANICAL GARDEN. 5251 Oak St. at W 37th. 55 acres (22 hectares) of former golf course have been converted into an immense garden showcasing 7500 taxa from six continents. An international **sculpture** collection is interspersed with the plants, while more than 60 species of **birds** can be seen amongst areas such as the Fragrance Garden, Children's Garden, Bonsai House, Chinese Medicinal Garden, or the Elizabethan Maze, which is planted with 3000 pyramidal cedars. Daily tours given at 2pm, or follow a self-guided tour tailored to show the best of the season. Flower & Garden Show is first weekend of June. *(From downtown take #17 Oak bus and get off at West 37th and Oak. ☎ 878-9274. Free parking. Mostly wheelchair accessible. Apr.-Sept. $6.50, ages 65+ $4, 13-18 $5, 6-12 $3.25, family $15; Oct.-Mar. up to half off. Open June to mid-Aug. 10am-9pm, mid-Aug. to Labour Day 10am-8pm, Labour Day-Sept. 30 10am-6pm, Oct.-Mar. 10am-4pm, Apr. 10am-4pm, May 10am-8pm.)*

BRITISH COLUMBIA

BLOEDEL FLORAL AND BIRD CONSERVATORY. In the center of Queen Elizabeth Park on Cambie and 37th Ave. a few blocks east of VanDusen. Journey from tropics to desert in 100 paces inside this 43m diameter triodetic geodesic dome constructed of plexiglass bubbles and aluminum tubing. The conservatory, maintained at a constant 18°C (65°F), is home to 400 varieties of exotic plants, 150 birds—60 species of finches, plus macaws and cockatoos—and koi. (☎ 257-8570. $3.75, ages 65+ $2.25, ages 13-18 $2.85, ages 6-12 $1.85, under 5 free. Open Apr.-Sept. M-F 9am-8pm, Sa-Su 10am-9pm; Oct.-Mar. daily 10am-5pm.)

UNIVERSITY OF BRITISH COLUMBIA (UBC)

The high point of a visit to UBC is the breathtaking ■**Museum of Anthropology.** The high-ceilinged glass and concrete building houses totems and other massive carvings, highlighted by Bill Reid's depiction of Raven discovering the first human beings in a giant clam shell. The actual site of the discovery is in the Queen Charlotte Islands (see p. 317). Free hour-long guided walks (11am and 2pm) pick through the maze of eras and modes of expression. Behind the museum, in a courtyard designed to simulate the Pacific islands, the free re-created village displays memorial totems and a mortuary house built by Reid and Douglas Cranmer. *(6393 NW Marine Dr., bus #4 or 10 from Granville St. Museum.* ☎ *822-3825 or 822-5087. Open M and W-Su 10am-5pm, Tu 10am-9pm; Sept.-May closed M. $7, students $4, seniors $5, under 6 free; Tu after 5pm free.)* Across the street caretakers tend to **Nitobe Memorial Garden,** the finest classical Shinto garden outside of Japan. *(*☎*822-6038. $2.75, ages 65+ and students $1.75, under 6 free. Open mid-Mar. to Oct. daily 10am-6pm; Nov.-mid-Mar. M-F 10am-2:30pm.)* The **Botanical Gardens** are a collegiate Eden encompassing eight gardens in the central campus, including the largest collection of rhododendrons in North America. *(6804 SW Marine Dr.* ☎*822-9666. $4.75, ages 65+ and students $2.50, under 6 free. Same hours as Nitobe Garden.)* In addition to its greenery, UBC has a public **swimming pool.** *(*☎*822-4521. $3.75, students $2.75. Open M-F 1:30-4:30pm and 8-10pm, Sa-Su 1-10pm.)* It also boasts a **Fine Arts Gallery** and free daytime and evening **concerts.** *(Gallery* ☎*822-2759. $3, students free. Concert* ☎*822-3113. To arrange a walking tour between May and August call* ☎*822-8687.)* Just east of campus in **Pacific Spirit Regional Park,** woods stretch from inland hills to the beaches of Spanish Banks. With 50km of gravel and dirt trails through dense forest make the park ideal for **jogging** and **mountain biking.** Grab free maps at the **Park Centre** on 16th Ave., near Blanca.

STANLEY PARK

Established in 1889 at the tip of the downtown peninsula, the 1000-acre **Stanley Park** (☎ 257-8400) is a testament to the foresight of Vancouver's urban planners. An easy escape from the nearby West End and downtown, the thickly wooded park is laced with cycling and hiking trails and surrounded by an 10km **seawall** promenade popular with cyclists, runners, and rollerbladers. *(To get to the park, take #23, #123, #35, or #135 bus. A free shuttle runs between major destinations throughout the park June-Sept. 10am-6pm.)*

■**VANCOUVER AQUARIUM.** The aquarium, on the park's eastern side not far from the entrance, features exotic aquatic animals. BC, Amazonian, and other ecosystems are skillfully replicated. Dolphin and beluga whales demonstrate their advanced training and intelligence by drenching gleeful visitors in educational wetness. The new Wild Coast exhibit allows visitors to get a close-up view of marine life. Outside the aquarium, an **orca fountain** by sculptor Bill Reid glistens black. *(*☎*659-3474; www.vancouveraquarium.bc.ca. Open July-Aug. daily 9:30am-7pm; Sept.-June 10am-5:30pm. Shows throughout the day from 10am-5:30pm. $14.50, students, ages 13-18 and seniors $12, ages 4-12 $9, 3 and under free.)*

WATER. The **Lost Lagoon,** brimming with fishies, birds, and the odd trumpeter swan, provides a utopian escape from the skyscrapers. **Nature walks** start from the **Nature House,** underneath the Lost Lagoon bus loop. *(Walks* ☎ *257-8544. 2hr. Su at 1pm. $5, under 12 free. Nature House open June-Aug. F-Su 11am-7pm.)* Farther into the park, **Beaver**

Lake is a place to paint water lilies and feed ducks. The park's edges boast a few restaurants, tennis courts, a cinder running track with hot showers and changing room, and an outdoor theater—the **Malkin Bowl** (☎ 687-0174)—and swimming beaches staffed by lifeguards. For warm, chlorinated water, take a dip in the Second Beach Pool. *(Next to Georgia St. park entrance. Pool ☎ 257-8370. $4, ages 13-18 $3, ages 65+ $2.40, ages 6-12 $2. Towels $1.72, lockers 25¢. Open May 19-June 10 M-F noon-8:45pm, June 11-Sept. 3 M-F 10am-8:45pm, May 19-Sept. 3 Sa-Su 10am-8:45pm.)* For free chlorinated water, kids can romp around the Variety Kids Water Park by Lumbermen's Arch.

FALSE CREEK AND GRANVILLE ISLAND

GRANVILLE ISLAND PUBLIC MARKET. Southwest of downtown under the Granville Bridge; intersperses trendy shops, art galleries, restaurants, and countless produce stands. *(From downtown, bus #50 "False Creek" or #51 "Granville Island" from Granville St. ☎ 666-5784. Open daily 9am-6pm; Jan. closed M.)* During the summer, the tiny False Creek Ferry and Aqua Bus carry passengers from the Aquatic Centre (see **Beaches,** below) to Granville Island and to Vanier Park (van-YAY) and its museum complex. *(☎ 684-7781. Ferries every 5min. as early as 7am to as late as 10:30pm; schedules available at the docks. $2, seniors and children $1. An Adventure Pass is available for $12, seniors $10, children $8; includes $15 of coupons and unlimited day travel on the boats.)*

GRANVILLE ISLAND BREWING COMPANY. Canada's first micro-brewery offers daily tours at noon, 2pm and 4pm. *(Under the bridge at the southern tip of the island. ☎ 687-2739. $7. Includes samples of 4 brews and a souvenir glass. Call for store hours.)*

MARITIME MUSEUM. The Aqua Bus at Vanier Park shares the Maritime Museum dock with historic vessels. The wood-and-glass A-frame museum on shore houses **R.C.M.P. St. Roch,** a schooner that patrolled the Northwest Passage in the 1940s and was the first to sail it in both directions; in 1950, she was the first to circumnavigate North America. Admission includes a 15min. documentary on the St. Roch and the opportunity to explore the decks of the ship. Also hands-on exhibits, paintings and photos of Vancouver's harbor in the early days, and exhibits on tugboats, fireboats, and pirates. *(1905 Ogden Ave. ☎ 257-8300. $7, youths and seniors $4, families $16; Tu half-price seniors. Open daily Victoria Day-Labour Day 10am-5pm; winter Tu-Sa 10am-5pm, Su noon-5pm. Last video shown at 3:45pm.)*

H.R. MACMILLAN SPACE CENTRE. Housed in the same circular building as the **Vancouver Museum,** the space center runs a motion-simulator ride, planetarium, and exhibit gallery, as well as laser-light rock shows. *(Bus #22 south on Burrard St. from downtown. 1100 Chestnut St. ☎ 738-7827. Open daily July-Aug. 10am-5pm, Sept.-June closed M. $13, students and seniors $10; laser-light show $9.25. Vancouver Museum ☎ 736-4431. Open daily 10am-5pm; winter closed M. $8, under 19 $5.50, seniors $7. Combined admission to both museums $17, youth $11.)*

BEACHES

Vancouver has kept its many beaches remarkably clean. Follow the western side of the Stanley Park seawall south to **Sunset Beach Park,** a strip of grass and beach extending all the way along **English Bay** to the Burrard Bridge. The **Aquatic Centre,** 1050 Beach Ave., at the southeast end of the beach, is a public facility with a sauna, gym, and a 50m indoor pool. *(☎ 665-3424. Call for public swim hours, generally M-Th 9am-4:20pm and 8pm-9:55pm, F 9am-4:20pm and 8:20-8:55pm, Sa 10am-9pm, Su 1-9pm. $4, ages 13-18 $3, ages 6-12 $2, ages 65+ $2.40.)*

Kitsilano Beach ("Kits"), across Arbutus St. from Vanier Park, is another local favorite for tanning and beach volleyball. For fewer crowds, more young 'uns, and free showers, visit **Jericho Beach** (head west along 4th Ave. and follow signs). North Marine Dr. runs along the beach, and a cycling path at the side of the road leads to the westernmost end of the UBC campus. Bike and hiking trails cut through the campus and crop its edges. West of Jericho Beach is the quieter **Spanish Banks;** at low tide the ocean retreats almost a kilometer, allowing for long walks on the flats.

Most of Vancouver's 31km of beaches are patrolled daily by lifeguards from late May to Labour Day between 11:30am and 9pm. Even if you don't dip a foot in the chilly waters, you can frolic in true West Coast spirit during summer weekend **volleyball tournaments,** offering all levels of competition. Scare up a team at the hostel, then call ☎ 291-2007 to find out where to play. Team entry fees from $40.

"Co-ed Naked Beach Volleyball" would make a fine t-shirt slogan, but you wouldn't wear it at **Wreck Beach.** Take entry trail #6 down the hill from SW Marine Dr. opposite the UBC campus. A steep wooden staircase leads to a totally secluded, self-contained sunshine community of nude sunbathers and guitar-playing UBC students. There are no lifeguards, but naked entrepreneurs peddle vegetarian-friendly foods, beer, and other awareness-altering goods for premium prices. Call **Wreck Beach Preservation Society** (☎ 273-6950) for more info.

▶ DAYTRIPS FROM VANCOUVER

EAST OF NORTH VAN. East of city center, the town of **Deep Cove** in North Vancouver luxuriates in saltiness, and sea otters and seals ply pleasant Indian Arm. **Cates Park,** at the end of Dollarton Hwy. on the way to Deep Cove, has popular swimming and scuba waters and makes a good bike trip out of Vancouver. Trails leave from Mt. Seymour Rd., and a paved road winds 11km to the top for access to hiking and biking. See also **Local Mountains,** p. 249. *(Bus #210 from Pender St. to the Phibbs Exchange on the north side of Second Narrows Bridge. From there, take bus #211 or 212 to Deep Cove. Bus #211 also leads to Mount Seymour Provincial Park.)*

■ LIGHTHOUSE PARK. If you only get out of Vancouver once, go to gorgeous **Lighthouse Park.** Numerous trails crisscross the 185-acre park, including an easy 2hr., 3km loop that covers most of the park. To reach one of the **best picnic spots in the world,** walk down the path toward the lighthouse, hang a left at the buildings, keep right at the fork in the trail, and walk to a large flat rock. Some **rock climbing,** consisting of sea cliff top-roping and bouldering, is located at Juniper Point on the west side of the park. *(Head across Lions Gate Bridge from Stanley Park and west along Marine Dr. for about 10km through West Van. 50km round-trip from downtown; blue bus #250 goes right to the park's entrance. For a park map stop by the West Van. Parks & Community Services Office at 750 17th St., 2nd floor. ☎ 925-7200. Open M-F 8:30am-4:30pm.)*

REIFEL BIRD SANCTUARY. Reifel Bird Sanctuary is on 850-acre Westham Island. The marshland supports 265 bird species, and spotting towers are set up for extended birdwatching. April, May, October, and November are the best months. *(Westham Island lies northwest of the Tsawwassen ferry terminal and 16km south of the city. ☎ 946-6980. Open daily 9am-4pm. $3.25, seniors and children $1.)*

LYNN CANYON. An idyllic setting that provides easy hiking for city escapists. Unlike the more famous Capilano (below), the suspension bridge here is free, uncrowded, and hangs 50m above the canyon. The park also offers more trails than Capilano; several are 10-20min., while longer hiking trails are also plentiful. Swimming, however, is not recommended; many have died over the years from the treacherous currents and falls. *(SeaBus to Lynn Canyon Park, in North Vancouver. Bus #229 from the North Vancouver SeaBus terminal to the last stop (Peters Rd.) and walk 500m to the bridge. ☎ 981-3103. Open summer 7am-9pm; spring and fall 7am-7pm; winter 7am-6pm.)*

CAPILANO SUSPENSION BRIDGE. You and every other Vancouver tourist will enjoy crossing the precarious Capilano Bridge. Although the bridge was built in 1889, it remains awe-inspiring, spanning 137m and swaying 70m above the river. Added highlights are the Totem Park, with 39 authentic totem poles, and the Little Big House, where native carvers work at their craft and perform native dances thrice daily. A few short trails meander through the surrounding old growth forest. Guided tours every 15min. in summer. *(10min. from town. Drive through Stanley Park, over the Lions Gate Bridge, north 1km. on Capilano Rd. From Hwy. #1 take Exit 14 and go north.5km. 3735 Capilano Rd. North Van. or take bus #246 from downtown to Ridgewood stop, walk 1 block* north to park. ☎ 985-7474; www.capbridge.com. Open in summer Su-Th 8am-8pm, F-Sa 8am-9pm; winter daily 9am-5pm. $12, senior $10, student $7.50, child 6-12 $3.25, under 6 free. CAA/AAA, transit 20% discount, HI members get student rate.)

LOCAL MOUNTAINS

Three local mountains loom above the city on the North Shore, bringing the locals out year round. In winter, all three offer night skiing and heavier snow than mountains farther from the ocean. Their size and impact on your wallet are much smaller than Whistler, which is a 2hr. drive north on Hwy. 99 (see p. 251). In summer, all offer challenging hiking and beautiful views of the city from the top.

GROUSE MOUNTAIN. The closest ski hill to downtown Vancouver has the crowds to prove it. The slopes are lit for skiing until 10:30pm from mid-November to mid-April. Take bus #236 from the North Vancouver SeaBus terminal, which drops passengers off at the Super Skyride, an aerial tramway open daily from 9am-10pm. (☎ 984-0661; snow report 986-6262. Lift tickets $35, youth $25, senior $19, child $15, night passes at a reduced rate. Tramway $17.50, seniors $15.50, ages 13-18 $12.) The steep 2.9km **Grouse Grind Trail** is popular among Vancouverites in the summer; it climbs 853m to the top of the mountain and takes a good 2hr. The Skyride back down costs $5.

CYPRESS BOWL. A little farther removed, Cypress Bowl in West Vancouver provides a less crowded ski alternative. It boasts the most advanced terrain of the local mountains on its 23 runs. Head west on Hwy. 1, and take Exit 8 (Cypress Bowl Rd.). A few minutes before the downhill area, the 16km of groomed trails at Hollyburn **cross-country ski area** are open to the public. In summer, the cross-country trails are excellent for **hiking** and **berry-picking**. (☎ 922-0825; snow report 419-7669; www.cypressbowl.com. Discount tickets available at Costco supermarkets.)

MOUNT SEYMOUR. Bus #211 from the Phibbs Exchange at the north end of the Second Narrows Bridge leads to **Mt. Seymour Provincial Park.** Trails leave from Mt. Seymour Rd., and a paved road winds 11km to the top. The Mt. Seymour ski area is the cheapest. However, its marked terrain is also the least challenging, although the spectacular back country is the preferred terrain of many several top pro snowboarders. (Midweek lift tickets $19, seniors $15, ages 6-12 $9; weekends and holidays $26, ages 6-12 $13, ages 13-18 $21, seniors $15.)

SECHELT PENINSULA ☎ 604

Vancouver Island's Sunshine Coast deserves its name. Tucked between the Strait of Georgia and Porpoise Bay, Sechelt (SEE-shelt) is one of BC's greatest secrets. Only 1½hr. by road and ferry from downtown Vancouver, this quiet seaside paradise remains miles away in attitude, lifestyle, and even climate. The region offers a rich array of outdoor activities: world-class kayaking, hiking, scuba diving, biking, and even skiing are close-by.

◾◪ ORIENTATION AND PRACTICAL INFORMATION. Sechelt is the largest community on the Sunshine Coast, 27km west of the **BC Ferries,** Langdale Ferry Terminal (☎ 886-2242 or 888-223-3779). The fare on the ferry between Langdale and Horseshoe Bay is only charged on the way from the mainland to Sechelt (40min.; 8-10 per day; $8, ages 5-11 $4, car $30; off-season slightly cheaper). **Malaspina Coach Lines** (☎ 885-3666) runs to **Vancouver** (2 per day, $10.75 plus ferry fare). **Sunshine Coast Transit System** (☎ 885-3234) buses run from Sechelt to the ferry terminal (adult $1.50, students and seniors $1). **National Tilden,** 5623 Wharf St., rents cars. (☎ 885-9120. From $50 per day; 25¢ per km over 100km; winter rates start at $44.) Hail a **Sunshine Coast Taxi** at ☎ 885-3666. The **visitors center** is located in the Trail Bay Centre at Trail Ave. and Teredo St. next to Home Hardware. (☎ 885-0662 or 877-633-2963. Open July to mid-Sept. M-Sa 9:30am-5:30pm, Su 10am-4pm; off season closed on Su.) **Trail Bay Sports,** at Cowrie St. and Trail Ave., rents mountain bikes and sells fishing gear and permits as well as other useful outdoor gear. (☎885-2512. Bikes $10 per hr., $45 per 8hr. Open summer M-Th and Sa 9am-6pm, F 9am-9pm, Su 10am-4pm; winter M-Sa 9:30am-5:30pm.) The **Sechelt Public Library,** 5797 Cowrie St., has **Internet access** for $1 per 30min. (☎885-3260. Open Tu 10am-5pm, W-Th 11am-8pm, F and Su 1pm-5pm, and Sa 10am-4pm.) **Laundromat: Sechelt Coin Laundry,** on Dolphin St. at Inlet Ave. Wash $1.75, dry 25¢ per 5min. (☎885-3393. Open daily 9am-9pm.) **Emergency:** ☎911. **Hospital: St. Mary's** (☎885-2224), on the highway, at the east end of town. **Post office:** On Inlet Ave. at Dolphin St. (☎885-2411. Open M-F 8:30am-5pm, Sa 8:30am-12:30pm.) **Postal Code:** V0N 3A0.

ACCOMMODATIONS AND CAMPING. Most of Sechelt's accommodations are pricey, but deals can be found. The comfortable **Moon Cradle Hostel,** 3125 Hwy. 101 across from the golf course, 10km east of Sechelt, is situated on 10 acres of woodland property with a firepit, sauna, laundry, Internet, and bike rentals ($5 per hr.). It can turn into a hangout for the locals, so idyllic silence isn't always the norm. (☎885-2070 or 877-350-5862. $20, students and seniors $17; private room $58; tenting sites $15, students and seniors $10.) **Eagle View B&B,** 4839 Eagle View Rd., 5min. east of Sechelt, has rooms with private bath, sitting room with TV/VCR and video collection, an ocean view, complimentary tea and biscuits, and delightful hosts. (☎885-7225. $45-50 singles, $65 double or twin with shared bath, $70 double with private bath.)

The provincial parks in the area are dreamy. The family-oriented **Porpoise Bay Provincial Park,** 4km north of Sechelt along Sechelt Inlet Rd./E Porpoise Bay Rd., offers a forested campground with toilets, showers, firewood, playground, and a lovely beach and swimming area. Near Angus Creek, where salmon spawn in late Oct.-Nov. (Reservations ☎800-689-9025. Wheelchair accessible. 84 regular sites, $18; cyclist campsites by the water $9. Gate closed 11pm-7am.) For more seclusion, **Roberts Creek Provincial Park,** 11km east of Sechelt, has private sites amid old growth Douglas Firs. (Pit toilets, firewood, water. Wheelchair accessible. 24 sites, $12.) **Smuggler Cove Provincial Park** has five primitive, free walk-in sites (pit toilets, no water). The sites are accessible by boat, and the cove is an excellent base for kayaking. Head west out of town towards Halfmoon Bay and turn left on Brooks Rd., which leads 3.5km to a parking area. The campsite is 1km along a trail.

FOOD. The **Gumboot Garden Cafe,** 1059 Roberts Creek Rd., 10km east of Sechelt in Roberts Creek, serves delicious meals with largely organic ingredients. Lunch and breakfast favorites include fries and miso gravy ($3.50) and Thai salad with chicken, salmon, or tofu ($6-7). A variable dinner menu is uniformly excellent and always includes vegan options. (☎885-4216. Open M-W 8:30am-6pm, Th-Su 9am-9pm.) In Sechelt, the **Old Boot Eatery,** 5520 Wharf St., serves up generous portions of Italian food and local hospitality; pasta entrees $9-15. (☎885-2727. Open M-Sa 11am-10pm; winter 11am-9pm.) **Wakefield Inn,** on the highway (number 6529) 5min. west of Sechelt, dishes out standard pub fare and live music with a great view of the ocean. (☎885-7666. Burgers $7-9; pints $4-5. Music F-Sa 9pm-1am.) For groceries, **Claytons,** in the Trail Bay Centre, sells Sechelt's by the seashore. The deli serves up a sandwich with all the toppings you want and any deli salad or soup for $5.50. (☎885-2025. Open M-Th 9am-7pm, F 9am-9pm, Sa-Su 10am-6pm.)

SIGHTS AND OUTDOOR ACTIVITIES. The eight wilderness marine parks in the protected waters of **Sechelt Inlet** make for fantastic sea kayaking and canoeing and offer free camping along the shore. **Pedals & Paddles,** at Tillicum Bay Marina, 7km north of town, rents vessels. (☎885-6440. Single kayaks $23 per 4hr., doubles $46; canoes $27. Full-day single kayaks $40, doubles $75; canoes $45.) The intersection of Sechelt and Salmon Inlets is home to the **S.S. Chaudiere artificial reef,** one of the largest wreck dives in North America. **Suncoast Dive Center** rents equipment, teaches lessons, and charters boats (☎740-8006; www.suncoastdiving.com. Basic rental $30 per day; full rental $75 per day; 1 day charter $75). On the other side of the peninsula, **Pender Harbor** offers equally impressive diving; Jacques Cousteau considered this site second only to the Red Sea. **Skookumchuck Narrows** is a popular destination by water or by land to view tidal rapids that bring waves standing 1.5m at peak tides. Tidal schedules are available at the Info Centre or at the trailhead. To get there, drive 54km west to **Earl's Cove** and then 4km towards **Egmont** (about 1hr.). From the parking area, it's a 4km walk to four viewing sites (allow 1hr.). The route to the first site is wheelchair-accessible.

Dakota Bowl and Wilson Creek 4km east of Sechelt have hiking and free cross-country skiing trails. From Sechelt, turn left on Field Rd. and drive 8km to the trailhead. Sechelt's lumber legacy has left it with an extensive system of former logging roads suitable for hiking and mountain biking. The intermediate **Chapman Creek Trail** passes huge Douglas firs en route to **Chapman Falls**. The trailhead is at the top of Havies Rd., 1km north of the Davis Bay Store on Hwy. 101, or access at Brookman Park on the highway. The **Suncoaster Trail** extends over 40km from **Homesite Creek,** near Halfmoon Bay northwest of Sechelt, through the foothills of the **Caren Range,** home of Canada's oldest trees (some as old as 1835 years).

Indoors, the **Sunshine Coast Arts Centre,** on Trail Ave. at Medusa St., showcases local talent in a log building. (☎885-5412. Open Tu-Sa 10am-4pm, Su 1-4pm. Admission by donation.) They also organize the Hackett Park Crafts Fair, held during the Sechelt's big event, the **Sunshine Coast Festival of the Written Arts,** which attracts talented Canadian and international authors to give **readings** (August 8-11, 2002). Panels are held in the **botanical gardens** of the historic Rockwood Centre, and tickets go early. (☎885-9631 or 800-565-9631. Grounds open daily 8am-10pm.) The **Roberts Creek Community Hall** (☎886-3868 or 740-9616), on the corner of the highway and Roberts Creek Rd., is an unlikely venue that attracts excellent musicians on weekends, from reggae to Latin funk. Tickets ($10-20) can be purchased at the **Roberts Creek General Store** (☎885-3400).

ALONG HWY. 99: SEA TO SKY HWY.

Winding around the steep cliffs on the shore of Howe Sound from Horseshoe Bay to Squamish and then continuing inland to Whistler, the Sea to Sky Hwy. (Hwy. 99) is one of the loveliest, most dangerous, and best loved drives in British Columbia. Sinuous curves combine with brilliant vistas of the Sound and Tantalus Range.

VANCOUVER TO WHISTLER

Fifty-two kilometers north of Vancouver, at the **BC Museum of Mining** in Britannia Beach, visitors can hop on a train and ride deep into a copper mine that has been inactive since 1974. (☎896-2233. Open May-Oct. daily 9am-4:30pm. $9.50; students and seniors $7.50, under 5 free. Add $3.50 for the Gold Panning tour.)

Numerous provincial parks line the rocky drive to Whistler, providing excellent hiking and climbing opportunities. One worth stopping for is **Shannon Falls,** just off the highway, 3km past the museum. The park affords a 2min. walk (350m) to a spectacular view of a 335m waterfall, the third highest in BC. Steep but well-maintained trails from the falls make for difficult **dayhiking** up to the three peaks of the **Stawamus Chief** (11km round-trip), the second largest granite monolith in the world, which bares a 671m wall of solid granite. The face of the Chief is a popular climb for expert hikers. **Squamish Hostel**, 38490 Buckley Rd., in downtown Squamish, is a common stopover for those tackling the local geography. In summer, the hostel is packed with wandering climbers, as the region between Squamish and Whistler boasts over 1300 excellent routes. (☎892-9240 or 800-449-8614 in BC. Shower, kitchen, linen. $15; private rooms $25.) At **Eagle Run,** a viewing site 4km north of the hostel along the Squamish River, thousands of bald eagles make their winter home along the rivers and estuaries of Squamish Valley. BC Parks runs a spotless campground 13km north of Squamish at **Alice Lake**. (Reservations ☎800-689-9025; www.discovercamping.ca. Showers, hot water, firewood. $18.50.) Nearby **Garibaldi Park** contains a vast number of stunning hikes, including an 18km (round-trip) trail up to **Garibaldi Lake.** The backcountry campgrounds at the lake provide further access to Black Tusk and Cheakamus Lake (trailhead at Rubble Creek parking lot, 25km north of Squamish). The **BC Parks District Office** in Alice Lake Park has trail maps. (☎ 898-3678. Open M-F 8:30am-4:30pm.) The **BC Forest Service office,** 42000 Loggers Ln., has maps of local logging roads and primitive campgrounds and sells the $10 permits needed to camp at them. (☎ 898-2100; www.for.gov.bc.ca/Vancouver/district/squamish. Open M-F 8:30am-4:30pm.)

WHISTLER ☎ 604

This skiers' and snowboarders' utopia is among the top ski destinations in the world, and for good reason: over 7000 acres of skiable terrain make it the largest ski area on the continent. The mountains are part of Garibaldi Provincial Park, and it takes little effort to get off the beaten path. When the snow melts, Whistler offers exceptional mountain biking, horseback riding, and white-water rafting. Whistler, the town, is currently bidding to host the 2010 Winter Olympics.

ORIENTATION AND PRACTICAL INFORMATION

Whistler is located 125km north of Vancouver on the beautiful, if dangerously twisty, Hwy. 99. Services are located in **Whistler Village,** most of which is **pedestrian-only. Whistler Creek,** 5km south on Hwy. 99, offers a smaller collection of accommodations and restaurants.

Greyhound Bus Lines: (☎ 932-5031 or 800-661-8747), in Vancouver. To **Vancouver** from the **Village Bus Loop** (2½hr.; 6 per day; $21, round-trip $42). The Activity Centre sells tickets.

BC Rail: ☎ 984-5246. **Cariboo Prospector** departs North Vancouver at 7am for Whistler Creek and returns at 6:40pm daily. $39 one-way. The train station is on Lake Placid Rd. in Creekside; free connecting bus service to the Village.

Whistler Taxi: ☎ 932-3333.

Tourist Office: Activity Centre (☎ 932-3928) in the Conference Centre provides maps and booking services. Open daily 9am-5pm. The **Chamber of Commerce** and **Info Centre** are in a log cabin at the corner of Hwy. 99 and Lake Placid Rd. in Creekside (☎ 932-5528; open 9am-6pm daily). Or call **Whistler/Blackcomb** (☎ 932-3434 or 800-766-0449; www.whistlerblackcomb.com).

Laundry: Laundry at Nester's, 7009 Nester's Rd. (☎ 932-2690). $2 wash, $1 for 20min. dry. Open 8am-8pm.

Weather Conditions: ☎ 932-5090.

Emergency: ☎ 911.

Police: 4315 Blackcomb Way (☎ 932-3044), in the Village.

Telecare Crisis Line: ☎ 932-2673.

Medical Services: Whistler Health Care Center, 4380 Lorimer Rd. (☎ 932-4911).

Internet Access: Whistler Public Library. Free, but long waits. Open M-Tu and Th 10am-8pm, F-Su 10am-5pm. For an arm at **Mailboxes Etc.** $5 per 30min.; $9 per hr (behind the Marketplace). For a leg at **Soapy's Internet Station,** 4369 Main St., $3.50 per 15min., $7.50 per 50min., laptop hookups $7 per hr. Open daily 10am-10pm.

Post Office: (☎ 932-5012), in the Village Marketplace. Open M-F 8:30am-5:30pm, Sa 8:30am-12:30pm. **Postal Code:** V0N 1B0.

ACCOMMODATIONS AND CAMPING

Whistler offers great hostels and campgrounds. The Forest Service office in Squamish (see p. 251) has maps for other camping options.

WHISTLER ■ 253

Whistler Hostel (HI), 5678 Alta Lake Rd. (☎932-5492). BC Rail from Vancouver stops right in front on request. 5km south of Whistler Village off Hwy. 99. The Rainbow Park bus runs to the Village ($1.50). The timber building has kitchen, fireplace, ski lockers, pool table, and sauna. Ski tuning performed on the premises. Bikes $18 per day. Canoes free on Alta Lake. Reserve ahead. Linens $1, towels 50¢. Bunks $20; nonmembers $24; under 13 half-price; under 6 free. Private rooms $10 surcharge.

The Fireside Lodge, 2117 Nordic Dr. (☎932-4545), 3km south of the Village. Caters to a quiet, easygoing crowd. The spacious and spotless cabin comes with the works: mammoth kitchen, lounge, sauna, coin-operated laundry, game room, storage (bring your own lock), and parking. More square footage to relax than to sleep. Check-in 3:30-8:30pm. 24 dorm beds. Apr. to mid-Dec. $20; mid-Dec. to Mar. $30.

Shoestring Lodge, 7124 Nancy Greene Dr. (☎932-3338), 1km north of the Village. Cable, private bath, laundry, and Internet. Use of kitchen for a small fee. In-house pub can lead to late-night ruckus outside. Free shuttle to slopes Dec.-Apr. Check-in 4pm. Check-out 11am. 4-person dorm $17-30; doubles $90-140; more expensive in winter.

Riverside Resort (☎932-5469), 2.5km north of the Village. Brand new campground with steep fees, but plentiful amenities: store, laundry, cafe, bike rentals, volleyball, horseshoe pits, game room, Internet ($3 per 15min.). $25 unserviced; $40 full hookups; $150 for 2-4 person cabin. Extra charges apply for more than 2 adults.

FOOD

Cheap food is hard-won in the Village with the exception of the popular **IGA** supermarket in the Village North (open daily 9am-9pm).

Zeuski's Taverna (☎932-6009), in Whistler Village's Town Plaza. Features hearty Mediterranean cuisine. Dinner prices are Olympian ($13-29). Falafel, souvlaki, and gyro lunches for $6-12. Open daily 11am-11pm.

South Side Deli, 2102 Lake Placid Rd. (☎932-3368), on Hwy. 99 by the Husky station 4km south of the Village. Be sure to try the B.E.L.T.C.H. (bacon, egg, lettuce, tomato, cheese, and ham). Open Th-Su 6am-10pm, M-W 6am-3pm.

Moguls Coffee Beans (☎932-4845). A tasty and thrifty option. Delectable home-baked goods ($2.25 or less) and sandwiches ($4.50). Open daily 6:30am-9pm.

OUTDOOR ACTIVITIES

WINTER SPORTS. Thirty-three lifts (15 of them high-speed), three glaciers, over 200 marked trails, and a mile (1609m) of vertical drop, makes **Whistler/Blackcomb** a top destination for snow enthusiasts. Parking and lift access for this behemoth are available at six points, with Whistler Creekside offering the shortest lines and the closest access for those coming from Vancouver. A **lift ticket** is good for both mountains. (☎932-3434 or 800-766-0449. June 11-Aug. 6 $39; multi-day discounts available.) A **Fresh Tracks** upgrade ($15), available every morning at 7am, provides a basic breakfast in the mountaintop lodge on Blackcomb along with the chance to begin skiing as soon as the ski patrol has finished avalanche control. **Cheap tickets** are often available at convenience stores in Vancouver, and rates are sometimes cheaper mid-week and early or late season. While Whistler offers amazing alpine terrain and gorgeous bowls, most **snowboarders** prefer the younger Blackcomb for its windlips, natural quarter-pipes, and 16-acre terrain park. Endless **backcountry skiing** is accessible from resort lifts and in Garibaldi Park's **Diamond Head** area.

> The BC Parks office in Alice Lake Park (see p. 251) has **avalanche** info. Avalanches kill people every year, and there are no patrols outside resort boundaries. Be safe, always file trip plans, and stay within the limits of your experience.

SUMMER ACTIVITIES. While skiing is God in Whistler and lasts until August on the glaciers, life goes on in the summer as the **Whistler Gondola** continues to whisk sightseers to the top of the mountain, providing access to the resort's extensive **hiking trails** and **mountain bike park** ($22 for hiking only, $30 for mountain bike park). Hiking trails tend to be short dayhikes, with lengths ranging from 20min. to 5-6hr. and most trails taking less than an hour to complete. For more info on trails and the multitude of other options—such as river rafting, off-road tours, jet boating and horseback riding—that make Whistler/Blackcomb famous in the summer, check their comprehensive web site at www.whistler-blackcomb.com or call the tourist info line (see **Tourist Office,** p. 252).

NORTH OF WHISTLER

PEMBERTON. It only takes 30min. of driving north on Hwy. 99 to leave the land where "economy class" is long forgotten and reach the underdeveloped town of Pemberton. The region's numerous glacial lakes lure fishermen like a fat nightcrawler. **Visitor information** is located in a booth on the highway. (☎894-6175. Open Th-M 9am-7pm.) You can pitch a tent or park an RV for $12 at the **Nairn Falls Provincial Campground,** 5km south of Pemberton on Hwy. 99. The campsite has hot water, wood, and a beautiful 3km (1hr.) round-trip hike to the falls (sturdy footwear recommended). You will, however, be lulled to sleep by the passing highway traffic. If you get hungry, grab a quick and scrumptious meal at the **Outpost Restaurant,** 2min. down Vine St. toward the center of town off Hwy. 99. (☎894-3340. Open M-F 11:30am-10pm, Sa-Su 9am-10pm; in winter closed M and at 9pm.)

JOFFRE LAKES. For a fantastic **day hike** 65km north of Whistler, climb to the **Joffre Lakes** along a popular 12km path round-trip that passes three glacially-fed lakes and affords spectacular views of Joffre Peak and Slalok Mountain (accessible in the summer months only, look for the entrance 32km north of Pemberton).

LILLOOET. Little traffic continues north along Hwy. 99 and the drive is eerily remote. **Lillooet** ("B.C's Little Nugget"), 135km north of Whistler, was originally Mile 0 of the historic **Cariboo Gold Rush Wagon Trail,** which led 100,000 gold-crazed miners north to Barkerville between 1862 and 1870. The town itself is small, but oozing with history. The **Chamber of Commerce** (☎256-4364; fax 256-4315) will help you find a place to crash. In the second weekend in June, the town celebrates its heritage during **Lillooet Days** with a host of events including a staged train robbery and mock trial and execution.

FARTHER NORTH. From Lillooet, Hwy. 99 meanders north another 50km snaking with the Fraser River until it meets Hwy. 97 11km north of **Cache Creek.** The weary can break halfway for trout fishing and swimming in **Crown Lake** beneath the red limestone cliffs of **Marble Canyon Provincial Park** (camping $12).

VANCOUVER ISLAND

Vancouver Island stretches almost 500km along continental Canada's southwest coast and is one of only two points in Canada extending south of the 49th parallel. The Kwagiulth, Nootka, and Coastal Salish shared the island for thousands of years until Captain Cook's discovery of Nootka Sound in 1778 triggered European exploration and infiltration. The current culture of Vancouver Island bespeaks its hybrid heritage, presenting a curious blend of totems and afternoon teas. The cultural and administrative center is Victoria, BC's capital, on its southernmost tip.

The Trans-Canada (Hwy. 1), leads north from Victoria to Nanaimo, the transportation hub of the island's central region. Outside of Victoria to Nanaimo, towns shrink in size as the wilderness takes over, creating a haven for hikers, kayakers, and mountaineers. Pacific Rim National Park, on the island's west coast, offers some of the most rugged and outstanding hiking in North America. On the northern third of the island, crumpets give way to clamburgers, and 4x4 pickups and logging caravans prowl the road.

NORTH OF WHISTLER ■ 255

256 ■ VANCOUVER ISLAND

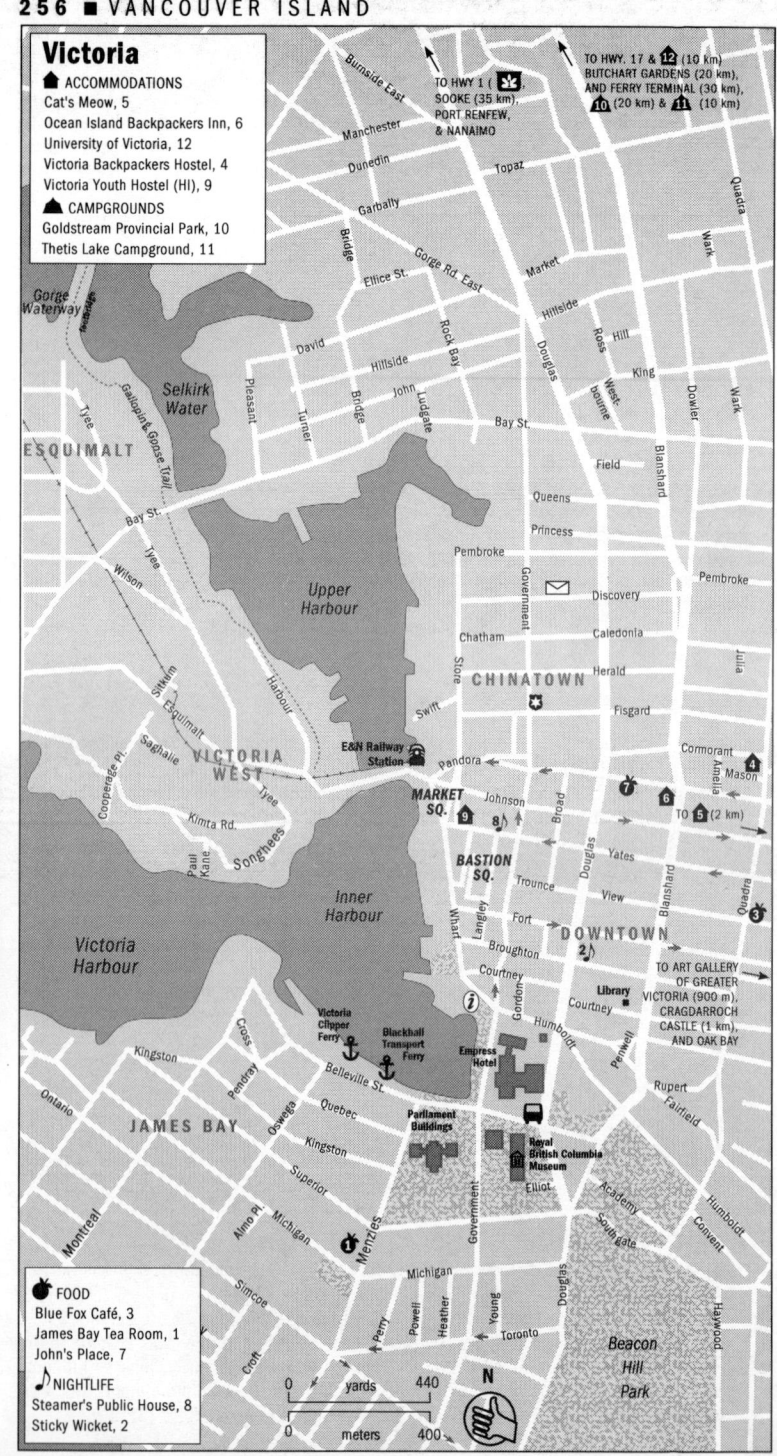

Victoria

ACCOMMODATIONS
- Cat's Meow, 5
- Ocean Island Backpackers Inn, 6
- University of Victoria, 12
- Victoria Backpackers Hostel, 4
- Victoria Youth Hostel (HI), 9

CAMPGROUNDS
- Goldstream Provincial Park, 10
- Thetis Lake Campground, 11

FOOD
- Blue Fox Café, 3
- James Bay Tea Room, 1
- John's Place, 7

NIGHTLIFE
- Steamer's Public House, 8
- Sticky Wicket, 2

VICTORIA ☎ 250

Although many tourist operations would have you believe that Victoria fell off Great Britain in a neat little chunk, its high tea tradition actually began in the 1950s to draw American tourists. Before the invasion of tea, Fort Victoria, founded in 1843, was a fur trading post and supply center for the Hudson Bay Company. But the discovery of gold in the Fraser River Canyon pushed it into the fast lane in 1858, bringing international trade and the requisite frontier bars and brothels. The government soon followed. Victoria became the capital in 1868.

Clean, polite, and tourist-friendly, Victoria is a homier alternative to cosmopolitan Vancouver. The namesake British monarch and her era of morals and furniture aside, Victoria is a city of diverse origins and interests. Galleries selling native arts operate alongside new-age bookstores, tourist traps, and pawn shops. Double-decker bus tours motor by English pubs while bike-taxis pedal past the markets, museums, and stores that make up the rest of downtown. Victoria also lies within easy striking distance of the rest of Vancouver Island's "outdoor paradise."

TRANSPORTATION

The **Trans-Canada Hwy. (Hwy. 1)** runs north to Nanaimo, where it becomes **Hwy. 19**, stretching north to the rest of Vancouver Island. The **West Coast Hwy. (Hwy. 14)** heads west to **Port Renfrew** and the West Coast Trail unit of the **Pacific Rim National Park**. The **Pat Bay Hwy. (Hwy. 17)** runs north from Victoria to Swartz Bay ferry terminal and the airport, 30min. from downtown. Driving in Victoria is relatively easy, but **parking** downtown is difficult and expensive, and you'll be playing Frogger with the tourists. Victoria surrounds the **Inner Harbour;** the main north-south thoroughfares downtown are **Government St.** and **Douglas St.** To the north, Douglas St. becomes Hwy. 1. **Blanshard St.,** one block to the east, becomes Hwy. 17.

Trains: E&N Railway, 450 Pandora St. (schedule ☎ 383-4324; general info and tickets 800-561-8630), near the Inner Harbour at the Johnson St. Bridge. 10% senior discount. 25% off when booked 7 days in advance. Daily service to **Nanaimo** (2½hr.; $23, students with ISIC $15) and **Courtenay** (4½hr.; $44, students with ISIC $29).

Buses: Laidlaw, 700 Douglas St. (☎ 385-4411 or 800-318-0818), at Belleville St. Laidlaw and its affiliates, **Pacific Coach Lines** and **Island Coach Lines,** connect most points on the island. To: **Nanaimo** (2½hr., 6 per day, $17.50), **Vancouver** (3½hr., 8-14 per day, $29) and **Port Hardy** (9hr., 1-2 per day, $93).

Ferries: BC Ferries (☎ 656-5571 or 888-223-3779; 7am-10pm operator 386-3431; www.bcferries.com). Service to all **Gulf Islands** (see p. 262). Ferries depart **Swartz Bay** to Vancouver's Tsawwassen ferry terminal (1½hr.; 8-16 per day; $8-9.50, bikes $2.50, car and driver $32-34). **Washington State Ferries** (☎ 381-1551 or 656-1831; in the US 206-464-6400 or 800-843-3779) depart from **Sidney** to **Anacortes, WA.** A ticket to Anacortes allows free stopovers along the eastward route, including the **San Juan Islands** (2 per day in summer, 1 per day in winter; US$9, car with driver US$41). **Victoria Clipper,** 254 Belleville St. (☎ 382-8100 or 800-888-2535), runs passenger ferries direct to **Seattle** (2-3hr.; 4 per day May-Sept., 1 per day Oct.-Apr.; US$79-125, seniors US$90-103, ages 1-11 $50-56). **Black Ball Transport,** 430 Belleville St. (☎ 386-2202), runs to **Port Angeles, WA** (1½hr.; 4 per day mid-May to mid-Oct., 2 per day Oct.-Dec. and mid-Mar. to mid-May; US$7.75, car and driver US$30, ages 5-11 US$4, bicycle US$3.50).

Public Transportation: BC Transit (☎ 382-6161; www.transitbc.com). City bus service with connections at the corner of Douglas and Yates St. Single-zone travel $1.75; multi-zone (north to **Swartz Bay, Sidney,** and the **Butchart Gardens**) $2.50; seniors $1.10 and $1.75; under 5 free. Day passes ($5.50, seniors $4) and free *Rider's Guide* at the library, from any driver, or with maps at **Tourism Victoria.** Disability Services for Local Transit (☎ 727-7811) is open M-Th and Su 7am-10pm, F-Sa 7am-midnight. **Bus #70** runs between downtown and the Swartz Bay and Sidney ferry terminals ($2.50).

258 ■ VICTORIA

Car Rental: Island Auto Rentals, 1030 Yates St. (☎384-4881). $25 per day, plus 12¢ per km after 100km. Must be 21 with major credit card. Insurance $13. The big companies with comparable rates are located at the bottom of Douglas St. near the Museum.

Taxis: Victoria Taxi ☎383-7111. **Westwind** ☎474-4747. $2.15 base, $1.30 per km.

🛈 PRACTICAL INFORMATION

Visitor Information: 812 Wharf St. (☎953-2033), at Government St. Also a Ticketmaster outlet. Open July-Aug. daily 8:30am-7:30pm; winter 9am-5pm.

Tours: Grayline, 700 Douglas St. (☎388-5248; www.victoriatours.com). Runs several tours in double-decker buses through different parts of the city ($17-97). **Historical Walking Tours** (☎953-2033) cover downtown in small groups, leaving from the visitors center. Tours daily in summer. Various durations and departure times. From $7.50-22.

Equipment Rental: Cycle BC Rentals, 747 Douglas St. (☎380-2453), guarantees best prices in town. Bikes from $6 per hr., $19 per day; scooters $12 per hr., $45 per day. Motorcycles available. Look for coupons at hostels and hotels. Open daily 9am-6:30pm in summer, otherwise 9am-5pm. **Harbour Rental,** 811 Wharf St. (☎995-1661), opposite the visitors center. Rowboats and single kayaks $15 per hr., $49 per day; doubles $25 per hr., $69 per day; canoes $19 per hr., $49 per day. Open daily 8am-10pm; winter 9am-5pm. **Sports Rent,** 611 Discovery St. (☎385-7368), rents camping equipment. Sleeping bags from $9, tents from $15, packs from $11. Open M-Sa 9am-6pm, Su 10am-5pm.

Laundromat and Showers: Oceanside Gifts, 102-812 Wharf St. (☎380-1777), beneath the visitors center. Wash $1.25, dry $1. Showers $1 per 5min. Open daily 7:30am-10pm.

Emergency: ☎911.

Police: 850 Caledonia (☎995-7654), at Quadra St.

Crisis Line: ☎386-6323. 24hr. **Rape Crisis:** ☎383-3232. 24hr.

Pharmacy: Shoppers Drug Mart, 1222 Douglas St. (☎381-4321). Open M-F 7am-8pm, Sa 9am-7pm, Su 9am-6pm.

Hospital: Royal Jubilee, 1900 Fort St. (☎370-8000).

Internet Access: $3 per hr. at the **Library,** 735 Broughton St. (☎382-7241), at Courtney St. Open M, W, F-Sa 9am-6pm; Tu and Th 9am-9pm. **Ocean Island Backpackers Inn** (see below). $1 per 15min.

Post Office: 621 Discovery St. (☎963-1350). Open M-F 8am-6pm. **Postal Code:** V8W 2L9.

🏠 ACCOMMODATIONS AND CAMPING

Victoria has a plethora of budget accommodations. A number of flavorful hostels and B&B-hostel hybrids make a night in Victoria an altogether pleasant experience. More than a dozen campgrounds and RV parks lie in the greater Victoria area. Reservations are wise in the summer.

■ **Ocean Island Backpackers Inn,** 791 Pandora St. (☎385-1788 or 888-888-4180), downtown. This colorful hostel boasts a better lounge than most clubs, tastier food than most restaurants, fantastic staff, and accommodations comparable to most hotels. Undoubtedly one of the finest urban hostels in Canada. Laundry, email, and free linen. Parking $5. 140 beds, 1-6 per room. HI or students $17.25, $20 otherwise; doubles $40-50. Weekly and monthly rates.

The Cat's Meow, 1316 Grant St. (☎595-8878). Take bus #22 to Fernwood and Grant St. A mini-hostel with 12 quiet beds, 3 blocks from downtown. Coin-op laundry, free street parking, discounts on kayaking and whale watching. Breakfast included. Closed 10:45am-4pm. $19; private rooms $40-45.

Selkirk Guest House, 934 Selkirk Ave. (☎389-1213), in West Victoria. Bus #14 along Craigflower to Tillicum; Selkirk is 1 block north. One coed dorm, free canoes, trampoline, treehouse, and a hot tub on the water. Kitchen, TVs in every room, laundry $1, free linen and towels. Breakfast $5. Dorm $20; single $65-85. Off season cheaper.

Victoria Backpackers Hostel, 1608 Quadra St. (☎386-4471), close to downtown. A funky old house with a small yard, lounge, and kitchen. Newly renovated dorms, lounge, and kitchen. Laundry $2, free linens, towels, soap. Reception M-F 8am-midnight, Sa-Su 10am-midnight. Dorms $15 or $40 for 3 nights; private rooms $40.

Victoria Youth Hostel (HI), 516 Yates St. (☎385-4511 or 888-883-0099), at Wharf St. downtown. Big and spotless barracks-style dorms. Foosball, pool, video games, TV room, and info desk. Kitchen, free linen. Storage $3 per week. Laundry $2, towel 50¢. Reception 24hr. Dorms July-Sept. $17, nonmembers $21; private rooms $4 more.

Goldstream Provincial Park, 2930 Trans-Canada Hwy. (☎391-2300; reservations ☎800-689-9025), 20km northwest of Victoria. Riverside area with dayhikes and swimming. Toilets, firewood. Follow the trail on the other side of the hwy. to a railway trestle in the woods. 167 gorgeous, gravelly sites. Sani-dump. Gates closed 11pm-7am. $19.

Thetis Lake Campground, 1938 W Park Ln. (☎478-3845), 10km north of the city center. Drive up Hwy. 1 to Colewood (Exit 10 from Victoria, or Exit 11 from up island) or take the Galloping Goose Trail. Popular among locals for cliff diving. Cliff-diving is not recommended by *Let's Go* or your mother. Toilets and laundry. Showers 25¢ per 5min., 90 sites, $16; 30 full hookups $20.

FOOD

A diverse array of food await in Victoria, if you know where to go. Ask locals for favored eats, or wander downtown to explore the many options. Many **Government St.** and **Wharf St.** restaurants raise their prices for the summer tourists. **Chinatown** extends from Fisgard and Government St. to the northwest. Coffee shops can be found on every corner. Cook St. Village, between McKenzie and Park Sts., offers an eclectic mix of creative restaurants. **Fisherman's Wharf,** at the end of Erie St., is hoppin' with the day's catch. For groceries, try **Thrifty Foods,** 475 Simcoe St., six blocks south of the Parliament Buildings. (☎544-1234. Open daily 8am-10pm.)

John's Place, 723 Pandora St. (☎389-0711), between Douglas and Blanshard St. Dishing up Canadian fare with a Thai twist plus a little Mediterranean flair. Try the veggie burger with sun-dried tomato pesto and mushrooms ($7.50). Extra selections on Thai night (M) and perogie night (W). Open M-F 7am-10pm, Sa 8am-4pm and 5-10pm, Su 8am-4pm and 5-9pm.

Blue Fox Cafe, 101-919 Fort St. (☎380-1683). Walk 3 blocks up Fort. St. from Douglas St. Locals' favorite for its tasty food. Breakfast all day, everyday; specials until 11am for under $5. Try the "Bubble & Squeak," sauteed veggies and panfries drowned in cheese and baked ($7). Open M-F 7:30am-4pm, Sa 9am-4pm, Su 9am-3pm.

James Bay Tea Room & Restaurant, 332 Menzies St. (☎382-8282), behind the Parliament Buildings. At James Bay, the sun never set on the British Empire. A trip to Victoria is improper without a spot of tea. The sandwiches and pastries that accompany tea service ($7.25) or high tea on Sunday ($10.25) are a lower-key version of the archaic High Tea served at the Empress Hotel. Open M-Sa 7am-8pm, Su 8am-8pm.

Cafe Mexico, 1425 Store St. (☎383-2233), has been voted the best Mexican in Victoria for 6 years running. You'll be ready to fiesta by the end of your meal, especially on Margarita Wednesday. Open summer Su-Th 11am-10pm, F-Sa 11am-11pm; winter Su-Th 11am-9:30pm, F-Sa 11am-10pm.

The Bistro, 714 Cormorant St. (☎381-1431). The Bistro has a menu as colorful as its decor. Vegetarian-friendly creations and breakfasts under $9. Open M-F 7:30am-5pm.

The Sour Pickle Cafe, 1623 Store St. (☎384-9390), serves a variety of burgers ($4-7) and omelettes ($5.50-6.50) in addition to inexpensive breakfast specials ($3, served until 11:30am). Open M-F 7:30am-4pm, Sa-Su 9am-4pm.

♪ ENTERTAINMENT

The **Victoria Symphony Society,** 846 Broughton St. (☎ 385-6515), performs regularly under conductor Kaees Bakels. The highlight of the season is the **Symphony Splash,** which is played on a barge in Inner Harbour. The performance concludes with fireworks and usually draws 50,000 listeners (first Su in Aug.; free). For the last 10 days of June, Victoria bops to **JazzFest.** (☎ 388-4423. $35 per day, or 5-day pass $90.) **Folkfest** hosts multicultural entertainment with food and dancing at Market Square and Ship's Point. (☎ 388-4728. Late June to early July. $2-12.)

On Tuesdays, first-run screenings at the **Cineplex Odeon,** 780 Yates St. (☎ 383-0513)—and virtually every other first-run theater in Canada—are discounted. To experience the cheapest movies available, visit **The Roxy,** 2657 Quadra St., an old airplane hangar turned movie theatre. (☎ 382-3370. $5 for 3 movies, seniors $2.50; Tu $2.50.) For offbeat and foreign films, head to the **University of Victoria's Cinecenta** in the Student Union. (☎ 721-8365. Bus #4, 26, 11, or 14. $6.75, seniors and kids $4.75, students $5.75, Sa-Su matinees $3.75.) In June, **Phoenix Theaters** (☎ 721-8000), at UVIC, puts on plays, as well as term-time live theater performances. Victoria goes Elizabethan when the **Annual Shakespeare Festival** lands in the Inner Harbour. (☎ 360-0234. Mid-July to mid-Aug.)

♣ NIGHTLIFE

Victorians may follow the metric system, but their beer is still sold by the pint. English pubs and watering holes abound throughout town. The free weekly *Monday Magazine,* out on Wednesdays, lists who's playing where and is available at hostels, hotels, and most restaurants.

Steamers Public House, 570 Yates St. (☎ 381-4340). Locals and visitors alike dance nightly to live music, from world-beat Celtic to funk. The best Su entertainment in town. Open stage M, jazz night Tu. Cover $3-5 at night, free M-Tu. Open Tu-Sa 11:30am-2am, Su 11:30am-midnight, M 11:30am-1am.

Suze, 515 Yates St. (☎ 383-2829). Trendy lounge and restaurant serves creative pizzas ($11.50-13.50) and Asian-inspired items such as the popular pad thai ($9). Nightly martini specials. 20% HI discount. Open Su-W 5pm-midnight, Th-Sa 5pm-1am.

Sticky Wicket, 919 Douglas St. (☎ 383-7137). A decent English-style pub, one of seven bars in the Strathcona Hotel. The Roof Top Bar has the only rooftop beach volleyball court for rent and serves great food. Downstairs, **Legends,** the adjacent club, occasionally brings in big names like Maceo Parker and Clarence "Gatemouth" Brown. Mainly plays Top 40. Pubs are free and serve food until 1am. Open M-Sa 11:30am-2am, Su 11:30am-midnight. Legends has $4 cover F-Sa; open M-Sa 9pm-2am.

Spinnakers Brew Pub, 308 Catherine St. (☎ 384-6613, office 384-0332). Take the Johnson St. bridge from downtown and walk 10min. down Esquimalt Rd., or stick to the waterfront and you'll walk right by it. The oldest brew pub in Canada is a great place to shoot pool and boasts the best view of the Inner Harbor. Open daily 11am-11pm.

◎ SIGHTS

If you don't mind becoming one with the flocks of tourists heading to the shores of Victoria, wander along the **Inner Harbour.** You'll watch boats come in and admire street performers on the Causeway as the sun sets behind neighboring islands.

■ **ROYAL BRITISH COLUMBIA MUSEUM.** This museum houses thorough exhibits on the biological, geological, and cultural history of the province. The First Nation exhibit features a totem pole room and an immense collection of traditional native art. The museum's **National Geographic IMAX Theater** runs the latest action documentaries on a six-story screen. **Thunderbird Park** and its many totems loom behind the museum and can be perused for free. *(675 Belleville St. Recording ☎ 387-3014; person 356-7226. Open daily 9am-5pm. $9; students, youths, and seniors $6; under 6 free. IMAX $10; seniors $8.50; youth $6.50; child $3.50. Combo prices available.)*

OUTDOOR ACTIVITIES ■ 261

BUTCHART GARDENS. The elaborate and world-famous Butchart Gardens, founded by Robert P.'s cement-pouring fortune, sprawl across 50 acres 21km north of Victoria off Hwy. 17. Immaculate landscaping includes the magnificent **Sunken Garden** (a former limestone quarry), the Rose Garden, Japanese and Italian gardens, and fountains. The gardens sparkle with live entertainment and lights at night. Outstanding fireworks on Saturday evenings in July and August draw out the locals. *(Bus #75 Central Saanich runs from downtown at Douglas and Pandora, $2.50, 1hr. The Gray Line, ☎ 388-6539, runs a round-trip, direct package for $26, youth $17.25, and child $7—includes admission to gardens; 35min. each way. Recording ☎ 652-5256; office 652-4422. Open daily July-Aug. 9am-10:30pm. $19.25, ages 13-17 $9.50, ages 5-12 $2, under 5 free.)*

BUTTERFLY GARDENS. Close to the Butchart Gardens, this enclosure devoted to winged insects is maintained at 20-28°C (80-85°F) and 80% relative humidity. Hundreds of specimens of over 35 species float around visitors' heads alongside canaries, finches, and cockatiels, while caterpillars munch on the profusion of tropical plants thriving in the moist environment. The gardens successfully breed giant Atlas Moths, which with a wingspan of up to 30cm (1 ft.) are the largest species of moth in the world. *(1461 Benvenuto Ave. Open Mar.-Oct. daily 9am-5pm. $8, seniors and students $7, ages 5-12 $4.50. 10% AAA or family discount.)*

PARLIAMENT BUILDINGS. The imposing **Parliament Buildings**, home of the Provincial government since 1898, stand opposite the Royal British Columbia Museum. The 10-story dome and vestibule are gilded with almost 50 oz. of gold. While the House is in session, swing by the **public gallery** and witness Members of the Legislative Assembly discussing matters of great importance. *(501 Belleville St. ☎ 387-3046. Open M-F 8:30am-5pm; Sa-Su for tours only. Free tours leave from the main steps in summer daily 9am-5pm, 3 times per hr.; call for off-season tour hours.)*

ART GALLERY OF GREATER VICTORIA. The **Art Gallery of Greater Victoria,** displays magnificent specimens from its 14,000 piece collection that covers contemporary Canada, traditional and contemporary Asia, North America, and Europe. It has the only Shinto shrine outside Japan. *(1040 Moss St. ☎ 384-4101. Open M-W and F-Sa 10am-5pm, Su 1-5pm, Th 10am-9pm. $5, students and seniors $3, M by donation.)*

VANCOUVER ISLAND BREWERY. After a few days of hiking, biking, and museum-visiting, unwind with a tour of the **Vancouver Island Brewery.** The 1hr. tour is both educational and alcoholic. *(2330 Government St. ☎ 361-0007. Tours F-Sa 3pm. $5 covers four 4 oz. samples and souvenir pint glass. Must be 19 to have samples.)*

◫ OUTDOOR ACTIVITIES

The flowering oasis of **Beacon Hill Park,** off Douglas St. south of the Inner Harbour, pleases walkers, bikers, and the picnic-inclined and borders the gorgeous Dallas Rd. scenic drive. The **Galloping Goose,** a 100km trail beginning in downtown Victoria and continuing to the west coast of Vancouver Island is open to cyclists, pedestrians, and horses. Ask for a map, which includes Transit access info, at the Info Centre. The trail is a part of the Trans-Canada Trail (still in progress), which will be the longest recreational trail in the world. When it is finished, it will cover 16,000km and stretch from Coast to Coast.

The **beach** stretches along the southern edge of the city by Dallas St. A particularly nice stretch of **white sand,** at Willows Beach, is located at Oak Bay—take Fort St. east, turn right on Oak Bay St. and follow to the end. Victoria is a hub for sailing, kayaking, and whale-watching tours. Whatever the activity, be it chartering a boat or bungee jumping, the folks at **Westcoast Activities Unlimited,** 1140 Government St., will help you find somewhere or someone to help you do it, free of charge. (☎ 412-0993. Open daily 8am-7:30pm.) **Ocean River Sports,** 1437 Store St., offers kayak rentals, tours, and lessons. (☎ 381-4233 or 800-909-4233. Open M-Th and Sa 9:30am-5:30pm, F 9:30am-7:30pm, Su 11am-5pm. Single kayak $42 per day, doubles $50; canoes $42. Multi-day discounts available.) Most whale-watching companies give discounts for hostel guests. **Ocean Explorations,** 532 Broughton St., runs tours in Zodiac raft-boats that visit the resident pods of orcas in the area. (☎ 383-6722. Runs Apr.-Oct. 3hr. tours $69, hostelers and children $49, less in early season. Reservations recommended. Free pickup at hostels.)

Pacific Wilderness, on Wharf St., near the train station, runs train tours from Victoria up-island. The narration on the trip will point out trestles, tunnels, and other sights on the two hour trip. (☎ 381-8600 or 800-267-0610. Departs Victoria 11am, and 2pm. $29, ages 6-12 $15, 5 and under $5, family $94.)

▶ DAYTRIP FROM VICTORIA: SOOKE

About 35km west of Victoria on Hwy. 14. To get to Phillips Rd. from the city, take bus #50 to the Western Exchange and transfer to #61. The potholes are located 5km north of Hwy. 14 on Sooke River Rd.

The Sooke Region Museum, 2070 Phillips Rd., just off the highway, houses a **visitors center** and delivers an excellent history of the area. (☎ 642-6351. Open daily July-Aug. 9am-6pm; Sept.-June Tu-Su 9am-5pm. Admission by donation.) The **Sooke Potholes** are a chain of deep swimming holes naturally carved out of the rock in the narrow Sooke River gorge. These popular and sun-warmed waters reputedly host some of the best cliff jumping in the area (*Let's Go* still does not recommend cliff jumping) and draws people from all over. (Access is through private property owned by **Deertrail Campground and Adventure Gateway** and costs $10 per vehicle; bikes and hikers free. ☎ 382-3337. 63 sites, $20; $15 additional nights. Includes entrance fee.) North of Sooke, Hwy. 14 continues along the coast, stringing together two provincial parks and their rugged, beautiful beaches: **Juan de Fuca Provincial Park,** home to **China Beach** and **Loss Creek.** China Beach campground has 78 drive-in sites. (☎ 800-689-9025. $12.) Walk-in camping on the beach is available at four beaches and two forest areas ($5 per person, per night). **French Beach Provincial Park** has tent sites. (☎ 391-2300. $12.) The **Juan de Fuca Marine Trail** starts at China Beach and heads north to Botanical Beach at Port Renfrew. Trails connect beaches with road, which is still far enough away to keep the seaside wild. Camping in wide open sites is free at the popular **Jordan River Recreation Area,** 10min. past French Beach. The **Galloping Goose** bike and horse trail (see **Outdoor Activities,** above) passes a day-use area and trails heading east and west across the island's southern tip. The **Sooke River Flats Campsite,** on Phillips Rd. past the museum, has open sites with a large picnic area, showers, toilets, and running water. On **All Sooke Day,** the third Saturday in July, the campsite hosts competitions centered around logging, sharp objects, and family fun. (☎ 642-6076. Gates locked 11pm-7am. Sites $15; sani-dump $5.) Blend in with the locals at **Mom's Cafe,** 2036 Shields Rd., in town. Driving from Victoria, turn right after the stoplight. (☎ 642-3314. Open daily 8am-9pm; winter Su-Th 8am-8pm, F-Sa 8am-9pm.)

NEAR VICTORIA: GULF ISLANDS

Midway between Vancouver and Victoria, the **Gulf Islands** are a peaceful retreat from urban hustle. While the beaches are uniformly rocky with few sandy retreats, the islands are known for a contagiously relaxing lifestyle, as well as excellent kayaking and sailing opportunities. The chain's five main islands, **Galiano, Mayne, Pender, Salt Spring,** and **Saturna,** are visited by BC Ferries at least twice a day.

SALT SPRING ISLAND ☎ 250

Named for a dozen brine springs discovered on its northern end, **Salt Spring** is the largest (185 sq. km), most populous of the islands and has the widest range of activities and accommodations. Inhabited by the Coastal Salish since 1800 BC, the island has been a refuge to many groups since. The first permanent residents were African-Americans who moved north from California in the 1850s. Salt Spring in the 1960s was a popular destination for American draft-dodgers, while in the 70s and 80s it lured retirees. Today, the island is a haven for artists whose medium of choice varies from pottery to painting to metals to wood.

ORIENTATION AND PRACTICAL INFORMATION.
Life on Salt Spring Island is centered around the small village of **Ganges;** all of the listings below are in Ganges unless otherwise specified. **BC Ferries** (☎ 386-3431 or in BC 888-223-3779; www.bcferries.bc.ca) from **Vancouver Island** arrive in **Fulford Harbor,** 14.5km south of Ganges, while ferries from **Vancouver** and the other Gulf Islands dock at the **Long Harbor** wharf, 6km northeast of town. In summer, the **Gulf Island Water Taxi** runs to Galiano and Mayne Islands each Wednesday and Saturday. (☎ 537-2510. $15 round-trip, bikes free. Departs 9am, returns 4:40pm.) **Silver Shadow Taxi** (☎ 537-3030) tends to the carless. **Budget Rent-A-Car,** 124 Upper Ganges Rd. (☎ 537-6099) is right beside Moby's (see **Food,** below). Rentals $60 per day with 100km free plus free pickup and delivery to any ferry terminal on the island. 10% student discount. Open daily 9am-5pm. The **Info Centre,** 121 Lower Ganges Rd., will help travelers find a place to stay. (☎ 537-5252. Open July-Aug. daily 9am-6pm, call for winter hours.) The **Bicycle Shop,** 131 McPhillips Ave., rents them for $5 per hr., $20 per 24hr; other time increments at negotiable, fair prices. (☎ 537-1544. Open Tu-F 9am-5pm, Sa 10am-4pm, Su 11am-3pm; call for winter hours.) **New Wave Laundry,** 124 Upper Ganges Rd. next to Moby's Marine Pub. (☎ 537-2500. Wash $2.50, dry 25¢ per 8min. Open M-Th 8am-10pm, T-Sa 8am-8pm, Su 9am-5pm.) **Public Showers:** beneath Moby's Marine Pub. ($1 per 5min.) **Pharmacy: Pharmasave,** 104 Lower Ganges Rd. (☎ 537-5534. Open M-Sa 9am-6pm, Su 11am-5pm.) **Internet Access: CorInternet Cafe,** 134 McPhillips Ave. (☎ 537-9132; $1 per 15min., youths and seniors 50¢ per 15min.; open Tu-Th 1-8pm, F-Su noon-5pm), or **Salt Spring Books,** 104 McPhillips Ave. (☎ 537-2812; 10¢ per min., $5 per hr.; open daily 8:30am-6pm in summer and 9:30am-5pm in winter). **Emergency:** ☎ 911. **Police:** (☎ 537-5555) on Lower Granges Rd., on the outskirts of town. **Post office:** 109 Purvis Ln. (☎ 537-2321), in the plaza downtown. Open M-F 8:30am-5:30pm, Sa 8am-noon. **Postal Code:** V8K 2P1.

ACCOMMODATIONS, CAMPING, AND FOOD.
Salt Spring offers a wealth of both food and B&Bs (from $70), despite its small size. The least expensive beds on the island are 8km south of Ganges in the **Salt Spring Island Hostel (HI),** 640 Cusheon Lake Rd.—look for the tree-shaped sign that says "Forest Retreat." In addition to three standard dorms in the comfortable home, the hostel's 10 fern-covered acres also hide three tepees that sleep three and two hand-crafted **treehouses** that sleep two to four. (☎ 537-4149. Rent bikes from $15 per day, scooters from $20 per 2hr. Open Apr. to mid-Nov. Tepees $16; dorms $16, nonmembers $20; treehouse double $60, nonmembers $70. Linens $2. MC only.) **Wisteria Guest House,** 268 Park Dr., is an oasis on an acre of garden near the village. It receives high recommendations for its delicious breakfasts and reasonable prices. (☎ 537-5899. $55-80.) The five inexpensive rooms at **Tides Inn,** 137 Lower Ganges Rd., overlook downtown Ganges. (☎ 537-1097. 24hr. reception. Restaurant downstairs. Double with shared bath $50.) **Ruckle Provincial Park,** 23.5km southeast of Ganges, has public camping. Its 78 walk-in sites on the unsheltered Beaver Point overlook the ocean. Dry toilets, free firewood. (☎ 391-2300 or 877-559-2115. $12.)

Follow your nose to **Barb's Buns,** which sells all kinds of baked goods including spelt bread and delicious chocolate hazelnut sticky buns ($2.75). Sandwiches $4-5. (☎ 537-4491. Open M-Sa 6am-5:30pm.) The **Tree House Cafe,** 106 Purvis Lane, delivers interesting and tasty sandwiches ($5-7) in the shade of an old plum tree and has open-mic Thursdays (7pm) in addition to live music every night in summer. (☎ 537-5379. 10% HI discount.) **Moby's Marine Pub,** 124 Upper Ganges Rd., a 5min. walk north of the village, is no typical harborside dive. It offers live jazz on Sundays and an open mic every other Wednesday. Pints and margaritas $5.25. (☎ 537-5559. Open M-Th 10am-midnight, F-Sa 11am-1am, Su 10am-midnight.) Score cantaloupes and Raisin Bran at **Thrifty Foods,** 114 Purvis Ln. (☎ 537-1522. Open June-Sept. daily 8am-9pm; Oct.-May 8am-8pm.)

SIGHTS. A self-guided **studio tour** introduces visitors to the residences of 36 artisans around the island; pick up a brochure at the visitors center (see **Visitor Information,** p. 263). Performances at the **ArtSpring,** 100 Jackson Ave. (☎537-2102), generally cost $12-25, but exhibitions are free. From October to April, two series run: Great Performances (classical), and ArtSwings! (jazz classics). Check the website for latest details at www.artspring.ca. The century-old **Fall Fair** (☎537-8840), held the third weekend of September, draws farmers from all over the islands to display their produce, animals, and crafts with pride. The **Saturday Market** is a smaller version of the fall fair held in downtown's **Centennial Park** from Easter to Thanksgiving and is a big deal on the island.

OUTDOOR ACTIVITIES. Wallace Island and **Prevost Island** are two excellent kayaking daytrips from Salt Spring. **Sea Otter Kayaking,** located on Ganges Harbor at the end of Rainbow Rd., rents boats to experienced paddlers only. They also run 2hr. introductory certification courses ($40), tours including 3hr. sunset ($35) and full-moon trips ($40), and multi-day excursions. (☎537-5678 or 877-537-5678. Singles $25 per 2hr., $55 per day; doubles $40 per 2hr., $80 per day. 15% discount for hostel guests. Open daily 9am-6pm in summer; reservations preferred in winter.) Five of Salt Spring's ten freshwater lakes are open for swimming. **Blackburn Lake,** 5km south of Ganges on Fulford-Ganges Rd., is one of the less crowded spots, and is clothing-optional. **Hiking** and **biking** options are limited on Salt Spring due to the small and residential nature of the islands. **Ruckle Provincial Park** offers 200 acres of partially settled land to explore and an 11km waterfront trail. **Mt. Maxwell,** 11km southwest of Ganges on Cranberry Rd., offers a stunning vista.

PENDER ISLAND ☎250

Pender is actually two islands, joined by a small bridge, that total 26km in length. With only 2000 residents, Pender lacks the kind of social focal point that Salt Spring's downtown provides, but has similarly exceptional kayaking and sailing.

ORIENTATION AND PRACTICAL INFORMATION. BC Ferries arrive at Otter Bay, on the larger North Pender Island. **Kayak Pender Island,** at the Otter Bay Marina, a five minute walk from the ferry terminal, rents to experienced paddlers. (☎629-6939. Single kayak $20 per 2hr., $40 per day, $20 per additional day; double $30 per 2hr., $60 per day, $30 per additional day. Guided tours from $35.) The **visitor center** is 1km from the ferry terminal. (☎629-6541. Open daily May-Aug. 9am-5pm.) The marina (☎629-3579) is also a convenient location to **rent bikes** ($5 per hr., $25 per day), take a **shower** ($1 per 4min.), or do **laundry** ($2.50). If stuck waiting for the ferry, the nearby **Pender Island Golf and Country Club,** 2305 Otter Bay Rd., offers nine holes. (☎629-6659. $19, club rental $10. Open daily in summer 8am-8pm.) The **post office, gas station, bakery** and **grocery store** are all located at the Driftwood Centre, on Harbour Rd. in the center of North Pender. The only **ATM** on the island is at the **AT General Store,** 5827 Schooner Way (☎629-6114), on North Pender Island. **True Value Foods,** in the Centre, allows customers to take out extra cash on a debit or credit card. (☎629-8322. Open daily 9am-8:30pm.)

ACCOMMODATIONS AND FOOD. Budget accommodations are not easy to come by in Pender. **Cooper's Landing,** rents beautiful cabins for a hefty fee (☎888-921-3111; www.cooperslanding.com. Cabin that sleeps 4 $120-170.) Campers have several options. **Prior Centennial Provincial Park** maintains 17 wooded sites 6km from the ferry on Canal Rd. near the bridge joining North and South Pender. (☎391-2300. Pit toilets. $12.) On South Pender, the more secluded **Beaumont Provincial Marine Park** requires a boat or 30 minutes of hiking from the road to reach its 15 beachside sites. ($5 per person.) For showers, head to the **Port Browning Marina** on North Pender at the end of Hamilton Rd.

(Off Harbour Rd. ☎ 629-3493. $10 includes use of facilities and pool.) **Mortimer Spit,** adjacent to the Landing, is one of the few sandy beaches on the islands. For a superior sandy experience, head to small **Irene Bay** on the west side of the North Island, at the end of Irene Bay Rd.

Outside of the grocery store, food is scarce. **Memories Restaurant at the Inn,** 4709 Canal Rd. (☎ 629-3353), bakes pizzas on homemade dough from 5:30-8:30pm nightly. The visitors center can make additional recommendations (see p. 264).

PACIFIC RIM NATL. PARK ☎ 250

The Pacific Rim National Park stretches along a 150km sliver of Vancouver Island's remote Pacific coast. The region's frequent downpours create a lush landscape, rich in both marine and terrestrial life, that has beckoned explorers for over a century. Hard-core hikers trek through enormous old growth and along rugged beach trails. Long beaches on the open ocean draw beachcombers, bathers, kayakers, and surfers year-round. Each spring, around 22,000 gray whales stream past the park. Orcas, sea lions, bald eagles, and black bears also frequent the area. The park comprises three distinct geographic regions. The southern portion is home to the **West Coast Trail** which connects the towns of Bamfield and Port Renfrew. The park's middle section—known as the **Broken Group Islands**—is comprised of roughly 100 islands in Barkley Sound. Finally, the northern region of the Park, known as **Long Beach,** is northwest of Barkley Sound. The villages of Ucluelet and Tofino are on the boundaries of this region.

WEST COAST TRAIL

A winding, 1½hr. drive up Hwy. 14 from Hwy. 1 near Victoria lands you in Port Renfrew. Spread out in the trees along a peaceful ocean inlet, this isolated coastal community of 400 people is the most easily accessible gateway to the world famous **West Coast Trail.** The West Coast Trail is a demanding, world-famous hike covering 75km along the southern third of the Pacific Rim National Park between Port Renfrew and Bamfield. The route weaves through primeval forests, waterfalls, rocky slopes, and rugged beach tracing the treacherous shoreline. The combination of foul weather and slippery terrain over a long distance means that only experienced hikers should attempt this trail, and never alone; each year dozens of people are rescued or evacuated by Park Wardens. The trail is regulated by a strict and unforgiving quota system; reservations are necessary to hike it. Each day between May 1 and September 30, 52 hikers are allowed to begin the journey from the two trailheads, Pachena Bay in the north and Gordon River in the south (26 from each trailhead; 20 reserved and 6 wait-listed). The max. group size is 10 people. For info on the illustrious trek, call Tourism at 800-435-5622 or Parks Canada at 726-7721, or write to Box 280, Ucluelet, BC, V0R 3A0. Hikers pay about $120 per person for access to the trail (reservation fee $25, trail use fee $70, ferry crossing fee $25). Seek out maps, information on the area, and registration info at one of the two **Trail Information Centres:** in **Port Renfrew** (☎ 647-5434), at the first right off Parkinson Rd. (Hwy. 14) once in "town"; or in **Pachena Bay** (☎ 728-3234), 5km from Bamfield. (Both open daily May-Sept. 9am-5pm.) David Foster Wayne's *Blisters and Bliss* is an excellent guide to the trail ($11).

TRANSPORTATION. West Coast Trail Express runs daily from **Victoria** to **Port Renfrew** via the **Juan de Fuca** trailhead. (☎ 477-8700; www.trailbus.com. May-Sept., 2¼hr., $35.) Buses also run from **Nanaimo** to **Bamfield** (3½hr., $55), **Bamfield** to **Port Renfrew** (3hr., $50), and **Port Renfrew** or **Bamfield** to **Nitinat** (2hr., $35). Reservations are recommended, and they can be made for beaches and trailheads along the route from Victoria to Port Renfrew. The **Juan de Fuca Express** operates a water taxi to Bamfield. (☎ 888-755-6578. $76.)

CAMPING AND FOOD. Accommodations are limited outside the park campgrounds, but you can drive to Sooke, near Victoria on Hwy. 14, for numerous B&B's. Near Port Renfrew and adjacent to the West Coast Trail registration office, the **Pacheedaht Campground** (☎ 647-5521) rents tent ($10) and RV sites ($16); hikers can use the Reserve Beach for $8 per night. To wash the trail dust off in Port Renfrew, use the public **shower** ($2 for 10min.) and **laundry** ($2), available at the **Port Renfrew Hotel** (☎ 647-5541). Almost all of the restaurants in Port Renfrew are inexpensive and offer the usual fare. The **General Store** on the main road into town basic groceries. If stocking up for any more than a daytrip, build your stores in Victoria. (☎ 647-5587. Open daily 10am-8pm, winter 11am-5pm.)

OUTDOOR ACTIVITIES. If you only want to spend an afternoon roughing it, visit the gorgeous **Botanical Beach Provincial Park.** Be sure to visit at low tide or don't expect to see much—info centers will have tide charts. Nature enthusiasts will delight in the many varieties of intertidal life. Botanical Beach forms one end of the 47km **Juan De Fuca Marine Trail,** connecting Port Renfrew with **Juan de Fuca Provincial Park** to the east. The trail, which can be traveled in four to six days, is an extension of the West Coast Trail, but also has excellent day use opportunities along the beach. There are a number of campsites along the way; overnight permits are required ($5 for a party of 4, self register at trailheads). For more information on the trail and day use information, look at the **map** in the Botanical Beach or China Beach parking lots for directions.

THE BROKEN GROUP

The **Broken Group's** 100 islands stretch across Barkley Sound and make for some of the best sea kayaking, as well as expensive, but high-biodiversity, **scuba diving.** This is the wettest spot on the island, so expect liquid sunshine.

PRACTICAL INFORMATION. Hours of logging roads or water travel are the only two ways into **Bamfield.** Gravel roads wind toward Bamfield from **Hwy. 18** (west from Duncan) and from **Hwy. 4** (south from Port Alberni). Be sure to watch for logging trucks. **West Coast Trail Express** (see above) runs daily from **Victoria** to **Bamfield** (4½hr., $55) and from **Nanaimo** to **Bamfield** (3½hr., $55); reservations are recommended. Because Bamfield lies on two sides of an inlet, water transit is necessary to cross town. **Alberni Marine Transportation** (☎ 723-8313 or 800-663-7192; Apr.-Sept.) operates a passenger ferry from **Port Alberni** to **Bamfield** (4½hr., $23) and **Ucluelet** (4½hr., $25). **Emergency:** 911 **Hospital:** ☎ 728-3312. **Post office:** Near the Bamfield Inn, by General Store. (Open M-F 8:30am-5pm.) **Postal code:** V0R 1B0.

ACCOMMODATIONS AND FOOD. Accommodations are limited; motels and B&Bs are expensive (singles $50-180, doubles $70-180, with the majority at the higher end), so making camp in the park is a better bet. The **Pachena Bay Campground** offers tree-rich sites just a short walk from the beach. (☎ 728-1287. Sites $24, sani-dump only $26, full hookups $31.) Eight islands in the archipelago contain primitive campsites ($5 per person.) The **T&T Market** offers groceries and supplies. (☎ 728-2000. Open daily 8am-8pm.)

OUTDOOR ACTIVITIES. While the Nuu-cha-nulth have navigated these waters for centuries, the Sound can be dangerous to those with less experience. A maze of reefs and rocky islands, combined with large swells, tidal currents, and frigid waters make ocean travel in small craft hazardous, but adventuresome. **Alberni Marine Transport** (see **Practical Information** above) and other operators transport paddlers from Ucluelet or Port Alberni to the Broken Group. (Alberni runs one per day M, W, F; 3hr.; $20.) For hikers who make it to **Bamfield** without traversing the West Coast Trail several **short hiking trails** pass through shore and forest at **Pachena Bay, Keeha Beach,** and the **Pachena Lighthouse.**

LONG BEACH

The northern third of Pacific Rim National Park begins where Hwy. 4 hits the west coast after a 90min. drive from Port Alberni. Ucluelet (yew-KLOO-let) remains a quiet fishing village until it floods with travelers every July and August. The more popular Tofino, with its tree-hugging populace, is an increasingly popular resort destination, attracting backpackers and wealthy weekend-warriors alike.

ORIENTATION AND PRACTICAL INFORMATION

The two towns of Ucluelet and Tofino lie 40km apart at opposite ends of the **Pacific Rim Hwy.**, separated by the lovely and trail-laden Long Beach. **Chinook Charters** (☎ 725-3431) connects **Victoria** and **Nanaimo** with Tofino and Ucluelet through Port Alberni. Two buses leave daily in summer from **Victoria** to **Tofino** (7hr., $55) via Ucluelet (6½hr., $53). The **Islandlink** (☎ 726-7790) connects Tofino with **Long Beach** and Ucluelet in the summer (6 per day; $10 round-trip to Long Beach, $12 to Ucluelet). **Lady Rose Marine Services** (☎ 723-8313 or 800-663-7192) operates a passenger freighter in summer from Port Alberni to Ucluelet (1 per day M, W, and F; 5hr.; $25). **Tofino Taxi** (☎ 725-3333) runs to Long Beach for $5. A trio of **Info Centres** guide visitors. The first is located where Hwy. 4 splits into a road to each town. (☎ 726-7289. Open daily Victoria Day to Labor Day 11am-7pm.) The Tofino **Info Centre** is at 351 Campbell St. (☎ 725-3414. Open July-Aug. daily 9am-5pm; winter hours sporadic.) Ucluelet's **Info Centre** is at 227 Main St. (☎ 726-4641. Generally open daily 10am-5pm; call for hours. Off-season weekends closed.) **Parks Canada Visitor Info** has two branches, one on the Pacific Rim Hwy. at the first right inside the park (☎ 726-4212; open mid-June to mid-Sept. daily 9:30am-5pm), and the other further in at Wickaninnish Beach. (☎ 726-7721. Open year-round daily 10:30am-6pm.)

The **CIBC Bank** is on 301 Campbell St. (**24hr. ATM;** no currency exchange. Open M-Th 10am-3pm, F 10am-4:30pm.) Get **Internet access** at the **Blue Raven Coffee House and Cyber Cafe** in Ucluelet. (☎ 726-7110. $2.50 per 20min. or $7 per hr. Open daily 7am-10pm.) **Storm Light Marine Station,** 316 Main St. (☎ 725-3342; open June-Oct. daily 9am-9pm, Nov.-May 10am-6pm), rents sleeping bags ($12 per day) and tents ($15 per day). **Fiber Options,** at the corner of 4th and Campbell, rents bikes for $6 per hr. or $25 per day, credit card required. (☎ 725-2192. Open June-Sept. daily 9:30am-10pm, Oct.-May 10am-6pm.) **Weather:** ☎ 726-3415. **Police:** 400 Campbell St. (☎ 725-3242). **Hospital:** 261 Neill St. (☎ 725-3212). **Post office:** 161 1st St., at Campbell. (☎ 725-3734. Open M-F 8:30am-5:30pm, Sa 9am-1pm.) **Postal Code:** V0R 2Z0.

ACCOMMODATIONS AND FOOD

Tofino is the place to be, but there are options in Ucluelet and outside of the park. In general, there is no free camping around, and food options are limited. Reservations for most accommodations are a must after mid-March.

IN UCLUELET. Prices are steep, especially in the summer. Travelers without reservations might get shut out of reasonably priced accommodations and forced into a motel room (singles from $75). The Info Centre gives out a pamphlet listing the many **B&Bs** in town. **Agapé,** 246 Lee St., 4km before town, is a treasure for the price and serves up gourmet breakfasts. Five languages spoken. (☎ 726-7073. Singles from $40; doubles from $55.) **Radfords,** 1983 Athlone St. (☎ 726-2662), off Norah St., is closer to town. It rents two quaint singles ($40) and a double ($80, $15 per additional guest), and offers fresh muffins, fruit, and a view of the harbor. **Matterson House Restaurant,** 1682 Peninsula Rd., has homemade Canadian fare. Locals love the $14 Matterson Chicken with raspberry cream sauce. (☎ 726-2200. Open daily 7:30am-9pm.) Taste the northwest in **Blueberries Restaurant's,** 1627D Peninsula Rd., $9 salmon burgers. (☎ 726-7707. Open daily 7:30am-9:30pm.)

IN AND AROUND THE PARK. While there are a number of private **campgrounds** between the park and the towns, they average at least $22 to camp and $30 for hookups. The ones on the Ucluelet side tend to be cheaper. If you miss the high prices in the Rockies, this is the place to relive the adventure! The **Park Superintendent** (☎ 726-7721) can be contacted year-round for advance information. **Ucluelet Campground,** off Pacific Rim Hwy. in Ucluelet, offers sites in the open (better for sun than for privacy) with showers and toilets. (☎ 726-4355. Showers $1 per 5min. Open Mar.-Oct. $23; full hookups $27.) **Greenpoint Campground,** 10km north of the park info center, is the only campground in the park itself and is often full. Greenpoint has 94 regular sites and 20 walk-ins and is equipped with toilets and fire rings. Despite swarms of campers in the summer, it offers hedge-buffered privacy. (☎ 726-4245. Reservations essential, call 800-689-9025. $20.) The **golf course** in the park often has private, showerless gravel sites ($15).

IN TOFINO. ■**Whalers on the Point Guesthouse (HI),** voted as best hostel in Canada by HI, has room for 64 (4 beds per room). Free sauna, billiards, linen, and harborside views. Turn right on 1st St. from Campbell St. and then left on Main St. (follow to West St.). Check inside for HI discounts around town. (☎ 725-3443. Check-in 7am-2pm and 4-11pm. $22, nonmembers $24; private rooms $66, $70) **Wind Rider Guesthouse,** 231 Main St., is all female (except for kids under 12) and drug and alcohol free. Gleaming kitchen, jacuzzi, and TV room make this a welcoming haven. (☎ 725-3240. Check-in 1-6pm. Free linen. Dorms $25; private room from $60.) Shop for groceries at the **Co-op,** 140 1st St. (☎ 725-3226. Open M-Sa 9am-8pm, Su 10am-6pm.) **Salals Co-op,** near 4th St. on Campbell, sells organic groceries and has an all-vegetarian menu that includes all-day breakfast ($4.50-10) and lunches for $6-8. (☎ 725-2728. Open daily 9am-9pm.) The **Common Loaf Bake Shop,** 180 1st St., is the best place in Tofino to relax with a paper and a cup of coffee. Thai and Indian dinners $7-9. (☎ 725-3915. Open daily 8am-9pm; winter 8am-6pm.) The adjacent and colorful **Alleyway Cafe,** 305 Campbell, has outdoor seating on driftwood benches. Breakfast is dished up all day until the place reopens as **Costa Azul** with Mexican dinners for under $10. (☎ 725-3105. Open daily 10am-2pm, then 5-9pm)

OFF ISLAND. On Vargas Island, 20min. off Tofino, the **Vargas Island Inn,** rents guest rooms in a classy lodge and two beach cabins. (☎ 725-3309. Tent sites $15, hostel beds $30, private rooms from $40, cabins from $30.) The boat shuttle is free for guests, but hikers can pay $25 and hike to **free camping** at Ahous Bay (no facilities). For some out of the way R&R try **Nielson Island Inn,** the only establishment on 20-acre Nielson Island, a 5min. boat ride from Crab Dock. Enjoy the benefits of a small kitchen (the owner will cook dinner with your ingredients), a lush yard, and a trail around the island. (☎ 726-7968. Free pickup. Singles $35; doubles $50.)

SIGHTS AND OUTDOOR ACTIVITIES

HIKING. Hiking is a highlight of the trip to the west side of the Island. The trails grow even more beautiful in the frequent rain and fog. **The Rainforest Centre,** 451 Main St. (☎ 725-2560), in Tofino, has assembled an excellent **trail guide** for Clayoquot Sound, Tofino, Ucluelet, the Pacific Rim, and Kennedy Lake (available by donation). Park passes cost $3 per 2hr. or $8 per day (available in all parking lots); seasonal passes are also available ($45). **Long Beach** is, fittingly, the longest beach on the island's west coast, and is the starting point for numerous hikes. The **Parks Canada Visitor Centre** and **Info Centres** (see **Orientation and Practical Information,** p. 267) provide free maps of nine hikes ranging from 100m to 5km in length. On the **Rainforest Trail** (two 1km loops), boardwalks off the Pacific Rim Hwy. lead through gigantic trees and fallen logs of old growth rainforest. **Bog Trail** (.8km) illuminates little-known details of one of the wettest, most intricate ecosystems in the park. You can even view the tiny carnivorous plants. Wheelchair accessible. **Big Trees Trail** (1hr.) winds through gigantic trees to **Meares Island,** a $20 boat ride from the 4th St. Dock (☎ 726-8361 or 725-3793).

SURFING AND KAYAKING. Exceptional **surf** breaks invitingly off **Long Beach** and **Cox Bay** (5km south of Tofino). These two coves funnel large and occasionally dangerous waves toward hordes of young diehards; just don't forget your wetsuit. **Live to Surf,** 1180 Pacific Rim Hwy., rents everything you could need. (☎725-4464. Full wet-suits $20; surfboard $25; bodyboard or skimboard $20; lessons available on request.) It is possible to kayak to Meares Island and throughout the sound, although the trailhead is difficult to find. **Pacific Kayak,** at Jamie's Whale Station (see above), provides a map, has the best rates in town, and rents to experienced paddlers. (☎725-3232. Singles $40 per day, doubles $65; multi-day discounts.)

WHALE WATCHING. Every March and April, gray whales migrate past the park and Clayoquot Sound north of Tofino. Six or seven stay at these feeding grounds during the summer. There are more tour companies than resident whales. **Jamie's Whale Station,** 606 Campbell St., just east of 4th St. in Tofino, runs smooth rides in large boats, but rough-riders choose Zodiacs to ride the swells at 30 knots. (☎725-3919 or 800-667-9913; www.jamies.com. Boats $80 per 3hr., students and seniors $70, youths $50. Zodiacs: adults and seniors $59 per 2hr., students $53.) They also have an outlet in Ucluelet at the bottom of Main St. Also see Hot Springs, below.

HOT SPRINGS. Hot Springs Cove, 1hr. north of Tofino by boat, is one of the least crowded hot springs in all of British Columbia. The **Matlahaw Water Taxi,** operated by the Hesquiaht First Nation, makes a run or two each day to the cove. (☎670-1106. $35 per person one-way.) The springs are near an exceptionally quiet and lush campground, and a footpath to more secluded beaches in the Maquinna Marine Park. (No showers. 15 private sites. $20.) **Seaside Adventures,** at 300 Main St. in Tofino, makes two 6hr. trips leaving in the morning and whale-watches on the way. All the whale watching companies have trips as well. (☎725-2292 or 888-332-4252. $90; students and seniors $80; children $60.)

UP ISLAND

To a Victorian, anything north of town constitutes being "up Island." 'Nuff said.

NANAIMO ☎250

Primarily a ferry terminal stopover for travelers en route to the rainforests of northern and western Vancouver Island, Nanaimo (na-NYE-moe) appears along the highway as a strip of motels, gas stations, and greasy spoons. While the city contains several beaches and parks, the semi-urban setting lacks the natural splendor of Vancouver Island's more secluded locations. The silver lining of city life is Nanaimo's ridiculous annual bathtub boat race and legalized bungee jumping.

ORIENTATION AND PRACTICAL INFORMATION

Nanaimo lies on the east coast of Vancouver Island, 111km north of Victoria on the **Trans-Canada Hwy. (Hwy. 1),** and 391km south of **Port Hardy** via the **Island Hwy. (Hwy. 19).** Hwy. 1 turns into **Nicol St.** and **Terminal Ave.** in Nanaimo before becoming Hwy. 19A. **Nanaimo Parkway** (Hwy. 19) circumvents the town.

- **Trains: VIA Rail,** 321 Selby St. (☎800-561-8630). To **Victoria** (1 per day, $20).
- **Buses: Laidlaw** (☎753-4371), at Comox Rd. and Terminal Ave. behind Howard Johnson Inn. To: **Victoria** (2¼hr., 6 per day, $20); **Port Hardy** (7½hr., 1-2 per day, $74); **Tofino** and **Ucluelet** (4hr., 2 per day, $33).
- **Ferries: BC Ferries** (☎753-1261 or 888-223-3779), at the northern end of Stewart Ave., 2km north of downtown. To Vancouver's **Horseshoe Bay** (1½hr.; 8 times per day; $8-9.50, car $24-34) and Tsawwassen terminals (2hr.; 4-8 per day; $9, car $30-32). The **Scenic Ferry** (☎753-5141) runs from the Maffeo-Sutton Park in downtown to Newcastle Island just offshore (on the hr. 10am-6pm; $5).

270 ■ UP ISLAND

Car Rental: Rent-A-Wreck, 227 Terminal Ave. S (☎ 753-6461). From $33 per day plus 16¢ per km after 150km. Must be 21 with major credit card. Free pickup. Open M-F 8am-6pm, Sa 9am-4pm, Su 10am-4pm.

Visitor Info: 2290 Bowen Rd. (☎ 756-0106), west of downtown. Head south from Terminal Ave. on Comox Rd. which becomes Bowen Rd.; or go north from Hwy. 19 on Northfield Rd. Open daily 8am-7pm, winter 9am-5pm.

Laundromat: 702 Nicol St. (☎ 753-9922), at Robins Rd. in Payless Gas Station. Open 24hr. $2.50 per load.

Equipment Rental: Bikes ($20 per day, $10 for Nicol St. Hostel Guests; $35 per week) available at **Chain Reaction,** in The Realm at 2 Commercial St. (☎ 754-3309. Open M-Sa 9:30am-6pm. In-line skates $15 per day, including all safety equipment.

Emergency: ☎ 911. **Police:** 303 Prideaux St. (☎ 754-2345), at Fitzwilliam St.

Crisis Line: ☎ 754-4447. 24hr.

Hospital: 1200 Dufferin Crescent (☎ 754-2141). Open 24hr.

Pharmacy: London Drugs, 650 Terminal Ave. S (☎ 753-5566), in Harbour Park Mall. Open M-Sa 9am-10pm, Su 10am-8pm.

Internet: Free at the **Library,** 90 Commercial St. (☎ 753-1154). Open M-F 10am-8pm, Sa 10am-5pm, Su noon-4pm.

Post Office: 650 Terminal Ave. S (☎ 741-1829), in Harbour Park Mall. Open M-F 8:30am-5pm. **Postal Code:** V9R 5J9

ACCOMMODATIONS AND CAMPING

Travelers should never be at a loss for a room in Nanaimo. Cheap motels are packed in like sardines along the main drag.

Nicol St. Hostel, 65 Nicol St. (☎ 753-1188). A quick walk from the ferry, bus station, or downtown. Living room, small tidy kitchen, laundry, bathrooms. Lots of freebies: paint for ongoing mural, parking, linens, and Internet. 25 beds; tent sites and ocean views in backyard. Reservations recommended. Dorms $17, doubles $34, tenting $10 per person, private cottage from $40.

Cambie Hostel, 63 Victoria Crescent (☎ 754-5323; fax 754-5582; www.cambiehostels.com). In a converted hotel downtown. Rooms have large bunk beds and private bathrooms. On top of a pub and cafe which features live music F-Sa until 1am. Free breakfast until 2pm. Free linen. $20, couples rooms available.

Living Forest Oceanside Campground, 6 Maki Rd. (☎ 755-1755), 3km southwest of downtown. 193 large, spacious sites with several amid cedars overlooking the ocean. Clean bathrooms. Showers $1 per 5min. Tent sites $17-19, full hookups $20-23.

Brannen Lake Campsites, 4220 Biggs Rd. (☎ 756-0404 or 866-756-0404), 6km north of the ferry terminal. Take Island Pkwy. (Hwy. 19). exit 24 onto Jingle Pot Rd., turn left onto Biggs Rd., roll past the Nanaimo Correction Centre, then look for signs. Shaded sites with moderate privacy on an active cattle ranch. Petting zoo. Showers $1. Sites $16, full hookups $19.

FOOD

The highway attracts dives and fast-food joints, many open late or 24hr. Nosh a Mr. Big or other groceries from **Thrifty Foods** in the Harbour Park Mall. (☎ 754-6273. Open daily 8am-10pm.) Nanaimo is known throughout Canada for the **Nanaimo bar,** a richly layered chocolate confection of extreme indulgence (see p. 271).

Charlie's Restaurant, 123 Commercial Dr. (☎ 753-7044). Downtown, large, windowed diner has prime people-watching territory. A full menu sports the regular fare for decent prices ($5 lunch specials). Breakfast all day. Open M-Sa 8am-4:30pm, Su 9am-3pm.

> **NANAIMO BARS** Originally sent in care packages from the United Kingom to hard-working sons in Nanaimo coal mines, these dense cakes travelled well on the overseas journey.
> **Layer 1:** ½ cup butter, ¼ cup white sugar, 1 egg, 1 tsp. vanilla, 1 tbsp. cocoa, 2 cups graham cracker crumbs, 1 cup unsweetend coconut, ½ cup walnut pieces.
> Combine butter, sugar, egg, vanilla, and cocoa, in the top of a double boiler, over medium heat, and stir until slightly thickened. Combine crumbs and coconut in a bowl, then pour the hot mixture over top. Stir, and then press into the bottom of a shallow 6x9 in. rectangular pan. Refrigerate.
> **Layer 2:** 2 tbsp. custard powder, 2 cups icing sugar, ¼ cup soft butter, 3 tbsp. milk.
> Blend the butter, sugar, milk, and powder until smooth. Spread over first layer.
> **Layer 3:** 5oz. semi sweet chocolate, 1 tbsp. butter.
> Melt chocolate and butter in double boiler. Spread the chocolate over layer 2. Chill.
>
> Yum. Heart attack in a dish—a worthy claim to fame for a small town.

Dar Lebanon, 347 Wesley St. (☎ 755-6524). Up Franklyn from City Hall, take a right on Wesley. A quiet respite from downtown. Sizeable pita sandwiches $5-8. Open M-Sa 10am-midnight, Su 4pm-midnight. 15% discount for Nicol St. Hostel guests.

Gina's Mexican Cafe, 47 Skinner St. (☎ 753-5411). Standard Mexican fare and creative items like the Don Juan, a veggie and cheese omelette in a grilled tortilla ($8). Vegetarian options. Open M-Th 11am-9pm, F 11am-10pm, Sa noon-10pm, Su noon-8pm.

SIGHTS AND EVENTS

SIGHTS. The **Nanaimo District Museum,** 100 Cameron Rd., pays tribute to Nanaimo's First Nation communities with an interactive exhibit on the Snun'muxw (SNOO-ne-moo) and a section on the coal mining origins of the town. (☎ 753-1821. Open M-Sa 9am-5pm. $2, students and seniors $1.75, under 12 75¢.) The **Bastion** up the street was a Hudson's Bay Company fur-trading fort, and it fires a cannon every weekday at noon. (Open July-Sept. W-M 10am-4:30pm.)

EVENTS. The multi-day **Marine Festival** will be held July 25-28, 2002, with many events leading up to the actual festival. Highlights include the **Bathtub Race,** in which contestants race tiny boats built around porcelain tubs with monster outboards they race from Nanaimo harbor, around Entrance and Winchelsea Islands, and finish at Departure Bay. Officials hand out prizes to everyone who makes it, and they present the "Silver Plunger" to the first tub to sink. The organizer of this bizarre and beloved event is the **Royal Nanaimo Bathtub Society** (☎ 753-7223).

OUTDOOR ACTIVITIES

BUNGEE JUMPING. Adrenaline-junkies from all over the continent make a pilgrimage to the **Bungy Zone,** at 35 Nanaimo River Rd., the only legal bungy bridge in North America. Plummet 42m (140 ft.) into a narrow gorge (water touches available); variations include a zipline, high-speed rappel, and the Swing. (☎ 716-7874 or 888-668-7874; nanaimo.ark.com/~bungy. $95, same-day jumps $35. 20% HI discount. Campsites $10 per person.) To reach the Zone, take Hwy. 1 south to Nanaimo River Rd. and follow the signs, or take the free shuttle to and from Nanaimo.

HIKING. Petroglyph Provincial Park, 3km south of town on Hwy. 1, protects carvings inscribed by Salish shamans. A menagerie of animals and mythical creatures decorates the soft sandstone. Rubbings can be made from concrete replicas at the base of the short trail to the petroglyphs. The serene **Newcastle Island Provincial Park,** accessible only by boat, has 756 automobile-free acres filled with hiking trails, picnic spots, and campsites. (☎754-7893. $9.50.) The **Shoreline Trail** that traces the island's perimeter offers great vantage points of Departure Bay. Ferries depart Maffeo-Sutton Park at the Sway-A-Lana Lagoon, near downtown. (☎753-5141. 1 per hr. 10am-6pm. $5 round-trip, seniors and kids $4; bikes $2, dogs free.)

WATER. The waters of **Departure Bay** wash onto a pleasant, pebbly beach in the north end of town on Departure Bay Rd., off Island Hwy. Jacques Cousteau called the waters around Nanaimo "The Emerald Sea," and they offer top diving opportunities. The **Nanaimo Dive Association** helps visitors find charters, lessons, or equipment. (☎729-2675) **The Kayak Shack,** 1840 Stewart Ave., near ferry terminal, rents kayaks, canoes, and camping equipment. (☎753-3234. Singles and canoes $10 per hr., $40; doubles $15 per hr., $60.)

HORNBY ISLAND ☎250

In the 1960s, large numbers of draft-dodgers fled the US to settle peacefully on Hornby Island, halfway between Nanaimo and Campbell River. Today, hippie-holdovers and a similarly long-haired and laid-back younger generation mingle on the island with descendants of 19th-century pioneers. Low tide on Hornby uncovers over 300m of the finest sand in the strait of Georgia. **Tribune Bay,** at the end of Shields Rd., is the more crowded of the two beaches (**Li'l Tribune Bay** next door is clothing-optional). The alternative, **Whaling Station Bay,** has the same gentle sands and is about 5km farther north, off St. John's Point Rd. On the way there from Tribune Bay, Helliwell Rd. passes stunning **Helliwell Provincial Park,** where well-groomed trails lead through old-growth forest to bluffs overlooking the ocean.

ORIENTATION AND PRACTICAL INFORMATION. There are two main roads on Hornby: the coastal **Shingle Spit Rd.** (try saying *that* 10 times fast) and **Central Rd.,** which crosses the island from the end of Shingle Spit. With light traffic and smooth roads, Hornby Island is easily explored on two wheels. The island has no public transit and is hard to cover without a bike or car. On-foot travelers have been known to ask friendly faces for a lift at Denman or on the ferry (*Let's Go* cannot recommend hitchhiking). The **Laidlaw** (☎753-4371) bus has a flag stop at **Buckley Bay** on Hwy. 19, where the ferry docks. **BC Ferries** (☎335-0323; www.bcferries.com) has sailings all day from **Buckley Bay** to **Denman** and from Denman to **Hornby** ($4.50-4.75 per adult; $15-17 with car). To reach the Hornby ferry, follow Denman Rd. all the way to end, on the other side of the island. The **visitors center** (☎335-0313; open daily 10am-3pm), and the **Hornby Island Off-Road Bike Shop** (☎335-0444; $8 per hr., $30 per day; children $5, $20; open daily 10am-5pm), are located in the island's **Ringside Market. Hornby Ocean Kayaks** transports kayaks to the calmest of seven beaches and provides guided tours, lessons, and rentals. (☎335-2726. Tours $30; full-day $65. Rentals $24 for 4hr.; $40 per day.) The island's only **24hr. ATM** is at the **Hornby Island Resort** (See **Accommodations and Food,** below). The **post office** is also at the Ringside Market in the Co-op. (Open M-Sa 9:30am-4:30pm; closed 1-1:30pm.) **Postal Code:** V0R 1Z0.

ACCOMMODATIONS AND FOOD. At the earthy heart of Hornby sits the grocery-bearing **Co-op** in the Ringside Market. (☎335-1121. Open daily 9am-6pm.) The colorful market, at the end of Central Rd. by Tribune Bay, is also home to artisan **gift shops** and two budget- and vegetarian-friendly restaurants. Most B&Bs cluster around the **Whaling Station, Galleon Beach, and Sandpiper Beach** areas and cost from $65-175 per night, with the majority in the $80-90 range. The **Hornby Island Resort,** right at the ferry docks, is a pub/restaurant/laundromat/hotel/campground. The fare at the resort's **Thatch Pub** is standard, but the view from the outdoor deck is not. The **Wheelhouse Restaurant,** with ocean views from a shared deck, has breakfasts from $9 and burgers for $7-8.50. (☎335-0136. Pub open daily 11:30am-midnight; live jazz every F night at 7pm. Restaurant open daily 9:30am-9pm. Campsites $20; hookups $19; Jan.-Mar. sites $14. Private rooms from $75.) **Tribune Bay Campsite,** on Shields Rd., offers 118 sites a quick walk from the island's popular beach. Showers, toilets, and playground. Reservations necessary July-Aug. (☎335-2359. Sites $24, power $27, cyclists with tent $19.) **Bradsdadsland Country Camp,** 1980 Shingle Spit Rd., offers standard tent sites. Campers bear the iron rule of quiet (only whispers after 11pm, no music ever) in exchange for privacy, clean sites, and stairs down to the ocean. Book as far in advance as possible. (☎335-0757. Toilets, laundry, showers. $36 for a waterfront site in July 13-Aug. 23, full hookups $39. Non-waterfront site $29. Dogs $7 per night.) The **Hornby Festival** celebrates classical music with a small touch of the popular variety for today's rambunctious youth. In early July, island residents offer a $15 walking tour of many local studios, homes, and galleries to raise money for the festival. For more information call the festival office. (☎335-2734; www.mars.ark.com/~festival. Performances $5-15, full pass $165.)

DENMAN ISLAND   ☎250

For those wanting to avoid Hornby Island's late-summer circus, **Denman Island** is a nice alternative. The Denman village center, perched above the Buckley Bay ferry terminal, offers most crucial amenities. **Denman Island General Merchants** houses the **visitors center,** the **post office** (postal code V0R 1T0; open 8:30am-4:30pm M-Sa), and basic groceries. (☎335-2293. Open M-Th 7am-9pm, F-Sa 7am-11pm, Su 9am-9pm; winter hours shorter.) Next door, the **Cafe on the Rock** serves delicious food at delicious prices. Full vegetarian breakfast $6, homemade pie $4, and sandwiches from $4. (☎335-2999. Open same hours as general store.) The ■**Denman Island Guest House/Hostel,** 3806 Denman Rd., offers a suspended wooden sphere with beds and the opportunity to support sustainable living. Hostel prices and atmosphere with more space than you need. Kitchen, with home-baked treats and hot tub. (☎335-2688; www.earthclubfactory.com. $17; private double or sphere, which sleeps 1-2, $50 with breakfast, $40 without. Bikes $10 per day.) You can pitch a tent at beach-side **Fillongley Provincial Park,** just off Denman Rd. halfway to the Hornby Ferry. (☎335-2325. Reservations recommended 800-689-9025. Pit toilets, water. $15.) You can camp for free at **Sandy** or **Tree Island** at the north end of the island. To get there, take a short hike along NW Rd. from the village center, a left onto Gladstone Way, and a hoof north toward the island with all the trees. (No campfires; access at low tide only.) The island's two lakes, Graham Lake and Chickadee Lake, offer fine freshwater swimming (access Graham Lake along Jemima Rd. and Chickadee along Lake Rd.).

COMOX VALLEY   ☎250

With fine hiking, fishing, and skiing, and the southern regions of Strathcona Provincial Park just an emu's trot away, the tourist season never ends in this self-proclaimed "Recreation Capital of Canada." The area's beaches, trails, and forested swimming holes would take weeks to explore. Sheltering the towns of Courtenay, Comox, and Cumberland, the Comox Valley boasts the highest concentration of artists in Canada and offers many free museums and galleries. In addition, the 1989 discovery of the 80-million-year-old "Courtenay Elasmosaur," which swam in the valley back when the valley was a lake, has transformed the region into a minor mecca of paleontology.

■⁊ **ORIENTATION AND PRACTICAL INFORMATION. Courtenay,** the largest town in the Valley, lies 108km (1hr.) north of Nanaimo on the **Island Hwy.** (Hwy. 19). In Courtenay, the Island Hwy. heading north joins **Cliffe Ave.** before crossing the river at 5th St., intersecting with **Comox Rd.,** and then once again heading north. **Laidlaw** (☎334-2475) buses run to **Port Hardy** (5hr., $64), **Victoria** (5hr., $40), and **Nanaimo** (2hr., $20) from Courtenay at 2663 Kilpatrick and 27th St. by the Driftwood Mall. The **Comox Valley Transit System** connects the valley's three towns. (☎339-5453. Buses run 6:40am-10:20pm. $1.25; seniors $1.) **BC Ferries** (☎888-223-3779; www.bcferries.com) links Comox with **Powell River** (1¼hr.; 4 per day; $8, car $22-25). The **Bar None Cafe** (see **Food,** below) has a **ride board.** The **visitors center,** 2040 Cliffe Ave., is in Courtenay. (☎334-3234. Open M-F 9am-6pm, Sa-Su 9am-5pm; shorter hours in winter.)

Comox Valley Kayaks, 2020 Cliffe Ave. beside the visitors center, rents, transports, and leads workshops and full-moon paddles. (☎ 334-2628 or 888-545-5595. Singles $35 per day, doubles $63. Open daily 10am-6pm; by appointment in winter.) Free **Internet access** at the **Library,** on 6th St. next to Thrifty's. (☎ 338-1700. Open M-F 10am-8pm, Sa 10am-5pm.) Wash up at **The Pink Elephant,** 339 6th St. (☎ 897-0167. Wash $1.75; dry 25¢ for 5min. Open M-F 8:30am-7pm, Sa-Su 9am-7pm.) **Emergency:** ☎ 911. **Police:** ☎ 338-1321. **Hospital:** ☎ 339-2242. **Weather:** ☎ 339-5044. **Post office:** 333 Hunt Place. (☎ 334-4341. Open M-F 8:30am-5pm.) **Postal Code:** V9N 1G0.

ACCOMMODATIONS AND FOOD.
The **Comox Lake Hostel,** 4787 Lake Trail Rd., about 8km from town, is within hiking distance of Strathcona Provincial Park. To get there, take 5th St. toward the mountains to Lake Trail Rd., turn west, and just keep going. (☎ 338-1914. Kitchen, laundry. Linen free. Downtown shuttle $3; ferry $6. Call ahead. Beds $16; tent sites $10 per person.) The new **Courtenay Riverside Hostel,** 1380 Cliffe Ave., allows a hostel stay right in town by the river and the park being developed around it. Private rooms available. (☎ 334-1938. Linen, towels, laundry. Dorms $16. Winter ski and stay package $50.) Campers hit **Kin Beach** campground, on Astra Rd., past the Air Force base in Comox. To get there turn left at the four-way stop in front of the base, then take your first right, and follow it for 5min. (☎ 339-6365. Tennis, pit toilets, water. 16 wooded sites, $7.50.) Despite the trek 25km north from Courtenay, family-oriented **Miracle Beach** on Miracle Beach Dr. is often full. (☎ 337-5720; reservations required 800-689-9025. Showers, toilets. Sites $19.) **Comox Valley Farmers' Market,** occurs three times per week at different locations: W at 4th St. and Duncan St., F at the Comox Marina, and Sa at the fairground on Headquarters Rd. (May-Sept. 9am-noon). Thaw an emu TV dinner from **Safeway** on 8th St. in Courtenay (open M-Sa 8am-9pm, Su 9am-9pm). The **Atlas Cafe,** 250 6th St., serves delicious quesadillas ($5.75-7) and light entrees. (☎ 338-9838. Open M-Th and Sa 8:45am-10pm, F 8:45am-11pm, Su 8:45am-9:30pm.) **Bar None Cafe,** 244 4th St. off Cliffe Ave. in Courtenay, stocks exceptional vegetarian fare. Open mic Tu-F 6-9pm. (☎ 334-3112. Open M-Sa 8am-7pm.)

SIGHTS.
The area's largest draw is **Mt. Washington** ski area, on the edge of Strathcona Provincial Park (see p. 276). It is only a 30min. drive to the base of the lifts from Courtenay, so staying in a cheap motel is a viable way to avoid the stratospheric prices on the mountain. The **Comox Valley Art Gallery,** 367 4th St., in Courtenay, is a focal point for the local arts community. (☎ 338-6211. Open July-Aug. M-Sa 10am-5pm, Sept.-June closed Su-M.) The **Queneesh Gallery,** 3310 Comox Rd., in front of the Comox Band big house, displays the work of some of the finest carvers of the coast Salish and Kwakwaka'wakw traditions on northern Vancouver Island. (☎ 339-7702. Open daily 10am-5pm. Jan.-Feb. closed Su-M.) Inquire at the **visitors center** about other galleries. Ponder the work of the Canadian military at the **Comox Air Force Museum** (☎ 339-8162), on the grounds of CFB Comox Base. The **Heritage Aircraft Park** houses post-WWII fighters and a retired Czechoslovakian MiG-21. (Open daily June-Aug. 10am-4pm; shorter hours in winter. Donation requested.) The **Cumberland Museum,** 2680 Dunsmuir Ave., displays exhibits on the coal-mining town that in 1920 was home to large Chinese and Japanese communities. (☎ 336-2445. Open daily 9am-5pm; winter closed Su. Admission by donation.)

OUTDOOR ACTIVITIES.
The snowmelt-fed **Puntledge River** at **Stotan Falls,** a long stretch of shallow waters racing over flat rocks, is a great place for **swimming;** test the current and depths before wading or jumping. Coming from Courtenay on Lake Trail Rd., turn right at the stop sign onto the unmarked road at the first "hostel" sign. Take the next left at the logging road Duncan Bay Main, cross the pipeline, then park on either side of the one-lane bridge. For longer trails through the woods try breath-taking **Nymph Falls,** upriver. From Duncan Bay Main, go left on Forbidden Plateau Rd. to the "Nymph" sign. **Horne Lake Caves Provincial Park,** 55km south of Courtenay off the Island Hwy., on Horne Lake Rd., offers superb caving tours for beginners (1½hr.; $15, children $12), and 5hr. tours involving crawlways and rappelling. (☎ 757-8687 or 248-7829; reservations www.hornelake.com. Tour $79. Must be 15.) **Tiderunner Charters** (☎ 337-2253 or 334-7116) rents boat and rods.

CAMPBELL RIVER   ☎ 250

The Big Rock covered with graffiti welcomes visitors to Campbell River, another of BC's many "Salmon Capitals of the World." *National Geographic* called Campbell River's incredible fishing and scuba diving "second only to the Red Sea." The number of gas stations and motels along the old Island Hwy. (Hwy. 19A) confirms Campbell River's role as the transportation hub of the island's north. It provides easy access to Strathcona Provincial Park, Port Hardy, and the Discovery Islands.

ORIENTATION AND PRACTICAL INFORMATION.
Campbell River lies 45km north of Courtenay on the **Island Hwy.** (Hwy. 19). **Laidlaw** (☎287-7151), at 13th and Cedar, sends buses to **Nanaimo** (4 per day, $24.75), and **Victoria** (4 per day, $44) as well as **Port Hardy** (1-2 per day, $58). **BC Ferries** (☎888-223-3779) runs to Quadra Island (all day; $4.50-4.75, cars $10.50-12, ages 5-11 $2.25-2.50). The **visitors center** is off the Island Hwy. near the Tyee Mall adjacent to the Marina. (☎287-4636. Open daily 8am-6pm; winter M-F 9am-5pm.) **Weather:** ☎287-4463. **Emergency:** ☎911. **Police:** ☎286-6221. **Crisis line:** ☎287-7743. **Hospital:** 375 2nd Ave. (☎287-7111).

ACCOMMODATIONS, CAMPING, AND FOOD.
B&Bs in Campbell River tend to be a bit expensive (singles $45-70; doubles $60-90), but the Info Centre can help you find a bed to sleep in. The best camping near town is at **Quinsam Campground**, in Elk Falls Provincial Park, on Hwy. 28, with space among firs. (Pit toilets. 122 sites, $12.) **Strathcona Provincial Park** (see p. 276) is next best, but slightly farther out of town. The **Beehive Cafe,** 921 Island Hwy., has a deck overlooking the water. Breakfast and lunch run $6 and up. For an amazing local treat try the smoked salmon bagel sandwich. (☎286-6812. Open daily 6:30am-10pm; winter 7am-8pm.) Shop for honey at **Super Valu** in the Tyee Mall. (☎287-4410. Open daily 8:30am-9:30pm.) To spice up your life while in town, sizzle by **Spice Island,** 2269 Island Hwy., in the Willow Point Plaza, on the main drag through town. They offer customized meat, seafood, or tofu Asian-influenced dishes with 5 levels of spiciness. (☎923-0011. Open Tu-Sa 4:30pm-closing.) Sockeye, coho, pink, chum, and chinook **salmon** are hauled in by the boatload from the waters of the Campbell River. The savvy can reap the fruits of the sea from **Discovery Pier** in Campbell Harbour, and the unskilled can at least buy rich ice cream and fro-yo on the pier, which has an artificial reef built to attract fish. (Fishing $2; rod rentals $2.50 per hr., $6 per half-day.) Get a **fishing license** ($6-8 per day) at the visitors center or any sports outfitter in town. A "salmon sticker" costs $6.50 extra.

SIGHTS AND OUTDOOR ACTIVITIES.
Tour the **Quinsam River Salmon Hatchery,** 4217 Argonaut Rd., and see a wealth of "natural" resources. The hatchery nurtures little fishies to adolescence. (☎287-9564. Open daily 8am-4pm.) **Scuba** gear rentals can be pricey and require proper certification, but **Beaver Aquatics,** 760 Island Hwy., offers a nifty $25 **snorkeling** package including suit, mask, snorkel, and fins, as well as a $50 full dive package. (☎287-7652. Open M-Sa 9am-5pm, Su 10am-2pm.)

DAYTRIP FROM CAMPBELL RIVER: QUADRA ISLAND.
Quadra boasts pleasing landscapes that rival her southern Gulf Island cousins, a European history that is older than that of most settlements on Vancouver Island, and a thriving First Nation community around Cape Mudge. Quadra is a 10min. ferry ride from Campbell River (see p. 275). **BC Ferries** sail to Quadra every hour on the half hour from Campbell River (see **Orientation,** above). **Quadra Foods** will satisfy your grocery needs and sell you a **fishing license.** (☎285-3391. Open daily 9am-8pm. Licenses $6-8 per day, $6.50 extra for salmon.) **Quadra Credit Union** (☎285-3327; **24hr. ATM**) and a **visitors center** with maps of island trails and rental info await at the first corner of Harper Rd. across from Quadra Foods. **Emergencies:** ☎911. **Police:** ☎285-3631. The **Kwagiulth Museum and Cultural Centre,** in the village of Cape Mudge, just south of Quathiaski Cove, houses a spectacular collection of potlatch regalia confiscated by the government early this century and not returned

until as late as 1988. (☎ 285-3733; www.island.net/~kmccchin. Open M-Sa 10am-4:30pm; in summer also Su noon-4:30pm. $3, seniors $2, children $1. Tours $1.) Weary travelers will find a welcome place to relax at the ■**Travellers' Rural Retreat**, where remarkable hosts welcome you into their home. Ask to see Jim's driftwood sculptures. (☎ 285-2477. Call for directions. $16.) Several minutes down Heriot Bay Rd. from the beauty of **Rebecca Spit Provincial Park** and **Heriot Bay**, the **We Wai Kai Campsite** lies on the water. (☎ 285-3111. Toilets, water, laundry, coin showers. Sites $15-17.) **Spirit of the West** rents kayaks and runs guided trips that explore Quadra Island's wildlife-rich shores and beyond. (☎ 800-307-3982; www.kayakingtours.com. Singles $50 per day; doubles $75. Full-day tour $89, includes lunch.)

STRATHCONA PROVINCIAL PARK ☎ 250

Elk, deer, marmots, and wolves all inhabit the over 2000 sq. km of Strathcona, one of the best-preserved wilderness areas on Vancouver Island. Strathcona is the oldest provincial park in BC. The park spans the land just west of the Comox Valley, reaching north to connect with Campbell River via Hwy. 28. It stretches from sealevel to the highest point on Vancouver Island, 2200m Golden Hinde.

■**☑ ORIENTATION AND PRACTICAL INFORMATION.** The park is accessible from Courtenay or Campbell River. The two **BC Parks** offices are on **Buttle Lake** (open summer only, F-Su 9am-4pm), on Hwy. 28 between Gold River and Campbell River, and **Mt. Washington/Forbidden Plateau,** outside Courtenay off Hwy. 19. For park info, contact BC Parks, District Manager, Box 1479, Parksville, BC, V9P 2H4 (☎ 954-4600).

☒☒ ACCOMMODATIONS AND CAMPING. The two frontcountry **campgrounds,** with 161 sites between them, are **Buttle Lake** and **Ralph River.** Both are on the shores of Buttle Lake and accessible by **Hwy. 28** and secondary roads (follow the highway signs). **Buttle Lake,** 50km from Campbell River (about 45min. of scenic, but winding driving), has comfortable sites, a playground, and sandy beaches on the lake (pit toilets; water; $15). Less crowded **Ralph River,** 75km (1½hr. drive) west of Campbell River, provides convenient access to the park's best hiking trails ($12). Five smaller marine campsites are accessible only by trails (pick up a map at the park entrance). The **Ark Resort,** 11000 Great Central Lake Rd., just west of Port Alberni, off Hwy. 4, rents canoes for the 35km water journey to the Della Falls trailhead (see **Outdoor Activities,** below) or provides a water taxi for $85 per person round-trip. (☎ 723-2657. Sites $19; rooms $45.) For outfitting and outdoor guidance on the doorstep of the park, **Strathcona Park Lodge,** 30km from Campbell River on Hwy. 28, offers equipment rental and experienced guides. The lodge's roomy wooden houses are lakefront, and the dining hall serves three buffet-style meals a day. (☎ 286-3122. Single kayaks $9 per hr., $37 per day; doubles $14 per hr., $53 per day; 17 ft. sailboats $20 per hr., $70 per day. Dining hall 7am-9am $10; noon-2pm $10, 5:30-7pm $17, summer 6-9pm a la carte.)

◪ **HIKING.** The park offers a great variety of trails of all lengths and difficulties. Visitors who wish to explore Strathcona's **backcountry areas** must camp 1km from main roads and at least 30m away from water sources; campfires are discouraged in the park. Those entering the undeveloped areas of the park should notify park officials of their intended departure and return times and should be well equipped (**maps** and **rain gear** are essential). Be sure to check back in with wardens upon your return.

Karst Creek Trail (2km, 45min.), passes limestone sinkholes and waterfalls, leaves from the Karst Creek day-use area. Easy.

Myra Falls Trail (1km, 20-40min.), starts 1km past Thelwood bridge at the S end of Buttle Lake at a signed parking area. The trail features a walk through old growth forest and a steep hill with loose rock on the way to the immense, pounding falls. Moderate.

Phillips Ridge (12km round-trip, 7-8hr.). Trailhead at the parking lot just south of the campsite along the highway. The trail leads to Arnica Lake and wildflower-strewn alpine meadows, passing two waterfalls and ascending 700m along the way. Difficult.

Elk River Trail (11km one-way, 4-6hr.). This popular trail starts just before Drum Lakes along Hwy.28; follow signs to trailhead on the left. A campsite at 9km has bear food caches. Trail gains 600m in elevation as it follows an old elk trail to Landslide Lake, where part of Mt. Colonel Foster fell into the water. Moderate.

OUTDOOR ACTIVITIES. Skiers and snowboarders hit the slopes just outside the park boundaries at **Mt. Washington,** to take advantage of the 10m of annual snowfall. The mountain is accessible from Courtenay; follow Cliffe St. to the end, take a right on 1st St., a left at the end of 1st, and then follow the signs. A few years ago one of the nearby lodges actually caved in from too much snow, and lifts have been known to be closed on occasion because of the excess snow. (☎338-1386; www.mtwashington.bc.ca. $44; over 65 and ages 13-18 $36; ages 7-12 $23; 6 and under free. Night Skiing F-Sa 4:30-9pm. $6, 6 and under free.) A lift is open in the summer to satiate the appetites of the vista hungry. ($10, youth and senior $8, under 6 free; with bike $15.) The mountain also offers 40km of cross country and snowshoe trails; the lodge offers rentals. (Alpine ski package $22; cross country $16; over 65 and ages 13-18 $12. Snowboards $36; snowshoes $9.)

THE PORT McNEILL AREA ☎250

The protected waters and plentiful fish of Johnstone Strait provide a fine summer home for orca pods. Mainland and island settlements near Port McNeill provide fine quiet waterside trips. Sighting charters run $60 for 3-4hr., but lucky visitors can glimpse orcas from the ferry between Port McNeill, Sointula, and Alert Bay, or even from the shoreline. For good whale-watching, head 25km south of Port McNeill to the boardwalk town of **Telegraph Cove.** Turn left south of town on the Island Hwy.; over the last 5km, it becomes an unpaved road. **North Island Kayaks,** in Port Hardy (see below), will drop off and pick up kayaks in the cove. (☎949-7707 or 877-949-7707. Kayaks $40 per day; doubles $60.)

Tiny Cormorant Island and the town of **Alert Bay** is home to a fabulously rich repository of native culture. The cultural legacy of several groups of the **Kwakwaka'wakw** peoples (ka-kwak-QUEW-wak; formerly known as the Kwakiutl or Kwagiulth) sets the fishing village apart from its aquatourist siblings. By the Big House stands a 173 ft. totem pole, the largest in the world. Two kilometers north of the ferry terminal, the pole towers over the **U'mista Cultural Centre,** which houses an astonishing array of Kwakwaka'wakw artifacts repatriated decades after Canadian police pillaged a potlatch. *U'mista* means "the return of a loved one taken captive by raiding parties." (☎974-5403. Open daily 9am-5pm; winter M-F 9am-5pm.) **Sointula,** on the coast of Malcolm Island, is a modern artist and fishing community with Finnish roots known for its December Christmas bazaar.

PRACTICAL INFORMATION. Laidlaw (☎956-3556) runs one bus per day to **Port McNeill** from **Victoria** (8hr., $91). **BC Ferries** (☎956-4533 or 888-223-3779; www.bcferries.com) runs from Port McNeill to **Sointula** on Malcolm Island (25min.) and **Alert Bay** (45min.; 6 per day; round-trip $5.50-6, car $13-15). **Visitors centers** are stationed at 351 Shelley Crescent in Port McNeill (☎956-3131; open daily 9am-5pm in summer) and 118 Fir St. in Alert Bay (☎974-5024; open daily 9am-6pm June-Sept.). To get to the visitors center in Port McNeill, follow Campbell Way off the Island Hwy. to the bottom, take a left on Broughton Pl., and then left onto Shelley. **Emergencies:** ☎911. **Hospital:** 2750 Kingcome Pl. (☎956-4461) in Port McNeill.

ACCOMMODATIONS AND FOOD. The **Sun Spirit Hostel,** 549 Fir St., in Alert Bay, remains a welcome spot to play piano and whale-watch from the roomy living room. (☎974-2026. $17, cash or traveler's checks only.) Beautiful camping, with a view of the mainland coastal range, is available across the island at **Bere Point Regional Park** near Sointula. (Pit toilets, no water. 12 sites, by donation.) The budget-mindful eschew island restaurants for the hardtack at **ShopRite Grocery,** 99 Fir St. (☎974-2777. Open M-Sa 9am-6pm, Su 10am-5pm.) The **Killer Whale Cafe,** in Telegraph Cove is all yellow cedar and stained glass. High prices and erratic service. (☎928-3131. Dinner from $11. Open daily 8am-2:30pm and 4-10pm.)

PORT HARDY ☎250

Port Hardy, an idyllic logging and fishing community, is the southern terminus for the BC Ferries route up the Inside Passage. The northernmost major town on the island, it has a vested interest in tourism. You will be welcomed by a chainsaw-carved sign, erected for the 1500 passengers who sleepily disembark the ferry every other night. These transients join a surge of fishermen preparing for unpredictable fall fisheries on the west coast of BC and a growing indigenous population drawn from more remote towns for schooling and employment.

TRANSPORTATION. Port Hardy, on Vancouver Island, is perched 36km north of Port McNeill and 238km (2½hr.) north of Campbell River on **Hwy. 19. Market St.** is the main drag, running through the shopping district and along a scenic **seaside path. Laidlaw** (☎949-7532), opposite the visitors center on Market St., runs to **Victoria** (8¾hr., $102) via **Nanaimo** (6hr., $83) each day at 9am and when the ferry arrives. **BC Ferries** (☎949-6722 or 888-223-3779; www.bcferries.com) depart 3km south of town at **Bear Cove,** for **Prince Rupert** (every other day June-Sept.; winter every Sa and 2nd W $53-106, car $124-218). The Discovery Coast Passage route between Port Hardy and **Bella Coola** runs from mid-June to mid-Sept. ($70-110, car $140-220). Book months ahead for cars. **North Island Taxi** (☎949-8800) services the ferry from all over town for $5.25 per person.

ORIENTATION AND PRACTICAL INFORMATION. To reach the **visitors center,** 7250 Market St., follow Hwy. 19 until the end and take a right on Market St. (☎949-7622. Open daily 8:30am-8pm; winter M-F 9am-5pm.) The **Port Hardy Museum** (see **Sights and Outdoor Activities,** below) also has in-depth info on the region. The **CIBC bank,** 7085 Market St., has a **24hr. ATM.** (☎949-6333. Open M-Th 10am-4pm, F 10am-6pm.) **North Star Cycle and Sports,** at Market and Granville St., rents bikes. (☎949-7221. $20 per day. Open daily 9:30am-6pm.) For all else, there's **Jim's Hardy Sports,** in the Thunderbird Mall on Granville St. (☎949-8382. Open M-Sa 9am-6pm, Su 10am-5pm; winter closed Su.) Diving rentals can be found at **North Island Diving and Water Sports,** at Market and Hastings St. (☎949-2664. Open Tu-Sa 11am-6pm.) Wash up at the **Shell Gas Station,** on Granville St. (☎949-2366. Wash $1.75; dry 25¢ per 7min. Open 24hr.) **Internet access** is $5 at the **library,** 7110 Market St. (☎949-6661. Open M, W, F noon-5pm and 7-9pm; Tu and Th noon-5pm). **Police:** 7355 Columbia St. (☎949-6335). **Crisis line:** ☎949-6033. **Hospital:** 9120 Granville St. (☎949-6161). **Postal code:** V0N 2P0.

FOOD. To stock up on groceries before the long ferry ride or trip down the island, **Glenway Foods,** 8645 Granville St. (☎949-5758), will satiate your needs. The burger is this town's budget meal. One of the best is $6 at **I.V.'s Quarterdeck Pub,** 6555 Hardy Bay Rd., on the scenic fishing dock. Their great vegetarian fare is balanced by F prime rib night ($15 with all the trimmings) and 25¢ W and Su wings. (☎949-6922. Open daily 11am-midnight.) The **Oceanside Restaurant & Pub,** 6435 Hardy Bay Rd., just down from I.V.'s at the Glen Lyon Inn, has a terrific view and serves 25¢ wings on W and F. (☎949-7115. Open daily 6:30am-9pm.) Your best breakfast bet is at **Snuggles Restaurant,** 4965 Byng Rd., by the Quatze River Campground. (☎949-7494. Full breakfast starting at $5. Open daily 7:30am-9:30pm.)

ACCOMMODATIONS AND CAMPING. The visitors center will reserve B&B rooms for free. (☎949-7622. Call ahead on ferry nights.) The ■**Dolphin House** B&B, 297 Harbor Rd., Coal Harbor, is a short excursion (20min.) from Port Hardy. This hidden gem offers incredible ocean views, an array of outdoor activities, and proximity to native villages. Take Island Hwy. 19 to Coal Harbor Rd., turn right at the coffee shop in town, and head past the whale bones. (☎949-7576. Free pickup from ferry, bus station, airport. Singles $50; doubles $60.) **This Old House,** 8735 Hastings downtown by the bus station and minutes from the beach, rents cozy rooms with balconies upstairs. (☎949-8372. Free linen, laundry. Backyard BBQ, shared bath. 5 hostel beds $20; singles $40; doubles $70.) The proprietors of **The Hudson's Home B&B,** 9605 Scott St., provide all the TLC and custom breakfasts you can handle. Hot tub, Internet, and pickup and drop-off from the bus station. (☎949-5110. Singles $50; doubles $65; mention *Let's Go* and get 10% off.) **Bonita B&B,** new on the scene, offers guests privacy and their own sparkling kitchen to use. (☎949-6787. Singles $50; double $65-70.) Quiet, wooded sites at **Quatse River Campground,** 8400 Byng Rd. (☎949-2395; toilets, showers, laundry; $14, full hookups $18) are a 25min. walk from town but just minutes from **Snuggles Restaurant** (see **Food,** below). Internet access $1.50 per 15min. The camp shares space with a **fish hatchery.** (☎949-9022. Tours are best Sept.-Nov.) Sites amid an overgrown garden at **Wildwoods Campsite** lie off the road to the ferry, a walk to the terminal, but a hike from town. (☎949-6753. $12, hookups $18.)

SIGHTS AND OUTDOOR ACTIVITIES. The **Port Hardy Museum and Archives,** is at 7110 Market St., beneath the library. The museum's sea-creature remnants, 19th-century Cape Scott pioneers' personal effects, 8000-year-old tools from Hardy Bay, and erudite curator merit a visit. (☎949-8143. Open Tu-Sa 11:30am-5:30pm; shortened hours in winter. Donation requested.) A 15min. drive from town brings picnickers to the hard sand of **Storey's Beach,** a good place to put in a kayak or stroll along the rocky shore. Turn left off the Island Hwy. when driving out of town onto Byng Rd. and then take a left on Beaver Harbour Rd. to the water. Nearby, the **Copper Maker,** 114 Copper Way, commissions some of the finest Kwakiutl carvers in the region. From Byng Rd., turn left onto Beaver Harbour Rd., right on Tsak'is Way, and right again. (☎949-8491. Call for hours.) Farther down Tsak'is Way, a ceremonial and community **bighouse** overlooks the sea from the heart of Fort Rupert village, a site inhabited by the Kwakiutl for thousands of years. **Petroglyphs** adorn rocks near **Fort Rupert;** ask at the museum for advice in locating them at low tide. At the north end of the village stands the decaying stone chimney of Fort Rupert, an outpost built in 1849 by the Hudson's Bay Company.

A map of logging roads from the visitors center will allow you to explore the **geological curiosities** of the region's limestone bedrock or just get out into the woods: Devil's Bath sinkhole, the Vanishing and Reappearing River, and several spelunkable caves are all located toward **Port Alice** (40min. from town). **Odyssey Kayaking** can equip and transport you. (☎902-0565. Singles $40 per day; doubles $60. Must be 19 and have one experienced paddler in your group.) The Port Hardy area is known for some of the world's best **cold-water diving. Sun Fun Divers** (☎956-2243; www.sunfundivers.com) rents gear ($60-80), and runs half-day ($60) and full-day ($80) trips out of Port Hardy and Port McNeill.

CAPE SCOTT PROVINCIAL PARK ☎250

Off the Island Hwy. just out of Port Hardy, 64km of gravel logging roads snake across the wild and wet North Island toward the Pacific coast and Cape Scott Provincial Park. Carry a good spare, keep your headlights on, and yield to the logging trucks. The mass of the park is only accessible by trails leading into it from the parking lot near San Josef Bay near the park entrance (follow signs from Holburg). Off the main road past Holberg, a 15min. drive down Ronning Main, leads to a rugged, 1hr. trail to a secluded sandy beach at **Raft Cove Provincial Park.** Remarkable **Ronning Garden,** the work of a turn-of-the-century botanically-crazed pioneer, is farther along and a 10min. hike off the main road (free). For more detailed info on the park, contact BC Parks (☎ 954-4600), or pick up the Cape Scott Provincial Park **pamphlet** at one of the visitors centers in the region, since none are available at this sporadically patrolled park (May-Sept.).

When hiking in the park be sure to prepare for wet weather. Along the trek in you can find old rusting relics from the two failed attempts to settle the area, one in 1897 and one in 1910, plus everything from old abandoned buildings to a cougar trap from the early 1900s. There are also nearly a dozen shipwrecks dating from 1860 off the 100km of ocean frontage. Some of the trails include the mellow 2½km (45min.), wheelchair-accessible trail route to **San Josef Bay** around a rocky corner on the second northerly beach campsites (pit toilets, water). Backpackers can also depart the parking lot for the 23.6km trail (8hr.) to **Cape Scott,** the spectacular northwestern tip of the island. A 100km trail connecting Port Hardy to Cape Sutil, the northernmost point on the island, is under construction but progress is slow due to financial difficulties. Once completed, this trail will offer a longer but more rewarding second option to access the park's scenery and history. Random wilderness camping is allowed for $5 per person per night June-Sept.; self-register at the trailhead. Call the District Office for season schedules at 954-4600. The beaches at **San Josef Bay** (2.5km, 45min. from parking lot) and **Nels Bight** (16.8km or 6hr. in; pit toilets) are the best for camping.

INTERIOR BRITISH COLUMBIA

From the jagged snow-capped Rocky Mountains, the Fraser River courses and hurdles its way through 1300km of canyons and plateaus on its journey toward a land more arid than the Pacific. The sweeping agricultural basin in the middle of BC between the Rockies and the Coast Range mountains sees much more sun than the coast and is a vacation hot spot for city-slickers and back-country adventurers alike. The Rockies form the boundary that was finally breached by rail lines to unite Canada, and the mountains still form a large part of western Canada's identity. Today they are home to hugely popular national parks and thousands of square kilometers of hiking, climbing, and camping. Bus and train routes cross the interior and pass by various means through the mountains.

FRASER RIVER CANYON

In 1808, Simon Fraser enlisted the help of native guides to make the perilous expedition down the river from Mt. Robson to Vancouver. Today's route from Cache Creek to Hope on the Trans-Canada Hwy. (Hwy. 1) makes his trailblazing seem like a distant dream. Up close, the canyon is a good place to feel small, with 200km of pounding rapids below and pine sprouting out of near-vertical rock walls above.

In quiet **Hope,** travelers will find a tranquil town despite its fame as the Chainsaw Carving Capital. Hope's location at the intersection of several highways ensures easy arrival and departure. The **Trans-Canada Hwy. (Hwy. 1)** originates in Vancouver, passes through Hope, then bends north to Yale and eventually Cache Creek, where it meets the **Cariboo Hwy. (Hwy. 97;** see p. 305). **Hwy. 7** runs west along the north bank of the Fraser River to Vancouver's suburbs. The **Crowsnest Hwy. (Hwy. 3)** winds east through breathtaking country through Manning Provincial Park, through Kootenay Country to Nelson, and over Crowsnest Pass into Alberta. The **Coquihalla Hwy. (Hwy. 5),** is a new toll road ($10) running north to Kamloops, and preferred by most heading to the Rockies in a hurry—it's faster as long as the miles of grueling 8% grade don't get the best of the cars.

FRASER RIVER CANYON ■ 281

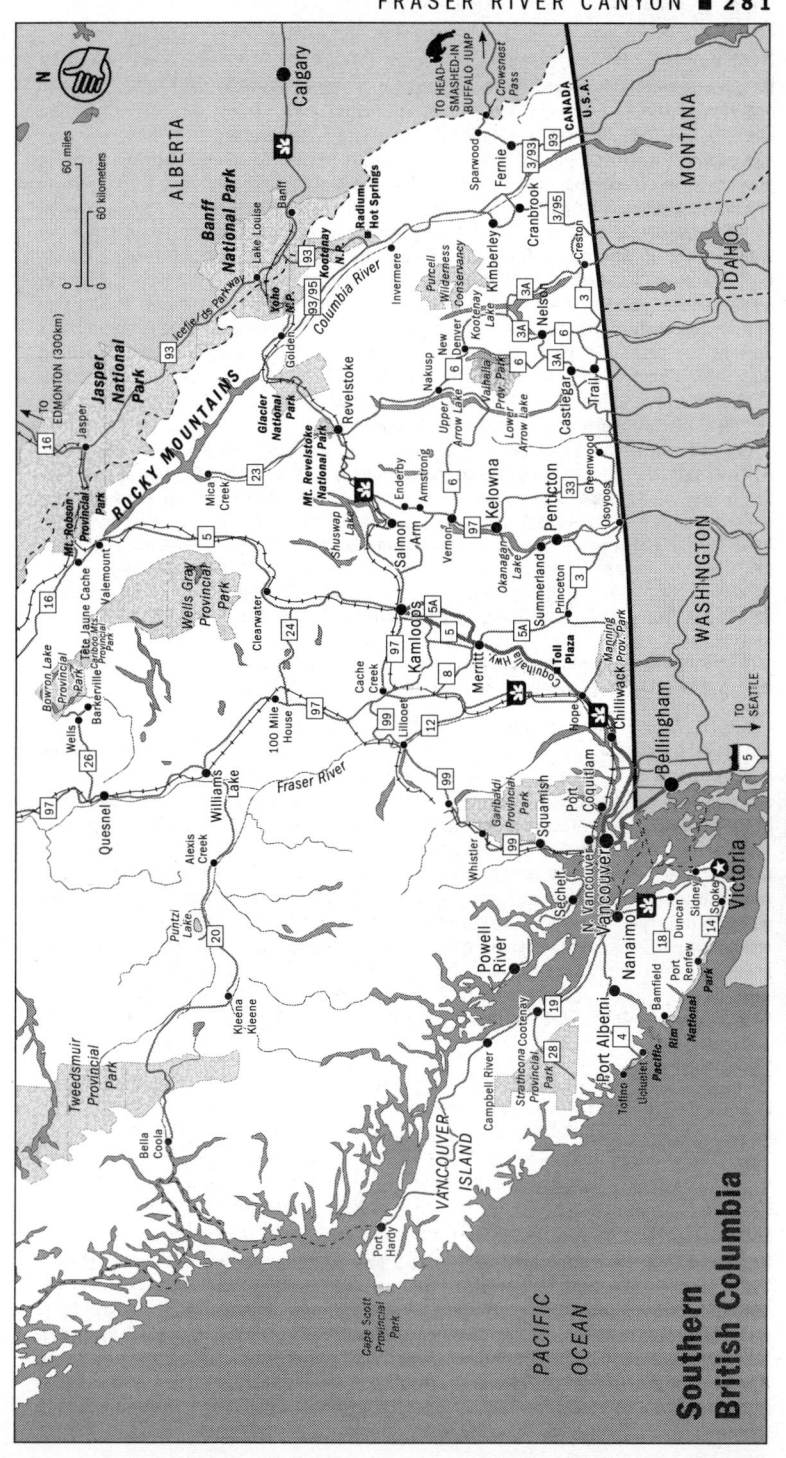

HOPE
☎ 604

Buses arrive in Hope at the **Greyhound** station, 677 Old Hope-Princeton Way (☎ 869-5522), a hub for bus travel throughout the region. Buses run north on the Coquihalla to **Kamloops** (2½hr., 3 per day, $30) then east to **Jasper** (8½hr., 2 per day, $85), **Banff** (10½hr., 3 per day, $89), and **Calgary** (12hr., 3 per day, $106); north on Hwy. 1 along the Fraser Canyon to **Cache Creek** (2¾hr., 2 per day, $28); east on Hwy. 3 to **Penticton** (3½hr.; 2 per day M-Sa, 1 on Su; $35) and points east; and west to **Vancouver** (2½hr., 6 per day, $20). Many try hitching north on Hwy. 1, where rides are reputedly easy to find (*Let's Go*, however, does not recommend hitchhiking). **Gardner Chev-Olds,** 945 Water Ave., rents cars. (☎ 869-9511. $40 per day, 7th day free. 13¢ per km after 100km. Must be 25 with credit card. Open M-Sa 8am-6pm.) The **Visitors Center,** 919 Water Ave. (☎ 869-2021 or 800-435-5622. Open 9am-5pm M-F.), provides the riveting, self-guided Rambo Walking Tour (*First Blood* was filmed here) and Arts & Carving Walking Tour, in addition to sharing info on Fraser River Canyon and Manning Park. **Police:** 690 Old Hope-Princeton Way (☎ 869-7750). **Post office:** 777 Fraser St. **Postal Code:** V0X 1L0.

If you're stuck in Hope for a night, there's a motel on every corner downtown ($45-55 singles). On the outskirts of town, **Holiday Motel,** 63950 Old Yale Rd. (☎ 869-5352; fax 869-3176), offers rooms starting at $34, tent and RV sites $12 including showers and hookups $20; all include a free breakfast sandwich. Campers can head for the big trees at the spacious **Coquihalla Campsite,** 800 Kawkawa Lake Rd., off 6th Ave., on the east side of town along the banks of the Coquihalla River. (☎ 869-7119 or 888-869-7118. Open Apr.-Oct. 122 sites $16; river sites $19; hookups $20.) Shop for groceries at **Buy and Save Foods,** 489 Wallace St. (☎ 869-5318. Open daily 8am-9pm, and until 10pm July-Aug.) Locals love the generous portions (big burgers from $4) at the **Home Too Restaurant,** 250 Fort St. (☎ 869-5241). **Mocachino's Coffee & Internet Cafe** allows you to surf the web for $8.50 per hr. (Open M-F 8am-6pm, Sa-Su 8:30am-6pm; in winter closed Su).

AROUND HOPE
☎ 604

A number of excellent hikes begin in or near Hope. Find the lush **Rotary Trail** (20min.) on Wardle St. at the confluence of the Fraser and Coquihalla Rivers. **Mt. Hope Loop** (45min.), offers an impressive view of the town and surrounding area. To reach **Lookout Trail** (3½-4hr. round-trip), turn right under the Hwy. 1 overpass at Old Hope-Princeton Way. A trail for hikers looking for more of a challenge. Pause for a pleasant diversion at **Kawkawa (a.k.a. Suckers) Creek,** off Union Bar Rd., enhanced in 1984 to aid the late summer and mid-fall salmon spawning. The boardwalk along the creek leads to a swimming hole and popular picnicking spot. **Manning Provincial Park.** 15min. east of Hope on Hwy. 3. has more extensive hiking options out of the four campgrounds in the rugged Cascade Mountains. (350 sites, $12-18.50.) **Paintbrush Nature Trail,** at Blackwall Peak is a rare opportunity to enjoy subalpine meadows (bloom late July to early August). Wheelchair accessible.

OTHELLO QUINTETTE TUNNELS. The **Coquihalla Canyon Recreation Area** is a 5-10min. drive out of Hope along Kawkawa Lake Rd. Here the **Othello Quintette Tunnels,** blasted through solid granite, provide mute evidence of the daring engineering that led to the opening of the **Kettle Valley Railway** in 1916. The dark tunnels lead to narrow bridges over whitewater shooting through the gorge. To get there, turn right on Othello Rd. off Kawkawa Lake Rd. and right again on Tunnel Rd.; allow 30min. to walk through the tunnels.

LADY FRANKLIN ROCK AND RAFTING. For an even closer view of the Fraser River, head 36km north on Hwy. 1 to the town of **Yale.** Take the first right after the stop light, then follow the gravel road for about 1km to a view of the majestic Lady Franklin Rock, which splits the river into two sets of heavy rapids. **Fraser River Raft Expeditions,** south of town, runs full-day whitewater trips almost daily on the Fraser and its tributaries. Travelers can stay the night in their oversized teepee or in the B&B. (☎ 863-2336 or 800-363-7238 for reservations. Class III-IV rapids; $110 includes lunch. Teepee $10 per night; customers free. B&B double $70.)

HELL'S GATE AIRTRAM. When Simon Fraser made his pioneering trek down the river, he likened one tumultuous stretch of rapids, 25km north of Yale on Hwy. 1, to the Gates of Hell where "no human beings should venture." The Hell's Gate Airtram, 43111 Hwy. 1, carries the vertigo-immune 500 ft. down into the canyon in four minutes. (☎867-9277. $10, seniors $8.50, ages 6-17 $6.50, families $26.50.) Acrophobes and budgeteers will prefer the nearby 1km trail down to the river.

KAMLOOPS ☎250

T'Kumlups, a Shuswap word meaning "where the waters meet," fits the town well, as it surrounds the convergence of the North and South Thompson rivers, and the heavily traveled Hwys. 5 and 1. Over 200 lakes lie within an hour's drive of town. That, combined with a fine hostel, outdoor live music in the summer, and numerous outdoor adventure opportunities, makes the town a great base for daytripping in the area, or a good way station on long highway voyages.

ORIENTATION AND PRACTICAL INFORMATION. Kamloops lies 356km east of Vancouver and 492km west of Banff, anchoring the junction of the heavily traveled Yellowhead (Hwy. 5) and Trans-Canada (Hwy. 1). **VIA Rail** (☎800-561-8630) trains stop at North Station, 11km north of city center off Hwy. 5, making three runs per week to **Vancouver** (8½hr., $92) and **Edmonton, AB** (15hr., $20). **Greyhound,** 725 Notre Dame Ave. (☎374-1212), departs Kamloops for **Vancouver** (4½hr., 5 per day, $49), **Jasper, AB** (6hr., 3 per day, $60), and **Calgary, AB** (9hr., 4 per day, $82). **Kamloops Transit System** (☎376-1216) buses cost $1.25. The **Visitors Center** is just off the Trans-Canada Hwy. (☎374-3377 or 800-662-1994. Exit #368. Open June-Aug. daily 9am-5pm; Sept.-May M-F 9am-5pm.) **Cycle Logical,** 194 Victoria St. (☎828-2810) rents bikes for $25 per day. **McCleaners,** 437 Seymour St. (☎372-9655), is a McLaundry. **Police:** 560 Battle St. (☎828-3000 or ☎911) in the City Center. Free **Internet access** at the **Public Library,** 466 Victoria St. (☎372-5145. Open Tu-Th 10am-9pm, M and F-Sa 10am-5pm, Su noon-4pm.) **Post office:** 301 Seymour St. (☎374-2444.; Open M-F 8:30am-5pm.) **Postal Code:** V2C 5K2.

ACCOMMODATIONS AND FOOD. The excellent ■**Kamloops Old Courthouse Hostel (HI),** 7 W Seymour St., is in fact a turn-of-the-century courthouse. The giant common room still sports a jury box, judge's bench, and witness stand, compensating for the tightly-packed dorm rooms. (☎828-7991. Check-in 8am-1pm and 5-10pm. 75 beds. $16, nonmembers $20, private rooms $5 surcharge.) Campers can set down for the night 8km east of the city center at **Kamloops View Tent & Trailer Park,** 1-4395 ETC Hwy. Forty sites are accompanied by showers, flush toilets, and laundry. (☎573-3255. Full hookups $25, tenting $16. A huge variety of foods lines Victoria St., the main strip downtown.) For the best breakfast in town, **Amsterdam Pancake House,** 369 Victoria St., serves Dutch-style *pannenkoeken* ($5-9) and $5-6 grilled sandwiches. (☎377-8885. Open daily 8am-3pm). **Zack's Coffees,** 377 Victoria St., sells exotic teas and coffees and $4 sandwiches. (☎374-6487. Open daily 7am-11pm.) **Steiger's Swiss Cafe and Pastries,** 359 Victoria St., gives succor to sweet tooths and satisfies fresh bread cravings. (☎372-2625. Open Tu-Sa 8am-5:30pm.)

SIGHTS. Every night in July and August at 7:30pm there is "Music in the Park," as bands perform in **Riverside Park** on the banks of the Thompson River. The **Wanda Sue Paddle Boat,** 2472 Thompson Dr., gets you up close and personal with the river on a 2hr. cruise. (☎374-7447. 1-3 cruises per day. $11.50, seniors $10.50, ages 6-12 $6.50.) **Secwepemc Museum and Heritage Park,** 355 Yellowhead Hwy., is devoted to preserving the culture and heritage of the Shuswap people. It contains the reconstructed remains of a 2000-year-old Shuswap village. Located near the site of a school from which the Canadian government removed native children as late as the 1970s, the museum is a testament to the endurance of the First Nations through sundry trials. (☎828-9801. Open June-Labor Day M-F 8:30am-8pm, Sa-Su 10am-6pm; Sept.-May M-F 8:30am-4:30pm. Summer $6, youths and seniors $4; off-season $1 less.) The **Art Gallery**, located in the same building as the library, has a flexible gallery space that exhibits both local work and traveling shows such as the recent "Gaugin to Toulouse-Lautrec: French Prints of the 1890s" from the National Gallery of Canada. (☎828-3543. Open M-W and F-Sa 10am-5pm, Th 10am-9pm, Su noon-4pm. $5, students and seniors $3, under age 6 free; Th 5-9pm voluntary donation.) The annual **Cattle Drive** (☎800-288-5850) gives you the opportunity to live an expensive Western dream from Gardens Creek Ranch to Kamloops. Would-be ranchers lacking mounts have to pay a hefty ransom for rentals. The cattle drive runs once a year in mid-July. Booking early is essential.

OUTDOOR ACTIVITIES. Sun Peaks, 1280 Alpine Rd., a 45min. drive north of Kamloops, is a powdery magnet for snowboarders and skiers. The mountain's large vertical drop (881m) and annual snowfall (559cm), as well as the six glades, justify the somewhat pricey tickets. In summer, the lift carries hikers and bikers up to trails and wildflower meadows. (☎800-807-3257. Hiking $12, seniors and ages 13-18 $11, ages 6-12 $9; mountain biking $26, seniors and ages 13-18 $22, ages 6-12 $12; winter $48, seniors $34, ages 13-18 $43, ages 6-12 $28.) Take Hwy. 5 north from Kamloops, turn right at Heffley Creek and continue 31km to Sun Peaks. The resort also hosts the annual **Ice Wine Festival** in mid-January. The **Stake Lake Trails** form a network of cross-country skiing terrain, with a good selection of beginner and intermediate options. Take Exit 366 from Hwy. 1 south of Kamloops, and follow Lac Le Jeune Rd. for 20min. Ask for a map at the visitors center or get one at the hut in winter. (Snow report ☎372-5514. $7 per day, $30 per 5 days. Summer usage for biking or hiking is free.) For more information on skiing, boat tours, mountain biking, rafting, and fresh water scuba diving in close proximity to Kamloops, contact the Kamloops Visitors Center.

For a an up-close look at the creatures inhabiting the area surrounding the rails, check the **Wildlife Park,** 15min. east of Kamloops along Hwy. 1, a non-profit organization devoted to rehabilitating local wildlife (☎573-3242; $6.75, ages 65 and up and 13-16 $4.75, ages 3-12 $3.75). Local climbers head out to **rock climb** at a crag about 25km weston Hwy. 1 out of Kamloops. Always in the shade, these 35 easy to moderate sport climbs offer a scenic view of Kamloops lake. Drop by **Ropes End** 975 B Laval Cres. (☎372-0645), climbing gym for more details.

SHUSWAP LAKE REGION ☎250

From the dugout canoes of the Shuswap to the house-boats and RVs of today's vacationers, the warm waters and productive fisheries of the sublime Shuswap Lake have attracted people for centuries. The area is a peaceful place to stay for the night or to stop and enjoy the scenery. Salmon Arm, a metropolis compared to the nearby villages, is still unexceptional but for its lakefront situation and its poster-perfect backdrop of rolling, forested mountains. Beware: if you are going to try and find your way through Salmon Arm off the highway, have a good map—the streets are more confusing than folding the map will be. The area is rich in camping and fishing opportunities, making it a popular vacation destination for British Colombians looking for a relaxing weekend getaway.

ORIENTATION AND PRACTICAL INFORMATION. Shuswap Lake is shaped like a sloppy, sideways 'H'. Coming from the west, Hwy. 1 hugs the northern arm of the lake before dipping south and following the southern arm east from Salmon Arm. The **Salmon Arm Transit System** (☎832-0191) has scheduled ($1.80, M-Sa) and door-to-door service ($1.50, M-F). **Visitors Center:** 751 Marine Park Dr. (☎832-6247 or 877-725-6667; fax 832-8382. Open May-Sept. M-Su 9am-7pm; Oct.-Apr. M-F 9am-5pm.) **Greyhound:** 50 10th St. SW (☎832-3962). **Shuswap Laundry:** 330 Ross St. (☎832-7300. Open daily 7am-10pm.) **Emergency:** ☎911. **Post office:** 370 Hudson St. NE. (☎832-3093. Open M-F 8:30am-5pm.) **Postal Code:** V1E 4M6. **Internet Access:** Free at the **Public Library** Picadilly Pl. Mall on 10th Ave. SW. (☎832-6161. Open M, W-Th, Sa 10am-5pm; Tu, F 10am-8pm.)

SHUSWAP LAKE REGION ■ 285

ACCOMMODATIONS AND CAMPING. **Squilax General Store and Caboose Hostel (HI),** 10km east of Chase, 8km west of Sorrento on Hwy. 1, sleeps travelers on board three Canadian National Railway cabooses. All three were specially outfitted for hosteling with kitchenettes and restrooms. Ample lounge space, showers, "sweat lodge," and laundry facilities are also part of the package. (☎ 675-2977. Linens $1. In summer, daily 9am-10pm check-in; off season M-Tu 5-10pm, W-Su noon-10pm check-in. 24 beds. $14, nonmembers $18. Tent sites by the river $8.) **B&Bs** are the way of Salmon Arm; for help finding a cheap one (prices range $45-100), visit or call the visitors center or Chamber of Commerce (see above). Campgrounds in Salmon Arm, especially those on Shuswap Lake, are often crowded and cramped. There are a handful of them on the lake side of Hwy. 1, about 10km west of Salmon Arm. For a much more peaceful stay, take the extra 30min. to drive to **Herald Provincial Park,** 27km northwest of Salmon Arm by following signs off Hwy. 1. The park maintains 119 campsites with a large swimming area and access to day hiking along Margaret Falls. (Reservations ☎ 800-689-9025. $18.50 includes firewood, hot showers, and toilets. See **Entertainment and Outdoor Activities,** below.)

FOOD. The best food deal for miles around awaits at the **Real Canadian Wholesale Club,** 360 Hwy. 1. Even the non-bulk items cost less than at a supermarket. (☎ 804-0258. Open M-F 9am-9pm, Sa 9am-6pm, Su 10am-5pm.) Farther west on Hwy. 1, **De Mille Fruits and Vegetables,** 3710 10th Ave. SW, markets local produce and, in August and September, incredible sweet corn. (☎ 832-7550. Open June-Sept. daily 8am-8pm; Oct.-May 8am-6:30pm.) To try Bannock, a type of bread eaten by natives, a stop at the **B&B Bannock Booth** is a must. It is located across the bridge on Squilax-Anglemont Rd., north of the hostel. The Smoked Salmon Bannock ($3) is sure to convert you. Or you can satisfy your sweet tooth at **Wee Willie's Deli,** 160 Lakeshore Dr. They also have freshly baked bread for making your own sandwiches. (☎ 832-3888. Open M-Sa 7:30am-5:30pm.)

ENTERTAINMENT AND OUTDOOR ACTIVITIES. **Caravan Farm Theatre,** 8km northwest of Armstrong and 45min. from Salmon Arm, presents top-notch performances during summer. Tickets are available from the Squilax General Store and Hostel. (☎ 546-8533. Call for show times, $6-12.) The Farm overflows with remnant hippie charm, organic produce, and musical instruments dangling from the trees. For an outstanding Native Dance Competition, see the Powwow in July; the visitors center has show times. The mystery of curds, is solved in a tour at **Gort's Gouda Cheese Factory,** 1470 50th St. SW. The tour is short and filled with tasty samples. Or, skip the tour and stock up on bargain cheeses and watch the cheese-making process through viewing windows, from cow to wax package. (☎ 832-4274. Tours mid-June to Aug. M-W and F 10am, store M-Sa 9am-5pm.)

Most of the area's outdoors attractions feature the waterways surrounding town, whether it be fishing for kokanee and rainbow trout in Lake Shuswap, or taking 10min. to walk through **Herald Park** (see **Accommodations,** above) to view the lovely **Margaret Falls**. For the latter, be careful to stay on the path, as the habitat is recovering from excessive trampling. Closer to town, many trails meander along the nature preserve on the banks of Lake Shuswap, where you can catch a glimpse of the rare Western grebe (Call Shuswap Lakes Tourism Assoc., ☎ 800-661-4800, for the date of this year's spring Grebe Festival). **Interior Whitewater Expeditions,** in Scotch Creek, leads 2hr. trips on the reasonably gentle (Class II-IV) **Adams River.** (☎ 800-661-7238. $44, under 16 $34; 15% HI discount.) The paths along the river can be hiked or mountain biked on an 18km round-trip trail. Take Squilax-Anglemont Rd. north across the bridge, just west of the Squilax General Store, and the trail heads upriver across the first narrow bridge on the road. Every four years, the salmon run on the Adams River is huge, so don't miss the big one in 2002.

THE OKANAGAN VALLEY

Known throughout Canada for its bountiful fruit harvests, the Okanagan (oh-kuh-NAH-gan) Valley lures visitors with summer blossoms, ample sun, plentiful wineries, and tranquil lakes. The Okanagan Connector (Hwy. 97C) links Vancouver to the valley in a 4hr. drive, making the valley a popular vacation destination among sun-starved coastal British Columbians. In the north, the quiet valley is rudely interrupted by an explosion of bloated shopping centers on Hwy. 97. Demure parks and beaches reward those who seek them out. Travelers looking to earn some cash can sign on to pick fruit at one of the many orchards stretching south from Penticton to the US border along Hwy. 97.

KELOWNA ☎ 250

In the heart of the Okanagan Valley, Kelowna (kuh-LOW-nuh) is one of Canada's richest agricultural areas. Its fruit stands, acclaimed wineries, and fabulous sunshine draw thousands of vacationing Vancouverites every summer. Those who visit this natural playground can enjoy a blend of chains and unique shops or while the day away on the shores of Okanagan Lake.

▛ TRANSPORTATION

Kelowna lies 400km east of Vancouver, 602km west of Calgary, and 86km north of Penticton on **Hwy. 97** at the eastern shore of Okanagan Lake. Hwy. 97, **Harvey Ave.** in town, runs east-west across the lake and bisects the town. The bridge across the lake features great views and terrible traffic snarls.

- **Buses: Greyhound,** 2366 Leckie Rd. (☎ 860-3835), just off Harvey Ave. next to the Best Western, runs buses to: **Vancouver, BC** (6½hr., 6 per day, $55); **Penticton, OR** (1½hr., 6 per day, $14); and **Calgary, AB** (10hr., 3 per day, $80).
- **Public Transportation:** Kelowna Regional Transit System (☎ 860-8121) services town. $1.25, students $1. Day passes $3.50-4.50. Runs M-Sa 6am-10pm, Su 9am-6pm.
- **Taxis: Kelowna Cabs** (☎ 762-2222 or 762-4444). 24hr. $1.60 base, $2.50 per mi.
- **Car Rental: Rent-A-Wreck,** 2702 N Hwy. 97 (☎ 763-6632) at Leathead Rd., will supply you the means to take on the town. From $30 per day, 12¢ per km over 100km. Must have a major credit card. Open M-Sa 8am-5pm, Su 9am-4pm.

▛ PRACTICAL INFORMATION

- **Tourist Office: Visitor Center,** 544 Harvey Ave. (☎ 861-1515). Brochures, bathrooms, and a doggie watering trough. Open M-F 8am-7pm, Sa-Su 9am-7pm.
- **Equipment: Sports Rent,** 3000 Pandosy St. (☎ 861-5699). Bikes $15-26 per day, in-line skates $1, kayaks $25, canoes $35. Open May-Sept. daily 9am-6pm, Oct.-Apr. 9am-8pm.
- **Internet Access: Kelowna Public Library,** 1380 Ellis St. (☎ 762-2800) offers 1hr. of free Internet access. Open M and F-Sa 10am-5:30pm, Tu-Th 10am-9pm; Oct.-May also Su 1-4pm. **Mind Grind Internet Cafe and Bookstore,** 1340 Water St. (☎ 763-2221), charges $3 for 30min., $5 per hr. Open June-Aug. daily 7:30am-11pm; Sept.-May M-Th 7:30am-10pm, F-Sa 7:30am-11pm, Su 8am-10pm. The **SameSun Hostel** offers access for $2 per 30min., and **Kelowna International Hostel** does the same (both see below).
- **Laundromat: Pandosy Laundry,** 2660 Pandosy St. Wash $1.50, dry 25 per 5min. Open M-F 8:30am-8pm, Sa 8:30am-6pm, Su 9am-5pm.
- **Emergency:** ☎ 911. **Police:** 350 Doyle Ave. (☎ 762-3300).
- **Hospital:** 2268 Pandosy St. (☎ 862-4000), 7 blocks south of Harvey Ave.
- **Post office:** 530 Gaston Ave. (☎ 763-4095). Open M-F 8:30am-5pm. **Postal Code:** V1Y 7G0.

ACCOMMODATIONS AND CAMPING

As Kelowna summers dry out thousands of soggy Vancouverites, be sure to make reservations or you'll be stuck in a chain hotel 5km out of town.

Kelowna International Hostel (HI), 2343 Pandosy St. (☎ 763-6024). Only 1 block from the beach in a restored home, this laid-back hostel is a budget dreamland. With keg parties and many movies, there's always something to do. Kitchen, laundry, Internet access ($2 for 30min.), pancake breakfast, and pickup from bus station. Reception 7am-11pm. Beds $16, nonmembers $18. Private rooms $37, nonmembers $40.

SameSun International Hostel, 245 Harvey Ave. (☎ 763-9814 or 877-562-2783), just a few blocks from the beach. Here, one-night stopovers often turn into week-long stays. The 4 keg parties each week, pub crawls, and day-trips are instrumental in this regard. Kitchen, laundry, and free pickup from bus terminal. Key deposit $10. Reception 8am-11pm. Call ahead if you'll arrive after-hours. Dorm beds $19.50, private rooms $49.

By the Bridge B&B, 1942 McDougall St. (☎ 860-7518), at the east end of Okanagan Lake Bridge, minutes from the lake. Cozy rooms, private baths, continental breakfast, and free bikes. Singles Oct.-May $47-57, June-Sept. $50-60; doubles $54-64, $65-75.

Bear Creek Provincial Park (☎ 494-6500 or 800-689-9025), 9km north of Hwy. 97 on Westside Rd., has shaded lakeside sites, a beach, and beautiful views. Line up at the crack of dawn for the lakeside sites. Showers and toilets are a plus. 122 sites, $19.

Fintry Provincial Park (☎ 800-689-9025), 34km north of Kelowna on Westside Rd., is similar to Bear Creek, but a twisting road discourages large trailers. Relatively unknown, Fintry is a great place to avoid the crowds. Toilets and water. 50 sites, $19.

FOOD

Kelowna overflows with fresh produce. Find juicy delights at the stands outside town along **Benvoulin Rd.** and **KLO Rd.,** or head south on **Lakeshore Dr.** to the u-pick cherry orchards. In town, the shelves groan beneath big carrots and cucumbers at **Safeway,** 697 Bernard Ave. (☎ 860-0332. Open daily 8am-midnight.) For all other fare, **Bernard Ave.** is lined with restaurants and cafes.

The Bohemian Cafe, 363 Bernard Ave. (☎ 862-3517). This cafe features delectable food in a spartan but comfortable atmosphere right on the main drag. Quiches and pasta run $5-6; huge sandwiches start at $5. Open M-F 7:30am-3:30pm, Sa 9am-3pm.

The Pier, 2035 Campbell Rd. (☎ 769-4777), just across the lake off Harvey Ave. An unassuming joint that serves up unbelievable daily specials: Tu 12oz. Sirloin steak ($7.50); Th 15¢ wings. Open Su-W 11am-midnight, Th-Sa 11am-1am.

Doc Willoughby's Downtown, 353 Bernard Ave. (☎ 868-8288). A new pub-style restaurant with live music from Celtic to blues on F-Sa nights. Food starts around $8. Hostelers get 20% off. Open M-Th 11:30am-11pm, F-Sa 11:30am-midnight, Su 4:30-10pm.

SIGHTS AND OUTDOOR ACTIVITIES

SAND AND WATER

The sun is Kelowna's main attraction, warming Okanagan parks and beaches for an average of 2000hr. per year. **City Park,** on the west end of downtown, is the principal lawn and beach from which to enjoy *el sol*, but **Boyce Gyro Park,** on Lakeshore Rd. south of the Okanagan Bridge, features prime beach volleyball locales. **Sports Rent,** a short walk from the lake, rents camping, boating, and sporting equipment (see **Practical Information,** above). **Kelowna Parasail Adventures,** 1310 Water St., at the docks of Grand Okanagan Resort north of City Park, transforms patrons into kites, floating them high above the lake. Other than wine festivals, Kelowna quiets down until mid-July, when the Regatta comes to town. The party surrounding the **Kelowna Regatta** (☎ 861-4754) has mellowed since 1988 when the regatta was shut down because of rioting, but the races still pack 'em in, and the good keep rolling.

HIKING, BIKING, AND SKIING

While the main attraction of Kelowna lies in Okanagan Lake, surrounding areas offer excellent opportunities for land-based fun. Hikers find trail opportunities throughout Okanagan Mountain Park, and bikers head to Wildhorse Canyon in the southern end of the park for technically challenging rides. One popular trail is **Kettle Valley Railbed** (12-41km, 2-8hr.), which passes through scenic Myra Canyon and then the only desert in Western Canada. It can be extended for a full-day adventure from Kelowna to Penticton. To get to the trail, take Chute Lake Rd. to the Chute Lake Resort and follow the signs to the Kelowna trailhead. Easy to moderate.

One hundred trails and over 1624 ft. of vertical drop greet powder hounds at family-friendly **Big White Ski Resort,** on a clearly marked access road off Hwy. 33, east of town. With two hostels and plenty of cheap eats surrounding the slopes, Big White is a great place for skiers on a budget. (☎765-3101; snow report 765-7669; www.bigwhite.com. Open mid-Nov. to late Apr. $48, ages 13-18 $40, ages 6-12 $25. Night-skiing 5-8pm, $16. Multi-day discounts. Skis $26; snowboard $35.)

WINE AND FRUIT

Over the past few years, the Okanagan valley has become the center of the British Columbian, and therefore Canadian, **wine** industry. Kelowna and surrounding area is home to 12 of the valley's more than 25 wineries, all of which offer tastings, and many of which have tours. Contact the visitors centers for a complete list of tours (i.e., How to Get Drunk for Free, Very Slowly), or call 868-WINE. Wine and cheese parties are common at the **Okanagan Wine Festival** (☎861-6654; www.owfs.com) for 10 days in early October, for four days at its lesser counterpart in late April, and for three days at the new **Icewine Festival** in late January. **Mission Hill,** 1730 Mission Hill Rd., on the west bank of Okanagan Lake, is the most respected local winery. To get there, cross the bridge west of town, turn left on Boucherie Rd., and follow the signs. Overlooking the lake, this large winery woos connoisseurs with its award-winning 1996 *Reserve* Chardonnay. Free tours explain the vinting process, and promise tastes for those over 19. (☎768-7611. Call for hours and tour times.) The posh **Summerhill Estate Winery** lets you taste five sparklers and join a tour to get a peek into the aging replica of the Cheops pyramid. Take Lakeshore Dr. to Chute Lake Rd. (☎800-667-3538. Open daily 10am-7pm; tours on the hr. 1-4pm.)

Kelowna Land and Orchard, 2930 Dunster Rd., off KLO Rd. on E Kelowna, is the town's oldest family-owned farm, and gives a 45min. hayride and tour that explains farming techniques and technologies. Kudos to those who can resist buying the tantalizing produce at the end of the tour. (☎763-1091. Open May-Oct. daily 8am-5pm; call for winter hours. $5.25, students $2, under 12 free.)

MUGGLES SPOT FANTASTIC BEAST. First reported in 1872, Ogopogo the sea monster is said to have pre-dated the native people' inhabitancy of the Okanagan Lake area. Now affectionately dubbed "Ogie" by the people of Penticton and Kelowna, the monster is a whopping 50ft. long with the head of either a horse, a bearded goat, or a sheep—slight discrepancies in the reports preclude certainty—and a worm-like body. Most of the Ogopogo sightings so far have been of several humps a few feet apart sticking out of the water. Between August of 2000 and September of 2001, a search for Ogopogo was conducted, with a prize of $2 million awarded for a verifiable sighting of the monster in Okanagan Lake. To check the results of the hunt, or to join a potentially new race for the booty, head to www.ogopogosearch.com. If you don't become an instant millionaire with a sighting of the *real* Ogopogo, you can still enjoy its image on the signs, sculptures, and blow-up dolls, peddled by the good people of Penticton and Kelowna.

PENTICTON ☎ 250

Close your eyes and imagine Florida. Replace the ocean with two turquoise lakes, the palm trees with old-growth spruce, and add mountains and hockey fans. Now open your eyes. Voila: Penticton. Indigenous peoples named the region between Okanagan and Skaha Lakes Pen-tak-tin, "a place to stay forever," but their eternal paradise has been transformed by heated pools and luxury hotels into one of Western Canada's biggest vacation towns, ushering in the Tourist Age to sleepy Penticton. It may well strain a budget to spend a weekend, let alone eternity, here.

TRANSPORTATION

Penticton lies 395km east of Vancouver at the junction of **Hwy. 3** and **Hwy. 97**, at the southern extreme of the Okanagan Valley. **Okanagan Lake** borders the north end of town, while smaller **Skaha Lake** lies to the south. **Main St.** bisects the city from north to south, turning into **Skaha Lake Rd.** as it approaches Skaha Lake.

- **Buses: Greyhound,** 307 Ellis St. (☎ 493-4101), runs buses to **Vancouver** (6-7hr., 6 per day, $52) and **Kelowna** (1½hr., 6 per day, $12). Open daily 6am-5pm.
- **Public Transportation: Penticton Transit System,** 301 E Warren Ave. (☎ 492-5602), services town. $1.50, students and seniors $1.20; day pass $3.25, students $2.75. Runs M-F 6:15am-10pm, Sa 8:30am-6:50pm, Su 9:40am-6pm.
- **Taxis: Courtesy Taxi,** (☎ 492-7778). 24hr. $2 base, $2.50 per mi.
- **Car Rental: Rent-a-Wreck,** 130 W Industrial Ave. (☎ 492-4447), rents cars from $40 per day, then 12¢ per km over 100km. Major credit card required. Open M-Sa 8am-5pm.

PRACTICAL INFORMATION

- **Tourist Office: Penticton Wine and Information Center,** 888 W Westminster Ave. (☎ 493-4055 or 800-663-5052; www.penticton.org), at Power St., The info center does not, unfortunately, serve wine. Open M-F 8am-8pm, Sa-Su 10am-6pm.
- **Equipment: Freedom: the Bike Shop,** 533 Main St. (☎ 493-0686). Bikes $30 per day, $5 HI discount. Open M-Sa 9am-5:30pm.
- **Laundromat**: **The Laundry Basket,** 976 W Eckhardt Ave., next to the golf course. Wash $1.50, dry 25 per 5min. Open daily 8am-8pm.
- **Internet Access: Penticton Public Library,** 785 Main St. (☎ 492-0024) offers free access. Open M, W, F, and Sa 10am-5:30pm, Tu-Th 10am-9pm. **Mousepad Coffee Bar,** 320 Martin St., charges $5 per hr. Open M-Sa 6am-10pm, Su 8am-8pm. **Net Werx,** 151 Front St. offers Internet access for $3 per 30min. Open M-F 10am-5pm, Sa 11am-4pm. Also at **Penticton Hostel** (see below) for $1 per 10min.
- **Hospital: Penticton Regional,** 550 Carmi Ave. (☎ 492-4000).
- **Emergency:** ☎ 911. **Police:** 1101 Main St. (☎ 492-4300).
- **Crisis Line:** ☎ 493-6622. **Women's Shelter:** (☎ 493-7233). 24hr.
- **Post Office:** 56 W Industrial Ave., (☎ 492-5769). Open M-F 8:30am-5pm. **Postal Code:** V2A 6J8.

ACCOMMODATIONS AND CAMPING

Penticton is a resort city year-round; cheap beds are few and far between and it's essential to make reservations in summer. If possible, avoid the expensive yet decrepit hotels that lurk along Skaha Lake Rd., and benefit from the beautiful hostel. As far as camping in Penticton is concerned, sardine companies might take a lesson on packing from the expensive campgrounds lining Skaha Lake.

- **Penticton Hostel (HI),** 464 Ellis St. (☎ 492-3992), is in a large house near the Greyhound stop, 10min. from the beach. Comfortable lounge, kitchen, and laundry facilities.

Free linen. No curfew. Reception 8am-noon and 5-10pm. Fills up June-Aug., and during ski season. 47 beds. $16, nonmembers $20; private singles $27, $32.

Riordan House, 689 Winnipeg St. (☎493-5997), rents enormous rooms with luxurious beds in an arts-and-crafts-style mansion. Breakfast of fresh scones and local fruits. Free pickup from Greyhound depot. Singles $50, lavish doubles with TV/VCR $60-85.

Okanagan Lake Provincial Park (☎800-689-9025), 24km north of town on Hwy. 97. 168 sites between the highway and the lake in 2 units. The north park is more spacious, and the beach is good for swimming. Free firewood, showers, and toilets. $19.

FOOD

Find your staples at **SuperValu Foods,** 450 Martin St. (☎492-4303. Open M-Sa 8am-8pm, Su 9am-6pm.) For more organic fare, accompanied by arts and crafts, the **Penticton Farmer's Market** flourishes every Saturday from June to October in Gyro Park at the corner of Westminster and Main St. (Open 8:30am-noon.) Finally, you can find your **fruits and vegetables** at family stands (look for signs on the side of the road) both north and south of town of Hwys. 97 and 3A. Stop by **Blue Magic,** 65 E Nanaimo for wraps and pitas ($7-10), or a $10 pizza topped with sauteed shrimp. (☎493-2227. Open M-F 11am-2pm and 5-9pm, Sa 11am-10pm.)

OUTDOOR ACTIVITIES

Long, hot summers and plenty of sport facilities (read: sand volleyball courts) make the lakes a popular hangout for the young. The Penticton tourist trade revolves around **Okanagan Lake,** but **Lake Skaha** at the other end of town has more sand and more volleyball nets. **Pier Water Sports,** 45 N Martin St. (☎493-8864), rents various vessels for those unwilling to express their manhood in the sand. Jet skis are $65 per hr. To avoid the crowds of youth, float down the river in a tube for a mere $10—chump change in expensive Penticton—courtesy of **Coyote Cruises,** 215 Riverside. (☎492-2115. Open in summer daily 9-11am.)

The **Skaha Bluffs,** southeast of town on Valley View Rd., have developed into a popular **rock-climbing** venue with pitches of varying difficulty. A resource for gear and advice is **Ray's Sports Den,** 215 Main St. They rent cross-country skis for $13 per day, and rock boots for $10, but not harnesses or other equipment. (☎493-1216. Open M-F 9:30am-6pm, Sa 9:30am-5pm, Su 10am-4pm.)

Heavy snowfalls make for excellent **skiing,** and **Apex Mountain Resort,** off an access road west of Penticton on Hwy. 3, has the best runs in the area. Apex has downhill, cross-country, and night **skiing** (W and F-Sa 4:30-9:30pm) on over 60 runs with a 2000 ft. drop, and a new half pipe and terrain park for boarders. (☎292-8222 or 877-777-2739, weather 492-2929 ext. 2000; www.apexresort.com. $38, ages 13-18 $32, ages 8-12 and 65-69 $25, under 7 or 70+ free. Ski $24 per day, snowboard $36.)

NELSON ☎250

Nelson is a little different from the other isolated 9000-person towns in the BC interior. While offering the same wide range of outdoor activities, the town of Nelson sports an off-beat attitude. The population of locals and seasonal transplants have made bongo drums and tofu accepted in these forested hills above Kootenay Lake, and businesses cater to the alternative rather than mainstream. Many find town a relaxation haven, but further mellowness awaits on the lake and slopes.

TRANSPORTATION

Nelson lies at the junction of **Hwy. 6** and **3A,** 624km southwest of Calgary, 454km southeast of Kamloops, and 657km east of Vancouver. From Nelson, Hwy. 3A heads 41km west to Castlegar. Hwy. 6 leads 65km south to the US border, where it becomes Washington Rte. 31, continuing 110 mi. south to Spokane.

Nelson

♠ **ACCOMMODATIONS**
Dancing Bear Hostel, 4
Duhamel Motel, 1
Nelson City Tourist Park, 2
Whitewater Ski Resort, 9

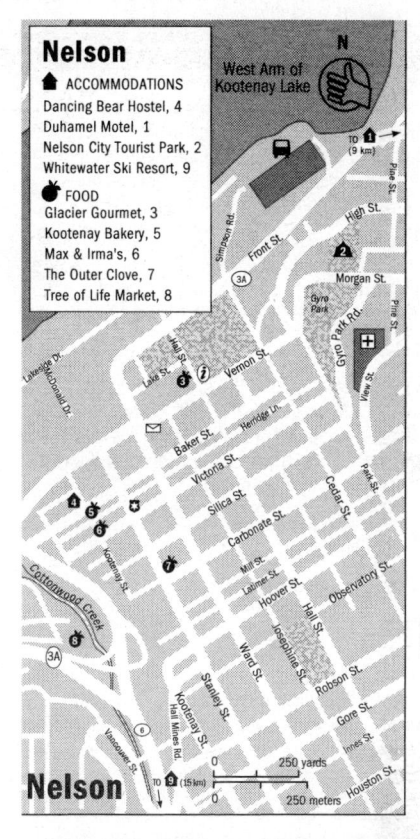

🍴 **FOOD**
Glacier Gourmet, 3
Kootenay Bakery, 5
Max & Irma's, 6
The Outer Clove, 7
Tree of Life Market, 8

Buses: Greyhound, 1112 Lakeside Dr. (☎ 352-3939), in the Chako-Mika Mall, runs buses to: **Vancouver** (12hr., 2 per day, $94); **Calgary, AB** (12hr., 2 per day, $85); **Banff, AB** (13½hr. with a 1-5am layover in Cranbrook, 1 per day, $70). Terminal open M-F 6am-8:30pm, Sa 6-11am and 4-8:30pm, Su 7:30-8:30am and 4:30-8:30pm.

Public Transportation: Nelson Transit Systems (☎ 352-8201) has 4 bus lines that cover the city and lake. $1-1.25. Runs M-F 7am-11:30pm, Sa-Su 8:30am-7:30pm.

Taxis: Glacier Cabs, (☎ 354-1111). $2 base, $2 per km in Nelson. 24hr.

Car Rental: Rent-a-Wreck, 524 Nelson Ave. (☎ 352-5122), in the Esso station. $38 per day, 12¢ per km after 200km; or $30 per day, 12¢ per km. Must have credit card.

🛈 PRACTICAL INFORMATION

Tourist Office: Visitor Information, 225 Hall St. (☎ 352-3433; www.discovernelson.com), provides an unusually good map of the city and surrounding area. Open July-Aug. daily 8:30am-8pm; Sept.-June M-F 8:30am-4:30pm.

Outdoor information is available at **West Kootenay Visitor Centre** (☎ 825-4723), in Kokanee Creek Provincial Park, 20km east of Nelson on Hwy. 3A. Helpful staff provides maps and trail info. Open June-Sept. Sa and Su 10am-4pm, July-Aug. daily 9am-9pm.

Equipment: The Sacred Ride, 213 Baker St. (☎ 354-3831) rents full suspension bikes for $35 per day, sells maps for $5, and offers free trail advice. Open M-Th, and Sa 9am-5:30pm, F 9am-6pm. **Gerick Cycle and Sports,** 702 Baker St. (☎ 354-4622). Rents bikes for $29 per day and cross-country ski packages for $15 per day. Open M-Th and Sa 9am-5:30pm, F 9am-9pm, Su 11am-4pm. In winter closed Su.

Internet Access: Nelson Library: 602 Stanley St. (☎ 352-6333). $2 per 30min. M, W, and F 1-8pm, Tu and Th 10am-6pm, Sa 11am-6pm. The **Dancing Bear Inn** (see below) charges $1 per 10min., and the **Flying Squirrel Hostel** (see below) has free access.

Laundromat: At the **Esso Station,** 524 Nelson St. (☎ 352-3534). Open Th-F 7am-10pm, Sa-W 7am-9:30pm. Wash $1.50, dry 25¢ per 10min.

Showers: Nelson City Tourist Park (see below). $2 for non-campers.

Police: 606 Stanley St. (☎ 352-2266). Next to the library.

Hospital: 3 View St. (☎ 352-3111). **Crisis line:** ☎ 352-3504. 24hr.

Emergency: Nelson does not have 911 service. **Ambulance:** ☎ 352-2112.

Post office: 514 Vernon St. (☎ 352-3538). Open M-F 8:30am-5pm. **Postal Code:** V1L 4E7.

ACCOMMODATIONS AND CAMPING

Dancing Bear Inn (HI), 171 Baker St. (☎352-7573). With an array of single bedrooms, polished wooden floors, and art on the walls, this hostel seems more like a B&B. Super-helpful staff. Laundry, kitchen, and Internet access $1 per 10min. No curfew. Check-in 4-10pm. Reception 7-11am. Reservations recommended June-Aug. $17, nonmembers $20, under 10 half-price. Private rooms $34-45, nonmembers $40-54.

Flying Squirrel Hostel, 198 Baker St. (☎352-7285 or 866-755-7433). More flamboyant than the Dancing Bear, this new hostel attracts outdoors-lovers. With Internet access, full kitchen, laundry, and free pickup from the bus station, they do it all. Reception 8am-noon and 4-9pm. Checkout by 11am. $17-20, private rooms from $39.

Kokanee Creek Provincial Park (☎825-4212; reservations 800-689-9025), 20km north of town on Hwy. 3A. Shaded, spacious sites with decent privacy are near the lake. Flush toilets, running water. Wheelchair accessible. 166 sites, $19.

Nelson City Tourist Park, on High St., is convenient for camping, backyard-style. Take Vernon St. to its eastern end, and follow signs. Flush toilets, water, showers. Wash $1, dry 50¢ for 30min. 40 sites, $15; electricity $18, with water $20.

FOOD AND NIGHTLIFE

Get basic groceries at **Extra Foods,** 708 Vernon St. (Open M-Sa 9am-9pm, Su 9am-6pm.) Fresh bread, vegan brownies, and organic goodies can be had from the **Kootenay Co-op and Bakery,** at 295 Baker St. (Bakery ☎352-2274. Open M-Sa 8am-6pm. Co-op ☎354-4077. Open M-Th and Sa 9:30am-6pm, F 9:30am-8pm.)

Baci's Bistro, 445 Baker St. (☎354-0303). Whet your appetite with the aromas of homemade Italian cooking filling the bistro; then satiate your food-lust with a big bowl of pasta made with your choice of sauce ($9-12) and a heavenly chocolate dessert ($4.50). Open M-F 11am-10pm, Sa-Su 11am-11pm.

Redfish Grill, 479 Baker St. (☎352-3456) has an eclectic menu with amazing food, all served alongside equally eclectic local artwork. Thai-influenced wraps start at $5.50 or, for the culinarily unadventurous, burgers run $6-8. Open daily 7am-1am.

The Outer Clove, 536 Stanley St. (☎354-1667). This "Garlic Cafe" puts garlic in everything from tapas ($4-8) to garlic ice cream ($2). For those with problems other than garlic breath, the vampire killer chili is only $7. Open M-Sa 11:30am-9pm.

Glacier Gourmet (☎354-4495), at the corner of Vernon St. and Hall St., has live music, with jazz and blues on F and Sa nights. The Gourmet accompanies its musical fare with filling, vegetarian-friendly meals (wraps and pita melts $6-7; pizzas $9-15). Open M 8:30am-7pm, Tu-Th and Su 8:30am-9pm, F 8:30am-11pm, Sa 10am-9pm.

Max and Irma's Kitchen, 515A Kootenay St. (☎352-2332), rescues quality 10 in. pizzas from a wood-fired oven ($10-13), and serves enticing sandwiches like croque monsieur for $8. Open Su-Th 11am-9pm, F-Sa 11am-10pm.

OUTDOOR ACTIVITIES

Bordering Nelson on the north, the watery **West Arm** seems huge, but it's just a tiny segment of enormous **Kootenay Lake.** Dolly varden, rainbow trout (up to 14kg according to local legend), and kokanee cruise the lake, while sturgeon up to 1.5m long inhabit the nearby **Kootenay River.** The best time to find the big ones is from Oct. to Feb., although most of the fish run about 15 lb. Licenses, bait, and a good place to begin are all at the **Balfour Dock,** 30min. north of town on Hwy. 3A.

HIKING
Some of the area's best hiking can be found in **Kokanee Glacier Provincial Park,** which is generally uncrowded because it's so hard to reach. Various entrances off Hwy. 3A north of Nelson are not regularly maintained; ask at the visitors center for details on these routes, or enter 19km north of town along bumpy Kokanee Creek Rd. For a complete list of trails, *Don't Waste Your Time in the West Kootenays*, is a trail guide published in 2000 by Voice in the Wilderness Press; available at the visitors center (see **Practical Information,** p. 291) and at bookstores.

- **Old Growth Trail** (2km, 1-2hr.) begins 12km up the Kokanee Creek Rd. from a trailhead on the left. Following the **Cedar Grove Loop,** this trail wanders through a cedar forest and offers views of the surrounding mountains and an old mining tramway. Easy.

- **Gibson Lake to Slocan Chief Cabin Trail** (10km round-trip, 3-4hr.) lies another 4m up Kokanee Creek Rd. at the Gibson Lake Trailhead. If you're parking a car there, wrap it with chicken wire to prevent damage from porcupines (more info at the West Kootenay visitors center). From trailhead, a 4km trail leads up and across the mountainside to **Kokanee Lake** and continues 3km to **Kaslo Lake** campground, which consists of 10 sites with pit toilets and good fishing. Another few kilometers along, the path reaches the 12-person **Slocan Chief cabin** below **Kokanee Glacier.** (Campgrounds $5. Cabin $15 per person or $30 for group.) Don't walk on glacier without a guide. Moderate.

- **Silver Spray Trail** (8km, several hours). On Hwy 31, take the Woodbury Creek turnoff 10km north of Ainsworth Hot Springs and drive 13km to the trailhead. This difficult trail passes through several avalanche areas and prime grizzly bear feeding areas en route to the Silver Spray Cabin (wood fireplace, sleeps 4-8) and the circa 1920s Violet mine and blacksmith shop. The views of the glacier are unbelievable. Strenuous.

HOT SPRINGS
Several kilometers northeast of Nelson, the **Ainsworth Hot Springs,** 3609 Hwy. 31, allows you to lounge or dip in a large soaking pool. If the heat doesn't soothe you, the high mineral content (highest of any hot springs in Canada) will work its healing magic. For a more natural spa experience, linger in the dark, humid caves at the springs' source. Then jump in the glacier-fed pool nearby for an invigorating jolt. (☎229-4212 or 800-668-1171. $7.50, all day $10.)

SKIING
In winter, the soft powder of **Whitewater Ski Resort,** 12km southeast of town off of Hwy. 6, draws skiers and boarders to 32 groomed runs, some of Canada's best bowls, and 1300 ft. vertical drop. Sporting an average snowfall of over 40 ft., Whitewater has over 12km of groomed cross-country trails. (☎354-4944 or 800-666-9420, snow report 352-7669; www.skiwhitewater.com. Lift tickets $37, ages 13-18 $28, ages 7-12 $21, under 7 free. Full package ski or snowboard rentals $25 per day.)

VALHALLA PROVINCIAL PARK ☎ 250

Valhalla stretches up from the crystal clear, trout-filled waters of Slocan Lake through a temperate rain forest of bewitching lushness to craggy alpine peaks. Once a homeland to the Sa-al-tkw't Indians, who left pictographs on the bluffs above the forest, the park is now largely given over to cougars, mountain goats, and golden eagles. Residents of nearby New Denver fought for years to have this treasure declared a protected park before their success in 1983. Much of the park is accessible only by boat, with the only road into the park leaving from the miniscule town of Slocan. Nine separate camping areas with bear caches and pit toilets are spread throughout the park to which no mechanized vehicles of any kind, including mountain bikes, are allowed. Dogs must be leashed and are only allowed in certain areas of the park; fires also are allowed only in designated areas and must be made with driftwood from the beaches. Many trails require expert-level route-finding skills; other trails offer moderate, clear paths through fields of brilliant green moss, over waterfalls, and past rock castles and crags.

ORIENTATION AND PRACTICAL INFORMATION

Valhalla lies on the west shore of Slocan Lake, 150km south of Revelstoke and 286km east of Kelowna. In the south, a bridge from **Slocan** provides access to southern trailheads, most at the end of long and bumpy forest roads. In the north, the town of **New Denver** provides food and shelter to weary wanderers as well as water taxi service to the northern trailheads (see Kingfisher Water Taxi, below). The two towns are linked by Hwy. 6, which runs north from Nelson. **New Denver,** way back in the 1940s, was the center of the Japanese internment camps set up by the Canadian government during WWII. The **Nikkei Internment Memorial Center,** located on the north end of town off Hwy 6. (follow the signs) has exhibits on the details behind the internment of nearly 20,000 Japanese-Canadians, many from the western region. Open May-Sept. daily 9am-5:30pm. $4, students and seniors $3.)

While several New Denver businesses provide a range of free informative brochures, the **visitors center** at the corner of 6th Ave. and Eldorado Ave. is the best source of information on the town itself; for **outdoor info,** visit the folks who led the crusade to preserve Valhalla as a national park, the **Valhalla Nature Center/Valhalla Wilderness Society,** 307 6th Ave. (☎358-2333. Open M-F 10am-5pm, Sa 11am-3pm.) If the office appears closed, knock anyway; someone working late may answer and provide you with their invaluable park trail guide ($4). To get to the park from New Denver, rent a canoe at **Sweet Dreams Guesthouse** ($45 per day or $160 per week; see **Accommodations,** below) or call **Kingfisher Water Taxi** (☎358-2334), which totes visitors from the dock for about $20. There is no 911 service for this area, including Valhalla park and New Denver. For emergencies call the **Police:** 407 Slocan Ave. (☎358-2222), south of 6th St. **Post office:** 219 6th Ave. (☎358-2611. Open M-F 9am-5pm, Sa noon-4pm.) **Postal Code:** V0G 1S0.

ACCOMMODATIONS AND FOOD

Those who don't wish to camp can stay at the **Sweet Dreams Guesthouse,** 702 Eldorado Ave. Take 6th Ave. toward the lake and turn left on Eldorado Ave. This B&B is located in a cozy country home with a beautiful view of the lake. Three-course dinners are available by reservation and run $13-19. (☎358-2415. Singles $45; doubles $65. Multiple-day rates are often available.) Another lodging option is the **Valhalla Inn,** on Hwy. 6 in town, which offers spare but spotless rooms just off the highway as well as a restaurant (entrees run $4-15) and a pub with $4 pints. (☎358-2228. Singles $55, doubles $60.) Convenient but unaesthetic camping is available at the municipal campground at **Centennial Park,** on the south side of town by the lakeshore between 3rd and 1st Ave. Forty small sites, most filled with RV toting boaters, cluster around showers and a boat launch. (Tents $13, on the water $14, electricity and water $16.) In Valhalla Park itself, several free sites are available.

Ann's Natural Foods, 309 6th St., has a small selection of groceries. (☎358-2552. Open M-F 9am-5:30pm, Sa 10am-4pm.) Meals await on 6th Ave., where the renowned **Appletree Cafe,** 210 6th Ave., holds court. The tiny cafe is home to a colorful local crowd, including the 90-year-old former mayor, who visits so regularly he has a permanently reserved table. The cafe promises "up to the minute gossip" and other essential small-town services including homemade soups ($3.50), and build-your-own $6-8 sandwiches. (☎358-2691. Open M-F 7am-4pm, Sa 11am-4pm.)

HIKING

Though an outdoor paradise, generally free of people, Valhalla requires certain precautionary measures of its explorers. First of all, most areas of the park require a $5 per day fee. The temperate rain forest of Valhalla is often wet, and hypothermia is a real concern, even in summer. Extra layers of warm clothing are a good idea. Be aware of the possibility of bear encounters. Most camping areas provide bear-proof food caches, but if none are available, bear-bagging supplies are necessary. Finally, remember that forest roads may be impassable as late as June due to snow. One popular activity, which arose in response to this problem, is to canoe along the lake's shore and camp near the beach.

- **Bannock Burn to Gimli Ridge** (4km, 2-3hr.). Turn off Hwy. 6 at Slocan City, cross the river and follow the gravel road 13km south. Turn right onto Bannock Burn Creek logging road and follow it to the parking lot. It is an unsurpassed hike with opportunities for world-class rock climbing. Camping is available along the trail. Moderate to strenuous.
- **Wee Sandy Creek Trail** (14.4km, day-long). The trail begins along the west shore of Slocan Lake with boat access only. An arduous trek along historic logging trails and through mountain goat and grizzly habitat. Near the end of the trail is a log shelter with a stove and fireplace, and a lake for fishing. Moderate to strenuous.
- **Evan's Creek Trail** (8km, 2-3hr.). Park on the Slocan City side of the Slocan River bridge, walk across, then turn right to walk 200m to the trailhead. The trail passes along the lakeshore and past moss-carpeted waterfalls. A cabin and tent pads are available at the creek, and ample fishing awaits at Cahill and Beatrice Lakes. Easy to moderate.

FERNIE ☎250

Those willing to travel the extra kilometer will be rewarded with the best snow around. A magnet for mountain bikers and snowboarders, Fernie combines the familiarity of small-town life with the breadth of outdoor activities found in Jasper and Banff. While not as familiar as Banff and Whistler, Fernie is increasingly attracting the attention of travel guides and snow-lovers. Summer-time Fernie offers everything you would expect from a city set in the Rockies: gorgeous hiking, superior mountain biking, and world-class trout fishing. Add to these a range of excellent, cheap hostels, and you have a treasure destined for discovery.

ORIENTATION AND PRACTICAL INFORMATION. Fernie is located on Hwy. 3 1hr. east of Cranbrook and 3½hr. southwest of Calgary. Local services cluster along Hwy. 3 and in downtown Fernie, 5km north of the ski resort. The **Visitors Center** is set beneath a wooden oil rig 1km east of town on Hwy. 3. (☎423-6868. Open July-Aug. daily 9am-7pm, Sept.-June M-F 9am-5pm.) **Greyhound**, 742 Hwy. 3 (☎423-6871), in the Park Place Lodge, runs two buses per day to **Vancouver** (17½hr., $90) and **Calgary** (6½hr., $42). **Fernie Transportation**, (☎423-9244 or 800-575-0405) runs two buses per day to **Calgary** (4hr., $50) and Cranbrook (1¼hr., $30) from Fernie and the Alpine Resort. **Kootenay Taxi** (☎423-4408) runs 24hr. and ferries powder-heads to the slopes in winter ($15 one-way). Fernie **lacks 911** service so in emergencies, contact an **ambulance** (☎800-461-9911). **Police:** 496 13th St. (☎423-4404). **Hospital:** The **Fernie District Hospital**, 1501 5th Ave. (☎423-4453). **Squeaky's Laundromat:** 1221 7th Ave. (☎423-6091), at 12th St. Wash $1, dry 25¢ per 5min. Open daily 8:30am-10:30pm. **Internet Access: Fernie Library**, 492 3rd Ave. offers access for $5 per hr. (☎423-4458. Open Tu-Th 11am-8pm, Sa-Su noon. Closed M, F, and Oct.-Apr. Su. **Raging Elk Hostel** has access for $1 per 10min. **Ski and See Adventure Lodge** offers free Internet access to guests. **Post office:** 491 3rd Ave. (☎423-7555). Open M-F 8:30am-5pm. **Postal Code:** V0B 1M0.

ACCOMMODATIONS AND FOOD. Ski and See Adventure Lodge, 301 2nd Ave. above the Grand Central Hotel is the latest addition to the Fernie travel scene. This new European-style hotel offers shared and private rooms, comfortable common areas, and a huge outdoor patio with a hot tub. (☎423-7367. Shared rooms $19, winter $30; private rooms $30, winter $60.) The **Raging Elk Hostel (HI),** 892 6th Ave., is a yellow and red converted motel providing dorm-style lodging and private rooms. In addition to the comfortable living quarters, it boasts a large common area, kitchen, laundry, **Internet access,** and a free pancake breakfast. Reservations are crucial during the December to April ski season. (☎423-6811. Reception daily 8-11am and 5-11pm. Summer $15, private bath $18; winter $18, nonmembers $22. Private rooms from $25 in summer and $60 in winter.) **Mount Fernie Provincial Park,** 3km south of town on Hwy. 3, offers 38 private and shaded sites as well as flush toilets and water. Find Rocky Mountain Original Coors and Pringles at **Overwaitea Foods** on 2nd Ave. (☎423-4607. Open Sa-Th 8am-8pm, F 8am-9pm.) **The Curry Bowl,** 931 7th Ave., offers "enlightened Asian cuisine" like curry ($8-12) and large bowls of noodles for $5. (☎423-2695. Open Tu-F 5-11pm, Sa-Su 4-11pm.) **The Arts Station,** 1st Ave. and 6th St., is a former train depot that acts as an gallery for local artists and serves homemade soups ($3) and sandwiches for $7. (☎423-4842. Open M-Sa 8am-4pm.) **Mug Shots Bistro,** 592 3rd Ave., is a small cafe serving up **Internet access** alongside its blueberry pancakes ($4.50), homemade sandwiches ($5.50-8), and $8 bag lunches. (☎423-8018. Open daily 7am-4pm.) Unwind after snowboarding at **The Grand Central Hotel,** 301 2nd Ave., with $4 pints, and Monday nights 15¢ wings. (☎423-3343. Open M-Sa noon-2am, Su noon-midnight.)

■ SKIING. The engine driving Fernie's expansion is the **Fernie Alpine Resort** and its 2500+ acres of feathery powder. With a 875cm/29 ft. annual snowfall, the Fernie Alpine Resort embarrasses the competition. Over 100 trails spread out across the Lizard Range, creating a winter wonderland of gullies, ravines, five alpine bowls, a terrain park, a vertical-drop, and tree-skiing. (☎423-4655, snow report 423-3555; www.skifernie.com. $54; students 18-24, ages 13-17, and 65+ $43; ages 6-12 $15.) **Fernie Sports,** 1191 7th Ave., on Hwy. 3, offers **ski and snowboard rental** packages for $22 and $25. (☎423-3611, www.fernie-esports.com. Open daily in winter 8:30am-6pm; summer M-F 10am-6pm, Sa 9am-5pm, Su 11am-4pm.)

■ OUTDOOR ACTIVITIES. The April thaw, while heralding the end of ski season, also uncovers Fernie's abundant hiking trails. Many trails leave from the Alpine Resort, where free maps are provided. The **Fernie Ridge Walk** (11 mi., at least 8hr.) begins in the parking lot of the ski resort and offers spectacular views of alpine meadows and jagged limestone peaks before returning to the valley floor. Cheaters can take the lift part way up the mountain in the summer ($8, bikes $3), but won't avoid the steep Snake Ridge or a 15m/50 ft. fixed-rope climb. 1000m/3300ft. gain. Strenuous. Fernie and the mountain resort offer varying trails. **The Guides Hut,** 671 2nd Ave., is happy to recommend equipment and trails, or rent front-suspension bikes. (☎423-3650 or 888-843-4885. Open Sa-Th 9:30am-5:30pm and F 9:30am-8pm; call for winter hours. $25 per day, $130 per week.) The **Bike Base,** 432 2nd Ave., and neighboring **Ski Base,** rent trade-ins at great prices. (☎423-6464. Open Sa-Th 9:30am-5:30pm, F 9am-8pm. Front-suspension $30 per day.) The Elk river and its tributaries provide 180km of world-class **fly-fishing** for bulltrout and cut-throat. Follow the crowd and fish along Hwy. 3, or head off the beaten path and farther along the river. A good start, the **Kootenay Fly Shop and Guiding Company,** 821 7th Ave., rents rods for $20 per day and sells maps and books for $10-17. (☎877-7423-4483. Open M-Sa 8:30am-5:30pm; July-Aug. also open Su.)

REVELSTOKE ☎250

In the 19th century, Revelstoke was a town straight out of an old western, complete with dust-encrusted misers maiming one another amid the gold-laden Selkirk and Kootenay Mountains. Located on both the Columbia River and the Canadian Pacific Railway, the town was born as a transfer station for boats and trains. Although still a stopover for travelers to the Rockies, Revelstoke is finally coming into its own. Excellent hostels, free outdoor entertainment in the town center and extensive outdoor pursuits make Revelstoke a particularly welcoming destination.

ORIENTATION AND PRACTICAL INFORMATION

Revelstoke is on the Trans-Canada Hwy. (Hwy. 1), 285km west of Banff, 210km east of Kamloops, and 565km east of Vancouver. The town is easily navigated on foot or by bike as evidenced by the lack of traffic and abundance of parking spaces downtown. **Mount Revelstoke National Park** lies just out of town on Hwy. 1.

Buses: Greyhounds depart from 1899 Fraser Dr. (☎837-5874). To get there, at the lights on Hwy. 1, turn away from the city center and take your first left. Open M-Sa 8am-7pm, Su 11am-1pm and 3-5pm. To **Calgary, AB** (6hr., 4 per day, $57); **Vancouver** (8-10hr., 5 per day, $69); and **Salmon Arm, BC** (1½hr., 5 per day, $17).

R Taxi: ☎837-4000.

Visitors Info: Visitors Center (☎837-3522), junction of Hwy. 1 and Hwy. 23 N. Open daily June-Aug. 9am-7pm; Sept.-May 9am-5pm. **Parks Canada** (☎837-7500), at Boyle Ave. and 3rd St. Open M-F 8:30am-noon and 1-4:30pm.

Bike Rental: High Country Cycle and Sports, 118 Mackenzie Ave. (☎814-0090; fax 814-0091). $7-8 per hr., $35-40 per day. Open 9:30am-5:30pm.

Laundry: Selkirk Laundromat, on 100 Boyle Ave. $5 per load. Open Oct.-Feb. 9am-8pm, otherwise daily 9am-5pm.

Emergency: ☎911. **Police:** 320 Wilson St. (☎837-5255).

Ambulance: ☎837-5885.

Hospital: Queen Victoria Hospital, 6622 Newlands Rd. (☎837-2131).

Internet Access: Free at the **Public Library,** 600 Campbell Ave. (☎837-5095; open Tu and F 1-8pm, W and Sa 10am-4pm, Th 1-5pm); **Bertz Outdoor Equipment and Cafe** (see **Food,** p. 298). $4 for 30min., $7 per hr.

Post Office: 307 W 3rd St. (☎837-3228). Open M-F 8:30am-5pm. **Postal Code:** V0E 2S0.

ACCOMMODATIONS AND CAMPING

Revelstoke Traveller's Hostel and Guest House (HI), 400 2nd St. W (☎888-663-8825), has an office across the street at 403 2nd St. W. This house has only 2-4 beds in each of its 26 clean rooms. Several kitchens, full bathrooms, and living room with TV. Free Internet access and 24hr. check-in. Pickup from the bus station. In winter, **$29 buys a bed *and* a lift ticket.** June to mid-Sept. $17, otherwise $15; nonmembers $19; singles $23-30; private rooms available. Tent sites $12-15, includes access to utilities.

Daniel's Guest House, 313 First St. E (☎837-5530), a 2min. walk from downtown. A home-turned-hostel, the comfortable beds, couch-filled common room, and porch make the place feel, well, homey. Kitchen, laundry ($1.50), satellite TV, 2 bathrooms, and free pickup from the bus station. 24hr. check-in. 20 beds in single-sex 6-person dorms and private rooms. Dorms $17; doubles $34; private rooms $30. HI discount; kids free.

Williamson's Lake Campground, 1818 Williamson Lake Rd. (☎837-5512 or 888-676-2267), 5km southeast of town on Airport Way. Farther from the hwy. than competitors, this simple ground is peacefully set on a popular swimming hole. Laundry, hot showers, and general store. Closed Nov. to mid-Apr. 41 sites, $14.50; 20 full hookups $18.

FOOD

The town's local market is **Cooper's Supermarket,** 555 Victoria St. (☎837-4372. Open daily 8am-9pm. For an option on the east side of town try **Southside Grocery,** 900 4th St. (☎837-3517. Open daily 9am-9pm.)

Chalet Deli and Bakery, 555 Victoria St. (☎837-5552), across the parking lot from Cooper's. Your best bet for lunch and baked goods. Offers a hot deli, pizza by the slice ($2.50), and sandwiches on fresh bread ($4.50). Open M-Sa 6am-6pm.

The Ol' Frontier Family Restaurant, 122 N Hwy. 23 (☎873-5119), at Hwy. 1 and 23 N, next to the visitors center. Serves ¼ lb. burger with the works and the "Ain't No Bull" mushroom-and-peppers veggie burger, each for $6. Open daily 5am-10pm.

Bertz Outdoor Equipment and Cafe, 217 Mackenzie Ave. (☎837-6575), will supply you with food, outdoor equipment, and advice on local climbing and mountaineering. Large bagel sandwiches ($4.50). See **Internet access,** above. Open in summer M-F 8am-5pm, Sa 9am-4pm, Su 10am-4pm; winter M-F 8am-5pm.

◉ ⚑ SIGHTS AND OUTDOOR ACTIVITIES

SIGHTS. Revelstoke Railway Museum, 719 W Track St., off Victoria Rd., tells of the construction of the Trans-Canada line, which was completed in 1885. Other exhibits include a real steam engine and a full passenger car. *(☎877-837-6060. In summer open daily 9am-8pm; spring and fall M-F 9am-5pm; winter M-F 1-5pm. $6, seniors 60+ $5, ages 7-16 $3, under 7 free.)* The mechanical marvels of the **Revelstoke Dam,** 5km north of Hwy. 1 on Hwy. 23, are illustrated in a free talking-wand tour. *(☎837-6515 or 837-6211. Open May to mid-June and mid-Sept. to mid-Oct. daily 9am-5pm, mid-June to mid-Sept. 8am-8pm. Wheelchair accessible.)*

SUMMER SPORTS. Canyon Hot Springs, between Mt. Revelstoke National Park and Glacier National Park on Hwy. 1, sports two spring-fed pools that simmer at 26°C and 40°C. (☎837-2420. May-June and Sept. 9am-9pm; July and Aug. 9am-10pm. $6.50, seniors and under 14 $5.50, under 4 free.) The neighboring **Apex River,** runs 2hr. and 4hr. whitewater rafting tours on the Illecillewaet's Class II-III rapids. (☎837-6376 or 888-232-6666. Open daily 9am-6pm. May-Sept. 2hr. $42, under 17 $32; 4hr. $69; 17% HI discount.) The 140 bolted routes on Begbie Bluffs offer exceptional **sport climbing.** *(From the small parking area almost 9km down 23 South from Hwy. 1, the bluffs are a 10min. walk; take the left fork.)* Rogers Pass and all the surrounding peaks offer a lifetime of opportunity to hone **mountaineering** skills year-round.

WINTER SPORTS. Winter in Revelstoke brings excellent **downhill skiing. Powder Springs Resort** (☎800-991-4455), is only 5km outside town and maintains one chairlift and 21 trails (2000 ft. vertical drop) on the bottom third of Mt. MacKenzie. Tickets cost $28-32, but inquire about money-saving accommodation packages (see **Revelstoke Traveller's Hostel and Guest House,** p. 297). Local companies offer heli-skiing and cat-skiing on the upper two-thirds of this and other local mountains. Ask at the Visitors Center for more information and where the cheapest equipment rentals can be found. Parks Canada (see **Practical Information,** p. 297) offers excellent advice on area nordic trails and world-class backcountry skiing.

MT. REVELSTOKE NATIONAL PARK. Adjacent to town, Mt. Revelstoke National Park furnishes a quick and satisfying nature fix with its astounding scenery. It is a favorite of mountain bikers and hikers. **Summit Cycle Tours** drives customers to the summit of Mt. Revelstoke and provides bicycles and a guided tour on the two-hour, 27km descent. *(☎888-700-3444. $54, under 16 $49; group discounts, 10% HI discount.)* There are two **back-country campgrounds** in the park (permit $6); get details from the **Revelstoke Parks Canada** office or the **Rogers Pass** visitors center (see p. 299). For hiking, two boardwalks off Hwy. 1 on the east side of the park access the trails. **Skunk Cabbage Trail** (1.2km, 30min.), leads through acres of stinking perfection: skunk cabbage plants tower at heights of over 1.5m. **Giant Cedars Trail** (500m, 15min.), has majestic trees over 600 years old growing around bubbling brooks. **Meadows in the Sky Parkway** (Summit Rd.) branches off Hwy. 1 about 1.5km east of town, leading to a 1km hike up Mt. Revelstoke to subalpine meadows. Shuttle available (summer only, 10am-4:20pm), wheelchair accessible.

GLACIER NATIONAL PARK ☎ 250

This aptly named national park is home to over 400 monolithic ice flows covering one-tenth of its 1350-square-kilometer area. The jagged peaks and steep, narrow valleys of the Columbia Range not only make for breathtaking scenery but also prevent development in the park. An inland rain (although it feels more like snow) forest, Glacier receives significant precipitation every other day in the summer, but the clouds of mist that encircle the peaks and blanket the valleys only add to the park's astonishing beauty. In late summer, brilliant explosions of mountain wildflowers offset the deep green of the forests. Avoid exploring the park in winter, as extreme winter conditions and avalanches could knock the unaware flat. Roger's Pass itself has quite a history, as it was the last, great obstacle overcome by the Canadian Pacific Railroad in 1882.

ORIENTATION AND PRACTICAL INFORMATION. Glacier lies 350km west of Calgary and 723km east of Vancouver. **Greyhound buses** make one trip from Revelstoke. (☎837-5874. $14.70, 1 hr.) For details on the park, including great trail suggestions, talk to the Parks Canada staff or buy a copy of *Footloose in the Columbias* ($2) at the **Roger's Pass Information Center,** on the highway in Glacier. (☎814-5232. Open daily mid-June to mid-Sept. 8am-7pm; mid-Nov. to Apr. 7am-5pm; May to early June and late Sept. to early Nov. 9am-5pm.) Daily **park passes** cost $4, ages 65+ $3, 6-16 $2, group of 2-7 $10 (see p. 37). For more info about Glacier, write to the Superintendent, P.O. Box 350, Revelstoke, BC V0E 2S0, or call 837-7500. In an **emergency,** call the **Park Warden Office.** (☎837-7500. Open daily 7am-5pm; winter hours vary; 24hr. during avalanche control periods.)

CAMPING. There are two campgrounds in Glacier: **Illecillewaet** (ill-uh-SILL-uh-way-et), 3½km west of Rogers Pass (wheelchair accessible, 60 sites open mid-June to early Oct.), and **Loop Brook** (20 sites), another 3km west on Hwy. 1 (open July-Sept.). Both offer toilets, kitchen shelters with cook stoves, and firewood. Sites $13. Backcountry campers must purchase a **backcountry pass** ($6 per day) from the Parks Canada office in Revelstoke (☎837-7500) or from the Rogers Pass Information Center. Food is limited in the park; stock up in **Golden** or **Revelstoke.**

OUTDOOR ACTIVITIES. Biking and **fishing** in Glacier are prohibited. **Backcountry skiing** at Roger's Pass and Balu Pass is reputed to be world-class. Contact the Roger's Pass Information Center for registration and info on areas and avalanche conditions. Glacier also boasts the **Nakimu Caves,** an extensive limestone wonderland open only to experienced cavers. Access to the caves is granted to 6-12 people per week by a lottery system; interested parties need to apply to the park superintendent (see **Orientation and Practical Info,** above) by early summer or hope for an empty spot at the last minute (not recommended). Traveling the caves, located off the Balu Pass Trail near the info center, is physically demanding, and guides are recommended ($20 per person; guides around $150 per group).

HIKING. More than 140km of rough, often steep trails lead from the highway, inviting mountaineers to penetrate the near-impenetrable. Eight popular hiking trails begin at the Illecillewaet campground.

> **Meeting of the Waters Trail** (2km one-way). A gentle hike that leads to the impressive confluence of the Illecillewaet and Asulkan Rivers.
>
> **Avalanche Crest Trail** (8.5km round-trip, 6hr.), offers spectacular views of Roger's Pass, Hermit Range, and Illecillewaet River Valley. The treeless slopes below the crest testify to the destructive power of winter snowslides and endanger the highway. 995m gain.
>
> **Balu Pass Trail** (10km round-trip, 4hr.). Trailhead is at the west edge of Rogers Centre parking lot, near Roger's Pass info station. The Ursus Major and Ursus Minor peaks provide the best chance of seeing wildlife. (*Balu* is Inuit for bear, while *Ursus* is Latin for it.) This trail is prime bear habitat; check with park wardens before embarking.

Copperstain Trail (16km, 6hr.). Beaver River Trailhead, 10km east of the Glacier Park Lodge uphill through alpine meadows. From early July to late August, the park staff run sporadic interpretive hikes at 8:30am. Contact the Visitors Center for details.

YOHO NATIONAL PARK ☎ 250

A Cree expression for awe and wonder, Yoho is the perfect name for this small, superlative park. It sports some of the most engaging names in the Rockies, such as Kicking Horse Pass, named after Captain John Hector who, struggling to find a mountain pass for the Canadian Pacific Railroad, was kicked in the chest by his horse. Driving down Yoho's narrow pass on Hwy. 1, visitors can see evidence of geological forces: massive bent and tilted sedimentary rock layers exposed in sharply eroded cliff faces, and natural rock bridges formed by water carving away the stone. Beneath these rock walls, Yoho overflows with natural attractions, including the largest waterfall in the Rockies—Takakkaw Falls—and the most illuminating discovery—500-million-year-old fossils—known to paleontologists.

■🗗 **ORIENTATION AND PRACTICAL INFORMATION.** Yoho runs on Mountain Time, one hour ahead of Pacific Time. The park lies on the Trans-Canada Hwy. (Hwy. 1), next to Banff National Park. Within Yoho, the town of **Field**, is 27km west of Lake Louise on Hwy. 1. **Greyhound** (☎800-661-8747), stops for travelers waving their arms on the hwy. at the Field junction as long as they call first. **Hostelling International** runs a shuttle connecting hostels in Yoho, Banff, and Jasper National Parks and Calgary ($8-65). The **Visitors Center** in Field is on Hwy. 1. (☎343-6783. Open daily in summer 8am-7pm; spring and fall 9am-5pm; winter 9am-4pm.) **Bike rentals:** see **Equipment Rental** for Banff. **Park passes:** $5, senior $4, child $2.50, groups $10. (Valid for Glacier and Revelstoke.) In case of **emergency**, call 911 in the Field area; the **Park Warden Office** (☎403-762-4506, 24hr.; 762-1473 for non-emergencies); or the **RCMP** (☎344-2221) in nearby Golden. **Post Office:** 312 Stephen Ave. (☎343-6365. Open M-F 8:30am-4:30pm.) **Postal Code:** V0A 1G0.

🏠🗗 **ACCOMMODATIONS AND CAMPING.** With one of the best locations of all the Rocky Mountain hostels, the ■**Whiskey Jack Hostel (HI),** 13km off the Trans-Canada on the Yoho Valley Rd., is the best indoor place to stay while taking in Yoho's sights. The hostel offers a kitchen, nightly campfires, indoor plumbing, propane light, easy access to Yoho's best high-country trails, and the splendor of the Takakkaw Falls right from the front porch. Reserve through the Banff Hostel. (☎403-762-4122. Open mid-June to mid-Oct. $14, nonmembers $18; see p. 357.)

The five official **frontcountry campgrounds** offer a total of 330 sites, all easily accessible from the highway. All sites are first come, first served, and only Monarch and Kicking Horse fill up regularly in summer. ■**Takakkaw Falls Campground,** is situated beneath mountains, glaciers, and the magnificent falls 14km up curvy Yoho Valley Rd. It offers only pump water and pit toilets, and campers must park in the Falls lot and haul their gear 650m to the peaceful sites. (Open late June until the snow flies. 35 sites, $13.) **Hoodoo Creek,** on the west end of the park, has kitchen shelters, running hot water, flush toilets, a nearby river, and a playground. (Open mid-May to early Sept. 30 sites, $13.) It lies just across the Trans-Canada Hwy. from **Chancellor Peak,** which has pump water and pit toilets. (Open late May to Sept. 58 sites, $13.) **Monarch Campground** sits at the junction of Yoho Valley Rd. and Hwy. 1. (Open late June to early Sept. 46 sites and 10 walk-ins, $13.) **Kicking Horse,** another km up Yoho Valley Rd., has hot showers, toilets, and is wheelchair accessible. (Open mid-May to mid-Oct. 86 sites, $18.) Reserve one of two backcountry **alpine huts** through the Alpine Club of Canada. (☎403-678-3200. $16.) The group campground at splendid **Lake O'Hara,** in the east end of the park, can only be reached by a 13km trail or on a park-operated bus. (Bus reservations ☎343-6433, up to 3 months in advance. Round-trip $12. Permit required for camping.)

◐ **FOOD.** The most convenient food stop in Yoho, and potentially a sit-all-day-stop, is the ⍟**Truffle Pigs Cafe and General Store,** on Stephen Ave. in Field. Basic foodstuffs, microbrews, wine, camping supplies, and local crafts line the walls, and the friendly owners push home-made food, including sandwiches ($4.25), breakfast ($4.50-7), and an eclectic, sophisticated dinner menu. (☎343-6462. Meals $8-15. Has only **ATM** in the area. Open daily 8am-10pm; winter M-Sa 10am-7pm.)

⚡ **OUTDOOR ACTIVITIES.** The Great Divide is both the boundary between Alberta and BC as well as between the Atlantic and Pacific watersheds. Here a stream forks with one arm flowing 1500km to the Pacific Ocean, and the other flowing 2500km to the Atlantic via Hudson's Bay. It is also the site of the **Burgess Shale,** a layer of sedimentary rock containing the world's most important animal fossils, imprints of the insect-like, soft-bodied organisms that inhabited the world's oceans prior to an intense burst of evolution known as the **Cambrian Explosion.** Discovered in 1909, the unexpected complexity of these 505-million-year-old specimens changed the way paleontologists thought about evolution. Larger, clumsier animals known as humans have since successfully lobbied to protect the shale from excessive tourism. Educational hikes led by the **Yoho-Burgess Shale Foundation** (☎800-343-3006), are the only way to see it. A full-day, 20km hike costs $45, under 12 $25. A steep 6km loop to the equally old and trilobite-packed **Mt. Stephen Fossil Beds** runs $25. (July to mid-Sept. only. Reservations required.) For easier sightseeing, follow the 14km of the Yoho Valley Rd. to views of the **Takakkaw Falls,** Yoho's most splendid waterfall, and the highest in the Canadian Rockies.

HIKING. The park's six **backcountry campgrounds** and 400km of trail make for an intense wilderness experience. Before setting out, pick up **camping permits** ($6 per person per day), maps, and the free *Backcountry Guide to Yoho National Park* at the visitors center. The park's finest terrain is in the Yoho Valley and is accessible only after the snow melts in mid- to late summer.

- **Wapta Falls** (4.8km round-trip). The trailhead is not marked on Hwy. 1 for westbound traffic as there is no left turn lane. Continue 3km to the west entrance of the park, turn around, and come back east. Highlights include seeing Kicking Horse River drop 30m.
- **Mt. Hunter Lookout to Upper Lookout** (12.8km). Provides an excellent view of the Kicking Horse and Beaverfoot valleys.
- **Emerald Triangle** (21.5km round-trip). The route travels through the Yoho Pass (see *Backcountry Guide*) to the Wapta Highline trail, Burgess Pass, and back to the start.
- **Iceline Trail** (via Little Yoho 19.8km, via Celeste Lake 17km). Starts at the hostel. Takes hikers through forests of alder, spruce, and fir and passes the striated rock and icy pools of Emerald Glacier.

KOOTENAY NATIONAL PARK ☎ 250/453

Kootenay National Park hangs off the Continental Divide on the southeast edge of British Columbia, bordering Alberta. Many visitors travel through Kootenay to get to or from Banff National Park on the majestic Banff-Windermere Hwy. (Hwy. 93), the first road across the Canadian Rockies. The federal government built the road in 1920 in exchange for the 8km of land on either side that now constitutes the park. Kootenay's biggest attractions is its lack of people: unlike Banff and Jasper, Kootenay has no development at all. The only civilization is Radium Hot Springs, on the park's western border. Instead, its stately conifers, alpine meadows, and pristine peaks hide in Banff's shadow, allowing travelers to experience the true solitude of the Canadian Rockies while still in a national park.

ORIENTATION AND PRACTICAL INFORMATION

Kootenay lies southwest of Banff and Yoho National Parks. **Hwy. 93** runs through the park from the **Trans-Canada Hwy.** in Banff to **Radium Hot Springs** (see **Hot Springs**, p. 303) at the southwest edge of the park, where it joins **Hwy. 95**. One **Greyhound bus** per day stops at the Esso station, 7507 W Main St. (☎347-9726. Open daily 7am-11pm.), at the junction of Hwy. 93 and Hwy. 95 in Radium Hot Springs on the way to Banff (2 hr., $22) and Calgary (3½ hr., $39). The **park information center** and **Tourism BC Info Centre** are both located at 7556 Main St. W in Radium. They supply free maps and the **backcountry hiking guide**. (☎347-9505. Open daily late May to late June 9:30am-4:30pm, July to early Sept. 9am-7pm.) The **Kootenay Park Lodge** operates another visitors center 63km north of Radium. (☎403-762-9196. Open July-Aug. 9am-8pm; reduced hours in June and early Sept.) The **Park Administration Office,** on the access road to Redstreak Campground, dispenses the backcountry hiking guide and is open in winter. (☎347-9615. Open M-F 8am-noon and 1-4pm.) **Ambulance:** ☎342-2055. **Emergency:** call the Banff Park Warden ☎403-762-4506 or call the **police** in either Invermere (☎342-9292) or in Radium Hot Springs (☎347-9393). **Hospital: Windermere District Hospital,** 850 10th Ave. (☎342-9201), in Invermere, 15km south of Radium on Hwy. 95. **Post office:** On Radium Blvd in Radium Hot Springs. (☎347-9460. Open M-F 9am-5pm.) **Postal Code:** V0A 1M0.

ACCOMMODATIONS AND FOOD

The **Misty River Lodge (HI),** 5036 Hwy. 93, is the first left exiting the park's West Gate. B&B upstairs ($69-79, 10% HI discount), dorms downstairs (☎347-9912. Dorms $16, nonmembers $21; private room with bath $42, nonmembers $65. Bike rental for $10 per day.) Downtown, Radium features over 30 other motels, with high-season doubles starting at $40. The park's only serviced campground is **Redstreak,** on the access road that departs Hwy. 95 near the south end of Radium Hot Springs, which boasts 50 fully-serviced sites, 38 with electricity only. Toilets, showers, firewood, and playgrounds. Arrive early to secure a spot. (Open mid-May through Sept. $17, full hookups $22.) **McLeod Meadows,** 27km north of the West Gate entrance on Hwy. 93, offers more solitude and wooded sites on the banks of the very blue Kootenay River, as well as access to hiking trails. (Open mid-May to mid-Sept. 98 sites. $13.) **Marble Canyon,** 87km north of the West Gate entrance, also provides more privacy with flush toilets. (Open June through Sept. 61 unserviced sites, $13.) From September to May, snag one of seven free winter sites at the **Dolly Varden** picnic area, 36km north of the West Gate entrance, which boasts free firewood, water, toilets, and a shelter. Ask at the visitors centers for details on **Crooks Meadow,** which is available for groups (75 people max.), and cheap ($8), unserviced camping in the nearby Invermere Forest District.

There is little affordable food in Kootenay, with the exception of a few basic staples at the **Kootenay Park Lodge.** Radium supports a few inexpensive eateries on Main St. The best selection of groceries is at **Mountainside Market,** 7546 Main St. E. (☎347-9600. Open M-Sa 9am-9pm, Su 9am-8pm.)

OUTDOOR ACTIVITIES

The 95km **Banff-Windermere Highway (Hwy. 93)** forms the sinuous backbone of Kootenay. Stretching from Radium Hot Springs to Banff, the highway follows the Kootenay and Vermilion Rivers, passing views of glacier-enclosed peaks, dense stands of virgin forest, and green, glacier-fed rivers. The wild landscape of the Kootenay River Valley remains unblemished but for the ribbon of road.

HOT SPRINGS

The park's main attraction is **Radium Hot Springs,** named after the radioactive element detected there in trace quantities. The crowded complex is responsible for the traffic and towel-toting tourists just inside the West Gate. Natural mineral waters fill two swimming pools—a hot one for soaking at 40°C (open 9am-11pm) and a cooler one for swimming at 27 °C (open noon-9pm). The hot pool is wheelchair accessible. (☎347-9485. Single entry $6, ages 3-17 and 65+ $5, family $17.50; winter $5, children and seniors $4.50, family $15. Lockers 25¢, towel rental $1.25, swimsuit rental $1.50.) The **Lussier Hot Springs** in Whiteswan Lake Provincial Park offer a more natural alternative to Radium's lifeguards and ice cream vendors. The springs flow directly from the riverbank into the Lussier River, and piled-up rocks form shallow pools that trap the water at varying temperatures. To find this diamond in the rough, turn onto the rough dirt logging road 66km south of Radium and follow it for 17km.

HIKING

The **Rockwall Trail** in the north of the park is the most popular backcountry area in Kootenay. All **backcountry** campers must stop at a visitors center (See **Orientation and Practical Info,** p. 302) for the hiking guide, which has maps, trail descriptions, and topographical profiles, as well as a mandatory **wilderness pass.** ($6 per person per night, $42 per season.) A number of shorter trails lead right off Hwy 93 about 15km from the Banff border. Two fire roads, plus all of Hwy. 93, are open for **mountain biking,** but Kootenay lacks the extensive trail systems of its larger siblings. Icy water and rock flour from glaciers make for lousy fishing.

- **Marble Canyon Trail** (750m, 15min.). Many tourists enjoy this path which traverses a deep limestone gorge cut by Tokumm Creek before ending at roaring falls.
- **Paint Pots Trail** (1.6km, 30min.). 3.2km south of Marble Canyon on Hwy. 93. This partially wheelchair-accessible trail leads to ochre springs rich in iron oxide. Tourist-heavy.
- **Stanley Glacier Trail** (5.5km, 4hr.). Starts 3.5km from the Banff entrance and leads into a glacier-gouged valley, ending 1.6km from the foot of Stanley Glacier. One of the hot springs' most astounding and therapeutic powers is their ability to suck travelers out of the woods, leaving Kootenay's many longer hiking trails uncrowded. Moderately difficult and considered the "best dayhike in the park."
- **Kindersley Pass** (16.5km). The 2 trailheads at either end of the route, Sinclair Creek and Kindersley Pass, are less than 1km apart on Hwy. 93, about 10km inside the West Gate entrance. Trail climbs more than 1000m. to views of the Columbia River Valley in the west and the crest of the Rockies in the east.

NORTHERN BRITISH COLUMBIA

Northern BC remains among the most remote and sparsely inhabited regions of North America. Averaging one person per 15 sq. km, the land's loneliness and sheer physical beauty are overwhelming. Native peoples have lived here for thousands of years, adapting their lifestyles and culture to patterns of animal migration and the uncompromising climate. White settlers began migrating West in the early 19th century, attracted by the wealth of natural resources. While furs were lucrative, it wasn't until several gold rushes hit, that stampedes rushed in to settle permanently. Since then, the lumber and mining industries have brought a steady flow eager to extract the wealth of the land. Despite some telltale signs of logging and mining, the land remains mainly unspoiled. Unfortunately the area is often blown through by travelers hell bent on Alaska. Their loss; the stark mountains, yawning canyons, roaring rivers and clear lakes are left all that more pristine for those who will stop to appreciate them.

ALONG HWY. 20: CHILCOTIN HWY.

WILLIAMS LAKE TO BELLA COOLA   ☎ 250

The allure of the Chilcotin Hwy. lies not in its lackluster endpoint of Bella Coola but in the rugged and scenic lands along the 457km highway (5-7hr. drive). Most of the drive is smooth sailing other than the unforgettable "hill"—the guardrail-less obstacle of 57km of gravel (see below). Leaving Williams Lake, the Chilcotin Hwy. heads west across the **Fraser River** and climbs briefly before flattening out through forests and pastures dotted with cattle ranches. Warning to unsuspecting travelers: cattle at large. Watch for them on roads to avoid unplanned barbecues.

    Alexis Creek (Km 110) **Nimpo Lake** (Km 300), and **Anahim** (Km 305) are stops with gas, cafe, lodging, and a general store. **Bull Canyon Provincial Park,** 8km past Alexis Creek, features fishing on the Chilcotin River as well as two dozen tent sites with pit toilets ($12). Lakeside resort turn-offs are sprinkled along the highway with a concentration worth visiting in **Puntzi Lake.** The best meal can be consumed in **Nimpo Lake** at the **Chilcotin's Gate.** (☎ 742-3720, Burgers $7-8, sandwich and fries $7, steak dinner $13. Open daily June-Sept. 6am-9pm; winter 7am-7pm.)

    Low-priced convenient camping is across the highway at **Vagabond RVs** but bring earplugs to sleep through the early morning take-offs of floatplanes. (Tent $10, RV $15, free shower, coin laundry.) **Nimpo Towing** aids the Chilcotin-traveler in need (☎ 742-3484, M-Sa 8am-6pm) or feeds the hungered traveler at the bakery and cafe (open M-Sa 6am-6pm). **Chilko River Expeditions** runs **rafting** expeditions along the Chilcotin and Chilko Rivers from Williams Lake lodging. (☎ 354-2056 or 877-271-7626. $100 for day trip.)

PUNTZI LAKE

A 5km turn-off along a gravel road at Chilanko Forks (Km 175) leads to the 9km long **Puntzi Lake,** surrounded by several affordable resort options. Activities include fishing for kokanee and rainbow trout and watching white pelicans in summer. Smiling owners dole out camp sites, cabins, and canoe rentals at **Puntzi Lake Resort** (☎ 481-1176 or 800-578-6804; cabins $45-85; sites $15, full hookups $17-19), **Barney's Lakeside Resort** (☎ 481-1100; cabins $40 for 2, $5 each additional person; sites $15), and **Jack & Faye's Place** (☎ 481-1169; cabins $50 for 2; extra adults $7.50; extra children $5.) Each has its specialty: custom-fit cabins at Puntzi Lake, hopping campground at Barney's Lakeside, and cream of the crop cabins with private baths and TV/VCR at Jack & Faye's.

PARKS

South of the Chilcotin Hwy. **Tsylos** (sigh-LOSS) **Provincial Park,** boasts Canada's first grizzly bear refuge, the glacier-fed, trout- and salmon-rich Lake Chilko. To reach the **Gwa da Ts'ih campground** on the north side of the park, turn off at Tatla Lake (Km 220), and drive 63km on washboard gravel roads (4-6hr. from Williams Lake). The highway enters the southern portion of **Tweedsmuir Provincial Park** (☎ 398-4414) at Heckman's Pass, 360km west of Williams Lake. The park protects the Atnarko River, Hunlen Falls, Monarch Glacier, and the colorfully streaked shield volcanoes of the Rainbow Mountains. Unfortunately, road-trippers' introduction to the park is 21km of gravel hell, known simply as "The Hill": a one-lane, no-barrier nightmare, with steep grades and sharp switchbacks descending travelers through undeniably spectacular views of the valley below (road conditions ☎ 900-565-4997). For decades, Hwy. 20 ended at **Anahim Lake,** 315km west of Williams Lake. In 1955, frustrated by government inaction, locals got two bulldozers, borrowed money, and finished the job themselves, earning the route its second name, the "Freedom Highway." After the hill, the highway is paved again for its most scenic 75km, following the **Bella Coola River** into town along the Hwy. 20 corridor through the rest of Tweedsmuir Park and into Bella Coola. Perhaps the biggest thing happening in Tweedsmuir is the terminus of the 25- to 30-day **Alexander Mackenzie Heritage Trail,** reserved for those hikers beyond hard-core and off the deep end. Its 420km stretch from **Blackwater River,** just west of Quesnel, across western British Columbia to **Burnt Creek Bridge** on Hwy. 20, traces the final leg of Mackenzie's 1793 journey across Canada to the West Coast. Mackenzie reached the Pacific more than a decade before Lewis and Clark, although the Americans continue to hog all the glory. For more moderate hiking, the southern end of the park overflows with opportunities. A multi-day trip can be had to **Hunlen Falls** (a difficult, grizzly inhabited 16.4km hike, 9hr.; trailhead access by 4WD across from Rainbow Range trailhead at top of "The Hill"). After hiking into the falls, visitors can rent canoes on the **Turner Lakes** ($25 per day), or walk the gorgeous **Ptarmigan Lake** loop (12km, 5hr.). Summertime daytrippers can explore **Rainbow Ridge Trail** (trailhead before "the hill," 8km one-way, 2-3hr.) or for a shorter trip follow the hour-long **Valley Loop/Burnt Bridge Trail** (5km round-trip, 1-2hr.) from the Mackenzie Heritage Trailhead (50km east of Bella Coola). The viewpoint overlooks the Bella Coola Valley. Call the park for details (see above).

BELLA COOLA

The pot of pewter at the end of the Chilcotin rainbow is the coastal village of Bella Coola, homeland of the Nuxalk Nation. Salmon fishery restrictions and the pull-out of the logging industry over the last two years have severely depressed the local economy making the town increasingly dependent on the tourism from the **BC Ferries'** *Discovery Passage* route that links Bella Coola with Port Hardy on the northern tip of Vancouver Island from mid-June to mid-September. (☎888-223-3779. Car $220. Adults $110, ages 5-11 $55, under 5 free.) The **visitors center** is located in the *Discovery Passage* office downtown. (☎799-5268, 800-863-1181. Open M, W, F 9am-4:30pm, Tu and Th 9am-6pm, Sa 2-6pm.) The **Shell Station,** across from the Valley Inn on McKenzie Rd., does repairs and has the only gas in town. (☎799-5314. Open daily 8am-8pm.) Getting a room in town is expensive, but the **Bella Coola Motel** downtown has camping on its large back lawn. (☎799-5323. Toilets, free showers. Tents $10; RV $12, no hookups.) For shaded and forested sites, head to **Gnome's Home Campground** and RV Park, in Hagensborg 16km east of Bella Coola along the highway. (☎982-2504. Toilets, showers, coin laundry. Sites $12; full hookups $15.)

For a bite to eat try the **Bay Motor Hotel** coffee shop on Hwy. 20 in Hagensborg or the small grocery store across the street. (☎982-2212. Open daily 6am-9pm; F and Sa to 6am-10pm.) In Bella Coola sit on the deck and eat similar fare or pricier dinner options at the **Bella Coola Valley Inn.** (☎799-5316. Open daily 7am-9pm.)

WILLIAMS LAKE TO QUESNEL ☎250

Williams Lake, 90km north of 100 Mile House, is the Cariboo's largest town, but certainly not its most appealing. Fortunately, it's easy to leave, with Hwy. 20 meandering 457km west to **Bella Coola** (see p. 304) and Hwy. 97 continuing north to the rough-hewn lumber towns of **Quesnel** and **Prince George.** The biggest thing happening in town is the celebration of its cowboy heritage over Canada Day weekend (July 1) with the **Williams Lake Stampede.** Festivities include a rodeo, mountain race, wild cow milking, barn dance, and live music. (☎800-717-6336. $11-15, cheaper if bought before June 14.) **Visitor information** in town is available on Hwy. 97. (☎392-5025. Open June-Aug. daily 9am-5pm; Sept.-May M-F 9am-4pm.) The town **library** at the corner of 3rd Ave. N and Proctor St. has free **Internet access** for 30min. (☎392-3630. Open Tu-Th 10am-8pm, F-Sa 10am-5pm.)

The **Slumber Lodge,** 27 7th Ave., is cheap with a small indoor pool, phones, and cable. (☎392-7116 or 800-577-2244. Singles $45; doubles $50.) For a cheap thrill, pitch tent on the **Stampede grounds** in the center of town. To get there, cross the bridge on Hwy. 20 from the junction with Hwy. 97 and take first right on Mackenzie Rd.; the grounds are on your right. (☎392-6585. $8, full hookups $15.)

HOW MUCH WOOD DOES BC CHUCK? About 76 million cubic meters a year. That's enough to bring BC 15.3 billion loonies from exports, employ a group of people three times the population of the Yukon (nearly 100,000), and dole out $4 billion in wages and salaries. The majority of BC's chopped riches make their way to Canada's North American next-door neighbor—the USA—in the form of softwood lumber. Before you get your tree-hugging self heading to BC to tie yourself to a sapling in protest, note this: it's been done before and with some success. As a result of such a protest, stringent forest management laws were passed leading to careful planning and reforestation efforts. Over 200 million baby trees are plopped in the soil each year, and tree planters earn their wages by the tree. Eat your heart out, Johnny Appleseed.

To escape the bustle, bask on the beach at **Blue Lake Holiday Campgrounds** (☎297-6505), turn off at Blue Lake Rd. 32km north of town and 3km up a gravel road. Campsites ($12) and canoes ($5 per hr.) on the bright blue-green lake are at your disposal. Corral your buckin' bronco and hightail it to the all-you-can-eat chock-full salad and hot entree buffet at **Fraser Inn**, Hwy. 97 north of intersection. (☎398-7055. Salad bar only $6, whole shebang $8. M-F 11am-1:30pm, Sa and Su 11am-4pm.) If looking to fill your saddlebag with an overflowing sub or wrap, the deli **Zesto's**, 86 3rd Ave. N, has every option under the western sun. (☎398-9801. Open M-Sa 8:30am-10pm, Su 10am-10pm.)

The 122km drive north to Quesnel can be a little dull, but those willing to subject their car to a little gravel can make it more interesting. About 35km north of Williams Lake, the **Soda Creek Townsite Rd.** splits from Hwy. 97 for 20km of rustic splendor alongside the **Fraser River.** The road returns to the highway several kilometers south of the free **Marguerite Ferry,** which shuttles drivers across the river to a gravel road paralleling Hwy. 97 for the remainder of the trip to Quesnel. (Open May-Oct. 5min., on demand 7-11:45am, 1-4:45pm, and 6-6:45pm.)

QUESNEL ☎250

The town of Quesnel (kwuh-NELL), 123km north of Williams Lake and 116km south of Prince George, takes great pride in its gold-driven past and forestry-propelled present. The town itself has little to offer but provides relatively close access to other options. After being welcomed into town by the world's largest goldpan on the north end of town on Hwy. 97, it's only a 10min. drive to **Pinnacles Provincial Park:** cross the river on Marsh Rd., then turn right on Baker Dr., and follow it for 5km. Park at the gate and a 1km walk leads to hoodoos—volcanic rock formations that look like giant sand dribble castles—and impressive views. Every third weekend of July, crowds flock to Quesnel for the wholesome family fun of **Billy Barker Days**, featuring a rodeo, live entertainment, and a "Crash-to-Pass" demolition derby. The logging industry maintains a very strong presence (and odor) in this industrial oasis. The visitors center has the scoop on mill tours at **West Fraser Lumber** (times arranged on demand).

ORIENTATION AND PRACTICAL INFORMATION. Highway 97 becomes Front St. in Quesnel and wraps along the river. One block over the main drag, Reid St., parallels Front St. in the "city centre." The **Greyhound** depot is on Kinshant between St. Laurent and Barlow. (☎992-2231 or 800-661-8747. Open M-F 6am-8pm, Sa 6am-noon and 6-7:30pm, Su 6-10:30am and 6-7:30pm.) Buses to **Prince George** (1½hr.; 3 per day; $19, students and seniors $17) and **Vancouver** (10hr.; 3 per day; $87, students and seniors $78). The **visitors center,** 705 Carson Ave., is just off Hwy. 97 at the south end of town. (☎992-8716 or 800-992-4922. Open July-Aug. daily 8am-6pm; mid-May to June and Sept.-Oct. daily 9am-4pm; Nov. to mid-May M-F 9am-4pm.) **Market and pharmacy: Safeway,** 445 Reid St., (☎992-6477. Open daily 8am-9pm.) **Free Internet access** at the **library,** 593 Barlow Ave. on two computers. Reserve in advance. (☎992-7912. Open Tu-Th 10am-8pm, F-Sa 10am-5pm.) **Emergency:** ☎911. **Police:** ☎992-9211. **Post office:** 346 Reid St. (☎992-2200. Open M-F 8:45am-5:15pm.) **Postal Code:** V2J 3J1.

ACCOMMODATIONS AND FOOD. With a nod to Quesnel's history, the **Gold Pan Hotel,** 855 Front St., north edge of downtown offers cheap rooms with dingy bedspreads but clean bathrooms, cable, coffee, and phones. (☎992-2107. Single $40, double $44.) Treat yourself to the **Caribou Hotel,** 254 Front St., downtown. Ten more bucks will land you a riverview, continental breakfast, TV, phone, and a jacuzzi bathtub. Request rooms 1-3 when a live band plays downstairs in the **pub** (☎992-2333 or 800-665-3200. Live music W-Sa. Open M-Sa 11am-1am, Su 11am-midnight. Check monthly calendar for nightly drink and food bargains.) Also, **drive-in liquor store** keeps the place hoppin'. For more ambience than the cheap RV parks on either end of town, **Robert's Roost Campground,** 3121 Gook Rd., 8km south of town and 2km off Hwy. 97, offers elegantly landscaped lakeside sites. Coin showers and laundry, a playground, and fishing; row boat and canoe rentals $5. (☎747-2015. Sites $17; full hookups $22.) Pub food can be found throughout Quesnel and south on Hwy. 97. A burlap-bag-ceiling alternative for any meal, **Granville's Coffee,** Front St., bakes gigantic ham and cheese muffins ($1.50), heaping sandwiches ($4.25), and $5 mac and cheese. (Open M-Sa 7am-10pm, Su 9am-10pm.)

SIGHTS AND OUTDOOR ACTIVITIES. The long-defunct mining town of **Barkerville,** 90km east of Quesnel along Hwy. 26, was established in 1862 after Billy Barker found gold on Williams Creek, sparking BC's largest gold rush. For the rest of the 19th century, Barkerville was the benchmark against which the rest of western Canada was measured. Since 1958 the town has been operated as an educational **"living museum,"** housing only residents who run the local B&Bs. (☎994-3332. Open daily 8am-8pm in summer. Two-day pass $8, students and seniors $6.25, youth $4.75, children $2.25, under 5 free. 30% off from late May to mid-June. Additional fee for shows and stagecoach rides.) One day is enough to see it all, but those staying a while might find services 8km away in the mining town **Wells.**

Bowron Lakes Provincial Park is a paddling paradise located 25km north of Barkerville. This necklace of lakes forms a 116km loop in the heart of the **Caribou Mountains.** Since the circuit takes most canoers 10 days to complete, the park service charges $50 per person to canoe the circuit and $25 per person to canoe the westside to Unna Lake (three to four days) to help maintain the 56 lakeside camping areas. Reservations required through **Super, Natural BC;** two walk-ons per day (☎800-435-5622). **Becker Lodge** rents canoes and kayaks (☎992-8864 or 800-808-4761; $130-230 for the circuit) as does the **Bowron Lake Lodge** (☎992-2733; $100-225). Both also offer camping and cabins within a stone's throw of the loop's starting point. Tent sites overlooking the lake are more private at Becker (tents $15, RVs $20) while lodging in the Bowron Lake motel is cheapest ($60).

Anyone traveling between Prince George and Quesnel on Hwy. 97 will live a better life for having stopped at **Cinema Second Hand General Store,** 32km north of Quesnel on Hwy. 97, the ultimate in highway-side general stores. Cash-strapped road warriors will find everything they need (except an actual cinema), plus a wide variety of things they could never possibly need, like old-fashioned snowshoes and disco LPs. The store also offers **free camping** with pit toilet. (☎998-4774. Open daily 9am-9pm.)

PRINCE GEORGE ☎250

Prince George stands at the confluence of the Nechako and Fraser Rivers, the banks of which have succumbed to the pulp and lumber mills that crowd the valley floor in an impressive display of industrial *forte*. Prince George is a crucial point of transport for goods and services heading in all directions, a true nerve center for the Northwest. But even with recent additions to the town—a civic center, a national university, and a Western League hockey team—Prince George is a stopover, not a destination.

ORIENTATION AND PRACTICAL INFORMATION

Hwy. 97 cuts straight through Prince George just to the west of the city center. **Hwy. 16** runs through the city center, becomes **Victoria St.** in town, and crosses Hwy. 97 to the south of town. Running the width of the city, **15th St.** is home to most of the shopping centers and terminates on the east end downtown.

Greyhound, 1566 12th Ave. (☎564-5454 or 800-661-8747), opposite the Victoria St. visitors center, runs to **Edmonton** (10hr., 2 per day, $99), **Vancouver** (12hr., 3 per day, $96), **Prince Rupert** (10hr., 2 per day, $92), and **Dawson Creek** (6hr., 2 per day, $54). Ticket office open M-Sa 6:30am-5:30pm and 8pm-midnight; Su 6:30-9:30am, 3:30-5:30pm, and 8pm-midnight. **BC Rail,** 1108 Industrial Way (☎561-4033), 2km south off Hwy. 97 at the end of Terminal Blvd., runs the scenic Cariboo Prospector to **Vancouver** (14hr.; M, Th, Sa at 7am; $212, over 59 $191, children $127; 3 meals included. Station open M-F 3-11:30pm, Su 6-10pm and M, Th, Sa 6-10am).

Visitor Information: Visitors Center, 1198 Victoria St. (☎562-3700 or 800-668-7646; www.tourismpg.bc.ca) at 15th Ave. Open M-F 8:30am-6pm, Sa 9am-6pm. Another center (☎563-5493) is at the junction of Hwy. 16 and Hwy. 97 beneath a huge "Mr. P.G." logger. Open daily May-Sept. 9am-8pm.

Equipment Rental: Centre City Surplus, 1222 4th Ave. (☎564-2400), rents and sells outdoor gear at competitive prices. Open M-Sa 9am-6pm, Su 11am-4pm.

Market: The Real Canadian Superstore, 2155 Ferry Ave. at Hwy. 16 (☎960-1335), is at its best with loads of fresh produce, aisles of bulk bins, ethnic foods, pharmacy, clothes, and gas. (Open M-F 9am-10pm, Sa 8am-10pm, Su 10am-8pm.)

Laundromat: Whitewash Laundromat is at 231 George St. Wash $1.25, dry 25¢ per 8min. Open M-Sa 7:30am-6pm.

Emergency: ☎911. **Police:** 999 Brunswick St. (☎561-3300).

Crisis Line: ☎563-1214. 24hr.

Hospital: 2000 15th Ave. (☎565-2000; emergency 565-2444).

Internet Access: Free 1hr. daily at the **library,** 887 Dominion (☎563-9251), near the Victoria St. visitors center. 12 computers. Open M-Th 10am-9pm, F-Sa 10am-5:30pm; winter Su 1-5pm. **Internet Cafe,** inside London Drugs in the Parkwood Mall at Victoria and 15th St. $3 per 30min. Open M-Sa 9am-10pm, Su 10am-8pm.

Post Office: 1323 5th Ave. (☎561-2568). Open M-F 8:30am-5pm. **Postal Code:** V2L 3L0.

ACCOMMODATIONS AND CAMPING

During the summer, the **College of New Caledonia Student Residence,** 3330 22nd Ave., turn off Hwy. 97 west of downtown and take second right, offers the best deal in town with clean rooms and a young crowd. Rooms include fridge, microwave. With kitchen, lounge, BBQ, and cheap laundry the price is unbeatable. (☎561-5849 or 800-371-8111. Linen $5. Wash $1.50, dry 50¢. $20; doubles $25.) To upgrade to a queen bed and cable TV, a good bet is the **Queensway Court Motel,** 1616 Queensway, one motel over from 17th Ave., close to downtown. Well-kept rooms come with fridges, microwaves, and cable. (☎562-5068. Singles $36; doubles $40.)

The **Log House Restaurant and Kampground,** located on the shores of Tabor Lake, pleases adults with its impeccable grounds, proximity to fishing, and a costly German-owned steakhouse. To reach this slice of Europe, head out of town on Hwy. 16 E; after 3km, turn right on "Old Cariboo Hwy.," left on Giscome Rd. and follow the signs (15min. from downtown). Rowboats ($6), canoes ($8), and pedal boats ($8) can be rented by the hour. (☎963-9515. Sites $15; full hookups $22; cabins with kitchenettes $45; teepees $10 per person.) To secure a bed and breakfast room, call the helpful **B&B Hotline** (☎888-266-5555).

FOOD AND NIGHTLIFE

Hard-pressed to escape chains and interchangeable pasta joints on George St., a few alternatives stand out. Freshness exudes from the **1085 Cafe** ("Ten 85"), 1085 Vancouver St., tucked away at 11th Ave. near the mall. Enjoy sushi ($5), wraps ($4-6), salads, or chai ($3.50) on the flowered patio. (☎ 960-2272. Open M and Sa 9am-4pm, Tu-F 7am-9pm.) Hit up hip **Javva Mugga Mocha Cafe,** 304 George St., for the best cup of joe in town. (☎ 562-3338. Open M-F 7:30am-5:30pm, Sa 8am-5:30pm.) An oasis for the big appetite, **Esther's Inn,** 1151 Commercial Crescent, off Hwy. 97 near 15th Ave., has an all-you-can-eat spread laid out next to a waterfall in the tropical dining area. Main dish theme varies. (Lunch $8.50, dinner M-Th $12, F-Sa $14. Open for lunch 11am-2pm, dinner 4-10pm.)

There's no shortage of taps flowing in Prince George. Pubs are aplenty, and a favorite, **JJ's Pub,** 1970 S Ospika, reminds its loyal Canadian crowd and visitors that "Canadians kick ass." (☎ 562-2234. Off 15th Ave. heading from Hwy. 97 to UNBC. Open 11am-midnight.) Cowboy hats congregate for live country rock at **Cadillac Ranch,** 1390 2nd Ave., and two-step under disco lights. (☎ 563-7720. Open M-Th 9pm-2am, Fr-Sa 8pm-2am.) Clubs and bars explode with college students during the academic year; in the summer, 20-somethings can be found in a line-up outside **Sgt. O'Flaherty's,** 770 Brunswick, at 7th Ave. under Crest Hotel, on Thursday nights when pints fill up for $2.50. Live music nightly. (☎ 563-0121. Open M-Sa 4pm-1am.)

SIGHTS AND EVENTS

PARKS. Fort George Park, on the banks of the Fraser River off 20th Ave., offers an expansive lawn, beach volleyball courts, picnic tables, and barbecue pits. It also makes a perfect starting point for the 11km **Heritage River Trail,** which wanders through the city and along the Fraser and Nechako Rivers. After meandering through **Cottonwood Island Nature Park,** off River Rd., the last few kilometers of the trail skirt industrial yards. Unless an industrial walk is your bag, finish with Cottonwood's leisurely riverside walking trails along the banks of the Nechako. For a bird's eye view of Prince George—the cement jungle—scramble up to **Connaught Hill Park,** home of picnic tables and ample frisbee-throwing space. To reach the park, scale the yellow metal staircase across 15th Ave. from the visitors center or take Connaught Dr. off Queensway. **McMillan Regional Park** is right across the Nechako River off Hwy. 97 North and features a deep ravine and a view of the city from the river's cutbanks. Two parks farther out of town have wide trails that are wheelchair accessible and double for cross-country skiing in the winter. **Forests for the World,** a tribute to the role of forests in Prince George life on nearby Cranbrook Hill, is only a 15min. drive from town and one of the prettiest parts of Prince George. To take advantage of the web of trails, pick up a map at the visitors center first. To get there, take Hwy. 97 North, turn left on 15th Ave., right on Foothills Blvd., left onto Cranbrook Hill Rd., and finally left on Kueng Rd. The trails at **Esker's Provincial Park** (☎ 565-6340), off Hwy. 97 (12km north) and 28km down Ness Lake Rd., circle three lakes.

FISHING. With more than 1500 lakes within a 150km radius, fishing is excellent near Prince George. The closest spot is **Tabor Lake,** where the rainbow trout all but jump into boats in spring and early summer. Tabor is east on Hwy. 16; follow the directions to the Log House Restaurant and Kampground described above. For a complete listing of lakes and licensing information, contact visitor information.

EVENTS. Imagine finding organic produce, baked goods, jams, salsas, and tofu concoctions in this town of chain food. Each Saturday these unexpected treats can be found on tables at the **Farmers Market** (☎ 563-3383), Courthouse Plaza on George Ave., May-September 8:30am-1pm. **Mardi Gras** (☎ 564-3737) lasts for 10 days in late February and features such events as snow golf, dog-pull contests, and bed races. You'll swear you're in New Orleans. **Sandblast** (☎ 564-9791) sends daring skiers down the steep, snowless Nechako Cutbanks on the third Sunday in August.

JOHN HART (HWY. 97): PRINCE GEORGE TO DAWSON CREEK

Travelers on their way to Mt. Robson or Jasper beyond will depart Prince George along the Yellowhead Hwy. (Hwy.16) leading east (see p. 310), while those bound for the Cassiar Hwy. (Hwy. 37) or the Queen Charlotte Islands will depart along the Yellowhead Hwy. leading west (see p. 326). Travelers continuing north will stick to Hwy. 97, called the John Hart Hwy., on its way out of town. Neon lights and strip malls become a distant memory a few kilometers into the 402km stretch from Prince George to Dawson Creek (Mile 0 of the Alaska Hwy.). The road cuts a lonely swath along a winding path through the forests of northern British Columbia. The first outpost of civilization is the micropolis of **Bear Lake,** 74km along Hwy. 97, which offers a motel, RV park, restaurant, and gas.

CROOKED RIVER AND WHISKERS POINT PROVINCIAL PARKS. Situated on **Bear Lake,** 2km south of town, **Crooked River Provincial Park** offers a great beach for swimming and picnicking, as well as 90 secluded, wooded campsites. The trails around the lake make this park well-suited for winter activities such as tobogganing, snowshoeing, and cross-country skiing. For park conditions or ski and weather info, call 562-8288 during business hours. (Campground ☎972-4492. Toilets. Gates locked 11pm-7am. $15.) **Whiskers Point Park,** 51km past Bear Lake, has the same lakefront charm and all the amenities as Crooked River on a slightly smaller scale. The park provides a boat launch for the large **McLeod Lake.** (Toilets. Gates locked 11pm-7am. $15.)

MACKENZIE. Blink and you'll miss **MacKenzie Junction,** 26km past Whiskers Point. From the junction, it's 149km to the next town of note, Chetwynd, and almost 80km to the next gas station, **Silver Sands Gas.** (☎ 788-0800. Open daily 9am-10:30pm.) The junction also provides a turn-off to the town of **MacKenzie,** 29km north on Hwy. 39, the largest town in the area and home to the closest hospital. Barring medical emergency, MacKenzie is probably not worth the detour unless it has been your life's dream to see the world's largest tree crusher.

CHETWYND. Pause to eat your picnic PB&J 115km before Chetwynd at **Bijoux Falls Provincial Park.** 300km from Prince George, **Chetwynd** is the Chainsaw Sculpture Capital of the World. It's worth cruising downtown to see what's not visible from the highway. Ask at the **visitors center** for a town guide to see what chopped wood dreams are made of. (☎401-4100. Open daily 9am-5pm.) **Wildmare Campground,** 5km before town along the highway, provides showers ($2), toilets, laundry facilities, and budget rates in lackluster sites. (☎788-2747. Tents $7; RV $17.) If clean and affordable is what you desire, head for the **Chetwynd Court Motel,** 5104 North Access Rd. right off Hwy. 94, offering TV and kitchenettes. (☎788-2271. Rooms $43.) After Chetwynd, Dawson Creek is 102km away.

MONKMAN PROVINCIAL PARK. Monkman Provincial Park (☎787-3407) covers a portion of the central Rocky Mountains and foothills. The park is home to the **Kinuseo Falls,** which are taller than Niagara Falls. Several dayhikes provide views and some easy paddling below the falls. BC Parks maintains 42 sites at **Kinuseo Falls Campground** on nearby Murray River. (Pit toilets, water, firewood. $12.) To reach Monkman, take Hwy. 29 south to the coal town of **Tumbler Ridge,** 94km from Chetwynd. Monkman is another 60km due south on a gravel road.

ALONG HWY. 16: YELLOWHEAD HWY.

PRINCE GEORGE TO MT. ROBSON ☎250

East of Prince George, the pristine terrain that lines the 319km of road to Mt. Robson gives little indication of the logging that drives the regional economy, thanks to scenic, sightline-wide strips of forest left untouched alongside the route. Lakeside campsites at **Purden Lake Provincial Park,** 59km east of Prince George, cost $15 with toilets and free firewood. (☎565-6340. One wheelchair-accessible site. Gate closed 11pm-7am.) **Purden Lake Resort** (☎565-7777), 3km east, offers cheap tent sites ($10), full hookups ($16-20), a cafe (open 7am-8pm), and the last gas before **McBride**, 140km east. Tenters can find refuge, toilets, showers, and laundry, at the **Beaverview Campsite**, 1km east of McBride. (☎569-2513. $13, partial hookups $17.)

From McBride, the Yellowhead weaves up the **Robson Valley,** part of the Rocky Mountain trench stretching north-south the length of the province. **Tête Jaune Cache** lies 63km east of McBride where Hwy. 5 leads 339km south to Kamloops and the Okanagan beyond. **Tête Jaune Motel and RV Park** offers no-frills lodging right off the highway. (☎566-9815. Showers $1. Camping $12; hookups $14.) Just 2km east of the intersection, the diminutive **Rearguard Falls** (a 20min. walk) mark the terminus of the chinook salmon's migration from the Pacific.

As Hwy. 16 continues east, the scenery reaches a crescendo at towering **Mt. Robson**, 84km west of Jasper and 319km east of Prince George. Standing 3954m tall, Robson is the highest peak in the Canadian Rockies; mountaineers reached its summit in 1913 only after five unsuccessful attempts. Less ambitious folk can appreciate the mountain's beauty from the parking lot and picnic site beside the **Mt. Robson Provincial Park Headquarters.** (☎566-4325, reservations 800-689-9025. Open June-Aug. daily 8am-8pm; May and Sept. 8am-5pm.) Sedentary types are accommodated at **Robson River Campground** and the larger **Robson Meadows Campground,** both opposite the headquarters ($17.50; toilets and hot showers). Five nearby **hiking trails,** ranging from 2km walks to 66km treks, are the park's main draws (backcountry camping permit $5 per person per night; under 13 free). The 22km trail to **Berg Lake** (two days; trailhead at the parking lot by Robson River 2km from the visitors center) is a luscious, well-maintained path along the milky-blue Robson River past Lake Kinney and **Valley of a Thousand Falls** (water, one hopes). Berg Lake is the highest of five **campsites** along the route which can be used as a base to explore options from alpine ridge-running to wilderness camping.

PRINCE GEORGE TO TERRACE ☎250

As Hwy. 16 winds its way westward 575km (8hr.) toward Terrace from Prince George, towering timbers gradually give way to the gently rolling pastures and the tiny towns of British Columbia's interior **Lakes District.** To escape city camping, stop 1½hr. outside Prince George at **Beaumont Provincial Park** (☎565-6490), on Fraser Lake, with 49 roomy sites, clean facilities, a playground, a swimming area, and firewood ($15).

BURNS LAKE

Hwy. 16 takes a turn at the town of **Burns Lake,** where almost every building is adorned with the likeness of a trout. A **visitors center,** right on the highway, is the best place to stop for fishing info with a brag board showing off pictures of the best local catches. The Burns Lake area boasts of its 3000 mi. of fishing shoreline although most fishermen drop a line from boat. They also have an obscene amount of camping and hiking info. (☎692-3773. Open July-Aug. daily 8am-7pm; winter M-F 9am-5pm.) Twenty-four kilometers south of town along Hwy. 35, forestry campsites are available at large **Francois Lake,** noted for rainbow and lake trout. (Pit toilets, no water. $8.) The strenuous **Opal Bed Trail** (2km one-way) leads to a creek bed lined with opals and agates, giving you by far the biggest bang for you hiking buck. From Hwy. 35 turn right onto Eagle Creek Rd., which runs 7km to a recreation site and the trailhead (30min. drive from Burns Lake).

HOUSTON

Houston lies 80km west of Burns Lake. Its Texas-scale contribution to the rampant superlativism of the late 20th century is the **world's largest flyrod** and local phallic symbol (20m long and over 365kg). Houston's **visitors center** offers a guide on how to realize your fishing fantasies. (☎845-7640. Open M-F 9am-8pm, Sa 9am-6pm, Su 9am-5pm; winter M-F 9am-5pm.) In the transition zone from cow country to an Alps-like landscape camp at **Tyhee Lake Provincial Campground.** The 55 well-maintained, private sites are 53km from Houston but near their share of hiking, fishing, swimming, and even showers. (☎800-689-9025; $17.50). **Smithers,** 64km northwest of Houston, is a fast-food haven with skiing on the slopes of Hudson Bay Mountain and plenty of food and accommodations.

NEW HAZELTON

The town of **New Hazelton** is 68km past Smithers, where **visitor information** consists of several pamphlets on the area's totem poles. (☎842-6071. Open daily May-June 9am-5pm, July-Aug. 8am-7pm.) The **'Ksan Village & Museum**, 7km along Churchill Ave. towards Old Hazelton, displays a rich collection of totem poles, longhouses, and artwork of the Gitskan and offers the only real reason to get off the highway at New Hazelton. Gitskan dancers perform every Friday at 8pm from July to August. (☎842-5544. $10, seniors and children 6-18 $6.50. Tours every 30min. Open daily July to mid-Aug. 9am-6pm; reduced hours in winter. Wheelchair accessible.) Another 44km west of New Hazelton is the junction with the Cassiar Hwy. (Hwy. 37; see p. 328) which leads 733km north to the Yukon Territory and the Alaska Hwy. (see p. 334). The **Petrocan** sells the last gas before Terrace. (☎849-5793. Open daily 7am-9pm.) For the remaining 97km (1hr.) to Terrace, Hwy. 16 winds along the base of the **Hazelton Mountains** and follows the thundering **Skeena River**.

TERRACE ☎250

An extended spell of bad weather and a highly disproportionate male-to-female ratio caused 3000 Canadian Army World War II troops stationed in Terrace to mutiny. For three weeks, disgruntled enlisted men ruled Terrace while officers took refuge in Prince Rupert, 144km to the west. Now, Terrace is known for its wildlife, habitat of the world's largest Chinook salmon (weighing in at 92½ lb.), and the infamous Kermodei bear, a member of the black bear family recognizable by a coat that ranges from light chestnut blond to steel blue gray in color. On arrival however, this wilderness utopia is dampered by the sense of overprocessed suburbia and fast food chains. For those who cannot live by fishing alone—seemingly a minority of the town's residents and visitors—Terrace's unique geography of plains and beaches sculpted by the Skeena River makes for scenic hiking.

◪ PRACTICAL INFORMATION. Terrace is 144km east of Prince Rupert on the Yellowhead Hwy. (Hwy. 16) and 91km southwest of the junction of the Yellowhead and the Cassiar Hwy. (Hwy. 37). **VIA Rail** (☎800-561-8630), sends three trains per week to **Prince Rupert** (2½hr., $24) and **Prince George** (10hr., $78). **Greyhound**, 4620 Keith St. (☎635-3680), runs twice daily to **Prince Rupert** (2hr., $20) and **Prince George** (8hr., $66). **Canadian Tire**, at 5100 Hwy. 16, will get your wheels back in action. (☎635-7178. Open M-F 7am-9pm, Sa 7am-6pm, Su 10am-5pm.)

The **visitors center**, 4511 Keith St., is off Hwy. 16 just east of town. (☎635-0832 or 800-499-1637. Open daily 9am-5pm; winter M-F 8am-4:30pm.) The **24hr. ATM** is in the city center at **Bank of Montreal**, 4666 Lakelse Ave. (☎615-6150). **Women's Resource Centre**, 4542 Park Ave., by the Aquatic Centre, has referral services, advocacy, lay counselling, and a library. (☎638-0228. Drop-in M-Th 10am-4pm.) **Richard's Cleaners**, 3223 Emerson St., has washers ($2), dryers (25¢ per 5min.), and **fake sun**. ($1.10 per min. ☎635-5119. Open daily M-Sa 7:30am-9pm, Su 8am-9pm.) **Terrace Aquatic Center**, on Paul Clark Dr., has pool, hot tub, saunas, and gym facilities. (☎615-3030. $4.50, students and seniors $2.40, ages 2-14 $1.75.) **Market** and **pharmacy** at **Safeway**, 4655 Lakelse Ave., has a bulk section you could live off of and produce. (☎635-7206. Open daily 8am-10pm.) For super cheap produce, and one-hour photo hit **The Real Canadian Wholesale Club**, located behind the visitors center off Hwy. 16. (☎635-0995. Open M-F 9am-9pm, Sa 9am-6pm, Su 10am-5pm). **Mills Memorial Hospital:** 4720 Haugland Ave. (☎635-2211). **Emergency:** ☎911. **Police:** 3205 Eby St. (☎635-4911). **Sexual Assault Crisis Line:** ☎635-1911. Staffed daily 8:30am-4:30pm. **Internet access** is free at the **library**, 4610 Park Ave. for 1hr.; call ahead. (☎638-8177. Open M 1-9pm, Tu-F 10am-9pm, Sa 10am-5pm, Su 1-5pm; closed Su in July and Aug.) Pay at **Van's News**, 4607 Lakelse, opposite the Coast Inn. (☎635-8899. $3 per 15min., $5 for 30min., $8 per hr. Open daily 8am-10pm.) **Post Office:** 3232 Emerson St. (☎635-2241). Open M-F 8:30am-5pm. **Postal Code:** V8G 4A1.

ACCOMMODATIONS, CAMPING, AND FOOD.
Motels in the $45-75 range abound along the highway outside of the city centre. **Kalum Motel,** 5min. west on Hwy. 16 is a bargain. (☎635-2362. Single or double $40. Big TV, local phone calls, coffee maker included. Kitchenettes $5 extra.) The **Alpine House Motel,** 4326 Lakelse Ave., is also removed from noisy downtown. Kitchenettes available for no extra charge. Take the Alternate Route across the one lane bridge as you enter on Hwy. 16 from the east. (☎635-7216 or 800-663-3123. Singles $45, doubles $55; Oct.-Apr. $10 less.) **Ferry Island Municipal Campground,** lies just east of Terrace on Hwy. 16 with big sites under big trees and lushly vegetated walking trails. The island's prime fishing spot is a short walk and lined with eager anglers. The community pool is half-price for Ferry Island campers. (☎615-3000. Pit toilets, water, firewood. Sites $12, hookups $14.) **Kleanza Creek Provincial Park** is the site of an abandoned gold mine, 19km east of the town on Hwy. 16, with sites nestled in towering evergreens along the rushing creek. (Pit toilets, water, firewood. $12.)

Terrace offers a handful of welcome breaks from the dreariness of highway diner cuisine. **Don Diego's,** 3212 Kalum St., is a fun, laid-back joint that serves Mexican, Greek, and whatever's in season. Fresh, new menu with each meal. (☎635-2307. Lunch $7-9. Dinner $9-15. Open M-Sa 11:30am-3pm, 5-9pm, Su 4:30-9pm.) For authentic and affordable Indian cuisine, drive 5min. west of town along Hwy. 16 to **Haryana's Restaurant,** in the Kalum Motel. Vegetarian entrees cost $9-12 and succulent chicken tikka masala is $13. (☎635-2362. Open M-Th 5-9pm, F 5-11pm, Sa 11am-11pm, Su 11am-9pm.) For a bite to eat after-hours or if you want to catch the game on TV with beer in hand, head to the **Back Eddy Pub,** 4332 Lakelse Ave., next to the Alpine House Motel. Chess boards and pool tables add class. (☎635-5336. Open daily 11am-midnight.)

SIGHTS.
Heritage Park Museum, perched above town on Kerby St. at Kalum St., houses countless artifacts from the pioneer era—including a working pump organ and an elaborate wreath made from human hair—perfect for pursuers of the grisly side of kitsch. (☎635-4546. Open daily May-Aug. 10am-6pm for 1½hr. tours. Last tour 4:30pm. $3, students and seniors $2, families $7.) The **Falls Gallery,** 2666 Hwy. 37, just east of town, has an impressive collection of native masks and art. Much of the artwork is for sale, with smaller souvenirs and jewelry available. Take the Hwy. 37 turn-off south towards Kitimat, and turn in the driveway before the Volkswagen dealer. (☎638-0438. Open daily 10am-5pm.) On Saturday mornings from May to October and on Wednesdays after 4pm, the **Farmer's Market** behind Lower Little Park sells what's homegrown and homemade (behind the library on Park St.).

Gruchy's Beach, 13km south of Terrace on Hwy. 37, is a 1.5km hike from the parking lot and is big, sandy, and begging to be picnicked upon. Check out the locals cliff-jumping at **Humphrey Falls.** Take Hwy. 37 south towards Kitimat and after about 35km turn left on a gravel road, then drive or walk to the water. The **Nisga'a Memorial Lava Bed,** Canada's youngest lava flow, lies 100km north of Terrace. To reach this 54 sq. km swath of moonscape, follow Kalum Lake Dr. (also called the Nisga'a Hwy.), which intersects Hwy. 16 just west of downtown, through the scenic valleys of the **Tseax** (T'SEE-ax) and **Nass Rivers.** At the end of the long trek, you can sleep amongst the lava for $12 in a BC Parks campground near the Lava Bed visitors center. **Hayatsgum Gibuu Tours,** leads 4hr. hikes and guided tours of the lava bed. (☎633-2150. Hikes May-Aug. W-Su 10am and 3pm; reservation required. $12, students $10, children $5.)

OUTDOOR ACTIVITIES.
The **Terrace Mountain Nature Trail** is a popular climb of moderate difficulty, beginning at Johnstone Ave. in the east end of town. The route (10km, 1½-2½hr.) offers spectacular views of plateaus and surrounding valley. For an easy stroll, visit the **Redsand Lake Demonstration Forest,** 26km north on West Kalum Forestry Rd., a well-maintained gravel route found 200m past the Kalum River Bridge west of town off Hwy 16. The three trails meander around beautiful Redsand Lake, and through a variety of forested areas.

314 ■ ALONG HWY. 16: YELLOWHEAD HWY.

Anglers can strap on their hip-waders and try their luck on the east shore of **Ferry Island** (see above). Ask for hot tips at the **Misty River Tackle Shop**, 5008 Agar Ave. (☎638-1369. Open M-Sa 7am-10pm, Su 8am-10pm; winter daily 7am-10pm.) In winter, groomed **cross-country** trails stretch halfway to Kitimat (about 30km down Hwy. 37) around the enigmatic (depth-testing has yet to detect its bottom) **Onion Lake** (☎798-2227 or 615-3000). World-class **downhill skiing** is but 35km west on Hwy. 16 at **Shames Mountain.** Locals go nuts every winter on Shames' double chair, t-bar, and handle tow, the 18 trails over 130 acres, and the 500m vertical drop.

PRINCE RUPERT ☎250

In 1910, railway magnate Charles Hays made a covert deal with the provincial government to purchase 10,000 acres of choice land at the western terminus of the Grand Trunk Pacific Railway. When the shady operation was exposed two years later, Hays was already under water—not drowned in his dire financial straits, but in the wreckage of the *Titanic*. The sole fruit of Hays' illegal labors was a town which, in a nationwide naming contest, was smacked with the shockingly bland "Prince Rupert" which belies the charming and youthful quality of the city today. The cool, water-front corner of town, Cow Bay, offers the highest density of establishments-not-to-be-missed, including the incredible **Cow Bay Cafe.** The rest of the city is a collection of privately owned ethnic restaurants and small businesses which are fighting the battle against the strip malls, fast food, and RV caravans that are subsuming the Yellowhead Hwy. With decent hiking and sea kayaking available in the area, Prince Rupert offers a brilliant combination of tasteful urbanism and access to the outdoors.

▐ TRANSPORTATION

Prince Rupert is a gateway to Southeast Alaska. Both BC Ferries from Vancouver Island and the Alaska Marine Hwy. from Bellingham (see p. 179) have made this town a stop on their coastal routes, providing access to nearby villages like Metlakatla (see p. 402), and farther ports in the Inside Passage. The only major road into town is the Yellowhead Hwy. (Hwy. 16), known as **McBride St.** within the city. At the north end of downtown, Hwy. 16 makes a sharp left and becomes **2nd Ave.** At the south end, Hwy. 16 becomes **Park Ave.,** continuing to the **ferry docks.** Avenues run parallel to the waterfront with McBride splitting the east from west. Building numbers ascend from this central point as well. Streets run perpendicular and ascend numerically from the waterfront. Much of the city's businesses are located on 2nd and 3rd Ave. with Cow Bay off to the right as you enter town.

Flights: Prince Rupert Airport is on Digby Island. The ferry and bus to downtown costs $11 (seniors $7, children $4) and takes about 45min. **Air Canada** (☎888-247-22620) runs 2-3 flights per day to **Vancouver** (booked 14 days in advance $378; under 25 and standby $208).

Trains: VIA Rail (☎627-7304 or 800-561-8630) at the BC Ferries Terminal. To **Prince George** (12hr., 3 per week, $100). A **BC Rail** (in BC ☎800-339-8752; elsewhere 800-663-8238 or 604-984-5500) train continues the next morning from Prince George to **Vancouver** (14hr., $212).

Buses: Greyhound, 6th St. at 2nd Ave. (☎624-5090). To **Prince George** (11 hr., 2 per day, $92) and **Vancouver** (24hr., 2 per day, $183). Station open M-F 8:30am-12:30pm and 4-8:45pm, Sa-Su 9-11am and 7-8:45pm.

Ferries: The docks are at the end of Hwy. 16, a 30min. walk from downtown. Ferry-goers may not park on Prince Rupert streets; check with the ferry company or visitors center for paid parking options. **Seashore Charter Services** (☎624-5645) runs shuttle buses between the terminal and the hotels and train station for $3. **Alaska Marine Hwy.** (☎627-1744 or 800-642-0066; www.akmhs.com) runs to **Ketchikan** (6hr., US$42) and **Juneau** (26hr., US$104). **BC Ferries** (☎624-9627 or 888-223-3779; www.bcferries.bc.ca). To **Queen Charlotte Islands** (6-7hr.; 6 per week; peak season $25, car

$93) and **Port Hardy** (15hr.; every other day; $106, car $218). Reserve for BC ferries well in advance. If the ferry is full you can get on the standby list over the phone.

Public Transportation: Prince Rupert Bus Service (☎624-3343) runs downtown Su-Th 7am-6:45pm, F until 10:45pm. $1, students 75¢; seniors 60¢; day pass $2.50, seniors and students $2. Buses from downtown leave from 2nd Ave. West and 3rd. About every 30min., the #52 bus runs to within a 5min. walk of the ferry terminal. Twice per day, a bus runs to Port Edward and the North Pacific Cannery. $2.50, students $2.

PRACTICAL INFORMATION

Visitor Information: (☎624-5637 or 800-667-1994) at 1st Ave. and McBride St., in a cedar building modeled after a traditional Tsimshian (SIM-shian) longhouse. Ask for maps and useful packets on accommodations, attractions, and trails. Open May 15 to Labour Day M-Sa 9am-8pm, Su 9am-5pm; winter M-Sa 10am-5pm.

Equipment Rental: Far West Sporting Goods (☎624-2568), on 3rd Ave. near 1st St., rents **bikes,** including lock and helmet. $8 per hr., $25 per day. Sells **camping gear.** Open M-Sa 9:30am-5:30pm. **Eco-Treks** (☎624-8311), on the dock in Cow Bay, rents **kayaks** and gear. Single $30 or double $45 for 4hr.; single $40 or double $70 per day. No rentals to novices or soloists. 3hr. guided tours for any ability level leave at 1 and 6pm with safety lessons for novices ($45).

24hr. ATM: Several banks along 2nd Ave. W. and 3rd Ave. W.

Market: Safeway, at 2nd St. and 2nd Ave. (☎624-2412), offers everything from a florist to a deli. Open daily 8am-10pm.

Laundromat: Mommy's Laundromat, 6th St. between 2nd and 3rd Ave. Offering the cheapest wash in the land: $1, dry 75¢ per 15min. Open daily 9am-9pm.

Pool: Earl Mah Pool, 1000 McBride St. (☎624-9000). Pool, sauna, showers, and gym for $4, $3 students. Call for schedule.

Emergency: ☎911. **Police:** 100 6th Ave. (☎624-2136).

Hospital: 1305 Summit Ave. (☎624-2171).

Internet Access: Library, 101 6th Ave. W at McBride St. (☎624-8618). Free 30min., Internet access then $2 per hr. Open M-Th 10am-9pm and F-Sa 10am-5pm. **Javadotcup,** (see **Food**), $3.50 per hr.

Post Office: (☎624-2353), in the mall at 2nd Ave. and 5th St. Open M-F 9:30am-5pm. **Postal Code:** V8J 3P3.

ACCOMMODATIONS AND CAMPING

Nearly all of Prince Rupert's hotels nestle within the six-block area defined by 1st Ave., 3rd Ave., 6th St., and 9th St. Everything fills to the gills when the ferries dock, so call a day or two in advance. Most motels are pricey—a single costs at least $60.

Andree's Bed and Breakfast, 315 Fourth Ave. E (☎624-3666), turn left on Fifth Ave. E. heading out of the town center; then left on Cotton and left on Fourth Ave. E. In a spacious 1922 Victorian-style residence overlooking the harbor and city. Watch sunsets from the deck. Singles $50; doubles $65; twins $70. $15 per extra person.

Eagle Bluff Bed and Breakfast, 201 Cow Bay Rd. (☎627-4955 or 800-833-1550), on the waterfront in the loveliest part of town. Attractively furnished with bright rooms and private deck on the bay. Singles $45; doubles $55; $10 extra for private bath. Each room with TV. Common kitchen area. No pets.

Pioneer Hostel, 167 3rd Ave. E (☎624-2334 or 888-794-9998), one block east of McBride St. A quasi-historic facade and modest, well-kept interior. Quite the deal. Microwave, TV, gazebo, BBQ. Laundry $3 wash and dry with soap. Showers for non-guests $3. Beds in shared room $17. Singles $20; doubles $35.

316 ■ ALONG HWY. 16: YELLOWHEAD HWY.

North Pacific Historic Fishing Village (☎ 628-3538), at the Cannery Museum in Port Edward. Live for cheap in the renovated cannery workers' quarters. Inconvenient without wheels. Stay in the Miki Bunkhouse as Japanese bachelors did, $10. Modest inn rooms with shared bath, $45. Small one bedroom units with kitchens, $65.

Prudhomme Lake, 20km east of town on Hwy. 16, run by BC Parks. Worth the drive to escape the RVs. Fishing, water, wood, and pit toilets. $12.

Park Avenue Campground, 1750 Park Ave. (☎ 624-5861 or 800-667-1994). 1km east of the ferry on Hwy. 16. An RV metropolis! Showers for non-guests $3.50. Laundry. Sites $10.50; RVs $13.50, with hookups $18.50.

FOOD

Cow Bay Cafe, 201 Cow Bay Rd. (☎ 627-1212), shares the waterfront corner of Cow Bay with Eagle Bluff B&B. Local patrons savor an ever-changing menu of gourmet delights. A trip to BC would be lacking without a heavenly fresh lunch ($8-9) and dinner ($12-16) here. Attempt to choose between ten smashing dessert creations daily ($4-5). Extensive wine list; a glass of tasty Australian or Chilean is $5. Reservations necessary. Open Tu noon-2:30pm, W-Sa noon-2:30pm and 6-8:30pm.

Opa, 34 Cow Bay Rd. (☎ 627-4560), upstairs. Funky pottery studio and sushi bar in old fishing net loft. Drink free tea out of handspun mugs. Spin a bowl at the in-house pottery studio, and while it's firing, hang out on the deck enjoying sushi. Tuna rolls ($3); miso soup ($1.50). Open Tu-F 11:30am-2pm and 5-9pm, Sa noon-3pm and 5-9pm.

Cowpuccino's, 25 Cow Bay Rd. (☎ 627-1395). Caffinate while taking in the cow pics from around the world. Don't just chew your cud! Try colossal muffins ($1), bagel sandwiches ($4.50), or Sex in a Pan $4.75. Open M-Sa 7am-10pm, Su 9am-9pm.

Rodho's (☎ 624-9797), on 2nd Ave. near 6th St. Huge menu of pleasing Greek entrees ($13-16), pastas ($8-9), and pizzas ($14 for a loaded medium). Open daily 4pm-1am. Will deliver, gratis.

Javadotcup, 516 3rd Ave. W (☎ 622-2822). Mod Internet cafe with speedy computers, coffee to give you a pick-me-up, and quick lunches ($3). Smoothies $3. Internet $3.50 per hour. Open M-Th 7:30am-10:30pm, F 7:30am-11pm, Sa 8am-11pm, Su 7:30am-10pm.

Galaxy Gardens, 844 3rd Ave. W (☎ 624-3122). One in a Chinese restaurant crowd. Western entrees from $7. Ginger chicken $13.50. Free delivery. Open daily 11:30am-10pm, F until 11pm.

SIGHTS AND OUTDOOR ACTIVITIES

Prince Rupert's harbor has the highest concentration of archaeological sites in North America. Archaeologists have unearthed materials from Tsimshian settlements dating back 10,000 years. **Archaeological boat tours** leave from the visitors center. (2½hr. tours depart daily mid June to early Sept. $26, children $14.) A local expert interprets several sites from the boat, with a stop at the village of **Metlakatla** (see p. 402) across the harbor. The **Museum of Northern British Columbia**, in the same building as the visitors center, documents the history of logging, fishing, and North Coast Tsimshian culture, and displays beautiful Tsimshian artwork. (☎ 624-3207. Open late May to early Sept. M-Sa 9am-8pm and Su 9am-5pm; mid-Sept. to late May M-Sa 9am-5pm. $5, students $2, children 6-12 $1; includes guided tour of collection, totem pole and heritage walking tours.) The **North Pacific Cannery** in Port Edward, 30min. away by car or bus, takes visitors back to the days when the salmon canning industry boomed in the area. Take the turn off from Hwy. 16 toward Port Edward, follow the winding road for 6km past town, and the cannery will be on your right. (☎ 628-3538. Open daily May 1-Sept. 30 9am-6pm. $7.50, student or senior $7, youth 6-18 $5. Includes several worthwhile tours.)

The best time to visit Prince Rupert may be during **Seafest** (☎624-9118), an annual four-day event planned for June 6-9, 2002. Surrounding towns celebrate the sea with parades, bathtub races, and beer contests. The **Islandman Triathlon** (☎624-6770; 1000m swim, 35km bike, 8km run) is also held around the time of Seafestivities and was won in 1997 by an intrepid *Let's Go* researcher. Later in June, Prince Rupert hops during the **National Aboriginal Day.**

A number of attractive small parks line the hills above Prince Rupert. Tiny **Service Park,** off Fulton St., offers panoramic views of downtown and the harbor beyond. An even wider vista awaits atop **Mt. Oldfield,** east of town, for serious hikers practicing the "buddy system" (8.4km, 5-6hr.). The trailhead is at Oliver Lake Park, about 6km from downtown on Hwy. 16. The **Butze Rapids trail** (5km, 2½-3½hr., trailhead across the highway) teaches walkers about plants and then plants them in front of rushing tidal rapids.

Sea kayaking around Prince Rupert pleases the beginner or the pro with much untouched shoreline and wildlife at the fingertips. **Eco-Treks** (see **Equipment Rental,** above) specializes in kayak introductions and also rents to the experienced who can hop in at Cow Bay, paddle north around Kaien Island—home to Prince Rupert—and brave the challenging Butze Reversing Tidal Rapids.

♪ ▨ ENTERTAINMENT AND NIGHTLIFE

Well, there's always the movies. The **cinema** at 2nd Ave. and 5th St. (☎624-6770) shows three features twice a night. ($6.50, children and seniors $3.25, cheap Tu $3.50.) Drinking establishments in Prince Rupert compete for ferry tourists and fishing boat crews. Come sundown, the town is a-crawl with sea life come to shore. The **Surf Club,** 200 5th St., attracts a younger set later in the evening with space to dance and alternating nights of live music and karaoke. (☎624-3050. Open M, Th-Sa 10pm-2am.) A relaxing brew in a swank setting with a magnificent vista of the sun over the sea awaits at the **Crest Hotel,** 222 1st Ave. W (☎624-6771).

The **Empress Hotel,** 716 3rd Ave. W (☎624-9917), has the best house band, but is not recommended for the pub-naive. **Shooters Bar and Grill** at The Commercial Inn, 901 1st Ave., and **Breaker's Pub,** 117 George Hills Way in Cow Bay overlooking the small boat harbor, are full of local color. (Shooters ☎624-6142. Open Su-M noon-midnight, Tu-Th noon-1:30am, F-Sa noon-2am. Breaker's ☎624-5990. Open M-Th 11:30am-midnight, F-Sa 11:30am-1am, Su noon-midnight.)

QUEEN CHARLOTTE ISLANDS/HAIDA GWAII

A full 130km west of Prince Rupert, two principal islands and 136 surrounding inlets form the archipelago known as "the Canadian Galápagos." Graham, the northern island, is home to all but one of the islands' towns, a particularly potent strain of hallucinogenic mushroom, and an eclectic population of tree-huggers, tree-cutters, First Nations people, and fishermen. Few tourist-huggers inhabit Haida Gwaii; in fact, locally drawn postcards poke fun at visitors. Yet, mellow, open inhabitants disinterestedly welcome those who have come to revel in the beauty, to photograph, to birdwatch, to fish, or to soul-search. To the south, hot springs steam from mountainous Gwaii Haanas (Moresby Island on many maps), where the massive wooden totem poles of the islands' first inhabitants decay. Remote wilderness envelopes kayakers and boaters who test these divine waters. The islands' chief employer is the timber industry, narrowly edging out the Canadian government. In the 1980s, the islands attracted global attention when environmentalists from around the globe joined the Haida Nation in demonstrations to stop logging on parts of Gwaii Haanas. In 1988, the Canadian government established the Gwaii Haanas (Gwaii-HAH-nus) National Park Reserve now managed co-operatively by the government of Canada and the Haida Nation.

318 ■ QUEEN CHARLOTTE ISLANDS/HAIDA GWAII

TRANSPORTATION

The **BC Ferry** from Prince Rupert docks at Skidegate Landing on Graham Island, which is between **Queen Charlotte City** (4km west of the landing), and the village of **Skidegate** (2km to the northeast). All of the towns of Graham Island lie along Hwy. 16, which continues north from Skidegate through **Tlell, Port Clements,** and **Massett**. Beware of the roadside-congregating Bambi hordes when trucking along. Each town has its own flare; the best bet for dining out and hostel accommodation is Queen Charlotte while hiking-haven, beach-combing bliss, and spunky lodging for about $24 can be had in Tlell and Massett. To the south, Moresby Island is home to **Sandspit** and the Islands' only commercial airport. From Skidegate Landing, 12 ferries per day make the 20min. crossing between the big islands. The lack of public transportation and the exorbitant cost of car rentals deter the faint of heart and light of wallet, but residents are supposedly generous in picking up hitchhikers, although *Let's Go* cannot recommend hitchhiking.

QUEEN CHARLOTTE CITY ☎ 250

Queen Charlotte City's central location and size make it the base for exploring both main islands, providing the only road link to the west coast of Graham Island. "Size" is relative, however; this community of just over 1000 people is not the city its name claims to be. Charlotte grew up around a sawmill, and logging is still its foremost industry. However, fishing and the government supply jobs as well.

TRANSPORTATION

Towns on the island line one waterfront road; in Charlotte that road is **3rd Ave.** Charlotte is 4km east (left) of the **ferry terminal.**

Ferries: BC Ferries (☎ 559-4485 or in BC 888-223-3779; www.bcferries.bc.ca), in Skidegate Landing, 3km east of Queen Charlotte City. To **Prince Rupert** (6hr.; July-Aug. 6 per week, Oct.-June 4 per week; $25, car $93, bike $6). Reserve at least 3 weeks in advance for cars; car fares do not include driver. Ferries also run between **Skidegate Landing** on Graham Island and **Alliford Bay** on Moresby Island (20min.; 12 per day; round-trip $4.75, car $12.60; off-season car $9.50; no reservations).

Taxis: Eagle Cabs (☎ 559-4461). $7-10 between Charlotte and the ferry terminal. Open Su-W 7am-9pm, Th-Sa 7am-late.

Car Rental: Rustic Rentals (☎ 559-4641), west of downtown at Charlotte Island Tire. Must be 21 with credit card. Will pick up at the ferry terminal in Skidegate. $39 per day, 15¢ per km. Office open daily 8am-7pm, but available 24hr.

Auto Repair: Charlotte Tire (☎ 559-4641), along Hwy. 33, provides 24hr. towing. Open daily 8am-7pm.

PRACTICAL INFORMATION

Visitor Information: (☎ 559-8316; fax 559-8952; www.qcinfo.com), on Wharf St. at the east end of town. Ornate 3-D map of the islands and a creative natural history presentation. The free *Guide to the Queen Charlotte Islands* has detailed maps. Holds **mandatory orientations** for visitors to Gwaii Haanas Park every day at 8am and 7:30pm (see **Gwaii Haanas** below). Open mid-May to mid-Sept. daily 10am-7pm; early May and late Sept. daily 10am-2pm.

Outdoor Information: Gwaii Haanas Park Information (☎ 559-8818; www.fas.sfu.ca/parkscan/gwaii), on 2nd Ave. off 2nd St. above city center. A trip-planning resource. Open M-F 8am-noon, 1-4:30pm. For registration info, see **Gwaii Haanas National Park Reserve,** p. 326. **Ministry of Forests** (☎ 559-6200), on 3rd Ave., at the far west end of

QUEEN CHARLOTTE CITY ■ 319

town, has info on Forest Service campsites and logging roads on both islands. Open M-F 8:30am-4:30pm. Get a saltwater **fishing license** at **Meegan's Store**, 3126 Wharf St. (☎559-4428). Open M-Sa 9am-6pm. Freshwater licenses are available only from the **Government Agent** (☎559-4452 or 800-663-7867), 1½ blocks west of the city center.

Equipment Rental: Premier Creek Lodge has bikes. $15 per half-day, $30 per full day.

Bank: Northern Savings Credit Union (☎559-4407), on Wharf St. The **24hr. ATM** is a life-saver; many businesses don't take credit cards. Bank open Tu-Th 10am-5pm, F 10am-5:30pm, Sa 10am-3pm. The only other bank is in Massett.

Market: Food is more expensive on the islands. Stock up off-island. The only Massett grocery is **City Centre Stores** (☎559-4444), in the City Centre Mall (open M-Sa 9:30am-6pm). **Isabel Creek Store**, 3219 Wharf St. (☎559-8623. Open M-Sa 10am-5:30pm), opposite the visitors center, offers more organic foods than you can shake a stick at.

Laundromat: 121 3rd Ave. (☎559-4444), in the City Centre Mall. Wash $1.50, dry 25¢ per 5min. Open daily 9am-9pm. Also at **Premier Creek Lodging** for $4 including soap.

Showers: Premier Creek Lodging will get you clean again for a precious $5, but the huge soft towel they throw in makes it worth it.

Emergency: ☎559-8484. **No 911. Ambulance:** ☎800-461-9911.

Police: 3211 Wharf (☎559-4421).

Pharmacy: (☎559-4310), downstairs in the hospital building. Open M-Tu and Th-F 10:30am-12:30pm and 1:30-5:15pm, W 1:30-5:15pm.

Hospital: (☎559-4300), on 3rd Ave. at the east end of town.

Internet Access: Free at the **Library**, 138 Bay St. (☎559-4518), under the community hall. Open M and W 2-5:30pm and 7-9pm, Sa 10am-noon and 1:30-5:30pm. Also available at **Premier Creek Lodging** for $3 per 20min.

Post Office: (☎559-8349), in the City Centre Mall on 3rd Ave. Open M-F 9am-5pm, Sa noon-4pm. **Postal Code:** V0T 1S0.

▓ ACCOMMODATIONS AND CAMPING

The accommodations of Queen Charlotte City are cozy and charming. During the summer, make reservations or arrive early in the day to secure a room.

▓ **The Premier Creek Lodging**, 3101 3rd Ave. (☎559-8415 or 888-322-3388). Ideal hostel facilities in a charming setting. Burl bunk beds in a creekside cottage behind the main hotel with shared kitchen, bath, common room, and campfire pit. For breakfast, scramble to the sunny breakfast room for a hot breakfast with garden herbs and fresh fruit ($5-8). Laundry $4. Bed in hostel $19; one double $38. Warm, clean rooms in hotel $30; with kitchenette $45. Large rooms with kitchen and couches, overlooking ocean $65 single, $75 double. One campsite $15. Credit cards accepted.

Dorothy and Mike's Guest House, 3125 2nd Ave. (☎559-8439), centrally located up the hill behind the downtown Rainbow Gallery. A standing hammock chair, stained pine interior, a library, breakfast, and kitchen use. Call ahead. Singles $45, doubles $60.

Joy's Campground (☎559-8890), halfway between the ferry terminal and Charlotte. Camp in Joy's waterfront backyard (which runs alongside 3rd Ave.), and drink from the spring. No toilets. To secure space, go to Joy's Island Jewelers, 3rd Ave., next to Sea Raven Restaurant. Tent sites $5; hookups $9; electrical $15.

Haydn-Turner Community Campground, 5min. drive west of town. Turn left down a short dirt road labeled "campground" as the main drag turns to gravel. Pleasant and forested. Water, firewood, pit toilets. 6 sites, $10. Walk-in beach front site $5.

320 ■ QUEEN CHARLOTTE ISLANDS/HAIDA GWAII

FOOD

Hanging by a Fibre (☎559-4463), on Wharf St., beside the Howler's building. Hang out in this artsy, popular coffeshop. Take in the local art shows that change each month and a Starving Artist lunch ($4) of fresh bread and soup—a culinary artist's creation. Wraps or quiche with salad ($8). Lunch served 11:30am-4pm. Open M-Sa 9am-5:30pm and Su noon-4pm

Howler's Bistro (☎559-8602), on 3rd Ave., serves each dish with festive flair. Dine on deck over the water. Fully loaded Howler burger or veggie burger $9, sandwiches $7, Mexican dishes $8-10, chicken or seafood dinners $10-18. Leave room for one of 5 flavors of cheesecake ($6). Open daily 11am-11pm; winter 11am-10pm. **Howler's Pub**, downstairs, is the only happenin' nightspot in town. Open daily 1pm-2am.

Oceana, 3119 3rd Ave. (☎559-8683), offers a huge menu of Asian cuisine ($10-14). Lunch specials ($6-10). Open daily 11:30am-2pm and 5-10pm.

Sea Raven, 3301 3rd Ave. (☎559-8583), offers an airy, sun-washed dining area and glimpses of the ocean through alder trees. Large seafood selection and the best salmon clam chowder on the island at $4.50 a bowl. Expensive at dinner ($15-21) but reasonable lunches ($7-10). Open daily 7am-2pm and 5-9pm.

Summerland Pizza and Steakhouse (☎559-4588), west on 3rd Ave. about 1km from the center of town, your local pizza joint with Mediterranean and Greek mixed in, turning out a huge menu to diners at picnic tables outside or in the non-descript dining room. Pizza lunch special $6. Sandwiches with fries $6-9. Steak, seafood, or Greek dinners $14-19. Open daily 11am-3pm, dinner 4:30-9pm.

SIGHTS

Few Haidas survived the smallpox plague of once-thriving villages in the southern islands in late 1800s. Still, today the Haida history of 10,000 years on the Queen Charlotte Islands, or "Haida Gwaii," which means "Islands of the People" remains alive. Six impressive cedar **totem poles** were raised in June 2001 on Second Beach, 1km east of the ferry landing on Hwy. 16, as a symbolic demonstration of the continuation of Haida culture. The locally carved poles represent each of the six southern Haida villages now in ruins that can be visited by boat in Gwaii Haanas Haida Heritage Site (see p. 326). Behind the totem poles a shed protects the 50 ft. cedar canoe, the **Lootaas,** carved for Vancouver's Expo '86 by renowned Haida artist Bill Reid (open M-F 9am-4:30pm). Next door the **Haida Gwaii Museum at Qay'llnagaay,** houses totem poles, contemporary Haida prints and carvings, and turn-of-the-century photographs from European exploration of the islands. (☎559-4643. Open June-Aug. M-F 10am-5pm, Sa-Su 1-5pm; May and Sept. closed Su; Oct.-Apr. closed Tu as well. $4, students and seniors $3, children under 12 free.)

The Haida town of **Skidegate,** known as "the village," lies 1km beyond the museum. This community of 695 people is the nexus of Haida art and culture. Residents are sensitive to tourists and expect that visitors will exhibit discretion and respect concerning local culture and practices. Many a bald eagle has perched upon the totem pole out front of the **Skidegate Community Hall** near the water, a Haida longhouse built in 1979 according to ancient design specifications. Visitors must get permission from the **Skidegate Band Council Office** (☎559-4496), between the Gwaii Coop and the Taawnaay gas station on the main highway, to photograph the cemetery or to camp and hike in certain areas; ask for details from the receptionist at the **Haida Gwaii Watchmen,** next to the museum. (☎559-8225. Open M-F 9am-noon and 1-5pm.)

OUTDOOR ACTIVITIES

Queen Charlotte also offers the only road access to the west coast of the island. Following 3rd Ave., it turns to gravel and multiple west coast destinations are listed on a sign less than a kilometer down the road. Multiple forestry recreation sites on Rennell Sound, about 27km down feisty lumber roads, provide a true escape into the wild ($8 permit for overnight use).

The **Spirit Lake Trail** network (several loops and 3km of trail, 1-2hr.) departs from a parking lot beside the George Brown Recreation Centre off Hwy. 16, in Skidegate. The network leads up a hill side and to the lake (1000m) where it breaks off into various loops that are all well maintained and clearly marked. Guide pamphlet available at visitors center. **Balance Rock** teeters on a roadside beach 1km north of Skidegate. A group of brawny loggers once failed in an attempt to dislodge the boulder, so it's unlikely to topple from its precarious perch.

Navigating the tangle of local logging roads is easier with a few good maps or assistance from the **Tlell Watershed Society** (see Tlell). Even on a two- or three-day hike, it's important to leave a **trip plan** with the visitors center or RCMP before setting out. The visitors center issues crucial information on **tides** and **scheduled logging road activity.** It's very dangerous for hikers or 4x4s to vie for trail space with an unstoppable logging truck.

TLELL   ☎ 250

Tlell (tuh-LEL), 40km north of Queen Charlotte City, is a line of houses and farms spread thinly along a 7km stretch of Hwy. 16. The quasi-town enjoys some of Graham Island's best beach vistas, plus a population of artisans who earn Tlell a reputation as the Charlottes' hippie zone. Tlell hosts its own Woodstock, **Edge of the World Music Festival,** in early July. Here the rocky beaches of the south give way to sand, and the Tlell River offers fishing and water warm enough for swimming.

PRACTICAL INFORMATION. Visitors center, outdoors information, and flora and fauna displays put together by Tlell Watershed Society at **Naikoon Park Headquarters,** right before the campground. (Open 11am-5pm. Closed Wednesday.) Check for schedule of programs. Tlell's **bookstore** is in the Sitka Studio, which shows local artists and sells art supplies if you are feeling inspired, at the end of Richardson Rd. (☎ 557-4241. Open daily 10am-6pm.) **Emergency/ambulance:** ☎ 800-461-9911, **no 911. Police:** (☎ 559-4421) in Queen Charlotte City. **Post office:** on Hwy. 16, 2km south of Wiggins Rd. (Open M-F 2:30-5:30pm.) **Postal code:** V0T 1Y0.

ACCOMMODATIONS AND FOOD. Sea breezes and birds singing in the spruces await at **Cacilia's B&B/Hltunwa Kaitza,** snuggled against the dunes just north of Richardson Ranch on the ocean side of the road. This may be the islands' nicest B&B, and is certainly the most distinctive. Friendly cats, driftwood furniture and toilet paper holders, and hanging chairs give character to the common living space roofed with giant spruce beams. Rooms are skylit, immaculate, and comfortable. (☎ 557-4664. Singles $40; doubles $60; grassy tent site and campfire pit near dunes $15.) Pitch a tent or park an RV at the beautiful **Misty Meadows Campground** in **Naikoon Provincial Park,** 2km beyond Cacilia's, just south of the Tlell River bridge. (Pit toilets, water, picnic tables, beach access. 14-day max. stay. $12.)

Lunch ($5-8) can be found at **Dress for Less,** 1km south of Richardson Ranch in a pink building. Sidle up to the pink coffee bar nestled among racks of vintage clothing. Enjoy your pick of local artist's wares, used clothes, or sip coffee on the deck. (☎ 557-2023. Open daily 9am-5pm.) Locals recommend "going to Port" for dinner but your best prices and selection on the island were back in Queen Charlotte City. Turn off for Port Clements, 22km north of Tlell, for a not-so-cheap dinner ($12-18) at an old diner, the **Hummingbird Cafe.** (Open Tu-Su 11am-3pm, 5-8pm.)

FALL AND RISE OF THE GOLDEN SPRUCE

For years, oddity-seekers of the world drove, biked, hiked, and ran to Port Clements, where the planet's only Golden Spruce basked in singular glory. Due to a rare genetic mutation, the 300-year-old tree contained only a fraction of the chlorophyll present in an ordinary Sitka spruce, causing its needles to be bleached by sunlight. The striking 50m giant glowed fiery yellow in the sun, beaming its way into Haida creation myths and horticulturists' dreams. In January 1997, however, a disgruntled ex-forestry worker arrived at the site with an axe and a mission. To protest the logging industry's destruction of British Columbia's forests, he chopped down the tree. These actions won him no prize for logic, but certainly drew province-wide attention.

While islanders reacted with astonishment at their beloved tree's untimely demise, the University of British Columbia revealed another shocker: there had been not one but *three* Golden Spruces—two, created in 1977 from clippings of the original, were growing peacefully in the botanical gardens of the UBC Victoria campus. University authorities donated these golden saplings to the Haida nation, and their future looks good. Concurrent with the fall of the Golden Spruce, an albino raven was born on the island, an event that locals took as a sign foretelling a continuation of the Spruce's three-century history.

HIKING. One of the most popular trails around Tlell leads to the **Pesuta Shipwreck,** the hulking remains of a 246-foot lumber barge that ran aground during a gale in 1928. The 2hr. hike to the site leaves from the Tlell River picnic area off Hwy. 16, just north of the river. When the trail branches, follow the "East Beach" sign up the ridge, or walk the whole way at low tide along the river. Hwy. 16 cuts inland just north of Tlell, leaving over 90km of incredibly pristine beach exclusively to backpackers. Allow 4-6 days to reach the road access at the north end of the route, 25km east of Massett. Before setting out on the **East Beach hike** register at Naikoon Provincial Park Headquarters (☎557-4390), in a brown building on the right side of the highway, just before the Tlell River bridge; call ahead. Tlell Watershed Society leads hikes throughout the island to local secret spots, such as Pretty John's Hike. Hikes are on island time so estimated return may be much later. (Call Berry Wijdeven for information ☎557-4709; www.tlellwatershed.org.)

MASSETT ☎250

At Mile Zero of the Yellowhead Hwy. (Hwy. 16), Massett's low-rise businesses and dilapidated houses present an initially underwhelming welcome. Yet some surprisingly eclectic establishments and truly odd people mingle within this rather drab collection of tired buildings. The mixture of loggers, Haidas, and hippies leads to the occasional culture clash and a sometimes volatile political and social scene. Spectacular scenery surrounds the town; the rainforest of Tow Hill and the expansive beachfront of the Blow Hole, east of town in Naikoon Provincial Park, more than justify the northward trek.

ORIENTATION AND PRACTICAL INFORMATION

Massett is about 108km (1¼hr. on a good, although narrow and deer-filled, road) north of Skidegate on Hwy. 16. To get downtown, take a left off the highway onto the main bridge, just after the small boat harbor. After the bridge, **Delkatla Rd.** is on the left. **Collision Ave.,** the main drag, is the first right off of Delkatla. To reach the campgrounds (see below), continue on Hwy. 16 without crossing the bridge.

Taxis: Vern's Taxi (☎626-3535). Open daily 8am-6pm.

Car Rental: Tilden Rentals, 1504 Old Beach Rd. (☎626-3318), at the Singing Surf Inn. From $40 per day; 25¢ per km. Must be 25. Open M-Sa 7am-9pm, Su 8am-9pm.

Car Repair: TLC (☎ 626-3756), on Collision Ave. Open daily 8am-6pm. 24hr. towing.

Visitor Information: Tourist Information Centre, Old Beach Rd. (☎ 626-3982 or 888-352-9242), at Hwy. 16. History, maps for bird watching, extensive Massett packet. Open daily July-Aug. 10am-8pm; Sept.-June F-M 9am-2pm. The **Village Office** (☎ 626-3955) has advice year-round. Open M-Th 9am-4pm, F noon-4pm.

Bank: Northern Savings (☎ 626-5231), Main St. north of Collision Ave. Only bank and **24hr. ATM** outside Queen Charlotte City. Open Tu-Th and Sa 10am-3pm, F noon-5pm.

Laundromat: (☎ 626-5007), just north of Collison on Orr St. Wash $1.75, dry $1.75. Open Tu-Sa 9am-9pm.

Pool: Massett Rec Centre (☎ 626-5507). Pay to use pool, fitness room, weights, and squash courts. Open M-F 8:30am-9pm, Sa noon-9pm, Su 3-9pm. $5, senior and children under 18 $2.50.

Internet Access: Free at the **Library** (☎ 626-3663), at Collison Ave. and McLeod St. 30min. limit. Call ahead. Open Tu 2-6pm, Th 2-5pm and 6-8pm, Sa noon-5pm. Available daily but costly ($4 per 20min.) at **tourist information centre** (see above).

Ambulance: ☎ 800-461-9911, **no 911. Police:** (☎ 626-3991), on Collison Ave. at Orr St.

Hospital: (☎ 626-4700; emergency 626-4711). The clinic (☎ 626-4702 or 626-4703) is on Hodges Ave., on the right just over the main bridge into Massett. Call ahead.

Post Office: (☎ 626-5155) on Main St. north of Collison. Open M-F 9am-5:30pm, Sa 1-4pm. **Postal Code:** V0T 1M0.

ACCOMMODATIONS AND CAMPING

Cheap campsites amid Massett's centuries-old trees and expansive waterways are plentiful. There is free **beach camping** on North Beach, 1km past Tow Hill, 30km east of Massett, in **Naikoon Provincial Park.** Look for signs marking the end of Indian Reserve property. Call ahead for favored indoor lodging.

Rapid Richie's Rustic Rentals (☎ 626-5472; www.beachcabins.com), 18km east of Massett on Tow Hill Rd. Self-sufficient accommodation on a wild northern beach. Six airy cabins with water collected from roof, propane lights, wood or propane heating, kitchen, cookstove, and pit toilets. Sleeps 2-4. $40-65 per day for 2; $10 per extra person. Reservations recommended.

Singing Surf Inn, 1504 Old Beach Road (☎ 626-3318 or 888-592-8886), next to visitors center before crossing bridge into Massettt. Another blah motel but when accommodations cost an arm and a leg, convenience wins. TV, kitchenette, and queen bed fit snugly. Single $49, double $55.

Copper Beech House, 1590 Delkatla Rd. (☎ 626-5441), at Collison Ave. by small boat dock. Dine off Beijing china, share a bath with carved wooden frogs from Mexico, and snuggle under comforters from Finland. Singles $75; doubles $100; loft in the garden shed $25 or make use of that shovel next to your pillow and stay for free.

Agate Beach Campground, 25km east of town in Naikoon Provincial Park, before Tow Hill. After 35min. of moss-swathed trees, this windswept fairyland clearing looks too good to be true. Right on the beach. Packed pretty tightly. Tent platforms, picnic shelter, firewood, water, clean pit toilets. Free clamming (see **Food,** below). 14-night max. stay. May-Sept. 32 sites, $12.

FOOD

Snatching great, big crabs is as easy pie on North Beach. A little more strenuous but still free (and potentially toxic) **razor clams** await as well. Call the **Department of Fisheries and Oceans** (☎ 626-3316) before harvesting the mollusks (see **Red Tide,** p. 32) then stop by on Christie St. (behind the visitors center) to pick up a free permit and harvesting tips. Lemons and seafood garnishes are sold at **Delmos Co-op,** on Main St., south of Collison Ave. (☎ 626-3933. Open M-Sa 10am-6pm.)

Moon Over Naikoon, 18km on the left on the Tow Hill Rd. The fruits of one man's beach-combing labor include whale bones, bleached animal skulls, bird wings, fossils, opals, and glass balls from Japanese fish nets. Edibles include whole wheat flaxseed bread ($5), melt-in-your-mouth butter tarts ($1), and marine-inspired soups and lunch dishes. Open F-M 11am-7 or 8pm.

Marj's (626-9344), on Main St. next to the post office. With the smoky ambiance of a crowded bar, this little diner is the heart of Massett town, where most of the village's problems are solved (or at least discussed) over all-day brekkie ($5-8), burgers ($6-8), a NY steak ($12), or a gargantuan slice of fresh pie ($3). Open daily 7am-3:30pm.

Sandpiper Gallery, 2062 Collison Ave. (☎626-3672). The owners happily *plaudern* with homesick Germans and serve a *lecker* chicken burger ($8). Open M-Sa 8:30am-9pm.

◼ SIGHTS AND OUTDOOR ACTIVITIES

Tow Hill, an incredible outcrop of volcanic basalt columns about 26km east of town, rises out of nowhere at the far end of Agate Beach, and presides over Massett as the area's reigning attraction. Continue 1km past Agate Back Campsite to **Tow Hill Viewpoint trailhead.** Like a fairy prance over the tar paper-covered boards up the mountain to a fabulous overlook (unless it's foggy) 100m above the rocky shoreline (30min. to ascend). On a clear day, miles of virgin beach and even the most southerly reaches of Alaska spread out below; sunsets are stupendous. On the way back down (10min.), take a detour to loop past the **Blow Hole** (25min.), a small cave that erupts with 15-foot high plumes of water at mid-tide.

Two less-traveled trails depart from the Tow Hill Viewpoint parking lot: an 11km beach walk to **Rose Spit** (2½-3hr. one-way) at the island's northeast corner, and a 10km hike on the **Cape Fife trail** (3½-4hr. one-way), which passes through some of the island's most varied vegetation with access to the East Coast Beach and the long hiking route out of Tlell (see p. 321). A lean-to at the end of the Cape Fife trail allows tireless backpackers to link the two routes, exploring the entire island in a 4-6 day trek. Inform **Naikoon Park Headquarters** (☎557-4390 in Tlell; see p. 321) before multi-day trips, and contact them for advice. Across the Hiellen River, **North Beach** is where Raven discovered a giant clam containing the first men in the Haida creation myth and where clam and crab catchers congregate today.

Closer to town, red-breasted sapsuckers, orange-crowned warblers, glaucous-winged gulls, and binocular-toting birdwatchers converge on the **Delkatla Wildlife Sanctuary,** off Tow Hill Rd. The best paths for observing 113 local species begin at the junction of Trumpeter Dr. and Cemetery Rd. Continue on Cemetery Rd. past the sanctuary to reach **Oceanview Cemetery,** in a lush green forest on the beach.

With over 600 residents, **Old Massett,** 2km west of town, is the largest Haida village on the Charlottes. Beyond a few modern totem poles, however, there's not much to look at; hold out for the **Haida Gwaii Museum** (see p. 320). Those who wish to visit abandoned Haida villages on Graham Island can request a free permit at the **Massett Band Council Office,** in the cedar-and-glass building at the east end of town. The council office also has information on local **Haida artists** with works for sale. (☎626-3337. Open M-F 8:30am-noon and 1-4:30pm.)

SANDSPIT ☎250

Sandspit is the only permanent community on Moresby Island. The town's endless ocean views and beachfront bald eagle crowd make the drive through town aesthetically pleasing. Mother Nature buffets the community with a perpetual west wind and provides sprawling sunsets over a porpoise-filled bay each evening. While Sandspit has limited culinary options, reasonably priced accommodations are plentiful and tend to fill up less quickly than those on Graham Island. This well-groomed hub houses the only commercial airport on the islands, and serves as a major launching point for kayak and boat trips to Gwaii Haanas National Park Reserve (see p. 326).

ORIENTATION AND PRACTICAL INFORMATION.
Having a car or bike is handy in Sandspit, since the town is spread over the long **Beach Rd.** parallel to the seashore. There isn't much traffic on the 13km road between Sandspit and **Alliford Bay,** where the ferry docks; those hitching to catch a late ferry report that it is often hard to find a ride. Bringing a bike over on the ferry is free, and the trip to town is an idyllic, easy, one-hour ride along the ocean.

Sandspit Airport is near the end of the spit on Beach Rd. **Air Canada** (☎ 888-247-2262) flies to **Vancouver** ($466, youth standby $160). **BC Ferries** (☎ 223-3779 or 888-559-4485; www.bcferries.bc.ca) runs between **Skidegate Landing** on Graham Island and **Alliford Bay** on Moresby Island (20min.; 12 per day; $4.75 round-trip, car $12.60, kayak or canoe $2, bikes free). **Eagle Cabs** runs a shuttle from the airport across to Queen Charlotte City twice per day. (☎ 559-4461 or 877-547-4461. One shuttle Sa. Reservations recommended. $14 includes ferry.)

Budget, 383 Beach Rd. (☎ 637-5688 or 800-577-3228), by the post office, rents autos for $50 per day plus 35¢ per km if you are 21 with a credit card. **Bayview Sales and Services,** at the west end of town, pumps gas and sells camping fuel. (☎ 637-5359. Open M-F 9am-noon and 3-7pm, Sa 9am-noon and 1-6pm, Su 9am-1pm and 6-8pm.) **Visitor and Outdoor Information** is available at the airport. Register and gather trail information or buy topographical maps here before heading into the park. **Park orientations** are held daily at 11am during the summer. (☎ 637-5362. Open mid-May to mid-Sept. 9am-6:30pm; May 1-16 and mid-Sept. to Sept. 30 daily 9am-1pm.) **The Trading Post,** on Beach Front Rd., before the gas station when heading out of Sandspit, sells fishing licences and outdoor gear. (Open M-Sa 9am-noon and 1-6pm.) The **Supervalu Supermarket,** 383 Alliford Bay, in the mini-mall near the spit, carries the only decent produce around and sells alcohol. (☎ 637-2249. Open M-Sa 9:30am-6pm, Tu 9:30am-7:30pm, Su 10am-4pm.)The **health clinic** is on Copper Bay Rd., in the school building. (☎ 637-5403. Open M-F 10am-noon.) After hours, call the **Queen Charlotte General Hospital** (☎ 559-4506). **Ambulance:** ☎ 800-461-9911. **Police:** (☎ 559-4421) in Queen Charlotte City. **Post office:** (☎ 637-2244), at Beach and Blaine Shaw Rd. Open M-F 9am-5pm, Sa 11am-2pm. **Postal code:** V0T 1T0.

ACCOMMODATIONS AND CAMPING.
Sandspit rooms are more affordable and less crowded than most on the islands. The **Seaport Bed and Breakfast,** just up the road toward Spit Point, offers island hospitality with guest pickup at the airport. Rooms in two cottages with kitchens and cable TV common rooms and a make-your-own breakfast of eggs and home-baked goods. Reservations are essential in summer. (☎ 637-5698. Singles $30; doubles $40.) Identical accommodations are provided by Bonnie's daughter two blocks away on Beach Rd. at **Bayside Bed and Breakfast** (☎ 637-2433). Not quite as homey but nearly as economical, **Moresby Island Guest House,** on Beach Rd. next to the post office, has eight rooms with shared washrooms, kitchen, and coin-operated laundry facilities. Make-your-own-breakfast is provided, but further kitchen use costs $10. (☎ 637-5300. Singles $30; doubles from $55; cots $15.) **501 RV and Tent Park,** 501 Beach Rd., has the only public showers on the island. (☎ 637-5473. Showers $1 per 2min. Open daily 8am-9pm. 5 tent sites $8, 10 hookups $10.)

Along the west coast of the island, BC Parks and the Forestry Service maintain two campgrounds. The first at **Mosquito Lake,** about 35km (1hr.) from **Sandspit,** is every tenter's dream with mossy sites in wooded seclusion. About another 7km down the road, **Moresby camp** has mowed sites with fewer bugs but the traffic of eager boaters heading off into Gwai Haanas. Both require an $8 permit. Follow Alliford Bay Main past the ferry docks to South Bay Main to Moresby Rd. to get there. **Grey Bay,** 20km south of town (30min. drive), offers a virtually uninterrupted expanse of sand. Twenty primitive forestry **campsites** line the long expanse of the beach giving tons of privacy, but arrive early on weekends ($8 permit only). Obtain directions and logging road activity updates at the visitors center.

🍴 **FOOD.** For all the golf you can handle ($20) and loaded burgers or veggie burgers ($6-8), head to **Willows Golf Course Clubhouse,** near the end of Copper Bay Rd. (☎637-2388. Open W-Su 11:30am-8pm.) More pleasant inside than out, **Dick's Wok Restaurant and Grocery,** 388 Copper Bay Rd., serves a heaping plate of fried rice ($9.50) next to a tank filled with monster goldfish. Dick also offers a limited selection of groceries. (☎637-2275. Open daily 5-10pm.) The **Sandspit Inn,** opposite the airport near the spit's end, houses the town's only **pub.** (☎637-5334. Open daily 11:30am-11pm, F-Sa until 1am.)

OUTDOOR ACTIVITIES AND EVENTS. Spectacular sunrises and sunsets reward those who wander to the end of the **Spit** where anglers surf-cast for silver salmon. Beachcombers should stay below the tide line if possible, since the spit is legally airport property. Several trails depart from the road between the ferry docks and the spit. In May take the easy stroll on **Onward Point trail** (30min.) to a grey whale watching outlook and the nearby fossil bed. The **Dover Trail** begins 40m west of the Haans Creek Bridge across from the small boat harbor and passes by giant cedars with ancient Haida markings (2hr.). The **Skyline Loop** runs an hour down to the shore over more difficult terrain. Although this trail system is marked, it goes through dense brush and crosses other trails, making the return trip difficult to follow.

Dirt logging roads lead south and west of town into some smashingly scenic areas. If you plan on using **logging roads** between 6am and 6pm during the week, you must check in at the visitors center for active logging status; in winter call Teal Jones (☎637-5323). Ten kilometers past where Copper Bay Rd. turns into gravel are the rocky shores of **Copper Bay,** a haven for bald eagles.

The roads are perfect for **mountain biking.** The closest rentals are in Charlotte, and bikes are allowed free on ferries. The 24km Moresby Loop is a popular route that runs from Sandspit down to an old train trellis over Skidegate Lake and on to an abandoned Cumshewa Inlet logging camp. Logging in the area has slowed, locals still celebrate **Logger Sports Day** in July. The festival features pole-climbing, caber-tossing, axe-throwing, and other vigorous lumber-related activities.

GWAII HAANAS NATIONAL PARK RESERVE/ HAIDA HERITAGE SITE

Rugged yet mystical. Harsh yet soothing. No, it's not a new scent from Calvin Klein—it's an island. Visitors lured to Gwaii Haanas (gway-HAH-nus) will be challenged physically and rewarded spiritually. Appropriately, the powerful Gwaii Haanas was born in a whirlwind of controversy. Provincially owned Crown Land for most of the 20th century, the territory has been disturbed only by sporadic logging and occasional tourist visits to deserted Haida villages. In the mid-80s, the timber industry, the Haida nation, environmentalists, and the provincial government came to heads over land use on the island. In 1988, the federal government interceded, purchasing the southern third of the Queen Charlotte Islands to create a National Park Reserve. A 1993 agreement united the Haida Nation and the Government of Canada in the management of Gwaii Haanas. The Canadian Parks Ministry now patrols the islands, while the Haida Gwaii Watchmen guide visitors with the goal of protecting their cultural heritage.

ORIENTATION

By air or by sea, each summer a few thousand visitors make the long ocean journey south from Moresby Camp (about 25km). **No trails** penetrate Gwaii Haanas and most exploration remains close to the 1600km of shoreline. While the 640km east coast consists of islands, inlets, bays, and sandy beaches, the seas on the rocky west coast pound, making travel treacherous. The serene, remote waters teem with marine life and birds, peaking in Burnaby Narrows with the highest density of animal and vegetable protein per square meter in the world. Not as far south, jellyfish and enormous, garishly colored starfish fill the waters of **Juan Perez Sound.** Haida people divide ecology into three. Sea, land, and sky are ruled by killer whale, bear, and eagle. Gaze up to see bald eagle nests in dead trees, cross your fingers and run across a transient killer whale pod, and paddle silently along shore at dawn to spot the strong-jawed sub-species of **black bears** unique to Haida Gwaii. The islands hold treasures as inspiring as the seascape. Old growth forest stands tall in **Hik'yah (Windy Bay),** where Haida stood up to loggers. Chains of lakes and waterfalls span Gwaii Haanas. At **Gandll K'in (Hotsprings Island),** three pristine seaside pools steam, soothing ocean-weary muscles.

Haida Gwaii Watchmen share the history of their culture at settlements being permitted to "return to the land," in keeping with Haida tradition. Totem poles slowly decay at **K'uuna (Skedans)** on Louise Island, north of Gwaii Hanaas, and the UNESCO World Heritage site of **Nan Sdins (Ninstints).** Both Haida villages were deserted after late-19th-century epidemics of smallpox and tuberculosis. At **T'aanuu (Tanu)** a moss grown longhouse village can be envisioned from the depressions and fallen poles. The grave of the recently deceased, famous Haida carver Bill Reid can be visited on the point next to the grave of the anonymous "Charlie."

PRACTICAL INFORMATION

Three hundred people can enter the park **without licensed tour operators** each year and face unique planning and preparation concerns. These experienced kayakers and small craft owners may reserve dates to enter and exit the park by calling **Super, Natural British Columbia** (in Canada and the US ☎ 800-663-6000; elsewhere 250-387-1642). Reservations cost $15 per person. The park also provides six standby entries daily, although if you secure one of these spots you still may not be able to enter the park for another couple of days. All visitors must attend the 1½hr. **orientation session** before they depart: these are held daily at 8am and 7:30pm at the **Queen Charlotte City visitor center** (see p. 318) and at 11am at the **Sandspit visitor center** (see p. 325) from May to September. Call at least a day ahead to arrange sessions. Park user fees are $10 per day (under 17 free; $80 max.). For a **trip-planning** package with a list of charter companies, contact **Parks Canada** (☎ 250-559-8818). Ask the park management about camping locations to avoid traditional Haida sites. Kayakers venturing into the park alone should file a **sail plan** with the **Prince Rupert Coast Guard** (call collect 250-627-3081). Contact **Fisheries and Oceans** (☎ 559-4413) before sampling shellfish. Freshwater fishing is not allowed; saltwater licenses are available in Charlotte (see p. 318).

Weather reports are broadcast on VHF channel 21. Two **warden stations** are staffed from May to September, at Huxley Island (about halfway down the park) and at Rose Harbour (near the south tip of Moresby Island). They can be reached on VHF channel 16. Five **watchmen sites** (VHF 6) are staffed during the same period, and will offer assistance upon request, although their role is not to act as tour guides. To visit a cultural site, contact the watchmen a day in advance. No more than 12 people are permitted ashore at any one time.

> **SIREN'S CALL** Pause from paddling. Cut off your Zodiak engine. Break the silence with a bull kelp horn! The long, strong plant material floating on the surface can be put to use to demonstrate—loud and clear—how your inner animal is being freed in these wilds (or at least how your inner child is free to partake in an arts and crafts break). Snatch a dislodged piece of the kelp, unfold your Swiss army knife, and slice it off at both ends to a length of 1-2 meters. You should see daylight through the ends. Now hold your horn in a "U" shape, buzz as you would to play a brass instrument, and suck face with one end of that slimy kelp. Hear it echo! Start a band: The Bullkelps.

OUTDOOR ACTIVITIES

To avoid the exposed north portion of Moresby Island and to begin your trip in shelter of coastal islands, **Moresby Camp,** on the west side of the island, is a logical place to enter the park. Check with the info center in Sandspit (see p. 324) before traveling the potentially hazardous logging roads to this access point. **Bruce's Taxi** will run you down the gravel roads to Moresby Camp. (☎637-5655. 1hr. $150 one-way; fits 7 people and 2 kayaks; pre-arranged pickup.) **Moresby Explorers** (☎800-806-7633) will transport kayakers, kayaks, and gear from Sandspit into Gwaii Hanaas ($125 per person to Juan Perez Sound) or to their float camp at the north edge of Gwaii Haanas to pick-up rental kayaks ($320 per week to rent and be transported). **Queen Charlotte Adventures,** 34 Wharf St. (☎559-8990 or 800-668-4288), in Queen Charlotte City, offers sea kayak rentals (singles $40 per day, $200 per week), marine transport ($135 from Queen Charlotte to Juan Perez Sound). A round-trip kayak voyage down the length of the Gwaii Haanas takes two weeks.

To experience Gwaii Haanas with less time and challenge, **tour operators** guide visitors and facilitate all logistics for entering Gwaii Haanas. Guided visitors do not have to make independent reservations or attend an info session. Run by energetic Doug Gould, **Moresby Explorers** (☎637-2215 or 800-806-7633; www.moresby-explorers.com), on Beach Rd. in Sandspit just west of Copper Bay Rd., offers chartered trips ($125, 2 days with overnight at float camp $350). Bombing along on Zodiaks with guides who know the waters like the back of their hands, visit Stellar sea lion haul-outs, Haida ruins, and secluded inlets and beaches. **South Moresby Air Charters** (☎559-4222) flies over many of the heritage sites.

APPROACHING THE YUKON

People exiting Northern BC take one of two routes. The Alaska Hwy. (Hwy. 97) hugs more to the eastern side of the province, while the Cassiar Hwy. (Hwy. 37) runs through the western portion of the north. The Cassiar is accessed from the south from Hwy. 16. A smattering of small towns line each road.

ALONG HWY. 37: CASSIAR HWY.

A growing number of travelers prefer the Cassiar Hwy. to the Alaska Hwy., which has become an RV institution. Built in 1972, the Cassiar slices through charred forests and snow-capped ebony peaks, passing scores of alpine lakes on its way from the Yellowhead Hwy. (Hwy. 16) in British Columbia to the Alaska Hwy. in the Yukon. Three evenly spaced provincial campgrounds right off the highway offer beautiful camping and lodges in the provincial parks section in the middle provide resort-like accommodation at prices lower than highway motels on the Alaska Hwy. Any waiter or lodging owner along the Cassiar's 718km will readily list its advantages: less distance, consistently intriguing scenery, and fewer crowds. On the other hand, services are scarce in many portions of the highway, and the Cassiar is less maintained. Large sections past Meziadin Junction are dirt and gravel and become slippery when wet. This causes little concern for commercial trucks roaring up and down the route, but keeps the infrequent service stops busy with overambitious drivers in need of tire repair. Driving at dawn, dusk, and on Sundays keeps you in sight of wildlife and out of the way of gravel-spitting behemoths.

HWY. 16 TO MEZIADIN JUNCTION

Just north of the junction of Hwy. 37 and Hwy. 16 stand the totem poles of **Gitwengak,** which relate the history of the First Nation fort that stood on nearby **Battle Hill** until 1800. The 2.5km **Kitwanga Loop Rd.,** 4km north of the junction, leads through Kitwanga to the **National Historic Park** where Battle Hill is located. Once equipped as a stronghold for the mighty warrior **Nekt,** Battle Hill has become demure in its old age. Its intricate tunnel system has given way to stairs and guided walkways. The totem poles in the small native village of **Gitanyom** lie another 19km to the north and 3km off the highway.

The first gas stop is 139km north at **Meziadin Lake General Store,** where produce, deli sandwiches, mail, and fishing stuff can be found. (☎ 636-2657. Open in summer daily 7am-11pm; winter 7am-9pm.) **Postal code:** V0J 3S0. **Meziadin Lake Provincial Park** (meh-zee-AD-in) lies another 16km north, with plenty of fishing but tightly packed sites. (Water, free firewood, and pit toilets. 66 sites $12.) The gravel sites are better geared to RVs, but tenters endure for the fishing; Meziadin Lake is one of three lakes in BC where salmon spawn.

Make minor **tire repairs,** grab gas, and shoot the bull with truckers at **Meziadin Junction.** (☎ 636-2390. Open daily 7am-9pm; winter 8am-7pm.) There is also an unremarkable but cheap **cafe.** (☎ 636-9240. Open daily in summer 7am-7pm.) Don't get confused by the "T" in the road. Turn right to **Whitehorse, YT,** which lies 953km (13-15hr. of solid driving, depending on your vehicle) to the north. Or, turn left to **Stewart, BC,** and **Hyder, AK,** which are 62km (45min. on paved roads) west, along Hwy. 37A. The road to Stewart and Hyder is known as the "Glacier Highway" because immense ice-tongues creep down so close to the road that drivers can feel the frigid air on their skin.

STEWART, BC AND HYDER, AK ☎ 250

"It's the prettiest place on earth," profess most Hyderites. Arriving along Hwy. 37A past towering glaciers and gushing waterfalls, most visitors need little convincing. **Stewart, BC,** is positioned in the jaws of one of the world's longest fjords among tidal flats. Its cross-border partner, the former ghost town of **Hyder, AK,** maintains its frontier character among stray horses taking refuge under eaves and porches. Although Hyder is technically in Alaska, its currency is Canadian (except at the US Post Office), its clocks tick to Pacific Standard Time, and its area code is 250. During International Days, from Canada Day to Independence Day (July 1-4), the two tiny communities erupt in an extravaganza of fellowship that is North America's longest birthday party, and visitors are heartily welcomed to bond in local bars. Stewart provides most modern amenities in contrast with Hyder, which sports frontier-style nightlife and dirt roads. Although the past economy has been based on mining and timber industries, with attractions like the world's largest road-accessible glacier, Hyder and Stewart are becoming a tourist center with the friendliness to keep folks coming back.

ORIENTATION AND PRACTICAL INFORMATION

Hwy. 37A becomes **Conway St.** in Stewart. It intersects **5th Ave.** which is the main drag on the waterfront and leads along the bay into Hyder. On your return from Hyder, beware: Canadian customs has begun patrolling the border to curb smuggling. Be prepared to show ID and be asked how long you were in "America." Humorless officers don't flinch at the typical response of "about 5 minutes."

- **Airplanes: Taguan Air** (☎ 636-2800) flies a mail plane which carries passengers to **Ketchikan** (45min., M and Th, $100). Call ahead.
- **Local Transportation: Seaport Limousines** (☎ 636-2622), in Stewart, drives to Terrace (4hr., daily 10am, $30) and takes sightseers to Salmon Glacier for $32 per person.

Auto Repair: PetroCan (☎ 636-2307; after hours ☎ 636-2456), at 5th Ave. and Conway, has the only gas in either town. Open daily 7:30am-8pm, repairs 8am-4:30pm. 24hr. road service.

Visitor Information: In **Stewart** (☎ 636-9224) on 5th Ave. heading to Hyder. Open June-Aug. daily 9am-7pm; winter M-F 1-5pm. In **Hyder** (☎ 636-9148), at the **Hyder Community Association Building;** bear right at the Sealaska Inn downtown. Open June-Aug. M 10am-2pm, Th noon-4pm.

Outdoor Information: Forest Service (☎ 636-2367), down the hall from Hyder visitors center. Open May 1-Sept. 15, usually 10am-2pm. Call ahead.

Bank: Canadian Imperial Bank of Commerce (☎ 636-2235). Open M and W noon-3pm. A **24hr. ATM** on 5th Ave. in Stewart is the only bank, by the post office.

Laundromat and Public Showers: Shoreline Laundromat (☎ 636-2322), on Brightwell and 6th, behind the post office. Wash $1.75, dry 25¢ per 4min. Showers $1 per 1½min. Open daily 7am-11pm. In Hyder, beside the **Sealaska Inn.** Wash $2, dry $1.75. Showers $3 per 8min. Open 24hr.

Emergency: ☎ 911. **Police:** (☎ 636-2233) at 8th Ave. and Conway St.

Ambulance: ☎ 800-461-9911. **Fire:** ☎ 636-2345.

Health Centre: (☎ 636-2221), at Brightwell and 9th. Open M-F 9am-5pm.

Internet Access: A cheap $2 per hr. at **Stewart Public Library** in the school, turn left on 9th Ave. as you drive into Stewart from highway. In June: M and Th 6-9pm; Su, Tu, and Th 1:30-4:30pm. In July and Aug.: M and Th 6-9pm; Tu, W, and F 1:30-4:30pm. **Toast Works,** see **Food,** below. $6 per hour.

Post Office: (☎ 636-2553) In Stewart, at Brightwell St. and 5th Ave. Open M-F 8:30am-5pm, Sa 9am-noon. **Postal Code:** V0T 1W0. In Hyder, 1 Hyder Ave. (☎ 636-2662), past the Community Building towards Fish Creek. US currency only. Open M-F 9am-1pm and 2-5pm, Sa 10:30am-12:30pm. **ZIP code:** 99923.

ACCOMMODATIONS AND FOOD

Reasonably priced B&Bs are popping up all over Stewart and Hyder. Get into the coastal spirit with the overwhelming number of nautical knick-knacks at **Anchor Down B&B,** the last house on 5th Ave. before heading to Hyder. For a small cost, you can soak in the big bathtub, relax on the comfy couch overlooking the bay, and then fill-up on Tami's fresh bread smeared in Nutella while Tony shares his fishing tales. (☎ 636-2789. Single $50, double $65, private cabin $75. Full breakfast included.) **Kathi's B&B,** at the corner of 8th and Brightwell, provides placid accommodations and a full breakfast. (☎ 636-2795. Singles $60; doubles $70.)

Stewart's **Rainey Creek Campground,** located at the end of Brightwell St., is orderly, quiet, and woodsy; putting-green quality grassy tent sites, forested sites with electricity, and impeccably clean showers. (☎ 636-2537. Showers $1 per 4min. Tents $11 for 2 people, $3 per extra person. Dry RV sites $15, sites with electricity $18.) Less appealing **Camp Runamuck,** in Hyder, has tent-sites ($10) next to the sani-dump, separated from a gravelly RV park (hookups $18) with coin showers and laundry in the **Sealaska Inn.** The Inn has cubicle-like, "sleeping rooms" and regular rooms. (☎ 636-2486 or 888-393-1199. Tents $10, hookups $18. Sleeping rooms with shared bath $34; singles $54; doubles $58.) It's upstairs from a night lounge famous for its wet t-shirt contests during **International Days.**

The **Bitter Creek Cafe,** in Stewart on 5th Ave., makes a stab at trendy, California-inspired fare in a great building adorned with historical photos and frontier appliances. (☎ 636-2166. Open May-Oct. daily 11:30am-2pm and 5-8pm; July-Aug. 8am-9pm.) Across the street, **Toast Works** has an interactive appliance bar and serves fruit smoothies. Two dollars will get you into toaster-lover's heaven, dedicated to the history of the toaster. (Open daily mid-May to mid-Sept. noon-5:30pm.) **Rainey Creek Bakery and Deli,** also on 5th Ave. will tempt you with low-priced, fresh-baked treats and breads. (☎ 636-2777. Open daily 8am-8pm.) **Cut-Rate Foods,** on 5th Ave. in Stewart, lives up to its name. (☎ 636-2377. Open daily 9am-9pm. No credit cards.)

MEZIADIN JUNCTION TO ISKUT ■ 331

INTERNATIONAL DAYS Celebrated in Stewart, BC, and Hyder, AK, International Days run from Canada Day, July 1st, to Independence Day, July 4th. The four days of wild festivities are kicked off by the wet t-shirt contest at the Sealaska. It features such events as the ax throw and the broom kick and culminates with the annual Bush Woman Classic. The strong-armed women of Hyder and Stewart come together to flex their muscles and to post the fastest time and highest accuracy over a course that includes hanging laundry, shooting a bear, chopping wood, diapering a baby, hauling pails of water, and finally sprinting while applying lipstick. Beware, these women take no prisoners, and spectators are often rallied into competing.

SIGHTS, NIGHTLIFE, AND OUTDOOR ACTIVITIES

SIGHTS. The Stewart Historical Society runs a **museum,** on Columbia St., which offers, among the usual suspects of stuffed wildlife, an exhibit on the Great Avalanche of '65 and a disturbing collection of photos documenting the 1981 filming in Stewart of *The Thing.* (☎636-2568. In winter call 636-9029 for appointment. Open mid-May to mid-Sept. daily 11am-7pm. $4, ages 6-12 $2, under 6 free.)

NIGHTLIFE. The principal activity in Hyder is sidling up to the bar in the historic **Glacier Inn** and asking to be "Hyderized." Over $45,000 in signed bills line the tavern walls, where early miners would tack up cash to insure themselves against returning to town too broke to buy a drink. A sign over the door reminds youth that the drinking age in the US is 21. (☎636-9092. Open 10am-sometime late; winter 2pm-whenever.) If you want to catch a ballgame on TV or master the Grand Lizard pinball machine, head over to the **Sealaska.** (Take a left at the "intersection," for your Hyderization. ☎636-2486. Open 11am til the wet t-shirts dry.)

OUTDOOR ACTIVITIES. Each year during the salmon spawning season (late July-Aug.), bears congregate at **Fish Creek,** 5 mi./8km down the road in Hyder, to feed on bloated, dying Alaskan chum salmon. Come early in the morning to avoid tourist crowds. The only maintained trail on the Hyder side is the **Titan Trail,** a challenging 16km (round-trip) hike up from the valley with creek crossings. It gains 1200m of elevation, becoming rocky and difficult toward the end (check with the Forest Service for trail conditions). Heading away from Hyder, the trailhead is on the right about half a mile past Fish Creek. Check with forestry gang for trail conditions and bear density. Eight miles/13km north of Stewart along Hwy. 37A, the **Ore Mountain Trail** is a shorter, but still challenging 4 mi./7km (round-trip) climb to a viewpoint overlooking the Bear River Valley.

Salmon Glacier, 20 mi./32km from Hyder on the Salmon River Rd., is the fifth-largest glacier in the world and the largest accessible by road. Beginning at Mile 19, the road creeps along a ridge almost directly above the glacier for several miles, providing eagle-eye views. The rocks above the road make for good hiking as the immense glacier lays beneath the setting sun. The road to the glacier is rocky and winding but navigable for most vehicles. There are many scenic pullouts. Check road conditions with the Forest Service and pick up a self-guided tour brochure. **Bear Glacier,** 22½ mi./35km east of Stewart, sits in plain and glorious view of Hwy. 37A. Most anglers let the bear population work the creeks and streams, but for a hefty sum, deluxe fishing boats can be chartered for the hour, day, or week. If you already possess boating prowess, you can rent your own craft.

MEZIADIN JUNCTION TO ISKUT   ☎ 250

This stretch of the Cassiar Hwy. has hands-down the best lodging and roadside bear-viewing around and also closest access to the two provincial parks. The area around the small village of **Iskut,** 256km north of Meziadin Junction, presents a range of resorts, earning it the unremarkable title, "Resort Capital of NW BC."

The first stop after the junction is 90km north at **Bell II Lodge,** the posh heli-skiing that caters to road trip enthusiasts in the summer searching for gas and food at reasonable prices. Big breakfast $8 and burgers $6-8. (☎604-881-8530 or 800-655-5566. Sites $10. RV hookups $22. Showers and dump station. Gas and coffee shop open daily 7am-10pm. Dining room open daily 7am-8pm.) Another 117km north is **Kinaskan Lake Provincial Park,** where an immaculately kept campground includes water, pit toilets, firewood, and a boat launch onto the rainbow trout-stocked lake. (Wheelchair accessible. 50 lakeside sites, $12.) At the far end of the lake is the head of a 24km hiking trail to **Mowdade Lake** in **Mount Edziza Provincial Park** (see below). There is gas, car repairs, lodging, boat rentals, and the last food for a while among the moose antlers of the "wilderness oasis" of **Tatogga Lake Resort,** another 25km north. Rustic, lake-front cabins with woodstoves $30, cabins with amenities $45 for one bed, $65 for two beds. Canoes $20 for 2hr., $40 per day. Boat and motor $65 per day. Meat lover's sandwich $4.50. (☎234-3526. Laundry $2.50 wash or dry, showers $3. Tent sites $10-12. RV hookups $18. Open daily May-Sept. 7am-10pm, winter 7am-7pm.) A stone's throw farther is the **Ealue Lake** (EE-lu-eh) turn-off on Spatsizi Rd., which leads to trailheads pointing deep into the virgin backcountry of the **Spatsizi Plateau Wilderness** (see below).

Even the most discriminating hostel connoisseurs heartily approve of ■**The Red Goat Lodge,** 3km south of Iskut on **Eddontenajon Lake.** The **hostel** in the basement of this lodge boasts a full kitchen, spacious common room, wood stove, coin showers, and laundry. The hosts' kids and llamas keep the place lively even when it's not packed. The **B&B** upstairs is equally impressive. (☎234-3261. Showers $1 per 3½min. Wash $2, dry $1. Hostel $15. B&B singles $65, doubles $85. Cabins $85-105.) Tent sites on the loon-inhabited lake. ($13; RV hookups $20. Canoes $10 per half-day. Rentals for trips on the **Stikine** and **Spatsizi Rivers** start at $35 per day.)

At Iskut, travelers can get gas and groceries at **Kluachon Centre.** (☎234-3241. Open daily June-Aug. 8am-10pm; winter M-Sa 9am-6pm, Su noon-5pm.) It doubles as the **post office** (open M, W, and F 9am-4pm, Tu 1-4pm). **Postal Code:** V0J 1K0.

Just north of Iskut, ■**Mountain Shadow RV Park and Campground** has lovely campsites nestled in the mountain forest near a trail to the lake or a hike into the woods. Sleeping cabin with electricity $45 or the Ritz of cabins with stocked kitchen and bathroom $65. Showerhouse is cute and clean with flush potties. (☎234-3333. Tent sites $15. RV electric hookups $18. Full hookups $20. Boat rental $15.)

DEASE LAKE ☎250

Dease Lake, 84km north of Iskut, became a Hudson Bay Company outpost in the late 1800s, although it had been long known by the local indigenous Tahltan as "Tatl'ah" ("Head of the Lake"). The settlement had its share of early gold rush glory in 1864 and 1873 and now serves as a rudimentary service center for northwestern BC. There's little to draw road-trippers to this town besides gas and food. The traveler in search of accommodations should stay outside of Dease Lake in resort-like, lake-front accommodations in the **Iskut** area that cost less and have more character.

❼ PRACTICAL INFORMATION. The **Dease Lake Tourist Information Office** is in the Northern Lights College, a small series of buildings on Cassiar in the middle of town (☎771-3900). The **Forest Service** (☎771-8100) occupies the building next door and offers info on local trails or campsites; call ahead. Fishing and camping supplies can be found at **McLeod Mountain Supply Ltd.,** on Boulder St. past **Tanzilla Bar.** (☎771-4699. Open M-Sa 9am-5pm, Su 10am-4pm.) Free **Internet access** is available at the Northern Lights College. (Open M-F 8:30am-noon and 1-4:30pm.) The **TD Bank** is in the Government building across the highway from the college. (Open M, W, and F 10am-noon and 1-3pm.) **Dease Gas Station** has **showers** ($4; includes towel, soap, and shampoo) and a **laundromat** (☎771-5600; wash $3, dry

NEAR DEASE LAKE: TELEGRAPH CREEK ■ 333

25¢ per 5min.; open daily 7am-8pm). The **Stikine Health Center** is just off the Cassiar at the north end of town. (☎771-4444. Walk-in M-F 8:30am-4:30pm.) **Police:** ☎771-4111. **Ambulance:** ☎771-3333. **Post office:** (☎771-5013), in the Dease Gas Station. Open M-F 8:30am-1pm and 2-5pm. **Postal Code:** V0C 1L0.

🍴🛏 ACCOMMODATIONS AND FOOD. The spacious, pine-furnished **Arctic Divide Inn,** right on the Cassiar, deserves accolades for its squeaky clean rooms with private bath, phones, TV, and access to a spotless shared kitchen. From the rugged staircase to the carefully positioned rock and mineral collection, the inn's decor is a welcome exception to regional drabness. (☎771-3119. Singles and doubles $65. Includes generous continental breakfast.) Camping in town leads to **Allen Lake.** From Boulder St., go left on 1st Ave. and follow it to the end ($8 camping permit only; no real sites, no water, pit toilets). Revellers take advantage of the campground's proximity to the smoky, dark **Tanzilla Bar.** (☎771-3131. Open noon-midnight, 1am on weekends.) Those without four-wheel-drive vehicles shouldn't park at the campground—the steep gravel driveway to the lake is likely to hold city cars hostage. Opt for camping outside of town to the south at the Tanzilla River Lion's Club Campground ($7 for a site with fire pit and pit toilets, $3 per bundle of wood) or drive an hour south for true camping paradise.

Northway Country Kitchen, or "the restaurant," offers big portions in a clean, spacious setting. Feel your arteries clog for only $9.50 with "pierogies & smokies," cheese-filled dumplings with four sizeable sausages. (☎771-4114. Open May-Oct. daily 7am-9pm.) Stock up on the best priced and fullest selection of **groceries** for quite a distance at the **Supervalu.** (☎771-4381. Open mid-June to Sept. daily 8am-8pm; winter M-Sa 9am-7pm, Su 9am-6pm.)

NEAR DEASE LAKE: TELEGRAPH CREEK

Lying 119km from Dease Lake on Telegraph Creek Rd., Telegraph Creek is the only remaining settlement along the **Stikine River** (stuh-KEEN). The highest navigable point on the Stikine, the site was an important rendezvous for the coastal Tlingit and interior Tahltan people. Telegraph Creek's 400 residents are still predominatley Tahltan. The community welcomes its infrequent visitors, but those keen to explore should seek permission from the **Tahltan Band** (☎235-3151) before crossing onto tribal lands. For **tire repair,** contact **Henry Vance** (☎235-3300). Mechanically adept locals have been known to help out those whose vehicles incur the substantial wrath of the Telegraph Creek Rd. Follow signs for Glenora to find the **health clinic** (☎235-3212 or 235-3171). **Police:** ☎235-3111. On your way to town, the **post office,** is on the right. (Open M and W 9:30-11:30am, Tu and Th 1-4pm, F 9:30-11:30am and 1-4pm.) **Postal code:** V0J 2W0.

The biggest attraction for thrill-seeking travelers is the 112km **Telegraph Creek Rd.** The gravel road is well maintained and offers magnificent views of the **Stikine Grand Canyon.** It is no place, however, to lug a clumsy RV or give a failed brake system a second chance. The second half of the road features 20% grades and hairpin turns along the steep obsidian outbanks of the Tuya and Stikine River canyons. Travelers should allow 2½hr. to drive each way, with ample time to de-frazzle in between. A rest stop, 88km from Telegraph Creek, offers a view of the canyon and a chance to speak words of encouragement to your beleaguered transmission.

The modern village of Telegraph Creek revolves around the historic **Stikine RiverSong.** Originally the Hudson Bay Company building near the neighboring tent city of **Glenora,** 12 mi. from Telegraph Creek, the RiverSong was disassembled in 1902 and moved to its present location. Today, the RiverSong acts as Telegraph Creek's hotel, cafe, gas station, and general store. Rooms are clean, with cedar finishing and a common kitchen. (☎235-3196. Showers $4. Open May-Sept. M-Sa 11am-7pm, Su noon-7pm. Singles $55; doubles $65; $10.50 per additional person.) Free **camping** is available 15 mi. toward Glenora past Winter Creek.

DEASE LAKE TO THE ALASKA HWY.

This stretch of highway follows the old Cassiar Gold Route, and dredges still in use can be seen along its length. **Moose Meadow Resort,** 85km north of Dease Lake, is a roomy lakeside campground with access to canoe routes. (Firewood, water, showers $2.50. Sites $8; cabins from $25.) **Jade City,** 113km past Dease Lake, offers free RV and tent sites in addition to an impressive jade stash. (Open daily 8am-9pm.) **Kididza Services,** at Good Hope Lake, 23km past Jade City, is the last gas for 98km, when you hit the Alaska Hwy. (☎239-3500. Open M-Sa 8am-9pm, Su 10am-4pm.) **Boya Lake Provincial Park** is 152km north of Dease Lake and the final campground before the Alaska Hwy. (85km), situated on a magnificent turquoise lake with a boat launch and swimming dock. Spacious, well-kept campsites please tenters and RV drivers with a book exchange box at the entrance. (Pit toilets, firewood, water. 45 sites, $12.) Having crossed into Yukon 3.5km back and reached the end of this 718km odyssey at the junction of the Cassiar Hwy. and the Alaska Hwy., travelers can grab showers, munchies, gas, and minor repairs at the **PetroCan Station,** which doubles as the office for the RV park and motel next door. (☎536-2794. Showers free, $3 for non-guests. Sites $12-14, full hookups $19. Shared bath; no TV or phone. Singles and doubles $40.) If the office is closed, check in at the **saloon.** (☎536-2796. Open daily 11am-midnight.) The station also operates a **24hr. laundromat** (wash $1.50, dry 50¢ per 14min.). Travelers can chomp on a Junction Melt ($8) at the **Junction 37 Cafe,** next to PetroCan. (☎536-2795. Open May-Oct. M-Sa 6am-midnight, Su 7am-10pm; winter 7am-10pm daily.) **Whitehorse** lies another 435km (5hr.) west on the Alaska Hwy. (see below).

HWY. 97: THE ALASKA HWY.

Built during World War II in reaction to the Japanese bombing of Pearl Harbor and the capture of two Aleutian Islands, the Alaska Hwy. served to calm Alaskan fears of an Axis invasion. Due to the speed with which it was built, the highway stands as one of the most incredible engineering feats of the 20th century. Army troops and civilians pushed from both ends—Dawson Creek and Fairbanks—and bridged the 2451km at Mile 1202 (near Beaver Creek) in 8 months and 12 days.

While the original one lane dirt track has evolved into a "highway," the potholes that develop after the winter thaw and the patches of loose gravel give drivers a taste of the good old days. In recent years, the US Army has been replaced by an annual army of over 250,000 tourists and RV-borne senior citizens from the US and Europe. Travelers in July, the busiest month, will face crowded campgrounds and seemingly endless RV caravans. The twists and turns of the highway, built to accommodate the terrain, make the caravan movement slower than molasses. They'll also be passed by the speediest semis the roads have ever known. In general, there's a trade-off between the excitement you'll find on the Alaska Hwy. and the speed with which you'll reach Alaska. For those with the time to stop, there are countless opportunities to hike, fish, and view wildlife off the highway. However, if your priority is to beat the quickest path to the Yukon border, the **Cassiar Hwy.** (Hwy. 37; see p. 328) may be a better route for you. Another scenic option is on the far side of the Yukon border, on the **Campbell Hwy.** (Hwy. 4; see p. 389).

For daily Alaska Hwy. road conditions call 867-667-8215. Mileposts put up along the highway in the 1940s are still used as mailing addresses and reference points, although the road has been rebuilt and rerouted so many times that they are no longer accurate. In BC and the Yukon, more dependable kilometer posts were installed in the mid-70s and recalibrated in 1990. Washouts sometimes occur in the spring, and other hazards include forest fires, falling rock, and construction delays. Motorists should always be aware of wildlife on the road, keep headlights on, carry spare tires and spare parts, and be prepared to slow down for graders, potholes, and general road breakup and gravel patches.

DAWSON CREEK ☎ 250

Mile 0 of the Alaska Hwy. is Dawson Creek, BC (not to be confused with Dawson City, YT or Dawson's Creek, *WB*). First settled in 1890, it was just another pipsqueak frontier village of a few hundred people among the flaming canola fields of Peace River. The town's status as a railroad terminus made it a natural place to begin building a 2600km highway. The 13,000-odd residents are serious about their home's role as the womb of the Alaska Hwy., and visitors who pause to enjoy the town's history and genuine hospitality can easily get caught up in the enthusiasm. Dawson draws a hardy Alaskan bound crew and caters more to the pure tourist than the outdoorsman.

ORIENTATION AND PRACTICAL INFORMATION

There are two ways to reach Dawson Creek from the south. From Alberta, drive northwest from Edmonton along **Hwy. 43**, through Whitecourt to Valleyview; turn left on **Hwy. 34** to Grande Prairie, and continue northwest on **Hwy. 2** to Dawson Creek for a total journey of 590km. From Prince George, drive 402km north on the John Hart section of **Hwy. 97** (see p. 310). Both drives take the better part of a day.

- **Buses: Greyhound,** 1201 Alaska Ave. (☎ 782-3131 or 800-661-8747), runs to **Whitehorse, YT** (20hr.; June-Aug. M-Sa; $182), **Prince George** (6½hr., 2 per day, $54), and **Edmonton** (8hr., 2 per day, $77). Open M-F 6am-5:30pm and 8-8:30pm; Sa 6-11am, 2:30-4:30pm, and 8-8:30pm; Su 6-10:30am, 3-4:30pm, and 8-8:30pm.

- **Visitor Information:** Stop at the **visitors center,** 900 Alaska Ave. (☎ 782-9595), next to the grain elevator, for daily road reports, maps to just about everything in the city, and a small museum (donation requested). Open daily May 15 to Labour Day 8am-7pm; winter Tu-Sa 9am-5pm.

- **Bank: CIBC** (☎ 782-4816), 10200 10th St. 24hr. **ATM.**

- **Internet access:** Free 1hr. at the **library,** 10 St. and McKellar Ave. (☎ 782-4661). Open Tu-Th 10am-9pm, F 10am-5:15pm, Sa and Su 1:30-5:15pm; closed Su summer.

- **Laundromat:** King Koin Laundromat, 1220 103rd Ave. (☎ 782-2395). Wash $2.50, double load $3, dry 25¢ per 5min. Limitless showers $2.75. Open daily 8am-9pm. At the **Mile 0 Campground,** loads are a buck a piece (see **Accommodations,** below).

- **Auto Repair: J&L Mechanical Services** (☎ 782-7832) does **24hr. road service.**

- **Market:** Groceries at **IGA,** 1100 Alaska Ave. (☎ 782-5766). Open daily 8am-11pm.

- **Hospital:** 1100 13th St. (☎ 782-8501). **Ambulance:** ☎ 782-2211.

- **Police:** (☎ 782-5211) at Alaska Ave. and 102nd Ave.

- **Post office:** (☎ 782-9429), at 104th Ave. and 10th St. Open M-F 8:30am-5pm. **Postal code:** V1G 4E6.

ACCOMMODATIONS AND CAMPING

Those willing to trade a few amenities for bargain prices, great location, and an offbeat aura should head straight for the historic **Alaska Hotel.** It is located above the Alaska Cafe & Pub (see **Food,** below) on 10th St., 1½ blocks from the visitors center. Sacrificing a bit of quality for character, comfortable rooms are carefully decorated, some with pictures of Marilyn and Elvis. (☎ 782-7998. Shared bath; no TV or phone. Singles $30; doubles $35; winter $5 less.) The newer **Voyageur Motor Inn,** 801 111th Ave., facing 8th Ave., offers motoring voyagers phones, cable TV, and fridges at no extra charge in sterile boxy rooms. (☎ 782-1020. Singles $45; doubles $50.) Pitch a tent if you want, but remember you are at Mile Zero of the Alaska Hwy. and every senior citizen with a 46-footer is on the verge of realizing their retirement dreams. The popular but RV-laden **Mile 0 Campground** is 1km west of Alaska Hwy. Adjacent to the Pioneer Village;

has free showers. (☎ 782-2590. Coin laundry $1.25. Sites $12; full hookups $17.) Campers can also head for the convenient **Alahart RV Park,** 1725 Alaska Ave., at the intersection with the John Hart Hwy. for free showers, a dump station, and laundry. The friendly owners rival the visitors center for maps and suggestions on entertainment and food. (☎ 782-4702. Sites $10; full hookups $20.)

FOOD

The **Alaska Cafe & Pub,** "55 paces south of the Mile 0 Post" on 10th St., serves excellent burgers and fries from $6. The pub offers live music nightly at 9pm (mostly country), and travelers can sing at Monday night karaoke amidst stuffed cougars, elk, and marmots. (☎ 782-7040. Open Su-Th 10am-10pm, F-Sa 11am-11pm; pub open daily noon-3am.) Eating too many sandwiches ($5) at **PotBelly Deli,** 1128 102nd. Ave., will give your tummy some chub too. Each night a new ethnicity inspires the chef. (☎ 782-5425. Open M-F 10am-7pm, Sa 10am-5pm.) Dine old-school style in **Mile One Cafe.** Select your entree from the chalkboard as you relive Dawson Creek in 1940s in the Pioneer Village. (See **Sights.** Open Tu-Su 8am-7pm.) Pick up a loaf for the road at the **Organic Farms Bakery,** 1425 97th Ave. From the visitors center, drive west along Alaska Ave. and take a right at 15th St. and you can't miss it; it's the biggest building in town. Breads are baked fresh from local grain and start at $1.70; cakes and cookies are also available. (☎ 782-6533. Open F 9:30am-5:30pm, Sa 9am-4pm.)

SIGHTS AND OUTDOOR ACTIVITIES

This town boomed during construction. Literally. On February 13, 1943, 60 cases of exploding dynamite leveled the entire business district save the **COOP** building, now Bing's Furniture, opposite the Mile 0 post. Travelers cruising through Dawson Creek can't miss the photo ops at **Mile 0 Cairn** and **Mile 0 Post** near the visitors center. Both commemorate the birth of the Alaska Hwy., and are within a stone's throw of the visitors center. The **Art Gallery** in the old grain elevator next door displays a photo essay on the Alaska Hwy. creation saga. (☎ 782-2601. Open daily June-Aug. 9am-5pm; winter Tu-Sa 10am-noon and 1-5pm.)

The **Pioneer Village** 1km west of Mile 0 is an excellent re-creation of Dawson Creek life from the 1920s to the 40s, with antique (read: rusted) farm equipment, an antler carver hard at work, nine gardens tended by the Horticultural Society, and a play area for children. (☎ 782-7144. Donation requested. Open May-Aug. daily 8am-8pm.) In early August, the town plays host to the **Fall Fair & Stampede** (☎ 782-8911) with a carnival, fireworks, chuckwagon races, and a professional rodeo.

Bird lovers will find much more to aim their binos at than the omnipresent magpies of the canola fields; just travel 10km out of town to the highland marshes of **McQueen's Slough** and follow the trail to the left across a boardwalk and around the water. Take Hwy. 49 east from the visitors center, turn left onto Rd. 3. (Rolla Rd.), and take the second left at the driveway across from the binocular signpost.

DAWSON CREEK TO FORT NELSON ☎ 250

The Alaska Hwy. between Dawson Creek and **Fort St. John** (76km and about 45min. up the Alaska Hwy.) offers little more than cows and rolling hills through a region more concerned with industry (natural gas, timber) than tourism. Ride a 10km loop of the Old Alaska Hwy. over the curved Kiskatinaw Bridge (the only original timber bridge still in existence), 28km from Dawson Creek, and you'll appreciate the condition of the new highway.

TAYLOR AND FORT ST. JOHN. In early August, gold-grubbers converge 20km south of Fort St. John in **Taylor** to pan for prizes and fame at the **World Invitational Gold Panning Championships** (☎ 789-3392) in Peace Island Park. **The Honey Place,** just south of Fort St. John, is home to the **world's largest glass beehive.** (☎ 785-4808. Open M-Sa 9am-5:30pm. Squeeze honey bear $3.) Fort St. John itself is hardly as abuzz with excitement, but it's your last chance at fast food. The **visitors center,** 9923 96th Ave., at 100th St., is adjacent to the park and museum. (☎ 785-3033. Open June-Aug. M-F 8am-8pm, Sa and Su 9am-6pm; winter M-F 8am-5pm.) Fort St. John takes deep pride in their gargantuan **North Peace Leisure Pool,** containing every imaginable aquatic delight. (☎ 787-8178. Wave pool, sauna, hot tub, water slide, and steamroom. $5; ages 13-18 $3.85; under 13 $2.75.)

SIKANNI. Sikanni River RV Park, at Alaska Hwy. Mile 160, has full amenities in a mountain setting. Grassy tent sites along the river have picnic tables and fire pits. (☎ 774-1028. Showers, toilets, laundry. $12; full hookups $19.) Best sites for camping along the way are at **Buckinghorse Provincial Park,** 27km from Sikanni, along the river but they are not so private (pit toilets $12). Two kilometers beyond **River Lodge** allows **free tenting** on its grassy lawn. (☎ 773-6468. Showers $3.)

FORT NELSON ☎ 250

Four hundred fifty-six of the highway's least exciting kilometers north of Dawson Creek, and 210km east of Toad River, is a bastion of natural resource extraction at Fort Nelson. The **visitors center,** in the Recreation Centre/Curling Rink on the north edge of town, provides **daily Alaska Hwy. road reports.** (☎ 774-6400. Open daily May-Sept. 8am-8pm.) Rest up at the **Mini-Price Inn,** 5036 51st Ave. W, one block off the highway near the visitors center. (☎ 774-2136. No phones. Cable TV. Singles $45; doubles $50; kitchenettes $5 extra.) By the **CIBC Bank** off the Alaska Hwy., the **Almada Inn** offers a free breakfast. (☎ 774-2844. Singles $60; doubles $70.)

The **Westend Campground,** across from the visitors center, has dusty sites in a pretty, wooded area, but the place is more RV-oriented than tent friendly. Showers ($1 per 9min.), a laundromat (wash $2, dry $1 per 30min.), and free car wash and firewood. (☎ 774-2340. Sites $13; full hookups $20.) There are slim pickins' for dining in Fort Nelson. **Dan's Pub,** at the southern end of town, offers nightly drink specials, pool, and an extensive menu in a dark pub. (☎ 774-3929. Open M-Th 11am-12:30am, F-Sa 11am-1:30am. After 8pm, 19+.)

Blue Bell Restaurant, opposite Dan's in the Blue Bell Inn, serves a $5 breakfast. (☎ 774-3550. Open M-Sa 6am-9pm, Su 8am-4pm.) The **Fort Nelson Heritage Museum,** across the highway from the visitors center, features an impressive (if unsettling) collection of stuffed local game, as well as remnants from the era of highway construction. (☎ 774-3536. Open daily 9am-6pm. $3, children 6-16 and seniors $2.) The **First Nations Craft Center,** is on 49th Ave. From 50th St., off 50th Ave. S, take a right on 49th Ave.; it's on the right. (☎ 774-3669. Open M-F 8:30am-4:30pm.)

FORT NELSON TO THE BC/YUKON BORDER

Small towns—usually composed of one gas pump, one $50-60 motel, and one cafe—pock the remainder of the highway to Whitehorse. Fortunately for the glassy-eyed driver, highway scenery improves dramatically after Fort Nelson.

STONE MOUNTAIN. About 150km north of Fort Nelson, the stark naked Stone Mountain appears. Next, Summit Lake lies below the highest summit on the highway (1295m). The neighboring **Stone Mountain Campground** makes a superb starting point for hiking in the area. (New-fangled composting outhouse, firewood, water. $12.) The steep Summit Peaks Trail begins across the highway from the campground, ascending 5km along a ridgeline to the breathtaking crest. A more moderate trail climbs 6km to the alpine Flower Springs Lake. Each hike takes about 5hr. round-trip. Gas and accommodations are available roadside 7km past the lake.

TOAD RIVER. Toad River, a town of 75, lies 45km north of Summit. The **Toad River Cafe** on the highway dangles some 5295 hats from the ceiling. (☎232-5401. Tasty burgers from $6. Headwear donations accepted. Open daily 6:30am-10pm; winter 7am-9pm.) An Alaska Hwy. odyssey—a grassy, RV and tent-friendly campground with private, brand-spanking new sites, **Poplars Campground and Cafe** springs up 5km after Toad River. (☎232-5465. Tents $12, full hookups $20.)

MUNCHO LAKE. Fifty kilometers north of Toad River, Muncho Lake Provincial Park delights even the weariest drivers. Muncho ("big lake" in Tagish) is a seven-mile-long azure mirror. **Strawberry Flats Provincial Campground** and **MacDonald Provincial Campground,** 8km farther on, provide the best camping in the area with sweet lakefront sites. (Pit toilets, fire wood, water. $12.) If you don't want to camp, stay at the **Muncho Lake Lodge,** 10km north of Strawberry Flats. Rooms are spacious. Outstanding service. (☎776-3456. Singles $45, tents $14, hookups $16.)

LIARD RIVER HOT SPRINGS. Near the 775km mark are the Liard River Hot Springs. These two naturally steamy and sulphurous pools are a phenomenal place to sooth a driver's derriere. For privacy and deeper water, skip the Alpha pool and head up to Beta. The park service manages campsites and free day-use of the springs. Arrive early as non-reservation campsites are in high demand. (Reservations ☎800-689-9025. Water, toilets, firewood. Gates closed 11pm-6am. $15.)

ALBERTA

> **ALBERTA'S... Drinking age:** 18. **Sales Tax:** 7% national sales tax (GST). **Traffic Laws:** Seatbelt required. Bicycle helmets required. **Capital:** Edmonton. **Tartan:** Forest green, wheat gold, sky blue, rose pink, coal black.

With its gaping prairie, oil-fired economy, and conservative politics, Alberta is the Texas of Canada. Petrodollars have given birth to gleaming, modern cities on the plains. In 1988, the Winter Olympics temporarily transformed Calgary into an international mecca, and the city hasn't stopped collecting tourist interest off the legacy yet. Calgary is also the stomping grounds for the Stampede, the world's largest rodeo and meeting place for the most skilled cowboys in the West. Alberta's capital, Edmonton, is slightly larger than Calgary, its hockey rival to the south, and serves as the trusty transportation hub for the stunning national and provincial parks that line the Alberta-British Columbia border.

For adventurous outdoor enthusiasts, Alberta is a year-round playground. Hikers, mountaineers, and ice climbers will find a recreational paradise in the Canadian Rockies in Banff, and Jasper National Parks and Kananaskis Country. Canoeing centers adjoin the lakes of northern Alberta and the Milk River in the south. The province boasts thousands of prime fishing holes, internationally renowned fossil fields, and centers of indigenous Canadian culture.

ALBERTA'S HIGHLIGHTS

THE ICEFIELDS PKWY. winds through breathtaking **scenery** between Banff to Jasper; this area is best seen on two wheels (see p. 362).

COWBOYS swagger into town for the **Calgary Stampede** (see p. 350).

DIG for dinosaurs bones in the **Badlands** (see p. 350).

SOAK away your sorrows and contemplate the meaning of life while pondering the view from **Miette Hot Springs** (see p. 367).

HIT the slopes at Lake Louise (p. 361).

EDMONTON ☎ 780

The provincial capital of Alberta may not have claim to the amazing scenery of Banff and Jasper or the spectacle that is the Calgary Stampede, but this popular travel destination has a variety of other things to offer a wide spectrum of tastes. Edmonton hosts the Canadian Finals Rodeo in November, and is home to the world's biggest shopping mall. A plethora of museums attracts children and art lovers, while the Saskatchewan River valley beckons to hikers and bikers. A perpetual stream of music, art, and performance festivals draws summer crowds to this self-proclaimed "City of Champions." All this combined with a happening strip on Whyte Ave. transforms Edmonton into a pleasant urban oasis near the almost overpowering splendor of the neighboring Rockies.

TRANSPORTATION

Although Edmonton is the northernmost major city in Canada, it's in the southern half of Alberta. The city lies 294km north of Calgary, an easy but tedious 3hr. drive on the **Calgary Trail (Hwy. 2).** Jasper is 362km to the west, a 4hr. drive on Hwy. 16. Edmonton's **streets** run north-south, and **avenues** run east-west. Street numbers

Alberta

increase to the west, and avenues increase to the north. The first three digits of an address indicate the nearest cross street: 10141 88 Ave. is on 88 Ave. near 101 St. **City center** is quite off-center at 105 St. and 101 Ave. The "Pedway" pedestrian walkways link businesses and sights on three levels.

Flights: The **airport** sits 29km south of town, an expensive cab fare away. The **Sky Shuttle Airport Service** (☎ 465-8545 or 888-438-2342) runs a shuttle downtown, to the university, or to the West Edmonton Mall for $11 ($18 round-trip). Cheapskates have been known to hop on a free airport shuttle bus taking travelers to downtown hotels.

Trains: The Greyhound is downtown. **VIA Rail**, 12360 121 St., a 10min. drive NW of downtown (info ☎ 422-6032 or 800-835-3037, reservations 800-561-8630), in the CN Tower with the huge red letters. 3 per week to **Jasper** (6hr.; $138, students $90) and **Vancouver, BC** (23hr.; $258, students $168). No train service to Calgary.

Buses: Greyhound, 10324 103 St. (☎ 420-2412). Open daily 5:30am-midnight. To **Calgary** (nearly every hr., $42), **Jasper** (5hr., 4 per day, $52), **Vancouver, BC** (14-16hr., 2 per day, $140), and **Yellowknife, NWT** (22½hr.; 2 per day M-F, winter 3 per week; $194). Locker storage $2 per day. **Red Arrow,** 10010 104 St. (☎ 800-232-1958), at the Holiday Inn. Open M-F 7:30am-8pm, Sa 8am-8pm. 10% discount with hosteling card. To **Calgary** (6 per day, $46) and **Fort McMurray** (2 per day, $54). The Edmonton International Youth Hostel (see p. 343) also sells tickets.

Public Transportation: Edmonton Transit (schedules ☎ 496-1611; info 496-1600; www.gov.edmonton.ab.ca). Buses and **Light Rail Transit (LRT)** run frequently throughout city. LRT is **free downtown** between Grandin Station at 110 St. and 98 Ave. and Churchill Station at 99 St. and 102 Ave. Runs M-F 9am-3pm and Sa 9am-6pm. $1.65, over 65 and under 15 $1.05. No bikes on LRT during peak hours traveling in peak direction (M-F 7:30-8:30am and 4-5pm). No bikes on buses. For info, contact Churchill **LRT station info booth** (open M-F 8:30am-4:30pm).

Taxis: Yellow Cab ☎ 462-3456. **Alberta Co-op Taxi** ☎ 425-8310. Both 24hr.

Car Rental: Budget, 10016 106 St. (☎ 448-2000 or 800-661-7027); call for other locations. From $46 per day, with unlimited km; cheaper city rates with limited km. Ages 21-24 $12 per day surcharge and must have major credit card. Open M-F 7:30am-6pm, Sa 8am-5pm, Su 9am-5pm. **National,** 10133 100A St. (☎ 422-6097). From $49 per day for unlimited km. Open M-F 7am-7pm, Sa 8am-4pm, Su 9am-5pm. Must be 21. Ages 21-25 mandatory $21 insurance and $10 surcharge per day.

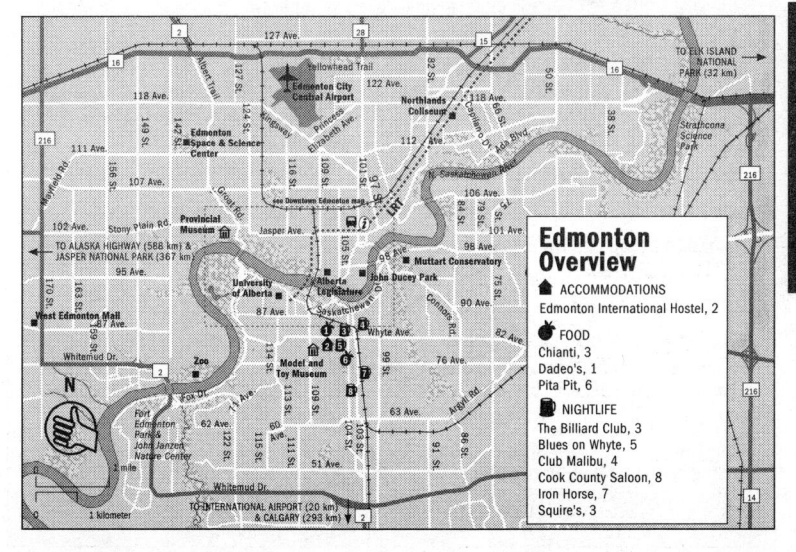

342 ■ EDMONTON

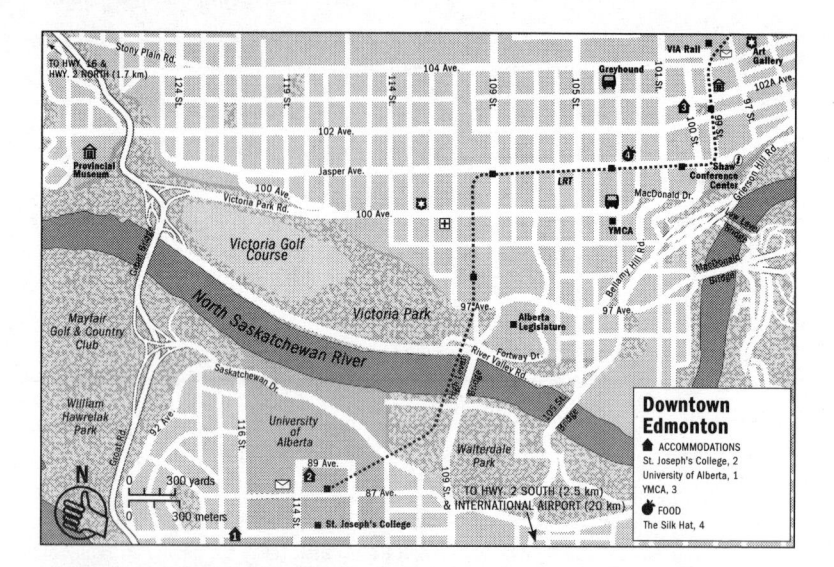

Downtown Edmonton
♠ ACCOMMODATIONS
St. Joseph's College, 2
University of Alberta, 1
YMCA, 3
● FOOD
The Silk Hat, 4

PRACTICAL INFORMATION

Visitor Information: Edmonton Tourism, Shaw Conference Centre, 9797 Jasper Ave. (☎496-8400 or 800-463-4667), on Pedway Level. Info, maps, directions. Open M-F 8:30am-4:30pm. Also at **Gateway Park** (☎496-8400 or 800-463-4667), on Hwy. 2 south of town. Both open daily 8am-9pm; winter M-F 8:30am-4:30pm, Sa-Su 9am-5pm. **Travel Alberta** (☎427-4321 or 800-661-8888). Province-wide info. Open M-F 7am-7pm, Sa-Su 8:30am-5:30pm.

Equipment Rental: The Edmonton International Youth Hostel (see **Accommodations,** below) rents bikes. $7 per half-day, $12 per day. **Campus Outdoor Centre** (☎492-2767), NW corner of the Butterdome at U of A, rents a variety of equipment for all seasons including cross-country skis ($7 overnight), camping equipment, and bikes ($15 per day). Open Apr.-Aug. M-Tu 9am-7pm, W 10am-5pm, Th-F 9am-8pm, Sa-Su noon-4pm; longer hours in winter.

Gay and Lesbian Services: Gay/Lesbian Community Centre, 10612 124 St. #103 (☎482-2855). Community listings, youth services, on-site peer counseling. Open M-F 7-10pm; events recording plays during non-business hours. **Womenspace** (☎482-1794) is Edmonton's lesbian group. Call for a recording of local events.

Emergency: ☎911. **Police:** ☎423-4567.

Crisis Line: ☎482-HELP. **Sexual Assault Centre,** ☎423-4121. Both 24hr.

Pharmacy: Shoppers Drug Mart, 11408 Jasper Ave. (☎482-1011), or by Whyte Ave. 8210 109 St. (☎433-2424). Open 24hr.

Hospital: Royal Alexandra Hospital, 10240 Kingsway Ave. (☎477-4111).

Internet Access: Dow Computer Lab, 11211 142 St. (☎451-3344), at the Odyssium (see **Sights,** below); free with admission. **Free** at the **library,** 7 Sir Winston Churchill Sq. (☎496-7000), 1hr. per day for a week. Open M-F 9am-9pm, Sa 9am-6pm, Su 1-5pm. $1 per 10min. at the **hostel** (see below).

Post Office: 9808 103A Ave. (☎944-3265), adjacent to the CN Tower. Open M-F 8am-5:45pm. **Postal Code:** T5J 2G8.

EDMONTON ■ 343

ACCOMMODATIONS

The hostel is the liveliest place to stay in Edmonton, while St. Joseph's College and the University of Alberta provide a bit more privacy. For B&B listings, contact **Alberta B&B Association**, 3230 104A St. (☎ 438-6048).

Edmonton International Youth Hostel (HI), 10647 81 Ave. (☎ 988-6836). Bus #7 or 9 from the 101 St. station to 82 Ave. You'd never know that this hostel is in a renovated convent, except for the abundance of private 2-person bedrooms with the dimensions of a nun's cell. Facilities include a kitchen, game room, lounge, new bathrooms, laundry, free linen, and a small backyard. Just around the corner from the clubs, shops, and cafes of Whyte Ave. Family rooms available. Internet access. Open 24hr. Check-in 3pm. $18, nonmembers $23; semi-private rooms $20, $25.

St. Joseph's College, 89 Ave. at 114 St. (☎ 492-7681), at the University of Alberta. Take the LRT and get off at University. The rooms here are smaller than those at the university. Library, huge lounges, rec room, laundry, free linen, and close to U sports facilities. Reception M-F 8:30am-4pm. Call ahead; the 60 dorms often fill up quickly. Rooms available early May to late Aug. Singles $30, with full board $50.

University of Alberta, 87 Ave. between 116 and 117 St. (☎ 492-4281), on the ground floor of Lister Hall. Generic dorm rooms. Game rooms available. Dry cleaning, kitchen, free Internet access, convenience store, and buffet-style cafeteria downstairs. Check-in after 3pm. Reservations strongly recommended. Rooms available late Apr.-Aug. Singles $28. Weekly or monthly rates available.

YMCA, 10030 102A Ave. (☎ 421-9622). A facility in the heart of downtown close to bus and rail stations. Free gym and pool facilities for guests. Secure 4th-floor rooms available for women and couples. Discounts for long-term stays and students. 3-night max. dorm stay. Dorm bunks $20; singles for men $35, for women $38.

FOOD

Little evidence can be found to support the theory that citizens of the self-labeled City of Champions kick off their day with a big bowl of Wheaties. Instead, Edmonton locals swarm into the coffee shops and cafes of the Old Strathcona area along Whyte (82) Ave., between 102 and 106 St.

Chianti, 10501 Whyte Ave. (☎ 439-9829). An old Strathcona post office gone authentically Italian. Chianti's name attests to its lengthy wine list. Daily specials, desserts, and coffees accompany an expanse of pasta, veal, and seafood dishes. Pastas $6.60-10; veal $10-13. M-Tu all pasta dishes $6. Open Su-Th 11am-11pm, F-Sa 11am-midnight.

The Silk Hat, 10251 Jasper Ave. (☎ 425-1920), beside the Paramount Theater. The oldest restaurant in Edmonton, with plenty of character. This diner in the heart of downtown serves a huge array of food, from seafood to veggie-burgers ($6.25) to breakfast all day. Happy Hour M-F 4-6pm. Open M-F 8am-5:45pm, Sa 10am-8pm.

Dadeo's, 10548A 82 Ave. (☎ 433-0930). Cajun and Louisiana-style food in exile from the bayou in this funky 50s diner. Gumbo $4.50. M-Tu Po' Boys $7. Su $4 for a pint or a plate of wings. Spicy dishes make diners sweat just right. Open M-W 11:30am-11pm, Th-Sa 11:30am-midnight, Su 3-10pm.

Grounds for Coffee and Antiques, 10247 97 St. (☎ 429-1920), behind the Edmonton Art Gallery. Small cafe and antique shop features coffee and hot and cold dishes, including daily specials, alongside old furniture and older trinkets. Hosts an occasional art exhibit. The Mideastern Combo ($5.65) is a favorite among local clientele. Open M-F 8:30am-5pm, Sa 10am-5pm.

Kids in the Hall Bistro, 1 Sir Winston Churchill Sq. (☎ 413-8060), in City Hall. This lunchroom is truly one-of-a-kind. Every employee, from waiter to chef, is a young person hired as part of a cooperative community service project. Various entrees ($5-10) and sandwiches ($5-7). Takeout available. Open M-F 8am-4pm.

ALBERTA

344 ■ EDMONTON

The Pita Pit, 8109 104 St. (☎435-3200). Delicious pitas takeout style, near Whyte Ave. Souvlaki $5.25. Students don't pay GST. Open Th-Sa 11am-4am, Su noon-3am, M-W 11am-3am.

🍸 NIGHTLIFE

Edmonton, like many big cities, has a variety of clubs, and like other Alberta cities, ample cowboy clubs. Many of the happening clubs are lined up along Whyte (82) Ave. in Old Strathcona. For club listings, see *Magazine*, published every Thursday and available in free stacks at cafes.

The Billiard Club, 10505 82 Ave. (☎432-0335), 2nd fl., above Chianti. A busy bar packed with a diverse crowd of young up-and-comings and some older already-theres. Pool tables, mellow back room, outdoor patio for self-contained socializers. Open daily 11:30am-2:30am.

Squire's, 10505 82 Ave. (☎439-8974), lower level. A popular bar with the college crowd. Specials every day, including M $2.50 bottles of Canadian, Tu $2 highballs, and Th half-price from 7-11pm. Peruse the picture wall of shame while you enjoy 9¢ wings on W. Open M-Sa 4pm-3am.

Blues on Whyte, 10329 82 Ave. (☎439-5058). If blues is what you want, blues is what you'll get. Live blues and R&B from top-notch performers every night, Sa afternoon jam 3-8:30pm. This joint may deserve its reputation as a biker bar; these blues are anything but sedate. 8 oz. glasses of beer for just $1. Open daily 10am-3am.

Cook County Saloon, 8010 103 St. (☎432-2665). Bring your hat and your best shitkickers to Edmonton's rootinest *and* tootinest country bar. W night dance lessons ensure that no one gets hurt. Happy Hour F-Sa 8-9pm. M oil wrestling. Hosts hot live concerts on many nights. Open W-Su 8pm-2am.

Iron Horse, 8101 103 St. (☎438-1907). A full restaurant turned top 40 dance club at night. A turn-of-the-century railway station now hosts live music Su, "Extreme Karaoke" Th, and "Love Train" (singles night) W. Large patio. Popular with a younger crowd. Happy Hour M-F 4-8pm. Open daily 11:30am-2am.

Club Malibu, 10310 85 Ave. (☎432-7300). This well-known dance club shows Edmonton's younger crowd how to party. Th 50¢ Coronas until 10pm, $2 everything all night; $1-3 drinks on F. Sa offers 25¢ bottles of Canadian beer until 10pm. M is ladies' night with male entertainers and more cheap drinks. Club Malibu also hosts some of the best DJs in the city. Open M and Th-Sa 8pm-3am.

🎵 ENTERTAINMENT

Edmonton proclaims itself "Canada's Festival City," with celebrations of some kind going on year-round. The **International Jazz City Festival** (☎432-7166; June 21-30, 2002) packs 10 days with club dates and free performances by top international and Canadian jazz musicians, coinciding with a visual arts celebration called **The Works.** (☎426-2122. June 21-July 3.) At the **International Street Performers Festival,** musical and acting talent combust and burst into a fireball of artistic activity, aesthetically scorching downtown's Winston Churchill Square. (☎425-5162. July 5-14.) **Klondike Days** are Edmonton's answer to Calgary's Stampede with chuckwagon racing, daredevil circus acts, parades, live entertainment, and the Taste of Edmonton showcase of culinary talent. (☎471-7210. July 18-27. See p. 350.) In August, the **Folk Music Festival** (Aug. 8-11), considered one of the best in North America, takes over Gallagher Park. Only a week later, all the world's a stage in Old Strathcona for the **Fringe Theater Festival,** when top alternative music and theater pours from parks, stages, and streets. This is the high point in Edmonton's festival schedule, and 500,000 travelers make their way to the city just to find the Fringe. (☎448-9000; www.fringe.alberta.com. Aug. 15-25.)

The Edmonton area hosts many entertaining **small-town rodeos.** On summer weekends there may be several; the $6-10 admission is negligible given the quality of competition. Where else can you watch leather-clad contestants wrestle with each other in the dirt, besides a sketchy bar? At the bullfights! Contact Travel Alberta (☎ 800-661-8888) for upcoming rodeos. For more information on all the festivals and events, visit www.tourism.ede.org.

👁 SIGHTS

WEST EDMONTON MALL. A blow against Mother Nature in the battle for tourists, the $1.3 billion **West Edmonton Mall** engulfs the general area between 170 St. and 87 Ave. No ordinary collection of stores, the World's Biggest Mall contains water slides, an amusement park with a 14-story roller coaster, miniature golf, dozens of exotic caged animals, over 800 stores, an ice-skating rink, 110 eating establishments, a full-scale replica of Columbus's *Santa Maria,* an indoor bungee jumping facility, a casino, a luxury hotel, a dolphin show, swarms of teenage mall rats, multiple movie theaters, and twice as many submarines as the Canadian Navy. One could, in theory, spend an entire vacation without leaving the Übermall's climate-controlled embrace. One note of caution: remember where you park. The world's largest mall also has the world's largest parking lot. *(☎ 444-5200. Bus # 1, 2, 100, or 111. Open M-F 10am-9pm, Sa 10am-6pm, Su noon-6pm. Amusement park and some other attractions stay open later.)*

FORT EDMONTON PARK. After worshiping at the temple of consumerism, take a breather at the **Fort Edmonton Park.** At the park's far end sits the fort, a 19th-century office building for Alberta's first capitalists, the fur traders of the Hudson Bay Company. Between the fort and the park entrance are three streets—1885, 1905, and 1920 St.—bedecked with period buildings from apothecaries to blacksmith shops, all decorated to match the streets' respective eras. Costumed schoolmarms and general store owners mingle with visitors, valiantly attempting to bring Edmonton's history to life. While at the fort, hike through birch groves and pet salamanders at the **John Janzen Nature Centre.** *(Park: On Whitemud Dr. at Fox Dr. Buses #2, 4, 30, 31, 35, 106, and 315 stop near the park.* ☎ *496-8787. Mid-May to late June open M-F 10am-4pm, Sa-Su 10am-6pm; late June to early Sept. daily 10am-6pm; rest of Sept. wagon tours only from M-Sa 11am-3pm, Su 10am-6pm. $7.75, seniors and ages 13-17 $5.75, ages 2-12 $4, family $23.50.* **Nature Centre:** *Open Jan. to mid-May M-F 9am-4pm, Sa-Su 1-6pm; mid-May to June M-F 9am-4pm, Sa-Su 11am-4pm; July to early Sept. M-F 10am-5pm, Sa-Su 11am-5pm; early Sept. to late Dec. M-F 9am-4pm, Sa-Su 1-4pm. $1.25, ages 13-17 and seniors $1, ages 2-12 75¢, family $3.75.)*

ODYSSIUM. The reincarnated Space and Science Centre still appeals to the curiosity of all ages with exhibits on the human body and the environment, plus Gallery of the Gross and the hands-on Crime Lab. Housed in a building shaped like an alien spacecraft, the largest **planetarium** dome in Canada features a booming 23,000 watts of audio, used during its laser light shows. The **IMAX theater** makes the planetarium seem like a child's toy. *(11211 142 St.* ☎ *451-3344. Open daily 10am-10pm. Day pass includes planetarium shows and exhibits: $10, students and ages 13-17 $8, ages 3-12 $7. General admission and IMAX show $16, students and ages 13-17 $12.75, ages 3-12 $11.25.)*

EDMONTON ART GALLERY. The **Edmonton Art Gallery,** 2 Sir Winston Churchill Sq., showcases work by both Canadian and international artists. Programs for 2002 include Jades (Jan. 25-Mar. 24), the Alberta Biennial (Jun. 21-Aug. 25), and Ukranian Avant-garde during Jun. 29-Sept. 15. *(☎ 422-6223; www.edmontonartgallery.com. Open M-W and F 10:30am-5pm, Th 10:30am-8pm, Sa-Su 11am-5pm. $5, students and seniors $3, ages 6-12 $2, under 6 free. Free Th after 4pm.)*

RIVER VALLEY. The best part of Edmonton would have to be the longest stretch of urban parkland in Canada. Edmonton's **River Valley** boasts over 50km of easy to moderate paved multi-use trails and 69km of granular or chip trail for hiking and cycling. Any route down the river leads to part of the linked trail system; pick up a map at the Ranger Station. *(12130 River Valley Road.* ☎ *496-2950. Open daily 7am-1am.)*

CALGARY ☎ 403

Mounties founded Calgary in the 1870s to control the flow of illegal whisky, but it was a different liquid that made the city great: oil. Today, petroleum fuels Calgary's economy and explains why the city holds the most corporate headquarters in Canada outside of Toronto. As the host of the 1988 Winter Olympics, Calgary's dot on the map grew larger; already Alberta's largest city, this thriving young metropolis is now Canada's 2nd fastest-growing city. No matter how big its britches, though, the city pays annual tribute to its original tourist attraction, the "Greatest Outdoor Show on Earth," the Calgary Stampede. For 10 days in July, the city dons cowboy duds and lets out a collective "Yeeha!" for world-class bareback riding, country music, Western art, and free pancakes.

TRANSPORTATION

Calgary is 126km east of Banff along the Trans-Canada Hwy. (Hwy. 1). It is divided into quadrants (NE, NW, SE, SW): **Centre St.** is the east-west divider; the **Bow River** splits the north and south sections. **Avenues** run east-west, **streets** run north-south, and numbers count up from the divides. Cross streets can be derived by disregarding the last two digits of the street address: 206 7th Ave. SW would be in the southwest quadrant on 7th Ave. at 2nd St. Downtown, the "+15" elevated walkway system facilitates pedestrian travel.

CALGARY ■ 347

Downtown Calgary

ACCOMMODATIONS
Calgary International Hostel, 4
University of Calgary, 1
YWCA, 3

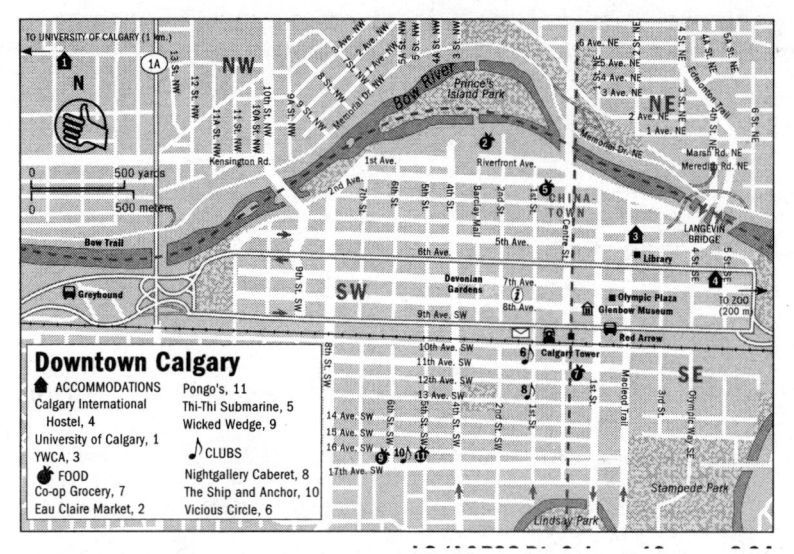

FOOD
Co-op Grocery, 7
Eau Claire Market, 2

Pongo's, 11
Thi-Thi Submarine, 5
Wicked Wedge, 9

♪ **CLUBS**
Nightgallery Caberet, 8
The Ship and Anchor, 10
Vicious Circle, 6

Flights: The **airport** (☎ 735-1372) is 17km northeast of the city center. Major airlines such as Air Canada, United, American, and Continental fly into Calgary International.

Buses: Greyhound, 877 Greyhound Way SW (☎ 265-9111 or 800-661-8747). To: **Edmonton** (3½hr., 8 per day, $43); **Banff** (1¾hr., 4 per day, $22); **Drumheller** (1¾hr., 2 per day, $24). Free shuttle from Calgary Transit C-Train at 7th Ave. and 10th St. to bus depot (every hr. near the half hour 6:30am-7:30pm). **Red Arrow,** 205 9th Ave. SE (☎ 531-0350). To **Edmonton** (7 per day, $46) and points north. 10% HI discount; student and senior rates. **Brewster Tours** (☎ 221-8242), from the airport or downtown to **Banff** (2½hr., 4 per day, $36) and **Jasper** (8hr., 1 per day, $71). 15% HI discount.

Public Transportation: Calgary Transit, 240 7th Ave. SW (☎ 262-1000). Open M-F 8:30am-5pm. C-Trains free in downtown zone. Buses and C-Trains outside downtown $1.75, ages 6-14 $1.10, under 6 free. Day pass $5, ages 6-14 $3. Book of 10 tickets $14.50, ages 6-14 $9. Runs M-F 6am-11pm, Sa-Su 6am-9:30pm. Tickets at the transit office, Safeway and Co-op grocery stores, and 7-11 and Mac's corner stores.

Taxis: Checker Cab, ☎ 299-9999. **Yellow Cab,** ☎ 974-1111.

Car Rental: Rent-A-Wreck, 113 42nd Ave. SW (☎ 287-1444). From $33 per day. 12¢ per km over 250km; 7th day free. Must be 21 with credit card. Open M-F 8am-6pm, Sa-Su 9am-5pm.

▐ PRACTICAL INFORMATION

Visitor Information: 220 8th Ave. SW (☎ 750-2397). Open daily 9am-5pm.

American Express: Canada Trust Tower, 421 7th Ave. SW (☎ 261-5085), on main floor.

Equipment Rental: Outdoor Program Centre at U of Calgary, 2500 University Dr. (☎ 220-5038), rents tents (from $8), canoes ($17), downhill skis ($15), and everything else outdoor-related. Open daily 8am-8pm. **Mountain Equipment Co-op** (☎ 269-2420) rents watercraft ($30-55 per day, including all safety equipment and paddles), camping gear ($9-21), rock and ice climbing gear ($8-22), and snow sports equipment ($8-35). Both companies have weekend specials.

Laundromat: Inglewood Laundromat, 1018 9th Ave. SE (☎ 269-1515). Open daily 9:30am-7pm. Wash $2, dry 50¢ for 7min.

Weather: ☎ 299-7878.

348 ■ CALGARY

Gay and Lesbian Services: Events, bars, clubs ☎234-9752. Counseling ☎234-8973.
Emergency: ☎911. **Police:** 133 6th Ave. SE (☎266-1234).
Pharmacy: Shopper's Drug Mart, 6455 S Macleod Trail (☎253-2424), in the Chinook Centre. Open 24hr.
Hospital: Peter Lougheed Centre, 3500 26th Ave. NE (☎291-8555).
Internet Access: At the **Calgary Hostel.** $2 per 20min. Also at the **Library,** 616 Macleod Trail SE (☎260-2600). $2 per hr. Open M-Th 10am-9pm, F-Sa 10am-5pm; mid-Sept. to mid-May also Su 1:30-5pm.
Post Office: 207 9th Ave. SW (☎974-2078). Open M-F 8am-5:45pm. **Postal Code:** T2P 2G8.

ACCOMMODATIONS

Lodging prices skyrocket when tourists pack into the city's hotels during the Stampede in July; call far in advance. Contact the **B&B Association of Calgary** for info and availability. (☎543-3900. Singles from $30; doubles from $50.)

■ **Calgary International Hostel (HI),** 520 7th Ave. SE (☎269-8239), near downtown. Go east along 7th Ave. from the 3rd St. SE C-Train station; the hostel is on the left just past 4th St. SE. This welcoming urban hostel has it all: clean kitchen, game room, lounge areas, laundry, email, and a backyard with BBQ. Linen $1. Free city tours on M, daily guest activities. Open 24hr. Wheelchair accessible. 120 beds. $16, nonmembers $20; Oct. 16-May 1: $15, $19. Private rooms $4 surcharge per person.

University of Calgary, the ex-Olympic Village in the NW quadrant, far from downtown if you're walking. Accessible by bus #9 or the C-Train. Popular with conventioneers and often booked solid. Coordinated through Cascade Hall, 3456 24th Ave. NW (☎220-3203), a 12min. walk from the University C-Train stop. Rooms available May-Aug. only. Open 24hr. Shared rooms $21; singles $34, with student ID (May and June only) $28; doubles with student ID $17; lavish suites with private bath about $44 per person.

YWCA, 320 5th Ave. SE (☎263-1550). Walk 2 blocks north of the 3rd St. SE C-Train station. 2 newly renovated residential floors. Women only. Singles from $40, seniors $36; doubles from $50, seniors $45. 150 beds available.

FOOD

The most gloriously satisfying and cheap food is located in ■**Chinatown,** concentrated around four blocks at the north end of Centre St. S and 1st St. SE. Six dollars buys a feast in Vietnamese noodle-houses and Hong Kong-style cafes, many of which don't close until the wee hours. Some budget chow-houses also hide out among the trendy, costlier spots in the popular **Kensington District,** along Kensington Rd. and 10th and 11th St. NW, as well as those on **17th Ave.** between 2nd St. SW and 14th St. SW. To get to Kensington, take the C-Train to Sunnyside or cross the Louise Bridge (9th St. SW and 10th St. NW). **Co-op Grocery,** 123 11th Ave. SE, sells groceries. (☎299-4257. Open daily 9am-10pm.) Restaurants, produce, international snack bars, and flowers grace the plaza-style, upscale **Eau Claire Market,** at the north end of 3rd St. SW. Five dollars fetches a filling plate for a picnic in nearby Prince's Island Park. (☎264-6450. Open M-Th and Su 7am-9pm, F-Sa 7am-10pm.

■ **Thi-Thi Submarine,** 209 1st St. SE (☎265-5452). Some people have closets larger than Thi-Thi, yet the shop manages to pack in 2 plastic seats, a bank of toaster ovens, and the finest Vietnamese submarines in Calgary. $2.75 will buy a 12-in. "super-sub." The veggie sub is an unreal $2. Open daily 10am-7pm.

Take 10 Cafe, 304 10th St. NW (☎270-7010). A local favorite, Take Ten attracts customers not by being the coolest place in Kensington, but rather by offering dirt-cheap, high-quality food. All burgers under $5.75. The owners also offer a variety of their native Chinese food ($6.25). Open Tu-Sa 9am-6pm, Su 9am-3pm.

Wicked Wedge, 618 17th Ave. SW (☎228-1024). Serves topping-heavy, large slices of pizza ($3.75) to Calgary's post-party scene. 3 varieties of pie dished out nightly. Open M-Tu 11am-1am, W-Sa 11am-3am, Su noon-midnight.

Pongo's, 524 17th Ave. SW (☎209-1073). A futuristic design grounds the consumption of a variety of Asian foods. Large portions. Try a huge helping of Pad Thai for $8. Patio and takeout available. Open Su-Th 11:30am-midnight, F-Sa 11:30am-4am.

Peter's Drive In, 219 16th Ave. NE (☎277-2747). On Hwy. 1 through town. One of the city's remaining old drive-ins. The hordes attest to the great food they serve. Drive-in or walk to the service window. Famous milkshakes $2.50. Open daily 10am-midnight.

NIGHTLIFE

Nightclubs in Alberta only became legal in 1990, and Calgary is making up for lost time. The city is crawling with bars and nightclubs that cater to the waves of visitors and young locals. Live music in Calgary ranges from national acts and world famous DJs to some guy with a guitar. The best areas in town for finding pubs, clubs, and live music are the Stephen Ave. Walk (8th Ave. SW), 17th Ave. SW, and 1st and 4th St. SW. Wherever you head, finding cheap liquor is not a problem. Many bars in town offer ridiculous drink deals. Last call in Alberta is at 2am, and is strictly observed. For listings of bands and theme nights, check *The Calgary Straight* or *Calgary's Ffwd*. Both come out on Thursday and are free. *Outlooks*, the city's gay and lesbian events publication, offers information on different bars. All are available at local clubs and cafes.

Nightgallery Cabaret, 1209B 1st St. SW (☎269-5924). One large dance floor, one bar, and a diverse program attract clubbers. Breaks out the best House in town at "Sunday Skool" and on Th. Reggae-Dub on M draws a slightly older crowd. Cover $5. Live music F and Sa. $1.50 highballs before 11pm. Open daily 8pm-3am.

Vicious Circle, 1011 1st St. SW (☎269-3951). Relaxing bar offers solid menu, colored mood lights and a disco ball, pool tables, and a variety of music in the background. All kinds of coffee, a full bar, and 140 martinis. Happy Hour all night Su. Summer patio seating. Open daily 11am-2am.

The Ship and Anchor, 534 17th Ave. SW (☎245-3333). Decked out with sailing paraphernalia, the Ship is a meeting place for the city's young and beautiful scurvy dogs. Eclectic music and patrons, decent food, a spacious patio, and a staff of aspiring actors keep this ship of fools afloat. Live music every 2nd W. Open daily 11am-2:30am.

Eau Claire Market IMAX (☎974-4629). Watch the latest larger-than-life adventure. Box office open M-F 11:30am-10pm, Sa and Su 10:30am-10pm. IMAX films $9, ages 65 and up $7.50, under 13 $6.50. Also at Eau Claire, Cineplex Odeon shows conventional films; call for times (☎263-3166).

SIGHTS

OLYMPIC LEFTOVERS. Over a decade later, Calgary still clings to its two weeks of Olympic stardom. Visit the **Canada Olympic Park** to learn about gravity at the site of the four looming ski jumps and the bobsled and luge tracks. The **Olympic Hall of Fame,** also at Olympic Park, honors Olympic achievements with displays, films, and a bobsled simulator. In summer, the park opens its hills and a lift to **mountain bikers.** (☎247-5452. *A 10min. drive northwest of downtown on Hwy. 1. Open daily 9am-9pm. $7 ticket includes chair lift and entrance to ski jump buildings, Hall of Fame, and icehouse. Guided tour $10, $35 per family. Mountain biking open May-Oct. daily 10am-9pm. Hill pass $7 for cyclists. Bike rental $12 per hr., $31 per day.)* Keep an eye out for ski-jumpers, who practice at the facility year-round. The miniature mountain (113m vertical) also opens up for recreational **downhill skiing** in winter. (Snow report ☎289-3700. $21.) The **Olympic Oval,** an enormous indoor speed-skating track on the University of Calgary campus, remains a major international training facility. Speed skaters work out in the early morning and late afternoon; sit in the bleachers and observe the action for free. (☎ 220-7890. *Public skating hours in summer daily 8-9:30pm. $4, children and seniors $2, family $9, under 6 free. Hockey skate rental $3.50, speed skates $3.75.*) Downtown, the **Olympic Plaza** was built for medal ceremonies and now holds special events such as **free concerts** every Wednesday noon in July and August. (*On 7th Ave. and 2nd St. SE.*)

PARKS AND MUSEUMS. Footbridges stretch from either side of the Bow River to **Prince's Island Park,** a natural refuge only blocks from the city center. In July and August, Mount Royal College performs **Shakespeare in the Park** (☎ 240-6374 or 240-6908. *Various matinees and evening shows; call for times.*) Calgary's other island park, **St. George's Island,** is accessible by the river walkway to the east or by driving. It houses the **Calgary Zoo,** including a botanical garden and children's zoo. For those who missed the wildlife in Banff and Jasper, the Canadian Wilds exhibit recreates animal habitats. For those who missed the Cretaceous Period, life-sized plastic dinosaurs are also on exhibit. (*Parking is off Memorial Dr. on the north side of the river.* ☎ 232-9300. *Open daily 9am-5pm. $12, seniors and under 17 $6, seniors half-price Tu-Th; reduced winter rates. 20% AAA and 10% HI discounts.*) The **Glenbow Museum** gathers mineral treasures, art, and native Canadian history all under one roof. Extensive collection of Native American art and material culture. (*130 9th Ave. SE.* ☎ *268-4100. Open Su-W 9am-5pm, Th-F 9am-9pm. $10, seniors $7.50, students and youth $6, under 6 free. 10% HI discount. Everyone $6 Th-F 5-9pm in summer; $3 F evenings in winter.*)

STAMPEDE. The more cosmopolitan Calgary becomes, the more tenaciously it clings to its frontier roots. The Stampede draws one million cowboys and tourists each summer. **Stampede Park,** just southeast of downtown, borders the east side of Macleod Trail between 14th Ave. SE and the Elbow River. From July 5-14, 2002, the grounds will be packed for world-class steer wrestling, bareback- and bull-riding, pig racing, wild cow-milking, and chuckwagon races. Check out the livestock shows, cruise the midway and casino, ride the rollercoaster, or hear live country music and marching bands. The festival spills into the streets at night, as bars and clubs get good and loud. Depending on your attitude, the Stampede will either be an impressive spectacle rekindling the Western spirit or an overpriced, slick carnival where humans assert their dominion over the lesser animals. Parking is ample and reasonably priced. The C-Train features a Stampede stop, and the walk isn't bad. (*Tickets and info* ☎ *269-9822 or 800-661-1767; www.calgarystampede.com. Gate admission $10, seniors and ages 7-12 $5, under 7 free. Rodeo and evening shows $21-55, rush tickets $10; on sale at the grandstand 1½hr. before showtime.*)

🧭 DAYTRIP FROM CALGARY: ALBERTA BADLANDS

Once the fertile shores of a huge ocean, the Badlands are now one of the richest dinosaur fossil sites in the world. After the sea dried up, wind, water, and ice molded twisting canyons into the sandstone and shale bedrock, creating the desolate splendor of the Alberta Badlands. The **Royal Tyrrell Museum of Paleontology** (TEER-ull), with its remarkable array of dinosaur exhibits and hands-on paleontological opportunities, is the region's main attraction. **Greyhound** runs from Calgary to **Drumheller** (1¾hr., 2 per day, $24), which is 6km southeast of the museum.

ROYAL TYRRELL MUSEUM OF PALEONTOLOGY. You won't lose the crowds at the museum but you might lose your sense of self-importance. The world's largest display of dinosaur specimens is a forceful reminder that *Homo sapiens* missed out on the first 2½ billion years of life on earth. From the Big Bang to the present, the museum celebrates evolution's grand parade with quality displays, videos, computer activities, and towering skeletons, including one of only 12 reconstructed *Tyrannosaurus Rex* skeletons in existence. Recently, the museum created a spooky gallery of the insect-like undersea creatures of the Burgess Shale. (*Secondary Hwy. 838. 6km northwest of Drumheller, which itself lies 138km northeast of Calgary. Get there by driving east on Hwy. 1 from Calgary, then northeast on Hwy. 9.* ☎ *403-823-7707 or 888-440-4240; www.tyrrellmuseum.com. Open daily Victoria Day to Labour Day 9am-9pm; Labour Day to Thanksgiving 10am-5pm; Thanksgiving to Victoria Day Tu-Su 10am-5pm. $8.50, seniors $6.50, ages 7-17 $4.50, under 7 free, families $20.*)

HEAD-SMASHED-IN BUFFALO JUMP Some 5700 years ago, plains-dwelling Blackfoot began using gravity to kill bison. Disguised as calves, a few men would lure a herd of the short-sighted animals into lanes between stone cairns. Hunters at the rear, dressed as wolves, then pressed forward, whipping the bison into a frenzy. When the front-running bison reached the cliff and tried to stop, the momentum of the stampede pushed them over the edge. The entire herd followed; hunters sought to prevent any animals from escaping, for they believed that survivors would warn other buffalo. Each year, the communities obtained food, tools, and clothing from the bodies of the bison. The particular cliffs of Head-Smashed-In Buffalo Jump were an active hunting site for a millennia, but only gained their modern name 150 years ago when a thrill-seeking warrior watching the massacre from under the cliff ledge was crushed by the falling stampede.

As European settlement spread over the plains, the bison that once numbered 60 million continent-wide were nearly extinct in 1881. A century later, the United Nations named Head-Smashed-In a UNESCO World Heritage Site. Ten-meter-deep beds of bone and tools make this one of the best-preserved buffalo jumps in North America. The magnificent interpretive center explores the hunting, history, and rituals of the Plains people. (☎ 553-2731. Open daily May 15 to Labour Day 9am-6pm; off-season 10am-5pm. $6.50, seniors $5.50, ages 7-17 $3, family $15, under 7 free.) A 10min. video reenactment of the hunt plays all day, and 2km of trails lead along and under the cliffs. Head-Smashed-In Buffalo Jump lies 175km south of Calgary and 18km northwest of Fort Macleod, on Secondary Rd. 785 off Hwy. 2.

DIGS. The museum's hugely popular 12-person **Day Digs** include instruction in paleontology and excavation techniques, and a chance to dig in a fossil quarry. The fee includes lunch and transportation, but all finds go to the museum. *(Weekends only in June; daily from July-Aug. Digs depart at 8:30am, returning at 4:30pm. $85, ages 10-15 $55. Reservations required; call the museum.)* See the paleontologists and Day Diggers sweating for their prey on a **Dig Watch**, a 1½hr. interpretive bus and walking tour of the quarry. They explain how the fossils are found and uncovered, and what happens to them afterwards. *(July-Aug. daily at 10am, noon, and 2pm. $12, ages 7-17 $8, under 7 free. Reservations recommended.)*

DINOSAUR PROVINCIAL PARK AND BADLANDS BUS TOUR. The Badlands, a UNESCO World Heritage Site, is the source of many finds on display at the Tyrrell Museum; more fossil species—over 300, including 35 species of dinosaurs—were discovered here than anywhere else in the world. The museum's **Field Station**, 48km east of the town of **Brooks** in **Dinosaur Provincial Park**, contains a small museum, but the main attraction is the **Badlands Bus Tour**. The bus chauffeurs visitors into a restricted hot spot of dinosaur finds. Many fossils still lie within the eroding rock; if you make a discovery, however, all you can take home with you are memories, Polaroids, and a Fossil Finder Certificate. The park's **campground** is shaded from summer heat, and grassy plots cushion most sites. Although it stays open year-round, the campground only has power and running water in summer. *(To reach the **Field Station** from Drumheller, follow Hwy. 56 south for 65km, then take Hwy. 1 about 70km to Brooks. Once in Brooks, go north along Hwy. 873 and east along Hwy. 544. 2hr. drive from Drumheller. Field Station ☎ 378-4342. Open daily Victoria Day to Labour Day 8:15am-9pm; Labour Day to Victoria Day M-F 9am-4pm. **Museum** admission $2.50, ages 7-17 and 65+ $1.50, under 7 free. Tours Victoria Day to Thanksgiving. 2-8 per day. $4.50, ages 7-17 $2.25, under 7 free. Reservations ☎ 378-4344. Sites $13, with power $15.)*

DINOSAUR-FREE ACTIVITIES. The Badlands also offer a variety of other recreational activities. The staff of **Midland Provincial Park** (☎ 823-1749), located halfway between the Tyrrell Museum and Drumheller, leads free 75min. natural history walking tours, departing from the museum one or two times per day. To see **hoodoos** in the making, go 15km east on Hwy. 10 from Drumheller. These limestone columns are relatively young: they still wear the stone caps that created the pillars by protecting them from erosion. In **Horseshoe Canyon**, about 20km west of Drumheller on Hwy. 9, **hiking and biking trails** wind below the prairie through red rock layers carved into bizarre, rounded formations. Several trails located in Dinosaur Provincial Park take hikers over and through the eroded landscape, including the **Coulee Viewpoint Trail** (.9km, 45min., moderate) and the **Cottonwoods Flats Trail** (1.4km, 2hr., easy), which weaves Deer River. Or, for a tamer look, gaze from the lookout just off the highway. More hiking can be done around the Tyrrell Museum. Carry plenty of water during hot weather, as it isn't called the Badlands for nothing. Be sure not to hop fences onto private property. Stock up on groceries at **IGA Market,** at N Railroad Ave. and Centre St. (☎823-3995. Open daily 24hr.)

NEAR CALGARY: KANANASKIS COUNTRY ☎403

Between Calgary and Banff lie 4200 sq. km of provincial parks and multi-use recreational areas collectively known as Kananaskis Country (KAN-uh-NASS-kiss). The area sweeps down from the Canadian Rockies through rolling foothills less than an hour from Banff, and contain a natural majesty comparable to the national parks with blissfully little of their crowds and none of the entrance fees (but expect to pay $1 for trail maps).

🛈 PRACTICAL INFORMATION AND ACCOMMODATIONS. Budget cuts and short staffing have hurt customer service at the **Barrier Lake Visitor Centre,** 6km south of Hwy. 1 on Hwy. 40. (☎673-3985. Call for hours.) Public transportation to Kananaskis is scarce. **Greyhound** stops at the **Rusticana Grocery,** 801 8th St. (☎678-4465), in Canmore. Four times per day to both **Banff** (25min., $8) and **Calgary** (1¼hr., $18). Unfortunately, Canmore is still a 25min. drive away. **Emergency:** ☎911.

Ribbon Creek Hostel, 24km south of the Trans-Canada Hwy. (Hwy. 1) on Hwy. 40. (turn right at Kananaskis Village, then follow signs for Ribbon Creek and the hostel. Sleeps 47.) Lots of hiking trails radiate from the site. Common room has a fireplace and comfy couches. Firepit, BBQ, volleyball court, hot showers, and huge kitchen. For reservations, call the Banff International Hostel. (See p. 357; ☎762-4122. Linen $1. $15, nonmembers $19. Private rooms $42, nonmembers $50.) The hostel has winter-time **lift ticket and lodging deals** with nearby Nakiska. Over **38 campgrounds** are accessible via K-Country roads (more than a dozen group campgrounds also exist). When traveling in areas with established backcountry campgrounds, visitors must use the areas provided. Backcountry permits are $3 per night and available at the visitors centers. Campsites cost $11-29 per night.

📖 HIKING. The University of Calgary runs extensive outdoor programs on campus and in Kananaskis Country in addition to their rental services (see **Equipment Rental,** p. 348). Day hikes start at $28, and mountaineering, and water and winter sports adventures are available.

The area is divided into eight sections; the three most popular are the meadows and forests of Bow Valley Provincial Park, with an office just off Hwy. 1 (☎673-3663; open M-F 8am-4:30pm), the grasslands of Elbow River Valley (☎949-4261) on Hwy. 66 near Bragg Creek, and the towering peaks of **Peter Lougheed Provincial Park** (☎491-6322), 1hr. south on Hwy. 40. Descriptions of Kananaskis Country's abundant activities give many outdoor enthusiasts goose bumps. With over 1000km of trails, hiking in K-Country can provide anything from a 1hr. quick fix to a full-blown Rocky Mountain High. Gillean Daffern's *Kananaskis Country Trail Guide*, published by Rocky Mountain Books and available at any area information center ($17), is a definitive source of info on longer trails. **1982 Canadian Mt. Everest Expedition Trail** (2km) starts at the White Spruce parking lot in Peter Lougheed Park 10km south of the visitors center. Climb through forest to a lookout point that provides a majestic view of both Upper and Lower Kananaskis Lakes. **Ribbon Creek Trail** (8km to falls, 10km to lake) passes through the waterfall-rich canyon land between Mt. Kidd and Mt. Bogart, arriving at the Ribbon Falls backcountry campground. (Start .5km south of the hostel parking lot. 350m elevation gain.)

THE ROCKIES ■ 353

⚠ OTHER OUTDOOR ACTIVITIES. Cliffs throughout the park offer excellent climbing opportunities. **Barrier Bluffs,** 6km south of the **Barrier Lake Visitor Centre,** has dozens of bolted routes up the wall. **Grotto Creek,** 1.9km from Grotto Mtn. on Hwy. 1A, follows powerlines then winds up a narrow canyon to vertical rock walls and a waterfall. Kananaskis is scaling back on trails open to bikes—check with the visitors centers for information. The foothills of the **Sibbald Area** in the northeast of K-country (30min. off Hwy. 1) offer wide expanses of terrain to **horseback riders, hikers,** and **cyclists,** while both the Peter Lougheed and the Kananaskis Valley Parks contain paved trails. A popular route for mountain bikers is **Skogan Pass,** winding along the power lines from Dead Man's Flats just north of Hwy. 1.

In the winter, the region's peaks draw a crowd of **ice-climbers** and Nordic and **backcountry skiers.** The **Canmore Nordic Centre** (☎403-678-2400; lodge open daily 9am-5:30pm), the 1988 Olympic Nordic skiing venue, offers 72km of **cross-country skiing** in the winter and mountain biking in the summer ($5 per day, ages 12-17 and 55+ $4, ages 6-11 $3). The **Nakiska ski area** was custom-built for Calgary's 1988 Winter Olympics. Its 28 mostly intermediate runs, 735m vertical drop, and extensive snowmaking make it a decidedly tamer choice than the hills at Banff and Lake Louise. (☎591-7777; snow report 244-6665; www.skinakiska.com. Open M-F 9am-4pm, Sa-Su 8:30am-4pm.)

THE ROCKIES

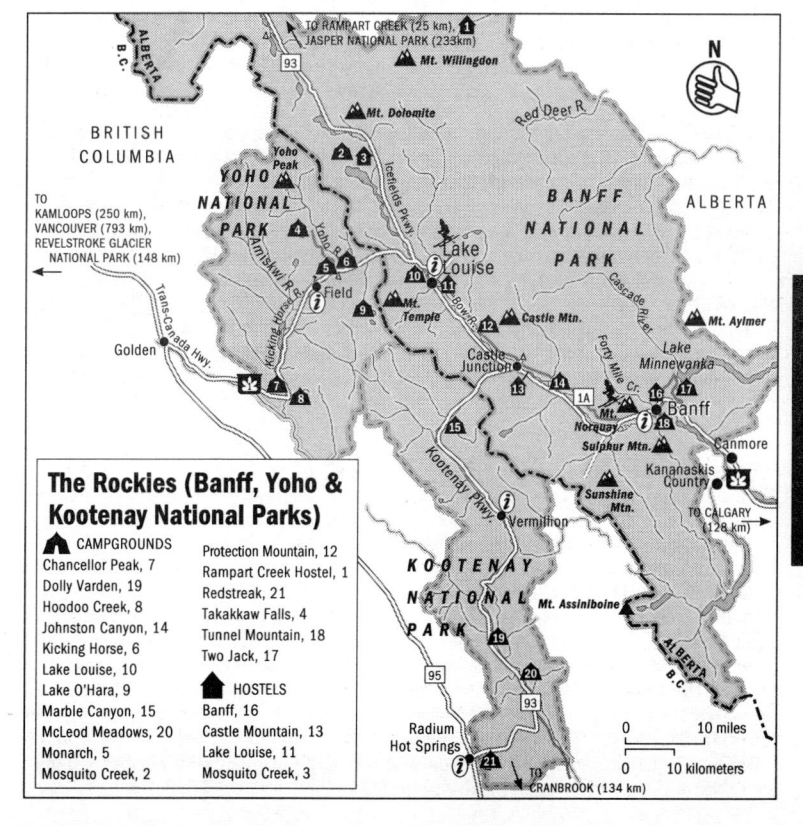

The Rockies (Banff, Yoho & Kootenay National Parks)

CAMPGROUNDS
Chancellor Peak, 7
Dolly Varden, 19
Hoodoo Creek, 8
Johnston Canyon, 14
Kicking Horse, 6
Lake Louise, 10
Lake O'Hara, 9
Marble Canyon, 15
McLeod Meadows, 20
Monarch, 5
Mosquito Creek, 2
Protection Mountain, 12
Rampart Creek Hostel, 1
Redstreak, 21
Takakkaw Falls, 4
Tunnel Mountain, 18
Two Jack, 17

HOSTELS
Banff, 16
Castle Mountain, 13
Lake Louise, 11
Mosquito Creek, 3

354 ■ BANFF NATIONAL PARK

The four national parks of the Canadian Rockies comprise one of Canada's top tourist draws, and with excellent reason. Every year, some five million visitors make it within sight of the parks' majestic peaks, stunning glacial lakes, and myriad varieties of wildlife. Thankfully, much of this traffic is confined to highway-side gawkers, leaving infinite backcountry trails and mountains in which to escape the flocks of tourists. Of the big two—Banff and Jasper—the latter feels a little farther removed from the droves of tourists. The hostels that line both parks are among the country's best, and usually are booked up as a result. It's also well worth diving into the quieter Yoho (see p. 300), Glacier (see p. 299), and Kootenay National Parks (see p. 301), as well as Kananaskis Country (see p. 301), the locals' free playground that separates Calgary from the Rockies.

TRANSPORTATION

BY CAR, BUS, AND TRAIN. Alberta's extensive highway system makes travel between major destinations easy, and provides the traveler with beautiful roadside scenery. The north-south **Icefields Parkway (Hwy. 93)** runs between **Banff** and **Jasper.** The east-west **Yellowhead Hwy. (Hwy. 16)** connects **Edmonton** with **Jasper,** and continues across British Columbia. The **Trans-Canada Hwy. (Hwy. 1)** completes the loop, linking **Calgary** with **Banff.** The easiest way to get here is to drive yourself or explore the bus options. **Buses** (Greyhound, Brewster, and Red Arrow) travel all of these routes; VIA Rail **trains** run from Edmonton to Jasper.

BY BIKE. Icefields Parkway is a popular trail, although the trip is best suited to experienced cyclists. Inquire at the rental shops (see **Equipment Rental,** below) about packaging services to get bikes back to their origins for one-way trips. The 291km separating Jasper and Banff is swelling with hundreds of glaciers, dramatic mountain peaks, and fantastic hostels well-spaced both on and off of the highway.

BY TOUR. Without a car, guided bus rides may be the easiest way to see some of the park's main attractions, such as the **Great Divide,** the **Athabasca Glacier,** and the spiral railroad tunnel. **Brewster Tours** offer 9½hr. guided tours on the Icefields Parkway. (☎762-6767. Mid-May to Oct. at 8:10am. $95, child $47.50. Spring and fall $72, child $36. 10% HI discount. A visit to the Columbia Icefields is $27 extra, $13.50 children.) **Bigfoot Tours** runs fun, two-day, 11-passenger van trips between Banff and Jasper with an overnight stop at the **Mt. Edith Cavell Hostel.** (See p. 365. ☎888-244-6673, in Vancouver 604-278-8224; fax 604-278-4881. $95, not including food or lodging.) They also run multiple other trips connecting Vancouver, Seattle, Kamloops, Whistler, Kelowna, and Revelstoke. All trips have three departures a week (daily connecting Seattle and Vancouver). Trips east stop at the **Squilax General Store Hostel** and trips west stop at the Old Courthouse Hostel in Kamloops.

BANFF NATIONAL PARK ☎403

Banff is Canada's best-loved and best-known natural park, with 6641 sq. km of peaks, forests, glaciers, and alpine valleys. It also holds the title of Canada's first National Park; it was declared so only days after the completion of the Canadian Pacific Railway in 1885. Its name comes from Banffshire, Scotland, the birthplace of the two Canadian Pacific Railway financiers who convinced Canada's first Prime Minister that a "large pecuniary advantage" might be gained from the region, and told him that, "since we can't export the scenery, we shall have to import the tourists." Their plan worked with a vengeance, but even streets littered with gift shops and chocolatiers cannot mar the beauty of the wilderness outside of the Banff townsite. Outdoors-lovers arrive with mountain bikes, climbing gear, skis, and snowboards, but a trusty pair of hiking boots remains the park's most widely-used outdoor equipment.

FLOUR POWER

Passing by the many lakes and streams in the Rockies, you may notice that they have an unusual color. When looking at the swimming-pool turquoise or glowing blue color of these watery features of the landscape, you might wonder if this is some kind of gimmick perpetuated by the park wardens to bring in the tourists. Many years ago, one visitor to Lake Louise claimed that he had solved the mystery of the beautiful water: it had obviously been distilled from peacock tails. Turns out he was a bit off the mark. The actual cause of the color comes from "rock flour." This fine dust is created by the pressure exerted by the glacier upon rocks trapped within the ice; the resulting ground rock is washed into streams and lakes in the glacial meltwater. Suspended particles trap all colors of the spectrum except for the blues and greens that are reflected back for your visual pleasure.

TRANSPORTATION

Banff National Park hugs the Alberta side of the Alberta/British Columbia border 128km west of Calgary. The **Trans-Canada Hwy. (Hwy. 1)** runs east-west through the park, connecting it to Yoho National Park in the west. The **Icefields Parkway (Hwy. 93)** connects Banff with Jasper National Park to the north and Kootenay National Park to the southwest. Civilization in the park centers around the towns of **Banff** and **Lake Louise**, 58km apart on Hwy. 1. The more serene **Bow Valley Parkway (Hwy. 1A)** parallels Hwy. 1 from Lake Louise to 8km west of Banff, offering excellent camping, hosteling, sights, and wildlife. The southern portion of Hwy. 1A is restricted at night in the late spring and early summer to accommodate the wildlife on the road. All listings apply to Banff Townsite, unless otherwise specified.

Buses: Brewster Transportation, 100 Gopher St. (☎ 762-6767). To: **Jasper** (5hr., $51); **Lake Louise** (1hr., $11); and **Calgary** (2hr., $36). Depot open daily 7:30am-9pm. Ages 6-15 half-price. See **The Rockies,** p. 353, for info on tours to, from, and in parks. **Greyhound** (☎ 800-661-8747) uses Brewster's station. 4 per day to **Lake Louise** (1hr., $12) and **Vancouver, BC** (14hr., $105); 5 per day to **Calgary** (1½hr., $22).

Public Transportation: The **Happy Bus** runs between the Banff Springs Hotel, the trailer area, and Banff Hostel on Tunnel Mountain Rd., as well as between the Tunnel Mountain Campground, downtown, and the Banff Park Museum. $1, children 50¢. Mid-May to Sept. 7am-midnight; late Apr. to early May and Oct.-Dec. noon-midnight.

Taxis: Banff Taxi, ☎ 726-4444. 24hr. **Lake Louise Taxi,** ☎ 522-2020. Runs 6am-2:30pm.

Car Rental: Available from several establishments with rates ranging from $48-$57 per day, with 100-150 free km. Ask at the visitors center for a comparison chart.

Tours: Bigfoot Adventure Tours (☎ 888-244-6673) runs fun 10-day trips from Vancouver to Jasper and Banff. Passengers are welcome to jump off and on either of the three vans that run per week (daily from July-Sept.). A $380 fee covers transportation, park fees, and a good laugh; but not the HI accommodations, food, or entertainment.

PRACTICAL INFORMATION

Visitors Center: Banff Visitor Centre, 224 Banff Ave. Includes **Banff/Lake Louise Tourism Bureau** (☎ 762-8421; www.banfflakelouise.com) and **Parks Canada** (☎ 762-1550). Open June-Sept. daily 8am-8pm; Oct.-May 9am-5pm. **Lake Louise Visitor Centre** (☎ 522-3833), at Samson Mall on Village Rd. Open mid-June-Sept. daily 8am-6pm; Oct.to mid-June 9am-5pm.

Equipment Rental:

Mountain Magic Equipment, 224 Bear St. (☎ 762-2591) is one of the few places in Banff to rent packages for Telemark ($25 per day) and mountaineering ($50 per day), along with the usual bike, ski, and snowboard rentals. Outdoor rock climbing lessons $25-60. 10% HI discount. Open Dec.-Mar. daily 8am-9pm, Apr.-Nov. 9am-9pm.

356 ■ BANFF NATIONAL PARK

Bactrax Rentals, 225 Bear St. (☎ 762-8177). Rents mountain bikes for $6-10 per hr., $22-36 per day. Bike tours $15 per hr. including all equipment. Ski packages from $16 per day, snowboard packages $28. 20% HI discount. Open Apr.-Oct. daily 8am-8pm, Nov.-Mar. 7am-10pm.

Performance Sports, 208 Bear St. (☎ 762-8222). Rents tents ($20-26 per day), fishing gear ($16-30 per day), cross-country ski or snowshoe packages ($12 per day, $31 for 3 days), avalanche packages ($23 per day), and snow or rainwear ($8-17 per day). 10% HI or Real Big Adventures discount. Open daily July-Aug. 9:30am-8pm, Sept.-June 10am-6pm.

Wilson Mountain Sports (☎ 522-3636) in the Lake Louise Samson Mall, rents bikes ($8 per hr.) as well as mountaineering packages ($35 per day), rock climbing packages ($15 per day), and camping and fishing gear. Sells fishing permits. Open daily mid-June to Sept. 9am-9pm, Oct. to Apr. 8am-8pm, May to mid-June 9am-8pm.

Laundry: Cascade Coin Laundry, 317 Banff Ave. (☎ 762-0165), downstairs in the Cascade Mall (past food court, by restrooms). Wash $2.50, dry 25¢ per 5min. Open M-Sa 8am-10pm, Su 8am-9pm. **Johnny O's,** 223 Bear St. (☎ 762-5111). $4.50 for wash and dry. Open daily 9am-10pm.

Weather: ☎ 762-2088

Road Conditions: ☎ 762-1450

Emergency: ☎ 911 (in Banff and all neighboring parks except Kootenay).

Police: Banff Police, ☎ 762-2226; non-emergency 762-2228. On Lynx St. by the train depot. **Lake Louise Police,** ☎ 522-3811; non-emergency 522-3812. **Banff Park Warden,** ☎ 762-4506; non-emergency 762-1470 (24hr.). **Lake Louise Park Warden,** ☎ 522-1200.

Ambulance: ☎ 762-2000.

Hospital: Mineral Springs, 301 Lynx St. (☎ 762-2222), near Wolf St. in Banff.

Internet Access: Library, 101 Bear St. (☎ 762-2611). Sign up days in advance. Closed Su from late May early Sept. **Cyber Web,** on the lower level of Sundance Mall (215 Banff Ave.); enter across from tourist office. (☎ 762-9226). Open daily 10am-midnight. $3 per 15min., $8 per hr., $5 per hr. from 9:30pm-close. For laptop hookups, open M-Th 10am-8pm, F 10am-6pm, Sa 11am-6pm, Su 1-5pm. $1 per 15min.

Post Office: 204 Buffalo St. (☎ 762-2586). Open M-F 9am-5:30pm. **Postal Code:** T0L 0C0.

▛ ACCOMMODATIONS

Finding a cheap place to stay in Banff is becoming increasingly difficult as the number of visitors soars into the millions every year. Townsite residents offer rooms in their homes, occasionally at reasonable rates ($75-140, winter $60-100). Check the list at the back of the *Banff and Lake Louise Official Visitor Guide*, available free at the visitors centers.

Mammoth **modern hostels** at Banff and Lake Louise anchor a chain of cozier hostels from Calgary to Jasper. **Rustic hostels,** the last three on the following list, provide more of a wilderness experience (read: no electricity or flush toilets), and often have some of the park's best hiking and cross-country skiing right in their backyards. HI runs a **shuttle service** connecting all the Rocky Mountain hostels and Calgary ($8-90). Wait-list beds become available at 6pm, and the larger hostels try to save a few stand-by beds for shuttle arrivals. Beds go quickly, especially during the summer, so make your reservations as early as possible. The hostels below are listed from south to north, and excluding Lake Louise, all reservations are made through Banff International at ☎ 762-4122 or online at www.hostellingintl.ca. Free reservations are held until 6pm, or can be guaranteed until later with a credit card.

■ **Lake Louise International Hostel (HI;** ☎ 522-2200), 500m west of the Info Center in Lake Louise Townsite, on Village Rd. toward the Park Warden's office. Ranked fourth in the world by HI, and rightly so. More like a resort than a hostel, it boasts a reference library, a stone fireplace, 2 full kitchens, a sauna, and a quality cafe. Internet access $2 per 20min. Hub for mountaineering tours. Linen or locker $1, towels 50¢. Check-in 3pm, check-out 10am. $23, nonmembers $27; private rooms available.

Rampart Creek Hostel (HI), 34km south of the Icefield Centre. Close to several world-famous ice climbs (including Weeping Wall, 17km north), this hostel is a favorite for winter mountaineers. Wood-burning sauna, full-service kitchen, creek water. Ask to see the spot overlooking the magnificent valley below. Linen $1. 2 coed cabins with 12 beds each. Closed Oct. 9-Nov. 7; closed Nov. 8-Dec. 19 M-W. $14, nonmembers $18.

Castle Mountain Hostel (HI), on the Bow Valley Parkway (Hwy. 1A), 1.5km east of the junction of Hwy. 1 and Hwy. 93, between Banff and Lake Louise. A smaller, quieter alternative to the hubbub of the Big Hostels. Friendly staff, hot showers, kitchen, laundry, and electricity. Comfortable common area with huge bay windows. A library, collection of games, and fireplace. Linen $1. Check-in 5-10pm; check-out 10am. Sleeps 28. Closed Apr. 16 to May 1; Oct. 9 to Nov. 6. $15, nonmembers $19.

Mosquito Creek Hostel (HI), 103km south of the Icefield Centre and 26km north of Lake Louise. Across the creek from the Mosquito Creek campground. Close to the Wapta Icefield. Enormous living room with wood stove, wood-burning sauna, kitchen, and pump water. 2 coed cabins of 12 beds each. Linen $1. Closed Apr. 16 to May 14, Oct. 9 to Nov. 6). $15, nonmembers $19; kids 7-18 half-price, under 6 free.

Hilda Creek Hostel (HI), 8.5km south of the Icefield Centre and the highest hostel in Canada at 2000m, at the base of Mt. Athabasca. Park across the street 100m north of the hostel and walk on the trail behind the divider. Some of the Icefield's best hiking and skiing lie just behind on Parker Ridge—in winter, ski directly from the hostel. Sauna, firepit, barbecue, full-service kitchen, and free toboggan. Propane heat and light; water at creek. Closed Oct.29 to Dec. 5; closed M-W Dec. 6-19. $14, nonmembers $18.

Banff International Hostel (HI; ☎ 762-4411), 3km uphill from Banff Townsite on Tunnel Mountain Rd. Walk or take Happy Bus from downtown ($1). This monster hostel has 3 lounges, kitchens, laundry facilities, and hot showers. Seasonal staff turnover can lead to inconsistent quality of service. Linen $1. Check-in 3pm. Check-out 11am. Sleeps 215. $21.50, nonmembers $25.50; better rooms in new building add $1.50.

CAMPING

As with the hostels, a chain of campgrounds stretches between Banff and Jasper. Extra-large, fully hooked-up grounds lie closer to the townsites; for more trees and fewer vehicles, try the more remote sites farther from Banff and Lake Louise. At all park campgrounds, a campfire permit (includes firewood) is $4. Sites are first come, first served; go early. The sites below are listed from south to north and have wheelchair access but no toilets or showers unless otherwise noted.

Tunnel Mountain Village, 4km from Banff Townsite on Tunnel Mountain Rd. With nearly 1200 sites, this facility is a camping metropolis. Trailer/RV area has 321 full hookups, Village 2 has 188 sites, and Village 1 houses a whopping 618 sites. Fires allowed in Village 1 only; all villages have showers. Village 2 is open year-round; 1 and 3 closed Oct. to early May. $17; power only $21; full hookups $24.

Two Jack, 13km northeast of Banff, across Hwy.1. Open mid-May to mid-Sept. The 381 sites in the main area ($13) have no showers or disabled access, while the 80 lakeside sites ($17) do.

Johnston Canyon, 26km northwest of Banff on Bow Valley Pkwy. (Hwy. 1A). Access to Johnston Canyon Trail (see below). Showers. Open mid-June to Sept. 140 sites, $17.

Protection Mountain, 15km east of Lake Louise and 11km west of Castle Junction on the Bow Valley Pkwy. (Hwy. 1A). 89 spacious and wooded sites (14 trailer) in a basic campground. Open late June through early Sept. Sites $13.

Lake Louise, 1½km southeast of the visitors center on Fairview Rd. On Bow River, not the lake. Plenty of hiking and fishing awaits near this tent city. Showers. 189 trailer sites with electricity only, open year-round; $21. 220 tent sites, open mid-May to Sept.; $17.

Mosquito Creek, 103km south of the Icefield Centre and 26km north of Lake Louise. 32 sites with hiking access. Pit toilets. Sites $10.

358 ■ BANFF NATIONAL PARK

Rampart Creek, 147km north of Banff, 34km south of the Icefield Centre, across the hwy. from Rampart Creek hostel and amazing ice climbing. Pit toilets. Open late June to Aug. 50 sites, $10.

🍽 FOOD AND NIGHTLIFE

Like everything else in the park, Banff restaurants tend toward the expensive. The Banff and Lake Louise hostels serve affordable meals in their cafes ($3-10). Groceries await at **Safeway,** at Marten and Elk St., just off Banff Ave. (☎762-5378. Open daily 8am-11pm.) Bartenders maintain that Banff's true wildlife is in its bars. Check the paper or ask at the visitors center to find out which nightspots are having "locals' night," featuring cheap drinks. Banff Ave. hosts more bars, restaurants, kitschy gift shops, ATMs and banks than there are mountains. The fun doesn't stop after Saturday night, either: Banff Sundays boast great nightlife.

- **Rose and Crown,** 202 Banff Ave. (☎762-2121), upstairs on the corner of Banff and Caribou. Ample room for drinking, dancing, and pool-playing ($1.25), even on busy nights. Couch-adorned living room for watching sports and live music every night at 10pm. Happy hour M-F 3:30-6:30pm. $2 cover Sa, Jam Night Su with happy hour 9pm-close. Open daily 11am-2am.

- **Laggan's Deli** (☎522-2017; fax 522-3299), in Samson Mall in Lake Louise. Always crowded; there's nowhere better in town. Thick sandwiches ($4-5) or fresh-baked loaves ($3). Open June-Sept. daily 6am-8pm; winter 6am-7pm. Cash or traveler's checks only.

- **Sunfood Cafe,** 215 Banff (☎760-3933), second floor of the Sundance Mall. A very relaxed vegetarian cafe hidden upstairs in a touristy mall. Veggie burger with the works $6.25. Daily specials, to go available, beer and wine. Open M-Sa 10am-8pm.

- **Aardvark's,** 304A Caribou St. (☎762-5500 or 762-5509). Does big business after the bars close. Skinny on seating. Thick slices of pizza $3. Small pie $6-9; large $13-21; buffalo wings $5 for 10. 10% HI discount on large pizzas. Open daily 11am-4am.

- **Aurora,** 110 Banff Ave. in the basement of Clock Tower Plaza (☎760-5300). This neon-lit ultra-modern club caters to the 25+ crowd with its diverse spaces—martini and cigar bar in back; house, hip-hop, and trance dance floor; sports area with big-screen; and 5 bars. Highballs and beers Sa. Open 9pm-2am.

- **Lux Cinema Centre,** 229 Bear St. (24hr. cinema info ☎762-8595). Fun for the whole family. Call for movies and times.

- **St. James's Gate,** 205 Wolf St. (☎762-9355). A laid-back Irish Pub with friendly staff. Ask the bartenders which of the 32 beers on tap to try. Live jigs and reels on F-Sa completes the Irish ambience. Open daily 11am-2am.

👁 SIGHTS

MUSEUMS. Visitors can purchase a pass to gain admission to all three of the following sites (mid-May to Sept. $11, seniors and students $7, family $28; Oct.-mid-May $7, seniors and students $4.50, family $15). The **Whyte Museum of the Canadian Rockies,** 111 Bear St., explores the history and culture of the Canadian Rockies over the last two centuries in the Heritage Gallery, while temporary exhibits focus on the natural history of the region. Displays include works done by Canadian painters. (☎762-2291. Open daily 10am-5pm; $6, students and seniors $4, 5 and under free.) The **Banff Park Museum National Historic Site** is western Canada's oldest natural history museum, with rooms of stuffed specimens dating to the 1860s. On Banff Ave. near the bridge. (☎762-1558. Open mid-May to Sept. daily 10am-6pm; Oct. to mid-May 1-5pm. Tours summer daily 2:30pm, weekends in winter. $2.50, seniors 65 $2, children $1.50.) Banff National Park would not exist if not for the **Cave and Basin Mineral Springs,** once rumored to have miraculous healing properties and the birthplace of National Park System. The **Cave and Basin National Historic Site,** a refurbished bath house built circa 1914, is now a small museum detailing the history and science of the site. Access to the low-ceilinged cave containing the original spring is inside the building. Five of the pools are the only home of the park's most endangered species: the small Banff Springs snail—*physella johnsoni*. (☎ 762-1566. *Open daily in summer 9am-6pm; winter 11am-4pm. Tours at 11am. $2.50, seniors $2, children $1.50.*) The **springs** are southwest of the city on Cave Ave. For an actual dip in the hot water, follow the egg smell to the Upper Hot Springs pool, a 40°C (104°F) sulfurous cauldron on Mountain Ave. (☎ 762-1515. *Open mid-May to mid-Oct. daily 9am-11pm; mid-Oct. to mid-May Su-Th 10am-10pm, F-Sa 10am-11pm. Summer rates $7.50, seniors and children 3-17 $6.50, families $21.50. Winter $5.50, seniors and children $4.50, families $15. Swimsuits $1.50, towels $1.25, lockers 50¢.*)

EVENTS. In summer, the **Banff Festival of the Arts** keeps tourists occupied. A wide spectrum of events, from First Nations dance to Opera, are performed from May to mid-August. Some performances are free; stop by the visitors center for a schedule. The **Banff Mountain Film Festival,** in the first week of November, screens films and videos that celebrate mountains and mountaineers. (For info, call 762-6301.)

◪ OUTDOOR ACTIVITIES

A visitor sticking to paved byways will see only a tiny fraction of the park. Those interested in the seemingly endless outdoor options can hike or bike on more than 1600km of trails. Grab a free copy of *Mountain Biking and Cycling Guide* or *Day Hikes in Banff* and peruse park maps and trail descriptions at information centers. For still more solitude, pick up the *The Banff Backcountry Experience* and an **overnight camping permit** at a visitors center and head out to the backcountry ($6 per person per day, up to $30; $42 per year). Be sure to check with the park wardens for current weather and wildlife updates.

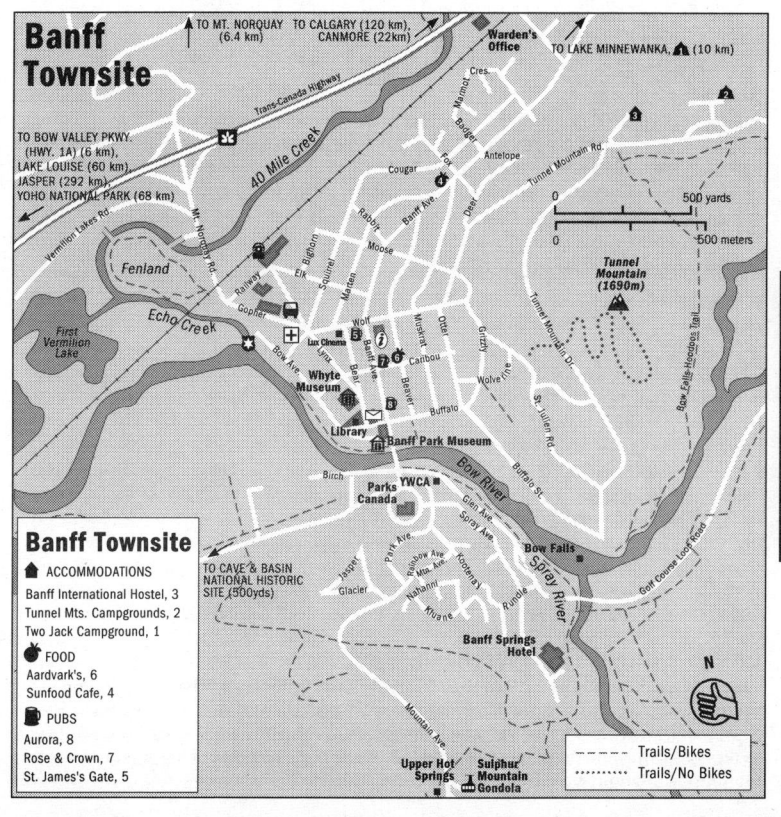

BANFF TOWNSITE AREA
HIKING
Two easy trails are within walking distance of Banff Townsite.

Fenland (2km, 1hr.). Follow Mt. Norquay Rd. to the outskirts of town, and look for signs across the tracks on road's left side. The trail winds through a flat area shared by beaver, muskrat, and waterfowl, but is closed for elk calving in late spring, early summer.

Tunnel Mountain (2.5km, 2hr.). Follow Wolf St. east from Banff Ave., and turn right on St. Julien Rd. to reach the head of the steep trail. Provides a dramatic view of the **Bow Valley** and **Mt. Rundle.** Tunnel Mountain has the unfortunate distinction of being the Rockies' smallest mountain.

Mt. Rundle (11km round-trip, 7-8hr.). The trail includes an exposed ridge known as the Dragon's Back, which leads to a scramble up scree slopes just short of the summit. The unrivaled vista is well worth the effort. The visitors center sells the warning-and-tip-packed *A Climber's Guide to Mount Rundle*. 1600m gain. Strenuous.

Johnston Canyon (5.5km). West of the Norquay Interchange on Hwy. 1, then 18km along the Bow Valley Pkwy. (Hwy. 1A). A very popular half-day hike. A catwalk along the edge of the deep limestone canyon runs 1.1km over the thundering river to the canyon's lower falls, then another 1.6km to the upper falls. The trail continues for a more rugged 3.2km to seven blue-green cold-water springs, known as the **Inkpots,** in an open valley above the canyon. More than 42km of trails beyond the Inkpots are blissfully untraveled and punctuated with campgrounds roughly every 10km.

Sulphur Mountain (5.5km, 2hr.). A moderate hike winds along a well-trodden trail to the peak of where a spectacular view awaits; the **Sulphur Mountain Gondola** doesn't charge for the 8min. downhill trip. (☎ 762-2523. Uphill $19, ages 6-15 $9.50, under 6 free.) The **Panorama Restaurant** (☎ 762-7486), perched atop the mountain, serves breakfast ($10) and lunch buffets ($13) from mid-May to mid-August.

BIKING
Biking is permitted on public roads, highways, and certain trails in the park. Spectacular scenery and a number of hostels and campgrounds make the **Bow Valley Parkway (Hwy. 1A)** and the **Icefields Parkway (Hwy. 93)** perfect for extended cycling trips. Every other store downtown seems to rent bikes; head to **Bactrax** or **Performance Sport** (see **Equipment Rental,** p. 355) for HI discounts. Parks Canada publishes brochures that describe trails and roadways where bikes are permitted (free at bike rental shops and visitors centers).

WATERSPORTS
Fishing is legal in most of the park's bodies of water during specific seasons, but live bait and lead weights are not. Get a **permit** and check out regulations at the info center. (7-day permit $6, annual permit valid in all Canadian National Parks $13.) **Bourgeau Lake,** a 7km hike in, is home to a particularly feisty breed of brook trout. Closer to the road, try **Herbert Lake,** off the Icefields Pkwy., or **Lake Minnewanka,** on Lake Minnewanka Rd. northeast of Banff. Lake Minnewanka Rd. passes **Johnson Lake,** where shallow warm water makes a perfect swimming hole.

Hydra River Guides runs **whitewater rafting** trips along the **Kicking Horse River.** (☎ 762-4554 or 800-644-8888; www.raftbanff.com. 22km, 2½hr. Up to Class IV+ rapids. $85, includes lunch, transportation, and gear; HI members $72.) **Blast Adventures** leads half-day, 1-2-person **inflatable kayak** trips on the rowdy Kananaskis River for $59 per person including transportation, gear, and snacks. (☎ 609-2009 or 888-802-5278; www.blastadventures.com. Full day rides $119, lunch included.)

LAKE LOUISE TOWNSITE AREA
The highest community in Canada (1530m), Lake Louise and the surrounding glaciers have often passed for Swiss scenery in movies and are the emerald in the Rockies' tiara of tourism. Once at the lake, the hardest task is escaping fellow gawkers at the posh **Chateau Lake Louise.** The chateau's canoe rentals at the chateau are more than steep ($30 per hr.).

OUTDOOR ACTIVITIES ■ **361**

> **THINGS THAT GO BANFF IN THE NIGHT** Bear sightings are common in the Canadian Rockies, but one black bear took it upon himself to give Banff residents an uncommon reminder of whose park it really is. Imaginatively known as Bear 16 (numbers are used to discourage personification), this ursine vagabond moved into town, disrupting everyday activity by foraging in front lawns and lazing in the road, blocking traffic. Bear 16 crossed the line when the scent from a bakery lured him too close to human territory. The park staff ultimately removed Bear 16 from the park, had him castrated, and relocated him to the Calgary Zoo.
>
> While most travelers to the park are eager to see its wildlife, few want as intimate an encounter as Bear 16 offered. The safest bet is to talk, sing, or yodel loudly while hiking, especially on windy days or near running water. The number of bear attacks actually ranks low among the total number of attacks by park animals; dozens of visitors are bitten each year by rodents pursuing human food. By far the most dangerous of Banff animals, however, are people—road accidents are the most common cause of death for large wildlife in the park.

HIKING

If you don't want to succumb to the prices, you can view the lake on several hiking trails that begin at the water's edge and have prime lookouts.

- **Lake Agnes Trail** (3.5km, 2½hr. round trip), and the **Plain of Six Glaciers Trail** (5.5km, 4hr. round trip) both end at teahouses and make for a lovely, if sometimes crowded, day hike. Open daily summer only 9am-6pm.

- **Moraine Lake,** 15km from the village, at the end of Moraine Lake Rd. and off Lake Louise Dr. (no trailers or long RVs). Moraine lies in the awesome **Valley of the Ten Peaks,** opposite glacier-encrusted **Mt. Temple.** Join the multitudes on the **Rockpile Trail** for an eye-popping view of the lake and valley and a lesson in ancient ocean bottoms (10min. walk to the top). Packs more scenic punch than its sister Louise; be sure to arrive before 10am or after 4pm to see the view instead of the crowds. If you don't visit Moraine, just get your hands on an old $20 bill; the Valley of Ten Peaks is pictured on the reverse.

- **Paradise Valley,** depending on which way you hike it, can be an intense dayhike or a relaxing overnight trip. From the **Paradise Creek Trailhead,** 2.5km up Moraine Lake Rd., the loop through the valley runs 18.1km through subalpine and alpine forests and along rivers (7½hr., elevation gain 880m). One classic backpacking route runs from Moraine Lake up and over **Sentinel Pass,** joining the top of the Paradise Valley loop after 8km. A **backcountry campground** marks the midpoint from either trailhead. Campers aren't the only admirers of the scenery: grizzly activity often forces the park wardens to close the area in summer. Check with the wardens before hiking in this area.

WINTER SPORTS

Winter activities in the park range from world-class ice climbing to ice fishing. Those 1600km of hiking trails make for exceptional **cross-country skiing** (**Morraine Lake Rd.** is closed to vehicle traffic in the winter, and is used for cross-country skiing, as are the backcountry trails) and three allied resorts offer a range of **skiing and snowboarding** opportunities from early November to mid-May. All have terrain parks for snowboarders. Shuttles to all the following three resorts leave from most big hotels in the townsites, and Banff and Lake Louise hostels typically have **ticket and transportation discounts** available for guests. Multi-day passes good for all three resorts are available at the **Ski Banff/Lake Louise** office, 225 Banff Ave., lower level, and at all resorts. Passes include free shuttle service and an extra night of skiing at Mount Norquay. (☎ 762-4561; www.skibanfflakelouise.)

- **Sunshine Mountain** (☎ 762-6500; snow report 760-7669; Calgary 277-7669; www.skibanff.com). Spreading across three mountains, with the largest snowfall (9.9m) in the area, this mountain attracts loyal followers to its 3168 acres. $54; students under 24, ages 13-17, and over 65 $43; ages 6-12 $16.

Lake Louise (☎522-3555; snow report in Calgary 244-6665, or in Banff 762-4766; www.skilouise.com). The second-largest ski area in Canada (4200 skiable acres), with amazing views, over 1000m of vertical drop and the best selection of expert (double-black) terrain, although simpler slopes cover plenty of the mountain. $54; students under 25 and adults over 65 $43; ages 6-12 $15.

Mt. Norquay (☎762-4421; fax 762-8133). A local's mountain: smaller, closer to town, and much less manic, with draws like Friday night skiing and 2-5hr. tickets. ($47; students, ages 13-17 and 55+ $37; ages 6-12 $16. Night-skiing $23; students, youth, seniors $21; ages 6-12 $12.)

SIGHTSEEING

The **Lake Louise Sightseeing Lift,** up Whitehorn Rd. and across the Trans-Canada Hwy. from Lake Louise, cruises up **Mt. Whitehorn.** (☎522-3555; fax 522-2095; www.skilouise.com. Open daily May-Sept. 8:30am-6pm, Oct.-Apr. 9am-4pm. Summer $17, students and seniors $15, ages 6-12 $9, under 6 free. To enjoy breakfast at the top, add $2; for lunch, add $6, under 6 $3.)

BANFF TO JASPER: ICEFIELDS PARKWAY (HWY. 93)

The Icefields Parkways began in the Great Depression as a work relief project. The 230km Parkway is one of the most beautiful drives in North America, heading north from Lake Louise in Banff National Park to Jasper Townsite in Jasper National Park. Drivers may struggle to keep their eyes on the road as they skirt stunning peaks, aquamarine glacial lakes, and highwayside glaciers.

⚑ PRACTICAL INFORMATION. Parks Canada manages the parkway as a scenic route, so all users must obtain a **Park Pass,** available at entrance gates and information centers. ($5, seniors $4; $10 per day, seniors $8; $70 per year for 2-7 persons. Valid at all Canadian national parks.) Free maps of the Icefields Parkway are available at park visitors centers in Jasper, Lake Louise, and Banff. They are also available at the **Icefield Centre,** at the boundary between the two parks, 132km north of Lake Louise and 103km south of Jasper Townsite. (☎780-852-6288. Open Apr. to mid-Oct. daily 9am-5pm.) Although the center is closed in winter, the Parkway is only closed for plowing after heavy snowfalls. Thanks to the extensive campground and hostel networks that line the Parkway, longer trips down the length of Banff and Jasper National Parks are convenient and affordable (see **Accommodations,** p. 357 and 365). Cyclists should be prepared to face rapidly changing weather conditions and some very steep hills.

⚑ OUTDOOR ACTIVITIES. The Icefields Parkway has 18 trails into the wilderness and 22 scenic points with spectacular views. **Bow Summit,** 40km north of Lake Louise, is the Parkway's highest point (2135m); there, a 10min. walk leads to a view of fluorescent aqua **Peyto Lake.** The Icefield Centre (see above) lies in the shadow of the tongue of the **Athabasca Glacier.** This gargantuan ice flow is one of six major glaciers that flow from the 200 sq. km **Columbia Icefield,** the largest accumulation of ice and snow in the Canadian Rockies. The icefield's runoff eventually flows to three oceans: the Pacific, Atlantic, and Arctic.

Columbia Icefield Snocoach Tours carries visitors over the Athabasca Glacier in monster-truck-like buses for an 80min. trip. (☎877-423-7433. Open daily Apr.-Sept. 9am-5pm; Oct. 10am-4pm. $27, ages 6-15 $13.50.) Visitors can also drive close and take a 10min. walk up piles of glacial debris to the glacier's mighty toe. Dated signposts mark the glacier's speedy retreat up the valley over the last century. For more tasty geological tidbits, sign up for an **Athabasca Glacier Icewalk.** Either of two tours runs each day at 11am except Su and Th; contact the Icefield Centre or Peter Lemieux. (☎780-852-3803. Tours run mid-June to mid-Sept. 3hr. Ice Cubed $40, ages 7-17 $20. "Ice Walk Deluxe" 5-6hr.; $45, ages 7-17 $22.)

The **Wilcox Pass Trail** begins 3km south of the Icefield Centre at **Wilcox Creek Campground** (see p. 364). The first 2.5km of the path climb onto a ridge with astounding views of Athabasca Glacier and Mt. Athabasca. The **Parker Ridge Trail** leads 2.5km away from the road and up above treeline, where an impressive view of the **Saskatchewan Glacier** awaits. The trailhead is 1km south of the **Hilda Creek Hostel** (see p. 357), and 8.5km south of the Icefield Centre.

JASPER NATIONAL PARK ☎ 780

Northward expansion of the Canadian railway system led to further exploration of the Canadian Rocky Mountains and the 1907 creation of Jasper, the largest of the National Parks in the region. The area went virtually untouristed until 1940, when the Icefields Parkway paved the way for the masses to appreciate Jasper's astounding beauty. The Parkway is popular with cyclists, making for a remarkable, albeit long, bike journey. In summer, caravans of RVs and charter buses line the hwy. jostling for the chance to take photos of surprisingly fearless wildlife. Because 40% of the park is above the treeline, most visitors stay in the sheltered vicinity of Jasper Townsite, smaller than its nearby counterpart. Every summer, the tourist influx quadruples the town's population to over 20,000. In the face of this annual bloat, Jasper's permanent residents struggle to keep their home looking and feeling like a small town. In the winter, crowds melt away, snow descends, and a modest ski resort welcomes visitors to a slower, more relaxed town.

TRANSPORTATION

All of the addresses below are in **Jasper Townsite,** near the center of the park at the intersection of **Hwy. 16,** which runs east-west through the northern reaches of the park, and the **Icefields Parkway (Hwy. 93),** which connects Jasper with Banff National Park in the south. Many bike shops rent one-way between the two parks. Hitching is popular and reportedly easy along the Parkway, but *Let's Go* does not recommend hitchhiking. The two front streets in Jasper hold all the shops and stores, while the hostels and campgrounds are a short hike out of town.

- **Trains: VIA Rail,** 607 Connaught Dr. (☎ 800-561-8630). 3 per week to **Vancouver, BC** (16½hr., $192), **Edmonton** (5hr., $138), and **Winnipeg, MB** (1 day, $210).

- **Buses: Greyhound** (☎ 852-3332), in the train station. To **Edmonton** (4½hr., 3 per day, $52) and **Vancouver, BC** (11½hr., 3 per day, $104), via **Kamloops, BC** (5hr., $59). **Brewster Transportation** (☎ 852-3332), in the train station. To **Calgary** (7½hr., $71) via **Banff** (5½hr., $51).

- **Taxis: Heritage Cabs** (☎ 852-5558). Flat rates from town to Jasper International Hostel ($11); and to the Maligne Canyon Hostel ($17).

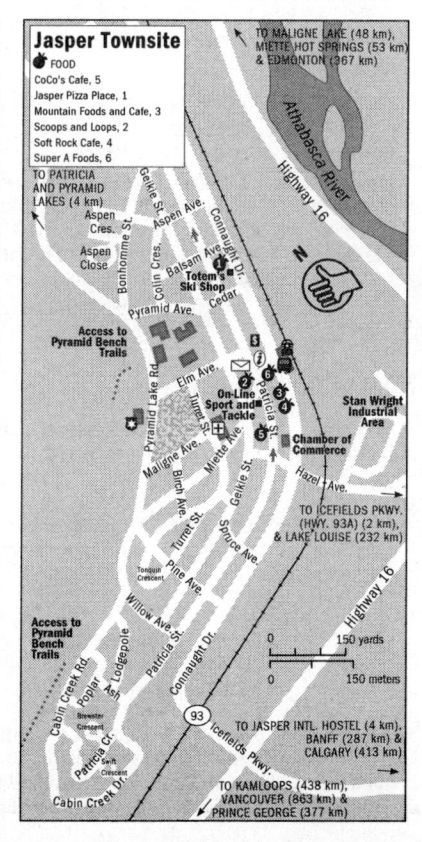

364 ■ JASPER NATIONAL PARK

Car Rental: Hertz (☎852-3888), in the train station. $50 per day, 24¢ per km after 100km. Must be 21 with credit card. Closed winter. **Budget** 638 Connaught Dr. (☎852-3222), in the Shell Station. $53 per day, 23¢ per km after 150km; 6hr. for $33 with 50km free and 23¢ per km thereafter.

Car Repair: Petro Canada, 300 Connaught Dr. (☎852-3366).

Tours: Bigfoot Adventure Tours runs trips between Vancouver and Jasper and Banff (see Banff).

PRACTICAL INFORMATION

Visitor Information: Park Information Centre, 500 Connaught Dr. (☎852-6176), has trail maps and offers free local calls. Open mid-June to early Sept. daily 8am-7pm, early Sept. to late Oct. and late Dec. to mid-June 9am-5pm.

Bank: CIBC, 416 Connaught Ave. (☎852-3391), by the visitors center. Open M-Th 10am-3pm, F 10am-5pm. 24hr. **ATM.**

Equipment Rental: Freewheel Cycle, 618 Patricia Ave. (☎852-3898; www.freewheel.ca). Hi-end mountain bikes $8 per hr., $24 per day, $32 overnight. Snowboard package $28 per day. Watch for twin-tip ski demo deals. Open in summer daily 9am-9pm; spring and fall 9am-6pm; call for winter hours. **Jasper International Hostel** also rents mountain bikes. $8 per half-day, $15 per day. Snowshoes $8 per day.

Laundromat and Public Showers: Coin Clean, 607 Patricia St. (☎852-3852). Wash $1.75, dry 25¢ per 5min. Showers $2 per 10min. Open daily 8am-9:30pm.

Weather: ☎852-3185. **Road Conditions:** ☎852-3311.

Emergency: ☎911. **Police:** 600 Pyramid Lake Rd. (☎852-4421).

Women's Crisis Line: ☎800-661-0937. 24hr.

Pharmacy: Cavell Value Drug Mart, 602 Patricia St. (☎852-4441). Open daily mid-June to Sept. 9am-10:30pm; Sept. to mid-June M-Sa 9am-9pm, Su 10am-7pm.

Hospital: 518 Robson St. (☎852-3344).

Internet Access: Soft Rock Cafe (see **Food,** below). $1 for 10min., $5 per hr. (10min. free with $8 food purchase). $5 per hr. charge at the **library** if you don't have an account, 500 Robson St. (☎852-3652). Open M-Th 11am-5pm and 7-9pm, F-Sa 11am-5pm. From Sept.-July, the **Adult Education Building** (631 Patricia St.) charges $2 per hr. Open M-F 9am-5pm.

Post Office: 502 Patricia St., (☎852-3041), across from the townsite green and the visitors center. Open M-F 9am-5pm. **Postal Code:** T0E 1E0.

ACCOMMODATIONS

The modern Jasper International Hostel, just outside Jasper Townsite, anchors a chain of **Hostelling International (HI)** hostels throughout Jasper National Park. The rustic hostels farther into the park offer fewer amenities, but lie amid some of Jasper's finest scenery and outdoor activities. HI runs a shuttle service connecting the Rocky Mountain hostels with Calgary. For reservations and info on all hostels, call the Jasper hostel. Reservations are necessary for most hostels in summer, but wait-list beds become available at 6pm. In winter, Jasper International, Athabasca Falls, and Maligne Canyon run normally; guests at other hostels must pick up the key at Jasper International and give a deposit. For couples or groups, a B&B may prove more economical (doubles $40-130; winter $30-95). Many are in town near the train station; ask for a list at the park information center or the bus depot.

Jasper International Hostel (HI; ☎852-3215 or 877-852-0781), also known as Whistlers Hostel, is 3km up Whistlers Rd. from Hwy. 93, 4km south of the townsite. Closest hostel to the townsite, but still a 7km walk. Attracts a gregarious breed of backpackers and cyclists. 84 often-full beds (get ready for some sharing—the women's dorm packs in

30 beds and the coed has 44). 3 private rooms available with at least 2 people, $10 surcharge. Credit cards accepted. 2am curfew. Sun Dog Shuttle (☎ 852-4056) runs from train station to hostel en route to Jasper Tramway ($3). $18, nonmembers $23.

Maligne Canyon Hostel (HI), on Maligne Lake Rd. just north of the Maligne Canyon parking lot across the street, 11km east of town off Hwy. 16. Small, recently renovated cabins sit on bank of Maligne River, with access to the Skyline Trail and the Maligne Canyon. Manager is on a first-name basis with several local bears. Electricity, fridge, pay phone, potable water. Closed W Oct.-Apr. Check-in 5-11pm, lockout 10am-5pm. 24 beds. $13, nonmembers $18.

Mt. Edith Cavell Hostel (HI), 12km up Edith Cavell Rd., off Hwy. 93A. Cozy quarters heated by wood-burning stoves. A postcard view of Mt. Edith Cavell and her glaciers, with easy access to the mountain and trails. Propane light, spring water (filter in the newly-painted kitchen), private wash area, firepit, and the best smelling outhouses in the park. Road closed in winter, but the hostel is open to anyone willing to pick up the keys at Jasper International Hostel and ski uphill from the hwy. 32 beds. Check-in 5-11pm, lockout 10am-5pm. $13, nonmembers $18; winter $10, nonmembers $15.

Athabasca Falls Hostel (HI; ☎ 852-5959), on Hwy. 93 just south of the 93-93A junction, 32km south of the townsite. A hostel in a quiet setting yet with the comforts of town—electricity, email, and ping-pong. However, the only running water around is at Athabasca Falls, a 500m stroll away (free showers await at Jasper Int'l). Propane heat. 44 beds in 3 cabins. Closed Nov., and Tu Oct.-Apr. $13, non-members $18.

Beauty Creek Hostel (HI; ☎ 852-3215), on Hwy. 93, 87km south of the townsite. On the banks of the glacier-fed Sunwapta River and close to the Columbia Icefields. A half km south of the 3.2km Stanley Falls trailhead. Poetry on the outhouse walls and views of the whole valley from the solar shower. 22 beds. Open late May to Sept. Check-in 5pm-11pm, lockout 10am-5pm. $12, nonmembers $17.

CAMPING

These government-run campgrounds are listed from north to south. Most are primitive sites with few facilities. All are first come, first served, and popular. Call the park info center (☎ 852-6176) for details. Fire permits are $4. All campgrounds except for Pocahontas and Wabasso also offer kitchen shelters.

Pocahontas, on Hwy. 16 at the northern edge of the park, 44km northeast of the townsite. Closest campground to Miette Hot Springs (see p. 367). Flush toilets. Open mid-May to mid-Oct. 130 sites and 10 walk-in tent sites. $13.

Snaring River, on Hwy. 16. 16km north of Jasper Townsite. 56 sites and 10 walk-in tent sites, dry toilets. Open mid-May to late Sept. $10.

Whistlers, on Whistlers Rd., 3km south of the townsite off Hwy. 93. This 781-site behemoth is the closest campground to Jasper Townsite and has all the amenities. Public phones, dump station, and showers. Open early May to mid-Oct. Wheelchair accessible. Sites $15; full hookups $24.

Wapiti, on Hwy. 93, 3.8km south of Whistlers, along the Athabasca River. Plentiful brush separates tenters from RVers. Pay phone, sani-dump, and coin showers. Electricity in 40 summer sites. Wheelchair accessible. 362 sites, $15-18. Winter, 91 sites $13-15.

Wabasso, on Hwy. 93A, 16km south of the townsite. Toilets, showers, sani-dump. Open late June to Labor Day. Wheelchair accessible. 232 sites. 6 riverside walk-ins. $13.

Mount Kerkeslin, on Hwy. 93, 36km south of the townsite. On the banks of the Athabasca River. Kitchen, toilets, pay phones. Open late June to Labor Day. 42 sites, $10.

Honeymoon Lake, is about 51km south of town near Sunwapta Falls and has a swimming area. Dry toilets and pay phones. Open late May to early Oct. 35 sites, $10.

Columbia Icefield, 109km south of the townsite. Lies close enough to the Athabasca Glacier to intercept an icy breeze and even a rare summer night's snowfall. Difficult and steep access road makes its sites tents-only. Dry toilets and pay phones. Open late May to early Oct. 22 sites and 11 walk-ins. $10.

366 ■ JASPER NATIONAL PARK

Wilcox Creek is at the southern park boundary, 111km south of the townsite. Dry toilets and pay phones. Open early June to mid-Sept. 46 sites. $10.

FOOD

Food prices in Jasper rise quickly from the affordable to the outrageous. However, cheap options can be found and lots of places offer good lunch deals. **Super A Foods,** 601 Patricia St., satisfies basic grocery needs at a central location. (☎852-3200. Open M-Sa 8am-11pm, Su 9am-10pm.) The larger selection and the bakery at **Robinson's IGA Foodliner,** 218 Connaught Dr., is worth the 5min. walk. (☎852-3195. Open daily 8am-10pm.) **Nutter's Bulk Foods,** 622 Patricia St., offers bulk snacks, vitamins, and fresh $5 sandwiches. (☎852-5844. Open daily 8am-11pm.)

- **Jasper Pizza Place,** 402 Connaught Dr. (☎852-3225). With draft and bottle beer, the Place turns bar-ish at night. Free delivery in Jasper area (min. order $5). Large wood-oven pizzas $9-13, sandwiches $3-8. 15% HI discount. Open daily 11am-midnight.

- **Mountain Foods and Cafe,** 606 Connaught Dr. (☎852-4050). Offers wide selection of sandwiches, salads, home-cooked goodies, and take-out lunches for the trail. Turkey focaccia sandwich and assorted wraps $7.50. Breakfast $5.50. Open daily in summer 8am-9pm, winter 8am-5pm.

- **Coco's Cafe,** 608 Patricia St. (☎852-4550). A small, vegetarian-friendly cafe downtown. Homemade items include tasty soups, baked goods, and the smoothies ($3.50). Breakfast wraps are served all day ($5.25). A variety of tasty sandwiches from $4.75. Open daily in summer 7am-8pm; winter 7am-6pm. HI 15% discount on meals.

- **Scoops and Loops,** 504 Patricia St. (☎852-4333). No ordinary ice cream parlor. Serves sandwiches ($3-4), sushi ($3-7), *udon* ($8). Open M-Sa 10am-11pm, Su 11am-11pm.

- **Soft Rock Cafe,** 622 Connaught Dr. (☎852-5850). Internet access, but no memorabilia signed by Britney. Baguette sandwiches $4.25-8. Breakfast all day: sizable omelette, homefries, and thick toast $8. Open daily 7am-11pm; winter 7am-7pm.

OUTDOOR ACTIVITIES

HIKING

Jasper National Park offers excellent day hiking, with a full slate of genuine tourists to accompany the experience. Short, gorgeous walks make the postcard perfect scenery of the Canadian Rockies easily accessible. For more info, get a copy of *Day Hikes in Jasper National Park.* As an alternative or supplement to hiking, check out The **Jasper Tramway** (☎852-3093) is 4km up Whistlers Rd. just past the Jasper International Hostel, which is 4km south of the townsite on Hwy. 93. Climbing 973m up Whistlers Mountain, the tramway leads to a panoramic view of the park and, on clear days, far beyond it. From the upper station you can join hikers on the Whistlers Trail for the last 200m elevation gain to the summit. ($19, ages 5-14 $9.50, under 5 free. Open daily Apr.13-May17 and Oct. 9:30am-4:430pm; May 18-June 25 and Sept. 9:30am-9pm; June 26-July 8:30am-10pm.) **Sun Dog Tours** (☎852-4056; fax 852-9663) offers a shuttle from town and tram ride to the top ($24).

- **Path of the Glacier Loop** (1.6km, 45min.). The trailhead is 30km south of the townsite; take Hwy. 93 to 93A to the end of the bumpy, twisty, 15km Mt. Edith Cavell Rd. One of the two paths featuring as a backdrop **Mt. Edith Cavell,** the glacier-laden peak named after an English nurse executed by the Germans for providing aid to the Allies during World War I. An easy path leading to a rewarding view of a receding glacier to a lake littered with icebergs. Open June-Oct.; no trailers or vehicles over 6m long.

- **Cavell Meadows Loop** (8km, 3-6hr.). Trailhead is same as Path of the Glacier Loop. A more strenuous ascent past the treeline and through a carpet of wildflowers (from mid-July to Aug.), with striking views of the towering north face and the Angel Glacier. Be careful to stay on the trail as steep cliffs make for dangerous slide conditions. 400m gain. Open June-Oct.; no trailers or vehicles over 6m long.

OUTDOOR ACTIVITIES ■ 367

Sulphur Skyline Trail (9.6km round-trip, 4-6hr.). This challenging hike enables the hardy to summit a peak in a day and attain views of the limestone Miette Range and Ashlar Ridge. The trail leaves conveniently from the parking lot of the Miette Hot Springs (see p. 367). If you have lunch at the peak, guard it from the courageous golden-mantled ground squirrels. Beware afternoon thunderstorms. 700m gain.

Maligne Canyon (2.1km one-way, 1-2hr.). The spectacular, over-touristed Maligne Canyon (mah-LEEN) is 11.5km east of the townsite on the Maligne Lake Rd. From the trailhead, a path follows the Maligne River as it plunges through a narrow limestone gorge. 5 footbridges afford viewing opportunities. 15km farther along the Maligne Lake Rd., the river flows into Medicine Lake, and the water escapes underground through tunnels in the porous limestone, re-emerging 15km away in springs along the Athabasca River, making this the longest known underground river in North America.

Whistlers Trail (7.9km one-way; 3-5hr. up, 2-3hr. down) is a strenuous hike beginning behind the Jasper International Hostel volleyball court. Don't forget extra layers; weather conditions change rapidly at the 2464m summit. 1200m gain.

MALIGNE LAKE

Maligne Lake, at the end of the road, is the longest (22km) and deepest (97m) lake in the park. A flotilla of water vessels allow escape from fellow tourists and the plastic geraniums of Maligne Lake Chalet. **Maligne Tours,** 627 Patricia St. (☎852-3370), rents kayaks ($85 per day) and leads canoe trips ($15 per hr.), horseback riding ($55 per 3hr. at 10am and 2pm), and interpretive hikes ($10 per hr.), as well as narrated scenic cruises (90min.; $35, seniors $29.75, children $17.50). Free maps to hiking trails are available at the Maligne Tours office or by the lake. The **Opal Hills Trail** (8.2km round-trip, 4-6hr.), starting at the northeast corner of the first parking area, winds through subalpine meadows and ascends 460m in only 3km to views of the lake. **Shuttle service** from Jasper to the area is available from Maligne Tours. (To the canyon $8; to the lake $12; round-trip with cruise $56; 3-6 per day, 8:30am-5:30pm.)

BACKPACKING

An extensive network of trails weaves through the park's backwoods, providing respite from tourist-land. The trails cover three different ecological regions. The **montane zone** (which includes Jasper Townsite) blankets valley floors with lodgepole pine, Douglas fir, white spruce, and aspen and hosts elk, bighorn sheep, and coyotes. Subalpine fir and Engelmann spruce share the **subalpine zone** with porcupines and marmots, while fragile plants and wildflowers struggle against mountain goats and pikas in the uppermost **alpine zone.** To avoid trampling endangered plant species, hikers should not stray from trails in the alpine area.

Kick off any foray into the wilderness with a visit to the visitors center in the townsite, where rangers distribute the free *Backcountry Visitors' Guide*. Overnight hikers need to register and pay the $6 per night fee, and many buy *The Canadian Rockies Trail Guide* ($15). Before hitting the trail, ask about road and trail closures, water levels (some rivers cannot be crossed at certain times of the year), and snow levels at high passes. The Icefield Centre (see p. 362) on Hwy. 93 at the southern entrance to the park, provides similar services.

HOT SPRINGS

The **Miette Hot Springs,** 42km north of the townsite on Hwy. 16, and 15km along the well-marked Miette Hot Springs Rd., blends heat therapy with a panoramic view of the surrounding limestone mountains. Originally a rudimentary log bath-house in 1913, the waters—the hottest in the Canadian Rockies—are now chlorinated and filtered before they arrive in three outdoor pools, at temperatures ranging from 39-41°C or 6-22°C. The road to Miette is, sadly, closed in winter. (☎866-3939. Open daily spring and fall 10:30am-9pm; summer 8:30am-10:30pm. $6, children and seniors $5; off-season $1 cheaper. Swimsuit $1.50, towel $1.25.)

SKIING

Winter brings 4m. of snowfall and plenty of opportunities to the slopes of **Marmot Basin.** 19km south of Jasper via Hwy. 93, 93A, and the Marmot Basin Rd. The upper half of the slope's 897m vertical drop is above the treeline, creating room for bowls and a modest snowboard park. (☎852-3816; www.skimarmot.com. Full-day lift ticket $49, 65 and over $35, ages 13-17 and students up to age 25 $41, ages 6-12 $20, under 6 free.) Bargain **ski rental** is available at **Totem's Ski Shop,** 408 Connaught Dr. (☎852-3078. Open daily winter 8am-6pm; summer 9:30am-10pm, ski package $9-20; snowboard package and boots $25; cross country skis from $9 per day.) **The Sports Shop,** 406 Patricia St., offers the same hours and ski rental prices and rents ice skates as well as camping and fishing equipment. (☎852-3654. Skates $4 per hr., $10 per day.) Maligne Lake offers **cross-country ski trails** from late November through May. **Everest Outdoor Stores,** 414 Connaught Dr., rents cross-country skis from $12 per day, downhill skis and boots $25-35 per day, and snowshoes $10 per day. (☎852-5902. Open daily 9:30am-10pm, winter 8am-6pm.)

FISHING

The key to finding a secluded **fishing hole** in Jasper is to hike somewhere inaccessible to cars. **Currie's,** in **The Sports Shop,** 406 Patricia St. provides gear, tackle and trim, and gives tips on good spots. (☎852-5650. Rental rod, reel, and line $10; fly $20. One-day boat or canoe rental $30; after 2pm $20, after 6pm $15. Pickup and drop-off service or guided trips available.) **Permits** are available at fishing shops and the Park Information Center ($6 per week, $13 per year).

OTHER OUTDOOR ACTIVITIES

Paul Valiulis teaches half-day ($59) and full-day ($89) rock courses (☎852-4161; www.icpeaks.com). **Peter Amann** teaches two-day introductory **rock climbing** classes. (☎852-3237. May-June and Sept. $150.) Both companies also lead ice climbing and mountaineering trips. **Gravity Gear** 618 Patricia St. (☎888-852-3155) offers rentals for mountain adventures. Multi-day discounts.

Rocky Mountain Unlimited, 414 Connaught Dr., serves as a central reservation service for most local outdoor businesses. They provide prices and recommendations for rafting, fishing, horseback riding, wildlife safaris, and all your outdoor pursuits. (☎852-4056. Open daily 9am-9pm; winter 9am-6pm.) **Whitewater** leads trips on the Athabasca River and the faster Sunwapta River. (☎852-7238. 2-3hr. From $40, under 12 half-price). Register by phone, or stop at the townsite car wash in the industrial park across the railroad tracks from Connaught Dr. **Rocky Mountain River Guides,** 600 Patricia St., in On-Line Sport and Tackle, offers a calmer ride. (☎852-3777. 2hr. $35.) **Boat rentals** are available at **Pyramid Lake Resort,** 7km from town off Pyramid Ave. from Connaught Dr. (☎852-4900. Open daily 8am, last boat out at 10pm. Canoes, kayaks, and pedal boats $15 for 1hr., $10 per additional hr., $55 per day; rowboats $25 for 1hr., $20 per additional hr.)

THE YUKON

> **YUKON TERRITORY'S...** **Drinking Age:** 19. **Capital:** Whitehorse. **Population:** 32,635. **Caribou Population:** 100,000. **Attempted Coups by the Underrepresented Caribou Population:** 5. **Area:** 478,970km^2. **Bird:** Raven. **Flower:** Fireweed. **Holiday:** Discovery Day, on the third Monday in Aug. For **emergencies** outside the Whitehorse area, 911 may not work; call the local police detachment or 867-667-5555.

The Yukon Territory lies at the end of a long drive along the Alaska Hwy. or the less-touristed Cassiar and Campbell highways. Here the land rises into ranges that stretch for kilometers and sinks into lakes that snake toward the Arctic Ocean. The dry land's lonely beauty and its purple dusk are overwhelming. Glaciation left much of the Yukon untouched, creating an ice-free corridor for vegetation, wildlife, and early hunters. Although summer here is still spectacular, Yukoners have been suffering payback for the ancient fair weather ever since, enduring what's often described as "nine months of winter and three months of bad snowmobiling." Fur traders in the 1800s came looking for faster routes and new partners. The gold seekers of 1898 came charging to Carcross from Skagway, then down the Yukon River to Whitehorse, Dawson City, and the goldfields beyond. A second territorial rush occurred during the course of the Alaska Hwy.'s construction. Logging, mining, and the federal government have since supported the region's economy. Yukon First Nations are presently negotiating with the federal government for land, self-government, and innovative projects to rebuild communities.

> ### THE YUKON TERRITORY'S HIGHLIGHTS
>
> **JAM** with musicians at the **Dawson City Music Festival** (see p. 388).
>
> **DIP** your toes in the Arctic Ocean after driving up the **Dempster Hwy.** (see p. 390).
>
> **FLY** over the **Kluane National Park** (see p. 379) to enjoy all its splendor.
>
> **RETRACE** prospectors foot steps on the Chilkoot Trail (see p. 379).
>
> **BASK** under the **aurora borealis** in the winter (see p. 377), and the **midnight sun** in the summer.

WHITEHORSE ☎ 867

Whitehorse was born during the Klondike Gold Rush, when the gold-hungry used it as a layover on their journey north. Miners en route to Dawson coined the name, claiming that whitecaps on the rapids downstream resembled galloping white stallions. With a population of 24,000, Whitehorse is home to 70% of the territory's population. The capital of the Yukon shifted here from Dawson in 1953, and now the majority of government employees call Whitehorse home. Although as urban a setting as can be found in the Yukon, Whitehorse attracts outdoors lovers of all ages who take advantage of the nearby rivers and trails.

TRANSPORTATION

Whitehorse lies 1500km north of Dawson Creek, BC, along the **Alaska Hwy.** (see p. 334), and 535km south of Dawson City. The city is an oblong grid of numbered avenues running north-south, parallel to the Alaska Hwy. Streets run east to west.

Flights: The **airport** is off the Alaska Hwy., southwest of downtown. **Air Canada** (☎888-247-2262 or 668-4466) flies to **Calgary** and **Edmonton, AB** ($579; youth stand-by, ages 12-24 $340) via **Vancouver, BC** (3 per day; $389 round-trip, youth standby $286). **Canada 3000** (☎888-226-3000 or 416-259-1118) flies cheap to **Vancouver** ($210) in summer.

British Columbia and the Yukon Territory
Beaufort Sea
Ivvavik Natl. Park
Vuntut Natl. Park
Tuktoyaktuk
ALASKA
Inuvik
Fort McPherson
Tsiigehtchic
Eagle Plains
Dempster Hwy.
Top of the World Hwy.
Dawson City
Klondike Hwy.
Mackenzie River
YUKON TERRITORY
Beaver Creek
Alaska Hwy.
Carmacks
Faro
Ross River
Burwash Landing
Destruction Bay
Haines Junction
Kluane Natl. Park
Whitehorse
Campbell Hwy.
NORTHWEST TERRITORIES
Carcross
Tatshenshini-Alsek Provincial Park
Skagway
Teslin
Haines
Atlin
Watson Lake
Juneau
Liard River
Telegraph Creek
Dease Lake
Muncho Lake
Toad
Stone Mountain
Fort Nelson
Cassiar Hwy.
Iskut
Spatsizi Plateau Wilderness
Kwadacha Wilderness
Hyder
Meziadin Jct.
Stewart
Fort St. John
ALBERTA
BRITISH COLUMBIA
Chetwynd
Dawson Creek
Prince Rupert
Hazelton
MacKenzie
Masset
Terrace
Yellowhead Hwy.
Burns Lake
Tlell
Queen Charlotte City
Sandspit
Prince George
Bowron Lakes Provincial Park
Edmonton
Gwaii Haanas Natl. Park
Queen Charlotte Islands (Haida Gwaii)
Tweedsmuir Provincial Park
Barkerville
Quesnel
Tête Jaune Cache
Willmore Wilderness
Bella Coola
Wells Gray Provincial Park
Jasper Natl. Park
Williams Lake
Cariboo Hwy.
Banff Natl. Park
Glacier Natl. Park
Yoho Natl. Park
Kootenay Natl. Park
N
PACIFIC OCEAN
Port Hardy
Kamloops
Revelstoke
Cache Creek
Salmon Arm
Whistler
Vancouver Island
0 150 miles
0 150 kilometers
Penticton
Nanaimo
Hope
Pacific Rim Natl. Park
Vancouver
Victoria
WASHINGTON
On this map, due north varies according to longitude.
8
5
9
2
6
1
3
4
37
97
16
20
99
95

Buses: The bus station is on the northeast edge of town. **Greyhound,** 2191 2nd Ave. (☎667-2223), runs to: **Vancouver, BC** (41hr., $314); **Edmonton, AB** (30hr., $246); **Dawson Creek, BC** (18hr., $174). **Dawson City** route run by **Dawson City Courier** (☎393-3334; 5hr.). No service to AK. Buses run late June to early Sept. M-Sa; rest of year M, W, and F departures. Open M-F 8am-5pm, Sa 4-8am. **Alaska Direct** (☎668-4833 or 800-770-6652), in the Greyhound depot, runs to: **Anchorage, AK** (15hr., 3 per week, $165); **Fairbanks, AK** (13hr., 3 per week, $140); and **Skagway, AK** (3hr.; reservation only; M, Th, and F. $50). In winter, 1 bus per week to above destinations.

Public Transportation: Whitehorse Transit (☎668-7433). Limited service to downtown, the airport, Robert Service campground, and Yukon College. Buses arrive and depart next to the Canadian Tire on Ogilvie St. Runs M-Th 6:15am-7:30pm, F 6:15am-10:30pm, Sa 8am-7pm. $1.50.

Taxis: Yellow Cab, ☎668-4811 or **Global Taxi,** ☎633-5300. Both 24hr.

Car Rental: Norcan Leasing, Ltd., 213 Range Rd. (☎668-2137; from western Canada 800-661-0445; from AK 800-764-1234). Cars from $50 per day, winter prices lower, 25¢ per km after 100km per day. Must be 21 with credit card.

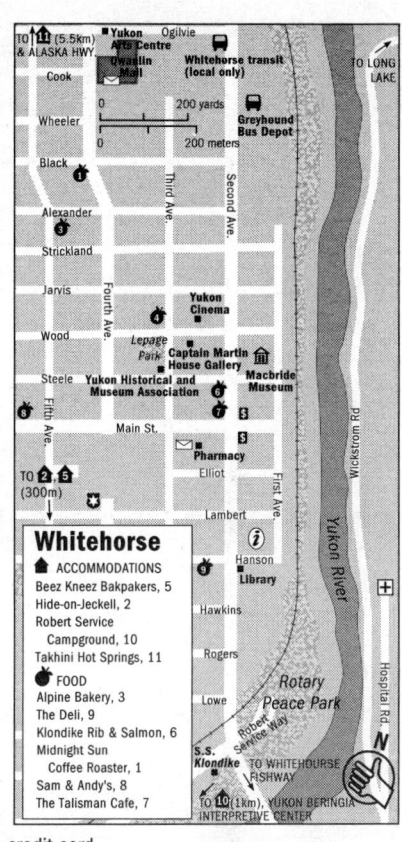

Auto Repair: Petro Canada, 4211 4th Ave. (☎667-4003 or 667-4366). Full service. Oil and lube about $40. Open daily 7am-10pm. Gas pumps open 24hr.

PRACTICAL INFORMATION

TOURIST, LOCAL, AND FINANCIAL SERVICES

Visitor Information: 100 Hanson St. off 1st Ave. (☎667-3084), in the conspicuous Tourism and Business Centre at 2nd Ave. Dazzling free 15min. film every half-hour daily. German, French, and Dutch spoken. Open daily mid-May to mid-Sept. 8am-8pm; winter M-F 9am-5pm.

Outdoor Information: Yukon Conservation Society, 302 Hawkins St. (☎668-5678), offers maps and great ideas for area hikes along with titles such as *The Yukon Hiking Guide* ($20). Open M-F 10am-2pm.

Equipment Rental: Several upscale equipment shops with staff who know a thing or two about the area line Main St. between 2nd and 3rd Ave. **Kanoe People** (☎668-4899), at Strickland and 1st Ave., rents mountain bikes ($15 per half-day), canoes ($25 per day), and kayaks (plastic $35 per day, fiberglass $45). Pickup 20km downstream $30. Open daily 9am-6pm.

24hr. ATM: Bank of Montreal (☎668-4200) or **CIBC** (☎667-2534), at the corner of Main St. and 2nd Ave.

Bookstore: Mac's Fireweed Bookstore, 203 Main St. (☎ 668-2434). Open daily 8am-midnight. Used books and also CDs and videos across from library at **Zack's New & Used Books,** 2nd Ave. and Hawkins (☎ 393-2614). Open M-Sa 11am-6pm, Su closed.

Market: Extra Foods, 4th Ave. and Ogilvie St. (☎ 667-6251), in the Qwanlin Mall. Open M-W and Sa 8:30am-7pm, Th-F 8:30am-9pm, Su 10am-6pm.

Laundromat: Public Laundromat at **Family Motel,** 314 Ray (☎ 668-5558), at 4th Ave. next to **Qwanlin Mall.** Wash $2, dry 25¢ per 5min.

Public Pool: Whitehorse Lions Pool, 4051 4th Ave. (☎ 668-7665), next to the High Country Inn. $4.50, seniors and children $2, students $3.50. Call for swim times.

EMERGENCY AND COMMUNICATION

Emergency: ☎ 911. **Police:** 4100 4th Ave. (☎ 667-5555). 24hr.

24hr. Refuge: Tim Horton's, 2210 2nd Ave. (☎ 668-7788), at the far northern end of downtown, 1 block from river.

Pharmacy: Shoppers Drug Mart, 211 Main St. (☎ 667-2485). Open M-F 9am-9pm, Sa 9am-6pm, Su 10am-6pm.

Hospital: Whitehorse General (☎ 393-8700) is across the river from downtown on Hospital Rd., just off Wickstrom Rd.

Internet Access: Library, 2071 2nd Ave. (☎ 667-5239), at Hanson. Free 30min. Internet access twice daily; reserve in advance or stop in for first come, first served 15min. computer. Open M-F 10am-9pm, Sa 10am-6pm, Su 1-9pm. **Wired Cabin,** 402 Hawkins (☎ 250-309-1225), at 4th Ave. $2 per 10min. or $5 per hr. Also scanning, CD burning, and color copies. Open daily 8am-midnight.

Post Office: General services, 211 Main St. (☎ 667-2485), in the basement of **Shopper's Drug Mart.** Open M-F 9am-6pm, Sa 11am-4pm. Also in Qwanlin Mall (☎ 667-2858) at 4th Ave. and Ogilvie St., in **Coffee, Tea and Spice.** Open M-Th and Sa 9:30am-6pm, F 9:30am-8pm. General delivery at 300 Range Rd. (☎ 667-2412). **Postal codes** for last names beginning with the letters A-L is Y1A 3S7; for M-Z it's Y1A 3S8. Open 10am-1:40pm and 2:15-4:45pm.

ACCOMMODATIONS AND CAMPING

Interchangeable motels around town charge upwards of $69, but fear not; the hostel and campground options are superb.

Hide on Jeckell Guesthouse, 410 Jeckell (☎ 633-4933), between 4th Ave. and 5th Ave., 1 block from Robert Service Way. Creativity flows out of this new accommodation, which is like summer camp gone bed and breakfast. Stay in the continent-themed room of your choice and pick your endangered species-labelled bed and fridge bin. Services included are endless: showers, coffee, kitchen use, bikes, Internet, local calls, linens, used books, lockers, BBQ night. No curfew. Open year-round. 22 beds, 6 rooms. $20. 10% discount for cyclists, 20% for tandem.

Beez Kneez Bakpakers Hostel, 408 Hoge St. (☎ 456-2333), off 4th Ave., 2 blocks from Robert Service Way. Weary bakpakers find refuge in this new hostel equipped with Internet, BBQ deck, washer ($2) and dryer ($2). 8 bunks, $20 each. $50 private room.

Robert Service Campground (☎ 668-3721), 1km from town on Robert Service Way along Yukon River. A home-away-from-home for university students who tan on lawn and sip espresso on terrace. Food trailer, firewood ($2), drinking water, showers ($1 per 5min.). Open late May to early Sept. Gates open 7am-midnight. 68 sites. $12 per tent.

Takhini Hot Springs (☎ 633-2706). Follow the Alaska Hwy. northwest from downtown about 10km, turn right on North Klondike Hwy., and left after 6.5km onto Takhini Hot Springs Rd. and drive to end 10km for tenting plus thermal relief. Separate $4-5.50 admission charge for daily pool use in winter or summer. Restaurant, showers, horseback riding ($20 per hour). Pools open May-Sept. daily 10am-10pm. 88 sites. $12.50, with electricity $15.

WHITEHORSE ■ 373

🍴🎵 FOOD AND ENTERTAINMENT

While Whitehorse gives the impression of catering only to the Alaska Hwy. driver craving fast food, hip musicians and tourists hungering for the frontier will find good grub, too. An excellent selection of cheap, top-quality fruits and veggies are to be found at **The Fruit Stand,** at 2nd Ave. and Black St. (☎393-3994. Open in summer M-Sa 10:30am-7pm.) Antipasta connoisseurs appreciate **The Deli,** 203 Hanson St., which peddles reasonably priced imported foods, meats, and olives. (☎667-7583. Open M-F 8:30am-5:30pm, Sa 9am-5:30pm.) ◪**Alpine Bakery,** 411 Alexander St., between 4th and 5th Ave., turns out exquisite bread. (☎668-6871. Open M-Sa 8am-6pm; winter closed M.) The health-crazed can live it up at **Three Beans,** 308 Wood St. (☎668-4908. Open M-F 10am-6pm, Sa 10am-5:30pm.) Those looking for bars can choose from a wide variety on Main Street. Most have nightly live music, and the scene varies from 20-year-old pop fans at **Lizard Lounge** to blues at **Discovery Bar** to Canadian rock at **Capitol Hotel.**

◪ **The Talisman Cafe,** 2112 2nd Ave. (☎667-2736). Decorated with local First Nations and local art. The veggie, ethnic food lover, and carnivore all will leave happy and full. Serves heaps of fresh food from Mexican to Middle Eastern to Yukoners for under $12. Open daily 9am-8pm.

◪ **Klondike Rib and Salmon Barbecue,** 2116 2nd Ave. (☎667-7554). In an old wall-tent structure, these down-home folks will call you "sweetie" and serve you friendly-like. Worth its weight in (Yukon) gold, the cobb salad lunch ($10) comes with a big ole hunk of homemade bread. Order from the "fuel list" to complement tasty fish and chips ($13). Dinner menu pricier. Open May to Sept. M-F 11:30am-9pm, Sa-Su 5pm-9pm.

Sam and Andy's, 506 Main St. (☎668-6994), between 5th and 6th. Tex-Mex on a jumpin' patio. Generous build-your-own fajitas are mid-range entrees ($12). Save money if you order veggie version. Thrifty Thursdays mean $1 draft, $2 pint. Open M-Sa 11am-11pm, Su 11am-10pm.

Midnight Sun Coffee Roaster, 4168 4th Ave. (☎633-4563). Offers every coffee drink under the sun to sip among stained-glass art in comfy chairs or in funky outdoor booths. Internet $3 for 30min., $5 per hr. Open M-F 7am-10pm, later on weekends.

👁 SIGHTS

YUKON BERINGIA INTERPRETIVE CENTRE. The aspiring paleontologist, archaeologist, or history buff will marvel at the recreation of the human and mammal migration to North America 24 millennia ago. (☎667-8855; www.beringia.com. On the Alaska Hwy., 2km northwest of the Robert Service Way junction. Open daily mid-May through Sept. 8:30am-7pm; winter Su 1-5pm and by appointment. $6, seniors $5, student $4.)

WHITEHORSE FISHWAY. If you think you're a weary traveler, meet the chinook salmon who swim 3000km upstream before reaching the fish ladder—designed to save them from death by dam. You're most likely to see them climbing the 370m ladder from late July through August. (2.4km from town, over the bridge by the S.S. Klondike. ☎633-5965. Open June W-Su 10am-6pm. Open early July to early Sept. daily 8:30am-9pm. Admission by donation. Wheelchair accessible.)

MACBRIDE MUSEUM. Local history finds a home here. Travel from a gold mining camp in the basement to the log cabin in the museum courtyard, built in 1899 by Sam McGee, whose demise and subsequent cremation has been immortalized by Robert Service, the Bard of the Yukon. (1st Ave. and Wood St. ☎667-2709. Open daily June-Aug. 10am-6pm; call for winter hours. $5, seniors $4.50, children 5-16 $3.50, under 5 free.)

S.S. KLONDIKE. The 1929 sternwheeler *S.S. Klondike* is restored and dry docked; it harkens back to the days when the river ran the Yukon. Wander the decks with a guide for 30min. (☎667-4511. Robert Service Way at Yukon River. Open June-Aug. daily 9am-7pm; May and Sept. 9am-6pm. $4, seniors $3.50, children $2.25, families $10.)

VISUAL ARTS. Government patronage and an inspired population make Whitehorse a northern epicenter of the arts. The Yukon Government's **permanent collection** is housed throughout the administrative and public spaces of the capital. (☎667-5264.) Pick up a free **ArtWalk** brochure at the visitors center, or at the nonprofit, Yukon artwork adorned **Captain Martin House Gallery.** (305 Wood St. ☎667-4080. Open M-F 10am-8pm, Sa 10am-5pm; Su noon-5pm; winter M-Sa 11am-5pm; closed Jan.) The Yukon's only public art museum, the **Yukon Arts Centre Art Gallery,** at Yukon College, hangs shows, typically showcasing Canadian contemporary art, every 6-10 weeks. (☎667-8578. Open June-Aug. M-F 11am-5pm, Sa-Su noon-5pm; Sept.-May Tu-F 11am-5pm, Sa-Su 1-4pm. Adult $3, students and seniors $2, children under 12 free. Su free.)

EVENTS. Two Whitehorse festivals draw crowds from all over the world: the **Yukon International Storytelling Festival** (☎633-7550) to be held May 30-June 2, and the **Frostbite Music Festival** (☎668-4921) in February. The **Commissioner's Potlatch** gathers indigenous groups and visitors in June for traditional dancing, games, artistry, and a feast. Locals, transients, and native artists perform for free at noon with **Arts in Lepage Park** on weekdays. (☎668-3136. Wood St. and 3rd Ave. From June to mid-Aug.) Call the **Yukon Arts Centre Theatre** for stage updates. (☎667-8574; www.yukonartscentre.org.) The **Yukon River** hosts the popular **Rubber Duckie Race** on Canada Day, July 1. (☎668-7979. $5 per duck. Proceeds go to charity.)

OUTDOOR ACTIVITIES

HIKING

There seem to be more trails around Whitehorse than people. Seasoned hikers can just wander, with heed to the bear population, of course. **Kluane National Park** (see p. 379) beckons from the west, but there is plenty of accessible dayhiking near town. *Whitehorse Area Hikes and Bikes* ($19), published by the **Yukon Conservation Society,** or the *Whitehorse Area Hikes* map ($10) are both available at **Mac's Fireweed Books.** Discover where to spot a golden eagle or the boreal birds with the aid of the **Yukon Bird Club** (☎667-4630) or take an easy-paced, free birding trip into the wetlands during the summer.

> **Grey Mountain.** Take Lewes Blvd. across the bridge by the S.S. Klondike, then take a left on Alsek Ave. Turn left again at the Grey Mt. Cemetery sign and follow the gravel road to its end. Partially accessible by gravel road. It is a fairly vigorous dayhike.
>
> **Miles Canyon Trail Network.** Take Lewes Blvd. to Nisutlin Dr. and turn right; just before the fish ladder, turn left onto the gravel Chadbum Lake Rd. and continue 4km up to the parking area. Parallels the Yukon River and is loved by joggers, bikers, and cross-country skiers alike. The Conservation Society leads free hikes daily July-Aug. Schedule available at office. Open M-F 10am-2pm.

JUSTICE TO GO, TRIBAL STYLE As in many remote regions, law in the Yukon is administered with a long arm. While Whitehorse is the seat of the territorial government, the work of frontier justice is carried out on the frontier: Once a week a judge, a clerk, and a recorder climb into a single-engine plane and depart for outlying towns, where a prosecuting and defending attorney will meet them, themselves arriving by car in long, cross-country odysseys between clients. Court is then set up in community centers and recreation halls. This system has evolved in recent years from a transplanted version of a courthouse's formal proceedings to a truer reflection of the traditions of the mostly indigenous communities it serves. Increasingly, elements of traditional justice are changing how community members are punished: friends and family are in more and more cases invited to sit down in a "sentencing circle," in which everyone has a say in how the criminal can be cared for and reintegrated into society. The circle has done amazing work, greatly reducing recidivism, and creating a team-building attitude in the makeshift halls of justice.

WATER

The **M.V. Schwatka,** on Miles Canyon Rd. off Robert Service Way, floats folks on a relaxing, historical ride through Miles Canyon. (☎ 668-4716. 2hr. cruises. 2pm daily from June to early Sept. 7pm tour added in July. $21, ages 2-10 $10.50, under 2 free. Wheelchair accessible.) **Up North Boat and Canoe Rentals,** 103 Strickland St., lets you paddle 25km to Takhini River or take a longer unguided or guided trip. (☎ 667-7035. 4hr. $30 each for two or $60 solo, including transportation.) An eight day trip on the Teslin River costs $200, but you can rent sea kayaks and canoes by the day ($25-30). The waterways around **Sanfu Lake** (1½hr. south of Whitehorse on the Atlin Rd.) are ideal for kayaking among tiny islands. **Tatshenshini Expediting,** 1602 Alder St., leads intense whitewater rides. Take the Alaska Hwy. north 2km, left on Birch, left on 15th St., which becomes Alder. (☎ 633-2742. Full-day $107.)

WINTER

In winter, the Whitehorse area is criss-crossed by 300km of groomed and ungroomed **snowmobile trails.** Up North Boat and Canoe Rentals (see above) rents snowmobiles and skis. Whitehorse is also a **cross-country skiing** paradise. The **Whitehorse Cross Country Ski Club,** beside Mt. McIntyre off Hamilton Blvd. near the intersection of Two Mile Hill and the Alaska Hwy., grooms 50km of world-class trails; 5km are lit at night. Club facilities include saunas and showers. (☎ 668-4477. Day passes $8, under 19 $4; 3 days $20, 5 days $35.) In February, "the toughest race in the world," or the **Yukon Quest 1000 Mile International Sled Dog Race** (☎ 668-4711), follows gold rush routes between Whitehorse and Fairbanks.

THE ALASKA HWY.: BC BORDER TO WHITEHORSE

WATSON LAKE   ☎ 867

Switchbacking between the Yukon and British Columbia, the Alaska Hwy. (see p. 334) winds through tracts of scorched forest—gray, skeletal trees mixed with new growth—that stretch in all directions. Just after it crosses into the Yukon for the second time, at Km 1021, the highway runs through **Watson Lake,** site of the zany **Sign Post Forest.** In the 1940s, a homesick WWII Army G.I. posted the mileage from Watson to his hometown of Danville, Illinois. As a panacea for your homesickness, wander the forest, and you'll likely find the distance to your hometown as 45,000 travelers have followed suit. The **visitors center** is hidden just inside this forest of signs along the Robert Campbell Hwy. (☎ 536-7469. Open May-Sept. daily 8am-8pm.) If finding the distance to your hometown fails to remedy your longing for home, email your pals for free on one of the computers at the new **library.** (☎ 536-7517. In the town office on Adela Trail. Open Tu-F 10am-8pm, Sa noon-6pm.)

Scan for mountain bluebirds on **Wye Lake** from the 3km boardwalk trail running from the Town Center to **Wye Lake Park.** Watson Lake also lures passersby with the **Northern Lights Centre** opposite the visitors center, which divulges scientific and cultural explanations of the aurora borealis. (☎ 867-536-7827. Exhibits free. Pay for 50min. shows 6 times daily. $10; seniors and students $9; children $6.)

The **Liard Canyon Recreation Site** on **Lucky Lake,** 8km before town, makes for great picnicking and swimming. A 2km trail down the canyon is a relaxing and scenic stroll. Accommodations in Watson Lake are plentiful but pricey. A budget traveler's best bet is the **Watson Lake Campground,** 3km west of town along the hwy. and then 4km down a well-marked gravel road, with primitive private sites ideal for tenting ($8 camping permit only). Campers can swim on the lake and hike several trails of varying difficulty. Or, continue out of Watson Lake 21km northwest to accommodations at the **Cassiar Hwy.** junction. Dining options in town are restricted

376 ■ THE ALASKA HWY.: BC BORDER TO WHITEHORSE

BRIGHT LIGHTS, NO CITY

Many travelers come to Alaska to get away from all the bright lights and noise of the big city, only to find themselves falling under the spell of the most awesome of natural light shows: the aurora borealis (the northern lights). Some bands of Native Americans believed these Christmas-colored clouds and arcs were the torches of spirits, lighting the way to heaven for those who had died a voluntary or violent death. Scientists, however, point the finger at violent solar flares which hit the earth, sweeping streams of electrically charged particles into the atmosphere. As the earth's magnetic field deflects these particles away from the Equator and up toward the poles, the particles enter the atmosphere and begin to glow. Oxygen atoms create either the brilliant yellow-green, or if higher in the atmosphere, a burning red. Ionized nitrogen particles cast a blue hue, while neutral nitrogen creates a cloud of purplish-red. But such scientific mumbo-jumbo can't detract from the supernatural mystery of the northern lights. A few onlookers claim to be able to even *hear* the lights overhead, although no scientist has yet to record these sounds or come up with an explanation. Some Inuit tribes interpreted these noises as the whisperings of the spirits. So prick up your ears as you next stare skyward, and you may discover that no matter how far away you think you've gotten from civilization, there might still be someone to spoil your quiet.

to highway fare. The **Pizza Place**, at the **Gateway Motor Inn**, is a somewhat pricey gem. Medium specialty pies start at $14, but ambitious eaters go right for the $21 "Yukoner," loaded with all manner of meats and vegetables. For the tighter budget, grille meals range from $6-8. (☎ 536-7722. Open daily 6:30am-10pm.) **Groceries** and an **ATM** can be had at **Tags Foods,** by the visitors center. (☎ 536-7422. Open daily 6am-midnight.) Gas pumps and convenience store open 24hr. CIBC Banking Center (☎ 536-7495) in the shopping center on the east side of the visitors center has a **24hr. ATM.** Next door is the **post office**. (Open M-F 8:30am-5:30pm, Sa 8:30am-12:30pm). **Postal Code:** Y0A 1C0.

Hardcore travelers **fish** for dinner. In mid-summer, grayling swim in the back eddies of tiny streams west along the Alaska Hwy., and both **Lucky Lake** (5½km east of town) and **Hour Lake** (at the east end of town behind the RCMP) are full of rainbow trout. Check in at the visitors center to purchase the appropriate permits.

Here at Watson Lake, the **Campbell Hwy.** (Hwy. 4) begins an alternate route into the Yukon Territory toward Whitehorse, via Ross River and Johnson's Crossing, or to Dawson City, via Ross River, Little Salmon, and Carmacks. For coverage of this wonderful side track, see p. 389. Km 1043 (or Mile 649) marks the Alaska Hwy.'s junction with the **Cassiar Hwy** (Hwy. 37; see p. 328) that leads south to the **Yellowhead Hwy** (Hwy. 16; see p. 310). For coverage of this junction, see p. 334.

TESLIN LAKE ☎ 867

About 260km west of Watson Lake, the **Dawson Peaks Resort** on **Teslin Lake** dishes up delectable burgers in its restaurant ($6) and offers a number of accommodation choices. (☎ 390-2244. Open daily 7:30am-10pm. Showers $2. Toilets, firewood, water. Sites $10; full hookups $18; canvas tent platforms $35; private cabins $79.) The friendly hosts lead **river runs** (4-5 days, $400), organize guided **fishing charters** ($50 per hr.), and rent canoes ($8 per hr.) and powerboats ($25 per hr.).

Teslin, 11km west of the resort, tells its story at the duly acclaimed **George Johnston Museum,** on the Alaska Hwy. at the west end of town. Born in Alaska in 1889, George Johnston was a Tlingit man who ran a trap line and a general store while experimenting with photography on the side. Johnston left a legacy of stunning photographs documenting Tlingit life in Teslin from 1910 to 1940. The museum also displays a moose skin boat, Teslin's first automobile (bought by Johnston when the town was roadless), and an excellent video about the Alaska Hwy.'s effect on native culture. (☎ 390-2550. Open daily mid-May to early Sept. 9:30am-5:30pm. $4, students and seniors $3.50, children 6-15 $2, families $10. Wheelchair accessible.) RV travelers bond over food and the earned free river boat and camping at **Muklak Annie's** 7km east of Teslin. There's nothing miniature about a mini-salmon plate ($15) or kids' portion ($9), but the big-eaters can pay ($18) for loads of salmon, all-you-can-eat salad, fresh rolls, coffee, and dessert. Ribs, porkchops, and burgers served as well on the checked cloths in the gift shop decor dining hall. (☎667-1200. Open daily 7am-9pm. All-you-can-eat full breakfast $8. Free campsite, house boat ride, RV wash, dump station, and water fill-up with meal. Showers $4, cabins with shared bath $40, motel $50.) From Teslin, the 183km (2hr.) drive to Whitehorse is interspersed with a few gas stops and provincial campgrounds.

CARCROSS ☎867

Carcross, shortened from "Caribou Crossing," perches on the narrows between Bennett and Nares Lakes, surrounded by snow-capped peaks and pristine waterways. When the woodland caribou population was larger, they passed through town as they crossed the shallow waters of Nares Lake, which lies just east of town. At the turn of the century, Carcross served as a link in the gold seekers' treacherous route between Skagway and the Yukon River, and during the 1940s as a supply depot for the construction of the Alaska Hwy. Now it serves as a place for a brief stopover on the scenic trip along the Klondike Hwy. between the more exciting towns, Whitehorse and Skagway. The town remains in picturesque disrepair with a fragment of the Whitepass Railway running through its heart. Shops cater to tour buses from the Skagway cruise ships.

ORIENTATION AND PRACTICAL INFORMATION. On the Klondike Hwy. (Hwy. 2), Carcross is 74km south of Whitehorse, YT, and 106km north of Skagway, AK. Turn right off the highway into the town. Don't blink, or you'll miss Carcross. **Atlin Express Buses** (☎250-651-7575) run to Atlin, BC (2hr.; $21, seniors $18, ages 5-11 $10.50, under 5 free) and Whitehorse (1¼hr.; $15, seniors $13, ages 5-11 $7.50, under 5 free). **Visitor information** and daily highway or weather reports are available inside the depot. (☎821-4431. Open daily mid-May to mid-Sept. 8am-8pm.) **Montana Services**, in the Shell Station on Hwy. 2, has **laundry, public showers,** and the only **ATM** in town. (☎821-3708. Open daily 7am-11pm, winter 8am-8pm. Wash $2.25, dry 25¢ per 4min. Shower $3.) The **library** on Tagish St. has free **Internet access.** (☎821-3801. Open M-Th noon-4:30pm.) A **health station** (☎821-4444) is inside the two-story red building behind the Caribou Hotel. **Ambulance:** ☎821-3333. **Police:** ☎821-5555 or 667-5555. The **post office,** with a free paperback exchange, is in the red-trimmed white building on Bennett Ave. (☎821-4503. Open M, W, and F 8am-noon and 2:30-4pm, Tu and Th 10-11:45am.) **Postal Code:** Y0B 1B0.

ACCOMMODATIONS AND FOOD. The Yukon Government maintains 14 **campsites** by the airstrip across Hwy. 2 from the Shell station with potable water, firewood, and pit toilets. (Requires an $8 Yukon government camping permit.) **Spirit Lake Wilderness Resort,** 10km north of town on Hwy. 2, has lakeside accommodations and rents canoes for $7.50 per hour. (☎821-4337. Toilets, free showers, coin laundry. Tent sites $13.50, with power $19.50; adorable cabins on the jade-colored lake $69 for 1-2 people, $79 for 3-4 people.) If you don't mind parking lots, **Montana Services** offers RV hook-ups ($10) and car tent sites ($5).

Just up the road from the Spirit Lake Resort (9km north of town) the **Cinnamon Cache,** with smiles as sweet as their buns, is a gem among Dall sheep and bluebirds. Homemade cinnamon buns, survival cookies for the trail (both $2.50), and soup and sandwiches make tummies happy. (☎821-4331. Open Feb.-Sept. daily 7am-7pm.) Your best bet in town is the small local operation **Koolsen Place** in the newly rebuilt **White Pass Warehouse** behind the depot. Watch the river wash by and munch on one of the few items on the menu. (Open daily 10am-7pm.)

THE CHILKOOT TRAIL A valuable coastal trade route protected by the Tagish and Tlingit for thousands of years, the Chilkoot Trail bore the great torrent of gold-seekers hungering for the Yukon interior in the late 1890s. First led by native packers and later accompanied by hordes of their fellow stampeders, north-country novices slogged back and forth 33 mi. between Skagway, Dyea, and Lake Bennett, transporting 1000 pounds of provisions each to satisfy Canadian officials that they were prepared for the country ahead. "It's hard enough to do the trail with just yourself to look after," complained one man. "Imagine looking after yourself, plus a half a ton of mining supplies and beef jerky. And a horse." Hikers take to the trail today for a rigorous 3-5 day hike past the horse skeletons and gold-rush relics that still litter the precipitous pass. The trail departs from the coast through a dramatic variety of climate, terrain, and vegetation, both above and below the timberline, before descending into the forests of northern British Columbia within reach of Lake Bennett and Carcross. For more hike info, see p. 430.

OUTDOOR ACTIVITIES AND SIGHTS. Legendary big-game guide Johnny Johns led countless trips out of the Carcross area in the direction of the Yukon Mountains, the Upper Rockies, and the Coastal Range, which are all visible from town. While outfitting companies such as his no longer operate, hiking in the Carcross area inspires justifiable acclaim. Pick up a copy of *Whitehorse Area Hikes and Bikes* at the visitors center or in Whitehorse before setting out. The most popular hike in the area is the **Chilkoot Trail** (see p. 434), a moderately difficult 3-5 day adventure beginning at Skagway and ending at the far end of Lake Bennett. The lake's two sandy beaches are understandably popular with locals in July and August. Overlooking the town, rough mining roads snake around Montana Mountain. To access them, follow Hwy. 2 south and take the first right after crossing the bridge. Take the first left and drive until you reach the washout. From there, it's all on foot to astounding views. (Round-trip 21km, 8hr. including drive, 1000 ft. gain.) The adventurous can play in the sand of an exposed glacial lake bottom in the world's smallest desert, Carcross Desert, 3km north of town on the highway.

KLUANE NATIONAL PARK ☎ 867

The Southern Tutchone (tuh-SHOW-nee) people named this area Kluane (kloo-AH-nee), meaning "place of many fish." They might also have mentioned that Kluane National Park is a place of many Dall's sheep, eagles, glaciers, and untouched mountain landscapes. Together with Glacier National Park and adjacent Wrangell-St. Elias National Park in Alaska (see p. 451) and Tatshenshini/Alsek Provincial Park in BC, Kluane is part of one of the world's largest protected wilderness areas. Canada's massive mountain range, the St. Elias Mountains, is divided into two separate ranges within the park. The smaller Kluane Range runs right along the Alaska Hwy. (p. 334). The soaring giants of the Icefield Range, including Canada's highest peak, Mt. Logan (5959m), and the most massive non-polar ice fields in the world are separated from the Kluane range by the Duke Depression. The ice-blanketed mountains of Kluane's interior are a haven for experienced expeditioners, but render two-thirds of the park inaccessible (except by plane) to humbler hikers. Fortunately, the northeastern section of the park (bordering the Alaska Hwy.) offers splendid, easily accessible backpacking, rafting, biking, fishing, and dayhiking. Many routes follow original Southern Tutchone and Tlingit trails and old mining roads left over from Kluane's brief and disappointing fling with the gold rush in 1904-05. Most ventures into Kluane begin from **Haines Junction**.

ORIENTATION AND PRACTICAL INFORMATION

Kluane's 22,015 sq. km are bounded by the **Kluane Game Sanctuary** and the **Alaska Hwy.** (Hwy. 1; p. 334) to the north, and the **Haines Hwy.** (Hwy. 3) to the east. **Haines Junction** (pop. 800), 158km west of Whitehorse at the park's eastern boundary, serves as the gateway to the park. There is also access to trails in the north of the park from **Sheep Mountain**, 72km northeast of Haines Junction on the Alaska Hwy.

Buses: Alaska Direct (☎800-770-6652, in Whitehorse ☎668-4833) runs a summer schedule from **Haines Junction** on Su, W, and F to **Anchorage, AK** (13hr., US$145); **Fairbanks, AK** (11hr., US$125); **Whitehorse, YT** (2hr., US$40); and **Skagway, AK** (16hr., 12hr. overnight in Whitehorse; US$50 plus CDN$40).

Auto Repair: Source Motors Ltd. (☎634-2268), 1km north of Haines Junction on the Alaska Hwy. Does just about everything and offers 24hr. emergency road service. Open M-F 7am-9pm, Sa-Su 9am-9pm.

Visitor Information: Kluane National Park Visitor Reception Centre (☎634-7207; www.parkscanada.gc.ca/kluane), on Logan St. in Haines Junction (Km 1635 on the Alaska Hwy.). Provides **wilderness permits** ($5 per night, $50 per season), **fishing permits** ($4 per day for Canadians, $5 for Americans; $15 per season for Canadians, $35 for Americans), **topographical maps** ($11), **trail and weather info,** and registers overnight visitors to the park. Open May-Sept. daily 9am-7pm; Oct.-Apr. M-F 10am-noon and 1-5pm. **Yukon Tourism** (☎634-2345) gives information on activities inside and outside the park. Open daily mid-May to mid-Sept. 8am-8pm. Inquire about guided tours in late June and Aug. The phoneless, wind-swept **Sheep Mountain Information Centre,** 72km north of town at Alaska Hwy. Km 1707, registers hikers headed for the northern area of the park. Sells hiking guides for $1 and rents bear canisters. Open daily May-Labour Day 9am-5pm. Overnight registrations until 4:30pm only.

Bank: Toronto Dominion (☎634-2820), in Madley's Store. Exchanges foreign currency and cashes traveler's checks. Open M-F 12:30-4:30pm. **ATM** available 8am-9pm daily.

Pool: (☎634-7105). Call for hours. Open late May to Sept.

Internet Access: Free at the **library** (book ahead if possible), located next door to Madley's. (☎634-2215. Open Tu-F 1-5pm and Sa 2-5pm.) Better hours but a fee at **Village Bakery.** (☎634-2928. $3 per 30 min. Open daily 7:30am-9pm in summer.)

Laundromat and Showers: Gateway Motel (☎634-2371), at the junction. Wash $2, dry 25¢ per 6 min. Shower $4. Open daily 8:30am-10pm. Comparable prices at **Kluane RV Kampground** (☎634-2709) with 24hr. access to laundry and showers on the meter, north on the Alaska Hwy. from the junction.

Emergency and Police: ☎634-5555; no 911. **Fire:** ☎634-2222. **Ambulance/Health Clinic:** ☎634-4444. Across from Madley's. Open M-F 9am-noon and 1-5pm.

Post Office: (☎634-3802), in Madley's. Open M-F 8:15am-noon and 1-5pm. **Postal Code:** Y0B 1L0.

ACCOMMODATIONS AND CAMPING

Camping by a gorgeous lakeside beats staying at a clean-but-forgettable hwy. motel or RV park any day (see also **Kluane Lake** below).

Stardust Motel, (☎634-2591). 1km north of town on the Alaska Hwy. The Stardust offers spacious rooms. Satellite TV, bath. No phones. Kitchenettes extra. Open mid-May to mid-Sept. Reservations recommended. Singles $55; doubles $65.

Bear Creek Lodge, (☎634-2301). 11km north of Haines Junction towards Sheep Mountain on the Alaska Hwy. Forgoing the location in town rewards the Kluane visitor with cheaper rooms. Ring bell for late arrivals. Singles from $50, doubles from $60.

Pine Lake, 7km east of town on the Alaska Hwy. Closest government-run campground to Haines Junction and very popular. Features a sandy beach with a swim float, a pit for late-night bonfires, and an interpretive trail along the river. Water, firewood, pit toilets. $8 with Yukon camping permit only.

KLUANE NATIONAL PARK ■ 381

Kathleen Lake Campground, National Park land off Haines Rd. 27km south of Haines Junction. Base for many of the area's hikes. Water (boil before drinking), toilets, fire pits, and firewood. Wheelchair accessible. Open mid-May to mid-Sept. 39 sites, $10.

FOOD

Haines Junction restaurants offer standard highway cuisine. But ooh, ahhh, the exception is the scrumptious ■**Village Bakery,** across from the visitors center, which serves up vegetarian options, mouth-watering baked goods, and beer. Substantial soups with bread ($3.50), sourdough cheese dogs ($2.25), sushi (on F only $4.50 for 5 pieces), and a superb rhubarb cranberry pie. Make reservations to enjoy live music and salmon–BBQs ($13) on Monday nights. (☎634-2867. Open daily May-Sept. 7:30am-9pm.) "We got it all"—the motto of **Madley's General Store**—is an understatement. Find power bars, star fruit, tackle, hardware, and a butcher block south of the junction. (☎634-2200. Open May-Sept. daily 8am-9pm; Oct.-Apr. 8am-6:30pm.) After a long day of soaking in all that Kluane National Park has to offer, kick back with a cold beer in front of the big screen TV or try your hand at pool in the bar at **Wong's Restaurant,** located in the Kluane Park Inn across the Alaska Hwy. from the information center. (☎634-2261. Open daily noon-2am.)

SIGHTS AND ENTERTAINMENT

Visit the **Kwaday Dan Kenji** traditional camp of the Champagne people, recently constructed with the help of local elders and enjoy a mug of fresh brewed tea ($1.25) on the willow chairs. Kwaday Dan Kenji is a few minutes east of the village of Champagne, situated 70km west of Whitehorse and 88km east of Haines Junction on the Alaska Hwy. Camping facilities on a natural meadow have pit toilets and fresh water ($10), and there is a guided tour of the traditionally-made shelters and animal traps. (Small shop with artifacts and local crafts open daily May-Oct. 9am-7:30pm. $10, children $6.)

The usually quiet hamlet of Haines Junction vivifies itself for back-to-back events. During the second weekend of June, music-loving rowdies from all over the area gather for "the function at the junction" to hear northern artists perform at the **Alsek Music Festival.** (☎634-2520; ask about the Kidzone for younger folk.) Only a week to recover for hosting the start of the 155 mi. **Kluane Chilkoot Bike Relay Race.** Ride it alone or in a team (☎634-7100).

HIKING

Kluane's trails are varied and very accessible. The visitors centers are great sources for trail maps, information, and conditions. A $1 pamphlet lists about 25 trails and routes ranging from 500m to 96km. Routes, as opposed to trails, are not maintained, do not have marked paths, are more physically demanding, and require backcountry navigation skills. Oddly-rendered beaver pictograms mark trailheads and park boundaries. Overnight visitors must register and pay at one of the visitors centers ($5 per night for adults), and use bear-resistant food canisters, which the park rents for $5 per night (with $150 cash or credit refundable deposit).

Dezadeash River Loop (DEZ-dee-ash, 5km). The trailhead is downtown at the day-use area across from Madley's on Haines Rd. This flat, forested trail will disappoint those craving the vertical, but it makes for a nice stroll. As always when in bear country, use a noise-maker or belt out tunes like *Lady Marmalade* to warn bears that you're coming.

Auriol Loop (15km, 4-6hr.). The trail begins 7km south of Haines Junction on Haines Rd. and cuts through boreal forest, leading to a subalpine bench (400m gain) just in front of the Auriol Range. Divided by a primitive campground halfway along, this is a popular overnight trip, although it can easily be hiked in a day without heavy packs.

King's Throne Route (10km round-trip). Difficult but rewarding dayhike with a panoramic view (1220m gain). It begins at the Kathleen Lake day-use area at the campground (see p. 381).

Sheep Creek Trail (10km round-trip). Down a short gravel access road just north of the visitors center for **Sheep Mountain**. A satisfying moderate dayhike (430m gain) and one of the better bets to see Dall sheep during the summer months. Sheep Mountain boasts more excellent hiking near the park's northern section. An easy 500m jaunt up to **Soldier's Summit** starts 1km north of the Sheep Mountain Info Centre and leads to the site where the Alaska Hwy. was officially opened on Nov. 20, 1942. The site pays homage to the "grunts and doughboys" who labored over the massive project during WWII and offers a nice view of Kluane Lake.

OTHER OUTDOOR ACTIVITIES

WATER
Anglers can readily put the park's many-fished reputation to the test at **Kathleen Lake** (see p. 381), home to lake and rainbow trout (catch and release only), grayling and rare freshwater Kokanee salmon (usually in season mid-May to early June). Less-crowded **St. Elias Lake** is an easy 3.5km hike from the trailhead, 60km south of Haines Junction on Haines Rd. **Pine Lake**, the popular territorial campground, is a good spot to put in the canoe for a paddle, as it is less windy than Kathleen Lake. Fishing here requires a Yukon permit from Madley's while Kluane waters require a **National Parks fishing permit,** available at the visitors center in Haines Junction (see **Bank**, p. 380).

TOURS
Guides are worth their weight in gold for area information, bear security, and navigation skills. In addition to guiding services, **PaddleWheel Adventures,** down the road from the Village Bakery, arranges flightseeing over the glaciers, hike-out helicopter rides to the Kluane Plateau, and full-day rafting trips on the Class III and IV rapids of the **Blanchard** and **Tatshenshini Rivers.** They also rent just about everything you might need to explore the park on your own, including tents, packs, and bear spray. (☎ 634-2683. Flightseeing $90 per person for 30min. flight over the Kaskawulsh. Rafting $100 per person including lunch. Helicopter rides vary depending on desires. Bikes $25 per day. Canoes $25 per day. Guides $150 per day for up to 6 people and $25 per additional person; fishing guides $150 per day for one person.) Call **Kluane Ecotours** for custom-fitted hiking, canoeing, or kayaking guides (☎ 634-2626. $75 per person; minimum $150 per day.)

MOUNTAIN BIKING
The **Alsek River Valley Trail,** which follows a bumpy old mining road for 14km from Alaska Hwy. Km 1645 to Sugden Creek, is popular for **mountain bikers** who crave rugged terrain. The rocky road crosses several streams before gently climbing to a ridge with a stellar view of the Auriol Mountains. More insider tips on the park's bike-friendly trails are available from PaddleWheel Adventures (see above).

WINTER ACTIVITIES
For winter use of the southern portion of the park, call ahead for snow conditions (☎ 634-7207) and stop by the visitors center for free, detailed maps of at least five cross-country ski routes. The Auriol, Dezadeash, and St. Elias trails (see above) are all local favorites. Bound through the trails with snowshoes, or pick-up dog-mushing regulations at the information center. Camping available at day-use area in town in the winter.

SHEEP MOUNTAIN TO ALASKA

KLUANE LAKE. The drive northwest from Haines Junction to the Alaska border is broken up by a smattering of pit stops, the most scenic of which lie along Lake Kluane. The lake's spectacular aquamarine color is due to suspended "glacier flour" particles in the water that reflect blue light waves. Spanning 478 sq. km, Kluane Lake is the largest in the Yukon. **Congdon Creek Campground,** at Km 1723 on the Alaska Hwy., is the nicest campground before the US border, with a long stone beach for evening strolls and breathtaking mountain views. Prime lakeside sites fill up early. (Water, pit toilets, firewood. 80 sites. $8 with Yukon casing permits.) If lake spots at the territorial campground are all taken or you prefer showers and laundry, continue south 6km to the equally beautiful **Cottonwood RV Park and Campground.** Sooth pot-hole-weary muscles in the hottub ($4 for 30min.) while the whipper-snappers play mini-golf. (No phone. Full hook-up $23; dry site $17.)

DESTRUCTION BAY. The small town of Destruction Bay, at Km 1743, earned its name when, in 1952, the tremendous wind that tunnels down the valley and off Kluane Lake destroyed the first village. These days, it's home to a gas station, motel, lounge, and cafe (all built low to the ground). **Destruction Bay Lodge** is a convenient spot to rest the rig and get some chow. (☎841-5332. Showers. Full hookups $19, sites $10.) Due to high winds, a strict **fire ban** is enforced in the town. A nurse is on call 24hr. at the **health clinic.** (☎841-4444. Open M-F 9am-4:30pm.)

BURWASH LANDING. Sixteen kilometers north of Destruction Bay is Burwash Landing, home to the world's largest gold pan at the **Kluane Museum of Natural History.** This noisy museum plays animal sound effects to accompany the Yukon's largest wildlife display and a collection of Southern Tutchone garb. (☎841-5561. Open daily late May and early Sept. 10am-6pm; June-Aug. 9am-9pm. $3.75, seniors $3.25, children 6-12 $2.) *Nlan* or stop, at Kluane First Nation's **Dalan Campground** for secluded campsites on the lake. (☎841-4274. Wood, water, pit toilets. 25 sites. $10.) Tenting or dry RV is free on **Burwash Landing Resort's** lawn or parking lot. The lakeside resort houses a diner in the lodge that serves up cheap and hefty portions beneath a Yukon-sized moose head on the wall. (☎841-4441. Open daily in summer 7am-11pm. Sandwiches $4-8. Showers $4. Hookups $16. Rooms with TV and private bath. Singles $70; doubles $80.)

Between Burwash and Beaver Creek, break up the monotonous mountain-viewing miles at **Pine Valley Bakery and RV** (Km 1845) and grab some grub, shower, gas, tire repair, or cheap lodging at this busy jack-of-all-trades stop. (☎862-7407. Open 24hr. mid-May to mid-Sept.)

BEAVER CREEK. The westernmost community (Km 1935) in Canada is by far the liveliest of all these roadside wonders. Get a sales pitch about Beaver Creek offerings, such as the oddly shaped historic church, at the new **visitors center.** (☎862-7321. Open daily in summer 8am-8pm.) Anything you need can be found at the log **1202 Motor Inn,** from camping ($10 dry, $15 power) and motel rooms ($35 for "plain jane" with shared bath, $65 for the works) to a grocery store, restaurant with giant-sized sandwiches ($6-8), and an ATM. (☎800-661-0540. Open daily 6:30am-1am.) A **heated indoor public pool** is open June to August (☎862-7702). Lodging is a steal at the **Beaver Creek Hostel** in the **Westmark Inn** (double inn rooms with a shared bath), which has a bar and rec room for fun. (☎862-7501. $20. May-Sept.)

ENTERING THE US. Past Beaver Creek, 20 mi. of hwy. and prime moose-viewing wilderness separate US and Canadian customs and immigration, although several signs and landmarks can be found at the official border on the 141st meridian. Alaska time is one hour behind Pacific time. Gas a few mi. into US territory is considerably cheaper than anything in Canada. From the border it's 80 mi. (1½hr.) to Tetlin Junction, where the Alaska Hwy. meets the Taylor Hwy. (see p. 521) and 92 mi. (2hr.) to Tok (see p. 520).

ALONG HWY. 9: TOP OF THE WORLD HWY.

The majestic 127km (1½hr.) highway deserves its name. Starting across the Yukon River from Dawson City, it climbs for several kilometers and then follows the spine of a series of mountains. The trip affords breathtaking views of the Southern Ogilvies and North Dawson range before connecting with the Taylor Hwy. at **Jack Wade Junction** in Alaska. Unmarked trails head into the bush from rest stops. The road is open May through September, although the mountainous Yukon-Alaska border crossing at Km 108 is only open 9am-9pm Pacific (i.e., Yukon) time. The only services on the Canadian side are the links to Top of the World Golf Course (☎ 867-667-1472), about 10km past the ferry. The 5min. ferry runs 24hr. from June to July (peak traffic 7-11am from Dawson and 2-8pm to Dawson). While the road on the Canadian side is well maintained, the potholed gravel on the American side will have you cursing Uncle Sam. Just over the border in the US, the **Boundary Cafe** sells snacks and will trade a gallon of gasoline for your soul (roughly US$2.50).

DAWSON CITY ☎ 867

Born in a frenzied lust for dust, Dawson City booms today by telling its own history. On August 17, 1896, three men stumbled upon thick ribbons of gold in a stream outside of today's Dawson City. Every prospector in the Klondike area descended upon Dawson within weeks, and as word of the discovery reached the United States, thousands of money-hungry American men began the treacherous trek north. Services quickly followed with merchants capitalizing on the dense population by opening shops, saloons, and hotels. For 12 glorious, crazy months from 1898-1899, this was the largest Canadian city west of Toronto, known as "the Paris of the North." After that year of frenzied claim-staking and legend-making, most of the once-eager gold seekers realized that the early birds had scooped up all the prime claims before their arrival. Restless, they packed up and followed the Yukon River to Nome, and Dawson City fizzled almost as quickly as it had exploded. Within a few years the rich ground had been exhausted, and arduous, slow hand-mining was no longer profitable for even the lucky Sourdoughs (original prospectors, or today, those who weather an Arctic winter). Dredges took over and corporate mining trudged on from its center in Bear Creek, 13km south of Dawson, until sputtering out in 1966. In the early 1960s the Klondike Visitors Association and the Canadian government set out to return Dawson City to its gold-rush glory, restoring dirt roads, long boardwalks, wooden store fronts, and in the process transformed it into the lively RV and college student destination that it is today.

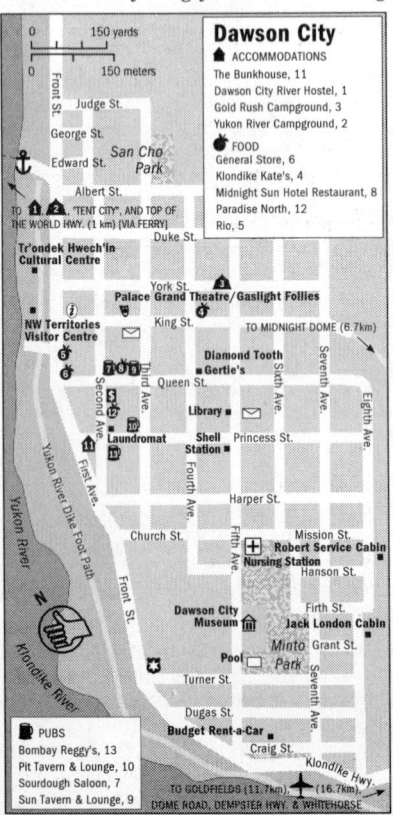

TRANSPORTATION

To reach Dawson City, take the **Klondike Loop (Hwy. 2)** 533km (6hr.) north from **Whitehorse,** or follow the majestic **Top-of-the-World Hwy. (Hwy. 9)** 108km east from the Alaska border (see **Taylor Hwy.,** p. 521).

Buses: Dawson City Taxi and Courier Service (☎ 993-6688), corner of 2nd and York. To **Whitehorse** (7½hr., June-Aug. M-F, $82.50). **Parks Hwy. Express** (☎ 888-600-6001) will take you across the "top of the world" and to **Fairbanks** (11hr., 3 daily, $125).

Cruise: Yukon Queen II River Cruises (☎ 993-5599), on Front St. next to the Keno. Office open daily 8am-8pm. Departs daily at 9am for **Eagle, AK** along the Yukon River. Includes hot meals and river stories (10-11hr. round-trip). One-way standby US$87, CDN$126; round-trip US$144, CDN$209; returns Eagle canoes US$50 (see p. 522).

Car Rental: Budget, 451 Craig St. (☎ 993-5644), in the Dawson City B&B. $60 per day, 20¢ per km after 100km. Free pick-up and delivery. Must be 21 with a credit card.

Auto Repair: Esso (☎ 993-5142) on the Klondike Hwy. (Hwy. 2) immediately before town. Open daily in summer 7am-11pm.

PRACTICAL INFORMATION

Visitor Information: (☎ 993-5566), at Front and King St. Movies, inexpensive tickets and pick-a-pack tour tickets (see **Sights**). Open mid-May to mid-Sept. daily 8am-8pm. The **Northwest Territories Visitors Centre** (☎ 993-6167) opposite, knows the Dempster Hwy. Open daily May-Sept. 9am-8pm.

Banks: Canadian Imperial Bank of Commerce, at 2nd Ave. and Queen. St. has a **24hr. ATM.** Open M-Th 10am-3pm, and F 10am-5pm.

Equipment Rental: Dawson City River Hostel (see **Accommodations,** p. 386). Bikes $20 and canoes $20 per day. Non-hostelers must use passport as deposit.

Bookstore: Maximilian's Goldrush Emporium (☎ 993-5486), on Front near Queen St., stocks every word ever written by local stars Jack London and Robert Service and postcards designed to incite the jealousy of friends and families. Open M-Sa 9am-8pm, Su 10am-8pm; winter M-Sa 9am-6pm, Su noon-6pm.

Laundromat and Public Showers: The Wash House Laundromat (☎ 993-6555), on 2nd Ave. between Princess and Queen. Wash $2.50, dry 25¢ per 4min. Showers $1 per 4min., towels 50¢. Open daily 9am-9pm; winter 10am-6pm.

Pool: (☎ 993-7412), on 5th next to Museum. Sunny new pool with whirlpool. Adults $4, college students $3.50, youth and seniors $3, child $2, family $9. Reduced after 8pm.

Weather: ☎ 993-8367.

Women's Shelter: (☎ 993-5086). 24hr.

Police: (☎ 993-5555 or 667-5555), at Front St. and Turner St., in southern part of town.

Ambulance: ☎ 993-4444.

Medical Services: Nursing Station (☎ 993-4444), at 6th Ave. and Church. Open M-F 8:30am-5pm.

Internet Access: Free 30min. at the **Library** (☎ 993-5571), in the school at 5th Ave. and Princess St. Call ahead. Open Tu-Th 10am-9pm, F-Sa 10am-5pm; winter Tu-Th 1-9pm, F-Sa noon-5pm. Also at **Grubstake** (☎ 993-6706), 2nd between King St. and Queen St. $5 per hr. Open Su-Th 10am-10pm, F-Sa until 11pm.

Post Office: (☎ 993-5342), 5th Ave. near Princess St. and Queen St. Open M-F 8:30am-5:30pm, Sa 9am-noon. The **Historical Post Office,** at 3rd and King St., gives historical service nearer downtown. Open daily noon-3pm and 3:30-6pm. **Postal Code:** Y0B 1G0.

ACCOMMODATIONS AND CAMPING

The hostel and campground on the west side of town, across the Yukon River, are by far the most attractive options in the trap that is Dawson City tourism. The **ferry** to float you and your wheels across is free and runs 24hr. Hop on at Front and Albert St., in the north end of town. The **tent city** in the woods next to the hostel remains popular with the town's summer college crowd, despite the $100 per person per summer price tag. Contact the **Northern Network of B&Bs** (☎993-5644) for the town's listings.

- **Dawson City River Hostel (HI;** ☎993-6823), across the Yukon River from downtown; take the first left off the ferry. Sun on lounge chairs overlooking the Yukon; bathe in wood-stove-heated creek water; stir-fry in the outdoor kitchen; or snuggle in the cozy lounge. Open mid-May to Sept. Beds $14, nonmembers $16.50; tent sites $9.50, additional tent occupants $7 per person; private rooms $35. No credit cards.
- **The Bunkhouse** (☎993-6164), on Princess at Front St. Clean wood-planked rooms and comfy firm beds. Best option actually *in* town. Singles $50, with bath $80; doubles $60, with bath $90; quads with bath $120. Open mid-May to mid-Sept.
  Yukon River Campground, first right off the ferry. Roomy, secluded sites are a haven for nature-lovers, who can peer at the peregrine falcons nesting across the river. Lacking hookups, it is an escape from the RV-mania across the river. Water, pit toilets.
  Gold Rush Campground (☎993-5247), at 5th and York St. Right downtown. Pure RV, baby. Laundry $3, dry $1.50. Shower $2 per 6min. Dump station. Hookups $23-26; pull-through sites $22; gravel tent sites $14.

FOOD

On Thanksgiving Day in 1898, a turkey in Dawson City cost over $100. Snag one today for much less at the **Dawson City General Store**, on Front St. (☎993-5475. Open M-Sa 8am-8pm, Su 10am-7pm.)

- **Paradise North** (☎993-5800), 2nd Ave. between Princess and Queen. Inexpensive breakfasts ($4), chock-full wraps in oven-fresh talami ($5-6), and loaded pizzas justify the name. Dine along the railing on the front porch and get tan at 9pm. The doors never close during Music Fest. Open M-Th 7am-10pm, F-Sa 7am-11pm, Su 9am-9pm.

NO, MA'AM, THAT'S NOT AN OLIVE IN YOUR MARTINI

When some people run across amputated body parts, they take them to a hospital for surgical reattachment. But for Capt. Dick Stevenson, the pickled human toe he discovered in a cabin in the Yukon could mean only one thing: a damn fine cocktail. The drink became famous and spawned the Sourtoe Cocktail Club, whose 14,000-plus members include a 6-month-old child and a 91-year-old toe-swallower. Aspiring initiates buy a drink of their choice and pay a small fee ($5) to Bill "Stillwater Willie" Holmes (Dick's replacement as keeper of the sourtoe), who drops the chemically preserved (er, pickled) toe in the drink. Then it's bottoms up, and the moment the toe touches your lips, you're in the club. "You can drink it fast, you can drink it slow—but the lips have gotta touch the toe." Listening to Stillwater Willie explain the club's sordid history and philosophize about life in the Yukon is in and of itself worth $5, but the fee includes a certificate and membership card; a commemorative pin or a book relating the saga of the sourtoe can be purchased separately for $5 each. Sourtoe initiations are held from 9-11pm nightly in the Sourdough Saloon at the Downtown Hotel (☎993-5346) on the corner of Queen and 2nd. A word of warning: Stillwater Willie may require that swallowed toes be replaced.

DAWSON CITY ■ 387

Klondike Kate's (☎ 993-6527), at 3rd and King St., in one of Dawson's oldest buildings. The favorite restaurant of Dawson Sourdoughs. Daily specials add to the full menu of pita wraps ($5), salads ($5-8), burgers ($8), and hummus plate ($6). Vegetarians and martini connoisseurs ($5.75) rejoice. Open mid-May to mid-Sept. daily 6:30am-11pm.

Rio (☎ 993-4683), on Front St. between King and Queen. Burger shack that attracts the summer college crowd with its funky patty creations and tasty fries ($8-9) and pool table on the deck. The best milkshakes in the north run $4. Open 11am-10pm.

Midnight Sun Hotel Restaurant (☎ 993-5495), 3rd and Queen St. Chinese entrees from $11. Burgers and more $5-8. Lunch smorgasbord on F ($10). Close enough to the lounge to hear locals belting out their favorite tunes at the hottest karaoke joint in town. (See **Debauchery**, p. 387.) Open Su-Th 6am-1am, F-Sa 6am-3am.

👁 SIGHTS AND ACTIVITIES

Parks Canada looms large in overseeing the sights of town. Scope information and buy ticket packages at the visitors center (see **Practical Information** p. 385).

GOLD. Nearly 16km of maintained gravel road follow Bonanza Creek to the former site of **Grand Forks**, which was chewed up when the dredges came through, leaving monster-size gopher tunnels. Along the way are **Gold Dredge #4**, a gigantic machine used to exhaust Bonanza Creek when corporate mining replaced hand-mining, and **Discovery Claim**, the site of the first discovery of gold in Dawson *(Gold Dredge #4: gold-info rich tours daily on the hour 9am-4pm, except 11am; $5. Discover Claim: interactive gold-staking program daily, 11am. $5).* **Goldbottom Mining Tours and Gold Panning,** 30km south of town, offers a tour of an operating mine and an hour of panning. *(☎ 993-5023. Open June to freeze-up daily 11am-7pm. $12.)* Pan for free at the confluence of the Bonanza and Eldorado Creeks beyond the Discovery Claim site, but panning anywhere else could lead to an unpleasant encounter with the owner of the claim you're jumping. Pans sold at local hardware store.

GHOST TOWN. Bear Creek, 13km south of town on the Klondike Hwy., is a ghost town of tools and machinery left behind when mining halted in 1966. *(Tours Su-F 1:30pm and 2:30pm. $5.)*

ROBERT SERVICE. Stop by Robert Service's cabin for an animated account of his life and poetry. If you still haven't had enough of the Yukon poet, catch **Robert Service readings** given by the magnificent Tom Byrne, who recounts the life of Robert Service as he weaves in Service's famous poems, "The Cremation of Sam McGee" and "The Shooting of Dan McGrew." The poems' wit and Byrne's story-telling make the show a feature attraction in Dawson. *(Cabin on 8th near Hanson. Free viewing 9am-noon and 1-5pm. Shows at 10am and 1:30pm. $5 includes Jack London talk. Shows at corner of Front St. and Prince. June-Aug. daily at 3pm and 8pm. $8, 10-16 $4, under 10 free.)*

JACK LONDON. Examine the traces of frontier literary genius Jack London at his **cabin**, where the great Californian author's life and brief stint in the Yukon are described in letters, photographs, and a talk by London fanatic and Canadian author Dick North. *(On 8th Ave. and Firth St. Open daily 10am-1pm and 2-6pm. 30min. tours daily 11:15am and 2:45pm. Exhibit and talk $2 or free with Robert Service cabin talk.)*

DEBAUCHERY. Diamond Tooth Gertie's, was Canada's first legal casino and the stuff movies are made of. Gamblers fritter the night away with roulette, blackjack, or Texas Hold 'em, against local legends such as Johnny Caribou and No Sleep Filippe. Madame Gertie belts out tunes and can-can dancing at 8:30pm, 10:30pm, and midnight. *(☎ 993-5575. At 4th and Queen St. Must be 19. Open nightly 7pm-2am. $6 cover or $20 season pass. No cover after 11pm. Happy hour midnight-2am.)* The **Gaslight Follies,** a high-kicking vaudeville revue, is held in **Palace Grand Theatre.** *(On King St., between 2nd and 3rd. ☎ 993-6217. Up to two shows nightly. Box office open daily 11am-9pm. $15-17, under 12 $7.50.)* As the night winds down, karaoke winds up at the **Sun Tavern and Lounge.** Young and old pack in to check out the local talent. Though no longer Dawson's roughest bar, the Sun is still no place to sip fruity

THE YUKON

drinks. *(At 3rd St. and Queen. ☎ 993-5495. Pints $4. Open daily noon-2am.)* See grown men cry to home-spun country tunes at **The Pit Tavern and Lounge.** Barnacle Bob plays the tavern from 4pm, and the much-acclaimed country and blues house band plays the lounge Wednesday to Saturday at 10pm. *(At the old Westminster Hotel on 3rd. ☎ 993-5339. Tavern open 9am-11pm; lounge noon-2am. Happy hour 4:45-5:45pm.)* For a less rowdy glass of sangria, head to the restored brothel, **Bombay Peggy's.** *(At 2nd St. and Princess. ☎ 993-6969. Happy hour 5-6pm, sangria pitchers $12 7-9pm. Open summer 2pm-1:30am, winter 4pm-1am.)*

TR'ONDEK HWECH'IN CULTURAL CENTRE. The **Tr'ondek Hwech'in Cultural Centre,** celebrated for its architecture since its completion in 1998, is a striking and innovative home for exhibits on First Nations culture. The center is open for visitors (donations welcome) to browse displays, watch videos, or participate in various cultural activities and demonstrations. *(On Front St. ☎ 993-6564. Open daily 10:30am-6pm. Tours of gallery and slide show $5. Offered 3 times a day.)*

DAWSON CITY MUSEUM. For a broader, less lyrical historical perspective, check out the **Dawson City Museum.** Exhibits on the region's geography, First Nations, first settlers, and the gold rush complement special films, demonstrations, and a children's exhibit of family heirlooms. Don't miss a 25min. film on Dawson the 1950s ghost town. *(On 5th Ave. in Minto Park. ☎ 993-5007. Open daily 10am-8pm. Wheelchair accessible. $5; student and seniors $4; family $12.)*

OUTDOOR ACTIVITIES. Dawson is a jungle-gym for outdoors people. Find trail maps for Moosehead slide and Midnight Dome at visitors center. The Dawson City River Hostel (see p. 386) sells topographical maps of the region ($12) and arranges four-day **canoe rentals** to Eagle, AK (US$110), or ten-day trips to Circle, AK.

🎵 EVENTS

A trip up the **Midnight Dome,** 7km along Dome Rd., just past the Esso gas station on the way into town, is a tradition on the **summer solstice,** on which the sun dips below the horizon for just 20min. around 12:30am. The Midnight Dome makes for a panoramic picnic spot or sunset photo op Drive up or take the steep 7km trail that ascends over 600m/1970 ft. leaving from the end of King St. (2hr. one-way, map at visitors center). Race it on the Saturday of Music Fest and then head riverside for a salmon barbecue.

During the third weekend of July, Gold Fever becomes Dance Fever as Canadians bust their move at the ■**Dawson City Music Festival** for three days of fantastic music and energy. Kid Fest events thrill the younger crowd. Tickets to see 20-plus pop, rock, and folk bands, go on sale in April, and usually sell out by mid-June. The ticketless eavesdrop outside venues and in the beer garden. (☎ 993-5584; www.dcmf.com. July 19-21, 2002. $70 for three days of workshops, performances, and dancing.) Mid-August sees Dawson explode in Sourdough charm during **Discovery Days** (Aug. 16-19, 2002) with a parade, pancake breakfasts, and an entire town in gold-rush period costume. Labour Day visitors will not want to pass up their chance to behold the **Great International Outhouse Race.** Teams of contenders tow occupied outhouses on wheels through the streets of Dawson. (Visitors Association ☎ 993-5575. Sept. 1, 2002.)

TOAST AND BRUSSEL SPROUT JELLY?!?!

Mmm...sweet like budd-ah! Little did you know that the margarine you've been slathering on your toast comes from canola—a relative of your childhood nightmares: brussel sprouts and cabbage. This yellow-flowered crop colors the fields of the Peace River area around Dawson Creek. "Canola" is a hybrid of the words "Canadian" and "oil." You can blame Canadian plant engineers—not your poor mother—for disguising the veggies this time. Aww...don't spit it out!

ALONG HWY. 4: CAMPBELL HWY.

In stark contrast with the Alaska Hwy., drivers on the Campbell Hwy. (Hwy. 4) feel like they are truly penetrating the wild and powerful north alone. They are following the footsteps of the highway's namesake, Robert Campbell, the first white man to brave the Yukon. From the south, the Campbell Hwy. runs 602km from **Watson Lake** to **Carmacks** (8hr.). With the towns along the highway turning into ghost-towns as mining ventures falter, only anglers, solitude-seekers, and wildlife buffs lured by Faro's eco-tourism venture on the road. From the tiny, largely native community of Ross River (originally a 19th-century fur-trading post), a finger of road cuts off towards the Northwest Territories (NWT) wilderness. Other roads off the Campbell service smaller mining and prospecting operations. Indeed, much of the activity and sparse settlement found along the Campbell seems to be dedicated to its maintenance; the 383km (5-5½hr.; no services on this stretch) of graded dirt road from Watson Lake in the south (on the Alaska Hwy.) to Ross River runs through wilderness broken only by year-round highway servicing camps. **This stretch is not to be taken lightly:** tires are sliced and windshields are cracked at high speeds. As you get closer to Ross River, you start to catch views of the velvet-puckered green Pelly Range to the south and strange, rounded, high dirt cliffs. On the way to Carmacks from Faro, the greatly improved road continues on high bluffs and eventually follows the Yukon River with some forceful views approaching town. Five government campsites lie on the route (Kms 80, 177, 376 at the turn-off for Ross River, 428 up toward Faro, and 517 on Little Salmon Lake. $8 permit camping only), and three more on the short Frenchman Rd. This branches off the Campbell at Km 551, near Carmacks, and leads 60km to the **Klondike Hwy.**

ROSS RIVER ☎ 867

Camping awaits just beyond the road to Ross River at **Lapi Canyon Territorial Campground,** above the river that flows between the sandy cliffs of the canyon. (Pit toilets, firewood, water. $8.) After traveling up from Watson Lake without a gas fill-up, the chevy will likely need a drink. Otherwise, there's no need to make the 10km detour to the depressed town of Ross River. The sole **gas station** doubles as a **general store** with groceries. (☎ 969-2212. Open daily 8am-6pm.) **Medical emergencies:** ☎ 969-4444. **Police:** ☎ 867-667-5555. From Ross River, you are 370km of gravel road and two campsites away from Watson Lake and the Alaska Hwy.

FARO ☎ 867

One hour northeast of Ross River and a jaunt down 10km of road will land you in the curious, almost-ghost-town of **Faro.** When active, the town's mine held the world's largest open-pit lead and zinc production complex. It was so big that attempts to reopen the mine today would drive world lead prices down below the unprofitable levels that forced it to close in 1997. If you do make the trip to Faro, you will enjoy the hospitality of the few remaining locals and some spectacular wilderness fit for good **fishing** and **hiking.** You may catch a view of rare black-and-white **Fannin sheep** from one of the town's specially constructed **viewing platforms.** The closest platform to town is at the corner of Blind Creek Rd. and Lorna Blvd.; ask at the visitors center for directions to others. The most impressive building in town, the **Campbell Region Interpretive Centre** (☎ 994-2288; open daily 8am-8pm), on the right as you enter town, illustrates the new attempt to boost the economy. It provides great info on geology, mining, First Nation habitation, and early fur-trading exploration of the area. Watch for special naturalist talks and presentations given at the center throughout the summer. To reach the **nursing station,** take a left on Bell Ave. off Campbell St. For the **police** (☎ 994-5555), turn right immediately upon entering town. The **post office** is on the left past Hoang's (open M-F 8:30am-5:30pm, Sa 8:30am-noon). If you need car repair, try **Shell.** (☎ 994-2538. **24hr. road service** ☎ 994-3019 or 994-2538.)

Camping can be found at the very private, yet painfully gravelly, **John Connolly RV Park,** across from the visitors center. (Toilets, hot showers $3 for non-guests. Sites $10, hookups $15.) A better place for tents, the **Johnson Lake Territorial Campground** lies 6.5km back toward the highway. (Pit toilets, pump water, and firewood. $8.) Otherwise, several blocks down the road from the visitors center, the owner of **Redmond's Hotel** (☎994-2430) might rent you a mighty nice room indoors for a steep $70 at the only hotel in town. **Hoang's** is the only restaurant in town, attached to the hotel on your left past the visitors center (open M-Sa 11am-8pm).

CARMACKS ☎867

Little Salmon Lake lies 85km before Carmacks offering awesome lakeside campsites. (Permit required. Pit toilets, firewood, water. $8.) Signs from here will guide you down the Campbell's paved 180km (2hr.) to **Faro**. Stop at **Eagle's Nest Bluff,** about 30km along the road, to hear the aspens rustle and get a high, wide-ranging view of the wide and easy Yukon River and surrounding lands. The end of the Campbell meets the North Klondike Hwy (Hwy. 2); turn left for Carmacks (2km). The final approach to Carmacks delivers in-town **camping** along the Nordenskiold River at the popular **Tantalus Public Campground,** and a meandering stretch of riverside boardwalk. (Pit toilets, water. $12.) The **visitors center** is beside the campground. (☎863-6330. Open M-F 8:30am-5pm.) Eat with local characters and work on becoming one at the **Gold Panner Cafe,** part of the Hotel Carmacks complex below the highway. (☎863-5221. Open daily 6am-10pm; winter reduced hours.) North of town, the new **Tage Cho Hudan Cultural Centre** preserves the Tutchone culture and displays the world's only mammoth snare model. (☎863-5830. Open daily 9am-5pm. Donation requested.) **Police** ☎863-5555; **Ambulance/health clinic:** ☎863-4444. From **Carmacks,** the smooth **North Klondike Hwy.** (Hwy. 2) runs 175km south to Whitehorse or 360km north to Dawson City.

APPROACHING THE NORTHWEST TERRITORIES: THE DEMPSTER HWY. ☎867

If you have ever dreamed of a day in which the sun never sets, or a sunset that lasted for hours before slowly flowing into a gorgeous sunrise, then the Dempster Hwy. will fulfill your Arctic Circle fantasies. The residents of the towns above the Arctic Circle shed their watches during the summer; while it may be perfectly fine to knock on your neighbors door at 2am, 10am may be late in the day. The experience is entirely worthwhile, but be prepared for wallet-slimming prices.

THE ROAD. Named after one of the most courageous officers in the Mounted Police, the Dempster Hwy. begins in the Yukon as Hwy. 5. It winds a spectacular 734km toward Inuvik, becoming Hwy. 8 when it crosses into the Northwest Territories (Km 465). Dempster completed his patrol route countless times over the years, following roughly the same 475 mi. path that now bears his name. Construction of the highway began in the 1950s when oil and gas were discovered near the Arctic Circle at Eagle Plains. Because much of the road is built on a 10m gravel bed to prevent the melting permafrost underneath from sinking the highway into marsh, the highway was finished decades after it was begun. It was not until 1979 that Canada's isolated Mackenzie River Delta towns of **Fort McPherson, Tsiigehtchic,** and **Inuvik** (ih-NOO-vik) finally had road access. These communities are largely indigenous Inuvialuit and Gwich'in .

THE REALITY. Like no other highway in North America, the Dempster presents its drivers with naked wilderness, unmolested by logging scars or advertisements. The challenge of battling the road and taking in the divine landscape makes driving the Dempster a religious experience: those who brave it across the Arctic Circle and the Continental Divide stare into the geological beginnings of the continent—and earn the right to write, "I did it!" in the dust coating their car. The road is not to be taken lightly. The Dempster's dirt and gravel are notorious for eating tires and cracking windshields. Parts of it are in great condition, while other

APPROACHING THE NORTHWEST TERRITORIES ■ 391

sections take on the appearance of a dry river bed. While the speed limit is posted at 90kmph, the rough road will punish you for going above 50-60kmph. The drive should be approached with careful planning. Services are limited to Klondike River Lodge (Km 0), Eagle Plains (Km 369), Fort McPherson (Km 550), and Inuvik (Km 734). Although a trip to Tombstone makes a pleasant overnight, the full drive takes at least 12hr. (two days each way to be fully and safely appreciated). The weather is erratic. Quick rainstorms or high winds can make portions of the route impassable (watch for flashing red lights that denote closed roads) and can disrupt ferry service to Inuvik for as long as two weeks, leaving travelers stranded.

☒ PRACTICAL INFORMATION. Road and Ferry Report (☎ 800-661-0752; in Inuvik 777-2678) provides up-to-date road info. The **NWT Visitor Centre** (see p. 385) in Dawson City has a free brochure and map of the highway, a short video, and reports from recent drivers. A full tank of gas, dependable tires (6-ply or better), a good spare or three, and emergency supplies (food, water, clothes, a first aid kit, and a can of gas) are necessary Dempster companions. The **Klondike River Lodge** (☎ 993-6892; open 7am-10:30pm) has full services and will rent you a gas can for $5 with a $15 deposit. Bring a sure-fire bug repellent (and some form of netting if camping), as the number of mosquitoes along the highway is staggering. If you lack wheels or doubt yours will survive the trip, **Dawson City Courier** (☎ 993-6688) drives up Mondays and Fridays and returns Wednesdays and Sundays for $225 each way.

SCENERY ORIENTATION. The spectacular first 150km of the Dempster pass through the crags of the **Ogilvie Mountains** renowned for their uncommon character as the only glacier-shaped mountain region along the highway. The dramatic peaks of the southern ranges gradually round out to the gentler, gravel-covered, unglaciated **Northern Ogilvies** near Engineer Creek (Km 194). The road then descends into forests and velvet tundra as it approaches the **Arctic Circle** (Km 405). The northernmost stretch of the Rockies, the Richardson Mountains, parallel the road in the distance. The trees become more stunted the farther north you go, a phenomenon due to the permafrost (ground frozen for more than two years) which covers much of the Yukon. The trees are forced to dig their roots in the "active layer" above the ice which becomes increasingly shallow. By the time you reach the tundra, simply dig a hole in the ground if you need to refrigerate anything. There are only a handful of settlements to distract drivers from the wonder of gazing.

TOMBSTONE. From Dawson some drivers make the range of igneous rock, Tombstone, a beautiful overnight destination. The **Interpretive Centre** at **Tombstone Campground** (Km 72) has wise staff, trails, and expansive displays including real specimens of local flora and fauna. For those continuing farther north, the center loans out a mile-by-mile written travelogue of the Dempster's natural history and wildlife: mountains and moraines, golden eagles, and the migrating **Porcupine caribou herd,** which at 150,000 head, is the largest in North America.

CAMPING. Several Yukon **government campgrounds** ($8) line the route north to Inuvik (Km 72, 194, 445). At the foot of Sapper Hill and Rock River, **Engineer Creek** (Km 194) provides the most scenic camping. Once in Northwest Territories, at **Nitainlii** (just before Ft. McPherson at Km 541) there is an excellent Gwich'in **interpretive center** and campground. (Center open June-Sept. daily 9am-9pm. Sites $15.)

> **DESTRUCKTION:** (deh-STRUK-shun) n. the act of semis racing along the Dempster Highway at high speeds, spitting gravel at the windshields of oncoming vehicular traffic. Vehicles can best avoid cracks from destrucktion by playing Dempster Chicken. Hug the center of the road and begin braking as the truck approaches, thus encouraging the steamroller to slow down. Before the truck passes, pull to the side of the road and stop so flying gravel will be less likely to crack the windshield.

BACKCOUNTRY. The mesmerizing landscape tempts **backcountry tripping** and demands the most vigilant take-nothing-leave-nothing ethic. The Ogilvie and Blackstone Rivers are favored by backcountry paddlers. *Paddling the Yukon* ($22, available at **Maximillian's**, see p. 385) is a comprehensive guide. Numerous mountain ridges that reach toward the road in the Northern Ogilivies are especially good for a straightforward manner of bushwhacking: following a ridge to the mountain. Only a handful of established paths access this wilderness. The road guide, *Along the Dempster* (p. 391), describes routes accessible from the highway in addition to the following highlights. Updated descriptions to routes that have become trails due to use, *Yukon's Tombstone Range and Blackstone Uplands: A Traveller's Guide* is well-worth the $20.

DAYHIKES. At Km 58, a small road behind the gravel pit becomes the **Grizzly Valley** trail (3hr. one-way), which leads through spruce forest to an alpine ridge with a fine view. The hike to **Tombstone Mountain** (known in Gwich'in as **Ddhah Ch'aa Tat**, "among the sharp, ragged, rocky mountains") begins just north of the interpretive centre or at Grizzly Creek, takes three to four days, and requires self-reliance, a compass, and topo maps. For a day-long adventure in the Northern Ogilvies, at Km 154 the **Mt. Distincta trail** ("Windy Pass") heads over craggy boulders to one of the area's highest peaks (1800m/5600 ft.). From the highway, walk southeast across a narrow ribbon of tundra to the base of the ridge. Follow the ridge south 6km, past a radio tower, and up a slope to the west to the true summit. From there, hike north 6km and then descend back to the highway where you will emerge 5km west of the trailhead. This trail rises about 1000m/3274 ft. **Sapper Hill,** with its yellow-gray ridge, is one of the best half-day hikes along the highway. It begins just after Engineer Creek (Km 194) and takes 4hr. Avoid walking along the fishbone crest of the ridge as the chunky limestone near the summit can be tricky to navigate.

EAGLE PLAINS HOTEL. Gas, food, a coin laundry and showers, and accommodations are available at the well-kept Eagle Plains Hotel, halfway to Inuvik at Km 369—a paragon of monopoly pricing in rooms with a comfy 70s decor. Rocky, parking lot-style camping is available. Gas in the summer of 2001 topped out at over a buck a liter, but the middle of nowhere is no time to be picky. The next pump is 197km away and the price is not much better. (☎993-2453. Singles $109; each extra person $14. $10, electrical $15.) Food at the hotel is of disarmingly good value. A Bushfire burger (onions, hot peppers and horseradish) with thick fries costs $8. (Restaurant open daily 7am-9pm. Lounge open daily 4:30pm-2am.)

ARCTIC CIRCLE. Just past Eagle Plains at Km 405, the Dempster crosses the Arctic Circle. Here lies an imaginary dotted line in the tundra. A sign provides photographic proof that you've reached the **Land of the Midnight Sun.**

NORTHWEST TERRITORIES. Set your watch to **Mountain Time** upon entering the Northwest Territories at Km 465. From mid-June to mid-October, **free ferries** cross Peel River (Km 539. Runs daily on demand) and Arctic Red River/MacKenzie River (Km 608. Runs daily. Departs from south shore 25min. past the hour 9am-12:25am.) In winter, cars can drive across the thick ice. No crossing is possible during fall freeze or spring thaw. Call 800-661-0752 for ice status.

INUVIK, NT ☎867

Inuvik ("living place") has 3200 residents mostly from two Arctic peoples; the Inuvialuit of the Beaufort Sea coast and the Gwich'in of the Mackenzie River Delta. During the long winter, Inuvik's houses are flamboyantly painted with bright colors and during the summer the community hosts a renowned ten-day Great Northern Arts Festival. While most shops try to operate on a night and day schedule, the town is usually out and about for the sun's lowest point in the sky (2:30am).

◪ PRACTICAL INFORMATION. Just about everything in town is on MacKenzie St., starting with the welcoming **Western Arctic Visitor Centre.** (☎777-4727. Open daily 9am-8pm.) Stop here on arrival and receive your **free Arctic Adventurer certificate** for driving the Dempster and visit its extensive display for a crash course on

INUVIK, NT ■ 393

the area. **Arctic Tire**, 80 Navy Rd., take left at first light in town, offers 24hr. road service and 24hr. gas pumps. (☎777-4149. Open M-Sa 8am-6pm.) Both the **CIBC bank** and the **post office** have **24hr. ATMs**. A great book selection and amazing topo maps are available at **Boreal Books**, 181 Mackenzie Rd. They also carry the coveted "We drove the Dempster Highway" bumperstickers. (☎777-3748. Open daily 10am-6pm.) **Free Internet access** at the **library**, 100 Mackenzie Rd., for 1hr. (☎777-2749. Open M-Th 10am-6pm and 7-9pm, F 10am-6pm, Sa-Su 2-5pm.) **Police:** ☎777-2935. **Ambulance:** ☎777-4444. **Inuvik Regional Hospital:** ☎777-8000.

ACCOMMODATIONS AND FOOD. The three hotels in town charge prices on the north side of outrageous. For an unparalleled Arctic experience, stay with twenty sled dogs at the **Arctic Chalet**. Walk your favorite dog in the summer or pay for a thrilling sled ride in the winter. Free canoe use; cars available. (Cozy single cabin $45; large cabins with kitchen, private toilet, and shared bathhouse from $85.) **Robertson's Bed and Breakfast**, 41 Mackenzie Rd., offers the cheapest rooms. (☎777-3111. Singles $70; doubles $80.) Pretty camping at **Chuk Campground**, right outside town. (☎777-3613. Showers, toilets. Sites $15, day use $5, electric hookups $20.) Caribou and musk-ox are northern meats to nibble in burger form, though the famed Arctic Char will cost you a pretty penny. The cheapest caribou and musk-ox burgers ($6-8) and greasy food at **To Go's**, 71 Mackenzie. (☎777-3030. Open M-Th 7am-midnight, F and Sa 9am-3am, Su 11am-11pm.) Try **The Backroom** and its take-out cousin **The Roost**, 120 MacKenzie, across from the Eskimo Inn, for variety, from heaping plates of Chinese food ($13.50), to the $12.50 caribou burger. (☎777-2727. Open daily in summer 5-11pm.) The **Cafe Gallery** serves baked goods (big muffins $2.50) and light lunches (sandwich and soup $10) in a studio with comfy chairs. (☎777-2888. Open M-Sa 8am-6pm, Su noon-6pm.) For a $7 breakfast and view of the **Igloo Church**, try **Sunriser Coffee Shop** at the Mackenzie hotel. (☎777-2861. Open daily 7am-6pm.) On a late night hit **The Zoo**, the Arctic's rowdy hotspot with tattooed bouncers and all in the Mackenzie Hotel. (Open daily 11am-2am. Dance party F and Sa.)

EVENTS AND OUTDOOR ACTIVITIES. Begun in 1989, the **Great Northern Arts Festival** brings over 100 artists and entertainers to Inuvik for performances, workshops, and a world-class art sale. (☎777-3536. July 12-21, 2002.) The festival draws the largest crowds of the year to Inuvik for workshops on braiding, carving and beading. The **Midnight Sun Tundra Nature Hike** (2hr. one-way) begins at the Marine Bypass Rd. on the north side of Inuvik and follows mountain ridges for 6km to **Three Mile Lake**. The ridges are a perfect spot to watch the sun in its lowest arc and to survey the **Richardson Range**. To explore the Mackenzie Delta contact **Western Arctic Adventures and Equipment**, 38 Sprucehill Dr. (☎777-2594), for canoes, kayaks, air charters, and trip-planning help. Canoes and kayaks can be "put in" behind the house for $35 a day with paddles, jackets, and friendly advice. **Arctic Nature Tours** (☎777-3300), beside the Igloo church, mobilizes outfitters and community contacts to lead nature and culture tours. Explore Inuvik (1½hr., $25); cruise the Mackenzie River and visit an Inuvialuit camp (4hr., 1hr. tour in camp, $75); tea and bannock with an elder (3½ hr., $65); or fly to Herschel Island Territorial Park to see abandoned whaling towns (5hr., $28). **Aurora Research College Research Centre** offers a naturalist's canoe tour of the Delta. At the research station, at Duck Lake St. and Mackenzie Rd., you can peruse the arctic library or catch a free slideshow on the region. (☎777-3838. Open M-F 8:30am-noon and 1-5pm. Tour 4hr.; summer M 6pm, Th 1pm; $32.)

THE LOST CITY OF INUVIK Around Inuvik, all the houses rest on pilings, though not, as one may suspect, to protect the abodes in case of flood. These high rises protect the ground and the precious permafrost beneath it from the heat houses radiate. Houses sitting on the ground risk melting the permafrost, thus sinking into their own foundations and gradually shrinking in height. The protective, temperamental permafrost, which varies in depth from a few centimeters to many meters, requires not only that houses be suspended awkwardly in the air, but also that water be kept in tanks above ground, so that the town does not disappear.

THE PANHANDLE

Southeast Alaska, known as "the Panhandle," spans 500 miles from the wet peaks of Misty Fiords National Monument (see p. 403), past the state capital of Juneau (see p. 418), to Skagway (see p. 430) and the foot of the Chilkoot Trail. Snow-capped coastal ranges separate it from the Interior and countless straits divide thousands of islands, inlets, and fjords, collectively known as the Inside Passage. Panhandle towns typically cling to narrow pockets of coast that provide little room for growth.

THE PANHANDLE'S HIGHLIGHTS

WRANGELL The ice-choked **Stikine River** and **Chief Shakes Hot Springs** are cold and hot, respectively, in a valley called a "Yosemite that keeps going..." (see p. 406).

JAM with folk fests, fiddles, and blues at **Juneau's Alaskan Hotel** (see p. 421).

EXPLORE hidden **Tlingit totem poles** in the forest around Sitka (p. 412).

SURF off the black sands, at Yakutat (see p. 435).

Boasting a mild, wet climate year-round, fantastic salmon runs, enormous halibut, the Tongass National Forest, and the largest old-growth temperate rainforest in the world, fishing and logging are the economic mainstays of the region. However, come summer, tourism is king. Cruise ships, charter boats, and ferries might clog the waterways, but it's still possible to slip away from the mayhem with a short hike to a quiet beach, cloud-swathed mountain, or lush rain forest. To avoid the cruise ship hordes (and the prices that go along with them) winter is the best time to travel. Unfortunately, many businesses close shop in winter due to little traffic. Wilderness camping is always free within the Tongass, and remote, well-maintained Forest Service cabins are a steal (from $25 per night), although many of these, along with some of the region's most vaunted sights—Misty Fiords, the Stikine River, LeConte Glacier, Glacier Bay—require fly-in or boat-in service. Such service can be expensive, but charter groups will often offer last-minute discounted fares for empty seats; good news for single travelers.

Russian fur-traders and missionaries made the Panhandle their headquarters in the 18th century. England, America, and British Columbia have all made claims to the area at one time or another. Much to their competitors' chagrin, the US trumped the game in 1867 by purchasing Alaska from Russia. Despite its European settlement, the Panhandle has truly been home to the Tlingit, Haida, and Tsimshian peoples. Traditionally divided into geographical areas called *kwaans*, many of the region's towns and villages are built upon these old Native settlements. Native culture and activism are very much alive in the Southeastern communities.

The Panhandle is accessible by boat and plane, but it is most often reached by the Alaska Marine Highway ferry system (see p. 398). The Alaska Marine Highway's late-night departures, delays, and occasional long layovers require patience and flexibility. By night, the deck is littered with mummy-bagged travelers camping under the stars to avoid pricey accommodations. By day, however, the views are spectacular—the Southeast is home to more bald eagles than anywhere else in the world and most of the humpback whales in the Pacific summer here.

KETCHIKAN ☎ 907

Ketchikan is the first stop in Alaska for cruise ships and would-be cannery workers and is popular despite its notoriously bad weather. An average of nearly 13½ ft. of "liquid sunshine" a year cannot deter visitors from enjoying the town's totem poles and rough n' tumble bar scene. Beyond the city limits, the Tongass National Forest and Misty Fiords National Monument (see p. 403) beckon outdoorsy types, or at least anyone willing to spend big bucks to see the wilderness from the window of a float plane or the deck of a charter boat.

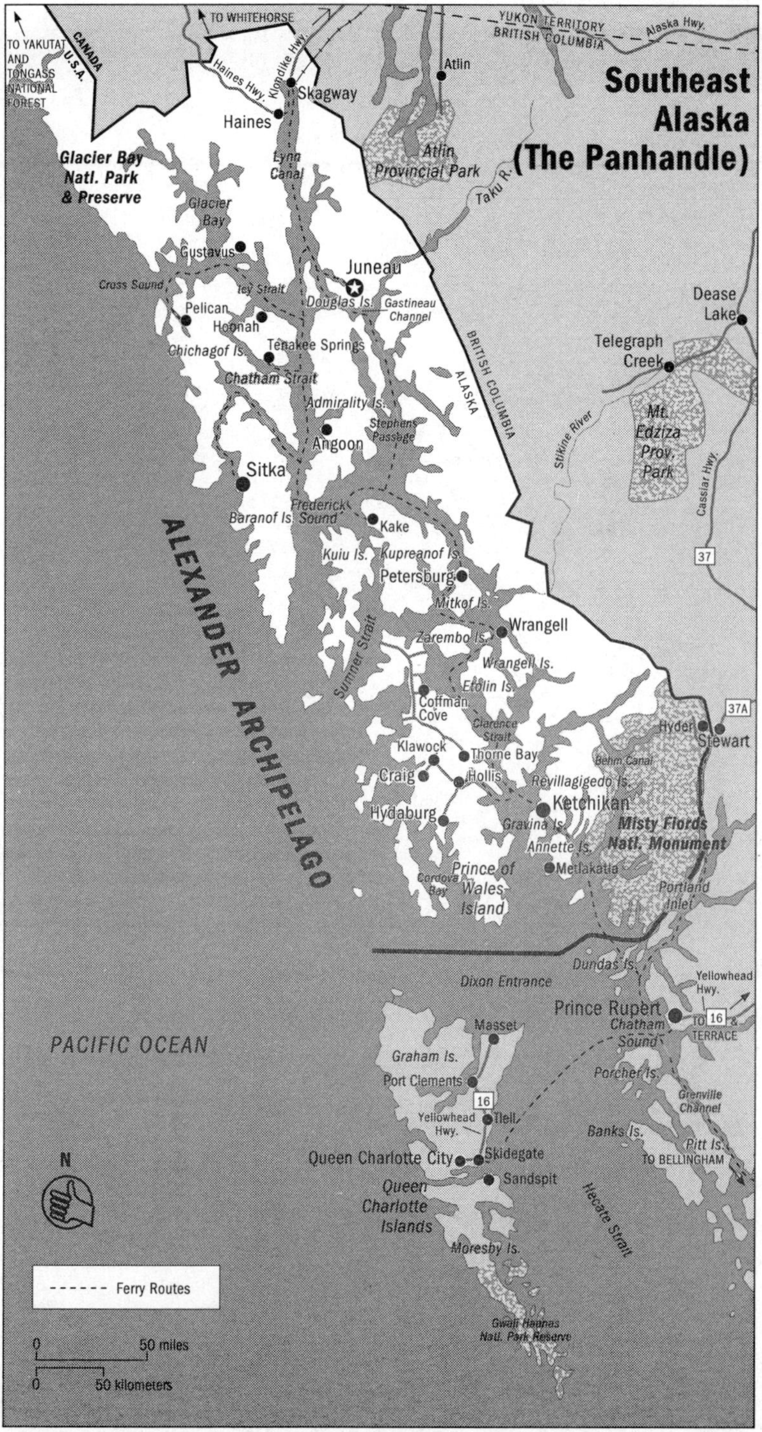
Southeast Alaska (The Panhandle)
TO WHITEHORSE
TO YAKUTAT AND TONGASS NATIONAL FOREST
CANADA
U.S.A.
YUKON TERRITORY
BRITISH COLUMBIA
Alaska Hwy.
Atlin
Haines Hwy.
Klondike Hwy.
Skagway
Haines
Glacier Bay Natl. Park & Preserve
Lynn Canal
Atlin Provincial Park
Taku R.
Glacier Bay
Gustavus
Juneau
Cross Sound
Icy Strait
Douglas Is.
Gastineau Channel
Pelican
Hoonah
Dease Lake
Chichagof Is.
Tenakee Springs
BRITISH COLUMBIA
ALASKA
Telegraph Creek
Chatham Strait
Admiralty Is.
Stephens Passage
Angoon
Stikine River
Mt. Edziza Prov. Park
Sitka
Cassiar Hwy.
Frederick Sound
Baranof Is.
Kake
ALEXANDER ARCHIPELAGO
Kuiu Is.
Kupreanof Is.
37
Petersburg
Mitkof Is.
Wrangell
Zarembo Is.
Sumner Strait
Wrangell Is.
Etolin Is.
Coffman Cove
37A
Hyder
Stewart
Clarence Strait
Klawock
Thorne Bay
Behm Canal
Craig
Hollis
Revillagigedo Is.
Hydaburg
Ketchikan
Gravina Is.
Misty Fiords Natl. Monument
Annette Is.
Metlakatla
Prince of Wales Island
Cordova Bay
Portland Inlet
Dundas Is.
Dixon Entrance
Yellowhead Hwy.
Prince Rupert
Chatham Sound
TO 16 & TERRACE
Masset
PACIFIC OCEAN
Graham Is.
Port Clements
Porcher Is.
Grenville Channel
16
Yellowhead Hwy.
Tlell
Banks Is.
Queen Charlotte City
Skidegate
Pitt Is.
TO BELLINGHAM
Sandspit
N
Queen Charlotte Islands
Hecate Strait
Moresby Is.
Ferry Routes
Gwaii Haanas Natl. Park Reserve
0
50 miles
0
50 kilometers

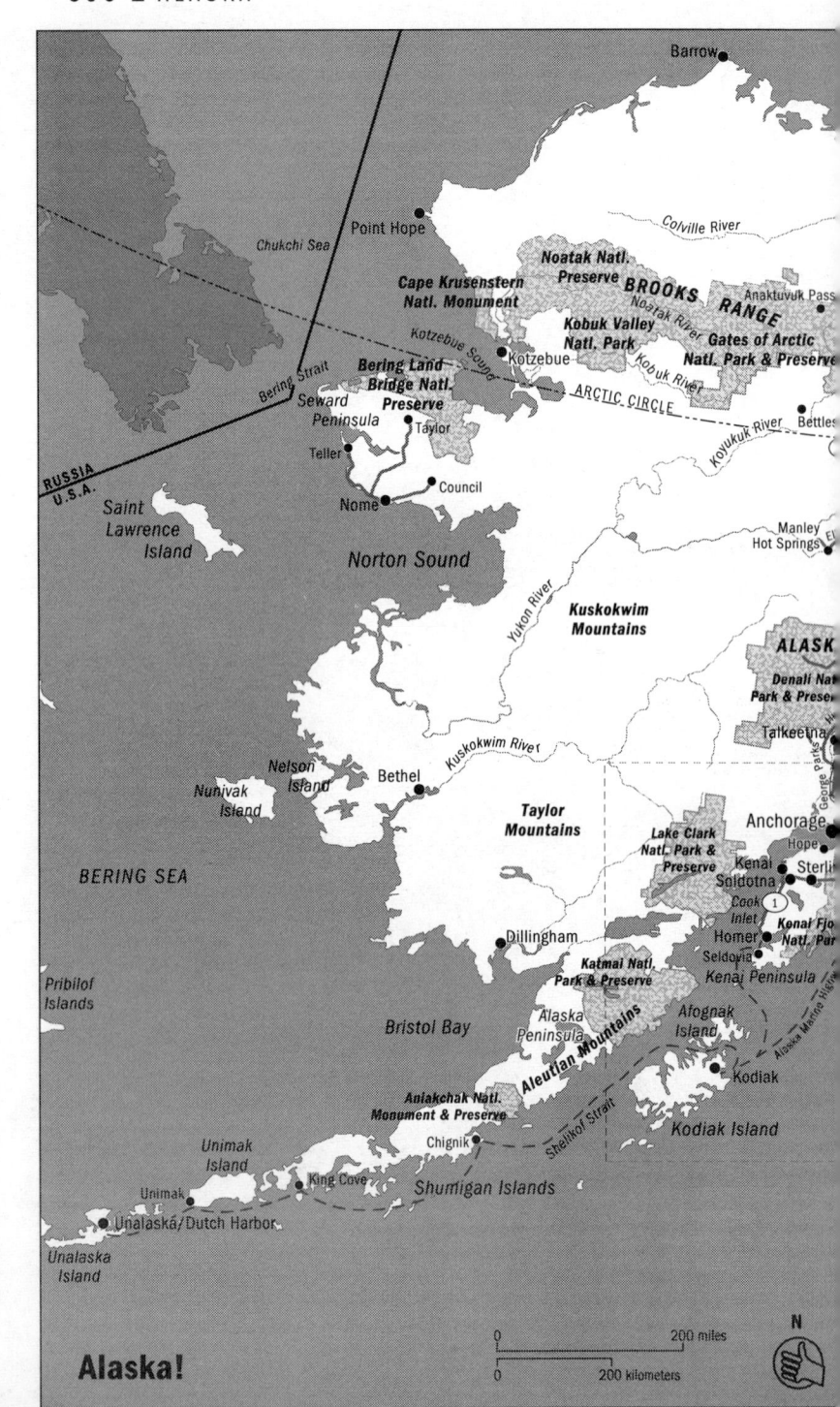

Alaska!

ARCTIC OCEAN
Beaufort Sea
Prudhoe Bay
Deadhorse
Mackenzie Bay
Tuktoyaktuk
Dalton Hwy.
Arctic National Wildlife Refuge
Arctic Village
ALASKA
YUKON TERRITORY
Inuvik
NORTHWEST TERRITORIES
8
Fort McPherson
Porcupine River
Fort Yukon
Beaver
Circle
U.S.A.
CANADA
Dempster Hwy.
Livengood
Steese Hwy.
Circle Hot Springs
6
5
YUKON TERRITORY
Fairbanks
Chena Hot Springs
Yukon-Charley Rivers Natl. Preserve
Eagle
Nenana
North Pole
Tanana River
Chicken
Hwy.
9
Dawson City
Delta Junction
Top-of-the-World Hwy.
Klondike Hwy
RANGE
Richardson Hwy
Taylor
2
5
6
Tok
Tetlin Junction
Denali Hwy
Mentasta Lake
Paxson
Tok Cutoff
4
Slana
2
Beaver Creek
Carmacks
Ross
Canol Rd
Campbell Highway
Glennallen
Nabesna
Faro
4
1
Copper Center
1
Burwash Landing
Chugach Mts.
Destruction Bay
Valdez
McCarthy/Kennicott
Haines Junction
Tagish Rd.
Whitehorse
Watson Lake
Cordova
Kluane Natl. Park
Carcross
Wrangell-Saint Elias National Park & Preserve
Chugach Natl. Forest
37
St. Elias Range
Atlin
Prince William Sound
Skagway
Yakutat
Haines
Cassiar Highway
Glacier Bay Natl. Park
Juneau
GULF OF ALASKA
Alaska Marine Highway
Gustavus
BRITISH COLUMBIA
Tenakee Springs
Chichagof Is.
Tongass Natl. Forest
Sitka
Petersburg
Wrangell
Baranof Is.
SEE SOUTHCENTRAL ALASKA MAP
Ketchikan
Prince of Wales Island
Metlakatla
PACIFIC OCEAN
SEE SOUTHEAST ALASKA MAP
Masset

398 ■ THE PANHANDLE

Ketchikan

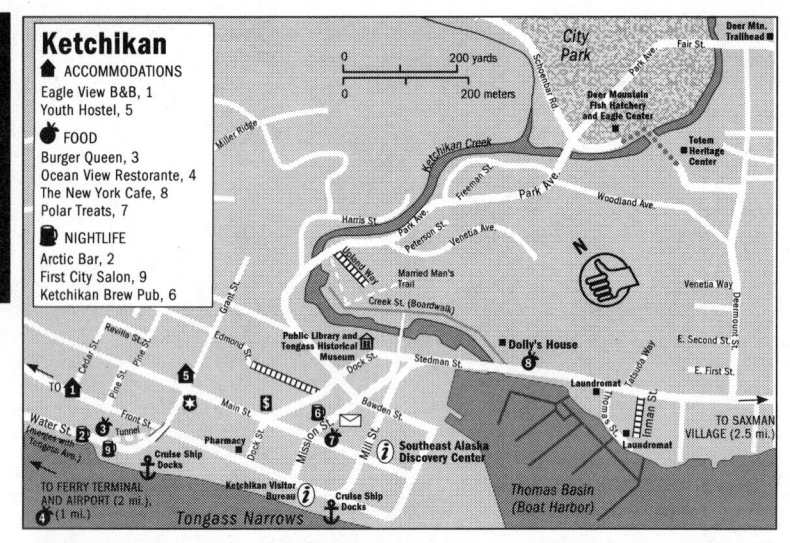

🏠 **ACCOMMODATIONS**
Eagle View B&B, 1
Youth Hostel, 5

🍴 **FOOD**
Burger Queen, 3
Ocean View Restorante, 4
The New York Cafe, 8
Polar Treats, 7

🍷 **NIGHTLIFE**
Arctic Bar, 2
First City Salon, 9
Ketchikan Brew Pub, 6

Three miles long and several hundred yards wide, Alaska's fourth-largest city with a population of approximately 14,800, stretches along the coast in typical Panhandle fashion. A revamped "historical district" is dressed for the tourists who support the newest growth industry, but parts of Ketchikan remain economically depressed. The adjustment to a tourism-based service economy has not been easy for many of the town's residents, who would prefer to turn back the clock to the days when fishing and logging were the only shows in town.

▌ TRANSPORTATION

Ketchikan rests on the west side of **Revillagigedo Island** (ruh-VIL-ya-GIG-a-doe), 235 mi. southeast of Juneau and 90 mi. northwest of Prince Rupert, BC. Reset your watch to Alaska Time, which is an hour behind Pacific Standard Time. Ketchikan caters to the travel elite, as evidenced by the location of the cruise ship docks (downtown) and the ferry docks (2 mi. north of town). Public transportation is inconvenient, but many sights are in walking distance. Renting a bike is a good idea to reach the sights outside of town.

Flights: A small ferry runs from the **airport,** across from Ketchikan on Gravina Island, to just north of the state ferry dock (every 30min., $2.50). From there, you can catch **"The Bus"** ($1.50, see below) or call a taxi ($9-10, see below) to get downtown. **Alaska Airlines** (☎800-225-2752), makes daily flights around Alaska and to **Juneau** (flights start at $100). **ProMech Air** (☎225-3845 or 800-860-3845), makes regular flights to Metlakatla, Prince of Wales Island, and other regional destinations. Much of the surrounding wilderness can be reached only by boat or float plane, for hire through the visitors center. **Island Wings** (☎225-2444 or 888-854-2444) and **Taquan Air** (☎225-8800 or 800-770-8800) will fly charter-flight routes for groups of 2 or more.

Ferries: Alaska Marine Highway (☎225-6181 or 800-642-0066; www.dot.state.ak.us), ferries dock 2 mi. north of the cruise ships on N Tongass Hwy. **"The Bus"** stops here (see below). To: **Wrangell** (5½hr., $24); **Juneau** (30hr., $74); and **Sitka** (18hr., $54).

Public Transportation: "The Bus" runs a loop between the airport parking lot near the ferry terminal, and the dock and Main St. downtown. Stops about every 3 blocks. M-Sa every 30min. 6am-9pm, Su every hr. 9am-3pm. $1.50; students, seniors, and children $1.25. Exact fare required. Schedules at visitors bureau (see **Visitor Info,** p. 399). A **free shuttle** runs from SEADC (see **Visitor Info,** p. 3) to **Walmart** every 30min.

Taxis: Alaska Cab (☎225-2133). **Sourdough Cab** (☎225-5544) and **Yellow Taxi,** (☎225-5555), offer charter rates ($25 per 30min.). From downtown to the ferry $8, downtown to Saxman $10. Check the Visitors Center for charter tours ($25 per 2hr.).

Car Rental: Alaska Car Rental (☎225-5000 or 800-662-0007), airport and in-town locations. Free local pick-up and delivery; unlimited mileage. Must be 21. **Southeast Auto Rental** ☎225-8778. Free delivery. Rates vary, but near $45 per day. Must be 25.

PRACTICAL INFORMATION

Visitor Information: 131 Front St. (☎225-6166 or 800-770-3300; www.visit-ketchikan.com), on the cruise ship docks. Offers maps, info and reservations on charter and touring companies, an ATM, public restrooms, and pay phones. Open daily 8am-5pm and when cruise ships are in. **Southeast Alaska Discovery Center (SEADC),** 50 Main St., is an essential stop for outdoor adventurers traveling anywhere in Southeast Alaska, with a housing trip planning room run by the **US Forest Service,** a bookstore, maps, brochures, and a knowledgeable staff. (☎228-6220; www.fs.fed.us/r10/tongass. Open May-Sept. daily 8am-5pm; Oct.-April Tu-Sa 8:30am-4:30pm.) **Southeast Reservations** (☎800-287-1607), does not contract with the cruise ships and is a good resource for finding high value in adventure trips.

Equipment Rental: Southeast Sea Kayaks (☎225-1258 or 800-287-1607), in the Visitors Center. Singles $35 per day, doubles $50 per day; cheaper rates for longer trips. $200 damage deposit. Trip planning available. **Alaska Wilderness Outfitting,** 3857 Fairview Ave. (☎225-7335), sells camping equipment and kits that include a Coleman stove, lantern, mess kit, cooler, and extras ($22 per day, $120 per week). Inflatable boats with outboard motors start at $82 per day. **Southeast Exposure,** 515 Water St. (☎225-8829). Bikes $6 per hr., $12 for 4hr., $22 per day. **The Great American Lumberjack Show** (☎225-9050 or 888-320-9049), on the boardwalk around the corner from the SEADC. Sportfishing equipment to use on-site ($20 per hr., $10 license). The brawny can also rent equipment to try lumberjack pole climbing ($10). Call ahead.

Bookstores: Village Source, 807 Water St. (☎225-7600). Open M-Sa 11:30am-5:30pm. **Parnassus** #5 Creek St. (☎225-7690) upstairs. M and Sa 9am-5pm, Tu-F 9am-6pm, Su 9am-3pm. **SEADC** also houses a bookstore (see above).

Laundromat/Public Showers: The Mat, 989 Stedman St. (☎225-0628), ¾ mi. from downtown, offers TV and play area. 10 lb. of laundry for $10. Showers $2.50 per 15min. Towels 75¢; soap 25¢. Open daily 6:30am-10pm. **Thomas Basin,** 124 Thomas St. (☎225-9274). Wash $2, dry $1.75, **Internet access** 25¢ per min., showers $2.90, espresso, snacks, and TV.

Weather: ☎800-472-0391.

Emergency: ☎911.

Police: ☎225-6631, at Main and Grant St. across from the hostel.

Pharmacy: Downtown Drugstore, 300 Front St. (☎225-3144). Open daily May-Sept. 8am-6:30pm, Oct.-Apr. 9:30am-6:30pm.

Hospital: Ketchikan General Hospital, 3100 Tongass Ave. (☎275-5171). 2 mi. north of town, just short of the ferry terminal.

Internet Access: Soapy's Station, 425 Water St. (☎247-9191), inside Sockeye Sam's by the tunnel. Open 8am-6pm or whenever a cruise ship is in. $3 per 15min., $5 per 50min. **Moggie's Mochas, Mugs & More,** 602 Dock St. $1 to log on, 10¢ per min. See **Thomas Basin,** above.

Post Office: (☎225-9601). Next to the ferry terminal. Open M-F 8:30am-5pm. There is a **substation** (☎225-7678), in the Great Alaskan Clothing building, on Mission St. near the library. Open M-Sa 9am-5:30pm. **ZIP Code:** 99901.

ACCOMMODATIONS AND CAMPING

Budget lodging is sparse in Ketchikan. The **Ketchikan Reservation Service** provides info on B&Bs. (☎ 800-987-5337; fax 247-5337. Singles from $69.) Few of these accommodations are wheelchair accessible. You'll have to hike or get a cab since the bus doesn't service these places. When you go, pack your tent and raingear, for as one local stated, "You won't catch a tan in Ketchikan." For more info on Forest Service campgrounds, call their reservations hotline (☎ 877-444-6777).

Ketchikan Youth Hostel (☎ 225-3319), at Main and Grant St. in the First Methodist Church. Two large dorms with cots available for families. Large kitchen and small bathrooms are impeccably clean. Free tea, cocoa, popcorn, and sometimes homemade cookies coax many to the common rooms at night. Linens $1.25. 4-night max. stay. Strict lockout from 9am-6pm, curfew 11pm. Open June-Aug. $10, nonmembers $13.

Eagle View Backpacker's Hostel, 2303 5th Ave. (☎ 225-5461). From Tongass, take Jefferson Ave. uphill, turn right on 5th Ave. Less than 1 mi. from ferry docks. Host Dale often meets guests at ferry. Kitchen, shared bath, deck, TV, and sauna. Great harbor views. 3 rooms with space for 5 males, 3 females, and one couple. Laundry $3 per load. Open Apr.-Oct., call for Nov.-Mar. $25 per person.

Signal Creek Campground (USFS), 5¼ mi. north of ferry dock, Mile 1.1 on Ward Lake Rd. Water, toilets, fire pits. Bring your fishing gear. Self-registration. Strict 14-day max. stay. Open early May to late Sept. Sites $10.

Last Chance Campground (USFS), 7½ mi. from the ferry dock, Mile 3 on Ward Lake Rd. Some wheelchair accessible sites. Self-registration. Reservations needed. Open late-May to early Sept. 19 RV-friendly sites $10.

FOOD

Grocery stores are your best bet for affordable food in this tourist town. **JR's**, closest to downtown at 407 Dock St., has a small selection. (Open daily 7am-11pm.) **Tatsuda's IGA**, at the corner of Stedman and Deermont stocks groceries, liquor, and deli products. (Open daily 7am-11pm.) **Carr's**, at the Plaza Shopping Center on Tongass near the ferry docks, is huge, has a pharmacy, and is open 24hr. Unless you catch your own, the salmon come at a price (starting at $17). If it's the salmon you came for, you're better off catching your own

Ocean View Restaurante, 1831 Tongass Ave. (☎ 225-7566). In a new location, this local favorite continues its tradition of good food and large portions, but now offers more seating and a gorgeous view. Italian and Mexican specialties start at $7. Free chips and salsa. If your view is better at home, they'll deliver. Reservations recommended. Open daily 11am-11pm.

New York Cafe, 207 Stedman St. (☎ 225-1800). At the south end of Creek St. Come for the incredible soup and healthy lunch specials (around $8) in this comfortable place to bide your time when locked out of the hostel. There is always a veggie option. Live music F-Sa nights. Internet access. Open M-F 6am-10pm, Sa-Su 6am-11pm.

Polar Treats, 410 Mission St. (☎ 247-6527). Tasty wraps and panini with veggie options ($7). Order half of the huge portion ($3.50) so you have room for the handmade ice cream. Will deliver for $1. Open M-F 11am-6pm, Sa-Su 11am-4pm.

Burger Queen, 518 Water St. (☎ 225-6060). North side of the tunnel. The best burgers in town were served out of a truck for 15 years. Now they are served in a building with less character but more seating. Get your burger ($5-8) delivered across the street to the Arctic Bar for a harbor view. Open daily 11am-7pm.

NIGHTLIFE AND ENTERTAINMENT

Among other works, Ketchikan's **First City Players** perform the bawdy *Fish Pirate's Daughter*, a melodrama about Prohibition-era Ketchikan, to sell-out crowds at the Main St. Theatre, 338 Main St. (☎ 225-4792. July-Aug. F 8pm, $15, students $12.) The annual **Timber Carnival** enlivens a boisterous 4th of July with speed-chopping, axe-throwing, and other fantastic lumberjack feats. On the second Saturday in August, the **Blueberry Arts Festival** brings art, food, music, and wackiness to the streets, when locals compete in slug races and chewing gum competitions

- **First City Saloon** (☎ 225-1494), ¼ mi. north of the tunnel on Water St. The youngest and most spacious hangout in town, where Guinness and a variety of microbrews are distributed liberally. Live local music Tu-Su. Open daily noon-2am.
- **Ketchikan Brew Pub,** 602 Dock St. (☎ 247-5221). The only beer brewed in town. With true local flavor, the owner Kevin hand-picks Sitka Spruce tips grown in Ketchikan, and steeps them in Spruce Tip Beer. The X-Tra Tuff is another favorite brew, served in winter and named after the rubber boots you'll see the locals sporting. If you bring any bottle that seals, they'll fill it for your beer-to-go. Open M-Sa 10am-2am, Su 12:30pm-2am.
- **Arctic Bar** (☎ 225-4709). A hop, skip, and stagger north of the downtown tunnel. Distinguished by their copulating bears logo. This is one of Ketchikan's most popular bars because of its deck with harbor view. Open daily until 2am.

SIGHTS

Every summer day, thousands of travelers tumble down gangplanks into Ketchikan, narrowly escaping horse-drawn carriages and charter fishing boats. The official walking tour does little to improve the lot of disoriented tourists, although the town has much to offer.

SAXMAN TOTEM PARK. Ketchikan's primary cultural attraction and Alaska's largest collection of totems. A Tlingit village founded in 1894, Saxman was only accessible by boat until a few decades ago. The community's longhouse is surrounded with brightly colored recent and historic carvings up to 150 years old. Each pole's story is described in a $1 guide, available at the **Saxman Arts Co-op** down the hill. Come during the day to view master carvers working at the **Edwin C. Dewitt Carving Center** next door to the park. *(2½ mi. SW of town on Tongass Hwy.; a short ride on the highway bike path or a $10 cab. Wheelchair accessible. Always open. Free.)*

TOTEM POLES. Totem Heritage Center presents 33 original 19th century totem poles and fragments collected within a 50 mi. radius of Ketchikan in their raw, unrestored state. This serves as an excellent introduction to totem carving traditions. *(Up Park St. on the hill above downtown. Open May-Sept. daily 8am-5pm; Oct.-Apr. Tu-F 1-5pm. Wheelchair accessible. $4.)* For more totem madness, check out the **Totem Bight State Historical Park** where totems look out from a more natural setting of forest to the sea. This is the only site in the area that allows visitors through an old longhouse. The structure of the longhouse was designed so that it could be taken apart and moved in one day with only the totems remaining. Consider biking and packing a picnic, since taxis operate on exorbitant charter rates of $55 round-trip. Go early to beat the tour buses. *(10 mi. north of the ferry docks on the N Tongass Hwy. Wheelchair accessible. Free.)*

DOLLY'S HOUSE. A remnant of Ketchikan's more colorful past. Dolly was the most famous Madame in the thriving red-light district where, as tour guides quip, sailors and salmon went upstream to spawn. Antiques sit in caches where she used to bootleg liquor during police raids. A woman of many talents, Dolly created the flowers on her shower curtain out of colored silk condoms from France. The Madame used to charge $3 to go upstairs. It now costs the blushing tourist $4. *(24 Creek St. ☎ 225-6329. Open daily 8am-5pm.)*

DEER MOUNTAIN TRIBAL HATCHERY AND EAGLE CENTER. Hatchery run by the Ketchikan Indian Corporation and offers a glimpse into modern fishing raise and release practices. Their pair of token captive eagles do little to protect the hatchery from the hoards of tourists that descend in late summer. Come in mid- to late June to see the adult salmon return. Hold your nose in July as the carcasses dry on shore. *(Located across the creek from the Totem Heritage Center. ☎ 225-6761. In summer open daily 8:30am-4:30pm. Wheelchair accessible. $7, $10 with admission to Totem Heritage Center.)*

OUTDOOR ACTIVITIES

The wilderness around Ketchikan offers boundless opportunities for the fisher, hiker, or kayaker. The SEADC Trip Planning room (see **Visitor Info,** p. 399) makes a great first stop. The US Forest Service (☎877-444-6767) maintains **cabins** ($25-45 per night) and **shelters** in the Tongass National Forest that can be reserved in advance. Be patient with the inefficient reservation system and act quickly; these cabins fill up fast. Many cabins are accessible only by boat or float plane.

HIKING. Many of the fishing, swimming, and outdoor activities are found along the hiking trails. Because the trail difficulty ranges from easy walk to strenuous climb, a tourist of any experience level can find a suitable trail.

Deer Mountain Trail (2½ mi. or 10 mi.). Walk ½ mi. up Ketchikan Lakes Rd. to the junction and the landfill. Turn left towards the mountain. Most hikers stop after 2½ mi., but the trail continues for 7½ more mi. past Blue Lake, John Mountain, Little Silvis Lake, and Beaver Falls Fish Hatchery to emerge 12 mi. south of Ketchikan at the Beaver Falls Powerhouse parking lot. During the latter 7½ mi., snow and ice remain even in the summer and the trail is less maintained. A steep climb yielding sparkling rewards, it gains 3350 ft. to the highest point. An A-frame cabin between Deer Mountain and John Mountain can be reserved through the Forest Service (☎877-444-6767). Open June-Sept.

Perseverance Lake Trail (2½ mi.). 100 ft. past the entrance to the 3C's Campground. A less strenuous, more family-oriented hike that climbs the 450 ft. to Perseverance Lake. The trail passes through muskeg, Sitka spruce, hemlock, and cedar, and the lake is great for trout fishing. Open Mar.-Nov.

Ward Lake (1 mi.). Head to the Signal Creek Campground for this easy walk around the grassy pond. Once there, outdoors activities abound. Bikers can explore surrounding logging roads; swimmers can take a dip in the cold pond; tanners lie on the sandy beach; and eaters feast at the picnic tables. Open year-round.

KAYAKING. A good secluded kayak route winds through the Naha Recreation Area to Jordan Lake on the northern part of the island. (See SEADC for more suggestions.) Southeast Sea Kayaks (see Practical Information, p. 399) picks up and drops off kayakers anywhere on the Ketchikan roads for $15 per person each way.

FLIGHTSEEING. Taquan Air will let you fly with the mail plane for cheaper rates than most. Ask for the Bush Pilot Tour to Hyder for the best viewing. Michelle at **Island Wings** will fly hikers and explorers to and from their trails or cabins. She is just as knowledgeable about the cabins as the Forest Service Personnel. *(Taquan Air starts at $89; Island Wings at $160. See Flights, p. 398.)*

METLAKATLA ☎907

Fifteen minutes by float plane from Ketchikan's cruise ship docks, Metlakatla, or "calm channel where the fog drifts in and out" in Tsimshian (SIM-she-an), is perched on the western flatlands of the **Annette Islands Reserve.** The Metlakatla Indian Community (pop. 1,603) is the island's only settlement and the state's only Native American reservation. The community struggled after losing its timber industry and is transitioning to the possibilities of mining, while trying to attract tourists to learn about their native culture. Sites such as the Fish Packing Company, Duncan Cottage Museum, and the Longhouse are open to tourists only during tours. **Traditional tribal dancing** is the finale worth waiting for. Tours are generally scheduled under contracts for cruise ships and run at varying times that often clash with the ferry and flight schedules. (Call the Tourist Director's Office in advance ☎886-8687, M-F 8am-4:30pm, $40). The view from atop **Yellow Hill** (named for the unique color of its rusting iron ore deposits) offers splendid vistas of Annette Island and a glimpse of Ketchikan on a clear day. The boardwalk trail begins 2 mi. out of town on Airport Rd. If overnighting, a permit is required, though the requirement is seldom enforced. **Uncle Fred's Inn** (☎886-5007), on Western Ave., past the long house, has attractive rooms for $85. **Camping** is free and generally acceptable out of sight of the road. Check with the **Municipal Offices** (☎ 886-4441), on Upper Milton St. first and tell the Metlakatla police where you are going.

Pro-Mech Air flies several 15min. trips a day from Ketchikan to "Met"; frequency and number vary, so call ahead. (In Metlakatla ☎ 886-3845, in Ketchikan ☎ 225-3845 or 800-860-3845. $66 round-trip, offers specials.) **Pacific Airways** (☎ 225-3500 or 877-360-3500) runs fewer flights for $45 round-trip. The **Alaska Marine Highway** (☎ 800-624-0066; www.dot.state.ak.us) visits the island six times a week and twice on Saturdays (1¼hr., $14). The ferry terminal is a short walk from town.

MISTY FIORDS NATIONAL MONUMENT ☎ 907

The jagged peaks, plunging valleys, and dripping vegetation of **Misty Fiords National Monument,** 20 mi. east of Ketchikan, make biologists dream and outdoor enthusiasts drool. Only accessible by kayak, power boat, or float plane, the 2.3-million-acre monument offers superlative camping, kayaking, hiking, and wildlife viewing. Walls of sheer granite, scoured and scraped by retreating glaciers, rise up to 3000 ft. and encase 3000 ft. deep saltwater bays. More than 12 ft. of annual rainfall and a flood of runoff from large icefields near the Canadian border feed the streams and waterfalls that empty into two long fjords, **Behm Canal** (117 mi.) and **Portland Canal** (72 mi. and one of wold's largest), on either side of the monument.

KAYAKING. Seasoned **kayakers** navigate the harsh currents between Ketchikan and Behm Canal and paddle straight into the monument. Transportation into the Fjords is provided by **Southeast Sea Kayaks** (see **Equipment Rental,** p. 399). They charge $150-300 for a drop-off and pickup at the entrance to the Fjords. A trip planning package, including maps and information on the area, is also available from them ($16). If there is room onboard, **Alaska Cruises,** 220 Front St. will shuttle kayakers into the Fjords. (☎ 225-6044. $200 for drop at the mouth of Rudyard Bay. Call ahead.) The folks at SEADC are a great resource for planning the trip yourself (see **Visitor Info,** p. 399). **Walker Cove, Punchbowl Lake,** and **Rudyard Bay,** off Behm Canal, are choice destinations for paddlers, although the waters are frigid and wide stretches of the coast lack good shelter or dry firewood.

CAMPING. Wilderness camping is permitted throughout the monument, and the Forest Service maintains four remote, free, first come, first served shelters and 14 cabins ($25). Steep hiking trails lead from cabins closer to the wildlife. Call far in advance to the **Misty Fiords Ranger Station** (☎ 225-2148) to help choose a cabin, or talk to the folks at SEADC (see **Visitor Info,** p. 399). To reserve cabins, call the Forest Service Hotline (☎ 877-444-6777).

PRINCE OF WALES ISLAND ☎ 907

Prince of Wales Island sits less than 30 mi. west of Ketchikan, beneath a thick temperate rainforest canopy broken by mountain peaks, patches of muskeg, and swaths of clear-cutting. **Tongass National Forest** and Native American tribal groups manage most of the island's real estate, which is criss-crossed with logging roads. Much of the island remains covered in virgin forest, while a fraction is regrowing.

Although it is difficult to access the pristine corners of the island, a Prince of Wales experience is not complete without a trip into the bush to one of the many remote forest service cabins. On an island this large–smaller only than Hawaii and Kodiak in the US—exploration requires a set of wheels. The 1800 mi. of logging roads are perfect for mountain biking or tooling around in an all-terrain vehicle. Rentals on the island are expensive; bring a bike or truck over on the ferry. Pricey charter companies reel in hunters, kayakers, and scuba divers, although independent travelers can set off on their own with maps and some help from the Forest Service (see **Accommodations,** below). Acquire permits for fishing and hunting, and know where tribal lands end and National Forest begins.

404 ■ THE PANHANDLE

There are three main towns on Prince of Wales: **Craig, Klawock,** and **Thorne Bay.** Craig is on the west side of the island with most of the tourist resources. The tribal community of Klawock lies 7 mi. north, while the more remote town of Thorne Bay is 43 mi. east of Klawock on the other side of the island. **Hollis,** where the ferry docks, is 31 mi. east of Craig and has only a mini-mart and a library. Come with a means of getting to Craig or call a taxi service. Craig was originally named "Fish Egg" for its commercial origins in the caviar industry. Services here cater to big-time fishermen and hunters who fork over lots of cash in exchange for the chance to take Black Bear or King Salmon trophies home with them. Others use Craig as a starting point for their exploration of Prince of Wales Island.

☏ TRANSPORTATION. Float planes fly directly into Craig from Ketchikan, although schedules vary; call for more detailed information. **Promech Air** (☏ 826-3845 or 800-860-3845) flies the route for $99 each way. **Pacific Airways** (☏ 877-360-3500) makes the trip for $89, but they offer fewer flights. The **Alaska Marine Highway** runs from Ketchikan to Hollis. (☏ 826-343; www.dot.state.ak.us. 2¾hr.; daily in summer; $24, ages 2-11 $12, car $41.) The new **Interisland Ferry** makes the 2½hr. route daily from Ketchikan. **Jackson Cab** (☏ 755-2557) runs between Hollis and Craig for about $25. **Klawock, Craig, Hollis Transporter** (☏ 826-3151; pager 755-3602) charges $25 for one person, but only $18 per person for two or more people. Call ahead for pick up, and leave plenty of extra time to get where you are going. **Holiday Rentals,** located at the TLC laundromat, rents cars for $50 per day plus 30¢ per mi. or for $75 per day with unlimited mileage. They also rent small skiffs (14 ft.) with an eight horsepower motor for $50 per day. (☏ 826-2966. Open daily 8am-8pm.) **Wilderness Rent-a-Car** located in Klawock, rents 4x4s. (☏ 800-949-2205 or 755-2691. $59 per day, 30¢ for every mile over 100 mi. Minimum age 25.) **Log Cabin Sporting Goods,** 1 Easy St., rents canoes and kayaks. You can also get your **hunting and fishing licenses** here. (☏ 826-2205. Open M-Sa 9am-5:30pm, Su 10am-4pm. Canoes $20 per day; single kayaks $40, doubles $50.)

🛈 PRACTICAL INFORMATION. Visitor information is available from the **Forest Service Office.** They give the skinny on caves, camping, 20 wilderness cabins, and recreation sites on the island at 9th Ave. and Main St. Craig. (☏ 826-3271. Open M-F 7am-5pm.) More info is available at the **Prince of Wales Chamber of Commerce** in Craig on Easy St. (☏ 826-3870. Open Tu-F 9am-4pm.) The **Wells Fargo Bank** (☏ 826-3040), by the post office on Craig-Klawock Hwy., in Craig and **Klawock IGA** have **ATMs. Voyageur Bookstore,** on Cold Storage Rd. in the Southwind Plaza deals in cappuccinos, books, music, and has **Internet** availability. (☏ 826-2333. Open M-F 7:30am-7pm, Sa 9am-7pm, Su 10am-5pm.) The **library** (☏ 826-3281) on 3rd St., has **free Internet access** if you sign up in advance. **TLC Laundromat** (See **Accommodations,** below) also has Internet access. (Open Tu-F 10-noon and 1-5pm, Sa noon-3pm. 300min. card for $20.) **Brown Bear** is a convenience store that also sells fishing gear. (Open daily 4am-midnight, in Klawock off the highway). **Emergency:** ☏ 911. **Police:** (☏ 826-3330), opposite the library. **State Police:** ☏ 755-2918. **Alicia Roberts Medical Clinic** (☏ 755-4800), is in Klawock, off the highway. **Post Office:** on Craig-Klawock St. beside the Thompson Supermarket. (☏ 826-3298. Open M-F 8:30am-5pm, Sa noon-2pm.) **ZIP Code:** 99921.

🛏 ACCOMMODATIONS AND CAMPING. Although most of the island falls within the free camping zone of Tongass National Forest, Craig is surrounded by private tribal lands where camping is **prohibited.** The **TLC Laundromat and Rooms,** on Cold Storage Rd. behind the supermarket, offers affordable, inviting slumber space with shared bath and public showers. (☏ 826-2966. Singles $40, doubles $50. Wash $2, dry 25¢ per 5min. Showers $2.50 per 5min. Open M-Sa 7am-8pm.) **Fish, Fur, and Feathers** (☏ 826-2309), behind the big fence on Beach Rd. in Craig, is a B&B offering doubles for $55 a night with a private bath. Other B&Bs start at $90. Call the Chamber of Commerce for information (See **Visitors Information,** p. 405).

Visits to **Tongass National Forest** may last up to one month, as long as campers spend no longer than two weeks at any one site. Contact the **Forest Service Station** in Craig (see **Practical Information,** above) or **Thorne Bay** (☎ 828-3304) for more information on the 20 **wilderness cabins** they maintain. (Advance reservations required. ☎ 877-444-6777; www.reserveusa.com. $25-45 per night.) A few cabins are road or trail accessible, but most are only reachable by boat or float plane. The Forest Service maintains two campgrounds on Prince of Wales Island: the newly built **Harris River Campground,** halfway between Hollis and Craig, and the **Eagle's Nest Campground,** halfway between Craig and Thorne Bay. Both campgrounds have toilets, water, cooking grates, picnic tables, and RV parking (sites $8 in summer).

❒ FOOD. Dockside, at the corner of Third and Front St., serves breakfast and lunch. Standard fare is massive omelettes for $6 and burgers for $7, but people come from near and far for their famous homemade pie for $3. (Open M-F 6am-3pm, Sa and Su 6am-9pm.) **Ruth Ann's,** on Front St., has affordable breakfast and lunch options ($6-8), but dinner prices skyrocket upwards of $18. (☎ 826-3377. Open daily 7am-9pm.) Find your (expensive) groceries at **Thompson House Supermarket** where you'll also find a salad bar, a deli, and a good spread of fruits and veggies. (☎ 826-3394. Open M-Sa 7:30am-8pm, Su 9am-7pm. On Craig-Klawock St.) **Papa's Pizza** in Craig is the only pizza joint in town, also serving hot sandwiches. 16 in. pie $14. Will deliver. (☎ 826-2244). **Healthy Generations** on Easy St. has a small menu for lunch ($6-10) as well as a natural foods and a vitamin selection.(☎ 826-4200 Open M-F 8am-6pm, Sa 10am-6pm).

OUTDOOR ACTIVITIES

HIKING. Although there isn't much hiking around town, the **Mt. Sunnahae Trail** (2hr.) connects with a boardwalk that goes all the way to the top of the mountain. Though often very slippery, the trail provides quality views. To get there, go out the road about one-quarter mile toward Klawock, and look for it on the left side of the road at the end of one of the guardrails. **One Duck Trail** (1½ mi.) is a short hike that climbs a steep 1200 ft. to outstanding views of the Klawock Mountains. It is off the Hydaburg Rd. 2 mi. south of the intersection with the Hollis-Klawock Hwy. A 3-sided shelter is located at the edge of the alpine vegetation zone. Contact Craig Parks and Recreation for more hiking ideas and trail conditions info (☎ 826-3405).

KAYAKING AND DIVING. Craig offers several locations to **launch kayaks** to tour Graveyard Island, Fish Egg Island, and Ballenas Islands. The **Sarkar** is a 15 mi. loop route which accesses five major lakes within a roadless area. The **Craig Dive Center,** offers a two-tank dive for groups of four. For canoe and kayak rentals in Craig, go to **Log Cabin Sporting Goods** (see **Transportation,** p. 404). **Launch kayaks** from the boat ramp at North Cove, the beach by the helipad on the south side of "old town", and the City Park on and near Graveyard Island. Contact Craig Ranger District for more ideas and tide conditions. **Sarkar** parking area is on Road 2050 in the parking lot for Sarkar Cabin. **Craig Dive Center** at 1st and Main St., in Craig ☎ 826-3481 or 800-380-3483. $125 per person.

SPELUNKING. One of the deepest known caves in North America, **El Capitan Cave** is one of the most striking sights of the island. There speleologists recently found grizzly bear bones, dated about 12,295 years old. Steep stairs lead to the cave entrance. Free 2hr. tours start behind the gate 150 ft. inside the cave, and require a hard-hat and flashlight (hard-hat provided, you provide the flashlight.) It's cold and damp inside, so dress accordingly. The cave is a 3hr. drive from Craig or Thorne Bay. Follow Forest Road 20 to Forest Road 15 and take a left for about a mile to the cave. (☎ 828-3304. Tours late May to early Sept. Th-Sa 9-11am, noon-2pm, 2-4pm; Children under seven not permitted. Call ahead for a schedule of tours and to make reservations with the Thorne Bay Ranger's Office.)

WRANGELL ☎ 907

Wrangell sits strategically on the wild and swift Stikine River, the fastest navigable river in North America. Wrangell is equally identified for its history of turbulent people, who sought the value of such a strong trading position. Petroglyphs from 2000-8000 years ago mark the first settlers of this region, the Tlingit, who prospered here because of the rich resources and "the great river" and remained here through Russian, British, and American rule, until fur traders and gold seekers took over the boisterous town. In 1879, John Muir described the town as "a lawless draggle of wooden huts," but revelled in calling the Stikine "a Yosemite that just kept going and going." Wrangell is now home to a community of about 2500, mostly loggers and fishermen, still in awe of the mighty Stikine. Hunters, kayakers, and trekkers are drawn to Wrangell's high mountains, filled with wildlife and surrounded by the blue ice of glaciers.

Anyone emerging from the ferry will probably first notice the row of children selling garnets. The first all-women's corporation in America mined these garnets to make hat pins and later sold to Fred Hanford, the mayor of Wrangell, who then willed the garnet mines to the Boys Scouts and the children of Wrangell. Many of the children here earn enough money for college by mining and selling the garnets. The town's attractions are convenient enough for a brief visit during a ferry layover, but plentiful enough to merit a longer stay. Note that locals take their day of rest very seriously: almost everything is closed on Sunday.

TRANSPORTATION

Wrangell rests on the northern tip of 30 mi. long Wrangell Island, 85 mi. north of Ketchikan, and 150 mi. south of Juneau. It is small and easily walkable. The **ferry** docks are at the north end of town; the **airport** is a mile and a half east, over the hill.

Flights: Alaska Air (☎874-3308 or 800-426-0333) is the only carrier with regular air service to and from Wrangell. Daily flights to: **Petersburg** ($87); **Juneau** ($129); and **Ketchikan** ($111). **Sunrise Aviation** (☎874-2319) offers flightseeing over the Stikine River ($300).

Ferries: Alaska Marine Highway (☎874-2021 or 800-642-0066), at Stikine Ave. and McCormack St. Frequent service to: **Sitka** (13hr., $42); **Juneau** (13-26hr., $62); and **Ketchikan** (6hr., $26). Open 1hr. before arrivals. Lockers 25¢.

Taxis: Star Cab (☎874-3622) and **Northern Lights Taxi** (☎874-4646). $5 to the airport, $8-10 to the Rainbow Falls Trail.

Car Rental: Practical Rent-A-Car (☎874-3975; fax 874-3911), on Airport Rd. near the airport. Compacts $43 per day, vans $55 per day; unlimited mileage. Must be 21.

PRACTICAL INFORMATION

Visitor Information: Chamber of Commerce (☎874-3901; www.wrangell.com), on Front St. by the cruise ship docks. Open M-F 10am-4pm or whenever a cruise ship is in. A huge calendar across the street lists events.

Outdoor Information: District Forest Service Station, 525 Bennett St. (☎874-2323), ½ mi. east of town, off Church St. and past the hospital. Maps and info on hiking, canoeing, kayaking. Provides information on local Forest Service cabins. Open M-F 8am-5pm.

Alaska Department of Fish and Game (☎874-3822), in the green Kadin Building on Front St., experts on available hunting and fishing. Call ahead for hours. **Ottesen's True Value** (☎874-3377), on Front St., sells licenses. Open M-Sa 8am-6pm, Su 10am-3pm.

Equipment Rental: Solo Cat Sports (☎877-874-2923), operates from the **Wrangell Tours** booth across from the Chamber of Commerce and is the place in town to rent kayaks. Singles $8 per hour, $28 for half-day, $40 per day. Canoes $36 for half-day, $52 per day. Bikes $9 per hour, $21 per day.

Internet Access: Library (☎874-3535), on Second St. Free, but must sign up ahead. Open M and F 10-noon and 1-5pm, Tu-Th 1-5pm and 7-9pm, Sa 9am-5pm.

Laundromat and Public Showers: Churchill Laundromat, on Front, near Shakes Island. Wash $2, dry 25¢. New machines. Showers $2.50 per 10min. Open daily 8am-8pm. **Thunderbird Laundromat,** 233 Front St. (☎874-3322). Same prices. Open daily 6am-8pm.

Emergency: ☎911.

Police: ☎874-3304. In the Public Safety Building on Zimovia Hwy.

Pharmacy: Stikine Drug, 202 Front St. (☎874-3422). Open M-F 10am-5pm, Sa 10am-2pm.

Hospital: ☎874-3356. At Bennett St. and 2nd Ave.

Post Office: (☎874-3714), at the north end of Front St. Open M-F 8:30am-5pm, Sa 11am-1pm. **ZIP Code:** 99929.

ACCOMMODATIONS AND CAMPING

Although it lacks the cruise ships and upscale hotels common in other Southeastern towns, Wrangell's accommodations are no more friendly to the pocketbook of the ferry traveler. Prices at some of the **B&Bs** are reasonable; call the **Chamber of Commerce** (see **Visitors Info,** above) for a list. If you've got a car or other means of transportation, well-maintained, well-located, free Forest Service campgrounds are the way to go. **Shoemaker Bay,** 5 mi. south of town, accommodates tenters and RVs. **Nemo,** 14 mi. south on Zimovia Hwy., sits on a ridge with breathtaking views of Zimovia Strait and the surrounding area. **Free forest service shelters** are first come, first served and are located only a few miles up the trail from the **Rainbow Falls trailhead** (see **Outdoor Activities,** below).

Wrangell Hostel, 220 Church St. (☎874-3534), 5 blocks from the ferry terminal in the Presbyterian Church; just look for the neon cross. Showers, kitchen, and common room with TV/VCR. Hostelers may join the men's group for a hot breakfast and Jesus talk, W. at 7am No daytime lockout. 11pm curfew extended for late ferry arrivals. Closed Sept. to early Jun. 20 foam mats on the floor $15.

Rooney's Roost (☎874-2026), at the corner of McKinnon and Church St., 4 blocks from the ferry terminal. Better looking on the inside than the outside, each of the rooms is decorated in rich color and has a unique personality. Large common rooms, big-screen TV. Full breakfast included. Free rides to airport and ferry. Call ahead for reservations. Single $60; double $75; double with private bath $95.

City Park, 1½ mi. south of town on Zimovia Hwy., immediately beyond the cemetery and baseball field. Picnic tables, shelters, drinking water, toilets, and a beautiful view of the water. One-day max. stay. Open Memorial Day to Labor Day. 8 free sites.

FOOD

Wrangell has limited food options, especially for vegetarians or picky eaters; the standard in town is pizza and burgers. Bobs' **IGA Supermarket,** 223 Brueger St. (☎874-2341), off Outer Dr., has groceries and the cheapest sandwiches in town for $3-5. (Open M-Sa 8am-8pm.) For bulk health food, head to **Homestead Natural Foods** (☎874-3462), half a mile north of town on Evergreen Ave., on the way to the petroglyphs. Call first on nice days in case Rosemary decides to close up and go kayaking. In June, vendors barbecued lunch specials to support the three Wrangell teenagers running to be 4th of July "Queen." **Diamond C Cafe** is local spot for early morning coffee and gossip. Specializes in breakfast; a plate of eggs and pancakes cost $6. (At Front St. and Outer Dr. ☎874-3677. Open daily 5am-3pm.)

408 ■ THE PANHANDLE

👁 SIGHTS AND EVENTS

There are a few worthwhile cultural attractions in town that could easily be seen in a day. Otherwise, the town has little to offer and travelers linger on the 9-hole golf course, along the river, or on hiking trails.

SHAKES ISLAND. If the ferry schedule gives you only 45min. in Wrangell, a walk out to Shakes Island is your best bet. Here you'll find a replica of turn-of-the-century Tlingit Chief Shakes's **tribal longhouse,** built during the Depression by the Civilian Conservation Corps without the aid of a sawmill or a single nail. Surrounding the longhouse are replicated **totem poles.** The ashes of Chief Shakes' nephew were placed in the original Bear totem pole. *(Walk south on Front St. toward the edge of town, past the Marine Bar, and when Front turns into Shakes St., follow it to the bridge and walk across. Contact Margaret (☎874-3747). Longhouse usually opens 30min. after a cruise ship docks. $2, by appointment $10. Totems can be visited anytime at no charge.)*

PETROGLYPH BEACH. This beach is an ancient archeological site with rock carvings made possibly 2000-8000 years ago. Petroglyph replicas are displayed on the boardwalk for making rubbings. Find the real thing by roaming the beach, where approximately 50 glyphs may be found. Killer Whale is to the right of the boardwalk, past the gray net shed. Continue to the right to find owl petroglyphs, visible under a large tree. *(¾ mi. north of town on Evergreen Ave. Best viewing 1hr. before and 1hr. after high tide. Wheelchair accessible. Free.)*

WRANGELL MUSEUM. A hodgepodge, cluttered collection of artifacts of daily living in Wrangell fill two rooms. The oldest Tlingit houseposts in existence are from Chief Shakes' longhouse and can be found at this museum. *(Located in the basement of the community center on Church St. ☎874-3770. Open May-Sept. M-F 10am-5pm, Sa 1-5pm. $3, under 16 free.)*

EVENTS. To break the monotony of dreary winter, the first weekend in February brings the **Tent City Festival** to Wrangell. Youthful locals proclaim the event to be "one big party," including beard-growing and long john contests. Mid-April brings the arrival of spring, bald eagle migration, sea lions, and the **Garnet Festival.** Events include informational speakers on wildlife, a golf tournament, and live bands. For the **Fourth of July,** Wrangell pulls out all the stops, boasting the largest, best celebration in the Southeast. Locals compete in the Soap Box Derby, log rolling, and other events, beginning on July 3rd.

🥾 HIKING

Wrangell's **Forest Service Station** offers free, guided flora and fauna excursions every Saturday during the summer, and is an invaluable trip-planning resource. In addition to information on hiking, biking, and kayaking, rangers have descriptions and access options for Forest Service cabins ($25-35) and shelters (free). Marie at **Rainwalker Expeditions** will conduct guided tours and hikes through some of the island's beautiful sites for $10 per hour or $60 per day. (☎874-2549. Includes transportation and bag lunch.) If you just want a ride to a campsite or trailhead, call her, and she may work something out for a reasonable price.

- **Mt. Dewey Trail** (½ mi. round-trip, 1hr.). Look for the sign on the right off Third St. The closest trail to town is this short, quiet, trail, which winds its way through hemlocks and cedars to the top of Mt. Dewey, overlooking the town and Zimovia Strait. To get to all the other trails around Wrangell you will need some sort of transportation.
- **Rainbow Falls Trail** (1½ mi., 4hr.). 3 mi. beyond City Park on Zimovia Hwy. The local favorite starts on the cool, spongy floor of an old-growth rain forest, and climbs a half-mile over boardwalk and 710 stairs to a scenic view of the 100 ft. Rainbow Falls. 500 ft. elevation gain.

North Wrangell High Country Trail (2½ mi. loop, 3-4hr.). At the large bridge on the Institute Creek Trail, approximately 2¼ mi. from Zimovia Hwy and the Rainbow Falls Trail trailhead. Newly built and well-maintained. It climbs into alpine and subalpine areas, with rewarding views of all of Southeast Alaska. The first 1¼ mi. is steep and then the trail levels off. One of the only loop trails available. 1100 ft. gain.

The Anan Creek Trail. 31 mi. south of Wrangell, access by boat or float plane. A mooring float is available for users of Anan Bay Recreation Cabin. Originally developed by Alaska natives for their summer fishing camp. Only accessible by boat or plane, the trail leads to excellent wildlife viewing at the **Anan Bear Observatory** during July and Aug. Forest service interpreters are on duty at the trailhead to brief you on safety instruction.

WATERSPORTS

Most sightseers spending a full day or more in Wrangell try to find their way up the Stikine River. Many kayak, but only very experienced paddlers should attempt to run it. The Forest Service has maps and info. There are six Forest Service cabins in the Stikine Delta and two bathing huts at **Chief Shakes Hot Springs,** a few miles upriver. For those with a few more days, the 160 mi. route on the Stikine River up to Telegraph Creek is a phenomenal trip of natural beauty and gold rush history. Unfortunately, because the rapid current makes upstream travel impossible, the only way to get to these and other attractions on the Stikine, such as **Shakes Glacier,** is by charter boat or plane. Single travelers may have better luck getting a group together. **Breakaway Adventures** (☎ 874-2488) charges $150 per person for daytrips up the Stikine to the bear observatory or to the glaciers, but often runs specials as low as $69; **Alaska Waters** (☎ 800-347-4462 or 874-2378) runs the same route for $145 and adds a little thrill and speed to the ride. Call ahead to either charter for special prices to Telegraph Creek. For more info on the twenty-plus charter boat services in Wrangell, as well as **whale-watching,** and **fishing** and **hunting** trips, contact the Chamber of Commerce.

PETERSBURG ☎ 907

While tourists and itinerant workers come and go every summer, the mainstays of Petersburg are the dependable salmon runs and generations of hardy fisherfolk who brave the winters here. Native Americans fished here first, but they never settled permanently. In 1897, Norwegian immigrant Peter Buschmann saw opportunity in the natural harbor, abundant fish, and ice from the nearby LeConte glacier, and built a cannery. Today Petersburg supports one of the world's largest halibut fleets and a strong Scandinavian legacy. The tiny Wrangell Narrows that lead to Petersburg spare the fishing town the cruise ship crowds that result in touristication. While there are relatively few cheap indoor accommodations, the plentiful summer work, nice hiking, and chance to see a Southeast fishing town at work, make it worth planting stakes and praying for sun.

TRANSPORTATION

Petersburg is on **Mitkof Island.** If you're looking for **Nordic Dr., Main St.,** or **Mitkof Hwy.,** you're probably on it: the main drag goes by all three. The **airport** is a mile east of the waterfront on Haugen Dr.; ferry docks are a mile south of downtown.

Flights: Alaska Airlines, 1506 Haugen Dr. (☎ 772-4255 or 800-426-0333), flies direct once a day to **Juneau** ($129) and **Seattle, WA** ($400). Next door, **LAB** (☎ 772-4300) flies 3 daily flights to **Juneau** ($131) and services **Kake** ($59). **Pacific Wing** (☎ 772-4258) runs 45min. flightseeing tours of LeConte Glacier ($80 per person for 3 people).

Ferries: Alaska Marine Highway (☎ 772-3855 or 800-642-0066), Mile 0.9 Mitkof Hwy. 1 mi. from the town center. Open 1hr. before ferry arrivals. To: **Ketchikan** (10hr., $42); **Sitka** (10hr., $20); **Wrangell** (3hr., $20); and **Juneau** (8hr., $48).

Harbormaster: (☎ 772-4688), at North Harbor. VHF channel 16.

Petersburg

Petersburg

♣ **ACCOMMODATIONS**
Nordic House B&B, 9
Petersburg B&B, 8
Tent City, 7

🍴 **FOOD**
Cold Coastal Storage, 4
Hammer and Wikan, 6
Kito's Cave, 2

● **OTHER**
Forest Service Office, 5
Glacier Laundry, 3
Tonka Seafoods, Inc., 1

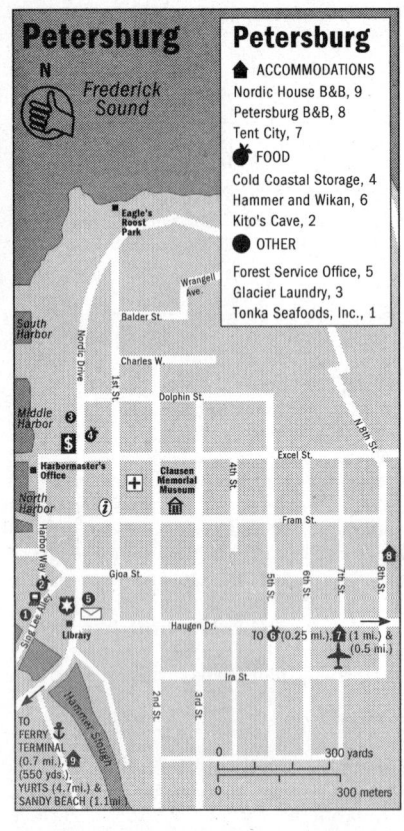

Taxis: City Cab (☎ 772-3003) and **Maine Cab** (☎ 772-6969). Rates start at $4 around town, $5 anywhere to Tent City.

Public Transportation: Stingy residents of Petersburg have been known to take advantage of the **Hammer & Wikan Supermarket Shuttle Service** (☎ 772-4246). Because the shuttle will pick up and drop off anywhere in town for free, these penny-pinchers buy their groceries and get a free ride all in one go. Use one of their courtesy phones at South, Middle, and North Harbors, or stop by their satellite store at 218 N Nordic Dr. to arrange a ride. Runs M-Sa 7am-8pm, Su 7am-7pm.

Car Rental: Scandia House (☎ 772-4281), 110 Nordic Dr. Rents cars ($52 per day) and skiffs ($160).

🛈 PRACTICAL INFORMATION

Visitor Information: (☎ 772-4636; www.petersburg.org) at 1st and Fram St. Open in summer M-Sa 9am-5pm, Su noon-4pm; winter M-F 10am-2pm.

Outdoor Information: Forest Service (☎ 772-3871), on 1st St., above old post office. Info on cabins, hiking, recreation. Open M-F 8am-5pm.

Dept. of Fish and Game (☎ 772-3801), Sing Lee Alley. Licenses available at **The Trading Union** (☎ 772-3881) on N Nordic Dr.

Equipment Rental: Northern Bikes (☎ 772-3978), next to the Scandia House. $4 per hr., $20 per day. Open M-Sa 11am-5pm, Su 10:30am-5pm. Call ahead.

Tongass Kayak Adventures, 106 N Nordic Dr. (☎ 772-4742), rents singles $45, doubles $50.

Laundromat: Glacier Laundry (☎ 772-4144), at Nordic and Dolphin. Wash $2, dry 25¢ per 5min. Open daily 6am-10pm.

Public Showers: The harbormaster at North Harbor (☎ 772-4688) has what are rumored to be the hottest showers in southeast Alaska ($1 per 7½min.). Also at **Glacier Laundry** ($2 per 7min.; towels $1), and **Tent City**.

Employment: Petersburg Employment Service (☎ 772-3791), at Haugen Dr. and 1st St. Petersburg is a great place to find temporary work in the canneries. Most jobs for the duration of summer; **day labor** occasionally needed. Open M-F 10am-2pm.

Emergency: ☎ 911.

Police: 16 S Nordic Dr. ☎ 772-3838.

State Police: ☎ 772-3100.

Hospital: Petersburg Medical Center (☎ 772-4291), at Fram and N 1st St.

Internet Access: Free at the **Library**, at Haugen and Nordic Dr. above the Fire Hall.; should sign up the day before. Open M-Th noon-9pm, F-Sa 1-5pm. **Chips** (☎ 772-2219), on Sing Lee Alley, peddles use of the Internet, scanners, and graphics programs for sending pics home to the family. $10 per hr. Open M-Sa 9am-10pm, Su noon-10pm, but call ahead, because the schedule varies. Also at Petersburg Bunk & Breakfast (see **Accommodations**).

Post Office: (☎ 772-3121), a block west of the airport on Haugen Dr. Open M-F 9am-5:30pm, Sa 11am-2pm. **ZIP Code:** 99833.

ACCOMMODATIONS AND CAMPING

It is a struggle to find a cheap room in Petersburg. Outside of Tent City and LeConte RV Park, the nearest campground, **Ohmer Creek,** is 22 mi. south of the ferries (water and pit toilets; $6). The **Raven's Roost Cabin,** 4 mi. up the Raven's Roost trail (see below), the only forest service cabin on Mitkof Island.

Petersburg Bunk & Breakfast, 805 Gjoa St. (☎ 772-3632), east of 8th St., between the airport and downtown. The cheapest beds in town. Ryn is an accommodating host who will help you make the most of your time in Petersburg. Free Internet. Breakfast with homemade bread. Laundry $3. Lockout 9am-5pm. Open May 15-Sept. 15. Groups of 4 or more accommodated in winter. $25, includes tax.

Nordic House B&B, 806 Nordic Dr. (☎ 772-3620), ½ mi. north of ferry terminal. Shared kitchen and bath. The sitting room view encourages dreams of bigger fish to fry. Free continental breakfast, best eaten on deck overlooking docks. Call weeks in advance. Singles $77; doubles $88.

Tent City (☎ 772-9864), on Haugen Dr. past the airport, 2 mi. from the ferry. Hordes of cannery workers bunk here in summer. Tenting is available atop the muskeg on wooden platforms. Amenities include a pay phone, 3 hotplates, a communal shelter, fire pits stocked with wood, water, toilets, 4 showers (75¢), and soda machines. Quiet hours 10pm-noon. Open May-Sept. $5 per night, $125 per month.

FOOD AND NIGHTLIFE

Although it's swimming in fish, Petersburg still charges a whole lot for seafood. Grocery shopping at **Hammer & Wikan,** 1300 Haugen Dr., earns a free shuttle ride (☎ 772-4246. Open M-Sa 7am-8pm, Su 7am-7pm. See **Public Transportation,** p. 410.)

Coastal Cold Storage, 306 N Nordic Dr. (☎ 772-4177). Serves fresh seafood at reasonable prices. The seafood burger is tasty and the daily specials are usually a treat. Reasonably priced ($5-11). Open M-Sa 7am-6pm, Su 7am-5pm.

Kito's Kave (☎ 772-3207), on Sing Lee Alley, is the liveliest place in town, catering to the young cannery workers. *Rolling Stone* once recognized Kito's for having the best Saturday Night music of any bar in Alaska. Locals are skeptical of this designation, but the bar still rules the roost. Open M-F 10am-2am, Sa 10am-3am, Su noon-2am.

Rincon Mexican Restaurant (☎ 772-2255), inside Kito's Kave. A local favorite for lunch or dinner. Large burritos, small prices. ($2-8) Open. M-Sa 11am-8pm, Su noon-8pm.

SIGHTS AND ENTERTAINMENT

This is one of the best places on the Panhandle to see a fishing town at work. The heart of the year-round operations is down at **North Harbor,** near the middle of town on Excel Ave., where you can wander the docks, talk to local fishermen, read the bulletin boards, and savor the smells. Just hanging out in the harbormaster's office is time well spent. Amateurs will discover that **jigging** for herring from the docks is alarmingly fun. Many of the fish processing companies will give tours to cruise ship passengers and other groups. A good way to see the industry from the food preparation side is a trip to Tonka Seafood. A tour runs daily at 1:30pm for groups of 6 or more. (☎ 772-3662 on Sing Lee Alley. $5, call ahead.) Petersburg is a major whale research site as well. Of approximately 1000 whales that summer in Southeast Alaska, about 500 feed in Frederick Sound, just north of Petersburg. **Kaleidoscope Cruises** (☎ 800-868-4373) will take you to see the whales with a retired marine biologist and Harrison Ford look-alike. This 8hr. science lesson comes at a high price, though ($180, min. group of two).

For those more interested in getting a taste of the past, the **Claussen Museum,** on Fram St. between 2nd and 3rd, has a couple of catch-all Petersburg exhibits, especially focused on the fishing industry and the town's Norwegian heritage. (☎772-3598. Open daily in summer 10am-4:30pm.)

A walk to **Sandy Beach** at low tide reveals 8000-year-old hidden treasures. Petroglyphs are found to the left of the cove and perfectly preserved ancient fish traps reach out from the mud. On the third full weekend in May, Petersburg joins in joyous celebration of Norway's 1905 independence from Sweden in its **Little Norway Festival.** Mock Vikings dance, sing, parade, hunt their own furs, wear horns, and sail in longboats in traditional Viking style. Stay away from open spaces on the **4th of July** in Petersburg: celebrations feature a **competitive herring toss.**

OUTDOOR ACTIVITIES

Wrangell's best outdoors options are kayaking and hiking. **Tongass Kayak Adventures** (see **Equipment Rental,** p. 410), rents sea kayaks and offers guided tours up Petersburg Creek (4hr. tours daily June-Aug.; $55 per person). **Pacific Wing** makes a 45min. flightseeing tour of the LeConte Glacier. (☎772-4258. $80.) Scandia House rents skiffs for $160. To set up a boat tour of the glacier (from $100), call the visitors center (see p. 410) or **Viking Travel,** 101 N. Nordic Dr. (☎772-3818 or 800-327-2571).

Only a handful of Petersburg's many trails are readily accessible by foot. The Forest Service has a free book of trail descriptions, maps of logging roads suitable for mountain biking, and makes reservations for cabins. For a less strenuous stroll around town, many people **walk the beach** beyond Eagle's Roost Park and out around Hungry Point. **Raven's Roost.** The two Petersburg trails, among others, begin at the state dock in the neighboring Kupreanof Island and are accessible only by boat. Many charter operators in town ferry folks across the narrows and rent skiffs, but this can cost more than $100. Try asking at the harbormaster's office for suggestions. Make sure you have a ride back to Miktof, though; residents on Kupreanof have grown impatient with unprepared visitors who knock on their doors to beg for a skiff ride back to town.

- **Raven's Roost Trail** (4 mi. one-way, 5hr.). Take Haugen Rd. out past the airport and make a right before Tent City. The trail starts by the orange and white water towers. Leads to a very popular cabin by the same name ($25), offering glimpses of the Coast Mountains across Frederick Sound on clear days. Beware the many bears.
- **Three Lakes Trail** (4½ mi., 2-3hr.). Drive south from Petersburg on the Mitkof Highway. The Three Lakes Loop Road meets the highway at both 10 mi. and 20 mi. from Petersburg. A boardwalk hike that makes a figure eight passing 4 lakes.
- **Blind River Rapids Trail** (¼ mi., 30min.). 15 mi. south of Petersburg on the Mitkof Hwy. Known for its salmon, this is the best place to walk with your fishing rod. New handicap accessible trails are in progress. Check with the Forest Service to see what is available.
- **Petersburg Lake Trail** (10½ mi.). Boat from Petersburg across the Narrows to the state dock on Kupreanof Island. You need a tide of 14 ft. or higher to reach the upper trailhead. The trail begins to the west of the dock and leads west up to Petersburg Lake, through a wilderness area to a Forest Service cabin. Follow the trail right up a small set of steps and for about 4 mi. until you get to the entrance of the Petersburg Creek-Duncan Salt Chuck Wilderness and high tide trailhead. Follow through the wilderness for another 6½ mi., crossing the creek as you go.
- **Petersburg Mountain Trail** (3½ mi. one-way, 4-5hr.). Leaves east from the same dock. A challenging trek ending with a steep climb (an anchored cable is there for assistance) to spectacular views of glaciers and coastal mountains from Narrows Peak.

SITKA ☎907

Though it is the most historic settlement of Russian America, Sitka was established as a Tlingit settlement for thousands of years before Russian traders founded the outpost in 1799 and made "New Archangel" the capital of Russian operations in America. The Tlingit refused to accept the unwelcome foreign inva-

SITKA ■ 413

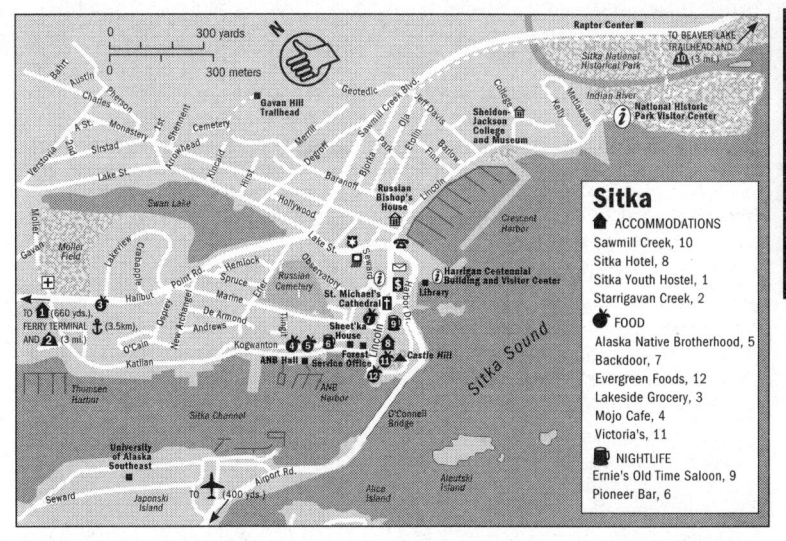

Sitka

🏠 ACCOMMODATIONS
Sawmill Creek, 10
Sitka Hotel, 8
Sitka Youth Hostel, 1
Starrigavan Creek, 2

🍴 FOOD
Alaska Native Brotherhood, 5
Backdoor, 7
Evergreen Foods, 12
Lakeside Grocery, 3
Mojo Cafe, 4
Victoria's, 11

🍸 NIGHTLIFE
Ernie's Old Time Saloon, 9
Pioneer Bar, 6

sion and fought for their land, until the Russians stymied their resistance and held the area until 1867, when political and economic reasons forced them into retreat. The sale of Alaska to the United States was finalized in Sitka on October 18 of the same year. Though visitors hustle to explore Sitka's Russian history, the town thrives independent of tourism, and a strong community of college students, leather-faced anglers, artists, and Tlingits share the town and its mountain peaks.

TRANSPORTATION

Sitka is one of the westernmost cities in the Southeast. As in all Southeast Alaskan towns, the **ferry terminal** is out of town—7 mi., to be exact. The **airport** is just a mile away across the O'Connell Bridge, on Japonski Island. The main drag is **Lincoln St.**, which connects the Sitka National Historical Park and Castle Hill.

- **Flights: Alaska Airlines** (☎966-2422 or 800-426-0333; www.alaskaair.com). To **Juneau** ($111, 3 daily) and **Ketchikan** ($153, 1 per day).

- **Ferries: Alaska Marine Highway,** 7 Halibut Rd. (☎747-8737 or 800-642-0066; www.dot.state.ak.us), 7 mi. from town. To **Ketchikan** (25hr., $58); **Petersburg** (10hr., $30); and **Juneau** (15hr., $30). Open 1hr. before arrival.

- **Local Transportation: Sitka Tours** (☎747-8443), meets most ferries ($5, round-trip $7) and planes ($3, round-trip $5) and will drop you off just about anywhere; call ahead for a ride from town. **Tribal Tours** maintains a **Visitors Transit System** (☎747-7290), that services the major attractions, although most sights are within easy walking distance of one another. $5 per day. Every 30min., M-F 12:30-4:30pm, mornings and weekends if cruise ships are in port.

- **Taxis: Sitka Taxi** (☎747-5001), and **Arrowhead Taxi** (☎747-8888). About $15 per person from Sitka to the ferry. $6 to the airport; 50¢ per additional person.

- **Car Rental: A&A Car Rental** (☎747-8228), on Sawmill Creek Hwy. Has the lowest rates. $44 per day, unlimited miles. Must be 21. Open M-F 8am-6pm, Sa 10am-2pm.

PRACTICAL INFORMATION

Visitors Center: A visitors center in the **Harrigan Centennial Building,** 330 Harbor Dr. (☎747-3225), has lots of printed information on sights and performance schedules. Open daily in summer from 8am until the cruise ships leave.

Sitka Convention and Visitors Bureau, 303 Lincoln St., suite 4 (☎747-5940; www.sitka.org). Open M-F 8am-5pm.

Outdoor Information: Sitka Ranger District, 201 Katlian #109, in the Totem Center (☎747-6671). Pick up detailed information on trails and info on Forest Service cabins ($35-45 per night). Open M-F 8am-5pm.

Fish and Game Dept., 304 Lake St. #103 (fishing ☎747-5355; hunting ☎747-5449). Open M-F 8:30am-5pm. **Mac's,** 213 Harbor Dr. (☎747-6970), sells licenses for both fishers and gamers. Open M-Sa 8am-7pm, Su 9am-5pm. The **fire station,** 209 Lake St. (☎747-3233), loans VHF radios for use on extended backpacking and kayaking trips to those who file a trip plan.

Banks: Nations Bank of Alaska (☎747-3226), on Lincoln St. behind the church. Open M-Th 9:30am-5:30pm, F 9:30am-6pm. **24hr. ATM.**

Equipment Rental: Southeast Diving and Sports, 105 Monastery St. (☎747-8279), rents 5-speeds and mountain bikes. $5 per hr., $20 per day. Open M-Sa 10am-5pm. **Yellow Jersey Cycle Shop,** 805 Halibut Pt. Rd. (☎747-6317), in the Pacific View Center, rents mountain bikes. $25 per day, $100 per week. Call for hours.

Sitka Sound Ocean Adventures (☎747-6375), in the blue bus by the Centennial Building, Single kayaks $25 per half-day, $30 per day; doubles $30 per half-day, $40 per day. Guided 2hr. tours, $50; skiffs for $130. Open daily 8am-5pm.

Baidarka Boats, 320 Seward St. (☎747-8996). Single kayaks $35 per half-day, $50 per day; doubles $50 per half-day, $85 per day; less for longer rentals. Half-day ($40-95) and full-day ($55-175) tours. Open M-Sa 8am-6pm.

Luggage Storage: The **fire station,** 209 Lake St., stores backpacks for free. The **Centennial Building,** 330 Harbor Dr., offers day storage only. The **ferry terminal** has lockers (25¢ for 24hr.), but they are only accessible when a ferry is in port.

Bookstore: Old Harbor Books, 201 Lincoln St. (☎747-8808). Marine charts, **topo maps,** info on local events. Open M-F 10am-6pm, Sa 10am-5pm, Su depends on the ships.

Laundromats and Public Showers: Duds 'n' Suds Laundromat, 906 Halibut Point Rd. (☎747-5050), convenient to the hostel. Wash $1.75, dry 50¢ per 10min. Shower $2 per 10min. Open M-F 7am-8pm, Sa-Su 8am-8pm.

Pharmacy: Harry Race Pharmacy, 106 Lincoln St. (☎747-8006). M-F 10am-5pm.

Hospital: Sitka Community Hospital, 209 Moller Dr. (☎747-3241). Take Halibut Pt. Rd. out to Moller Dr., take a right, and the hospital is across from the ballfields.

Internet Access: Kettleson Memorial Library, 320 Harbor Dr. (☎747-8708). Open M-Th 10am-9pm, F 10am-6pm, Sa-Su 1-5pm. Free access for those who call or show up early. The **Sheldon-Jackson College's** library (☎747-5259), has free Internet on 4 computers, although its weekly hours are more limited. Call ahead.**Highliner Coffee** (☎747-4924), off Lake St. at the Seward Square Mall ($5.25 per 30min., $8.40 per hr).

Post Office: 338 Lincoln St., (☎747-8491). Open M-Sa 8:30am-5:30pm. **ZIP code:** 99835.

ACCOMMODATIONS AND CAMPING

The two park service campgrounds are both far away. The visitors bureau has a list of Sitka's many **B&Bs** (from $60). **Sitka Sound Ocean Adventures** (☎747-6375) rents a floating cabin that sleeps 10, equipped with a skiff and kayaks.

Sitka Youth Hostel (HI), 303 Kimshan St. (☎747-8356), in the United Methodist Church at Edgecumbe St. Find the McDonald's 1 mi. out of town on Halibut Point Rd., then 2mi. up Peterson St. to Kimshan. Free pie and tea in the kitchen, VCR in the common room, free local calls. Basement dorms with cots are uncharacteristically comfortable. Strict lockout M-Sa 9:30am-6pm and Su 9am-6pm. Curfew 11pm. 3-night max. stay or until the next ferry leaves. Open June-Aug. $10, nonmembers $13 plus tax.

Sitka Hotel, 118 Lincoln St. (☎ 747-3288). Convenient downtown location. Established in 1939, this Victorian-style hotel offers comfortable and simple rooms with small bathrooms. Free cable and local calls. Laundry machines available. Reserve 2 months ahead. Shared bath, $55 single, $60 double. Private bath $15 extra.

Sawmill Creek Campground (☎747-4216), 8½ mi. south of town. Take Halibut Point Rd. to Sawmill Creek Rd., and follow Sawmill Creek to the pulp mill; take left spur for 1½ mi. Trees, stream, solitude, picnic tables, firerings, pit toilets, and fishing in nearby Blue Lake. Treat water from the creek. Quiet hours. 14-night max. stay. 11 sites. Free.

Starrigavan Creek Campground, at the end of Halibut Point Rd., 1 mi. past the ferry, 7 mi. from town. Secluded RV and tent sites near an estuary boardwalk trail. Water, pit toilets. 14-night max. stay. No vehicles in or out 10pm-7am. Wheelchair accessible. 30 sites $8. Open Memorial Day to Labor Day.

FOOD AND NIGHTLIFE

Find groceries, a pharmacy, and liquor at **Lakeside Grocery,** 705 Halibut Point Rd. (☎747-3317. Open daily 6am-midnight.) **Evergreen Natural Foods,** 2 Lincoln Rd., sells granola. (☎747-6944. Open summer M-Sa 9am-6pm, Su noon-4pm.)

Alaska Native Brotherhood (ANB) Hall, 205 Katlian Ave. (☎747-3359). Since its founding by Christian Sitka natives in 1914, the ANB has stood for interracial understanding and native community development. Lunches of traditionally-prepared local fish and game are good and cheap ($5), and proceeds go to scholarships for local Native youth. Mouth-watering fry bread $1. Open in summer M-F noon-5pm.

The Mojo Cafe, 256 Katlian Ave. (☎747-0667). Eclectic baked delights and diverse lunch specials greet taste buds with attitude. The lunch specials are best and are usually $3. Vegetarian-friendly. Open M-F 6:30am-2pm.

Victoria's (☎747-3288), next to the Sitka Hotel on Lincoln St. Large breakfast starts early for the fishermen (pancakes $4). Lunch serves loaded burgers with toppings like guacamole and salsa for $7. Salmon burgers are $9. Dinner is more expensive. Open daily 4:30am-9pm.

The Backdoor, 104 Barracks St. (☎747-8856), behind Old Harbor Books. Popular hostelers' hangout with local art and poetry readings, 12 oz. Buzzsaw (coffee with espresso) $2.25; homemade soup with bread $4. Open M-Sa 7am-5pm; Su 9am-3pm.

Pioneer Bar, 214 Katlian St. (☎747-3456). Weathered fishers rest here after a hard day, celebrate here on a good day, and come for company on the days in between. The bartender is an ex-commercial fisherwoman who can help you find the best fishing spots. Don't be tricked into ringing the bell at the bar or else it's a free round on you. $4 pints. Open M-Sa 8am-2am, Su noon-2am.

Ernie's Old Time Saloon, on Lincoln St. across from the Pioneer Home, has room enough for revelling fishers and rowdy hostelers on the weekends. Live hoe-down country sets everyone a-hoppin' Th-Su. Pool, darts. Pints $3.50. Open daily until 2am.

SIGHTS AND EVENTS

Sitka is one of the few cities in southeastern Alaska with indoor attractions that serve as more than just an excuse to get out of the rain. The multi-faceted history of the place manifests itself in the plethora of sights of cultural interest.

ST. MICHAEL'S CATHEDRAL. When Sitka was the Russian empire in Alaska, the cathedral was its center. Today, it holds 400-year-old icons and some belongings of its founder, Bishop Innocent. Though it was originally built in 1848, the cathedral burned in 1966 and was rebuilt by the town. Many original pieces were salvaged for this 80%-Tlingit congregation. (☎747-8120 or 747-3560. *Cathedral services open to public; conducted in English, Tlingit, and Old Church Slavonic. Vespers Sa 6:30pm, full service Su 10am. Generally open Tu-Th 9am-4pm, F 9am-12:30pm, and according to cruise ship schedules.*)

RUSSIAN BISHOP'S HOUSE. This former house of Bishop Innocent's stands sturdily and proudly as one of the four remaining Russian colonial buildings in Alaska. It was built with the finest materials and methods known at the time. Not one nail was used in construction of the walls, and only the brightest and gaudiest French wallpapers were used for decor. The Chapel of the Annunciation upstairs is laden with ornamentation and is the highlight of the tour. *(Two blocks past the cathedral on Lincoln St. Open mid-May to early Oct. daily 9am-1pm and 2-5pm; call for off-season access. Tours every 30min. $3; free for children under 12 and seniors.)*

SHELDON-JACKSON MUSEUM. Located on the compact Sheldon-Jackson College campus, this building houses a world-class collection of Athabascan, Aleutian, Inuit, and Northwest Coast Native American cultural artifacts. These include daily summer demonstrations from visiting Native artists. *(Located at 104 College Dr., east of town on Lincoln St. ☎ 747-8981. Open daily in summer 9am-5pm; $4, under 18 free. Winter Tu-Sa 10am-4pm, free.)*

SITKA NATIONAL HISTORIC PARK. The leisurely path through woods and along the shore's tidal pools leads to 11 totem poles and the site of the **Tlingit Fort** where the hammer-wielding Chief Katlean and his men nearly held off the Russians in the battle for Sitka. At the **Southeast Alaskan Native American Cultural Center,** carvers and weavers demonstrate their crafts. *(Located ½ mi. east of St. Michael's on Lincoln St. ☎ 747-6281. Trails open daily 6am-10pm. Visitors and cultural centers open daily 8am-5pm.)*

CASTLE HILL. Having served as the location for Baranov's administration of Russian America, this is the official site of the Russian sale of Alaska. The site provides an easily accesible view of the cathedral and the town. *(At the west end of Lincoln St. Open daily 6am-10pm.)*

OTHER SIGHTS. Eagles are to Sitka what pigeons are to Trafalgar Square. A good place to watch them is Thomsen Harbor when the fishing boats come in. Bald eagles and owls recovering from injury are sheltered at the Alaska Raptor Rehabilitation Center on Sawmill Creek Rd. *(☎ 747-8662. Open daily 8am-5pm. $10, children under 12 $5.)* Occupying a spot in Centennial Hall is the quirky Isabel Miller Museum, featuring information about little-known Alaskan World War II history and the purchase of Alaska from the Russians. *(☎ 747-6455. Open daily 9am-5pm. Donations appreciated.)* Also in Centennial Hall, the all-female New Archangel Dance Company performs traditional Siberian jigs for cruise ships. *(☎ 747-5516. Call for the week's schedule. $6.)* Sheet'KaKwaan Naa Kahidi Community House features tribal dances, songs, and stories for educational purposes. *(200 Katlian St. next to the Pioneer Home. ☎ 747-7290 or 888-270-8687. Schedules posted in the Centennial Building. $6.)*

EVENTS. In 1972, the organizers of the **Sitka Summer Music Festival** raised just enough funds to buy one-way tickets to Sitka for performers and covered the return flights with their revenues. Throughout the first three weeks of June, the festival, one of Alaska's most popular musical events, will draw 15 of the world's best classical musicians for a chamber music series. *(☎ 747-6774. All shows $14, under 18 $7.)* Other annual events include the **Russian Christmas** celebration on January 7, the **Gathering of the People** in April (a cultural exchange with native dance groups from across Alaska), and the **Whalefest,** the first week in November. The visitors center has more info.

◼ OUTDOOR ACTIVITIES

HIKING. The Sitka area offers excellent **hiking** opportunities of various ranges in difficulty. The Sitka Ranger Office has detailed information about each trail and its conditions. They can also direct you to a number of **remote trails** in the region, most accessible only by boat or floatplane, and many leading to wilderness cabins ($25-45 per night).

Mt. Verstovia Trail (5mi. round-trip, 5hr.). The trailhead is about 2 mi. east of town on Sawmill Creek Hwy., next to Rookie's Sports Bar and Grill. Provides a steep hike boasting the best panoramic views of the area. There are 192 small wooden markers leading to the top. Vegetation changes dramatically from hemlock forest, to subalpine meadows, to a rocky alpine area. If you continue to Arrowhead (confusingly named Verstovia on the USGS map), the elevation gain jumps from a 2550 ft. gain to 3300 ft.

Indian River Trail (11 mi. round-trip, 5hr.). Take Sawmill Creek Rd. out of town and turn on Indian River Rd. before the bridge. After traveling a short distance to the parking lot, walk around the gate and follow the road about a ½ mi. to its end at the pumphouse. The most consistent trail in rain or fair weather. Views are less dramatic than steeper trails, but finding the base of Indian River Falls pleases many. Spawning salmon are visible in late summer and early fall. 700 ft. gain.

Harbor Mountain/Gavan Hill Trail (6 mi. one-way, 4-6hr.). If you choose to continue on Harbor Mountain, prepare for a long day, as access to the road at the trail end is blocked by construction that adds another mile to the trip. Check the Rangers Office for updates. The Gavan Hill Trail begins at the end of Baranof St., near downtown. More strenuous hike but easier to access. The majority of the ascent is stairs, making the hike reminiscent of a stairmaster workout. The perseverant are rewarded by a sensational view of the sound. Farther along, on Harbor Mountain, are the ruins of a WWII lookout.

Beaver Lake Trail (2mi. round-trip, 1hr.). Take Sawmill Creek Rd. 5½ mi. east. Turn left across from the pulp mill onto the uphill gravel road. Go 1½ mi. to the Sawmill Creek Campground. The trailhead is across the bridge over the creek on the south side of the open area. This boardwalk trail is the easiest of the popular trails. Platforms overlooking the serene lake offer great fishing. A boat is available for public use.

Mt. Edgecumbe Trail (13 mi. round-trip, 8-12hr.). Accessible only by boat, about a ½hr. skiff ride from Sitka. The trailhead is behind Fred's Creek cabin on the southeastern shore of Kruzof Island. Full-day clamber to the crater of Sitka's very own dormant volcano. A shelter sits 4 mi. up the trail. The last 3 mi. of the hike are steep and end at the timber line. To reach the crater rim, continue straight up. Stunning views and a close look at eons-old red volcanic ash reward you at the summit. 3000 ft. gain.

KAYAKING. Sitka is a beautiful place to kayak because of its clear waters that allow the kayaker to spy purple, orange, and yellow starfish as well as other wildlife along the coast. Due to its proximity to the open ocean, kayaking here requires more caution and forethought than on the inside passage. For good advice on routes and to rent any equipment, contact Sitka Sound Ocean Adventures (☎747-6375). Alternatively, the water can be viewed in a more leisurely manner, namely by motorized sightseeing. Over 30 **charter operators** vie to separate you from Sitka and your money. The cheapest option is the $49 trip run by Sitka Wildlife Quest (☎888-747-8101; runs W, Sa, and Su). The visitors center has info on such options as deep-sea fishing, whale-watching, flightseeing, and wilderness drop-offs.

TENAKEE SPRINGS ☎907

The third-largest town on the largely uninhabited Chichagof Island, Tenakee Springs' one street is a dirt path populated by children pushing grocery-laden wheelbarrows, older fisherman lolling outside the mercantile, and ATVs traveling under 10 m.p.h. Residents thrive on the slow pace of this close-knit community of 100, and are quick to welcome visitors, even those heavy of pack and light of wallet. The few things to do here include sitting in the hot spring, talking to the locals, walking to Indian River, and sitting in the hot spring some more.

☛ PRACTICAL INFORMATION. Both **Alaska Seaplanes** (☎789-3331), and **Wings of Alaska** (☎736-2247), fly daily to and from Juneau ($80). The state ferry *LeConte* makes a short stop in Tenakee twice a week on its route between **Juneau** and **Sitka** (7-8hr.; $24 each way). There are **no banks** in Tenakee and limited groceries. The **post office** is right off the dock. (☎736-2236. Open M-F 7:30am-noon and 12:30-4pm, Sa 7:30-11:30am.) **ZIP Code:** 99841.

418 ■ THE PANHANDLE

ACCOMMODATIONS AND FOOD. The only affordable option is to rent one of **Snyder Mercantile's** six cabins. Each cabin is within steps of the hot spring and overlooks the water. Basic cabins sleep one to two comfortably ($50); a larger cabin sleeps four to five ($55). A $70 cabin sleeps seven, with carpeting, fireplaces, and—my stars—a flush toilet. Reservations at least a month in advance are essential in summer. (☎736-2205. Outside toilet, cooking facilities, no bedding, credit cards accepted.) **Camping** around Tenakee is bear-intensive; Chichagof Island has about one bear per sq. mi.; only Admiralty Island has a denser population. Walking from the ferry dock, make a right turn on the dirt street. After about three-quarters of a mile, a boardwalk to the left leads to **Indian River.** Camping is technically not permitted along this trail, but there are tent sites, a shelter, and a picnic table. If there have been bear sightings, though, it isn't wise to camp near the river. Big brown bastards have been known to torment tenters during the night.

Food options apart from the salmonberries along the path include **Snyder Mercantile,** next to the ferry dock, which stocks a limited supply of groceries. (Open M-Sa 9am-noon and 1-5pm, Su 9am-2pm.) **Thyme's Two Bakery,** bakes bread and cinnamon rolls, and serves basic sandwiches for lunch. (☎736-2305. In the Shamrock Building. Open Th-M 7:30am-2pm; Th-Su in winter.)

THE HOT SPRING. What better way is there to meet the locals than naked in a tub? Tenakee's namesake and epicenter is a natural sulfuric hot spring that feeds the public bathhouse at the end of the ferry dock. You won't find this unglamorous blue building on any postcards, but natives, miners and fishers have been soaking out aches and worries in these therapeutic 106°F (41°C) waters for more than a century. Visitors can get in on the town gossip by bathing when the spring is busiest, which is at the start of each new gender shift. Bathers are required to be naked and reasonably clean. (Women-only 9am-2pm and 6-10pm; men-only 2-6pm and 10pm-9am. Free; donations accepted at Snyder Mercantile.)

SIGHTS AND OUTDOOR ACTIVITIES. The rocks 15min. out from shore by kayak are home to dozens of **seals, land otters, and sea lions.** More seasoned paddlers ply **Tenakee Inlet,** at the end of which a 100-yard portage leads to **Port Frederick Inlet** and the town of **Hoonah.** This 40-mile trip offers unbroken shorelines, hidden coves, and local wildlife. Only the experienced should attempt it, since the waterways are often subject to high winds and bears are likely at beachside campsites. Kayaks are not available for rent and must be brought over on the ferry ($9). For **chartered expeditions** to fish, view wildlife, and learn about the area from someone who has been on the water around Tenakee all his life, contact **Jason Carter** (☎736-2311). Jason runs half- and full-day trips, and transports kayaks. Fishing and hunting licenses are available at **Snyder Mercantile.**

JUNEAU ☎907

A Tlingit man named Kaawa'ee led two men, Joe Juneau and Richard Harris, to gold nuggets in a nearby creek in the 1800s. Word spread, the Gold Rush began, and Juneau became one of the world's greatest hard-rock mining capitals and the first town founded after the U.S. purchase of the territory. Juneau is still quite literally built upon the products of its mines (tailings were poured into Gastineau Channel to serve as a foundation for the downtown area). It possesses one of the most eclectic mixes found in Alaska, made of a combination of adventurers, fishers, politicians, and business leaders. Juneau attracts about 640,000 tourists a year off cruise ships and about 100,000 independent travelers. Unfortunately, businesses cater to the majority. Luckily, there are great escapes to easily accessible trails, nearby Mendenhall Glacier, and Glacier Bay.

JUNEAU ■ 419

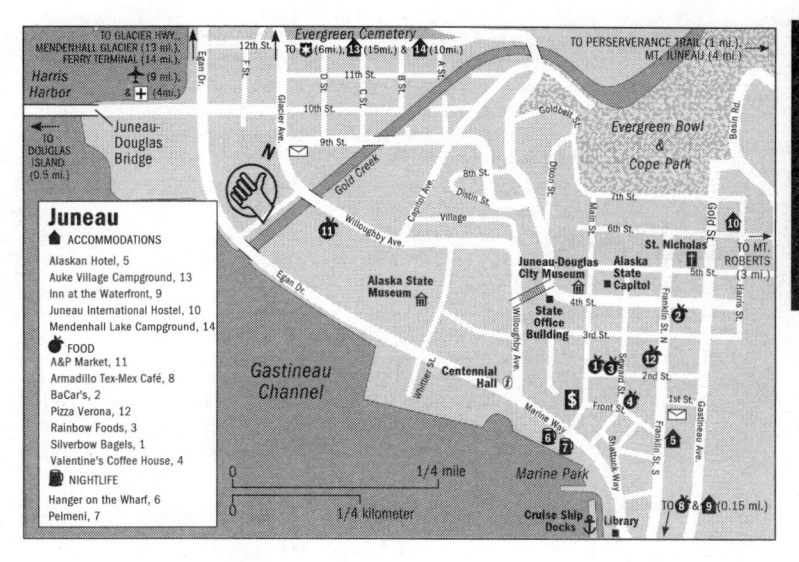

Juneau

◆ ACCOMMODATIONS
- Alaskan Hotel, 5
- Auke Village Campground, 13
- Inn at the Waterfront, 9
- Juneau International Hostel, 10
- Mendenhall Lake Campground, 14

◆ FOOD
- A&P Market, 11
- Armadillo Tex-Mex Café, 8
- BaCar's, 2
- Pizza Verona, 12
- Rainbow Foods, 3
- Silverbow Bagels, 1
- Valentine's Coffee House, 4

◆ NIGHTLIFE
- Hanger on the Wharf, 6
- Pelmeni, 7

TRANSPORTATION

Juneau sits on the Gastineau Channel opposite Douglas Island, 650 mi. southeast of Anchorage and 900 mi. northwest of Seattle. **Franklin St.** is the main drag downtown. **Glacier Hwy.** connects downtown, the airport, the residential area of the Mendenhall Valley, and the ferry terminal. Although cruise ships pull into port downtown, the ferry docks and the airport are both out in the boonies (14 and 9 mi., respectively). Buses are inconvenient and inefficient.

Flights: Juneau International Airport, 9 mi. north of town on Glacier Hwy. **Alaska Airlines** (☎ 789-0600 or 800-426-0333; www.alaska-air.com) flies to: **Anchorage** ($260); **Ketchikan** ($153); or **Gustavus** ($39). **LAB Air** (☎ 789-9160 or 800-426-0543), and **Wings of Alaska** (☎ 789-0790), fly smaller planes to smaller destinations in the region, as well as servicing **Gustavus. Hotel Express** ☎ 463-6916, shuttles between the airport and downtown hotels for every Alaska Airlines flight. $8 for one, $12 for two, $5 each for 3 or more. Schedules posted in hotels. The Baranoff is closest to the hostel. Check hotel lobbies for pick-up times; call for reservations. See **Buses,** below, for less frequent but cheaper transport to and from the airport.

Ferries: Alaska Marine Highway, 1591 Glacier Ave. (☎ 465-3941 or 800-642-0066, M-F 7:30am-4:30pm; fax 277-4829). Ferries dock at the Auke Bay terminal, 14 mi. northwest of the city on Glacier Hwy. To: **Ketchikan** (18-36hr., $74); **Sitka** (9hr., $26); and **Haines** (4½hr., $24). Most have cabins, but reserve them in advance; for Juneau-Ketchikan, these start at $29. Lockers 25¢ per 48hr. Open 3hr. before all departures.

Buses: Capital Transit (☎ 789-6901) runs about hourly from downtown to Douglas Island, Mendenhall Valley, and Auke Bay. From the airport, take the hourly express service from the terminal's north end. M-F 8:10am-5pm. Evenings and weekends, catch the non-express from Nugget Mall, a 10min. walk; ask at the airport for directions. The stop closest to the ferry dock is 2 mi. away, across from DeHart's General Store. Schedules at municipal building, airport, the Visitors Center, in the library, and on buses. $1.25, under 5 free; exact change only. Runs M-Sa 7am-10:30pm, Su 9am-6:30pm.

Taxis: Taku, ☎ 586-2121. **Alaska,** ☎ 780-6400.

Car Rental: Rent-A-Wreck, 9099 Glacier Hwy. (☎ 789-4111), next to the airport. $35 per day, 15¢ per mi. after 100 mi. Must be 21. Free pickup. If paying cash, there is a $200 damage deposit. Open M-F 8am-6pm, Sa-Su 9am-5pm. **Evergreen Ford** (☎ 789-9386), near the airport. Cars $40 per day. Free pickup weekdays. Open M-F 8am-6pm, Sa 9am-5pm. Call at least 2 weeks in advance for both companies June-Aug.

PRACTICAL INFORMATION

Visitor Information: Visitors Center, 101 Egan Dr. in Centennial Hall (☎586-2201 or 888-581-2201; www.traveljuneau.com). Open June-Sept. M-F 8:30am-5pm, Sa-Su 9am-5pm; Oct.-May M-F 9am-5pm. The **Capital City Weekly** (www.capweek.com), available at the center, has the lowdown on free local events.

Outdoor Information: Copies of trails are available at the **Visitors Center** (see above). **Foggy Mountain Shop** (see below) gives more genuine advice. For trail conditions, call the **trail hotline** (☎856-5330). **Alaska Dept. of Fish and Game,** 1255 W 8th St. (☎465-4112; licensing 465-2376), close to the bridge. Open M-F 8am-5pm. **Sport fishing hotline** (☎465-4116).

Outdoor Equipment: Mountain Gears, 126 Front St. (☎586-4327), next to McDonald's. Mountain bikes $6 per hr., $25 per day, $35 overnight. Open M-F 10am-6pm, Sa 10am-5pm. **Juneau Outdoor Center** (☎586-8220), on Douglas Island, delivers kayaks anywhere in the area. Singles $35; doubles $50. Flexible return time. They also rent tents and camping gear for various rates. Open daily Apr.-Sept. 8am-6pm. Gear for purchase available at the high-end **Foggy Mountain Shop,** 134 N Franklin St. (☎586-6780). Open M-Sa 9am-6pm, Su noon-5pm. **Outdoor Headquarters,** 9131 Glacier Hwy. (☎789-9785 or 800-478-0770), in the airport shopping center, is less expensive. Open M-F 9am-7pm, Sa 9am-6pm, Su 10am-5pm; variable in winter.

Banks: On Sa, only banks by the airport are open. **AlaskaUSA,** 8201 Glacier Hwy. (☎789-1361), is the closest. 24hr. ATM at Seward and Front St. and Seward and 2nd.

American Express: 8745 Glacier Hwy. (☎800-770-2750 or 789-0999). Open M-F 10am-7pm, Sa 10am-6pm.

Luggage Storage: The **Alaskan Hotel** stores bags (see p. 421). The hostel (see **Accommodations** below) offers free, unlocked storage. Lockers at ferry terminal are less convenient (see **Transportation** above).

Bookstore: Hearthside Books, 254 Front St. (☎789-1726), caters to all tastes. Variable hours due to cruise ships, usually 9am-8pm during summer. **The Observatory,** 235 2nd St. (☎586-9676), sells used and rare books, as well as old maps. Open M-F 10am-5:30pm, Sa noon-5:30pm.

Gay/Lesbian Information: Southeast Alaska Gay and Lesbian Alliance (☎586-4297). Juneau has about the only "out" gay and lesbian community in southeast Alaska, and SEAGLA is trying to raise awareness in the community by starting a Gay Pride Carnival. SEAGLA publishes *Perspective,* available at **Rainbow Foods** and **Silverbow Bagel.**

Laundromat and Public Showers: Dungeon Laundrette (☎586-2805), at 4th and Franklin. Wash $1.50, dry $1.50; free detergent, bring quarters. Open daily 8am-8pm. **Alaska Laundry,** 1114 Glacier Ave. (☎586-1133), offers showers ($2) and laundry. Wash $2, dry $1 for 20min.

Weather: ☎586-3997.

Emergency: ☎911.

Police: 6255 Alaway Ave. (☎586-2780). Drive northwest from town on Glacier Hwy. (not Egan Rd.) about 6 mi., make a left on Alaway (before the K-Mart).

Crisis and Suicide Prevention Hotline: ☎586-4357.

Rape and Abuse Crisis Line (AWARE): ☎800-478-1090. 24hr.

Pharmacy: Juneau Drug, 202 Front St. (☎586-1233), across from McDonald's. Open M-F 9am-9pm, Sa-Su 9am-6pm.

Hospital: Bartlett Regional, 3260 Hospital Dr. (☎586-2611), off Glacier Hwy., halfway between downtown and the airport.

Internet Access: The **Juneau Public Library** (☎586-5249) sits over parking garage at confluence of Marine Way and S Franklin St. Free **Internet;** call ahead to reserve. Open M-Th 11am-9pm, F-Su noon-5pm. The **State Library,** on the 8th floor of the State Office Building (at the end of 4th St.), has Internet access with less wait. Open M-F 9am-5pm. The **Juneau Hostel** and **Pelmeni** also have free Internet for patrons (see **Accommoda-**

tions and **Nightlife**, below). **Soapy's Station** (☎ 586-8960), in the Senate Building at the corner of Front and Franklin. $5 for 50min. Cheap prepaid phone cards and copies.
Post Office: 127 Franklin St. Open M-F 8:30am-4:30pm, Sa-Su 9am-2pm. **ZIP Code:** 99801.

ACCOMMODATIONS AND CAMPING

Affordable accommodations are limited; book ahead if possible. The **Alaska B&B Association** (www.accommodations-alaska.com) can help you find a room (from $65). The two beautiful Forest Service campgrounds are easily accessible by car.

Juneau International Hostel (HI), 614 Harris St. (☎ 586-9559), at 6th St. Follow signs up the steep hill on Franklin St. Spacious house with comfy common room, kitchen, laundry (wash $1.25, dry 75¢) and filled with friendly backpackers. Do your chore or be swept out the door. Strict lockout 9am-5pm. Midnight curfew. **Free Internet.** 3-night max. stay if full, which this popular hostel often is. $10 advance deposit by mail for phone reservations. 48 beds. $7, nonmembers $10.

Alaskan Hotel, 167 Franklin St. (☎ 586-1000 or 800-327-9347), in heart of downtown. This restored 1913 hotel is from the days of tiny bathrooms. Furnished with antiques, kitchenettes and TVs. Laundry machines for guests. Bar features live tunes Th-Sa and dancing. Rooms with shared bath $60, private bath $80. Weekly rates for $225.

Inn at the Waterfront, 455 S Franklin (☎ 586-2050). Across from cruise ship parking lot; sign out front says Summit Restaurant. Constructed in 1898 and served as a brothel until 1958. Rumor has it that the Inn is haunted within its dark hallways. Small, bright rooms and clean, renovated bathrooms ease the mind. Reserve well in advance and request a front room. Free continental breakfast. 14 rooms start at $60 with shared bath, $80 for private bath; winter rates $40 and up. Weekly rates available.

Mendenhall Lake Campground, Montana Creek Rd. From town, Take Glacier Hwy. north 10 mi. to Mendenhall Loop Rd., and take a right on Loop Rd. Turn left on Montana Creek after 3½ mi. Bus drivers stop within 1½ mi. upon request (7am-10:30pm only). 6 mi. from ferry. Stunning views, close to glacier and the West Glacier Trail (see below). Firepits, water, toilets, showers, free firewood. No reservations. 14-night max. stay. Open June to mid-Sept. 60 sites. Tents $10, RVs $20.

Auke Village Campground (☎ 586-8800), 15 mi. from town on Glacier Hwy. (1½ mi. west of the ferry docks). 12 secluded sites near a scenic beach. Firepits, water, toilets, tables. No reservations. 14-night max. stay. Open early May to late Sept. $8, seniors $4.

FOOD

Juneau has the most diverse culinary options in southeastern Alaska. **Juneau A&P Market,** 631 Willoughby Ave., near the Federal Building, is the place to go for one-stop grocery shopping, an extensive salad bar ($2.60 per lb.), and an **ATM.** (☎ 586-3101. Open daily 5am-11pm.) For organic produce, check out **Rainbow Foods,** at 2nd and Seward St. (☎ 586-6476. Open M-F 9am-7pm, Sa 9am-6pm, Su noon-6pm.)

Silverbow Bagels (☎ 586-9866) and **The Back Room** (☎ 586-4146), 120 2nd St., at the intersection with Main. These two establishments are housed in the same purple building and have a working, symbiotic relationship. Silverbow Bagels is home to the oldest operating bakery in Alaska. Their breads (made fresh M-Sa; around $3 per loaf) and bagels (80¢) are staples. Sandwiches ($5-7) are quality noontime chow. (Open M-F 7am-5:30pm, Sa 8am-4:30pm, Su 9am-3:30pm.) **The Back Room** restaurant has a trendier feel and picks up where Silverbow leaves off, serving brunch (Sa 8am-2pm, Su 9am-2pm), lunch (Tu-F 11:30am-2pm), and dinner (Tu-Sa 5:30pm-9pm). Prime dishes such as perogies ($8) or indonesian peanut pasta ($12). Movies every Tu, Th, and Sa night ($3 or $5 food minimum); theme changes monthly.

Pizza Verona, on Franklin St. (☎ 586-2816). This classic Italian restaurant uses hand-tossed, homemade dough to make their popular pies. ($3 slices; $12 for 12 in. pie). Seafood or pasta entree specials are often excellent and start around $12.

Armadillo Tex-Mex Cafe, 431 S Franklin St. (☎586-1880). Across from cruise ship docks. Southwest paintings and plastic armadillos watch over fast, saucy service and hot, spicy food. Locals rave about the Thai Chicken, while tourists come for the nachos. Heaping entrees $9-14. Home-brewed beers. Open M-Sa 11am-10pm, Su noon-9pm.

Valentine's Coffee House and Bakery, 111 Seward St. (☎463-5144). Provincial flavor in the heart of the capital. Fresh-baked calzones $6; salads $5; sandwiches $6. All sorts of breads and veggie options. Open M-F 7am-5:30pm, Sa 8am-4pm.

BaCar's (☎463-5091), at the corner of Franklin and 4th. This restaurant is a hidden secret among locals. Breakfast is most affordable and portions are generous. Two huge pancakes ($4) will fuel the hungry hiker. Open W-Su 6am-3pm.

SIGHTS AND EVENTS

ALASKA STATE MUSEUM. An excellent museum that sets the standard for presenting and interpreting Native Alaskan artifacts. Provides in-depth exhibits on natural and state history. The first floor introduces visitors to the history and culture of Alaska's major native groups. Upstairs houses Alaska's maritime history, Russian Alaska, and contemporary art. *(395 Whittier St. ☎465-2901. Open mid-May to mid-Sept. Daily 8:30am-5:30pm; mid-Sept. to mid-May Tu-Sa 10am-4pm. $3, under 18 free.)*

JUNEAU DOUGLAS CITY MUSEUM. Reminisce about Juneau's golden years and its early mining history. *(On the corner of 4th and Main St. ☎586-3572. Open mid-May to Sept. M-F 9am-5pm, Sa-Su 10am-5pm; Oct. to mid-May F-Sa noon-4pm and by appointment. $3 in summer, seniors and under 19 free, free in winter.)*

GASTINEAU SALMON HATCHERY. Between mid-July and September it is packed with tourists and horny fish. Impressive views of the spawning ladder and a brief talk are both available outside for free. *(2697 Channel Dr. ☎463-5113. Open M-F 10am-6pm, Sa-Su noon-5pm. Indoor aquarium $3, children $1.)*

ALASKA BREWING CO. Free samples! The free tour is brief and probably won't impress you as much as the ale. *(5429 Shaune Dr. Request the city bus to stop at Kosco; turn onto Anka Rd. from the Glacier Hwy., then make a right onto Shaune Dr. ☎780-5866. Bring ID. Tours every 30min. May-Sept. M-Sa 11am-5pm; Oct.-Apr. Th-Sa 11am-4:30pm.)*

SHRINE OF ST. THERESE. This quiet, tree-shrouded park 23 mi. north of town on the Glacier Hwy., on a small island connected by a causeway to the shore, offers splendid views of the Chilkat Mountains. Beaches and the hike-accessible **Eagle Glacier** are also this way, but no public transport is available.

PERFORMING ARTS. Talented local and visiting musicians, from guitar-strumming folkies to Salsa bands that get the whole crowd dancing, put on **free concerts** at Marine Park on the waterfront by the cruise ship docks. *(Summer F 7-8:30pm.)* The **Alaska Folk Festival** brings free, all-night jam sessions to Centennial Hall. *(☎364-2658. April.)* **Juneau Jazz and Classics** enlivens various venues including a shipboard "blues cruise." *(☎463-3378. May.)* The **Perseverance Theater** puts on quality local theater, and plays workshopped there have ended up on Broadway. *(914 3rd St. On Douglas Island. ☎364-2421.)*

HIKING

Juneau's trail system is extensive. The visitors center in town as well as the Mendenhall Glacier Visitors Center offer free, printed information on trails. Local bookstores and outfitters have lots of insight and thorough descriptions. As always, beware of bears and dress in layers to prepare for elevation changes.

Mt. Roberts Trail (4½ mi. one-way, 5hr.). To get the best view of the city, head up the trail to the summit of Mt. Roberts (3576 ft.). A steep climb, where the higher elevations reveal panoramic views up the Gastineau Channel and Mt. Juneau. Many hikers choose to stop at the 2½ mi. mark where a Father Brown's Cross stands. A tramway also offers access to the vista but requires $20 round-trip. Hikers can ride down for $5 or a $5 purchase at the gift shop. Begins at the end of 6th St., up a stairway, 2½ mi. to the Cross (2500 ft.), 3 mi. to Gastineau Peak (3700 ft), 4½ mi. to Mt. Roberts summit (3800 ft.).

West Glacier Trail (6¾ mi. round-trip, 5-6hr.). Request that the bus take you as close as possible to the West Glacier Trail. From the Mendenhall Loop Rd., take Montana Creek Road and veer right, following signs for Skater's Cabin. Entrance to the trail is at the end of the road from the parking lot. This much-vaunted trail yields stunning views of **Mendenhall Glacier** from the first step to the final outlook. The hike parallels the glacier, crosses a creek, and appears to end at an overlook. The trail continues up the rocks and ends above the timberline. A primitive route continues to Mt. McGinnis, but is only recommended for experienced hikers with an ice axe. 1300 ft. gain.

Perseverance Trail (6 mi. round-trip, 3-4hr.). Take Gold St. to Basin Rd. The trail starts at the cul-de-sac. This easy, wheelchair-accessible trail leads to the ruins of the Silverbowl Basin Mine and booming waterfalls. Avalanche danger in winter and early spring; call the Forest Service (see p. 420) for trail conditions. 700 ft. gain.

Mt. Juneau Trail (4 mi. round-trip). About 1 mi. from the trailhead, the trail peels left from the Perseverance Trail. Not recommended for the faint of heart or clumsy of foot: the path gets very slippery near the top, where there are no trees to grab. 3600 ft. gain.

OTHER OUTDOOR ACTIVITIES

Known as "the poor man's Glacier Bay," **Tracy Arm** offers much of the spectacular beauty and wildlife at nearly half the cost. This day cruise leads through Stephen's Passage to Tracy Arm Fjord for glimpses of wildlife and icy waters. The ships pass blue icebergs that offer safety to nursing harbor seal pups. The tour's climax is the stop at the Sawyer Glacier, where passengers gawk at the 10 mi. long sheet of ice and listen for the "white thunder" of pieces calving into icebergs. **Auk Nu Tours,** 76 Egan Dr., is the biggest tour company and has a naturalist on-board. (☎800-820-2628. 8hr. tour $110, under 18 $70; includes lunch and snacks, larger boat.) **Adventure Bound,** 245 Marine Way, runs a mid-sized boat, carrying 37 passengers and knowledgeable staff. (☎463-2509 or 800-228-3875. 8hr. tour. $100, under 18, $60.)

There are many excellent trails for **mountain biking,** but off-road is sometimes prohibited. Check with **Mountain Gears** for difficulty ratings and suggestions. Very few companies run **kayak** tours of the area, and it'll cost you. Most kayakers make the trip to Glacier Bay and spend their time in the East Arm. For those who remain in Juneau, **Juneau Outdoor Center** rents kayaks and gives lessons and information.

Southeast Alaska's only **ski area,** community-owned **Eaglecrest,** on Douglas Island, offers chutes, bowls, and marked runs. (☎586-5284. $25 per day, high-schoolers $17, under 12 $12. Ski rental $20, children $14.) The Eaglecrest ski bus departs from the Baranof Hotel at 8:30am and returns at 5pm on winter weekends and holidays (round-trip $6). In summer, the Eaglecrest **Alpine Summer Trail** is a good way to soak in the mountain scenery of virtually untouched Douglas Island

NIGHTLIFE

No real surprises here: the biggest city in the Southeast has the best nightlife. Local musical talent is surprisingly good.

Alaskan Hotel, 167 Franklin St. (☎586-1000). This bar attracts locals, tourists, and musicians in what used to be the most popular parlor of the red light district. Open mic night on Th is always packed. Live cajun and blues tunes on weekend. Open mic. night on Th is a local favorite. $4.50 pints. Su-Th noon-1am, F-Sa noon-3am.

Hangar on the Wharf (☎586-5018), in the Wharf on Marine Way. Capital clientele have their name engraved on their bar stools. On W night, local musicians strum laid-back tunes on acoustic guitar, while local bands play F-Sa. 110 beers served, including many microbrews. Great views of the water. Open Su-Th until midnight, F and Sa until 2am.

Pelmeni, in the Wharf on Marine Way. Only restaurant in town to stay open late for the hungry post-bar crowd. The only food is a $5 bowl of Russian dumplings stuffed with ground sirloin; the Russian name for the dish is the restaurant's namesake. Good with or without the extra spice. **Free Internet access.** Open M-Th until 1:30am, F-Sa until 3:30am. Open for lunch and dinner.

GUSTAVUS ☎ 907

The gateway to the gateway to Glacier Bay National Park, Gustavus is ignored by tourists on the way to Bartlett Cove, where trips into the Bay originate. Friendly locals are quick to reveal the secrets of the land, however, and their enthusiasm for the outdoors is infectious. Come prepared. There are no banks, ATMs, or liquor stores in Gustavus, so bring your booze and money with you. Although last-minute food stuffs can be picked up at Bear Track Mercantile, if you're planning a trip here, or even a one-night stay, bring provisions with you. Besides the Fireweed Gallery (☎ 697-2325; open M-F 1-5pm and by appointment), most everything to see and do in Gustavus is outside en route to Glacier Bay. Gawk from the boat dock at 360° views of mountain vistas, and get to the fjords.

ORIENTATION AND PRACTICAL INFORMATION. Gustavus is situated on a crossroads called "Four Corners," the intersection of Gustavus Rd. and State Ferry Rd., known by locals as "the road" and "the other road." **Glacier Bay Lodge** and **Bartlett Cove,** the entrance to the park, lie 10 mi. west of Four Corners; the **airport** lies 1 mi. east and the ferry arrives 1 mi. south. Gustavus is accessible only by boat or plane. The cheapest way to get there is via **Alaska Airlines** (☎ 697-2203 or 800-426-0333; $42 one-way from Juneau). **Skagway Air** (☎ 983-2218) flies from Gustavus to Haines or Skagway for $90. **Wings of Alaska** (☎ 697-2201 or 800-478-9464) offers direct flights to Haines ($108) and Juneau ($80). **Auk Nu Tours** runs a 2hr. ferry that departs Juneau daily at 11am. (☎ 800-820-2628. $45, round-trip $85. You may check your kayak for $40 or bike for $10.) Once in Gustavus, a **bus** from the Glacier Bay Lodge (see p. 425) meets most flights and rolls on to Bartlett Cove ($10). **TLC Taxi** (☎ 697-2239) charges $12 for one, $20 for two, and $8 per person if there are three or more of you, plus $5 per bike and $10 per kayak. **Bud** (☎ 697-2403) rents midsize cars for $60 a day. There is no visitors center in Gustavus, but you can ask questions at the **Gustavus Visitors Association** (☎ 697-2475). Otherwise, **Icy Passages** is the informative Gustavus paper; the community bulletin board is posted in front of **Bear Track Mercantile.** A volunteer-run **library** sits on Gustavus Rd. near the airport and is possibly the only library in Alaska that requires visitors to take their shoes off at the door. (☎ 697-2350. Open M and W 7-9pm, Tu 1-5pm, Th 10am-noon, F 1:30-3:30pm, Sa noon-4pm.) If injured, visit the **Gustavus Community Clinic** (☎ 697-3008). **Emergency:** ☎ 911. **Post office:** ☎ 697-2202, next to library. Open M-F 8am-noon and 1:30-4pm, Sa noon-2pm. **ZIP Code:** 99826.

ACCOMMODATIONS AND FOOD. Gustavus offers little in the way of budget accommodations. There are **no campgrounds** in Gustavus, although tenters sometimes crash on the beach near the ferry dock; the free campgrounds at Bartlett Cove aren't too far away and are the destination for most anyway. **Good River Bed and Breakfast** lends bikes, fishing gear, and rain gear and has a beautiful garden and cozy bedrooms with handmade quilts (☎ 697-2241). The only provider of (expensive) groceries in town is **Bear Track Mercantile,** a quarter-mile south of Four Corners. (☎ 697-2358. Open M-Sa 9am-7pm, Su 9am-5pm.) The **Strawberry Point Cafe** next door makes filling sandwiches for $6-8. (☎ 697-2227. Lunch Tu-Sa 11:30am-3pm. Dinner F-Sa 5:30-8pm.) The **Bear's Nest Cafe,** a quarter-mile north of Four Corners, serves lasagna, enchiladas (both $12), and espresso ($1.50). Expect $20 dinners. (☎ 697-2440. Open daily 11am-8pm.)

🌲 OUTDOOR ACTIVITIES. Wolf Track Expeditions (☎ 697-2326), on State Ferry Rd., offers **bike rentals** for $15 per day, whale watching charters for $100, and a combined bike rental and shuttle service to Couverden Point on Chichagof Island, across the Icy Straits, for $165. **Hikers** can walk the beach from Gustavus to Bartlett Cove in a long day. The trip is easiest at low tide and bears may join you for portions of the trip (see p. 40). Kayakers can also depart Gustavus instead of Bartlett's Cove; contact **Sea Otter Kayaks.** (☎ 697-3007. Singles $40 per day; doubles $50, less for longer trips. Includes tide tables, dry bags, boots.) Hard-core **golfers** tee off at the nine-hole **Mt. Fairweather Golf Course** (☎ 697-2214) year-round.

GLACIER BAY NATIONAL PARK ☎ 907

The landscape of Glacier Bay changes daily as about a dozen of its glaciers advance and retreat at geologically rapid speeds. Only 200 years ago, the Park Headquarters was completely covered in ice. Now, the daily cruise takes visitors a few hours to reach spectacular views of icebergs and glaciers. Besides glacier gawkers, the park attracts outdoor purists to the wild backcountry and isolated inlets, accessible only by boat or float plane. The bay is divided into two inlets: the westward **Tarr Inlet** reaches north to the termini of the **Grand Pacific** and **Margerie Glaciers,** while the eastward **Muir Inlet** ends at the faces of the **Muir** and **Riggs Glaciers.** Harbor seals, humpback whales, orcas, puffins, and Arctic terns share the icy waters with kayakers. **The Fairweather Range,** to the west, is the highest coastal range in the world and humbles the soul.

🚌 TRANSPORTATION. Getting to **Bartlett Cove,** the principle access point to the bay, is relatively easy. A plane or ferry takes visitors to **Gustavus** (see p. 424), and from there a taxi or shuttle (about $10) goes to **Glacier Bay Lodge** and the **Visitor Information Center** at the **National Park Service office,** both close to the campground in the immediate Bartlett Cove area. Transportation upbay is costly. Cruising and kayaking are the two main options. The standard cruise is convenient and popular, although Glacier Bay is becoming popular for kayakers seeking extended backcountry itineraries. Backcountry hiking and kayaking are also possible in the Dry Bay area, as is **rafting** down the Alsek River. For info contact the **Yakutat District Office** of the National Park Service, P.O. Box 137, Yakutat, AK 99689 (☎ 784-3295).

🗺️🛈 ORIENTATION AND PRACTICAL INFORMATION. The park offers great opportunities for independent explorers. The **Crystal Fjord** transports kayakers and hikers to four drop-off points. Reserve through the **Glacier Bay Lodge.** (☎ 697-2225 or 800-451-5952. One-way $84, round-trip $168, bay pass $188.) Because there are boat quotas in the summer, people with their own boats must call ahead to the **National Park Service Office** (☎ 697-2230) to book a visit. Other cruise ships and charter flightseeing tours operate from outside the park boundaries—get a full list of these by writing to the **Superintendent** (☎ 907-697-2230), P.O. Box 140, Gustavus, AK 99826-0140.

Any visit to the park begins at the **Visitor Information Station.** Tidal shifts of 25 ft. in as little as 6hr., a high population of brown bears, and no maintained campsites or trails outside the park's headquarters create a challenging environment for the explorer and should not be taken lightly. Rangers give a mandatory backcountry orientation, advise you of areas restricted by conservation or bear activity, and distribute permits and bear-proof food caches. Additional maps and wildlife info are available at the information center on the second floor of the Glacier Bay Lodge. (The **Station** is 10 mi. north of Gustavus, a quarter-mile past Glacier Bay Lodge, next to the dock in **Bartlett Cove.** ☎ 697-2230. Open daily 7am-9pm.)

🏠⛺ ACCOMMODATIONS AND CAMPING. The Glacier Bay Lodge is the center of tourist activity, housing a restaurant, comfy couches by the fire, visitor information, and nightly Ranger talks. All of these features are accessible to the camper and dormer. Showers ($1 per 5min.) and laundry ($2 wash, $1.25 dry) are adjacent to the Lodge. The best bet for food is to bring your own groceries from Juneau and have dinner on the beach. Dinner entrees at the Lodge ($15-$30) are mostly unreasonable, but the deck menu ($6-$8) serves nachos built in the shape of the Fairweather Mountains and large sandwiches until 9:30pm. Some visitors opt to stay in nearby Gustavus (see p. 459), and enjoy being in closer proximity to the locals.

Backpackers and kayakers can stay in the free **campground** in the lush forest that meets the shore of the bay. The 25 sites are rarely full. (¼ mi. from the dock. Outhouses, water. Register at the Visitors Station.) **Backcountry camping** is permitted throughout the park. Look for clearings off-shore, as tides change quickly and be sure to find a low-impact tent site. Those without a tent can collapse in comfortable dorm beds at the Glacier Bay Lodge ($28).

OUTDOOR ACTIVITIES. The options are endless for this enormous and underused park. **The Spirit of Adventure** is owned by the Lodge (see above) and offers a daily **boat tour** up the Tarr Inlet with a enthusiastic naturalist crew on board. Most visitors choose this 8hr. tour and few are disappointed. Wildlife sightings and views of glaciers calving are part of the daily routine. ($157. Includes lunch. Sightseeing and lodging packages are also available.) **Fjord Air** (☎ 697-2377) and **Air Excursions** (☎ 697-2375), offer aerial views of the glaciers deeper into the park and offer phenomenal views on clear days. From $75 for a 1½hr. tour.

Kayaking is the best way to explore the backcountry over several days. Paddlers revel in the park's landscape. Most wilderness travelers prefer the East Arm of the bay, because it is off-limits to motorized traffic, and most importantly, cruise ships that create large wakes. Many also enjoy the closer trip to the **Beardslee Islands** for fantastic wildlife. Head to the **Visitor Station** for registration, tidal charts, and bear containers. **Kayak rental** is available at **Sea Otter Kayaks.** (☎ 967-3007. Singles $40 per day; doubles $50. Includes rain gear, drybags, and charts.) **Glacier Bay Sea Kayaks** has similar rates. (☎ 697-2257. Has multi-day rates.) **Alaska Discovery** (☎ 800-586-1911) has guided one-day kayak trips from Bartlett Cove to the Beardslee Islands.

There are three short and fairly easy hiking trails near the lodge: **The Forest Trail** (1 mi.), **Bartlett River Trail** (4 mi., round-trip), and **Bartlett Lake Trail** (4 mi.). All are designed with the meandering nature-viewer in mind, rather than the thrill-seeking climber. The Lodge keeps a schedule of ranger-led walks. There are no other trails throughout the park. Backcountry hiking is accessible only by boat or plane, and is difficult and disorienting because of the thick forest. Beware of Devil's Club, the large-leafed spiny picker plant. Other backcountry hikes require ice-climbing gear, or skis and should only be approached by experienced climbers. Inquire at the visitor information station for suggestions.

HAINES ☎ 907

Snow-capped mountains and crystal blue waters surround Haines with breathtaking beauty. Called "the sunny spot of the Southeast," Haines gets *only* about 60 inches of precipitation. Haines is also very accessible, as a boat-bound traveler will attest at his or her first sight of RVs for weeks. Still, the town has cut back on its cruise ships and is complimented by travelers for its lack of crowds and for its genuineness. The coastal town is connected to the Interior, like Skagway, by a mountain pass traditionally protected by the coastal Tlingit and interior Athabascans, and now paved and well-traveled by people from all over. A site of cultural importance to Tlingits throughout Southeast Alaska, the tribal village of Klukwan remains in a strategic riverside location, isolated from Haines.

TRANSPORTATION

Haines lies on a thin peninsula between the **Chilkat** and **Chilkoot Inlets,** just southwest of Skagway on the Chilkoot Inlet. **Main St.** and the **Haines Hwy.** and their perpendiculars, **2nd** and **3rd Avenues** define downtown. Fort Seward lies to the south. Below this peninsula, two inlets merge into **Lynn Canal.** There are US (☎ 767-5511) and Canadian (☎ 767-5540) **customs offices** at Mile 42 of the Haines Hwy. (open daily 7am-11pm). Travelers must have valid proof of citizenship to enter Canada. Rental cars are not always allowed across the border.

Flights: Wings of Alaska (☎766-2030) offers the best rates to **Juneau** ($80). **LAB Air** (☎766-2222) and **Skagway Air** (☎983-2218) fly to **Skagway** ($40). "Skag" Air also services **Gustavus** ($90). All airlines provide free shuttle service to and from town.

Buses: R.C. Shuttles (☎877-479-0079) departs Mountain View Motel Tu 9am for **Fairbanks** ($130); stops in **Tok** ($80) and **Delta Junction** ($110).

Ferries: Alaska Marine Highway (☎766-2111 or 800-642-0066; www.akmhs.com). Terminal on Lutak Rd., 4 mi. from downtown. 1 per day to **Juneau** (4½hr., $28) and **Skagway** (1hr., $20). Parking for ferry passengers $5 per day, $25 per week. The **Haines-Skagway Water Taxi** (☎766-3395) departs from the south side of town and makes 2 trips per day between the 2 towns. $22 one-way, $35 round-trip; bikes $5. Will stop for wildlife. **Fast Ferry** makes 4 trips per day for $45 round-trip (☎766-2100).

Taxis: The New Other Guy's Taxi (☎766-3257). $8 single fare between ferry or airport and downtown; $5 per person.

Car Rental: Eagle's Nest Car Rental (☎766-2891 or 800-354-6009), at Eagle's Nest Motel, west of town on the Haines Hwy. $45 per day, plus 35¢ per mi. over 100 mi. Must be 25 with a credit card.

Car Repair: Charlie's Repair, 225 2nd Ave. (☎766-2494). Open M-F 8am-5pm.

PRACTICAL INFORMATION

Visitor Information: On 2nd Ave. near Willard St. (☎766-2234 or 800-458-3579; www.haines.ak.us). Open M-W and F 8am-8pm, Th 9am-10pm, Sa-Su 9am-6pm.

Outdoor Information: State Park Information Office, 259 Main St. (☎766-2292), above Helen's Shop between 2nd and 3rd Ave. Open Tu-Sa 8am-4:30pm, but call ahead. The **Fish and Game** folks are in the same building. Open M-F 9am-5pm.

Equipment Rental: Sockeye Cycle (☎766-2869), on Portage St., above the cruise ship docks in Ft. Seward. Bikes $6 per hr., $20 for 4hr., $30 for 8hr.; helmets and locks included. From here, the man who began the Kluane-Chilkat Bike Relay guides trips. Open in summer M-Sa 9am-6pm, Su 1-5pm. **Tanani Bay Kayak and Canoe Rentals** (☎766-2804), near the corner of Union and Front St., rents single kayaks $18 per day, doubles $26; canoes $12 per day. Pickup and delivery. Call for hours. **Alaska Sport Shop** (☎766-2441), sells fishing licenses. Open M-Sa 8:30am-6pm, Su 10am-4pm; winter M-Sa 9am-5:30pm.

Bank: First National Bank of Anchorage, on Main St., is the only bank in town. Open M-Th 10am-4pm, F 10am-5pm. **24hr. ATM.**

Bookstore: The Babbling Book (☎766-3356), on Main St. near Howser's Supermarket. Open M-Sa 10am-5:30pm, Su noon-5pm; call for winter hours.

Laundromat and Public Showers: Port Chilkoot Camper Park, see p. 428. **Pair-a-Dice** (☎766-2953), on Main St. near Front St. Wash $2, dry 25¢ per 7min. Showers $2. Open daily 8am-8pm; winter 8am-6pm. **Haines Quick Laundry,** behind the Outfitter on Haines Hwy. Wash $2.50, dry $1.50. Showers 25¢ per min. up to 15min.

Weather: ☎766-2727.

Emergency: ☎911.

Police: (☎766-2121), on Haines Hwy. between 2nd and 3rd Ave.

Rape and Abuse Crisis Line: ☎800-478-1090.

Medical Services: Health Clinic (☎766-2521), on 1st Ave. next to the visitors center.

Internet Access: The **Library** (☎766-2545), on 3rd Ave. offers 20min. free. Sign up early. Open M and W 10am-9pm, Tu and Th 10am-4:30pm and 7-9pm, F 10am-4:30pm, Sa-Su 1-4pm. **Mountain Market** (see **Food,** below). Free.

Post Office: On Haines Hwy., between 2nd Ave. and Front St. Open M-F 9am-5:30pm, Sa 1-3pm. **ZIP Code:** 99827.

ACCOMMODATIONS AND CAMPING

The weather is better in Haines than almost anywhere else in Southeast Alaska, making camping a pleasure. In addition to private campgrounds, there are several state campgrounds (with water and toilets) around town. **Chilkat State Park,** 7 mi. south on Mud Bay Rd., has guided nature walks and good king salmon and halibut fishing (32 sites, $5). **Chilkoot Lake,** 10 mi. north of town on Lutak Rd., provides views and sockeye salmon (32 sites, $10). **Mosquito Lake,** 27 mi. north on Haines Hwy., earns its name in late summer. (13 sites, $6.) Call the State Park Information Office (reservations ☎877-444-6767).

- **Bear Creek Camp and International Hostel** (☎766-2259), on Small Tracts Rd., 1½ mi. out of town. From downtown, follow 3rd Ave. out Mud Bay Rd. to Small Tracts. A ring of cabins is settled in a remote, but accessible, location. Call ahead for ferry terminal pickup. Bathhouse and kitchen. Laundry available. Tent sites behind cabins. No curfew. Bikes $10 per day. Sites $8; dorms $14; cabins $38. TV and movies available.
- **Hotel Hälsingland** (☎766-2000 or 800-542-6363). Located in Fort Seward, down the hill from where 3rd Ave. meets Mud Bay Rd. This old officers' quarters is made up of small, simple rooms with large windows and shows its age. Open May-Sept. and during Nov. for the Bald Eagle Festival. Singles $49; doubles $59; private bath starts at $74.
- **Portage Cove,** almost a mile south of town on Beach Rd. Backpackers and cyclists only. Tenters share a grassy space overlooking the water. Rarely crowded. Water, pit toilets. 7-night max. stay.
- **Port Chilkoot Camper Park** (☎766-2000 or 800-542-6363), opposite Hotel Hälsingland. Gravelly, crowded sites, but well-maintained. Water, dump station, laundry, and coin showers. Open Apr.-Sept. 60 sites, $8; full hookups $18.

FOOD

Creative sandwiches and burritos are beginning to replace steak and potatoes on Haines's menus. **Howser's Supermarket,** on Main St., is the town's grocer. (☎766-2040. Open daily 8am-9pm.) You may find dungeness crab on the dock, but salmon ($5-7 per lb.) and prawns ($10-13 per lb.) are always at **Bell's Seafood,** on 2nd Ave. under the Old City Jail and Firehouse sign. (☎766-2950. Open Su-Tu and Th-Sa 9am-6pm, W 9am-10pm.)

- **Mountain Market** (☎766-3340), at Haines Hwy. and 3rd Ave. Haines's extensive health food grocery store and cafe serves overflowing sandwiches loaded with your requested veggies and the most wholesome ingredients in town ($3-4), with soup ($7). Free Internet access. Open M-F 7am-7pm, Sa-Su 7am-5:30pm; winter daily 7:30am-6pm.
- **Wild Strawberry,** 138 2nd Ave. (☎766-3608), off Haines Hwy. The gourmet sandwiches come at decent prices for the quality. Try the Lynn Canal, halibut with cheese, onion, mushroom, and focaccia ($7), or the salad bar ($5) on the deck. The seafood is fresh and caught by the owners. Open M-F 7am-9pm, Sa-Su 8am-9pm.
- **Fireweed Bakery and Cafe** (☎766-3838), on Blacksmith Rd., up the hill behind Lutak Lumber, near Ft. Seward. Just try and resist the enticing baked goods ($1-3). Lunch specials average a pricey $12, but calzones and the occasional buffalo burger are more reasonable ($8). Service can be slow during lunch hour. Open M-Sa 7am-9pm.
- **Bamboo Room** (☎776-2800), on 2nd Ave. near Main St. No bamboo in sight. More frequently seen are fishermen in for a hearty breakfast (omelette, $8). Lunch specials ($7-9) are not so special, where entrees are standard. Open daily 6am-midnight.

SIGHTS AND ENTERTAINMENT

FORT WILLIAM SEWARD. The fort was built on the south side of town to assert American presence during times of increasing mining. It was the first permanent Army post in Alaska, with troops arriving in 1904. With duties including shoveling snow and watching for fires, the post quickly became known as a gentle assignment. "Even among men with the most modern arms, time is the hardest thing to kill," lamented one observer in a 1907 newspaper. After WWII, an attempt to turn the fort into a commune failed. Today, Fort Seward's colonial-style buildings remain on display, but are now mostly B&Bs and private living quarters. The replicated **Totem Village** (☎ 766-2160; in summer 766-2004) and a tribal house host **salmon bakes.** The village is home to Sea Wolf Studio-Gallery, where Tlingit artist Tresham Gregg carves masks. (☎ 766-2540. Open M-F 9am until the last ship leaves.) In the Alaska Indian Arts Center, carvers work in open workshops. (☎ 766-2160. Call for hours.)

AMERICAN BALD EAGLE FOUNDATION AND NATURAL HISTORY MUSEUM. A room of 180 stuffed Alaskan wildlife animals allows you close-up viewing. (At the intersection of Haines Hwy. and 2nd Ave. ☎ 766-3094. Open Sept.-May Sa and Su 1-4pm, M-W 9am-5pm, Th 9am-10pm. $3, ages 7-12 $1, under 7 free.)

THE SHELDON MUSEUM. A small room showcases collected relics and antiques from the community. The museum is interesting to those looking for more information on the military and missionary history of the town, but may be a bit boring to others. (Front St., downtown. ☎ 766-2366. Open Sa-M 1-6pm; T-W 10am-noon and 1-6pm; Th-F 10am-noon, 1-6pm, and 7-9pm. $3.)

BARS. The three main watering holes in town are **The Fogcutter** on Main St., opposite the bank; **Harbor Bar,** by the small boat harbor; and the **Hälsingland Hotel Bar.** In a unique system, all of them close depending on where the action is: once the party-spot has established itself sometime after midnight, the favored barkeep calls the other two bars and they close up early. A good bet is to start at the Fogcutter for a wide selection on tap and 50¢ pool. (Harbor and Hälsingland Hotel Bar open around 8am, Fogcutter opens at 5am.)

FESTIVALS. The biggest annual event in Haines is the **Alaska Bald Eagle Festival** (Nov. 6-10, 2002), when thousands of eagles gather on the Chilkat River. A winter salmon run provides food for hungry eagles; feeding eagles provide food for hungry photographers. Contact the **American Bald Eagle Foundation Center** (☎ 766-3094) for more information. Haines becomes party central in early summer with a **Craft Beer and Home-Brew Festival** (May 17-18, 2002) and an Alaskan **Mardi Gras** (the first weekend of June). If wheels are your thing, but hogs aren't, team up for the **International Kluane to Chilkoot Bike Relay** (June 15, 2002). The 153 mi. course covers the Haines Hwy. from Haines Junction, YT, to Haines, AK, with checkpoints every 20 mi. to relieve saddle soreness. **Sockeye Cycle** (see p. 427) has more info. The Bald Eagle Music Festival and State Fair is a major attraction throughout the region (Aug. 8-12, 2002).

OUTDOOR ACTIVITIES

The **Haines Hwy.** winds 40 mi. from Haines into the **Chilkat Range,** running north through the Yukon, with views guaranteed to blow you through the back of your Winnebago. The world's highest concentration of bald eagles congregates each November in the **Chilkat Bald Eagle Preserve,** 19 mi. up the highway.

BIKING. The Haines vicinity is a great place for biking, especially along the Haines Hwy., which runs out of town and offers access to a variety of sights and activities. Considering that bikes from **Sockeye Cycle** (p. 427) can run over $30 per day, it's best to bring a bike on the ferry or, better yet, pedal in from Canada.

WATER. A favorite swimming hole is **Chilkoot Lake,** 10 mi. north on Lutak Rd. The Chilkat is a late August salmon run, and is choice for canoeing and kayaking. Call **Tanani Bay** (p. 427) for rentals and tips. **Deishu Expeditions** (☎ 800-552-9257) runs guided tours in the area, some up around the Davidson glacier. **Chilkat Guides** runs a rafting trip down the Tsirku river for eagle viewing in isolated surroundings. Enthusiastic staff steer the rafts down the shallow, cold river. (☎ 766-2491. $75.)

FLIGHTSEEING. Haines is actually closer to the glaciers of Glacier Bay than the town of Gustavus (see p. 424). Views of all-white mountain peaks and miles and miles of glaciers trick the eyes into believing one has traveled back in time to an ice age. Although most of the small airlines also cater to their clients' flightseeing needs, **Mountain Flying Service** is the most hospitable crew and specializes in this business. Each tour is well worth the money. (1hr. $115; 80min. $159; 2hr. $259.) Glacier landings ($75 extra) are also available, but are at the discretion of the pilot. There is a two person minimum for all flights.

HIKING

Haines' surrounding mountains are stunning and views from their summits are superb. Ask for the free *Haines is for Hikers*, at the visitors center.

Mt. Ripinsky Trail (4½ mi. one-way, 6-8hr.). Follow 2nd Ave. north, then take Young St. uphill, veer left at the fork in the road. Pass a wooden water tank and enter Skyline Estates. Follow the power lines. The trailhead is on the left in front of a gate. This 3463 ft. summit offers panoramic views of snow-capped peaks, glacial fields, and alpine meadows. Weather can make the top especially slippery, requiring good boots.

Mud Bay Road (2¾ mi. one-way, 3½hr.). Follow 3rd Ave. south, then follow Mud Bay Rd. for about 3 mi. The trailhead is at the top of a bank across from the parking area. This is the steep (1760 ft. gain), direct route to the summit. Follow the steep trail and turn right at the intersection with the Lily Lake trail. The trail follows old-growth forest to open muskeg and excellent views.

Seduction Point Trail (7 mi. one-way, 9-10hr.). Take Mud Bay Rd. out of Haines 7 mi. to Chilkat State Park. Time the last part of the hike along **David's Cove** to coincide with low tide. Offers birds, beaches, ocean bluffs, berry picking, wildflowers, and alluring views of **Rainbow** and **Davidson Glaciers.** Camping along the trail is permitted. No water.

Battery Point Trail (2hr.). Trailhead is 1½ mi. from the City Dock. Follow Beach Rd. east around Portage Cove. Turn right at the end of the road. Follow the Battery Point trail for about a mile and continue straight to open meadow and beaches. This is the easiest and briefest hike, but still accesses serene shoreline.

SKAGWAY ☎ 907

Skagway's fascinating past, eccentric local population, and arresting location make visiting worthwhile. The rich history began thanks to gold mines and persists due to cruise lines. The winter population of 850 swells to 1600 summer residents, and the tourist-centric Broadway board sidewalk is trampled by nearly 800,000 visitors each year. Five hundred miles from Skagway, in August 1896, a Tlingit man named Skookum Jim was washing a pan in a tributary of the Klondike River when he discovered strips of gold so thick they looked "like cheese in a sandwich." By October, 20,000 stampeders from Skagway had set off for the site of Jim's discovery. As gold fields were exhausted, Skagway's shrunken population persisted beside an empty port at the terminus of the hastily engineered White Pass railway. Today the railroad carries tourists to see historic Broadway St. or hike the Chilkoot Trail.

TRANSPORTATION

At the northernmost tip of the Inside Passage, Skagway is a terminus of the **Alaska Marine Hwy.** Skagway is also at the end of the **Klondike Hwy.** (Rte. 98 in AK and Hwy. 2 in YT), 113 mi. (2½hr.) south of Whitehorse and 66 mi. (1½hr.) south of Carcross. Canadian and US **customs** are passable 24 hours a day, although the US office is not staffed from midnight to 6am. Although there are no services between Skagway and Carcross, the coastal scenery and deep ravine views once the road crosses into BC make focusing on the road a tough

SKAGWAY ■ 431

feat. **Haines** is 15 mi. away by water, 360 mi. by land. The **ferry** dock is at the southern end of downtown. Skagway's main drag, **Broadway St.**, runs inland from the docks with **Spring St.** on the right, and **State** and **Main St.** on the left. Numbered **avenues** intersect the streets, ascending from the water. The road into town runs straight to State St.

Flights: Skagway Air Service (☎ 983-2218), on Broadway between 4th and 5th Ave., flies 8 times per day to **Haines** (10min., $40), **Juneau** (45min., $80), and **Gustavus** (1hr., $90) and tours **Glacier Bay** (1½hr., 2 person min., $125). Open daily 7am-9pm; winter 7am-5pm.

Trains: White Pass and Yukon Route (☎ 983-2217 or 800-343-7373; www.whitepassrailroad.com), on 2nd Ave. One of North America's steepest and most scenic railroads. Round-trip daily excursions to White Pass Summit ($82) or Lake Bennett ($128 on Su, M, and F; $156 on Sa). Also accesses remote trailheads (see **Outdoor Activities**, p. 434). Train and bus service daily to **Whitehorse, YT** (5hr.; 8am; $95, ages 3-12 are half-price for all fares). Buses may not be wheelchair accessible. Reservations recommended.

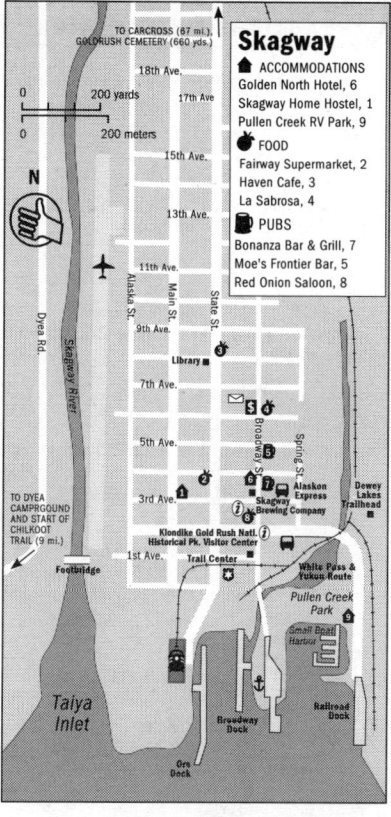

Skagway

♦ **ACCOMMODATIONS**
Golden North Hotel, 6
Skagway Home Hostel, 1
Pullen Creek RV Park, 9

● **FOOD**
Fairway Supermarket, 2
Haven Cafe, 3
La Sabrosa, 4

● **PUBS**
Bonanza Bar & Grill, 7
Moe's Frontier Bar, 5
Red Onion Saloon, 8

Buses: Alaska Direct (☎ 800-770-6652) runs vans by appointment from the ferry terminal, visitors center, and hostel to **Whitehorse, YT** (3½hr.; $50, round-trip $90). Connections on W, F, and Su to **Fairbanks** ($190) and **Anchorage** ($215); requires an overnight stay in Whitehorse (accommodation not provided). **Alaskon Express** (☎ 983-2241 or 800-544-2206), in the Westmark Inn on 3rd Ave. between Broadway and Spring St., runs in summer once daily to **Whitehorse, YT** (3hr., 8:45am, $46) and from mid-May to mid-Sept. Su and W to **Anchorage** ($219) and **Fairbanks** ($216). Both trips require overnighting in Beaver Creek, YT (23hr.; accommodation not provided but reduced rate at Westmark Inn available).

Ferries: Alaska Marine Highway (☎ 983-2941 or 800-642-0066). Beware dockside ticket office's erratic hours. Open when the ferry is in, 1:30-3:30pm. Ferry schedule also varies; check online: www.state.ak.us/ferry. Typically, in July and Aug. 6 per week leave for **Haines** (1hr.; $19 for walk-on, $28 for small vehicle, $33 for large) and **Juneau** (6½hr.; $35). **Water Taxi** (☎ 983-2083 or 888-766-3395). Open May-Sept. daily 7:30am-4:30pm. Buy tickets at Dijon Delights, on Broadway at 5th Ave. Runs twice per day to **Haines** (1hr.; $24, round-trip with 4hr. stopover $45; under 12 half-price).

Local Transportation: SMART (☎ 983-2743) runs shuttles year-round 7:30am-9pm, making stops on Broadway for a maximum fare of $3. Other local pick-up or drop-off accommodated. Call for reservations.

Car Rental: Sourdough Van & Car Rentals (☎ 983-2523, in AK 800-478-2529), 6th Ave. at Broadway. From $57 with unlimited mileage. Drop-offs at Haines and Whitehorse by arrangement. Must be 21 with credit card.

🛈 PRACTICAL INFORMATION

Visitor Information: Skagway Convention and Visitors Bureau (☎ 983-2854; www.skagway.org), on Broadway off 2nd Ave. in historic **Arctic Brotherhood Hall**, constructed of a reputed 10,000 pieces of driftwood. Open May-Sept. daily 8am-6pm; Oct.-Apr. M-F 8am-5pm. **Klondike Gold Rush National Historical Park** (☎ 983-2921), at 2nd Ave. and Broadway. Free exhibits and 45min. walking tours at 9, 10, and 11am, and at 2 and 3pm; self-guided tour brochures available. Open June-Aug. daily 8am-8pm; May and Sept. 8am-6pm.

Outdoor Information: The Parks **Trail Center** (☎ 983-3655) on Broadway sells **overnight permits** for Canadian side of Chilkoot trail. (CDN$35, under 16 CDN$17.50.) Knowledgeable staff prepare hikers. Open late-May to mid-Sept. daily 8am-4:15pm. Eminently knowledgeable staff at **The Mountain Shop** (see **Equipment Rental**) can also provide advice on local outdoors opportunities.

Bank: National Bank of Alaska (☎ 983-2265), at Broadway and 6th Ave. Open M-F 9:30am-5pm. 24hr. **ATM.**

Equipment Rental: The Mountain Shop (☎ 983-2544), on 4th Ave. between Broadway and State St., rents water, snow, camping, and Chilkoot gear at reasonable rates. Kayaks $40 per day, snowshoes $5, tents $20, and camp stoves $6. Rates reduced for multiple day usage. **Sockeye Cycle** (☎ 983-2851), on 5th Ave. off Broadway St. From $6 per hr. or $30 per day. Open daily May-Sept. 9am-6pm. **Sourdough Van and Car Rentals** (see above) rents bikes for $10 per day. **Skagway Hardware** (☎ 983-2233), on Broadway St. at 4th Ave., sells fishing permits ($10 per day) and outdoor gear. Open mid-Apr. to Sept. M-F 8am-6pm, Sa and Su 8am-5pm; winter M-Sa 8am-5pm.

Market: **You Say Tomato,** (☎ 983-2784), on State St. at 9th Ave. sells dry, natural meals by the pound, groceries, fresh produce, and nutritional supplements. Tons of organic goods and fresh bread. 15% discount on bulk orders. Open Apr.-Oct. M-Sa 10:30am-7:30pm, Su noon-5pm; call for winter hours. **Fairway Supermarket** (☎ 983-2000), at 4th Ave. and State St., sells groceries. Open M-Sa 8am-9pm, Su 8am-6pm; winter M-Sa 9am-6pm, Su 10am-4pm.

Bookstore: Skagway News Depot (☎ 983-3354), Broadway between 2nd Ave. and 3rd Ave. Open daily 8:30am-7pm.

Internet Access: Free at the **Library** (☎ 983-2665) at 8th Ave. and State St. (one terminal for research, one for email). Book ahead. Open M-F 1-9pm, Sa 1-5pm. Several expensive pay-by-the-hour operations as well.

Laundromat: Services Unlimited Laundromat (☎ 983-2595), at 2nd Ave. and State St. attached to the gas station. Wash $2, dry 25¢ per 5min. Open daily 7am-9pm, last load 7:30pm; winter 8am-6pm.

Public Showers: Garden City RV Park (☎ 983-2743), on State and 15th Ave. 75¢ per 5min.

Emergency: ☎ 911.

Police: (☎ 983-2232) on State St. towards the water past 1st Ave.

Hospital: Skagway Medical Service (☎ 983-2255; emergency 983-2418) on 11th Ave. between State and Broadway. Clinic open M-F 9am-noon and 1-5pm.

Post Office: (☎ 983-2330), at Broadway and 6th, next to bank. Open M-F 8:30am-5pm. **ZIP Code:** 99840.

🏠 ACCOMMODATIONS

Several reasonably priced and unique accomodations are reason enough for the non-cruise ship passenger to visit the town. Make reservations unless you're camping. Dyea, 9 mi. away, has the only free tenting.

SKAGWAY ■ 433

Skagway Home Hostel, P.O. Box 231 (☎983-2131). On 3rd Ave. near Main St. Home sweet home invites you into their family. Shared kitchen. Sign up for dinner before 4:30pm ($5; free if you cook). Showers, kitchen, bike use, and plenty of Chilkoot Trail stories and advice. Sheets and towels $1. Laundry $3. No credit cards. Chore required. Check-in 5:30-9pm. No lockout. Curfew 11pm (late ferries accommodated). Reservations advised (by mail only). Beds $15; double $40.

Golden North Hotel (☎983-2491), at 3rd Ave. and Broadway St. The classiest affordable hotel in Southeast Alaska and the oldest hotel in the state (est. 1898). Each room in a period style, with canopy beds and antique furniture. Ghost in Room 24. Singles $65, with bath $95; doubles $75, with bath $105.

Dyea Camping Area, 9 mi. northwest of Skagway on winding Dyea Rd., near start of Chilkoot Trail. Well maintained. Pit toilets, treat the water, no showers. Tough drive is hard on RVs. 14-night max. stay. 22 spacious, woodsy sites. Free.

Pullen Creek RV Park (☎983-2768), on 2nd Ave. by the harbor. Small and noisy, but convenient, with a pretty, unobstructed view of the mountains. Bathrooms, coin shower. No open fires. $12 for a tent, $4 extra for vehicle; hookups $22.

FOOD

Skagway's status as a cruise ship magnet can make eating and shopping pricey. Look in the right places, and you'll find quite a bit of spunk and flavor at a low cost.

La Sabrosa, on Broadway and 6th Ave. (☎983-2469). Sneak behind the large green building and find a local gem, kept secret from the cruise ship mobs. A fat, meaty burrito ($9) is a challenge to finish, while the salad ($6) and sandwich ($7) options are sure to delight. Rocket shake ($4.50). Open M-F 6am-4pm, Sa-Su 7am-2pm.

Red Onion Saloon (☎983-2222), on Broadway between 2nd and 3rd Ave. At Skagway's classiest former bordello, built in 1898, the bawdy waitresses entertain the daytime tourist crowd. Tasty sandwiches ($6-8); pizzas ($7). The dinner scene is much more mellow Live music. Many Alaskan beers on tap (pint $4.25). Open daily 10am-late.

Haven Cafe, State St. and 9th Ave. (☎983-3553). The one stop espresso shop in town far enough from crowds that you can settle in on the couch and enjoy a book. Goodies (scones $2), panini sandwiches ($8), and delectable desserts (cake $5) are options. Sundays 8pm-midnight is open mic. Open M-Sa 6am-10pm; Su 6am-midnight.

Corner Cafe, (☎983-2155), at 4th Ave. and State St. Head here for basic grub and relaxed open-air seating that helps dissipate the smoke. Listen to that fryer sizzle! Stack of buttermilk pancakes $4, burgers $6-8. Open daily 6am-8pm.

SIGHTS AND ENTERTAINMENT

KLONDIKE. Many of the pristine buildings from the 1900s on Broadway St. are leased to local businesses by the Park Service as part of the **Klondike Gold Rush National Historical Park.** Guided walking tours or a self-guided tour map available (see **Visitor Information** above). Polish up on gold rush trivia and Alaskan culture at the **Skagway Museum and Archive,** housed in the oldest and newest granite building in Alaska on 7th Ave. and Spring Street. (☎983-2420. Open M-F in summer 9am-5pm, Sa and Su 1-5pm. $2, students $1, under 12 free.)

GOLD RUSH CEMETERY. The **Gold Rush Cemetery,** about a 1½ mi. from town, retains an eerie serenity rare in other gold rush monuments. Take State St. to the parking lot before the bridge and follow the dirt road. A short trail from the cemetery leads to **Lower Reid Falls,** which cascades 300 ft. down the mountainside. **Dyea,** once Skagway's flourishing sister-city, sinks beneath June's blooming fields of irises and lilies.

THE CLEANEST CON MAN IN THE NORTH

Skagway's most notorious ne'er-do-well, Jefferson Randolph "Soapy" Smith, got his name from his favorite scam, the "soap game." He would sit on a street corner selling a chance to pick a bar of soap from his collection for an outrageous $5. Each bar had some bill wrapped around it, with the bar and bill wrapped in cloth to obscure the denomination. With thousands of prospectors roaming the streets of Skagway any given day, it never took long before a crowd gathered, and some impetuous spenders would step forward to buy bars. As luck would have it, those first two or three invariably held very large bills and triggered a buying frenzy. Most purchasers ended up with only a bar of soap and a single greenback. The two or three lucky fellows (a.k.a. his accomplices) would meet up with Soapy later and return the planted bills for a handsome payoff. Ultimately, Soapy Smith wasn't such a bad sort: he donated money to the community for a new church, started an adopt-a-dog program, and rarely robbed locals. In appreciation of his peculiar brand of philanthropy, the town named him a Marshal of the 4th of July parade in 1898. A few days later, Soapy died in a shoot-out, taking his adversary down with him. While Soapy was buried outside the limits of the town cemetery, the fickle public gave his killer a choice plot and a tombstone inscribed, "He gave his life for the honor of Skagway." Today, Soapy's spirit is celebrated each July at a debaucherous evening gathering called Soapy's Wake.

BARS. The Skagway bar scene on Broadway is driven by water-weary tourists in the day and tourist-weary locals in the night. Skagway bars have on occasion had last call approaching 4am, but bars typically close near midnight. For ribald history, hit the **Red Onion Saloon**, Skagway's first bordello built in 1898 and a popular bar with an enviable collection of bed pans. Come for live afternoon jazz (courtesy of cruise ship musicians), a tour upstairs with Madame Chilkoot, or a game of pool. (☎ 983-2222. Open May-Sept. daily 10am-late.) For less ambience but Skagway brews, the **Skagway Brewing Company** in the Golden North Hotel serves up six drafts from its in-house microbrewery. The **Oosic Stout** ($4) is named for the bone of a male walrus's nether regions. (Open daily May-Sept. 11am-closing.) **Bonanza Bar** is as American as apple pie with a game on the big-screen TV and sports jerseys on the wall. Pints from $4 and pitchers from $12.50. Open mic on W nights. Open daily May-Sept. 10am-midnight. **Moe's Frontier Bar**, on Broadway between 4th and 5th Ave., offers an escape from the hectic Broadway tourist scene. If dark and smoky is what you're looking for, Moe's will fit the bill to a tee. Beer in a can is $2.75, in a bottle from $3.25. Yee-haw! (☎ 983-2238. Open Apr.-Sept. 9am-late, winter 11am-late.)

ART. Skagway's history is nearly overshadowed by its souvenir shops. **Inside Passage Arts**, at Broadway between 4th and 5th Ave., is an artist-run gallery that sells indigenous crafts. (☎ 983-2585. Open daily May-Sept. 9am-7pm.) Bone carvings and fossilized ivory chronicle the history of Alaska in the free museum behind the showroom at **Corrington Alaskan Ivory**, at 5th Ave. and Broadway St. (☎ 983-2580. Open May-Sept. daily 9am-6pm.)

OUTDOOR ACTIVITIES

CHILKOOT TRAIL

Skagway offers both phenomenal day hikes and multi-day trips. The highly acclaimed **Chilkoot Trail** starts at the nearby Dyea Camping Area. Backpackers on the Chilkoot benefit from the Alaska National History Association's complete *Hiker's Guide to the Chilkoot Trail* ($2), available at the Trail Center. Hikers must register at the Trail Center to use any portion of the Chilkoot. Reservations for the Chilkoot are accepted for the coming year starting in January and are recommended if hiking in July to August. Fifty people per day are allowed to cross the pass into Canada, and there is space for only eight walk-ons. Hikers are advised to allow 3-6 days to hike the Chilkoot, although the record is only 16 hours. After a safety spiel at the trail center and swearing on the Blarney Stone to abide by the Chilkoot rules, the adventure begins. Rangers are stationed at the Dyea Trailhead, Sheep Camp, and Lindeman City. Upon completion, hikers must go to Canadian customs in Fraser, BC (☎867-821-4111), or Whitehorse, YT. (☎867-667-3943. CDN$35 for the whole trail, CDN$18 for children. Reservations CDN$10.)

In Whitehorse (☎800-661-0486 or 867-667-3910), persistence pays off in making reservations. Get information in Skagway, too (☎907-983-3655; open daily 8am-4:15pm). There are a number of ways to get between Skagway or Carcross and the Chilkoot trailheads at Dyea and Bennett Lake. **Frontier Excursions** (☎983-2512) and **Dyea Dave** (☎983-2731) run taxis between Skagway and Dyea ($10) and between Skagway and the road access end at Log Cabin ($25 for both drop and pickup). **The White Pass & Yukon Route** runs trains between Skagway and Lake Bennett, the traditional end. (☎983-2217. $65. Reservations required.)

GLACIERS

Outdoor accessibility knows no limit in Skagway—glaciers can be reached easily, and cabins await visitors. The White Pass & Yukon Railroad (see Trains) drops the glacier-bond at Laughton Glacier (easy 2½ mi. hike from Milepost 14, $54 round-trip) and Denver Glacier (5½ mi. hike from Milepost 6, $27 round-trip). Reservations for the Laughton Cabin (1½ mi. from train stop) or the noisier, Caboose Cabin (at Denver train stop) are through the U.S. Forest Service. (☎586-8751 or 877-444-6777. $35. Pit toilets, no water.)

DEWEY LAKE

Although the Chilkoot Trail is the marquee name in Skagway hiking, shorter local trails have inspiring views and less traffic. The **Dewey Lake Trail System** provides some of the best nearby hiking, from a 2hr. stroll to a strenuous climb to alpine lakes at 3700 ft./1130m. Pick up a free guide to the local hikes at the **Trail Center, The Mountain Shop,** or **visitors center** (see **Outdoor Information,** p. 432). To reach the trails, walk east along 2nd Ave. and follow the dirt path just before the railroad tracks to the left. Look for trailhead signs on the right. Narrow, tree-lined **Lower Dewey Lake** lies less than a mile up the trail. After passing the outhouse, hikers find refuge from the railroad, helicopter, and cruise ship noise. One trail branches to the lake (2 mi./3km), and another heads to **Icy Lake** and **Upper Reid Falls** (1½ mi./2.5km). Both walks are gentle, with little change in elevation. A third trail to **Upper Dewey Lake** branches off the Icy Lake trail near the northern end of Lower Dewey Lake. The first section of the trail (2¼ mi./3.5km) is brutal until the climb mellows out into switchbacks to the site of the lake, in a stunning amphitheater of peaks. The total ascent from town takes 2-3hr. A cramped cabin with space for 4 with bunks is available on a first-come, first served basis. The best tenting sites are along the far shore. **Fishing** is available at both Dewey Lakes. The **Skyline Trail** leads up AB Mountain named for the pattern created by spring meltwater on its face. Both the directions to the trailhead and the trail itself are confusing; pick up a **Skagway Trail Map** at the Trail Center or at the Klondike Gold Rush National Historical Park Visitor Center (see **Visitor Information,** p. 432). From town, it's about 5 mi. to the panoramic 3500 ft. summit; allow 4-5hr. for the steep ascent. A free **camping permit** is necessary in the Skagway area and is available at the police station.

YAKUTAT ☎907

The people of Yakutat live, eat, and breathe fish. King, sockeye, and silver salmon as well as halibut, steelhead, and rainbow trout are caught in large numbers here. Grown men (and a few women) act like giddy children at an amusement park when they reach Yakutat's isolated and plentiful shores for world-class sportfishing. The community survives on the fishing industry and the tourism it creates. This is old-time Alaska with a hearty population of 800, and is ringed by the highest coastal mountains in the world and flanked by alarmingly active ice. Hubbard Glacier to the north is the largest tidewater glacier in the world. While Yakutat's ocean-front weather can be treacherous (frequent storms bring up to 200 in. of rain and 200 in. of snow yearly), hardy surfers come here for some of the best waves in Alaska. Wrangell-St. Elias National Park (see p. 451) and Glacier Bay (see p. 425) lie to the west and east, respectively, and much land around Yakutat is in the Tongass National Forest. Backpackers beware: budget travel has yet to establish itself in Yakutat. Food here is the most expensive in the Panhandle. Moreover, the weather usually makes camping a cold, wet proposition. On a sunny day, though, the 180° views of jagged peaks will be salve to your pocketbook's wounds.

TRANSPORTATION. Yakutat is the northernmost village in the Panhandle. It sits on **Phipps Peninsula,** enclosing **Yakutat Bay,** the only protected harbor on the Gulf of Alaska between the "mainland" and the Panhandle. The **airport** is 5 mi. south of the ferry dock and downtown, on Monti Bay. Destinations are fairly spread out and require a vehicle. Most folks in Yakutat give directions by landmarks, not street names. Yakutat is the smallest community in the world with daily jet service. **Alaskan Airlines** (☎784-3366 or 800-426-0333) Flights #61 and #66 do the honors, stopping in on their way between **Seattle** and **Anchorage.** Short hops to **Juneau** ($153) and **Cordova** ($235) are also available. Once a month in summer, the **Alaska Marine Highway** stops in on its way from Juneau to Valdez. **Sunset Taxi** runs 24hr. (☎784-3773. $11 airport to downtown.) **Situk Leasing** meets flights and rents beat-up old trucks that suit Yakutat's dirt roads, for $65 per day. (☎784-3316. Unlimited mileage; must have insurance and major credit card.)

PRACTICAL INFORMATION. The **Yakutat Chamber of Commerce** (☎784-3933; www.yakutatalaska.com) has an office in the **National Park Service Ranger Station/Visitors Center** on Mallott Ave. that serves Wrangell-St. Elias and Glacier Bay National Parks. (P.O. Box 137. ☎784-3295. Open M-F 8am-5pm, but call ahead.) Get info on wilderness cabins at the **Yakutat Ranger District Forest Service,** on Ocean Cape Rd. (☎784-3359. Open M-F 8am-5pm.) The **Alaska Dept. of Fish and Game** office is near the airport. (☎784-3255. Open M-F 8am-5pm.) **Yakutat Hardware,** on Mallott Ave. downtown, sells licenses, hunting tags, gear, and supplies. (☎784-3203. Open M-Sa 10am-5:30pm.) **Weapons North** (☎784-3363) also sells licenses. **Alaska Pacific,** on Mallott Ave., is the only bank in town. (☎784-3991. Open M-Th 10am-3pm, F 10am-5pm.) **Monti Bay Foods** has the **ATM. Yakutat Lodge** has a coin laundry and charges $7 per shower. **Weather:** ☎800-662-6622. **Emergency:** ☎911. **Police:** (☎784-3206) in the hangar-shaped Public Safety Office on Max Italio Dr. **Pharmacy:** 24hr. Health Center, under Forest Service office. (☎784-3275. Pharmacy open M-F 9am-noon and 1-4:30pm.) **Post office:** (☎784-3201), on Mallott Ave. Open M-F 9am-5pm, Sa 9am-1pm. **ZIP code:** 99689.

ACCOMMODATIONS AND FOOD. Lodges and B&Bs cater to wealthy sport fishermen and offer expensive packages including food, vehicles, boats, and guides. **Yakutat Lodge,** next to the airport, rents rustic cabins that sleep four or more. This is the cheapest room in town, although it is a testosterone-dominated, father-son fishing joint. (☎784-3232. $25 per person; $50 min.) **Bay View Lodge** overlooks Monti Bay and provides comfy beds and the best food in town. ($50 per person. ☎784-3341. No credit cards.) About 3 mi. from the airport, **Cannon Beach** stretches 10 mi. bordering the Pacific tides and could provide some isolated camping. The old-growth forest on the beach provides shelter, both to you and the bears—be careful. Take a left a quarter-mile from the airport onto the gravel road, follow it 2 mi. over the bridge, through the forest and onto the beach.

The **Glass Door Bar,** on Mallott Ave., stays open nightly until folks clear out and is the only non-lodge bar in town. Serving mostly the town regulars, visitors are a welcomed change. (☎784-3331. Pints $3, pitchers $8.) **Mallott's General Store,** on Max Italio Dr., a quarter-mile from the turn-off after Monti Bay, is where locals get groceries, boots, and books. (☎784-3355. Espresso window open from 6am. Store open daily 8am-8pm; winter M-Sa 8am-7pm, Su 10am-3pm.) **Monti Bay Foods,** the purple building across from the post office, also sells groceries.

SIGHTS AND OUTDOOR ACTIVITIES.
Fairweather Days in August is a large town event with small bands, arts and crafts, and local excitement hosted on Cannon Beach. The town **dump** is a favorite place to view bears and eagles, though it may not be what the tourist had in mind for scenery. Beware: even though these beasts look tame, they are still wild. Keep your distance, or stay in the car. Hiking is good at **Harlequin Lake,** an easy, three-quarter-mile hike that leads to fantastic views of icebergs and **Hubbard Glacier.** (At the end of Dangerous River Rd. Allow 40min. round trip.) On a clear day, **Yakutat Glacier** is also visible. Reserve the Harlequin Lake Forest Service cabin for an overnight stay. Beware, very big bears are known to roam these parts (see p. 40). Surfers watch for rolling turquoise waves breaking off **Ocean Cape,** nicknamed "the graveyard," or **Point Munoz** on Khantaak Island along **Cannon Beach's** 10 mi. stretch. Jack at **Icy Waves Surf Shop** (☎784-3226) offers advice and sells wetsuits and boards; you'll need a 3-5mm wet suit for the 40-50°F water.

Although no **kayak or canoe** rentals are available in town, extensive waterways in the region are great for kayaking and canoeing. The Forest Service can suggest some spectacular trips for experienced paddlers. Camping is permitted on some of the islands of Monti Bay, but experienced paddlers can venture farther afield. A long portage to **Russell Fjord** makes way for a trip up to **Hubbard Glacier.** The **Arhnklin, Dangerous,** and **Awke Rivers** run parallel to shore up to **Dry Bay,** the western end of **Glacier Bay National Park.** Some fishing charter services will transport backpackers and kayakers along the Puget Peninsula toward Hubbard Glacier, or across Yakutat Bay to the eastern end of **Wrangell-St. Elias National Park. Gulf Air** flies backpackers and rafters to Wrangell-St. Elias, Glacier Bay, and the interior regions of **Yakutat Forelands Wilderness Area.** (☎784-3240. About $270 per hr. for fly-ins and **flightseeing.**) Contact the Chamber of Commerce for a list of charter operations. The Forest Service and the National Park Service have info on local hikes and cabins. Trippers bring their own gear and provisions.

CENTRAL ALASKA

> **ALASKA'S...Capital:** Juneau. **Population:** 626,932. **Area:** 586,412 mi.² **Motto:** We're way bigger than Texas and have more oil! **Real Motto:** North to the Future. **Flower:** Forget-me-not. **State Fish:** King salmon. **Tree:** Sitka spruce. **Mineral:** Gold. **Gem:** Jade. **Sport:** Dog mushing. **Holiday:** Alaska Day, Oct. 18. **Drinking Age:** 21.

Southcentral Alaska stands alone as the region by which many outsiders gauge the entire state. As the transportation hub, Anchorage can be a daunting undertaking, with strip malls and skyscrapers vying for a skyline dominated by mountain ranges. Major highways shuttle hordes of tour and camper buses from site to site come summer, while long winters enshroud locals in a blanket of quiet lasting just long enough for them to forget the rush they'll soon encounter. The twin towns of Kenai and Soldotna hold the sport fishing title, clogging the peninsula's highways in the manner of the Cook Inlet salmon lined fin-to-fin in the glacial waters.

Oil and fishing dominate the economy, and as the history of the 49th state has gone, so have its fortunes. Boom and bust has always been the name of the game

Southcentral Alaska

438

in Alaska, a fact that hasn't changed in the last two hundred years. Many say the Klondike gold rush of 1898 was only the first in a string, from the liquid gold of the pipeline boom, to ocean gold pulled up in the form of king crab pots out of the Bering Sea. The last ten years have seen the near-destruction of Alaska's commercial fishing industry due to the governmental regulations and fishery-depletion that have strangled towns like Kodiak that depend solely on the strength of their catch, while the North Slope's black gold pumps quietly into Valdez each year. The boomtimes are never far off though, whispering of natural gas pipelines, exploding fish populations, and coastal drilling from distant shores. This is a land of many names and faces, each with a unique history and future, tenuously tied to one another.

CENTRAL ALASKA'S HIGHLIGHTS

GLACIERS calve into the waters in Cordova (see p. 465).

DENALI'S breathtaking peak must be enjoyed, whether from up close or from afar, whether by car, by foot, or by plane (see p. 497).

ALASKAN MICROBREW FESTIVAL combines hot water and hops in early August at **Chena Hot Springs Resort** (see p. 517).

GODLINESS is next to the Shoup glacier in Valdez where Sunday services are held afloat at the foot of the ice (see p. 461).

ANCHORAGE ☎907

Alaska's foremost urban center and only metropolis, Anchorage's 260,000 residents compose two-fifths of the state's population. Not the most scenic of city designs, Anchorage nevertheless sits as the hub of travel and commerce for a state that has moved swiftly and decidedly into the 21st century, breaking barriers and stereotypes along the way. Long winters are softened by a mild coastal climate that significantly harshens only 40 mi. inland, and long summer days stretch out over Cook Inlet and the Chugach Mountains that encircle the "Anchorage Bowl."

It's impossible to pigeon-hole such a diverse city, with strong Alaskan native and Pacific island populations that shrug the wild Alaskan image, an image otherwise not dismissed by its coffee shops, high rises, and museums. Anchorage may only be a momentary jumping point for many travelers, but locals know they're within shouting distance of any outdoor adventure, and still undeniably urbane.

▐ TRANSPORTATION

Anchorage is the transportation hub of southcentral Alaska, 127 mi. (2½hr.) north of Seward on the **Seward Hwy.** (Rte. 9), 358 mi. (6hr.) south of Fairbanks on the **George Parks Hwy.** (Rte. 3), and 304 mi. (6hr.) west of Valdez along the **Glenn Hwy.** (Rte. 1) and **Richardson Hwy.** (Rte. 4). The city sprawls across some 50,000 acres of the Anchorage Bowl, framed by military bases **Fort Richardson** and **Elmendorf Air Force Base** to the north, the **Chugach Mountains** to the east, and the **Knik** and **Turnagain Arms** of the **Cook Inlet** to the west and south. Downtown Anchorage is laid out in a grid: numbered avenues run east-west, with addresses designated east or west from **C St.** North-south streets are lettered alphabetically to the west and named alphabetically to the east of **A St.** The rest of Anchorage spreads out along the major highways. The **University of Alaska Anchorage** lies on 36th Ave., off Northern Lights Blvd. Buses run infrequently and the city is too spread out to walk everywhere. Renting a bike is a wise move, as trails connect most of the city.

Flights: Anchorage International Airport (☎266-2437). Serviced by 8 international and 15 domestic carriers, including **Delta** (☎800-221-1212), **Northwest Airlines** (☎800-225-2525), **United** (☎800-241-6522), and **Alaska Airlines** (☎800-426-0333). Small airlines like **ERA Aviation** (☎800-866-8394 or 248-4422 in town) have cheap deals. Nearly every airport in Alaska can be reached from Anchorage, directly or via Fairbanks.

440 ■ ANCHORAGE

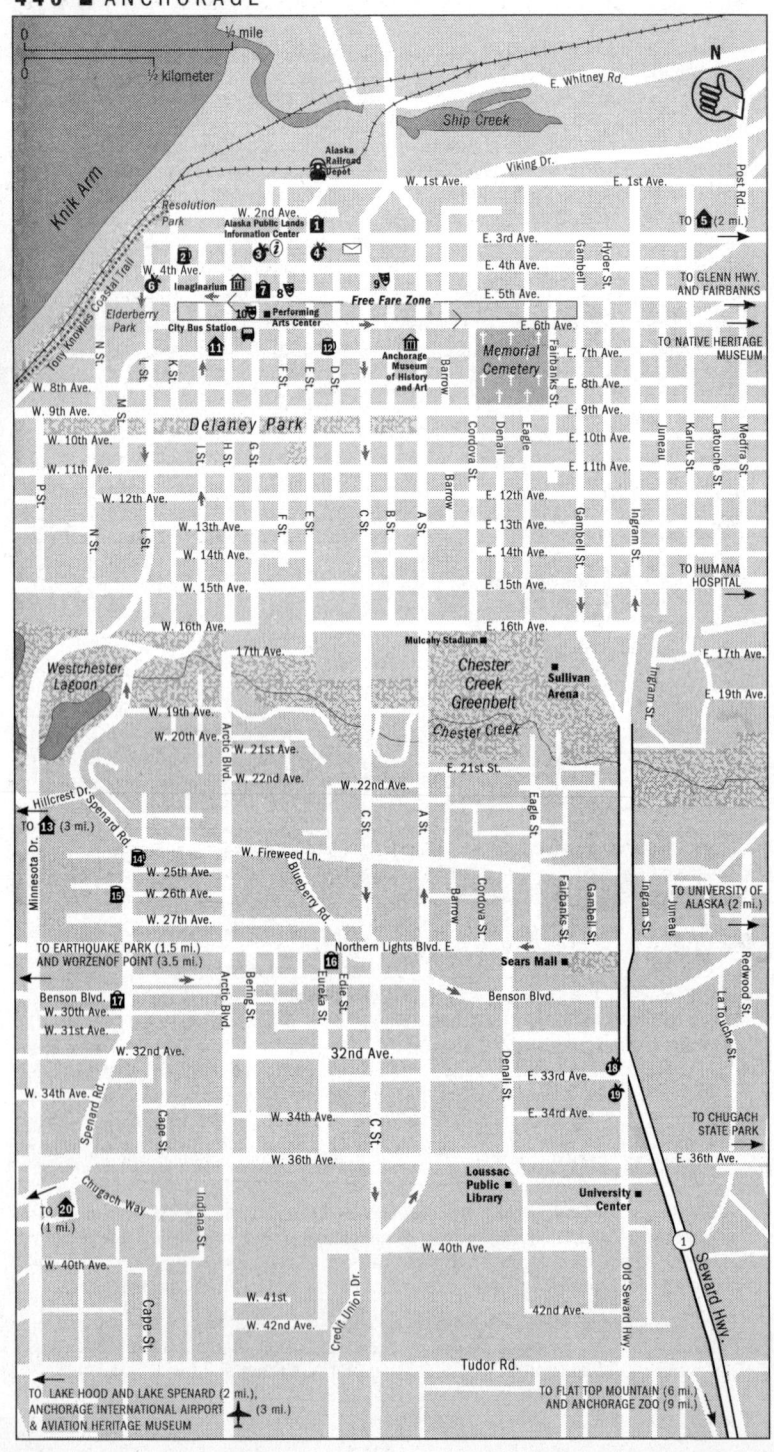

Anchorage

🏠 **ACCOMMODATIONS**
Anchorage Guesthouse, 13
Hostelling International, 11
International
    Backpacker's Hostel, 5
Spenard Hostel, 20

🍎 **FOOD**
Great Harvest Bread Co., 18
M.A.'s Gourmet Dogs, 3
Moose's Tooth, 19
Snow City Café, 6
Sweet Basil Café, 4

🍺 **PUBS**
Bears Tooth, 15

Bernie's Bungalow Lounge, 12
Chilkoot Charlie's, 14
Pioneer Bar, 2

🛍 **SHOPPING**
Mammoth Music, 17
The Rage Vintage Clothing, 7
Salvation Army Thrift Store, 16
Saturday Market, 1

🎭 **THEATRES**
Alaska Experience Theater, 10
Cyrano's Off Center
    Playhouse, 9
4th Avenue Theatre, 8

Trains: Alaska Railroad, 411 W 1st Ave., downtown (☎265-2494; outside AK 800-544-0552; www.alaskarailroad.com). 1 per day to **Seward** (4hr., $60), **Fairbanks** (12hr., $175) via **Talkeetna** (3hr., $75) and **Denali** (8hr., $125). No service to Seward in winter. Bikes up to $20. Tickets can be bought on board, but it's wise to book ahead. Station open M-F 5:30am-5pm, Sa-Su 5:30am-1pm.

Buses: Grayline Alaska (☎800-544-2206). Daily to **Valdez** (10hr., $71). 2 per week to **Skagway** ($219; overnight in **Beaver Creek**).

Homer Stage Lines (☎563-0800). To **Homer** (M-Sa; $48 one-way, $85 round-trip; service decreases Sept.-Apr.). **Parks Highway Express** (☎479-3065 or 888-600-6001), runs daily to **Denali** ($35) and **Fairbanks** ($55) May-Sept. Call for winter service. For buses along the **George Parks Hwy.**, see p. 505.

Ferries: Alaska Marine Highway, 605 W 4th Ave. (☎800-642-0066; www.akhms.com), in the Old Federal Building. No terminal, but ferry tickets sold and reservations granted. Open daily 7:30am-4:30pm; winter M-F 7:30am-4:30pm.

Public Transportation: People Mover Bus (☎343-6543), in Transit Center on 6th Ave. between G and H St. **Free fare zone** bordered by 5th Ave., Gambell St., 6th Ave., and L St. Runs hourly M-F 6am-10pm; less often Sa-Su. $1, ages 5-18 50¢, over 60 25¢. Transit Center sells tokens (90¢), day passes ($2.50), schedules ($1), and maps (50¢). Open M-F 8am-5pm.

Taxis: Yellow Cab (☎272-2422). **Checker Cab** (☎276-1234). **Alaska Cab** (☎563-5353). About $15 from the airport to downtown, $8 to Spenard Hostel.

Car Rentals: Airport Car Rental, 502 W Northern Lights Blvd. (☎277-7662). $50 per day with unlimited mileage. Must be 21; $5 per day extra if under 25. Credit card or cash deposit. Open M-F 8am-8pm, Sa-Su 8am-6pm. **Affordable Car Rental,** 4707 Spenard Rd. (☎243-3370), opposite the Regal Alaskan Hotel. $39 per day, $330 per week; unlimited mileage. Must be 22 with major credit card. Free drop-off and pickup.

Ride Board: At the Anchorage Youth Hostel (see **Accommodations,** p. 442).

🛈 PRACTICAL INFORMATION

TOURIST AND LOCAL SERVICES

Visitor Information: (☎274-3531; events 276-3200) on W 4th Ave. at F St. In the old sod-roofed cabin, or a new building behind. The **bike trails guide** ($3.50) is helpful. Open daily June-Aug. 7:30am-7pm; May and Sept. 8am-6pm; Oct.-Apr. 9am-4pm. Also at the airport (☎266-2437 or 266-2657), in the domestic terminal near the baggage claim, and in the international terminal at the central atrium.

Outdoor Information: Alaska Public Lands Information Center, 605 W 4th Ave. (☎271-2737; www.nps.gov/aplic/center), in the Old Courthouse Bldg. between F and G St. Here the **Park Service, Forest Service, Division of State Parks,** the **Fish and Wildlife Service,** and the **Alaska Marine Highway** reservation desks reside under one glorious roof. Popular topo maps ($4-7), regional Alaskan exhibits, and live presentations on Alaska's outdoor attractions. Open daily 9am-5:30pm. All the **maps** you could ever want live at the **United Stated Geological Survey Office (USGS),** 4230 University Dr. (☎786-7011) located on the University of Anchorage campus in Grace Hall. Take bus #11, 36, 45; get off by Providence Hospital or on campus.

442 ■ ANCHORAGE

Equipment Rental: Downtown Bicycle Rental, 333 W 4th St. (☎279-5293), between C and D St., 5 blocks from the Coastal Trail (see p. 445). Bikes $15 for 3hr., $19 for 5hr., $29 per day. Credit card required. Open daily 8am-6:30pm.

The Bike Exchange, 211 E 4th (☎276-2453), between Barrow and Cordova. $20 per day. Open M-F 11am-7pm, Sa noon-6pm.

Recreational Equipment, Inc. (REI), 1200 Northern Lights Blvd. (☎272-4565), near Spenard. Everything you'll need for the backcountry, including a wealth of top maps ($4-10), plus rentals for a myriad of outdoor gear (canoes $40 first day, $22 after; kayaks $50, $30). Open M-F 10am-9pm, Sa-Su 10am-6pm.

Alaska Mountaineering and Hiking (AMH), 2633 Spenard (☎272-1811), between Northern Lights and Fireweed. For finding hiking or climbing partners, tons of rentals, and great outdoor advice. Open M-F 9am-7pm, Sa 9am-6pm, Su noon-5pm.

Bookstore: Metro Music and Book Store, 530 E Benson Blvd., (☎279-8622), across from **Carrs** and **Sears**. A good place to hang out on a rainy afternoon. Bus #3 or #4, get off at Benson and C St., walk east on Benson, in the strip mall on the right.

Services for the Disabled: Challenge Alaska, ☎344-7399.

Gay and Lesbian Helpline: (☎258-4777). Open daily 6-11pm.

Laundromat: K-Speed Wash, 600 E 6th St. (☎279-0731), at Fairbanks. Wash $1.75, dry 25¢ per 5min. Open M-Sa 7am-10pm.

Public Showers: Fairview Community Recreational Center, 1121 E 10th St. (☎343-4130), between Karluk and Latouche. A 15min. walk from downtown. Untimed showers $2. Open M-F 8am-10pm, Sa 8am-9pm, Su 1-6pm.

Weather: ☎936-2525. **Motorists' and Recreation Forecast:** ☎936-2626. **Marine Weather:** ☎936-2727. **Road Conditions:** ☎273-6037.

EMERGENCY AND COMMUNICATION

Emergency: ☎911.

Police: 4501 S Bragaw (☎786-8500). 24hr.

Rape Crisis Line: (☎276-7273 or 800-478-8999). 24hr. Office at 1057 W Fireweed #230 at Spenard St. Bus #6, 7, and 60. Open M-F 8am-5pm.

Hospital: Columbia Alaska Regional Hospital, 2801 DeBarr Rd. (☎276-1131). 24hr. emergency (☎264-1222). **Providence Hospital,** 3200 Providence Dr. (☎562-2211). 24hr. emergency (☎261-3111).

Internet Access: Loussac Library (☎343-2975), at 36th Ave. and Denali St. is a great local library and an architectural oddity. Bus #2, 36, or 60; stops out front, #75 stop at C St. and 36th is within ½ block. Free 1hr. **Internet access.** Open M-Th 10am-8pm, F-Sa 10am-6pm; winter also Su noon-6pm. **Oscar's Roast and Smoke,** 508 W 6th Ave. (☎868-3028). $2 per 15min. Open M-F 10am-9pm, Sa-Su noon til the crowds leave. **Traveler's Web,** 245 W 5th St. (☎277-6969). $1 per 10min. Open M-Sa 9:30am-6pm.

Post Office: (☎800-275-8777), at W 4th Ave. and C St. on lower level of the banana-yellow mall. Open M-F 10am-5:30pm. **Stamp machine** 24hr. **Zip Code:** 99510

⋔ ACCOMMODATIONS AND CAMPING

Anchorage has large hostels, some with more drawbacks than others. Hotels, B&Bs, and even "cheap" motels are expensive, especially downtown. Try **Alaska Private Lodgings** (☎258-1717; open M-Sa 9am-6pm) or the **Anchorage reservation service** (☎272-5909) for out-of-town B&Bs (from $70). Tent options are available outside of town; just keep your eyes peeled and make sure you're not on private or military land. Try the gravel pull-outs on the western limits of Northern Lights Blvd. after it becomes a rural two-lane road. Pick up **Camping in the Anchorage Bowl** (free) at the visitors center for crowded in-town options, or head to nearby **Chugach State Park** (☎354-5014). Call ahead for directions to any of their sites.

> **LET'S MUSH** The celebrated Iditarod dog sled race begins in Anchorage on the first weekend in March. Dogs and their drivers ("mushers") traverse a trail over two mountain ranges, along the mighty Yukon River, and over the frozen Norton Sound to Nome. State pride holds that the route is 1049 mi., in honor of Alaska's status as the 49th state, but the real distance is closer to 1150 mi.
> The Iditarod ("a far-off place") Trail began as a dog sled supply route from Seward on the southern coast to interior mining towns. The race commemorates the 1925 rescue of Nome, when drivers ferried 300,000 units of life-saving diptheria serum from Nenana, near Fairbanks, to Nome. The first race, in 1967, was a 27 mi. jaunt; by 1973, the first full race was run in 20 days. Today, up to 70 contestants speed each year from Anchorage to Nome, competing for a $450,000 purse.
> The race has come under fire from animal rights activists because of the hardships borne by the dogs, some of whom die en route to Nome. Nevertheless, the race goes on, and Anchorage turns out in force for the ceremonial start downtown. For more info, contact the Iditarod Trail Committee (☎376-5145; www.iditarod.com), Dept. M, P.O. Box 870800, Wasilla, AK 99687, or visit the Iditarod Headquarters (with museum, video presentations, gift shop, and free admission) at Mile 2.2 Knik Rd. in Wasilla.

Anchorage Guesthouse, 2001 Hillcrest Dr. (☎ 274-0408). Bus #3, 4, 6, 36, or 60 from downtown; get off at West High School, and go west on Hillcrest. Guests take pride in the elegant kitchen and common area, and gladly earn their keep with a chore. Bikes $2.50 per hr., $20 per day. Free breakfast. $5 key deposit. Wash, dry $1.50 each. Internet $8 per hr. No alcohol. 1-week max. stay. Bunks $25. Private room $65.

Spenard Hostel, 2845 W 42nd Pl. (☎248-5036). Bus #7 from downtown to first stop past Gweenie's. On Spenard, turn west on Turnagain Blvd., then left onto 42nd Pl. Originally a commune, this friendly house still retains its original character without sacrificing cleanliness. Guests love the 3 lounges, kitchens, big yard, and Internet. Reception 9am-1pm and 7-11pm. 6-day max. stay. Chore requested; free stay for 3hr. work. $15.

International Backpackers Hostel, 3601 Peterkin Ave. (☎274-3870). The Parks Highway Express and Denali Shuttle buses stop here every day. Bus #45 or #76 from downtown to Mountain View Carwash on Commercial Ave. Turn left on Taylor and right at the stop on Peterkin. Towels $1, laundry (about $3). Bike rental $10 per day (15min. bike from downtown). $10 key deposit. Borealis shuttle travels to and from airport (15min.; $14 for 1, $17 for 2). Dorms $15. Sites $10, $2 for each extra person.

Hostelling International, Anchorage, 700 H Street. (☎276-3635). In the heart of downtown, between 7th and 8th Ave. 95 beds that are always close to full make this a somewhat hectic environment, but like they say...location, location, location. Wash, dry $1 each. Bike rental free from 10am-5pm with $10 deposit. Two large kitchen areas adjacent to TV, common room. Dorms $16, nonmembers $19; private rooms $40.

FOOD

Anchorage presents the most affordable and varied culinary fare in the state. **Great Harvest Bread Company,** 570 E Benson Blvd., in Benson Mall, stocks excellent fresh bread; loaves run $4-7, but hefty slices with all the butter and honey you can muster are free. (☎274-3331. Open M-Sa 7am-6pm.) **Carr's** sells groceries 24hr. in the Aurora Village Shopping Center, 1650 W Northern Lights Blvd., the Sears Mall, 600 Northern Lights Blvd., or 1340 Gambell.

Moose's Tooth, 3300 Old Seward (☎258-2537). Bus #2 or 36 to corner of the Old Seward and 36th. Named for one of Denali's neighbors, this relaxed joint serves an array of pizzas (personal $9) and brews ($3.75) as hearty as the climbers who come here. Hot bands usher in new brews on the first Th of every month. Be prepared to wait in this popular joint. Open M-Th 11am-midnight, F-Sa noon-1am, Su noon-midnight.

Sweet Basil Cafe, 335 E St. (☎ 274-0070). The cafe's CEO is a black labrador retriever named Buba, yet it's the owner-chefs who must wake up bright and early to make the fresh pastries, breads, and pastas. Killer vegetable and fruit juices ($3.50), smoothies, and lunches ($6). Open year-round M-F 7:30am-4pm, Sa 9am-4pm.

Snow City Cafe, 1034 W 4th St. (☎ 272-2489), at L St. Art-bedecked and acoustically blessed by live music F-Sa. One of the best breakfasts in town, served until 4pm. Open M-Tu 7am-4pm, W-Su 7am-4pm and 5-9pm; winter weekends begin one hour later.

Wings N' Things 529 I St.(☎ 277-9464), on the 5th Ave. corner. These buffalo wings are spiced to order, even coming with a special "warning" should the bold/crazy patron decide for the nukes (BBQ, medium, and hot for the standard folk). 10-piece wings $7, 6 in. subs from $5. Open M-W 9am-3pm, Th-Sa 9am-10pm.

M.A.'s Gourmet Dogs (☎ 278-3647), at corner of 4th and G St. in front of the old federal building. PBS and *USA Today* called it one of the best hotdog stands in America. Hotdogs, polish sausage, or reindeer sausage $3.25. Open Apr.-Sept. 10:30am-4:30pm.

🎵 ENTERTAINMENT

The visitors center (☎ 276-3200) provides a calendar of events. **Cyrano's Off Center Playhouse,** at 413 D St., between 4th and 5th, contains a cafe, a bookshop, the stage of the **Eccentric Theatre Company,** and a cinema that screens foreign and art films. Storytellers spin Alaskan tales here on summer afternoons, along with poetry readings, and film discussion groups. Check the cafe for the events schedule. (☎ 274-2599 or 263-ARTS. Theater at 7pm, summer F-Tu, winter Th-Su. Tickets $15; students $10.) The **Alaska Experience Theater,** 705 W 6th Ave., shows "Alaska the Greatland," a 40min. presentation of scenery, wildlife, and Alaskan culture projected on a 180° omniscreen (think IMAX). The theater's **earthquake exhibit** rumbles for a full 15 fun-filled minutes. (☎ 276-3730 or 272-9076. Movie on the hour 9am-9pm. $7, ages 5-12 $5. Earthquake exhibit every 20min. 9am-9:30pm. $5, ages 5-12 $4. Both $10, ages 4-12 $7.) The **4th Avenue Theatre,** 630 4th Ave., 1 block west of the Log Cabin Visitors Center, is restored to its 1940s decor. This, the first million-dollar building in Anchorage, hosts trolley tours and concerts. The nightly musical (8pm) is free with a trolley tour. (☎ 257-5609. Tours of town start at $10.)

The **Anchorage Bucs** (☎ 561-2827) and the **Anchorage Glacier Pilots** (☎ 274-3627) play baseball against teams like the Hawaii Island Movers and the Fairbanks Goldpanners in **Mulcahy Stadium,** at 16th and Cordova. Packed with some of the best college talent in the nation, Cordova boasts a sports history, including Mark McGwire, John Olerud, and Tom Seaver, all of whom played here before making it big.

🌙 NIGHTLIFE

Microbrews gush from Anchorage's taps like oil through the Pipeline, fueling a nightlife that can be both laid-back and rowdy, depending on your flavor.

Bears Tooth, 1230 W 27th St. (☎ 276-4200), at Spenard. Bus #7, get off at Chilkoot Charlies and walk to 27th. Recently renovated, this brew pub-theater offers an alternative to the standard bar scene. Catch recent flicks while enjoying your favorite pint ($3.75). Pizza $2.50 per slice. A balcony for those under 21. $2 cover for movie.

Pioneer Bar, 739 W 4th. Ave.(☎ 276-7996), near the corner of 4th and A St., downtown. Two pool tables, dart boards, and a shuffleboard table start to go unnoticed as the weekend nights wear on and the drinks keep coming. Bottles $3. Open daily noon-2am.

Bernie's Bungalow Lounge, 626 D St. (☎ 276-8808), at 7th St. Relax in a swingback chair as you sip your lemon drop martini ($5), puff on a cigar ($3-10), or play bocci at Anchorage's newest hot spot. Frequented by the young and retro. Outdoor patio and lawn. Live music or DJ Th-Sa. Open in the summer noon-2am, winter 3pm-2am.

Chilkoot Charlie's, 2435 Spenard Rd. (☎ 272-1010), at Fireweed. Bus #7. If defiling yourself in front thousands is a pastime, you've found the place. "Koots" is a critical rite of passage for all tender-foots. Come for the space. Come for the sawdust. Don't come for the class. $1 drink specials until 10pm. Escalating cover from 8pm ($2-5). 21+. Open Su-Th 10:30am-2:15am, F-Sa 11am-2:45am.

👁 SIGHTS

▨ ANCHORAGE MUSEUM OF HISTORY AND ART. Probably the finest museum in the state. Permanent exhibits of Native Alaskan artifacts and art mingle with national and international works. Once you're in, you could easily stay the entire day. *(121 W 7th Ave. at A St. ☎ 343-4326 or 343-6173; www.anchoragemuseum.org. Open May-Sept. daily 9am-6pm, Tu-Th 9am-9pm. Tours daily at 10, 11am, 1, and 2pm. One-hour films daily at 11am and 3pm. $6.50, seniors and military $6, under 18 free. $2 donation requested.)*

▨ THE ALASKA NATIVE HERITAGE CENTER. Great informational displays of the five Alaskan native traditions come with daily cultural shows and dances in this new heritage center. Walk around the recreated lodgings outside and learn how each tradition sustained itself in the past and even today. *(8800 Heritage Ctr. Dr. ☎ 330-8000 or 800-315-6608; www.alaskanative.net. From the Glenn Hwy., first right off the North Muldoon exit. Open daily 9am-6pm. Dance and music performances daily at 3pm. Adults $20, ages 7-16 $15, 6 and under free.)*

THE ALASKA AVIATION HERITAGE MUSEUM. Situated next to what is by far the largest float plane base in the world, this museum conveys the impact that air travel has had on the history of exploration and settlement in the state. See rare planes from the 1920's, or read up on the history of the WWII campaign throughout the Aleutian islands. *(4721 Aircraft Dr. Take the Lake Hood Exit off International Airport Rd. and turn left onto Aircraft Dr. ☎ 248-5325; www.alaskaairmuseum.com. Open daily 10am-6pm. $8, seniors $6, ages 7-12 $4, under 7 free; military and AAA members $6.)*

ALASKA ZOO. If you don't see Alaska's animals in the wild—a challenge, indeed—you can spot them at the Alaska Zoo. Binky the Polar Bear mauled a tourist here in 1994 and became something of a local hero. The cub that survives him, Ahpun (ah-poon), will hopefully be just as popular. *(4731 O'Malley Rd. Turn toward mountains off Seward Hwy., or take Minnesota which becomes O'Malley. ☎ 346-2133 or 346-3242. Open daily 9am-6pm. $8, seniors $7, ages 12-17 $5, 3-11 $4.)*

🅽 OUTDOOR ACTIVITIES

Watching over Anchorage from Cook Inlet is **Mt. Susitna,** known to locals as the "Sleeping Lady." Legend has it that this marks the resting spot of an Athabascan maid who dozed while awaiting her lover's return from war. When peace reigns in the world, she will awake. Anchorage locals are lucky to have easy access to some of the most beautiful country the state has to offer. From mountain peaks to coastal waterways, you are never more than a quick ride from great outdoor activities. Just 30min. south along the **Sterling Hwy.** (Rte. 9), skiing awaits at **Girdwood** (see p. 449); the drive past the tidal bores of **Turnagain Inlet** shouldn't be missed (see p. 448); 2hr. south on the Seward and across the Sterling, the Kenai River supports unstoppable fishing near **Cooper Landing** (see p. 490). Hikes near Exit Glacier, flightseeing tours, and a tour of the **Kenai Fjords National Park** are still more reasons to venture south (see p. 471). North of town, Talkeetna offers access to Denali, and routes to Glennallen promise views of the **Wrangell Mountains** (see p. 452).

IN TOWN

Walk, skate, or bike to the **Tony Knowles Coastal Trail,** which is a 13 mi., wheelchair-accessible, paved track that skirts Cook Inlet on one side and the backyards of Anchorage's upper crust on the other. The heavily traveled trail is one of the best urban bike paths in the country, groomed in winter for **cross-country skiing.** Pick up the trail on 2nd Ave. or Elderberry Park on the west edge of downtown. The coastal trail's southern terminus ends at **Kincaid Park** (see Biking, below), a haven for cross-country runners and mountain bikers in the summer, only to be taken over by nordic skiers come snowfall.

WATER ACTIVITIES

Nancy Lake State Recreation Area, just west of the Parks Hwy. (Rte. 3) at Mile 67.3, and just south of **Willow,** is well known for its **canoeing.** The **Lynx Lake Loop** takes two days, weaving through 8 mi. of lakes and portages with designated campsites along the way. The loop begins at Mile 4.5 of the Nancy Lake Parkway, at the Tanaina Lake Canoe Trailhead. For **canoe rental** or **shuttle service** in the Nancy Lake area, call **Tippecanoe.** (☎ 495-6688. Open Th-Tu 9am-6pm. Canoes $33 per day, $53 for 2 days; $78 for 4-7 days; shuttle free for backpackers.) **Lifetime Adventures,** at the Eklutna Campground, rents **bikes** and **kayaks.** (☎ 746-4644. Bikes $8 for 2hr.; $15 for 4hr.; $25 per day. Double kayaks from $25 per half-day, $45 per day.) **NOVA Riverrunners** runs whitewater rafting down the **Matanuska Valley.** (☎ 800-746-5753. 4hr. Class III and IV trip $75.)

SKIING AND SNOWBOARDING

Skiing and **snowboarding trails** weave around Anchorage. **Alyeska Ski Resort** is a short drive away along the Seward Hwy. (Rte. 9; see **Girdwood,** p. 449), offering world-class terrain. **Hatcher Pass** to the north, and **Turnagain Pass** to the south, both contain some of the best backcountry skiing in the region (for Turnagain Pass see **Seward Hwy.,** p. 448.) North of Wasilla and Palmer, the best alpine skiing in the Hatcher Pass area is off of **Archangel Rd.** The pass is also a training ground for the U.S. Olympic nordic team, as its elevation garners it some of the first snow each year and groomed cross-country trails in winter. Check at **AMH** and **REI** (see **Anchorage, Equipment Rental** p. 442). At the end of Raspberry Rd. and the Tony Knowles Coastal Trail lies **Kincaid Park,** the largest cross-country skiing area in the US and popular after-work stop for hundreds of skiers from the Anchorage bowl.

HIKING

In 1969, a grassroots organization headed by a 19-year-old asked for and got almost every square inch it proposed for the 495,000-acre **Chugach State Park.** The park surrounds the city on three sides and has enough land and trails to keep an avid hiker busy for years. Check out the **Park Headquarters** (☎ 345-5014) at Mile 115 of the Seward Hwy. to learn about fees and usage information. Call to reserve any of the park's public use cabins. (☎ 800-280-2267. $25 per night plus a $8.25 reservation fee.) Campgrounds here are the area's most accessible (see **Accommodations and Campgrounds,** p. 442). Chugach has 25 established **dayhiking** trails, which leave from different points in Anchorage and along the Glenn Hwy.

> **Flattop Mountain** (3½ mi., 4hr.). Take O'Malley, the continuation of Minnesota, toward the mountains off the Seward, turn right on Hillside, left on Upper Huffman for 4 mi. to the Glen Alps Trailhead mile, then turn right onto Toilsome and drive 2 mi. to the flight of steps on the right side of the parking lot. Provides an excellent view of the inlet, the mountains of the Aleutian Chain, and during (rare) clear episodes, Denali. Flattop is the most frequently climbed mountain in Alaska, with a steep and occasionally slippery 3½ mi. hike to its crowded summit. Parking $5; bus #92 drops you off at the foot of a 2000 ft. battle up to the trail. 4500 ft. elevation gain.
>
> **O'Malley Peak** (8 mi. round-trip, 5-8hr.). From the Flattop parking lot, follow signs to the Powerline Trail and turn east. After ¼ mi., turn left at the Middle Fork Loop Trail. After following the trail down to the footbridge at Campbell Creek, take the unmarked right fork to go to O'Malley Peak. A less crowded trail that towers over 5000 ft. above town, which offers views that rival any in the park. Moderately difficult.
>
> **Bird Ridge.** Drive south on the Seward Hwy. to the trailhead at Mile 102, just south of Indian. A sign marks the trailhead parking lot on the highway. A commanding position offers jaw-dropping views across Turnagain Arm in this fairly difficult but short climb.

BIKING

A multitude of trails for bikers of all skill levels surround Anchorage, both in the city and along the more well-maintained trails of **Chugach State Park**. The trails of **Kincaid Park** are an excellent collection of rolling hills and hard cornering that all riders find enjoyable. Follow the Raspberry Rd. entrance into the **chalet** lot and check out the trail maps that rate trails by difficulty and length. The **Bird Creek** trails offer bikers a fun romp through a dense forested valley along old logging roads. Head south of Anchorage at Mile 100.4 of the Seward Hwy., turn left at the Bird House Bar and travel down a gravel road for ¾ mi. to the trailhead.

ALONG RTE. 1: GLENN HWY. ☎ 907

The Glenn Hwy. and the George Parks Hwy. (Rte. 3; see p. 505) are one and the same for the first 37 mi. north of Anchorage until Palmer, when they separate. From this point, the Parks turns northwest to Denali and eventually to Fairbanks, and the Glenn Hwy. continues another 152 mi. east to Glenallen (see p. 452). From there it runs into Tok and the Richardson Hwy. (Rte. 4).

ANCHORAGE TO PALMER

Leaving Anchorage on 6th Ave., the highway traces the western edge of **Chugach State Park. Eklutna (ee-KLOOT-na) Historical Park** is at Mile 26 about half a mile off the Eklutna Exit and houses the remains of a Dena'ina (or Tanaina) village that dates back to 1650. The park is an example of the more recent confluence of Russian Orthodox and Athabascan traditions in Alaska. The small log structure of **Old St. Nicholas Russian Church** was used for services until 1962 and remains the oldest standing building in greater Anchorage. The restored cemetery is home to many brightly painted **spirit houses**. The village is accessible through the gift shop; a guided tour departs every 30min. or so. (☎ 688-6026. Open mid-May to mid-Sept. daily 8am-6pm. $6, under 6 free.)

From Eklutna, the Glenn Hwy. heads into the **Matanuska Valley**. The Roosevelt administration relocated 200 families here during the Great Depression, hoping to promote agricultural growth. The project worked and the settlers watched in astonishment as the long summer daylight produced vegetables big enough to feed a ship. The valley is still famous for its produce, legal and illegal: those in the know claim that **Matanuska Valley Thunderfuck** is some of the world's best marijuana. Let's Go does not recommend getting thunderfucked.

PALMER

After passing the turn-off for the George Parks Hwy. (Rte. 3, see p. 505), the Glenn Hwy. rolls eastward into the agricultural hamlet of Palmer, home every August to the **Alaska State Fair** (☎ 745-4827), which has awarded ribbons to vegetables larger than most adults. Past winners have included a 303 lb. squash and a 347 lb. pumpkin. Palmer's **visitors center**, 723 S Valley Way, provides info on the valley's plethora of outdoor opportunities. Currently undergoing construction, the road to **Hatcher Pass** is expected to be finished for the 2002 summer. The area offers excellent hiking, mountain biking, camping, rock climbing, and nordic skiing (inquire at Palmer visitors center). In autumn, after the fair, the center displays specimens of the region's freakishly big legumes. (☎ 745-2880. Open May to mid-Sept. daily 8am-7pm.) ▓**Vagabond Blues**, 642 S Alaska St., four blocks from the visitors center, is Palmer's artsy alternative to agriculture. This bar/restaurant has an entirely vegetarian menu, live music, and an open wall for local upstart artists. (☎ 745-2233. Live music F-Sa 8-10pm, tickets around $18. Open M-Th 7am-9pm, F and Sa 8am-11pm, Su 9am-5pm.) If a bed is what you desire, try the **Alaska Choice Inn Motel** (☎ 745-1505), at Mile 40 of the Glenn Hwy. Singles and doubles start at $65. For info on **B&Bs** in the area (starting at $50-60), contact the visitors center. After hours, they leave a list of available rooms out front next to the courtesy phone. Most backpackers find their way to the hostel in nearby Wasilla.

A unique, **domesticated musk ox farm** flanks Archie Rd., a few miles from the Parks Hwy. turn-off at Mile 50 of the Glenn Hwy onto Archie Rd. Introduced from Greenland in 1934, Palmer's prehistoric oxen are prized for their *qiviut* (KIV-ee-oot), or petal-soft fleece. (☎745-4151. Open daily 9am-7pm. Tours every 30min. $8.50; students $7.) The musk oxen's ungulate cousins play their games at the **Reindeer Farm**, on the Bordenburg Butte Loop Rd. off the Old Glenn Hwy., 11 mi. from its southern junction with the main Glenn Hwy, where you can hand-feed the affable beasts. (☎745-4000. Open May to mid-Sept. daily 10am-6pm. $5.)

PALMER TO GLENNALLEN

The **Matanuska Glacier** is visible near Mile 100 as the highway narrows and begins to wind, and drivers divide their time between scanning the colored ridge lines for Dall sheep, marveling at the glacier, and watching the road. After turning off at Mile 102 and paying an entrance fee at the **Matanuska Glacier Park Resort,** you can walk on the ice of the "Mat"—the most accessible glacier in the US. (☎745-2534. $8; seniors $6, children 6-14 $4.) For those with a desire for adventure, **MICA Guides** (☎800-956-6422) offers an introductory 1½hr. glacier trek complete with equipment and a glaciology lesson ($30 per person, 4 person min.), as well as more involved trips for those wishing to pursue the snowy experience.

Mile 113 is home to the **Sheep Mountain Lodge,** where road-weary travelers can rejuvenate themselves by relaxing in the hot tub or wood sauna, or by hiking one of the nearby trails. The cabins offer private baths and provide the perfect weekend retreat. The restaurant serves three meals a day for $6-8. (☎745-5721 or 877-645-5121. Bunks $15.) Those seeking the comfort of a trail can hike along the **Belanger Creek-Nelchina River.** The trailhead at Mile 126.4 heads 1½ mi. to Eureka Creek, eight miles to Goober Lake, and 9 mi. to the Nelchina River. Simply look for the little hiker sign. The highway climbs to the **Eureka Summit** (3322 ft.), Mile 129, where the river unfolds in the valleys below. The **Little Nelchina State Recreation Site,** at Mile 137.5, has free creek-side campsites, toilets, and firepits, but no water. The **Kamping Resort of Alaska** (☎822-3346), at Mile 153, is an all-purpose rest stop. At Mile 160, the turn-off for **Lake Louise Recreation Area,** 19 mi. off the highway, provides access to services and fishing licenses. This area is known for trout, cross-country skiing, and plump berries. **Ryan Lake,** at Mile 149, is known for grayling and rainbow trout. Big grayling await in the **Tolsona Creek** at Mile 173.

ALONG RTE. 9: SEWARD HWY.

Considered one of America's most scenic roads, the Seward Hwy. out of Anchorage provides spectacular views of mountain and water as it twists and turns its way along the **Turnagain Arm** of **Cook Inlet,** an area known for dramatic tidal fluctuations second only to Canada's Bay of Fundy. Miles of the arm are uncovered at low tide, only to be inundated by 10 ft. **bores,** walls of water created as the 15 mph tide races in. The bore tides reach Turnagain Arm about two hours after low tide in Anchorage; consult the Daily News for a tidal report. The Seward Hwy. is narrow and has many blind turns; drivers stopping to view animals near the highway cause accidents—use the turnouts and keep those headlights on.

> ❗ The area exposed at low tide turns into **extremely dangerous quicksand.** Regardless of its cement-like composition when the water is out, visitors are warned that numerous deaths have occurred due to the sand's suction capabilities when wet, trapping the unlucky adventurer in the Arm's tidal waters. **Do not walk on the sand!**

Potter Marsh, just miles outside of Anchorage (Seward Mile 117.4), is a tranquil bird sanctuary and a magnet for wildlife photographers. The info station, located in a train car next to **The Chugach State Park Headquarters,** at Mile 115.2, will help you navigate the innumerable trails along the Seward. (☎345-5014. Open M-F 8am-noon and 1-4:30pm.) Dall sheep sightings are virtually guaranteed, so keep your eyes peeled for white dots on the cliffs around Mile 110. **Beluga Point,** at Mile 110.4, is so named because of the white whales that frequent the area in search of smelt.

Immediately to the left off the Girdwood turn-off at Mile 90 is the **Chugach National Forest Glacier Ranger District Office,** which is an office, not a visitors center. If you missed the park headquarters or are coming from the south, rangers can still provide info on hikes in the national forest which stretches from just south of Anchorage to Prince William Sound. (☎ 783-3242. Open M-F 7:30am-5pm.) The turn-off for the next visitors center is another 10 mi. down the Seward Hwy. in **Portage** (see p. 450). There are well-marked trails at nearly every turn-off and a paved bike path which runs parallel to the highway.

Kayakers are in luck in this creek-rich region. **Bird Creek,** at Mile 101.2, is a narrow Class V run. (Hike up the trail to put in, and take out at the highway). **Ingram Creek,** at Mile 75.2, is another Class V chute with challenging waterfalls. **Class V Whitewater** (see **Girdwood,** p. 449) offers rafting and kayaking trips and information on every bit of moving water around. With snow depths that can exceed 12 ft. in the winter, **Turnagain Pass,** at Mile 68.5, is a backcountry skier and snowmachiner's mecca. There are bathrooms and an emergency phone at the turn-off at the pass. The Alyeska Resort (see **Girdwood,** p. 449) runs just off the highway.

GIRDWOOD ☎ 907

Tucked in at the base of Mt. Alyeska and encircled by the Chugach Mountains, Girdwood's charm comes from its sense of humor. With possibly the highest rates of preferred unemployment in the U.S., this bohemian mess of a hamlet has successfully avoided the development of Anchorage only 35 mi. north and retained its comfortable character. You won't find souvenir shops in this town, only fine restaurants, hiking, skiing, mountain vistas, and wonderful, slightly toasted people.

PRACTICAL INFORMATION. Girdwood Ski and Cyclery, (☎ 783-2453), on the Alyeska Hwy., rents **bikes** ($25 per day), snow shoes ($15 per day), and telemark and cross-country skis ($25-30 per day) and provides a wealth of local knowledge for all season sports. About a quarter-mile up Crow Creek Rd., you'll find the **Double Musky Inn,** which has been called one of Alaska's best restaurants. A steep Cajun-style dinner ($18-30) shouldn't distract you from the Double Musky pie ($4) and the garden outside. (☎ 783-2822. Open Tu-Th 5-10pm, F-Su 4:30-10pm.) There is free **Internet access** at the **municipal library,** in the school at the end of Hightower Rd., a left turn off the Alyeska Hwy. (☎ 783-2565. Open Tu 1-6pm, W 1-8pm, Th 10am-3pm, F-Sa 10am-6pm.) A left turn off the Alyeska Hwy. onto Hightower Rd. (look for signs indicating "New Townsite") leads to "downtown" Girdwood. For supplies, visit **Crow Creek Mercantile.** (☎ 783-3900. Open M-F 7am-midnight, Sa-Su 8am-midnight.) Past the mercantile is a **health clinic** (☎ 783-1355). Further on lies the **post office.** (☎ 783-2922. Open M-F 9am-5pm, Sa 9am-noon.) **ZIP code:** 99587.

ACCOMMODATIONS AND FOOD. The **Girdwood-Alyeska Home Hostel** is a rustic wooden cabin in a wide valley hemmed in by mountains. From the Seward Hwy., drive 2½ mi. down the Alyeska Hwy. and turn right on Timberline Dr., and right again on Alta. The hostel, on the left, has 11 beds. No hot showers—instead they boast the traditional Alaskan cleansing, the sauna. (☎ 783-2099. Reservations encouraged. Sheets $1. $12.) Showers, swimming, and a hot tub are available ($5) at the **Alyeska Prince Hotel.** Below the resort, turn left at the end of the Alyeska Access Rd. then turn right up the hill on Olympic to visit the **Bake Shop.** Folks statewide sing the praises of its sourdough ($3), bottomless bowls of soup ($4.50), and monstrous sweet rolls for $3. (☎ 783-2831. Open Su-F 7am-7pm, Sa 7am-8pm.) **Chair 5 Restaurant and Bar,** around the corner from the post office, serves the cheapest dinner in town, including small pizzas (from $7.50), burgers ($6.75), and steak or seafood entrees ($14). This local hangout boasts a perfect jukebox, 50¢ pool table, and many microbrews. (☎ 783-2500. Open daily 11am-10pm; bar open until 2am.)

450 ■ ALONG RTE. 9: SEWARD HWY.

OUTDOOR ACTIVITIES. Class V Whitewater (☎783-2004; www.alaskanrafting.com) leads moderate to truly intense rafting, kayaking, and fishing trips from $50. If you've ever wondered where all the hippies went, they're at the **Girdwood Forest Festival** (☎566-3039), a free, three-day outdoor fair every July 4th weekend. Non-stop musical acts on two stages, crafts and artwork from local artists, tasty—if pricey—cuisine, and beautiful people of all ages gather in the woods. Also see **Outdoor Activities** in Portage.

PORTAGE ☎907

One might wonder why Portage is on the map. Flattened by the 1964 Good Friday earthquake, the town has done little to rebuild itself and is now primarily an access road for the Chugach State forest and the town of Whittier. The well-paved **Portage Glacier Hwy.**, beginning at Seward Mile 78.9, runs for five of its miles through the magnificent **Portage Valley.** Four roadside glaciers carve through the steep walls of the valley and into the nearby ocean. The **Begich and Boggs Visitor Center**, at Mile 5, provides ranger-led **iceworm safaris** to Byron Glacier in search of mysterious, miniscule, ice-dwelling, algae-eating beasts, as well as exhibits on glaciers and the Whittier tunnel. A transparent observation tunnel in sight of water-bound and bizarrely blue glacial ice makes this visitors center one of the most kid-friendly around. (☎783-2326. Safaris May-Sept. Tu and Sa at 4pm. Open daily 9am-6pm; winter Sa-Su 10am-4pm. **Free.**) **Portage Glacier** has receded almost half a mile since the building's construction, so you have to drive through the first tunnel en route to Whittier to see the it. The only other way to view the glacier is to take a **Portage Glacier Cruise.** (☎783-2983. 1hr. May-Sept. 5 per day 10am-4:30pm. $25.)

CAMPING. In the national forest, camping is free anywhere that isn't an official campground or otherwise marked. About four miles off the highway, two state-run **campgrounds—Black Bear** (tents $10) and **Williwaw** ($12)—have water, toilets, bear-proof food lockers, and views of the glacier. With 12 wooded sites, **Black Bear** is the more tent-friendly of the 2, compared with **Williwaw's** 50+ paved pull-ins (☎877-444-6777; www.reserveusa.com).

SKIING. Great cross-country skiing can be found at Moose Meadows between the airstrip and the ski resort, and at Winter Creek, just north of Moose Meadows. **Alyeska Ski Resort** has 7 chairlifts and a 3934 ft. vertical drop of world-class skiing. (☎754-7669. Open Nov.-Apr. as snow conditions permit. Half-day $31, full-day $44; ages 14-17 $22-26, ages 8-13 or 60-69 $19, under 8 and over 69 $7.) A tram goes up in the summer for lunch. ($19; without lunch $16. Children $7, seniors $15.) Intrepid hikers can ride the tram down for free, but no bikes are allowed.

HIKING. Several easy, enjoyable hikes depart the Portage Hwy. **Moose Flats** has fishing ponds and interpretive displays along a wooden boardwalk, and **Middle Glacier** and salmon-spawning areas are accessible from **The Williwaw Nature Trail** that begins at **Williwaw Campground.** For more trail info, contact Chugach National Forest Office, 3301 C St., Anchorage 99503. (☎271-2500. Open M-F 8am-5pm.)

> **Crow Pass** (3 mi.). Drive 2 mi. east on the Alyeska Hwy., turning left (north) on Crow Creek Rd. Follow 7 mi. to trailhead. The most spectacular short hike in Girdwood climbs from the end of Crow Creek Rd. to a spectacular view of **Raven Glacier.** The trail continues 21 mi. past **Crow Creek in Chugach State Park** to the **Eagle River Visitor Center**.
>
> **Winner Creek Trail**, at the terminus of the Alaska Hwy., turn left onto Arlberg Rd., following signs to the Alaska Prince Hotel. Follow signs for trailhead from the hotel parking lot. This hike leads through lush spruce-hemlock forest at an easy pace, passing over the spectacular **Winner Creek Gorge** before ending at an historic mining cabin.

Moraine Nature Trail (1½ mi., 30min.). This wheelchair accessible loop has fine views of the glacier and the lush, green valley. Trail begins past the Portage Glacier Visitor Center near the restrooms.

Byron Glacier Trail (2 mi.,1hr.), is spectacular, beginning in an alder forest and continuing past the rushing Byron Creek to a snowfield near the foot of the glacier. Beware of avalanches. Park in the Glacier Cruise lot and walk out the south end of the parking lot.

◉ **THE TUNNEL.** The new attraction at the end of the road is the tunnel providing vehicle access to the town of **Whittier** located in **Prince William Sound.** Originally built as a military supply route between Anchorage and Whittier which was founded as an oil depot and army camp due to its deep-water harbor, the tunnel opened to vehicles on June 7, 2000—the same day train service from Portage ended. This, the longest highway tunnel in North America, caused great controversy throughout its construction. Costing huge sums of money, it opened up access to a town of roughly 300 that was initially poorly equipped to deal with the influx. The tunnel is only open to one direction of traffic at a time, so check out the schedule at the visitor's center or at www.dot.state.ak.us/whittier.tunnel to avoid long waits. Hourly service begins at 6am (one-way passenger vehicles $15).

HOPE

Settled at the turn of the century as a Gold Rush offshoot, the town of Hope sits at the end of the Hope Hwy., just past Turnagain Pass off the Seward Hwy. 18 mi. in, the Chugach Mts. push Hope into Turnagain arm, making it visible to motorists between Anchorage and Girdwood. Few amenities exist in this town of 200, which is primarily used for its access to the immensely popular **Resurrection Pass Trail,** and other hiking and biking trails. (At about Hope Hwy. Mile 16 take a left onto Palmer Cr. Rd., and a right half a mile later. Northern trailhead is at the end of this; 4 mi.) **Gull Rock** is a popular long day hike or overnight with both coastal and forest scenery along its flat, 10 mi. round-trip trail. (Accessible from Porcupine Campground at the terminus of the Hope Hwy. A popular bike trail as well, see **Girdwood, Practical Info** (p. 449) for bike rentals. Camping $10.)

WRANGELL-ST. ELIAS NATIONAL PARK ☎907

In a state where the enormous is commonplace, Wrangell-St. Elias remains unique. The largest national park in the US, it is so big that six Yellowstone National Parks could fit within its boundaries. The Wrangell, St. Elias, Chugach, and Alaska ranges all converge within its 13.2 million acres. Nine of the 16 tallest peaks in the United States can be found here, led by Mt. St. Elias, which at 18,008 ft., kowtows only to Denali. Also of interest is Mt. Wrangell, a huge, active shield volcano that last erupted in 1900 and today often emits steam visible to motorists on the Glenn Hwy. Beyond towering peaks and extensive glaciers, Wrangell-St. Elias teems with wildlife. Bears, Dall sheep, caribou, moose, sea lions, and a host of birds all make the park their home. With only two rough roads that penetrate its interior and almost no established trails, Wrangell keeps most tourists at bay. Only a fraction of Denali's visitor load even make it within park boundaries, much less into the mind-bogglingly beautiful backcountry. The land that surrounds the two roads into the park was prospected for copper and gold at the turn of the 20th century. Mining ruins, reeling railroad trestle bridges, and homesteaders' cabins still remain. Whereas McCarthy Rd. hikers should inquire about tracts of private property to avoid trespassing, those who venture farther into the backcountry may find themselves literally where no one has ever walked before.

PRACTICAL INFORMATION

Wrangell-St. Elias is in the southeast corner of Alaska's mainland, bordered by the **Copper River** to the west, the Yukon's **Kluane National Park** to the east (see p. 379), and **Yakutat Bay** to the southeast. The two routes to the park's interior are the **Nabesna Rd.** (see p. 453), which extends 46 mi. from Slana into the park's northern portion, and the challenging **McCarthy Rd.** (see p. 455), which shakes, rattles, and rolls 61 mi. from Chitina (CHIT-nuh) to McCarthy. If you don't have a set of wheels, or don't want to jeopardize those you have, **Backcountry Connection** shuttles people up the road to McCarthy for around $80 from Chitina (see p. 456). **Charter flights** into the bush from McCarthy, Nabesna, or Yakutat start at around $175 per person (round-trip), and increase in price, depending on the destination. There are numerous airfields that flight companies service for backcountry drop-offs. Dayhikers generally set out from points along or at the termini of the Slana-Nabesna or Chitina-McCarthy roads.

CAMPING

Camping is allowed anywhere in the park except on private property (check with ranger stations). For overnight trips, rangers request a written itinerary. There are **ranger stations** in and around the park. (All open May-Sept. daily; limited hours in winter.) The **park headquarters** is in **Copper Center**, south of Glennallen. (☎822-7261. Open daily 8am-6pm). Additional outposts are **Chitina** in the west (☎823-2205; open daily 10am-6pm); **Slana** in the north (☎822-5238; open daily 8am-5pm); and **Yakutat** in the east (☎-784-3295; open 8am-5pm). Additional info booths are at the park-run campground near **McCarthy** and at **Kennicott** in the Jurick Building (see below; open daily 8am-8pm). Both sell topographic maps ($10, quadrants $4).

OUTDOOR ACTIVITIES

Backcountry hikers in Wrangell-St. Elias will meet untouched wilderness; they must be seasoned trippers with extensive experience in route-finding, stream-fording, glacier-crossing, and survival skills. All hikers and campers (even in the McCarthy-Kennicott area) should be aware of the park's large **brown and black bear populations**; take appropriate precautions. All backcountry trekkers should come prepared with wilderness first-aid knowledge. The closest **medical care** is to the west in Glennallen and to the east in Yakutat. Evacuations (even by air) are difficult. Anyone entering the park should come ready with supplies, since services are limited in and near the park.

Mountaineers and climbers will revel in the park's many glaciers, icefields, and mountains. Most popular and vaunted among the peaks are **Sanford, Drum, Blackburn,** and **St. Elias.** The Copper and Chitina rivers offer the best **rafting** opportunities in the park. **Kayakers** can navigate some of the inland rivers and streams, but the bays, inlets, and coasts in the Yakutat (see p. 435) and Icy Bay areas are perhaps the park's most beautiful and under-used waterways. **Cross-country skiing** or **snowshoeing** is best in March, April, and May—after the winter's most severe cold weather, but before the snow has melted off the lowlands. **Mountain bikers** will rush to the networks of wagon roads around McCarthy and Kennicott.

GLENNALLEN ☎ 907

Glennallen itself isn't a destination, but serves as a base for entering **Wrangell-St. Elias National Park** (see p. 451) and for the fishing in rivers 20 mi. north or 14 mi. south of town; the marshy local land is better for hunting mosquitoes than for hiking, and much of it is privately owned. Glennallen stands 115 mi. (2½hr.) north of Valdez on the Richardson Hwy. (see p. 519) and 189 mi. (3½hr.) east of Anchorage

INTO THE PARK: SLANA AND THE NABESNA RD. ■ 453

on the Glenn Hwy., making it a stop for countless RVs. The two roads that lead into Wrangell-St. Elias are conveniently close. The **Nabesna Rd.** lies 75 mi. to the north (see p. 453), and the turn-off for **Edgerton Hwy.** (leading to the **McCarthy Rd.**; see p. 455) is 32 mi. south on the Richardson.

🛈 PRACTICAL INFORMATION. The **Wrangell-St. Elias Park Headquarters,** is 9 mi. south of Glennallen off the Richardson Hwy. (☎822-5235; www.nps.gov/wrst. Open daily 8am-6pm; winter 8am-4:30pm.) A fountain of **visitor information** on Wrangell-St. Elias and the surrounding area, and pamphlets on lodging and fishing in the Copper River Valley, flows under a log cabin's sod roof at the intersection of the Glenn and Richardson Hwy., on the east side of town. (☎822-5558. Open daily May 15-Sept. 15 8am-7pm.) **Winter** visitor information is available at the Chamber of Commerce on the Richardson Hwy., in the Ahtna building. (☎822-5558. Open daily 10am-4pm.) **National Bank of Alaska** is located off the Glenn Hwy. at Birch Rd. **24hr. ATMs** are located in the bank and at the **Hub Maxi Mart,** at the highway intersection. The **library,** 1½ mi. west of the crossroads on the Glenn Hwy., on Ballpark Rd. has **free Internet access.** (☎822-5226. Open Tu-Th 1-6pm, F 1-8pm, Sa 11am-6pm.) The **laundromat** is next to Park's Place. Wash $2, dry 25¢ for 10min. (Open daily 6am-11pm.) **Road Conditions:** ☎822-5511. **State Police:** ☎822-3263. The **Crossroads Medical Clinic** is 1 mi. west of the crossroads on the Glenn (☎822-3203; open M-Tu and Th-F 9am-5:30pm, W 11am-5:30pm.) The **post office** is on Glennallen Schools Rd., two blocks east of the Caribou Hotel, north of the Hwy. (☎822-3273. Open M-F 9am-5pm, Sa 9am-noon.) **ZIP Code:** 99588.

> **❗ PRIVATE PROPERTY.** Local Athabascan tribes own a large amount of land returned to them through the Alaska Native Claim Settlement Act of 1971. Since then, trespassing has been a significant problem. Much land that lines the Richardson Hwy. to the north and south of Glennallen, including some river access on the Gulkana, Klutina, and Copper Rivers, is Ahtna land, and some of it is not marked. Before camping or fishing, check in with the Ahtna Inc. Headquarters, across from the visitors center, which sells maps and has info on camping and river access. (☎822-3476; www.ahtna-inc.com. Open M-F 8am-5pm.)

🏠🍴 ACCOMMODATIONS AND FOOD. Northern Nights Campground and RV Park, a half-mile west of the crossroads on the Glenn Hwy., has 18 wooded sites for RVs, and five tent sites. (☎822-3199. Water and pit toilets. Tents $10; hookups $19.) **Carol's B&B,** on the right side of Birch St. off the Glenn Hwy. about a 1½ mi. west from the visitors center, serves a "true Alaskan breakfast" with sourdough pancakes and moose sausage. (☎822-3594 or 822-3600; fax 822-3800. Singles $60; winter $40-50; couples $75. For info on other affordable B&Bs, contact the Chamber of Commerce (☎822-5558). The **Caribou Hotel Annex,** behind the Caribou Cafe at Glenn Hwy. Mile 187, has the cheapest rooms in town with grimy bathrooms and poor ventilation. (☎822-3302 or 800-478-3302. Singles $49; doubles $59.) The only supermarket around for park-bound trippers is **Park's Place Groceries,** just west of the crossroads on the Glenn Hwy. Try their loaded deli sandwiches. (☎822-3334. Sandwiches $5. Open M-Sa 7am-10pm, Su 8am-10pm.) There are several restaurants in town, but only the **Rendezvous Cafe,** located half a mile north of the crossroads on the Richardson Hwy., does the trick. Munch on a huge sandwich ($9) or the all-you-can-eat salad bar for $6. (☎822-5353. Open daily 6am-10pm.)

INTO THE PARK: SLANA AND THE NABESNA RD.

TRANSPORTATION. Underappreciated and underused, this second road into Wrangell-St. Elias National Park is shorter (1½hr.), more scenic, slightly less bone-jarring than the McCarthy Rd., and offers access to nearly a dozen established trails of varying lengths and difficulties. The turn-off for the Nabesna Rd. is located at **Slana** (rhymes with "bandana"), 65 mi. southwest of Tok (see p. 520) on the Tok

Cutoff. Slana is the place to make last-minute preparations for a journey into the park, since **Nabesna,** at the end of the 46 mi. road, is little more than a mining ghost town populated by one family. The gravel Nabesna Rd. is passable for most cars in summer; ask at the ranger station about the water levels of the three or four streams that cross the road. It's best to charge through low water at between 10 and 25 mph to avoid getting mired in wet gravel, but use your best judgement as the nearest auto help is not readily accessible.

◘ PRACTICAL INFORMATION. The **Slana Ranger Station,** right off the Tok Cutoff, sells topo maps ($10, quadrants $4) and provides info on weather, road conditions, bear behavior, and everything else. (☎ 822-5238. Open 8am-5pm; winter by appointment.) For **emergencies,** call **911** or stop by a ranger station. Slana's **post office** is 1 mi. down Nabesna Rd. (Open M, W, and F 9am-1pm.) **ZIP Code:** 99586.

◘◘ ACCOMMODATIONS AND FOOD. Stop in to see Jay and Debbie at **Midway Services,** about 1 mi. northeast of the Nabesna Cutoff (on the Tok Cutoff) where the **"tent camping,** coffee and bullshit are **free."** They'll also gladly supply groceries, showers, coin laundry, **Internet access, fishing permits,** and minor car repairs. (☎ 822-5877. Open M-Sa. 10am-6pm. Showers $3. Internet $5 per 30min. RV sites $10.) If you're not sleeping for free in the mountains and need to snooze in Slana, **Hart D Ranch,** down the Nabesna Rd. next to the post office, has camping and showers. (☎ 822-3973. Showers $5 or free with stay. Tents $18, hookups $20, cabin $49.) Nestled in the forest, family-run **Huck Hobbit's Homestead Retreat and Campground** rents cabin bunks and tent sites. The secluded two- and six-person cabins sport trapping decor, are heated with wood-burning stoves, and are filled with relics from the last federal homestead. A fresh spring and solar shower provide cold and hot water, respectively. The friendly owners cook meals for guests with advance notice and rent **canoes** for use on the Slana River. (☎ 822-3196. Breakfast $7, dinner $10. Canoes $35 per day, including drop-off and pickup. $15, with linen $20. Tents $2.50.) To get there, head south on the Nabesna Rd., turn left at Four Mile Rd., then take the first right; follow the signs to the trailhead and hike in three-quarters of a mile (or call ahead for an ATV lift).

In miniscule Nabesna, the Ellis family charges $5 per day for parking, and runs the **End-of-the-Road Bed and Breakfast** with bunks (for large parties only), singles, and doubles. (☎ 822-5312; last-ditch messages 822-3426. Bunks $20; singles $50; doubles $65.) The family also runs **horseback riding, hunting trips,** and an **air taxi.** (Trips 3-5 days. From $450 per person. Flightseeing $78 per person for 1hr., 2 people min.; round-trip fly-ins from $200 per person. Package rates available.)

◘ HIKING. The Slana Ranger Station has a full list of **hikes** beginning at Nabesna or along the road. Most are ATV trails and are flat, wet, and muddy; they serve well as access points into the mountains along the road. Be wary of bears and mosquitos in the brushy areas, and savor the rare opportunity to sing as loudly and poorly as you want, while dousing yourself head to toe with bug dope.

Like every place else in the Wrangells, the best, most pristine hiking is in the backcountry, where you will see few, if any, other people. Popular fly-in destinations in the Nabesna area are **Grizzly Lake, Jeager Mesa,** and **Cooper Pass;** climbers prefer **Mt. Gordon, Nabesna Glacier,** and **Copper Glacier.**

> **Skookum Volcanic Trail** (5 mi. round-trip, 6-8hr.). Trailhead leaves from Mile 36.2. Highly popular and recently cleared by the Sierra Club, the trail rises about 2000 ft. up a forested alluvial fan. It follows rock cairns along a stream and into the tundra-covered tussocks in the crater of extinct Skookum Volcano. At the windy pass you can camp or continue alongside another creek down to the road again. Moderately strenuous.
>
> **Caribou Creek Trail** (4 mi., 2-3hr.). Park in the gravel quarry at Mile 18.9 and walk to the trailhead at Mile 19.2. A walk weaving across the creek 3 times before coming upon an old tin cabin with first come, first served bunks. From this cabin you can forge your own trails into the surrounding Mentasta Mountains, some of which offer good views of Mt. Blackburn, Mt. Wrangell, and Mt. Sanford on clear days. Easy.

Lost Creek Trail (21 mi., 2-4 days). Starts at Lost Creek Trail at Mile 31 and loops back to Trail Creek Trail at Mile 29. Trackless ridge-walking with gorgeous glimpses of alpine meadows, canyons, Dall sheep, and a 6000 ft. pass. The 2 creeks are not directly connected; secure a detailed map and chat with the rangers before setting out. Map skills are essential. Strenuous.

INTO THE PARK: THE MCCARTHY RD.

CHITINA. Chitina (CHIT-nuh) lies at the western gates of Wrangell-St. Elias. Once the largest town in Alaska and heralded as its future capital, Chitina bucked the yoke of greatness. When the copper mines dried up in the 1930s, the town virtually disappeared, too. What's left is a flower child community of about 110 year-round residents. The town has a **ranger station** (☎ 823-2205; open daily 10am-6pm) and also a **post office** (☎ 823-2225; open M-F 8am-4pm, Sa 10am-2pm). The last fuel stop on the McCarthy Rd. is at the **general store.** (☎ 823-2211. Open daily 7am-10pm.) Nightlife is comprised of several nondescript bars. The **It'll Do Cafe,** an obscure grub spot in a run-down shack serves up the basic greasy spoon fare for reasonable prices. (☎ 823-2244. Open W-M 8am-8pm.) Penniless campers will delight in the spacious, free **campground** across the **Copper River** (pit toilets, no water).

KENNICOTT RIVER. Starting at Chitina, the McCarthy Rd. follows the old railbed of the Copper River & Northwestern Railway for 61 mi. to the Kennicott River. Roadwork has improved what was once arguably the roughest state road in Alaska. Cars should take it slow (30 mph is safe for most parts of the road), watch for protruding rail ties, and carry at least one spare tire. The 2-3hr. trip to McCarthy rewards unflappable drivers with views of the Copper River Delta.

NUGGET CREEK. At Mile 13.5, a small wagon-wheel sign on the left marks the Nugget Creek/Kotsina Rd. The **Nugget Creek Trail** begins 2½ mi. up this road, immediately across Strelna Creek. This unremarkable 14 mi. ATV route leads to a first come, first served **public-use cabin** at the foot of beautiful Mt. Blackburn and the Kuskulana Glacier. Stream crossings may prove difficult; be prepared to turn back. Dayhikes from here pursue the canyons of Nugget Creek and the mining ruins in the hills behind the cabin. The Nugget Creek/Kotsina Rd. will also lead you to the **Dixie Pass Trail** which follows Strelna Creek through scenic canyons and a narrow, breathtaking pass over the mountains. This route joins the **Kotsina Trail,** which leads back to the road in a 45 mi. loop.

KUSKULANA RIVER. At Mile 17, the Kuskulana Bridge passes 238 ft. above the raging **Kuskulana River.** Summer thrill-seekers can **bungee jump** from the bridge thanks to **Club Way North.** (☎ 783-1335. Call ahead. One jump $50, 2 jumps $80.) Jumps are free if you jump naked, but the rope burn...After jolting and rattling for 44 mi. more, the road terminates on the western edge of the Kennicott River, where travelers going on to McCarthy must cross a footbridge and walk a half-mile farther. A **Park Service information desk** is located three-quarters of a mile before the river on the north side; all the rangers are residents and give frank advice. (Open daily mid-May to mid-Sept. 8am-8pm.) The parking lot at the Copper Point Tram Station beside the river charges $6 per day.

MCCARTHY AND KENNICOTT ☎ 907

Deep in the heart of Wrangell-St. Elias National Park, abandoned log-hewn buildings and roads straying off to points unknown bear witness to the boom towns past of McCarthy and Kennicott. In the early 1900s, thousands of miners swarmed to the site of the purest copper ore ever discovered, a vein running between the Kennicott Glacier and McCarthy Creek. In its heyday, the Copper River and Northwest Railway (CR&NW), jokingly dubbed the "Can't Run and Never Will," transported nearly $200 million of copper ore. During this boom, McCarthy sprouted as a free-wheeling, sin-celebrating alternative to stick-in-the-mud Kennicott, a company town where strict rules of conduct were enforced. In 1938, operations came to a halt, and the last train out marked the end of an era. Since the establishment of the national park in 1980, McCarthy has been revived as the hub of the summer tourist industry, and Kennicott provides visitors with a look into the area's mining history, as well as access to popular hikes.

PRACTICAL INFORMATION. Backcountry Connection (☎822-5292 or 800-478-5292) runs 15-passenger **vans** daily from **Glennallen** (4hr.; $70, round-trip same day $99, different day $105) and **Chitina** (3hr.; $55, round-trip same day $80, different day $90) to McCarthy. **Wrangell Mountain Air** flies to McCarthy twice daily from **Chitina** and farther afield by arrangement. (☎554-4411 or 800-478-1160. www.WrangellMountainAir.com. Round-trip $140.) A cost-cutting transportation option from Anchorage is to take the mail plane operated by **Ellis Air Taxi,** which leaves Anchorage at 8am on Wednesday and Friday only. (☎822-3368. Round-trip $400.) Relatively regular traffic makes hitchhiking the road a possibility, although getting stranded is another. *Let's Go* does not recommend hitchhiking. The road to town stops at the Kennicott River; carrying heavy gear across the footbridge is a self-evident hassle. Many McCarthy locals still get their water from **Clear Creek,** fill your water bottles at your own risk and please use the many outhouses as the town is very concerned about protecting this water source.

The first building you'll pass houses the **McCarthy-Kennicott Historical Museum,** filled with mining pictures and artifacts. A walking tour map is available here. (Open daily in summer 9am-6pm. Suggested donation $1.) Kennicott is 4 mi. north of McCarthy along the road, or a bit farther on the **Old Wagon Trail** (a moderately strenuous, uphill bike to Kennicott. 45-60min., see McCarthy campgrounds for rentals). Its recommended that bikers save the **Wagon Trail** for the trip back as its uphills can make it difficult to outride the mosquitoes. Kennicott is the gateway to the **Root Glacier** and home to the spooky ruins of the old **mill.** A **shuttle** runs the 5 mi. road between the towns. (9am-7:30pm. Round-trip $10.)

ACCOMMODATIONS AND FOOD. The cheapest and most convenient accommodations in the area are at or near the end of the McCarthy Rd. Several campgrounds line the side of the road. The **Glacier View Campground** has campsites, showers, and serves nondescript barbecue food (burgers $6) all day long. (☎554-4490. Showers $5. Open daily Memorial Day to Labor Day 7am-10pm. Sites $10.) **Bike rentals** here are the area's cheapest. ($10 per half-day, $20 per day.) Right next to the bridge and closest to town, **Copper Point Campground** has sites back in the woods with pit toilets and water or out by the river and away from the bugs ($10). Since most of the land around McCarthy and Kennicott is privately owned, camping is prohibited in most areas east of the river. If in doubt, check with a Park Service employee. Six miles north of McCarthy and 2 mi. north of Kennicott, a Park Service **campground** with no amenities overlooks the Root Glacier. The few, small tent sites on the hillside are hard to find but some have stunning views. Regardless of where you camp, be sure to keep a tight camp, set up 50 ft. off trail, and store food in bins and cars. Bear sightings have been on the increase in recent years. McCarthy's cheapest beds, six-person cabins, and a cozy common room await a quarter-mile before the river on the left at the **Kennicott River Lodge and Hostel.** (☎554-4441, winter 479-6822. Rooms $25; cabins $85; showers $5 with room, $7 without.) The food in town is expensive due to the cost of delivery to this remote location; bring groceries with you. **The Potato,** next to McCarthy Air, serves up spicy breakfast food, a strong cup-a-joe, and good tunes from 7:30am-4pm. Try the spudniks and gravy ($5).

OUTDOOR ACTIVITIES

FLIGHTSEEING. If you go flightseeing anywhere in Alaska, do it here. Even a short flight to 16,390 ft. Mt. Blackburn and the surrounding glaciers offers magnificent views. In addition to its scheduled flights, **Wrangell Mountain Air** (see **Practical**

Information, above), makes a 35min. tour of the amazing icefalls of the Kennicott and Root Glaciers ($60). The best bargain is a 70min. trip up the narrow Chitistone Canyon to view the thundering Chitistone Falls and on to a slew of glaciers and peaks ($105 per person; min. 2 people). **McCarthy Air** specializes in fly-in charters and flightseeing and offers equally enthralling tours for comparable prices. (☎554-4440 or 888-989-9891. 35min. for $50, 1hr. for $100; min. 2 people.)

ADVENTURE TRIPS. Copper Oar and **St. Elias Alpine Guides** run a comparable day-long **whitewater rafting** trip down the Class III Kennicott River with a flightseeing jaunt back from Chitina. (**Copper Oar** ☎554-4453 or 800-523-4453. $235. **St. Elias** ☎554-4445 or 888-933-5427. $245). **Kennicott-McCarthy Wilderness Guides** (☎800-664-4537) lead 3hr. tours of Kennicott that give visitors their only chance to see inside a 14-story mill ($25). A fully-serviced backcountry trip will cost participants about $150-200 per day. A popular choice is a day of **ice climbing** (about $100) and **glacier hiking** ($50-100 depending on length).

MOUNTAIN BIKING. Wagon trails between McCarthy and Kennicott and into the bush are great for riding. One good route is the semi-strenuous 9 mi. ride along the wooded **Nizina Rd.,** beginning across McCarthy Creek and continuing to the Nizina River. There the fractured Old Nizina River Bridge rests, a victim of glacial flooding. The **Nugget Creek Trail** is a well-defined path that gains significant elevation in its 34 mi. round-trip, making it a fairly strenuous ride. **Nugget Creek** begins 13½ mi. east of Chitina on the McCarthy Rd. The creek road leads to the north; park out of the way and expect a 5-7hr. ride. See above for bike rentals.

DAYHIKES. The **Root Glacier Trail** (2-3hr.) begins in Kennicott, 2 mi. from the glacier itself, and runs alongside the glacier for 2 mi. past a Park Service campground (see above). Exercise extreme caution if you choose to climb onto the glacier where the gravel covers it; these areas are very slick, and deep crevasses await hikers with careless footwork. Reach the trailhead by following Kennicott Rd. to its end and continuing along to the glacier and campground. The steep **Bonanza Peak Trail** is a gem, climbing 4000 ft. over 4 mi. to a commanding view of the Kennicott and Root Glaciers and the Donoho Peak between them. To access this strenuous trail, continue a quarter-mile east of Kennicott and take a right at the junction.

BACKCOUNTRY

As is true of most parts of Wrangell-St. Elias, the best hikes in the McCarthy area are backcountry hikes along routes established by miners from decades past and by millennia of game. Accessible hiking trails depart town and the McCarthy Rd. At Mile 13.5 of the McCarthy Rd., outside Chitina, a small wagon-wheel sign on the left marks the Nugget Creek/Kotsina Rd. For descriptions of the **Nugget Creek Trails** and 45 mi. **Dixie Pass Trail-Kotsina Trail** loop, which can be accessed from the same point, stop at the Chitina Ranger station for the National Park Service **trip reports.** The darling of backcountry McCarthy is the **Goat Trail,** an early miners' route from McCarthy to the Chisana gold fields. The trail starts at **Skolai Pass,** home to the Golden Horn and the Hole in the Wall glaciers, and traverses the ridge high above Chitistone Canyon and Falls, one of the park's most spectacular features. The route continues 25 mi. to Glacier Creek with fantastic views of the Wrangell and St. Elias mountain ranges. The **Goat Trail** requires crossing the sometimes-impassable Chitisone River. Check with rangers for river conditions which change daily and be prepared to turn back if necessary. Round-trip fly-ins with a drop-off in Skolai and pickup at Glacier Creek start at $195 per person with a two-person minimum. Talk with rangers at Slana or Copper Center when planning a backcountry trip. Many require fly-in drop-offs and cover unmarked trails, so plan ahead.

PRINCE WILLIAM SOUND

George Vancouver lays his mark once again; this time the namesake was the son of the third son of King George III. The Sound now lies within the Chugach National Forest, and provides ample natural resources. Oil makes this world go around, and shipping focuses around Valdez, the southern terminus of the Alaska Pipeline. Efforts continue in the Sound to recuperate from the oil spill in 1989.

VALDEZ ☎ 907

The northernmost ice-free port in Alaska, Valdez is the terminus of the Alaska pipeline, and oil runs the show. Natural and human disaster has fixed Valdez in the popular imagination. The 1964 Good Friday earthquake, an 8.6 on the Richter scale, gathered 100-foot tall waves that hammered the docks and flooded the town. Exactly 25 years later, disaster struck the relocated settlement again when the infamous Exxon *Valdez* tore open the Bligh Reef. Although no oil actually made it into the port, 11 million gallons spread across 1640 sq. mi. of Prince William Sound, and over 1500 mi. of shoreline, wreaking havoc on the ecosystem. The $2 billion dollar clean-up lasted over three years and tripled the town's population.

Disaster, however, has failed to mar the allure of Valdez. College-aged adventurers annually seek very small fortunes in canneries, or "slime houses," while sports fishermen seek the catch outright. A handful of backpackers pass through, camping in the hills outside the city and exploring its misty forests and streams. An absurd amount of snow—330 in. on average—makes Valdez "The Snow Capital of Alaska," and draws the winter purists seeking powder dreams.

TRANSPORTATION

Valdez lies in the northeast corner of Prince William Sound, 304 mi. (6hr.) east of Anchorage. From Valdez, the spectacular **Richardson Hwy.** (Rte. 4, see p. 519) runs 119 mi. north through Thompson pass to Glennallen (2½hr. from Valdez), where it intersects with the **Glenn Hwy.** (Rte. 1, see p. 447) running southeast to Anchorage and northeast to Tok. The Richardson Hwy. enters Valdez on the east side of town, becoming **Egan St.**, the main drag. Most of downtown Valdez lies on **Egan St., Fairbanks, Pioneer Dr.** and **North Harbor Dr.**, all of which run east-west between the north-south **Hazelet** and **Meals Ave.**

Flights: The airport is 4 mi. from town on Airport Rd. off Richardson Hwy. **ERA Aviation** (☎835-4282) flies to **Anchorage** (40min.; M-Sa 3 times per day, Su 2 times per day; $104-130).

Buses: Gray Line (☎800-544-2206) departs the Westmark Hotel for **Anchorage** daily (10hr., 8am, $70). **Parks Highway Express** (☎888-600-6001; www.alaskashutle.com) runs 3 times a week to **Fairbanks** ($79).

Ferries: Alaska Marine Highway (☎835-4436 or 800-526-6731; www.akferry.com), at the city dock at the end of Hazelet Ave. Service to **Bellingham, WA** (almost once a week, $351) via **Juneau** (1½ days, $102; ages 6-11 $51).

Taxi: Valdez Yellow Cab, ☎835-2500.

Car rental: Valdez-U-Drive (☎835-4402), at the airport. Cars, trucks, and vans $44-89 per day. 25¢ per mi. after the first 100 mi. Must be 25 or 21 with insurance.

PRACTICAL INFORMATION

Visitor Information: (☎835-2984, 835-4636, or 800-770-5954) at Fairbanks St. and Chenega. Open daily 8am-8pm; winter M-F 9am-5pm. Free tour and lodging calls.

Outdoor Information: Most fishing stores sell **fishing licenses** and offer free advice. Check with **Fish Central** (see below) or any local bartender or bouncer for the hot spots.

Employment: Alaska Employment Service (☎835-4910), on Meals Ave. in the Courthouse, Room 22. Open May-Sept. M-F 8am-noon and 1-4:30pm.

Equipment Rental and Sales: The Prospector, 141 Galena Dr. (☎835-3838), beside the post office, has an immense supply of outdoor/sportsman gear. Open M-F 8am-9pm, Sa 8am-8pm, Su 9am-6pm; opens and closes an hour earlier in winter.

Beaver Sports, 316 Galena Dr. (☎835-4727), opposite the post office, carries high-quality backpacking and climbing gear. Cross-country ski, snowshoe, and bike rentals. Bikes $6 per hr.; $16 per 6 hr.; $20 per day 1-4 days all rentals with $250 deposit. Open M-Sa 10am-7pm; winter 10am-6pm.

Fish Central, 217 N Harbor Dr. (☎835-5090), rents boats and rods.

Anadyr Adventures 217 N Harbor Dr. (☎835-2814), next to Fish Central, rents kayaks. Singles $45 per day for 2 days, $35 each day after; doubles $65 1st day, $55 each day after. Cash deposit or credit card required.

Banks: First National Bank of Anchorage, 101 Egan Dr. (☎834-4800). **24hr. ATM.**

Library: 260 Fairbanks Dr. (☎835-4632), beside the museum. Outstanding 3-floor library, with well-stocked Alaska Room and a selection of free books. **Free 1hr. Internet access;** call ahead. Open M and F 10am-6pm, Tu-Th 10am-8pm, Sa noon-5pm.

Laundromat and Public Showers: Like Home Laundromat, 121 Egan St. (☎835-2913). Wash $1.50, dry 25¢ per 7min. $4 for 10min. shower with towel, soap, and shampoo. Open daily 8am-11pm.

Weather: ☎835-4505.

Emergency: ☎911.

Police: ☎835-4560.

Pharmacy: Village Pharmacy (☎835-3737), in the same building as Eagle Quality Center at Pioneer Dr. and Meals Ave. Open M-Th 9am-6pm, F 9am-7pm, Sa 10am-1pm.

Hospital: Valdez Community Hospital, 911 Meals Ave. (☎835-2249).

Post Office: (☎835-4449), at Galena Dr. and Tatitlek St. Open M-F 9am-5pm, Sa 10am-noon. **ZIP Code:** 99686.

ACCOMMODATIONS

Finding a roof in Valdez can be expensive and time-consuming. The visitors center provides non-prioritized options, brochures, and a phone. Next to the fast-filling hostel, the cheapest indoor options are B&Bs (from $60). The free reservation center, **One Call Does It All** (☎835-4988 or 888-304-4988; www.alaska.net/~onecall), arranges B&Bs (as well as glacier tours, rafting trips, fishing charters, rental cars, and helicopter rides) and gives friendly advice on any of the local happenings. Valdez forbids camping in non-designated areas, but insolvent sojourners sometimes camp illegally along Mineral Creek, a 15min. walk from downtown. To explore the beautiful canyon, take Mineral Creek Dr. from Hanagita St., stay straight as the road turns to gravel, and cross the stream. Follow the left hand trail or stay on the road in the canyon. For free camping, most turn-offs at least 5 mi. out of town on the **Richardson** should be fair game (see p. 519).

Valdez Hostel, 139 Alatna St. (☎835-2155). Friendly, centrally located year-round hostel. Slightly cramped and chaotic, but by far the best deal in Valdez. Kitchen. Washer, dryer 75¢ each. Free local calls. 2-week max. stay. No lock-out or curfew. Parks Highway Express stops here. $2 off with HI. 12 beds. $22.

Blessing House B&B (☎835-5333 or 888-853-5333), at the corner of Meals Ave. and Dadina. Near downtown, the friendly hosts have 5 cheery rooms ($65-85), continental breakfast, and they give their guests complete use of their kitchen and a piano.

Blueberry Lake State Recreation Site, 24 mi. up the Richardson Hwy. from town. Camp, hike, and fish in the mountains near the top of Thompson Pass. May have snow late into the season. Pit toilets, water. 15 well-spaced sites. Sites $12.

Captain Jim's Glacier Campground (☎835-2282). With a natural waterfall and full picnic area, Capt. Jim's rests against the mountains 1 mi. past the airport. Turn north at the blinking light 3 mi. outside of town. Pit toilets, water. 101 RV and tent sites $10. Store all food in cars or away from tents due to bear activity.

FOOD AND NIGHTLIFE

Low key drinking and eating abounds in Valdez. The **Eagle Quality Center** (☎835-2100), at 313 Meals Ave. and Pioneer Dr., peddles grocery store items 24hr.

Lisa's Kitchen (☎835-5633). Lisa's trailer, currently located on the southeast corner of Egan St. and Meals Ave. will reward the famished with miraculous, tangy Mexican grub. A *por favor* and *gracias* may earn Lisa's good graces and more salsa for your portion. Vegetarian options available. Burritos $5.50. Open May-Aug. M-Sa 11:30am-8pm.

Mike's Palace (a.k.a. Pizza Palace), 201 N Harbor Dr. (☎835-2365). Good seafood and great pizza keep locals happy at the harbor side. Sit down for Greek, American, Mexican, and Italian fare with great soup ($3), burgers ($5), halibut ($14), and 12 in. pizza ($9). Open daily 11am-11pm. Closes at 10pm in winter.

Alaska Halibut House, 208 Meals Ave. (☎835-2788). The closest thing to fast-food in Valdez, the Halibut House offers up some of the cheapest fresh seafood in the state. It ain't glamorous, but it's quick. Catch of the day $5, halibut basket (huge!) $9.

Pipeline Club, 112 Egan St. (☎835-4332). With a local flavor that isn't too over-the-top, the Pipeline serves up cold Alaskan brews in a comfortable setting. Shoot some pool with a local cannery worker, or ask the bouncer where the fishing hot spots are while kicking back to live music. Su-W 1pm-midnight, Th-Sa 1pm-1am.

SIGHTS AND EVENTS

VALDEZ MUSEUM. This small museum packs an impressive informational punch for its size with excerpts from prospectors' diaries, exhibits on the Good Friday disasters, and an entire bar from Old Town. *(217 Egan St. ☎835-2764. Open May-Sept. M-Sa 9am-6pm, Su 9am-5pm; Oct.-Apr. M-F 10am-5pm, Sa noon-4pm. $3, seniors $2.50, ages 14-18 $2, under 14 free.)*

THE VALDEZ (MUSEUM) ANNEX. The large turquoise building before the ferry terminal features the '64 quake with a 40min. video, and displays models of Valdez prior to the quake. *(436 S Hazelet St. Follow Haselet St. to the waterfront. ☎835-2764. Open daily Memorial Day-Labor Day 9am-4pm. $1.50.)*

ALASKA CULTURAL CENTER. The largest private collection of Native Alaskan artifacts is housed here alongside a 15min. earthquake video that plays every hr. *(At airport. ☎834-1690. Open daily 11am-7pm. Call for winter hours. $4, under 12 $2.)*

THE PIPELINE. At the business end of the 800 mi. journey of the Alaska Pipeline from Prudhoe Bay (see p. 530) lies the **Valdez Marine Terminal. Valdez Tours** provides the only way to view the terminal without top secret clearance. The tour strikes a gusher in visitors' wallets with a dry 2hr. tour. The tours depart from the **Pipeline Visitor Center.** The center yields free pipelinalia and construction-related films. On the drive from Glennallen the pipe can be seen snaking through the wilderness. *(212 Tatitlek St. ☎835-2686. Tour $15, ages 6-12 $7.50, under 6 free. Visitors center free.)*

THEATER. The Prince William Sound Community College Theatre Conference, at the Civic Center in June, sponsors workshops with guest playwrights, performances, and a contest with five $1000 prizes for new playwrights. *(☎834-1612; www.uaa.alaska.edu/pwscc. Submit plays to PWSCC Theatre Conference, Box 97, Valdez, AK, 99686. Prices to be announced for 2002.)*

VALDEZ ■ 461

FESTIVALS AND EVENTS. Gold Rush Days are a feast for budget travelers. The visitors center hosts a free salmon and halibut fry, fashion show, dance, traveling jail bus, bed races, and an **ugly vehicle contest** (first W-Su in Aug.). Valdez makes the most of winter and its immense amounts of snow with the annual **Snowman Festival** (☎835-2330), during the first weekend in March. Amid snowmen, a drive-in movie is projected onto a giant snowbank. Make sure to wear your "frosty fever" buttons during festival days for good deals at local establishments. The **King and Queen of the Hill Snowboard Competition** will take place in 2002; last year's contest was cancelled at the last moment (☎277-0205; www.kingextreme.com). Competitors at the **Valdez Ice Climbing Festival** (☎835-5182) scale the frozen waterfalls of Keystone Canyon, and the 150 mi. **Quest for the Gold Sled Dog Race** (☎835-2984) lasts three days each winter. Call the visitors center for more info.

OUTDOOR ACTIVITIES

FISHING. Fishing is the big draw for many of Valdez's summer visitors. Derbies boast big prizes all summer (call the Chamber of Commerce at 835-2330 and compare prices), but pink and silver salmon bite as close as the town docks through August. Ask at **Fish Central** (see **Equipment Rental**, p. 459) for nearby hot spots.

PADDLING. Kayaking in Prince William Sound is the best way to travel. Moving along at a good clip with enough time to savor the sights, an extended trip among towering mountains and calving glaciers is enough to draw the queasiest landlover out on the seas. Both **Anadyr Adventures** (see **Equipment Rental**) and **Pangaea Adventures**, 101 N Harbor Dr. offer similar half- and full-day sea kayaking trips. (☎835-8442 or 800-660-9637. Half-day: 3hr. Duck Flats $55; 6hr. Gold Creek Coast $75. Full-day: 8-10hr. trips start around $50. Multi-day and mothership supported packages navigate inner channels to remote glaciers. River kayakers will thrill to the Class IV middle portion or the Class IV upper stretch of the Tsaina River. **Keystone Adventures** (☎835-2606 or 800-328-8460) leads kayaking and **rafting** trips, including a 4½ mi. (45min.; $35) route on the Lowe River through Class II and III rapids and past the vast Bridal Veil Falls, or get dressed up in a dry suit and helmet for the Class IV Tsaina run ($70). Be prepared to swim.

TOURS. By boat, helicopter, or plane, for a hefty price, visitors can view Prince William Sound's most prized possession: **Columbia Glacier.** The best budget option is the ferry (see **Ferries**, p. 458), which pauses in front of the face of the 3 mi. wide **Columbia Glacier** for 10min. on its way to and from Whittier ($64). For private tours, call **One Call Does It All,** 241 N Harbor Dr. (☎835-4988 or 888-304-4988), a free reservation and info service that will match you with trips with rates in your range.

CHURCH. The **Chapel of the Sea** allows the pious and penniless aboard the *Lu-Lu Belle* for a 1hr., non-denominational church service in the Sound. Show up Sunday by 7:45am at the dock adjacent to the Westmark Hotel. (☎800-411-0090. First come, first served. 65 seats. Free, but offering is collected.)

HIKING. Local hiking is first rate. Inquire at the visitors center or **Beaver Sports** for more info on further hiking opportunities in Valdez.

- **Solomon Gulch Trail,** (3¾ mi. round-trip). Begins 150 yards northeast of the hatchery on Dayville Rd. toward the Alyeska Terminal. Covers 2 steep inclines, ending at Solomon Lake with excellent views of Valdez Bay and the pipeline. The more rigorous **Goat Trail,** farther from the city, follows a Native Alaskan footpath that was once the only route from Valdez to the Interior. As it weaves through Keystone Canyon, the trail follows the Lowe River past glimpses of waterfalls.

  Mineral Creek Trail (8 mi.). Pull off the highway at Bridalveil Falls and follow the posted directions. First 6 mi. accessible by car along a gravel road and easily accessible by car at Mile 18.2, just north of downtown. A gentle 2 mi. round-trip footpath leads farther through the mountains past waterfalls and wildlife to the **Old Gold Mine.**

Shoup Bay Trail (12 mi.). Starts from the parking area located on the left at the west end of Egan St. Leads along the mountainside with views of the bay and distant mountains, but is muddy and mosquito-infested in places. About 6 mi. in, this fairly level trail crosses Gold Creek. A mile-long turn-off to the right leads to spectacular waterfalls. Another 6 mi. along the trail leads to a remarkable view of the distant **Shoup Glacier.**

SKIING. Valdez's plentiful snowfall and prime coastal location, warming up to a balmy 25°F in January, make the town a **skier's paradise.** Experienced skiers and snowboarders charter helicopters to **Mt. Odyssey** and any of the other 450 designated heli-skiing runs, or drive and "snow machine" (Alaskan for "snowmobile") to **Thompson Pass** to ski back. **Cross-country ski trails** lead to the left and right off Mineral Creek Rd. or along the road itself. Advanced runs are in the Tsaina Valley at the north base of Thompson Pass. Moderate trails begin at the Coast Guard Housing on Anchor Crest St. at the western end of town. For more details, pick up the free *Winter Guide* at the visitors center.

CORDOVA ☎ 907

Surrounded by rugged mountains and waters teeming with salmon, Cordova lures nature lovers and anglers alike. Accessible only by sea and air, the town of 2800 has preserved blissfully uncrowded hiking, biking, skiing, bird-watching, and fishing opportunities. Bumper stickers reading "Keep the Copper River Delta Wild" advertise the community's opposition to the proposed connection of Cordova with the Interior's road network. A dearth of cruise ships keeps Cordova a town with a small-volume tourist industry. Cordova will leave you with plenty of room to roam. The only drawback is the weather: many cloudy days and 150 in. of annual precipitation make this a damp paradise. June is the best month for staying dry.

▛ TRANSPORTATION

Cordova, on the east side of Prince William Sound at **Orca Inlet,** starts at the shore and climbs up the steep hillside. **Railroad Ave.** begins at water level, and numbered streets parallel the ocean. **First St.** is the downtown shopping district and leads out of town to the ferry terminal. Railroad Ave. becomes **Copper River Hwy.** out of town toward the airport and the Childs Glacier.

Flights: The **airport** is 13 mi. east of town on the Copper River Hwy. **Alaska Airlines** (☎ 424-3278 or 800-426-0333) flies once per day to **Juneau** ($235) and **Anchorage** ($129). They also contract **Era Aviation** (☎ 800-866-8394) to fly 3 more times per day to **Anchorage** for the same fare. The **Airport Shuttle** (☎ 424-3272) meets scheduled flights and runs to town for $10.

Ferries: Alaska Marine Highway (☎ 424-7333 or 800-642-0066; www.akmhs.com), 1 mi. north of town on Ocean Dock Rd., off 1st St. Regular service to **Valdez** (5½hr., $32) and **Whittier** (7hr., $62).

Taxis: Wild Hare Taxi Service, ☎ 424-3939.

Car Rental: Cordova Auto Rentals (☎ 424-5982), at the airport. $65 per day; unlimited free mileage. Big cars $80 per day. Hefty taxes added. Must be 21 with a credit card.

▛ PRACTICAL INFORMATION

Visitor Information: Cordova Historical Museum, 622 1st St. (☎ 424-6665). Open Tu-Sa 10am-6pm, Su 2-4pm. **Cordova Chamber of Commerce** (☎ 424-7260), on 1st Ave., opposite Cordova Realty. Open M-F 10am-noon and 1:30-5:30pm.

Outdoor Information: Forest Service Cordova District Ranger Station (☎ 424-7661), on 2nd St. between Browning and Adams, on the 2nd fl. Research Forest Service **cabins** here. Open M-F 8am-5pm. **Fishing licenses** are available at **Davis' Super Foods** (☎ 424-7681), on 1st St. Open M-Sa 7:30am-9pm, Su 9am-8pm.

CORDOVA ■ 463

Equipment Rental: Cordova Coastal Outfitters (☎ 424-7424), on the dock in the small boat harbor. Mountain bikes $15 per day; single kayaks $35 per day, doubles $50; skiffs (fishing gear and gas included) $115 per day; Zodiacs with motor $95; camping equipment, too. **Cordova Auto Rentals** rents canoes for $35 per day.

Bookstore: Orca Book Store (☎ 424-5305), on 1st St. Small but with ample room on the balconies for reading. Houses a collection of 1st edition Alaskan books. Open M-F 7am-5pm, Sa 8am-5pm. No credit cards.

Laundromat and Showers: Club Speedwash, in the alley behind the Club Bar on 1st St. Wash $2, dry 25¢ per 15min. Open daily 8am-8pm. **Harbormaster,** 602 Nicholoff Way (☎ 424-6400). Dry $3 per 10min. Tokens available M-F 8am-5pm and other irregular hours. Call ahead. Showers open 24hr.

Emergency: ☎ 911.

Police: (☎ 424-6100). Beside the post office on Railroad Ave.

Pharmacy: Cordova Drug Co. (☎ 424-3246), on 1st St. Open M-Sa 9:30am-6pm.

Hospital: 602 Chase Ave. (☎ 424-8000), off Copper River Hwy., just out of town in the building with the big orange roof.

Internet Access: At the **Library** (☎ 424-6667), on 1st St., next to the museum. Open Tu-Sa 1-8pm. Free, but slow. **Laura's Liquor** (☎ 424-3144), on 1st St. by the library. $5 for 15min., 20¢ per min. thereafter. Also has espresso, smoothies, and the namesake.

Post Office: (☎ 424-3564), at Council St. and Railroad Ave. Open M-F 10am-5:30pm, Sa 10am-1pm. **ZIP Code:** 99574.

ACCOMMODATIONS AND CAMPING

Although Cordova has several cheap options for rooms, the city and surrounding area is amazingly devoid of places to pitch a tent or park an RV. The **City RV Park,** 1 mi. from downtown on Whitshed Rd., offers minimal space and maximal noise. These sites are mainly used by summer cannery workers. (☎ 424-6400. Sites $3, RV hookups $12.) The residents of **Hippie Cove,** about 1½ mi. out of town past the ferry terminal, may help friendly backpackers find a place to camp down in the peaceful bay, even though camping there is illegal. The next closest option is **Childs Glacier,** 50 mi. from town on Copper River Hwy. The sites allow you to listen to the glacier calve and thunder throughout the night. They have pit toilets and no water for $5. Contact the Forest Service (☎ 424-7661) to find out whether **day-use sites** closer on the highway may be open for overnight use. It is also legal to camp on any land that falls within the **Chugach National Forest**—again, check with the Forest Service.

Alaskan Hotel and Bar (☎ 424-3299), on 1st St. Look for the upside-down sign. This building carries a history as rich as the town, but shows its age. Above the muffled sounds of the bar's jukebox, these rooms are simple, spacious, and centrally located. Singles and doubles $35, with private bath $55; add $10 for 3 or more people.

The Lighthouse, 514 1st St. (☎ 424-3581 or 424-3134), behind The Salvation Army. A beacon to budget travelers in search of clean, new rooms and privacy. The rooms are off the street and include a large kitchenette, private bath, two double beds, TV and phone. May-Sept. $60, mid-Sept. to Apr. $50. No credit cards.

Northern Nights Inn (☎ 424-5356), at 3rd St. and Council Ave. Rooms filled with antiques reflect the times of a previous copper-era millionaire. The house has 4 rooms, $65 and up, including a private kitchen and bath. Serves as a quiet hideaway, uphill from town. Winter rates start at $50. Bikes $12 per day.

FOOD

The food situation in Cordova is dicey and pricey. By day, lunches are fairly reasonable; by night, what joints are still open charge nearly $20 for a mediocre meal. If possible, buy and cook your own dinner. The best selection of groceries is the colossal **A.C. Value,** on Nicholoff St., in the small boat harbor. (☎ 424-7141. Open M-Sa 7:30am-10pm, Su 8am-9pm.)

Baja Taco (☎ 424-5599). In a red bus by the small boat harbor sits a woman who can add some spice to your life. Fish tacos with fresh halibut ($2.75) are outstanding. Breakfast burritos ($6.50) get the job done. Outdoor cafe tables allow you to linger. Open May-Sept. (weather permitting) M-Tu 8am-4pm, W-Sa 8am-8pm, Su 10am-8pm.

Killer Whale Cafe (☎ 424-7733), on 1st St. in the back of the groovy Orca Bookstore. Next to every other town's earthy espresso-steeped cafe, this stands out. Decks overlook the books here. Homemade soup and croissant $4; killer sandwiches $6-9. Open M-F 7am-4pm, Sa 8am-3:30pm.

SIGHTS, EVENTS, AND NIGHTLIFE

The **docks** are always bustling. Near Cordova Coastal Outfitters is a good place to see nets being mended, and you can see fish being processed at the canneries toward the ferry terminal. If it's raining (and it probably is), dry off in the **Cordova Historical Museum,** 622 1st St., in the same building as the library. The museum has preserved iceworms (little black critters that dwell on glaciers), plus Prince Willie, a leatherback turtle who strayed several thousand miles and wound up in a local fisherman's net. Check out the hilariously dramatic "Story of Cordova," shown daily at varying times. The museum also boasts an old printing press, and a replica of the living quarters aboard a 1953 fishing boat. (☎ 424-6665. Open Tu-Sa 10am-6pm, Su 2-4pm. $1 suggested donation.)

Cordova's nightlife is concentrated at the **Alaskan Hotel and Bar,** where the juke box plays into the wee hours. The original oak bar has been hospitable to local fishermen since 1906. Come here for a friendly drink—or several. The juke box blares into the wee hours. (☎ 424-3288. Open M-Th 8am-2am, F-Sa 8am-4am, Su 10am-2am.) In the dead of winter, Cordovans escape cabin fever by honoring the little squirmers who love the dark days and cold temperatures. **The Iceworm Festival** breaks loose the first weekend in February and includes a parading 100-foot iceworm propelled by Cordova's children and the coronation for the ever-sought-after title, Miss Iceworm Queen (☎ 424-3982). The **Copper River Delta** that surrounds the Copper River Hwy. is the largest contiguous wetland area in western North America, and supports the largest accumulation of shore birds in the world (about 14 million) during the second week of May, when birdwatchers flock to the annual **Shorebird Festival** (call the visitors center at 424-6665 for details).

OUTDOOR ACTIVITIES

The fish are always biting in the freshwater and saltwater surrounding Cordova. Fishing is best along **Orca Inlet Rd.,** on the **Eyak River,** or at **Hartney Bay.** Kings return May-June, coho Aug-Sept., sockeye in late May-June. Contact **Fish and Game** for details (☎ 424-7535). In Prince William Sound and Orca Inlet, kayaking is spectacular and the weather is often nicer out at sea, away from the mountains behind Cordova that draw the rain from the clouds. **Cordova Coastal Outfitters** (see p. 463) offers guided tours, drop-offs, gear rental, and advice. ($65 for 4hr., $95 for 8hr.)

For **surfing,** the water here is warmer than in nearby Yakutat, although the waves are somewhat less spectacular. The best breaks can be found off of **Hinchinbrook Island, Hook Point,** and **Strawberry Beach.** You'll need to find a boat ride there, but can stay at the **Hook Point** Forest Service cabin. Call local board-shaper David Parsons of **Surfboards Alaska** (☎ 424-3524) for advice and gear.

The oldest chairlift in Alaska swings over a mere three runs at **Mt. Eyak Ski Area.** (☎ 424-7766. Open Dec. 25-snow melt. Lift tickets $15). Excellent **cross-country skiing** is free along the Mt. Tripod Trail and farther down the Copper River Hwy. at the Muskeg Meander Ski Trail. In the dark months, the adventurous go **ice skating** on Lake Eyak.

HIKING

The only choice for a hike close to town is to walk up Browning Ave. to the ski trail. The top of the trail has exceptional views. Hiking in the Copper River Delta is often wet and tough, but the neighboring **Chugach Mountains** provide well-maintained dry trails and excellent climbing opportunities. Check with the Forest Service for a great free pamphlet on hiking around Cordova.

Crater Lake Trail (2½ mi. one-way, 2hr.). Trailhead 1½ mi. from Cordova on Power Creek Road, just beyond the city airstrip on the north side of Eyak Lake. A popular hike and difficult scramble that leads to views of the Copper River Delta, Prince William Sound, and the Chugach Mountains, as well as to the Crater Lake alpine bowl. Crater Lake connects with the Power Creek Trail through Ridge Route Intertie. 1500 ft. elevation gain.

Ridge Route Intertie (6 mi., 12mi. for the entire loop between Crater Lake and Power Creek). Trailhead at the end of Crater Lake Trail or at Mile 3 of Power Creek. This is the connecting trail between Crater Lake and Power Creek. Views from the ridge are outstanding. A shelter is available on the ridge, midway. 1000 ft. gain from Power Creek.

Power Creek Trail. Trailhead 7 mi. from Cordova on Power Creek road, north of Eyak Lake; 5 mi. to Power Creek Cabin, 9 mi. to Crater Lake. The trail passes through diverse scenery, with lots of waterfalls, a hanging glacier, and berry-picking. Bears enjoy the berries too, so beware. The trail begins moderately and as it reaches the ridge becomes very difficult. Allow plenty of time, wear rubber boots, and consider reserving the Forest Service Cabin. The connecting trail begins 3 mi. from the trailhead at Alice Smith cutoff trail and ends at Crater Lake. 1500 ft. gain. Call 877-444-6777 to reserve the cabin.

McKinley Lake (2½ mi. one-way, 2hr.). Access trailhead at Mile 21.6 of Copper River Hwy. The Lucky Strike Mining Co. began the construction of this trail in 1927. It is an easy walk, or bike, that leads through forest to the lake for great fishing. A rougher trail continues past the lake to the deserted mine. Take caution of nails, old boards, and collapsing mine shafts. Little elevation change. Two cabins can on the lake can be reserved (☎877-444-6777).

DAYTRIP FROM CORDOVA: CHILDS GLACIER

CHILDS GLACIER. One of the most stupendous road-accessible sights in Alaska, Childs Glacier stands 300 ft. tall and calves actively throughout summer months, as the Copper River's currents rise boldly. Twenty-story chunks of ice plunge into the silty waters with great thunder. The largest calvings can send 20 ft. waves over the observation area on the opposite bank of the river a quarter-mile away. Splintered trees and boulders strewn throughout the woods are testament to the power of these inland tsunamis. Although falls of this size are uncommon (occurring perhaps once per season), they are unpredictable and viewers should be prepared to run. It is also prohibited to harvest salmon flung into the woods by the waves (called "glacier fishing"). Visitors have a hard time tearing themselves away from the sight, always afraid to miss "the big one" as they head towards the parking lot and hear the thunder from afar. The **Million Dollar Bridge**, only a few hundred yards from the viewing area, was considered an engineering marvel in 1910 because of its placement between two active glaciers. **Miles Glacier** has retreated, but Childs is now less than a half mile away. The bridge was heavily damaged in the 1964 earthquake, but a creative patch job keeps it standing. Daredevils drive across at their own risk, although there is nothing to see on the other side.

The combined splendor of the delta and the glacier make the expensive trip worthwhile. If traveling with a group, rent a car, pack a lunch (there's no food anywhere on the highway), and make a glorious day of it. *Let's Go* does not recommend hitchhiking and those who do have been known to get stranded since Childs is not a major tourist attraction. **Copper River and North West Tours,** run by the folks at Northern Nights Inn (see p. 463), runs several all-day bus trips every week. Their tour lasts hours, with a lengthy lunch stop at Childs. (☎424-5356. $35 per person, $40 with lunch. Call for schedule.) They'll also drop and pickup hikers anywhere along the highway for $1 per mi.

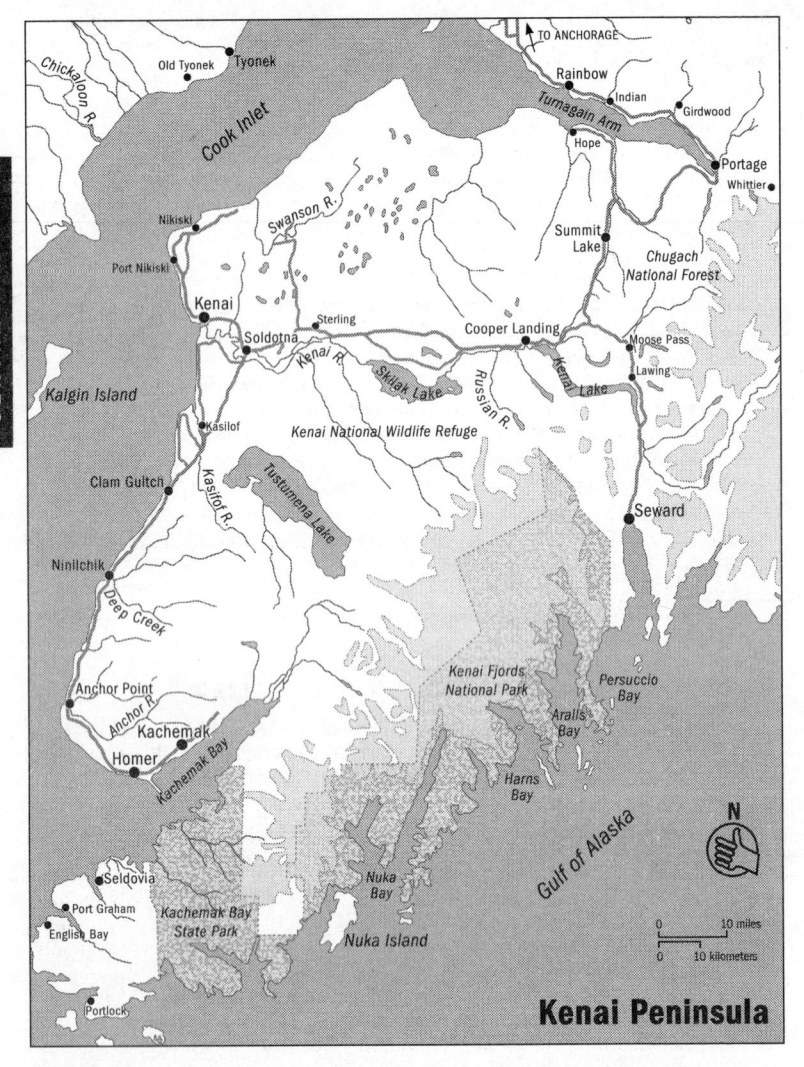

KENAI PENINSULA

Many visitors spend their whole trip to Alaska in the Kenai Peninsula due to its endless wildlife, heart-stopping scenery, and fantastic fishing. South of Anchorage, the Seward Hwy. (Rte. 9), runs to Seward and the Sterling Hwy. (Rte. 1), branches off to Homer, skirting Chugach National Forest, Kenai Fjords National Park, and the Kenai National Wildlife Refuge. On the western edge, snow-capped volcanoes reflect in the blue waters of Cook Inlet, while on the southern coast, glaciers reach out like enormous icy tongues from the Harding Ice Field to the sea.

SEWARD ☎ 907

Named for the Secretary of State who oversaw the purchase of Alaska from Russia in 1867, Seward was chosen as the terminus of the Alaska railroad for its ice-free, deep-water port. The lush alpine trails of Chugach National Forest and hulking tidewater glaciers of Kenai Fjords National Park see a massive wave of summer tourists that locals proudly welcome. Whale-filled emerald waters and abundant halibut and salmon draw still more visitors, and bald-eagles share the skies with exotic seabirds. Hikers, kayakers, sailors, and anglers: rejoice!

TRANSPORTATION

Seward is 127 mi. south of Anchorage on the scenic **Seward Hwy.** (Rte. 9) which turns into 3rd Ave. in town. Most services and outdoor outfits cluster in the small-boat harbor on **Resurrection Bay.** The more charming **downtown** is nine blocks farther south on the Seward Hwy. and one block east on 4th Ave., between Railroad and Madison Ave.

Flights: The airport is 2mi. north of town on the Seward Hwy. **FS Air Service** (☎248-9595) flies twice a day M-Sa and once on Su to **Anchorage** (30min., $59). **Scenic Mountain Air** (☎224-9152) offers charters.

Ferries: Alaska Marine Highway (☎224-5485 or 800-526-6731), follow Port Ave. to train tracks and take a right. To **Homer** (25hr., $106) via **Kodiak** (13hr., $66) and **Valdez** (11hr., $60).

Trains: Alaska Railroad (☎800-544-0552; www.akrr.com), at the north edge of town opposite the 3 renovated railroad cars. Trains leave daily in summer at 6:45pm for **Anchorage** (4½hr.; $55, ages 2-11 half-price). The train is generally accommodating to visitors taking in the glacier cruises (see **Kenai Fjords Nat'l Park,** p. 471).

Buses: Park Connection (☎800-266-8625; www.alaskacoach.com). **Katchemak Bay Transit** (☎235-3795) runs daily to **Homer** (5hr., $40), **Soldotna, Kenai, Cooper Landing** (1½-2½hr., $35-40), and **Anchorage** (3½hr., $35).

Public Transportation: Seward's trolley has designated stops throughout town. $2, all day $4, ages 6-15 half-price. Runs daily 10am-7pm. Group tours available.

Taxis: Glacier Taxi, ☎224-5678.

Car Rental: U-Save (☎800-254-8728), based out of Bell in the Woods B&B 6 mi. out of Seward. Compacts $60 per day, 100 free mi., 30¢ each additional mi. Must be 21. Required under-25 insurance $8 per day. Major credit card or $250 deposit. **Harbor Rentals** (☎224-8801 or 877-533-8801), has a similar deal and also rents vans and motor scooters. Provides group rates for shuttle services to Anchorage and towns on the Kenai. They also provide **Luggage Storage** $1.50-$5 per day.

PRACTICAL INFORMATION

Visitor Information: Seward Chamber of Commerce (☎224-8051), at Mile 2 on the Seward Hwy. Pictures and prices of accommodations and free calls within Alaska. Open M-F 8am-6pm, Sa 9am-6pm, Su 9am-4pm. **The Harbor Train Station General Information** (☎224-8747). This privately run info center has updated B&B vacancies and will reserve transportation, charters, and accommodations for free. Open daily in summer 9am-9pm; winter reduced hours.

Outdoor Information: Kenai Fjords National Park Visitor Center (☎224-3175 or 224-2132; www.nps.gov/kefj), at the small-boat harbor. A 12min. sideshow on the park is shown upon request and a short film on a ranger's crossing of the Harding Icefield is shown every 2hr. 10am-6pm. Open daily 8am-7pm; winter M-F 8am-5pm. The **Seward Ranger Station,** 334 4th Ave. (☎224-3374 or reservations 877-444-6777; www.reserveusa.com), at Jefferson St., has the skinny on cabins. Open M-F 8am-5pm.

Employment: Seward Employment Center (☎224-5276), 5th Ave. and Adams St., in the City Building. Lots of work available. Open M-F 9am-noon and 1-4:30pm.

Equipment Rental: The Fish House (☎224-3674), opposite the harbormaster, rent rods for $10. $50 cash or credit card deposit required. Tips and instructions free. Open daily 6am-9pm. **Bike rentals** available from **Seward Bike Shop** (☎224-2448) by the Harbor Train Station. Half-day $15-18, full-day $27-32. Open daily 9am-7pm.

Laundromat and Public Showers: Seward Laundry (☎224-5727), at 4th Ave. and C St., is the only laundromat in town and gets very crowded. Wash $2.50, dry 25¢ per 4min. Showers $5 per 15min. with towel and soap. Open M-Sa 8am-8pm, Su noon-6pm. Showers are available 24hr. at the **harbormaster**. $2 per 7min. Change available in the harbormaster's office, but only until 5pm.

Road Conditions: ☎800-478-7675.

Emergency: ☎911.

Police: (☎224-3338) at 4th and Adams. Provides a **24hr. refuge.**

Crisis Line: Seward Life Action Council, ☎224-3027 or 888-224-5257.

Hospital: Providence Seward Hospital (☎224-5205), at 1st Ave. and Jefferson St.

Pharmacy: Seward Drug, 224 4th Ave. (☎224-8989). Open M-Sa 9am-6pm. Reward yourself after the trek with a treat at the in-store soda fountain.

Internet Access: Seward Community Library (☎224-3646), at 5th and Adams. Free 30min.; call ahead. Open M-F noon-8pm, Sa noon-6pm. **Grant Electronics,** 222 4th Ave. (☎224-7015). $8 per hr. **Harley's Hogs & Dogs,** across from Grant's on 4th. $2 per 15min. Have a hot dog and espresso from a Hell's Angel as you type.

Post Office: (☎224-3001) at 5th Ave. and Madison St. Open M-F 9:30am-4:30pm, Sa 10am-2pm. **ZIP Code:** 99664.

ACCOMMODATIONS AND CAMPING

Seward has a host of reasonable housing and camping options, contributing to its popularity as a destination. **Connections** (☎224-5695, info line 800-844-2424; www.alaskaview.com) is a general reservation number for accommodations and trip bookings. You can also try the Harbor Train Station General Information number (see **Visitor Information,** above). The Chamber of Commerce has a sheet of available rooms listed for the week and a photo binder so you can check them out before you call. **Moose Pass,** at Mile 29.5, has 4 campgrounds. (Call to reserve ☎877-444-6777; www.reserveusa.com. $10-13.) If nothing else is available, there are plenty of pull-off spots along **Exit Glacier Rd.** Most are on the river side, with excellent views of the valley.

Kate's Roadhouse (☎224-5888), 5½ mi. outside town on the Seward Hwy. Huge continental breakfast with home-baking. Free shuttle service, bikes, car cleaning station, local calls, laundry, bedding, and towels. Shared baths including Alaska's only outhouse with heat and a flush toilet. Some local buses will drop off and pick up. Dorms with breakfast are the best deal in town. Dorms $17; private rooms $59.

Moby Dick Hostel (☎224-7072; www.mobydickhostel.com), at 3rd Ave. between Jefferson and Madison St. Conveniently located. Single-sex rooms, and view of Mt. Marathon. Showers and kitchen. Linen $2. Office open 9-11am, 5-10pm. $17; private room $45.

Fjords RV Park. Down Exit Glacier Rd. a half-mile, on the right. Clean, wooded sites in an open, old-growth forest. Tents $8 plus $5 per extra tent; RV's $10-15.

Municipal Waterfront Campground, along Ballaine Rd. between Railway Ave. and D St. Fish from your front door. Showers and extra toilets at the harbormaster. 2-week max. stay. Check-out 4pm. Open May 15-Sept. 30. Sites $6; RV sites $10, hookups $15. Week-long rate available.

FOOD

Although affordable, Seward's food is not its forte. The fish is fantastic when it is fresh. Stock up on groceries at the **Eagle Quality Center,** 1907 Seward Hwy., at Mile 1.5. (☎224-3698. Open 24hr.)

Railway Cantina, 1401 4th (☎224-8226), on the corner of 4th and N Harbor. Fillerup for $8 and under. Don't miss the halibut tacos ($7) complete with chips, mexican slaw, and your choice of six homemade salsas. Veggie options a plenty. Have a Corona with that for $3.50. Open daily Jan.-Oct. 11am-8pm.

Bakery at the Harbor, (☎224-6091), across from the harbormaster. A great breakfast stop for the hungry sailor. Slide in for a breakfast burrito ($3.50) or loaf of homemade bread ($4) and watch 'em clean the day's latest catch across the street.

Resurrect Art Coffee House Gallery, 320 3rd Ave. (☎224-7161), in a converted Lutheran church. Lattes so good they're sinful ($2.50). Sip Italian soda ($1.50) at the altar-turned-art-display or play a boardgame in the balcony-turned-loft. Open M-Th 7am-10pm, F-Sa 7am-midnight, Su 7am-6pm.

Red's (☎224-5995), at 3rd and Van Buren St. Best burgers in town cooked in a white school bus fronted by picnic tables. Try the halibut burger ($7)—it doesn't get any fresher than here. Open M-Sa 11am-9pm.

NIGHTLIFE

With the long hours of daylight in summer, outdoor activities can continue into the wee hours of the morning. When done with the seas or the trails, nightowls head downtown to the local watering holes which are concentrated in the blocks between Railway Ave. and Jefferson St. and 5th and 3rd.

New Seward Saloon (☎224-3095), on 5th. Mosey on up to the wooden bar and take a step back in time. If there were a hotspot for Seward's younger set, you'd find it here. Try one of the collection of martinis ($7), a tiny tini ($5.25), or sip a tankard of Long Island Ice tea through a 2 ft. straw as you pick your tunes from the huge CD collection. Microbrews $3.75. Open daily May-Oct. noon-2am, Nov-Apr. 5pm-2am.

Yukon Bar (☎224-3063), at 4th Ave. and Washington St., draws a young crowd with its frequent live music (Th-M). The Mt. Marathon race originated with a drunken bet here (see **Sights,** below). Pin a dollar to the ceiling lest you someday return with an empty wallet. Pool tables, micro-brew pints $3.75, open mic (M). Open daily noon-2am.

The Pit (☎224-3006), Mile 3.5 on the Seward Hwy. After downtown closes at 2am, head out of town to The Pit to hang with the late, late crowd. Take advantage of 5am drinks with shuffleboard and a great deck to enjoy the midnight sun.

SIGHTS AND ENTERTAINMENT

ALASKA SEALIFE CENTER. Opened in 1998 to state-wide anticipation the Sealife Center has become one of Seward's prized attractions. Created in the black wake of the Exxon *Valdez* oil spill, the $56 million research center gives visitors a glimpse of underwater Alaska and the research that documents it. While this is an active lab, not an ordinary aquarium, visitors can touch the starfish and watch tufted puffins, stellar sea lions, and harbor seals in large outdoor habitats. Immerse yourself in the unusual educational experience it provides. Visiting professors and resident biologists discuss current research, and kid-friendly programs include tours, films, sleep-overs in front of the tanks, and craft activities. *(At the end of downtown on Railroad Ave. between 3rd and 4th Ave.* ☎*224-6300 or 800-224-2525; www.alaskasealife.org. Open May-Sept. daily 8am-8pm; Oct.-Apr. W-Su 10am-5pm. $12.50, ages 7-12 $10. Children under 6 free. Family and group discounts available.)*

RESURRECTION BAY HISTORICAL SOCIETY MUSEUM. A nice quick bang-for-your-buck with plenty of traditional Alaskan artifacts and earthquake memorabilia. Stop-in during the evening on M, W, or F for a show on the history of the Iditarod Trail. *(In the Senior Center at 3rd Ave. and Jefferson St.* ☎ *224-3902. Open June to Labor Day daily 9am-5pm; call for winter openings. Museum $3, ages 5-18 50¢. Evening show $3.)*

POLAR BEAR JUMP-OFF. Seward's test of physical endurance is on the third weekend of January, when the three-day **Seward Polar Bear Jump** raises money for the American Cancer Society by plunging participants into the frigid waters of Resurrection Bay.

RACES. Seward's principal insanity-inducing annual event is the **Mountain Marathon.** Alaska's oldest footrace (only the Boston Marathon is older in the US) began after a tipsy sourdough challenged a barmate to get up and down Mt. Marathon (3022 ft.) in under an hour: the modern men's record is 43min., the women's 50min. Every year on July 4th hundreds of competitors run, slide, fall, and bleed up and down the mountainside. Brave runners buy their tickets by the end of February, but a handful are auctioned off on July 3rd. Accommodations and all available tent space fill up early (☎ 224-8051; $30). In its 10th year, the annual **Lost Lake Breath of Life Run,** covers 16 mi. over what may be the most beautiful trail race around. Don't worry about tiring, you'll be too busy rubber-necking your way through alpine vistas. Benefits go to cystic fibrosis research (☎ 224-3537). The **Exit Glacier 5K and 10K Run** begins in mid-May (☎ 224-4054).

FISHING. The annual **Silver Salmon Derby** creates a splash for nine days from the second Saturday in August. The elusive tagged fish is worth $100,000. No one has caught the slippery salmon since 1980, when Japanese tourist and lucky bastard Katsumi Takaku nabbed it from the city docks (☎ 224-8051). You can also try your luck at the longer **Seward Jackpot Halibut Tournament** which runs from mid-May-August with weekly prizes for the largest fish (☎ 224-8051).

OUTDOOR ACTIVITIES

The trails between Seward and its northern neighbor, **Portage,** are some of the most spectacular in the entire state. You really can't go wrong anywhere in Alaska, and the **Chugach National Forest** is no exception (see p. 450). Although many of these routes take days, portions of some can be turned into easily accessible dayhikes. Be advised that snow may exist at higher elevations well into July and weather in the area can change rapidly. Bring rain gear and extra layers. **Public cabins,** located throughout the forests and on several islands, sleep four to eight, and have tables and wood stoves, but no water, electricity, or mattresses. (Reserve at ☎ 877-444-6777; www.reserveusa.com. $25-45. $10 cancellation fee.) The many **Ranger Stations** in the area are your best bet for trail conditions and public cabin info (see **Visitor Information,** p. 467).

HIKING

The **Exit Glacier** area of **Kenai Fjords National Park** (see p. 471) provides several hikes of varying degrees of difficulty. Lost Lake, Resurrection Pass and Johnson Pass may all be snowed in on their upper stretches well into July. Be sure and check the conditions and pack accordingly before heading out. For detailed topos of these and other, shorter hikes, the **Kenai National Wildlife Refuge Topo** is an excellent, waterproof guide ($10 at the Portage Glacier Visitor Center; see p. 450).

> **Caines Head Trail** (5 mi., several hours with an optional overnight). This popular trail weaves its way along the coastal beaches of Resurrection Bay for 5 mi., ending at the mouth of Seward's bay. 2½ mi. past Caine's Head's north beach, trailheads lead to the abandoned Fort McGilvary. After 1½ mi., there is a 2½ mi. stretch negotiable only at low tide. Most hikers stay overnight before returning in order to catch the next low tide. Consult visitors centers, the newspaper, or outfitters for tide information and a detailed map of the area as several attractions lie on side trails. (Turn right at the end of 3rd. Ave. and follow the gravel road for 3 mi. to Lowell Point.)

- **Mt. Marathon.** You don't *need* to be half-crazy to get to the top of the mountain. There is a far more pedestrian, although still strenuous, route that leads to a glorious view of the sea, town, and surrounding mountains. (From 1st Ave. and Jefferson St., take Lowell St. to reach the trail, which begins with a steep ascent up a rocky stream bed.)
- **Lost Lake Trail** (16 mi., 1-2 days). A strenuous but extremely pretty dayhike or overnight trip, leading the hiker through dense forest to alpine meadows and back down over and into Seward. Though it can be done in a day, it's best to stretch the views out with an overnight stay in the hills. The trail is open to mountain bikers in the summer and cross-country skiers in the winter. (The north trailhead is at Mile 17 of the Seward Hwy. Follow signs to Primrose Campground.)
- **Resurrection Pass Trail** (39 mi., 3-5 days). North trailhead: turn south at Mile 16.2 of the Hope Hwy. on Palmer Cr. Rd. Take the right fork onto Resurrection Cr. Rd. and continue 4 mi. to trailhead. South Trailhead: head to Sterling Hwy. Mile 52. The true path to illumination is a favorite among mountain bikers and weekend hikers—expect to see an eighth of Anchorage's population along this trail on any given Saturday. This easy grade leads to several public use cabins and designated campsites.
- **Johnson Pass Trail** (23 mi., 2-3 days). The trail, which starts steeply and then levels off, provides an ideal way to view different Kenai Peninsula ecosystems as it passes through a spruce forest, rises into shrubby subalpine regions, and finally extends into alpine tundra. (The north trailhead starts at Seward Hwy. Mile 64; go south on a gravel road a quarter-mile to the trailhead. The south trailhead lies at Seward Hwy. Mile 32.5.)

FISHING AND MUSHING

Salmon and halibut fill the bay, and grayling and dolly varden can be hooked in the streams and lakes right outside of town. Best of all, fishing is free from the shore or docks. Charters abound for both halibut and salmon; prices start at $95, with all gear provided. To reach **IdidaRide Sled Dog Tours**, turn left on Exit Glacier Rd. at Seward Hwy. Mile 3.7, continue 3½ mi., take a right on Old Exit Glacier Rd., and follow the signs for the next half-mile. IdidaRide's owner, Mitch Seavey, competes in the Iditarod every year—you can help train his dogs in the summer by providing deadweight. (☎224-8607 or 800-478-3139. Full tour 1¼hr.; 5 daily; $34, under 12 $15. Kennel tour $15, children $7.50. Call for reservations.)

KENAI FJORDS NATIONAL PARK ☎907

Covering more than half of 607,805-acre Kenai Fjords National Park, the Harding Icefield spills its 32 frozen rivers out into the Gulf of Alaska along one of the most stunning stretches of coastal land in the world. This icefield, several thousand feet thick, engulfs over 60 mi. of mountain range in its slow recession, dropping house-sized blocks of ice into waters teeming with otters, sea lion, porpoise, whale, and hundreds of bird species. The wildlife alone is enough to warrant an extended stay among these icy waters, which are sadly unnavigable to the novice kayaker. The lay traveler can revel in the park's glory by foot, tour boat, kayak, or plane.

HIKING

Hikes begin at **Exit Glacier**, the only road-accessible glacier in the park, 9 mi. west on a spur from Mile 3.7 of the Seward Hwy. A **shuttle** runs here four times per day from downtown Seward (☎224-5770; $20 round-trip), and the park entrance fee is good for a week ($5 per car, $2 on foot). From the **Ranger Station** at the end of the road, a leisurely three-quarter-mile stroll leads to the outlandishly blue glacier. The first half-mile is wheelchair accessible. Rangers lead free, leisurely 45 minute **guided walks** to the glacier. The **Harding Ice Field Trail** begins at the parking lot on a paved trail, and climbs 3000 ft. over 4 mi. to a storm shelter, and just a bit farther for an astonishing view of the **Harding Ice Field.** The glimmering 300 sq. mi. of ice is 3000-5000 ft. deep and the source of over 40 glaciers. The trail is steep and often muddy or snow-covered depending on conditions. If the snow isn't gone, brush up on your route finding skills and add an hour or so to the normal 5-6hr. hiking time. Good boots with gaiters and a walking stick are recommended. If you still want to touch the ice, but can do without the incredible incline, try the more moderate quarter mile **Overlook Trail** which starts where the paved trail ends and provides direct access to the glacier.

TOURS

Boat cruises are the easiest way to see the park. All companies run basically the same trips, the difference being the size of boat and quality of food included. The longest and most expensive cruises access either **Aialik Bay** or the **Northwestern Fjord**. Both routes pass forested islands full of seabirds and coastal mountains striped with waterfalls and streams. The half-day cruises seek wildlife inside Resurrection Bay. **Kenai Fjords Tours** are informative. (☎224-8068 or 800-478-8068; www.kenaifjords.com. To Northwestern Fjord 9½hr.; $139, children $69. Holgate Glacier 6hr.; $109, children $54.) **Major Marine Tours** brings along a ranger and serves the best all-you-can-eat salmon and prime rib buffet on the water for $12. (☎224-8030 or 800-764-7300. To Holgate Glacier $109, children $54.) Both companies also offer a variety of tours within Resurrection Bay, including overnighters, and it pays to shop around for just the right type of trip (the cheapest start at $54). **Renown Charters and Tours** (☎224-3806 or 800-655-3806) runs similar cruises for about the same prices. **Mariah Tours** uses smaller boats for a more intimate effect. (☎224-8623 or 800-270-1238. Max. 16 passengers.) Pick up a list of charters at the Chamber of Commerce or **The Fish House** (see **Fishing and Mushing,** p. 471). **Scenic Mountain Air** skims over the crevasses of the glaciers and soars high above the ice field, (☎288-3646 or 224-9152. 1hr. tours from $99 per person. Air taxi and drop off service also available.) as does **Kenai Fjords Air Tours.** (☎224-1060. 1½ hr., $125.)

KAYAKING

Experienced kayakers can water taxi to islands and cabins. Contact the rangers in Seward for advice and resources. The inexperienced don't enjoy a high ratio of sea time to expense, nevertheless skimming along at water level is the best way to take it all in. **Sunny Cove Sea Kayaking** offers a joint trip with **Kenai Fjords Tours,** including the wildlife cruise, a salmon bake, kayaking instruction, and a two and half hour wilderness paddle. (☎345-5339. 8hr. $149-59.) **Kayak and Custom Adventures Worldwide** leads trips including paddling instruction and rents kayaks to the experienced. (☎258-3866 or 800-288-3134; www.KayakAK.com. Singles $30 per day, doubles $55.)

HOMER ☎907

Oh how we all long to live among the unfettered and unemployed, a combination which suits the amiable population of this smokey little town quite well. If you descend upon Homer from the Sterling Hwy., glimpses of misty mountains and crackling glaciers give way to the Gulf of Alaska, which draws a large portion of Homer's population out each day for commercial and sport fishing. With more halibut charters than you can shake a stick at, and one of most active fishing ports in Alaska, you'd expect a salty, calloused folk. Quite to the contrary, the other half lives in suspended 1960s animation, feeding a thriving community in a strange union of counterculture and working folk. So stay for the fish, or stay for the feel; either way Homer has a knack for keeping its visitors longer than they expect.

⌐ TRANSPORTATION

Surrounded by 400 million tons of coal, Homer rests on **Kachemak "Smokey" Bay,** named for the mysteriously burning deposits that first greeted settlers. The town is on the southwestern coast of **Kenai Peninsula,** on the north shore of the bay, and extending into the bay along an improbable 4½ mi. tendril of sand, gravel, and RVs known as **the Spit.** The rugged, beautiful wilds and hiking trails of **Kachemak Bay State Park** lie across the bay, where the southern end of the **Kenai Mountains** reaches the sea. Also on the south side of the bay is the artist/fishing colony of **Halibut Cove,** the sparsely populated **Yukon Island,** the **Gull Island** bird rookery, and the Russian-founded hamlet of **Seldovia** (see p. 496).

Homer

ACCOMMODATIONS
International Backpackers Hostel, 2
Karen Hornaday Park, 1
Seaside Farm, 10
Spit Municipal Camping, 9
Sunspin Guest House, 4

FOOD
Cafe Cups, 3
Duncan House, 11
Eagle Quality Center, 7
Two Sisters Bakery, 8
Young's Oriental Restaurant, 6

NIGHTLIFE
Alice's Champagne Palace, 5
Homer Brewing Co., 12

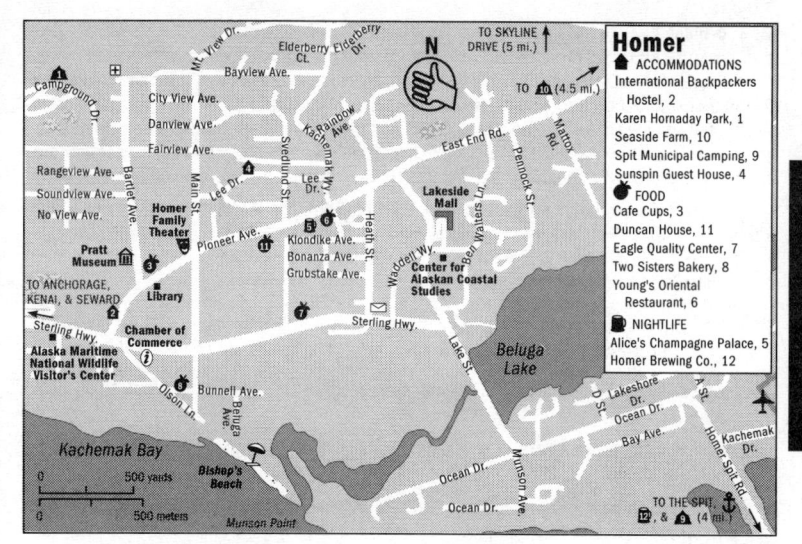

Across the Kenai peninsula, 226 mi. from Anchorage, the **Sterling Hwy.** (Hwy. 1) becomes the **Homer Bypass** as it enters downtown Homer. The Sterling changes names again to become **Ocean Dr.** and then veers right in its final transformation into the **Homer Spit Rd.** as it moves out into the bay. The heart of Homer lies in a triangle defined by the shoreside Homer Bypass, the downtown drag **Pioneer Ave.**, and the cross-cutting **Lake St.** The walk from downtown to the Spit takes more than an hour. Reports say hitching is easy, though *Let's Go* doesn't recommend it.

Flights: Follow signs from Ocean Dr. just before it becomes Spit Rd. to reach the airport. **Era Aviation** (☎ 800-866-8394) flies to **Anchorage** (6 per day, one-way $85-110). **Homer Air** (☎ 235-8591) flies to **Seldovia** (15min., many per day, round-trip $60). **Smokey Bay Air**, 2100 Kachemak Dr. (☎ 235-1511), flies to Seldovia just about hourly (round-trip $60). Both **Homer** and **Smokey Bay Air** are located ½ mi. down Kachemak Dr., the first left at the beginning of the Spit Rd.

Buses: Homer Stage Line, 1242 Ocean Dr. (☎ 235-2252), next to Quicky Mart. To **Soldotna** (1½hr.; 1 per day M-Sa; $25, $45 round-trip), **Anchorage** (5½hr.; 1 per day M-Sa; $48, round-trip $85), and **Seward** (4hr.; M, W, and F; $40, $75 round-trip). $5 extra for drop-off at Anchorage Airport. Runs regularly Memorial Day to Labor Day with decreased service continuing in the off season.

Ferries: Alaska Marine Highway (☎ 235-8449 or 800-382-9229). Office and terminal just before the end of the Spit. To **Seldovia** (1½hr., Tu, $40 round-trip); **Kodiak** 9½hr.; Su, M, Tu; $106 round-trip); and once per month to **Dutch Harbor** in the Aleutian Islands (1 week, $532 round-trip). Open M-Sa 7am-5pm and when ferry is in port.

Local Transport: Homer Trolley (☎ 235-2345) runs a route from the **Wildlife Refuge Visitors Center** to the **Spit** and back through downtown every 2hr. 10am-6pm. $3 per ride, $9 for a day pass. Listen for the bell.

Taxis: Chux Taxi (☎ 235-2489). To downtown from the airport ($5) or ferry ($10). **Kache-cab** (☎ 235-1950), offers the same prices.

Car Rental: Polar (☎ 235-5998 or 800-876-6417 until 9pm). Economy size $56 per day, 33¢ per mi. after 100 mi., 7th day free. Must be 21 with credit card. Open daily 7:15am-9:30pm.

474 ■ KENAI PENINSULA

⚡ PRACTICAL INFORMATION

Visitor Information: (☎235-7740; www.homeralaska.org), near Main St. Local and long-distance courtesy phone. Be sure to pick up the Chamber of Commerce's exceptionally useful visitor's guide. Open June to Labor Day M-F 9am-8pm, Sa-Su 10am-6pm; Labor Day to May M-F 9am-5pm. It helps to be aware that these visitors centers are likely to only recommend establishments that are chamber of commerce members.

Outdoor Information: Alaska Maritime National Wildlife Refuge Visitor Center, 509 Sterling Hwy. (☎235-6961), next to the Best Western Bidarka Inn. Wildlife exhibits highlight the immense seabird population around Homer. Leads 1hr. bird and tide pool walks twice a week and shows videos upon request. Open daily May-Sept. 9am-5pm.

Southern District Ranger Station (☎235-7024), 4 mi. out of town on the Sterling Hwy. has info on the park across the bay. Catch 'em when they're open F-Su 1-6pm. Call first in winter. **Fishing licenses** ($10 for 1 day, $20 for 3 days) available from many local stores. **Alaska Department of Fish and Game,** 3298 Douglas St. (☎235-8191), near Owen Marine. Open M-F 8am-5pm.

Employment: Alaska State Employment Service, 270 W Pioneer Ave. (☎235-7791; www.jobs.state.ak.us/jobseeker). Open M-F 8:30am-noon and 1-5pm.

ATM: Eagle Quality Center (24hr.; see **Food,** below). **Salty Dawg Saloon,** on the Spit. and several banks around town.

Equipment Rental: Chain Reaction (☎235-0750), in the Lakeside Mall. Bikes $15 per half-day, $25 per full day. Open M-Sa 9am-6pm, Su 10am-5pm. Numerous outfits on the Spit rent fishing gear, clamming rakes, and shovels, including **Sportsman's Supplies** (☎235-2617), in the white building on the Spit by the Fishing Hole. Salmon or halibut poles $10 per 24hr., clamming gear $5 a day. Open daily in summer 7am-9pm.

Laundromat and Public Showers: East End Laundry, near **Seaside Farm** on East End Rd., just before the Tesoro. Wash $2.50, dry 25¢ for 7min., showers $2 for 7min. **The Washboard,** 1204 Ocean Dr., before the Spit. (☎235-6781). Same prices as East End except for their cozy, private shower rooms. 30min. for $3.50.

Weather: ☎235-5600.

Emergency: ☎911.

Police: 4060 Heath St. (☎235-3150), off Pioneer Ave.

Women's Crisis Line: (☎235-7712 or 235-8101 after hours). 24hr.

Hospital: South Peninsula Hospital, 4300 Bartlett (☎235-8101), off Pioneer St.

Internet Access: Free 30min. per day at the **Library,** 141 Pioneer Ave. (☎235-3180), near Main St. Open M, W, F-Sa 10am-6pm, Tu and Th 10am-8pm. Also free at **K-Bay Cafe,** 5941 East End Rd. (☎235-1551) 3½ mi. out of town on E End Rd. in the Kachemak Building Center. Open M-F 6am-6pm, Sa-Su 8am-5pm.

Post Office: (☎235-6129), off Homer Bypass. Open M-F 8:30am-5pm, Sa noon-2pm. General delivery only held for 10 days. **ZIP Code:** 99603.

🏕 ACCOMMODATIONS AND CAMPING

Affordable accommodations are not hard to come by in Homer. **The Bookie** (☎888-335-1581) and the **Homer's Finest B&B Network** (☎800-764-3211) can aid you in your search, as there is an endless supply of B&Bs in the $70-90 range.

■ **Seaside Farm,** 58335 East End Rd. (☎235-7850 or 235-2670), 4½ mi. out of town on East End Rd. A bit of a hike or a $9 cab from town, though hitching is reportedly easy (*Let's Go* cannot recommend hitching). A clover field for camping with one of Homer's finest views of the bay. Enjoy a covered outdoor common area, kitchen, hammock, and international visitors around the campfire. Sometimes you can trade work for lodging (1hr. of work=tent space, 2hr.=bunk). Open May-Labor Day. Bunks $15. Tent sites $6. Private cabins $55. Discounts available for extended stays.

International Backpacker's Hostel/Inn (☎235-2463), on Pioneer near Pratt Museum turn off. Attractive bunks and a common area with a stupendous view of the Spit and mountains. Linens included. Internet and laundry facilities available. Both the Homer Stage Line and Kachemak Bay Transit stop here. Bunks $18; private doubles $50.

Sunspin Guest House, 358 Lee Dr. (☎235-6677 or 800-391-6677). From Pioneer Ave., take Kachemak Way toward the bluff to Lee Dr. on the right. Convenient to downtown. Clean and warm decor. Linens and continental breakfast included. Beds $28.

Karen Hornaday Park, within 1 mi. of downtown. From Pioneer St., go uphill on Bartlett St., left on Fairview, right on Campground Rd. Most sites grassy, secluded, and spacious. Water, pit toilets, and a great playground. Tents $6, RVs $10.

Spit Municipal Camping, 3735 Homer Spit Rd. (☎235-1583), sites line the approach to the Spit, but registration is at the booth across from the fishing hole. A giant gravel parking lot at seaside. Terrific views can be marred by fleets of RV's and tent-uprooting winds. Water, toilets. Tents $6, $36 a week; RVs $10, $60 a week.

FOOD

Homer provides ample opportunity to escape the hamburger and fries or fish and chips doldrums of the rest of the peninsula. From the markets to the restaurants, both the variety and the quality provide welcome refreshment. Eating in? Try the huge **Eagle Quality Center,** 90 Sterling Hwy. (☎235-2408. 24hr.) **Smoky Bay Natural Foods,** 248 W Pioneer Ave., has outstanding produce. (☎235-7252. Open daily 9am-7pm.) On the Spit, salmon bite at the **Fishing Hole.** Fresh seafood can be purchased directly from fishing boats or retail. **His Catch Seafoods,** 1411 Lakeshore Dr., across from Homer News, lets its fresh salmon and halibut go for around $6.50 per lb. They also offer it smoked and will ship anywhere. (☎235-7101 or 800-215-1701. Open 4:30am-4:30pm.) Wash it down with free samples or a nostalgic jug of locally brewed Broken Birch Bitter from the **Homer Brewing Company,** 1562 Homer Spit Rd. (☎235-3626. Open M-Sa 11am-8pm, Su noon-6pm.) Mmmm...beer.

- **Two Sisters Bakery,** 106 W Bunnell (☎235-2280), off Main St. near the water. A meeting place for artists, the wayward, and locals. A cinnamon bun and coffee ($3.50) will get you going in the morning. Steaming bowls of soup ($5.50) tickle the senses; chatty locals excite the mind. Open M-Sa 7am-8pm.

- **Duncan House,** 125 E. Pioneer (☎235-5344). In a town that prides itself on eccentricity, Duncan House tops 'em all by remaining somewhat common. Fill up with a down-home breakfast and lunch menu (biscuits and gravy $4.75) while nosing in on the old-timers' fishing gossip. Open M-W 7am-2pm, Th-Sa 7am-9pm, Su 8am-2pm.

- **Cafe Cups,** 162 Pioneer Ave. (☎235-8330). Expect offbeat servings of food and atmosphere that'll both leave you strangely satisfied. Soup seems to be a popular draw in town, so get it with the bread and salad for $7. Open daily 11am-9pm.

- **Young's Oriental Restaurant,** 565 E Pioneer Ave. (☎235-4002). A 20 ft. buffet of Chinese and Japanese sends Young's shooting ahead in the race for All-you-can-eat Asian Buffet Champion (11am-3:30pm $7.55; 3:30-9pm $10.55). Open daily 11am-10pm.

ENTERTAINMENT AND NIGHTLIFE

Check the *Homer News* for live theater and other performance schedules. The **Homer Family Theater,** at Main St. and Pioneer Ave., features current Hollywood blockbusters. (☎235-6728. $6, seniors and under 11 $3.) With a healthy mixture of young wanderers and salty fishermen, Homer nightlife can range from the absurd to incredibly late absurd as there is no enforced curfew. The **Salty Dawg Saloon,** under the log lighthouse near the end of the Spit, is something of an Alaskan landmark with sawdust-covered floors and long communal tables that breed tall tales and arm wrestling competitions. (☎235-9990. Open 11am-whenever.) **Alice's Champagne Palace,** 196 Pioneer Ave., is a wooden barn that hosts live music Wednesday to Saturday. See Alaska's pride, **Hobo Jim,** rock the house every Wednesday night as old and young dance like fools and yell along to down-home Alaskan tunes. (☎235-7650. Pints $4, pool 75¢. No cover. Open M-Sa 2pm-5am.)

476 ■ KENAI PENINSULA

> **ARSON FISH STRIKE AGAIN** On July 1st, 1998, the Homer Spit suffered one of the worst disasters since it sank 30 ft. in the '64 Good Friday quake. At Icicle Seafood's processing plant, an ammonia leak and a pilot flame combined to blow the roof 30 ft. in the air—momentarily restoring it to its former height. Luckily, there were no casualties, but the Spit was closed down for three days. Hundreds of cannery workers lost jobs they'd only had since the day before. The result was a massive party the night of the disaster. The plant has yet to be rebuilt, and the question of whether or not to do so will affect Homer in the coming years. Will a steady stream of young college students hard-up for cash still flock here? Time will tell, and in the meantime, Homer's salmon and halibut will breathe that much easier.

SIGHTS AND EVENTS

SIGHTS. The **Pratt Museum**, 3779 Bartlett St. (☎ 235-8635), has been called one of the best of its size in the country and holds an impressive display of local art and artifacts, with displays on homesteader cabins, the oil spill, arts of the Inuit and Denali peoples, and marine mammals. Check out the live video feed of the McNeal bears during salmon season. (Open daily 10am-6pm; Oct.-Dec. and Feb.-Apr. Tu-Su noon-5pm. $6, seniors $5.50, under 18 $3. Wheelchair accessible.) Homer's residents take art seriously—even the supermarket sometimes has a gallery. Pick up *Downtown Homer Art Galleries* for info on current exhibits. The **Center for Alaskan Coastal Studies**, 708 Smokey Bay Way, off Lake St. across from Lakeside Mall, has a small exhibit on marine life and offers natural history and seabird tours across Kachemak Bay in conjunction with the **Carl E. Wynn Nature Center** on East Skyline Drive. The Nature Center also offers a free **Thursday Evening Lecture Series** from late June to August at 7pm. (☎ 235-6667. Open M-F 10am-5pm.)

EVENTS. Homer is often billed the Halibut Capital of the World, and the **Homer Jackpot Halibut Derby** is responsible for a lot of that hoopla. The competition runs from May 1 to Labor Day, and offers over $150,000 in prize money. Pull up a tagged fish and you can win from $500 to $10,000. Tickets ($7) are available in local charter offices on the Spit. Homer is blessed each year with an enormous seabird migration, and even more fortunate to bring all those birdwatchers together for the **Homer Shorebird Festival** (☎ 235-7337), during the second week in May for educational workshops and other exciting events. On the last Sunday in July, KBBI (☎ 235-7721) stages the fabulous all-day **Homer Folk Festival** at the town commons, featuring blues, rock, and bluegrass.

OUTDOOR ACTIVITIES

THE SPIT. Nearly everyone who comes to Homer spends some time on the **Homer Spit**. Don't expect sandy beaches: the 5 mi. strip of land sinks under the weight of tourists, RVs, charter companies, and the gift shops that love them. The real reason to visit the Spit is to take in (or take part in) the flurry of fishing activity. Between 4 and 6pm, the returning charters weigh in and display their massive catches, and successful fishers always appreciate an audience.

FISHING. As many as 90 halibut charter boats leave the Spit each day. Choosing one, like fishing itself, can be a crap shoot, although most charter companies are reputable businesses. Expect to pay around $170 for a full-day charter with all tackle and bait included. You can book a boat through **Central Charters** (☎ 235-7847 or 800-478-7847), near the middle of the Spit, but your best bet is to ask around. **The Bookie** can take care of charters, too, but keep in mind that booking outfits only advertise for companies that are in contract with them. They also book kayak trips, flightseeing, and lodgings, at no charge. (☎ 235-1581 or 888-335-1581. Open in summer daily 6am-9pm; phone service in winter.) For those without the cash to chase the big ones, there's always the **fishing hole** near the start of the Spit, where anyone who can hold a rod can probably catch a salmon.

HIKING. The best **hiking** is across the bay at **Kachemak Bay State Park** (see below). In and around Homer, take the moderate 6½ mi. **Homestead Trail** with jaw-dropping views of the Bay. Pick up a trail guide from the visitors center or the maritime center to better identify the arctic star flowers, marsh violets, green rein orchids, and other wildflowers blooming along the way. The trail is accessible from any of three access points: take Roger's Loop Rd. off the Sterling across from the Bayview Inn to the marked trailhead sign; or take Diamond Ridge Rd. off West Hill Rd. to the trail sign; or drive past the reservoir on Skyline Dr. off West Hill to a parking lot and trail sign. With miles of coastline to explore, **beach walks** are a great way to get around and enjoy the view. Walking west from **Bishop's Beach Park,** you can the stroll by a sea otter rookery at Mile 3 and highway access after 7 mi. Head downhill on Main, turn left at Bunnell, then right on Beluga to get to the parking lot.

NEAR HOMER: KACHEMAK BAY STATE PARK

Kachemak Bay State Park, Alaska's first, is one of the largest coastal parks in the country, containing 375,000 acres of beaches, tide pools, mountains, glaciers, and one of the northernmost temperate rainforests in the world. Forty miles of trail system throughout the park pack an impressive punch into what can be a largely untrampled area due to its location. The **Grewink Glacier Trail,** one of the easiest hikes in the park, winds through tall stands of spruce and cottonwood up to the glacier's lake and outwash. With the right winds, you might even be able to snag a passing iceberg. The trail begins north of Glacier Spit at the east end of Kachemak Bay, and the 6½ mi. round-trip can easily be hiked in 2-3hr. If you're up for outstanding views of Kachemak Bay, the **China Poot Peak Trail** offers a stout outing, climbing over 2,000 ft. from shore to skyline. Only experienced and equipped climbers should continue up the 500 ft. summit spur from the rocky bench at the "Lower Summit." Trail begins at China Poot Lake. Allow for 3-5hr. of strenuous hiking on its 4½ mi. round-trip. The only way to access the park is via water or air taxi. **Inlet Charters** (☎ 235-6126 or 800-770-6126), on the Spit across from the harbormaster, books trips with several water taxi companies. **Mako's Water Taxi** (☎ 235-9055) charges around $50 per person for the round-trip. The park's trail system winds around indefinitely, so pick up the **hiking trails** pamphlet ($1) at the visitors center for more options.

Rainbow Tours offers a pricey, full-day tour of **whale watching** that continues back by **Gull Island,** home to murres, cormorants, guillemots, a few puffins, and about a zillion gulls. (☎ 235-7272. Tour 9am-6pm. $125, lunch included.) **Mako's** also rents kayaks only for use on the non-Homer side of the bay. (Single $85 per day, double $150. Prices include round-trip taxi from the spit.)

KATMAI NATIONAL PARK

Words cannot adequately explain the haunting emptiness left in the wake of the 1912 eruption of Novarupta Volcano. On June 6, this century's largest volcanic eruption began, and it didn't stop for 60hr. A 25 mi. column of ash shot violently out of the earth, and a wave of semi-molten rock, gas, and steam charged down the valley at 100 mph. Dr. Robert Griggs visited the valley four years later on a National Geographic expedition, only to be stunned by the sight of a river of ash, in some places hundreds of feet deep and "full of hundreds, no thousands—literally tens of thousands—of smokes curling up from its fissured floor." So the **Valley of Ten Thousand Smokes** was christened, and Griggs successfully convinced President Woodrow Wilson to declare Katmai a national monument in 1918.

As amazing as the Valley of Ten Thousand Smokes is, many people come to Katmai without seeing it. They come instead to **Brooks Camp,** 23 mi. from the valley, for the region's chief draw: brown bears. Katmai's bears are drawn to her shores and streams for the same reason commercial fishers crowd Bristol Bay each season—sockeye salmon. The largest sockeye (red) salmon run in the world charges up the bay's six rivers each year, providing an abundant food source for the bears combing the banks of the **Brooks River.** The bear-viewing platform at Brooks Falls allows visitors to watch up to 20 bears at a time. The facilities are open from June 1 to September 17. Use of the backcountry is free, although a $10 **day-use fee** is required for visitors taking advantage of Brooks Camp bear-watching and camping facilities (see below). To find out more, stop at the Alaska Public Lands Info Center in Anchorage (☎271-2737; see p. 441). The visitors center in King Salmon is helpful, as is the ranger at Brooks Camp. Jean Bodeau's *Katmai* ($15), available at Cook Inlet Book Co. in Anchorage (see p. 441), and at the King Salmon visitors center, is a comprehensive guide to the park's trails, routes, and climbs.

KING SALMON ☎907

While King Salmon, 300 mi. from Anchorage and 20 mi. from Brooks Camp, is the gateway to Katmai National Park, many travelers going to Katmai spend little time here between their flights. Both King Salmon and nearby Naknek (12 mi. west) are home to the world's largest sockeye (red) salmon fishery out of Bristol Bay. Every year, the six rivers flowing into the bay are flooded by the run and the accompanying commercial boats. Services in King Salmon are spare and overpriced.

The **King Salmon Visitors Center,** by the airport, is a great source of info for Katmai and the King Salmon area. with a rich library and 60 wildlife videos. (☎246-4250. Open May-Sept. daily 8am-5pm; Nov.-Apr. M-F 9am-5pm.) The **King Salmon Mall** opposite the airport has a **24hr. ATM** in the National Bank of Alaska. **Mels Diner** (☎246-7629), in the King Salmon Mall, has Internet access for 20¢ per min. The trailer here houses a **laundromat** and **public shower** run by the **King Ko Inn** across the street. (☎246-3377. Wash $2.50, dry 25¢ per 4min. Untimed showers $5 with soap and towel. Open Mar.-Oct. 24hr.) Grab a pricey bite (burgers around $9) at the **Coho Cafe** (☎246-3378; open daily 7am-10pm) part of the King Ko, or stock up across the street at the **City Market Deli** (☎246-6109), a small grocery with the basics. If you need a place to crash, **Dave's World** (☎246-3353), a 160-acre campground, will do the trick. Camping is $8 per night, plus a $5 round-trip ferry ride across the river (located at the public docks, 1 mi. east of the airport). Cheap beds are nonexistent in King Salmon. **King Ko Inn's** (see above) trailer annex is the most affordable ($90 per night). **Post office:** It is 2 mi. east of the airport. (☎246-3396. Open M-F 8am-4:30pm, Sa 9:30-11am.) **ZIP code:** 99613.

BROOKS CAMP ☎907

Brooks Camp via King Salmon provides direct access to Katmai National Park. Several flight companies have packages to get you there, and all operators charge about the same amount for King Salmon-Brooks Camp flights ($140 round-trip). **Alaska Airlines** (☎800-426-0333) and **Pen Air** (☎800-448-4226) operate a partnership service, and fly five or six times a day to King Salmon from Anchorage (1hr.; see below) and **Katmai Air** (☎800-544-0551) flies from there to Brooks Camp on a float plane (20min. $420 round-trip.) **C-Air** (☎246-6318) and **Branch River Air** go on to Brooks Camp ($140 round-trip). **Katmailand Lodge,** in Brooks Camp, rents kayaks ($12 per hr., $50 per day) and canoes ($6 per hr., $36 per day). They also rent waders ($7 per day), spin and fly rods ($10 per day), and sell licenses ($10 per day). **Katmailand** (☎243-5448 or 800-544-0551) runs a pricey lodge and dining room at Brooks Camp, and rents **cabins** with bunks, toilets, and showers, for astronomical sums, even for four people ($116 per person), and are almost always full. **Brooks Campground** technically holds 60 people, but this may entail sharing a tent site with another group. The campground is enclosed in an electric fence, and has water, outhouses, food caches, and shelters for cooking in the rain. Call or write for advance reservations ($5 per night) and to secure **day use permits** ($10 per day) at 800-365-2267 or **NPRS,** P.O. Box 1600, Cumberland, MD 21502. The antler-adorned lodge has a large stone fireplace and serves **buffet-style** breakfasts ($12), lunches ($14), and dinner ($22). The bar (open 4pm-1am) serves Alaskan Amber (pints $4.75). Hot beverages $1. The lodge **Trading Post** (open daily 8am-5:30pm) sells sodas, film, white gas, and camp food at—yup—very high prices.

BROOKS CAMP ■ 479

⚠ OUTDOOR ACTIVITIES IN THE PARK

THE VALLEY OF TEN THOUSAND SMOKES. Currently, the Katmailand **bus tour** ($79 with bagged lunch, $72 without, $42 one-way), is the only way to get to the valley. Trips fill up and should be booked ahead. The bus leaves daily at 9am (meet at lower platform on Brooks River at 8:30am) and returns at 4:30pm. A 23 mi. scenic dirt road into the park, ending at the **Three Forks Overlook Cabin,** offers an amazing view of the valley which includes **Baked Mt.** and **Mt. Katmai.** Upon arrival, a knowledgeable park service ranger gives talks on area ecology and geology and leads a 2hr. hike down the 1½ mi. **Ukak Falls** trail. If you plan on biking, let the bus service know ahead and they'll work out a way to accommodate you for a ride out or back if needed. The unlocked ranger cabin at the end of the road has emergency supplies, a bunk, and a scrapbook with great pictures and articles about the valley.

From the end of the bus ride, Katmai really needs several days to be fully appreciated. One trail leading into the Valley begins from the right side of the road a half-mile before the ranger cabin. It begins on a relatively steep descent through alders and willows until opening up into the great ashen valley. A shallow stream crossing of the **Windy River** is required. The flat trail through soft ash and pumice along the hauntingly beautiful **River Lethe** leads to a perfect camping spot at a large draw by a creek. The trail basically disappears once in the valley, but orientation isn't a worry with peaks on either side. A ranger cabin on **Baked Mt.** can offer shelter from high winds, but expect to be kicked around quite a bit, so make sure your tent can handle it. **Novarupta Volcano** (site of the 1912 explosion) is 13 mi. back and within range of **Mt. Katmai,** which sunk in the eruption, creating **Crater Lake** in its caldera. Backcountry travelers should be sure to talk with rangers at the Brooks Camp station and learn about special considerations needed in and around the valley and beyond (i.e. bears, river crossings in the Valley of Ten Thousand Smokes). If you only have a day in the valley, the **Ukak Falls Trail** is a 3 mi., 2½ mi. round-trip with 700 ft. elevation loss and gain. The only established trail from the cabin, it leads down to the falls and crazy views of the gorge. A short, flat, quarter-mile side trail offers an eery view of the **Windy River, Snake River,** and **River Lethe** confluence. (The tour bus allows plenty of time for hikers to check out both routes.) For an extended stay in the valley, bring eye protection and a handkerchief. Winds can be fierce and ash can kick up into black-outs, making hiking and set-up very difficult.

BEAR VIEWING. If you can't get to the valley, you could spend days at the bear-viewing platform (unless it is crowded). A trail leads from the Trading Post across a wooden bridge to the **Lower Platform;** check in with a ranger who will radio ahead to the falls platform before you set out. (Be prepared: the region is almost as ranger-intensive as bear-intensive.) The road leads a quarter-mile to a flat half-mile trail leading off on the right and turning into a raised, bear-safe walkway to the **Upper Falls Platform.** Let the viewing begin. Nowhere else in the world can you see so many bears from so close and still be safe. There are ethical issues involved in erecting permanent structures along the banks of such a feeding ground, yet the park service has chosen to localize the destruction of the area as much as possible.

HIKING. The only established trail from Brooks Camp, the moderate, 4 mi. **Mt. Dumpling Trail** leaves from the campground and encounters a steep initial 1½ mi. through poplar forest with high brush cranberries (in late August) providing a panorama of Brooks Lake, Naknek Lake, and Iliuk Arm. On a clear day, the route through alders and willows into the open tundra will reward you with a killer view of all the volcanic peaks in the valley all the way to King Salmon (a round-trip to the first overlook at 1½ mi. takes 1½hr.; to the trail's end at 2400 ft., 5-6hr.). The quick and easy **cultural walk** covers about a half-mile before coming to a reconstructed *inna* ("dwelling" in Sugpiak-Alutiiq), housed in an unlocked cabin, which can be a good way to kill some time. Placards tell about the Dena'ina and Yupik peoples that historically called this area home.

KODIAK ISLAND

In this century, Kodiak Island has been rocked by earthquakes, engulfed by *tsunamis*, coated in crude from the Exxon *Valdez*, and blanketed in nearly 2 ft. of volcanic ash. Much of the island is still covered in thick spruce forests dripping with moss, and Kodiak's peaks open up into wild, geranium-speckled meadows. Tiny islands and rock outcroppings poke out of the whale-filled waters. As the site of the Kodiak National Wildlife Refuge, the island is home to more than 3000 Kodiak brown bears, the world's largest carnivorous land mammal. The refuge's 800 mi. of coastline encircle the island's sharp inland peaks, pushing Kodiak's human population onto the eastern shore. Rich surrounding waters have historically made the island's fishing fleet one of the most productive in the state, drawing young people each summer to work in its canneries. Islanders take seafood seriously, and until recently, tourism has been only an afterthought.

KODIAK ☎ 907

Pressing out on the eastern edge of the island, the town of Kodiak is one that lives and dies by the sea. Swarming throughout the Gulf of Alaska, the island's lifeblood is and will remain to be the very waters that surround it, and as the ocean ebbs and flows, so does Kodiak's fortune. The last 10 years have seen politics and regulations tie the hands of the fishing industry and cripple an economy that is vital to the survival of all coastal towns, Kodiak in particular. It has survived nonetheless, a testament to the strength and tenacity of its people. As one cabbie said, "fishing's like gambling, sometimes you win, sometimes you lose." Though the town's troubles are not a distant memory, cruise ships are beginning to venture into port, and sports fishermen and adventure seekers are starting to discover the fish and wilderness. So Kodiak and its residents weather this storm and always look ahead.

TRANSPORTATION

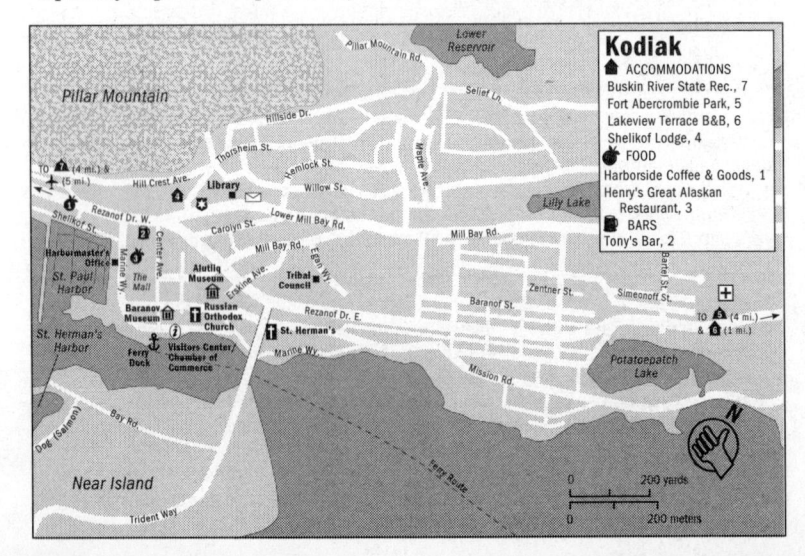

The city of Kodiak is on the eastern tip of Kodiak Island, roughly 250 mi. south of Anchorage. Paved and rutted gravel roads run 100 mi. along the scenic coastlines north and south of the city. **Chiniak Rd.**, which heads south for 42 mi., makes an especially impressive trip. In town, the main drag is **Center St.**, which starts at the ferry terminal and heads inland, ending at the intersection with **Rezanof Dr.** to the left and **Lower Mill Bay Rd.** to the right. The cluster of downtown shops and most of the good restaurants are within a 5min. walk from the ferry.

Flights: The **airport** is 5 mi. southwest of town on Rezanof Dr. **Alaska Airline's** (☎800-252-7522), offers commuter service, **Era Aviation** (☎800-866-8394), flies to Anchorage 7 times daily (1hr.; $130-175, round-trip $250-350). **Island Air** (☎486-6196 or 800-478-6196) offers 4 flights per day to destinations on Kodiak Island such as **Old Harbor** ($61) and **Larsen Bay** ($68).

Ferries: Alaska Marine Highway (☎486-3800 or 800-526-6731). Ferries depart Kodiak May-Sept. 1-3 times per week; less frequently in winter. The terminal is next to the visitors bureau, on the waterfront. Open M-F 8am-5pm, Sa 8am-4pm, Su 9am-1pm, and when ferries are in. To **Homer** (9½hr., $53), **Seward** (13hr., $59), and **Valdez** (29hr., $108). 5-day round-trip to the **Aleutian Islands** (1 per month, $222).

Taxis: A&B Taxi (☎486-4343). $3 base, $2 per mi.

Car Rental: Rent-a-Heap, at the airport (☎486-5220; open daily 6:30am-11pm) and downtown at Port Gifts (☎486-8550; open daily 9am-7pm). Rents cars for $35 per day, 35¢ per mi. Must be 25. **Avis** (☎487-2264) rents to those 21-25 for $64 per day for a compact.

PRACTICAL INFORMATION

Visitors Information: Kodiak Island Convention and Visitors Bureau, 100 Marine Way (☎486-4782; www.kodiak.org), in front of the ferry dock. The friendly help here can point you in the right direction for many of your needs; ask for their restaurant, lodging, and car rental printouts. Open daily 8am-5pm and for most ferry arrivals; winter M-F 8am-noon and 1-5pm, Sa-Su 10am-4pm.

Outdoor Information: Fish and Wildlife Service and **National Wildlife Refuge Visitor Center,** 1390 Buskin River Rd. (☎487-2600), just outside Buskin State Recreation Site, 4 mi. southwest of town on Rezanof Dr. Wildlife displays, films, and info on Kodiak National Wildlife Refuge and its cabins. Excellent, free hiking guide. Open M-F 8am-4:30pm, summer also Sa noon-4:30pm. **State Department of Parks,** 1200 Abercrombie Dr. (☎486-6339), at Fort Abercrombie. Info on state parks and campgrounds, as well as on public-use cabins on Shuyak Island and Afognak Island. Open M-F 8am-5pm, Sa 1-5pm; winter M-F 8am-4:30pm. Free 2-3hr. **Audubon Hikes** weekends mid-Apr. to mid-Sept. Meet at the ferry dock; range from whale watching to strenuous climbs. Schedules at the visitors center. Swing by the visitors center for a schedule of the upcoming **Naturalist Programs,** each Sa at 7pm.

Fishing Information: Alaska Department of Fish and Game, 211 Mission Rd. (☎486-1880). Open M-F 8am-4:30pm. **Licenses** are available at local sporting goods stores.

Equipment Rental: 58° North, 1231 Mill Bay Rd. (☎486-6249), about 2 mi. from the ferry. Take Upper Mill Bay until it turns into Mill Bay. Rents bikes ($25 per 24hr.) and gear; great resource for hiking and biking trail info. **Mack's Sports Shop,** 117 Lower Mill Bay Rd. (☎486-4276), across from McDonald's and the police station. Rods, guns, and tips. Rent rods for $15 a day plus $130 deposit. Open M-Sa 7am-7pm, Su 9am-5pm.

Banks: First National Bank on the corner of Center and Mill Bay has a **24hr. ATM,** as well as the **First Union** at the inland end of Center Ave. **ZIP Code:** 99615.

Employment: Alaska State Employment Service, 309 Center St. (☎486-3105), in Kodiak Plaza. First stop for fish-canners. Open M-F 8am-5pm.

Laundromat and Public Showers: Ernie's, 218 Shelikof (☎486-4119), opposite the harbor. Wash $3, dry 25¢ per 4min. Showers $4, towel $1. Open daily 8am-8pm. Last wash at 6:30pm; last shower 7pm.

Emergency: ☎911.

Police: 217 Lower Mill Bay Rd. (☎486-8000).

Crisis Line: ☎486-3625. **Women's Crisis Line:** ☎486-6171.

482 ■ KODIAK ISLAND

Hospital: 1915 W Rezanof Dr. (☎ 486-3281), 1 mi. northeast of town. On call 24hr.

Internet Access: Library, 319 Lower Mill Bay Rd. (☎ 486-8686). Free 1hr. **Internet access.** Open M-F 10am-9pm, Sa 10am-5pm, Su 1-5pm. **The Treasury** (☎ 486-0373), located next to AC Center. $2.50 per 30min. and normally lenient with charges if you keep it short. Open M-F 8am-8:30pm, Sa 9:30am-8:30pm, Su 10am-5pm.

Post Office: 419 Lower Mill Bay Rd. (☎ 486-4721). Open M-F 9am-5:30pm. **Downtown Contract Station** (☎ 486-5761), in the AC Value Center (see **Food and Nightlife,** below). Open M-Sa 10am-6pm.

ACCOMMODATIONS AND CAMPING

Kodiak has no hostels, no true budget accommodations, and a brutal 11% hotel tax in town, 6% outside of town. There are a couple of cheap motels close by and several nice, somewhat affordable B&Bs farther out. Finding a room becomes almost impossible when the airport shuts down due to bad weather, which happens often. Some law-defiers pitch up on Near Island, but otherwise there is no free camping in town. The state runs two nice **campgrounds** (see below), but camping is perfectly silent and free on any trail outside of town.

- **Lakeview Terrace B&B,** 2426 Spruce Cape Rd. (☎ 486-5135). Travel 2 mi. northeast of town at the bottom of Benny Benson Dr., on Mission Lake. Cable TV, shared bath, breakfast, and playful dog. Singles $60; doubles $80.

- **Fort Abercrombie State Park** (☎ 486-6339), 4 mi. northeast of town on Rezanof-Monashka Rd. Built around the site of WWII cannon emplacements, the carpeted forest, dripping moss, ocean cliffs, and trout-stocked lake are worth the extra trek into town. Water, toilets, no hookups. 7-night max. Open to motor traffic in summer only; walk-ins year-round. 13 sites, $10.

- **Shelikof Lodge,** 211 Thorsheim Ave. (☎ 486-4141), up the street to the right of McDonald's, 3 blocks from the ferry. Remodeled motel; green rooms with cable TV. Courtesy airport shuttle. Singles $65; doubles $70.

- **Buskin River State Recreation Site** (☎ 486-6339), 4½ mi. southwest of town, off Rezanof Dr. Water, pit toilets, RV dump station. Closer to the airport and the Buskin River, where over 50% of Kodiak's sport fish are caught. 14-night max. stay. 15 sites, $10.

FOOD AND NIGHTLIFE

Food is not Kodiak's strong suit. In fact, the several fast food options in town may appear especially tempting for lack of anything else. Groceries can be purchased 2 mi. from town at **Safeway,** 2685 Mill Bay Rd. (☎ 486-6811. Open daily 6am-midnight.) In the heart of town **AC Value Center** also sells groceries. (☎ 486-5761. Open M-Sa 7am-10pm, Su 8am-9pm.) **Cactus Flats Natural Foods,** 338 Mission St., sells vitamins, too. (☎ 486-4677. Open M-Sa 10am-6pm.) The bar scene in town is rowdy between those drying their heels and Coast Guard troops from the nearby station; if action is your thing, Kodiak nights can dish it out.

- **Martha's Place** (☎ 654-0752) could be anywhere, but always close to town. Ask any local where she is, and you'll soon be gorging yourself on a spicy steak burrito ($8.50) and wondering how you'll down that extra taco (from $3). Herbivores welcomed, too.

- **Harborside Coffee and Goods,** 216 Shelikof (☎ 486-5862). Proximity to the harbor draws the summer fishing crowd. Tea comes in a big, beautiful earthenware mug ($1). Make free local calls on the house phone. Soup and bread $4.50. Open M-Th 6:30am-9pm, F and Sa 6:30am-10pm, Su 7am-8pm.

- **Henry's Great Alaskan Restaurant** (☎ 486-8844), in the mall on Marine Way. The all-you-can-eat pork ribs and pint of Alaskan Amber for $15 might be the big winner after a hard day sliming. Order up when the bell rings: a friendly just bought the house a round. Open M-Th 11:30am-9:30pm, F-Sa 11:30am-10:30pm, Su noon-9pm. Bar until 11pm.

Tony's Bar (☎ 486-9489), in the alley beside AC Center. Claims to be Kodiak's biggest navigational hazard with over a million drinks spilled in an otherwise friendly, laid-back atmosphere. Bottled beer $3-4, cocktails $4. Pool, darts, and a super bowling game. Live rock music F-Sa. Open daily 11am-2:30am.

SIGHTS AND ENTERTAINMENT

ALUTIIQ MUSEUM AND ARCHAEOLOGICAL REPOSITORY. Housing displays and artifacts dating to 4600 BC document the culture of the Alutiiq. The museum was built with restoration funds from the Exxon *Valdez* oil spill and is supported by Alaska's native corporations. The Alutiiq building also doubles as the home-base for more than 800 archaeological expeditions on the island, attempting to piece together this culture's rich heritage that has been nearly wiped out by Russian fur traders, European explorers, and the American fishing industry. Visitors can volunteer to help on extensive archeological digs on Kodiak and neighboring islands during June and July. *(215 Mission Rd. ☎ 486-7004; www.alutiiqmuseum.com. Open M-F 9am-5pm, Sa 10am-5pm. $2, under 12 free.)*

CHURCHES. The **Holy Resurrection Russian Orthodox Church**, just behind the museum, serves the oldest parish in Alaska. Built in 1794 and rebuilt after a fire shortly before WWII, its elaborate icons date to the early 1800s. *(385 Kashevanof Cir. ☎ 486-3854. Services are open to the public, although the schedule varies. Tours given upon request; donation requested.)* Another block past the church on Mission, **St. Herman's Theological Seminary** and one of three Orthodox seminaries in the US, houses a small museum, a number of religious objects, as well as a wonderful replica of the old chapel that used to stand down the road. The tiny **Chapel of St. Herman** is made entirely of wood, down to the pegs that hold it together. *(Both the seminary and chapel open M-Sa 10am-4pm, Su noon-5pm.)*

BARANOV MUSEUM. Housed in a storehouse for sea otter pelts built in 1808, the oldest Russian structure standing in Alaska and the oldest wooden structure on the US West Coast. It displays a collection of Russian and Native Alaskan artifacts and a walrus skull complete with tusks. The library has photos and literature ranging from the Russian period to the present. *(101 Marine Way, across from the visitors center. ☎ 486-5920. Open Memorial Day to Labor Day M-Sa 10am-4pm, Su noon-4pm; Labor Day to Jan. and Mar. to Memorial Day M-W and F 10am-3pm, Sa noon-3pm. $2; under 12 free.)*

SPORTING EVENTS. The five-day **Kodiak Crab Festival** celebrates a bygone industry with parades, fishing derbies, and kayak, bike, foot, crab, and survival suit races. The festivities culminate with the **Chad Ogden Ultramarathon,** a superhuman race along 43 mi. of hilly roads from Chiniak to Kodiak. *(☎ 486-5557. May 23-27, 2002.)* The absurd **Pillar Mountain Golf Classic** is Alaska's answer to the Masters: one par-70 hole. The tee is at the base of Pillar Mountain; the snowy green is at the 1400 ft. summit. *(www.chiniak.net/pillar; Mar. 31-Apr. 1, 2002. $50 entry fee.)* The **Bear Country Music Festival,** brings 100 rock, blues, jazz, Cajun, Russian, and world musicians together at the Kodiak Fairgrounds, from noon-1:30am and around the campfire until dawn. Contact Jerimiah Myers between 7 and 8pm Alaska time for more info. *(☎ 486-6117. July 19-20, 2002. Tickets F $10, Sa $15; camping $10 for the weekend.)*

OUTDOOR ACTIVITIES

Largely due to the motivation of a growing local contingent, more varied and exciting outdoor options are sprouting up throughout the island. Where else in Alaska, let alone the Lower 48, can you surf and ski in the same day, kayak among whale and otter along pristine coastal waters, or beat your ass to dirt on miles of challenging mountain bike trails? This island is literally teeming with outdoor opportunities throughout the year and is a warranted destination for any enthusiast.

HIKING

Hikes around Kodiak generally come in one flavor: slog straight up though burning legs and try not to injure yourself on the downhill flail.

Termination Point (6 mi.), begins at the end of Monashka Bay Rd. and ends in the parking lot. No defined trailhead, though it would be difficult to get lost. Easy, flat hiking offers a welcome respite to the bipeds. Cross the creek and head to the **beach,** where hikers can either stroll in the sand or choose one of several paths that parallel the water.

Barometer Mountain (2 mi., 2hr.). Head west out of town on Rezanof Dr., and take the first right past the end of the airport runway up a broad ATV trail. After passing through a stand of thick alders, the trail climbs steadily along a steep grassy ridge before arriving at the summit. On the rare clear day, hikers can take in a view stretching from the Kenai Peninsula to the Alaska Peninsula at the top. 2500 ft. gain. Strenuous.

FISHING

The island's 100 mi. road system gives access to several good **salmon streams.** In Kodiak, surfcasting into Mill Bay at high tide often yields a pink or silver. The **Buskin River,** just outside town, receives a good run of reds and silvers each year, and the fortunate baiter might pull a dolly varden or steelhead out. On the way to Pasagshak, the **American** has pinks, chum, and a late run of silvers. The **Pasagshak River** itself is a popular joint in that the rare king salmon gets lifted, along with a healthy supply of silvers and reds to complement the scenery. If the rivers beat you down, cast your flies into any of the lakes off the road system, all of which are stocked with trout by Fish and Game (many people do not know this, so keep quiet). **Mack's Sport Shop** will rig you up (see **Practical Info**), and almost any store in town sells licenses. Kodiak offers a variety of fishing charter trips, but most of the companies are operated out of people's homes or boats. The visitors center has brochures, and the sporting goods stores can advise you.

KAYAKING

Guided **sea kayaking** trips come eye-to-eye with sea otters, puffins, bald eagles, and, on lucky days, encounter giant Kodiak bears from a comfortable distance. **Kodiak Kayak Tours** explore Near Island and Mill Bay. Trips typically start at 9am and 2pm. No experience is necessary; call at least a day ahead. (☎486-2722. Tours 3hr. 9am and 2pm. 2-person min. Call ahead. $45.) **Mythos Expeditions** (☎486-5536) runs similarly priced trips as well as more expensive trips to Shuyak and Afognak Islands. They also rent kayaks and provide water taxi service.

MOUNTAIN BIKING

A love-hate relationship exists between ATVers and bikers on "the rock." Digging deep ruts, clearing fragile flora, and many times reducing trail to a boggy mess, four-wheelers can rapidly destroy what was an untouched trail. Bikers do owe some debt of gratitude, however, as those same fuel-injected monsters cleared out miles of awesome, challenging trail throughout the island. Rentals, gear, and great advice are available from Tim, the owner of **58° North** (see **Practical Info.**). Definitely pick up the *Kodiak Mountain Bike Guide: The Joys of Riding on "The Rock"* ($3), before you head out and get an idea of where you're going. There really are no easy rides in Kodiak, so be sure and inquire about certain trail features from experienced riders before heading out.

Russian Ridge Trail. Head straight up Maple St. as it becomes Pillar Mountain Rd. and turns to gravel. Just after the gravel quarry take a right, where you'll find the trails a popular route due largely to its proximity to town. After a steady climb, you drop into dense, mossy forest on an obvious and somewhat technical trail. After spitting out onto Monashka Bay Rd., choose between a leisurely ride along the pavement, or a more challenging adventure through a rolling footpath in and out of Kodiak's neighborhoods.

Burma Road Trail. Drive or bike 4½ mi. out of town on Rezanof Dr. West to Anton Larson Bay Rd. Turn right and go ½ mi. to Busking Bridge No. 6. On the far side of the bridge, take the second left where you'll either park or find the trail. While less technical, Burma is a classic ride along an old WWII road linking the Buskin River area with Bell's Flats, through a mountain pass. Unless the trail is dry or frozen, watch out for nasty puddles.

BACKCOUNTRY SKIING

Having no ski lifts has forced the locals to venture into untouched areas, expeditions which have yielded great rewards. The town itself may mire in rain and slush year-round, but this makes for perfect ski conditions throughout the island's high country. April through July is recognized as the most stable season, with many areas retaining snow through August. You've gotta "earn your turns" on Kodiak though, so expect an average approach of 2hr. for most runs outside of town. **Pyramid Mountain,** right off Anton Larson Bay Rd. has the most highly traveled slope, while the backside of the **Three Sisters** (falsely labeled Devil's Prong on USGS maps) opens wide for bowl skiing, touring, and steeps. Make **Orion's** your one-stop shop for the latest conditions, directions, gear, and knowledgeable advice. (☎ 486-8380. Open M-Sa 11am-6pm. Just uphill from **58° North.**) Part-owner Steve Wielebski is an endless source of info and enthusiasm (☎ 486-6790) and may even direct you toward partners/guides for your first go. Trails to most of the areas are not clearly marked, and snow conditions may be unstable, so make sure to inquire locally, and **bring your own gear** as there are no ski rental outfits on the island.

DRIVING

If you have wheels, the 42 mi. coastal drive to **Chiniak** presents beautiful seascapes of small offshore islets bathed in fog, and dozens of mufflers lying along the rough road. Pick up Kodiak's visitor guide for mile-by-mile descriptions of several longer drives on the island, as well as a walking tour of downtown Kodiak. Take the turn-off for Pasagshak Bay Road at Mile 30 of the Chiniak for great hiking, fishing, and camping, and, at the end of the road, one of the prettiest bays on Kodiak. Mile 12.5 on Pasagshak Bay Rd. is Kodiak's best surfing spot with the best breaks in winter. **Orion's** (see above) sells surfboards.

KODIAK NATIONAL WILDLIFE REFUGE

Kodiak National Wildlife Refuge encompasses the western two-thirds of Kodiak Island. Since this is a refuge rather than a park, human recreational use is of secondary concern; no trails or roads lead into the region, and there are no official campgrounds. The refuge **visitors center** (see p. 481) introduces this remarkable area with videos and informational exhibits.

Hiking into the refuge would demand a 20 mi. or more trek crossing several mountains, while a flight to Larsen Bay ($110 round-trip) will put you in range of the backcountry. Although the refuge contains seven public use **cabins,** only three can be reached by boat; the others require an expensive float plane ride (around $450). The cabins with a kerosene heater and an adjacent pit toilet rent for $20 a night and sleep four to five. Two cabins, **Blue Fox Bay** and **Uganik Bay,** are wheelchair accessible. Call or write the visitors center for more information (see above). Any cabin can be booked by mail through the refuge visitors center. Applications are processed in the first week of January for dates in April-June, the first week in April for July-Sept., and the first week in July for Oct.-Dec. Not all dates get booked, but it is wise to plan ahead; call the refuge visitors center for an application. It goes without saying that with so many bears wandering around it is especially important to store food properly and to be noisy when hiking.

Most visitors come to Kodiak to see the enormous bears. The numerous "guaranteed" brown-bear-viewing packages run $350-400 for a 3-4hr. float plane tour. Some of the prime viewing areas have visitor quotas, and reservations are made months ahead of time. Call the refuge visitors center or ask at the visitors center in town for permits and suggestions on the cheapest way to get close to the animals. A worthwhile alternative is a similarly priced plane trip to Katmai (see p. 477), where bears can be seen at closer range in as remarkable a setting.

ALEUTIAN ISLANDS

At the fiery boundary between two tectonic plates, the string of snow-capped volcanoes of the Alaska Peninsula and the Aleutian Islands stretches more than 1000 miles into the desolate North Pacific toward the coastal waters of Kamchatka, Russia. The Aleutians are one of the most remote locations on earth, and the lava-scarred cones on these green but treeless isles are abused by some of the world's most vicious storms. Recent findings on Hog Island, support a hypothesis that the ancestors of today's Aleuts migrated here from Asia by moving from island to island, rather than across the Bering Land Bridge formed later.

Travellers stand awe-struck at the rugged beauty of these islands, and the commanding hand the ocean has in daily life. Southeasterly weather patterns drive in from the brutally cold waters of the Bering Sea, numbing the senses and outbound flights for days. But, the waters also support an abundance of life. Nutrients kick up from the depths of the Pacific onto the Bering's shallow shelf, creating a feeding ground for all species and providing subsistence and commerce for over 8000 years of human habitants. Perched on the world's edge, the Aleutians have only recently been explored by adventurers. The outdoors will gradually bring more tourists, but the Aleutian's natural beauty will remain.

> **WHEN WWII CAME TO ALASKA.** On June 3rd, 1942, the Japanese began to bomb the Aleutian Islands and occupied Attu and Kiska in an attempt to divert American forces from the southern Pacific. The US responded by constructing the Alaska Hwy. and stationing nearly 60,000 soldiers on Unalaska. The remains of their occupation still mark the landscape—the last base is only now being gradually decommissioned. With as little as 24 hours notice, the US Army evacuated Aleut residents from many of the islands, ostensibly in the interest of safety, although Caucasians were allowed to remain. In the inhumane conditions of their exile, up to 25% of the displaced Aleuts perished. Roughly 70% returned to find their property destroyed by American soldiers, and whole villages were abandoned. This is a little-known and shameful piece of American history, officially silenced until the passage of the Civil Liberties Act of 1988, when the Aleuts were offered an official apology and granted financial compensation.

TRANSPORTATION

The only two ways of reaching the Aleutian Islands are alarmingly expensive. A one-way **flight** from Anchorage to Dutch Harbor, the largest town on the Aleutians, costs about $450 and is only serviced by **Alaska Airlines** (☎ 800 252-7522). A one-way fare on the **Alaska Marine Highway** from Homer takes four days and costs $532 round-trip (children 2-11 $261, bikes/kayaks $39 extra). This route is serviced only six times per year between April and September. Clear days promise unique panoramas, and an on-board naturalist gives regular presentations on the plants and wildlife visible from the ship. The ferry stops briefly at small towns, from fishing villages to prefabricated cannery quarters, before reaching Dutch Harbor. Unfortunately, it only stops here for about 5hr. (from 6:30am-11:45am) before turning around and heading back. The boat has showers, water, and a dining room with limited hours and food (breakfast $5-7, lunch $6-10, dinner $9-13); bringing provisions from Homer is a good idea. Passengers lay their sleeping bags and pitch their tents on deck. Call well in advance to rent a cabin. Stock up on Dramamine before leaving. While the weather is mildest in July, the *M/V Tustumena* still weathers 5- to 15-foot seas—it is not called the "Vomit Comet" for nothing.

UNALASKA AND DUTCH HARBOR ☎ 907

Isolated at the western limit of the Alaska Marine Highway's ferry service, Dutch Harbor and Unalaska (un-uh-LAS-ka), are as remote a community of 4100 as you'll find in North America. The name Unalaska comes from the original Aleut name for the area, "Agunalaksh." When the Russians came to the island, this evolved into "Ounalashka," and since 1890, the current name has persisted. Dutch Harbor is a port with its own post office and ZIP code. An Unalaskan suburb has been built on the smaller Amaknak Island, about 2 mi. from downtown Unalaska, and oftentimes is also called Dutch Harbor because it is from this island that the harbor is accessed. The two islands are connected by the **Bridge to the Other Side.**

The king crab boom of the late 1970's brought hordes of wide-eyed and hungry young men to the Bering Sea's cruel waters. Skyrocketing crab prices were met by a still unexplained eruption in harvestable crab, creating what many Alaskans call the "second gold rush." Sometimes pocketing $20,000 in a week's work, this boomtime mentality along with weeks of sea-time fostered a hard-drinking, hard-living population. While that edge may not be so strong today, Unalaska and Dutch Harbor hold the last of the cowboys, men who work and live in the most dangerous conditions imaginable. Unalaska has been the nation's top port for pounds of seafood caught and value of fish and crab delivered since 1988, and over 90% of the community depends on the fishing industry.

Unalaska is not a haven for the budget traveler, due to its remoteness and the unusually high incomes of the sport fisherfolk who are the port's most frequent visitors—over $130 million in seafood passes through this port annually. But the view of treeless, snow-capped, green mountains soaring thousands of feet from the bay's chilly blue waters may be a worthwhile investment.

■♬ ORIENTATION AND PRACTICAL INFORMATION. Unalaska lies about 300 mi. from the tip of the Alaska Peninsula and 800 air miles from Anchorage. It is in the same time zone as the rest of the state. The **airport** is about a quarter-mile from City Dock on the main road into town, and is served by **Pen Air** (☎581-1383 or 800-442-0333) and **Alaska Airlines** (☎581-1380 or 800-426-0333). Planes sometimes don't fly in or out for a week at a time due to fog or wind. The **Alaska Marine Highway** (☎800-526-6131) departs City Dock, 1½ mi. from Dutch Harbor and 2½ mi. from Unalaska to **Homer** (4 days, about once a month, $532 round-trip). **Taxi service** is available from *eight* companies (all equally pricey)—locals are as baffled by that number as we are (**Aleutian Taxi** ☎581-1866). The ride to town costs $12-14.

Visitor Information is available upstairs in the grey building next to the Parks Culture and Recreation Community Center on the corner of 5th and Broadway. (☎581-2612; www.arctic.net/~updhcvb. Open M-F 9am-5pm, Sa 9am-3pm.) The **Ounalashka Corporation,** 400 Salmon Way, in a low, orange-roofed building nearby, sells required **hiking and camping permits** and is working on developing a trail map. Pick up the visitor's guide, a map of town, and an Aleutian WWII National Historic Area Map and Guide here. (☎581-1276. Open M-F 8am-noon and 1-5pm.) Jeff, at **Aleutian Adventure Sports** (☎581-4489 or 888-581-4489), at 4th and Broadway, rents mountain bikes ($25 per half-day, $35 per day, $125 weekly) and cross-country skis ($20 per day) along with great advice and directions for any outdoor adventures on or around the island.

Parks Culture and Recreation Community Center, on 5th St. across the Lliuliuk River from the post office, provides untimed showers, free local calls, indoor swimming and track, weight room, pool tables, video games, and parlor games. (☎581-1297. Open M-F 7am-10pm, Sa 8am-10pm, Su noon-9pm. $4.) **Lliuliuk Family and Health Services** is in a big gray building just down the street from the police station. (☎581-1202; after-hours 581-1233. Open M-F 8:30am-6pm, Sa 1-5pm.) **Emergency:** ☎911. **Police:** 29 Safety Way (☎581-1233), just off Airport

Beach Rd., on the Unalaska side. **Library:** On Elanor Dr., past the Unalaska post office. (☎581-5060. Free **Internet access.** Open M-F 10am-9pm, Sa-Su noon-6pm.) **Post office:** Unalaska, 99685 (☎581-1232); Dutch Harbor, 99692 (☎581-16570). Both offices are open M-F 9am-5pm and Sa 1-5pm. **Bank and ATM:** Next to the Dutch Harbor post office.

ACCOMMODATIONS AND FOOD. Once again: it ain't cheap. The visitors center keeps a list of accommodations. Ninety percent of the land is owned by native corporations, and a fee is required for access. (Land-use $6 per day; camping $11 per night.) If the Corporation (see above) is closed, purchase land-use permits from patrol trucks. **Summer Bay,** a 7 mi. hike from the ferry, is a popular unserviced camping spot. To camp closer to the town, walk up a hill directly behind the Unalaska **post office** and camp on the rise up top. From here you'll have a commanding view over town, Iliuliuk Bay. The prevailing winds are strong, so be sure your tent is sturdy; gusts have been recorded at up to 170 mph here, strong enough (as local legend has it) to blow the car door off a VW Bug, depositing it on a hillside where it has sat for over a decade.

Linda's Bunkhouse is nicer than the name suggests with sparkling private rooms, shared baths, and a lounge with TV, fridge, and microwave. (☎581-4357. Meals are sometimes available for $10. Free bike delivery when renting from **Aleutian Adventure Sports.** Singles $55; doubles $75. Wash $2, dry $2.) From the airport, follow the Airport Rd. past the Dutch Harbor post office and take the first left, about a half-mile down the road, on Gilman. The Bunkhouse is next to the Peking restaurant.

Eagle Quality Center, in Dutch Harbor next to Grand Aleutian, sells over-priced groceries, but their deli (sandwiches $5) has some of the cheapest food in town. (☎581-4040. Open daily 7am-11pm.) Fresh or frozen crab or fish can be bought straight from any seafood company: **Alyeska** (☎581-1211); **Royal Aleutian** (☎581-1671); **Westward** (☎581-1660); or **Unisea** (☎581-1258). Prices fluctuate season to season depending on availability, so call first to see what they have and how much it'll cost. If you'd rather be served, check out the restaurants near Broadway and 2nd on Unalaska, or make the wise choice and head to ◪**Amelia's,** on Airport Beach Rd., next to the Eagle grocery. With a menu the size of mainland Alaska, Amelia serves up burgers ($9), Mexican, and Greek omelettes ($9), and $10 burritos. (☎581-2800. 15min. walk from the airport.)

SIGHTS. If it's sunny and clear when you arrive, hastily see **Outdoor Activities,** below. Otherwise, the brand new **Museum of the Aleutians,** just past the Ounalashka Corporation building on Salmon Way, provides a colorful history of the entire Aleutian chain. (☎581-5150. Open June-Sept. M-Sa 10am-5pm, Su noon-5pm; winter W-Su 11am-4pm. $2.) Archeological digs are ongoing and visitors can frequently visit sites, some within 200 yards of the museum.

In Unalaska on Beach Front Rd., the impressive **Holy Ascension Orthodox Church,** built in 1824-27 and expanded in 1894, is one of the oldest standing Russian-built churches in the US. This area was the thriving center of Orthodox missionary activity in Alaska. The once-dilapidated church became a National Historic Landmark in 1970 and is in the process of extensive restoration. Services (Sa 6:30pm, Su 10am) are open to the public and are conducted in English, Russian, and Aleut. To view the church when services are not in session, ask the visitors center (see **Orientation and Practical Info,** p. 487). **A.L.E.U.T Tours** (☎581-6001 or 391-1747) and **Extra Mile Tours** (☎581-6171) offer another opportunity to view the relics. Tours during the ferry layover are around $40, take 2-3hr., and cover WWII. They fill quickly, so call ahead or talk to the Purser onboard the boat. The **Unalaska Cemetery and Memorial Park,** a mile past the church or 4 mi. from the City Dock on the eastern edge of Unalaska, present a description of the Japanese air attacks of June 1942. If you haven't seen enough bald eagles, head to the landfill on Sommer Bay Rd. or the Westmark Cannery at Captains Bay. In town on a Wednesday night?

OUTDOOR ACTIVITIES. A **land-use pass** is required for venturing off the main roads. Purchase one at the visitors center or the Ounalashka Corporation ($6 per day, see **Practical Info**, p. 487). It's wise to rent a bike from **Aleutian Adventure Sports** ($35 per day, see **Practical Info**), which often greets the ferry. If you have the luxury of time, explore the extensive backcountry opportunities; you may run into wild horses and feral cows. Even on local treks prepare for sudden weather changes.

HIKING. If you have the good fortune to be in Unalaska on a sunny day, make haste to hike to the top of **Mt. Ballyhoo,** just behind the airport, so named by temporary resident Jack London. Trail starts behind the airport hangars and is clearly visible from the base. Allow 45min. to reach the summit, and another hour or more down the backside. Ferry passengers can walk along the ridge for another 20-30min. past the summit, and still easily return to catch the boat. The summit affords one of the most mind-bogglingly beautiful sights in the entire universe. Superlative overkill is not possible here: amazing gold, red, and black rock formations jut out of a sheer cliff that drops 1634 ft. to the translucent green water of the ocean below, and the 6880 ft. **Mt. Makushin Volcano** can be seen steaming on clear days. Following the ridge off Ballyhoo's backside leads to **Ulakta Head National Historic Area** and WWII bunkers on the cliffs. Just before the bridge to Unalaska (30min. walk from the ferry) sits **Bunker Hill,** which was heavily fortified during WWII. Following either the construction road clockwise from behind the hill or the beach counter-clockwise to reach the old trail, a quick but steep 420 ft. climb leads to a large concrete bunker affording a great view of the surrounding bays and mountains.

If you happen to miss your ferry back and have a month to play with, the **Ugadaga Bay Trail** is an easy-to-moderate, extremely scenic trail passing waterfalls and steep-walled valleys along what was an ancient portage route for the Unangan people between Unalaska and the small outer islands. In colder weather, it may require crossing a snowfield. The marked trailhead begins on the right side of a small pond at the top of Overland Dr. (a continuation of Broadway), 2½ mi. from downtown. A perfect overnight would be to hike the **Agamgik Bay Trail,** which starts from Humpy Cove past Summer Bay on Summer Bay Rd. This flat 4½ mi. trail follows a river bed for the first half, before dropping into gorgeous Agamgik Bay. The bay offers some sheltered camping and a great view of Eagle Rock. The trailhead begins at the pull-off on the right. Allow 2hr. one-way on this relatively flat trail.

BIKING. With no trees and old WWII access roads criss-crossing the island, Unalaska is a perfect spot to explore on bike. Expect steep hills and creek crossings; virtually every flat spot on the island is taken up by the village itself. The **Overland Trail** to **Summer Bay** is a good introduction, climbing switchbacks along the Ugadaga Bay trail to Summer Bay Lake before hooking back around and down to the road system leading to town. Climb Overland Rd., passing the Ugadaga Bay trailhead on top. Follow the road down to Summer Bay Lake where it leads to Summer Bay Rd. and back to town. All 13½ mi. are on good road, so expect 3-4hr. of moderately challenging riding. This is a city-owned right of way, so you do not need a permit for the trail. If that isn't enough, true masochists can jump on the **Pyramid Peak Trail,** combining a difficult climb with a challenging downhill over its 7 mile route. Expect some bike-toting time on this trail, or else you might be nursing some war wounds. Access Pyramid Peak from Captain's Bay Rd., turn left and onto trail at Westwood Seafoods. Initially well-maintained, stay left at two trail splits, passing through a gated trailhead. Be sure to stop off at **Aleutian Adventure Sports** and talk to Jeff before heading out. A virtual fountain of information, he'll be happy to give directions, advice, gear, etc.

BY WATER. There will never be a better spot to go on a **halibut charter.** Companies all have comparable rates (half-day $90, full-day $165), and can be booked through the visitors center or the Grand Aleutian gift shop. Trips are almost always full, so book well in advance. The kayaking from Unalaska is some of the finest you'll find in the Bering Sea. Unfortunately, there is no place to rent kayaks on the island, but

Aleutian Adventure Sports offers all sorts of trips ranging from 4-5hr. paddles to a tour of bird- and history-rich Hog Island to multi-day surveys of the Akutan Volcano and hot springs and mountaineering and hiking adventures.

ALONG RTE. 1: STERLING HWY. ☎907

The Sterling Hwy. begins 90 mi. south of Anchorage at the **Tern Lake Junction.** From here, the highway runs 66 mi. west to the Twin Cities of **Soldotna** and **Kenai** passing wonderful hiking, camping, and fishing in **Chugach National Forest** and the **Kenai National Wildlife Refuge** on the way. From Soldotna, the highway runs south on the western side of the peninsula along **Cook Inlet** (see p. 495), ending after 75 mi. at the town of **Homer** (see p. 472). The Sterling passes through moose country, so drivers should be cautious. Mile markers measure the distance from Seward.

COOPER LANDING ☎907

Shortly after its intersection with the Seward Hwy., the Sterling passes the aquamarine **Kenai Lake,** which stretches in a giant Z through the Chugach Range. The next 120 mi. of highway, from Cooper Landing to Anchor Point, parallel some of the most spectacular **salmon fishing** anywhere. The king in this town has fins and swims in streams. Laundry, showers, and an **ATM** are available at **WildWash** at Mile 47.5. (☎495-1888. Wash $2.25, dry $1.75 per 10min. Showers $3. Open daily 8am-midnight.) For dolly varden and free camping, turn left onto Snug Harbor Rd. after the Kenai River Bridge and drive 3½ mi. on the dirt road. Park in the gravel lot adjacent to the large orange and white powerlines and scramble down to the lake. In another 10 mi., on Snug Harbor Rd., is trout-teeming **Cooper Lake** with more remote free camping. During the summer runs, Cooper Landing and surrounding campgrounds take on a carnival atmosphere, as fishermen line up on the banks of the Kenai River to try their luck. It's not unusual to see anglers "combat fishing," standing shoulder-to-shoulder filling their baskets. Above the tackle shop rests **Sandy's Cafe** (☎595-1802), serving breakfast and lunch for around $6.

Fishing charters in the $90-200 range abound. A cheaper option for salmon is the **ferry trip** to the opposite bank of the Kenai River, which yields comparable views and access to good fishing. The boat uses cables and current to carry it across at Sterling Mile 55. Parking is $7, so take advantage of the gravel pull-outs just before and after the entrance ($6, ages 3-11 $3). Be forewarned that restrictions on fishing (bag limit, type of tackle, etc.) vary often within very small areas. Licenses are available at most grocery and fishing stores. **Kenai Lake Tackle,** at Mile 47.1, sells licenses, guides trips, and rents gear (☎595-2248; rods and waders $10). The Kenai River offers several places to **whitewater raft** without substantially risking life and limb. Some of these floats are as scenic as Class III river-running gets. Outdoor outfits generally supply lunch and gear on full-day trips, but anglers should buy their own licenses beforehand. **Alaska Wildland Adventures** at Mile 50.1 offers a variety of half- and full-day rafting trips. (☎595-1279 or 800-478-4100. $45-195, children $29-69.) The **Alaska River Company** (☎595-1226; www.alaskariverscompany.com) offers rafting, fishing, and hiking tours starting at $40. Other than the ferry, the most economical way to get on the water is with **Run Wild's** half-day scenic raft trip. (☎595-2000 or 888-836-9027. $39.)

KENAI NATIONAL WILDLIFE REFUGE ☎907

From Cooper Landing, the Sterling Hwy. stretches 50 mi. to **Soldotna,** with services at Cooper and Sterling. It runs alongside the chock full o' fish Kenai River and through the two million acres of the Kenai National Wildlife Refuge. The peninsula is prime moose territory—the area was originally designated the Kenai National Moose Refuge in 1941. Hiking trails within the refuge are some of the most popular in the state, as droves of adventurers shuttle from Anchorage and every weekend to walk, bike, run, and ski over 200 mi. of highly accessible and well-maintained paths. Let's not forget the famous fishing areas, spectacular canoe routes, and free camping everywhere.

KENAI NATIONAL WILDLIFE REFUGE ■ 491

ORIENTATION AND PRACTICAL INFORMATION

For fishing regulations, trail conditions, and information it is wise to check out one of the visitors centers. The **Kenai National Wildlife Refuge Visitor Contact Station,** at Sterling Mile 58, is close to many of the campgrounds and trailheads. This log cabin station sells maps ($3-5) and other outdoor literature. (Open May-Sept. daily 9am-6pm). The **State Park Headquarters,** located in Sterling off the Sterling Hwy. at Mile 85, 3½ mi. down a paved road toward the Morgan's Landing campsite ($10 per night; toilets, water), has info on cabins, campsites, and trails. (☎262-5581. Open M-F 8am-5pm, Sa-Su 10am-5pm; winter M-F 8am-4pm, closed holidays.) The **Kenai National Wildlife Refuge Headquarters and Visitors Center** is in Soldotna off the Sterling Hwy. between Miles 96 and 97; turn left on Funny River Rd., then take an immediate right and follow the signs. *Refuge Reflections,* their free publication, gives detailed fishing, hiking, and canoeing tips. The center shows nature films daily and leads a host of hikes, talks, and kid-friendly exhibits. A 10min., wheelchair-accessible, self-guided nature walk also leaves from the center. (☎262-7021. Open M-F 8am-5pm, Sa-Su 9am-6pm; winter M-F 8am-4pm, Sa-Su 10am-5pm.)

CAMPING

Free **campgrounds** with boat launch, water, and toilets are located on the lakes for which they are named. Look along Swanson River Rd. at **Dolly Varden Lake, Rainbow Lake,** along the Skilak Loop Rd. at **Kelly Lake, Engineer Lake,** and **Lower Skilak Lake,** or **Watson Lake,** directly off the Sterling at Mile 71. Other free camping options abound along the loop and on lakes throughout the system although they are less developed. For info on these campgrounds, call the Soldotna visitors center (☎ 262-7021) or check out the park paper, *Refuge Reflections.* **Alaska Canoe and Campground** (☎262-2331), Mile 84 in Sterling, rents canoes (half-day $24, full-day $40, 3 or more days $30 per day), bikes ($35 per day) and fishing gear, as well as RV ($14) and tent sites ($7). To protect those precious canoes, they'll shuttle renters to their area of choice for 60¢ per mi., a fair rate considering their proximity to Swan Lake Rd. (1½ mi.), the primary trailhead for canoe trips in the vicinity.

OUTDOOR ACTIVITIES

As beautiful as Alaskan hiking can be, the southern reaches of the refuge are primarily flat and boggy. No worries for the adaptable adventurist, though; these waterways are teeming with all species of fish, reachable by motorboat, foot, and a beautiful system of canoe trails. Winter recreation includes snowshoeing, snowmachining, backcountry ice-fishing, and cross-country skiing at the Kenai Golf Course. Call the visitors center for resources.

PADDLING

The refuge, lying north of the Sterling Hwy., boasts some of the best **canoeing** networks in Alaska. The **Swan Lake System** contains 30 lakes interconnected by waterways and portages, forming a possible 60 mi. of canoeing, though many less demanding routes exist. Find it at Mile 16.4 of the Swanson River Rd., turn right onto Swan Lake Rd. and continue 3½ mi. to the West Entrance, or an additional 6 mi. to the East Entrance. The more challenging **Swanson River System** connects 40 lakes with 46 mi. of the Swanson River for a trail system of over 80 mi. through marshy wetlands. Recommended for more experienced paddlers. Pick up The Kenai Canoe Trails ($19) or the Kenai Nat'l Wildlife Refuge topo map for a guide to these areas and stop at **Alaska Canoe and Campground** for advice. The **Swanson River** trailhead is 2½ mi. from the Swan Lakes East Entrance.

492 ■ ALONG RTE. 1: STERLING HWY.

HIKING

Fuller Lakes Trail (5½ mi. round-trip, 4-7hr.). At Mile 56.9, a dirt pull-out points directly to the trailhead. After a challenging first mi. of steady ascent through dense forests, striking views highlight the glimmering Lower Fuller Lakes and the lush Kenai Mountains and precede slightly easier hiking above treeline. Moderately strenuous. 1400 ft. gain.

Kenai River Trails provide a moderate alternative and access to the river. Both the upper and lower trails are accessible from Skilak Lake Rd. at Mile 58. The **upper trail** (5½ mi. round-trip) starts at Mile 2.2 of Skilak Lake Rd. The **lower trail** (4½ mi. round-trip) begins at Mile 3 of Skilak Lake Rd. Plenty of **bears** keep the moose company.

FISHING

Fish for Arctic char from the banks of Finger Lakes and Silver Lake. Dolly varden swim near the banks of Paddle Lake and the Kenai River. There are rainbows along the shores of Paddle, Forest, Eugumen, and Upper and Lower Ohmer Lakes. Red and silver salmon ply the ever popular Kenai River.

SOLDOTNA ☎ 907

Soldotna spreads its strip mall tentacles for several miles along the northern stretch of the Sterling Hwy. One of the urban blemishes on the face of the peninsula, the town supplies groceries and camping gear to those interested in fishing and to travelers en route to elsewhere.

ORIENTATION AND PRACTICAL INFORMATION. Soldotna's **visitors center,** just over the Kenai River on the way south to Homer, has pamphlets on fishing and recreation possibilities in the area, a phone for local use, and free canoe route maps. (☎ 262-9814. Open daily 9am-7pm.) **Wilderness Way,** 2 mi. east of town, is well stocked with high-quality backpacking, biking, kayaking, and canoeing gear. (☎ 262-3880. Open M-Th 9am-6pm, F-Sa 9am-8pm, Su noon-6pm.) The **Sports Den** sells gear and licenses and rents everything you need to catch the big one. They also run guided fishing and trophy hunting trips and are a stellar source of outdoor info. (☎ 262-7491. Canoes $35 per day. Rod and reel $10 per day. Open daily mid-May to Aug. 8am-7pm; Sept. to mid-May M-Sa 10am-6pm.) **Road conditions:** ☎ 262-9228. **Hospital:** 250 Hospital Pl. (☎ 262-4404). **Post office:** 175 N Binkley St. (☎ 262-4760. Open M-F 8:30am-5pm, Sa 10am-2pm.) **ZIP code:** 99669.

ACCOMMODATIONS AND FOOD. Camping is available pretty much everywhere along the Sterling Hwy., especially by **Skilak Lake Rd.** (see **Kenai Wildlife Refuge,** p. 490). With the exception of the Kenai-Russian River, Upper Skilak Lake, and Hidden Lake Campgrounds ($5-10), camping within the refuge is free. The empty-handed angler's luck won't improve much in the way of eats around Soldotna as the multitude of fast-food joints create a virtual tractor beam for even the most stringent calorie-counter.

The **Hogg Heaven Cafe,** right before the Kenai bridge, serves up tasty omelettes and greasy burgers adjacent starting at $5. Give the Kalifornia avocado burgers a shot ($8). The most comfortable and affordable lodging in the Twin City area is actually in **Sterling,** which is a short drive from Soldotna, and a bit longer one from Kenai (worth the drive). To get to **Jana House** turn down Swanson River Rd. at Mile 83.5 of the Sterling Hwy. and follow it a quarter-mile. Cavernous bunk rooms with a kitchen and bathrooms so fancy you'll wish you had them at home. (☎ 260-1451. Shuttle picks up in Soldotna and Kenai. Linens included. Open 24hr. June-Oct. Full RV hookups $12; tents $8; bunks $22; private rooms $50, $10 per additional person.)

KENAI ☎ 907

What do you get when you cross a strip mall with an RV park full of fish? The twin towns of Kenai and Soldotna are Alaska's best answer to this smoke and pit-stop clouded vision. The Kenai River, by many accounts the best king salmon fishing in the world, lures unending swarms of tourists, weekenders, and die-hards to its jade green waters every summer to try their luck at the yearly run of salmon flowing in from the waters of Cook Inlet.

Perched on a bluff overlooking the place where the Kenai River empties into Cook Inlet, Kenai has a magical view of the Aleutian-Alaska Range and its prominent volcanoes, Mt. Redoubt and Mt. Augustine, on a clear day. First inhabited by the Dena'ina Indians, then colonized by Russian fur traders and missionaries at the end of the 19th century, and eventually fortified by the American military in the 1940s, Kenai culture bears the signs of its varied past.

TRANSPORTATION

Kenai, on the western Kenai Peninsula, is 158 mi. from Anchorage and 96 mi. north of Homer. The town can be reached via **Kalifornsky Beach Rd.,** which joins the **Sterling Hwy.** (Rte. 1) just south of Soldotna, or via the **Kenai Spur Rd.,** which runs north from Soldotna and west to Kenai. Kalifornsky mile markers measure distance from Kenai, while the Kenai Spur mile markers measure from Soldotna.

Flights: Airport 1 mi. north of downtown. Take Kenai Spur Rd. to Willow St. and follow signs. **Alaska Airlines** commuter service, **Era Aviation** (☎800-426-0333), has near hourly service to **Anchorage** (30min., $62-70).

Buses: Homer Stage Line (☎262-4585). 1 per day June-Aug M-Sa. Service decreases in the off season. To **Anchorage** (4hr., $35) and **Homer** (1½hr., $25). **Kachemak Bay Transit** (☎235-3795) runs to **Anchorage** ($40) and **Homer** ($25).

Taxis: Inlet Cab, Kenai ☎283-4711; Soldotna ☎262-4770. $1.60 base, $2 per mi.

Car Rental: Great Alaska Car Company (☎283-3469). Prices vary by month peaking in July when they start from $45 per day, $270 per week. Unlimited mileage for multiple day rentals. Must be 21 with credit card.

Car Repair: Alyeska Sales and Service, 200 Willow St. (☎283-4821). Open M-F 8am-6pm, Sa 9am-5pm.

PRACTICAL INFORMATION

Visitors Information: Visitor and Cultural Center, 11471 Kenai Spur Hwy. (☎283-1991; www.visitkenai.com), just past the corner of the Spur Rd. and Main St. Hiking trail guide ($1), *Free and Inexpensive Things to Do in Kenai* (free), traditional artifacts, films on area development in the small museum, and an art exhibit if you're lucky. (Museum $3, students free). Open M-F 9am-8pm, Sa 10am-7pm, Su 11am-7pm; winter M-F 9am-5pm, Sa-Su 10am-4pm.

Outdoor Information: For info on **Lake Clark National Park and Preserve,** across Cook Inlet from Kenai, call the **superintendent** in Anchorage (☎271-3751), or the park ranger (☎781-2218; 8am-5pm). **Lee's Alaska Booking Service,** 1000 Mission Ave. (☎283-4422), provides info on local fishing, charters, and tours; rents gear and sells licenses. The **Kenai National Wildlife Refuge Headquarters** is 15min. away, in Soldotna (see p. 490).

Employment: Alaska Employment Service ☎283-2900. Dial-a-Job ☎283-2924.

Library: 163 Main St. Loop (☎283-4378). Free **Internet access.** Open M-Th 10am-8pm, F-Sa 10am-5pm, Su noon-5pm.

Laundromat and public showers: Wash-n-Dry (☎283-8473), at Lake St. and Spur. Wash $1.75, dry 25¢ per 7min. Untimed showers $4 plus tax. Open daily 8am-10pm.

Emergency: ☎911.
Police: 107 S Willow St. (☎283-7879).
Crisis Line: ☎283-7257. 24hr.
Women's Services: Resource Center, 325 S Spruce St. (☎283-9479). Hotline and shelter. Open M-F 9am-5pm.
Hospital: Central Peninsula General Hospital, 250 Hospital Pl. (☎262-4404).
Post Office: 140 Bidarka St. (☎283-7771). Open M-F 8:45am-5:15pm, Sa 9:30am-1pm. **ZIP Code:** 99611

ACCOMMODATIONS

There are few inexpensive lodgings in Kenai; the numerous B&Bs begin at $70. **The B&B Association** (☎888-266-9091) has all the listings and rates. **Lee's Alaska Booking Service** (☎283-4422) arranges rooms at no charge. **Camping** is available at the city campsite located at Mile 10 of the Spur Rd. (tents $8). **Katmai Hotel,** 10800 Kenai Spur Hwy., part of the Katmai Pines Lodge, 1 block from downtown. (☎283-6101 or 800-275-6101. Small rooms with nice decor and cable. Singles $79; doubles $89.) **Beluga Lookout RV Park and Lodge,** 929 Mission St. Take Main St. toward the water and go right on Mission St. Prime location on the bluff. Scan the sea for belugas from the lounge or gaze at the volcanoes across the inlet. (☎283-5999. Coin laundry $1.50. Showers $2. Full hookups $20.)

FOOD

There are fast food options aplenty on the Spur Rd. just before town. **Carr's Quality Center,** in the Kenai Plaza next to K-Mart on the Kenai Spur Rd., has a bakery, pharmacy, fruit, natural foods, and fast food. (☎283-6300. 24hr. grocery.) Buy fresh fish along the Bridge Access Rd. just before it meets the Spur.

Veronica's Coffee House (☎283-2725), at the end of Mission Rd. opposite the Russian church. Friendly service in a historically homey building decorated with paintings and overlooking the inlet. Half sandwich and cup of soup $6. Live folk Sa. Open M-Sa 8am-8pm, Su 10am-5pm.

Old Town Village Restaurant, 1000 Mission Ave. (☎283-4515). Housed in a restored 1918 cannery building which was moved from Sitka. Old Town is known for its seafood dinners (from $13), salad bar ($5), and hearty Su brunch (10am-2pm; $10). Open M-Th 11am-9pm, F-Sa 11am-10pm, Su 10am-8pm.

Little Ski-Mo's Burger-n-Brew (☎283-4463), on Kenai Spur Rd. across from the visitors center. A staggering array of burgers in a lodge-like interior, complete with fireplace. Twin Cities burger (with egg, bacon, cheddar, and sprouts) $6.50. 2 scoops of ice cream only 65¢. Open M-Th 10am-10pm, F 10am-11pm, Sa 8am-11pm, Su 8am-9pm.

New Peking, 145 S Willow St. (☎283-4662), off Kenai Spur Rd. Savor the all-you-can-eat lunch buffet ($7; M-Sa 11:30am-2pm) in a lush Far Eastern setting. Mongolian BBQ summer evenings ($13). Open M-F 11am-10pm, Sa 3-10pm.

SIGHTS AND OUTDOOR ACTIVITIES

VISITOR TOUR. The visitors center provides a map of the half-mile, wheelchair-accessible walking tour of **Old Town Kenai.** The highlight of the tour is the **Holy Assumption Russian Orthodox Church,** on Mission St. off Overland St. Built in 1846, then rebuilt in 1896, this National Historic Landmark contains 200-year-old icons. Tours are given upon request; call for more info. (☎283-4122. *Open in summer M-Sa 11am-4pm. Public services Sa 6pm and Su 10am.*)

COOK INLET. Breathtaking **Cook Inlet** is framed by smooth sand, two mountain ranges, and volcanic **Mt. Augustine** and **Mt. Redoubt.** The best places to admire the view are at the state recreation area or at the beach at the end of Spruce Dr. The beach is also a great place to watch beluga, salmon, and eagles. The best time to see whales is 2hr. before or after high tide. If you coordinate with the arrival of the fishing boats, you may see a freeloading seal or sea lion as well.

CAPTAIN COOK STATE RECREATION AREA. Premier views of the inlet and the Alaska-Aleutian Range make for a lovely picnic on a bluff or beach. You can swim or wet your line for trout and arctic char at **Stormy Lake** and the downstream end of the **Swanson River Canoe Trail** begins nearby. *(At the northern end of the Kenai Spur Rd., 25 mi. from town. Campsites $10 feature water and pit toilets.)*

NIKISKI. The **North Peninsula Recreation Center** in Nikiski houses a geodesic-domed indoor pool for rainy days (expect many), a hockey rink, a ski trail, a paved path (wheelchair accessible), outdoor volleyball and tennis courts, and picnic area. *(12½ mi. north of Kenai at Mile 23.4 of the Spur Rd. ☎ 776-8472 or 776-8800. Open 7am-5pm and 6-9pm. $3, seniors $2. Alaska's largest waterslides $6.)*

FISHING. Check at the visitors center or **Lee's** (see above) for **charter** info (prices are comparable to those in Soldotna). Most are located along Bever Loop Rd. off the Spur or Angler Dr. off Bever if you feel like walking in. Anglers can do their thing on any public land along the **Kenai River,** where the majority of fishing takes place. Beginners should ask at fishing shops (most of which are in neighboring Soldotna on the Sterling Hwy; see **Soldotna, Orientation and Practical Info**) for recommended locations to avoid accidentally damaging the banks of the river and jeopardizing fish habitat. **Licenses** are available at gas stations, groceries, or outfitters. If salmon aren't your thing, **Swanson River** and **Stormy Lake,** in the Captain Cook Recreation Area, contain rainbow trout, silver salmon, and arctic char.

NINILCHIK ☎ 907

From Kenai, the Sterling Hwy. (Rte. 1) winds through shoreline forest on a bluff overlooking the Cook Inlet. It affords fantastic views across the inlet of Mt. Redoubt and Mt. Iliamna, both volcanoes that rise over 10,000 ft. and have erupted in the last 50 years. The highway winds into the town of Ninilchik, a Russian hamlet best known for its combat-fishing king run. Although nearby **Clam Gulch** (Mile 117.4) is a clammers paradise, *do not* eat shellfish harvested in the area without assurances from health authorities that they are toxin-free. Take Mission off the Sterling and drive through the old part of town for a step back in time.

The **General Store,** at Sterling Mile 137, sells groceries, fishing, clamming supplies, and has the town's only **ATM.** (☎567-3378. Open M-Th 7am-11pm, F 7am-midnight, Sa-Su 6am-midnight.) The **Alaskan Angler RV Park,** on Kingsley at Mile 135 of the Sterling, rents clamming gear for $3 per day and rubber boots for $4. (☎567-3393 or 800-347-4114. Office open Apr.-Sept. daily 9am-9pm. Tent sites $10; electric hookups $19; full hookups $24.) Their **showers** ($2 for 10min., with towel) and **laundromat** (wash and dry each $1.50) are open **24hr.**

For scenic dining, take Mission off the Sterling and follow signs for the beach and cannery to the **Boardwalk Cafe.** This seaside spot can't get much closer—it literally hangs over the beach. Menu highlights include homemade pie ($2.75) and great seafood soup. ($2.50; ☎567-3388. Open daily May-Sept. 8am-8pm.) The **Inlet View** bar, at Mile 134.5, is a laid-back local hangout that stays open really late. (☎567-3337. Pints $3.50. Open daily 10am-5am.) **Deep Creek Packing** (☎567-3396), at Mile 137, sells and gives bite-sized **free samples** of different kinds of smoked fish.

The supremely pleasant ⬛**Eagle Watch Hostel (HI)** is 3 mi. east of town on Oil Well Rd., which starts just before the Tesoro gas station. Although the building is spacious and clean, views of the Ninilchik River snaking its way through the valley will keep you smiling. Always eagles (as advertised) and sometimes moose and bears can be seen from the deck. A BBQ, showers, phone, clam shovels, fishing rods, tree swing, new mattresses, and playful dog seal the deal. (☎ 567-3905. Linen $2, no sleeping bags. Towels 50¢. Lockout 10am-5pm. 11pm curfew enforced. $10; nonmembers $13. Cash or traveler's checks.)

The several **state campgrounds** near Ninilchik have water and toilets. Sites along the river are $10; sites along the beach are $5. Superb spots in the **Ninilchik State Recreation Area** overlook the inlet less than a mile north of town. The nearby, beach-level **Deep Creek Recreation Area** (not the Deep Creek Campground) is one of the most popular campgrounds on the peninsula; turn west about a quarter-mile south of Deep Creek. Locals claim that the area has saltwater king salmon fishing; dolly varden and steelhead trout ply the waters, too ($10, day-use parking $5).

SELDOVIA ☎ 907

It would seem that Seldovia was founded on the wings of a small Homer migration (for Homer, see p. 472). Talking with residents and walking its streets, the attitude and ambience seem much the same. Nonetheless, this sleepy, isolated hamlet has carved itself out as a proud stepping stone to the Alaskan waters, and retains a charm that is not lost on the daily cruise-boat tourists who descend upon its kitschy shops and espresso machines. Unmatched views and embarrassingly-good halibut fishing serve to bring its visitors back for more, time and again.

▐? PRACTICAL INFORMATION. All you could ever want to know about Seldovia can be found on their award-winning web site, www.seldovia.com. The **airport** is less than 1 mi. out of town on Airport Ave. **Homer Air** (☎ 235-8591) and **Smokey Air** (☎ 235-8591) both fly frequently to Homer for around $60 round-trip. The **Alaska Marine Highway** (☎ 235-8449 or 800-382-9229) chugs from Homer to Seldovia once per week (1½hr., Tu 10:30pm, one-way $20), lingering for only 4hr. before heading back. Two **tour boats** also cruise daily to Homer. **Rainbow Tours** offers the least expensive service and gives you 5hr. to see the town before pushing off. (☎ 235-7272. Round-trip $50.) **Jakalof Bay Express** provides a friendly ferry to the Jakalof dock, a 9 mi. bike ride from "downtown" Seldovia. Bringing a bike costs $5, a kayak $10. (☎ 235-6384. $45 round-trip.) Susan Springer, owner of **Herring Bay Mercantile** (☎ 234-7410), on Main St., and author of *Seldovia, Alaska*, is happy to share her wealth of knowledge. **Charles Bike Rental,** next to the hotel on Main St., rents bikes. (☎ 234-7641. Open daily Mar.-Sept. 7am-4:30pm. $8 per hr., 3hr. $15, full-day $25.) **Kayak'atak,** with an office in Herring Bay Mercantile on Main St., rents kayaks for single or multiple day trips. (☎ 234-7425. Call between 8am-10pm. Single kayaks $50 per day, each additional day $35; doubles $75, $55.) Bring money to Seldovia; there are no banks, and not all establishments accept credit cards. **Laundromat and Showers: Harbor Laundromat,** on Main St. (☎ 234-7420. Open daily 11am-7pm. Showers $4 per 10min., towel and soap included. Wash $2.50-5, dry 25¢ per 6min.) **Emergency:** ☎ 911. **Police:** ☎ 234-7640. **Clinic:** ☎ 234-7825. (Open M, W, F 9am-4pm.) **Post office:** ☎ 234-7831. at Main and Seldovia St. (Open M-F 9am-5pm.) **ZIP code:** 99663.

▐▐ ACCOMMODATIONS AND FOOD. Try www.seldovia.com for full listings with pictures. At the end of Main St. by the boardwalk, **Dancing Eagles Lodge** offers some small rooms and a beautiful private cabin, along with a private extension of the town boardwalk, a hot tub, and a terrific view of the bay. (☎ 234-7627. Rooms from $65, doubles $110. Cabin with full kitchen and bath $175 for 2, $50 per additional person.) The best deals for groups are the pleasant, newly furnished, multi-room, converted apartments with TV and kitchenette at the **Main St. Market and Inn.** (☎ 234-7631. Sleeps 4-6 all for the same rate. Street view $110; water view $140.) **Outside Beach,** and **Wilderness Park,** both 1 mi. from town and adjacent, offer camping and close encounters with sea otters. Turn left off Jakalof Bay Rd. at the "Narrow Road" sign or hike the **Otterbahn Trail** (see below) to get to the beach.

The Main Street Market, stocks a modest supply of groceries, hardware, tackle, liquor, and pharmaceuticals. (☎234-7633. Open M-Sa 9am-8pm, Su noon-5pm.) Frozen dairy treats, hot showers, and laundry services mingle in bizarre but happy matrimony at the sparkling **Harbor Laundromat** (see **Practical Information,** above). **The Buzz,** 231 Main St., serves coffee, espresso, and great food in a nice rainy-day loitering space. Cinnamon rolls ($2.75), local art, and friendly company abound. (☎234-7479. Open Mar.-Sept. M-Sa 6am-5pm, Su 7am-4pm.) The **Crab Pot Cafe,** on Main St. next to the post office, is a small grocery that serves sandwiches (half $5, whole $8) sells fishing licenses, and hosts theme dinners Thursday to Saturday for $12.50 and up. (☎234-7435. Open Apr.-Dec. M-Sa 9am-7pm, Su noon-7pm.)

SIGHTS AND OUTDOOR ACTIVITIES. Seldovia's quiet, colorful homes, friendly locals, and beautiful harbor make for lovely strolls. The Seldovia Native Association runs the **Berry Kitchen/Museum,** which has a small case of native artifacts. Watch through the display window as they whip and package their famous preserves, throwing together everything from fireweed jelly to their strangely enticing kelp preserves (open daily 10am-5pm).

The **Otterbahn Hiking Trail,** starting at the Susan B. English School near Winifred Ave. a half-mile from town, winds a moderate 1 mi. to the cliffs and tidal pools of Outside Beach, passing through old growth and floral meadows. It grants a spectacular view of the volcanoes on clear days. The ride to **Jakolof Bay** can be a great bike trip on a good day as it winds through tall spruce and over a rolling dirt road. Shoreline Dr. terminates at Jakolof Bay Rd., which will take you the 9 mi. to the bay. The **Seldovia Native Corporation,** 328 Main St., owns much of the land above the reservoir and between the Jakalof dock and town, so secure a hiking and camping permit before exploring. (☎234-7625. Open M-F 8am-5pm. $1 per day.)

INTERIOR ALASKA

Banked by the remote Brooks Range to the north and the towering peaks of the Alaska Range to the south, Alaska's expansive interior covers over 166,000 sq. mi. of the wildest and most untouched land in the world. While Fairbanks remains the second most populated city in the state, the majority of settlements throughout the interior are "bush" towns. These small hamlets are populated primarily by Athabascan Indians and are accessible only by small, propeller-operated planes. A proud people, the Alaskan Natives have built their lifestyle and culture around Alaska's rugged interior in all its beauty, expanse and unforgiving conditions. Time has seen the passage of gold rushes, a Cold War, and oil booms, but none have affected the nature of the interior. Even a colossal undertaking such as the Alaska Pipeline construction of the 1970s could do nothing more than brush the surface.

"Big" describes most everything in Alaska, and the interior is no new story. Everything from the unofficial state bird (the mosquito), to Denali and the Alaska Pipeline is huge. While today you can come to the interior expecting soft beds and warm handshakes, the true adventurer will find a majestic expanse of nature in all its untamed beauty and reality. To get you there, the Parks Hwy. from Anchorage to Fairbanks, the Glenn Hwy. from Anchorage east to Glenallen and the Yukon, and the Alaska Hwy. from the Yukon northwest to Fairbanks are the only accessible roads into the interior. The less well-maintained Denali Hwy. is a more scenic east-west alternative for the adventurous.

DENALI NAT'L PARK AND PRESERVE ☎907

Denali's six million acres of snowcapped peaks, braided streams and glacier-carved valleys are interrupted only by a lone gravel road less than 100 mi. long. Visitors to the park are guests of the countless grizzly bears, moose, caribou, wolves, Dall sheep, raptors, and wildflowers that thrive here. Over one million

498 ■ INTERIOR ALASKA

humans invite themselves to the park every year, but there is little the crowds can do to take away from the glory of the park's vast and pristine wilderness. The park's centerpiece, Denali, only adds to the splendor. With 18,000 of its 20,320 ft. above the surrounding lands, it is the world's tallest mountain from base to peak. Although the US Geological Survey names the peak "Mt. McKinley," most Alaskans know it as Denali. Denali is so big that it manufactures its own weather: when moist air from the Pacific Ocean collides with the cold mountaintop, sudden storms encircle the summit. Since Denali's face is only visible about 10% of the time in summer, many visitors to the park never actually see the peak. Those who venture far from the park's few paths will find themselves as the explorers did: in a pristine, but often inhospitable, land and climate.

In summer, especially between mid-June and mid-August, crowds and lines at the entrance are unavoidable. Shuttle buses into the park only run from late May until mid-September, so the window of relatively crowd-free access is small. Mid- to late August is an excellent time to visit—fall colors peak, berries ripen, mosquito season has virtually ended, and September's snows have not yet arrived. Be sure to check out the park's newspaper, the *Alpenglow*, as soon as you get there. It has all the vital information that will help you avoid the lines at the visitors desk. Making advance reservations for campsites and shuttle buses will spare you a day or two of waiting for permits and tickets upon arrival at the park.

> Visiting or traveling in Denali during the winter presents many possible hazards and should only be attempted by experienced travelers. Before any winter travels in Denali, visit the Park Headquarters at Mile 3.2 on the left side of the park road. (☎ 683-2294. Open M-F 8am-4:30pm.)

TRANSPORTATION

The park is easily reached by road or rail. Anchorage lies 237 mi. south and Fairbanks 120 mi. north along the **George Parks Hwy.** (Rte. 3; see p. 505). The rough **Denali Hwy.** (Rte. 8; see p. 504) meets the Parks Hwy. 27 mi. south of the park entrance at Cantwell, and extends 136 mi. east to Paxson. Anyone with permission to overnight can ride the flat-rate **camper buses** (see **In The Park,** p. 499).

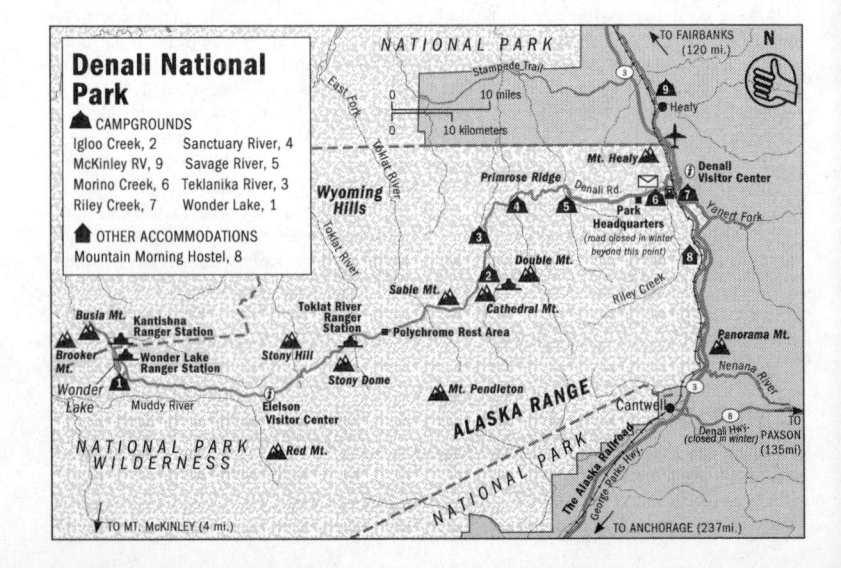

Denali National Park

▲ CAMPGROUNDS
Igloo Creek, 2   Sanctuary River, 4
McKinley RV, 9   Savage River, 5
Morino Creek, 6   Teklanika River, 3
Riley Creek, 7   Wonder Lake, 1

🏠 OTHER ACCOMMODATIONS
Mountain Morning Hostel, 8

Buses: Many of the buses that ply the Parks Hwy. will drop off and pick up at trailheads along the park's edge with advance notice. **Parks Highway Express** (☎ 888-600-6001) runs daily to **Anchorage** (5hr., $42) and **Fairbanks** (3½hr., $27). **Alaska Tourquest** (☎ 344-6667) makes the run daily from Anchorage for $25.

Trains: Alaska Railroad (☎ 265-2494 or 800-544-0553) stops at Denali Station, 1½ mi. from the park entrance. Open daily 10am-5pm. Scenic ride to **Fairbanks** (4½hr., $50 peak season, $40 value) and **Anchorage** (8hr.; $125 peak, $100 value). Ages 2-11 50% off; under 2 free. Mid-Sept. to mid-May the train runs weekly at reduced rates.

AT THE ENTRANCE

The free **Riley Creek Loop Bus** (30min., 6am-9pm) runs between the visitors center, the Denali Park Hotel, the Alaska Railroad station, the Horseshoe Lake trailhead, and the Riley Creek campground. Schedules are posted at each stop. Chalet-owned **courtesy buses** run from what was the Denali Park Hotel to the chalet near Lynx Creek Pizza, and to McKinley Village (6 mi. south of the park entrance) from 5am to midnight. **Caribou Cab,** complete with antlers on the roof, is at ☎ 683-5000.

IN THE PARK

In order to limit human impact on the land and wildlife, only the first 14 mi. of the park road are accessible by private vehicle (no special permit necessary). The remaining 75 mi. are open only to bicycles and park-run buses. In summer, two services travel the park's interior in rehabilitated school buses.

Shuttle buses carrying talkative tour guides leave from the visitors center, stop when any passenger spots a large mammal, and turn back at various points along the road (daily 5am-6pm; ages 13-16 50% off, under 13 free). All travel times are round-trip: **Toklat,** Mile 53 (6hr., $17); **Eielson,** Mile 66 (8hr., $23); **Wonder Lake,** Mile 85 (11hr., $30); and **Kantishna,** Mile 89 (13hr., $33). Most buses are wheelchair accessible, but be sure to inform them of your specific needs when making a reservation. A ticket allows you to get on and off the bus as you please to take side hikes, naps, or photos. For those who don't make it into the backcountry, this is a great way to see the park, and wildlife sightings are all but guaranteed. **Camper buses** ($18.50), transport only those visitors with campground or backcountry permits, have extra room for gear and **bikes,** and move faster than the shuttle buses and with less narration. Ask at the visitors center for a complete schedule. Both camper and buses stop to pick up pedestrians anywhere along the road back. **Bicyclists** must keep to the road and only the road, although they can sometimes travel it even when it's closed to other vehicles. Backcountry travelers must leave bikes locked up at the racks provided at campgrounds.

MCKINLEY OR NOT MCKINLEY—THAT IS THE QUESTION

History has not been kind to William McKinley, 25th president of the United States. Washington, D.C. has no McKinley Memorial. Few have celebrated McKinley's birthday since he last marked the occasion himself in 1901.

In Alaska, however, an attempt was once made to memorialize McKinley in a form that would dwarf Mt. Rushmore. In 1896, William A. Dickey, a Princeton-educated prospector, named the highest mountain in North America "Mt. McKinley" to honor the then new presidential candidate and his support of the gold standard. Of course, the mountain had a name long before any Ivy League Republicans laid eyes on it. Athabascans of the interior had long called the 20,320 ft. giant Denali ("the Great One").

At 18,000 ft. from base to summit, Denali has the greatest total altitude gain of any mountain in the world. Mt. Everest—originally Sagarmatha or Jomolungma—is higher above sea level but rises only 11,000 ft. from its base on the Plateau of Tibet. In 1980, an official effort to rename Mt. McKinley failed, but the land on which it stands was designated Denali National Park as a compromise. Today, almost everyone ignores the US Geological Survey and uses the original name.

Most shuttle tickets and campground spots are purchased in advance by phone. Nevertheless, those willing to wait in line can purchase their tickets up to the day of, if available. A set of **binoculars** (bring a pair or purchase at the visitors center for $20+) is recommended for viewing wildlife along the road, or else you'll be prying them out of your neighbor's hand.

PRACTICAL INFORMATION

Entrance Fee: Payable at the time of reservation (campground or shuttle). $5 per person for 7 days.

Visitor Information: Denali Visitor Center (☎ 683-2294; www.nps.gov/dena/home), half a mile from the Parks Hwy., is the essential one-stop info and permit shop. Their free publication, the *Alpenglow*, contains park regulations, rates and history, and schedules of ranger-led events, including interpretive walks, dog sled demonstrations, and campfire talks. A worthwhile 15min. **slide program** presents the history of Denali (repeats every 30min.). Most park privileges are distributed on a first-come, first-served basis. Lockers 50¢ per day. Open Memorial Day to Labor Day 7am-8pm; open late Apr. to Memorial Day 10am-4pm and Memorial Day to late Sept. 10am-4pm. Lines form for shuttle tickets by 6:30am. All references below are to this center. **Eielson Visitor Center,** 66 mi. into the park, is accessible only by shuttle bus. Friendly rangers lead informative 45min. **tundra walks** daily at 1:30pm. No food is available. None. Running water and flush toilets. Open daily mid-June to Sept. 9am-7pm. Ranger Stations are located at **Kantishna, Toklat River, Igloo Creek,** and **Sanctuary River.** The park **headquarters** is located near **Riley Creek.**

Bank: None in the park or vicinity. **Wally's Service Station,** 11 mi. north of the park entrance in Healy, has a temperamental **ATM.** There is one in the gas station by **McKinley RV and Campground,** and at the **Totem Inn,** both also in Healy. Most park services accept credit cards.

Mountaineering Information: Talkeetna Ranger Station, in Talkeetna (see p. 506).

Equipment Rental: Denali Outdoor Center (☎ 683-1925 or 888-303-1925; www.denalioutdoorcenter.com), at Parks Hwy. Mile 238.9, just north of the park entrance. Bikes half-day $25, full-day $40, 5 or more days $35 per day.

Laundromat: McKinley Campground (☎ 683-2379), in Healy, 11 mi. north of the park entrance. Wash $2.50, dry $1.75. Tokens sold June-Aug. daily 8am-10pm; winter 8am-8pm. Machines available 24hr.

Internet Access: At the **Black Bear Coffee House.** $3 first 15min. $2.50 per each additional 15min. See Food below for hours.

Emergency: ☎ 911.

Medical Services: Healy Clinic (☎ 683-2211), 12 mi. north and a half-mile east of the park on Healy Spur Rd. in the same building as the community center. Open May-Sept. M-F 9am-5pm; Oct.-Apr. M-F 10am-3pm. On call 24hr.

Post Office: (☎ 683-2291). Next to what was the Denali Hotel, 1 mi. from the visitors center. Open May-Sept. M-F 8:30am-5pm, Sa 10am-1pm; Oct.-Apr. M-Sa 10am-1pm. **ZIP Code:** 99755.

ACCOMMODATIONS AND CAMPING

Campers must obtain a **permit** from the visitors center and may stay for up to 14 nights in park campgrounds. Free permits are available on a first come, first served basis one day in advance. Sites at four of the seven campgrounds can be reserved in advance. Reservations are strongly recommended; without one, prepare to camp or stay outside the park for at least one night. Sixty-five percent of shuttle tickets and all of the campsites at **Riley Creek, Savage River, Teklanika,** and **Wonder Lake** can be reserved from February up until the day before travel. (☎ 800-622-7275 or 272-7275. Open daily 7am-5pm.) Permits for remaining sites are available two days in advance at the visitors center on a first come, first served basis. The visitors center opens at 7am, and the early bird gets the permit. There is a $4 non-refundable fee for campground reservations, and there is a $6 fee per site or bus ticket to change your reservations. RV amenities are sparse in Denali: there are no hookups and only one dump station (at Riley Creek). RV drivers can pay $12 per night to park at Riley Creek, Savage River, or Teklanika River, or they can head to any of the RV parks near the park entrance. All campgrounds within the park are wheelchair accessible, except for Igloo Creek and Sanctuary River. Unless otherwise noted, all campgrounds are open May-September. Options farther from the park include several motels in Healy (just over 11 mi. north of the park entrance) and a series of bed and breakfasts located off the Healy Spur Rd.

- **Denali Mountain Morning Hostel** (☎ 683-7503 or in Alaska 866-D-HOSTEL; www.hostelalaska.com). 13 mi. south of the Park entrance, these rustic hand crafted cabins sit nestled between the eastern borders of Denali Park and the Talkeetna Mountains. The owners are eager to give outdoors advice for the park itself and the surrounding area. Clean rooms, full kitchen, showers, groceries, **free Park shuttles** (call for schedules), outdoor gear rentals and sales (backpacker kit $30 first day, $7 additional days). Bunks $22, ages 5-13 $17. Semiprivate and private rooms start at $50. Tent sites $15. Reservations strongly recommended.

- **Riley Creek,** Mile 0.4 Denali Park Rd. The only year-round campground in Denali. All sites assigned at the visitors center. Close to the highway and the visitors center, Riley Creek is louder and more congested than the other campgrounds. Piped water, flush toilets, and sewage dump. No water in winter. 100 sites. $12.

- **Morino Creek,** Mile 1.9 Denali Park Rd., next to the train tracks. 60 2-person sites for backpackers without vehicles. Water, chemical toilets. No open fires (stoves only). Nearest showers at the Mercantile. Many backpackers stay here while they wait for permits and check out the park on the buses. Sites $6.

- **Savage River,** Mile 13 Denali Park Rd. High, dry country with easy access to popular Primrose Ridge. 33 sites. Complimentary shuttle to and from the visitors center. Flush toilets and water. Last area accessible by car without an access permit. $12.

- **Sanctuary River,** Mile 23 Denali Park Rd. Quiet, wooded campsite with river and mountain. Chemical toilets, no fires (stoves only). Accessible only by bus. 7 tent sites. $6.

- **Teklanika River,** Mile 29 Denali Park Rd. Popular with members of the Winnebago tribe. Piped water and flush toilets. Accessible by shuttle bus or by vehicle with permit. 3-night min. for vehicle campers. Vehicles are permitted only to drive in and to drive out and must remain parked for the duration of the stay. 53 tent and RV sites. Sites $12.

- **McKinley RV and Campground** (☎ 683-2379), 11 mi. north of the park entrance, in Healy. Provides the most wooded spots in that area. Hookups and dumping for RVs. Showers $2. Laundry (see **Practical Information**). A convenience store has an ATM. The office is located in the gas station convenience store. Register year-round 10am-8pm. Tents $16.25; RVs $22-27.

FOOD

Denali is expensive, and local grocery options are limited. Wise is the traveler who stocks up in Fairbanks or Wasilla. **McKinley Mercantile** can be found at the Riley Creek Campground. (☎ 683-9246. Open daily 7am-9:30pm.) The **Denali General Store** (☎ 683-2920; open daily May-Sept. 8am-10pm), 1 mi. north of the park entrance, also stocks groceries (be prepared to pay $4 for a loaf of bread). Once you board the park bus, there is no food available anywhere past the hotel.

- **Black Bear Coffee House** (☎ 683-1656), 1 mi. north of the park entrance in the center of a long row of log cabin storefronts. The most affordable and fulfilling food stop near Denali as well as the only place to get online (see **Practical Information** above). The coffee's hot and strong, and served up with freshly baked goods. Espresso ($2), chunky homemade soup ($3.50), breakfast ($6.50), and half-sandwich with chips ($6). Open daily May-Sept. approx. 7am-10pm.

Denali Smoke Shack (☎683-7665), north of the park entrance on the hill just after the Nenana river bridge. Real Alaskan barbecue. The Smoke Shack's hip young waitstaff, friendly dog, great views, and large vegetarian menu make it a local favorite. Popular late-night scene with a full bar. Lunch $5-9; dinner starts at $9. Open daily 7am-3am.

McKinley Creekside (☎683-2277), 13 mi. south of the park entrance and across the highway from the hostel (see **Accommodations and Camping**), the Creekside offers slightly more reasonable rates than those nearer to the entrance along with highly edible fare among a more local crowd. Chow on a hot sandwich ($8-9), chug a brew or espresso and take the waiter up on dessert. Open daily May-Sept. 6am-10pm.

HIKING

The shuttle bus affords excellent views and wildlife-sighting opportunities, but the real Denali lies beyond the road. Past Mile 14 there are **no trails.** The park's backcountry philosophy rests on the idea that independent wandering creates more rewards and less impact than would a network of trails or routes. In an effort to disperse hikers as widely as possible, rangers will not recommend specific routes, although they will suggest areas that meet hikers' desires and abilities. Topographical maps are available at the visitors center.

DAYHIKING

A must. You can begin dayhiking from anywhere along the park road by riding the shuttle bus to a suitable starting point and asking the driver to let you off. Don't feel obligated to get off at one of the designated rest stops (about every hour or so along the way); drivers will be happy to drop you off anywhere that isn't restricted due to wildlife. Once you've wandered to your heart's content, head back to the road and flag down a shuttle bus heading in your direction. The first couple of buses may be full, but it's rare to wait more than 30min. for a ride. Be sure to check when the last buses will be passing your area in order to guarantee a ride back. Stream crossings and bushwhacking are inevitable if you plan to get far from the road: good boots, long pants, and gaiters are all advisable.

For those waiting on shuttle tickets, great dayhiking is accessible from many shuttle stops. **Polychrome Overlook** at Mile 47 offers a spectacular 360° view of the park and grants easy ridge access for those looking to gain some altitude. From the **Toklat River** stop at Mile 53 the wanderer can choose between a hike north up the river valley, or south into the larger drainage. Hikes following the many river systems are generally easier to negotiate and cover ground more quickly than bushwhacking. The visitors center is a great resource for planning dayhikes. Though the rangers won't recommend specific hikes, if you come with an idea of what you'd like to do (ridges, glaciers, peaks, etc.), they are likely to point you in a good direction. Deeper within the enormous and uniformly stunning park, recommendations become much harder to make and much less useful; your best bet is to spend a little time with the helpful staff and literature back at home base. A few easy-to-moderate trails are maintained around the park entrance. **Horseshoe Lake Trail** is 1½ mi. round-trip with lovely mountain views, and the lake is popular with moose. **Roadside Trail** runs 2 mi. from the hotel toward Park Headquarters, where the sled-dog demonstrations are held. **Mt. Healy Overlook Trail** is more challenging and starts from the hotel parking lot. The 5 mi. round-trip climbs 1700 ft. to an impressive view of the valley at 3400 ft. and takes 3-4hr. The particularly ambitious can continue up the ridge to the 5700 ft. summit. More information on entrance area trail hikes is available in the *Alpenglow*.

Discovery hikes are guided 3-5hr. hikes, departing on special buses from the visitors center. Topics vary; a ranger might lead you on a cross-country scramble or a moose trail excursion, providing a comprehensive introduction to local wildlife, flowers, and geological formations. The hikes are free but require reservations and a bus ticket. More sedate 45min. **tundra walks** leave from Eielson Visitor Center daily at 1:30pm, and many other talks and naturalist programs are posted at the visitors center.

EXPLORING THE BACKCOUNTRY

The road barely scratches this wilderness, and the wildlife doesn't seem quite so wild through a bus window. With no major cities for 300 mi. in any direction, camping in Denali's backcountry is an experience like no other. Only 2-12 backpackers can camp at a time in each of the park's 43 units. Overnight stays in the backcountry require a **free permit,** available no earlier or later than one day in advance at the **backcountry desk** in the visitors center. The **quota board** there reports which units are still available. Type-A hikers line up outside as early as 6:30am to grab permits for popular units. Some units may be temporarily closed after a fresh wildlife kill or bear encounter. The **Sable Pass** area has been off-limits to hikers since 1955 due to bear activity.

The park covers a variety of terrain, with varying implications for hiking. **River bars** are level and rocky, offering very good footing for hikers but potentially difficult stream crossings. **Low tundra,** in brushy, soggy areas above the treeline, is not easily navigable and makes for exasperating hiking under insect-infested conditions. **Alpine tundra** (or **dry tundra**), is higher and drier which means fewer mosquitoes. Generally, the southern reaches of the park contain dry tundra and river bars opening wide vistas of the park. The northern reaches are brushier but include high points with incredible views of the Mountain. Some of the most enjoyable hiking and wildlife-viewing awaits in the middle of the park near the Toklat River and Polychrome Pass.

Backcountry campers must stay within their registered unit, pitching tents at least half a mile from the road and out of sight. A compass (not available at the visitors center) and **topographical maps** ($4) are essential. Before they head out, campers receive a short introduction to bear management, and are required to spend some quality time with the center's interactive **backcountry simulator.** This allows virtual hikers to learn about a number of potentially dangerous wilderness situations. All but two zones require that food be carried in a 3 lb. plastic **bear-resistant food container (BRFC),** available for free loan at the backcountry desk. Be sure to leave space in your backpack. Backcountry hikers *will* cross streams, whack bushes, and battle mosquitoes: gaiters and head nets are luxuries to consider. Denali's backcountry provides ideal conditions for **hypothermia.** With the park's many rivers, streams, and pools, your feet *will* get wet. Under these conditions, hypothermia sets in quickly; talk with rangers about prevention and warning signs.

Mosquito repellent is an extremely wise investment for anyone going into Denali's backcountry. These annoying insects have the ability to turn a pleasant bushwhack into a fly-swatting, arm-swinging, itch-fest.

OTHER OUTDOOR ACTIVITIES

BIKING

Unlike private vehicles, **bicycles** are permitted on the entire length of the park road, making them a perfect way to escape the shuttle-bus ticket blues. Park at Savage River and ride into the heart of Denali. The park road is 90 mi. long, crossing four mountain passes, so if you're not up to the 180 mi. round-trip, feel free to turn back at anytime. Most of the road is unpaved, so thicker tires work best. Off-road biking is not permitted anywhere in the park. For bike rental info, see **Practical Information,** p. 500.

RAFTING

Several **rafting** companies run the Class III rapids of Denali's Nenana River. The stretch is swift, splashy, and scenic. Most companies provide drysuits—something you'll need if you take a spill into the 36°F (2°C) water. The **Denali Outdoor Center** (**DOC**; see Practical Information p. 500) boasts the most experienced guides on the river. (Canyon run $55 per person, $75 for 4hr. The DOC also runs guided **kayak** tours ($75), with no experience necessary; tours include a free shuttle. Open daily May-Sept. 8am-9pm.)

FLIGHTSEEING
Flightseeing tours are a wonderful way to see the Mountain, especially on a clear day, but ironically, the park is not the best place to do this. **ERA Helicopters Flightseeing Tours** (☎683-2574, www.eraaviation.com) offers mountain viewing as well as guided helihiking ($300), but the town of Talkeetna is closer to the Mountain and has companies that offer cheaper trips.

WINTER SPORTS
Cross-country skiing, snowshoeing, and **dog sledding** allow visitors to see the park during the winter. Despite 20hr. nights and temperatures below -40°C, many people of perfect mental health consider winter the most beautiful time of year in Denali. If you plan to travel through Denali in the winter, you are strongly encouraged to stop by the visitors center to tell them your route. For the safety of rangers and travelers alike, rangers request route info and expected completion dates.

DENALI HWY. (RTE. 8)   ☎907

The breathtaking Denali Hwy. runs west from **Paxson**, 80 mi. (1¼hr.) south of Delta Junction on the Richardson Hwy. (Rte. 4), to **Cantwell**, 27 mi. (30min.) south of the Denali National Park entrance. Along the way, it skirts the foothills of the Alaska Range to the north and Talkeetna Mountains to the south, amid countless lakes and streams teeming with trout, burbot, and grayling. Fortunately for solitary sorts, the highway's 115 mi. of gravel scare away most tour buses, RVs, and other wayward travelers. Pristine free campgrounds and unique geological formations along the way make the road a destination in itself. Bullet-riddled road signs attest to the popularity of hunting in this area, but hikers, fishermen, bird watchers, and archaeologists also frequent the region. The highway itself, and many of the trails that branch off it, particularly in the Tangle Lakes district (see below), are ideal for mountain biking. The Denali Hwy. is **closed** from October to mid-May. Except for the 21 mi. west of Paxson, it is entirely gravel. Most vehicles can expect to keep a pace of 30 mph. **Mile markers**, where they exist, measure the distance from Paxson. **Gas and services** are available at Mile 20 and Mile 82. **Emergency:** ☎911 **State Trooper:** ☎768-2202 (Cantwell).

TANGLE LAKES
The **Tangle Lakes National Register District,** between Mile 17 and 37, serves as a base for mountain bikers, ATVers, and birders. Pick up the Bureau of Land Management's free *Trail Map and Guide to the Tangle Lakes* at the **Tangle River Inn** (see below) for details. Archaeological sites in the area contain evidence of some of the first human settlements in North America, some of which are at least 10,000 years old. For more info contact the **Bureau of Land Management** (BLM; ☎822-3217). Three established campground exist along the highway, yet any anxious camper could feasibly set up shop almost anywhere along the highway. At Mile 21 the scenic **Tangle Lakes Campground** (free; toilets, water pump) provides easy access to the 30 mi., 2-3 day, **Delta River Canoe Route,** which has one difficult stretch of Class III rapids and one portage. Takeout is at Mile 212.5 of the Richardson Hwy. The **Upper Tangle Lakes Canoe Route** is an easier 9 mi. paddle beginning at **Tangle River** and ending at **Dickey Lake**, also the starting point for the extended **Middle Fork of the Gulkana Canoe Route**. The helpful *Delta* and *Gulkana* brochures are available from the BLM and most establishments along the highway. The **Tangle River Campground** (Mile 21.7) and **Brushkana Campground** (Mile 104) offer similar services, in spite of a $6 fee at the latter. The owner of the **Tangle River Inn**, at Mile 20 across the highway from the boat launch, homesteaded the area by dog sled before the highway was built. Private rooms and beds in a shared room with a common room with pool table, TV, and VCR are popular; book ahead. The inn offers a cafe, bar, gas, and canoe rental. (☎822-3970, winter 895-4022. Canoe $3 per hr., $24 per day. Private room $45.) Fishers as well as flora and bird fans flock to the

Tangle Lakes Lodge, at Mile 22. The owners have the lowdown on the area's wildlife and canoe routes. (☎ 822-4202. Canoes $3 per hr. and $30 per day. Rooms up to four $75, $10 extra with canoe for night.) The area hosts 140 different species of birds, including the arctic warbler and Smith's longspur (see www.alaskan.com/tanglelakes/cklist.htm for a **birding checklist**), and some of the best car-accessible arctic fishing in the state.

TANGLE LAKES TO CANTWELL

Spectacular mountain scenery lines the rest of the highway, interrupted only by an occasional roadhouse or cafe. The trailhead at Mile 35 begins the short, level trail to the **Maclaren Summit** (4086 ft.), from which the **Maclaren River** is visible flowing from the **Maclaren Glacier**, with the Alaska Range and wildflowers all around. The scenic 8 mi. **Osar Lake Trail** begins at Mile 37 and is ideal for mountain biking. At Mile 80, the highway crosses the beautiful **Susitna River.** The turn-off at Mile 130, 5 mi. east of Cantwell, grants an excellent view of Denali on clear days. At Cantwell, the highway meets the more heavily-traveled George Parks Hwy. (see p. 505); Denali National Park is 30 min. north, and Anchorage is 3½ hr. to the south.

ALONG RTE. 3: GEORGE PARKS HWY. ☎ 907

Thirty-five miles out of Anchorage, the George Parks Hwy. splits from the Glenn Hwy. (Rte. 1) and runs 322 mi. north to Fairbanks, linking Alaska's two largest cities. A drive on "The Parks" is a visual feast. Moose sightings, wolf crossings, and spectacular views on the approach to Denali make it a worthwhile trip in itself. Its two lanes are paved and in good condition, except for a few frostheaves. Drivers heading north from Anchorage can stop in at the **Mat-Su Visitor Center**, on the Parks Hwy. just after it splits from the Glenn Hwy., for some friendly advice on where to stop along the way. (☎ 746-5000. Open mid-May to mid-Sept. daily 8:30am-7pm.) Bluegrass and folk music festivals take place in towns up and down the highway at the end of July and beginning of August.

TO TALKEETNA ☎ 907

Wasilla, at Mile 39.5, is home to the **Iditarod race headquarters and museum,** 2¼ mi. off the Parks on Knik Goose Bay Rd., where visitors can learn all about the famous race, watch a video, admire the trophies, and take a short ride on a dog-drawn wheeled buggy. (☎ 376-5155; www.iditarod.com. Open mid-May to mid-Sept. daily 8am-7pm; Sept.-May M-F 8am-5pm. Free. Sled rides, weather permitting June-Aug. $5 for about 5min.) The race has always started in downtown Anchorage, but since 1980 the state Department of Transportation has refused to issue permits for the teams to travel the Glenn Hwy. So, after the official start of the race on the first Saturday of March, dogs and rider take an anticlimactic truck ride and the race restarts in Wasilla on that Sunday morning.

The **Wasilla Backpackers Hostel,** 3950 Carefree Dr., off Campbell St. at Parks Hwy. Mile 39, after undergoing some renovations this past winter, is now equipped with a spacious guest kitchen for its diverse crowd. Other features include flowers, a hammock, porch horseshoes, and basketball. The owners have plenty of enthusiastic advice on nearby hiking, biking, and canoeing opportunities. Mountain bikes are available for $20 per day. (☎ 357-3699. Laundry $1, drying $1. Internet access $3 per 30min., $5 per hr. 14 singles $22. Major credit cards accepted.)

The **Museum of Transportation** is ¾ mi. off the Parks on Neuser Rd. near Mile 47. While all of the planes, motor toboggans (snowmobiles), cars, and school buses in the main room actually run, *Let's Go* can't guarantee the first hang glider used from the summit of Denali is still in working order. The planes, trains, and automobiles outside are full of Alaska Railroad history. (☎ 376-1211. Open May-Sept. daily

9am-6pm; call ahead in the winter. $5, students and seniors $4, family $12.) Next door, you can ride a **model steam train** run by the Alaska Live Steamers. (☎373-6411. Open 10am-5pm every first and third weekend of the month. $2 per ride.) The **Nancy Lake** campground, located in Willow at Mile 64 down Buckingham Place Rd., is one of the most picturesque of the many campgrounds along the Parks, with over 30 first come, first served lakeside sites. (Pit toilets, well. $10.)

TALKEETNA ☎907

Talkeetna (tah-KEET-nah) is a Tanaina word meaning "rivers of plenty" and an apt name for this eclectic settlement plunked down at the confluence of the Talkeetna, Susitna, and Chulitna Rivers. The convergence of old and new Alaska are more evident in this town as anywhere throughout the state. Because of its proximity to Denali—only 60 mi. by air to the north—Talkeetna is the flight departure point for would-be climbers of the Mountain. Every year between April and June, over 1200 mountaineers from around the globe converge on Talkeetna, creating an improbable international village and a run on accommodations. The climbing community is an unlikely departure from what used to be a gritty mining hamlet, but both lifestyles have contributed to this offbeat and worthwhile stop.

TRANSPORTATION

Talkeetna lies at the end of the **Talkeetna Spur Rd.**, which runs 14 mi. northeast off the Parks Hwy. from Mile 98.5. The town is 113 mi. north of Anchorage, 139 mi. south of the Denali National Park entrance, and 260 mi. south of Fairbanks.

Trains: The **Alaska Railroad** station (☎800-544-0552; www.alaskarailroad.com) is a covered platform half a mile south of town. Trains run mid-May to mid-Sept. Peak season is June 5-Sept. 3. Value season May 14-June 4 and Sept. 4-19. To: **Denali** (4½hr.; 1 per day; $70 peak, $56 value); **Anchorage** (3½hr.; 1 per day; $75 peak, $60 value); and **Fairbanks** (9hr.; 1 per day; $100 peak, $80 value). Purchase tickets on board if seats are available.

Buses: Parks Highway Express (☎888-600-6001; www.alaskashuttle.com) stops at the Talkeetna junction, where taxi service will take you the remaining 14 mi. ($18 cab ride, $6 each additional person). Runs once per day mid-May to late Sept. to **Anchorage** (2hr.; $34, round-trip $53) and **Fairbanks** (7hr., $54, round-trip $84) via **Denali** (4hr., $39, round-trip $64). Call for winter service info. **Talkeetna Shuttle Service** (☎888-288-6008) has daily service to Anchorage right from town. Runs mid-Apr. to July. Additional trips during climbing season. $50, round-trip $90. **The Park Connection,** run by Alaska Tour and Travel (☎800-266-8625) drops off in town during climbing season. Once per day to **Anchorage** (11am, $41), and **Denali** (6:30pm, $41 each way).

PRACTICAL INFORMATION

Visitor Information: Talkeetna Mountain Shop (☎733-1686), at Main St. and Spur Rd. Info on air charters and walking tours. Open Apr. to mid-Sept. daily 8am-6pm.

Outdoor Information: Talkeetna Ranger Station (☎733-2231; fax 733-1465; www.nps.gov/dena/home). Turn left at the terminus of Main St.; the station is on the left. With plenty of information and weather reports, the station is a great place to plan any kind of trip to Denali. Climbers must be registered 60 days in advance. Registration fee $150. Open mid-May to Aug. daily 8am-6pm; Sept. to mid-May M-F 8am-4:30pm.

Equipment Rental: The **Talkeetna Outdoor Center** (☎733-4444), toward the end of town on Main St., sells mountaineering gear and some camping gear, and provides outdoor information. (Open mid-Apr. to mid-Oct. daily 9am-6pm; open on demand in the off season.) **Crowley Guide Services** (☎733-1279), on Main St., sells, rents, and repairs mountain bikes, and offers information. **Busy Bikes** (☎232-5334), in a tin shed on the airport corner, rents bikes as well. Half-day $15, full-day $25.

Banks: There are **no banks** in town, but there is an **ATM** ($1.50 surcharge) at **Nagley's Store** on Main St. (see **Food and Nightlife**) and at the **Three Rivers Tesoro** gas station on Main St. Open daily 8am-9pm.

Laundromat and Public Showers: At the **Three Rivers Tesoro** gas station (☎ 733-6212), on Main St. Wash $2, dry 25¢ per 6min. Showers $2 per 8min. Open daily 8am-9pm.

Emergency: ☎ 911.

State Police: Just past the Talkeetna Alaska Lodge (☎ 733-2256), Mile 13, Spur Rd.

24hr. Crisis Line: ☎ 746-4080.

Medical Services: Sunshine Community Health Clinic (☎ 733-2273 or 24hr. emergency 733-2348), 9 mi. from town on Spur Rd. Open M-Tu and Th-F 9am-6pm, W 1-6pm, Sa 9am-5pm.

Internet Access: Free at the **Library** (☎ 733-2359), 1 mi. from town on Spur Rd. Open Tu and W 11am-6pm, F and Th 11am-7pm, Sa 10am-5pm.

Post Office: (☎ 733-2275). In town on Spur Rd. Open M-F 9am-5pm, Sa 10am-2pm. **ZIP Code:** 99676.

ACCOMMODATIONS AND CAMPING

Indoor accommodations can fill up quickly during climbing season (Apr.-June). Memorial Day (the fourth weekend in May) is also a particularly busy time for the campgrounds, so plan ahead.

Talkeetna Hostel International (☎ 733-4678; www.akhostel.com). Turn off Spur Rd. by the airport onto 2nd St. Turn left on "i" street; it's the 3rd house on the right. A short walk from town, airport and rail, the rates include a kitchen, free hot drinks in the morning, and a common area with TV and wood stove. Internet access $10 per hr. 1 shared bath. 5-night max. stay. Closed Oct.-May. Comfy bunks $23; private doubles $55, add $1 if paying by credit card.

Talkeetna Roadhouse (☎ 733-1351). Centrally located at Main and C St. Built in 1917, it is the oldest building in town still in use. The living room of this cozy establishment features soft couches, old books, a guitar, and a piano that opens into the dining area. 4 shared bathrooms. During climbing season, reservations should be made well in advance. Bunks $21; singles $48; doubles downstairs $63 or upstairs $90.

Talkeetna River Adventures (☎ 733-2604). Turn right off Spur Rd. at the airport, then turn left. Look for signs. Clean and quiet, in a wooded area. Water, outhouses, and easy river access. Showers $3. Open May-Sept. Sites $12. Major credit cards accepted.

River Park Campground, at the end of Main St. Because of its close proximity to town, it may not always be serene. Outhouses. First come, first served. $12.

FOOD AND NIGHTLIFE

Nagley's Store on Main St. stocks groceries and sells a latte for little more than $1 and footlong hotdogs for $2.50. (☎ 733-3663. Open Su-Th 8am-10pm, F-Sa 8am-11pm; in winter closes 1hr. earlier.) The **Three Rivers Tesoro** gas station (see **Orientation and Practical Information**) also sells groceries.

Talkeetna Roadhouse Cafe (see **Accommodations and Campgrounds,** above), offers family-style dining livened up with local banter and tall tales. Hearty breakfast $7. Sandwiches $6. The cafe has great baked goods to go along with a strong cup of coffee or tasty homemade soup. Open Apr.-Sept. daily 6:30am-3pm; Dec.-Mar. Sa-Su 6:30am-3pm; closed Oct.-Nov.

West Rib, on Main St., where "climbers peak when they're on top," proudly serves tasty musk-ox and caribou burgers ($8). Grab a game of pool as you enjoy an Alaskan beer ($4) in a beer garden. Open daily in summer noon-close; in winter noon-midnight.

Fairview Inn offers bands on weekends and live music nightly. Party down with the locals if the trophy mounts (caribou and bearskin) don't scare you off. BBQ in summer. Burgers $5.50. Beer $2. Open daily noon to late (often as late as 5am in the summer).

Main Street Cafe (☎ 733-1275). Quick eats for any meal. Sit inside or out on the deck. Either way, try breakfast ($3-6). Talkeetna Cheese Steak ($5) and Oriental Chicken Salad ($9). Open daily 8am-10pm; in winter, closed M.

SIGHTS AND EVENTS

The **Talkeetna Historical Society Museum**, off Main St. between C and D St., includes the town's oldest cabin and a dramatic scale model of the Mountain. (☎ 733-2487. Open May-Sept. daily 10:30am-5:30pm; Oct.-Apr. Sa-Su 11am-5pm. $2.50.) For life-size dioramas highlighted by authentic Alaskan noises, follow the moose tracks through the light-hearted **Museum of Northern Adventure**, on Spur Rd. near Main St. (☎ 733-3999. Open daily in summer 10am-6pm. $2, seniors and under 12 $1, family $5.) Alaska's annual answer to Woodstock takes place at Parks Hwy. 102 during the first weekend in August in the form of the **Talkeetna Bluegrass Festival**. Alaska's biggest campout features a talented line-up of state bands and promises a wacky good time, rain or shine. The second weekend in July brings Talkeetna's increasingly famous **Moose Dropping Festival** (www.moosedrop.com) sponsored by the Historical Society. Thousands flock here to enjoy the two-day festival complete with parade, live bagpipes, trade in various moose-nugget novelties, and a moose dropping toss.

Early December brings the **Wilderness Women Contest**, with such events as wood-chopping, salmon-fishing, target-shooting, beverage serving, and sandwich making; skills vital for life on the frontier.

OUTDOOR ACTIVITIES

FLIGHTSEEING

Because of Talkeetna's proximity to Denali, flights from here are cheaper than those found directly outside the park itself. If the weather cooperates, these flights are worth every penny and will leave you itching for more. Flights come in two standard flavors: a 1hr. flight approaching the Mountain from the south, and a 1½hr. tour that circumnavigates the peak. Landing on a remote glacier at the base of Denali ups the cost but is an available addition for almost all flights. One-hour trips cost $100-120 per person. The 15-30min. glacier stop-off (often at a climbing base camp) costs an additional $35-45 per person. All flights are weather-dependent, with most companies offering flights over the rugged Talkeetna Mountains to the south if Denali weather is uncooperative. Many companies, including **Doug Geeting Aviation** offer discounts to groups of four or five (☎ 733-2366 or 800-770-2366). **K2 Aviation** (☎ 733-2291 or 800-764-2291), **McKinley Air Service** (☎ 733-1765 or 800-564-1765), and **Talkeetna Air Taxi** (☎ 733-2218 or 800-533-2219) offer standard services, plus a variety of other specialized trips. All flight services suspend glacier landings in mid-July due to unsafe and unpredictable snow conditions. If you come to Talkeetna hell-bent on flightseeing, be prepared to wait a few days for the clouds to break. Call the flight outfits regardless of the weather in town; the mountains can bask in sun while clouds smother Talkeetna.

FISHING AND RIVER TOURS

Operations abound in the waterways around town. **Talkeetna River Guides**, on Main St., offers fishing tours and 2hr. float trips that grant views of Denali and wildlife. (☎ 733-2677 or 800-353-2677; www.talkeetnariverguides.com. Fishing half-day $129, full-day $175; float trip $54.) **Mahay's Riverboat Service** (☎ 800-736-2210; www.mahaysriverboat.com), on Main St. just before downtown, also offers fishing charters and leads tours geared more toward education. ($45, ages 2-12 $22.50). Take the 6hr. Devil's Canyon tour and try your hand at gold panning ($175). **Tri-River Charters** (☎ 733-2400), next to the post office, runs fishing charters along the Talkeetna River and offers drop-off services and equipment rentals.

BIKING

Opportunities for mountain biking in the general vicinity of Talkeetna are abundant, with the Talkeetna River Trail as a gem among these. This trail leads the biker through a wide and easy-to-follow, wooded path, intersecting with the Talkeetna River and Larson Creek for excellent fishing. This trail may lead to some bushwhacking and river crossings which can be negotiated easily by carrying your bike. (Traveling north, turn right onto Comsat Rd. (unmarked) at Mile 12 of the Talkeetna Spur Rd. Drive to its end and park out of the way. Enter ski trails and follow to the right, climbing a rutted hill. Stay on the established trail until Mile 7.6 at "Y," continue right to Larson Creek.)

TALKEETNA TO NENANA ☎ 907

From Talkeetna, the Parks Hwy. begins a gradual ascent into the Alaska Range and offers some of the finest views of Mt. McKinley available from the ground. The road winds northward from here across the Alaska Range, passing over steep canyons and through **Broad Pass** (Mile 201), the scenic high point of the drive. **Denali National Park** (see below) is about 30min. past the turn-off for the **Denali Hwy.** (Rte. 8; see p. 504). North of the National Park, the highway follows the **Nenana River** for about 70 mi. to Nenana.

OUTDOOR EXCURSIONS

The **South Denali Viewpoint,** near the entrance to Denali State Park, offers a spectacular profile of the 20,320 ft. peak and keeps drivers from running off the road. The turn-off to the viewpoint is just a few miles from the **Ruth Glacier,** but may not be worth the trip when it's cloudy. **Denali State Park** (☎ 745-3975), Miles 132-168, offers plenty of hiking trails solitude. Two pleasant **campgrounds,** both with toilets and drinking water, are accessible from the highway: **Troublesome Creek** at Mile 137.2 (10 tent sites; $5) and **Byers Lake** at Mile 147. (☎ 745-3975 or 269-8000 for PUC reservations. 66 sites for tents and RVs, $10. 2 public-use cabins.) A few short hikes put this site a cut above the rest. Canoe and kayak rentals are available from **Susitna Expeditions** (☎ 800-891-6316). For the weary traveler looking for a bed, the **Byers Creek General Store.** (☎ 357-2990. At Mile 144. 8 bunks. $25; a private cabin with great views of the Alaska Range, $65. Showers $4, free with stay. Wash $2, dry $1.) Just past Byers lake, visit the **Alaska Veteran's Memorial** and the **Denali State Park Visitor Information Center** for the view, the Alaskan history, and local outdoor lore. (Open daily Memorial Day-Labor Day 9am-6pm.) The **Denali Viewpoint North,** 10min. north of the state park, provides a breathtaking evening for those looking for a place to camp (sites $10, RVs free) or simply look at the mountain.

ON THE 51ST DAY OF CHRISTMAS, MY TRUE LOVE GAVE TO ME... The town of North Pole, AK, celebrates Christmas 365 days a year. Santa officially came to town in 1953, when the sleepy village of Moose Crossing changed its name to woo toy manufacturers. Town planners hoped that corporations would rush north for the privilege of displaying "made in the North Pole" on their products, but to no avail. The North Pole's 1700 residents, most of them military personnel stationed at nearby Fort Wainwright, have carried on nonetheless, transforming their town into a shrine to the jolly fat man. St. Nicholas Dr. runs into Santa Claus Ln. Bus stops, lampposts, and shopping malls all reflect the Christmas theme. Holiday cheer is mandatory. The US Postal Service even redirects Santa's mail—20,000 letters a year—to North Pole, and the merry old elf has recruited North Pole schoolchildren to help answer it. Best of all, anyone can get a personalized letter from Kris Kringle himself. Just send the recipient's name, age, sex, full mailing address, brothers' and sisters' names, favorite hobby, and anything special you would like Santa to write. The ruddy-cheeked old elf demands only $5 in return. His official address is 325 S. Santa Claus Ln., North Pole, AK 99705.

NENANA

Nenana (ne-NAH-na), 53 mi. south of Fairbanks, has played host to the **Nenana Ice Pool** since 1917. Bored out of their skulls during the long winter, residents of Alaska and the Yukon bet on the precise minute when the Nenana River will thaw in the spring. The 2001 pot climbed to $300,008. Call 832-5446, email tripod@ptialaska.net, or write P.O. Box 272, Nenana, 99760, to place a $2 bet. If waiting for the ice to break doesn't hold your interest, you may want to just move on to the **Two Choice Cafe**, located on A St., which actually has several choices: burgers ($6), ice cream cones ($1.50), and much more. (☎ 832-1010. Open May-Oct. daily 7:30am-3pm.) For a bed and "family-style" dining, the **Rough Woods Inn and Cafe** (☎ 832-5299) at the corner of 2nd and A St. will order up reasonable breakfast and lunch prices ($6-9) to compensate for dinner ($11-28). Rooms start at $55; major credit cards accepted.

FAIRBANKS ☎ 907

Had E.T. Barnette not run aground near the junction of the Tanana and Chena Rivers and not decided on the spur of the moment to set up a trading post, and had Felix Pedro, an Italian immigrant-turned-prospector, not unearthed a golden fortune nearby, Fairbanks might never have been born. But it did, and they were, and today, Fairbanks stands unchallenged as North American civilization's northernmost hub. In this rough-and-tumble town, men noticeably outnumber women, the streets are filled with four-wheel-drive steeds, and the beer flows as freely as the Chena's muddy waters. The University of Alaska has brought "northern scholarship" and a coffee shop culture to northwest corner of the city's large suburban area. It seems, though, that liberal student voices are drowned out in the great conservative chorus of local neuvo-frontierspeople.

▐▀ TRANSPORTATION

Fairbanks lies at the junction of three major routes: Prudhoe Bay lies 500 mi. north along the gravelly **Dalton Hwy.** (Rte. 11, see p. 528), Anchorage lies 358 mi. south along the **George Parks Hwy.** (Rte. 3, see p. 505), and Delta Junction lies 98 mi. southeast of Fairbanks along the **Richardson/Alaska Hwy.** (see p. 519). Downtown proper is somewhat lost in semi-urban sprawl, but the highest concentration of services lies within a square formed by four thoroughfares: **Airport Way** to the south, **College Rd.** to the north, **Steese Expwy.** to the east, and **University Ave.** to the west. The city center lies along **Cushman St.**, north of Airport Way. Fairbanks is a **bicycle-friendly** city with wide shoulders, multi-use paths, and sidewalks.

> **Flights:** The airport is 5 mi. southwest of downtown on Airport Way. **Alaska Air** (☎ 452-1661) goes to **Anchorage** ($135, round-trip $255) and **Juneau** ($280, round-trip $328). Booking well ahead results in much lower fares. Other carriers include **Delta, Northwest,** and **United. Frontier Flyer Service** (☎ 474-0014) and **Larry's Flying Service** (☎ 474-9169) fly large prop planes into the Bush. Fares change frequently. **Airlink Shuttle** (☎ 452-3337) runs a shuttle service. Airport to downtown $7.

> **Trains: Alaska Railroad,** 280 N Cushman (☎ 456-4155 or 800-544-0552), behind the Daily News-Miner building. An excellent way to see the wilderness rather than the Alaskan highways. From mid-May to mid-Sept., 1 train per day to **Anchorage** (12hr., $175) via **Denali National Park** (4hr., $50). From mid-Sept. to mid-Oct. and from early Feb. to mid-May, a train leaves for **Anchorage** once per week ($140). Ages 2-11 half-price. Depot open M-F 7am-3pm, Sa-Su 7-11am, and for evening arrivals.

> **Buses: Parks Highway Express** (☎ 479-3065 or 888-600-6001) departs each day at 9am to **Denali** (3½hr.; $27, round-trip $47) and **Anchorage** (9hr.; $55, round-trip $100), and 3 times per week to **Glenallen** (2½hr.; $45, round-trip $85) and **Valdez** (8hr.; $62, round-trip $117). Pickup at the visitors center, Billie's Backpackers Hostel (see **Accommodations,** below), and elsewhere upon request. **Alaska Direct** (☎ 800-770-6652) runs 3 buses per week from the downtown bus terminal at 5th and Cush-

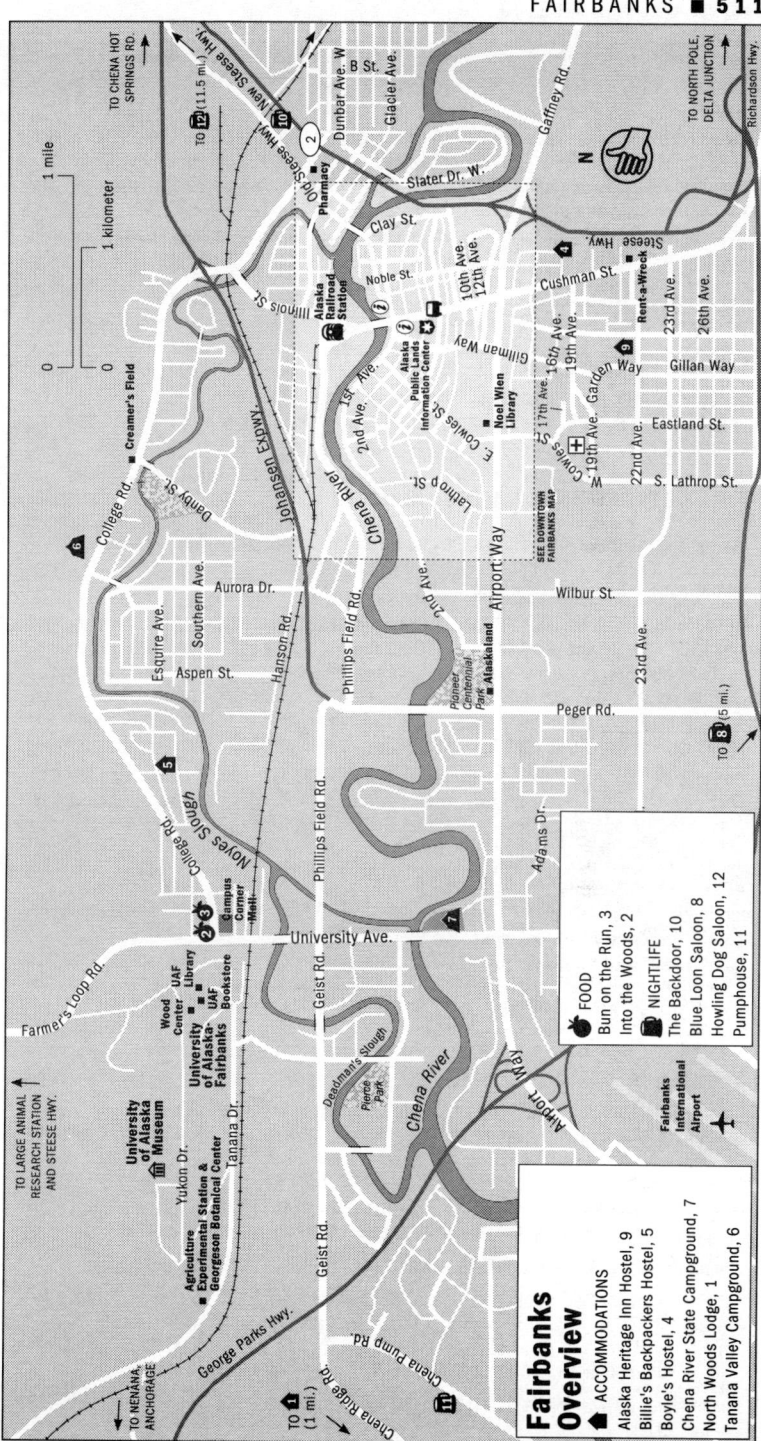

FAIRBANKS ■ 511

Fairbanks Overview

ACCOMMODATIONS
Alaska Heritage Inn Hostel, 9
Billie's Backpackers Hostel, 5
Boyle's Hostel, 4
Chena River State Campground, 7
North Woods Lodge, 1
Tanana Valley Campground, 6

FOOD
Bun on the Run, 3
Into the Woods, 2

NIGHTLIFE
The Backdoor, 10
Blue Loon Saloon, 8
Howling Dog Saloon, 12
Pumphouse, 11

512 ■ ALONG RTE. 3: GEORGE PARKS HWY.

man to **Tok** (4½hr., $40), **Whitehorse, BC** (15hr., $120), and **Anchorage** (12½hr., $65). Grayline's **Alaskon Express** (☎451-6835 or 800-544-2206) runs to **Skagway** (overnight, 3 per week, $212) or **Whitehorse, BC** (overnight, 3 per week, $170).

Public Transportation: Municipal Area Commuter Service, MACS (☎459-1011), at 5th Ave. and Cushman St. $1.50; under 18, over 65, and disabled 75¢; under 5 free. Day pass $3. Service generally M-F 7am-8pm and more limited on Sa; no buses on Su. Schedules available at the visitors center and post office.

Taxis: King Diamond Taxi (☎455-7777), $1 base, $2.20 per mi. **Fairbanks Taxi** (☎452-3535), $1 base, $2 per mi.

Road Conditions: ☎456-7623.

Car Rental: National companies offer free mileage, but won't allow driving on dirt roads; small companies charge hefty mileage fees. Call months ahead. **Rent-a-Wreck**, 21055 Cushman St. (☎452-1606). $39 per day, 30¢ per mi. after 100 mi. Must be 21 with credit card. No gravel highways. **U-Save Auto Rental**, 333 Illinois (☎452-4236). $35 per day, 26¢ per mi. after 100 mi. Must be 21 with credit card or $250 cash deposit. Under 25 extra $3 per day plus $500 deposit. Only the Dalton Hwy. is off limits.

🛈 PRACTICAL INFORMATION

Visitor Information: Convention and Visitors Bureau, 550 1st Ave. (☎456-5774 or 800-327-5774), at Cushman. Free local calls. Open daily 8am-8pm; winter M-F 9am-5pm. **Fairbanks Events Hotline:** ☎456-4636.

Outdoor Information: Alaska Public Lands Information Center, 250 Cushman #1A (☎456-0527), in the basement of the Old Federal building at Cushman and 3rd. Invaluable resource for use of all public lands throughout the state. Free daily films and exhibits, as well as an Alaska Natural History Association bookstore. Maps of all kinds. Open daily 9am-6pm; winter Tu-Sa 10am-6pm.**The Wood Center** at UAF has resources for trails throughout Alaska and is loves to help visitors plan trips.

Outdoor Equipment: 7 Bridges Boats & Bikes (☎479-0751) rents both. Canoes $30 per day, $100 per week. Bikes $10-15 per day, weekly rates negotiable. **Rocket Surplus**, 1401 Cushman St. (☎456-7078), vends military surplus camping supplies. Open M-F 9am-6pm, Sa 10am-6pm, Su 10am-5pm.

Bookstore: Gulliver's New and Used Books, 3525 College Rd. (☎474-9574), in the Campus Corner Mall, has a huge selection of reading and free **Internet access** in its Second Story Cafe. Open M-F 9am-10pm, Sa 9am-8pm, Su 11am-6pm.

Laundromat and Showers: B&C (☎479-2696), at University Ave. and College Rd., in Campus Corner Mall. Wash $2.25, dry 25¢ per 8min. Showers $3, towels 50¢. Open M-Sa 7:30am-9:30pm, Su 8am-9:30pm.

Weather: ☎452-3553.

Emergency: ☎911.

Police: 656 7th Ave. (☎459-6500), at the intersection with Cushman.

State Troopers: ☎451-5100.

Crisis Line: ☎452-4357 or 800-478-7273. Info on **gay and lesbian groups.**

Pharmacy: Fred Myer Pharmacy, 19 College Rd. (☎456-2151), at Steese, across from the Bentley Mall. Open M-F 9am-9pm, Sa 10am-7pm, Su 10am-6pm.

Hospital: Fairbanks Memorial, 1650 Cowles St. (☎452-8181), south of Airport.

Internet Access: See **Bookstore** above; **Noel Wien Library**, 1215 Cowles St. (☎459-1020), at Airport Way. Free 15min. slots are available; 1hr. blocks should be reserved in advance by phone. Open M-Th 10am-9pm, F 10am-6pm, Sa, 10am-5pm, open Su in winter. **Kinko's** (☎456-7348) 418 3rd St. $12 per hr., or $.20 per minute.

Post Office: 315 Barnette St. (☎452-3203). Open M-F 9am-6pm, Sa 10am-2pm. **ZIP Code:** 99707.

Downtown Fairbanks

ACCOMMODATIONS
Fairbanks Hotel, 1

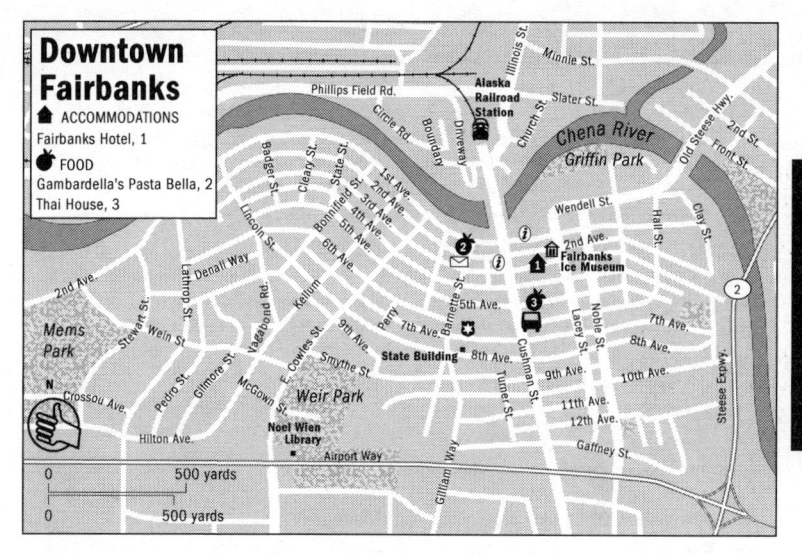

FOOD
Gambardella's Pasta Bella, 2
Thai House, 3

ACCOMMODATIONS AND CAMPING

Although hostels and campgrounds abound in Fairbanks, there are precious few affordable hotel rooms to be had. **Fairbanks Hotel** 517 3rd Ave. (☎456-6411), is downtown and newly remodelled with an Art Deco motif ($55-110). The visitors bureau has info on the many **B&Bs,** most starting around $70.

- **Boyle's Hostel,** 310 18th Ave. (☎456-4944). Rooms are spacious and tidy with comfy bunks. Cabins outside are really beds-in-a-shed, but are surprisingly suitable. 2 large kitchens and TVs in every room. Showers and laundry. No curfew or lockout. Dorms $18, $25 for private double; outside cabins $15 per person. Monthly rates available.

- **Billie's Backpackers Hostel,** 2895 Mack Blvd. (☎479-2034). Red bus to Westwood and College, then walk a block off College to Mack Rd. This place has a little bit of everything: a radio, 2 kitchens, files of travelling info, outdoor garden, deck, and 2 songbirds in a cage. 10 bunks in co-ed rooms; 4 of them near the kitchen are only for the immodest, $20. Tent space $15. Private double with jacuzzi $50. No curfew or lockout.

- **North Woods Lodge** (☎479-5300 or 800-478-5305; fax 479-6888). From town, take Chena Pump Rd. out 2 mi. past the Parks Hwy. overpass, turn right onto Roland Rd., and then take another right onto Chena Hill Dr. ¼ mi. up on the right. A wooded hideaway a fair distance from town offers sleeping space on the floor of a loft ($15) and private cabins (starting at $45).

- **Alaska Heritage Inn Youth Hostel,** 1018 22nd Ave. (☎451-6587). Take Cushman to 22nd Ave., then go west to the green and white building on the right with a totem pole in front. Rooms are clean, but dim and bland. Common room with TV, picnic area, showers. Breakfast $3. Quiet hours from 11pm. No curfew. Beds $17, nonmembers $18. Private rooms from $45. Tent spaces $11.

- **Chena River State Campground,** north of Airport Way on University Ave. Landscaped, popular recreation site with boat launch and volleyball court, as well as nature trail. Campsites are along the river. 5-night max. stay per vehicle. 56 walk-in sites, $10-15.

- **Tanana Valley Campground,** 1800 College Rd. (☎456-7956), behind the farmer's market by the fairgrounds. Near Aurora Ave. on the red bus route. Noisy, but grassy and secluded in town. Laundry $2 wash and $2 dry. Showers $3 for non-campers. Tent sites $8; RV sites $12; hookups $15.

514 ■ ALONG RTE. 3: GEORGE PARKS HWY.

◘ FOOD

On Airport Way and College Rd., the northernmost franchises of almost every fast-food chain in existence lure burger lovers to their artery-blocked doom 24hr. a day. **Carr's,** 526 Gaffney (☎452-1121) and **Safeway** (☎479-4231), at University Ave. and Airport Way supply groceries. The **Farmers Market** at the fairgrounds at Aurora and College sells abnormally large local vegetables in mid- to late summer and early fall. (☎456-3276. Open W 11am-6pm, Sa 9am-4pm.)

■ **Bun on the Run,** a trailer in the parking lot between Beaver Sports and the Marlin on College Rd. across from Campus Corner Mall. Few, if any, are disappointed with the scones, meringues, and, of course, the buns that the whimsical pink trailer produces. Devour a sandwich ($5) at a nearby picnic table. Open M-F 7am-6pm, Sa 9am-4pm.

■ **Gambardella's Pasta Bella,** 706 2nd Ave. (☎456-3417), at Barnette. You're not in Alaska anymore...Italian music, authentic dishes, flowers on the patio...and hiking boots on the customers. Guess you are still in Alaska. Subs or small pizzas $6-9. Open M-Sa 11am-10pm. Reservations recommended in summer. Dinner prices higher.

Into the Woods, 3560 College Rd. (☎479-7701). A respite from the busy street, this cabin houses a used book collection and rooms with fireplace. Outdoor music in the summer jams with hippies. Open M, Tu 6pm-midnight, W-Su noon-midnight.

Thai House, 526 5th Ave. (☎452-6123), just east of Cushman in the heart of downtown. The spiciest and most authentic Thai joint in town—The Kao Khew Wan Neur seasoned with green curry and basil ($7) for lunch and ginger dishes like Pad-ped Sam-sahai ($12) for dinner are the chef's favorites. Open M-Sa 11am-10pm.

🎟 EVENTS

GOLDEN DAYS. In mid-July Fairbanks citizens don old-time duds and whoop it up for Golden Days, a celebration of Felix Pedro's 1902 discovery that sparked the Fairbanks gold rush. The celebration is full of venders and special daily events. Watch out for the traveling jail; without a silly-looking pin commemorating the event (sold at most stores), an unknowing tourist may be imprisoned and forced to pay a steep price to spring free. For more details, contact the visitors bureau.

SHAKESPEARE THEATER. Off Steese Hwy, turn onto Fairhill, then left onto Birch Hill. During the first three weeks of July, the **Fairbanks Shakespeare Theater** puts on a play from the Bard's portfolio in the idyllic setting of Birch Hill Recreation Area. *(North of town off Steese Hwy.* ☎ *457-7638. $16, students $12, under 10 free.)*

TANNA VALLEY STATE FAIR. A traditional country fair with rides, lots of food, and competitions for biggest cabbage and cutest baby. Suggestions for replacing them with biggest baby and cutest cabbage have so far been ignored. If you're lucky, you'll be chosen to compete in the **kiss the cow contest,** although the cow is unfairly prohibited from judging. *(The first 2 weeks in August. Fairground at intersection of College Rd. and Aurora.* ☎ *452-3750. $7; seniors and ages 6-17 $3.)*

UM, HONEY IS IT...COLD IN HERE? The thick blanket of snow that envelops Alaska in the winter months shields the state from the flood of tourism that washes over it in the summer. Those who brave the Alaskan winter come for the intense skiing and snowboarding opportunities. And for the luck. Japanese tradition has it that good luck will follow the couple whose marriage is consummated under the northern lights. The dead of winter thus finds Fairbanks deserted except for the locals and a few blushing Japanese newlyweds.

WORLD ICE ART CHAMPIONSHIPS. Competitors from all over the world come to use the specially harvested and unusually clear ice that Fairbanks provides. Each contestant gets two days to make their masterpiece, but they remain on display until April 1. A kid's park is complete with ice slides and caves to play in. (☎ 451-8222. March 6-24, 2002.).

SPORTING EVENTS. In winter, February's **Yukon Quest Sled Dog Race** runs between Fairbanks and Whitehorse, ending in Fairbanks on odd years. The Quest is considered more extreme, colder, and dammit, more Alaskan than the famous Iditarod. There are fewer dogs, fewer stops, and less concern for human welfare. For info, contact the Yukon Quest Business Office, 558 2nd Ave. (☎ 452-7954).The second week in March, the **Limited North American Championship Sled Dog Race** (☎ 488-1357) draws almost 80 teams annually and runs through Fairbanks.

Summer Solstice Events. The summer solstice inspires some wild activity in Fairbanks. The Fairbanks Goldpanners play their annual **Midnight Sun Baseball Game** on the solstice itself (June 21, 2002). The game begins as the sun dips at 10:30pm, features a short pause near midnight for the celebration of the midnight sun, and ends at about 2am, in full daylight. The **Goldpanners** play more than 30 home games throughout the summer and have won five Alaska league national championships since 1970. Barry Bonds played here (perhaps the source of his fetish for large gold jewelry). Games are played at **Growden Memorial Park** (☎ 451-0095), near Alaskaland. The **Yukon 800 Marathon Riverboat Race** sends high-horsepower competitors in low-slung powerboats on an 800 mi. quest up the Tanana and Yukon Rivers to the town of Galena and back (☎ 488-4627). On June 21st, thousands will join in the **10km Midnight Sun Run** (☎ 452-8351), to run, walk, or compete in the costume division. In September, Fairbanks hosts the annual **World Eskimo-Indian Olympics,** in mid- to late July. For a true sports spectacular, see Native Alaskans from all over the state compete for three days in traditional tests of strength, balance, and survival. Witness the ear pull, traditionally played to prepare for frostbite. Sinew is wrapped around the ears of contestants, who then tug to see who can endure the most pain. Ears have been pulled off in this event. (☎ 452-6646. Daily pass $6, season pass $20.) If you miss this event, the University's museum has daily exhibitions for $6. The **Equinox Marathon** (☎ 452-8531), is one of the five most rigorous in the nation. About 300 hearty competitors run 26.2 mi. up Ester Dome, sometimes in frigid conditions, gaining 3500 ft. in elevation.

🔵 SIGHTS

■ UNIVERSITY OF ALASKA MUSEUM. Fairbanks' proudest institution holds one of the top ten visitor attractions in the state. The museum is at the top of a hill overlooking the flat cityscape and distant mountains (even Denali on a clear day). Exhibits include displays on the aurora borealis, gold collections, a thorough look at the Aleut/Japanese evacuation during WWII, and indigenous crafts. Blue Babe, a 36,000-year-old steppe bison recovered from the permafrost, would be truly foolish to miss. Daily summer programs on varying topics are worth the extra $6. Free 2hr. **campus walking tours** begin in front of the museum M-F at 10am, June-Aug. *(Museum ☎ 474-7505. A 10min. walk up Yukon Dr. from the bus stop at Wood Campus Center, or take a shuttle from the visitor parking lot. Open June-Aug. daily 9am-7pm; daily May and Sept. 9am-5pm; Oct.-Apr. M-F 9am-5pm. $5, seniors $4.50, ages 7-17 $3.)*

FAIRBANKS ICE MUSEUM. These ice sculptures are far more impressive than your average cornucopia or swan. View through the glass, or walk inside exhibits (15°F) to experience a Fairbanks winter. A thorough film shows the experts at work. Exhibits change seasonally. *(Around the corner from the visitors center on 2nd Ave. ☎ 451-8222. Open daily 10am-6pm. $8, seniors $7, ages 6-12 $5, under 6 free.)*

516 ■ ALONG RTE. 3: GEORGE PARKS HWY.

LARGE ANIMAL RESEARCH STATION. Be sure to sit upwind of the university's research station, which offers a rare chance to see baby musk oxen and other Arctic animals up close. If you miss the tour, grab some binoculars and ogle the musk ox, and reindeer from the viewing stand on the road. *(Take Farmer's Loop to Ballaine Rd. turn left on Yankovich; farm is 1 mi. up on the right.* ☎ *474-7207. Tours June-Aug. Tu, Th, Sa at 11am and 1:30pm; Sept. Sa 1:30pm. $5, students $2, seniors $4.)*

GEORGESON BOTANICAL GARDENS. Demonstration gardens show off bursting colors of Alaskan flowers and vegetables are delightful to walk through on a clear day. Benches and picnic areas coax you to stop and smell the flowers. *(On Tanana Dr., west of the museum.* ☎ *474-1944. Open 8am-8pm with guided tours F at 2pm. Suggested $1 donation.)*

▲ OUTDOOR ACTIVITIES

Fairbanks is geared towards biking and running paths, most of which run through the university campus. Maps for **multi-use trails** are available at the Wood Center, in the UAF Student Activities Office. **Cross-country skiing trails** cross near the UAF campus, and several begin and end at the University museum. Anyone looking for excursions into the wild will need to travel out of town (see **Nearby Fairbanks** below). Trip planning advice is available at the Wood Center or the Alaska Public Lands Information Center (see **Practical Information**, above). Near Fairbanks, the **White Mountains National Recreation Area** has trails and cabins accessible from the Steese and Elliott Hwy., north of Fox, and the **Chena River State Recreation Area** (see **Near Fairbanks,** below) has a variety of multi-use trails. Maps for both areas are available at the Alaska Public Lands Info Center (see p. 512). One popular place for nature trails is found in **Creamer's Field.** Take your binoculars along these nature walks to observe the migratory waterfowl in this refuge. (At College and Danby Rd. Guided walks are led Sa and W at 9am and Tu, Th at 7pm. ☎ 452-5162)

For skiing, **Moose Mountain,** 20min. northeast from Fairbanks, grooms over 30 trails. Take Sheep Creek Rd. to Murphy Dome Rd. Make a right onto Moose Mt. Rd. (☎ 479-4732. $23, ages 7-12 $18, free in Moose Meadow only. Rentals $20, under 12 $15. Open Th-Su 10am-5pm, or dusk.) Another option, 30min. north of Fairbanks and holding over 20 trails, is **Mt. Aurora Ski Land,** 2315 Skiland Rd. Take a right onto Fairbanks Creek Rd. off the Steese Hwy. (Rte. 6) at Mile 20.5, then turn left. (☎ 389-2314. Lift tickets $24, students and military $20, ages 13-17 and seniors $17, ages 7-12 $10, under 6 and over 70 $5. Rentals $20, students, military, and seniors $15. Open Nov.-April. 10am-dusk.)

♪ NIGHTLIFE

This is a good town to get pined in. Not so many hikes, but lots of cheap beer and plenty of time to kill. Women are often heartily welcomed to the nightlife scene, given that the population mix of the military presence and the general Alaskan stats put them in the minority.

- **Howling Dog Saloon** (☎ 457-8780), 11½ mi. north of town on the Steese (Rte. 6), at the intersection of the Old and New Steese Hwys. in the "town" of Fox. A mean-looking band, volleyball, and horseshoe by the midnight sun keep the party rolling through the night. Live music W-Sa. Open May-Oct. Su-Th 4pm-2am, F-Sa 4pm-4am.
- **Blue Loon Saloon,** 2999 Parks Hwy. (☎ 457-5666), 5 mi. south of town on the Parks Hwy., near **Ester.** Nights vary here between dancing with go-go dancers to lounging on the couches and watching a movie. The grille serves burgers ($6), nachos ($7), and entrees ($9-14) throughout the night. Cover $3. Open Su-Th 5pm-1am, F-Sa 5pm-3am.
  - **The Pumphouse** (☎ 479-8452), at Mile 1.3 on Chena Pump Road. A calmer clientele sips their drinks on the deck to enjoy the view of the Chena River. Karaoke night on W gets much rowdier. Open M-Sa 11:30am-2pm and 5pm-1am. Su 9am-2pm.

The Backdoor, behind Jeffrey's restaurant at the intersection of Trainer Gate Rd. and the Steese Hwy. Mix $5 pitchers (all draft beers including Newcastle and Sam Adams) with $1 shots and you get a full batch of the young and drunk. Foosball, and pool tables ensure that there's inebriated fun for everyone. Open daily until 2am.

NEAR FAIRBANKS ☎ 907

A short drive in any direction from Fairbanks plunges travelers into genuine Alaskan wilderness. Fish or look for wildlife in a river basin, hike up a ridge to view the Brooks or Alaska Ranges, and, after a long day, soak your sore muscles in hot-spring-fed pools. Maps and detailed info on hikes are available at the Alaska Public Lands Info Center in Fairbanks (see p. 510).

FISHING AND CAMPING

Along the **Chena River,** graylings are common, and king salmon run in late July and early August. The **Chatanika River,** which runs along the Steese Hwy. (Rte. 6) between Miles 29 and 39, teems with shellfish and northern pike. Call Fish and Game (☎ 459-7200) for more info. Chena Hot Springs Rd. branches off the Steese Hwy. (Rte. 3) at Mile 5. The **Chena River State Recreation Area** (☎ 451-2695) spills across Chena Rd. between Miles 26 and 51, encompassing almost 400 sq. mi. of wilderness and offering outstanding fishing, hiking, and canoeing. Tent sites (pit toilets, water; $10) convenient to Chena Hot Springs Rd. are at the quiet, secluded **campgrounds** of **Rosehip** (Mile 27), **Tors Trail** (Mile 39), and **Red Squirrel** (Mile 43).

HIKING

Maps and info on all these trails are available at the Public Lands Office in Fairbanks (see p. 512), **Tacks' General Store** at Mile 23 of Chena Hot Springs Rd., and at the Chena Hot Springs Resort. (Open daily 8am-8pm; also a post office.)

Granite Tors Trail (15 mi. round-trip, 6-10hr., 2500 ft. gain). At Mile 39 of Chena Rd., across the street from Tors Trail campground. The trail climbs gradually through birch, aspen, spruce, and eventually past the treeline to a peak topped by giant granite pillars ("Tors"). Blessed with fantastic views of Chena Dome and Flat Top Mountain, this could be a long dayhike or a leisurely overnight affair spent at a shelter at the Granite Tors.

Angel Rocks Trail (3½ mi. round-trip, with 6½ mi. spur to Chena Hot Spring; 3-4hr.; 750 or 2000 ft. gain). Near Mile 49 on Chena Hot Springs Rd. This trail follows the Chena River before turning for a climb alongside the Angel Rocks, prominent granite slabs that offer views of the river valley and the Alaska Range. This loop makes a wonderful family hike and has spawned numerous spur trails through the bush. A further scramble up the treeless ridge will offer even better views.

Chena Dome Trail (29 mi., 3-4 days). Lower Chena Dome Trailhead is at Mile 49.1 Chena Hot Springs Rd.; the Upper Chena Dome Trailhead is at Mile 50.5. Follow rock cairns above treeline. Open to mountain bikers and equestrians, this is the most spectacular trail in the park that follows the high, rocky rim of the Angel Creek Valley. The climb from either trailhead is a steep one, and park rangers advise backpackers planning on covering the entire loop to begin at the northern trailhead. Those out for just the day can reach good views within 3 mi. of either trailhead.

CHENA HOT SPRINGS

Fifty-seven miles northeast of Fairbanks steams the bubbling pools of **Chena Hot Springs Resort.** In winter, scores shiver their way to the resort for prime northern lights viewing from the "Aurorium," although many park their RVs at the resort in summer to see wildlife and to soak on a cool day. The resort caters to a crowd who prefers chlorine and jets in their "natural" hot springs, yet is isolated enough to attract wildlife. Day use of the hot pools comes at a price. (Open 7am-midnight. $10, under 18 $7, free if staying in a room.) The resort's **restaurant** serves standard expensive restaurant fare (open daily 7am-10pm). Nearby are hiking/biking trails, over 30 mi. of cross-country skiing trails, and fine fishing (after the spring thaw). The resort rents bikes ($7.50 per hr., $25 per day). Early in August, the resort plays host to an annual **Alaskan microbrew festival.**

Rooms at the Chena Hot Springs Resort are unkind to the pocketbook, but **campsites** are available by the river. (☎ 451-8104; Fairbanks office 452-7867. In summer doubles $125; suites $170. Showers $3; water and dump station. Sites $20; dry RV sites $40.) The resort is a good place to amass info on a number of activities (snowmobiling, dog sledding, rafting, fishing), but it's not the only option for spending the night in the park. The **Angel Creek Lodge** (☎ 369-4128), at Mile 50 on the Chena Hot Springs Rd., provides more affordable accommodations. Its six rustic cabins sleep 3-5 people, have electricity and access to free showers and a sauna ($45-100). A cafe, liquor store, and bar are open to any and everyone. The place bustles in February as a checkpoint on the **Yukon Quest Sled Dog Race** (see p. 378).

FROM FAIRBANKS: STEESE HWY. (RTE. 6)   ☎ 907

The Steese Hwy. heads northeast out of Fairbanks and runs 162 mi. to the town of **Circle** on the **Yukon River.** Just 5 mi. outside Fairbanks, the Steese meets **Chena Hot Springs Rd.** (see p. 517), where a right turn brings you toward Chena River Recreation Area and the Chena Hot Springs. The **Elliott Hwy. (Rte. 2)** comes hard on the heels of the Chena Rd., at Mile 11 in **Fox.** Make a right turn at the intersection to stay on the Steese. Fox is the last place to fuel up for the next 117 mi. of the Steese until the town of **Central** (and gas is far from cheap in Central). For the next 20 mi. past Fox, the highway winds through boreal forest, past two ski resorts, and into a region of stunted spruce and fir trees known as taiga. At Mile 16.5 is the **Felix Pedro Monument,** a plaque honoring Pedro's 1902 discovery of gold in the creek across the highway. Both of the "highways" are gravel roads and require slow driving. Some car rental companies will not allow their cars on these roads.

CAMPING. The **Upper Chatanika River Campground,** at Mile 39, provides secluded, woodsy campsites ($10). **Cripple Creek Campground,** at Mile 60, offers good fishing and recreational goldpanning. (Sites $6. Walk-ins $3.) At Mile 45.4, soon after the road turns to gravel, the **Long Creek Trading Post** stands on the left side of the Hwy. The Post runs a shuttle service for paddlers and their canoes and rents canoes ($30 per day). They also have a small general store and liquor store, and a bathhouse with laundry and an RV park with dump station. (☎ 389-5287. Open daily 9am-9pm.) Hiking trails to overlooks of **Davidson Ditch,** a 90 mi. system that carried water from the Chatanika River to Fairbanks, are wheelchair accessible. At about Mile 70 the road begins to climb consistently into the highway's nicest scenery. The **White Mountain National Recreation Area** and the **Steese National Conservation Area** lie side-by-side to the north. Mile 85 brings outstanding views from **Twelvemile Summit.** At Mile 107, the highway passes over **Eagle Summit,** one of the most challenging points on the **Yukon Quest International Sled Dog Race,** and also where the panoramic view of peaks and fragile tundra is well worth a stop.

OUTDOOR ACTIVITIES. Chatanika River Canoe Trail parallels the Steese for nearly 30 mi. The easygoing stream is a clear Class II; its only treacherous obstacles are low water and overhanging trees. (Both campgrounds have access to the river.) Traveling from a headwater stream to a twisting river, **Birch Creek** creates Class I, II, and III rapids. Both ends by Steese Hwy. at Mile 94.5 and 140.4. Allow 7-10 days for the 126 mi. No guides lead **gold panning** demonstrations here, but the gold is yours if you find it. Stay within the restricted limits. Check with the Public Lands Office for guidance. Take Steese Hwy. to Mile 57, go 6 mi. north on US Creek Road. Large white signs mark the 4 mi. stretch of Nome Creek where recreational panning is allowed. Access requires at least one ford of Nome Creek.

Pinnell Mountain Trail is the most spectacular and popular hike in the vicinity of Fairbanks. The 27 mi. trail is rugged and exposed, and while it gains little elevation, it remains entirely above treeline and passes among alpine tundra flora. With proper timing, you can bask in the midnight sun (June 17-23, 2002), witness an explosion of wildflowers (late June), or watch caribou migration in the valleys below (Aug.-Sept.). Although it can be hiked either way, starting at Mile 107 eliminates some of the grueling uphill sections. Most hikers hitch back to their cars. Even if you don't have time to schlep 27 mi., a scramble up either end of the trail is worthwhile. Get to the trail at Mile 86 and 107 on Steese Hwy. Two 4-wall shelters are available between Mileposts 10 and 11 and between Mileposts 17 and 18 of the trail. Allow three days for the entire trip. For more info on this and other trails, call the Bureau of Land Management in Fairbanks at 474-2200.

CENTRAL AND CIRCLE HOT SPRINGS ☎ 907

Central (Mile 127), a pit-stop town of about 400 summer residents, is anything but central. The **Central Motor Inn** serves nondescript sandwiches ($6) and dinners (from $8), offers laundry (wash and dry $2 each) and showers for $3. (☎ 520-5228. Open daily from 8am.) **Gas** is available here and at **Crabb's**, down the street.

From Central, the road gets considerably worse, winding its way down towards the **Yukon River Flats Basin.** Unless you are planning to float the mighty **Yukon River** or urinate into its great waters—an activity inexplicably favored by some tourists—there is little reason to drive the highway's final 34 mi. to **Circle.** Instead, follow the signs and veer right after downtown Central to the **Circle Hot Springs.** The springs are just 8 mi. from Central, and provide a pleasant and uncrowded reward for those who make the long drive. The pool here is outdoors, surrounded by woods, and is up to 12 ft. deep. A day pass for non-guests at the **Arctic Circle Hot Springs Lodge** is $5 (open 8am-midnight). The pool is open all hours, but is "clothing optional" after midnight. The lodge is charming, historic, boasts piping-hot spring-fed toilets, and is haunted by a ghost—"a real prankster." The rooms are costly, but the lodge has a hostel on the fourth floor next to its library and provides campsites. The hostel rooms are individual sleep spaces with very low-slanted ceilings and no beds, but those who stay there get free use of the pool. (Singles $75; doubles $100. Dorms first person $20; each extra adult $15; under 9 $7.50. Each room fits up to 4 people. Sites $5; RV sites $10; electrical $15.) The dining room serves tasty sandwiches for $4-7 and dinner entrees for $10-16. (Open 8am-8pm.) **Cold Rush** offers an abundance of ice cream in a homemade waffle cone for $3.50. (Open M-F 2-4pm and 6-9pm.)

ALONG RTE. 2: THE ALASKA HWY.

DELTA JUNCTION ☎ 907

Aptly named the Crossroads of Alaska, Delta Junction is located at the intersection of the **Alaska Hwy. (Rte. 2),** which leads 108 mi. southeast to **Tok,** and the **Richardson Hwy. (Rte. 4),** which runs 95 mi. northwest to Fairbanks and 27 mi. south to Valdez (see p. 458). Moreover, the huge post in front of the **visitors center** declares this site in Delta Junction the terminus of the Alaska Hwy., although Fairbanks argues otherwise. (☎ 895-5068. Open early May to mid-September daily 8am-8pm.) Here, at milepost 1422, you can buy a macho certificate of Alaska Hwy. completion for $1 or, for $2, play the "Delta Deep Freeze Classic." The guess nearest to the date and time of the coldest winter temperature in the upcoming December to February wins half the proceeds. A 1920s buffalo importation scheme is responsible for Delta Junction's free-ranging buffalo herd, the largest in the US. Glimpse the mighty bison from across the fence at the buffalo ranch four mi. up Clearwater Rd. (7 mi. toward Tok on the Alaska Hwy., on your left).

Services are the last for miles: **Hendrick's Auto Parts,** is 3 mi. north of junction (☎895-4221. Open M-Th 9am-6pm, F 9am-5pm, Sa 9am-3pm.) **National Bank of Alaska** (☎895-4691), half a mile north of visitors center on the left has a **24hr. ATM.** The **post office** is across the highway. (☎895-4601. Open M-F 9:30am-5pm, Sa 10:30am-noon.) **Emergency:** ☎911. **State police:** ☎895-4344. **Health Clinic:** Off Richardson Highway 1½ mi. north of junction (☎895-5100). **Internet access:** Free at the library, located on the right past post office (☎895-4102. Open Tu-Th 10am-6pm, Sa 10am-4pm.) **Zip Code:** 99737.

Nearby state park areas have camping ($10, water and pit toilets), in addition to hiking, biking, canoeing, and fishing. **Delta State Recreation Site** (25 sites), half a mile north, and Big Delta Historical Park (23 sites in parking lot, $5), 8 mi. north are nearest to town center. **Clearwater Lake** (17 sites), at the end of Clearwater Rd. off the Alaska Hwy. toward Tok, offers birdwatching during migrations of waterfowl and Quartz Lake, 12 mi. north on the Richardson, is known for sport fishing (16 sites). Laundry and showers available 2 mi. north at Smith's Green Acres RV Park and Campground, which has shaded sites, vehicle washing, and a playground. (☎895-4369. Tents $10; dry RV $13; electric hookups $17; full hookups $21.)

The **Alaska Steakhouse and Motel,** just south of the crossroads, is an option for small, cheap rooms. (☎895-5175. Single with shared bath $45; double $65.) Pay a bit more for bigger rooms, more satellite TV channels, coffee, and tidiness at **Alaska 7 Motel.** (☎895-4848. Single $64; double $70.) Across the hwy., the speciality of **Buffalo Center Drive-in** is buffalo—in burger form ($7.25)—or viewed for free in wildlife form out back. (☎895-4055. Open M-Sa 11am-10pm, Su noon-9pm.) Break into the **IGA Food Cache** north on Richardson Hwy. (☎895-4653. Open M-Th 7am-9pm, F-Sa 7am-10pm, Su 8am-8pm.)

TOK ☎907

Originally a base camp for the construction of the Alaska Hwy. (Rte. 2) and Glenn Hwy./Tok Cutoff (Rte. 1), Tok (TOKE) calls itself "Main Street Alaska," sitting at the intersection of these two main roads at Mile 1314. Like many small towns along the highway, Tok is summer tourist-oriented and no place for the RV-shy. Tok, named in honor of a WWII US Army battalion's pet husky, revives its affection for sled dogs every winter in late March with the Race of Champions (☎883-6874), the last major dog race on the Alaska circuit. In summer, the Burnt Paw Shop offers free dog team demonstrations. (☎883-4121. M-Sa 7am-10pm.)

Tok is only 12 mi. east of the Alaska Hwy.'s intersection with the Taylor Hwy. (Rte. 5) at Tetlin Junction (see p. 521). Tok is 206 Alaska Hwy. miles southeast of Fairbanks, and is the halfway point on the 600 mi. drive from Whitehorse, YT, to Anchorage. **Alaska Direct** (☎800-770-6652) buses leave from Texacoon W, F, and Su to Fairbanks (4hr., $40), Anchorage (7hr., $65), and Whitehorse, YT (9½hr., $80).

The largest Alaskan log building houses the **visitors center** and its overwhelming collection of area brochures at the junction (☎883-5775. M-Sa 8am-7pm, Su 10am-5pm.) To find out more about Alaskan lands and waters, walk next door to the **Alaska Public Lands Information Center** (☎883-5667; www.tokalaskainfo.com. Open daily June-Aug. 8am-7pm; Sept.-May M-F 8am-4pm.) Across the highway, the **Tetlin National Wildlife Refuge Headquarters** provides info on the preserve. (☎883-5312. Open M-F 8am-4:30pm.) **Bike rental and repair** at Alaska Biking Adventures located at Cleft of Rock B&B west on Alaska Hwy. (☎883-4219. $5 per hr., $15 per day.) **24hr. ATM:** Young's Chevron at the junction, ☎883-2821. **Emergency:** ☎911. **Police:** ☎883-5111. **Health Clinic:** Half a mile down Tok Cut-off. (☎883-5855. Open M-Th 8am-5pm, F 8am-noon.) **Post office:** At the junction. (☎883-2025. Open M-F 8:15am-5:45pm, Sa 10am-3pm.) **Internet access:** All Alaska Gifts, at the junction. (☎883-5081. $6 per hour. Open daily 7:30am-10pm.) **Zip Code:** 99780.

An alternative to the pricey motels are the state campgrounds outside of town and the abundance of RV parks in town or the quiet, tent cabin **Tok International Youth Hostel,** 8 mi. towards Delta Junction in a pine forest (☎883-3745. $10 YHA members, $13 nonmembers.)

Serene **Moon Lake Recreation Site** (18 mi. west on the Alaska Hwy., $10) mutates into a noisy swimming hole and jet-ski haven for locals with warm summer weather. Earn a free RV or tent site after gorging on an all-you-can-eat dinner grilled to perfection at ▒**Gateway Salmon Bake,** on the Alaska Hwy. at the east end of town. (☎883-5555. Open mid-May to mid-Sept. M-Sa 11am-9pm, Su 4-9pm. Showers $2. Sites $10; free with $17 salmon or halibut dinner, or $12 chicken dinner.) Plate-sized sour-dough pancakes ($2.50) at **Sourdough Campground,** 1½ mi. down Tok Cutoff. (☎883-5543. Cafe open daily 7-11am.)

Locals swear by **Fast Eddy's** for the most bang for your buck. Burgers are $5, sour cream and chive fries $3.25, well-stocked fresh fruit and veggie salad bar $5.50. (☎883-4411. Open daily 6am-midnight.) **Fruit Cache** at Golden Bear RV Park has an unusually large selection of produce that traveled 44hr. by truck from Seattle (Open M-Sa 8am-8pm, Su 1pm-8pm). **Three Bears Food Center** doubles as a hardware store with food available in giant-sized packages. (☎883-5195. Open daily in summer 7am-11pm; winter M-Sa 8am-9pm, Su 8am-7pm.)

Don't rush off to the Canadian border. East of Tok before the border, the Tetlin National Wildlife Refuge offers hiking, boating, fishing, and hunting. Free camping at two campgrounds on serene lakes around 50 mi. into the refuge at the Lakeview Campground and Deadman Lake Campground. A sod-roofed visitors center near the border has an observation deck for an expansive view of the refuge (☎778-5312. Open Memorial Day to Labor Day M-F 8am-4:30pm.)

ALONG RTE. 5: TAYLOR HWY. ☎907

The Taylor proves that the term "highway" is used very loosely in the north. The Hwy. follows the track of an old horse and wagon trail. Not much seems to have changed since the path's construction through the hilly wilderness of Alaska's richest and earliest (circa 1886) gold fields. With dirt or gravel roadbeds and countless hairpin turns, the Taylor Hwy. is definitely not for the timid. The road will, however, lead you to the remains and modern incarnations of the gold mining towns of Forty Mile, Wade Creek, and Chicken Creek, as well as historic dredges, some beautiful camping, and scenic rivers with fishing potential.

TETLIN JUNCTION TO EAGLE

Beginning at **Tetlin Junction,** 12 mi. east of **Tok** (see p. 520), the highway is initially pleasant, with wide, smooth lanes. At Mile 96, the highway intersects another good route, the **Top-of-the-World Hwy.** (Hwy. 9; see p. 384), which continues 79 mi. east to **Dawson City, YT** (see p. 384). The Taylor continues north 64 mi. through worsening roads to the tiny town of **Eagle** (see below). The drive from Tetlin Junction to Eagle takes about 4½hr. Camping overnight along the way or in Eagle would make for a comfortable two-day round-trip.

THE BORDER. If you decide to cut off towards Dawson City, be prepared to cross the US/Canada border. (Open daily May-Sept. 8am-8pm Alaska time.) Make sure to have proof of citizenship. No scheduled buses run the Taylor, although there is boat service between Eagle and Dawson City (see p. 522). Some car-less travelers hitchhike, but sparse RV traffic makes this difficult; for safety's sake, *Let's Go* does not recommend hitchhiking. Gas and food are available only at the **Boundary Cafe,** just west of the border, and in **Chicken,** at Mile 66. From **Mile 0,** the Taylor Hwy. gradually climbs to over 3500 feet as it rolls toward 5541 ft. Mt. Fairplay. The woodsy **West Fork Campground** lies at Mile 49. (Pit toilets, water. 25 sites. $8.)

CHICKEN. The megalopolis of **Chicken,** rumored to have received the named after local miners couldn't spell their first choice, "Ptarmigan," lies at Mile 66. Without a phone or a flushing toilet, Chicken has little to offer the weary traveler. Each summer, Chicken's population explodes with an influx of gold miners from its usual 15 to upwards of 50. The **Chicken Creek Saloon** is a great hole in the wall to cool off your engine. The walls are decorated with hats and rather random pieces of clothing left by many passers-by. Take a moment to pet Tucker, the three legged dog that lost a fight with a GMC truck. (Open 8am-whenever.) RV parking ($10), pricey gas ($2 per gallon) and tire repair (hallelujah! about $20) can be found at the **Goldpanner**, on the Taylor south of the "downtown" turn-off. (Open daily May-Oct. 8am-8pm.) In good weather, half-hour walking tours of old ghost-town Chicken leave three times per day (for groups of four or more) from in front of the store; they are the only way to see the original mining cabins (donations encouraged). The Goldpanner also loans out pans for free gold-panning at one well-panned stretch of water. Next to the Saloon, the pricey **Chicken Creek Cafe** serves up burgers and sandwiches from $7. Two weighty flapjacks ($4.75) or a wiener with potato salad ($6) are more reasonable deals. (Open daily 8am-6pm; cold food served in the bar until midnight.) The cafe also hosts a nightly **Salmon Bake** (in summer 4-8pm; $15). Tenters and RVs can set up on the lot next to the cafe for free, although the site is less than ideal. The **Chicken Mercantile Emporium** pushes souvenirs aplenty and also sells gas. (Open daily in summer 8am-8pm.)

HIKING. Just past Chicken, at Mile 68, is a Bureau of Land Management **ranger station,** and an easy to moderate three-mile, two-hour round-trip **hike** along Mosquito Fork River towards an old dredge. Take the mosquitoes seriously. Another eight miles north on the highway (Mile 82) will land you at **Walker Fork Campground.** (Water, pit toilets, fishing. 20 riverside sites. $8.)

MINING RELICS. The **Jack Wade Dredge,** a huge machine used for placer mining, lies rusting away next to the Hwy. at Mile 86. The deteriorated dredge's safety is dubious, but that doesn't stop travelers from wandering around its eerie skeleton. From this point until Eagle, evidence of mining, large and small-scale, abounds. At Jack Wade Junction, the road forks north for Eagle and east for Dawson via the Top-of-the-World Hwy. For the last 64 mi. from the Eagle Junction, the road tightropes and snakes along mountainsides and canyons over **Forty Mile River,** another popular, although difficult, spot for rafters to put in (see **Eagle,** below, for outfitters). This last portion of the highway can be an arduous, two-hour test of drivers' grit, making you wonder if the tiny town at the end is really worth it. It is.

EAGLE ☎ 907

Before the Taylor Hwy. opens in the summer, this unpretentious wilderness town is connected to the outside world only by sled dog or air. Eagle is no tourist mecca, lacking a town water and sewage system and a police department. Eagle's heyday was in 1899, when the Secretary of War established a military base here to keep the town's booming gold rush population in check. In 1901, Eagle became the Interior's first incorporated city. The military went south after the mining fizzled, but unlike other forts along the Yukon, several of Fort Egbert's buildings and paraphernalia remained untouched by marauding miners. Eager Eagle-ites have quick grins and plenty of tales about pioneer great-grandmothers to share with travelers passing through. They also have more enthusiasm for their town and way of life than perhaps any other northern community; during the long winters, when the only access is by plane, they proclaim: "We're not snowed in. You're snowed out!"

🛈 PRACTICAL INFORMATION. The Taylor Hwy. closes from mid-October until at least mid-May. **Tatonduk Air** (☎ 547-2249) flies twice a day except Sunday to **Fairbanks** (1¼hr.; $93). There is **no bank, no ATM,** and **only Bo takes credit cards.** Bo Fay, the proprietor of **Telegraph Hill Services,** on the Taylor Hwy., is an unofficial visitor center. He readily provides coffee, conversation, gas, car repairs, and an indispensable map. (☎ 547-2261. Open daily 8am-6pm; winter 9am-5pm.) The real **visitor**

center and the **Yukon-Charley Rivers National Preserve Headquarters,** at the end of 1st St., left off the main road toward the old airstrip, provides the lowdown on canoe trips to Circle and beyond. (☎547-2233. Open daily in summer 8am-5pm.) The **Eagle Trading Co.,** on Front St. by the river, carries hardware, groceries, and supplies. In the evening, the whole town gathers on the benches out front. (☎547-2220. Open daily in summer 8am-8pm; winter 10am-6pm.) In an **emergency,** call the **Village Public Safety Officer** at ☎547-2300. **Post office:** On 2nd St. at Jefferson. (☎547-2211. Open M-F 8:30am-4:30pm.) **ZIP code:** 99738.

ACCOMMODATIONS, CAMPING, AND FOOD. The **Eagle Trading Co.,** on Front St., also has hot showers ($4), laundry (wash $4 per double load, dry 25¢ per 5min.), RV hookups ($15), and clean rooms with porches overlooking the river. (☎547-2220. Singles $50; doubles $60. Open daily in summer 8am-8pm; winter 10am-6pm.) Campers will rejoice upon finding the **Eagle BLM Campground,** a one-mile hike past Fort Egbert, or the first left after Telegraph Hill Services. Several short hiking trails start here. Ask Bo—he knows. (No water, pit toilets. Sites $8; seniors $4.) The **Riverside Cafe** serves the usual but with a view of the Yukon River. (☎547-2250. Breakfast all day. Lunch $6-7. Open daily May-Oct. 7am-8pm.)

SIGHTS. No visit to Eagle is complete without the 3hr. **walking tour,** offered by the **Eagle Historical Society and Museum.** The tour includes visits to the courthouse and Fort Egbert, which can't be viewed otherwise. Examine well-preserved relics of frontier life, from a birch bark canoe to experimental (failed) horse snowshoes. (☎547-2325. $5; under 12 free. Tour daily in summer at 9am from Courthouse Museum at 1st and Berry St. Call to arrange an alternate time.) Locals run yearly foot races up the copper-colored bluff above town and back down in 30 minutes. The line can be **hiked** in a more leisurely couple of hours. Figuring out where the trail starts can be confusing. Ask around town to guarantee success.

FLOATING FROM EAGLE. The 1979-mile-long Yukon River is the fourth longest river in North America and has the fifth largest flow volume of any river on earth. No other American river is as undeveloped, and navigating its entire length has become a cult experience. The trip takes three to four months and ends 1200 miles from Eagle near Nome at the Bering Sea. If four months sounds too daunting, the 154-mile trip between Eagle and Circle (see p. p. 519) takes only four to six days. The river runs through the **Yukon-Charley Rivers National Preserve** and some of Alaska's wildest country, but remains relatively calm the whole way. Campers do their best to avoid bears and countless mosquitoes by pitching tents on the gravel bars along the river. For detailed info, visit the Eagle Visitor Center or write the National Preserve, P.O. Box 167, Eagle, AK 99738. **Eagle Canoe Rentals** will set you afloat for the five-day trip to Circle. (☎547-2203. $165; equipment return included.) Getting back is up to you, but flights to Fairbanks are available from Eagle and Circle, as is the daily river trip from Eagle to Dawson City on the *M/V Yukon Queen* (5hr., US$117; canoe or kayak $20).

> **MY CAR'S STUCK 5 MILES UP THE ROAD. DO YOU HAVE AN ATM?** In the winter of 1905, the Norwegian explorer Roald Amundsen hiked several hundred miles across northern Canada into Eagle when his ship became locked in the ice floes of the Arctic Ocean. Amundsen used Eagle's new telegraph to cable his government for money, then mushed back to his ship and successfully completed the first journey from the Atlantic to the Pacific through the hitherto unthinkable Northwest Passage. Amundsen Park, on 1st St. at Amundsen, commemorates his voyage with a glistening silver globe etched in relief.

ARCTIC ALASKA ☎ 907

The farthest northern reaches of Alaska are home to some of the most unique and precious ecosystems in the world. They scrape out an existence in some of the world's harshest weather. Months pass in the winter without the sun peaking above the horizon, yet in the dead months the barren sky is lit by one of the most magical natural phenomena, the aurora borealis. Polar bears ride ice floes and hundreds of thousands of caribou roam freely. The Alaskan communities are few and far between, accessible only by plane, boat, or snowmobile. Life changes very little in the North: many Inupiat communities rely on the same subsistence methods as their distant ancestors. On the flip side, the difficulty of the Arctic lifestyle means that not much remains constant. Companies come and go, schedules are erratic, and consistency and reliability have a whole new meaning north of the Arctic Circle. Hours we list below are somewhat consistent, but there is little guarantee that things will be the same a year from now.

Any travel in this remote landscape will be expensive. All supplies must be shipped in from Fairbanks, Kotzebue, or Nome, and stores stock for their residents; a general store does not cater to the backcountry hiker. While some communities are open and friendly, others are close-mouthed and less welcoming. There are more than 14,000 sq. mi. of protected wilderness in Northwest Alaska, comprising 11% of the land administered by the National Park Service. This is wilderness at its wildest, accessible to only the most dedicated, experienced (not to mention propertied) outdoors people. Daunting as the Arctic sounds, a venture into its natural beauty and complete solitude is unforgettable.

✦ ORIENTATION

Arctic Alaska is separated from the Interior by the **Brooks Mountain Range**, which stretches from the Canadian border to the Chukchi Sea. Peaking at 10,000 ft., the 150-million-year-old range was named after Alfred Hulse Brooks, former head of the Alaskan branch of the United States Geological Survey. The Brooks are considered one of the most remote and inhospitable areas in the world, through which only the equipped and experienced should travel. Waters from the Brooks drain to the north, south, and west. The greatest river is the **Noatak**, flowing from the heart of the mountains, and then arcing a full 90° before spilling into **Kotzebue Sound**.

Beyond the Brooks lies the Arctic Slope. Continuously ensconced by permafrost (up to 2000 ft. underground in places), the Slope's terrain is markedly different from its mountainous border. The lay of the land is relatively flat, criss-crossed by braided streams and occasional lakes. Many lakes are oriented northwest, reflecting the prevailing winds. This frozen land thaws in the summer, becoming a soggy bog that is not pleasant for hiking. Receiving less than eight inches of precipitation annually, the parched Arctic Slope is a desert. Yet while the combination of cold and dryness makes the land sound particularly inhospitable, it has in fact been inhabited on and off for the past 27,000 years.

Along Alaska's westernmost coast (not including the Aleutians) the towns of **Nome** and **Kotzebue** perch precariously. They are nestled among a trove of protected lands: **Bering Land Bridge National Park, Kobuk Valley National Park, Gates of the Arctic National Park and Preserve, Noatak National Preserve,** and **Cape Krusenstern National Monument.** On the eastern side of the plethora of parks and preserves, sit the small town of **Bettles** and the Nunamiut Eskimo village, **Anaktuvuk Pass.** More remote and desolate communities lie along the northernmost coast of Alaska. **Prudhoe Bay** and **Deadhorse** are the terminus of the **Dalton Hwy.** (p. 528) and the origin of the Alaska Pipeline. Their connection to a roadway makes them much less expensive. To the east lies the most controversial tract of land in Alaska, the **Arctic National Wildlife Refuge.** West of Prudhoe Bay, inaccessible by any overland route, lies **Barrow,** the northernmost community in the US. Contacting the National Parks office and local towns you intend to visit will facilitate your travels.

✈ TRANSPORTATION

Bush planes are to the Arctic as cars are to the Lower 48. What few roads there are do not connect to the Interior and are often in poor repair. The exception is the **Dalton Hwy.** (p. 528), running from Fairbanks up to Prudhoe Bay. From Anchorage, **Alaska Airlines** (☎800-252-7522; www.alaskaairlines.com) services **Nome** (2½hr., $310 one-way) and **Kotzebue** (3hr., $310 one-way). The web site www.alaskaflight.com can get you price estimates for routes in the Arctic including the price of transporting your gear. **Fairbanks** to **Bettles** (1½hr., $140, 60¢ per lb.), **Fairbanks** to **Anaktuvuk Pass** (2hr., $170, 80¢ per lb.). Since 1979 **Bering Air** (☎443-5464; www.beringair.com) has offered comprehensive flights from both Kotzebue and Nome. They offer return tickets, triangle tickets, and flagstops at villages on unscheduled days. They also offer occasional flights to the Russian Far East and are the only scheduled service from Nome to Kotzebue (1hr., $175 one-way). Besides Bering Air, flight options from Nome include **Baker Aviation** (☎443-3081), **Cape Smythe Air Service** (☎443-2414), **Evergreen Helicopters** (☎443-5334), and **Grant Aviation** (☎443-4650). **Arctic Wilderness Lodge** (☎376-7955) offers fly-in services in the Brooks Range, Gates of the Arctic, and the Alaska National Wildlife Reserve from Prudhoe Bay. In Bettles, **Bettles Lodge** operates **Bettles Air Service** (☎692-5111 or 800-770-5111; www.bettleslodge.com) which offers fly-ins to the Brooks Range and Gates of the Arctic National Park. Prices start at $350 per hr., and are dependent on distance and the weight of you and your gear.

🏛 NATIONAL PARK OFFICES

Arctic National Wildlife Refuge (☎456-0250), P.O. Box 20, 101 12th Ave., Rm. 236, Fairbanks, AK 99701.

Bering Land Bridge National Preserve (☎443-2522), P.O. Box 220, Nome, AK 99762.

Cape Krusenstern National Monument (☎442-8300), P.O. Box 1029, Kotzebue, AK 99752.

Gates of the Arctic National Park and Preserve (☎456-0281), P.O. Box 74680, Fairbanks, AK 99707.

Kobuk Valley National Park (☎442-8300), P.O. Box 1029, Kotzebue, AK 99752.

Noatak National Preserve ☎442-8300.

BETTLES   ☎907

The region in which Bettles is located has been occupied by several Native groups in the course of time, including the Koyukon Athabascans and Kobuk, Selawik, and Nunamiut Eskimos. "Old Bettles" was founded by Gordon Bettles during the 1899 gold rush, and was actually located 7 mi. from the present day town site. From 1901-1956 Bettles was the terminus for the Koyukon River barge. The town relocated when the FAA built a runway to support the US Navy in exploring National Petroleum Reserve 4. Work opportunities flourished, attracting both white and native settlers. Today the village is primarily white and has a 90% employment rate, both uncharacteristic traits for rural villages. The town is accessible by road during the winter, meaning that goods and services are much cheaper than in other Bush towns. The **Hickel Trail**, a 30 mi. road, links residents to the Dalton Hwy. but is only accessible by snowmachine in winter (see p. 528). The Koyukuk River is the other main transportation route in the summer (although there is no barge service). The Park Service also operates the helpful **Gates of the Arctic Field Station**. (☎692-5494. Open June-Aug. M-F 8am-5pm; call for hours Sept.-May.) The **post office** sometimes closes for lunch. (☎692-5236. Open M 8am-5pm, Tu-W 8am-3pm, Th-F 8am-2pm, Sa 1-4pm.) **ZIP code:** 99726.

Bettles Lodge, which runs **Bettles Air Service** (see p. 525), has been declared a National Historic Site, but still rents rooms and acts as a trip planner. (☎ 800-770-5111; www.bettleslodge.com. Main lodge singles $115; doubles $135; triples $165. Aurora Lodge singles $135; doubles $160; triples $195.) At the lodge, the **Bettles Trading Post/Sourdough Outfitters** (see above) sells expensive groceries.

NOME ☎ 907

Nome owes its existence to the "three lucky Swedes" who discovered gold on nearby Anvil Creek in 1898, and its name to the poor penmanship of a British sailor. Baffled as to what to call this barren, weather-beaten camp at the edge of the sea, he scribbled "Name?" on his map. Cartographers back in England got his vowels confused, and the rest is history. Nome is home to a population of 4000, over half of which is Native Alaskan. Those who can afford to get here will find untamed wilderness accessible by road, refreshingly non-commercialized relics of mining history, and a culture centered around the Iditarod dog sled race and the Midnight Sun Festival.

█ PRACTICAL INFORMATION. Nome's **airport** is 2 mi. west of town. **Checker Cab** (☎ 443-5211) and **Village Taxi** (☎ 443-2333). Rates are similar ($3 point to point in town, $5 to the airport). The **Alaska Cab Garage** (☎ 443-2939) and **Aurora/Stampede Vehicle** (☎ 443-3838) have similar prices, letting go of a 2WD truck for around $75 per day. **Visitors center** (☎ 443-6624; www.nomealaska.org) is on Front St. across from city hall. The **National Park Service** (☎ 443-2522), on Front St. in the Sitnasuak Native Corporation Building, can provide info on the Bering Land Bridge National Park and Preserve, other Western Alaska national parks, and local hiking. Since credit cards are not widely accepted, you may need to visit the **Wells Fargo,** at 250 Front St. (☎ 443-2223). The **Carrie M. McClaine Memorial Museum** (223 Front St.) should give you a little background on the fast and furious history of a town that once had no less than 44 functioning saloons on Front St., the kind of environment that welcomed the company of notables like Jack London, Wyatt Earp, and Herbert Hoover (when he was a mining engineer). Free, with suggested $2 donation. The **Kegoayah Kozga Library** (☎ 443-6627), above the museum on Front St., has free **Internet access.** (Open M 5-8pm, Tu-Th noon-8pm and F-S noon-6pm.) At the **Recreation Center** (☎ 443-5431), at the northern edge of town on 6th Ave., you can play basketball, pump some iron, and shower on slow days ($4 admission). To check the **weather** call 443-2321 or press the button on the magic box outside the visitors center. **Emergency:** ☎ 911. **Police:** ☎ 443-5262. **Hospital: Norton Sound Health Corporation** (☎ 443-3311), at the corner of 5th and Bering St. **Post Office:** 240 E Front St. (☎ 443-2401). **ZIP Code:** 99762.

█ ACCOMMODATIONS AND FOOD. Beds in Nome can be costly. **Weeks Apartments,** 697 3rd. Ave. at G St., offers clean rooms with TV, kitchen, private bath, and private washer and dryer. (☎ 443-3194 or 800-448-3194. Singles $60; doubles $80; $10 per extra person. Call ahead.) The **Polaris Hotel,** has modest rooms at affordable rates. (☎ 443-2000. Singles with shared bath $40 and $5 key deposit; doubles with private bath $80.) **Free camping** is permitted on the flat, sandy beaches, 2 mi. east of town on Front St., past the sea wall. The land is privately owned, but gold panning and tent camping are allowed; enjoy the company and hope to fall asleep despite the drone of their sluices. If you have a car, try **Salmon Lake State Campground,** at Mile 38 of the Taylor Hwy. (see **Outdoor Activities,** below).

Stock up on groceries at **Hanson's Safeway** (☎ 443-5454), on Bering St. **Corner Market** (☎ 443-5940), at 4th and K St., also carries groceries. The rowdy **bars** in town, grouped on Front St., are always packed with locals. The **Polar Cub,** on Front St.

isn't a bad option with daily specials for under $9, better than most spots in town (fish and chips $10). **Twin Dragon** (☎ 443-5552), at the corner of Front St. and Steadman, has a bright, well-decorated interior. Extremely fresh vegetables—how'd they do that? Look for lunch specials or nab the sweet and sour pork ($9).

SIGHTS AND EVENTS. Isolation from the rest of the world makes people do strange things. The **Midnight Sun Festival** on June 23-24, 2001 celebrates the summer solstice with a parade, BBQ, simulated bank robbery, and a street dance, among other silliness. On Labor Day, the **Great Bathtub Race** sends wheeled bathtubs, filled with water, soap, and bather, hurtling down Front St.

The biggest event of the year, the **Iditarod** is accompanied by an entire month of festivals from late February to late March when the town comes under a near-constant attack of events celebrating the race, and thousands of out-of-town spectators journey in for the finish. Local accommodations book nearly a year in advance, and the town's population nearly doubles (☎ 800-545-6874; www.iditarod.com). The world's foremost dog sled race begins each year in Anchorage on the first Saturday in March and finishes here two or three weeks later (the current record is under 10 days) beneath the log arch by City Hall. The **Bering Sea Ice Golf Classic,** is held two weeks after the race start in March on the frozen ocean. Contestants use bright orange balls and face a number of unique hazards: ice crevasses, bottomless snow holes, and frosted greens. Course rules dictate: "If you hit a polar bear (Endangered Species List) with your golf ball, you will have three strokes added to your score. If you recover said ball, we will subtract five strokes." Two of the holes are in **Nome National Forest** (a "seasonal forest" consisting of donated Christmas trees frozen into holes drilled in the treeless tundra).

OUTDOOR ACTIVITIES. Branching out into the surrounding wilderness, Nome's three highways are a godsend for the adventurous traveler. Although entirely gravel, all are generally well-maintained. According to the visitors bureau, hitchers can usually find rides fairly easily on weekends up the Taylor or Council Hwy., when many Nome residents head in that direction. There are excellent **fishing** rivers along the highways, including the **Nome** and **Pilgrim Rivers.** Bring mosquito repellent or curse the day you heard of Nome.

Nome's outskirts are home to the remnants of abandoned **gold dredges.** The closest, **Swanberg's Dredge,** is about 1½ mi. from downtown on Front St., en route to the **Taylor Hwy.** The Taylor (a.k.a. Kougarok Rd.) heads north from Nome for 85 mi., then peters out without reaching any particular destination. Along the way is **Salmon Lake,** near Mile 38. Popular with locals, the lake offers fantastic fishing and primitive campsites. At Mile 53.6, an unmarked 7 mi. road leads to the **Pilgrim Hot Springs** area. The Catholic Church ran an orphanage here from 1917 to 1941, and many of the buildings are intact and undisturbed. This is private land, but the visitors bureau can provide the name and number of the caretaker for permission to soak in the hot springs. The **Kigluaik Mountains** are accessible via this highway, and offer good hiking and wildflower viewing.

The **Council Hwy.** runs 73 mi. from Nome to **Council,** a ghost town and summer home for Nome residents, accessible only by boat from the end of the road. En route, the highway goes around **Cape Nome,** passing beaches, fishing camps, and the fascinating **Last Train to Nowhere** at Mile 33, a failed railroad (with engine and cars) that sits rusting on the tundra. The **Nome-Teller Hwy.** winds 72 mi. west from Nome to the tiny fishing village of **Teller,** home to Iditarod legend Joe Garnie.

BERING LAND BRIDGE NATIONAL PRESERVE

Nome is also one of two departure points to the **Bering Land Bridge National Park and Preserve,** a testament to the once thousand-mile-wide land bridge now sunk beneath the shallow waters of the Bering Sea. The **Serpentine Hot Springs,** just inside the southern border of the park and about 30 mi. from the end of the Taylor Hwy., is the most popular destination. A primitive bathhouse contains the 140-170°F water and is open year-round. The most common way to get there is by snowmobile in the winter. In summer, a charter flight can be taken to **Taylor;** from there, Serpentine lies 8 mi. over the tundra. Contact the Park Service office in Nome (☎443-2522) for topographic maps and more info.

KOTZEBUE ☎907

On the tip of the **Baldwin Peninsula,** 160 mi. northeast of Nome and 25 mi. north of the Arctic Circle, Kotzebue (KOTZ-ih-boo) is principally a transportation and commercial hub for native settlements and other small communities in Alaska's Arctic Northwest. The wind-buffeted village has little to offer independent travelers except access to three remote and wild national park lands, all above the Arctic Circle. The **Northwest Alaska Native Corporation (NANA)** has its headquarters here. It takes a ton of money to reach Kotzebue, and $20 more earns admission to the **NANA Museum's Iñupiaq Program** (☎442-3301), which teaches native dance and the ceremonial blanket toss.

The **airport** is on the west end of town, a 10min. walk from Kotzebue's modest downtown. **Polar Cab** runs lucratively around town (☎442-2233). The **Visitors Center and National Park Service** is two blocks from the airport on 2nd Ave. (☎442-3760 or 442-3890. Open daily 9am-6pm.) The center is a stop-off for the busloads of tourists staying at the local expensive hotel, but also has maps and info about charters, along with a 15min. video about the parks and preserves that are serviced from Kotzebue. The **Wells Fargo Bank** (☎442-3258) is at 2nd and Lagoon. Camping is difficult in Kotzebue. Some visitors befriend locals and pitch tents in their backyards. Others make their way to the fish camps 1 mi. either way on the beach. Call the visitor center for B&B options. **Hanson's,** on Shore Ave., stocks the usual groceries, but be warned: a gallon of milk costs $5.50. The two restaurants in Kotzebue sit side by side on Shore Ave., both serving American and Chinese. **Bayside Restaurant** (☎442-3600) is your best bet with windows overlooking the whitecaps. Try the Alaskan omelette ($10) with reindeer sausage. **Internet access** is free at the **Chukchi Community College Library** on 3rd Ave., after Bison St.

DALTON HWY. (RTE. 11) ☎907

The Dalton Hwy. parallels the Alaska Pipeline from Fairbanks to the Arctic Circle, then reaches all the way to Deadhorse and the gates of Prudhoe Bay, an oil field on the Arctic Ocean. Before considering the drive, check your wallet to see if a tour is within your means. The **Northern Alaska Tour Company** (☎474-8600; www.northernalaska.com) offers a daytrip from Fairbanks to the Arctic Circle boundary (departs 6:30am, returns 11pm; $130), and a three-day trip to Prudhoe Bay including everything but meals ($650). These pricey tours are the best way to view the area while preserving both your car and your sanity—and a flat tire halfway up the Dalton would be a far worse financial drain, anyway.

The entire Dalton Hwy. was opened to the public on January 1, 1995. Truckers predominate; a tiny number of RVs, a handful of 4WD vehicles, and an occasional motorcyclist constitute the tourist traffic. Some hitchers proceed on the logic that nobody would leave a person stranded in the middle of nowhere, yet truckers almost always do. The road is passable in a standard passenger car at speeds under 45mph, but it's unwise to try it. The sharp gravel road is interrupted by rocks, boulders, and ditches, and most rental packages won't cover cars north of the Arctic Circle. The drive *is* breathtaking, although almost entirely without services. Bring two spare tires, a rabbit's foot or other superstitious talisman, extra gas, tools, clothing, food supplies, and drinking water. Being towed to Fairbanks costs around $7 *per mile.* The 498 mi. highway takes about four days round-trip.

FAIRBANKS TO THE ARCTIC CIRCLE   ☎ 907

A drive up the Dalton Hwy. begins with an 84 mi. jaunt from Fairbanks along the **Elliott Hwy.** to Mile 0 of the Dalton. Savor the pavement as you head out of Fairbanks—it's the last blacktop you'll see for almost 900 mi. The Dalton crosses the **Yukon River** at Mile 56, 140 mi. from Fairbanks. On the north side of the river is **Yukon Ventures,** one of the highway's two (count 'em, two) service stations, which sells gas, rents rooms, and has a small cafe. (☎ 655-9001. Open daily Apr.-Nov. 7am-9pm. Shared bath. Singles $65, doubles $100.)

As it gains elevation, the road winds through its first alpine region: at Mile 97.5, it passes **Finger Rock** to the east and **Caribou Mountain** to the west. The **rest area** just past Finger Rock is an ideal place to calm pothole-jarred nerves and enjoy views of the Brooks Range. Next comes the **Arctic Circle** (Mile 115), the southernmost point at which the sun does not set on the longest day of the year. A recently constructed pull-off has several picnic tables and presents four displays on the Arctic seasons (summer, winter, winter, and winter). Thousands hunger for the enormous Arctic Circle sign photo-op, and the spot offers good, free camping. Most folks are satisfied with merely reaching the Arctic Circle, and quickly retreat to Fairbanks. From here, the road only gets worse.

ARCTIC CIRCLE TO DEADHORSE   ☎ 907

Continuing north over Gobblers Knob (1500 ft.), the Dalton rattles past Prospect Camp and Pump Station No. 5, before heading over the Jim River and the South Fork of the Koyukuk River. A popular rafting trip is the middle fork of the Koyukuk River; many put in at **Coldfoot,** leaving their cars by the airstrip and arranging to be picked up 90 mi. down river in Bettles and flown back (contact the **Coldfoot visitors center,** below, for more info; for Bettles charters and outfitters, see p. 525). Coldfoot has the last services before Prudhoe Bay, 240 mi. away. A mining town that once boasted a gambling hall, two roadhouses, seven saloons, and ten prostitutes, Coldfoot was named for the group of prospectors who briefly considered wintering above the Arctic Circle and then headed south again. Just north of town, the **Coldfoot Visitors Center** is a resource for travelers eyeing the Brooks Range. (☎ 678-5209. Open daily 10am-10pm; daily slide presentations 8pm.) Otherwise the settlement is really only "the northernmost truck stop in North America." Gas flows 24 hours a day, the tire shop is on call until midnight, and the **Coldfoot Cafe** (☎ 678-5201) serves hot, expensive food around the clock in summer. The **Slate Creek Inn** (☎ 678-5224) rents RV sites (hookups $30) and has pay **showers** ($5). Eight miles north, the **Marion Creek Campground** rents sites in muskeg forest (water and pit toilets; $8). Away from Alaska access roads, **camping** is free. Send news of your journey from the **post office.** (☎ 678-5204. Open M, W, F 10am-6pm; winter 1:30-6pm.) **ZIP code:** 99701.

Twelve miles north of Coldfoot, a turn-off at Mile 188.6 leads 3 mi. to the intact gold-mining village of **Wiseman,** subject of Robert Marshall's 1933 work, *Arctic Village.* Perhaps the wildest road-accessible frontier town in Alaska, Wiseman is home to many of the canine stars in the movie version of *White Fang*—including White Fang himself. There is a modest **museum** here. (Open daily in summer 3-5pm.) **Boreal Lodge** rents **cabins.** (☎ 678-4566. Singles $50; doubles $70.) From Wiseman, the highway continues into the heart of the **Brooks Range,** a region frequented by moose, bear, caribou, and hawks. At Mile 235, the last tree along the highway—a majestic, surprisingly tall spruce—marks the beginning of the steep and awe-inspiring ascent toward **Atigun Pass** (4752 ft.). The highway cuts steeply into the mountainside as it approaches the snow-covered pass, offering spectacular views. Over the mountains lies the long descent toward the Arctic Ocean.

> **OLD PILOTS AND BOLD PILOTS, BUT NO OLD, BOLD PILOTS** Alaska has the highest per capita ownership of small planes, the greatest number of pilots, the highest number of float planes, and one of the nation's busiest airports (in Anchorage). Throughout much of the Interior, small planes aren't simply the best way to get there; they're the only way. Some of the state's most colorful lore is steeped in aviation—like the story of Alaska's third governor, who broke both ankles crash-landing his small plane to avoid endangering the children playing on the airstrip. Tales of unusual landings are as common as tales of unusual cargo: bush pilots have been known to transport canoes, beer, furniture, pizza, and even moose to the farthest reaches of the state.

The mountains gradually flatten into tundra, perpetually brown except during a short flourish in July and August. Its surface of bumps and moss lumps, called tussocks, covers water trapped beneath the frozen ground. The terrain is wet, soggy, and makes for difficult walking, although it supports wildlife not found below the Brooks Range: musk oxen, arctic fox, snow owls, and tundra swans. Even during summer, the temperature rises to only 43°F (5°C).

Ten miles from the highway's end, coastal fog enshrouds the sun and the temperature plummets. Deadhorse appears on the horizon and, three miles later, Prudhoe Bay (see below). You're there. The Arctic Ocean. The northernmost point accessible by road in North America. Fun, eh? Now you just have to get back.

DEADHORSE AND PRUDHOE BAY ☎ 907

Deadhorse, on the southern perimeter of Lake Colleen, got its name from the motto of the company that shipped the road-building materials north: "We'll haul anything, even a dead horse." The airstrip here is serviced by **Alaska Airlines** (☎ 800-252-7522; from Fairbanks $285 each way). Staples are sold in the **Arctic Caribou Inn.** (☎ 659-2368. Open daily 10:30am-9pm. Rooms from $120.) Register at the hotel for tours of **Prudhoe Bay,** the area of company-owned oil fields that flank the Arctic Ocean, otherwise inaccessible to the public. The tour (2½hr.; daily at 8:15am and 1:30pm; $60) brings visitors to Mile 0 of the pipeline at Pumpstation No. 1 and the shore of the Arctic Ocean. A shortened version passes through the oil fields en route to the ocean (80min.; 11am, 4:30pm, and 6pm; $25). Be aware that this is a dry "community." In an **emergency,** call the ARCO operator at 659-5300; there are no public emergency services. They have a **post office.** (☎ 659-2669. Open daily 1-3:30pm and 6:30-9pm). **ZIP code:** 99734.

ARCTIC NATIONAL WILDLIFE REFUGE

Covering a vast swath of the northeast, the isolated 31,100 sq. mi. of the Arctic National Wildlife Refuge (ANWR) encompass the calving grounds of the teeming Porcupine caribou herd and the Brooks Range's highest mountains. The question of drilling for oil has jettisoned this remote land into the milieu of politics in the Lower 48. Drilling would likely produce 2 million barrels of oil and reduce US dependence on foreign oil, generate jobs, and create income for the Inupiat Natives. Opposed to the drilling are environmentalists who fear a negative impact. Those in favor of drilling point to the already-successful arctic drilling at Prudhoe Bay that has had relatively little impact on the surrounding environment. US President George W. Bush supports recovering the oil, and it seems likely that drilling will occur eventually.

BARROW ☎ 907

Huddled on flat brown tundra next to the icy waters of the Chukchi Sea, Barrow endures some of the harshest conditions in the world: months without a hint of sunlight, temperatures below zero (-60°F), and windchills even lower.

50°F makes for a balmy summer day and the tundra wind always blows, so don't forget your jacket and a warm hat! Barrow is the northernmost point on the North American mainland, almost 330 mi. north of the Arctic Circle. As early as 2000 BC, the native Inupiat roamed the area. Today, 60% of the 4500-person population is still Inupiat. As in ancient times, bowhead whaling remains an economic mainstay and a central part of the culture, with extensive hunts in the fall and spring. Ancient and modern customs coexist—the native Inupiat language is spoken as much as English, and visitors will see fresh seal meat and bear hides hung out to dry beside $30,000 cars. This blend gives Barrow a distinct flavor, and attracts daring tourists every year. After dipping their toes in the chilly arctic water and taking several pictures of Inupiat dancing, however, most travelers content themselves with the fact that they've been to the "top of the world," then head back south, leaving the locals to face a winter of permafrost and pervasive gray.

TRANSPORTATION AND PRACTICAL INFORMATION. As with all true bush communities, Barrow is only accessibly by plane. Buy a ticket far in advance; the earlier the reservation, the cheaper. **Alaska Airlines** (☎852-8822 or 800-462-0333) flies three times in the summer and twice per day Sa-Su and in the winter from **Fairbanks** ($376 round-trip) and **Anchorage** ($437 round-trip). A **package tour** can actually be the cheapest way to see Barrow. Call the **Northern Alaska Tours Company** for info. (☎800-474-1986. Day tours from: **Fairbanks** $395, **Anchorage** $565. Overnight tours are also available.) Although the town is walkable, **Alaska Taxi** (☎852-3000), **City Cab** (☎852-5050), or **Arcticab** (☎852-2227) will take you anytime, anywhere, in town for a flat rate of $5. Three **buses** make loops around town every 20min. Flag one down anywhere along the route. The public TV station shows where the bus is en route ($1, seniors free). The **library** is located at the **Heritage Center** (see **Sights and Events,** below) has free Internet and is open noon-9pm. **Emergency:** ☎911. **Police:** ☎852-6111. On Kiogak St. **Crisis Line:** ☎852-0311. 24hr. **Hospital:** (☎852-4461), at the end of Agvik St. **Post Office:** On Laura Madison St. (☎852-6800). Open M-F 10am-5pm, Sa 9am-1pm. **ZIP Code:** 99723.

ACCOMMODATIONS, CAMPING, AND FOOD. Accommodations in Barrow are outrageously expensive; if you're planning on staying the night, be prepared to pay an arm and a leg. Harsh weather and bears make camping a purgatory, but die-hard tenters can camp along the rocky beach. The **Airport Inn**, P.O. Box 933, is one block from the airport on Momegana St. and has friendly and informative staff. At $115 per night they have the cheapest rooms in town. (☎852-2525.) N.A.R.L. (Navy Arctic Research Lab) is out of the way, in Browerville, but is on the bus route and occasionally rents its dorms ($65).

Although costly, Barrow's **food** options are surprisingly diverse and almost all deliver. Chinese/American, Mexican, Japanese, and Italian cuisines all come at high prices, as the location dictates. **Pepe's** (North of the Border) serves standard tacos and burritos for $3-9, entrees $10-15 and is owned by Fran, who seconds as the Easter Bunny of East St. Louis. (☎852-8200. Open 6am-5pm.) The **Stuaqpak** or "big store" is the **AC Value Center** on the corner of Ahkovak St. and Laura Madison St—a large and modern grocery store offering all (well, most) of the conveniences of home at prices which reflect the distance the items have traveled (gallon of milk, $8). A full **food court** offers some of the cheapest eats in town and the one and only coffee bar. (☎852-6711. Open M-Sa 7am-10pm, Su 9am-9pm. 6 in. sub $5.) **Ken's**, 1721 Ogrook St., above Cape Smythe Air, serves the best breakfast in town. (☎852-8888. Omelettes start at $8.50; Chinese dishes from $15. Open M-Sa 7am-midnight, Su 7am-10pm. Breakfast served all day.)

SIGHTS AND EVENTS.
Barrow itself is a sight with 84 straight days of light (or dark, depending on the season). Simply being about as far north as north goes is the most memorable part for many travelers. With the exception of the arduous trek to Point Barrow, all of Barrow's sights can easily be seen in a day with the aid of the bus system. To reach Point Barrow, the northernmost tip of the continent, continue 5 mi. north after the end of Stevenson St. Leave notice with someone before you go. Walking the beach can be very dangerous because of polar bears and Arctic foxes. If you see a polar bear, leave immediately. A safer and speedier way to touch the northernmost point is to hire a vehicle. Frank or Joe (☎ 852-1462) or John (☎ 852-3800) offer $60 tours to Point Barrow in a hummer. Arctic Tours runs similar trips, but includes mushing in the cold weather (☎ 852-6874).

The **North Slope Borough Inupiat Heritage Center** located at the corner of C Ave. and Ahkovak St. has exceptional exhibits on the history of whaling. The center includes historical displays, traditional arts, and a library. (☎ 852-4594. Open M-F 9am-5pm.) Joe the Waterman (and Dana Carvey look-alike) opens his **private museum** in his home by appointment when he's not out on deliveries. A stuffed polar bear and musk-ox greet the visitors at the door (☎ 852-5131; donation requested).

Hollywood as the locals call it, is about 16 mi. south of town, along the coast, and is the site of the Will Rogers/Wiley Post plane crash site as well as where a Disney movie was filmed. Relics from the plane hang in the Cape Smythe Airport in town. If trekking miles out of town seems arduous (and it is), simply walking around town, looking at the whale meat out to dry, noticing the ice basements cut out of the ground for storage, meeting the people, and posing by the icy shore gives the tourist a sense of the kind of life and mentality that is Barrow.

MILEAGE (DISTANCES)

	Anchorage	Calgary	Dawson City	Edmonton	Fairbanks	Portland	Prince George	Prince Rupert	Prudhoe Bay	Seattle	Spokane	Vancouver	White-horse	San Fran.
Anchorage		2160 mi.	515 mi.	1975 mi.	358 mi.	2610 mi.	1678 mi.	1605 mi.	847 mi.	2435 mi.	2578 mi.	2145 mi.	724 mi.	3153 mi.
Calgary	3478km		1747 mi.	184 mi.	2038 mi.	859 mi.	493 mi.	950 mi.	2527 mi.	738 mi.	443 mi.	609 mi.	1436 mi.	1514 mi.
Dawson City	829km	2812km		1562 mi.	393 mi.	2197 mi.	1390 mi.	1192 mi.	882 mi.	2022 mi.	2200 mi.	1764 mi.	327 mi.	2830 mi.
Edmonton	3180km	296km	2515km		1853 mi.	1043 mi.	461 mi.	906 mi.	2342 mi.	790 mi.	628 mi.	722 mi.	1251 mi.	1698 mi.
Fairbanks	576km	3281km	633km	2983km		2455 mi.	1668 mi.	1483 mi.	489 mi.	2313 mi.	2456 mi.	2137 mi.	602 mi.	3121 mi.
Portland	4202km	1383km	3537km	1679km	3953km		733 mi.	1208 mi.	2977 mi.	175 mi.	400 mi.	318 mi.	1886 mi.	655 mi.
Prince George	2701km	794km	2238km	742km	2686km	1180km		434 mi.	2074 mi.	558 mi.	663 mi.	486 mi.	983 mi.	1437 mi.
Prince Rupert	2584km	1529km	1919km	1459km	2388km	1945km	699km		1972 mi.	1033 mi.	1230 mi.	901 mi.	881 mi.	1880 mi.
Prudhoe Bay	1363km	4068km	1420km	3771km	787km	4793km	3339km	3175km		2802 mi.	2975 mi.	2541 mi.	1091 mi.	3610 mi.
Seattle	3920km	1188km	3255km	1271km	3724km	282km	898km	1663km	4511km		282 mi.	143 mi.	1711 mi.	808 mi.
Spokane	4151km	713km	3542km	1011km	3954km	644km	1067km	1980km	4790km	454km		400 mi.	1987 mi.	1055 mi.
Vancouver	3453km	981km	2840km	1162km	3440km	512km	782km	1451km	4091km	230km	644km		1450 mi.	973 mi.
Whitehorse	1166km	2312km	527km	2014km	969km	3036km	1583km	1418km	1756km	2755km	3199km	2334km		2519 mi.
San Fran.	5076km	2438km	4556km	2734km	5025km	1055km	2314km	3027km	5812km	1301km	1699km	1567km	4056km	

APPENDIX

Travel Cheep.

Visit **StudentUniverse** for real deals on student and faculty airline tickets, rail passes, and hostel memberships.

StudentUniverse.com Real Travel Deals

800.272.9676

INDEX

A

AAA (American Automobile Association) 52
Aberdeen, WA 204
accommodations 33
Adams, Bryan 20
aerogrammes 43
airplane travel
  fares 44
  standby 47
Alaska
  Aleutian Islands 486
  Central Alaska 438
  employment service 59
  Interior Alaska 497–523
  Kenai Penisula 466–472
  Kodiak Island 480–485
  Panhandle 394–437
  Prince William Sound 458–465
  purchase of 14
  state parks. See state parks, Alaska
Alaska Hwy. 334
  in Alaska 519
  in the Yukon 375–383
Alaska Marine Hwy. 53
Alaska Native Claims and Settlement Act 17
Alaska Railroad 49
AlaskaPass 54
Albany, OR 109
Alberta 339–368
  Calgary 346–352
  provincial parks. See provincial parks, AB
  The Rockies ??–368
Alberta Badlands, AB 350
alcohol and drugs 30
Alert Bay, BC 277
Aleut 13
Aleutian Islands, AK 486–490
Alutiiq 483
Alvord Desert, OR 140
American Express 26, 27, 28, 52
Amtrak 49
Anchorage, AK 439–447
animals
  Kermodei bear 312
  land otters 418
  sea lions 418
  seals 418
animals, interesting
  Banff Springs snail 359
  icewoms 464
Appendix 533
Arctic Alaska 524–532

Arctic Circle 391, 529
Ashford, WA 214
Astoria, OR 87
ATM cards 27

B

B&Bs 36
Mt. Bachelor, OR 124
backpacks 40
Bamfield, BC 266
Bandon, OR 104
Banff National Park 354–362
Banff-Windermere Hwy. (Hwy. 93), BC 302
Barkerville, BC 307
Barrow, AK 530
BC Ferries 54
beaches
  Irene Bay 265
  Jericho Beach, BC 247
  Kitsilano Beach, BC 247
  Li'l Tribune Bay 272
  Long Beach 267
  Miracle Beach 274
  Mortimer Spit 265
  North Beach, BC 324
  Sandy Beach, AK 412
  Spanish Banks 247
  Tribune Bay 272
beaches, nude
  Blackburn Lake, BC 264
  Wreck Beach, BC 248
Bear 16 361
Bear Lake, BC 310
bears 41
Beaver Creek, YT 383
beaver fever 32
bed and breakfasts 36
beer. See breweries 5
Bella Coola, BC 305
Bellingham, WA 179–181
Bend, OR 122
Bering Land Bridge National Park, AK 527
Bill, Lightnin' 222
Bingen, WA 83
Birch Bay, WA 181
Black Ball Transport 54
Blackcomb Mt., BC 253
Blaine, WA 181
BLM. See Bureau of Land Management
Blue Mountains, OR 132
Boxing Day 2
breweries
  general info 5
  Juneau, AK 422
  Skagway, AK 434

Vancouver, BC 261
British Columbia 233–338
  Approaching the Yukon 328
  Fraser River Canyon 280–285
  Gulf Islands 262–265
  highlights 233
  Interior 280–303
  Northern 303, 317
  Northern Vancouver Island 254
  Pacific Rim National Park 265
  provincial parks. See provincial parks, BC
  Queen Charlotte Islands 317–328
  Sea to Sky Hwy. (Hwy. 99) 251–254
  Sechelt Peninsula 249
  Shuswap Lake Region 284
  Vancouver 235–249
  Vancouver Island 254–280
  Victoria 257–262
Brookings, OR 105
Brooks Camp, AK 478
Brooks, AB 351
bungy jumping 271
Bureau of Land Management (BLM) 39
Burgess Shale 301
Burns Lake, BC 311
Burwash Landing, YT 383
Buschmann, Peter 409
Bush 524–532
bush pilots 530
Butchart Gardens 261

C

CAA (Canadian Automobile Association) 52
Calgary, AB 346–352
calling cards 43
Campbell Hwy. (Hwy. 4), YT 389
Campbell River, BC 275
camping 37
Canada Day 2
Canadian Pacific Railroad 233, 299
Canmore, AB 352
canneries 59
Cannon Beach, OR 92
Cantwell, AK 504
Cape Alava, WA 201
Cape Flattery, WA 201
Cape Perpetua 99
Cape Scott Provincal Park 279

535

536 ■ INDEX

Capilano Bridge, BC 248
capitals of the world
  bear viewing 479
  Chainsaw Sculpture 310
  Cranberry 105
  Halibut 476
  largest flyrod 311
  microbrewery 75
  Salmon 275
Captain Cook 254
car rentals 52
Carcross, YT 378
Cariboo Gold Rush Wagon Trail 254
Carnes, Natalie 346
The Cascades, WA 206-224
The Cascades, OR 122
Cassiar Hwy. (Hwy. 37), BC 328
Center for Wooden Boats 167
Central Alaska 438-532
Central, AK 519
Charleston, OR 102
cheeses, famous
  Gort's Gouda, BC 285
  Harris Walsh 213
  Tillamook cheddar 95
Chelan, WA 217
Chena River State Recreation Area 517
Chetwynd, BC 310
Chicken, AK 521
Chilcotin Hwy. (Hwy. 20), BC 304
children and travel 57
Chilkoot Trail 3, 379, 434
Chiniak, AK 485
Chitina, AK 455
Circle, AK 519
Cirrus 27
Citicorp 26
Clarkston, WA 133, 232
Clayoquot Sound, BC 269
climate 2
climbing
  Fernie, BC 296
  Kamloops, BC 284
  Kananaskis Country, AB 353
  Mt. St. Helens, WA 210
  Olympic National Park (for guides, see Port Angeles), WA 198
  Mt Rainier, WA 216
  Rampart Creek Ice Walls, AB 358
  Revelstoke, BC 298
  Skaha Bluffs, Penticton, BC 290
  Smith Rock State Park, OR 127
  Stawamus Chief, BC 251
  Valhalla Provincial Park, BC 295
Clinton, WA 177
Coldfoot, AK 529

Columbia River Estuary, WA 205
Columbia River Gorge, OR 82-86
Columbus Day 2
Comox Valley, BC 273-274
competitions, odd
  $1,000 prize for new plays 460
  bathtub race
    on land 527
    on sea 271
  Bering Sea Ice Golf Classic 527
  buffalo chip toss 132
  caber toss 326
  ear pull 515
  herring toss 412
  kinetic sculpture race 109
  kiss the cow 514
  Miss Iceworm Queen 464
  moose dropping toss 508
  Nenana Ice Pool 510
  outhouse race 388
  Pillar Mountain Golf Classic 483
  rubber duckie race 374
  silly boat race 271
  slug race 401
  ugly vehicle contest 461
  wild cow milking 305
  World Invitational Gold Panning 336
con men
  "Gassy Jack" Deighton 245
  "Sneaky" Steve Davis 530
  "Soapy" Smith 434
  "Wild" Bill Gates 168
Concrete, WA 221
consulates 22
Continental Divide 300
Cooper Landing, AK 490
Coos Bay, OR 102
Cordova, AK 462
Corvallis, OR 108
Council Travel 46
Council, AK 527
Coupeville, WA 177
Courtenay, BC 273
Cowlitz Valley, WA 211
Crater Lake National Park, OR 128
credit cards 27
Crosby, Bing 230
Cumberland, BC 273
customs 25
cybercafes 44

D

Dalles, OR 83
Dalton Hwy. (Rte. 11), AK 528
Dawson City, YT 384
Dawson Creek, BC 335
Deadhorse, AK 530

Dease Lake, BC 332
debit cards 27
Deep Cove, BC 248
Delta Junction, AK 519
Dena'ina 447, 493
Denali Hwy. (Rte. 8), AK 504
Denali National Park, AK 497-504
Denman Island 273
Destruction Bay, YT 383
Diablo, WA 223
Die, Imperialist Pig! 185
disabled travelers 56
Discover 1-8
Discover Card 27
diseases 31
Doe Bay, WA 187
dorms 37
Dosewallips, WA 197
driving permits 51
drugs and alcohol 30
Drumheller, AB 350
Dutch Harbor, AK 487

E

Eagle Run, BC 251
Eagle, AK 522
Easter 2
Eastsound, WA 187
Edmonton, AB 339-345
Elgin, OR 133
Elliott Hwy. (Rte. 2), AK 518, 529
email 44
embassies 22
emergency medical services 31
Enterprise, OR 133
environmentally responsible tourism 41
Ester, AK 516
Eugene, OR 110
exchanging money 26
extreme sports 4
Exxon *Valdez* 458, 483

F

Fairbanks, AK 510-516
Fairhaven, WA 179
False Creek, BC 247
Federal Express 28, 42, 43
Fernie, BC 295, 310
festivals 21
Field, BC 300
Fields, OR 139
fire lookouts 38
First Nations Land Management Act, 1999 18
flightseeing
  Denali, AK 504
  Glacier Bay, AK 430
  Ketchikan, AK 402

INDEX ■ 537

Kluane Icefields, YT 382
Lakhanti Glacier, AK 412
Petersburg, AK 412
Stikine River, AK 406
Yakutat, AK 437
Florence, OR 100
Flying Death. See Head-Smashed-In Buffalo Jump
Forest Service 38
Fort Clatsop National Memorial 89
Fort McPherson, NWT 390
Fort Nelson, BC 337
Fort St. John, BC 336
Fox, AK 518
Fox, Terry 242
Fraser River Canyon, BC 280–285
Frenchglen, OR 139
Friday Harbor, WA 183

G

Ganges, BC 263
Gates, Bill 168
gay travelers 55
General Delivery 42
George Parks Hwy., AK 505–510
giardia lamlia 32
Girdwood, AK 449
Gitskan 312
Glacier Bay Nat'l. Park, AK 425–426
Glacier Hwy., BC 329
Glacier National Park, BC 299
glaciers
  Bear, BC 331
  Childs, AK 465
  Copper, AK 454
  Davidson, AK 430
  Grand Pacific, AK 425
  Grewink, AK 477
  Hubbard, AK 437
  Kokanee, BC 293
  LeConte, AK 412
  Mendenhall, AK 423
  Muir, AK 425
  Riggs, AK 425
  Root, AK 457
  Ruth, AK 509
  Salmon, BC 331
  Shakes, AK 409
  Skagway, AK 435
  Yakutat, AK 437
Glenn Hwy. (Rte. 1), AK 447
Glennallen, AK 452
Glenora, BC 333
goats, rampaging 196
Gold Beach, OR 106
Golden Spruce 322
Golden, BC 300
The Gorge, OR 82
Government Camp, OR 80
Grand Coulee Dam, WA 218

Grants Pass, OR 115
Granville Island, BC 247
gray whales 102
Grayland, WA 204
Greyhound Bus Lines 49
guesthouses 36
Gulf Islands, BC 262–265
  Pender Island 264
  Salt Spring 262
Gustavus, AK 424–425
Gwaii Haanas National Park Reserve, BC 17, 326
Gwich'in 390, 392

H

Haida 326, 394
Haida Gwaii Watchmen 320
Haines Junction, YT 380
Haines, AK 426–430
Head-Smashed-In Buffalo Jump, AB 351
health 30
heatstroke 31
Hells Canyon, OR 133
highways
  Rte. 20, WA 220, 224
  Banff-Windermere (Hwy. 93), BC 302
  Campbell (Hwy. 4), YT 389
  Cassiar (Hwy. 37) 328
  Chilcotin (Hwy. 20), BC 304
  Dalton (Rte. 11), AK 528
  Denali (Rte. 8), AK 504
  Elliott (Rte. 2), AK 518, 529
  Glacier, BC 329
  Hwy. 16 329
  Icefield (Hwy. 93), AB 362
  Island Hwy. (Hwy. 19) 269
  John Hart (Hwy. 97), BC 310
  Parks, George (Rte. 3), AK 505–510
  Sea to Sky (Hwy. 99), BC 251–254
  Seward (Rte. 9), AK 448
  Steese (Rte. 6), AK 518
  Sterling (Rte. 1), AK 490–497
  Taylor (Rte. 5), AK 521–523
  Top-of-the-World (Hwy. 9), YT 384
  Trans-Canada (Hwy. 1) 269
  U.S. 26, OR 80
  Yellowhead Hwy. (Hwy. 16) 310
hiking equipment 39
Hines, OR 137
holidays 2
Homer, AK 472
Hood River, OR 83
Mt. Hood, OR 122
Hoodsport, WA 197
Hope, BC 282
Hoquiam, WA 204

Hornby Island, BC 272
Hostelling International (HI) 34
hostels 34
hot springs
  Aisworth, BC 293
  Alvord, OR 140
  Canyon, BC 298
  Chena, AK 517
  Chief Shakes, AK 409
  Circle, AK 519
  Cougar, OR 114
  Hart Mountain, OR 140
  Lakeview, OR 142
  Liard River, BC 338
  Lussier, BC 303
  Miette, AB 367
  Pilgrim, AK 527
  Radium, BC 303
  Serpentine, AK 527
  Sol Duc, WA 200
  Takhini, BC 372
  Tenakee Springs, AK 418
  Tofino, BC 269
Hyder, AK 329

I

Icefields Parkway (Hwy. 93), AB 362
Iditarod 443
Iditarod. See sled dog racing.
Imnaha, OR 134
Independance Day 2
insurance 32, 53
Interior Alaska 497
Interior BC 280–303
International Driving Permit (IDP) 51
International Student Identity Card (ISIC) 24
International Teacher Identity Card (ITIC) 24
Internet 44
Internet resources 62
Inuvialuit 390, 392
Inuvik, NWT 390, 392
Invermere, BC 302
ISIC card 24
Iskut, BC 331
Island Hwy. (Hwy. 19), BC 269
Islandman Triathlon, BC 317
Issaquah, WA 169
ITIC card 24

J

Jack Wade Junction, AK 384
Jasper National Park, AB 363–368
John Hart Hwy. (Hwy. 97), BC 310
Johnston, George 377

538 ■ INDEX

Joseph, OR 133
Juneau, AK 418–423

K

Kachemak Bay, AK 477
Kananaskis Country, AB 352
Katmai Nat'l Park, AK 477–479
Kelowna, BC 286
Kenai Fjords National Park, AK 471
Kenai Peninsula, AK 466–472
Kenai, AK 493
Ketchikan, AK 394
King Salmon, AK 478
Klamath Falls, OR 128
Kluane National Park, YT 379
Kodiak Island, AK 480–485
Kodiak National Wildlife Refuge, AK 485
Kodiak, AK 480
Kootenay National Park, BC 301
kosher food 57
Kotzebue, AK 528
Kwagiulth 233
Kwakiutl 277, 279
Kwakwaka'wakw 233

L

La Grande 133
Labor/Labour Day 2
Lake Crescent 200
lakes
 Alice, BC 251
 Berg, BC 311
 Buttle, BC 276
  See also Tuttle 276
 Byers, AK 509
 Crater, OR 128
 Crown, BC 254
 Dease, BC 332
 Dewey, AK 435
 Ealue, BC 332
 Eddontenajon, BC 332
 Francois, BC 311
 Garibaldi, BC 252
 Gibson, BC 293
 Harlequin, AK 437
 Kaslo, BC 293
 Kokanee, BC 293
 Kootenay, BC 292
 Mowdade, BC 332
 Muncho, BC 338
 Okanagan, BC 290
 Onion, BC 314
 Ptarmigan, BC 305
 Puntzi, BC 304
 Redsand, BC 313
 Shuswap, BC 284
 Skaha, BC 290
 Tangle, AK 504
Lakes District, BC 311
Lakeview, OR 140
lentils 232
lesbian travelers 55
Lewis and Clark 14, 63
Lightnin' Bill. See Bill, Lightnin'
Lillooet, BC 254
Lincoln City, OR 96
London, Jack 387
Long Beach Peninsula, WA 204
Long Beach, BC 267
loonie 26
Lopez Island, WA 189
lost passports 23
Lostine, OR 133
Lyme disease 32

M

MacKenzie, Alexander 233
mail 42
Makah 201
Marblemount, WA 221
marijuana 30, 240
Matanuska Valley Thunderfuck 447
Marrowstone Island, WA 195
Martin Luther King, Jr. Day 2
Masset, BC 322
MasterCard 27
McKenzie Junction, BC 310
McKenzie Pass, OR 114
McKenzie, BC 310
Memorial Day 2
Metlakatla, AK 402
Meziadin Junction, BC 329
Mima Mounds, WA 178
Minam, OR 133
minority travelers 57
Misty Fiords National Monument, AK 403
M.L.K. Day 2
Model Mugging 29
Moose Pass, AK 468
Morton, WA 206
Mossyrock, WA 206
Mount St. Helens, WA 206
mountain biking
 Banff National Park, AB 360
 Bend, OR 124
 Canmore, BC 353
 Columbia River Gorge, OR 86
 Corvallis, OR 110
 Denali Hwy., AK 504
 Denali Park Rd., AK 503
 Fernie, BC 296
 Haines, AK 429
 Juneau, AK 423
 Kluane National Park, YT 382
 Kootenay, BC 303
Petersburg, AK 412
Prince of Wales Island, AK 403
Sandspit, BC 326
Sechelt Peninsula, BC 251
Sisters, OR 127
Whistler, BC 254
mountains
 Augustine, AK 495
 Mt. Bachelor, OR 124
 Baked Mt., AK 479
 Blue Mountains., OR 132
 Chugach, AK 465
 Mt. Everest, Nepal 499
 Grouse, BC 249
 Mt. Hood, OR 122
 Joffre Peak, BC 254
 Marathon, AK 471
 McGregor Mtn., WA 220
 Mt. Katmai, AK 479
 Mt. Maxwell, BC 264
 Norquay 362
 Norquay, AB 362
 Mt. Rainier, WA 214
 Redoubt, AK 495
 Mt. Robson, BC 311
 Mt. St. Helens, WA 206
 Mt. Seymour 249
 Slalok Mountain, BC 254
 Steens Mtn., OR 139
 Strawberry Mtn., OR 143
 Mt. Sunnahae, AK 405
 Sunshine, AB 361
 Mt. Washington, BC 274
Mt. Revelstoke National Park, BC 298
Mt. Susitna, AK 445
musk ox farm 448

N

Nabesna Glacier, AK 454
Nabesna, AK 454
Naches, WA 225
Nanaimo Bars 271
Nanaimo, BC 269–271
national forests, U.S. 39
 Mt. Baker-Snoqualmie, WA 181
 Chugach, AK 490
 Deschutes, OR 123
 Fremont, OR 141
 Gifford Pinchot, WA 208, 214
 Mt. Hood, OR 81
 Malheur, OR 143
 Mt. Baker-Snoqualmie, WA 214, 220, 221
 Nome, AK 527
 Ochoco, OR 138
 Olympic, WA 174
 Siskiyou, OR 105
 Siuslaw, OR 99
 Tongass, AK 405
 Umatilla, OR/WA 132, 232
 Wallowa, OR 133
 Wenatchee, WA 214
 Willamette, OR 112

INDEX ■ **539**

national monuments, U.S.
  Diamond Craters, OR 138
  Misty Fiords, AK 403
  Mount St. Helens, WA 206
  Newberry 126
  Oregon Caves, OR 116
national parks, Canada 37
  annual passes 38
  Banff, AB 354–362
  Glacier, BC 299
  Gwaii Haanas, BC 326
  Jasper, AB 363–368
  Kluane, YT 379
  Kootenay, BC 301
  Mt. Revelstoke, BC 298
  Pacific Rim, BC 265–269
  Yoho, BC 300
national parks, U.S. 37, 38
  Bering Land Bridge, AK 527
  Crater Lake, OR 128
  Denali, AK 497
  Glacier Bay, AK 425–426
  Katmai National Park, AK 477
  Kenai Fjords, AK 471
  Klondike Gold Rush Historical, AK 433
  North Cascades, WA 220, 222, 224
  Olympic, WA 190–204
  Mt. Rainier, WA 214
  San Juan Historical, WA 186
  Sitka National Historic Park, AK 416
  Wrangell-St. Elias, AK 451
national preserves, U.S.
  Yukon-Charley Rivers, AK 523
national recreation areas, U.S.
  Lake Chelan, WA 220
  Oregon Dunes, OR 100
  Ross Lake, WA 220
  White Mountain, AK 518
national wildlife refuges, U.S.
  Arctic 530
  Hart Mountain National Antelop Refuge 140
  Kenai, AK 490
  Kodiak, AK 485
  Malheur, OR 138
  Nisqually, WA 176
  Willapa, WA 204
native culture 4
  arrival of europeans 12
Neah Bay 201
Nelson, BC 290
Nenana, AK 510
New Hazelton, BC 312
Newberry Nat'l. Monument 126
Newport, OR 97
Ninilchik, AK 495
Nisga'a 17
Nome, AK 526
Nootka 233

Nootka Sound, BC 254
North Bend, OR 102
North Cascades National Park, WA 220, 224
North Cascades, WA 224
North Pole, AK 509
Northern BC 303–338
northern lights viewing 517
Northwest Territories 392
Nunavut 18
Nuu-cha-nulth 233, 266
Nuxalk 305

O

Okanagan Valley, BC 286–290
Okanogan, WA 224
Olga, WA 187
Olmsted, Frederick Law 167, 175
Olympia, WA 171–176
Olympic Peninsula, WA 190–204
orcas 277
Orcas Island, WA 179
Oregon 63–145
  Columbia River Gorge 82
  Oregon Coast 86–106
  Portland 65–82
  state parks. See state parks, OR
Oregon Caves National Monument 116
Oregon Country Fair 113
Oregon Dunes National Recreation Area, OR 100
Oregon trail 14
Otter Crest Loop, OR 97
Oysterville, WA 205

P

Pacific City, OR 96
Pacific Crest Trail 3, 121, 130, 220
Pacific Rim National Park, BC 265–269
  Long Beach 267
  West Coast Trail 265
packing 33
Palmer, AK 447
PAM (Portland Art Museum) 73
Panhandle, AK 394–437
parasailing
  Kelowna, BC 287
Parks Canada 38
passports 23
Paxson, AK 504
Pemberton, BC 254
Pender Island, BC 264
pensions 36
Penticton, BC 289

Petersburg, AK 409–412
phones 43
Pig War 185
PIN (personal identification number) 27
PLUS 27
Plush, OR 140
Pomeroy, WA 232
Port Edward, BC 316
Port Hardy, BC 278
Port McNeill, BC 277
Port Renfrew, BC 265
Portage, AK 450
Portland, OR 65–82
prescription drugs 30
presidents
  Eisenhower, Dwight D. 51
  McKinley, William 499
Presidents Day 2
Prince George, BC 307
Prince of Wales Island, AK 403
Prince Rupert, BC 314
Prince William Sound, AK 458
Prineville, OR 126
provincial parks, AB 38
  Bow Valley 352
  Dinosaur 351
  Midland 351
  Peter Lougheed 352
provincial parks, BC 39
  Bear Creek 287
  Beaumont 311
  Beaumont Marine Park 264
  Botanical Beach 266
  Bowron Lakes 307
  Boya Lake 334
  Bull Canyon 304
  Cape Scott 279
  Crooked River 310
  Elk Falls 275
  Esker's 309
  Fillongley 273
  Flintry 287
  French Beach 262
  Garibaldi 252
  Goldstream 259
  Helliwell 272
  Herald 285
  Horne Lake Caves 274
  Joffre Lakes 254
  Juan de Fuca 262, 266
  Kinaskan Lake 332
  Kinaskan, BC 332
  Kleanza Creek 313
  Kokanee Creek 292
  Kokanee Glacier 293
  Manning 282
  Marble Canyon 254
  Meziadin Lake 329
  Monkman 310
  Mount Edziza 332
  Mt. Fernie 296
  Mt. Robson 311
  Naikoon 322
  Newcastle Island 271

540 ■ INDEX

Okanagan Lake 290
Petroglyph 271
Pinnacles 306
Porpoise Bay 250
Prior Centennial 264
Purden Lake 310
Raft Cove 279
Rebecca Spit 276
Roberts Creek 250
Mt. Robson 311
Ruckle 263, 264
Mt. Seymour 248
Smuggler Cove 250
Strathcona 276
Tatshenshini/Alsek 379
Tsylos 304
Tweedsmuir 304
Valhalla 293
Whiskers Point 310
Whiteswan Lake 303
Prudhoe Bay, AK 530
Puget Sound, WA 171

Q

Quadra Island, BC 275
Queen Charlotte City, BC 318
Queen Charlotte Islands, BC 317–328
　Gwaii Haanas NP 326
　Masset 322
　Queen Charlotte City 318
　Sandspit 324
Queen Marie of Roumania 84
Quesnel, BC 306
Quilcene, WA 197

R

rafting
　Adams R., BC 285
　Alsek R., AK 425
　Athabasca R., BC 368
　Banff National Park, BC 360
　Bend, OR 125
　Blanchard R., YT 382
　Chilcotin R., BC 304
　Fraser R., BC 282
　from Seattle, WA 168
　Hells Canyon, OR 133
　Illecillewaet, BC 298
　Klickitat R., OR 213
　Koyukuk R., AK 529
　Nenana R., AK 503
　Skagit R., WA 223
　Snake R., OR 137
　Sun R., OR 125
　Sunwapta R., BC 368
　Tatshenshini R., YT 382
　White Salmon R., OR 213
Mt. Rainier Nat'l. Park, WA 214
Randle, WA 206
red tide 32

Redmond, OR 126
Reid, Bill 20, 246, 320
Rememberance Day 2
Revelstoke, BC 296
Revillagigedo Island, AK 398
Riis, Jacob 167
rivers
　Adams, BC 285
　Apex, BC 298
　Arhnklin, AK 437
　Awke, AK 437
　Bella Coola, BC 304
　Blackwater, BC 305
　Chilko, BC 304
　Dangerous, AK 437
　Fraser, BC 304
　Kootenay, BC 292
　Maclaren, AK 505
　Nass, BC 313
　Ralph, BC 276
　Sanctuary, AK 501
　Savage, AK 501
　Skeena, BC 312
　Spatsizi, BC 332
　Spokane, BC 227
　Stikine, BC 332
　Teklanika, AK 501
　Toad, BC 338
　Tseax, BC 313
Rockaway Beach, OR 93
The Rockies. See Alberta and BC
rodeos
　Billy Barker Days, Quesnel, BC 306
　Calgary Stampede 350
　Central Washington State Fair, Yakima, WA 226
　Dawson Creek, BC 336
　Pendleton Round-Up 132
　Sedro Woolley Loggerodeo, WA 221
　Sisters, OR 127
　Toppenish Powwow 226
　Williams Lake Stampede, BC 305
　Winthrop, WA 223
Rogue River, OR 116
Ross Lake, WA 223
Royal Nanaimo Bathtub Society 271
　See also competitions, odd. 271
RVs 41

S

Salem, OR 106
Salish 233
Salt Spring Island, BC 262
San Juan Islands, WA 182–189
Sandspit, BC 324
Santa Claus 509
Sea to Sky Hwy. (Hwy. 99) 251–254
Seaside, OR 90

seat belts 51
Seattle, WA 146–163
Sechelt Peninsula, BC 249
Sedro Woolley, WA 221
Seldovia, AK 496
self defense 29
Seward Hwy. (Rte. 9), AK 448
Seward, AK 467
Shakespeare Festival, OR 120
Shanghai Tunnels 74
shellfish poisoning 32
Shuswap Lake Region, BC 284
Sisters, OR 126
Sitka, AK 412–417
Skagway, AK 430–435
ski areas
　Alyeska, AK 446
　Apex Mountain, BC 290
　Mt. Ashland, OR 121
　Mt. Aurora Ski Land, AK 516
　Mt. Bachelor, OR 124
　Mt. Baker, WA 182
　Big White, BC 288
　Blackcomb, BC 253
　Cypress Bowl, BC 249
　Discover 4
　Eaglecrest, AK 423
　Mt. Eyak, AK 464
　Fernie Alpine, BC 296
　Grouse Mt., BC 249
　Hudson Bay Mt., BC 311
　Lake Louise, AB 361
　Nakiska, AB 352
　Powder Springs, BC 298
　Revelstoke, BC 298
　Rogers Pass, BC 299
　Sandblast (No Snow), BC 309
　Mt. Seymour, BC 249
　Shames Mt., BC 314
　Sun Peaks, BC 284
　Mt. Washington, BC 277
　Whistler, BC 253
　Whitewater, BC 293
Skidegate, BC 320
Skookum Jim 430
Slana, AK 453
sled dog racing
　Iditarod 443, 505, 527
　Limited North American Championship 515
　Quest for the Gold 461
　Yukon Quest 375, 515
Smith Rock State Park 127
Smith, Jefferson "Soapy" 434
Smithers, BC 311
Snake River, OR 137
Snoqualmie, WA 168
Snun'muxw 271
Sointula, BC 277
Soldotna, AK 492
solo travel 55
Sooke, BC 262

INDEX ■ 541

Sourdoughs 384
Sourtoe Club 386
South Slough Reserve, OR 103
Southern Tutchone 379
speed limits 51
spelunking
 Ape Cave, WA 209
 El Capitan Cave, AK 405
 Oregon Caves, OR 116
Spokane, WA 226
spotted owl 18
Springfield, OR 110
Squamish, BC 251
St. George's Island 350
STA Travel 46
standby flights 47
Stanley Park, BC 246
state parks, AK 38
 Chilkat 428
 Chugach 446, 448
 Denali 509
 Kachemak Bay 477
 Kachemak Bay State Park, AK 477
 Totem Bight Historical 401
state parks, OR 39
 Ainsworth 70
 Beacon Rock 84
 Beverly Beach 98
 Boardman 106
 Bullard's Beach 104
 Cape Blanco 105
 Cape Kiwanda 95
 Cape Lookout 95
 Cape Meares 95
 Champoeg 70
 Clyde Holliday 142
 Crown Point 84
 Depoe Bay 97
 Devil's Lake 96
 Ecola 93
 Emigrant Springs 131
 Fort Stevens 88
 Golden and Silver Falls 103
 Harris Beach 105
 Humbug Mountain 105
 Oswald West 94
 Shore Acres 104
 Silver Falls 107
 Smith Rock 127
 South Beach 98
 Sunset Bay 103
 Tumalo 123
 Umpqua Lighthouse 101
 Valley of the Rogue 115
 William M. Tugman 101
state parks, WA 39
 Beacon Rock 86
 Deception Pass 179
 Fort Canby 205
 Fort Casey 178
 Fort Columbia 205
 Fort Ebey 178
 Fort Flagler 195
 Fort Worden 196
 Ike Kinswa 211
 Lake Chelan 218
 Lake Cushman 197
 Larrabee 180, 181
 Limekiln 186
 Millersylvania 174
 Moran 187, 188
 Peace Arch 181
 Rasar 221
 Riverside 228
 Rockport 221
 Seaquest 209
 South Whidbey 178
 Spencer Spit 189
 Mt. Spokane 228
 Twenty-Five Mile Creek 218
Steese Hwy. (Rte. 6), AK 518
Steese National Conservation Area, AK 518
Stehekin, WA 219
Sterling Hwy. (Rte. 1), AK 490–497
Stewart, BC 329
Stonehenge Replica 85
Student Universe 46
studying abroad 58–59
suggested itineraries 6
superlatives
 Let's Go picks 5
 best picnic spot 248
 biggest mall 345
 highest concentration of archaeological sites 316
 highest waterfall 301
 largest Caribou herd 391
 largest carnivorous land mammal 480
 largest chinook salmon 312
 largest dino bones display 350
 largest glass beehive 337
 largest wooden clear-span structure 95
 longest underground river 367
 most rigorous marathon 515
 smallest park 73
surfing
 Long Beach 269
 Ocean Cape, AK 437
 Point Munoz, AK 437
 See also *Apocalypse Now*
Mt. Sustina, AK 445

T

Takakkaw Falls, BC 301
Talkeetna, AK 506–509
Taylor Hwy. (Rte. 5), AK 521–523
Taylor, BC 336
Telegraph Cove, BC 277
Telegraph Creek, BC 333
telephones 43
Teller, AK 527
Tenakee Springs, AK 417–418
Terrace, BC 312
territorial parks, YT 39
Teslin Lake, YT 377
Tetlin Junction, AK 521
Thanksgiving 2
Thomas Cook 27
Three Capes Loop, OR 95
ticks 32
Tillamook, OR 94
time zones 44
Tlell, BC 321
Tlingit 13, 394, 401, 416, 426, 429
 longhouse 408
 totems 401
Tofino, BC 267
Tok, AK 520
Tollgate, OR 133
Toonie 26
Top of the World Hwy. (Hwy. 9), YT 384
Toppenish, WA 226
totem poles 16
trails, long
 Alexander Mackenzie Heritage, BC 305
 Chilkoot 379, 434
 Chilkoot Trail 3
 Desert Trail, OR 140
 Discover 3
 Juan de Fuca Marine 266
 Mt. Healy Overlook 502
 Pacific Crest 121, 130, 220
 Pacific Crest Trail 3
 West Coast 265
 West Coast Trail 3
trains 49
Trans-Canada Hwy. (Hwy. 1) 269
travel agencies 46
traveler's checks 26
treeplanting 59
triathlons, won by Let's Go researchers 317
Tsiigehtchic, NWT 390
Tsimshian 394
Tumbler Ridge, BC 310
Tutchone 390
Twisp, WA 224

U

Ucluelet, BC 266
Unalaska, AK 487
United Indians of All Tribes Foundation 167
universities
 British Columbia (UBC) 246
 Calgary 348
 Gonzaga 230
 Oregon (U of O) 114
 Portland State (PSU) 73
 Simon Fraser, BC (SFU) 240
 Washington State (WSU, Wazoo) 230
Up Island, BC 269

542 ■ INDEX

V

Valdez, AK 458
Vally of Ten Thousand Smokes 479
valuables, protecting 29
Vancouver Island, BC 254–280
Vancouver, BC 235–249
  accommodations 239
  daytrips 248
  entertainment 242
  music, theater, and film 242
  nightlife 243
  practical information 238
Vashon Island, WA 176
vegetarian food 57
Veneta, OR 113
Veterans Day 2
VIA Rail 49
Victoria Day 2
Victoria, BC 257–262
vineyards 5
Visa 27
visas 24
volunteering abroad 60

W

Wallowa Mountains, WA 133
Wapato, WA 225
Washington
  Cascades 206–224
  Eastern Washington 224–232
  North Cascades (Rte. 20) 220–224
  Pacific Coast 204–205
  Puget Sound 171–176
  San Juan Islands 182
  Seattle 146–163
  state parks. See state parks, WA
Washington State Ferries 54
Wasilla, AK 505
water, purifying 32
Watson Lake, BC 375
weather 2
web resources 62
Wells, BC 307
Wenaha-Tucannon Wilderness, WA 232
West Coast Trail 3
West Coast Trail, BC 265
  Gordon River 265
  Pachena Bay 265
Western Union 28
whale watching
  Long Beach, BC 269
  Wrangell, AK 409
Whidbey Island, WA 177
Whistler, BC 252
Whitehorse, YT 369
wilderness 40
Willapa Bay, WA 204
Williams Lake, BC 305
Willow, AK 446
windsurfing
  Columbia River Gorge 85
wineries. See vinyards 5
wines, odd 89
Winter Olympics 252
Winthrop, WA 223
Wiseman, AK 529
women travelers 55
World Eskimo-Indian Olympics 515
world wide web 62
Wrangell, AK 406
Wrangell-St. Elias National Park, AK 451–457

Y

Yakima, WA 225
Yakutat, AK 435
Yale, BC 282
Yellowhead Hwy. (Hwy. 16), BC 310
Yoho Nat'l Park, BC 300
Yukon Approaches
  Alaska/Alcan (Hwy. 97) 334
  Cassiar Hwy. 328
  from BC 328
  Hwy. 16 329
Yukon River, YT 384
Yukon Territory
  Alaska Hwy. 375–383
  territorial parks 39
Yukon-Charley Rivers National Preserve, AK 523

Z

Zillah, WA 226

ABOUT LET'S GO

FORTY-TWO YEARS OF WISDOM

For over four decades, travelers crisscrossing the continents have relied on *Let's Go* for inside information on the hippest backstreet cafes, the most pristine secluded beaches, and the best routes from border to border. *Let's Go: Europe*, now in its 42nd edition and translated into seven languages, reigns as the world's bestselling international travel guide. In the last 20 years, our rugged researchers have stretched the frontiers of backpacking and expanded our coverage into the Americas, Australia, Asia, and Africa (including the new *Let's Go: Egypt* and the more comprehensive, multi-country jaunt through *Let's Go: South Africa & Southern Africa*). Our new-and-improved City Guide series continues to grow with new guides to perennial European favorites Amsterdam and Barcelona. This year we are also unveiling *Let's Go: Southwest USA*, the flagship of our new outdoor Adventure Guide series, which is complete with special roadtripping tips and itineraries, more coverage of adventure activities like hiking and mountain biking, and first-person accounts of life on the road.

It all started in 1960 when a handful of well-traveled students at Harvard University handed out a 20-page mimeographed pamphlet offering a collection of their tips on budget travel to passengers on student charter flights to Europe. The following year, in response to the instant popularity of the first volume, students traveling to Europe researched the first full-fledged edition of *Let's Go: Europe*. Throughout the 60s and 70s, our guides reflected the times—in 1969, for example, we taught you how to get from Paris to Prague on "no dollars a day" by singing in the street. In the 90s we focused in on the world's most exciting urban areas to produce in-depth, fold-out map guides, now with 20 titles (from Hong Kong to Chicago) and counting. Our new guides bring the total number of titles to 57, each infused with the spirit of adventure and voice of opinion that travelers around the world have come to count on. But some things never change: our guides are still researched, written, and produced entirely by students who know first-hand how to see the world on the cheap.

HOW WE DO IT

Each guide is completely revised and thoroughly updated every year by a well-traveled set of nearly 300 students. Every spring, we recruit over 200 researchers and 90 editors to overhaul every book. After several months of training, researcher-writers hit the road for seven weeks of exploration, from Anchorage to Adelaide, Estonia to El Salvador, Iceland to Indonesia. Hired for their rare combination of budget travel sense, writing ability, stamina, and courage, these adventurous travelers know that train strikes, stolen luggage, food poisoning, and marriage proposals are all part of a day's work. Back at our offices, editors work from spring to fall, massaging copy written on Himalayan bus rides into witty, informative prose. A student staff of typesetters, cartographers, publicists, and managers keeps our lively team together. In September, the collected efforts of the summer are delivered to our printer, who turns them into books in record time, so that you have the most up-to-date information available for your vacation. Even as you read this, work on next year's editions is well underway.

WHY WE DO IT

We don't think of budget travel as the last recourse of the destitute; we believe that it's the only way to travel. Our books will ease your anxieties and answer your questions about the basics—so you can get off the beaten track and explore. Once you learn the ropes, we encourage you to put *Let's Go* down and strike out on your own. You know as well as we that the best discoveries are often those you make yourself. When you find something worth sharing, please drop us a line. We're Let's Go Publications, 67 Mount Auburn St., Cambridge, MA 02138, USA (feedback@letsgo.com). For more info, visit our website, www.letsgo.com.

DOWNLOAD

Let's Go: Amsterdam
Let's Go: Barcelona
Let's Go: Boston
Let's Go: London
Let's Go: New York City
Let's Go: Paris
Let's Go: Rome
Let's Go: San Francisco
Let's Go: Washington, D.C.

For Your PalmOS PDA

Pocket-sized and feature-packed, Let's Go is now available for use on PalmOS-compatible PDAs. **Full text, graphical maps,** and **advanced search capabilities** make for the most powerful and convenient Let's Go ever.

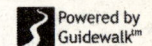

go and buy it at mobile.letsgo.com

Powered by Guidewalk™

PalmOS is a registered trademark of Palm, Inc.

Will you have enough stories to tell your grandchildren?

Yahoo! Travel

Do You Yahoo!?

CHOOSE YOUR DESTINATION SWEEPSTAKES

No Purchase Necessary.

Explore the world with Let's Go® and StudentUniverse!
Enter for a chance to win a trip for two to a Let's Go destination!

Separate Drawings! May & October 2002.

GRAND PRIZES:
Roundtrip StudentUniverse Tickets

✓ Select one destination and mail your entry to:

- ☐ Costa Rica
- ☐ London
- ☐ Hong Kong
- ☐ San Francisco
- ☐ New York
- ☐ Amsterdam
- ☐ Prague
- ☐ Sydney

Choose Your Destination Sweepstakes
St. Martin's Press
Suite 1600, Department MF
175 Fifth Avenue
New York, NY 10010-7848

Let's Go

Restrictions apply; see offical rules for details by visiting Let'sGo.com or sending SASE (VT residents may omit return postage) to the address above.

* Plus Additional Prizes!!

Name: _____
Address: _____
City/State/Zip: _____
Phone: _____
Email: _____

Grand prizes provided by:

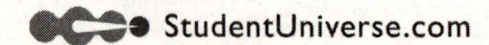

StudentUniverse.com   Real Travel Deals

Drawings will be held in May and October 2002. NO PURCHASE NECESSARY. These are not the full official rules, and other restrictions apply. See Official Rules for full details.
To enter without purchase, go to www.letsgo.com or mail a 3"x5" postcard with required information to the above address. Limit one entry per person and per household.

Void in Florida, Puerto Rico, Quebec and wherever else prohibited by law. Open to legal U.S. and Canadian residents (excluding residents of Florida, Puerto Rico and Quebec) 18 or older at time of entry. Round-trip tickets are economy class and depart from any major continental U.S. international airport that the winner chooses.
All mailed entries must be postmarked by September 16, 2002 and received by September 27, 2002.
All online entries must be received by 11:59 pm EDT September 16, 2002.

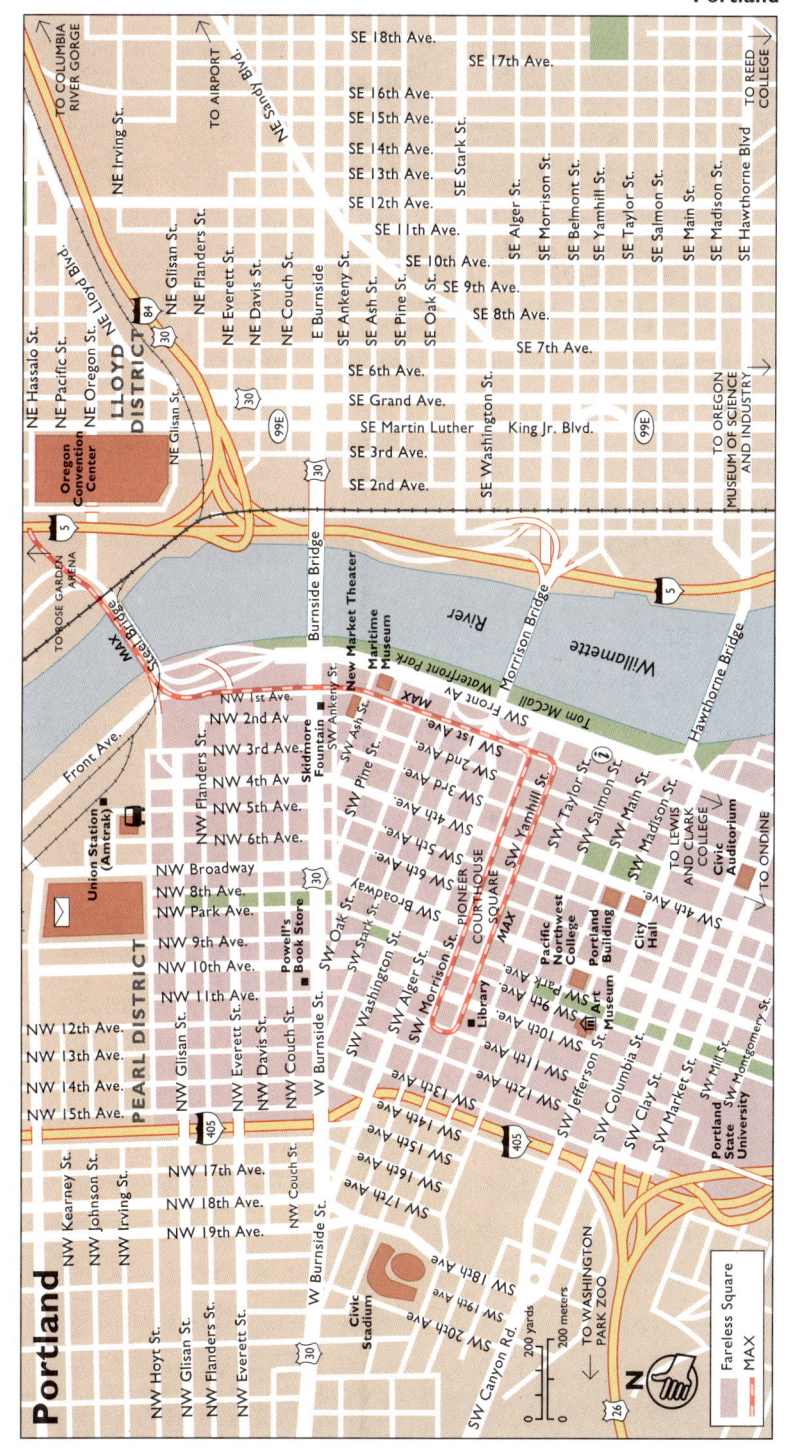

Portland

Seattle

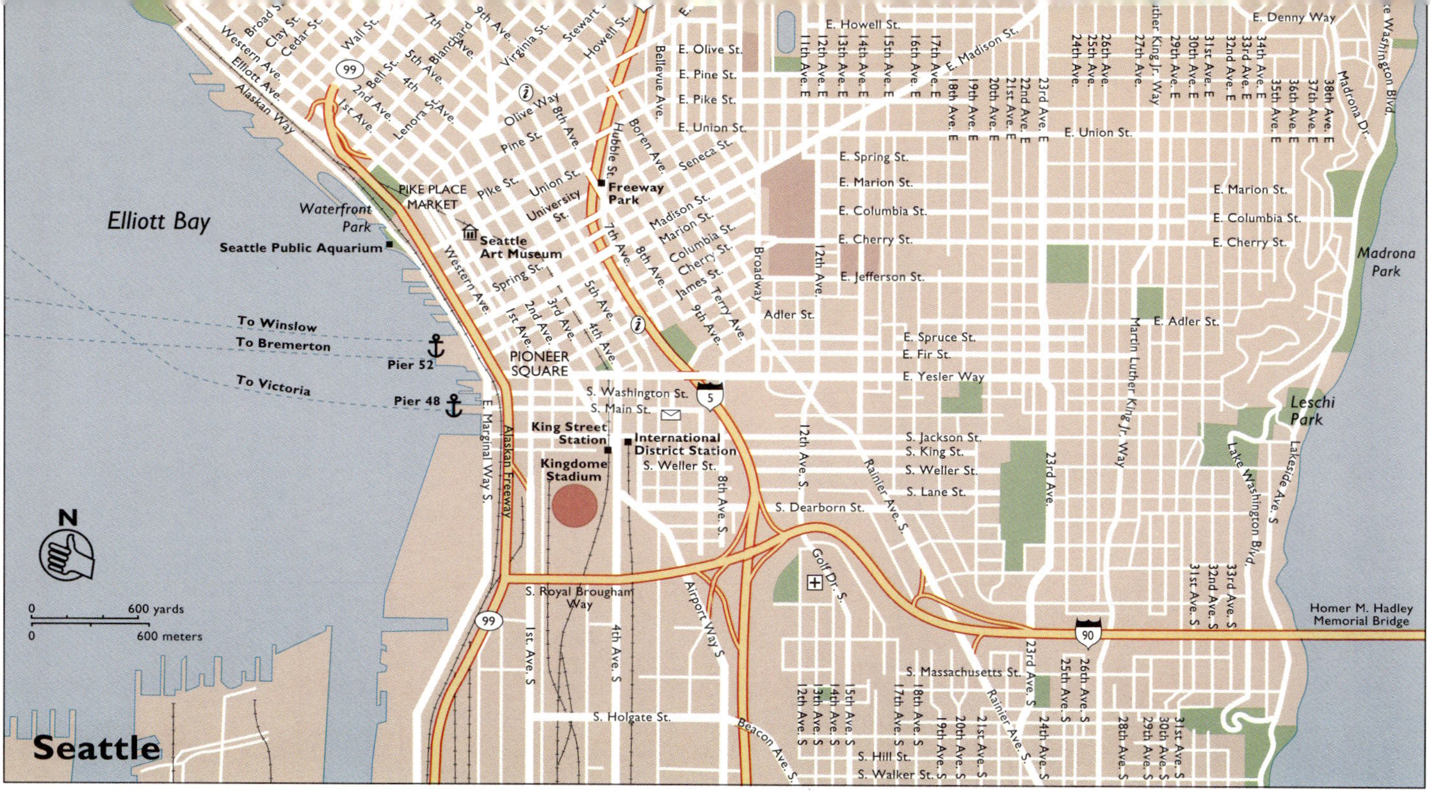

Vancouver

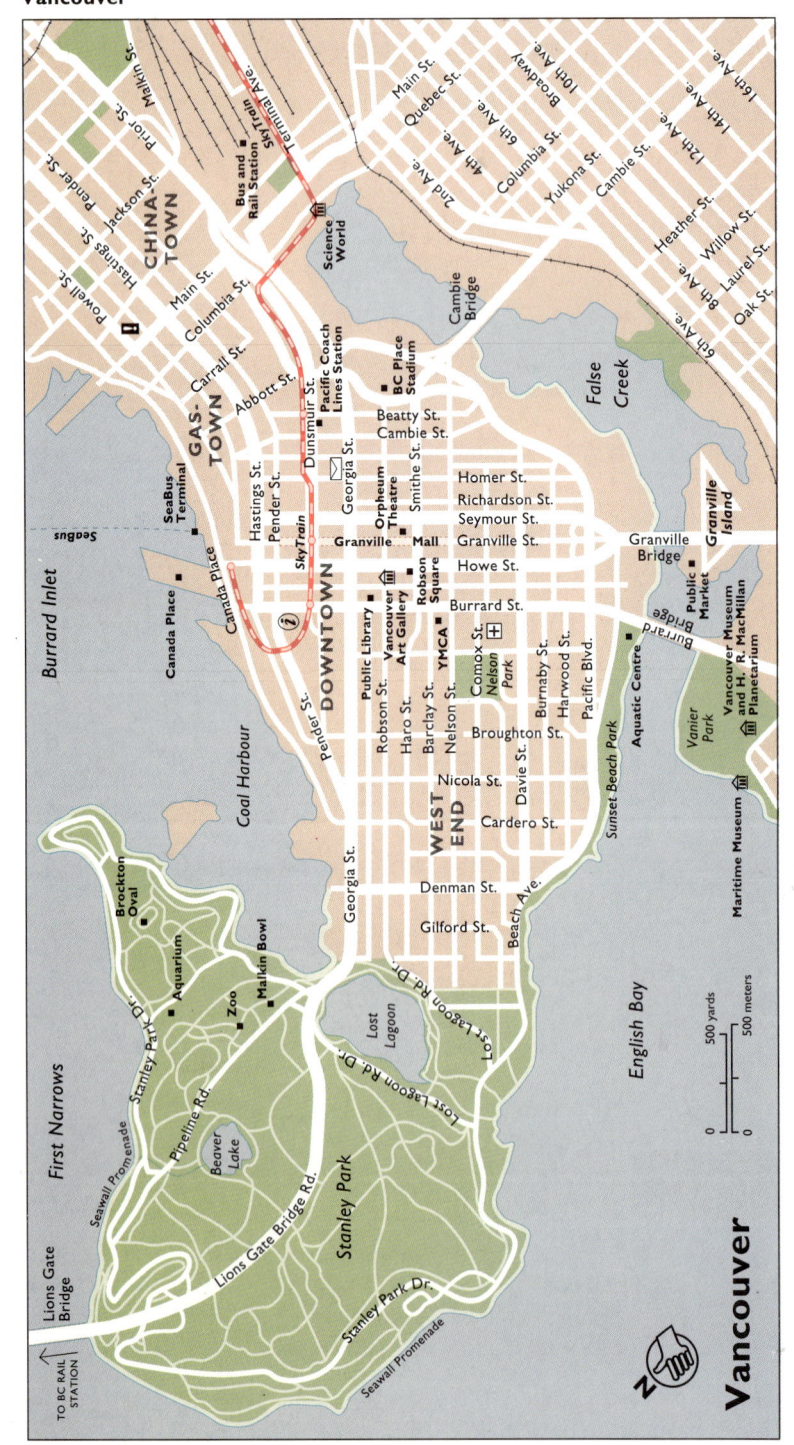